DISCARDED

College of Notre Dame Library
Belmont, California

International Marketing Data and Statistics 1994

International Baracuta Code
all rights reserved 2008

International Marketing Data and Statistics 1994

Euromonitor Plc, 87-88 Turnmill Street, London EC1M 5QU

College of Notre Dame Library
Belmont, California

INTERNATIONAL MARKETING DATA AND STATISTICS 1994
First published 1975
Eighteenth edition 1994

Researched and published by
EUROMONITOR
87-88 Turnmill Street
London EC1M 5QU
Great Britain

Telephone: (071) 251 8024
Telex: 262433
Fax: (071) 608 3149

EUROMONITOR INTERNATIONAL INC
111 West Washington Street
Suite 920
Chicago
Illinois 60602, USA

Tel: (312) 541 8024
Fax: (312) 541 1567

International Marketing Data and Statistics 1994

A CIP catalogue record for this book
is available from the British Library

ISBN: 0 86338 529 X

ISSN: 0308-2938
© Euromonitor Plc 1994

Printed in Great Britain by BPCC Wheatons Ltd, Exeter

Ref.
HA
42
.I56

This document is strictly copyright. Reproduction in any form whatsoever is prohibited and libraries should not permit photocopying without prior arrangement.

Table of Contents

Countries are described in alphabetical order under the following regional headings: North America, South America, Caribbean, Central America, South Asia, Japan, ASEAN/NICs, East/SE Asia, Australasia, Pacific, Middle East, North Africa, West Africa, East/Central Africa and Southern Africa.
Each entry includes:
Population, Languages spoken, Currency, Head of State, Head of Government, Ruling Party, Main Urban Areas, Political and Economic Developments

List of Charts

Foreword

International Marketing Data and Statistics is a compendium of statistical information on the countries of the Americas, Asia, Africa and Oceania. Published annually, it provides a wealth of detailed and up-to-date statistical information relevant to international market planning. The information is regularly updated and held on an international database of market information comprising 24 subject areas.

Published annually since the mid-1970s, **International Marketing Data and Statistics** or IMDAS is now in its 18th edition. The data coverage includes a considerable number of fourteen- and fifteen-year trendings, which permit the analysis of socio-economic trends over a longer time span as a basis for forecasting. The inclusion of figures for the most recent complete year (in this edition, 1992) for key parameters ensures that up-to-date information is available for analysis.

In addition to major countries, the country coverage includes smaller international countries and states. Although the availability of statistical information on these countries is limited and they are minor markets, it assists in building up a more comprehensive picture of the total international market and will be of interest to academic users.

The data are presented in spreadsheet form and in several sections a number of extrapolated tables have been included, together with several illustrative graphs.

A consolidated summary section includes spreadsheets showing key parameters for fifteen major sub-regions, giving comparisons with the major European economic entities.

The handbook contains a full alphabetical index, and we have included a list of major sources of information on international markets. Readers requiring detailed guidance on sources of information are referred to the *International Directory of Marketing Information Sources* (Euromonitor, 1988) and the *International Directory of Non-Official Statistical Sources* (Euromonitor, 1990) for more comprehensive listings.

A companion volume of marketing data, *European Marketing Data and Statistics* (EMDAS) is also available in the same format.

As multinational companies extend their activities and developing countries and regions play an increasingly important role in international trade, statistical information on the countries of the world will become an essential prerequisite for forward planning. **International Marketing Data and Statistics** aims to provide such a compilation in a handy format which allows easy access to key data drawn from hundreds of market sources and Euromonitor's own extensive information resources. Euromonitor is currently extending its research programme in the world's emerging markets (concentrating firstly on Eastern Europe, Latin America and South-East Asia), and has already published several new reports and marketing handbooks concentrating on these areas.

Several of the databases in this 18th edition of **International Marketing Data and Statistics** are still in a formative stage and will be expanded and developed over subsequent editions. User comments are welcomed. Also, whilst the editors have made every effort to ensure accuracy, Euromonitor cannot accept responsibility for any errors which may have occurred.

GUIDE TO USING THIS HANDBOOK

1. Scope of the Handbook

International Marketing Data and Statistics (IMDAS) is a statistical yearbook of business and marketing information. This edition features a compilation of up-to-date and detailed marketing statistics on 24 principal subject areas. These sectors are stored on a database of international marketing information and are regularly updated by Euromonitor's research team.

The sections of IMDAS cover a wide variety of marketing topics, ranging from socio-economic trends and background information through to key consumer marketing parameters. There are also sections covering consumer expenditure, retailing, advertising, consumer market sizes and household composition. Key agro-industrial trends covering energy, automotives, industrial output and agricultural resources are included.

The final section includes regional consolidations for 15 major sub-regions of the world, including comparisons with the major economic entities of Western and Eastern Europe.

In IMDAS 1994, each statistical tabulation presents comparative information, either in the form of fourteen-year (in some cases fifteen-year) trendings, or single-year data for the latest year available. All the countries are listed down the left-hand column, grouped into regional entities. Where appropriate and available, regional totals and averages are included.

The country listing is either the full matrix or a "key countries" listing. This is dependent on data availability or relevance.

Where data is in values, units have been generally been left in national currencies unless initially compiled in US dollars. However the spreadsheets on which the data is stored facilitate calculations in US dollars. These are calculated only for the latest year available (usually 1991 and 1992) as fluctuations in exchange rates and contrasts in rates of inflation render year-on-year conversions meaningless.

In addition, calculations have been made where deemed appropriate to show growth rates over a 14- or 15-year period, and per capita data. These permit rapid cross-comparisons between countries, regions and markets.

Using IMDAS 1994 is easy. Whatever topic is of interest, you simply look up the relevant tables (using the list of contents or index) and the table will show the relevant data for all countries. The heading shows the relevant section, title summary and title of the table, and unit. A guide to the sources used in the compilation of the data appears at the foot of the table, while any relevant notes are collected together at the end of each section.

The aim of IMDAS is to locate in one handbook the essential statistical information relevant to international market planning. The handbook will save the busy marketeer or researcher hours of time trawling through statistics from many sources and provides a wealth of hard-to-get information drawn from many sources. Business users and librarians will find the handbook especially useful.

2. Subject Coverage

IMDAS 1994 is presented in 25 separate sections or "databases" which have all been specially updated by Euromonitor for this new edition. The subjects have been selected as those most appropriate for strategic planning and international market analysis, covering both background marketing parameters and detailed consumer market information. The 24 product databases are discussed below (the final section features regional summaries drawn from the main body of the book).

01 Marketing Geography

This database features a summary of basic data (population, area, main cities, currency, language(s), religion(s), economic and political structure, heads of state and government and last election results) for each country covered.

02 Demographic Trends and Forecasts

This database features 20 statistical compilations covering population trends, vital statistics, urbanisation, demographic analysis by age and sex, and population forecasts. Much of the data is in 14- and 15-year trends, forming a basis for forecasting and projections.

03 Economic Indicators

This database features 13 tables of key economic data, again with several 14- and 15-year trend tables. The main economic indicators are all covered, including GDP, GNP, inflation, money supply, public and private consumption, government finance and exchange rates.

04 Finance and Banking

This section features five tabulations showing data from 1980-1992 and covering bank assets, liabilities, claims and interest rates.

05 External Trade

This section features ten tables giving a cohesive and structured trade overview covering total imports and exports and external trade breakdowns by origin/destination and commodity.

06 Labour Force Indicators

This nine-table database covers the key employment indicators including numbers employed, unemployed and hours of work. The structure of the labour force by industry sector, age group and status is included for latest years available.

07 Industrial Resources and Output

This section provides key industrial indices for a 15-year period and includes output tables covering major industrial materials.

08 Energy Resources and Output

This section consists of fourteen tables on energy supply and demand. Coverage extends to household energy consumption and includes a number of tables trended over ten or more years.

09 Defence

This section features some key data on defence spending and personnel.

10 Environmental Data

This section includes five tables covering various environmental factors. New data have been included this year on emissions of carbon dioxide as well as on the consumption of chlorocluorocarbons (CFCs).

11 Consumer Expenditure Patterns

This section comprises fourteen tables providing data on total consumer expenditure and consumer spending in all key sectors. Most of the data are presented in 15-year trends with growth rates and 1991 dollar comparisons.

12 Retailing and Retail Distribution

This section includes fifteen tables covering retail sales and channels and breakdowns for different retail sectors.

13 Advertising Patterns and Media Access

This database features nine tables covering advertising expenditure data and a range of media data.

14 Consumer Market Sizes

This section gives per capita consumption and retail market sizes in eleven tables for 1991/92. The information for the main countries is drawn from Euromonitor's market information database, which will form the basis for the forthcoming companion volume, *Consumer International* (1st edition planned for publication in early 1994).

15 Consumer Prices and Costs

Trends in consumer prices and selected international living costs are portrayed in three tables of data.

16 Housing and Household Facilities

This section comprises six tables of comparative statistics on households. Data on housing stock and household composition are included together with available data on household ownership of selected consumer durables.

17 Health and Living Standards

This database comprises seven tables covering major health indicators (including a table on the number of reported AIDS cases).

18 Literacy and Education

A range of literacy and educational statistics are included in this five-table section.

19 Agricultural Resources

This section presents key data on land use and the output of various agricultural products. There are eight tables on the database, mostly including figures for 1991.

20 Communications

This four-table section features information on telecommunications.

21 Automotives

This eight-table database covers the circulation, manufacture and sales of cars, commercial vehicles and two-wheelers.

22 Transport Infrastructure

This eleven-table database covers major movements in the road, rail, air and shipping transport sectors.

23 Tourism and Travel

This database consists of six tabulations covering tourism values and movements, tourist accommodation and its usage.

24 Cultural Indicators

This section includes four tables covering available data on libraries, museums and book publishing.

3. Data Coverage

Each of the statistical compilations is presented in one of four data periods:

(1) A 16-year trend table from 1977-1992, with data for each country drawn from the same consistent source. In some cases, some intermediary years have been excluded for reasons of space, mainly 1978/79 and/or 1981/82.

(2) A different period trend, eg 1980-1992 (13-year trend) or a recent period (eg 1982-1991 or 1983-1992) where only certain periods are available.

(3) Latest year available, with the years differing between countries. These are used where the information is drawn from occasional studies, eg a census, or where statistical offices vary in the speed of publishing statistics.

(4) A single year, eg 1992, where space does not permit trends or where an interactive range of information is provided (eg imports by origin, GDP by origin etc).

The statistics in this volume are as available during the compilation period (June-October 1993). Data for 1992 (in some cases provisional or estimated) have been included where possible. However consolidations across the world tend to take time and much of the data is to 1991. Various one-off surveys cover earlier years only.

4. Country Coverage

The country coverage of IMDAS extends over 158 countries. Due to a lack of separate gathered data on the newly-emergent republics of Eritrea, Kazakhstan, Kyrgyzstan, Tajikistan, Turkmenistan and Uzbekistan, these countries do not appear in the main matrix; however, they are featured in the Marketing Geography section and will form part of the main tables in future years.

The 152 countries appearing in the main matrix are grouped in 15 regional entities as follows:

North America
Canada — United States of America

South America
Argentina — Guyana
Bolivia — Paraguay
Brazil — Peru
Chile — Suriname
Colombia — Uruguay
Ecuador — Venezuela
French Guiana

Caribbean
Anguilla — Grenada
Antigua — Guadeloupe
Aruba — Haiti
Bahamas — Jamaica
Barbados — Martinique
Bermuda — Netherlands Antilles
British Virgin Islands — St Kitts
Cayman Islands — St Lucia
Cuba — St Vincent & Grenadines
Dominica — Trinidad and Tobago
Dominican Republic

Central America
Belize — Mexico
Costa Rica — Nicaragua
El Salvador — Panama
Guatemala — Puerto Rico
Honduras

Central Asia
Kazakhstan — Turkmenistan
Kyrgyzstan — Uzbekistan
Tajikistan

South Asia
Afghanistan — Nepal
Bangladesh — Pakistan
Bhutan — Sri Lanka
India

Japan

ASEAN and the NICs
Brunei — Philippines
Hong Kong — Singapore
Indonesia — South Korea
Macau — Taiwan
Malaysia — Thailand

East and South-East Asia
Cambodia — Myanmar
China — North Korea
Laos — Vietnam
Mongolia

Australasia
Australia
New Zealand

Pacific

American Samoa	Papua New Guinea
Fiji	Solomon Islands
French Polynesia	Tonga
Guam	Tuvalu
Kiribati	Vanuatu
Nauru	Western Samoa
New Caledonia	

Middle East

Bahrain	Lebanon
Egypt	Oman
Iran	Qatar
Iraq	Saudi Arabia
Israel	Syria
Jordan	United Arab Emirates
Kuwait	Yemen

North Africa

Algeria	Mauritania
Chad	Morocco
Djibouti	Niger
Eritrea	Somalia
Ethiopia	Sudan
Libya	Tunisia
Mali	

West Africa

Benin	Guinea
Burkina Faso	Guinea-Bissau
Cameroon	Liberia
Cape Verde	Nigeria
Côte d'Ivoire	Sao Tomé e Príncipe
Equatorial Guinea	Senegal
Gabon	Sierra Leone
Gambia	Togo
Ghana	

Eastern and Central Africa

Angola	Mauritius
Burundi	Réunion
Central African Republic	Rwanda
Comoros	Seychelles
Congo	Tanzania
Kenya	Uganda
Madagascar	Zaire
Maldives	

Southern Africa

Botswana	South Africa
Lesotho	Swaziland
Malawi	Zambia
Mozambique	Zimbabwe
Namibia	

For some sections, only major markets are featured. These are drawn from the following list of 28 key countries:

Argentina	Mexico
Australia	New Zealand
Brazil	Nigeria
Canada	Pakistan
Chile	Peru
China	Philippines
Colombia	Singapore
Ecuador	South Africa
Hong Kong	South Korea
India	Taiwan
Indonesia	Thailand
Israel	United States of America
Japan	Venezuela
Malaysia	Vietnam

5. Sources

International Marketing Data and Statistics is based on an extensive and ongoing programme of research into international markets and industries. A network of market analysts and researchers work to pull together available data on socio-economic patterns, market conditions and trends, living standards and background information relevant to business, export and market planning.

The principal sources used in the compilation of IMDAS are as follows:

-International organisations, such as the United Nations, OECD, and the International Monetary Fund.

-National statistical offices in each country.

-International and national trade and industry associations.

-Industry study groups and unofficial research publishers.

-Euromonitor's own research publications, including one-off reports and statistical compilations.

-Original research specially commissioned for the handbook, including consumer research, trade interviews and retail surveys.

A guide to the main sources used in the compilation of each table is included at the foot of each table. For reasons of space the main sources are only briefly cited; in some cases, many different publications are used in the preparation of just one table. For example, we may have extracted data from publications by the national statistical offices for all the countries covered in order to compile one table. In other cases, statistical compilations are from secondary sources which have in turn used a number of sources.

A brief guide to the main sources used in each of the 24 product databases follows.

01 Marketing Geography

Information mainly drawn from the business press, data from the yearbooks of the national statistical offices and various informal studies on the countries covered.

02 Demographic Trends and Forecasts

Drawn mainly from the statistical yearbooks of the national statistical offices supplemented with UN data and population forecasts.

03 Economic Indicators

The principal international sources are The World Bank and the International Monetary Fund (IMF). National statistical offices (yearbooks, national accounts) and economic bulletins by leading banks are also used.

04 Finance and Banking

The major source of comparative financial data is the IMF's *International Financial Statistics.*

05 External Trade

The IMF, OECD and United Nations track external trade flows in some detail. National statistical yearbooks are also utilised.

06 Labour Force Indicators

The primary international source is the International Labour Office, which publishes both a statistical yearbook and quarterly bulletins.

07 Industrial Resources and Output

Mainly drawn from UN and OECD publications. Various industry sectors are covered by associations as stated.

08 Energy Resources and Output

This compilation draws mainly on the UN, OECD, and various industry publications.

09 Defence

Sources include the International Institute of Strategic Studies and the IMF.

10 Environmental Data

Drawn largely from OECD sources and publications of the Food and Agriculture Organisation of the United Nations, and the World Resources Institute.

11 Consumer Expenditure Patterns

Drawn from the national accounts of each country (generally published by the national statistical offices). Euromonitor estimates have been used to reach levels of consolidation.

12 Retailing and Retail Distribution

Reference was made to *Retail Trade International* (Euromonitor 1992), also original new research. Primary sources include retail trade censuses (various countries) by national statistical offices, retail trade associations, major retailers etc.

13 Advertising Patterns and Media Access

Drawn from various media study groups, advertising associations and agents in various countries.

14 Consumer Market Sizes

Drawn from Euromonitor's consumer market database; primary sources include trade associations and industry leaders in all countries.

15 Consumer Prices and Costs

Mainly from the International Monetary Fund and the OECD; living costs from the International Labour Office.

16 Housing and Household Facilities

Compiled from various publications from national statistical offices, UN publications and incorporating Euromonitor estimates and calculations.

17 Health and Living Standards

The main sources are the World Health Organisation (yearbooks, various publications) and the OECD.

18 Literacy and Education

The main source is UNESCO with data from national statistical offices incorporated as available.

19 Agricultural Resources

Mainly based on the publications of the FAO.

20 Communications

Mainly based on UN data.

21 Automotives

Drawn from various motor trades organisations and compilations from the same.

22 Transport Infrastructure

Based on various UN publications; the International Civil Aviation Organisation; the International Road Federation; Union Internationale des Chemins de Fer (UIC) and Lloyd's Register of Shipping.

23 Tourism and Travel

A compilation sourced from the World Tourism Organisation, OECD and Euromonitor's own research.

24 Cultural Indicators

Mainly drawn from the UN, UNESCO and national statistical offices.

6. List of Abbreviations

ADB	Asian Development Bank
ASEAN	Association of South-East Asian Nations
EC	European Community
EFTA	European Free Trade Association
FAO	Food and Agriculture Organisation of the United Nations
GATT	General Agreement on Tariffs and Trade
IAA	International Advertising Association
IBRD	International Bank for Reconstruction and Development (World Bank)
ICAO	International Civil Aviation Organisation
IEA	International Energy Authority
ILO	International Labour Office
IMF	International Monetary Fund
IRF	International Road Federation
ITU	International Telecommunication Union (a UN agency)
MVMA	Motor Vehicle Manufacturers Association
OECD	Organisation for Economic Co-operation and Development
SMMT	Society of Motor Manufacturers and Traders
UIC	Union Internationale des Chemins de Fer
UN	United Nations
UNESCO	United Nations Educational, Scientific and Cultural Organisation
WHO	World Health Organisation
WTO	World Tourism Organisation
EAP	Economically active population
GDP	Gross domestic product
GNP	Gross national product
NGL	Natural gas liquids
NIC	Newly Industrialising Country
PDR	People's Democratic Republic
SITC	Standard International Trade Classification
'000	thousand
ha	hectare
kg	kilogramme
km	kilometre
km2	square kilometre
KTOE	thousand tonnes of oil equivalent
kWh	kilowatt hours
m2	square metre
m3	cubic metre
mn	million
MTOE	million tonnes of oil equivalent
MW	megawatt
R/P	reserves/production
TMTOE	thousand million tonnes of oil equivalent

7. International Map

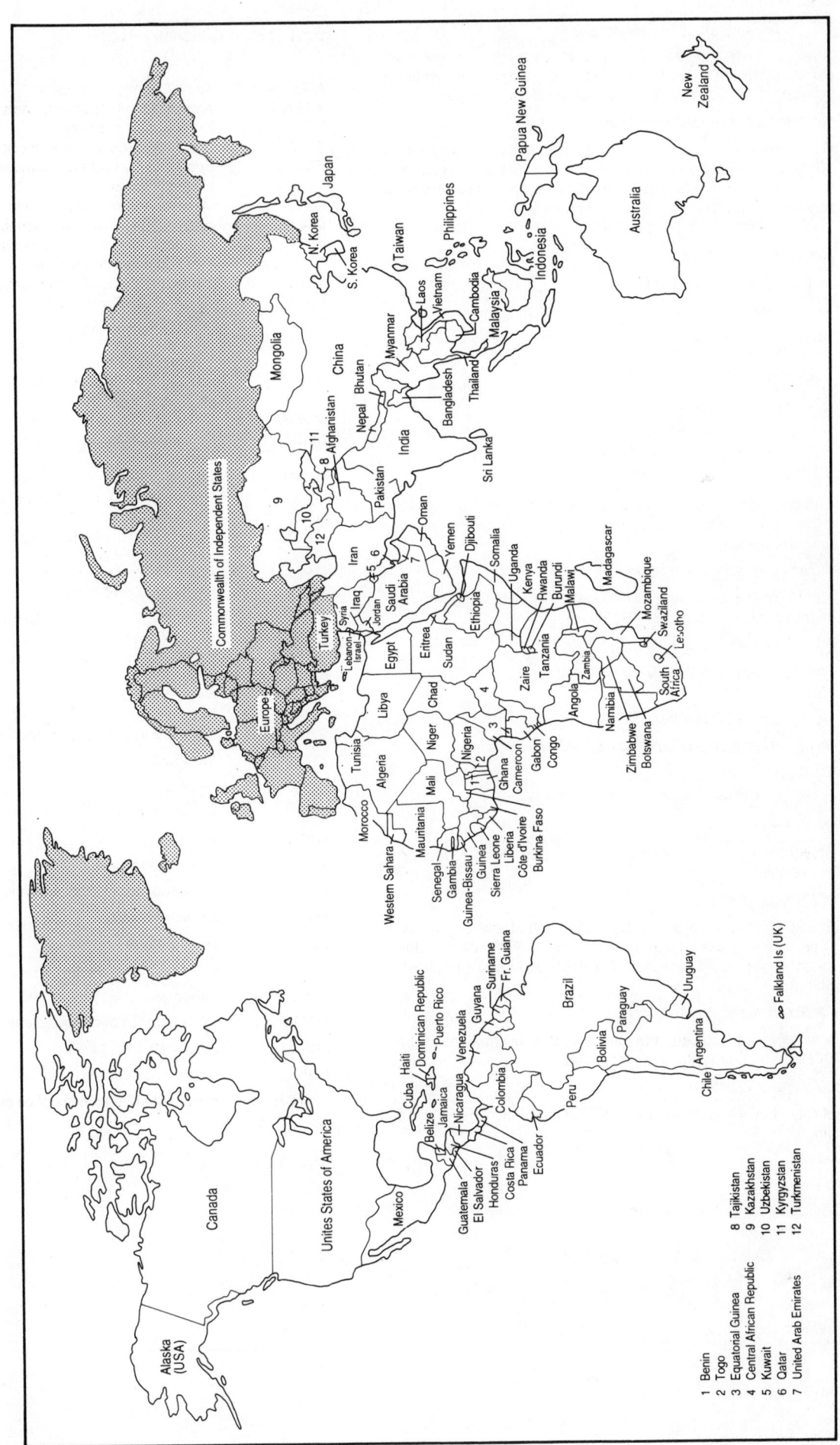

1 Benin
2 Togo
3 Equatorial Guinea
4 Central African Republic
5 Kuwait
6 Qatar
7 United Arab Emirates

8 Tajikistan
9 Kazakhstan
10 Uzbekistan
11 Kyrgyzstan
12 Turkmenistan

KEY INTERNATIONAL MARKET INFORMATION SOURCES

1. Introduction

This section identifies the major information sources for researching the international market. The listings are not intended as exhaustive; rather, we aim to list some of the main international and national organisations publishing statistics, to locate some of the principal non-European libraries and to identify the main general business contacts.

Readers are referred to several other Euromonitor publications for further information on international sources:

International Directory of Marketing Information Sources (Euromonitor, 1988)

This handbook presents information on official sources including further detail on national statistical offices, together with listings of market research companies, online databases, trade associations, trade journals, and general business contacts throughout the world. (For equivalent information on Europe, the reader is referred to the companion *European Directory of Marketing Information Sources*, Euromonitor, 1991. The forthcoming *World Directory of Business Information Sources*, which will be published in early 1994, will combine the coverage of both of the above publications,)

World Directory of Business Information Libraries (1st edition, Euromonitor 1993)

This is a new directory detailing over 2,500 of the major libraries in the world that provide public access business information.

Consumer USA (2nd edition, Euromonitor, 1992)

Consumer Japan (2nd edition, Euromonitor, 1993)

Primarily handbooks of consumer market data, these regularly updated publications list the major official and non-official sources providing information on consumer markets across the United States and Japan respectively.

International Directory of Non-Official Statistical Sources (Euromonitor, 1990)

This directory provides details of over 1,000 regularly produced statistical information publications from unofficial and semi-official organisations throughout the world, with special emphasis on the major industrialised nations including the USA, Canada and Japan. (The companion volume, *European Directory of Non-Official Statistical Sources*, was published in its second edition in 1993.)

Asian Advertising, Marketing and Media Data

Latin American Advertising, Marketing and Media Data (both new publications planned for 1994)

Following the established format of *European Advertising, Marketing and Media Data* (2nd edition, Euromonitor, 1992), these handbooks will examine advertising expenditure patterns, media availability and basic consumer marketing parameters in the Asian and Latin American markets, and each will also provide an extensive directory section with details of the leading agency and media operators, major advertisers and useful sources for further information.

World Retail Directory and Sourcebook (Euromonitor, 1991; second edition to appear during 1994)

This directory includes detailed information on over 1,200 retail information sources worldwide.

Asia: A Directory and Sourcebook (Euromonitor, 1993)

South America: A Directory and Sourcebook (Euromonitor, 1993)

These handbooks, which together with the 1992 publication *Eastern Europe: A Directory and Sourcebook* form a new series from Euromonitor, provide a detailed guide to key official and non-official business information sources in their respective regions.

2. Official International Organisations

African Development Bank
Address: 01 BP 1387 Abidjan 01, Côte d'Ivoire
Telephone: 204444
Fax: 227839
Telex: 23717
Publisher of statistical series: As above

ALADI (Asociación Latinoamericana de Integración)
Address: Cebollati 1461, Casilla de Correo 577, Montevideo, Uruguay
Telephone: (02) 401121, 401128
Fax: (2) 490649
Telex: 26944
Publisher of statistical series: CENCI (Centro de Estadísticas Nacionales y Comercio Internacional del Uruguay, Sección ALADI)
Obtaining publications: from CENCI, Casilla de Correo 1510, Montevideo, Uruguay; tel. (02) 954578 or 952930

Arab Fund for Economic & Social Development (AFESD)
Address: PO Box 21923, Safat, 13080 Kuwait
Telephone: 2451580
Fax: 2416758
Telex: 22153

Arab Industrial Development Organisation
Address: Al-Saadoon Street, PO Box 3156, Baghdad, Iraq
Telephone: (1) 7187059/60
Telex: 3823 AIDO IK
Publisher of statistical series: as above
Obtaining publications: from address above
Publications: AIDO collects national statistical data compiled from ministries of industry in Arab countries, and prepares a regularly updated statistical publication

Arab Monetary Fund
Address: PO Box 2818, Abu Dhabi, United Arab Emirates
Telephone: (2) 215000
Fax: (2) 326454
Telex: 22989 AMF EM
Publisher of statistical series: as above
Obtaining publications: from address above
Guides to publications: *Arab Monetary Fund: publications catalogue* (annual, free)

Arab Organisation for Agricultural Development
Address: PO Box 474, Khartoum, Sudan
Telephone: (11) 78760/78761/78762/78763/78764
Telex: 22554 AOAD SD
Publisher of statistical series: as above
Obtaining publications: from address above
Guides to publications: some details given in free brochure about the Organisation

Asian and Pacific Coconut Community
Address: PO Box 1343, Jakarta Pusat, Indonesia
Telephone: (21) 510073
Fax: (21) 52051260
Telex: 62863 APCC IA
Publisher of statistical series: as above
Obtaining publications: from address above
Guides to publications: free brochure

Asian Development Bank
Address: PO Box 789, 1099 Manila, Philippines
Telephone: (2) 632 4444; (632) 711 3851 for international calls
Fax: (632) 741 7961
Telex: 63587 ADB PN
Publisher of statistical series: Economics and Development Resource Center at above address
Obtaining publications: from the Information Office, Asian Development Bank, at the above address

Guides to publications: free sales list of ADB publications; free list of the ADB Statistical Report Series (available from the Economics Office); *Reference manual: concepts, definitions and statistical foundations of data used by ADB* (free)

Association of South East Asian Nations (ASEAN)
Address: 70A Jalan Sisingamangaraja/PO Box 2072, Jakarta, Indonesia
Telephone: (21) 712272
Fax: (21) 7398234
Telex: 47214 ASEAN JKT
Publisher of statistical series: as above
Obtaining publications: from the ASEAN Secretariat, at the address above
Guides to publications: *ASEAN Selected Statistics 1982-1988* (1990); free list of current publications available

Banque Centrale des Etats de l'Afrique de l'Ouest
Address: Avenue Abdoulaye Fadiga, BP 3108, Dakar, Senegal
Telephone: 231615, 231042
Publisher of statistical series: as above
Obtaining publications: from address above

Caribbean Community and Common Market (CARICOM)
Address: Bank of Guyana Building, PO Box 10827, Georgetown, Guyana
Telephone: (2) 69280
Fax: (2) 56194
Telex: 2263 CARISEC GY
Publisher of statistical series: Statistical Section, Caribbean Community Secretariat
Obtaining publications: from the Secretariat at the above address
Guides to publications: list of CARICOM publications in print (free)

Central American Common Market (CACM)
Address: 4a Avda 10-25, Zona 14, Apolo Postal 1237, 01901 Guatemala City, Guatemala
Telephone: (2) 682151
Fax: (2) 681071
Telex: 5676
Publisher of statistical series: as above

The Commonwealth
Address: Commonwealth Secretariat, Marlborough House, Pall Mall, London SW17 5HX, England
Telephone: (071) 839 3411
Fax: (071) 930 0827
Telex: 27678
Publisher of statistical series: As above

Council of Arab Economic Unity
Address: PO Box 1, Mohammed Fareed, Cairo, Egypt
Telephone: 755321
Fax: 754090
Publisher of statistical series: Arab Central Bureau of Statistics and Documentation, General Secretariat, Council of Arab Economic Unity, at the above address
Obtaining publications: from the above address

Eurostat (Statistical Office of the European Community)
Address: BP 1907, rue Alcide de Gasperi, L-2929 Luxembourg-Ville
Telephone: 43011
Fax: 436404
Telex: 3423 COMEUR LU
Publisher of statistical series: Office for Official Publications of the European Community, BP 103, 2 rue Mercier, L-2985 Luxembourg-Ville; telephone 499281; fax 488573; telex 1324 PUBOF LU
Obtaining publications: directly from the Office for Official Publications of the European Community (see above), or through sales and subscriptions offices in individual countries; in the UK these are HMSO and, as sub-agent, Alan Armstrong Ltd, 2 Arkwright Road, Reading RG2 0SG, telephone (0743) 751769
Guides to publications: regular information on publications given in *Eurostat news* (quarterly), *Catalogue of Eurostat publications* (annual, free from sales and subscriptions offices)

Food and Agriculture Organisation of the United Nations (FAO)
Address: Via delle Terme di Caracalla, I-00100 Rome, Italy
Telephone: (06) 5797-1
Fax: (06) 5797-3152
Telex: 610181 FOODAGRI I
Publisher of statistical series: as above
Obtaining publications: from sales agents (HMSO in the UK), or from the Distribution and Sales Section of the FAO at the address above for countries without agents
Guides to publications: *FAO books in print* (annual catalogue of FAO publications in English); *List of documents*, listing publications in all languages expected to be of a reasonably lasting nature

Fundación de Investigaciones Económicas Latinoamericanas
Address: Esmeralda 320, Piso 4°, 1343 Capital Federal, Argentina
Telephone: (0541) 356127/359270
Fax: (0541) 317466/317470
Publisher of statistical series: as above
Obtaining publications: from address above

General Agreement on Tariffs and Trade (GATT)
Address: Centre William Rappard, 154 rue de Lausanne, CH-1211 Geneva 21, Switzerland
Telephone: (022) 739 5208
Fax: (022) 731 5458
Telex: 412324 GATT CH
Guides to publications: GATT publications are included in the general *Catalogue of United Nations publications* (see main United Nations entry). There is also a guide, *GATT Publications*, published annually

Instituto Centroamericano de Investigación y Tecnología Industrial/Central American Research Institute for Industry
Address: Avenida la Reforma 4-47, Zona 10, Apartado Postal 1552, Guatemala City, Guatemala (also regional offices in other countries covered, ie Costa Rica, El Salvador, Honduras, Nicaragua)
Telephone: (02) 310631/317466
Telex: 5312 ICAITI GU
Obtaining publications: from address above
Guides to publications: list of publications available

Inter-American Development Bank
Address: 1300 New York Avenue, NW, Washington, DC 20577, USA
Telephone: (202) 623 1397
Fax: (202) 623 1403
Publisher of statistical series: as above
Obtaining publications: from address above

International Bank for Reconstruction and Development - IBRD (World Bank)
Address: 1818 H St NW, Washington, DC 20433, USA
Telephone: (202) 473 7561
Fax: (202) 473 8347
Telex: 248423
Obtaining publications: Publications Sales Unit, Dept E, at the above address; or from 66 avenue d'Iéna, F-75116 Paris, France; or from national stockists
Guides to publications: World Bank Catalog of Publications

International Chamber of Commerce
Address: 38 Cours Albert 1er, 75008 Paris, France
Telephone: (1) 495 32828
Fax: (1) 495 32942
Telex: 650770

International Civil Aviation Organisation
Address: 1000 Sherbrooke Street West, Suite 400, Montréal, QC H3A 2R2, Canada
Telephone: (514) 285 8219
Telex: 24513
Fax: (514) 288 4772
Publisher of statistical series: as above
Obtaining publications: from the Document Sales Unit at the above address, or from several addresses abroad (United Kingdom: Civil Aviation Authority, Printing and Publications

Services, Greville House, 37 Gratton Road, Cheltenham, Gloucestershire GL50 2BN)
Guides to publications: ICAO Publications and Audio Visual Training Aids

International Cocoa Organisation
Address: 22 Berners Street, London W1P 3DB, UK
Telephone: (071) 637 3211
Fax: (071) 631 0114
Telex: 28173 ICOCOA G
Publisher of statistical series: as above
Obtaining publications: from the address above
Guides to publications: Quarterly Bulletin of Cocoa Statistics

International Energy Agency
Address: 2 rue André-Pascal, F-75775 Paris Cedex 16, France
Telephone: (1) 45248200
Telex: 620160 OCDE F
Fax: (1) 45248500
Publications: Energy policies and programmes of IEA countries (annual), *Annual oil market report, Quarterly oil and gas statistics, Annual oil and gas statistics, Energy prices and taxes* (quarterly), *Energy Statistics and Balances of OECD Countries* (annual), *Energy Statistics and Balances of Non-OECD Countries* (annual)
Notes: IEA is an autonomous body within the framework of OECD; for details on obtaining publications, etc see OECD entry

International Labour Office (ILO)
Address: 4 route des Morillons, CH-1211 Geneva 22, Switzerland
Telephone: (022) 799 6111
Fax: (022) 798 6358
Telex: 415647 ILO CH
Obtaining publications: from International Labour Office Publications at the above address or from branch offices in ca. 40 countries
Guides to publications: ILO Publications (quarterly in English, French, Spanish, German, Russian, Arabic and Chinese), *Catalogue of ILO Publications in Print*

International Monetary Fund (IMF)
Address: 700 19th St, NW, Washington, DC 20431, USA
Telephone: (202) 623 7430
Fax: (202) 623 7201
Obtaining publications: from Publications Unit at the above address. In the UK the publications may be obtained from HMSO or Microinfo Ltd, telephone (0420) 86848
Guides to publications: IMF publications are included in the general *Catalogue of United Nations publications* (see United Nations entry); there is also a publications brochure, *IMF Publications Catalogue,* available from the above address

International North Pacific Fisheries Commission
Address: 6640 Northwest Marine Drive, Vancouver, BC V6T 1X2, Canada
Telephone: (604) 228 1128
Fax: (604) 228 1135
Publisher of statistical series: as above
Obtaining publications: from address above
Guides to publications: INPFC Statistical Yearbook

International Pepper Community
Address: 3rd floor, Wisma Bakrie, Jl H R Rasuna Said Kav Bl, Kuningan, Jakarta Selatan, Indonesia
Telephone: (21) 510192/510212 ext 439
Fax: (21) 5200401
Telex: 62218 BAKROS IA
Publisher of statistical series: International Pepper Community Secretariat
Obtaining publications: from the Secretariat at the above address
Guides to publications: Pepper News (monthly news letter) plus *Pepper Statistical Yearbook* (annual)

International Sugar Organisation
Address: 1 Canada Square, Canary Wharf, London E14 5AE, UK
Telephone: (071) 513 1144
Fax: (071) 513 1146
Telex: 24143 G
Publisher of statistical series: as above

Obtaining publications: from address above
Guides to publications: Statistical Bulletin (monthly) plus *ISO Sugar Yearbook* (annual)

International Telecommunication Union (ITU)
Address: Place des Nations, CH-1211 Geneva 20, Switzerland
Telephone: (022) 730 511
Fax: (022) 733 5194
Telex: 421000
Guides to publications: List of publications (twice a year)

Northwest Atlantic Fisheries Organisation
Address: PO Box 638, Dartmouth, NS B2Y 3Y9, Canada
Telephone: (902) 469 9105
Telex: 019-31475 CA
Publisher of statistical series: as above
Obtaining publications: from the Secretariat at the above address
Guides to publications: leaflets and price list available

OECD (Organisation for Economic Co-operation and Development)
Address: 2 rue André-Pascal, F-75775 Paris Cedex 16, France
Telephone: (1) 45248200
Fax: (1) 45248500
Telex: 640048 OCDE F
Publisher of statistical series: as above
Obtaining publications: all orders should be addressed to OECD Publications Services at the main address above
Guides to publications: OECD publications (annual catalogue) and quarterly supplements. *Just out. News from OECD,* a monthly bulletin, also lists publications appearing during the current month and is available regularly free on request

Organisation of American States
Address: General Secretariat, 1889 F St NW, Washington DC 20006, USA
Telephone: (202) 458 3000
Telex: 440118
Publisher of statistical series: as above
Obtaining publications: from the Sales and Promotion Unit, Department of Publications at the above address, or from agencies

Organisation of Arab Petroleum Exporting Countries (OAPEC)
Address: PO Box 108, Majlis ash-Sha'ab, 11516 Cairo, Egypt
Telephone/fax: (2) 354 2660
Telex: 21158
Publisher of statistical series: as above
Obtaining publications: from Information & International Relations Department at the above address
Guides to publications: Annotated list of OAPEC publications (annual, free)

Organisation of Petroleum Exporting Countries (OPEC)
Address: Obere Donaustrasse 93, A-1020 Vienna, Austria
Telephone: (01) 211120
Fax: (01) 264320
Telex: 134474 A
Publisher of statistical series: as above
Obtaining publications: OPEC Department of OPECNA and Information at the above address
Guides to publications: sales list available

South Pacific Bureau for Economic Co-operation
Address: PO Box 856, Suva, Fiji
Telephone: 312600
Fax: 14204
Telex: 2229 SPECSUVA FJ
Publisher of statistical series: no statistical series published
Obtaining publications: no statistical series, but other publications available from address above
Publications: mainly technical and trade reports; also a directory of aid agencies, two monthly newsletters and an annual report

Southern African Development Community (SADC)
Address: Private Bag 0095, Gaborone, Botswana
Telephone: 51863
Telex: 2555

United Nations
Address: Palais des Nations, CH-1211 Geneva 10, Switzerland;
Room DC-2-853, United Nations, New York, NY 10017, USA
Telephone: (022) 734 6011/731 0211 (Geneva); (212) 963 8302
(New York)
Fax: (022) 740 0931 (Geneva); (212) 963 4116 (New York)
Telex: 289696 (Geneva); 126171 (New York)
Publisher of statistical series: as above
Obtaining publications: can be bought directly from the Sales
Sections in Geneva (orders from Europe, Africa and the Middle
East) or in New York (orders from North and South America, Asia
and the Pacific); also available from worldwide bookshops, agents
or distributors (lists available from Sales Sections). The UK agent
is HMSO, POB 276, London SW8 5DT (trade and mail orders
only) or 49 High Holborn, London WC1V 6HB (callers only) and
other HMSO bookshops
Guides to publications: *Catalogue of UN publications* (annual,
free) lists all publications currently in print of UN bodies and
affiliated agencies whose publications are sold by UN Sales
Sections). *UNDOC: current index (United Nations Documents
Index)* is issued ten times a year and gives comprehensive
coverage of UN documentation, on a subscription basis

**United Nations Conference on Trade and Development
(UNCTAD)**
Address: Palais des Nations, CH-1211 Geneva 10, Switzerland
Telephone: (022) 734 1473/740 0921
Fax: (022) 740 0931
Telex: 289696 CH
Publisher of statistical series: as above
Obtaining publications: most UNCTAD documents are first issued
as mimeographed documents, some of which are later reissued in
printed form and become sales publications. Sales publications
are obtained from the usual UN Sales Sections or agents (see
main UN entry); occasional copies of mimeographed UNCTAD
documents may be obtained from the UNCTAD Editorial Section
at the address above (stocks permitting), quoting the document
number. Subscription orders for mimeographed documents should
be sent directly to the Geneva Sales Section. The complete output
of UNCTAD is also available on microfiche from UN Sales
Sections
Guides to publications: UNCTAD sales publications are included
in the general *Catalogue of United Nations publications*. There is
also an annual *Guide to UNCTAD publications*, which contains
entries in English, French and Spanish and is available from the
UNCTAD Reference Unit, Conference Affairs Service, at the
above address

United Nations Economic Commission for Africa
Address: Africa Hall, PO Box 3001, Addis Ababa, Ethiopia
Telephone: (1) 517200
Telex: 21029
Fax: (1) 514416
Publisher of statistical series: as above
Obtaining publications: available from United Nations Sales
Sections, as described in main United Nations entry
Guides to publications: details included in main *Catalogue of
United Nations publications*

**United Nations Economic Commission for Latin America and
the Caribbean**
Address: Naciones Unidas, Avda Dag Hammerskjöld, Casilla
179d, Santiago, Chile
Telephone: (2) 2085051
Fax: (2) 2080252
Telex: 340295
Publisher of statistical series: as above
Obtaining publications: from main UN Sales Sections as
described in main UN entry; orders from Argentina, Brazil, Bolivia,
Chile, Ecuador, Peru, Paraguay and Uruguay may be sent to
Unidad de Distribución, CEPAL, at the address above
Guides to publications: details of CEPAL publications in English
are included in the English version of the *Catalogue of United
Nations publications*; full details of items published only in Spanish
are given in the Spanish catalogue. There is also a free leaflet
from CEPAL, *Publicaciones de la CEPAL*

United Nations Economic Commission for Western Asia
Address: PO Box 927115, Amman, Jordan
Telephone: 694351
Fax: 694981
Telex: 216917

**United Nations Economic and Social Commission for Asia
and the Pacific**
Address: United Nations Building, Rajdamner Avenue, Bangkok
10200, Thailand
Telephone: (2) 2829161/200
Fax: (2) 2829602
Telex: 82315 ESCAP TH or 82392 ESCAP TH
Publisher of statistical series: as above
Obtaining publications: available from United Nations Sales
Sections as described in main United Nations entry
Guides to publications: details of publications are included in the
main *Catalogue of United Nations publications* (see main UN
entry)

**United Nations Educational, Scientific and Cultural
Organisation (UNESCO)**
Address: 7 place de Fontenoy, F-75700 Paris, France
Telephone: (1) 45681000
Fax: (1) 45671690
Telex: 204461
Guides to publications: UNESCO publications are included in the
general *Catalogue of United Nations publications* (see main UN
entry)

United Nations Industrial Development Organisation (UNIDO)
Address: Vienna International Centre, PO Box 300, A-1400
Vienna, Austria
Telephone: (01) 211310
Fax: (01) 232156
Telex: 135612 A
Publisher of statistical series: as above
Obtaining publications: from UN Sales Sections and agents, as
described in main UN entry
Guides to publications: UNIDO publications are included in the
main *Catalogue of United Nations publications*, and leaflets on
some publications/services are available from UNIDO at the
address above

World Health Organisation (WHO)
Address: Avenue Appia, CH-1211 Geneva 27, Switzerland
Telephone: (022) 791 2111
Fax: (022) 788 0746
Telex: 415416
Obtaining publications: Direct from WHO or HMSO in the UK
Guides to publications: *Catalogue of publications* (free)

World Tourism Organisation (WTO)
Address: Capitan Haya 42, E-28020 Madrid, Spain
Telephone: (91) 571 0628
Fax: (91) 571 3733
Telex: 42188 OMT E
Publisher of statistical series: as above
Obtaining publications: from address above
Guides to publications: *Publications catalogue* (annual, free)

3. National Statistical Offices

AFGHANISTAN
Central Statistics Authority
Address: Block 4, Macroraion, Kubul
Telephone: (93) 24883
Publisher of statistical series: as above

ALGERIA
Office National des Statistiques
Address: 8 rue des Moussebiline, BP55 Algiers
Telephone: (2) 647790/1/2
Telex: 52620
Publisher of statistical series: as above
Obtaining publications: from the address above
Guides to publications: *Catalogue des publications*

ANTIGUA & BARBUDA

Ministry of Finance and Trade
Address: High St, St Johns
Telephone: 462 4860
Fax: 462 1622

ARGENTINA

Instituto Nacional de Estadística y Censos, Secretaría de Planificación
Address: Hipolito Yrigoyen 250, Piso 12, 1310 Buenos Aires
Telephone: (01) 33 7872
Telex: 21952 MINEC AR
Publisher of statistical series: as above
Obtaining publications: from the above address
Guides to publications: Nómina de publicaciones (free sales list)

AUSTRALIA

Australian Bureau of Statistics
Address: PO Box 10, Belconnen, Canberra, ACT 2616
Telephone: (06) 252 7911
Fax: (06) 251 6009
Telex: 71 (06) 262020 AA
Publisher of statistical series: as above
Obtaining publications: from address above
Guides to publications: Catalogue of Publications and Products 19.. (annual, free); *Australian Bureau of Statistics Publications to be released in (Year)* (annual, free); *Publications issued in [name of month]* (monthly, on subscription); *Catalogue of small area statistics Australia* (biennial, priced)

BAHAMAS

Central Bank of the Bahamas
Address: Frederick St, PO Box N-4868, Nassau
Telephone: 322 2193
Fax: 322 4321
Telex: 20115
Publisher of statistical series: as above
Obtaining publications: from address above
Guides to publications: List of publications (free)

BANGLADESH

Bangladesh Bureau of Statistics
Address: 14/2 Topkhana Rd., Dhaka
Telephone: (2) 409871
Publisher of statistical series: as above
Obtaining publications: by post, from address above; publications may also be obtained personally by cash payment from all Regional Statistical Offices of BBS situated at headquarters of former districts, leading booksellers in Dhaka and the following BBS Sale Centres: Shed No 10, Bangladesh Secretariat, Dhaka (telephone (2) 23000/23921/22081) and Ansari Building (2nd floor), 14/2 Topkhana Road, Dhaka (telephone (2) 283503)
Guides to publications: price list of publications is available

BOLIVIA

Instituto Nacional de Estadística
Address: Plaza Mario Guzmán Aspiazu No 1, La Paz, Casilla 6129
Telephone: (02) 367443
Fax: (02) 354230
Telex: 3505

BARBADOS

Barbados Statistical Service
Address: National Insurance Bldg, Fairchild St, Bridgetown
Telephone: 427 7841
Publisher of statistical series: as above

BOTSWANA

Central Statistics Office
Address: Private Bag 0024, Gaborone
Telephone: 352200
Fax: 352201
Publisher of statistical series: as above

Obtaining publications: from the Government Printer, Private Bag 0081, Gaborone, telephone 353202
Guides to publications: none

BRAZIL

Fundaçao Instituto Brasileiro de Geografia e Estatistica - IBGE
Address: Rua Gen Canabarro 666, 20271 Maracana Rio de Janeiro RJ
Telephone: (021) 284 4597
Telex: (021) 34128 IBGEBR
Publisher of statistical series: as above
Obtaining publications: from Antonio Penteado, Gerente, Gerencia de Marketing - GEMAR, Av. Beira Mar 436, 6° andar, 20021 Rio de Janeiro, RJ; tel. (021) 533 3094, telex (021) 30939

BRUNEI

Statistics Section
Address: Economic Planning Unit, Ministry of Finance, Bandar Seri Begawan
Telephone: (2) 241991
Fax: (2) 226132
Telex: 2676 EPUMOF BU
Publisher of statistical series: as above
Obtaining publications: from Information Section, Department of Broadcasting and Information, Jalan Residency, Bandar Seri Begawan; telephone (2) 21872, telex 2614 BRUGOV BU
Guides to publications: price list available

BURUNDI

Service National des Etudes et Statistiques
Address: Ministère du Plan, BP 1156, Bujumbura
Telephone: (2) 12149/25593/22635
Publisher of statistical series: as above
Obtaining publications: from address above
Guides to publications: none

CAMEROON

Direction de la Statistique et de la Comptabilité Nationale
Address: Ministère du Plan et de l'Aménagement du Territoire, Yaoundé
Telephone: 220788
Telex: 8203
Publisher of statistical series: as above
Obtaining publications: from address above

CANADA

Statistics Canada/Statistique Canada
Address: Ottawa, ON K1A OT6
Telephone: (613) 990 8116
Fax: (613) 952 1013
Telex: 053 3585 CA
Publisher of statistical series: as above
Obtaining publications: by mail order from Publication Sales, Room 1710, Main Building, at above address. Publications may also be ordered through regional offices in St John's, Halifax, Montréal, Ottawa, Sturgeon Falls, Toronto, Winnipeg, Regina, Edmonton and Vancouver, or from authorised bookstore agents or other booksellers. Enquiries may be made to any of the regional reference centres (for addresses see Statistics Canada entries in the section on libraries)
Guides to publications: Current publications index (annual catalogue, priced, giving details of all publications except those over ten years old, out of print or discontinued more than one year previously; details of excluded publications are contained in a *Historical catalogue of Statistics Canada publications*; *Selected publications: Statistics Canada* (quarterly, priced); *The Daily* (daily, priced, includes list of titles of publications released); *Infomat* (weekly digest, priced, includes a complete list of publications released during the week)

CHILE

Instituto Nacional de Estadísticas
Address: Avoda Bulnes 418, Casilla 498-3, Corrego 3, Santiago
Telephone: (02) 699 1441

CHINA

State Statistical Bureau, People's Republic of China
Address: 38 Yuetan Nanjie, San Li He, Beijing
Telephone: (1) 81 7410
Telex: 22778 FASSB CN
Publisher of statistical series: China Statistics Publishing House, at the address above; telephone (1) 81 7841
Obtaining publications: from the publisher

COLOMBIA

Departamento Administrativo Nacional de Estadística (DANE)
Address: Apartado Aéreo 80043, Santa Fe de Bogotá, DC
Telephone: (01) 222 1100
Fax: (01) 222 2107
Telex: 44573
Publisher of statistical series: Fondo Rotatorio-DANE, at above address
Obtaining publications: from the División de Promoción, Ventas y Distribución, at the above address
Guides to publications: details of publications given in the quarterly *Boletín de estadística*

ECUADOR

Instituto Nacional de Estadística y Censos
Address: Av. 10 de Agosto no 229, Quito
Telephone: (02) 519597/519320/519130
Fax: (02) 513557
Telex: 21421 INEC ED
Publisher of statistical series: as above
Obtaining publications: from address above
Guides to publications: sales list available

EGYPT

Central Agency for Public Mobilisation and Statistics
Address: PO Box 2086, Nasr City, Cairo
Telephone: (02) 604632
Telex: 92395

ETHIOPIA

Central Statistical Office
Address: PO Box 1143, Addis Ababa
Telephone: (1) 113010
Publisher of statistical series: as above
Obtaining publications: from address above
Guides to publications: free sales list available

FIJI

Bureau of Statistics
Address: PO Box 2221, Government Buildings, Suva
Telephone: 315144
Fax: 303656
Publisher of statistical series: as above
Obtaining publications: from the Government Printer, Printing and Stationery Department, PO Box 98, Suva
Guides to publications: sales list available

GAMBIA

Directorate of Information and Broadcasting
Address: 14 Hagan St, Banjul
Telephone: 27230

GHANA

Central Bureau of Statistics
Address: PO Box 1098, Accra
Telephone: (21) 66512
Telex: 2001 STAR ACCRA GH
Publisher of statistical series: as above
Obtaining publications: from address above

GUATEMALA

Dirección General de Estadistica
Address: 8a Calle 9-55, Zona 1, Edificio America, Guatemala City
Telephone: (02) 26136
Publisher of statistical series: as above
Obtaining publications: from the address above

Guides to publications: sales list available
Publications: statistical yearbook and bulletin, plus general publications on population and census, industry, trade, finance, prices

HONG KONG

Census and Statistics Department
Address: 19/F, Wanchai Tower I, 12 Harbour Road, Hong Kong
Telephone: (5) 445175
Publisher of statistical series: as above
Obtaining publications: orders by post and periodical subscriptions should be sent to the Publications (Sales) Office, Information Services Department, Baskerville House, 2/F, 13 Duddell Street. Publications may be purchased in person from the Department itself at the above address or from the Government Publications Centre, General Post Office Building, G/F., Connaught Place, Central
Guides to publications: *How to obtain statistics*, a free guide which includes a list of publications with brief annotations

INDIA

Central Statistical Organisation
Address: Department of Statistics, Ministry of Planning, Sardar Patel Bhavan, Parliament St, New Delhi-110001
Telephone: (11) 353626
Publisher of statistical series: as above
Obtaining publications: from the Controller of Publications, Civil Lines, Delhi-110054 or authorised agents
Guides to publications: *Guide to official statistics*, which describes recurrent publications and discusses methods of data collection etc; *Statistical system in India*, which outlines the historical development of the system and gives information on statistical offices, personnel etc

Directorate General of Commercial Intelligence and Statistics
Address: 1 Council House Street, Calcutta 700001
Telephone: (33) 283111
Telex: 217902 DGCI&S IN
Publisher of statistical series: Controller of Publications, Ministry of Urban Development, Government of India, Civil Lines, Delhi-110054; tel. (11) 252527/222631/227821
Obtaining publications: from the publisher
Guides to publications: *A guide to current official statistics of trade, shipping and customs and excise revenue of India*

INDONESIA

Central Bureau of Statistics
Address: Jalan Dr Sutomo 8, PO Box 3, Jakarta
Telephone: (21) 363366
Telex: 45159, 45169, 45325, 45375, 45385
Publisher of statistical series: as above
Obtaining publications: from Untuk Diserahkan Kepada, Koperasi Biro Pusat Statistik, Kotak Pos 3, Jakarta Pusat (10002)
Guides to publications: *Daftar buku terhitan/List of publications*

IRAN

Statistical Centre of Iran
Address: Dr Fatemi Avenue, Corner of Rahiye Moayei, Tehran 14144
Telephone: (21) 655061-9
Telex: 088 213233 AMAR IR
Publisher of statistical series: as above
Obtaining publications: from the Bureau of Supervision and International Relations, Statistical Centre of Iran, at the above address
Guides to publications: catalogue of publications is available in Farsi (Persian)

IRAQ

Central Statistical Organisation
Address: Ministry of Planning, Karradat Mariam, ash-Shawaf Sq, Baghdad
Telephone: 537 0071
Telex: 212218

ISRAEL

Central Bureau of Statistics
Address: Hakirya, Romema, Jerusalem 91130
Telephone: (02) 211400
Publisher of statistical series: as above
Obtaining publications: as above
Guides to publications: list of selected publications in English available; catalogue appears annually in Hebrew only

JAMAICA

Planning Institute of Jamaica
Address: 39-43 Barbados Avenue, Kingston 5
Telephone: 926 1480
Fax: 926 4670
Telex: 3529
Publisher of statistical series: Statistical Institute of Jamaica, Printing Unit, 84 Hanover Street, Kingston; telephone 922 8371
Obtaining publications: from the sales office only; 9 Swallowfield Road, PO Box 643, Kingston 5
Guides to publications: publications list and a small *Catalogue of publications and services* available

JAPAN

Statistics Bureau, Management and Coordination Agency, Government of Japan
Address: Kasumigaseki 3-chome, Chiyoda-ku, Tokyo 100
Telephone: (03) 581 6361
Fax: (03) 527 3118
Publisher of statistical series: as above
Obtaining publications: from the Government Publications Service Centre, 1-2-1 Kasumigaseki, Chiyodaku, Tokyo 100
Guides to publications: List of recent publications prepared by the Statistics Bureau, Management and Coordination Agency (free leaflet); *A guide to Statistics Bureau and Statistics Center* (1990; a guide to their organisation and functions, including details of topics covered by the various censuses and surveys)

JORDAN

Department of Statistics
Address: PO Box 2015, Amman
Telephone: 24313
Telex: 24117 STATIS JO
Publisher of statistical series: as above
Obtaining publications: from address above
Guides to publications: price list of periodical publications available

KENYA

Central Bureau of Statistics
Address: PO Box 30266, Nairobi
Telephone: (2) 333970
Publisher of statistical series: as above
Obtaining publications: from the Government Printer, Haile Salassie Avenue, PO Box 30746, Nairobi
Guides to publications: free sales list available; catalogue also available from Government Printer

KUWAIT

Central Statistical Office, Ministry of Planning
Address: PO Box 26188, Safat 13122, Kuwait City
Telephone: 242 8200
Fax: 243 0464
Telex: 22468 TAKHTET KT
Publisher of statistical series: as above
Obtaining publications: from the Department of Publication, Research and Training of the CSO at the above address
Guides to publications: Guide to statistical publications (free); List of publications issued by Central Statistical Office (free)

LIBERIA

Bureau of Statistics
Address: Ministry of Planning and Economic Affairs, PO Box 9016, Monrovia
Telephone: 222622
Telex: 44374 MINPLAN LI

Publisher of statistical series: as above
Obtaining publications: from the Ministry of Planning and Economic Affairs at the above address
Guides to publications: none

LIBYA

Census and Statistical Department
Address: Secretariat of Planning, 40 Sharia Damascus, 2nd floor, Tripoli
Telephone: 31731

MACAU

Direcçao de Serviços de Estatística e Censos
Address: Rua Inácio Baptista, Caixa postal no. 3022, Macau
Telephone: 550935
Fax: 30782
Publisher of statistical series: as above
Obtaining publications: from address above
Guides to publications: *User's Guide of Macau Statistics* free list of publications

MADAGASCAR

Banque des Données de L'Etat
Address: BP 485, Antananarivo
Telephone: 21613

MALAWI

National Statistical Office
Address: PO Box 333, Zomba
Telephone: 522 377
Publisher of statistical series: as above
Obtaining publications: from the address above
Guides to publications: lists of publications printed on the back pages of the *Monthly statistical bulletin*

MALAYSIA

Department of Statistics Malaysia (Jabatan Perangkaan Malaysia)
Address: Wisma Statistik, Jalan Cenderasari, Kuala Lumpur 50514
Telephone: (03) 292 2133
Publisher of statistical series: as above
Obtaining publications: from the above address, orders to be marked for the attention of the Sales Section; some regional publications (marked in the Department's *List of publications*) must be purchased from branch offices in Sabah and Sarawak
Guides to publications: *List of publications* (annual, free)

MAURITIUS

Central Statistical Office
Address: Toorawa Centre, cnr Sir Seewoosagur Ramgoolam and J. Mosque Sts, Port Louis
Telephone: 42088
Publisher of statistical series: as above
Obtaining publications: from address above
Guides to publications: leaflet available

MEXICO

Instituto Nacional de Estadística, Geografía y Informatica
Address: Av. Prolongación Héroe de Nacozari No. 2301, Sur CP 20290 Ciudad Industrial, Aguascalientes
Telephone: (491) 687 4691/2911
Publisher of statistical series: as above
Obtaining publications: from the headquarters address or from a network of regional offices (leaflet available giving a full list)
Guides to publications: *Catalogo de publicaciones INEGI*, plus leaflets on some individual publications

MOROCCO

Direction de la Statistique
Address: Charia Ma-Al-Ainain, BP 178, Rabat
Telephone: 73606
Telex: 32714 M
Publisher of statistical series: as above
Obtaining publications: from the address above

Guides to publications: Catalogue des publications de la Direction de la Statistique (annual, free)

MYANMAR

Central Statistical Organisation
Address: Ministry of Planning and Finance, Yangon
Telephone: (1) 76066
Publisher of statistical series: as above
Obtaining publications: from address above

NEW ZEALAND

Department of Statistics
Address: Aorangi House, 85 Molesworth St., Wellington 1
Telephone: (4) 495 4600
Fax: (4) 472 9135
Telex: 31313 STATSWN NZ
Publisher of statistical series: as above
Obtaining publications: from Publication Services at the above address, or through Government bookshops; enquiries about availability, cost etc are also dealt with by Publication Services. Standing orders and subscriptions are available through the Government Printing Office, Publishing Warehouse, PO Box 14277, Kilbirnie, Wellington, telephone (4) 872169/877018
Guides to publications: Statistics - publications catalogue (annual, free); *Statistics - product index* (free annual list of services and products of the Department); *Micrographics catalogue* (free list of all information available on microfiche); *Statistics - the people to ask* (free list published six-monthly showing who to ask for information on particular subjects within the Department)

NIGERIA

Federal Office of Statistics
Address: 7 Okotie-Eboh St, SW Ikoyi, Lagos
Telephone: 682935
Publisher of statistical series: as above
Obtaining publications: from address above
Guides to publications: sales list available

OMAN

Oman Directorate-General of National Statistics
Address: Development Council, PO Box 881, Muscat
Telephone: 698900
Telex: 5384

PAKISTAN

Federal Bureau of Statistics
Address: Statistics Division, 1-Sindhi Muslim Co-operative Housing Society, Karachi-3
Telephone: (021) 439101/439246
Publisher of statistical series: as above
Obtaining publications: non-priced publications are available from the Federal Bureau of Statistics (Publication and Publicity Section) at the above address; priced publications are obtainable from the Manager of Publications, Federal Publications Branch, Government of Pakistan, Stationery and Forms Office Building, University Road, Karachi-5, telephone (21) 411127 or 411586, or agents (agents include all Pakistan Missions abroad)
Guides to publications: Catalogue of publications (usually annual, free). New publications are also notified in the *FBS newsletter* (monthly)

PAPUA NEW GUINEA

National Statistical Office
Address: PO Wards Strip, Waigani
Telephone: 271705
Telex: 22144
Fax: 255057
Publisher of statistical series: as above
Obtaining publications: from address above
Guides to publications: sales list available

PARAGUAY

Dirección General de Estadística y Censos
Address: Humaitá 473, Asunción
Telephone: (21) 47900

Publisher of statistical series: as above
Obtaining publications: from address above
Guides to publications: none

PERU

Instituto Nacional de Estadística
Address: Avenida 28 de Julio 1056, Lima 1
Telephone: (41) 320237

PHILIPPINES

National Census and Statistics Office
Address: Solicarel 1, Magsaysay, Blvd., Cnr Ampil, PO Box 779, Manila
Telephone: (2) 613645
Fax: (2) 610794
Publisher of statistical series: as above
Obtaining publications: from address above or from Asia World Data Marketing Factors, 92-C South Avenue (Timog), Diliman, Quezon City, telephone 922 9968/922 6843
Guides to publications: sales list issued by Asia World Data Marketing Factors

QATAR

Central Statistical Organisation
Address: Ministry of Information, PO Box 5747, Doha
Telephone: 497497
Telex: 4552
Publisher of statistical series: as above
Obtaining publications: from address above
Guides to publications: none
Publications: No charge is made for any publications, except for postage

RWANDA

Direction Générale de la Statistique
Address: BP 83, Kigali
Telephone: 5665
Publisher of statistical series: as above
Obtaining publications: from the address above
Guides to publications: subscription leaflets available

SAUDI ARABIA

Central Department of Statistics, Ministry of Finance
Address: PO Box 3735, Riyadh
Telephone: (1) 402 9120/5360
Telex: 201021 FINANS SJ
Publisher of statistical series: as above
Obtaining publications: from address above
Guides to publications: none

SENEGAL

Direction de la Statistique
Address: Centre Compatable Andre Peytavin, rue Charles Laisne et ave Carde, BP 452, Dakar
Telephone: 226550
Telex: 61203
Publisher of statistical series: as above
Obtaining publications: from address above

SEYCHELLES

Department of Information and Telecommunications
Address: Union Vale, PO Box 321, Victoria
Telephone: 24220
Fax: 25339
Telex: 2320
Publisher of statistical series: as above
Obtaining publications: from address above
Guides to publications: price list available

SINGAPORE

Department of Statistics
Address: Office: 8 Shenton Way, 10-01 Treasury Building, Singapore 0106. Correspondence: Maxwell Road, PO Box 3010, Singapore 9050
Telephone: 3209686

Fax: 320 9689
Telex: 63001
Publisher of statistical series: as above
Obtaining publications: from the Department; there is also a sales outlet: Singapore National Printers Ltd (Publications Sales Division), 8 Shenton Way, B1-07 Treasury Building, Singapore 0106
Guides to publications: sales list available

SOUTH AFRICA

Central Statistical Service
Address: Steyns Arcade, 274 Schoeman St, Private Bag X44, Pretoria, 0001
Telephone: (12) 3108911
Fax: (12) 3108500
Telex: 320450 or 320173 SA
Publisher of statistical series: Government Printer, Private Bag X85, Pretoria 0001, telephone (12) 3239731
Obtaining publications: Publications obtainable from the Government Printer, Statistical news releases from the Central Statistical Service
Guides to publications: User guide, free brochure giving brief description of the publications and statistical news releases

SOUTH KOREA

National Bureau of Statistics, Economic Planning Board
Address: 90 Gyeongun-dong, Jongro-gu, Seoul 110-310
Telephone: (2) 7202788/7202789
Fax: (2) 7364298
Telex: 23202 DPMEPB K
Publisher of statistical series: as above
Obtaining publications: from the Korean Statistical Association, Room 512, Gohap Building, 89-4 Gyeongun-dong, Jongro-gu, Seoul

SRI LANKA

Department of Census and Statistics
Address: PO Box 563, 6 Albert Crescent, Colombo 7
Telephone: (1) 565291
Publisher of statistical series: as above
Obtaining publications: from The Superintendent, Government Publications Bureau, Colombo 1
Guides to publications: Annotated bibliography of the Departmental publications (priced)

SUDAN

Department of Statistics
Address: Ministry of Finance, PO Box 700, Khartoum
Telephone: 77003

SYRIA

Central Bureau of Statistics
Address: Abdel Malek Bin Marwan Str., Melki Quarter, Damascus
Telephone: (11) 335830/33
Telex: 411099 STC SY
Publisher of statistical series: as above
Obtaining publications: directly from the Central Bureau of Statistics
Guides to publications: list of publications and prices available

TAIWAN

Bureau of Statistics, Directorate-General of Budget, Accounting and Statistics, Executive Yuan
Address: 2 Kwang Chow Street, Taipei 10729
Telephone: (2) 3117147
Fax: (02) 3319925
Publisher of statistical series: as above
Obtaining publications: from the DGBAS, 1 Chung Hsiao East Road, Section 1, Taipei; some publications also available from other sales agents (details given under those publications)
Guides to publications: lists available in some publications, including *National conditions of the Republic of China* and *Monthly statistics of the Republic of China*

TANZANIA

Bureau of Statistics
Address: Ministry of Planning and Economic Affairs, Dar es Salaam
Telephone: (51) 22722, 28147
Publisher of statistical series: as above
Obtaining publications: from address above

THAILAND

National Statistical Office
Address: Larn Luang Road, Bangkok 10100
Telephone: (2) 281 3022
Fax: (2) 281 3814
Publisher of statistical series: as above
Obtaining publications: from address above
Guides to publications: sales list available

TRINIDAD AND TOBAGO

Central Statistical Office
Address: 23 Park Street, PO Box 98, Port of Spain
Telephone: 625 3705
Publisher of statistical series: Central Statistical Office Printing Unit, at above address
Obtaining publications: from above address, or from Government Printers
Guides to publications: List of publications

TUNISIA

Institut National de la Statistique
Address: 70 rue EC-CHAM, BP 260, 1002 Tunis-Belvedère
Telephone: (1) 282500
Publisher of statistical series: as above
Obtaining publications: list available
Publications: statistical yearbooks and monthly bulletin; surveys on population and census, trade, income and expenditure

UNITED ARAB EMIRATES

Ministry of Planning
Address: PO Box 1134, Sharjah
Telephone: (6) 22704
Publisher of statistical series: as above
Obtaining publications: the Ministry does not sell its publications, but copies are available locally free of charge; the Director of Publications is Mr Rashid Abd Al-Rahman Laflity
Guides to publications: none

UNITED STATES OF AMERICA

Bureau of the Census
Address: US Department of Commerce, Washington, DC 20233
Telephone: (301) 763 4100
Telex: 892536 (Department of Commerce)
Publisher of statistical series: as above
Obtaining publications: some publications (marked in catalogues) are available from Customer Services, Data User Services Division, at the above address; all others are available from the US Government Printing Office (GPO), Washington, DC 20402, telephone (202) 783 3238
Guides to publications: Census catalogue and guide (annual, free, describing all products); *Monthly product announcement* (free monthly listing of new products)

URUGUAY

Centro de Estadísticas Nacionales y Comercio Internacional (CENCI-Uruguay SRL)
Address: Misiones 1361, Piso 2, Esc. 17, Montevideo
Telephone: (02) 952939/954578
Publisher of statistical series: as above
Obtaining publications: from address above

Dirección General de Estadística y Censos
Address: Cuareim 2052, Montevideo
Telephone: (02) 201105
Publisher of statistical series: as above

Obtaining publications: from address above
Publications: statistical yearbook and monthly bulletin; demographic publications; quarterly and annual industrial surveys

VENEZUELA

Oficina Central de Estadística e Informatica
Address: Av. Boyacá, Edif. Fundación La Salle, (Maripérez), Caracas
Telephone: (2) 782 1133
Fax: (2) 782 2243
Telex: 21241
Publisher of statistical series: as above
Obtaining publications: publications available from various government ministries and offices; list available from OCEI at the above address
Guides to publications: Price list available with titles of main publications

VIETNAM

General Statistical Office
Address: Hanoi

ZAMBIA

Central Statistical Office
Address: PO Box 31908, Lusaka
Telephone: (1) 211231
Telex: 40430
Publisher of statistical series: as above
Obtaining publications: from address above
Guides to publications: free sales list available

ZIMBABWE

Central Statistical Office
Address: Kaguui Bldg, Fourth St PO Box 8063, Causeway, Harare
Telephone: (4) 706681
Publisher of statistical series: as above
Obtaining publications: from the address above
Guides to publications: price list of statistical publications currently available

4. Major Business Libraries

ALGERIA

Bibliothèque Nationale
Address: 1 Av. Frantz Fanon, 16000 Algiers
Telephone: (2) 631049
Enquiries: Mohamed Aissa-Oumoussa (director)
Availability: open to the public
Hours: 08.30 - 20.30 Saturday to Thursday
Stock: material in Arabic, French, and English covering North Africa, Arabic countries, Europe, particularly France. 188,000 journal titles, 360,000 books, microfilms
Services: photocopying, loans, enquiry service
Publications: Bibliographie de l'Algérie (2 p.a.; US$22)
Notes: The library is due to move to a purpose-built building at the end of 1993.

ANTIGUA AND BARBUDA

Organisation of Eastern Caribbean States (OECS), Economic Affairs, Secretariat Documentation Centre
Address: PO Box 822, St John's, Barbuda
Telephone: (809) 4623500
Fax: (809) 4621537
Telex: 2157 ECONSEC AK
Enquiries: Sue Evan-Wong (manager, documentation centre), Claudette de Freitas (documentalist)
Availability: for reference only
Hours: 08.30 - 16.30 Monday to Friday
Stock: covers agriculture, tourism, manufacturing, industry, trade, trade policies, energy with special reference to the OECS. Material in English. Includes annual and financial accounts for organisations within the OECS sub-region; company and trade directories (Caribbean); trade journals; other journals; statistics

(OECS and other Caribbean countries); books (8,000); local, OECS regional, Caribbean newspapers; audio-visual materials
Services: photocopying, enquiry service, database searches
Publications: Current Awareness Bulletin (quarterly); *Select Bibliography* (semi-annually)

ARGENTINA

Banco Central de la República Argentina, Biblioteca Dr Raul Prebisch
Address: Reconquista 266, 1003 Capital Federal
Telephone: (1) 394 9031 or (1) 394 9021, ext 561
Telex: 33-24031 BCFEX AR, 33-24035 BCATD AR
Enquiries: Alfredo C Rodriguez, Departamento de Biblioteca y Publicaciones
Stock: covers banking, economics, industrial policy, demography etc

Biblioteca de la Fundación de Investigaciones Económicas Latinoamericanas (FIEL)
Address: Esmeralda 320, Piso 4°, 1343 Capital Federal
Telephone: (1) 351733
Fax: (1) 3962727
Availability: open to the public
Hours: 09.00-13.00, 14.00-17.00 Monday to Friday
Stock: 5,000 volumes covering economics, social sciences, mathematical economics, agricultural economics etc
Services: photocopying, online searches

Biblioteca "Estanislao S Zeballos"
Address: Br. Oroño 1261, 2000 Rosario, Santa Fé
Telephone: (042) 212287, 218642, 219833, 45598, exts 53, 54
Enquiries: Oscar Matías López (Director)
Availability: open to the public, free of charge
Hours: 07.00-21.00 Monday to Friday, 07.00-13.00 Saturday
Stock: over 107,000 books and 1,000 periodical titles covering economics, accountancy, business administration, statistics
Services: home borrowing, to teachers and university graduates only
Publications: Boletín de Obras (bulletin on accessions); *Síntesis Bibliografica de Publicaciones Periódicas* (index to periodical publications); *Aportes Bibliograficos* (bibliographical contributions)

Biblioteca INDEC (Instituto Naciónal de Estadística y Censos)
Address: Avda Julio A Roca 609, PB 1067, Buenos Aires
Telephone: (01) 343 0072
Fax: (1) 343 0564
Enquiries: Mabel Saccavino de Roca
Availability: open to the public
Hours: 13.30-18.30 Monday to Friday
Stock: statistical material, census and sample census material
Services: loans, enquiry service

Instituto Torcuato di Tella, Biblioteca de Ciencias Sociales
Address: 11 de Setiembre 2139, 1428 Buenos Aires
Telephone: (01) 7817051/53
Fax: (01) 786 2636
Enquiries: Ricardo Rodríguez Pereyra (Director)
Availability: private library, but open to external users for reference purposes
Hours: 09.00-17.00 Monday to Friday
Stock: 60,000 books and 1,400 periodical titles in the field of social sciences
Services: photocopying, online searches, inter-library loans

Presidencia de la Nación, Secretaría de Planificación, Biblioteca
Address: Hipólito Yrigoyen 250, Piso 8°, Of. 801/C, 1310 Buenos Aires
Telephone: (01) 331 1121 (direct line), (01) 346411 exts 443, 605 (via switchboard)
Enquiries: Araceli García Acosta (Director), Morín Mastandrea (Head of Documentation Centre), Stella Zoppi (Head of Library)
Availability: open to the general public
Hours: 14.00-18.00 Monday to Friday
Stock: project evaluation (1,300 volumes), economic and social planning (about 3,000 volumes), economics (about 5,000 volumes); coverage includes industrial, agricultural, transport sectors etc. Deposit library for World Bank publications
Services: inter-library loans, selective bibliographies

Publications: *Boletín bibliográfico* (annual bibliographic bulletin); *Bibliografía evaluación de proyectos* (bibliography of project evaluation)

Universidad Nacional de Cordoba, Biblioteca Mayor, Centro de Documentación
Address: Obispo Trejo 243, Casilla Correo 63, 5000 Córdoba
Telephone: (051) 46323/24442
Fax: (051) 37841
Telex: 51822 BUCOR AR
Enquiries: Coralia Oro, Elena Rodriguez, Lilia Montenegro
Availability: open to the public: identity document required
Hours: 08.00-20.00 Monday to Friday
Stock: about 160,000 books and 3,560 periodical titles. Includes internal and external trade statistics published by the Instituto Naciónal de Estadística y Censos, industrial and internal trade statistics published by the Secretary of State for Industry and Trade, and export statistics published by the Ministry of Industry of Industry, Trade and Mining
Services: bibliographies, reference, loans, telex
Publications: *Boletín de la Biblioteca*; *Memoria anual*; *Tesis de la Escuela de Bibliotecarios de la Universidad Naciónal de Córdoba* (theses of the Cordoba University School of Librarianship)

Universidad Nacional de la Plata, Biblioteca Pública
Address: Plaza Rocha 137, 1900 La Plata
Telephone: (021) 214109
Telex: 31151 BULAP AR
Enquiries: Prof. Rosa Z Pisarello
Availability: open to the public without restrictions
Hours: 07.30-21.00 Monday to Friday, 08.00-12.30 Saturday; closed in January
Stock: about 500,000 volumes of books and 450,000 volumes of periodicals covering all subjects; special collection of newspapers from nineteenth century to current year
Services: photocopying, loans, reference, local head of CONICET network of scientific information
Publications: *Informaciones*; occasional bibliographies

AUSTRALIA

Australian Bureau of Statistics Library
Address: PO Box 10, Belconnen, ACT 2616
Telephone: (06) 252 6090
Fax: (06) 253 1404
Telex: 62020 AA
Enquiries: Margaret Pitt (Chief Librarian)
Availability: not open to the general public, but the reading room may be used by prior arrangement for material not available elsewhere. Small libraries in the State Offices are open to the public; their collections are mostly ABS publications
Hours: 09.30-16.00 Monday to Friday
Stock: about 38,000 monographs and 8,000 active serials; subjects covered include statistical methodology, material with statistical content with emphasis on Australia and the Pacific and South-East Asia regions and the major industrial countries, economics and social matters relevant to the collection of statistics, computers and computing. Also an archive collection of all ABS publications, the state statistical agencies prior to integration with the Commonwealth Office and all colonial official statistics
Services: inter-library loans, database searches
Publications: several bulletins, mainly for internal use

Australian Customs Service Library
Address: 117 Clarence Street, 7th Floor, PO Box 8, Sydney, NSW 2001
Telephone: (2) 270 7135
Fax: (2) 226 5995
Telex: 21882 AA
Enquiries: the Librarian
Availability: open to the public for reference; borrowing restricted to department personnel and inter-library lending
Hours: 08.30-16.15 Monday to Friday
Stock: 5,000 monographs and 250 periodicals, covering customs administration, personnel management, Australian law; collections of Australian Tariff and Industries Assistance Commission Reports
Services: photocopying, inter-library loans, reference enquiries

Australian Graduate School of Management
Address: PO Box 1, Kensington, NSW 2033
Telephone: (2) 662 0390
Fax: (2) 662 2451
Enquiries: Pamela Taylor
Availability: open to the public (limited seating available)
Hours: 08.00-19.00 Monday, Tuesday, Thursday, 08.00-.18.00 Wednesday, Friday, 12.00-.18.00 Saturday
Stock: 20,000 monographs and 800 serials, 40,000 annual reports of Australian and New Zealand companies
Services: photocopying, loans, inter-library loans, enquiry service, online searches
Publications: *Australian Business Ranking Index* and index to Australian financial data routinely available in the press and online

Australian National University, Library
Address: GPO Box 4, Canberra, ACT 2601
Telephone: (06) 249 5111
Fax: (06) 249 0734
Telex: 62760 NATUNI AA
Enquiries: C R Steele (University Librarian)
Availability: primarily for use of members of the university, but open to general public for reference, subject to approval by the Librarian
Hours: main reading rooms open 09.00-22.00 Monday to Thursday, 09.00-17.00 Friday, 13.00-18.00 Saturday, Sunday
Stock: total of about 1.5 million volumes; includes collection in printed and electronic form of government publications in the Official Documents Collection
Services: loans, enquiry service (free of charge), photocopying and online searching (charged for)
Publications: occasional papers on library topics

Australian Wool Corporation, Library
Address: PO Box 4867, Melbourne, Victoria 3001 (369 Royal Parade, Parkville, Victoria 3052)
Telephone: (3) 341 9416
Telex: 30548 AA
Availability: open to the public
Enquiries: Mr Henning Rasmussen
Availability: open to the public, preferably by appointment
Hours: 09.00-17.15 Monday to Friday
Stock: 2,500 monographs, 1,700 periodicals, 6,500 pamphlets, 100 videos; covers economics, fashion, management, marketing research, statistics, textile industry and trade, wool
Services: photocopying, inter-library loans, bibliography compilation, reference service
Publications: daily current awareness list, bibliographies and reading lists, video catalogue

National Library of Australia
Address: Parkes Place, Canberra, ACT 2600
Telephone: (06) 2621111
Fax: (06) 257 1703
Telex: 62100 LIBAUST AA
Enquiries: (62) 621266
Availability: open to the public; readers' tickets are required only for the Petherick (Advanced Studies) Reading Room and for the Rare Books and Manuscripts Reading Room
Hours: 09.00-21.00 Monday to Thursday, 09.00-16.45 Friday & Saturday, 13.30-16.45 Sunday. Some specialised reading rooms not open evenings and weekends
Stock: over 4.5 million volumes including microforms, plus serials, newspapers, manuscripts, pictorial items, music scores, films and videos, and oral history and folklore tapes. Includes government and official publications from Australia and overseas. Particular emphasis on Australia
Services: reference services, inter-library loans, online searches, exhibitions, national bibliographical services, and management of the National Bibliographic Database (accessed through the Australian Bibliographic Network)
Publications: many publications, listed in *National Library of Australia publications in print*; *Current awareness bulletins: area studies* (irregular, free)

Patent, Trade Marks and Designs Office Library
Address: Librarian, Patent Office, PO Box 200, Scarborough House, Woden, ACT 2606

Telephone: (06) 283 2304 (librarian), (06) 283 2305 (inter-library loans)
Telex: 61517 COMPAT AA
Enquiries: Ms Jean Geue (Librarian)
Availability: open to the public
Hours: 10.00-16.00 Monday to Friday
Stock: 14,000 books and 1,500 journals; covers all science, all technology, patents, trade marks and designs - stock includes official patent journals from all countries with a patent system. Patent abstracts and specifications are held by the Documentation Service
Services: copies of patents from Sales Unit, (62) 83255

State Library and Information Service of Western Australia, Business Information Centre
Address: Alexander Library Building, Perth Cultural Centre, Perth, WA 6000
Telephone: (9) 427 3111
Fax: (9) 427 3256
Telex: 92231 WAINF AA
Enquiries: Peter Bloomfield, Carol Smith
Availability: open to the public
Hours: 09.00-17.30 Monday, Friday, 09.00-21.45 Tuesday to Thursday, 14.00-17.30 Saturday, Sunday; staffed 09.00-17.00 Monday to Friday
Stock: national and international trade directories, telephone directories, financial newspapers and journals (international collection), containing financial, company and commodity information. Sources of company information, eg *Moody's International Manual, Principal International Businesses, Australian Graduate School of Management company annual report file* (on microfiche), *Sydney Stock Exchange Research Service on Australian Companies*
Services: free confidential information service, photocopying (self-service coin machine)

State Library of New South Wales
Address: Macquarie Street, Sydney, NSW 2000
Telephone: (2) 230 1414
Fax: (2) 233 2003
Telex: 121150 NSW GLH AA72233
Enquiries: Therese Lake (2) 230 1602
Availability: reading rooms open to the public; use of special collections requires a reader's ticket
Hours: General Reference Library: 09.00-21.00 Monday to Saturday, 14.00-18.00 Sunday; Mitchell Library: 09.00-21.00 Monday to Friday, 09.00-17.00 Saturday; Dixson Library: 09.00-17.00 Monday to Friday, by appointment
Stock: about three million items including special collections. General Reference Library strong in applied science and technology, bibliography (published and automated), modern history, biography, government publications
Services: photocopying, inter-library loans; online searches available to business, industry, government departments, organisations and individuals

Publications: Annual report; Directory of services; Research Service bibliographies (lists of bibliographies produced and recorded on cards); selected bibliographies are published

State Library of Queensland
Address: William Street, Brisbane, Queensland 4000
Telephone: (7) 221 8400
Telex: 41731 STLIBQ AA
Enquiries: Brian Patterson
Availability: open to the public
Hours: 10.00-21.30 Monday to Friday, 10.00-17.00 Saturday, 13.30-17.00 Sunday and public holidays
Stock: substantial bookstock covering many fields of industry, commerce and technology; reference collection includes directories, handbooks, yearbooks, indexes and abstracts, statistical publications, Australian and overseas telephone directories. Large collection of periodical and serial titles as well as government publications from official sources in Australia and overseas, plus strong collection of publications from international organisations, eg OECD, EC, UN and its allied agencies. Also

major Australian newspapers and selected overseas titles
Services: photocopying, inter-library loans, enquiry service, online searches

State Library of South Australia
Address: PO Box 419, North Terrace, Adelaide, South Australia 5001
Telephone: (8) 223 8911; 223 8735 (Reference), 223 8768 (Lending)
Telex: 82074 PUBLIB AA
Enquiries: Kaj Lindstrom (Reference Manager), Michael Talbot (Research Services Librarian)
Availability: access to the collections for reference is free and universal
Hours: 09.30-18.00 Monday, 09.30-21.30 Tuesday to Friday, 09.30-17.00 Saturday, 13.00-17.00 Sunday
Stock: 470,000 monograph volumes, 16,000 bound serials, 84,000 map sheets, covering all subject areas to representative level (except law and medicine). Ready reference collection includes business directories, trade directories, product directories (such as *Kompass* and *Thomas Register*), update service publications on tax and law (such as *Australian Company Law*), and international telephone directories
Services: photocopying, photographic and micrographic reproduction of collection items, limited special loans, phone and personal enquiry service, online searches (DIALOG, AUSINET, WILSONLINE)
Publications: Pinpointer: current subject guide to popular periodicals (bimonthly index and annual cumulation); occasional publications in history and bibliography

State Library of Victoria, Business Information Service
Address: 328 Swanston Street, Melbourne, Victoria 3000
Telephone: (3) 669 9845
Enquiries: Kerrie Carstensen (Business Information Librarian)
Availability: open to the public without restrictions
Hours: Business Information Service: 09.00-17.00 Monday to Friday; State Library of Victoria: 10.00-22.00 Monday to Friday, 10.00-18.00 Saturday, Sunday
Stock: extensive collection of Australian directories; emphasis on statistics and product/company information. Australian government publications and Australian newspapers collected in depth
Services: enquiry and research service, including online searching; inter-library loans

Technology and Industrial Development Authority
(formerly Department of Industrial Development)
Address: 8th Floor, 170 St George's Terrace, Perth, WA 6000
Telephone: (9) 327 5555 ext 608/593
Fax: (9) 327 5542
Telex: 95681 DEVWA AA
Enquiries: Mrs Janine Douglas
Availability: open to the public for reference and research only; public may not borrow directly from library, but must make use of inter-library loans service through their own local or company library
Hours: 08.15-16.30 Monday to Friday
Stock: over 6,000 monographs, 200 journals, reports, cassettes, videos, newspapers, Australian Bureau of Statistics material, annual reports, Departmental publications; covers manufacturing, Australian industries, economics, management, defence, marketing, technology, CAD/CAM, QA, QC
Services: photocopies, facsimile transmission, microfiche reader/printer, online searches (AUSINET, VIATEL, ABN, DIALOG), loans, reference service, current awareness service
Publications: Library bulletin

University of Melbourne Library
Address: University of Melbourne, Parkville, Victoria 3052
Telephone: (3) 344 5377
Fax: (3) 348 1142
Telex: 30815 AA
Enquiries: Information Services Librarian
Availability: open to the public; borrowing privileges only available to University members, and approved borrowers
Hours: term: 08.45-23.00 Monday to Thursday, 08.45-18.15 Friday, 13.00-17.00 Saturday, Sunday; summer vacation:

08.45-17.00 Monday, Tuesday, Thursday, Friday, 08.45-21.00 Wednesday
Stock: about 2.48 million volumes
Services: photocopying, loans, reference service, online searches, inter-library loans
Publications: infoguides on holdings and services; *University of Melbourne Library collection development policy; Annual report*

University of New South Wales, Library. Social Sciences and Humanities Library
Address: PO Box 1, Kensington, NSW 2033 (location: Anzac Parade, Kensington, NSW 2033)
Telephone: (2) 697 2659/2677/2222/2670
Fax: (2) 662 1203
Telex: 20467 UNITECH AA
Enquiries: Patricia Howard (Social Sciences and Humanities Librarian)
Availability: open to members of the public, but only members of the University may borrow
Hours: 08.30-22.00 Monday to Thursday, 08.30-18.00 Friday, 12.00-18.00 Saturday, Sunday and public holidays; reduced hours during vacations, ie July, December-February
Stock: total stock 1.4 million volumes, Social Sciences and Humanities Library stock about 500,000 volumes. Subjects covered include economics, accounting, business, marketing, organisational behaviour, industrial relations, finance, banking, computerised information systems. Australian census and statistical publications held in hard copy and microfiche
Services: reference services, loans (university members only), photocopying, online computer searches (on cost recovery basis), inter-library loans (university members only)

BAHAMAS

Nassau Public Library
Address: Shirley Street, PO Box N-3210, Nassau
Telephone: 322 4907
Enquiries: Vanrea Thomas-Rolle (Director)
Availability: open to residents by annual subscription and to visitors by deposit and subscription
Hours: 10.00-21.00 Monday to Friday, 10.00-17.00 Saturday
Stock: about 60,000 volumes, with special emphasis on local materials, Bahamas Government documents (and fiction). Caribbean materials quite extensive. Stock includes general marketing and business materials
Services: photocopying, loans, enquiry and research service, reservations

BAHRAIN

Manama Public Library
Address: PO Box 43, Manama
Telephone: 258400 ext 212
Telex: 9094
Enquiries: Directorate of public library
Availability: open to the public
Hours: 12 hours daily except Friday
Stock: 160,000 volumes
Services: photocopying, loans, enquiry service, microfiche
Publications: Monthly newsletter

University of Bahrain Library
Address: PO Box 1082, Manama
Telephone: 682748
Telex: 9258 UCOBAH BN

BANGLADESH

Bangladesh Institute of Development Studies Library
Address: E-17, West Agargaon, Sher-E-Bangla Nagar, Dhaka-7 (PO Box 3854)
Telephone: (2) 313536/325041-2/02
Fax: (2) 813023
Enquiries: Serajul Haque (Chief Librarian)
Availability: reading facilities are free; associate membership is available on payment of requisite fee
Hours: 07.30-17.00 Saturday to Thursday
Stock: 100,000 volumes on all aspects of social science, including some collections on marketing and business information
Services: photocopying, loans, enquiry service, abstracting, bibliography
Publications: about 100 bibliographies on different aspects of social sciences

National Library of Bangladesh
Address: Sher-E-Bangla Nagar, Agargaon, Dhaka 1207
Telephone: (2) 326572/313969/312733
Enquiries: Md. Shahabuddin Kahan (Assistant Director)
Availability: open to all, but should register as member of the library
Hours: 09.00-14.00 Saturday to Thursday
Stock: collections cover all subjects
Services: photocopying
Publications: publish the national bibliography and an index to periodical articles

BARBADOS

Barbados Export Promotion Corporation, Trade Information Centre
Address: Pelican Industrial Park, St Michael
Telephone: 427 5752/5/8/9
Telex: 392 2486 WB
Fax: 427 5867
Enquiries: Peggy Griffith (Assistant Director Operations), Veona Maloney (Librarian/Marketing Adviser)
Availability: intended to meet the needs of Barbadian exporters, but also used by researchers and students
Stock: general data on overseas markets, economic and trade statistics, names of manufacturers, importers and distributors overseas, information on individual products in over 100 selected product periodicals
Services: enquiry service by telephone, letter or personal visit; photocopying, telex and translation facilities; fashion information service on the men's, women's and children's fashion industry

Central Bank of Barbados Library
Address: Treasury Bldg, PO Box 1016, Bridgetown
Telephone: (809) 436 6870
Telex: 251

Central Public Library
Address: Coleridge Street, Bridgetown
Telephone: 426 1744
Availability: open to the public; all services available to visitors
Hours: 09.00-17.00 Monday to Saturday
Stock: includes a reference department

BOLIVIA

Centro de información y documentación del sector informal urbano (CIDSIU)
Address: Casilla de Correo 8630, La Paz
Telephone: (2) 360223
Enquiries: Maria Renee Rivero Flores
Availability: open to the public for reference only
Hours: 08.30 - 15.30 Monday to Friday
Stock: covers small businesses; retail trade, credit, employment, commercialisation, law, handicrafts and business; the material is in Spanish and English. The stock includes financial and company information for Bolivia; company and trade directories for Latin America; statistics; books (700); newspapers
Services: photocopying; searches; services

BOTSWANA

Botswana National Library
Address: Private Bag 0036, Gaborone, Botswana
Telephone: 352288/352397
Enquiries: the Director
Availability: open to the public without restriction
Hours: 09.00-18.00
Stock: total of 45,000 adult non-fiction books, including about 900 on business and marketing. The Gaborone library maintains the major collection of reference books in the National Reference Library, which includes books published in Botswana acquired by legal deposit; it is also a deposit library for publications of the United Nations and its agencies

Services: photocopying, enquiry service
Publications: *National bibliography of Botswana*; *BONESA* (current information on the library service in Botswana)

BRAZIL

Banco do Brasil SA - CACEX, Setor de Documentaçao
Address: Praca Pio X, 54-Sobreloja, 20091-040 Rio de Janeiro RJ
Telephone: (021) 216 0324
Telex: (021) 23753 BBSA BR, (021) 51178 BBSA BR
Enquiries: Rosane Nicolau Santos
Availability: open to the public
Hours: 10.00-16.30 Monday to Friday
Stock: 10,250 book titles and 298 periodical titles, specialising in foreign trade and related subjects: economy, statistics, legislation etc
Services: photocopying, enquiry service
Publications: *Boletim de documentaçao* (quarterly index to periodical articles)

Biblioteca Karl A Boedecker, Fundaçao Getúlio Vargas, Escola de Administraçao de Empresas de Sao Paulo
Address: Avenida Nove de Julho 2029, 01313 Sao Paulo, SP
Telephone: (011) 284 2311 exts 252/215
Telex: (011) 53148 FGVE BR
Enquiries: José Domingos de Brito
Availability: open to the public for reference and for telephone enquiries
Hours: 08.30-22.00 Monday to Friday, 09.00-17.30 Saturday
Stock: 8,000 books and 530 current periodicals covering administration, economics and marketing
Services: photocopying, loans, enquiry service
Publications: *Boletim bibliográfico* (list of recent acquisitions); *Sumário de periódicos* (current contents of periodicals)

Biblioteca Nacional, Seçao de Informaçao Documental
Address: Avenida Rio Branco 219, 20042 Rio de Janeiro, RJ
Telephone: (021) 240 8929
Fax: (021) 2204173
Telex: (021) 22941 BR
Enquiries: Eliane Perez
Availability: open to the public
Hours: 09.00-20.00 Monday to Friday, 09.00-15.00 Saturday
Stock: about seven million volumes, covering all subjects
Services: reference, reproduction (photocopying and microfilm), inter-library loans, information service
Publications: *Bibliografia Brasileira*

FEA/USP, Serviço de Biblioteca e Documentaçao
Address: Universidade de Sao Paulo, Faculdade de Economia e Administraçao, Av. Luciano Gualberto 908, CP 11.498, CEP 05508 Cidade Universitária, Sao Paulo, SP
Telephone: (011) 211 0411 ext 294
Enquiries: Márcia Bizarro Batista (Librarian)
Availability: open to the public
Hours: 07.30-22.00 Monday to Friday, 09.00-15.00 Saturday
Stock: about 64,000 volumes of books, 17,000 volumes of periodicals, 9,000 serials covering economics, administration and accounting
Services: photocopying, loans
Publications: *Boletim da Biblioteca da Faculdade de Economia e Administraçao*

Federaçao das Câmaras de Comércio Exterior
Address: Rua da Candelária 9, 7° andar, Sala 701, Rio de Janeiro, RJ
Telephone: (021) 203 1229 exts 210/236
Telex: 21141 BR, 21454 BR
Enquiries: Roberto Figueira Dalcin
Availability: open to the public
Hours: 09.00-18.00 Monday to Friday
Stock: business directories, literature on foreign trade, magazines

Fundaçao Biblioteca Nacional
Address: Av Rio Branco 219, 20040-008 Rio de Janeiro
Telephone: (21) 2409229
Fax: (21) 2204173
Telex: 2122943
Enquiries: Elaine Perez (librarian)
Availability: open to the public: identity document required

Hours: 09.00 - 20.00 Monday to Friday, 09.00 - 15.00 Saturday
Stock: the collection has approximately 8 million items (books, newspapers, records, maps, manuscripts, photos, etc) covering all subjects
Services: photocopying, bibliographies, documental services, online searches
Publications: *Bibliografia Brasileira* (US$20)

Fundaçao Instituto Brasileiro de Geografia e Estatística (IBGE)
Address: Rua General Canabarro, 666 Maracana, 20271 Rio de Janeiro
Telephone: (021) 248 6470
Fax: (021) 228 9575
Telex: (021) 2134128
Enquiries: Maria Beatriz Pontes de Carvalho
Availability: open to the public
Hours: 09.00-17.00 Monday to Friday
Stock: about 40,000 volumes, 3,000 serial titles, 6,000 maps, pamphlets, reflecting the publications of the Institute in the field of geography and national statistics
Services: photocopying, loans for staff only
Publications: include *Bibliografia das bibliografias existentes na Biblioteca Central do IBGE* (bibliography of bibliographies held in the library); *Documentaçao censitária existente na Biblioteca Central do IBGE* (census documentation held in the library); *Bibliografia sobre recenseamento no Brasil* (bibliography on the Brazilian census)

There are also a large number of state and territorial centres where IBGE publications may be consulted; a full list is available from the IBGE. The IBGE database SIDRA (Sistema IBGE de Recuperaçao Automatica) is available online; facilities are available for access at the following centres as well as at the central Rio de Janeiro library above:

Address: Serviço de Divulgaçao e Biblioteca, Edificio Venâncio II, 1° andar, 70302 Brasília, DF
Telephone: (061) 223 1359

Address: Delegacia de Pernambuco, Rua do Hospício 387, Boa Vista, 50000 Recife, PE
Telephone: (081) 222 0513, (081) 231 0811 ext 11

Address: Delegacia de Minas Gerais, Rua Oliveira 523, Cruzeiro, 30000 Belo Horizonte, MG
Telephone: (031) 223 0554 ext 5

Instituto de Economia Agricola, Serviço de Biblioteca e Documentaçao
Address: Avenida Miguel Stefano 3.900, CP 8114, 04301 Sao Paulo, SP
Telephone: (011) 275 3433 exts 229/233
Telex: (011) 22784 DNSC BR
Enquiries: Cleusa Batista Pastori
Availability: open to the public
Hours: 09.00-17.30 Monday to Friday
Stock: specialises in agricultural economics, also covers rural sociology. About 4,600 book titles, 2,400 periodical titles (1,150 current ones)
Services: photocopying
Publications: all kinds of bibliographies on agriculture and economics

Pontifícia Universidade Católica do Rio de Janeiro, Divisao de Bibliotecas e Documentaçao
Address: Rua Marquês de Sao Vicente 225, 22453 Rio de Janeiro, RJ
Telephone: (021) 552 9744
Telex: (021) 31048 BR
Enquiries: Laura Maia de Figueiredo (Head Librarian)
Availability: open to the public for reference only; borrowing only for students, teaching and administrative staff of the university
Hours: 08.30-21.30 Monday to Friday
Stock: over 168,000 books and nearly 3,000 journal titles covering many subjects, including administration and economics
Services: photocopying

CANADA

Alberta Economic Development & Trade
Address: Sterling Place, 9940 106th St, 8th Floor, Edmonton AB T5K 2P6
Telephone: (403) 4274957
Fax: (403) 4270610
Telex: 037 42815
Enquiries: Donna M Gordon
Availability: open to the public for reference only
Hours: 08.15 - 16.30 Monday to Friday
Stock: covers Alberta economic conditions and trends, Canadian economic conditions and trends, Alberta industry trends, Canadian industry trends, international trade (particularly as it relates to Alberta) and small business and entrepreneurship. Material is in English and the trade material is international in coverage. It includes annual reports for major Canadian and US companies; annual reports for some international companies; Canadian and American company and trade directories; directories for other countries (company); trade journals (Canadian and American); major business journals (emphasis on current business news); statistics (complete microfiche collection of Statistics Canada; also Alberta Bureau of Statistics documents); books (7,000 volumes); newspapers; audio-visual materials. Online access - Dialog, InfoGlobe, Infomart
Services: interlibrary loans (staff only); computer searches (staff only); compilation of bibliographies (staff only)
Publications: table of contents; new accessions list

Bank of Canada, Library
Address: 234 Wellington Street, Ottawa, Ontario K1A 0G9
Telephone: (613) 7828625
Fax: (613) 7828655
Enquiries: Sheila Bradley (chief librarian) (+1 613 7828343)
Availability: restricted access. Students need a letter of introduction from their library
Hours: 08.45 - 17.00 Monday to Friday
Stock: covers economics, banking, business, finance, monetary theory. Includes publications of Central Bank, Bank for International Settlements and Canadian banks. 35,000 books, 6,000 journals, Canadian trade directories, Canadian banks' annual reports, Canadian statistics (extensive historical collection), economic working papers
Services: interlibrary loans, photocopying, reference services. Online access to Dialog, Infomart, QL, Lexis/Nexis; CD-ROM access to ABI/Inform, Canadian Business and Current Affairs, IntlEC

Bibliothèque Nationale du Québec
Address: 125 rue Sherbrooke Ouest, Montréal PQ H2X 1X4
Telephone: (514) 8731100
Fax: 5148734310
Enquiries: Philippe Sauvageau (président-directeur général), Geneviève Dubuc (directrice des communications)
Availability: open to those over 18 or with college education
Hours: Saint-Sulpice and Aegidius-Fauteaux buildings: 09.00 - 17.00 Tuesday to Saturday (June to August, Monday to Friday); Marie-Claire Daveluy building: 09.00 - 17.00 Tuesday to Friday
Stock: general coverage including social sciences. Material in French. Includes journals, statistics (Québec), books (350,000 approximately), newspapers (local), microforms (337,000). Online access - SOQUIJ, SDM, DOBIS, IRIS (BNQ database), REFCATSS
Services: photocopying (self-service); printing microforms
Publications: *Bibliographie du Québec, liste mensuelle des publications québécoises, 1968 - Bibliographie du Québec 1821-1967*
Notes: Catalogue of BNQ publications available from: 1700 rue Saint-Denis, Montréal, Québec, Canada H2X 3K6, or by calling +1 514 8731100 ext 158, Freephone: +1 800 3639028

Business Library
Address: 510-155 Carlton Street, Winnipeg, MB R3C 3H8
Telephone: (204) 945 2036
Fax: (204) 945 2804
Telex: 07587833 MANITRADE CA
Enquiries: John W G Giesbrecht (Manager)
Availability: open to the public; intended to serve Government personnel (from the Industry, Trade and Technology Department and the Business Development and Tourism Department), the general business public and academics within business disciplines
Hours: 08.30-16.15 Monday to Friday
Stock: book collection of nearly 20,000 catalogued volumes plus reference documents and unnumbered government documents, reports etc covering mainly business, marketing, economics, international trade, tourism and public policy. Reference Unit of approximately 500 titles includes many specialised business materials; the Serials Unit includes over 300 industry, business and trade specific titles
Services: reference services, online searches (including DIALOG, CAN/OLE, BRS, INFOGLOBE, HANSARD), inter-library loans, orientation seminars and tours, technical information referral, liaison with other professionals in given industry fields, photocopying, audio-visual
Publications: annotated in-house current awareness lists, program literature for two key government portfolios, promotional literature designed for small business entrepreneurs

Canadian Exporters' Association Library
Address: 99 Bank Street, Suite 250, Ottawa, ON K1P 6B9
Telephone: (613) 238 8888
Fax: (613) 563 9218
Enquiries: Claudette Bourdon (Librarian)
Availability: open to the public for reference; there is a charge for borrowing privileges
Hours: 09.00-17.00 Monday to Friday
Stock: is a specialised extensive export-oriented library of over 5,000 texts, periodicals, papers and up to date foreign country export marketing reports
Services: loans, enquiry service

Economic Council of Canada Library
Address: mailing address: PO Box 527, Station B, Ottawa, ON K1P 5V6; location: 16th Floor, 320 Queen St, Ottawa, ON K1A 1G1
Telephone: (613) 952 1832
Fax: (613) 952 2171
Enquiries: Leonard Bonavero (Library Manager)
Availability: open to the public
Hours: 08.00-17.00 Monday to Friday
Stock: approximately 25,000 volumes covering economics, statistics and some banking. Is a depository library for Statistics Canada and also has the entire collection of Economic Council of Canada publications
Services: photocopying, loans, enquiry service, online searches, tailor-made bibliographies
Publications: monthly accessions list; list of material as yet uncatalogued received in the previous month

Export Development Corporation
Address: PO Box 655, 151 O'Connor Street, Ottawa, ON K1P 5T9
Telephone: (613) 598 2701
Fax: (613) 237 2690
Telex: 0534136
Enquiries: A James (Librarian)
Availability: open to EDC staff and those of other government departments only
Hours: 08.15-17.00 Monday to Friday
Stock: 700 serial titles, 6,000 annual reports, 4,000 monographs. Annual reports of official export credit agencies
Services: photocopying, inter-library loans, online searches, microform reader/printer
Publications: Acquisition list (monthly)

Industry, Science & Technology Canada
Address: Ottawa, ON K1A 0H5
Telephone: (613) 954 2728
Fax: (613) 954 1894
Telex: 0534123
Enquiries: R Segall (Manager, Library Services Division)
Availability: open to the public for reference
Hours: 09.00-17.00 Monday to Friday
Stock: collection covering industry, Canadian business and small business; includes collection of Canadian annual reports and complete collection of Statistics Canada publications
Services: photocopying, loans, reference services, online

searching (for Departmental employees); photocopying available for visitors
Publications: Recent additions/Acquisitions récentes; bulletin

Industry, Science & Technology Canada
Address: 800 Victoria Square, PO Box 247, Montréal, QC H4Z 1E8
Telephone: (514) 283 7274
Telex: 05560768
Enquiries: Nicole Beaudry
Availability: open to the public for reference
Hours: 08.30-12.00, 13.00-17.30 Monday, Wednesday, Friday
Stock: 10,000 documents covering industry, economy, statistics, regional development, tourism, trade, public administration
Services: reference, inter-library loans
Publications: Acquisitions monthly

Metropolitan Toronto Reference Library
Address: 789 Yonge Street, Toronto, ON M4V 2G8
Telephone: (416) 393 7148
Telex: 0622232 INTLX TOR CA
Enquiries: Margot Hewings (Manager, Business, Social Sciences and Municipal Reference Department)
Availability: open to the public
Hours: 10.00-21.00 Monday to Thursday, 10.00-18.00 Friday, Saturday, 13.30-17.00 Sunday (closed Sundays May 1 - October 15)
Stock: over 76,000 books and 1,500 corporation files, 7 newspapers, over 900 periodicals and nearly 600 vertical files. Covers economics, labour, management, corporations, banking and finance, taxation, trade and industry. Special collections of government documents, business and trade directories, statistical sources and company information; statistical sources include historical and current Statistics Canada collection, international and national yearbooks and UN and OECD world trade statistics
Services: photocopying (fees charged), inter-library loans, letter enquiries, centralised online searches
Publications: bibliographies on business topics (occasional, free)

National Library of Canada/Bibliothèque nationale du Canada
Address: 395 Wellington Street, Ottawa, Ontario K1A 0NA
Telephone: (613) 995 9481
Fax: (613) 943 1112
Enquiries: Paul McCormick (acting assistant director)
Availability: open to the public
Hours: (reference and information services division) 08.30 - 17.00 Monday to Friday
Stock: covers Canadian studies, the social sciences and the humanities with emphasis on collecting Canadian and Canada-related (Canadiana) published material and sound recordings. Material mainly in English and French. Some Canadiana publications are published in other languages. Online access to Badaduq, BRS, Canlaw, CAN/OLE, Datatimes, Datastar, Dialog, Dow Jone, Envoy, Epic, Infoglobe, Infomart, Insight, QL, Questel, RLIN, SDM Systems, Utlas, Wilsonline. CD-ROM facilities include Bibliodisc, CBCA, Ulrich's, PAIS, StatCan, Canadian Register, US GPO, CD Education, HMSO publications. Comprehensive company and financial information for Canada; selective Canadian annual reports. Similar information for other countries obtained from online systems. Market research reports including industry profiles, published by Industry, Science and Technology Canada. Comprehensive collection of company and trade directories for Canada and the US; major titles only for other parts of the world. 461,485 books. Extensive collection of Canadian newspapers, Selective collection of newspapers from abroad. Canadian microforms, major foreign microform sets, newspapers on microform, audio-visual Canadiana sound recordings.

Ottawa Public Library
Address: Main Library, 120 Metcalfe Street, Ottawa, ON K1P 5M2
Telephone: (613) 236 0301
Fax: (613) 567 4013
Telex: 0533621
Enquiries: Miss Margaret McMain
Availability: open to the public
Hours: 09.30-21.00 (winter) 09.30-20.00 (summer) Monday to Thursday, 09.30-18.00 Friday, 09.30-17.00 Saturday, 13.00-17.00

Sunday (from Sunday after Thanksgiving up to and including second Sunday in May)
Stock: Reference Library stock includes official gazettes, directories of large Canadian cities, telephone books for London, Paris, over 140 Canadian and 40 US cities; large business and investment collection includes many Canadian corporate annual reports; large collection of periodicals and indexes, and newspapers from Canada, the US, UK and France
Services: loans, inter-library loans, reference department, photocopying facilities
Publications: bibliographies, booklists, general information brochures on reference services, computer literacy etc

Statistics Canada
Statistics Canada, the national statistical service, has 10 regional reference centres providing a wide range of services, including a library at each centre. Users can consult (and purchase) Statistics Canada publications, microcomputer diskettes, microfiche, maps and other products; public copying facilities for printed materials and microfiche are available, and all centres have facilities to retrieve information from Statistics Canada's computerised data retrieval systems, CANSIM and Telichart. Regional centres are in the following locations:

Newfoundland and Labrador

Address: Advisory Services, Statistics Canada, 3rd Floor, Viking Building, Crosbie Road, St John's, NF A1B 3P2
Telephone: (709) 772 4073; toll free service: Zenith - 07037

Maritime Provinces

Address: Advisory Services, Statistics Canada, 3rd Floor, Sir John Thompson Building, 1256 Barrington Street, Halifax, NS B3J 1Y6
Telephone: (902) 426 5331; toll free service: (1-800) 565 7192
Fax: (902) 426 9538

Québec

Address: Advisory Services, Statistics Canada, Guy Favreau Complex, 200 Dorchester Blvd West, Suite 412, East Tower, Montréal, QC H2Z 1X4
Telephone: (514) 283 5725; toll free service: (1-800) 361 2831

National Capital Region

Address: Central Inquiries Service, Statistics Canada, Lobby, R H Coats Building, Tunney's Pasture, Ottawa, ON K1A 0T6
Telephone: (613) 990 8116; toll free service: dial the toll free number for the province from which you are calling

Ontario

Address: Advisory Services, Statistics Canada, 10th Floor, Arthur Meighen Building, 25 St Clair Avenue East, Toronto, ON M4T 1M4
Telephone: (416) 973 6586; toll free service: (1-800) 268 1151
Fax: (416) 973 7475

Nipissing Region

Address: Advisory Services, Statistics Canada, Civic Administration Centre, 225 Holditch Street, Sturgeon Falls, ON P0H 2G0
Telephone: (705) 753 4888; toll free service: dial the number given above for Ontario

Manitoba

Address: Advisory Services, Statistics Canada, 6th Floor, General Post Office Building, 266 Graham Avenue, Winnipeg, MB R3C 0K4
Telephone: (204) 949 4020; toll free service: (1-800) 542 3404

Saskatchewan

Address: Advisory Services, Statistics Canada, Suite 900, 2002 Victoria Ave., Regina, SK S4P 0R7
Telephone: (306) 780 5405; toll free service: (1-800) 667 7164
Fax: (306) 780 5403

Alberta and Northwest Territories

Address: Advisory Services, Statistics Canada, 2nd Floor, Hys Centre, 11010-101 Street, Edmonton, AB T5H 4C5
Telephone: (403) 420 3027/8; toll free service: (1-800) 222 6400; NWT call collect: (403) 420 2011

British Columbia and Yukon

Address: Advisory Services, Statistics Canada, 3rd Floor, Federal Building, Sinclair Centre, 757 West Hastings Street, Vancouver, BC V6C 3C9
Telephone: (604) 666 3691; toll free service: (1-112800) 663 1551 (South and Central British Columbia), Zenith 08913 (Yukon and Northern British Columbia)
Fax: (604) 666 4863

There are also 48 Full Depository Libraries across Canada which carry all Statistics Canada publications, as they automatically receive all federal government publications free of charge. These are mainly university, public and legislative libraries, and a full list is available from Statistics Canada. Three of the libraries for which full details are given in this chapter are Full Depository Libraries: Metropolitan Toronto Reference Library, University of Toronto and York University

Tourism Reference & Documentation Centre

Address: Tourism Canada, 4th Floor East, 235 Queen Street, Ottawa, ON K1A 0H6
Telephone: (613) 954 3943
Fax: (613) 952 7906
Availability: open to the public; material collected primarily to assist the tourism industry and staff of Tourism Canada, but is freely available to other government agencies and the general public
Hours: 08.30-16.30 Monday to Friday
Stock: over 7,000 books and documents, including research papers, statistical surveys, journals, conference proceedings, bibliographies etc, plus reference materials including yearbooks, business directories, newsletters and trade papers
Services: loans (within Canada) except reference material and rare publications, inter-library loans, bilingual bibliographic information storage and retrieval system using keywords
Publications: acquisition list

University of Toronto, Faculty of Management Library

Address: Room 310, 246 Bloor Street West, Toronto, ON M5S 1V4 Canada
Telephone: (416) 978 3421
Enquiries: Mrs Ruth Tolmie
Availability: open to the general public for reference; only people with current University of Toronto library cards may borrow materials
Hours: 08.45-21.00 Monday to Thursday, 08.45-18.00 Friday, 10.00-17.00 Saturday, 13.00-17.00 Sunday
Stock: close to 40,000 items, including bound periodicals; over 400 current subscriptions to business journals; circulating book collection covers accounting, marketing, organisational behaviour and finance; vertical file collection on certain Canadian industries. The main University of Toronto library is also a full depository library for Statistics Canada publications
Services: limited services provided to patrons without University of Toronto affiliation

York University Government Documents/Administrative Studies Library

Address: 113 ASB, 4700 Keele Street, North York, ON M3J 1P3
Telephone: (416) 736 5139
Fax: (416) 736 5687
Enquiries: Vivienne Monty (Head), D K Varma (Administrative Studies Librarian)
Availability: open to the public (borrowing privileges restricted)
Hours: 09.00-22.30 Monday to Thursday, 10.00-17.00 Friday, Saturday, 13.00-20.00 Sunday
Stock: Canadian federal and provincial documents, publications of international governmental agencies and foreign countries; business reference collection, business periodicals and reserves placed by Administrative Studies faculty. York University library is a full depository library for Statistics Canada publications
Services: photocopying, loans, enquiry service, online searches, instruction in sources of information, compiling bibliographies, research consultation
Publications: research guides, annotated bibliographies and information source lists, aids to publications in high interest topics

CHILE

Biblioteca Banco Central de Chile

Address: Agustinas 1180, Santiago
Telephone: (02) 670 2758
Fax: (02) 698 4847
Telex: 246569 CENBC CL
Enquiries: Beatriz Medina Lois
Availability: open to the public without restriction
Hours: 09.00-13.30 Monday to Friday
Stock: 16,000 volumes; specialises in economics and finance, and provides statistical data on the Chilean economy, eg foreign trade, production, indices, monetary statistics etc
Services: photocopying, loans, enquiry service, online searches
Publications: internal publications only

Biblioteca del Congreso Nacional

Address: Clasificador de Correos 1199, Santiago; location of reference service is: Compañía 1175, Santiago; location of cataloguing and online searches: Huérfanos 1117. 3rd, Santiago
Telephone: (02) 696 0509 (General Reference Service)/696 2111 ext 356/362 (periodicals)/698 1110 (Legislative Reference)/696 6872 (Accounting and Suppliers)
Fax: (02) 696 1143 (reference)/696 4233 (online service)
Enquiries: José Miguel Vicuña (Librarian), Eliana Navarro (data processing), Alicia Zambrano (Information Officer), Carmen Morandé (periodicals), Neville Blanc (legislative reference)
Availability: open to adults, aged 18 or over, but especially for lawyers, law students, professors, researchers
Hours: 09.30-20.00 Monday to Friday
Stock: 850,000 volumes of monographs, 7,000 volumes of serials; includes several serials of particular interest in the fields of economics, trade etc
Services: loans, enquiry service, online searches, microfilming, photocopying
Publications: *Boletín bibliografico*; *Revista de legislación*; *Bibliografías especiales*; *Fe de entradas del depósito legal*

Biblioteca Nacional de Chile

Address: Avenida Libertador Bernardo O'Higgins no 651, Clasificador 1400, Santiago
Telephone: (02) 383206/383373/338957
Fax: (02) 381975
Enquiries: Ursula Schadlich Schonhals
Availability: open to the public
Hours: 09.00-20.00 Monday to Friday, 09.00-15.00 Saturday
Stock: three million volumes in humanities, social sciences, history, literature etc
Services: photocopying, loans, enquiry service
Publications: *Bibliografía nacional*

Biblioteca ODEPLAN (Oficina de Planificación Nacional)

Address: Ahumada 48, Piso 4°, Santiago
Telephone: (02) 698 0104/ 722033 ext 340
Telex: 341400 ODEPLA CK
Enquiries: Señora Carolina Sánchez Edwards
Availability: open to adults aged 18 or over, students in higher education or equivalent; must have identity card
Hours: 08.30-13.00 Monday to Friday
Stock: 11,200 volumes of monographs, 760 periodical titles (362 current titles); covers economic and social planning, demography, industry, Chilean legislation. Depository library for publications of the World Bank and Chilean publications at government level, ie publications of the Central Bank, ministries, Instituto Nacional de Estadísticas, etc
Services: photocopying, loans, inter-library loans
Publications: acquisitions bulletin and bulletin of periodical publications received

CEPAL Biblioteca

Address: Casilla 179-D, Santiago
Telephone: (02) 485051 exts 2337/2338
Telex: 441054
Enquiries: Carmen Vera Arendt (Chief Librarian)
Availability: open to the public
Hours: 14.30-17.30 Monday to Friday
Stock: over 50,000 books and 3,000 periodical titles on economic and social development. Includes CEPAL documents and UN

publications
Services: enquiry service, online searches
Publications: CEPAL index (annual); also acquisitions lists, bibliographies etc (full list available)

Instituto Nacional de Estadisticas, Biblioteca
National Institute of Statistics, Library
Address: Avda Bulnes 418, Casilla 7597, Correo 3, Santiago
Telephone: (2) 6991441 ext 207
Fax: (2) 6712169
Enquiries: Sergio Miranda Perez
Availability: open to the public
Hours: 09.15 - 16.45 Monday to Thursday
Stock: covers statistics dealing with population, employment, housing, education, economics, law, prices, tourism, transport, industry, commerce, environment, health, social security etc. The material is mainly in Spanish. Stock includes 27,000 volumes; newspapers; microfiche (census material)
Services: photocopying; facilities for readers to use own computers; loans, enquiry service
Notes: Unpublished statistics may be obtained for a fee.

CHINA

Beijing Library (National Library)
Address: North Side, Zizhuyuan Park, Haidian District, Beijing
Telephone: (1) 841 5566
Coverage: all kinds of Chinese publications, including 24 minority languages
Activity: information service, photocopying, exhibitions, lectures and international exchanges

Beijing University Library
Address: Haidian District, Beijing
Telephone: (1) 282 471-3263
Telex: 22239 PKUNI CN
Stock: 4 million volumes, 6,200 current periodical titles covering liberal arts, natural sciences, applied sciences and social sciences

Fudan University Library
Address: 220 Handan Lu, Shanghai
Telephone/fax: (21) 544 1995
Telex: 33317 HUA FUCN
Coverage: philosophy, economics, politics, law, journalism, Chinese and foreign languages, history, mathematics, physics, chemistry, biology, computer sciences, etc
Activity: photocopying, information, exchanges

Hunan University Library
Address: Yuelushan Lu, Changsha, Hunan Province
Telephone: 82821
Stock: covers natural and social sciences, including business management
Services: interlibrary loans; photocopying

Library of Chinese University of International Business and Economics
Address: Xiaoguan, Andingmenwai, Beijing
Telephone: (1) 462161
Coverage: world economics, international trade, foreign language, reference books
Activity: photoduplication, information services, domestic and international exchange

Library of the People's University of China
Address: Beijing
Telephone: (1) 283985/285431
Enquiries: Professor Dai Yi (Honorary Librarian), Mr Yang Dong-Liang (Deputy Librarian)
Availability: open to the public
Hours: 08.00-18.00 Monday to Saturday (reading rooms open till 22.00)
Stock: coverage includes economics (political economics, world economics, history of Chinese and Western economics), industrial economics and statistics, agricultural economics, business economics and labour affairs, finance, demography

National Library of China
Address: 39 Baishiqiao Road, Beijing 100081
Telephone: (1) 8415566
Fax: (1) 8419291

Telex: 222211 NLC CN
Availability: open to the public
Stock: a comprehensive collection of about 14,000,000 volumes
Services: facilities for reading, photocopying, loans, enquiries and computerised data retrieval
Publications: Documentation (quarterly); *National bibliography of China*; *Bulletin of new books in foreign languages*; *Union catalogue of periodicals*

Shanghai Institute of Foreign Trade Library
Address: 620 Gubeilu, Shanghai
Telephone: (21) 518181
Coverage: economics, international trade, law etc.

Shanghai Jiaotong University Library
Address: 1954 Huashan Lu, Shanghai
Telephone: (21) 370147
Stock: covers science and technology, including management science. 861,000 volumes, 10,000 periodicals

Shanghai Library
Address: 325 West Nanjing Road, Shanghai
Telephone: (21) 563176
Services: interlibrary loans, special lectures, exhibitions, photocopying, information services and international exchanges

COLOMBIA

Biblioteca CEDE, Universidad de los Andes
Address: Centro de Estudios sobre Desarrollo Económico, Universidad de los Andes, Cra. 1 Este No. 18A-10, Apdo Aéreo 4976, Bogotá
Telephone: (01) 284 9911 Ext 2464
Fax: (01) 281 5771
Enquiries: Elsie Duque de Ramirez MLS
Availability: open to the public: identity document required
Hours: 08.00-18.00 Monday to Friday
Stock: relevant to the study of economic development
Services: photocopying, enquiry service
Publications: full list of the publications of the Centre available

Biblioteca Luis Angel Arango
Address: Banco de la República, Calle 11 no 4-14, Bogotá
Telephone: (01) 282 7516
Fax: (01) 281 5830, (01) 282 7946
Telex: 44736, 44889
Enquiries: Lina Espitaleta de Villegas
Availability: open to the public: identity document required
Hours: 09.00-21.00 Monday Saturday, 08.00-14.00 Sunday
Stock: covers all areas of knowledge, with about 400,000 titles. Includes reference collection and collection of Colombian books
Services: reference, inter-library loans, photocopying, bibliographies
Publications: acquisitions lists

Centro de Documentación, Instituto de Fomento Industrial
Address: Calle 16 #6-66 piso 14, AA 4222, Bogotá
Telephone: (01) 283 8753
Telex: 044642
Enquiries: Gloria Estrada de Asensio (Librarian)
Availability: open to the public
Hours: 14.00-17.00 Monday to Friday
Stock: about 5,200 books, 4,100 documents, 85 current periodical subscriptions and 860 reports (ie company reports); covers economic and industrial development, finances
Services: photocopying, loans, enquiry service
Publications: weekly bibliographic bulletin (a current awareness service)

Centro de Información Económico Social de Bogotá
Address: Edificio Carrera 9a no 16-21, AA 29824, Bogotá
Telephone: (01) 284 7528, (01) 281 9900 exts 268/269/270/288
Telex: 45574 CACBO CO
Enquiries: Alonso Franco Botero
Availability: open to the public
Hours: 09.00-13.00, 14.00-17.00 Monday to Friday
Stock: 500 serial titles, 6,000 documents, 9,000 clippings. Contains economic and social information on Colombia and the rest of the world; special collections on external trade and Latin America

Services: photocopying, loans, enquiry service; information network
Publications: union catalogue of economic and social information in Colombia

Escuela Superior de Administración Pública (ESAP), Biblioteca
Address: Diagonal 40, No 46A-37 (CAN), Apdo Aéreo 29745, Bogotá
Telephone: (911) 2020311
Fax: (1) 224251
Enquiries: Jairo Mora
Availability: open to the public subject to an institutional introduction letter
Hours: 08.00 - 20.30 Monday to Friday, 08.00 - 17.00 Saturday
Stock: covers public administration, political science, economics. Material in Spanish (95%), English and French, covering mainly Colombia. 700 journal titles on administration, public administration, political science and economics. Colombian statistics. 20,000 volumes. 2,000 microfiche
Service: bibliographical searches in the library's databases (ESAPMUN: statistical information about Colombian municipalities; HEMER: journal articles and REDOC: bibliographical information covering public administration)
Publications: CONTAP (contents of periodical publications)

Hemeroteca Luis López de Mesa
Address: Banco de la República, Calle 11 no 4-41, Barrio La Candelaria, Bogotá
Telephone: (01) 282 7516, (01) 243 9100 exts 276/282/231
Enquiries: Elsa Martínez C., Cilma Rodriguez
Availability: open to the public: identity document required
Hours: 09.00-21.00 Monday to Friday, 08.00-20.00 Saturday, 08.00-18.00 Sunday
Stock: 8,000 titles of serial publications, 2,000 periodical titles; covers mainly economics, administration, money and banking, also social sciences, humanities, science and technology; material from all countries, but with emphasis on Colombia
Services: photocopying, inter-library loans, telephone and written enquiries, bibliographies, current contents service etc
Publications: Catalogo general; Catalogo de publicaciones/areas; Boletín cultural y bibliografico, etc

UNIANDES, Biblioteca General
Address: Carrera 1 18A-10, Apdo Aéreo 4976, Bogotá
Telephone: (1) 2866309
Fax: (1) 2841890
Telex: 42343 UNAND CO
Enquiries: Angela María Mejía de Restrepo
Availability: free access for university students, staff, professional and researchers
Hours: 08.00 - 18.00 Monday to Friday, 08.00 12.00 Saturday
Stock: general coverage. Material is mainly in Spanish, English and French and covers Latin America, North America, Europe and Asia. It includes company and trade directories (national), statistics (national), books (280,000 volumes), local, national and international newspapers, microfiche, audio-visual materials, computer programs, trade journals (Latin America, North America, Europe, Asia). Online access - Dialog, CD-rom - Econline, dissertation abstracts
Services: photocopying
Publications: news-sheets (bi-annual), acquisition lists (monthly)

Banco Central de Costa Rica, "Alvaro Castro J" Library
Address: Apartado 10.058 - 1000, San José, Costa Rica
Telephone: 334233 exts 287/550
Telex: (376) 2163 CR, 3457 CR
Enquiries: Licda. Deyanira Vargas de Bonilla
Availability: open to the public, especially to students; home loans only for Bank employees
Hours: 09.00-16.00 Monday to Friday
Stock: about 40,000 volumes specialising in economics, business administration and statistics
Services: inter-library loans, photocopying, enquiry service on economic material
Publications: Lista de recientes adquisiciones (monthly list of acquisitions); current awareness service for periodicals

Institut Africain pour le Développement Économique et Social, INADES-documentation
Address: BP 8, Abidjan 08
Telephone: 441594
Fax: 440641
Enquiries: Yves Morel (Director)
Availability: open to the public by annual subscription
Hours: 08.00-12.00, 15.00-19.00 Monday to Saturday (closed Tuesday morning and Saturday afternoon)
Stock: documentation centre specialising in the following subjects relating to Africa: economic and social development, including politics, agriculture, socio-cultural change etc
Services: enquiry service, photocopying
Publications: Fichier-Afrique (article index); manuals on running a documentation centre

Cairo University, Institute of Statistical Studies & Research, Library
Address: 5 Tharwat St, Orman, Cairo
Telephone: (2) 713161
Fax: (2) 3482533
Enquiries: Prof Samir K Ashour (vice dean)
Availability: open to the academic staff and students of the institute
Hours: 08.30 - 17.00 Saturday to Wednesday, except in summer vacation and winter recess; 09.00 - 15.00 in summer vacations and winter recess
Stock: covers statistics, mathematics, demography and population studies, econometrics, biometrics, psychometrics, mathematical economics, reliability studies, computer science, operations research, economic planning, agricultural statistics. Material in Arabic and English covering the Middle East.
Services: photocopying, microfilm reader
Publications: The Egyptian Statistical Journal (bi-annual; US$15 p.a.); The Egyptian Computer Journal (bi-annual; US$15 p.a.); The Egyptian Population & Family Planning Review (bi-annual; US$15 p.a.); Proceedings of the Annual Conference (in 5 parts; US$50 p.a.)

Centre d'Etudes et de Documentation Economique, Juridique et Sociale
Address: 22 Al Fawakah Street, Mohandessine, Dokki, Cairo
Telephone: (2) 361 1932
Fax: (2) 349 3578
Telex: 93088 CEFEC UN
Enquiries: Soheir Imam Rizkalla
Availability: open to the public for reference; loans exclusively for researchers
Hours: 09.00-14.00 Monday, Thursday, Friday; 09.00-12.00 Tuesday; 09.00-18.00 Wednesday
Stock: 8,000 books covering social sciences (history, economy, law and politics), Egypt in the nineteenth and twentieth centuries, Egyptian literature, the Middle East (especially Sudan)
Services: photocopying

National Library of Egypt (Dar Al-Kutub Al-qawmia)
Address: Corniche El Nil, Boulaq, Cairo
Telephone: (2) 775000/775649/77509
Enquiries: Saad Mohamed Rashid (Director General)
Availability: open to the public
Hours: 09.00-18.00 daily in summer, 09.00-17.00 in winter; closed Fridays and official holidays
Stock: over 839,000 titles
Services: photocopying, microfilming, enquiry service
Publications: Legal deposit bulletin; Egyptian books in print; Information bulletin; GEBO publications list (GEBO = General Egyptian Book Organisation)

ETHIOPIA

Addis Ababa University Library System
Address: PO Box 1176, Addis Ababa
Telephone: (1) 115673, (1) 110844 ext 253
Telex: 0980-21205
Enquiries: Getachew Birru (University Librarian)
Availability: open to the public upon registration as members, for which a deposit is required
Hours: 08.00-22.00 Monday to Saturday, 15.00-21.00 Sunday
Stock: about half a million items, including non-print material
Services: photocopying, reference services, loan services
Publications: accession lists, bibliographies on various subjects

Central Statistical Office Library
Address: PO Box 1143, Addis Ababa
Telephone: (1) 115818
Availability: open to the public
Stock: includes the Office's publications and some unpublished material

National Bank of Ethiopia, Documentation Division
Address: PO Box 5550, Addis Ababa
Telephone: (1) 515823
Fax: (1) 514588
Enquiries: Mr Getachew Bebrewold
Availability: open for government business only
Hours: office hours Monday to Friday
Stock: covers banking, economics, agricultural policies, rural development, finance, statistics, capital markets. The collection includes a special Ethiopian collection. The stock is in English and includes company and trade directories, statistics (UN, IMF, FAO World Bank, EC), books (30,000) and newspapers
Publications: quarterly bulletin; annual report; recent additions

FIJI

Fiji Trade and Investment Board, Trade Information Centre
Address: 1st Floor, Velop House, 371 Victoria Parade, PO Box 2303, Government Buildings, Suva
Telephone: 315988
Telex: 2355 FTIB FJ
Availability: provides information services to locals as well as the region on trade related matters
Stock: monographs, including buyers' guides, directories etc; bibliographies; periodicals
Publications: Information Centre new acquisitions

GHANA

Ghana Library Board
Address: PO Box 663, Accra
Telephone: (21) 662795/665083
Enquiries: Director of Library Services
Availability: open to the public on payment of 100 Cedis subscription for adults and students
Hours: 08.00-19.00 Monday to Friday, 08.00-16.00 Saturday
Stock: covers all subjects; maintains a commercial library, which stocks patents, dictionaries etc
Services: loans, enquiry service, photocopying
Publications: Annual report of the Ghana Library Board; Ghana national bibliography; 25th anniversary brochure of the Ghana Library Board

GUATEMALA

Biblioteca Naciónal de Guatemala
Address: 5a Avenida 6-27, Zona 1, Guatemala
Telephone: (02) 122443
Fax: (02) 1539071
Enquiries: Lic. María Luisa Mulet de Cerego
Availability: open to the public
Hours: 12 hours daily, Monday to Friday
Stock: includes section on Guatemala, reference section and a foreign section
Services: photocopying

GUYANA

Bank of Guyana Library
Address: PO Box 1003, Georgetown
Telephone: (2) 63261/63256
Fax: (2) 72965
Telex: 2267 GY
Enquiries: Mrs Wenda R Stephenson
Availability: open to the public at librarian's discretion
Hours: 08.00-12.15, 13.30-16.30 Monday to Thursday, 08.00-12.15, 13.30-17.00 Friday
Stock: about 7,357 books and 540 periodicals (including annual reports); covers mainly social sciences but also law and science, eg computer science, mathematics etc
Services: inter-library loans, loans, enquiry service
Publications: Bank of Guyana Annual Report; Bank of Guyana Library List of Additions; staff publications

National Library
Address: 76/77 Main and Church Streets, Georgetown
Telephone: (2) 62690/62699
Enquiries: Mrs Joan L Christiani
Availability: open to the public
Hours: 09.00-18.30 Monday to Friday, 09.00-12.00 Saturday
Stock: over 192,000 volumes covering all subjects; includes small collection of books and periodicals on business and marketing
Services: photocopying, loans (personal and inter-library), enquiry service
Publications: Guyanese National Bibliography

HONG KONG

American Library
Address: United Centre, 1/F, 95 Queensway, Hong Kong
Telephone: 5299661/5202060
Availability: open to the public
Hours: 10.00 - 18.00 Monday to Friday
Stock: emphasis on US government and politics, business and economics, society and education
Services: local interlibrary loan service provided; photocopying; reference and borrowing; access to online databases

City Hall Reference Library
Address: Urban Council Public Libraries, Edinburgh Pl, Hong Kong
Telephone: 5228219
Fax: 8772641
Telex: 60645 UC USD HX
Enquiries: Miss Agnes Lee Ching-hing
Availability: open to the public
Hours: 10.00 - 19.00 Monday to Thursday; 10.00 - 21.00 Friday; 10.00 - 17.00 Saturday; 10.00 - 13.00 Sunday
Stock: comprehensive subject coverage. Special collections include: Hong Kong Stock Exchange Collection; World Bank Depository Collection; Hong Kong Collection; United Nations Depository Collection. Material is in Chinese and English with international coverage (emphasis on Hong Kong and South East Asia). Stock includes company annual reports (Hong Kong); market research reports (EIV and Hong Kong Bank Business Profile Series); company and trade directories (wide coverage); trade journals (Hong Kong); other journals (international coverage); statistics; 200,000 volumes on business and finance; newspapers; microforms and audio-visual materials. CD-ROM - ABI/Inform; Disclosure Worldscope Global; Million Dollar Disc; OZ on Disc; Wilson Business Abstract; Standards & Poor's Corporations
Services: photocopying of non-copyrighted material (HK$0.50 per A4 size copy); print-out of microform and CD-ROM databases (HK$1.50 per copy); enquiry service (free of charge), online database search services

Hong Kong Polytechnic Library
Address: Hong Kong Polytechnic, Hunghom, Kowloon
Telephone: 766 6857
Fax: 765 8274
Telex: 38964 POLYX HX
Enquiries: Mr Barry Burton (Librarian); Mrs W M Mok (Acting Information Services Librarian)
Availability: limited access for the public: senior staff from

commercial, industrial or governmental organisations needing information for their work may request help from the Library; library tickets are issued on a subscription basis
Hours: 09.00-22.00 Monday to Friday, 09.00-17.00 Saturday, 13.00-18.00 Sunday (09.00-17.00 in pre-exam or exam periods)
Stock: one of the largest collections of scientific, engineering and business materials in the Far East; total of over 590,000 items, and over 10,000 serial titles. Comprehensive collection of newspaper clipping files for materials related to Hong Kong
Services: photocopying, inter-library loans, online search
Publications: Hongkongiana - an index to selected Hong Kong periodicals; Directory of Professional Associations and Learned Societies in Hong Kong (biannual)

Hong Kong Trade Development Council Reference Library
Address: Convention Plaza, 36-39th Floors Office Tower, 1 Harbour Road, Wanchai
Telephone: 584 4333
Fax: 824 0249
Telex: 73595 CONHK HX
Availability: open to manufacturers and traders, etc
Hours: 09.00-18.00 Monday to Friday, 09.00-13.00 Saturday
Stock: trade statistics, market surveys, product reports, trade directories, introductions to overseas markets, yearbooks, information about local and overseas companies
Publications: Overseas market news (monthly, contains latest local market trends and product news from overseas offices)

Regional Council Public Libraries
Address: Head Office, 38 Sai Lau Kok Rd, 6/F Tsuen Wan, Central Library, Tsuen Wan New Territories
Telephone: 92203068
Fax: 415 8211
Enquiries: Alex Ng or Thomas Wong
Availability: 23 libraries open to all members of the public
Hours: most libraries open six days a week and for 56 hours
Stock: comprehensive stock of over 1.6 million items of book and non-book material covering all subject areas, including commerce and industry, marketing and business information
Services: free borrowing, reference enquiry service, photocopying (at Sha Tin Central Library and Tuen Mun Central Library only), inter-library loans
Publications: select booklists, bibliographies, guides

Stock Exchange Library
Address: Far East Exchange Building, 8 Wyndham Street, Central
Telephone: 526 6833

INDIA

Connemara (State Central) Public Library
Address: Pantheon Road, Egmore, Madras 600 008
Telephone: (44) 811151
Enquiries: Mrs Shereen Ahmed (chief librarian)
Availability: a public library, open to any resident of Madras City
Hours: 08.00-20.00 Sunday to Saturday
Stock: collection of books and periodicals covering all subjects; the library receives all publications of the UN
Services: photocopying, inter-library loans, home delivery, text book wing for students
Publications: Quarterly list of selected English books (ie those added to stock); *Bibliography of Tamil books* (monthly, with annual cumulation)

Delhi Public Library
Address: S P Mukerji Marg, Delhi 110006
Telephone: (11) 233990/2512682/2512382
Enquiries: R K Sharma (Director)
Availability: free to the public, open access
Hours: 08.30-20.00 Monday to Saturday
Stock: book stock of over 800,000 volumes on almost all subjects
Services: loans, inter-library loans, information service, photocopying facilities, special library services eg Braille Library, Hospital Library etc
Publications: annual progress reports

Directorate of Economics and Statistics, Ministry of Agriculture
Address: Library, Room 26, Directorate of Economics and Statistics, Ministry of Agriculture, Krishi Bhavan, New Delhi 110001
Telephone: (11) 388911/408
Enquiries: Anita Sharma (Librarian)
Availability: Departmental library, but also open to the public
Hours: 10.00-17.00 Monday to Friday
Stock: economics and statistics
Services: inter-library loans, enquiry service
Publications: Gleaning from the press (daily bulletin)

Federation of Indian Chambers of Commerce and Industry, FICCI Library
Address: Federation House, Tansen Marg 1, New Delhi 110001
Telephone: (11) 3319251 (11 lines)
Fax: (11) 3320714
Telex: 0312546, 03162521
Enquiries: Mrs Maud Nathan
Availability: open to the public
Hours: 10.00-17.15 Monday to Friday, 10.00-13.30 Saturday
Stock: covers commerce, trade and industry
Services: photocopying, loans, enquiry services
Publications: bibliographies of leading articles

Gokhale Institute of Politics and Economics Library
Address: Poona 411 004
Telephone: (212) 54287
Enquiries: Mrs A Ogale (Documentation Officer)
Availability: apart from the Institute staff and students, the library is open to graduates on payment of a membership fee
Hours: 11.00-17.30 Monday to Friday, 07.30-11.30 Saturday; summer (16th April-31st May): 07.00-12.00 Monday to Saturday
Stock: 226,000 books covering economics, sociology and politics
Services: photocopying, inter-library loans, enquiry services
Publications: the Institute issues many publications and a full list is available; includes bibliographies

Gujarat Vidyapith Library
Address: Gandhi Bhavan, Ashram Road, Ahmedabad 380014
Telephone: (272) 446148
Enquiries: K L Shah
Availability: open to the public, on payment of a small deposit and production of a guarantor's signature on a prescribed form
Hours: 09.00-19.00 all days except public holidays
Stock: collection built on the humanities and social sciences; over 700 periodicals including over 60 in the field of economics and several in the field of agriculture and agricultural economics. (Also special Gandhiana collection.)
Services: documentation, microfilming, inter-library loans, enquiry service, bibliographical services, photocopying, online computer searching etc
Publications: many bibliographies (full list available); a catalogue of articles published in Gujarati language; a catalogue of dissertations submitted by students

Indian Statistical Institute Library
Address: Documentation and Information Science Division, 203 Barrackpore Trunk Road, Calcutta 700 035
Telephone: (33) 526694 (5 lines)/528596 (3 lines)/527694 (4 lines)
Telex: 0212210 STAT IN
Enquiries: Dr Jogesh Misra (Chief Librarian)
Availability: serves students of higher classes and teachers and researchers of any institute/college/university in India by enrolling them as an institutional member; students and research scholars may also use the resources for a short period
Hours: 10.00-20.00 weekdays, 10.00-18.00 holidays
Stock: over 185,000 items; subject coverage includes statistics, economics, econometrics, marketing and business information
Services: photocopying, microfilming, microfiche etc; inter-library loans, enquiry services
Publications: bibliographies and indexes are compiled on demand from the research scientists of the institute

Jawaharlal Nehru Library
Address: Kurukshetra University, Kurukshetra 132119
Enquiries: K S Dalal (Librarian)
Availability: persons not belonging to the University may be admitted to the library under special conditions and on payment of a small fee

Hours: 07.00-19.00 summer, 09.00-20.00 winter, 11.00-18.00 holidays and Sundays; open throughout the year except for 6 days
Stock: over 650,000 books and bound periodicals volumes, and over 1800 periodicals received annually. Strengths in social sciences and humanities, with a special collection on East African and Soviet Studies to support area study centres
Services: photocopying, inter-library loans, enquiry service

Jawaharlal Nehru University Library
Address: New Mehrauli Road, New Delhi 110067
Telephone: (11) 650005/667676/667557 ext 370
Telex: 73167 JNU IN
Enquiries: V B Nanda (University Librarian)
Availability: open to faculty, post graduate students and research scholars only
Hours: 09.00-22.00 every day except four days a year
Stock: about 350,000 volumes covering all subjects including economics and international trade and development; includes government publications, publications of international organisations. 2000 journals on active subscription list
Services: photocopying, loans, press clippings, reference service
Publications: SUCHIKA (monthly index of social science articles); *J.N.U. dissertation index; India & World Affairs : A Bibliography* (database on India's Foreign Policy, 1947 to date)

Jayakar Library
Address: c/o University of Poona, Ganeshkhind, Poona 411007
Telephone: (212) 50064 ext 35
Enquiries: Dr S G Mahajan
Availability: open to the public with prior permission
Hours: 11.00-18.00; 08.00-21.00 during examination period
Stock: over 300,000 volumes (including bound volumes of periodicals) covering all postgraduate and research subjects
Services: photocopying, loans, enquiry service
Publications: Monthly list of documentation on social sciences; also catalogues of theses and dissertations, manuscripts and incunabula

National Council of Applied Economic Research
Address: Parisila Bhavan 11, Indraprastha Estate, New Delhi-110002
Telephone: (11) 3317861-68
Telex: 3165880 NCAR IN
Enquiries: N J Sebastian
Availability: open to the public, for reference only
Hours: 09.30-17.30 Monday to Friday
Stock: covers economics, energy, agriculture, rural development, industry, transportation; holds monographs, reports, serials, press clippings, company annual reports, statistical publications, UN documents etc, as well as the NCAER's own publications. Special collection of Census of India publications. Stock of about 56,000 books and reports; receives 540 journal titles
Services: access to bibliographic database of Indian economic literature, continuously updated
Publications: Artha suchi (quarterly index of Indian economic literature, the printed product from the database listed under *Services*)

National Productivity Council
Address: Lodi Road, New Delhi 110003
Telephone: (11) 690331/690332
Telex: 031-66059 NPC IN
Enquiries: S N Vig (information officer)
Availability: open to the public, for reference only
Hours: 09.00-17.30 Monday to Friday
Stock: over 15,000 books, 300 journal titles currently received; covers productivity, plant engineering, fuel efficiency, behavioural sciences, HRD, marketing, rural technology etc
Services: photocopying, inter-library loans, reference service, bibliographical service
Publications: bibliographies on topics relevant to the work of the Council

National Social Science Documentation Centre
Address: Indian Council of Social Science Research, 35 Ferozeshah Road, New Delhi-110001
Telephone: (11) 385959/383091/381571
Telex: 3161083 ISSR IN

Enquiries: Sh S P Agrawal (Director)
Availability: open to bonafide research scholars
Hours: 09.30-18.00 every day except three national holidays (26 Jan, 15 Aug, 2 Oct)
Stock: 30,000 books, research reports and theses; 100,000 back files of periodicals; 2,500 current acquisitions of periodicals. Covers social sciences
Services: photocopying, compilation of short bibliographies (both charged for); reference and referral services, consultancy, translation
Publications: Research information series (full list of titles available; includes indexes, bibliographies, union lists of periodicals)

INDONESIA

Airlangga University Library
Address: Jalan Oharmawangsa Dalam, Surabaya 60286, East Java
Telephone: (31) 40826/44509
Telex: 31138 UNAIR IA
Enquiries: Mrs. Drs. Parlinah Moedjono
Availability: open to students, lecturers and employees of the University; others need permission from the Chief Librarian
Hours: 07.30-20.00 Monday to Thursday, 07.30-11.00 Friday, 07.30-12.30 Saturday
Stock: covers most subjects; includes over 12,000 book titles and about 30 periodical titles in the field of social sciences
Services: photocopying, loans, enquiry service, offline computer searches
Publications: accession list (every two weeks, arranged by subject in Indonesian and English)

Brawijaya University Library
Address: Jalan Mayjen Haryono 169, Malang
Telephone: 51611 ext 171
Enquiries: Soejono
Availability: limited access for members of the public
Hours: 08.00-13.00, 16.00-20.00 Monday to Saturday
Stock: 60,000 books and 340 journals in the fields of law, economics, administration, agriculture, animal husbandry, fishery, engineering and medicine
Services: photocopying, loans
Publications: accession list

Gadjah Mada University Library
Address: Bulaksumur, PO Box 16, Yogyakarta
Telephone: 274 3163, or 88688 ext 494
Telex: 25135 IA
Enquiries: Mrs Murianti Pranowo (Chief Librarian)
Availability: open to the public
Hours: 08.00-13.00, 16.00-21.00 Monday to Thursday, 08.00-11.00, 16.00-21.00 Friday, 08.00-12.00, 16.00-21.00 Saturday
Stock: collection covers all subjects, consisting of over 300,000 volumes. Marketing and business information are available in the Economics Faculty Library
Services: photocopying, enquiry service, local inter-library loans; online searches
Publications: bibliography (monthly) and newsletter, both in Indonesian

IRAN

National Library of Iran
Address: 30 Tir Street, Tehran 11364
Telephone: (21) 673315/673564
Fax: (21) 281667
Enquiries: the Director
Availability: open for reference only to researchers, professors, scholars and students
Hours: 07.30-19.00
Stock: about 167603 volumes of Persian and Arabic printed books and 120,000 volumes in other languages; over 1,000 Persian and Arabic periodical titles, 1,400 Persian and Arabic newspaper titles, 700 periodicals in other languages. Acquires two copies of each book published in Iran and receives Government publications directly from the publishers

Services: acts as referral centre nationally and internationally; enquiry service
Publications: National bibliography of Iran

IRAQ

National Library
Address: Bab-el-Muaddum, PO Box 14340, Baghdad, Iraq
Telephone: (1) 4164190/4164199
Enquiries: Abdul Hameed El-Alawchi
Availability: open to the public
Hours: 08.00-17.00 Saturday to Thursday
Stock: all subjects
Services: photocopying, internal loans, enquiry service
Publications: Iraqi national bibliography; Al-Maktabah el-Arabiah (journal)

ISRAEL

Israel Institute of Productivity
Address: 4 Szold Street, (PO Box 33010), Tel Aviv 61330
Telephone: (03) 430231/430315/216890
Fax: (03) 216892
Enquiries: Mrs Avie Sommer, Mrs Larissa Feiger, Miss Pnina Kibrit
Availability: open to staff, students and affiliated members of the Institute as a lending and research library; open to the public at large for research on the spot and by subscription
Hours: 08.00-16.00 Sunday to Thursday; 08.00-13.00 Friday
Stock: 26,800 books, 250 periodicals, focusing on all aspects of production engineering, different facets of management including building management, labour relations and behavioural science, marketing, computing
Services: loans, enquiry service

Tel Aviv University, Library of Social Sciences and Management
Address: PO Box 39654, Tel Aviv 61396
Telephone: (03) 6409361
Fax: (03) 6409527
Telex: 342171 VERSY IL
Enquiries: Mrs Hadasa Ron
Availability: open to the public by annual subscription
Hours: 09.00-20.45 Sunday to Thursday
Stock: 1,500 periodical subscriptions, 100,000 volumes of books, covering management, finance, marketing, computers, economics, sociology, insurance, public administration, political science and labour studies
Services: photocopying, loans, reference; online computer searching planned in the near future
Publications: monthly list of new acquisitions

JAMAICA

Jamaica Library Service
Address: 2 Tom Redcam Drive, Kingston 5, Jamaica
Telex: 92-63310-2
Enquiries: Mrs Sybil Iton (Director)
Availability: open to the public
Hours: headquarters open 09.00-17.00 Monday to Friday; public libraries open 09.00-19.00 Monday to Friday, 09.00-13.00 or 09.00-17.00 Saturday
Stock: over 1,204,000 volumes covering all subjects
Services: photocopying, inter-library loans, enquiry service
Publications: Annual report; Statistical report of the Jamaica Library Service; Additions to stock; bibliographies, etc

National Library of Jamaica
Address: 12 East Street, Kingston, Jamaica
Telephone: 922 0620/5533
Enquiries: The Director
Availability: open to the public for reference use only
Hours: 09.00-17.00 Monday to Friday; 09.00-13.00 Saturday; closed Saturday during July and August
Stock: the library collects all material published in Jamaica, by Jamaicans, and about Jamaica. Stock includes monographs, serials (including periodicals and newspapers) and audio-visual publications, plus clippings files, on Jamaica and the West Indies
Services: photocopying, microfilming, reference, research and referral; online computer searching being planned for local and overseas databases
Publications: Jamaican national bibliography (quarterly); occasional bibliography series, etc

JAPAN

International Development Center of Japan, Library, Research and Development Division
Address: Shuwa Daini Toranomon Bldg, 21-19 Toranomon 1-chome, Minato-ku, Tokyo 105
Telephone: (03) 502 3911
Telex: J25338 DEVCENT
Enquiries: Miss Keiko Sanae, Miss Kaori Ohtake
Availability: books in the open stacks are freely available for use in the reading room
Hours: 10.00-12.00, 13.00-17.00
Stock: specialises in regional and economic features of developing countries, with emphasis on works relating to economic development, economic development studies, project evaluation etc. 25,000 books and 380 periodicals
Publications: IDCJ working paper series

Management and Co-ordination Agency, Library of the Statistics Bureau
Address: 19-1 Wakamatsu-cho, Shinjuku-ku, Tokyo 162
Telephone: (03) 202 1111 ext 485 (reading room), ext 486 (information unit)
Availability: open to the public
Hours: reading room: 09.15-16.45 Monday to Friday, 09.15-12.00 Saturday; information unit: 09.30-16.30 Monday to Friday, 09.30-12.00 Saturday
Stock: 103,000 volumes of Japanese books and 58,000 volumes of foreign books; stock covers a wide range of statistics of Japan and foreign countries, ie demography, economy, industry, health and welfare, education
Services: photocopying service available in the reading room (charged for), during the following hours: 10.00-11.30, 13.30-15.00 Monday to Friday, 10.00-11.00 Saturday
Publications: Catalogue of foreign books; Catalogue of Japanese books; Catalogue of foreign serials; Catalogue of Japanese serials; Annual catalogue of books added to the library

National Diet Library
Address: 10-1 Nagatacho 1 chome, Chiyoda-ku, Tokyo 100
Telephone: (03) 3581 2331
Fax: (03) 35979104
Telex: 2225393 NADLB
Enquiries: Director, Library Co-operation Department
Availability: open to anyone aged 20 or over, both Japanese and foreigners
Hours: 09.30-17.00 Monday to Saturday
Stock: about five million volumes of books and about 115,000 serial titles. Is the sole depository library in the country, receiving several copies of all government publications and publications of local public entities, and one copy of all private publications. Also has large numbers of overseas science and technology serials and social science books, and a collection of foreign government publications and publications of international organisations
Services: photocopying, loans, reference service
Publications: many publications, including *Japanese national bibliography* (weekly, annual, quarterly index); *Japanese periodicals index. Humanities and social science* (quarterly); *Catalog of the histories of companies and economic organisations in the National Diet Library; Accession list - Chinese and Korean language publications* (irregular); *Accession list - foreign language publications* (monthly); *Materials on Asia - accession list and review* (monthly); *Statistical abstracts of Japan* (annual)

National Institute for Research Advancement (NIRA), Centre for Policy Research Information
Address: Mitsui Building, 37th Floor, 2-1-1 Nishi-Shinjuku, Shinjuku-ku, Tokyo 163-04
Telephone: (3) 33443371
Fax: (3) 33451449
Telex: 2325332 NIRA J
Enquiries: Mikio Sono
Availability: open to the public by appointment only
Hours: 10.00 - 12.00, 13.00 - 17.00 Monday to Friday

Stock: covers economics, financial policy, public finance, business, labour, industry and commerce, law, political science, social science, society and technology and engineering. The material is mainly in English with international coverage. It includes information on policy research institutes (worldwide); journals; statistics; books (16,500); newspapers
Services: photocopying (minimal charge)
Publications: NIRA's World Directory of Think Tanks 1993 (¥10,000); *Nira Library International Crossroads* (distributed publication)
Notes: A list of NIRA publications is available.

Otaru University of Commerce Library, Reference Division
Address: 3-5-21 Midori, Otaru, Hokkaido 047
Telephone: (0134) 231101 ext 555
Enquiries: Chuji Matsumoto (Director), Hajime Murakami (Chief Officer), Toshimichi Hamada (Reference Librarian)
Availability: open to the public, for reference only
Hours: 09.00-17.00 Monday to Friday, 09.00-12.30 Saturday
Stock: over 162,000 books in the field of social sciences, including about 93,000 in Japanese and Chinese and 69,000 in other languages; over 2,200 Japanese periodical titles and about 650 foreign periodical titles; also about 14,500 books on agriculture and industry
Publications: bibliographies and catalogues

Research Institute for Economics and Business Administration, Library
Address: Kobe University, Rokkodai-cho, Nada-ku, Kobe 657
Telephone: (078) 881 1212 exts 3618, 3619
Enquiries: Tetsuji Maeda
Availability: open to the public
Hours: 09.00-17.00 Monday to Friday
Stock: 184,000 volumes of books, 2,500 periodical titles, 320,000 microfiche sheets; covers economics and business administration
Services: photocopying

Tokyo Metropolitan Central Library
Address: 5-7-13 Minamiazabu, Minato-ku, Tokyo 106
Telephone: (03) 34428451
Fax: (03) 34428919
Enquiries: Shuichi Kato
Availability: open to anyone aged 16 or over
Hours: 13.00-20.00 Monday, 09.30-20.00 Tuesday to Friday, 09.30-17.00 Saturday, Sunday and public holidays
Stock: over one million books and over 8,800 periodical titles
Services: photocopying, enquiry service
Publications: Catalog of foreign books in the Tokyo Metropolitan Central Library

JORDAN

Council of Arab Economic Unity
Address: PO Box 925100, Amman
Telephone: (6) 643268
Telex: 21900 WEHDA JO
Enquiries: Mrs Haifa Sharaiha (Librarian)

Greater Amman Public Library
Address: PO Box 182181, Amman
Telephone: (6) 637111
Telex: 21969 AMCITY JO
Enquiries: Farouk Mo'az (City Librarian)
Availability: open to the public
Hours: 08.00-17.00 (closed Fridays and official holidays)
Stock: 170,000 volumes on all subjects, including Arabic and English publications
Services: photocopying, loans, enquiry service

University of Jordan Library
Address: University of Jordan, Amman
Telephone: (6) 843555, (6) 843666 ext 3135
Telex: 21629 UNVJ JO
Enquiries: Dr Hani al-Amad (Director), Mr Izzat Zahidah (Deputy Director)
Availability: open to the public; refundable deposit required for borrowing
Hours: 08.00-20.00 Saturday to Wednesday, 08.00-17.00 Thursday
Stock: over 504,000 volumes covering all subjects, in various

languages. Depository library for publications of the UN and its agencies. Is the largest library in Jordan
Services: photocopying, loans, enquiry service, bibliographies, reference service, microfilming, literature search, professional lectures
Publications: Index of Arabic References; Index of Foreign References; Index of Microfilmed Manuscripts; Al-Maktaba (monthly newsletter); *Index of Dissertations; Index of Periodicals; Reader's Guide*

KENYA

Kenya National Library Service
Address: PO Box 30573, Nairobi
Telephone: (02) 725550, 725551
Enquiries: Francis W Ochden (Librarian)
Availability: public library open to all Kenyan citizens and visitors
Hours: 09.30-17.00 Monday to Friday, 09.00-13.00 Saturday
Stock: 250,000 items in main lending and reference library; East Africana collection, Kenyana collection
Services: loans, enquiry service, book post service
Publications: National bibliography; Kenya periodicals directory

KUWAIT

British Council Library
Address: 2 Al Arabi Street, Al Mansouriyah, PO Box 345, 13004 Safat
Telephone: 2520067/8
Fax: 2520069
Enquiries: Dr Thelma S Cruz
Availability: open to the public (membership)
Hours: 09.00 - 13.00, 16.00 - 20.00 Saturday; 09.00 - 13.00 Thursday
Stock: covers general interest, education, culture. Material in English and includes company and trade directories (UK); journals; 10,000 books; local and British newspapers; audio-visual material. CD-ROM facilities
Services: photocopying
Notes: The Kuwait British Council Library is the only English lending library in the country.

LEBANON

Centre d'Etudes et de Recherches sur le Moyen-Orient Contemporain (CERMOC), Bibliothèque
Address: Rue de Damas, PO Box 2691, Beirut
Telephone: (1) 640695/4
institute
Enquiries: Jean Hannoyer (director), Nada Kettaneh (librarian)
Availability: open to the public
Hours: Monday to Friday
Stock: material on the contemporary Middle East, particularly Lebanon, Beirut, Jordan, Palestine. 9,000 books, 200 journals, statistical publications. Material in French, English and Arabic

LIBYA

Garyounis University, Central Library
Address: PO Box 1308, Benghazi, Libya
Telephone: (61) 29713
Telex: 40175 UNIGAR LY
Enquiries: Ahmed M Gallal
Availability: open to the public with special permission
Hours: 07.00-18.00
Stock: about 250,000 volumes; 1,200 periodical titles, plus large number of microfilms and microfiches
Services: photocopying, loans

MALAWI

Malawi National Library Service
Address: PO Box 30314, Capital City, Lilongwe 3
Telephone: 783700
Fax: 783560
Enquiries: R S Mabomba, M A Ngaunje
Availability: open to the public
Hours: 09.00-17.30 Monday to Friday, 08.30-12.00 Saturday
Stock: total stock of 150,000 volumes on all subjects. Includes Malawi Collection in the Headquarters Reference Library, which

contains a copy of most publications printed in Malawi and a representative number of publications about Malawi from other sources

Services: lending, reference, photocopying; distribution agency for book donations

Publications: National Library Service annual report; National Library Service staff newsletter; Books about Malawi (bibliography)

National Archives of Malawi Library

Address: PO Box 62, Zomba
Telephone: 522922, 522184
Enquiries: D D Najira
Availability: open to the public for reference
Hours: 07.30-12.00, 13.00-17.00 Monday to Friday, 08.00-11.30 Saturday
Stock: 20,000 books, 160 periodical titles, 300 microfilms on a wide range of subjects. The Library is the only legal deposit library in the country and receives a copy of every publication printed in Malawi, including all Government publications etc
Services: photocopying, enquiry services
Publications: Malawi national bibliography (annual)

National Statistical Office Library

Address: PO Box 333, Zomba
Telephone: 522111/522377
Fax: 523130
Telex: 44015 CENSUS MI
Enquiries: Mr M R E Makwemba
Availability: open to the public by appointment only
Hours: 07.30 - 17.00 Monday to Friday
Stock: covers statistics including economic, financial trade, demography, markets, tourism, health, housing etc. The material is in English and covers Africa, Asia, Europe and the USA. It includes financial and company information, journals, statistics, books, national newspapers

University of Malawi Libraries

Address: PO Box 280, Zomba
Telephone: 522222
Enquiries: Steve S Mwiyeriwa
Availability: open to the public on payment of K25 annual subscription
Hours: 08.00-22.00 Monday to Friday, 08.00-12.00 Saturday, 13.00-17.00 Sunday
Stock: there are four separate libraries, including the Polytechnic Library, which contains about 41,200 volumes on commerce, business studies and engineering; the Bunda College of Agriculture Library, with 29,000 volumes; the Chancellor College Library, which has 200,000 volumes covering pure and social sciences, arts and humanities
Services: photocopying, loans, enquiry service and Kammzu College of Nursing with 15,000 volumes covering nursing and allied health sciences
Publications: Annotated bibliography of agriculture in Malawi; Union list of periodicals; University of Malawi accessions bulletin; Directory of Malawi Libraries (1990)

MALAYSIA

Asian and Pacific Development Centre, Library and Documentation Centre

Address: Pesiaran Duta, Box 12224, 50770 Kuala Lumpur
Telephone: (03) 2548088 ext 119
Telex: 30676 APDEC MA
Enquiries: Ms Siti Rafeah Shamsudin
Availability: open to staff of the APDC, officials from Malaysian government ministries, diplomatic missions, local and foreign researchers from institutions and universities and the private sector
Hours: 08.00-16.30 Monday to Friday
Stock: about 37,000 volumes of books, mainly covering agriculture, economic development and planning, energy, management, public enterprises, regional cooperation, rural development, trade and industry, training and women in development; refers to countries in the Asia and Pacific region in particular and the world in general. Collection also includes materials on specific subjects published by the UN and its

agencies, pamphlets, over 450 periodical titles, about 300 newsletter/bulletin titles, newspaper clippings. Special collection of APDC documents; the LDC is also a depository library for World Bank and South Pacific Commission publications
Services: include reference, loans, inter-library loans, photocopying, current awareness, SDI
Publications: Taxation patterns and policies in South-East countries: a bibliography; Publications on population programme management: a bibliography; South Pacific: a bibliography; Civil service in Asia: a bibliography; Rural industries: a bibliography; Rural energy planning: a bibliography

MARA Headquarters Library

Address: MARA (Majlis Amanah Rakyat - Trust Council for the People), 232 Jalan Abd. Rahman, 50609 Kuala Lumpur, West Malaysia
Telephone: (03) 2915111 ext 1417
Telex: 30316 MARA MA
Stock: anything related to business, eg industry profiles, reports, seminar/conference working papers

Ministry of Trade and Industry, Library

Address: 6th Floor, Ministry of Trade and Industry, Block 10, Government Offices Complex, Jalan Duta, 50622 Kuala Lumpur
Telephone: (03) 2546022/2548044 exts 431/722
Enquiries: Azeemunnisa Bte Abdul Majid
Availability: open to students, researchers specialising in industrial and commercial information on Malaysia, and civil servants; must bring a letter of reference from place of work or study
Hours: 08.00-16.15 Monday to Friday, 08.00-12.30 Saturday
Stock: about 11,600 books classified by the Standard Index for Trade Classification and 150 titles of magazines and newsletters. Subjects covered are trade, industry, commerce, statistics, management, law, shipping, SITC products, materials under countries, economy and finance. Special collection of import and export statistics of Malaysia
Services: reference enquiries, research enquiries, inter-library loans, circulation services, photocopying, TV and video services, current awareness services
Publications: accession list of current serials

National Library of Malaysia, Reference Division

Address: Tingkat 1, Wisma Sachdev, Jalan Raja Laut, 50572 Kuala Lumpur
Telephone: (03) 2923144/2923270/2923348/2923491
Fax: (03) 2917436
Telex: 30092 NATLIB MA
Enquiries: Director General, National Library of Malaysia
Availability: open to the public
Hours: 09.00-18.00 Tuesday to Friday; 09.00-17.00 Saturday; 09.30-17.00 Sunday
Stock: Books 625,432 volumes; Serials 16,432 titles; Manuscripts 1,338 volumes; Microfilm 4,835 reels; Microfiche 21,593 sheets; plus tapes, cassettes, maps and posters
Services: photocopying, loans, reference enquiry service, online searches
Publications: Bibliografi perniagaan dan industri (bibliography on business and industries); *Bibliografi perdagangan dan perindustrian* (bibliography on trade and industries); *Bibliografi mengenai pelaburan* (bibliography on investments)

Sabah State Library

Address: 88572 Kota Kinabalu, Sabah
Telephone: (088) 54333/54243/ 54493
Fax: (088) 233167
Telex: 80236 SASLIB MA
Enquiries: Mrs Adeline Leong (Director)
Availability: open to the public
Hours: 09.00-21.00 Monday to Friday, 09.00-17.00 Saturday, 09.00-13.00 Sunday
Stock: about 523,000 books; large reference and information collection, business collection, about 300 current magazine, periodical and newspaper subscriptions from all over the world
Services: loans, photocopying, enquiry service
Publications: accession lists, bibliography of the local collection, annual report

University of Malaysia Library
Address: Lembah Pantai, 59100 Kuala Lumpur
Telephone: (03) 7576887
Fax: (03) 7573661
Telex: 37453 MA
Enquiries: Mrs Khoo Siew Mun (Chief Librarian)
Availability: open to the public for reference and research on application to the Librarian; payment of registration fee, annual subscription and for membership card required, except sometimes for occasional visits
Hours: Main Library (term-time): 08.00-22.30 Monday to Friday, 08.00-15.30 (22.30 during period 2 of Semester II) Saturday and Sunday; closed public holidays, except period 2 of Semester II; varying hours for other parts of the library, eg Bound Periodicals Library, Current Periodicals Room, National Collection Division; reduced hours during semester breaks and long vacations
Stock: total of about one million items on all subjects and over 7,000 current periodical titles. General textbook collection; reference collection, including directories, indexes etc; conference proceedings. Special collections: East Asian Collection; Official Publications Collection; the National Collection and also the Arabic and Tamil Collections
Services: include loans, inter-library loans, enquiry service (contact Reader Services Division for enquiry service)
Publications: Kekal abadi (quarterly newsletter); *Senarai perolehan baru* (monthly accessions list of the Main Library); *Senarai Asia tenggara* (quarterly accessions list of South-East Asian materials in the Main Library);*Koleksi Asia Timur : Senarai Perolehan Baru* (quarterly accessions list of Chinese books); *Senarai Buku-buku Arab yang Diperolehi*; (biannual accessions list of Arabic books); *Senarai Buku-Buku Tamil* (quarterly list of Tamil books); also many bibliographies, listings and other works (complete list contained in *Guide to the Library*)

Universiti Utara Malaysia, Library
Address: Bandar Darulaman, 06000 Jitra, Kedah
Telephone: 772066
Telex: 42052 MA
Enquiries: Azizan Husain
Availability: open to the public, for reference only
Hours: 08.00-22.00 Saturday to Wednesday, 08.00-12.45 Thursday
Stock: about 30,000 volumes; subjects covered include economics, management, business and accounting as well as other subjects taught in the University
Services: photocopying, loans, enquiry service, online computer searching, inter-library loans
Publications: accession lists, bibliographies

MAURITIUS

Development Bank of Mauritius, Archives Department
Address: Petite Rivière
Telephone: 2334299/2334469
Enquiries: Dr Paul Henry Sooprayen (chief archivist)
Availability: open to the public on payment of moderate fee
Hours: 09.00 - 13.30 Monday to Friday; 09.00 - 12.00 Saturday
Stock: covers economic, political and social history of Mauritius. 10,000 books, 7,000 journals, statistics, local newspapers, company information for Mauritian companies
Services: photocopying, enquiry service
Publications: Annual report (20 rupees), *Quarterly memorandum of books* (free)

University of Mauritius Library
Address: Reduit, Mauritius
Telephone: 541041 ext 229
Fax: 454 9642
Telex: 4621 UNIM IW
Enquiries: B R Goordyal
Availability: open to the public on application; free access for study and consultation
Hours: 09.00-18.00 Monday to Friday, 09.00-12.00 Saturday
Stock: about 95,000 volumes; coverage includes accounting, banking, business studies, economics, executive and secretarial practice, law, public administration, local government, agriculture,

engineering, pure sciences
Services: photocopying, loans, enquiry service, microfilming
Publications: list available on request

MEXICO

Banco Nacional de Comercio Exterior, SNC
Address: Cerrada de Malintzin 28, Colonia del Carmen, Coyoacán, 04100 Mexico, DF
Telephone: (5) 688 1168
Telex: 017-71-070 BANCOMEXT ME
Enquiries: Lic. Maria Teresa Cornejo Gallegos
Availability: open to the public
Stock: library with about 5,000 books and 150 periodical subscriptions; also an Information Centre with about 18,000 documents and 100 periodical subscriptions. Specialises in materials on foreign trade, including directories, statistics, tariffs, market reports for specific products and countries

Camara Nacional de la Industria de Transformación
Address: Technical Information Center, San Antonio no. 256, Esq. Patriotismo Col. Ampliación Napoles, 03849 Mexico, DF
Telephone: (5) 563 3400 ext 131/136
Enquiries: Jorge Pineda Palacios (Manager, Technical Information Center)
Availability: open to the general public, students and industrialists
Hours: Monday to Friday
Stock: technical information and industry information
Services: photocopying service

Centro de Información sobre Comercio Exterior
Address: San Fernando 37, Tlalpan, 14050 Mexico, DF
Telephone: (5) 6556011, (5) 6525377 ext 1060/1061
Telex: 1777569 INFO ME
Services: information services on foreign trade
Publications: acquisition bulletin and *Alert*

INFOTEC
Address: San Fernando 37, Tlalpan, 14050 Mexico, DF
Telephone: (5) 655 6011 ext 1152/1143
Fax: (5) 568 9921
Telex: 1777569 INFO ME
Enquiries: Miss Guadalupe Carrión-Rodriguez
Hours: 09.00-18.00 Monday to Friday
Stock: about 7,300 books, including catalogues, directories, dictionaries, handbooks etc. Covers mostly technical subjects, but also contains material on statistics, management, innovation and technological development
Services: photocopying, loans, enquiry service, computer search service, consultancy service and training activities
Publications: monthly current awareness service, covering 13 areas including petrochemicals, pharmacy, strategic planning, administration, food, chemicals

Instituto de la Integración Iberoamerica, SC
Address: Camelia 329, Col. Florida, Mexico, 01050 DF
Telephone: (5) 548 0629/1073
Enquiries: Montserrat Alvarez Trejo
Availability: open to the public
Hours: 10.00-14.00, 17.00-20.00 Monday to Friday
Stock: economics and social subjects
Services: photocopying
Publications: some publications on economic topics

Instituto Tecnológico Autónomo de México, Biblioteca "Lic. Raúl Bailleres Jr"
Address: Río Hondo No.1, Col. Progreso Tizapán, Del. Alvaro Obregón, 01000 Mexico, DF
Telephone: (5) 550 9300 ext 110/109
Enquiries: José Orozco Tenorio
Availability: open to the public, but with some restriction on the services; if the external user obtains a library ID he is entitled to all services
Hours: 08.00-21.30 Monday to Friday, 08.00-12.00 Saturday
Stock: about 70,000 volumes and 500 periodicals on business administration, economics, computing, law, accounting and mathematics; special collection on the economic history of Mexico, depository library for the statistical publications of the

Mexican government
Services: all circulation services, inter-library loans, SDI, online computer searches, current awareness etc

MOROCCO

Centre National de Documentation
Address: Charii Maa Al Ainain, Haut-Agdal, BP 826, Rabat
Telephone: (7) 774944
Fax: (7) 773134
Telex: 310-52 M
Enquiries: Ahmed Fassi Fihri (Director)
Availability: open to the public
Hours: 08.30-12.00, 14.30-18.30 Monday to Friday
Stock: covers all subjects
Services: online computer searches, photocopying, production of microfilm and microfiche
Publications: include indexes in the fields of agriculture, management, economics, and some reference works. Full list available

Direction de la Statistique
Address: Charia Ma-Al-Ainain, BP 178, Rabat
Telephone: (7) 73606
Fax: (7) 73042
Telex: 32714 M
Availability: open to the public
Stock: includes all the publications of the Ministry of Planning, of which the Direction de la Statistique is a part

NEW CALEDONIA

South Pacific Commission
Address: BP D5, Nouméa Cedex, New Caledonia
Telephone: 262000/262011
Telex: 3139 NM SOPACOM
Fax: 263818
Enquiries: The Librarian
Publications: Statistical Bulletin/South Pacific Economies: statistical summary; *South Pacific Epidemiological and Health Information Service (SPEHIS)*

NEW ZEALAND

Auckland Public Library
Address: Lorne Street, Auckland 1; mailing address: PO Box 4138, Auckland
Telephone: (9) 3770209
Fax: (9) 3077741
Enquiries: Marion Saunders (City Librarian)
Availability: open to the public
Hours: 09.30-20.00 Monday to Thursday, 09.30-21.00 Friday, 09.30-17.30 Saturday (no borrowing after 13.00), 13.00-17.00 Sunday (reading only)
Stock: includes New Zealand reference collection, concentrating on the Auckland area; New Zealand, Australian, British and ISO standards as well as selected United States standards; overseas and New Zealand telephone and business directory collection; manuals collection consisting of motor vehicle and electrical appliances, New Zealand and overseas statistics, and marketing research collection
Services: all public library services, including online searching of local and overseas databases

Department of Statistics
Address: Aorangi House, 85 Molesworth Street, Wellington
Telephone: (4) 4954708
Fax: (4) 4729135
Telex: 31313 STATSWN NZ
Enquiries: Janet Upton
Availability: open to the public for research/reference purposes
Hours: 08.30-16.35 Monday to Friday
Stock: complete series of the Department's publications; 2,000 serial titles, many from overseas statistical organisations on exchange agreements; approximately 400 book titles covering social sciences, economics, management, computer technology, mathematics etc
Services: for the public: initial help tracing information, photocopying; for Departmental staff: all special library services, including photocopying, loans, reference requests, overseas

database searching, online searching
Notes: The Department has three other offices which have a small time series of publications available for study (usually three to five years, but often longer); they are in the following locations:
Address: Goodman Fielder Wattie Building, 70 Symonds St., Auckland
Telephone: (9) 3031055
Fax: (9) 790859
Address: Norwich Union Building, Cnr Bond/Rattray Streets, Dunedin
Telephone: (3) 477 7511
Fax: (3) 477 5243
Address: Winchester House, 64 Kilmore St, Christchurch
Telephone: (03) 793700
Fax: (03) 792554

DSIR Library Centre (Department of Scientific and Industrial Research)
Address: Private Bag 13, Petone
Telephone: (4) 666919 ext 8361
Telex: 74-3814
Fax: (4) 690117
Enquiries: Monica Hissink (Chief Librarian), or Reference/Liaison Section
Availability: open to the public during working hours; some charges for services levied
Hours: 08.00-17.00 Monday to Friday
Stock: collection of about 6,000 serial titles, 500 metres of books, 100 metres of standards and 700 metres of abstracts. Subjects covered are chemistry, physics and engineering, industrial processing and information technology, plus a small collection of non-scientific/technical titles of general science, business and economics; marketing and business information is small, but growing as the need to market services increases. Trade literature is selectively collected in the areas of electronics, instruments, components and laboratory equipment
Services: photocopying, inter-library loans; most items available for loan, some restrictions on loans of reference and abstract material; telephone and personal enquiry services; access to a number of DSIR databases including the DSIR union catalogue of 30,000+ records and SIRIS, the index to New Zealand scientific and technical literature (primarily DSIR publications), of about 13,000 records; also access to 14 overseas online database host systems, including DIALOG, ESA, Pergamon-InfoLine, BRS and ORBIT
Publications: Libra database monthly index (list of new publications received by all DSIR libraries for the current month); *DSIR bibliographic network publication*; occasional contributions to items in *Science information papers* series

National Library of New Zealand, Information Service
Address: Private Bag, Wellington
Telephone: (4) 743032
Telex: 30076 NZ
Enquiries: Christopher Keyse (Head of Reference Services)
Availability: open to all members of the public, although the public are encouraged to use their own local or institutional libraries first; reference only (lending available through inter-library loans)
Hours: 09.00-17.00 Monday to Friday
Stock: 500,000 monographs; all subjects covered, but concentrating on social sciences, humanities and New Zealand materials. Approximately 45,000 serial titles (including monographs in series); all subjects covered including technical, marketing and business. Separate reference collection contains large collection of national and international business directories
Services: photocopying, inter-library loans, referral service, online searches, enquiry service, facsimile transmission
Publications: bibliographies, pamphlets

New Zealand Institute of Economic Research, Library
Address: PO Box 3479, Wellington
Telephone: (4) 472 1880
Fax: (4) 472 1211
Enquiries: Mrs Margaret Malan
Availability: the Institute library serves its research staff and members primarily, but members of the public may use the library by arrangement

Hours: 09.00-15.00 Monday to Friday
Stock: bookstock about 1,000 titles and about 150 journal subscriptions, covering economics
Services: photocopying, enquiry service
Publications: the Institute publishes: *Quarterly predictions*; *Quarterly survey of business opinion*; research monographs and discussion papers

New Zealand Tourist and Publicity Department, NZTP Library
Address: 256 Lambton Quay, Wellington; mailing address: Private Bag, Wellington
Telephone: (4) 728860 exts 8770/8727
Fax: (4) 781736
Enquiries: Senior Librarian
Availability: open to the public on a restricted basis; resources to be used in-house or via interloan system
Hours: 08.30-17.00 Monday to Friday
Stock: 330 journal titles, 4,000 books; emphasis on tourism, but includes marketing, management, media, public relations and New Zealand texts
Services: photocopying, loans, enquiry service, online searches
Publications: annual catalogue; *International Visitors Survey (IVS)* (annual); *Domestic Travel Survey (DTS)* (biennial); *Internal Visitor Forecasts* (annual)

Reserve Bank of New Zealand Economics Library
Address: PO Box 2498, Wellington
Telephone: (4) 472 2029
Fax: (4) 473 8554
Telex: 3368 NZ
Enquiries: Liz Castle (Librarian) or Noelle Heap (Assistant Librarian)
Availability: open to the public
Hours: 08.30-17.00 Monday to Friday (from 09.00 to the public)
Stock: approximately 600 periodicals on a standing order basis (includes those on gratis or exchange basis); about 25,000 books, including research papers, working papers from various universities, polytechnics, etc, covering all aspects of economics, econometrics, finance, central banking areas; personnel and management collection rapidly growing
Services: photocopying (minimum service, usually for interloan requests only); computer and manual searches on request; material lent to personnel from outside institutions; requests/enquiries in person and by telephone are assessed and either answered or redirected
Publications: fortnightly list of recent additions and selection of indexed articles (of a general nature) is circulated amongst Bank staff, and sent to outside organisations requesting it; bibliographies compiled on request, as time allows

SATIS (Scientific and Technical Information Service, part of the National Library of New Zealand)
Address: PO Box 12264, Wellington; PO Box 4138, Auckland; PO Box 933 Hamilton; PO Box 22-260 Christchurch
Telephone: (4) 743000
Telex: 30076 NZ
Enquiries: Helen Meehan (SATIS Manager)
Availability: SATIS is an information search service for businesses
Hours: operates under normal business hours in all the libraries where it is situated
Stock: utilises all New Zealand collections for the benefit of its clients
Services: enquiry service; in-depth search service on demand, providing photocopies, inter-library loans, computer searching, fax, courier and postal delivery
Publications: pamphlets

University of Auckland Library
Address: Private Bag 92019, Auckland
Telephone: (9) 373 7999
Fax: (9) 373 7401
Telex: 21480 NZ
Enquiries: Peter Durey (Librarian); Information Desk (ext. 8044)
Availability: open to the public for reference purposes
Hours: term: 08.30-23.00 Monday to Thursday, 08.30-20.00 Friday, 09.00-17.00 Saturday, Sunday; vacation: 09.00-17.00 Monday to Friday, 09.00-12.00 Saturday
Stock: 1.2 million volumes, 14,000 periodicals, covering arts,

social sciences, science, law, engineering, fine arts, architecture and medicine; collection of New Zealand company reports
Services: photocopying, online computer searches
Publications: various aids to the use of the collections

NIGERIA

Bendel State Library
Address: 17 James Watt Road, P.M.B. 1127, Benin City
Telephone: (52) 21457/200810/241457
Enquiries: Mr Daniel O Oboro
Availability: open to the public, free access
Hours: 08.00-20.00 Monday to Friday, 08.00-19.00 Saturday
Stock: total collection of about 454,700 covering all subject areas
Services: loans, reference services, printing and binding services and bookselling
Publications: Bendel Library journal

Central Bank of Nigeria, Lagos
Address: Research Library, Central Bank of Nigeria, Tinubu Square, Lagos, PMB 12194
Telephone: (1) 660100, exts 160/420/409
Telex: 21350 CEBANK NG
Stock: specialises in economics, money and banking
Services: provide bibliographies, undertake literature searching
Publications: New additions list with index of articles; *Cumulative index to economic and financial reviews*

Centre for Management Development, Library for Management Studies
Address: Management Village, Shangisha, PMB 21578, Ikeja, Lagos
Telephone: (1) 901120-29
Fax: (1) 961167
Enquiries: Mrs Uyai Ray Ekpu
Availability: open to supervisors, managers, chief executives within the public and private sectors of the economy, and staff of the CMD; non-staff pay annual registration fee
Hours: 08.00-18.00 Monday to Friday, 08.00-13.00 Saturday
Stock: about 20,000 items excluding bound journals, Government and company publications. Areas covered: management theory and techniques, management education and research, management development and training, management of public enterprises, small business management, management consulting, management in individual industries and in the public service. Separate serials library with over 400 journal titles and press cuttings file
Services: photocopying, loans, enquiry service, inter-library loans etc; current awareness services
Publications: bibliographies, subject profiles

Hezekiah Oluwasanmi Library
Address: Obafemi Awolowo University (formerly University of Ife), Ile-Ife
Telephone: 036230, 2290-2299 (10 lines) ext 2287
Enquiries: J O Dipeolu (University Librarian), Ms L Quamina-Aiyejina (Reference Librarian)
Availability: open to registered students and staff of the University. Special permission given to staff, postgraduate students, and research workers of other universities and institutions (local and international) with proper identification
Hours: term: 07.30-21.30 Monday to Friday, 07.30-15.30 Saturday, 13.30-21.30 Sunday; vacation: 07.30-17.30 Monday to Friday, 07.30-15.30 Saturday
Stock: 325,750 volumes, about 6,900 periodical titles and 39,800 works in microform; subjects covered include public administration, management, accounting, international relations, agriculture, social sciences and technology
Services: photocopying, loans, reference enquiries
Publications: Annual report; annual abstracts of theses and details of research in progress

Institute of Management and Technology
Address: PMB 01079, Enugu
Telephone: (42) 331015
Enquiries: F C Ekpelba
Availability: open to the public, with permission from the chief librarian
Hours: 07.30-20.00 Monday to Friday, 08.00-13.00 Saturday

Stock: covers management, technology, engineering, technical teacher education and mass communication
Services: photocopying, loans, enquiry service
Publications: Students' handbook; Bulletin; New accessions

Lagos Island Local Government, Central Library, Lagos
Address: 48 Broad Street, Lagos, Lagos State
Enquiries: Mrs O M Ogundiya (Director of Library Services)
Availability: open freely to the public
Hours: 09.00-20.00 Monday to Friday, 09.00-16.30 Saturday
Stock: 100,000 volumes covering all areas of knowledge
Services: lending, reference etc

Library Board of Kaduna State
Address: PMB 2061, Kaduna
Telephone: (62) 210322/242590/214417/217478
Enquiries: J A Maigari (Director)
Availability: open to the public without charge
Hours: 08.00-20.00 Monday to Friday, 08.00-14.00 Saturday
Stock: over 112,000 volumes covering all subjects
Services: photocopying, loans, enquiry service
Publications: newspaper indexes, annual reports, current awareness bulletins, readers' guide, guide to libraries in Kaduna State

National Library of Nigeria
Address: 4 Wesley Street, PMB 12626, Lagos
Telephone: (1) 800040-42/634704/656590/656591
Telex: 20117 TDS NG
Enquiries: Muazu Wali (Director)
Availability: open for reference only to anyone aged 16 or over
Hours: 09.00-19.00 Monday to Friday, 09.00-13.00 Saturday
Stock: General Collection of about 68,330 titles, about 19,600 titles of Nigerian official documents, about 13,650 titles of Nigerian monographs, plus UN, Organisation of African Unity documents and other documents from abroad. Includes about 1,000 titles covering marketing and business information, plus serial titles
Services: photocopying, enquiry service, inter-library loans
Publications: full list available; includes *National bibliography of Nigeria; Nigerbiblios* (quarterly); *Afribiblios* (twice a year),

University of Nigeria, Nnamdi Azikiwe Library
Address: University of Nigeria, Nsukka
Telephone: (42) 771911 ext 59
Telex: 51496 ULIONS NG
Enquiries: S C Nwoye
Availability: open to University staff and students, and researchers from outside the University
Hours: 08.00-22.30 Monday to Friday
Stock: over 400,000 monographs and over 80,000 serials. Large special collections division including UN and government documents
Services: photocopying, loans, enquiry services
Publications: Nsukka library notes; Uxilan

PAKISTAN

Federal Bureau of Statistics Library
Address: Federal Bureau of Statistics, Government of Pakistan, 1-S.M.C.H. Society, Karachi-3
Telephone: (021) 439101/439268
Telex: 23491 FBSPK
Enquiries: Senior Librarian
Availability: open to the public
Hours: summer: 08.00-14.30, winter 08.30-15.00 all working days except holidays
Stock: covers economics, statistics, mathematics and allied subjects; obtains books, periodicals, research reports by purchase, exchange arrangements and donations from various organisations in Pakistan and abroad, including several United Nations agencies
Publications: Catalogue of library books; indexes and bibliographies

Liaquat Memorial Library
Address: Education and Culture Department, Government of Sindh, Stadium Road, Karachi-5
Telephone: (021) 415765
Enquiries: I A S Bokhari
Availability: open to the public

Hours: Saturday to Thursday
Stock: 100,000 volumes, including about 610 books on marketing and about 315 on business
Services: photocopying, inter-library loans
Publications: Pakistan national bibliography; catalogues of books on special subjects

Pakistan Institute of Development Economics, Library
Address: POB 1091, Islamabad
Telephone: (51) 812440/453
Fax: (51) 210886
Telex: 5602 PIDE PK
Enquiries: Zafar Javed Naqvi
Availability: open to the public for research purposes only
Hours: 08.00 - 14.00 Monday to Friday
Stock: mainly in English, covers economic and social development, demography, computer science and library and information science. Online access
Services: loans; photocopying; enquiry service
Publications: Pakistan Development Review (quarterly); *Lectures in Development Economics* (a series No.1-No.8); *Essays in Islamic Economic Philosophy* (series No.1-No.4); *Research Reports and Monographs*

State Bank of Pakistan, Central Directorate Library
Address: I I Chundrigar Road, PO Box 5714, Karachi 74000
Telephone: (21) 2417928
Fax: (21) 2417865
Telex: 2754/23730 SBPK PK
Enquiries: Syed Abad Ali (chief librarian)
Availability: researchers are allowed on request
Hours: 09.00 - 13.30 Saturday, 09.00 - 16.00 Sunday to Thursday, closed Friday
Stock: covers economics and related subjects, especially Islamic economics. 66,000 books, annual reports of central banks, journals, local, national and international newspapers
Services: photocopying
Publications: Economic Literature: A Select Bibliography (annual); *Central Acts and Ordinances, Government of Pakistan: An Index* (1834-1979), 1981 (58p); *Pakistan Economy: A Select Bibliography - Index of Periodicals Articles* (1974-1981) 1985 (150p); *United Nations Publications in State Bank of Pakistan Library: A Catalogue, 1981* (200p); *Government of Pakistan's Publications in State Bank of Pakistan Library: A Catalogue, 1981* (72p); *Matbuwat-E-Islami (Urdu): Books on Islam in (SBP) CD Library, 1986* (164p)

PANAMA

Biblioteca de Estadística y Censo
Address: Dirección de Estadística y Censo, Contraloría General, Apartado 5213, Panama 5, Panama
Telephone: 640777 exts 269/203
Enquiries: Iris Victoria Jaspe
Availability: open to the public
Hours: 08.30-16.30 Monday to Friday
Stock: about 58,500 volumes, mainly consisting of statistical material, including economic and census material; covers Panama, other countries and international organisations
Services: enquiry service, reference, loans, photocopying
Publications: Publicaciones mas importantes recibidas en la Biblioteca (monthly list of important acquisitions); special bibliographies

Biblioteca Nacional de Panama
Address: Cl. 21 Este Bis No. 1265, Zona 3, Panama, Apartado 2444
Telephone: 624777/620393
Enquiries: Profesor Algis Borrero E. (Director)
Availability: reader's ticket available to researchers, national and foreign students, and readers in general
Hours: 08.30-19.30 Monday to Friday, 09.00-16.00 Saturday
Stock: about 50,000 Panamanian titles, about 900,000 volumes of national periodical and serial publications, about 200,000 volumes of foreign works
Services: reference, photocopying, national bibliographies, inter-library loans
Publications: national bibliographies

PAPUA NEW GUINEA

National Library Service of Papua New Guinea
Address: PO Box 5770, Boroko
Telephone: 256200
Telex: 22234 NE
Enquiries: Jane Huseby (Reader Services Librarian)
Availability: open to the public, including borrowing privileges
Hours: 09.00-17.00 Monday to Friday, 09.00-13.00 Saturday, 13.00-16.00 Sunday
Stock: includes comprehensive Papua New Guinea collection, consisting of about 30,000 items (books, periodicals, government documents, maps etc either produced in Papua New Guinea or produced elsewhere about Papua New Guinea); rest of stock also includes about 35,000 items in reference collection and about 850 titles of newspapers and magazines. Main emphasis not on business and marketing, but tries to collect general interest materials in these areas as related to Papua New Guinea, Oceania and Australasia
Services: photocopying, telephone and personal reference queries; online computer searches done by National Library of Australia
Publications: Papua New Guinea national bibliography; National union list of serials; Directory of libraries in Papua New Guinea; Selective index to Times of Papua New Guinea; Checklist of current Papua New Guinea serials; National Library Service 16mm Film Catalogue; Selective Index to Paradise Magazine; Papua New Guinea Motu-Koita Bibliography; A Checklist of the Islands of Papua New Guinea

Public Library Service of PNG, Central Library
Address: POB 3161, Port Moresby
Telephone: 211442
Fax: 251331
Telex: 22234
Enquiries: Mrs Lisbeth Manjin
Availability: open to the public
Hours: 09.00 - 17.00 Monday to Friday, 09.00 - 13.00 Saturday, 13.00 - 16.00 Sunday
Stock: covers all subjects. Material is in English and Pidgin. It includes company and trade directories (Hong Kong); 10,500 books; newspapers
Services: photocopying (10 toea per copy)
Notes: This is a small library that comes under the National Library Service of Papua New Guinea (qv).

PERU

Biblioteca Nacional del Peru
Address: Avenida Abancay 4 C. S/N, Apartado 2335, Lima
Telephone: (014) 287690 ext 20
Enquiries: Sr Juan Mejía Baca (Director)
Availability: open to the public
Hours: 09.00-21.00 Monday to Friday, 09.00-13.00 Saturday
Stock: about 3,161,800 bibliographic units
Services: photocopying, microfilm, photography
Publications: Anuario bibliografico Peruano; Boletín de la Biblioteca Nacional; Fenix: revista de la Biblioteca Nacional

ESAN Documentation Centre
Address: Escuela de Administración de Negocios para Graduados, Alonso de Molina 1698, Apartado 1846, Lima 100
Telephone: (014) 351760 ext 357; (014) 363710
Enquiries: Isabel Olivera R. (Director)
Availability: serves faculty, researchers and students of the School; also open to the business community
Hours: 09.30-20.00 Monday to Friday, 09.30-16.00 Saturday
Stock: 30,000 volumes of books, 10,000 volumes of documents, 900 current periodical titles, 2,000 volumes of other materials. Covers management, accounting, economics, finance, marketing, information services, international commerce
Services: reference services, literature searches, bibliographies, user orientation, SDI, loans, photocopying, online searches (for periodicals only), enquiry service
Publications: INF SEL (bibliographical bulletin with abstracts)

PHILIPPINES

Asian Development Bank Library
Address: 2330 Roxas Blvd, Pasay 1300 Metro Manila
Telephone: (2) 834 4444
Fax: (2) 741 7961
Telex: 23103 ADB PH, 40571 ADB PM, 63587 ADB PN
Enquiries: Mrs Andrea P Carlos (Administrative Officer)
Availability: open to the public; must bring letter of introduction, and limited to two researchers per institution at any one time
Hours: 08.30-17.30 Monday to Friday
Stock: 38,183 volumes of books, 228,759 pamphlets, 539 periodical titles, 11 local newspaper titles, 73 foreign newspaper titles. Covers economics, banking and finance, management and business, geography, government and history
Services: loans, reference service, bibliographical services, inter-library loans, photocopying, online computer searches (DIALOG)
Publications: ADB Library bibliography series; Selected index to periodicals; Subject catalogue to books in the ADB Library; Current alphabetical list of periodicals in the ADB Library; Subject guide to the periodicals collection of the Library; Bibliography on the Asian Development Bank; ADB Publications catalogue; Key indicators of developing member countries of ADB (annual); *EDRC Statistical report series* (irregular)

Asian Institute of Management Library
Address: 123 Paseo de Roxas Street, Llgaspi Village, Makati, Metro Manila; PO Box MCC PO Box 898, Makati, Metro Manila
Telephone: (2) 874011 Loc. 211/214
Fax: (2) 817 9240
Telex: 63778 AIM PN
Enquiries: Victorina E Alba (Chief Librarian)
Hours: 08.00-midnight Monday to Friday, 08.00-17.00 Saturday, 15.00-midnight Sunday
Stock: 35,000 volumes of general collection and reference materials covering all areas of business management; special collections include Industry Information Collection, which includes information sources on different industries in the Philippines and other ASEAN countries, collection of ASEAN statistical documents
Services: photocopying, loans, enquiry service
Publications: Industry Information Collection index (annual); *AIM Library recent acquisitions list* (quarterly, free). Many other publications by the Institute itself (full list available)

College of Business Administration Library
Address: University of the Philippines, Diliman, Quezon City
Telephone: 971935
Enquiries: Ms Zenaida M Galang (Librarian-in-Charge)
Availability: bona fide students, University employees; government workers and employees; and by special permit to non-UP graduates, scholars and researchers
Hours: 09.00-20.30 Monday to Friday, 09.00-12.00, 13.00-17.00 Saturday
Stock: covers accounting, business policy and administration, business law, finance, marketing, production, business economics; total of about 25,000 volumes
Services: photocopying, reference service, readers services, indexing
Publications: new acquisitions list; *The Philippine Management Review*

Manila City Library
Address: Room 372, Third Floor, City Hall Building, Manila
Telephone: (2) 408810
Enquiries: Filemon L Gecolea (Chief Librarian III)
Availability: main and branch libraries freely open to the public
Hours: 08.00-17.00 Monday to Friday
Stock: about 70,000 books on various subjects, including materials on marketing and business published by local and foreign authors and agencies
Services: circulation and reference services
Publications: annual compilations of author and subject indexes to local periodical literature subscribed to by the library

National Economic and Development Authority Library
Address: Edsa, Quezon City
Telephone: (2) 966556, 971852

Telex: 29058 RCA PHILCOM
Enquiries: Mrs Elenita M Salvatierra (Supervising Economic Information Specialist)
Availability: open to the public; due to limited seating capacity, college students are admitted on a limited basis
Hours: 08.00-12.00, 13.00-17.00 Monday to Friday
Stock: majority of the collection covers economics, economic planning, economic development, regional planning, project management, social development and information technology; statistical reference materials covering economic and business information
Services: circulation, inter-library loans, enquiry service
Publications: bibliographies on various subjects prepared on request

National Library of the Philippines

Address: T M Kalaw Street, Manila
Telephone: (2) 505132/584361
Telex: 40726 NALIB
Enquiries: Mrs Narcissa V Muñasque
Availability: open to the public; present TNL ID card to checker of each reading area
Hours: 09.00-18.00 Monday to Saturday
Stock: over a million items in three reading areas, plus theses and dissertations collection
Services: photocopying, enquiry services
Publications: Philippine national bibliography; various research guides to the collections

Sycip, Gorres, Velayo & Company, Library

Address: 105 de la Rosa Street, Makati Commercial Center, Makati, Metro Manila
Telephone: (2) 817 0301
Telex: 22160 SGV PH
Enquiries: Celia S Samson
Availability: caters generally for the information needs of SGV staff, but also open to outside researchers who are referred by the school or company they are affiliated to
Hours: 08.00-18.00 Monday to Friday, 08.00-12.00 Saturday
Stock: 44,000 books, 350 periodical and serial titles, 60 cassette tapes; covers accounting, auditing, marketing, economics, management, law and taxation and other business related fields
Services: loans, enquiry service, METAFILE database for information retrieval, SDI services (eg circulation of annotated monthly list of acquisitions, bibliographies of basic books in particular subjects etc)
Publications: SGV journal; SGV newsletter; SGV financial studies

University of the East Library

Address: C M Recto Avenue, Manila
Enquiries: Mrs Sarah C de Jesus (Chief Librarian)
Availability: open to the public; must bring referral from respective librarians
Hours: 08.00-20.00 Monday to Friday
Stock: 250,000 volumes of books, 15,000 volumes of bound periodicals; covers wide range of subjects, including social sciences and agriculture
Services: photocopying services, bibliographic services

University of the Philippines, School of Economics, Library

Address: Diliman, Quezon City
Telephone: (2) 982044
Fax: (2) 991929
Enquiries: Rosemarie G Rosali
Availability: open to the public
Hours: 08.00 - 17.00 Monday to Friday, 08.00 - 12.00 Saturday
Stock: covers economics, quantitative methods, industrial organizations, technological change, industry studies, manpower, labour, population. 63,000 books, 460 journals, statistics, company information for local and some foreign companies. Material in English
Services: interlibrary loans; photocopying; enquiry service; referrals; bibliographic service
Publications: Philippine Economic Bibliography; Bibliography of theses and dissertations

PUERTO RICO

Biblioteca Regional del Caribe y de Estudios Latinoamericanos

Address: Apartado Postal Núm. 21927, Estación de la Universidad, San Juan 00931
Telephone: 764 0000 ext 3319
Enquiries: Almaluces Figueroa (Head)
Availability: open to the public (but closed stacks)
Hours: 07.00-17.00 Monday to Friday, 08.00-12.00 Saturday
Stock: about 159,200 volumes
Services: photocopying, loans, enquiry service

QATAR

National Library

Address: PO Box 205, Doha
Telephone: 429955
Fax: 429976
Telex: 4743 QANALI
Enquiries: M H Al Nassr
Availability: open to the public
Hours: 07.00-13.00, 15.00-18.00 (winter), 06.00-12.30, 15.30-18.30 (winter), Saturday to Thursday
Stock: 120,000 volumes of Arabic books on all subjects, 22,000 volumes of non-Arabic books
Services: loans, microfilm, bibliography etc
Publications: Qatar national bibliography (annual); Arabian Gulf: a selected bibliography; Catalogue of Qatar National Library (several volumes)

SAUDI ARABIA

Institute of Public Administration Library

Address: PO Box 205, Riyadh 11141
Telephone: (1) 461612 ext 599
Fax: (1) 4792136/6313442/8268881
Telex: 401160 IPADMN SJ, 404360 IPADMN SJ
Enquiries: Mostafa Sadhan
Availability: open to the public
Hours: 07.30-14.30 Saturday to Wednesday
Stock: 93,444 books in Arabic, 68,962 books in English, 47,900 Saudi Government documents, 4,400 government publications, 395 Arabic periodical titles, 412 current English periodical titles. Most periodical titles are in the fields of economics and management, with several on political science/international affairs as well
Services: photocopying, loans, enquiry service, online searches
Publications: Information sources on Saudi Arabia (a bibliography of materials in English, including directories, books, periodical articles, government publications etc contained in the library); Periodicals holdings list (Arabic periodicals); Periodicals holdings list (English periodicals); Bibliography of Saudi Government publications in IPA Documents Center (Arabic); Bibliography of IPA publications (Arabic)

Islamic Development Bank, Library

Address: PO Box 5925, Jeddah 21432
Telephone: (2) 6361400
Fax: 6366871
Telex: 601137/601407 ISDB SJ
Enquiries: Dr Helmi M Foudeh
Availability: open to the public
Hours: 07.30 - 15.30 Saturday to Wednesday; 09.00 - 13.30 Thursday
Stock: covers banks and banking, economics, finance, law, energy, Islamic studies, management, history and biography, transfer of technology, agriculture, computer science, library and information science, Islamic Fiqh and Shareea. Special collections include Islamic economics, banks and banking. Material is in Arabic, English and French and covers all 45 Islamic countries. It includes annual reports for financial institutions; directories (national and international); journals; statistics; books (23,000); newspapers; market research reports. Online access - Dialog. CD-ROM - the library has more than 30 CD-ROMs including Computer Select, Books in Print.

Services: photocopying, loans, enquiry service, facilities for readers to use own computers
Publications: Acquisition list

King Saud University Libraries
Address: PO Box 22480, Riyadh 11495
Telephone: (1) 476 1155, (1) 477 4379
Telex: 401019 KSU SJ
Enquiries: Dr Saad A Al-Rashid (Dean)
Availability: open to the public
Hours: 07.00-21.00 five days a week
Stock: stock of about 538,800 titles, including 6,550 periodical titles and 15,300 titles of government publications. Includes the library of the College of Administrative Sciences, part of the Central Library since 1985. Stock includes official publications from Saudi Arabia and other countries and international organisations, newspapers, Arab and non-Arab periodicals and Arab and non-Arab reference works
Services: photocopying, loans, enquiry service
Publications: include bibliographies, union lists of periodicals, abstracts; full list available

Saudi Consulting House Library
Address: PO Box 1267, Riyadh 11431
Telephone: (1) 448 4688/4533/4588/4677 ext 117
Telex: 401152 DEVIND SJ, 404380 S C H SJ
Enquiries: M. Fazlul-Haq (Research Librarian)
Availability: open to the public for reading and reference purposes, otherwise exclusively for the employees of Saudi Consulting House
Hours: 07.00-15.00 Saturday to Wednesday
Stock: strong in business management and marketing, but covers all subjects except fiction; 400 research studies on microfilm, receives Saudi Government publications, 150 films on marketing and management
Services: photocopying, loans, enquiry service, company information
Publications: printed catalogue, occasional and annual bibliographies

SENEGAL

Bibliothèque Universitaire Centrale de Dakar
Address: BP 2006, Dakar-Fann
Telephone: 246981
Fax: 242379
Enquiries: Henri Sene
Availability: open to the public
Hours: 08.00 - 20.00 Monday to Saturday
Stock: covers social sciences and humanities, law and economics with an accent on African problems. Company and trade directories, trade journals, statistics, national and international newspapers, microforms, computer programs. Material mainly in French
Services: photocopying, interlibrary loan, enquiry service, CD-ROM access
Publications: catalogue of periodicals; catalogue of academic dissertations

SIERRA LEONE

Bank of Sierra Leone
Address: PO Box 30, Freetown
Telephone: (22) 26501-10
Telex: 3232 SL
Stock: reference collection
Services: provides reference services

SINGAPORE

Department of Statistics Library
Address: Maxwell Rd, POB 3010, Singapore 9050
Telephone: 5336121

Institute of Southeast Asian Studies
Address: Heng Mui Keng Terrace, Pasir Panjang, Singapore 0511
Telephone: 7780955 ext 404
Telex: 37068 ISEAS RS
Enquiries: Ms Patricia Liru Pui Huen
Availability: open to own staff; applications for use welcome from persons conducting research on South-East Asia
Hours: 08.30-17.00 Monday to Friday, 08.30-13.00 Saturday
Stock: 81,659 volumes of books and bound periodicals, 9,472 reels of microfilm, 99,376 microfiches, 6,990 documents, 466 maps and 1,914 current serials, 77,642 audio-visual materials; covers modern South-East Asia, particularly stability and security, economic development and political and social change
Services: photocopying, loans, enquiry service
Publications: list of publications available; some relevant ones include: *ASEAN: a bibliography* (1984); *ASEAN: a bibliography II*; *Japan and Southeast Asia: a bibliography of historical, economic and political relations*; *Laos: a bibliography*; *Malaysian, Singapore and Brunei newspapers: an international union list* (forthcoming); *ASEAN and China: some recent references* (free); *ISEAS subscriptions to economic and banking periodicals* (free); *New Arrivals (Accessions List) (1988-)*; *Southeast Asia: census checklist/statistics checklist* (forthcoming)

National Library, Singapore, Business, Science and Technology Section, Reference Services Division
Address: Stamford Road, Singapore 0617
Telephone: 3309664/5
Fax: 3309611
Telex: 26620 RS
Enquiries: Head, Reference Services Division
Availability: open to members of the public
Hours: 09.00-20.00 Monday to Saturday
Stock: about 40,000 volumes covering business, management, marketing, advertising, economics, computers, science and technology. Includes trade directories, national and international statistical publications, local and foreign newspapers and periodicals, Singapore government publications, UN agency publications (eg FAO, UNIDO, World Bank), in-house and published indexes to periodical and newspaper articles
Services: reprography, inter-library loans, telephone and mail enquiries, referral service for online computer searching
Publications: Information resources and services for the food and beverage manufacturing industry (leaflet); *Information services for industry and commerce* (leaflet); *Food technology*; *Retail business*

National Productivity Board Resource Library
Address: NPB Building, 2 Bukit Merah Central, Singapore 0315
Telephone: 2786666 ext 3924
Telex: 36047 RS
Enquiries: Mrs Shirley See-Toh, Ms Glenda Leong
Availability: open to the public on a subscription basis
Hours: 08.30-22.00 Monday to Friday, 08.30-17.00 Saturday
Stock: about 12,000 books, 2,000 audiovisual items, 200 serial titles, 1,000 newsletters and annual reports; covers productivity, human resource management, labour management relations, training, engineering productivity, management, small and medium enterprises etc
Services: fully integrated computerised library system, providing online enquiry, circulation, cataloguing, acquisitions, serials management; also online DIALOG service, photocopying, sales of publications and videos, productivity information service (PINS)
Publications: monthly accession lists, in-house subject bibliographies

National University of Singapore
Address: 10 Kent Ridge Crescent, Singapore 0511
Telephone: 7723640
Telex: RS 33943 UNISPO VMID SCL
Fax: 7786301
Enquiries: Mrs P Wai Chee Hochstadt (Chief Librarian)
Availability: personal and corporate membership is approved on a case-by-case basis; reading or reference privileges granted to users on application
Hours: term: 08.00-22.00 Monday to Saturday, 09.30-16.30 Sunday and public holidays; long vacation (April-June): 08.30-17.00 Monday to Friday, 08.30-13.00 Saturday
Stock: 1,589,600 volumes of books and bound periodicals, 16,100 current periodical titles, 47,200 audiovisual items, 31,900 reels/164,900 fiches of microfilm/microfiche. Special Singapore/Malaysia collection, with over 43,000 volumes of books, bound journals and newspapers, theses, company reports, newspaper clippings and pamphlets. The Library also acts as a

European Reference Centre for the Commission of the European Communities
Services: photocopying, loans, enquiry service, online computer searches (including DIALOG and Pergamon Financial Data Services, ORBIT Search Service, STN and Profile Info)
Publications: include *Index to periodical articles relating to Singapore, Malaysia, Brunei and ASEAN* (regular publication); *Annual report* (in the *National University Singapore annual report*); accessions lists (monthly); *Catalogue of the Singapore/Malaysia Collection*; indexes, bibliographies, booklists

Singapore International Chamber of Commerce Reference Library
Address: 6 Raffles Quay, No 05-00 Denmark House, Singapore 0104
Telephone: 2241255 ext 21
Telex: 25235 INTCHAM RS
Enquiries: Miss Tho Swee Ping
Availability: open to Chamber members and foreign visitors
Hours: 08.30-16.30 Monday to Friday, 08.30-12.30 Saturday
Stock: 3,400 items, including the Chamber's publications, reports, trade directories, statistics, publications on customs, banking and shipping; trade, industrial, economic journals and publications, market reports, country reports, press cuttings, industrial standards and Government Gazettes
Services: loans, photocopying (for Chamber members); databank system to be available soon

Singapore Trade Development Board Library
Address: 1 Maritime Square No 10-40, World Trade Centre, Telok Blangah Road, Singapore 0409
Telephone: 2719388
Telex: 28617/28170 TRADEV RS
Enquiries: Miss Oei Huang Pi, Miss Doreen Lian
Availability: open to all business users only
Hours: 08.00-18.00 Monday to Friday, 08.00-13.00 Saturday
Stock: about 10,000 book titles, 700 titles of periodicals, newsletters and newspapers. Subjects covered are marketing, international trade, trade statistics, trade fairs, market reports, country reports, trade directories, yellow pages, company reports, publications on commodities, products etc
Services: photocopying, current awareness service, audio-visual facilities, enquiry service
Publications: Recent additions to the library; Singapore Trade Statistics Imports and Exports (both monthly)

SOUTH AFRICA

Central Statistical Service Library
Address: 270 Schoeman St, Private Bag 44, Pretoria, 0001
Telephone: (12) 3108490
Fax: (12) 3108504
Enquiries: Mrs M M Hugo
Availability: open to the public
Hours: 07.15 - 13.45
Stock: covers statistics, economics, demography. Material is in English with international coverage. It includes journals (covering statistics, economics, demography); statistics (South Africa statistics and international statistics); books (6,000); local newspapers. Online access - Sabinet, Staticat
Services: photocopying, loans, enquiry service, SDI services
Publications: Literature Review - free; *UNDOC Review* (guidelines on official statistics by the United Nations) - free

Durban Municipal Library
Address: PO Box 917, Durban 4000
Telephone: (31) 3006911
Fax: (31) 3006301
Enquiries: Director Libraries or Principal Librarian, Reference Services
Availability: open to the public
Hours: 09.00 - 18.00 Monday to Friday; 08.30 - 13.00 Saturdays
Stock: general subject coverage but with good coverage of South African law and government publications, economics and management. 650,000 books, 550 journals, local, national and international newspapers, South African company information
Services: photocopying (20c per page); loans; enquiry service (includes current awareness service)

Johannesburg Public Library
Address: Market Square, Johannesburg 2001
Telephone: (11) 836 3780
Fax: (11) 838 7366
Enquiries: The Director, Library of Museum Services
Availability: open to all
Hours: open Mondays to Saturdays, hours vary according to use made of department or branch; open 09.99-19.30 (17.00 Saturday) or less
Stock: about 1.5 million volumes covering all subjects in reference and lending departments. The Reference Library receives over 6,300 journals and has special collections in the fields of commerce and insurance; major South African and overseas newspapers can be consulted in the Newsroom
Services: photocopying, loans, enquiry service
Publications: Index to South African periodicals (annual, on microfiche, covering about 450 periodicals; available for consultation in the reference library)

South African Library
Address: PO Box 496, Queen Victoria Street, Cape Town 8001
Telephone: (21) 246331/246320
Fax: (21) 244848
Telex: 5722604
Enquiries: P E Westra (Director)
Availability: open to all members of the public who wish to conduct bona fide research and to 3rd year and postgraduate students
Hours: 09.00-18.00 Monday to Friday; 09.00-13.00 Saturday
Stock: 600,000 volumes, 160,000 bound periodicals, 8,000 current periodicals, 35,000 bound newspapers, 350 current newspapers and many special collections. Is the national reference and preservation library with legal deposit privileges, specialising in the humanities; all marketing and business publications published in South Africa are automatically received in the library. Has comprehensive sets of local and overseas newspapers and periodicals
Services: photocopying, microfilming, inter-library loans, photographic service, enquiry service
Publications: Quarterly bulletin of the South African Library (articles on the library, its collections and subjects of Africana interest); *Grey* bibliographies, general series, reprint series, indexes on microfiche, annual report. Printed catalogue available on request

State Library
Address: PO Box 397, Pretoria
Telephone: (12) 218931
Fax: (12) 325 5984
Telex: 322171 SA
Enquiries: Mrs M A Botha (Assistant Director), Mrs V Smith (PR Officer)
Availability: open to the public without restrictions. Study Section provides a library service for students who do not have access to other library facilities
Hours: 08.00-16.00 Monday to Friday; 08.00-12.00 Saturday (Study Section only)
Stock: about two million items, mainly legal deposit material or material of South African interest; all South African directories are held as well as annual reports of companies listed on the Stock Exchange
Services: photocopying, inter-library loans, reference, computer searches, indexing, joint catalogues
Publications: include: *SANB: South African national bibliography* (quarterly with annual cumulations); *Bibliography of overseas publications about South Africa* (bi-annual); *Directory of Southern African libraries*; full catalogue available

Wits Business School Library/John S Schlesinger Library
Address: University of Witwatersrand, PO Box 98, Wits 2050
Telephone: (11) 643 6641 ext 141
Fax: (11) 643 1623
Enquiries: D J Kruger
Availability: open to the public; individual membership R25 pa, corporate membership (10 people) R800 pa
Hours: 08.30-20.00 Monday to Thursday, 08.30-17.00 Friday, 08.30-12.30 Saturday
Stock: approximately 12,000 books and 200 journals covering all

aspects of business administration, student MBA research reports, local information, company annual reports; limited selection of government publications - others held in the university's Government Publications Library

Services: photocopying, loans, enquiry service, online searches (including DIALOG, ORBIT, Pergamon InfoLine), inhouse computer database of MBA research reports, linkup with SABINET (the national computerised cataloguing and bibliographic network)

Publications: Business School publications: *Fact and opinion papers*; *Business Alert*; *Management insights*

SOUTH KOREA

Central National Library

Address: 100-177, 1-Ga, Hoe-Hyeon-Dong, Jung-Gu, Seoul
Telephone: (2) 752 3722/3713, (2) 753 8536
Enquiries: Mr Soon-Ho Choo
Availability: open to the public free of charge
Hours: 06.00-21.00 all days except national holidays
Stock: about 1.3 million volumes on all subjects
Services: general public library services
Publications: *Korea national bibliography*; *Library journal*; *Bibliographic index of Korea*; *Union catalogue of foreign books in Korea*; *Classified catalogue*

Korea Productivity Centre

Address: CPO Box 834, Seoul
Telephone: (2) 785 5868, (2) 555 5868
Telex: 27672 KPCNTR K
Availability: loans only to staff and enterprises enrolled as KPC members, but material available for reference to anyone
Stock: about 20,000 books, including about 4,000 volumes of research and study reports. Collects theory of management and economics, case studies of good productivity performance, surveys of industrial and technological development, current statistics, business management and industrial policy information etc. Also collects productivity-related data published by foreign productivity centres

SRI LANKA

Ceylon Institute of Scientific and Industrial Research

Address: PO Box 787, 363 Banddhaloka Mawatha, Colombo 7
Telephone: (1) 693807/698624
Fax: (1) 686567
Telex: 22933
Enquiries: Miss C L M Nethsingha (Head, Information Service)
Availability: open for reference to any accredited enquirer; loans available with membership (application must be approved by employer)
Hours: Monday to Friday
Stock: 28,000 volumes on science and technology
Services: photocopying, loans, enquiry service
Publications: *Current technical literature* (indexing service); *Food digest*; *Energy digest*; bibliographies

Colombo Public Library

Address: Central Library, Ananda Coomaraswamy Mawatha, Colombo 7
Telephone: (1) 691968
Enquiries: MDH Jayawardhana (Chief Librarian)
Availability: open to the public
Hours: 08.00-18.30 all days except Wednesdays and public holidays
Stock: Reference Library available. Library stock includes newspapers, periodicals; the Library is also a depository library for the FAO

Department of Census and Statistics Library

Address: No. 11/1 Independence Avenue, Colombo 7
Telephone: (1) 598445
Enquiries: M D H Goonatillake (Librarian), A Kathiravelu (Information Officer)
Availability: open to the public for reference
Hours: 08.30-16.15 Monday to Friday
Stock: covers agriculture, economics, computer science, mathematics, demography and statistics, with over 50,000 books

and periodicals. Special collections of trade directories, publications on imports and exports and other publications on trade statistics

Services: photocopying, inter-library loans, enquiry service
Publications: *Annotated bibliography of the Departmental publications*; *List of current acquisitions and guide to periodical literature*; *List of latest Departmental publications*

Industrial Development Board Library, Industrial Information Service

Address: 615 Galle Road, Katubedda, Moratuwa
Telephone: (1) 505 exts 326, 327, 450, 394
Enquiries: Mrs Sharmini M Tennekoon
Availability: open to the public for reference; loans to members of staff only
Hours: 08.30 - 16.30 Monday to Friday
Stock: 15,000 volumes on economics, industrial development, management, workshop technology, marketing management, food, energy, rubber, engineering, computers and data processing; stock includes publications of the UN and its agencies
Services: industrial information service, monthly current awareness service, bibliographies, documentation bulletins, monthly accession lists for members
Publications: many publications on individual industries etc

Library, Centre for Industrial Technology Information Services (CITIS)

Address: No. 45 St. Miichael's Road, Colombo 3
Telephone: (1) 421256 exts 326/327/450/394
Enquiries: Mrs Sharmini M Tennekoon
Availability: open to the public for reference; loans to members of staff only
Hours: 08.30-16.30 Monday to Friday
Stock: 16,000 volumes on economics, industrial development, management, work shop technology, marketing management, food, energy, rubber, engineering, computers and data processing; stock includes publications of the UN and its agencies
Services: industrial information service, monthly current awareness service, bibliographies, documentation bulletins, monthly accession lists for members
Publications: many publications on individual industries etc

National Library of Sri Lanka

Address: Independence Avenue, Colombo 7
Telephone: (1) 698847/685199/ 685197/ 687582
Fax: (1) 685201
Enquiries: M S U Amarasiri (director)
Availability: for research purposes only
Hours: 09.00 - 17.00 Tuesday to Saturday
Stock: covers social sciences, humanities, science and technology, library and information science. Material is in English, Sinhala and Tamil. It includes journals; books; local newspapers; microforms; audio-visual material. CD-ROM - Science Citation Index, Library and Information Abstracts
Services: interlibrary loans; photocopying; enquiry services; referral service
Publications: *Sri Lanka National bibliography*; *Library News*; *Sri Lanka (ISBN) Publishers Directory*

National Museum Library

Address: PO Box 854, Sir Marcus Fernando Mawatha, Colombo 7
Telephone: (1) 93314
Enquiries: Miss K V S F de Soysa
Availability: open to members; membership card issued on completion of application form. Members include persons engaged in research on Sri Lanka
Hours: 09.00-17.00 daily except Fridays and public holidays
Stock: about 600,000 publications, 4,000 periodical titles and 3,700 palm leaf manuscripts. All publications on marketing and business published in Sri Lanka are available, as this is a legal deposit library
Services: photocopying, enquiry service
Publications: *Sri Lanka periodical index*; *Sri Lanka periodical directory*; special bibliographies on various subjects relating to Sri Lanka

SWAZILAND

Swaziland National Archives Library
Address: PO Box 1461, Mbabane
Telephone: (194) 42633
Telex: 2270 WD
Enquiries: Michael W K Gyimah
Availability: open to the public on completion of an access application form and its approval by the Director of the Archives
Hours: 08.00-16.00 Monday to Thursday, 08.00-15.30 Friday
Stock: 3,200 volumes consisting of: publications of Government departments of Swaziland from 1968 onwards; Government reports; publications of the High Commissioners of Basutoland, Bechuanaland Protectorate and Swaziland; British official publications on Swaziland pre-1968; local periodicals and serials. Currently building a special collection on southern African countries with emphasis on Swaziland in the fields of social sciences and the arts
Services: photocopying, inter-library loans, enquiry service

SYRIA

Assad National Library
Address: PO Box 3639, Malki Street, Damascus
Telephone: (11) 719151/722409
Telex: 419134 ASALIB SY
Enquiries: Ghassan Lahham (Director General)
Availability: open to the public, mainly intended for researchers
Hours: 09.00-20.00 Saturday to Thursday
Stock: about 86,000 books in Arabic, English, French, Russian and German covering all subject fields
Services: photocopying, enquiry service, online computer searches on DIALOG and Datasolve
Publications: National bibliography; Analytical index of Syrian periodicals

Institut Français d'Etudes Arabes, Bibliothèque
Address: PO Box 344, Damascus
Telephone: (11) 330214/331962
Fax: (11) 247887
Telex: 412272 IFEAD SY
Enquiries: Olivier Dubois, Claude Salane
Availability: open to researchers, university professors, postgraduate students
Hours: Monday to Saturday 08.00 - 13.00, 16.00 - 19.00
Stock: covers social sciences, Arabic studies. It is in many languages and covers Middle and Near East. It includes journals, statistics (Syria), books (32,000), microforms
Services: photocopying, no outside loans
Publications: Bulletin d'Etudes Orientales (annual)

TAIWAN

China External Trade Development Council (CETDC), Trade Data Library
Address: 7th floor, 333 Keeling Rd, Sec1, Taipei
Telephone: (2) 725 5200
Fax: (2) 757 6653
Telex: 21676 CETRA TP
Availability: open to local and foreign businessmen
Stock: together with CEDTC libraries in Taichung and Kaohsiung has more than 30,000 reference items, including information on basic trade, trade systems, trade law, taxes, industrial and market reports and specialised products; the three libraries are linked by computer and the computer system is updated regularly with information from factories, foreign buyers, domestic suppliers and customs authorities

Chueh Sheng Memorial Library
Address: Tamkang University, Tamsui, Taiwan 25137
Telephone: (2) 622 7821; 621 5656 ext 282
Enquiries: Prof. Shih-Hsion Huang (Director)
Availability: open to anyone with a valid ID
Hours: 08.30-22.00 Monday to Saturday, 09.00-17.00 Sunday
Stock: 400,000 volumes and 1,200 current periodical titles; coverage includes business and management. There is a Taiwan Special Collection

Services: photocopying, inter-library loans, reference and referral services, online searches, OCLC, CD-ROM etc
Publications: include How to use the Library: a handbook

National Central Library
Address: 20 Chungshan S. Road, Taipei 10040
Telephone: (2) 361 9132
Enquiries: Chen-ku Wang
Availability: open to the public, minimum age 19 for card holders
Hours: 09.00-21.00 daily
Stock: one million volumes covering all subjects including social sciences; reference collection
Services: photocopying, inter-library loans, enquiry service, online searches
Publications: Chinese national bibliography (monthly, annual and five-year cumulations); Index to periodical literature in the Republic of China (quarterly with annual cumulation); Catalog of publications of the Executive Yuan, ROC (quarterly); Index to Chinese official gazettes (quarterly); also several individual publications, including Union catalogue of Western language serials in humanities and social sciences in the ROC

National Cheng-Chih University, Chung-Cheng Library
Address: MuCha, Taipei
Telephone: (2) 9398335 ext 318
Enquiries: Louise Ching-Ju Tsang
Availability: open to any adult; home loans restricted to university teachers, students and staff members
Hours: 08.00-22.00 Monday to Friday, 08.00-16.00 Saturday
Stock: about 403,000 book titles, 2,290 periodicals etc; includes material on statistics, economics, management and marketing
Services: photocopying, loans, enquiry service
Publications: National Cheng-Chih University information services handbook

TANZANIA

Bank of Tanzania, Research Library
Address: PO Box 2939, 10 Mirambo Street, Dar-es-Salaam
Telephone: (51) 2129 ext 227
Telex: 41024 BENKUU TZ
Enquiries: Ivan Charles Nyongo
Availability: staff library; permission required for use by others
Hours: Monday to Saturday
Stock: over 1,000 book titles, over 50 periodical titles; covers banking, economics, monetary economics, statistics and money
Services: photocopying, enquiry service, loans
Publications: Library accession list

Iringa Regional Library
Address: Uhuru Avenue, PO Box 172, Iringa
Enquiries: M M Kaudura (Regional Librarian)
Availability: open to the public
Hours: Monday to Friday 09.30 - 18.30; Saturdays 09.30 - 12.30pm
Stock: covers all subjects. 69,000 books, Tanzanian statistics
Publications: abstracts of various subjects of national interest eg. agriculture, industry, health

THAILAND

Bank of Thailand, Library and Information Centre
Address: 273 Samsen Road, Bangkok 10200
Telephone: (2) 282 7985/8909
Enquiries: Mrs Chantana Kornkovit (Chief, Library and Information Centre)
Availability: open to the public for reference only
Hours: 08.30-16.30 Monday to Friday
Stock: 50,000 books, documents, audiovisual items and microforms and 1,000 periodicals on economics, money and banking, finance, accounting, commerce, management, computers
Services: photocopying, enquiry service
Publications: Library list of new books; Weekly list of selected articles from periodicals

Department of Industrial Promotion Library
Address: Rama VI Road, Phaya-Thai, Bangkok 10400
Telephone: (2) 245 9300/9429/9433, (2) 2464301-4 ext 547
Telex: 20562 DEPIPRO TH

Enquiries: Mrs Phanorat Sitthipranee, Miss Surinthrou Samanmit
Availability: special library, open to the public
Hours: 08.30-16.30 Monday to Friday
Stock: covers industry and technology, especially industry, with special collections on medium, small, cottage and handicraft industries and new manufacturing business. About 2,000 books in English and 1,500 books in Thai
Services: telephone enquiries, inter-library loans, indexes and clippings
Publications: monthly accessions list, Thai language indexes

Economic and Social Commission for Asia and the Pacific (ESCAP), Library
Address: United Nations Bldg, Rajadamnern Av, Bangkok 10200
Telephone: (2) 2829161
Telex: 82392 ESCAP
organisation
Stock: covers inland waterways, statistics, railway transport, road transport, tourism, telecommunications, environment. Includes journals; books; microforms.

National Institute of Development Administration, Library and Information Center
Address: Klong Chan, Bangkapi, Bangkok 10240
Telephone: (2) 377 7400-9, 377 9660-9 ext 282/283; (2) 377 5481
Enquiries: Miss Nitaya Berananda (Director), Miss Patcharee Mamanee (Associate Director), Miss Siriporn Suwanna (Head of Reader's Services)
Availability: reference and information services open to the public
Hours: 08.00-18.30 Monday to Friday, 10.00-15.00 Saturday and Sunday
Stock: Social Science collection; 170,000 books, 1289 periodical titles, 8,300 copies of pamphlets and documents and 22 newspaper titles
Services: include reference and information services, inter-library loans, current awareness service, abstracting and indexing, photocopying, computer search service
Publications: many publications, including *Directory of social sciences sources* (1986), guides to NIDA publications and bibliographies

Ramkhamhaeng University Library
Address: Bangkapi, Bangkok 10240
Telephone: (2) 318 0920, (2) 314 3375
Telex: 72515 UNIRAMA TH
Enquiries: Mrs Sutana Vongthongson
Availability: open to the public
Hours: 07.30-18.00 Monday to Friday, 08.30-16.30 Saturday, Sunday (longer hours one month before final examinations)
Stock: 360,000 volumes of books, 1,015 periodical titles, 18 newspaper titles
Services: readers' advisory service, reference service, inter-library loans, bibliography compilation, photocopying, library orientation etc
Publications: *Bibliography of social science* (based on materials in the Library); *Ramkhamhaeng University Library newsletter*; *Ramkhamhaeng University Library bulletin*

Thai National Documentation Centre
Address: 196 Phahonyothin Road, Bang Khen, Bangkok 10900
Telephone: (2) 579 1121-30 exts 219/310
Telex: 21392 TISTR TH
Enquiries: Mrs Nongphanga Chitrakorn
Stock: specialises in science and technology; includes standard specifications, British patent abridgements, bibliographies etc
Services: photocopying, enquiry service, translations service, inter-library loans etc
Publications: many publications, including accessions lists, guides to and directories of Thai scientific and technical literature, bibliographies etc

TRINIDAD AND TOBAGO

Central Statistical Office Library
Address: 23 Park Street, Port of Spain
Telephone: (809) 625 3705
Availability: open to the public for reference
Stock: includes the publications of the Central Statistical Office

Export Development Corporation Library
Address: Export House, 17 Richmond Street, Port of Spain
Telephone: (809) 623 3591-4, 623 6022
Telex: 22646, 2273 WG
Enquiries: Debra Rahamatali (Co-ordinator, Information Service)
Hours: 08.00-16.30 Monday to Friday
Stock: covers export trade, product development, international organisations, international statistics and international economic relations

South Trinidad Chamber of Industry and Commerce Library
Address: Room 313, Cross Crossing Shopping Plaza, Cross Crossing, San Fernando
Telephone: 657 9077, 652 5613
Enquiries: Anne Phillip (General Manager)
Hours: 08.00-16.00 Monday to Friday
Stock: covers trade, international economics and business

Trinidad and Tobago Chamber of Industry and Commerce (Inc), Information Centre
Address: 31 Frederick Street, PO Box 499, Port of Spain
Telephone: 623 1561/3
Hours: 08.00-16.00 Monday to Friday
Stock: covers trade and industry

Trinidad and Tobago Management Development Centre, Management Development Centre Library
Address: Second Floor, Salvatori Building, Port of Spain, Trinidad, Trinidad and Tobago
Telephone: 623 1961/3
Fax: 623 2111
Enquiries: Joyce H Williams (Librarian)
Hours: 08.00-16.00 Monday to Friday
Stock: covers management, marketing, production, management accounts, industrial relations and computer science

University of the West Indies, Main Library
Address: St Augustine, Trinidad
Telephone: 662 2002 (enquiries)
Fax: 662 9238
Telex: 24520 UWI WG
Enquiries: Mr O O Ogundipe
Availability: library open to all registered students at the University and to academic, research and senior administrative University staff; members of the public may be admitted according to their specific needs at the discretion of the Librarian
Hours: term and Easter vacation: 08.30-22.00 Monday to Thursday, 08.30-17.00 Friday, Saturday; other vacations: 08.30-18.30 Monday, 08.30-17.00 Tuesday to Friday, 08.30-12.30 Saturday
Stock: about 237,900 monographs, 8,180 microtexts, 4,900 current serial titles, 40,200 bound volumes of serials, etc; covers social sciences, including management studies and economics, as well as humanities, agriculture, life sciences, engineering, physical sciences. Special collections of West Indiana and UN documents
Services: loans, inter-library loans, reference services, current awareness services, photocopying, online searches
Publications: bibliographic series, periodicals lists, information bulletins, guides to services and facilities, teaching aids; *List of references to literature held*; *Accessions list (Caribbean studies)*; *CARINDEX* (index to social sciences and humanities material) etc

UGANDA

Institute of Public Administration, Deposit Library/Documentation Centre
Address: PO Box 20131, Lugogo, Kampala
Telephone: (41) 59581
Enquiries: Remy Ogwang-Ameny
Availability: open to participants on courses held at the Institute and staff of the Institute, public and private sectors
Hours: 08.00-22.00 Monday to Friday, 08.00-13.00 Saturday
Stock: about 12,000 volumes of books, 150 journal titles, newspapers, Government documents, eg budget speeches, statutory instruments, district planning committee minutes etc; microfiche, microfilms
Services: loans, enquiry service, photocopying services, user training, consultancy and liaison services

Ministry of Commerce, Export & Import Licensing Division, Library
Address: East African Development Bank Building, Plot no. 4 Buganda Road, PO Box 6877, Kampala
Telephone: (41) 233311-3, (41) 259944
Telex: 61085 UG
Enquiries: Nsamba Boaz
Availability: open to the public free of charge
Hours: 08.00-12.45, 14.00-17.00 Monday to Friday
Stock: 1,000 items, including trade journals and directories, market surveys, catalogues and Government publications. Main subjects covered are international business references, transport, commercial arbitration, marketing and distribution
Services: photocopying, enquiry service
Publications: Trade information services; accession lists and bibliographies (unpublished)

UNITED ARAB EMIRATES

Centre for Documentation and Research
Address: PO Box 2380, Abu Dhabi
Telephone: (2) 345371/212900
Telex: 22414 CULCEN EM
Enquiries: to the Director
Availability: open to the public by academic introduction
Hours: 08.00-13.00 Saturday to Thursday
Stock: specialises in Gulf affairs; based on archival documents of all powers with activities in the Gulf in modern times
Publications: Catalogue of archives

UNITED STATES OF AMERICA

Advertising Research Foundation
Address: 3 East 54th Street, New York, NY 10022
Telephone: (212) 751 5656
Fax: (212) 319 5265
Enquiries: Elizabeth Proudfit (Information Center Manager)
Availability: limited to members only; membership is open to companies
Hours: 08.00-17.00 Monday to Friday
Stock: comprehensive collection of material relevant to advertising and marketing research. 600 subject files, 150 periodicals and 1,500 books
Services: photocopying and search facilities available for members
Publications: (of the Foundation): *Journal of Advertising Research;* monographs, bibliographies and research studies. Publications are available to members and non-members

Baker Library - Harvard University Graduate School of Business Administration
Address: Soldiers Field, Boston, MA 02163
Telephone: (617) 495 6405, (617) 405 6361
Enquiries: Mary Chatfield (Librarian)
Availability: open to students, faculty and staff of Harvard Business School and Harvard University; HBS graduates and Associate Companies may apply for a privilege card, other companies may purchase a card
Hours: 08.15-midnight Monday to Thursday; 08.15-19.00 Friday; 10.00-19.00 Saturday; 11.00-midnight Sunday
Stock: the largest business library in the world, with 500,000 volumes, 325,000 microfiche, 10,000 rolls of microfilm and 6,500 active serial titles. Corporate information: annual reports, 10-K and other SEC filings for major US companies, plus annual reports for many foreign companies. Also special collections including record manuscript from over 1,300 firms and China trade correspondence, HBS Archives, and Kress collection of pre-1850 economics materials
Services: photocopying, loans, enquiry service, online searches
Publications: Recent additions to Baker Library (monthly); *Core collection: an author and subject guide* (annual index to the reading room collection); *Current periodical* publications in Baker Library (annual); *Working papers in Baker Library: a quarterly checklist* (list of extensive collection from institutions in the US, UK, Australia and other countries); also bibliographies and guides for business-related materials, including

"mini-lists" of sources for various subjects, eg basic US statistical sources, basic foreign statistical sources, sources of information on foreign countries

Boston Public Library
Address: Kirstein Business Branch, 20 City Hall Ave, Boston, MA 02108
Telephone: (617) 5230860
Enquiries: Dolores Schueler
Availability: open to the public
Hours: 09.00 - 17.00 Monday to Friday
Stock: covers business. It includes company information for US companies; stockbroker reports (US); company and trade directories (international coverage); journals (400 titles); statistics; 47,000 books; local, national and international newspapers; microforms.
CD-ROM facilities - ABI/Inform, Compact Disclosure, Standard & Poor's, F&S (US and international); Moody's (US and international; Infotrac's Business Index
Services: photocopying machines available for public to use at 10 cents a copy

Brooklyn Public Library, Business Library
Address: 280 Cadman Plaza W, Brooklyn, NY 11201
Telephone: (718) 780 7800

Bureau of the Census
Current publications of the Bureau (described in the section on national statistical offices) are kept for reference at 12 regional offices, and 47 Department of Commerce district offices. Regional offices have information services specialists who are able to answer questions about census and survey data. The regional offices are at the following locations:

Address: 1375 Peachtree Street NE, Rm 645, Atlanta, GA 30309-3112
Telephone: (404) 881 2274

Address: 441 Stuart Street, 10th floor, Boston, MA 02116
Telephone: (617) 223 0226

Address: 230 South Tryon Street, Suite 800, Charlotte, NC 28202
Telephone: (704) 371 6144

Address: 55 East Jackson Boulevard, Suite 1304, Chicago, IL 60604
Telephone: (312) 353 0980

Address: 1100 Commerce Street, Room 3E27, Dallas, TX 75242
Telephone: (214) 767 0625

Address: 7655 W Mississippi Ave PO Box 26750 Denver CO 80226
Telephone: (303) 236 2200

Address: Federal Building and US Courthouse, 231 West Lafayette Street, Room 565, Detroit, MI 48226
Telephone: (313) 226 4675

Address: One Gateway Center, 4th and State Streets, Kansas City, KS 66101
Telephone: (913) 236 3731

Address: 11777 San Vicente Boulevard, Room 810, Los Angeles, CA 90049
Telephone: (213) 209 6612

Address: Federal Office Building, 26 Federal Plaza, Room 37-130, New York, NY 10273
Telephone: (212) 264 4730

Address: William J. Green Jnr. Federal Building, 600 Arch Street, Room 9244, Philadelphia, PA 19106
Telephone: (215) 597 8313

Address: Lake Union Building, 1700 Westlake Avenue, North, Seattle, WA 98109
Telephone: (206) 442 7080

California State Library
Address: Library & Courts Bldg, 914 Capitol Mall, Box 942837, Sacramento, CA 94237-0001
Telephone: (916) 6540183
Fax: (916) 6540064
Availability: open to the public
Stock: general research collection covering amongst other areas

business, applied science and technology, population, public administration and statistics. 695,000 volumes, 9,600 journals, federal and state government document depository
Services: interlibrary loans; photocopying; online access

Chicago Board of Trade Library
Address: 141 West Jackson Blvd., Suite A-339, Chicago, IL
Telephone: (312) 535 8990
Enquiries: Rita Macellaio
Availability: open to the public for reference purposes
Hours: open to the public 13.30-16.00; library open 07.00-16.00 CST
Stock: 3,500 books, 550 bound periodical volumes, 400 journals and serials, 17 newspapers and nine charting services; specialises in commodity futures and options. Collection includes the Chicago Board of Trade *Statistical yearbook* from 1858, plus regulations, annual reports and statistics from other exchanges, plus other commodity industry sources
Services: DIALOG information service (for CBT members only), inter-library loans
Publications: Chicago Board of Trade commodity futures trading bibliography (annual); the CBT also publishes statistical annuals on the futures market and many other works related to commodities, as well as the periodical *Review of research in the futures markets* (at least three times a year)

Dun and Bradstreet Inc, Business Library
Address: 99 Church Street, New York, NY 10007
Telephone: (212) 285 7304

International Franchise Association, IFA World Resource Center
Address: 1350 New York Ave NW, Suite 900, Washington DC 200005
Telephone: (202) 6288000
Fax: (202) 6280812
Enquiries: Nancy L Minter (director, research)
Availability: open to the public by appointment only
Hours: 08.30 - 17.30 Monday to Friday
Stock: covers franchising material. Primarily in English. 100 specialised business periodicals; 350 books
Services: photocopying available for small charge
Publications: Franchising World (bi-monthly periodical); *Franchising in the Economy* (annual); and numerous other publications produced by IFA

Export-Import Bank of the US Library
Address: 811 Vermont Avenue, NW, Washington, DC 20571
Telephone: (202) 566 8320
Fax: (202) 566 7524
Enquiries: Ms T McGill
Availability: open to the public by appointment only
Hours: 08.30-16.30 Monday to Friday
Stock: 1,200 serial titles, 20,000 volumes. Covers international trade and finance; collection includes comprehensive statistical data from various central banks, export credit documentation, plus a complete collection of Economist Intelligence Unit country reports
Services: inter-library loans. No public photocopying

Federal Trade Commission Library
Address: 6th Street and Pennsylvania Avenue, NW, Washington, DC 20580
Telephone: (202) 236 2395
Enquiries: Suzanne B Perella
Availability: open to the public; the library serves the Federal Trade Commission, other government agencies, universities and colleges, private firms and the general public
Hours: 08.30-17.00 Monday to Friday
Stock: Covers law, business, economics, consumer protection, specialising in anti-trust and consumer protection. Resources include Moody's, Dun and Bradstreet, and Standard and Poor's services, Predicast indexes, trade and professional journals, state industrial directories, annual reports of New York Stock Exchange and American Stock Exchange companies, census materials, telephone directories and newspapers
Services: photocopying, inter-library loans, reference services
Publications: bibliographies; monthly bulletin of news and recent acquisitions, etc

Indiana University Business-School of Public and Environmental Affairs Library
Address: Bloomington, IN 47405
Telephone: (812) 335 1957
Enquiries: Mr Nels Gunderson
Availability: open to the public; identification card necessary
Hours: 08.00-22.30 Monday to Friday, less hours at weekends and during the summer
Stock: 135,000 volumes; collection primarily devoted to business, economics, management, finance, accounting, public administration, environment, labour, transportation systems and energy
Services: photocopying, loans, enquiry service, online searches
Publications: guides to the library and its resources

James Jerome Hill Reference Library
Address: Fourth and Market Streets, St Paul, MN 55102
Telephone: (612) 227 9531
Fax: (612) 222 4139
Enquiries: Denise Carlson (Reference Services Supervisor)
Availability: this is a privately supported, non-profit business and economics library, open to the public
Hours: 09.00-21.00 Monday to Thursday, 09.00-17.30 Friday, Saturday (winter); 09.00-20.00 Monday, Tuesday, 09.00-17.30 Wednesday to Friday (summer, Memorial Day to Labor Day)
Stock: specialises in management, business, economics, finance and related subjects, and in local and regional business information. Also has a special collection of manufacturing standards
Services: document delivery, inter-library loans, computer searching, in-depth research
Publications: The Directory of Minnesota Business and Professional Associations (annual); *Index to Minnesota Business Periodicals* (monthly)

Johnson Graduate School of Management Library, Cornell University
Address: 413 Malott Hall, Ithaca, NY 14853-4201
Telephone: (607) 255 3389
Availability: Open to the Cornell University community. Companies may purchase a privilege card
Stock: 160,000 volumes, 640,000 microfiche

Library of Congress
Address: Independence Avenue at First St, SE, Washington, DC 20540
Telephone: (202) 287 5108
Telex: 7108220185 LIB CON
Enquiries: Jean E Tucker (Assistant Public Affairs Officer)
Availability: reading rooms open to the public over high-school age
Hours: most reading rooms, including the Social Sciences (which includes business) and the Newspaper and Current Periodical Room (including government publications) open 08.30-21.30 Monday to Friday, 08.30-17.00 Saturday and 13.00-17.00 Sunday; some specialised reading rooms are open for fewer hours
Stock: apart from general collections in the main reading room (works deposited for copyright and a large amount of foreign acquisitions), the Social Science Reading Room provides a reference service on and access to materials in subjects including business, economics, finance etc and major abstracting and indexing services in the social sciences, plus some current periodicals
Services: reference service, photocopying, online information retrieval
Publications: numerous publications, including *Library of Congress information bulletin* (bi-weekly); a full catalogue, *Publications in print*, is available

Lockwood Memorial Library, State University of New York at Buffalo
Address: Amherst, NY 14260
Telephone: (716) 636 2818

Los Angeles Public Library
Address: 630 West 5th Street, Los Angeles, CA 90071
Telephone: (213) 612 3320
Enquiries: Robert Reagan (Public Relations Director)

Availability: open to the public
Hours: Central library and 62 branch libraries open varying hours, Monday to Saturday
Stock: the Central Library contains a business and economics collection (171,512 volumes), a municipal reference collection (87,188 volumes) and a social sciences and education collection (248,302 volumes); it is also a depository library for government documents
Services: photocopying, loans, enquiry service, online searches
Publications: many publications

National Chamber Foundation Library
Address: US Chamber of Commerce, 1615 H Street, NW, Washington, DC 20062
Telephone: (202) 463 5448/9
Enquiries: Rose Racine
Availability: open to the public by appointment only
Hours: 08.30-17.00 Monday to Friday
Stock: 5,000 books, including complete collection of *Nation's Business* magazine and *Business Advocate*
Services: enquiry service, loans
New York Public Library
Address: Economic and Public Affairs Division, Fifth Avenue and 42nd Street, New York, NY 10018
Telephone: (212) 930 0800
Availability: open to the public
Stock: The system includes more than 6.5 million book volumes, 13.4 million miscellaneous volumes, 3.5 million microforms

New York State Library
Address: Cultural Education Center, 100 Madison Avenue, Albany, NY 12230
Telephone: (518) 474 5943 (banking, finance, commerce, business, marketing, etc); (518) 474 5124 (accounting, management, personnel relations)
Telex: TWX/TELEX (110 baud) 710 441 8770
Enquiries: Stephanie Welden or Christine A Bain (reference services), Darrell Welch (inter-library loans)
Availability: open to the public
Hours: 09.00-17.00 Monday to Friday
Stock: a major research library, with good coverage in almost all areas of concern, although collections are generally at the support level rather than research level. Subjects covered include advertising, corporations (including foreign ones), management, manufactures, marketing, census, economics, foreign trade; is a regional depository for USGPO publications from nearly every government agency, and has comprehensive indexes to US government statistics. Also a depository for publications of New York State, and has large collections of publications of other states and of the United Nations, plus a comprehensive collection of abstracts and indexes
Services: photocopying, photostatting, paper copies from roll film or microfiche, microfiche duplication; loans of monograph material; ready-reference service; online searches
Publications: *Business libraries in New York State: a brief guide for business, professional and research users*, and many other publications

New York University, Leonard N Stern School of Business Library
Address: 2nd Floor, 19 Rector Street, New York, NY 10006
Telephone: (212) 285 6231
Fax: (212) 797 5349

Newark Public Library, Business Library
Address: 34 Commerce Street, Newark, NJ 07102
Telephone: (201) 733 7779
Enquiries: Mr Leslie P Rupprecht
Availability: open to the public
Hours: 09.00-17.30 Monday to Friday, 09.00-13.00 Saturday (closed Saturday during the summer)
Stock: subjects covered are business conditions and history, insurance, investments, marketing and salesmanship, money and banking; business holdings include business and industry in the US and abroad, plus New Jersey material, especially on the Newark area. Holdings include 13,000 books, 700 current periodicals (including trade journals, general business periodicals), 4,000 current directories (including foreign industrial

and trade directories as well as US ones), 13,000 reports (US and some foreign), 1,200 volumes of services (eg Moody's and Standard and Poor's), 162 bound newspapers, subject files on most business subjects (statistics, research reports, pamphlets and clippings) and federal government publications and state documents
Services: telephone reference service, photocopying, online searches

Ohio State University, Commerce Library
Address: 1810 College Rd, Columbus, OH 43210
Telephone: (614) 422 2136
Stock: collection of over 130,000 volumes and 1,250 periodicals

Purdue University, Management and Economics Library
Address: Krannert Graduate School of Management, West Lafayette, IN 47907
Telephone: (317) 4942920
Fax: (317) 4949007
Availability: open to the public
Stock: covers business, management, economics, industrial relations, marketing and finance. Special collections on business cycles and rare books in economics and business. 160,000 volumes, 4,000 annual reports, 1,220 journals, microforms and clippings
Services: interlibrary loans; photocopying; access to online databases

Rochester Public Library, Business Economics and Law Division
Address: 115 South Avenue, Rochester, NY 14604
Telephone: (716) 428 7328

Standard and Poor's Corporation
Address: Central Inquiry Unit, 25 Broadway, New York, NY 10004
Telephone: (212) 209 1199
Fax: (212) 514 7016
Enquiries: Ms Linda Payne (Librarian)
Availability: library not open to the public (although nominally open to subscribers), but anyone with a need for financial data may telephone. Some free services, but generally small fees are charged
Hours: 09.00-16.30 Monday to Friday
Stock: disclosure documents on paper and microfiche from 1967 for companies traded on US exchanges, and annual reports for publicly held companies; Standard and Poor's publications and many others for stock and bond quotes, periodicals and US government publications
Services: photocopying, enquiry service, online searches
Publications: monthly *Library notes*

Thomas J Watson Library of Business/Economics
Address: Columbia University, 130 Uris Hall, New York, NY 10027
Telephone: (212) 854 7803

United Nations Center on Transnational Corporations, Advisory and Information Services Division
Address: United Nations, New York, NY 10017
Telephone: (212) 754 1234
Telex: 661062 UNCTNC
Enquiries: E Ward (Transnational Corporations Affairs Officer; Advisory and Information Services Division)
Availability: agency staff; other UN agency staff; external users
Stock: 5,000 monographs; 100 volumes of legislation; 400 serial publications; statistics; 100,000 corporate reports. Covers investments, transnational corporations, economic development, economic aspects, investment policy, economic legislation, social behaviour, accounting, economic statistics. Worldwide geographical coverage
Services: loans (staff only), searching external databases, compilation of reference lists, information analysis, enquiry service (by letter or telephone)

University of Alabama Business Library
Address: PO Box 2937, Tuscaloosa, AL 35487-2937
Telephone: (205) 348 6096
Availability: open to the public
Hours: 07.45-midnight Monday to Friday, 09.00-19.00 Saturday, 13.00-midnight Sunday
Stock: 150,000 volumes covering marketing, economics,

accounting, real estate, taxation, international business, advertising, labour relations, personnel, arbitration, business law, banking, investments, transportation, insurance; annual report collection of US and foreign companies
Services: photocopying, inter-library loans, reference service, online searches

University of California, Los Angeles, John E Anderson Graduate School of Management, Library
Address: 405 Hilgard Ave, Los Angeles, CA 90024-1460
Telephone: (213) 8253138
Availability: open to the public for reference only
Stock: covers business, management, finance, personnel management, marketing. Special collections of rare books in business and economics. 140,000 books, 2,800 journals, extensive collection of company annual reports
Services: interlibrary loans; photocopying; fee-based online search service

University of Chicago Library, Business-Economics Department
Address: 1100 East 57th Street, Chicago, IL 60637
Telephone: (312) 702 8740
Enquiries: Jennette S Rader
Availability: open to persons not affiliated with the University of Chicago by special arrangement
Hours: varied hours during the school year
Stock: 375,000 volumes covering all business subjects

University of Illinois, Commerce Library
Address: 101 Main Library, 1408 Gregory Drive, Urbana, IL 61801
Telephone: (217) 3333619
Fax: 2440098/2446649
Enquiries: M Balachandran
Availability: material available for use in the library. Residents of the state of Illinois can check materials out of the library
Hours: 08.00 - 23.00 Monday to Thursday, 08.00 - 18.00 Friday, 10.00 - 17.00 Saturday, 13.00 - 23.00 Sunday
Stock: covers accountancy, business administration, economics, finance, regional planning, sociology and psychology, labour and industrial relations, communications, agricultural economics and computer science. It includes some 63,000 books in the Commerce Library, journals (840 titles), company and trade directories, stockbroker reports, statistics (OECD, UN, World Bank); newspapers; an extensive collection of annual 10-K, 10-Q and proxy reports for most American companies (in the case of the top 500 companies an almost complete run of annual reports available). Online access -Dialog, BRS, Electronic Bulletin Board, FEDFLASH, FRED. CD-ROM facilities include ABI/Inform, CD/Corporate, CIS Statistical Masterfile, Predicasts FxS Index plus Text, PAIS (Public Affairs Information Service), Regional Economic Information System
Services: international interlibrary loans; photocopying (10 cents a copy); microfilm/microfiche copying (10 cents a copy); online searches on DIALOG/BRS provided on a cost-recovery basis

University of Pennsylvania, Lippincott Library
Address: Van Pelt-Dietrich Library Center, 3420 Walnut St, Philadelphia, PA 19104-6207
Telephone: (215) 8985924
Fax: (215) 8982261
Enquiries: Michael Halperin (head librarian)
Availability: open to the public but restricted access at some times
Hours: 08.30 - 23.45 Monday to Thursday; 08.30 - 19.45 Friday; 10.00 - 19.45 Saturday; 12.00 - 23.45 Sunday (shorter hours in vacations)
Stock: business research library serving the Wharton School and the University of Pennsylvania. Stock covers business, finance, marketing, real estate and entrepreneurship. 200,000 volumes, 4,000 journals, collection of hard copy and microfiche annual reports and associated documents for US companies
Services: online catalogues, company information on CD-ROM, online access to BRS, Datastar, Dialog, Lexis/Nexis and Reuters

US Department of Commerce, International Trade Administration, New York District Office Library
Address: 26 Federal Plaza, New York, NY 10278
Telephone: (212) 264 0630
Enquiries: Reference Section

Availability: open to the public
Stock: ca. 3,000 volumes and 80 current periodicals, plus vertical files, covering domestic and foreign trade and related subjects including economics, marketing, foreign companies

West Virginia University, College of Business & Economics, Bureau of Business Research
Address: 209 Armstrong Hall, Box 6025, Morgan Town, WV 26506
Telephone: (304) 2935837
Fax: (304) 2937061
Enquiries: Randy Childs
Availability: open to the public on a limited basis. Some information requests may necessitate a fee
Hours: 08.00 - 12.00, 13.00 - 16.30 Monday to Friday
Stock: covers regional economics, travel and tourism, business, Federal Statistical Agencies and West Virginia State Agencies. It includes business and economic journals; statistics (major US and West Virginia series); books (3,000); local and national newspapers. Online computerised Bulletin Board. CD-ROM - Compustat, BEA, Census
Services: business and economic data (fee for some searches)
Publications: Journal of Small Business Management ($30.00 individual, $50.00 library); *County Census Profiles* ($6.00 each); *County Data Profiles* ($10.00 each)

URUGUAY

Banco Hipotecario del Uruguay, Biblioteca
Address: Daniel Fernández Crespo 1508, Montevideo
Telephone: (02) 403884
Telex: 6224 BHU UY
Enquiries: Bibga. Cyr Ruth Torres
Availability: open to the public for reference
Hours: 12.00-18.00 Monday to Friday
Stock: covers law, economics, information science and architecture
Services: photocopying, loans (to staff only), enquiry service, bibliographies on request, online computer searches

Dirección General de Estadística y Censos
Address: Cuareim 2052, Montevideo
Telephone: (02) 201105
Enquiries: Maria Emilia Guarnaschell
Availability: open to the public for reference only
Hours: 5 hours daily, Monday to Friday
Stock: covers statistics, economics and demographics
Services: photocopying

VENEZUELA

Biblioteca Técnica Científica Centralizada
Address: Avenida Libertador, Edificio Fudeco, Diagonal con el Complejo Ferial, Apartado 254, Barquisimeto, 3001-A, Estado Lara
Telephone: (051) 538022
Fax: (051) 544394
Telex: 51314 VC
Enquiries: Celmira Tirado E
Availability: open to the public
Hours: 08.00-12.00, 14.00-17.30 Monday to Friday
Stock: a scientific and technical library, including social sciences
Services: photocopying, loans

Centro Interamericano para el Desarrollo Regional (CINDER), Biblioteca
Address: Calle 69 N° 15D-32, Apartado Postal 1304, Maracaibo 4001-A
Telephone: (061) 516953/517336
Fax: (061) 523504
Telex: 61101 VC
Enquiries: Lourdes Crespo Herrera
Availability: open to the public, eg university students, researchers, postgraduate students from the Centre, professors
Hours: 08.00-12.00, 14.00-18.00 Monday to Friday
Stock: includes material on regional development, administration and Latin American regional development

Services: photocopying, computer search services
Publications: Boletin de nuevas adquisiciones (acquisitions bulletin, for internal use of the Centre)

Centro Latinoamericano de Administración para el Desarrollo (CLAD), Centro de Documentación
Address: Apartado Postal 4181, Caracas 1010-A
Telephone: (02) 922395
Fax: (02) 918427
Telex: 29076 SCLAD VC
Enquiries: Nuria Cunill
Availability: open to the public
Hours: 09.00-17.00 Monday to Friday
Stock: 10,000 non-conventional documents, 2,000 books, 1000 reference documents, 300 periodicals; covers public administration (main subject), administrative reform, public enterprises, management training, public management, local government and administration, citizen participation
Services: photocopying, bibliographies, online searches, SDI
Publications: Boletin de resumenes (quarterly, abstracts bulletin); *Boletin de alerta* (bimonthly, current awareness); *Selección de documentos clave* (biannual, key documents selection); *Serie eventos CLAD. Informes finales* (irregular, report of activities of CLAD)

Ernesto Peltzer Library
Address: Banco Central de Venezuela, Esq. de Carmelitas, Caracas 1010, Apartado Postal 2017
Telephone:(02)829811-829860exts 1422/1240/1235/1423/1618/1617
Telex: 28251/2/3 VC
Fax: (02) 811437
Enquiries: Lic. Elsa Carmauta Querecuto (Librarian)
Availability: open to the public (university members, researchers and professionals), and to Bank employees
Hours: 08.00-20.00 Monday to Friday
Stock: 90,000 titles, specialising in economics and finance, but also including some material on marketing, business, management etc
Services: photocopying (free of charge), loans to Bank employees; connected with NOTIS (Northwestern online total integrated system)
Publications: Boletin bibliografico B.C.V. (Central Bank of Venezuela bibliographic bulletin); *Bibliografía especializada* (specialised bibliography in various areas connected with economics and finance); the library also distributes publications edited by the Central Bank of Venezuela

Instituto de Comercio Exterior, División de Información, Biblioteca
Address: Avenida Libertador, Centro Comercial Los Cedros, La Florida, Caracas 1050
Telephone: (02) 729961-69, exts 348/380
Telex: 22630 ICEVE CARACAS VC
Enquiries: Teresa Arcila de Cádiz, Marla Herrera, María Nur Tejeda (librarians); Nelsón González, Alberto Vera, Norelis Blanco (commercial information specialists)
Availability: open to business personnel and students
Hours: 10.00-13.00, 14.00-17.00 Monday to Friday (open to students 14.00-17.00 Tuesday to Thursday)
Stock: about 5,000 monograph titles and 2,500 periodical titles; principal subjects are market studies, country studies, foreign trade, tariffs, foreign trade statistics of Latin America, USA, Canada, Europe. Reference works include guides, directories of exporters/importers, dictionaries etc and legislation on trade.
Services: photocopying, loans to members of the Institute; library is in the process of being incorporated into the Latin American commercial information network (la Red de Información Comercial Latinoamericana)
Publications: Boletin selectivo de noticias comerciales (weekly summary of notices of opportunities for trade)

Oficina Central de Estadística e Informatica, Centro de Documentación e Información
Address: Avenida Boyaca, Edificio Fundación La Salle, PB-3, Maripérez, Caracas
Telephone: (02) 782 1133 exts 150-173
Fax: (02) 782 2243

Telex: 21241
Enquiries: Nohelia Rivas de Silva
Availability: open to the public
Hours: 08.15-19.45 Monday to Friday
Stock: statistical material covering censuses, demographics, industry, foreign trade and finance
Services: enquiry service, sale of publications
Publications: public catalogue and Kardex; for publications edited by the Office see entry in the section on national statistical offices
There are also branch offices in the capital cities of each state where the Office's publications may be consulted; the state, town and telephone numbers of these offices are shown below:

Anzoategui: Barcelona; telephone 772332/761449
Apure: San Fernando de Apure; telephone 22661/24513
Aragua: Maracay; telephone (043) 542654
Barinas: Barinas; telephone 21704
Bolivar: Ciudad Bolívar; telephone (085) 226155 ext. 367
Carabobo: Valencia; telephone (041) 87207/51009
Cojedes: San Carlos; telephone 31369/332398
Falcon: Coro; telephone 516721/591487
Guarico: San Juan de los Morros; telephone 36680
Lara: Barquisimeto; telephone (051) 514432/514071
Merida: Mérida; telephone (074) 520004/528723
Miranda: Los Teques; telephone 42769/611564
Monagas: Maturín; telephone (091) 22290/54351
Nueva Esparta: Porlamar; telephone 615346/422256
Portuguesa: Guanare; telephone 55180/510342
Sucre: Cumaná; telephone (093) 24120/651141/23442
Tachira: San Cristóbal; telephone (076) 434581/446591/445070
Trujillo: Trujillo; telephone 31288/32943
Yaracuy: San Felipe; telephone 22075
Zulia: Maracaibo; telephone (061) 75907/223422
T F Amazonas: Puerto Ayacucho; telephone 21388
T F Delta Amacuro: Tucupita; telephone 21100

ZAMBIA

Dag Hammarskjold Memorial Library
Address: Mindolo Ecumenical Foundation, PO Box 21493, Kitwe
Telephone: (2) 214572/211488/215198/211269
Telex: 52050 ZA
Enquiries: Elijah F Sakala (Head Librarian)
Availability: free to MEF and sister institution students, and by annual subscription to external and other library users
Hours: 09.00-17.00 Monday to Friday, 09.00-12.00 Saturday
Stock: over 40,000 books on various subjects, including social sciences and government collections. Collection of 16mm films, slides, maps, tapes and video cassettes. An archive was established in 1976 to store important & historical documents in the ecumenical movement
Services: interlibrary loan, photocopying, enquiry services
Publications: Monthly acquisitions

United Nations Institute for Namibia Library
Address: PO Box 33811, Lusaka
Telephone: (1) 2164681
Telex: 410962 ZA
Enquiries: Prem Kulleen (Librarian)
Availability: open only to students and staff of the Institute. Facilities are extended to researchers in Namibia on application
Hours: 08.00-21.00 Monday to Friday
Stock: 12,000 books, 40,000 UN documents, 200 periodical titles; covers social sciences and Namibiana
Services: loans, photocopying, enquiry service, indexing and abstracting
Publications: Accessions list (quarterly); *Namibia abstracts* (irregular); *Namibia studies series*

ZIMBABWE

Bulawayo Public Library
Address: PO Box 586, Bulawayo, Zimbabwe
Telephone: (9) 60966
Enquiries: R W Doust
Availability: public subscription library
Hours: 09.00-17.30 Monday to Friday, 09.00-12.30 Saturday
Stock: approximately 75,000 books in central library, three

branches and mobile library. Reference department includes business and technical directories from the USA, UK and southern and central Africa. Lending department includes selected books on marketing, advertising, business management etc
Services: photocopying, loans, inter-library loans, current bibliographies
Publications: Bulawayo Book News (biannual); *Triennial report*

Central Statistical Office
Address: PO Box 8063, Causeway, Harare
Telephone: (4) 706681 ext 131
Stock: publications of the CSO, government statistical publications from other countries, publications of international organisations
Publications: Accession list

National Free Library of Zimbabwe
Address: 12th Ave S Park, PO Box 1773, Bulawayo
Telephone: (9) 62539
Telex: 33128 ZW

Enquiries: Miss D E Barron
Availability: open to all Zimbabweans aged 16 or over who have completed four years of secondary education
Hours: 10.00-17.30 Monday to Friday, 09.00-12.30 Saturday
Stock: 86,000 volumes of non-fiction, concentrating on educational and technical information
Services: photocopying, loans, inter-library loans, enquiry service
Publications: Shelfmark (bi-monthly bulletin of recent acquisitions)

Zimbabwe National Chamber of Commerce, Trade and Information Centre
Address: PO Box 1934, Harare
Telephone: (4) 708611
Telex: 2531 ZW
Enquiries: Miss Melver Mubataripi (Trade and Information Officer)
Availability: open to the business community
Hours: 08.00-16.45 Monday to Friday
Stock: business directories of foreign countries, trade bulletins from other chambers of commerce, buyers' guides and any publications with trade related information
Services: export enquiries, import enquiries, enquiries concerning domestic trade in Zimbabwe, enquiries on how to start a business
Publications: Commerce magazine (monthly); *Newsletter* (fortnightly); *Trade opportunities bulletin* (monthly); *Daily tender bulletin*

5. Foreign Trade and Export Departments

PAN-REGIONAL ORGANISATIONS

Association of African Trade Promotion Organisations (AATPO)
Address: BP 23, Tangiers, Morocco
Telephone: (9) 41687
Telex: 33695
Main contact: Farouk Shakweer (secretary general)
Publications: African Trade (monthly); *Directory of Trade Information Sources in Africa; Directory of Food Importers and Exporters in Africa*; various market studies
Notes: 26 member states

Caribbean Association of Industry and Commerce (CAIC)
Address: Musson Bldg, Hincks Street, PO Box 259, Bridgetown, Barbados
Telephone: (809) 4366385
Fax: (809) 4369937
Telex: 2473
Main contact: Pat Thompson (executive director)
Notes: Consists of chambers of commerce in 17 countries; aims to encourage economic development through the private sector
Publications: CAIC News (fortnightly), Business Wave (6 a year)

Caribbean Community and Common Market (CARICOM)
Address: Bank of Guyana Bldg., POB 10827, Georgetown, Guyana
Telephone: (2) 69280
Fax: (2) 56194
Telex: 2263

Main contacts: Edwin Carrington (secretary-general); Frank Abdulah (dep. secretary-general)
Notes: Promotes economic co-operation between member states through the Caribbean Common Market; encourages functional co-operation in areas such as education, health, transport etc; co-ordinates foreign policies. Member states:

Antigua and Barbuda, Bahamas, Barbados, Belize, Dominica, Dominican Republic, Grenada, Guyana, Haiti, Jamaica, Montserrat, St Kitts-Nevis, St Lucia, St Vincent and the Grenadines, and Trinidad and Tobago

Caribbean Development Corporation
Address: Reduit, Gros Islet, POB 619, Castries, St Lucia
Telex: 6222

Central American Common Market (CACM)
Address: 4a Avenida 10-25, Zona 14, Apdo Postal 1237, Guatemala City, Guatemala
Telephone: (2) 682151
Fax: (2) 681071
Telex: 5676
Main contact: Rafael Rodriguez Loucel (secretary-general)
Publications: Carta Informativa (monthly); *Anuario Estadistico Centro-americano de Comercio Exterior; Cuaderno de la SIECA*
Notes: Promotes inter-regional trade, carries out studies in industrial sector, advises on energy plans and marketing. Members are Costa Rica, Guatemala, El Salvador, Honduras and Nicaragua

Colombo Plan for Co-operative Economic and Social Development in Asia and the Pacific
Address: 12 Melbourne Ave, POB 596, Colombo 4, Sri Lanka
Telephone: (1) 581813
Fax: (1) 581754
Telex: 21537
Main contact: John Ryan (director of Colombo Plan Bureau)
Publications: Colombo Plan Newsletter (monthly); annual report; Development Perspectives (biennial)
Notes: Reviews economic and social development of the region and promotes co-operation among the 26 member countries

Confederation of Asian-Pacific Chambers of Commerce and Industry
Address: 10th Floor, 122 Tun Hua North Road, Taipei 10590, Taiwan
Telephone: (2) 7163016
Fax: (2) 7183683
Telex: 11144
Main contact: Johnson C Yen (director-general)
Notes: Holds biennial conferences; compiles and disseminates trade and business information. Members consist of national chambers of commerce of Australia, Bangladesh, Brunei, Hong Kong, India, Indonesia, Japan, Korea, Malaysia, New Zealand, Pakistan, Papua New Guinea, Philippines, Singapore, Sri Lanka, Taiwan, Thailand and Vietnam

Economic Community of Central African States (CEEAC)
Address: BP 2112 Libreville, Gabon
Main contact: Pierre Buyoya (President)
Notes: Promotes co-operation between member states by abolishing trade restrictions and standardising tariffs. 11 member states

Economic Community of West African States (ECOWAS)
Address: 6 King Cross V Road, POB 12745, Lagos, Nigeria
Telephone: (1) 636841
Telex: 22633
Main contact: Dr Abass Bundu (secretary general)
Notes: Promotes trade and economic, social and cultural co-operation and development between member states (Benin, Burkina Faso, Cape Verde, Côte d'Ivoire, Gambia, Ghana, Guinea-Bissau, Liberia, Mali, Mauritania, Niger, Nigeria, Senegal, Sierra Leone, Togo)

Latin American Integration Association (LAIA)
Address: Cebollati 1461, Casilla 577, Montevideo, Uruguay
Telephone: (2) 401121
Fax: (2) 490649
Telex: 26944

Main contact: Antonio de Cerqueira Antanes (secretary general)
Notes: Aims at encouraging regional trade and co-operation between member states, and the gradual establishment of a free trade area
Publications: Sintesis ALADI (monthly), Ambito Empresarial (monthly), annual reports and trade statistics

Preferential Trade Area for Eastern and Southern African States (PTA)
Address: PO Box 30051, Ndeke House Annexe, Lusaka, Zambia
Telephone: 229725
Fax: 252524
Telex: 40127
Main contact: Bingu Wa Mutharika
Notes: Aims at promoting economic co-operation and trade in the region, provides institutional mechanisms for facilitating trade. 18 member states.
Publications: PTA Trade Information Newsletter (monthly), official Trade and Investment Journal, PTA Traders Directory

South Pacific Bureau for Economic Co-operation
Address: GPO Box 856, Suva, Fiji
Telephone: 312600
Fax: 302204
Telex: 2229
Main contact: Ieremia T Tabai (secretary general)
Publications: SPEC Activities (monthly); *Trade and Industry Scene* (monthly); annual reports
Notes: Aims to facilitate continuing co-operation and consultation between members on trade, economic development, transport, tourism, etc. Promotes trade and export activities

South Pacific Commission
Address: BP D5, Nouméa Cedex, New Caledonia
Telephone: 262000
Fax: 263818
Telex: 3139
Main contact: Ati George Sokoman (secretary general)
Notes: The commission provides technical advice, training and assistance in economic, social and cultural development to countries of the region

South Pacific Trade Commission
Address: Level 6, 50 Park Street, Sydney, NSW 2000, Australia
Telephone: (2) 2835933
Fax: (2) 2835948
Telex: (1) 70342
Main contact: William T McCabe (trade commissioner)
Publication: South Pacific Trade Development Programme (monthly)
Notes: Funded by Australian government. Aims to identify and develop markets in Australia for exports from the Pacific islands

Union Douanière et Économique de l'Afrique Centrale (Customs and Economic Union of Central Africa)
Address: BP 969, Bangui, Central African Republic
Telephone: 610922
Telex: 5254
Main contact: Thomas Dakayi Kamga (secretary general)
Notes: Six member states: Cameron, Central African Republic, Chad, Congo, Equatorial Guinea, Gabon
Publications: Annuaire du Commerce Exterieur de l'UDEAC, Bulletin des Statistiques Générales (quarterly)

West African Economic Community (CEAO)
Address: Rue Agostino Neto, BP 643, Ouagadougou, Burkina Faso
Telephone: 306187
Telex: 5212
Main contact: Mamadou Haidari (secretary general)
Publications: Intégration Africaine (two per year); annual report
Notes: Promotes trade and regional economic co-operation and integration between member states (Benin, Burkina Faso, Côte d'Ivoire, Mali, Mauritania, Niger, Senegal)

AFGHANISTAN

Ministry of Commerce
Address: Darulaman Watt, Kabul
Telephone: (93) 41041
Telex: 234

ALGERIA

Centre National Algérien du Commerce Extérieur
Address: 24 Bordj El-Kiffan, BP 571, Algiers
Telephone: (2) 627044
Telex: 52763
Main contact: Zahir Abder-Rahim (director general)

Ministry of Commerce
Address: 44 rue Muhammad Belouizdad, Belcourt, Algiers
Telephone: (2) 633366
Telex: 52768
Main contact: Mostefa Benammar (minister)

AMERICAN SAMOA

Office of Economic Development and Planning
Address: Pago Pago 96799
Telephone: 6335155
Fax: 6334195
Main contact: Lydia Faleafine (Director)

ANGOLA

Commercial Services Department
Address: Largo Diogo Cao, CP 1337, Luanda
Notes: State trading organisation with branches throughout Angola

Exportang, UEE
Address: Rua dos Enganos 1a, CP 1000, Luanda
Telephone: (1) 332363
Telex: 3318
Notes: State exports agency

Importang, UEE
Address: Calçada do Municipio 10, CP 1003, Luanda
Telephone: 337994
Fax: 392787
Telex: 3169
Main contact: Simao Diogo Da Cruz (General Manager)
Notes: State agency for co-ordination of imports

Ministry of Foreign Trade
Address: Largo Kinaxixi 14, Luanda
Telephone: 344525
Telex: 3282
Main contact: Dr Emanuel Moreira Carneiro (minister)

ANTIGUA & BARBUDA

Antigua and Barbuda Chamber of Commerce and Industry
Address: Cross and Redcliffe Sts, PO Box 774, St John's
Telephone: 462 0743
Fax: 462 4575

Ministry of Finance and Trade
Address: High St, St John's
Telephone: 4624860
Fax: 4621662
Main contact: Molwyn Joseph (director)

ARGENTINA

Asociación de Importadores y Exportadores de la República Argentina
Address: Avda Belgrano 124, 1°, 1092 Buenos Aires
Telephone: (1) 3420010
Fax: (1) 3421312
Telex: 25761
Main contact: Fernando A Raimondo (president)

Camara de Comercio Exterior de la Federación del Comercio e Industria
Address: Avenida Cordoba 1868, Rosario, Santa Fé
Telephone: (042) 213896
Main contact: Eduardo C Salvatierra (president)
Notes: Deals with import/export

Camara de Exportadores de la República Argentina
Address: Ave Roque Saenz Peña 740, 1º, 1035 Buenos Aires
Telephone: (01) 497583
Fax: (01) 461000
Telex: 22910 CAMEX AR

Main contact: Daniel Brunella (president)
Publication: En Contacto (monthly)
Notes: Founded 1943; 408 members. Organises trade promotions, missions and seminars; provides research and information services

Consejo Federal de Inversiones
Address: San Martin 871, 1004 Buenos Aires
Telephone: (01) 3135557
Fax: (01) 3134486
Telex: 21180
Main contact: Ing. Juan José Ciacera (secretary-general)
Notes: Regulates domestic and foreign investment

Consejo Nacional Económico y Social
Address: Maipú 972, 1006 Buenos Aires
Telephone: (01) 3127649
Notes: National economic and social council

AUSTRALIA

AIDC Ltd (Australian Industry Development Corporation)
Address: Level 33, AIDC Tower, 201 Kent Street, Sydney, NSW 2000
Telephone: (2) 2355155
Fax: (2) 2355195
Telex: 23107
Main contacts: Sir Gordon Jackson (chairman); Arthur W O'Sullivan (managing director)
Notes: Public company. Promotes development of Australian industries; provides finance and financial services. Maintains library. Branches in Melbourne, Perth, Adelaide, Brisbane and Canberra

Australian Institute of Export
Address: Export House, 2nd Floor, 22 Pitt Street, Sydney, NSW 2000
Telephone: (2) 2411745
Main contact: Mrs M Miroslio (director)
Publication: Export Handbook (annually)
Notes: Promotes study of export practice and technique. Divisions in Queensland, South Australia, Tasmania, Victoria and West Australia

Department of Trade
Address: Edmund Barton Bldg, Kings Ave, Barton, ACT 2600
Telephone: (62) 723911
Telex: 62193
Main contact: Michael Duffy (minister)
Notes: Offices in Adelaide, Brisbane, Darwin, Hobart, Melbourne, Perth and Sydney

South Australian Exporters' Association Inc
Address: Industry House, 12 Pirie Street, Adelaide, SA 5000
Telephone: (8) 2124691
Telex: 88370
Main contact: M J Deare (executive officer)
Publications: Export News and Opportunities (six a year); *South Australia Exporters' Association Members' Directory* (every two years)

Tasmanian Development Authority
Address: 134 Macquarie Street, Hobart, Tasmania 7000
Telephone: (02) 2308011

Trade Practices Commission
Address: POB 19, Belconnen, ACT 2616
Telephone: (62) 641166
Telex: 62626
Main contacts: W R McLomas (chairman); W J Coad (deputy chairman)
Publications: Small Business and the Trade Practices Act, various brochures and guides

Notes: Deals with possible breaches of Trade Practices Act, advises businessmen and consumers of their rights and responsibilities under the Act

BAHRAIN

Ministry of Commerce and Agriculture
Address: POB 5479, Bahrain Tower, Government Road, Manama
Telephone: 531531
Telex: 9171
Main contact: Habib Ahmad Qassein (minister)

Ministry of Development and Industry
Address: POB 1435,Manama
Telephone: 291511
Fax: 271468
Telex: 8344
Main contact: Yusuf Ahmad ash-Shirawi (minister)

BANGLADESH

Association of Development Agencies in Bangladesh
Address: House 46a, Road 6a, Dhanmaudi R/A, Dhaka
Telephone: (2) 313318
Telex: 642940
Publications: Adab Sangbad (monthly, Bengali); *Adab News* (six a year, English)

Bangladesh Co-operative Marketing Society
Address: 9d Motijheel Commercial Area, Dhaka-1000

Export Promotion Bureau
Address: 122-4 Motijheel Commercial Area, Dhaka-2
Telephone: (2) 232245
Fax: (2) 833167
Telex: 642204
Main contact: Abu Syeed Chowdhury (vice-chairman)
Notes: Subsidiary of Ministry of Commerce; regional offices in Chittagong, Khulna and Rajshahi; branches in Comilla, Sylhet, Bogra and Barisal

Ministry of Commerce and Industries
Address: Shilpa Bhaban, Motijheel Commercial Area, Dhaka
Telex: 642201
Main contacts: M Ahmed Bablu (minister of industries), M A Munim (minister of commerce)

Trading Corporation of Bangladesh
Address: HBFC Building, 22 Purana Paltan, Dhaka-500
Telephone: (2) 325030
Telex: 642217
Main contact: A K M Aizul Islam

BELIZE

Belize Export and Investment Promotion Unit
Address: 7 Cork St, PO Box 291, Belize City
Telephone: (2) 44913
Fax: (2) 30755
Telex: 121
Main contact: Hugh Fuller (general manager)

Department of Economic Development
Address: PO Box 42, Belmopan
Telephone: (8) 22526
Fax: (8) 23111
Main contact: Humberto Paredes

BENIN

Ministry of Foreign Affairs and Co-operation
Address: BP 318, Cotonou
Telephone: 300400
Telex: 5200
Main contact: Guy Landry Haziume (minister)

Ministry of Trade, Crafts and Tourism
Address: BP 2037, Cotonou
Telephone: 315258
Telex: 5040
Main contact: Gado Girigissou (minister)

BHUTAN

Export Development Corporation of Bhutan
Address: Industrial Estate, Phuntsholing
Telephone: 2530
Telex: 890312
Notes: Manages exports on behalf of government. Branches in Phuntsholing, Gomtu and Calcutta, India

National Commission for Trade and Industry
Address: Thimphu
Telephone: 22403
Main contact: HM Druk Gyalpo Jigine Singye Wangchuck (chairman)
Notes: Regulates industrial projects

BOLIVIA

Ministry of Industry, Trade and Tourism
Address: Av Camacho, Esq Bueno, Casilla 1372, La Paz
Telephone: (02) 372044
Telex: 3259
Main contact: Fernando Campero Prudencio (minister)

BOTSWANA

Ministry of Commerce and Industry
Address: Private Bag 004, Gaborone
Telephone: 353024
Fax: 371539
Telex: 2674 TRADE BD
Main contact: Ponatshego H K Kedikilwe (minister)
Notes: Operates the Trade and Investment Promotion Agency (*main contact:* Mrs D T Tibone, Director); also operates Trade and Investment Information Service

BRAZIL

Conselho de Desenvolvimento Comercial (CDC)
Address: Ministry of Infrastructure, Bloco R, Esplanada dos Ministérios 227, 70044 Brasilia, DF
Telephone: (061) 2230308
Telex: (061) 2537
Notes: Commercial development council

Consello Nacional do Comercio Exterior (CONCEX)
Address: Fazenda 5° andar, Gabinete do Ministro, Bloco 6, Explanada dos Ministerios, 70.048 Brasilia, DF
Telephone: (61) 223 4856
Telex: 1142
Main contact: Namir Selek (executive secretary)
Notes: responsible for trade policy and the control of export activities

Ministry of Industry and Commerce
Address: Esplanada dos Ministérios, Bloco K, 70000 Brasilia, DF
Telephone: (061) 215 4300
Fax: (061) 225 7230
Telex: 1066
Main contact: José H Castelo Branco (minister)

BURKINA FASO

Ministry of External Relations
Address: BP 7038, Ouagadougou
Telex: 5222
Main contact: Leandre Bassole (minister)

Ministry of Trade and Supplies
Address: BP 365, Ouagadougou
Main contact: Mamadou Touré (minister)

Office National du Commerce Exterieur
Address: Ave Leo Frobénius BP 389, Ouagadougou
Telephone: 311300/311302/306224
Fax: 311469
Telex: 5258 BF
Main contact: Zabramba Benoît (managing director)
Notes: National external trade organisation

Office de Promotion de l'Enterprise du Burkina
Address: BP 94, Ouagadougou
Telephone: 990540

Telex: 5226
Main contact: Dieudonné Nikiema (managing director)
Notes: State agency for the development of industrial enterprise

BURUNDI

Ministry of Industry and Trade
Address: Bujumbura
Telephone: (2) 25330
Main contact: Albert Muganga (minister)

Office National du Commerce
Address: Bujumbura
Notes: State trading organisation controlling international commercial operations

CAMBODIA

KAMPEXIM
Address: Phnom-Penh
Notes: Handles imports and exports

Ministry of Trade
Address: Phnom-Penh
Main contact: Nhim Vanda (minister)

National Trade Commission
Address: Phnom-Penh
Main contact: Tang Saroem (president)

CAMEROON

Centre National du Commerce Extérieur
Address: BP 2461, 1er étage, Immeuble ONCPB, Douala
Telephone: 421679
Telex: 5585
Main contact: Louis Wansek (director)
Notes: Export development organisation

Ministry of Industry and Commerce
Address: Yaoundé
Telephone: 234040
Fax: 222704
Telex: 8638
Main contact: Patrice Mand (minister)

CANADA

Canadian Commercial Corporation
Address: 50 O'Connor Street, Ottawa, ON K1A 0S6
Telephone: (613) 996 0034
Fax: (613) 995 2121
Telex: 053 4359
Main contacts: H J Millington (Pres); P Théberge (Vice-Pres)
Notes: Government-owned. Aims to assist in development of trade between Canada and other nations

Canadian Exporters Association
Address: 99 Bank St, Suite 250, Ottawa, ON K1P 6B9
Telephone: (613) 238 8888
Fax: (613) 563 9218
Main contacts: L James Taylor (president); Clement Stour (director of communications)
Publications: Export News/Digest (bi-monthly)

Canadian International Development Agency
Address: 200 Promenade du Portage, Hull, QC K1A 0G4
Telephone: (613) 997 5456
Telex: 053 4140
Main contacts: Margaret Catley-Carlson (president); William McWhinney (vice-president)
Notes: Aims to foster international co-operation and enhance Canada's interests in the world, including food aid, funds for non-governmental organisations and support for business

Department of External Affairs
Address: Lester B Pearson Bldg, 125 Sussex Drive, Ottawa, ON K1A 0G2
Telephone: (613) 995 1851
Fax: (613) 996 9288
Telex: 053 3745
Main contacts: John Crosbie (minister for international trade); J M Weekly (director-general, Trade Policy Bureau)

Publication: Business Directory of Canadian Trade Representation
Notes: Maintains library

Department of Finance-Information Services
Address: 140 O'Connor Street, Ottawa, ON K1A 0G5
Telephone: (613) 992 1575
Fax: (613) 996 2690
Telex: 053 3336
Notes: Maintains library. Provides information for importers and exporters on international trade controls

Export Development Corporation
Address: 151 O'Connor Street, POB 655, Ottawa, ON K1P 5T9
Telephone: (613) 598 2500
Telex: 053 4136
Main contact: Sylvain Cloutier (chair and president)
Publication: EDC Today (six a year)
Notes: Provides insurance and bank guarantee services to Canadian exporters and arranges credit for foreign buyers. Maintains library

Investment Canada
Address: 235 Queen Street, PO Box 2800, Station D, Ottawa, ON K1P 6A5
Telephone: (613) 995 0465
Notes: Aims to promote and facilitate investment in Canada by domestic and foreign companies, undertakes research and analysis

CAPE VERDE

Ministry of Foreign Affairs
Address: Praça 10 de Mayo, CP 60, Praia, Sao Tiago
Telephone: 310
Telex: 6070
Main contact: Silvino da Luz (minister)
Publications: Boletin Informativo (weekly)

Ministry of Industry, Commerce and Tourism
Address: Unidade de Promoçào Industrial, PO Box 145 Praia, Sao Tiago
Telephone: 613949
Telex: 6035
Main contact: Dr Manuel Casimiro de Jesus Chantre (minister)

CENTRAL AFRICAN REPUBLIC

Ministry of Trade and Industry
Address: Bangui
Telephone: (61) 4488
Telex: 5215

CHAD

Ministry of Commerce and Trade
Address: BP 453, N'Djamena
Telephone: 515656
Main contact: Mahamat Habib Doumtoum (minister)

Société Nationale de Commercialisation du Tchad
Address: N'Djamena
Telex: 5227
Main contact: Marbrouck Natroud (director)
Notes: State import/export agency also responsible for marketing and distribution

CHILE

Dirección General de Relaciones Económicas Internacionales - Pro-Chile
Address: Avda Bernardo O'Higgins 1315, 2⁰ Casilla 14087 Correo 21, Santiago
Telephone: (02) 6960043, 6962543
Fax: (02) 6960639
Telex: 240836 PROCH CL
Main contact: Augusto Ainat Del Solar
Notes: Government export agency

CHINA

All-China Federation of Industry and Commerce
Address: 93 Beiheyan Dajie, Beijing 100006
Telephone: (1) 5736677
Fax: (1) 5122631
Telex: 22044
Main contacts: Rong Yiren (chairman)
Notes: Promotes overseas trade relations

Beijing Foreign Trade Corporation
Address: Building 12, Jianguomenwai Street, Beijing 150022
Telephone: (1) 5001315
Fax: (1) 5001668
Telex: 210064
Main contacts: Wu Yutian (chairman)
Notes: Controls import/export

China Council for the Promotion of International Trade
Address: 1 Fuxingmenwai St, Beijing 100860
Telephone: (1) 867229, 8013344/1522
Fax: (1) 8011370
Telex: 22315 CCPIT CN
Cable: COMTRADE BEIJING
Main contact: Jia Shi (chairman)
Publications: China's Foreign Trade; China's Exports; China Trade Promotion Review (weekly, Chinese)
Notes: Set up in 1952 as a non-governmental economic and trade organisation. Aims to promote economic and trade relations between China and other countries. Sponsors and arranges exhibitions. CCPIT's membership covers individuals, enterprises, organisations and associations involved in trade and commerce. Branches throughout China

China Economic & Trade Consultants Corporation
Address: B-12 Guanghua Road, Jianguomen Wai, Beijing 100020
Telephone: (1) 5052255 (Exchange) 5051580
Fax: (1) 5051571, 5051572
Telex: 22506 CTSUL CN
Notes: Offers trade and market information. Hosts foreign economic and trade delegations

China Economic & Trade Foreign Trade Bureau
Address: 190 Chaoyangmennei Dajie, Beijing
Telephone: (1) 554808
Telex: 22470
Cable: 8571 BEIJING
Notes: Branch in Shanghai

China Export Bases Development Corporation
Address: 28 Donghou Xiang, Andingmenwai, Beijing
Telephone: (1) 462902/461184
Telex: 22168 MFTPK CN
Notes: Promotes production of export commodities and establishment of joint venture enterprises with foreign investors. Branches in Fuzhou and Shanghai

China Industry-Commerce-Economic Development Corporation (INCOMIC)
Address: 93 Bei He Yan Dajie, Beijing
Telephone: (1) 554231
Telex: 22044
Main contacts: Hu Ziang (chairman), Zon Siyu (president)
Notes: Promotes exports and imports, offers consultancy service

Fujian Foreign Trade Corporation
Address: 1 Shangbin Road, Fuzhou
Telephone: (591) 34018/34246 (Import Department: (591) 34471)
Notes: Handles import business as entrusted by domestic departments. Acts as agent for foreign firms

Guangdong Foreign Trade Development Corporation
Address: 774 Dongfeng Dong Road, Guangzhou
Telephone: (20) 775148/755313/756049/776838
Fax: (20) 766025
Telex: 44508 GDFTD CN

Liaoning Foreign Trade Corporation
Address: 135 Stalin Road, Dalian
Telephone: 23041 (Import Department: 26892)
Telex: 86141 LFTC CN

Notes: Handles import business entrusted by domestic organisations, acts as distributor, agency for foreign firms, handles consignment trade and after-sales service on commission

Ministry of Commerce
Address: 45 Fuxingmennei St, Beijing 100801
Telephone: (1) 668581
Telex: 20032
Main contact: Hu Ping (minister)

Ministry of Foreign Economic Relations and Trade
Address: 2 Dongchangan Jie, Beijing 100731
Telephone: (1) 553031
Telex: 22168
Main contact: Li Lanqing (minister)
Notes: Operates Centre for Market and Trade Development within its International Trade Research Institute

Shanghai Foreign Trade Corporation
Address: 27 Zhongshan Dong Yi Lu, Shanghai (Import Department: 27 Zhongshan Road E1, Shanghai)
Telephone: (21) 3217350
Telex: 33034

Notes: Handles imports, consignment sales, exhibitions, fairs and after-sales service on commission. Acts as distributor and agency for foreign firms and manufacturers on commission

State Administration for Industry and Commerce
Address: 8 Sanlihe Dong Lu, Xichengqu, Beijing 100820
Telephone: (1) 8013300
Fax: (1) 862771
Telex: 222431 SAIC CN
Main contact: Ren Zhonglin (director)
Notes: Overseas internal trade

State Economic Commission
Address: Sanlihe, Fuxingmenwai, Beijing
Telephone: (1) 868521
Main contact: Lu Dong (minister in charge)

Tianjin Foreign Trade Corporation
Address: 80 Qufu Road, Tianjin
Telephone: 32630

COLOMBIA

Fondo de Promoción de Exportaciones (PROEXPO)
Address: Calle 28, No 13A-15, 35°-42°, Apdo Aéreo 240092, Santa Fe de Bogotá, DC
Telephone: (1) 269 0777
Fax: (1) 282 5071
Telex: 44452
Main contact: Dr Caros Caballero Argaiz

Ministry of Economic Development
Address: Carrera 13, No 28-01 5°-9° Santa Fé de Bogotá, DC
Telephone: (01) 258 1409
Fax: (01) 281 1103
Telex: 44508
Main contact: Miguel Merino Gordillo (minister)

COMOROS

Ministry of Foreign Affairs and Co-operation
Address: BP 428, Moroni
Telephone: 2306
Telex: 219
Main contact: Saïd Athoumane (minister)

Office National du Commerce
Address: BP 763, Moroni
Telephone: 730958
Telex: 241 PUBLIC KO
Main contact: MCHANGAMA Lilie Djohou (trade officer)

CONGO

Ministry of Trade
Address: Palais du Peuple, Brazzaville
Telephone: (83) 1827
Telex: 5210
Main contact: Alphonse Poati (minister)

Office Nationale du Commerce
Address: BP 2305, Brazzaville
Telephone: 834399
Telex: 5309
Main contact: V Enoussa Ncongo (director-general)
Notes: Import and distribution agency

COSTA RICA

Costa Rican Investment and Development Co (CINDE)
Address: Apdo 7170, 1000 San José
Telephone: 200036
Fax: 204750
Telex: 3514
Main contact: Luis Gamboa Arguedas (president)

Ministry of Foreign Trade
Address: Llancuna 12°, Avda Central, Calle 5, San José
Telephone: 5910
Fax: 239328
Telex: 2936
Main contact: Roberto Rojas Lopez (minister)

COTE D'IVOIRE

Ministry of Trade
Address: BP V142, Abidjan
Main contact: Ferdinand Kacou Angora Angba (minister)

CUBA

Ministry of Foreign Trade
Address: Infanta No. 16, Vedado, Havana
Telephone: (7) 709341
Fax: (7) 76234
Telex: 511174
Main contact: Ricardo Cabrisas Ruiz (minister)

DJIBOUTI

Chambre Internationale de Commerce et d'Industrie
Address: BP 84, Djibouti
Telephone: 351070
Telex: 5957
Main contact: Said Ali Coubeche (president)

Ministry of Commerce, Industry and Transport and Tourism
Address: BP 1846, Djibouti
Telephone: 351682
Telex: 5871
Main contact: Ahmed Ibrahim Abdi (minister)

DOMINICA

Ministry of Trade and Industry
Address: Government Headquarters, Kennedy Avenue, Roseau
Telephone: 82401
Main contact: Charles Maynard

THE DOMINICAN REPUBLIC

Secretariat of State for Industry and Commerce
Address: Edif de Oficianas Gubernamentales 3°, Avda México, Santo Domingo, DN
Telephone: 685 5171
Main contact: Rafael Bello Andino (secretary of state)

ECUADOR

Fondo de Promoción de Exportaciones
Address: Juan León Mera 130 y Avda Patria, Casilla 163, Quito
Telephone: (2) 564900
Fax: (2) 562519
Telex: 2193
Main contact: Daniel Ocampo

Ministry of Industry, Trade and Integration
Address: Juan León Mera y Roca, Quito
Telephone: (02) 527988
Telex: 2166
Main contact: Mauricio Pinto Mancheno (minister)

EGYPT

Ministry of Foreign Trade
Address: Lazoughli Square, Cairo
Telephone: (2) 25424
Main contact: Yusri Ali Mustapha (minister)

EL SALVADOR

Ministry of Economy
Address: Paseo General Escalón 4122, Apdo 0119, San Salvador
Telephone: 243000
Fax: 981965
Telex: 20269 ISCE SAL
Main contact: Arturo Zablah (minister)
Notes: provides free *Statistical Bulletin of Foreign Trade*; plus a wide range of statistical information and services, including directories, periodicals, market studies and assistance to exporters/importers

EQUATORIAL GUINEA

Empresa General de Industria y Comercio
Address: Malabo
Notes: State import/export agency

Ministry of Foreign Affairs and Co-operation
Address: Malabo
Telephone: 3220
Main contacts: Santiago Eneme Ouono (minister)

ETHIOPIA

Africa Trade Centre
Address: UNECA, POB 3001, Addis Ababa
Telephone: (1) 447200
Publications: *Flash on Trade Opportunities* (quarterly); *African Trade Bulletin* (2 pa)

Ethiopian Import and Export Corporation
Address: POB 2313, Addis Ababa
Telephone: (1) 512400
Telex: 21009, 21235
Fax: (1) 514396
Main contact: Aschenaki G. Hirrot

Ministry of Trade
Address: POB 1769, Addis Ababa
Telephone: 448200
Main contact: Yosef Kumelo (minister)

FIJI

Fiji Trade and Investment Board
Address: 3rd floor, Civic House, Town Hall Rd, PO Box 2303, Govt. Bldgs, Suva
Telephone: 315988
Fax: 301783
Telex: 2355
Main contact: Asesela Ravuvu

Ministry of Trade and Commerce
Address: Government Bldgs, Suva
Main contact: Harold Powell (minister)

FRENCH POLYNESIA

Association pour la Formation et le Développement en Polynésie
Address: Immeuble FARA, rue E Ahnne, BP 455, Papeete
Telephone: 426683
Main contacts: H Devay (president); J Wild (director-general)

Chambre de Commerce et d'Industries de la Polynésie Française
Address: BP 118, Papeete
Telephone: 420344
Fax: 435184
Telex: 274
Main contact: Gérard Afo (president)

GABON

Centre Gabonais du Commerce Extérieur
Address: BP 3906, Libreville
Telephone: 761167
Telex: 5347
Main contact: Michel Teale
Publication: *L'Economiste Gabonais* (quarterly)

Ministry of Foreign Affairs and Co-operation
Address: BP 2245, Libreville
Telephone: 762270
Telex: 5255
Main contact: Pancaline Bongo (minister)

GAMBIA

Ministry of Finance and Economic Affairs
Address: The Quadrangle, Banjul
Telephone: 28291
Fax: 28060
Telex: 2264
Main contact: Omar Sey (minister)

National Trading Corporation of The Gambia
Address: POB 61, 1-3 Wellington Street, Banjul
Telephone: 28395
Telex: 2252
Main contacts: Momodou Cham

GHANA

Ghana Export Promotion Council
Address: Public House, PO Box M146, Accra
Telephone: (21) 228813
Fax: (21) 668263
Telex: 2289
Main contact: Kwesi Ahwoi

Ghana National Trading Corporation
Address: PO Box 67, Accra
Telephone: (21) 664871
Notes: Organises exports/imports and distribution of commodities

Ministry of Trade
Address: PO Box M47, Accra
Telephone: (21) 665421
Telex: 2105
Main contact: Edward Falia (minister)

GRENADA

Marketing and National Importing Board
Address: Young Street, St. George's
Telephone: 440 3191
Fax: 440 4152
Telex: 3435
Main contact: Finton De Bourg (Chairman)

GUADELOUPE

Agence pour la Promotion Industrielle de la Guadeloupe (APRIGA)
Address: BP 1229, 97184 Pointe-à-Pitre
Telephone: 834897
Fax: 902187
Telex: 919780 GL

GUATEMALA

Comité Co-ordinador de Asociaciones Agrícolas, Comerciales, Industriales y Financieras (CACIF)
Address: Edif. Cámara de Industria de Guatemala, Ruta 6, No 9-21, Zona 4, Guatemala City
Telephone: (02) 310651
Telex: 6133
Main contact: Rafael Pola
Notes: Co-ordinates the work of member chambers, particularly on the organisation of free enterprise

GUINEA

Importex-Enterprise Nationale Import-Export
Address: BP 152, Conakry
Telephone: 442813
Telex: 625
Main contact: Mamadou Bobo Dieng (director)
Notes: State import/export agency

Ministry of Trade, Transport and Tourism
Address: Conakry
Telephone: 444512
Telex: 652

GUINEA-BISSAU

Ministry of Trade and Industry
Address: Bissau
Main contact: Luís Oliveira Sanca (minister)

GUYANA

Ministry of Trade, Tourism and Industry
Address: Urquhart St, Georgetown
Telephone: (2) 62505
Telex: 2288
Main contact: Michael Shree (minister)

HAITI

Ministry of Commerce and Industry
Address: Rue Legitime 8, Champ-de-Mars, Port-au-Prince
Main contact: Jean Robert Delsoin (minister)

HONDURAS

Ministry of Economy and Commerce
Address: Edif. Salame, 5a Avda, 4a Calle, Tegucigalpa
Telephone: 223251
Telex: 1396
Main contact: Carlos Chain (minister)

HONG KONG

Hong Kong Exporters Association
Address: 825 Star House, Salisbury Road Tsinnshatsui, Kowloon
Telephone: 430 9851
Fax: 730 1869
Telex: 57905
Main contacts: Andrew Koo (chairman), Judy Ip (executive secretary)

Hong Kong Trade Development Council
Address: 36-39th Floor, Convention Plaza,1 Harbour Road, Wanchai
Telephone: 584 4333
Fax: 824 0249
Telex: 73595 CONHK HX
Main contacts: Lydia Dunn (chairman), Jack So (executive director)
Publications: Hong Kong Enterprise (monthly); *Hong Kong Trader* (monthly); *Hong Kong Apparel, Hong Kong Toys, Hong Kong Jewellery, Hong Kong Watches & Clocks, Hong Kong Household, Hong Kong Gifts & Premiums, Hong Kong Garments & Accessories* (all biannual); *Hong Kong Electronics* (four a year); annual guide in eight languages
Notes: Established in 1966 as a semi-official body responsible for promoting and developing world trade with Hong Kong. Through its Trade Promotion Programme, organises displays of Hong Kong products, participation in international trade fairs, etc. Offices throughout the world

Industry Department
Address: 14th Floor, Ocean Centre, 5 Canton Road, Kowloon
Telephone: 722 2573
Fax: 730 4633
Telex: 50151
Main contact: J F Yaxley (director)

Trade Department
Address: Trade Dept Tower, 700 N Road, Kowloon
Telephone: 789 7555

Fax: 789249
Telex: 45126
Main contact: N W H MacLeod (secretary for trade and industry)

INDIA

Federation of Indian Export Organisations
Address: 4/2 SIRI Institutional Area, Hauz Khas, New Delhi 110016
Telephone: (11) 6851310
Telex: 3173194
Main contacts: Viremdara P Punj (president), Chandrakant G Rao (secretary-general)

Indian Institute of Foreign Trade
Address: B-21 Institutional Area, South of IIT, New Delhi 11016
Telephone: (11) 655124
Notes: Researches problems of foreign trade, conducts market surveys, disseminates information

Industries and Commerce Association
Address: ICO Association Road, POB 70, Dhanbad 826001, Bihar
Telephone: (326) 2639
Main contacts: P K Agarwalla (president), D D Banerjee (assistant secretary)

Ministry of Commerce
Address: Transport Bhavan, New Delhi 110011
Telephone: (11) 301 6664
Fax: (11) 371 0518 *Telex:* 3166527
Main contact: Dr Subramanian Suamy (minister)
Publication: Journal of Industry and Trade (monthly, English)

State Trading Corporation of India
Address: Jawahar Vyapar Bhavan, Tolstoy M, New Delhi 110001
Telephone: (11) 331 3177
Fax: (11) 332 6741
Telex: 3165734
Main contact: Sudhir Jayantilal Mulji (chairman)
Notes: Government imports/exports agency

Trade Development Authority
Address: POB 767, Bank of Baroda Building, 16 Parliament Street, New Delhi 110001
Telephone: (11) 332 0214/8161/8241/8218
Telex: 31-65155 ADEPT-IN
Main contacts: K Kipgen (executive director); P K Bhandari (joint chief-in-charge - TI & S Division)
Notes: Promotes exports, helps importers by arranging supply source contacts. Branches in Frankfurt, New York, Tokyo and Dubai

INDONESIA

Commercial Advisory Foundation in Indonesia (CAFI)
Address: Jalan Profolinggo 5, POB 249, Jakarta 10002
Telephone: 324487
Main contacts: R Ng S Sosrohadikoesoemo (chairman), Dick Hage (managing director)
Notes: Offers information, consultancy and translation services

Importers Association of Indonesia (GINSI)
Address: (Arena Pekan Raya Jakarta), Pinta Timur, PO Box 2744/JKT, Jakarta Pusat 10110
Telephone: (21) 360643/367269/343297
Telex: 46793 GINSI IA
Main contacts: Mr Daryatmo, Gen.(Ret.) (chairman)

Ministry of Trade
Address: Jalan Moch, Ikhwan Ridwan Rais 5, Jakarta Pusat
Telephone: (21) 348667/366318 (minister); (21) 348666 (junior minister)
Fax: (21) 374361 (minister); (21) 342875 (junior minister)
Main contact: Dr Arifin M Siregar (Minister); Dr J Soedradjad Djiwandono (Junior Minister)

National Development Planning Agency (Bappenas)
Address: Jalan Taman Suropah 2, Jakarta 10310
Telephone: (21) 334811
Fax: (021) 3105374

Telex: 61333
Main contacts: Purwanyo (chairman), Dr Saleh Afiff (vice-chairman)

IRAN

Ministry of Commerce
Address: Tehran
Notes: Minister: Abdolhossein Vahadji

IRAQ

Ministry of Trade
Address: Khulafa St, Khullan Sq, Baghdad
Telephone: (1) 887 2682
Telex: 212206
Main contact: Muhammed Mahadi Salih (minister)

ISRAEL

The Israel Export Institute
Address: Rehov Hamered Street, POB 50084, Tel Aviv 61500
Telephone: (3) 5142830
Fax: (3) 5142902
Telex: 35613

Ministry of Industry and Trade
Address: PO Box 229, 30 Rehov Agron, Jerusalem
Telephone: (2) 750111
Fax: (2) 245110
Telex: 25211
Main contact: Moshe Nissim (minister of Industry and Trade)
Notes: Export Market Research Department, 29 Hamered Street, Tel Aviv 68125; telephone (3) 630965, telex 341623

JAMAICA

Jamaica National Export Corporation
Address: 8 Waterloo Road, PO Box 645, Kingston
Telephone: 926 1200
Telex: 2124
Notes: Set up by the Ministry of Foreign Affairs to promote Jamaica's export trade

Ministry of Foreign Affairs and Foreign Trade
Address: 85 Knutsford Blvd, Kingston 5
Telephone: 926 4220
Fax: 929 6733
Telex: 2114
Main contact: David Coore (minister)

JAPAN

Council of All-Japan Exporters Association
Address: Kikai Shinko Kaikan Building, 5-8 Shibakoen 3-chome, Minato-ku, Tokyo
Telephone: (03) 434 6801

Economic Planning Agency
Address: 3-1 Kasumigaseki, Chiyoda-ku, Tokyo
Telephone: (03) 581 0261
Main contact: Wataru Hiiraizumi (director-general)

Industry Club of Japan
Address: 4-6 Marunouchi 1-chome, Chiyoda-ku, Tokyo
Telephone: (03) 3281 1711
Fax: (03) 3281 1797
Main contacts: Bumpei Ohtuki (president), Takashi Dai (executive director)

Institute of Foreign Exchange and Trade Research
Address: 9th Floor, Nichiginmae Building, 4 Nihonbashi Hongoku-cho 3-chome, Chuo-ku, Tokyo 103
Telephone: (3) 241 7721
Main contact: Tasuku Ikegami (managing director)

Japan External Trade Organisation (JETRO)
Address: 2-5 Toranomon 2-chome, Minato-ku, Tokyo 105
Telephone: (03) 3582 5522
Fax: (03) 587 0219
Telex: 24378
Publications: Focus Japan (monthly); *Tradescope* (monthly); *Japan Trade Directory* (annual)
Main contacts: Shoichi Akazawa (chairman), Shiro Miyamoto (president)
Notes: Provides information for foreign firms, investigates foreign markets, organises exhibitions. 31 domestic offices, 77 foreign offices in 58 countries. In the United Kingdom contact Japan Trade Centre, 6th Floor, Leconfield House, Curzon Street, London W1Y 7FB; telephone 071-493 7226

Japan Foreign Trade Council (Nihon Boeki-Kai)
Address: World Trade Center Building, 6th Floor, 4-1 Hamamatsu-cho 2-chome, Minato-ku, Tokyo 105
Telephone: (03) 3435 5952
Fax: (03) 3435 5967
Main contacts: Yohei Mimura (president), Masao Saito (executive managing director)

Japanese Association for the Promotion of International Trade
Address: Nippon Building, 5th Floor, 2-6-2 Otemachi, Chiyoda-ku, Tokyo
Telephone: (03) 3245 1561
Telex: 28471
Main contacts: Y Sakurauchi (president); Takamaru Morita (chairman)
Notes: Promotes Japanese private sector trade with People's Republic of China, Democratic People's Republic of Korea, Vietnam and Albania

Ministry of International Trade and Industry
Address: 1-3 Kasumigaseki, Chiyoda-ku, Tokyo
Telephone: (03) 3501 1511
Telex: 22916
Main contact: Hikaru Matsunaga (minister)
Notes: Library office in Kobe

Osaka Municipal Information Centre for Business and Trade
Address: 1-4 Semba-chu, Higashi-ku, Osaka
Telephone: (06) 262 3261

Tokyo Foreign Trade Association
Address: Tokyo Trade Center Building, 2nd Floor, 7-8 Kaigan 1-chome, Minato-ku, Tokyo
Telephone: (03) 438 2026
Fax: (03) 433 7164
Publication: Buyer's Guide of Tokyo (annually)

Tokyo Trade Center
Address: 7-8 Kaigan 1-chome, Minato-ku, Tokyo
Telephone: (03) 434 4241
Fax: (03) 434 4648
Telex: 27189
Publication: Tokyo Trade News (monthly)

World Trade Center of Japan
Address: World Trade Center Building, 37th Floor, 4-1 Hamamatsu-cho 2-chome, Minato-ku, Tokyo
Telephone: (03) 435 5651

JORDAN

Ministry of Trade and Industry
Address: POB 2019, Amman
Telephone: (6) 663191
Fax: (6) 603721
Telex: 21163
Main contact: Ziad Farns (minister)

KENYA

Industrial and Commercial Development Corporation
Address: Uchumi House, PO Box 45519, Nairobi
Telephone: (2) 29213
Telex: 22429
Main contacts: W Ntimama (chairman); J Simba (executive director)

Kenya External Trade Authority
Address: PO Box 43137, Nairobi
Telephone: (2) 333555
Fax: 226036
Telex: 22468 KETA
Main contact: Frederick L N Amiani (director)

Kenya National Trading Corporation
Address: Uchumi House, City Square, PO Box 30587, Nairobi
Telephone: (2) 29141
Telex: 22298
Main contacts: S Ogessa (chairman); E C Kotut (managing director)

Ministry of Commerce and Industry
Address: Haile Selassie Ave, PO Box 47024, Nairobi
Telephone: 340010
Main contact: Arthur Magugu (minister)

KUWAIT

Ministry of Commerce and Industry
Address: PO Box 2944, 13030 Safat, Kuwait City
Telephone: 2463600
Fax: 2424411
Telex: 22682
Main contact: Dr Abdullah Rashid Al-Hajiri

Ministry of Trade and Industry
Address: POB 2944, Safat, Kuwait City
Telephone: 246 3600
Fax: 242 4411
Telex: 22682
Main contact: Nasser Abdullah Arrodham (minister)

Laos

Ministry of Trade and Tourism
Address: rue Nongbone, Vientiane
Main contact: Vanthong Sengmuong (minister)

Société Lao Import-Export
Address: 43-47 Lanexang Road, Vientiane
Telephone: 2944
Fax: 5753
Telex: 4318
Main contact: Kanhkeo Saycocie (director)

LEBANON

Ministry of Economy, Trade, Industry and Oil
Address: Beirut
Main contact: Marwen Hamedeh (minister)

LESOTHO

Ministry of Trade and Industry
Address: PO Box 747, Maseru 100
Telephone: 322802
Fax: 310121
Telex: 4384
Main contact: Moletsane G Mokoroane (minister)

LIBERIA

Ministry of Commerce
Address: PO Box 9041, Monrovia
Telephone: 222040
Telex: 44331
Main contact: E Shaw (minister)
Publication: Journal of Commerce, Industry and Transportation

LIBYA

Secretariat of the General People's Committee for Economy and Trade
Address: Benghazi
Main contact: Farhat Sharnanah (secretary)

MACAU

Government Trade Department
Address: Luso International Bldg, Rua Dr Pedro José Lobo 1-3, Macau
Telephone: 378224
Telex: 88413 DPE OM
Fax: 590309

MADAGASCAR

Ministry of Commerce
Address: Antaninarenina, 101 Antananarivo
Telephone: (2) 27292
Telex: 22378
Main contact: Henri Rasamoelina (minister)

Société Nationale de Commerce
Address: BP 3187, 101 Antananarivo
Telex: 55623
Main contact: Andriamaniraka Ralison (director-general)
Notes: National import/export agency

MALAWI

Malawi Export Promotion Council
Address: Delamere House, Victoria Avenue, PO Box 1299, Blantyre
Telephone: 620499
Telex: 44589 EXPORT MI
Fax: 635429-33
Main contact: Mr J B L Malange (general manager)
Publications: Export Information Bulletin, Malawi Buyer's Guide (monthly)
Notes: Statutory body responsible to Ministry of Trade, Industry and Tourism. Promotes exports, gathers trade information and statistics, organises Malawi participation in international trade fairs, trains businessmen/women in export management

Ministry of Trade, Industry and Tourism
Address: PO Box 30366, Capital City, Lilongwe
Telephone: 732711
Fax: 732551
Telex: 44873
Main contact: Dalton S Katopola (minister)

MALAYSIA

Malaysian Export Trade Centre
Address: Ground Floor, Wisma PKNS, Jalan Raja Laut, 50350 Kuala Lumpur
Telephone: (03) 292 8122/8279/8351
Telex: 33721
Main contact: Tuan Syed Hamzah bin Syed Othman

Malaysian Industrial Development Authority
Address: 3rd-6th and 9th Floors, Wisma Damansara, Jalan Semantan, POB 10618, 50720 Kuala Lumpur
Telephone: (03) 255 3633
Fax: (03) 255 7970
Telex: MIDA MA 30752
Main contacts: Tan Sri Zianal Abidin Sulong (chairman); Dato' N Sadasivan (director-general)
Notes: Government's principal agency for the promotion and co-ordination of industrial development activities in Malaysia; eight regional offices and 14 overseas centres

Ministry of Trade and Industry
Address: Block 10, Government Offices Complex, Jalan Duta, 50622 Kuala Lumpur
Telephone: (03) 254 0033
Fax: (03) 2550827
Telex: 28017
Main contact: Datin Paduka Rafidah Aziz (minister)

MALDIVES

Ministry of Trade and Industries
Address: Ghaazee Bldg, Malé 20-05
Telephone: (32) 3668
Fax: 323756
Main contact: Ilyas Ibrahim (minister)

State Trading Organisation
Address: No 7 Haveeree Higun, Malé
Telephone: 325485
Fax: 325218
Telex: 66006
Main contacts: Ilyas Ibrahim (managing director); Moosa Ismail (director)
Publication: Trade Information News Sheet (monthly, Dhwehi and

English)
Notes: State-sponsored commercial and financial organisation. Handles majority of imports

MALI

Ministry of Finance and Trade
Address: BP 234, Bamako
Telephone: 225687
Telex: 2559
Main contact: Soumano Sacko (minister)

MARTINIQUE

Agence pour le Développement Economique de la Martinique
Address: 26 rue Lamartine, BP 803, 97244 Fort-de-France
Telephone: 734581
Fax: 724138
Telex: CHAMCO 912946 MR

MAURITANIA

Bureau d'Achats pour la République Islamique de Mauritanie
Address: BP 272, ave de Président J F Kennedy, Nouakchott
Telephone: 51057
Telex: 810
Main contact: D Diabira (director-general)
Notes: Import/export organisation

Ministry of Trade
Address: BP 183, Nouakchott
Telephone: 52138
Telex: 540
Main contact: Dia Abderrahman (minister)

Société Nationale d'Importation et d'Exportation
Address: BP 290, ave Bourguiba, Nouakchott
Telephone: 51472
Telex: 561
Main contacts: Dewahi Mohamed Saleck (president); Moussa Fall (director-general)

MAURITIUS

Mauritius Export Development and Investment Authority
Address: B.A.I. Bldg, 2nd floor, 25 Pope Hennessy St, PO Box 1184, Port Louis
Telephone: 2087750
Fax: 2085956
Telex: 4597
Main contact: Fakhra Currimjee (chairman)

Ministry of Industry
Address: New Government Centre, Port Louis
Telephone: 2011221
Fax: 2128201
Telex: 4249
Main contact: Beergoonath Ghurburrun (minister)

MEXICO

Asociación Nacional de Importadoren y Exportadores de la República Mexicana (ANIERM)
Address: Monterrey 130, Col-Roma-Cuauhtémoc, 06700 Mexico, DF
Telephone: (5) 5648618
Fax: (5) 5845317
Telex: 1772443
Main contact: Rodrigo Guerra

Secretariat of State for Trade and Industrial Promotion
Address: Alfonso Reyes 30, 10° Col. Condesa, 06170 Mexico, DF
Telephone: (5) 286 1757
Fax: (5) 2861543
Telex: 1775718
Main contact: Héctor Hernández Cervantes (minister)

MONGOLIA

Ministry of Foreign Trade
Address: 24 Nairamdalyn Gudamzh, Ulan Bator
Main contact: Jamsrangiyn Dulmaa (minister)
Publication: Foreign Trade of Mongolia (annual, English and Russian)

MOROCCO

Ministry of Trade, Industry and Tourism
Address: Ave Tadla Aviation, Mabella, Rabat
Telephone: (7) 751532
Fax: (7) 751739
Telex: 32025
Main contact: Abdullah al-Azmani(minister)

MOZAMBIQUE

IMBEC
Address: Rua da Mesquita 33, CP 4229, Maputo
Telephone: (1) 421455
Fax: (1) 423650
Telex: 6350
Notes: Government agency for import of consumer goods

Ministry of Foreign Trade
Address: Praça 25 de Junho, Maputo
Telephone: (1) 426091
Telex: 6372
Main contact: M Aranda da Silva (minister)

MYANMAR

Ministry of Trade
Address: 228/240 Strand Road, Yangon
Telephone: (1) 87034
Fax: (01) 89578
Telex: 21338
Main contact: U Khin Maung Gyi (minister)

NEPAL

Ministry of Commerce
Address: Kathmandu
Main contact: Sahana Pradhan (minister)

National Trading Co. Ltd
Address: POB 128, Teku, Kathmandu
Telephone: (1) 211962
Fax: (1) 225151
Telex: 2211
Main contacts: Sher B Pandey (chairman); G M Maskey (general manager)
Notes: Government-owned. Handles distribution and many imports. Branches in all major towns

Trade Promotion Centre
Address: POB 825, Lal Durbar, Durbar Marga, Kathmandu
Telephone: (1) 524771
Fax: (1) 521637
Telex: 2302
Main contact: S R Bhandary (chairman)
Notes: Government-owned

NEW CALEDONIA

Chambre de Commerce et d'Industrie
Address: BP M3, Nouméa
Telephone: 272551
Telex: 3045 NM
Fax: 278114
Main contacts: Arnold Daly (president); Georges Giovannelli (general manager)
Publications: Bulletin de liaison et d'information économique (quarterly); *Doc-Info* (bimonthly)

NEW ZEALAND

Ministry of Commerce
Address: Ministry of Commerce Bldg,33 Bowen Street, Wellington
Telephone: (4) 4720030
Fax: (4) 4734638
Telex: 31530
Publication: miscellaneous reports relating to New Zealand commerce and energy policy

New Zealand Bureau of Importers/Exporters
Address: Parnell House, 470 Parnell Road, Auckland
Telephone: (9) 771272
Telex: 2151

New Zealand Export/Import Corporation
Address: Ground Floor, Cornwall House, 23 Raroa Road, Lower Hutt PO Box 30-783, Lower Hutt
Telephone: (4) 667337
Fax: (4) 667227
Telex: NZ 31081
Main contacts: Mr Alastair M S Davis (general manager)
Notes: Undertakes export and import of goods and services. Performs trade promotion activities and offers advisory service

NICARAGUA

Ministry of Foreign Cooperation
Address: Apdo 4595, Managua, JR
Telephone: (02) 61796
Telex: 1367
Main contact: Dr Alejandro Martinez Cuenca (minister)
Notes: Foreign trade is a state monopoly in Nicaragua

NIGER

Ministry of Commerce, Industry and Transport
Address: BP 12130, Niamey
Telephone: 734382
Telex: 5467
Main contact: Amadou Nouhou (minister)

Société Nationale de Commerce et de Production du Niger
Address: BP 615, Niamey
Telephone: 732841
Fax: 735771
Telex: 5222
Main contact: Ali Alidou (managing director)
Notes: State import agency

NIGERIA

Ministry of Trade
Address: Abuja
Main contact: Senas John Ukpanah (minister)

Nigerian Export Promotion Council
Address: (Headquarters) 103 Lewis St, Lagos
Telephone: (9) 2341624
Fax: (9) 2341624
Telex: 91510
Main contact: Executive Director
Notes: Regional offices; Lagos, telephone (1) 803320-4; Kano, telephone (064) 624711; Port Harcourt, telephone (084) 330620

Nigerian Institute of International Trade (NIIT)
Address: PO Box 2931, Ikeja, Lagos

NORTH KOREA

Korean Committee for Promotion of International Trade
Address: Central District, Pyongyang
Main contact: Pak Se Chan (secretary-general)

Ministry of Foreign Trade
Address: Pyongyang
Main contact: Choe Jong Gun (minister)

OMAN

Ministry of Commerce and Industry
Address: POB 550, Muscat
Telephone: 799500
Fax: 794238
Telex: 3665
Main contact: Salim bin Abdullah al-Ghazali (minister)

PAKISTAN

Export Promotion Bureau
Address: Finance and Trade Centre, Shahrahe-Faisal, Karachi
Telephone: (21) 511494
Fax: (21) 215380
Telex: 23877
Main contact: Abdul Aziz Yaqoob (chairman)

Ministry of Commerce
Address: Block A, Pakistan Secretariat, Islamabad
Telephone: (51) 825078

Fax: (51) 825241
Telex: 5859
Main contact: Mohammed Khan (minister)

Trading Corporation of Pakistan
Address: Press Trust House, 11 Chundrigar Road, Karachi
Telephone: (21) 511016
Fax: (21) 515389
Telex: 2784
Main contact: Dr Mohammed Malik (chairman)

PANAMA

Ministry of Commerce and Industry
Address: Apdo 9658, Panama 4
Telephone: 274177
Fax: 275604
Telex: 2256
Main contact: Roberto Alfaro (minister)

PAPUA NEW GUINEA

Department of Trade and Industry
Address: Central Government Offices, Kumul Avenue, Wards Strip, Waigani
Telephone: 271094
Fax: 271750
Telex: 23310
Main contact: David Mai (minister)

Investment Promotion Authority
Address: POB 5053, Boroko
Telephone: 217311
Fax: 212819
Main contacts: Nigel Agonia (managing director)
Notes: Statutory body. Promotes, supervises and regulates foreign investment

PARAGUAY

Ministry of Industry and Commerce
Address: Av Espana 323, Asunción
Telephone: (21) 204693
Fax: (21) 210570
Telex: 259
Main contact: Dr Ubaldo Scavone (minister)

PERU

Ministry of Industry, Commerce, Tourism and Integration
Address: Calle 1 Oeste, Corpac, San Isidro, Lima 27
Telephone: (014) 407120
Telex: 20194
Main contact: Alfonso Bustamente Y Bustament (minister)

PHILIPPINES

Chamber of International Trade
Address: Room 904, L&S Bldg, 1414 Roxas Blvd, Ermita, Metro Manila
Main contact: Ramon P Tambunting (president)

Department of Trade and Industry
Address: Trade and Industry Bldg, 361 Gil J Puyat Ave. PO Box 2303, Makati, Metro Manila
Telephone: (2) 818 5701
Fax: (2) 856487
Telex: 14830
Main contact: Rizalino Navarro (minister)
Publications: numerous including *Direction of Trade & Foreign Trade Profile; Key Industrial Indicators*

Philippines International Trading Corporation
Address: Philippines International Centre, Tordesillas St, Salcedo Village, Makati, Metro Manila 3116
Telephone: (2) 8189801
Telex: 63745
Main contact: Raul A Boncan (president)

QATAR

Ministry of Finance, Economy and Trade
Address: POB 83, Doha
Telephone: 461444
Fax: 413617
Telex: 4233

RWANDA

Ministry of Commerce and Industry
Address: BP 476, Kigali
Telephone: 73875
Publications: Situation Economique du Rwanda (two a year)

SAO TOMÉ AND PRINCIPE

Ministry of Trade
Address: Sao Tomé
Main contact: Carlos B Gomez (minister)

SAUDI ARABIA

Ministry of Commerce
Address: POB 1774, Airport Rd, Riyadh 11162
Telephone: (1) 401 2222
Fax: 403 8421
Telex: 401057
Main contact: Dr Sulaiman Abd al-Aziz as-Sulaim (minister)

SENEGAL

Ministry of Trade
Address: BP 439, Dakar
Telephone: 221444
Telex: 482
Main contact: Abdourahmane Toure (minister)

SEYCHELLES

Department of Planning and External Relations
Address: National House, PO Box 656 Mont Fleuri
Telephone: 24688
Fax: 24845
Telex: 2260
Main contact: Danielle de St. Jorre

Seychelles Marketing Board
Address: Oceangate House, PO Box 516, Victoria
Telephone: 24444
Telex: 2368
Main contact: France Albert René

SIERRA LEONE

Ministry of Trade and Industry
Address: Ministerial Bldg, George Street, Freetown
Telephone: 225211
Telex: 3218
Main contact: Franklyn Kargbo (minister)

SINGAPORE

Economic Development Board
Address: #24-00 Raffles City Tower, 250 North Bridge Rd, Singapore 0617
Telephone: 336 2288
Fax: 3396077
Telex: 26233
Main contact: Philip Yeo (chairman)
Notes: Statutory board implementing and planning government's industrialisation programme

Ministry of Trade and Industry
Address: Treasury Building, 8 Shenton Way, Singapore 0106
Telephone: 225 9911
Fax: 3209260
Telex: 24702
Main contact: Suppiah Dhanabalan (minister)

Trade Development Board
Address: 1 Maritime Sq, Telok Blangah Rd, 10-40 World Trade Centre, Singapore 0409
Telephone: 271 9388
Fax: 274 0770

Telex: 28617
Main contacts: Alan Yeo (chairman); Yeo Seng Teck (chief executive officer)

World-Wide Import-Export Promotion Centre
Address: PO Box 503, Marine Parade Post Office, Singapore 9144
Telephone: 443 5246
Fax: 241 3982
Telex: 55708 IPCCP RS
Publications: Business Opportunities (monthly); *International Trade Promotion Guide*; trade directories

SOLOMON ISLANDS

Ministry of Commerce
Address: POB G26, Honiara
Telephone: 21140
Telex: 66311
Main contact: Alfred Maetia (minister)

SOMALIA

Ministry of Commerce
Address: Mogadishu
Telephone: (1) 33089
Main contact: M Said Mahmud (minister)

National Agency for Foreign Trade
Address: PO Box 602, Mogadishu
Main contact: Jama aw Muse (director-general)

SOUTH AFRICA

South African Foreign Trade Organisation
Address: PO Box 782706, Sandton 2146
Address: 8833737
Fax: 8836569
Telex: 424111
Main contact: RA Norton

Ministry of Trade and Industry and Tourism
Address: PB X274, Pretoria 0001
Telephone: 4612480
Main contacts: Derek L Keys (minister)

SOUTH KOREA

Federation of Korean Industries
Address: 2nd Floor, FKI Bldg, 28-1 Yoido-dong, Yongdeungpo-gu, Seoul
Telephone: (2) 780 0821/0830
Fax: (2) 784 1640
Telex: FEKOIS K25544
Main contact: Yoo Chang-Soon (chairman)
Publication: Korean Business Review (quarterly)
Notes: Conducts research on domestic and overseas economic trends; sponsors conferences

Korean Trade Promotion Corporation
Address: 159 Samsung-dong, Kangham-ku, CPOB 123, Seoul
Telephone: (2) 551 4181
Fax: (2) 551 4477
Telex: 23659
Main contact: Sun-Ki lee
Notes: Promotes Korea's exports, attends to the needs of foreign businessmen, participates in international trade fairs, compiles market information; 75 overseas branches

Korean Traders Association
Address: World Trade Center, Korea Bldg, 10-1 Hoehyon-dong 2-ga, Chung-gu, Seoul
Telex: 24265
Main contacts: Duck-woo Nam (chairman); Sun-ki Lee (vice-chairman)
Notes: Provides foreign businessmen with information, contacts and advice

Ministry of Trade and Industry
Address: 1 Jungang-dong, Gwachon City, Kyonggi Province
Telephone: (02) 503 9405

Fax: (02) 503 9496
Telex: 24478
Main contact: Lee Bong-Suh

Small and Medium Industry Promotion Corporation
Address: 27-2 Youido-dong, Yongdungpo-gu, Seoul
Telephone: (2) 783 9611/9618
Telex: 25542
Main contact: Chong-yul Yoo (president)

SRI LANKA

All Ceylon Trade Chamber
Address: 212/45, 1/3 Bodhiraja Mawatha, Colombo 11
Telephone: (1) 432428
Main contact: Y P Muthukumarana (general secretary)

Greater Colombo Economic Commission
Address: POB 1768, 14 Sir Baron Jayatilleke Mawatha, Colombo 1
Telephone: (1) 434403-5, 435407-9, 435027, 547531
Fax: (1) 547995
Telex: 21332 ECONCOM CE, 21428 DG GCEC CE
Main contact: Nissanka Wijewardane (director-general)
Notes: Promotes investment and administers Export Processing Zones, at Katunayake and Biyagama

Industrial Development Board of Ceylon
Address: 615 Galle Road, Katubedda, Moratuwa
Telephone: 605326
Fax: 607002
Telex: 22625
Main contacts: W Anton Fernando (chairman); C Shanmugalingam (general manager)

Ministry of Trade and Shipping
Address: 21 Rakshana Mandlraya, Vauxhall Street, Colombo 2
Telephone: (1) 35601
Telex: 21245
Main contact: A R Mansoor (minister)
For information, contact Trade and Shipping Information Service, POB 1525, Colombo 2; telephone: (1) 35277, main contact: S De Silva (director)
Publication: Business Lanka (quarterly)
Notes: Collects and disseminates commercial information and provides advice to exporters

Sri Lanka Export Development Board
Address: 310 Galle Road, Colombo 3
Telephone: (1) 573044
Telex: 21457
Main contact: J A D de Lanerolle (chairman)

Sri Lanka Importers, Exporters and Manufacturers Association
Address: POB 1050, 28 Rajamalwatle, Colombo 15
Telephone: (1) 523854
Fax: (1) 696321
Telex: 21494
Main contacts: David J O Perera (president); William J T Perera (honorary general secretary)

SUDAN

Ministry of Trade
Address: Khartoum
Telephone: (11) 730030
Telex: 22329
Main contact: Dr Ibrahim Obaidullah (minister)

State Trading Corporation
Address: PO Box 211, Khartoum
Telephone: (11) 78555
Telex: 22355
Main contact: E Tom (chairman)

SURINAME

Ministry of Economic Affairs
Address: Kleine Waterstraat 4, Paramaribo
Telephone: 75080
Telex: 119

Centre for Industrial Development and Export Promotion
Address: Rust en Vredestraat 79-81, PO Box 1275, Proniotion, Paramimbo
Telephone: 74830
Telex: 285
Main contact: R A Leter (manager)

SWAZILAND

Ministry of Commerce and Industry
Address: PO Box 451, Mbabane
Telephone: 43201
Fax: 43833
Telex: 2232
Main contact: Barnabus Mhlongo (minister)

Swaziland Commercial Board
Address: PO Box 509, Mbabane
Telephone: 42930
Main contact: J M Fakudze (managing director)

SYRIA

Ministry of Economy and Foreign Trade
Address: Damascus
Telephone: (11) 113513
Telex: 411928
Main contact: Muhammad al-Imadi (minister)

TAIWAN

Board of Foreign Trade
Address: Ministry of Economic Affairs, 15 Foochow St, Taipei
Telephone: (2) 3517271/3510286
Telex: 19884
Main contact: Vincent C Siew (director-general)

China External Trade Development Council (CETDC)
Address: 333 Keelung Rd, 4th-8th floors, Sec 1, Taipei 10548
Telephone: (2) 757 6297
Fax: (2) 757 6653
Telex: 21676 CETRA
Main contact: Agustin Ting-Tsu Liu (secretary general)
Publications: Taiwan Products (monthly); *Exports of the Republic of China; Imports of the Republic of China* (both annual)
Notes: Main trade promotion organisation in Taiwan. Founded in 1970 by business associations and supported by the government

Chinese National Federation of Industries
Address: 12th Floor, 390 Fu Hsing South Rd, Sec 1, Taipei
Telephone: (2) 703 3500
Fax: (2) 703 3982
Telex: 14565
Main contacts: Koo Chen-fu (chairman); Ho Chun-yih (secretary general)
Notes: Forum for discussion of country's industrial sectors. Aims to promote economic development

Far East Trade Service Inc. (FETS)
Address: 4-8F, CETRA Tower, 333 Keelung Rd., Sec. 1, Taipei 10548, Taiwan
Telephone: (02) 738 2345
Fax: (02) 757 6653
Telex: 21676 CETRA
Notes: Founded in 1971 to assist the China External Trade Development Council (qv) in promoting Taiwanese products and provide trade services abroad

Industrial Development and Investment Centre
Address: 4 Chung Hsiao West Road, 19th floor, Sec 1, Taipei
Telephone: (02) 389 2111
Fax: (02) 392 6835
Telex: 10634 INVEST
Main contact: John Chang-I Ni (director)
Notes: Assists investment and planning. Deals with foreign investment in the three export processing zones of Kaohsiung, Nantze and Taichung

Taipei World Trade Center
Address: Taipei World Trade Center, 5 Hsinyi Road, Sec. 5, Taipei
Telephone: (02) 725 1111

Publications: Trade Opportunities in Taiwan (weekly); numerous other trade publications
Notes: Founded in 1980 by the CETDC (qv) and various business enterprises to offer trade services and information to international traders

TANZANIA

Board of External Trade
Address: PO Box 5402, Dar es Salaam
Telephone: (51) 33524
Fax: 36303
Telex: 41408
Main contact: Mbaruk K Mwandoro (director-general)
Notes: Responsible for trade promotion

Ministry of Industries and Trade
Address: PO Box 9503, Dar es Salaam
Telephone: (51) 27251
Telex: 41689 INDIS TZ
Main contact: Cleopa David Msuya (minister)
Publications: Foreign Trade News Bulletin (two a year)

Zanzibar State Trading Corporation
Address: PO Box 26, Zanzibar
Telephone: 30271
Fax: 31550
Telex: 57208
Main contact: Abdulrahman Rashid (general manager)

THAILAND

Board of Trade of Thailand
Address: 150 Rajbopit Road, Bangkok 10200
Telephone: (2) 221 0555/1827/9350, (2) 2229031, (2) 2232069
Fax: (2) 225 3995
Telex: 84309 BOT TH
Main contact: Dr Yukta na Thalang (chairman); Mr Prayoon Talerngsri (executive director)
Publications: Board of Trade of Thailand's Trade Directory 1990-1991; list of Thai importers/exporters classified by product and by country.

Ministry of Commerce
Address: Sanamchai Road, Bangkok 10200
Telephone: (2) 220 0855
Fax: (2) 226 3318
Telex: 82389
Main contact: Uthai Phimchaichon (minister)

TOGO

Ministry of Trade
Address: rue du Commerce, Lomé
Telephone: 210909
Main contact: Poulpou Mensah David Defanti (minister)

Société Nationale de Commerce
Address: BP 3009, Lomé
Telephone: 213118
Telex: 5281
Main contact: Jean Ladoux (director-general)
Notes: State import organisation

TONGA

Office of the Ministry of Labour, Commerce and Industries
Address: PO Box 110, Nuku'alofa
Telephone: 23688
Fax: 23887
Telex: 66265
Main contact: Kinikininilau Tutoatasi Fakafanua (Secretary for Labour, Commerce & Industries)

TRINIDAD AND TOBAGO

Trinidad and Tobago Industrial Development Corporation
Address: 10-12 Independence Square, Port of Spain
Telephone: 6237291
Fax: 6259124
Telex: 22255

Main contacts: Bertrand Doyle (chairman); Jack Balkissoon (general manager)
Notes: Promotes the development of new industries

Trinidad and Tobago Export Dvelopment Corporation
Address: Export House 10-14, Philipps St, PO Box 582, Port of Spain
Telephone: 6236022
Fax: 6270050
Telex: 22646
Main contact: Oscar Alonso

TUNISIA

Ministry of National Economy
Address: 7 rue du Royaume d'Arabie, Saoudile, 1035 Tunis
Telephone: 285134
Telex: 14341
Main contact: Sadok Chaabane (minister)

Centre de Promotion des Exportations
Address: 28 rue Ghandi, 1001 Tunis
Telephone: 350344
Fax: 353683
Telex: 14716
Main contact: Kamel Belkahia

UGANDA

Ministry of Commerce, Industry and Co-operatives
Address: PO Box 7103, Kampala
Main contact: Richard Kaijuka (minister)

Uganda Advisory Board of Trade
Address: PO Box 6877, Kampala
Telephone: (41) 33311
Telex: 61085
Main contact: J G Sentogo-Dungu (secretary)
Notes: Import and distribution agency

Uganda Export Promotion Council
Address: PO Box 5045, Kampala
Telephone: 259779
Telex: 61391
Main contact: Henry Njakoojo

UNITED ARAB EMIRATES

Dubai Trade Centre Management
Address: POB 9292, Dubai International Trade Centre, Dubai
Telephone: (4) 472200
Telex: 47474

Ministry of Economy and Commerce
Address: POB 901, Abu Dhabi
Telephone: (2) 215455
Fax: (2) 215339
Telex: 22897
Main contact: Said Ghobash (minister)

UNITED STATES OF AMERICA

American Association of Exporters and Importers
Address: 11 West 42nd Street, New York, NY 10036
Telephone: (212) 944 2230
Fax: (212) 382 2606
Main contact: Eugene J Milosh (president)
Publication: International Trade Alert (weekly) plus numerous reports
Notes: Represents interests of exporters and importers to government, customs and other trade regulation bodies

American Economic Development Council
Address: 4849 North Scott Street, Suite 22, Schiller Park, IL 60176
Telephone: (312) 671 5646
Main contact: Edward J Collins Jnr (president)
Publications: AEDC Newsletter (monthly); *Legislative Affairs Report* (monthly); *Economic Development Review Journal* (two a year)

Federal Trade Commission
Address: Pennsylvania Avenue and 6th Street, NW, Washington, DC 20580

Telephone: (202) 326 2000
Main contact: Janet D Steiger
Notes: Investigates monopolies, offers legal advice, seeks to guarantee fair trade practices

US Council for International Business
Address: 1212 Avenue of the Americas, New York, NY 10036
Telephone: (212) 354 4480
Main contacts: Abraham Katz (president); J G Clarke (chairman)
Publications: monthly newsletter; *ICC Business World* (quarterly)
Notes: Promotes open system of international trade, represents business interests in the major economic institutions and to government

US Department of Commerce
Address: 14th Street, between Constitution Avenue and E Street, NW, Washington, DC 20230
Telephone: (202) 377 2000
Fax: (202) 377 5270
Publication: *Commerce Business Daily*; various directories
Notes: Promotes US business, conducts research, provides export assistance. Houses **International Trade Administration** which aims to promote international trade, and provides information and advice, publishes *Business America Magazine* (fortnightly)

VANUATU

Ministry of Economic Affairs
Address: PMB 051, Port Vila
Telephone: 22913
Fax: 23142
Telex: 1040
Main contact: Serge Vohor (minister)

VENEZUELA

Instituto de Comercio Exterior (ICE)
Address: Centro Comercial Los Cedros, Avda Libertador, Apdo 51852, Caracas 1050
Telephone: (2) 729960
Fax: (2) 716061
Telex: 21838
Main contact: Miguel Rodriguez Mendoza
Notes: Exports institution responsible to the Ministry of Foreign Affairs

VIETNAM

Ministry of Commerce
Address: 31 Trang Tien, Hanoi
Telephone: 254915
Telex: 254075
Main contact: Le Van Triet (minister)
Notes: Directs and controls all foreign trade activities

VIRGIN ISLANDS (BRITISH)

Chief Minister's Office
Address: Trade and Investment Promotion Dept., Chief Minister's Office, Road Town, Tortola
Telephone: 494 5007/3701 ext. 241
Fax: 494 4435
Telex: 7959 CENAB VB
Notes: statistical information obtained from Development Planning Unit (address as above)

YEMEN

Ministry of Trade and Supply
Address: San'a
Main contact: Abd Ar-Rahman Ba Fadhel (minister)

ZAIRE

Department of Industry
Address: Immeuble ONATRA, BP 8500, Kinshasa-Combe
Telephone: 22945
Telex: 21232
Main contacts: Fernand Tala Ngai (state commissioner)

ZAMBIA

Ministry of Commerce and Industry
Address: PO Box 31968, Lusaka
Telephone: (1) 213767
Telex: 45630
Main contact: Alfeyo Hambayi (minister)

National Import and Export Corporation
Address: PO Box 30283, Lusaka
Telephone: 2288018
Fax: 252771
Telex: 44490
Main contacts: E Kaunga (chairman); P Chisang (managing director)

ZIMBABWE

Ministry of Industry and Commerce
Address: Private Bag 7708, Causeway, Harare
Telephone: (4) 702731
Telex: 26368 TRADE ZW, 24472 TRADE ZW
Main contact: Chris Ushewokunze (minister); Mr S K Hwindingwi (deputy secretary export promotions)
Publications: *Zimbabwe Export Directory*; *Digest of Statistics* (quarterly) and *Statistical Yearbook* (every two years)

Section One
Marketing Geography

North America

Canada

Population ('000)   27,440 (1992)
Urban Population (%)   76.5 (1986)
Land Area (km²)   9,922,385
Language/s   English (60.6%), French (24.3%),
                    American Indian (0.4%), Other European
                                             (14.7%)
Religion/s   Mainly Christian
Currency   Canadian dollar (C$ = 100 cents)
Head of State   HM Queen Elizabeth II
Head of Government   Jean Chrétien
Ruling Party   Liberal Party

Main urban areas	Population
Toronto	3,893,046
Montréal	3,127,242
Vancouver	1,602,502
Ottawa (capital)	920,857
Edmonton	839,924
Calgary	754,033
Winnipeg	652,354
Quebec	645,550
Hamilton	599,760

(1990)

The Dominion of Canada comprises a federation of 12 provinces and territories, each of which exercises considerable political autonomy over its own affairs. The Northwest Territories are to be divided so as to create an Indian territory, to be known as Nunavut. Québec, which is French-speaking, voted in 1992 against a move for secession from the Federation. The House of Commons in Ottawa has 295 members and the Senate (Upper House) 107. A Governor-General represents the monarch.

The elections of October 1993 brought a spectacular defeat for the Progressive Conservative Party, which had ruled the country since 1984, but which retained only two seats in the Commons after a disastrous campaign. The Liberal Party, which had held only 82 seats previously, increased its representation to 178 and went on to form the new government. Meanwhile the secessionist Bloc Québecois became the official opposition with 54 seats, and the Reform Party won 52. The left-wing New Democratic Party retained only eight of its 44 seats. There were two independents.

High levels of spending in the 1980s, coinciding with a contraction in mineral and raw material prices, left Canada with a serious overspending problem which the Government has sought to meet with tight fiscal policies and high taxes. The Government is hoping to improve its trade relationship with the United States, in the light of the proposed North American Free Trade Agreement, but in the autumn of 1993 the future of the plan was still uncertain. Social and political tensions have been raised by the high level of unemployment during the early 1990s.

United States of America

Population ('000)   255,082 (1991)
Urban Population (%)   73.7 (1990)
Land Area (km²)   9,363,130
Language/s   English
Religion/s   Mainly Christian
Currency   US dollar (US$ = 100 cents)
Head of State   President Bill Clinton (January 1993)
Head of Government   President Bill Clinton
Ruling Party   Democratic Party

Main urban areas	Population
New York	7,323,000
Los Angeles	3,485,000
Chicago	2,784,000
Houston	1,631,000
Philadelphia	1,586,000
San Diego	1,111,000
Detroit	1,028,000
Dallas	1,007,000
Phoenix	983,000
San Antonio	936,000
San Jose	782,000
Baltimore	736,000
Indianapolis	731,000
San Francisco	724,000
Jacksonville	672,971
Columbus	632,910
Milwaukee	628,088
Memphis	610,337
Washington, DC (capital)	606,900
Boston	574,283

(1990 census)

The United States has an executive President, elected for a four-year term of office by universal suffrage, who then selects and directs his own Cabinet ("Administration"). The US Congress comprises a 435-member House of Representatives, elected every two years, and a 100-member Senate, which serves for six years but a third of which is re-elected every two years. The country has a strong federal structure, and devolves its legal and fiscal system to a considerable extent.

At the presidential elections held in November 1992, the Democrat candidate Bill Clinton defeated the incumbent George Bush, receiving 43% of the popular vote and 370 electoral college votes. In the legislative elections held at the same time the Democrats maintained control of both chambers of Congress: they won 259 seats in the House of Representatives (Republicans 175, Independents 1), and 57 in the Senate (compared to 43 for the Republicans).

With the largest economy in the world, the USA has been able to exert considerable influence in both political and strategic terms over the last 50 years. Its economy is highly diversified, although somewhat prone to government interference and indeed to protectionism. In the 1990s, public attention is moving away from European trade partnerships and toward new arrangements with Canada and Latin America.

South America

Argentina

Population ('000)   33,101 (1992)
Urban Population (%)   86.1 (1991)
Land Area (km²)   2,777,815
Language/s   Spanish
Religion/s   Roman Catholic (90%)
Currency   Peso argentino (P = 100 centavos =
                                        10,000 australes)
Head of State   President Carlos Menem
Head of Government   President Carlos Menem
Ruling Party   Justicialist Party

Main urban areas	Population
Buenos Aires (capital)	11,382,002
Córdoba	1,166,932
Rosario de Santa Fé	1,096,254
Mendoza	728,966
La Plata	644,155
San Miguel	626,143
Mar del Plata	523,178

(1990 estimates, including suburbs)

Argentina has an executive President who is elected every six years, and who is answerable to a 254-seat Chamber of Deputies and a 46-seat Senate. The country has undergone a radical change of direction since the early 1980s, when the military junta which had ruled for most of the 1970s was deposed. Argentina comprises a Federal District, 23 provinces and the National Territory of Tierra del Fuego, all of which enjoy varying degrees of autonomy.

Elections took place in May 1989 for 127 of the 254 seats in the Chamber of Deputies, in which the Justicialist Party (the Peronist party led by the then opposition leader Carlos Menem) obtained 44.6% of the votes, compared with 28.9% for the Radical Civic Union Party (UCR); this left the Justicialists with enough deputies to form only a minority government, however. Presidential elections on the same day produced a slim majority (51.7%) in favour of Menem, who was thus appointed.

Argentina's economic recovery from the sharp slump of the 1980s has been particularly noticeable in recent years, as the corruption and exploitation which were once endemic have been gradually eradicated. The country's political rehabilitation has helped to cement its future resources among its foreign investors, and it appears set for firm growth. A major programme of privatisations was announced in 1993. But inflation and the attendant currency risks are still a serious problem.

Bolivia

Population ('000)	7,524 (1992)
Urban Population (%)	50.9 (1990)
Land Area (km²)	1,098,575
Language/s	Spanish (official, although a majority speak Indian languages: Quechua or Aymara)
Religion/s	Roman Catholic (65%)
Currency	Boliviano (= 100 centavos)
Head of State	President Gonzalo Sánchez de Lozada
Head of Government	President Gonzalo Sánchez de Lozada
Ruling Party	Acuerdo Patriótica, a broad coalition of the Movimiento de la Izquierda Revolucionaria and the right-wing Acción Democrática Nacionalista.

Main urban areas	Population
La Paz (administrative capital)	1,049,800
Santa Cruz	615,122
Cochabamba	377,259
Oruro	200,000
Sucre (capital)	95,635

(1988)

Bolivia has an executive President who is elected every four years by universal suffrage, together with the 130-member Chamber of Deputies and the 27-member Senate. Each of the country's nine departments has its own administration, governed by a prefect who is in turn appointed by the President. Bolivia's political past has been exceptionally turbulent, with over 180 coups d'état in the years between independence in 1825 and 1980; in 1993 major constitutional reforms were being discussed.

Congressional elections were held in June 1993, when the ruling MNR obtained 52 seats in the Lower House and 17 in the Senate, compared with 35 seats and 8 seats for its coalition partner, the AP. The UCS obtained 20 Lower and one Upper house seat, and the MBL won 7 Lower but no Upper house seats.

Bolivia's economy remains stricken by crisis and uncertainty, despite the potential wealth in its hills. This is partly because of political mismanagement over the last four decades, but also partly due to the failure of farmers and others to co-operate effectively with one another. With no tourism industry of any size, and with a poor external image, it has had difficulty in obtaining international aid.

Brazil

Population ('000)	156,275 (1992)
Urban Population (%)	75.5 (1991)
Land Area (km²)	8,511,965
Language/s	Portuguese
Religion/s	Mainly Roman Catholic (90%)
Currency	Cruzeiro (CR $=100 centavos)
Head of State	President Itamar Franco (December 1992)
Head of Government	President Itamar Franco
Ruling Party	National Reconstruction Party leads a coalition

Main urban areas	Population
Sao Paulo	9,700,111
Rio de Janeiro	5,487,346
Belo Horizonte	2,103,330
Salvador	2,075,392
Brasilia (capital)	1,841,028
Fortaleza	1,708,741
Recife	1,335,684
Porto Alegre	1,254,692
Curitiba	1,248,395
Nova Iguaçu	1,246,775
Belém	1,235,625
Goiâna	998,471
Manaus	996,716
Campinas	835,070
Sao Luis	781,374
Sao Gonçalo	720,704
Maceió	699,760
Guarulhos	679,400
Santo André	610,430
Natal	606,276

(1991 estimates, including suburbs)

Brazil has an executive President who is elected by popular mandate for a term of five years, and who is answerable to a bicameral National Congress. Whereas the Senate's 72 members are elected for eight years, with one-third or two-thirds coming up for re-election every four years, the Chamber of Deputies is elected by universal suffrage every four years; its size may vary, but is usually around 490. In December 1992 the incumbent President Collor de Mello resigned after being impeached on charges of corruption and drugs activity. Work began in October 1993 on a major review of the constitution, intended to increase the country's appeal to foreign investors.

Congressional elections were held in October and November 1990, when the Collor parties obtained 257 of the 498 contested seats: the National Reconstruction Party won 41, the Liberal Front Party 92, the Social democrats 40, the Labour Party 33, the Liberal Party 15, and the Christian Democrats 21. However, the opposition Brazilian Democratic Movement won 109 seats, and there were more than a dozen other parties elected.

Brazil's economy remained in deep crisis throughout 1993, with international confidence waning as the inflationary spiral started to worsen again after the respite of the early 1990s. Meanwhile, the country adopted an openly defiant stance toward its external creditors, raising fears in many quarters. In June 1993, as inflation reached 29% per month, the currency was downgraded by a factor of 1,000, and an ambitious privatisation programme was set in train.

Chile

Population ('000)	13,599 (1992)
Urban Population (%)	84.9 (1991)
Land Area (km²)	751,625
Language/s	Spanish
Religion/s	Mainly Roman Catholic (85%)
Currency	Chilean peso (P = 100 centavos)
Head of State	President Patricio Aylwin Azócar
Head of Government	President Patricio Aylwin Azócar
Ruling Party	Christian Democratic Party

Main urban areas	Population
Santiago (capital)	4,545,784

(1992)

Chile, a former Spanish colony, was a parliamentary democracy before it was seized in 1973, in a coup which established Gen. Augusto Pinochet as President, ruling largely by decree. In 1989, however, constitutional reforms led to elections in which an executive President would be elected for a four-year term, and Pinochet was soon voted out of office. President Aylwin has made sincere attempts to distance himself from the former military administration, but he will not be standing for re-election in December 1993. There is a 47-member Senate and a 120-member Chamber of Deputies, elected for four years.

The congressional elections of December 1989 gave the right-wing alliance around the Christian Democrats 22 of the 38 elected seats in the Senate, and a working majority among the 120 in the Chamber of Deputies. At the same time Aylwin scored a clear win over the non-party Pinochet supporter, Hernán Büchi, in the presidential elections. In Aylwin's absence, the Christian Democrat candidate Eduardo Frei Ruiz Tagle was regarded as almost certain to become President after the elections of December 1993.

Economic decline in the1980s, under the last years of the Pinochet regime, has been comprehensively reversed by the new administration, and yet the need for tough restrictions on spending remain. Fortunately Aylwin has the continuing support of much of the population for his painful reform programmes. However, much may ultimately depend on the resolution of Chile's serious agricultural disputes with the United States.

Colombia

Population ('000)	34,198 (1992)
Urban Population (%)	68.0 (1988)
Land Area (km²)	1,138,915
Language/s	Spanish
Religion/s	Roman Catholic (95%)
Currency	Colombian peso ($ = 100 centavos)
Head of State	President César Gaviria Trujillo
Head of Government	President César Gaviria Trujillo
Ruling Party	Liberal Party

Main urban areas	Population
Bogotá (capital)	4,150,000
Medellín	1,660,000

(1992 estimates)

Colombia has an executive President who answers to a 102-member Senate and a House of Representatives with 161 elected members. The Constitution was under review in 1993, but the process was briefly interrupted in 1992 as the President briefly declared a state of emergency over allegations that government officials had been implicated in the violent escape of Pablo Escobar Gaviria, the leader of the country's largest drugs cartel. In May 1993 Gaviria agreed terms for his re-arrest.

The municipal elections of March 1992 produced a notable setback for the ruling Liberal Party, and showed clear support for opponents of the Government's soft line on drug traffickers. Some 70% of the electorate in Bogotá abstained.

Colombia's traditional dependence on its coffee crop, its main export earner, has been shifting in recent years toward a more diversified agricultural structure: the agricultural system is, however, badly in need of reform. Colombia has vast and still under-exploited reserves of minerals.

Ecuador

Population ('000)	11,118 (1992)
Urban Population (%)	55.4 (1990)
Land Area (km²)	263,950
Language/s	Spanish (also Quechua Indian)
Religion/s	Roman Catholic (80%)
Currency	Sucre (S = 100 centavos)
Head of State	President Sixto Durán Ballén (August 1992)
Head of Government	President Sixto Durán Ballén
Ruling Party	Social Christian Party (PSC) leads a multi-party coalition of the right.

Main urban areas	Population
Guayaquil	1,508,444
Quito (capital)	1,100,847

(1990 census)

Ecuador has an executive President who is elected by universal suffrage for a single, unrenewable four-year term. He appoints his own Cabinet and reports to a 77-member Congress, 12 of whose members are elected by national ballot for a four-year term while the remainder are appointed by regional assemblies for a two-year term. The 20 provinces enjoy a substantial degree of political autonomy.

Elections were held in May 1992 to the 77-seat Congress, in which the PSC secured 21 seats, the Ecuadorian Roldoist Party 13, Republican Unity Party 12 and the Communist Party six seats. The ruling Democratic Left Party won a mere seven seats in the new body and was thus removed from power. There were five independents.

The oil price falls of the 1980s plunged Ecuador's economy into a crisis from which it has yet to emerge to any satisfactory extent. The Government was too slow in reacting to the loss of its incomes with a cutback in spending, and a massive external debt developed; in the 1990s, the unemployment rate alone confirms the need for caution about growth prospects in the short and indeed medium term. The Government has tried to counter with a Foreign Investment Directive (1993) which waives many former requirements of foreign investment.

French Guiana

Population ('000)	110 (1992)
Land Area (km²)	91,000
Language/s	French
Religion/s	Mainly Roman Catholic (75%)
Currency	French franc (FF = 100 centimes)
Head of State	President François Mitterrand (France)
Head of Government	Elie Castor
Ruling Party	Parti Socialiste Guyanais

Main urban areas	Population
Cayenne (capital)	41,667

(1990)

French Guiana is an external department of France and is therefore governed to a considerable degree from Paris. The country sends deputies to the French Assemblée Nationale, and is represented at the European Community. Since being accorded regional status in 1974, however, it elects its own 31-member Regional Council for a term of six years, with responsibility for economic and social planning. Other executive power rests in a 16-member General Council.

The last full elections were to the French Assemblée Nationale in 1988, in which the Socialists returned one delegate and the Rassemblement pour la République returned one "dissident" member.

French Guiana's economy remains one of the most neglected in Latin America; its dependence on Paris has not always proved to its advantage, and it has proved difficult to attract foreign investors. At present, therefore, France is likely to continue to be its main economic mainstay.

Guyana

Population ('000)	1,072 (1992)
Urban Population (%)	34.6 (1990)
Land Area (km^2)	214,970
Language/s	English
Religion/s	Christian (50%), Hindu (33%), Muslim (10%)
Currency	Guyana dollar (G$ = 100 cents)
Head of State	Cheddi Jagan (October 1992)
Head of Government	Sam Hinds
Ruling Party	The People's Progressive Party

Main urban areas	Population
Georgetown (capital)	200,000

(1992 estimate)

Guyana, an independent member of the Commonwealth, has a semi-executive President who in fact exercises considerable powers. The country was for many years so firmly identified with the policies of the ruling PNC that it amounted to a single-party state. Rising tensions surrounding the former President, Desmond Hoyte, prompted him in December 1991 to declare a state of emergency, in an attempt to quieten his opponents.

The last full election was held in October 1992, when Desmond Hoyte's People's National Congress lost its strong parliamentary majority to the People's Progressive Party. Since the 1985 election the Hoyte administration had been racked by claims of ballot-rigging, and the "free and fair" elections promised for 1991 had been postponed. Even so, the 1992 election still left the PPP with only a one-seat majority. PPP voters are predominantly Indian in origin, whereas Afro-Caribbeans tend to support the PNC.

Guyana's overspent economy is currently undergoing a period of change as the pseudo-one-party policies of the Hoyte regime are dismantled. The Government has, however, announced ambitious plans for an industrial restructuring.

Paraguay

Population ('000)	4,520 (1992)
Urban Population (%)	42.8 (1982)
Land Area (km^2)	406,750
Language/s	Spanish, Guarani
Religion/s	Mainly Roman Catholic (90%)
Currency	Guaraní (G = 100 centimos)
Head of State	Gen. Juan Carlos Wasmosy (1993)
Head of Government	Gen. Juan Carlos Wasmosy (1993)
Ruling Party	Asociación Nacional Republicana - Partido Colorado

Main urban areas	Population
Asunción (capital)	825,000

(1992 estimate)

The Republic of Paraguay has an executive President who is directly elected by universal suffrage for a five-year term of office, and who answers to a bicameral national Congress comprising a 45-member Senate and a 80-member Chamber of Deputies - both similarly elected for five years. In elections to the Chamber of Deputies, the party which receives the most votes is automatically granted two-thirds of the seats in both Houses. Constitutional reforms are under discussion, however.

Congressional elections were held in May 1993, when the Colorado Party won 43% of the vote and assumed its 40 Lower House seats and its 20 Upper House seats. Its main rival was the Partido Liberal Radical Auténtico (Authentic Radicals), which made strong progress to win 32 Lower and 17 Upper House seats; the Encuentro Nacional (National Encounter Party) won 8 Upper House and 8 Lower House seats. Presidential elections were held, also in May 1993, when Wasmosy outpointed Domingo Laíno of the Authentic Radicals to win 40.9% of the vote against 32.1%. Caballero Vargas of the National Encounter Party obtained 23% of the vote.

The economy remains in the lower to middle range of Latin American countries, with the impetus for change being only weakly felt at present. Heavy external debts are still a major problem.

Peru

Population ('000)	22,454 (1992)
Urban Population (%)	72.4 (1990)
Land Area (km^2)	1,285,215
Language/s	Spanish, Quechua, Aymara
Religion/s	Mainly Roman Catholic
Currency	New sol (S = 100 céntimos)
Head of State	President Alberto Fujimori (1990)
Head of Government	Oscar de la Puente Raygada
Ruling Party	Cambio 90, a coalition of independents, was formed in 1990 to back Fujimori.

Main urban areas	Population
Lima (capital)	6,601,000
Arequipa	634,500
Trujillo	532,000
Callao	515,200

(1992 estimate)

Peruvian politics entered a new and uncertain phase in May 1992, when President Alberto Fujimori declared what he termed a presidential coup. With army backing, he suspended the Constitution, disbanded Parliament and imposed direct rule from the Presidency. Ordinarily, the President is elected by universal suffrage for a term of five years, and reports to the 240-member Congress (180 in the Lower House and 60 in the Upper House), which is also elected by universal suffrage for a five-year term.

Following the presidential coup of May 1992, elections were held in November, when the Cambio 90 coalition gained 44 seats in the new 80-member Democratic Constituent Congress. The main opposition parties boycotted the elections, however.

Peru's diversified economy has not been immune to the pressures arising from uncertainty about the validity or the powers of the regime. With the presidential coup of 1992, and the introduction of rule by decree, investment is likely to prove even harder to attract for the country, which was already overloaded with debt.

Suriname

Population ('000)	416 (1992)
Land Area (km²)	163,820
Language/s	Dutch
Religion/s	Christian, Hindu, Muslim
Currency	Suriname guilder (Sf = 100 cents)
Head of State	President Ronald Venetiaan (September 1991)
Head of Government	Jules Adjodhia
Ruling Party	The New Front for Democracy and Development is the ruling coalition

Main urban areas	**Population**
Paramaribo (capital)	240,000

(1992 estimate)

The Republic of Suriname gained its independence from the Netherlands in 1975, and continued for some years to receive aid. In the late 1970s, however, the country was plunged by corrupt government into a protracted civil war, against which background a succession of coups and counter-coups took place. The situation had eased by 1993, however, following another military coup in December 1990. The executive President is chosen by an electoral college, as is a Prime Minister who answers to a 51-member National Assembly elected by popular vote.

A general election was held in May 1991, when 30 of the 51 seats in the National Assembly were won by a broad-based multi-ethnic coalition, the New Front for Democracy and Development. Campaigning for a form of commonwealth status vis-a-vis the Netherlands, the New Front defeated the ruling Suriname National Party, which won only 12 seats, and another coalition named the Democratic Alternative, which also favoured commonwealth status, won the remaining nine seats.

Suriname's economy has been damaged, though not entirely devastated, since the mid-1980s by the ongoing civil disturbances and by the slump in world prices for bauxite, its chief export product. With the restoration of political calm, some improvement has been seen, which seems sustainable in the 1990s.

Uruguay

Population ('000)	3,131 (1992)
Urban Population (%)	89.1 (1991)
Land Area (km²)	186,925
Language/s	Spanish
Religion/s	Mainly Roman Catholic (77%)
Currency	New Uruguayan peso (= 100 centésimos)
Head of State	President Luis Alberto Lacalle Herrera (1990)
Head of Government	President Luis Alberto Lacalle Herrera
Ruling Party	Partido Nacional

Main urban areas	**Population**
Montevideo (capital)	1,305,400

(1992 estimate)

Uruguay has an executive President who is elected every five years, together with a 99-member House of Deputies and a 31-member Senate. The political system was effectively suspended from 1973, when a military dictatorship took over the country, until 1985, when civilian rule was restored.

In the November 1989 elections, the first full poll since 1971, the Blanco Party (later known as the Partido Nacional) gained 13 of the 31 Senate seats and a majority of the 99 seats in the House of Deputies. Yet it was frequently outvoted by the Frente Amplio (Broad Front), which won most votes in the capital Montevideo. Indeed, this split between town and country is one of the most enduring features of the political system.

During the 1980s Uruguay's economy stagnated, and towards the end of the decade was dogged by exceptionally high levels of inflation. The Government has introduced an economic adjustment plan, including raised taxes and cutbacks in the social security sector, combined with privatisation measures, in a bid to meet stringent new economic targets.

Venezuela

Population ('000)	20,720 (1992)
Urban Population (%)	84.0 (1990)
Land Area (km²)	912,045
Language/s	Spanish
Religion/s	Mainly Roman Catholic (90%)
Currency	Bólivar (= 100 centimos)
Head of State	President Ramon José Velasquez (June 1993)
Head of Government	President Ramon José Velasquez
Ruling Party	Acción Democrática

Main urban areas	**Population**
Caracas (capital)	3,435,795
Maracaibo	1,400,643
Valencia	1,274,354
Maracay	956,656
Barquisimeto	787,359
Ciudad Guayana	542,707

(1990)

Venezuela has an executive President who is directly elected for a five-year term, and who answers to a 49-member Senate and a 201-member Chamber of Deputies, also elected for five years. The country has an extensively devolved political structure, with 20 autonomous states and 72 dependencies. In recent years the country's failure to address the economic problems of the 1980s has generated widespread discontent which has periodically degenerated into violent dissent: there was a failed coup attempt against the President Carlos Andrés Peréz Rodriguez (1989) in February 1992, and in May 1993 he was suspended on corruption charges.

Regional and municipal elections were held in December 1992, at which the ruling Acción Democrática was decisively rejected, even though the results were unclear. However the party refused to concede defeat, and continued with a minority government. Presidential elections were due to be held in December 1993. President Velazquez has called for the creation of a separate, elected Prime Minister.

Having enjoyed a huge boom during the 1970s on the back of steep oil price rises, Venezuela's economy was plunged into recession in the 1980s by the Government's failure to acknowledge in time the consequences of a continuing spending boom. The failure of the economy since then has been compounded by organisational failings which have aroused serious resentment against the authorities. The Government maintains strict price controls even on the private sector.

Caribbean

Anguilla

Population ('000)	9 (1992)
Land Area (km²)	91
Language/s	English
Religion/s	Mainly Christian
Currency	East Caribbean dollar (EC$ = 100 cents)
Head of State	HM Queen Elizabeth II
Head of Government	Emile Gumbs
Ruling Party	Anguilla National Alliance

Main urban areas	Population
The Valley (capital)	500

(1992 estimate)

As a Dependent Territory of the United Kingdom, ultimate sovereignty rests with the British monarch, although in practice the Chief Minister governs. Until 1980 Anguilla was technically a part of St Christopher (St Kitts)/Nevis/Anguilla, but this proved to be an unhappy union, since the Anguillans repudiated the St Kitts administration. The 1982 Constitution came into operation in May 1990.

In the general elections of February 1989, the ruling ANA was returned to power with three seats in the seven-member Parliament: it then entered a coalition with one independent member. The Anguilla United Party won two seats and the Anguilla Democratic Party took the remaining one.

Anguilla's fast growing domestic industries have done only little to limit its dependence on remittances from Anguillans employed in other countries, or on grants from the British Government. That said, however, its range of activity is sufficiently broad to provide a reasonable degree of protection from disasters in any one area.

Antigua

Population ('000)	66 (1992)
Land Area (km²)	442
Language/s	English
Religion/s	Mainly Christian
Currency	East Caribbean dollar (EC$ = 100 cents)
Head of State	HM Queen Elizabeth II
Head of Government	Rt Hon Vere C Bird
Ruling Party	Antigua Labour Party

Main urban areas	Population
St John's (capital)	38,000

(1992 estimate)

As a member of the British Commonwealth, the British monarch is the titular head of state. In practice, the Prime Minister appoints the British Governor (currently Sir Wilfred Ebenezer Jacobs). Legislative authority is vested in the 17-member parliament, and a 17-member Senate (Upper House) which is appointed by the Governor-General.

The 1989 elections to the 17-member House of Representatives resulted in a convincing win for the ruling ALP, which has held power since 1976 and which obtained 15 of the seats. The opposition United National Democratic Party obtained only one seat despite winning 31% of the vote, and the Barbuda People's Movement won the remaining seat.

Antigua's generally booming economy is so based on one activity - tourism - that some degree of vulnerability is inevitable. However, the island's image is being undermined by complaints of high prices and corruption - the result of a chronic labour shortage.

Aruba

Population ('000)	60 (1992)
Land Area (km²)	193
Language/s	Dutch, Papiamento, Spanish, English
Religion/s	Mainly Roman Catholic
Currency	Aruban guilder
Head of State	HM Queen Beatrix (Netherlands)
Head of Government	Nelson Oduber
Ruling Party	The Movimento Electoral di Pueblo leads a coalition with the Partido Patriotico Arubano and the Acción Democratico Nacional.

Main urban areas	Population
Oranjestad (capital)	

Aruba, which was formerly part of the Netherlands Antilles and which is hence an overseas territory of the Netherlands, became a separate political entity in January 1986, and is due to achieve full independence in January 1996.

Aruba's economy has had a difficult launch from the security of its once close relationship with the Netherlands. Having been forced, effectively, to concentrate on tourism as its main line of development, it requires major investment to take the decision further. Meanwhile, the scope for developing the financial services sector has been reduced by bilateral tax evasion agreements involving the United States.

Bahamas

Population ('000)	267 (1992)
Land Area (km²)	13,865
Language/s	English
Religion/s	Mainly Christian
Currency	Bahamian dollar (B$ = 100 cents)
Head of State	HM Queen Elizabeth II
Head of Government	Hubert Ingraham
Ruling Party	Free National Movement

Main urban areas	Population
Nassau (capital)	190,000

(1992)

The Bahamas are an independent member of the British Commonwealth, in which a British-appointed Governor-General exercises only nominal powers. The Prime Minister and his Cabinet are answerable to a 49-member House of Assembly (Lower House of Parliament) and to a 16-member appointed Senate. Elections to the House of Assembly are normally held every five years.

General elections were held in August 1992, in which the Progressive Liberal Party (PLP) Government of Lynden Pindling failed to obtain a fifth term of office, having obtained only 16 of the 49 seats in the enlarged House of Assembly, The opposition Free National Movement achieved a landslide victory with all of the remaining 33 seats, and went on to form a government under Hubert Ingraham.

The Bahamas' apparently well-balanced economy, together with its close relationship with both the USA and Western Europe, appear to lend a high degree of stability. There are rising political tensions, however, and the tightening of US pressure on banking legislation may add to the growing problems in the coming years. In 1993 the Government announced plans to privatise many of the country's major state-owned interests.

Barbados

Population ('000)	265 (1992)
Urban Population (%)	44.8 (1990)
Land Area (km²)	430
Language/s	English
Religion/s	Mainly Christian
Currency	Barbados dollar (BD$ = 100 cents)
Head of State	HM Queen Elizabeth II
Head of Government	Hon. L. Erskine Sandiford
Ruling Party	Democratic Labour Party

Main urban areas	Population
Bridgetown (capital)	7,670

(1992 estimate)

Barbados, an independent member of the Commonwealth, has a 28-seat House of Assembly whose members are elected by universal suffrage for a term of five years, and a 21-member Senate. The sovereign, Queen Elizabeth II, is represented by a Governor-General, who appoints the Prime Minister on the advice of Parliament.

General elections to the House of Assembly were held in January 1991, when the Democratic Labour Party of L. Erskine Sandiford won 18 of the 28 seats, down from 20 in 1986. The Barbados Labour Party won 10 seats, having obtained 40% of the vote, while the National Democratic Party, a DLP splinter group, failed to win any seats.

The country's domestic problems have added to the sense of foreboding being expressed in some quarters about the economic future. High unemployment is only partly offset by a heavy dependence on expatriate remittances, and the continuing slackness in the international oil markets, together with the weakness of the US dollar, have combined to depress prospects.

Bermuda

Population ('000)	60 (1992)
Land Area (km²)	54
Language/s	English
Religion/s	Mainly Anglican/Episcopal
Currency	Bermudan dollar (BD$ = 100 cents)
Head of State	HM Queen Elizabeth II
Head of Government	John Swan
Ruling Party	United Bermuda Party

Main urban areas	Population
Hamilton (capital)	6,000

(1992 estimate)

Bermuda, a British Dependent Territory, has a 40-member House of Assembly which exercises legislative authority, and which is elected by universal suffrage for a term of five years. There is also an 11-member Senate whose members are nominated by the Governor. The Governor also appoints the Prime Minister, on the basis of advice from the House of Assembly, and the Premier then appoints his own Cabinet.

General elections were held in February 1989 to the House of Assembly, in which the United Bermuda Party won 23 of the 40 seats - a marked deterioration from 1985, when it had won 31 seats. The Progressive Labour Party, which supports total independence from the UK, raised its electoral share from seven seats to 15, while the National Liberal Party and the Independent Environmentalist Party each won one seat.

Bermuda's economy is among the most affluent in the Atlantic/Caribbean nexus, thanks largely to the large number of offshore investment funds based on the islands. Yet the country's close dependence on the twin pillars of tourism and financial services renders it vulnerable to economic change.

British Virgin Islands

Population ('000)	17 (1991)
Land Area (km²)	153
Language/s	English
Religion/s	Mainly Christian
Currency	US dollar (US$ = 100 cents)
Head of State	HM Queen Elizabeth II
Head of Government	Hon. H. Lavity Stoutt
Ruling Party	Virgin Islands Party

Main urban areas	Population
Road Town (capital)	2,510

(1992 estimate)

The British Virgin Islands, a United Kingdom Crown Colony, are governed to a large extent by the local assembly (Legislative Council), despite the presence of a Governor appointed by the Crown who formally presides over an Executive Council. The Legislative Council has nine elected members as well as the Speaker and the Attorney General.

In the general elections of September 1986, the Virgin Islands Party obtained a substantial majority over the United Party of Conrad Maduro. New elections were due to take place in late 1992.

Cayman Islands

Population ('000)	25 (1989)
Land Area (km²)	259
Language/s	English
Religion/s	Mainly Christian
Currency	Cayman Islands dollar (CI$ = 100 cents)
Head of State	HM Queen Elizabeth II
Head of Government	Governor Michael Gore
Ruling Party	There are no official political parties in the Cayman Islands

Main urban areas	Population
George Town (capital)	13,150

(1992 estimate)

The Cayman Islands, which were a dependency of Jamaica until 1962, have been a United Kingdom Dependent Territory ever since. The 1972 Constitution awards all executive power to the Governor and the eight-member Executive Council (of which four members are elected by the Legislative Assembly, with the Governor and the other three ex officio members). The Legislative Assembly is elected by universal suffrage for a term of five years. A move introduced in 1987 granted resident Cayman Islanders certain electoral privileges over immigrants.

Elections to the Legislative Assembly were last held in November 1992, when all the candidates presented themselves as independents.

The country's liberal taxation and financial regulation policies have won it both popularity and notoriety over the years. Affluence is high, thanks to the considerable revenues from import duties and other fee incomes, but the Cayman Islands' dependence on financial services means that they remain a little vulnerable to shifts in the regulatory environments of their offshore competitors. The currency is often stronger than the US dollar, a factor which periodically impacts on the tourism sector.

Cuba

Population ('000)	10,808 (1992)
Urban Population (%)	73.1 (1989)
Land Area (km²)	114,525
Language/s	Spanish
Religion/s	Mainly Roman Catholic
Currency	Cuban peso (P = 100 centavos)
Head of State	President Fidel Castro Ruz (1976)
Head of Government	President Fidel Castro Ruz
Ruling Party	Partido Comunista de Cuba

Main urban areas	Population
Havana (capital)	2,152,000

(1992 estimates)

Constitutional changes in 1992 have not altered the country's official commitment to the creation of a communist society, such as the administration which Castro has been running since the 1950s. Indeed, the executive President's powers have now been enhanced so as to allow him to declare a state of emergency at any time. However, the National Assembly of Popular Power (Parliament), which is currently appointed by the country's 14 provincial assemblies, will henceforth be elected in a national secret ballot, probably starting in 1993.

The country's first direct elections to the legislature took place in March 1993, when all 589 official candidates for the 589 seats were successful. The claimed turnout was 99.6%.

Cuba's centrally planned and rigidly collectivist economy is experiencing decline as foreign investors remain wary of an island which would normally be considered to have considerable natural potential. However, a growing number of US interests have declared themselves willing to take the risk of offending the US Government; Washington's response is likely to be crucial.

Dominica

Population ('000)	72 (1992)
Land Area (km²)	751
Language/s	English
Religion/s	Mainly Roman Catholic (80%)
Currency	East Caribbean dollar (EC$ = 100 cents)
Head of State	President Clarence Seignoret
Head of Government	Dame Mary Eugenia Charles
Ruling Party	Dominica Freedom Party

Main urban areas	Population
Roseau (capital)	20,755

(1991 census)

Dominica, an independent republic within the Commonwealth, is formally ruled by an executive President, who in practice hands most of his legislative authority to the Prime Minister and her Cabinet. There is a unicameral House of Assembly, whose 30 members include nine appointed members, but whose other members are elected by universal suffrage for a five-year term. The House then elects the President, for a maximum of two five-year terms. Dominica is considering political union with Grenada, St Lucia and St Vincent and the Grenadines.

Elections were held in May 1990 to the House of Assembly, when the ruling Dominica Freedom Party won an unexpectedly narrow victory with only 11 of the 21 elected seats. The newly formed Dominica United Worker's Party won six seats, while the Labour Party of Dominica finished third with four seats.

Despite an abundance of natural advantages, Dominica's economy remains among the weakest in the Caribbean, and at present there are few indications of an imminent upturn. Expatriate labour is a major source of income. Moreover, the country's fate depends to a large extent on the development of the European Community's policy on banana imports, a factor over which the country has little real control.

Dominican Republic

Population ('000)	7,471 (1992)
Urban Population (%)	49.9 (1982)
Land Area (km²)	48,440
Language/s	Spanish
Religion/s	Roman Catholic (80%)
Currency	Dominican Republic peso (RD$ = 100 centavos)

Head of State	President Joaquin Balaguer (1986)
Head of Government	President Joaquin Balaguer (1986)
Ruling Party	Partido Reformista Social Cristiano

Main urban areas	Population
Santo Domingo (capital)	2,430,000

(1992 estimate)

The Dominican Republic is ruled by an executive President who is elected for a four-year term by universal suffrage, and who answers to a 120-member Chamber of Deputies and a 30-member Senate - all elected similarly for a four-year term. The country comprises a total of 26 provinces, each of which is run by an appointed governor, and also the Distrito Nacional around the capital Santo Domingo.

The last full election took place in May 1990, when the ruling PRSC lost its control of the Chamber of Deputies, obtaining only 42 of the 120 seats, compared with 44 for the opposition Partido de la Liberación Dominicana, 32 for the Partido Revolucionario Dominicano and two for the Partido Revolucionario Independiente; it did, however, retain control of the Senate, with 16 of the 20 seats, and continued in power.

The economy remains fundamentally weak, with the Government being forced to implement politically unpopular austerity measures in an effort to put its overspent economy back on the road to stability. Still, it has been able to attract foreign investment from Asia and from the United States, and this has helped to create employment while assisting in the diversification of the manufacturing sector.

Grenada

Population ('000)	105 (1992)
Land Area (km²)	345
Language/s	English
Religion/s	Roman Catholic (60%), Anglican (20%)
Currency	East Caribbean dollar (EC$ = 100 cents)
Head of State	HM Queen Elizabeth II
Head of Government	Nicholas Brathwaite (1990)
Ruling Party	National Democratic Congress

Main urban areas	Population
St George's (capital)	7,000

(1992 estimate)

As an independent member of the Commonwealth, Grenada is essentially self-governing, with the Crown being represented by a Governor-General. The Prime Minister is answerable to a 15-member Parliament elected by popular mandate for a term of five years. There is also a 13-member Senate, appointed by the Governor-General.

The general elections of March 1990 produced an inconclusive result, with the NDC winning seven of the 15 seats in the House of Representatives, and with the Grenada United Labour Party of the former Prime Minister Sir Eric Gairy obtaining four seats: the National Party obtained two seats and the New National Party another two. However, Brathwaite accepted an offer of coalition from the National Party and established a Cabinet which has proved susceptible to deep rifts on policy matters.

Grenada's economy is suffering to some extent from the legacy of its very large debts built up in the past. Unemployment is high, and the country relies heavily both on workers' remittances from abroad and on grant aid from the UK. In 1992 the Government announced an IMF-sponsored reform programme aimed at reducing the country's debt burden.

Guadeloupe

Population ('000)	342 (1992)
Land Area (km²)	1,780
Language/s	French
Religion/s	Mainly Roman Catholic
Currency	French franc (= 100 centimes)
Head of State	François Mitterrand (France)
Head of Government	Dominique Larifla
Ruling Party	Fédération guadeloupienne du parti socialiste

Main urban areas	Population
Les Abimes	23,889
Basse Terre (capital)	14,107

(1990 census)

As a part of the French Antilles, Guadeloupe is an external department of France and is governed to a considerable degree from Paris. The country sends deputies to the French Assemblée Nationale, and is represented at the European Community. Since being accorded regional status in 1974, however, Guadeloupe elects its own 41-member Regional Council for a term of six years, with responsibility for economic and social planning. Other executive power rests in a 42-member General Council.

The last full elections were to the French Assemblée Nationale in 1988, in which the Socialists returned two delegates, the Communists one and the Rassemblement pour la République one.

Guadeloupe's perennial trade deficit is only partially covered by its tourism revenues, and for the most part the country is forced to rely on remittances from France.

Haiti

Population ('000)	6,784 (1992)
Urban Population (%)	30.2 (1991)
Land Area (km²)	27,750
Language/s	French, Creole
Religion/s	Roman Catholic (75%)
Currency	Gourde (G = 100 centimes)
Head of State	Vacant
Head of Government	Marc Bazin (appointed June 1992) resigned in June 1993
Ruling Party	Movement for the Establishment of Democracy in Haiti

Main urban areas	Population
Port-au-Prince (capital)	1,300,000

(1992 estimate)

Haitian politics currently remain split between the supporters of the exiled former president Jean-Bertrand Aristide - the last elected president - and the minority administration of the National Front for Change and Democracy which overthrew him using military force in September 1991. From the USA Aristide has attempted to organise a comeback; meanwhile the political system remains in abeyance, and most foreign diplomats have boycotted the new regime. In October 1993 an upsurge of armed violence broke out among anti-Aristide factions opposing the the return of the President. An international trading blockade was thereupon imposed by the UN.

Elections were held in January 1993, but were so widely boycotted by opposition parties that they were considered null.

The economy is currently at an extremely low ebb after the failure of the national government to rectify the structural weaknesses bequeathed by its dictatorial and generally corrupt predecessors. Despite manifestations of support from the United States for the (now deposed) Aristide, aid has seldom been forthcoming in large amounts.

Jamaica

Population ('000)	2,595 (1992)
Urban Population (%)	52.3 (1985)
Land Area (km²)	11,425
Language/s	English
Religion/s	Mainly Christian
Currency	Jamaican dollar (J$ = 100 cents)
Head of State	HM Queen Elizabeth II
Head of Government	Rt Hon. Percival Patterson (March 1989)
Ruling Party	People's National Party

Main urban areas	Population
Kingston (capital)	643,801

(1991)

Jamaica, an independent member of the Commonwealth, is ruled by a Prime Minister and Cabinet who are drawn from a 60-member House of Representatives (Lower House), elected by universal suffrage for a five-year term. The Governor-General, who represents the Crown, has only formal functions. There is a 21-member Senate (Upper House), whose functions are mainly advisory. The constituency character of the electoral system means that parliamentary representation is often out of proportion to the levels of actual electoral support.

General elections to the House of Representatives were held in March 1993, when the People's National Party of Percival Patterson won a landslide victory, obtaining 54 of the 60 parliamentary seats, while the Jamaican Labour Party won only 6 seats. However, the PNP did less well in urban centres than in the contry as a whole.

Jamaica's economy retains many characteristics of a socialist state, with nationalised industries still present in abundance. However, the private sector is gaining ground. Severe overspending in the 1970s and 1980s has been largely rectified, but as a result the economy remains weak with extremely high unemployment.

Martinique

Population ('000)	333 (1992)
Land Area (km²)	1,079
Language/s	French
Religion/s	Mainly Roman Catholic
Currency	French franc (= 100 centimes)
Head of State	President François Mitterrand (France)
Head of Government	Claude Lise
Ruling Party	Fédération Socialiste de la Martinique (associated with the French Socialist Party) leads a coalition.

Main urban areas	Population
Fort de France (capital)	101,540

(1990 census)

As an external department of France, Martinique is governed to a considerable degree from Paris. The country sends deputies to the French Assemblée Nationale, and is represented at the European Community. Since being accorded regional status in 1974, however, Martinique elects its own 41-member Regional Council for a term of six years, with responsibility for economic and social planning. Other executive power rests in a 42-member General Council.

The last full elections were to the French Assemblée Nationale in 1988, in which the Socialists returned three delegates and other left-wing organisations one. Elections to the Regional

Council took place in October 1990, when the socialists won 18 of the 41 seats. The Parti progressiste de Martinique obtained 14 seats, and the separatist Mouvement indépendantiste martiniquaise won seven seats.

Martinique, like many other French overseas territories, has occasionally felt left out of the mainstream of the decision-making process with regard to its own economy, although it has achieved a better development than most. Tourism appears the most profitable way ahead, and the most likely solution to the country's perennial trade deficit.

Netherlands Antilles

Population ('000)	199 (1992)
Land Area (km²)	993
Language/s	Dutch, Papiamento, English, Spanish
Religion/s	Mainly Christian
Currency	Netherlands Antilles guilder (N Fl = 100 cents)
Head of State	HM Queen Beatrix (Netherlands)
Head of Government	Mary Liberia Peters (1988)
Ruling Party	Nationale Volkspartij/Partido Nashonal di Pueblo leads a coalition with the Unión Patriótico Bonairiano

Main urban areas	Population
Willemstad (capital)	

The Netherlands Antilles is a Dutch overseas dependency, in which the Dutch monarch rules through an appointed governor; in practice, the country enjoys a high degree of political autonomy, and is edging toward independence; Aruba, which was part of the group until 1986, will become fully independent in 1996. The country has a unicameral Parliament (Staten), which is elected by universal suffrage for a four-year term.

Elections to the Staten were held in March 1990, when Mary Liberia Peters' centre-right coalition was re-elected, although voting patterns were determined largely by geography rather than politics. The NVP won seven seats in Curaçao, against three for the Frente Obreroi Liberashon, two for the social democratic Movimentu Antijas Nobo, and one each for the Democratische Partij and the Nos Patria. In Bonaire, the UBP won all three seats, on St Maarten the Democratic Party and the Patriotic Alliance each one one, on Saba the WIPM won the single seat and on St Eustatius the DPE won the single seat.

The slump in the economy has been only partially offset by rises in tourism revenues, and in 1992 it was difficult to see how the country could regain the high level of foreign investment needed to restructure its economy. Tightening world prices for oil processing may put its own industry in jeopardy, although this is far from certain.

St Kitts

Population ('000)	42 (1992)
Land Area (km²)	261
Language/s	English
Religion/s	Mainly Anglican
Currency	East Caribbean dollar (EC$ = 100 cents)
Head of State	HM Queen Elizabeth II
Head of Government	Dr Kennedy Simmonds
Ruling Party	People's Action Movement

Main urban areas	Population
Basseterre (capital)	14,900

(1992 estimate)

St Kitts (St Christopher and Nevis) has been a fully independent member of the Commonwealth since 1983. The Crown is represented by a Governor-General who appoints the Prime Minister and Cabinet in accordance with the wishes of Parliament. The unicameral National Assembly consists of a speaker, three senators appointed by the Governor-General, and 11 members who are elected by universal suffrage for a term of five years. The island of Nevis has a separate eight-member legislature and a Cabinet with certain internal powers.

In the 1989 elections to the National Assembly, the People's Action Movement obtained six of the 11 elected seats, while the St Kitts-Nevis Labour Party won two, the Nevis Reformation Party two, and the Concerned Citizens' Movement one. The result was seen as a disappointment to the island of Nevis, where there was speculation that it would increase the pressure for a secession from the federation.

St Kitts has recently been trying to diversify its economy away from the traditional reliance on farming, with an effort to develop the tourism sector and the cotton textiles industry. Living standards are low by the standards of the region, however.

St Lucia

Population ('000)	140 (1992)
Land Area (km²)	616
Language/s	English
Religion/s	Mainly Roman Catholic (82%)
Currency	East Caribbean dollar (EC$ = 100 cents)
Head of State	HM Queen Elizabeth II
Head of Government	John G M Compton
Ruling Party	United Workers' Party

Main urban areas	Population
Castries (capital)	51,994

(1991 census)

St Lucia, a member of the Commonwealth, is one of the Windward Islands group which favours political integration with Dominica, Grenada and St Vincent and the Grenadines. The 17-member legislature is elected by universal suffrage for a term of five years. In recent years the Compton Administration has come under attack for what its political opponents have called "benevolent dictatorship" or "clientism"; Compton was, however, comfortably returned to his post in 1992, and appeared to be gaining in popularity.

The April 1992 elections to the 17-member Parliament produced a clear win for the UWP, which won 11 seats compared with only nine in 1987. The St Lucia Labour Party won the remaining six seats, with the Progressive Labour Party none.

St Lucia is trying, like many other Caribbean islands, to diversify its economy in the face of growing pressure on the commodity markets. Standards of living are fair, and tourism is seen as one of the main opportunities for wider employment.

St Vincent & the Grenadines

Population ('000)	109 (1992)
Land Area (km²)	389
Language/s	English
Religion/s	Mainly Christian
Currency	East Caribbean dollar (EC$ = 100 cents)
Head of State	HM Queen Elizabeth II
Head of Government	James Mitchell
Ruling Party	New Democratic Party

Main urban areas	Population
Kingstown (capital)	15,679

(1991 census)

St Vincent and the Grenadines has been a Commonwealth member since independence from the UK in 1979. The Crown is represented by a Governor-General who appoints the Prime Minister in accordance with the wishes of Parliament. The unicameral National Assembly consists of six appointed senators and 15 members who are elected by universal suffrage for a term of five years. The country is one of the Windward group which are considering a formal political integration at some time in the future.

Elections to the National Assembly were held in May 1989, when the New Democratic Party won all 15 of the elected seats, with more than 66% of the votes cast. Indeed, the opposition Labour Party lost all three of the seats which it had held before the election, while the Movement for National Unity and the United People's Movement failed to elect any candidates. Voter turnout was 71%.

The country's economy has been expanding, like those of its neighbours, in an attempt to diversify away from basic commodities, but growth has been slow in recent years. Living standards are moderate by the standards of the Caribbean.

Trinidad and Tobago

Population ('000)	1,265 (1992)
Urban Population (%)	69.1 (1990)
Land Area (km²)	5,130
Language/s	English (official); French, Spanish, Hindi and Chinese are also spoken
Religion/s	Roman Catholic (34%), Hindu (25%), Anglican (15%), Islam (6%)
Currency	Trinidad and Tobago dollar (T$ = 100 cents)
Head of State	President HE Noor Mohammed Hassan-Ali
Head of Government	Patrick Manning
Ruling Party	The People's National Movement

Main urban areas	Population
Port-of-Spain (capital)	60,450

(1992 estimate)

The Republic of Trinidad and Tobago is an independent member of the Commonwealth in which the executive President is elected by Parliament for a term of five years. Legislative power rests with the bicameral Parliament, comprising a 31-member Senate and a 36-member House of Representatives; whereas the House is elected by universal suffrage for five years, the Senate is appointed - 16 by the Prime Minister, six by the Leader of the Opposition, and nine by the President. Tobago has its own 12-member House of Assembly, with some autonomous powers.

General elections were held in December 1991, when the People's National Movement won 21 of the 36 seats and thus roundly defeated the National Alliance for Reconstruction, led by Arthur Robinson, which had governed since 1986 but which now retained only two of its 33 seats. This was a direct reversal of the 1986 result, in which the PNM had won only three seats. In the 1991 poll the United National Congress Party became the country's biggest opposition party with 13 seats, compared with only one seat in 1986.

With one of the highest per capita incomes in the Caribbean, Trinidad and Tobago has a diversified economy with strengths in oil, farming, manufacturing and tourism. Nevertheless, the political disquiet of the last few years has worried some of the country's foreign investors.

Central America

Belize

Population ('000)	189 (1992)
Land Area (km²)	22,965
Language/s	English (official); Spanish is the mother tongue of 15% of the population
Religion/s	Mainly Christian (Roman Catholic 60%)
Currency	Belize dollar (BZ$ = 100 cents)
Head of State	HM Queen Elizabeth II
Head of Government	George Price
Ruling Party	People's United Party

Main urban areas	Population
Belize City	44,800
Belmopan (capital)	4,400

(1992)

Belize, an independent member of the Commonwealth since 1981, has a bicameral National Assembly comprising a 28-member House of Representatives, elected by popular vote for a five-year term, and an eight-member Senate whose members are appointed by the Governor-General. In September 1991 the country opened formal diplomatic relations with Guatemala, which had previously maintained a formal claim on the whole territory of Belize. The possibility of political union with Dominica, St Lucia and St Vincent and the Grenadines remains under discussion.

General elections to the 28-member National Assembly were held in September 1989, when the PUP unexpectedly defeated the ruling United Democratic Party with 15 seats, based on a tiny electoral majority of 50.9%. The UDP, which won the remaining 13 seats, had polled 49% of the vote, and five of its ministers lost their seats. After the election one UDP member announced his intention to support the PUP in the Assembly.

Belize remains one of the poorer countries in the Caribbean, and offers only a limited prospect as a consumer market at present. Still, the improvement of relations with Guatemala and the USA may produce some change in this respect.

Costa Rica

Population ('000)	3,161 (1992)
Urban Population (%)	53.6 (1990)
Land Area (km²)	50,900
Language/s	Spanish
Religion/s	Roman Catholic
Currency	Colón (= 100 céntimos)
Head of State	President Rafael Angel Calderón Fournier (1990)
Head of Government	President Rafael Angel Calderón Fournier
Ruling Party	Partido Unidad Social Cristiana

Main urban areas	Population
San José (capital)	296,625

(1991)

Costa Rica has an executive President who is elected by universal suffrage for a term of four years, and who answers to the 57-member Legislative Assembly, also elected for four years. The President is assisted by two Vice-Presidents, and appoints the Cabinet personally. A Labour Council was formed in 1991 to address the growing trade union pressure for a reform of the labour and social market.

In the Legislative Assembly elections of February 1990, the PUSC won 29 of the 57 seats, overturning the rule of the Partido de Liberación Nacional, which obtained only 25 (down from 29 in 1985). Three seats were won by smaller parties, of which one was left wing and the other concerned mainly with regional matters. In the presidential elections on the same day, Calderón Fournier was returned with 51.4% of the vote, against 47.3% for the PLN leader Carlos Manuel Castillo.

Despite its generally high relative standard of living, the general dissatisfaction with government performance indicates that a period of possible instability may be approaching. This would be particularly regrettable in view of the generally fair balance of the economy, and its central role in the politics of the region.

El Salvador

Population ('000)	5,508 (1992)
Urban Population (%)	44.8 (1989)
Land Area (km²)	21,395
Language/s	Spanish
Religion/s	Roman Catholic (87%)
Currency	Salvadorean colón (C = 100 centavos)
Head of State	President Alfredo Cristiani Burkard (1989)
Head of Government	President Alfredo Cristiani Burkard (1989)
Ruling Party	Alianza Republicana Nacionalista (Arena)

Main urban areas	Population
San Salvador (capital)	520,000

(1992 estimate)

The executive President is elected by universal suffrage for a term of five years, and answers to a unicameral Legislative Assembly whose membership was expanded from 60 to 84 seats in March 1991.

The March 1991 elections produced a narrow victory for the ruling Arena Party, which won 44.3% of the vote but obtained only 39 of the 84 seats in the Legislative Assembly. The Partido Demócrata Cristiano won 26 seats, while the Partido de Conciliación Nacional won nine and the Convergencia Democrática eight seats. The Unión Democrática Nacionalista and the Movimiento Auténtico Cristiano each won one seat.

The Government has embarked on a reform programme that includes privatising the country's inefficient large companies - the Salvadorean Coffee Company, the entire banking system and perhaps the national airline. Yet the main obstacle to growth is still the severe disruption of the infrastructure that occured during the years of civil war, which will take many years to repair. An improving relationship with the United States will play an important role.

Guatemala

Population ('000)	9,744 (1992)
Urban Population (%)	42.0 (1990)
Land Area (km²)	108,890
Language/s	Spanish, Indian dialects
Religion/s	Mainly Christian (Roman Catholic 75%, Protestant 25%)
Currency	Quetzal (Q$ = 100 centavos)
Head of State	President Ramiro de Léon Carpio (June 1993)
Head of Government	President Ramiro de Léon Carpio (June 1993)
Ruling Party	Movimiento para Acción y Solidaridad leads a minority coalition.

Main urban areas	Population
Guatemala City (capital)	1,095,677

(1991, excluding suburbs)

Guatemala is a republic with an executive President who is elected by popular mandate for a five-year term. Of the 116 members in the unicameral National Congress, 87 are directly elected and the remainder appointed according to a system of proportional representation. Guatemala has now renounced its claim to the territory of Belize, but it still faces a virtual US trade embargo in consequence of alleged human rights abuses. In May 1993 the then President Jorge Serrano Elias mounted a "self-coup" like that of the Peruvian President Alberto Fujimori (qv), in an attempt to reinforce his authority; but he then surrendered power peacefully to President Ramiro de Léon Carpio, the present incumbent.

Elections to the National Congress were held in November 1990, with a second round in January 1991. The eventual result, as announced, gave the Christian Democrats only 28 seats, compared with 41 for the Union del Centro Nacional, 18 for the Movimento para Acción y Solidaridad, 12 for the Partido por el Adelantamiento Nacional, 11 for the right-wing PID/FRG/FUN coalition, one for the left-wing AP5/PSD coalition, and one for the Partido Revolucionario.

Guatemala's economy appears broadly based and potentially sturdy; the only factor holding it back, in fact, is the political uncertainty which continues to pervade the country. Allegations of human rights abuses, as long as they last, will do little to remedy this situation.

Honduras

Population ('000)	5,462 (1992)
Urban Population (%)	44.3 (1991)
Land Area (km²)	112,085
Language/s	Spanish (English is first language in certain areas)
Religion/s	Mainly Roman Catholic
Currency	Lempira (L = 100 centavos)
Head of State	President Rafael Leonardo Callejas (1989)
Head of Government	Gen. Lazaro Malario Avila Soleno (1992)
Ruling Party	Partido Nacional

Main urban areas	Population
Tegucigalpa (capital)	620,000

(1992 estimates)

Honduras has an executive President who is directly elected by popular mandate for a four-year term. He and his Cabinet are answerable to a 128-member National Assembly. In practice, the Administration relies heavily on the support of the armed forces.

Elections were held in November 1989 to the National Assembly, when the right-wing PN won 71 seats, although it had obtained only 51% of the votes: the Partido Liberal de Honduras won 43% of the votes but only 55 seats, while the Partido de Innovación y Unidad won two seats. President Callejas was elected shortly afterwards, having obtained only barely more than half the vote in the presidential elections of the same month.

The tough austerity measures being implemented by the Government have restrained the potential for domestic growth in the short term, although they may enhance the longer-term prospects. Development is held back by a weak infrastructure.

Mexico

Population ('000)	89,540 (1992)
Urban Population (%)	72.6 (1989)
Land Area (km²)	1,972,545
Language/s	Spanish (95%), Indian languages (Náhuati, Maya, Zapotec, Otomí, Mixtec)
Religion/s	Mainly Roman Catholic (91%)
Currency	Mexican peso (= 100 centavos)
Head of State	President Carlos Salinas de Gortari (1988)
Head of Government	President Carlos Salinas de Gortari
Ruling Party	Partido Revolucionario Institucional

Main urban areas	Population
Mexico City (capital)	8,236,960
Guadalajara	1,628,617
Nezhualcóyotl	1,259,543
Monterrey	1,064,197
Puebla	1,054,921
León	872,453
Ciudad Juárez	797,679
Tijuana	742,686
Aguascalientes	719,650
Mexicali	602,390
Culiacá	602,114
Acapulco	592,187
Mérida	557,340
Chihuahua	530,487
San Luis Potosí	525,819
Aguas Calientes	506,384

(1990 census, excluding suburbs)

Mexico, a parliamentary democracy with an executive President, has one of the longest democratic traditions in Latin America; yet its politics have been dominated so completely since 1917 by the PRI that it has a virtually one-party character. The President is elected for a six-year term by universal suffrage, and the Federal Chamber of Deputies every three years. There is also a 64-member Senate, elected for six years, and numerous regional parliaments which exert considerable powers of autonomy.

In the congressional elections of August 1991, the ruling PRI won 320 of the 500 seats in the Chamber of Deputies, including 290 of the 300 seats which were filled on a direct basis - the remainder being elected under proportional representation. The Partido Acción Nacional won 89 seats, while the Partido de la Revolución Democratica saw its vote shrink by 75% and won only 41 seats. The Partido del Frente Cardenista de Reconstrucción Nacional, the Partido de la Revolución Mexicana and the Partido Popular Socialista won 42 seats between them.

The rapid growth of the Mexican economy in recent years reflects the strength of its ties with the United States, which takes optimum advantage of Mexico's freeport facilities and its in-bond (Maquiladora) industrial zones, which make export foods free of duty. Economic reform since 1987 has installed a considerable degree of macro-economic stability and a large reduction of outstanding foreign debt.The country's fundamental strengths lie in its location and in its oil reserves.

Nicaragua

Population ('000)	4,131 (1992)
Urban Population (%)	61.0 (1991)
Land Area (km²)	148,000
Language/s	Spanish (English in certain coastal areas)
Religion/s	Mainly Roman Catholic (90%)
Currency	Córdoba oro (gold córdoba) (C = 100 centavos)
Head of State	President Violeta Barrios de Chamorro (1990)
Head of Government	President Violeta Barrios de Chamorro
Ruling Party	Unión Nacional Opositora

Main urban areas	Population
Managua (capital)	730,000

(1988, estimate)

Nicaragua's modern history began in 1979, when the left-wing Frente Sandinista de Liberación Nacional overthrew the Somoza dynasty which had ruled since the 1930s; a US blockade followed, and a civil war started which cooled only slightly after the 1990 elections brought a centre-right government to power. The 1987 Constitution provides for an executive President, directly elected for a six-year term, and for a unicameral National Assembly (Parliament), elected by universal suffrage every six years.

The legislative elections of February 1990 produced a crushing defeat for the ruling Sandinistas, which won only 40% of the vote against 55% for the centre-right Unión Nacional Opositora.

The gradual stabilisation of the political situation appears likely to encourage back some of the many investors who have avoided the country for many years. However, external debts remain extremely high.

Panama

Population ('000)	2,515 (1992)
Urban Population (%)	52.9 (1990)
Land Area (km²)	78,515
Language/s	Spanish (English is widespread)
Religion/s	Mainly Roman Catholic
Currency	Balboa (B$ = 100 cents)
Head of State	President Guillermo Endara Galimany (1990)
Head of Government	President Guillermo Endara Galimany
Ruling Party	Alianza Democrática de Oposición Civilista

Main urban areas	Population
Panama City (capital)	413,505

(1990 census)

The 1983 Constitution provides for an executive President who is elected by universal suffrage for a term of five years, and for a unicameral National Assembly whose 67 members are also elected for five years at a time. Panamanian politics have changed considerably since the removal in 1989 of Gen. Manuel Noriega, who was able to run a sophisticated and corrupt drugs operation because he combined the Presidency with a senior military position: in December 1991 the Assembly approved a constitutional amendment which abolished the national army.

There were no parliamentary elections until January 1991, when a handful of by-elections were held. They showed a fine balance between Endara's Alianza Democrática de Oposición Civilista and the Coalición para la Liberación Nacional, which had supported Noriega.

Panama's economy is undergoing a transitional period after the downfall of the disgraced Noriega regime, and it will remain dependent on the goodwill of the United States for some time to come. However, changing US legislation is eroding its scope as a financial centre, a factor which is likely to mean consumer affluence remaining at best static in the 1990s.

Puerto Rico

Population ('000)	3,580 (1992)
Urban Population (%)	66.8 (1980)
Land Area (km²)	8,960
Language/s	Spanish, English
Religion/s	Mainly Roman Catholic (81%)

Currency	US dollar (US$ = 100 cents)
Head of State	Governor Pedro Rossello (January 1993)
Head of Government	Governor Pedro Rossello
Ruling Party	Partido Popular Democrático
Main urban areas	**Population**
San Juan (capital)	2,000,000

(1992 estimate)

The Commonwealth of Puerto Rico, an external territory of the United States, has a Resident Commissioner who is elected by universal suffrage for a four-year term, and who has a non-voting seat in the US House of Representatives. Executive authority is vested in an elected Governor and his Cabinet, while legislative power rests with the bicameral Legislative Assembly - comprising a 27-member Senate and a 53-member House of Representatives, both popularly elected for a four-year term.

The legislative elections of November 1992 gave the ruling PNP 20 of the 27 seats in the Senate and 36 of the 53 seats in the House of Representatives. A referendum held in December 1991 came out overwhelmingly for closer integration with the USA - a move which prompted the then Governor Hernández Colón to tender his resignation in protest.

As a trust territory of the United States, Puerto Rico has come to rely heavily on its close relationship with its larger neighbour. Yet its development has remained at a low level generally, and it depends on migrant labour in the USA for much of its economic wellbeing.

Central Asia

Kazakhstan

Population ('000)	16,793 (1991)
Land Area (km^2)	2,717,300
Language/s	Kazakh
Religion/s	Islam
Currency	Rouble
Head of State	President Nursultan Nazarbayev (1991)
Head of Government	Sergei Tereshchenko
Ruling Party	Socialist Party of Kazakhstan (the former Communist Party)
Main urban areas	**Population**
Alma Ata (capital)	1,160,500
Karaganda	630,000

(1992 estimate)

Kazakhstan declared its independence only in October 1990, having tried in vain to campaign for the vanishing Soviet Union, and it remains controlled by the Socialist Party of Kazakhstan, the renamed Communist Party. The state has a 360-member Supreme Soviet, which is elected by universal suffrage, and an executive President who has been similarly elected in recent years, but who was formerly the Chairman of the Supreme Soviet. A new constitiution was introduced in January 1993, creating a smaller parliament with full-time members.

Elections to the Supreme Soviet were held in March 1990 (i.e. before independence), when the ruling Communist Party was re-elected almost unopposed.

Despite its historical role as one of the breadbaskets of the old Soviet Union, Kazakhstan remains underdeveloped and under-organised. As part of the effort to make the agricultural sector more efficient, the government announced in 1993 its intention to privatise all farms by 1995. It also required than henceforth 30% of all foreign currency earnings should be paid to the state.

Kyrgyzstan

Population ('000)	4,421 (1991)
Land Area (km^2)	198,500
Language/s	Kyrgyz
Religion/s	Islam
Currency	Som (= 200 roubles)
Head of State	President Askar Akayev
Head of Government	Tursunbek Chyngyshev
Ruling Party	Erkin Kyrgyzstan Democratic Party
Main urban areas	**Population**
Bishkek (capital)	628,500

(1992 estimate)

Kyrgyzstan attempted, like Kazakhstan, to defend the former Soviet political system, and declared independence only in December 1990. Thereafter, however, it rejected communism quickly: the pro-reform politicians initiated an ambitious economic reform programme. The country has an executive President who is elected by universal suffrage for a maximum of two five-year terms, and who leads a Cabinet of Ministers which has been much reduced in size since February 1991. The Supreme Soviet has 350 directly elected members. A new constitution was adopted in May 1993, in which early ambitions to implement an Islamic state were dropped.

Legislative elections were held in February 1990, long before independence, when the then Communist Party won a resounding and almost unopposed victory. Presidential elections took place in October 1991, when Askar Akayev was appointed. Economic progress has been hampered by the instability of the Russian economy, which still influences many of the smaller ex-Soviet republics, and the weakness of the rouble which is still the main measuring stick for the currency, the som. Hence the lack of confidence in the som. In January 1993 however Kyrgyzstan reached an agreement with Western credit institutions for a $300 million loan, in order to pursue its free market reforms. The country inherited a foreign debt of $800 million from the former Soviet Union, for which, in October 1992, Russia agreed to take responsibility.

Tajikistan

Population ('000)	5,357 (1991)
Land Area (km^2)	143,100
Language/s	Tajik
Religion/s	Mainly Islam
Currency	Rouble
Head of State	Imamoli Rakhmanov
Head of Government	Abdulmalik Abdullodzhanov
Ruling Party	Communist Party of Tajikistan
Main urban areas	**Population**
Dushanbe (capital)	605,000

(1992 estimate)

Tajikistan declared its independence from the Soviet Union relatively late, in August 1991, and has changed less than many other ex-Soviet states. The Communist Party still retains its political power, despite having been briefly banned, and nearly all opposition is from Islamic parties - four of which were also banned in June 1993 after allegations of terrorism. The country has an executive President who has been elected since November 1991 by universal suffrage, and a 230-member Supreme Soviet.

The last elections to the Supreme Soviet were held in March 1990, before independence, when the Communist Party scored an overwhelming victory. The Presidential elections of November 1991 resulted in the controversial appointment of Rakhmon Nabiyev, a communist from the Brezhnev era - a period now disowned by most Communist Party members.

Tajikistan has few significant economic activities other than farming, producing mainly livestock products. Its mountainous terrain has made it suitable for hydro-electric development, and sales of power make a small contribution to the external economy.

Turkmenistan

Population ('000)	4,254 (1993)
Land Area (km²)	488,100
Language/s	Turkmen
Religion/s	Mainly Islam
Currency	Rouble (to be replaced by the manat)
Head of State	President Saparmurad Niyazov (October 1990)
Head of Government	President Saparmurad Niyazov
Ruling Party	Democratic Party of Turkmenistan
Main urban areas	**Population**
Ashkhabad (capital)	517,200

(1993 estimate)

Turkmenistan declared its independence from the Soviet Union in October 1991, fairly late in the dissolution of the former state, and like Tajikistan it is still ruled by the Communist Party, albeit under the new name of the Democratic Party of Turkmenistan. The 1991 Constitution allows for an executive President, who is the Chairman of the Supreme Soviet, and who was first elected by that body, although he was subsequently confirmed by popular vote. The 50-member Majlis exercises legislative power, and is elected for five years.

The last elections to the Majlis were held in November-December 1992, when the Democratic Party of Turkmenistan won most of the seats. President Niyazov was re-elected unopposed in June 1992, obtaining 99.5% of the vote. The new People's Council, set up as a new supervisory body under the new Constitution adopted in May, met for the first time in December 1992.

Uzbekistan

Population ('000)	20,739 (1991)
Land Area (km²)	447,400
Language/s	Uzbek
Religion/s	Mainly Islam
Currency	Rouble. The central bank will shortly issue its own currency.
Head of State	President Islam Karimov (1990)
Head of Government	Abdulkhashim Mulatov (May 1993)
Ruling Party	People's Democratic Party
Main urban areas	**Population**
Tashkent (capital)	2,310,000

(1992 estimate)

Uzbekistan, a predominantly Sunni Muslim state within the former USSR, has an executive President who is directly elected by universal suffrage for a term of five years. He answers to a 500-seat Supreme Soviet. Uzbek politics have changed less than those of many other republics, since the outgoing communist administration has effectively been re-elected in its entirety, with religious groups offering the only serious organised competition. There have been calls for reform in recent years, but the republic still retains an inflexible attitude.

The last full elections to the Supreme Soviet were in March 1990, before independence, when the ruling Communist Party (now reformed as the PDP) was generally uncontested. By December 1991, when free presidential elections were held, the Communist Party chairman Islam Karimov still won 86% of the vote. Islamic groups are important in Uzbek politics.

The economy is based on a traditional centrally planned system, with few moves towards reform introduced.The loss of subsidies from the central Government, which had previously underpinned the economy, means that for the short term at least prospects for growth are minimal. However, new policies introduced in 1993 have encourage the creation of joint ownership programmes.

South Asia

Afghanistan

Population ('000)	19,060 (1992)
Urban Population (%)	17.7 (1988)
Land Area (km²)	636,265
Language/s	Dari (Persian dialect), Pushtu. Also a number of minority languages
Religion/s	Mainly Islam
Currency	Afghani (= 100 puls)
Head of State	President Burhanuddin Rabbani (December 1992)
Head of Government	Gulbuddin Hekmatyar (June 1993)
Ruling Party	Hezb-i-Islami
Main urban areas	**Population**
Kabul (capital)	1,090,000

(1992 estimate)

Afghanistan's political system has made a significant recovery from the confusion into which it was thrown by the removal of the Soviet-backed President Najibullah in 1992, and his replacement by a regime sympathetic to the mujaheddin. Yet factions within the mujaheddin remain locked in bitter conflict; the Jamiat-i-Islami faction which orginally replaced Najibullah was overturned by the rival Hezb-i-Islami faction in June 1993. Legislative authority rests with the National Assembly (Meli Shura), most of whose members are elected although some 30 are direct presidential appointments. In practice, power now rests with the Islamic Jihad Council, a Sunni mujaheddin organisation. An Economic Council was formed in July 1992 to address the country's severe economic problems.

In the National Assembly elections of 1988, the only candidates were those who stood for three organisations within the ruling National Front of Afghanistan: mujaheddin delegates refused an invitation to enter the polls.

The economy has yet to make an adequate recovery from the crisis of the 1980s, and in 1992 the lack of internal cohesion among the mujaheddin has hindered progress since the removal of the communist authorities. Increases in international assistance and trade co-operation with Pakistan are viewed as possible sources of future growth.

Bangladesh

Population ('000)	119,290 (1992)
Urban Population (%)	13.8 (1986)
Land Area (km²)	144,000
Language/s	Bengali
Religion/s	Islam
Currency	Taka (= 100 poisha)
Head of State	President Abdurrahman Biswas (1991)
Head of Government	Begum Khaleda Zia
Ruling Party	Bangladesh Jatiyabadi Dal (Bangladesh Nationalist Party)

Main urban areas	Population
Dhaka (capital)	3,637,892
Chittagong	1,566,070
Khulna	601,051

(1991 census)

Bangladesh is an independent member of the Commonwealth, with an executive President. President Mohammed Ershad, who seized power in 1982, declared himself President for life but was deposed in 1990 after allegations of corruption, and a system of election by popular mandate was brought in. Legislative authority rests in the 330-seat Jatiya Sangsad (Parliament), 300 of whose members are elected.

The February 1991 elections to the Jatiya Sangsad resulted in a substantial victory for the BNP, the party founded by the widow of Maj.-Gen. Zia Rahman who was assassinated in 1981. The BNP had boycotted the 1988 elections, but won 140 of the 330 seats, while the Awami League, a broadly socialist alliance, won 84 seats; the Jatiya party of the disgraced President Ershad won 35 seats; the Islamic Jamaat-i-Islami won 18; the Bangladesh Communist Party won five; and the Krishak Sramik won 4. Another eight seats went to independents, or to others of the 79 parties contesting the election.

Bangladesh, although rigorous enough in its enforcement of often painful correction programmes, has nevertheless failed to raise its average earnings far above the subsistence level. This is partly because of government problems in the 1980s, but is also due to the extremely rapid rate of population growth and recurrent natural disasters which have struck the country. Its progress in the 1990s is likely to depend to a large extent on its ability to retain current levels of international trade flows. In 1993 the Government announced a round of major tax increases, accompanied by deep cuts in public spending.

Bhutan

Population ('000)	1,610 (1992)
Land Area (km²)	46,620
Language/s	Dzongkha (Tibetan dialect). English is also widely used and there are a number of local dialects
Religion/s	Mahayana Buddhist
Currency	Ngultrum (Ng = 100 chetrum)
Head of State	HM King Singye Wangchuk
Head of Government	HM King Singye Wangchuk
Ruling Party	There are no legal political parties in Bhutan

Main urban areas	Population
Thimphu (capital)	29,000

(1992 estimate)

The Kingdom of Bhutan is a hereditary limited monarchy in which the King shares power with the Council of Ministers, the Tshogdu (National Assembly) and the chief priest of the Buddhist religion in Bhutan (Je Khempo). The 151-member Tshogdu has the power to vote the King out of office, and is required to pass a vote of confidence in him every three years. The King has let it be known in recent years that he favours a gradual democratisation of the political process; indeed, he has threatened to abdicate if nothing substantial is agreed.

There are no general elections in Bhutan. Delegates to the Tshogdu are elected in their various constituencies as and when the need arises, and are not allowed to represent political groups.

The apparent inflexibility of the political regime is mirrored by its insistence on adhering to the principle of the five-year plan - now discredited in most other parts of the region. However, the current emphasis is on building new roads and other communications links, to improve the country's international standing.

India

Population ('000)	879,550 (1992)
Urban Population (%)	25.7 (1991)
Land Area (km²)	3,166,830
Language/s	Hindi, English, 14 recognised regional languages
Religion/s	Mainly Hindu
Currency	Indian rupee (Rs = 100 paise)
Head of State	President Shankar Dayal Sharma (July 1992)
Head of Government	PV Narasimha Rao (June 1991)
Ruling Party	Congress I Party

Main urban areas	Population
Bombay (Greater)	12,571,720
Calcutta	10,916,272
Delhi (capital)	8,375,188
Madras	5,361,468
Hyderabad	4,280,261
Bangalore	4,086,548
Ahmedabad	3,297,655
Poona	2,485,014
Kanpur	2,111,284
Nagpur	1,661,409
Lucknow	1,642,134
Surat	1,517,076
Jaipur	1,514,425
Kochi	1,139,543
Coimbatore	1,135,549
Vadodara	1,115,265
Indore	1,104,065
Patna	1,098,572
Madurai	1,093,702
New Delhi (capital)	294,149

(1991 census, including suburbs)

India is essentially a federation of 25 states and seven union territories, spanning extremes of terrain and climate, and encompassing a very large number of ethnic groups. Ethnic and religious clashes characterise national politics at every level. The President holds all executive power, and appoints the Prime Minister and his Cabinet on the basis of election results to the Lok Sabha (Parliament). The Lok Sabha has 545 seats while the Rajya Sabha (Council of States) has 245 members.

Elections in the various states take place at regular intervals, and often produce sharply differing results from those at national level. The last national elections were in May and June 1991, when Congress I won 226 of the 545 elected seats, compared with 119 for the Bharatiya Janata Party, 55 for the Janata Dal, 35 for the Communist Party (Marxist), 14 for Telegu Desam, 13 for the other Communist Party, 11 for the All-India Anna Dravida Munnetra Kazhagam and 34 for other parties; numerous other seats were not filled, sometimes because of electoral violence.

India's vast economy remains poorly co-ordinated and is growing only slowly, hampered by the extremely high population growth rate; it nevertheless achieves a notable degree of self-sufficiency. Periodic extremes in the weather cause not only food shortages but also internal disruption.

Nepal

Population ('000)	20,580 (1992)
Urban Population (%)	7.12 (1986)
Land Area (km²)	141,415
Language/s	Nepali, Maithir, Bhojpuri
Religion/s	Hindu (90%)
Currency	Nepalese rupee (N Rp = 100 paisa)

Head of State	HM King Birendra Bikram Shah Dev (1972)
Head of Government	Girija Prasad Koirala
Ruling Party	Nepalese Congress Party
Main urban areas	**Population**
Kathmandu (capital)	255,000

(1992 estimates, including suburbs)

The Kingdom of Nepal is a constitutional monarchy in which the King, as the "symbol of Nepalese nationality and the unity of the people of Nepal", has extensive powers. He appoints 10 of the 60 members in the National Council (Rashtriya Sabha) - 15 of the remainder being chosen by an electoral college, and 35 being elected by the House of Representatives (Pratinidhi Sabha). The 205 members of the latter are elected by universal adult suffrage for a five-year term. Political parties were banned from 1960 to 1990.

The first free elections for 32 years were held in May 1991, when Koirala's Nepalese Congress Party won 110 of the 205 seats, against 69 for its main challenger, the United Nepal Communist Party. The United People's Front won nine seats, the Nepal Sadbhavana Party six, the National Democratic Party (Chand) three, the Nepal Mazdoor Islam Party and the Communist Party two each, and the National Democratic Party (Thapa) one seat. Three seats went to independents.

Nepal's difficult political situation has been matched by its economic problems, and in the early 1990s it appears unlikely that a rapid improvement can result. High domestic unemployment forces many men to seek work over the border in India; however, living standards remain fair by the standards of the region, especially in Kathmandu. The rupee was floated for the first time in February 1993.

Pakistan

Population ('000)	119,107 (1992)
Urban Population (%)	28.2 (1991)
Land Area (km²)	803,940
Language/s	Urdu is the official language, but is only in everyday use among about 8% of the population. Other languages in more general use include Punjabi (48%), Pushto (13%), Sindhi (12%), Saraiki (10%); English is also widely spoken
Religion/s	Islam (97%)
Currency	Pakistani rupee (R = 100 paisa)
Head of State	President Farooq Ahmed Khan Legari (November 1993)
Head of Government	Mrs Benazir Bhutto (October 1993)
Ruling Party	Pakistan People's Party
Main urban areas	**Population**
Karachi	7,500,000
Lahore	3,500,000
Faisalabad	1,104,209
Rawalpindi	794,843
Hyderabad	751,529
Multan	722,070
Gujranwala	658,753
Peshawar	566,248
Islamabad (capital)	350,000

(1992, estimate)

Pakistan, an independent member of the Commonwealth, has an executive President who is elected by universal suffrage, and who reports to an elected Parliament. In practice, the army is seldom far from the decision-making process, as few presidents have been able to contradict its interest for long. Pakistan's Constitution declares it to be an Islamic state, a fact most recently expressed in the banning of bank interest charges by an Islamic court. 1992-1993 brought a bitter power struggle between the President, who attempted to remove the Prime Minister, and the Prime Minister Nawaz'Sharif.

The last full elections to the National Assembly were held in October 1993, when the Pakistan People's Party won 86 of the 207 seats reserved for Muslim organisations, compared with only 45 in 1990. The Islamic Democratic Alliance, which had hitherto ruled with 106 seats, won only 72. The remaining seats were won by independents. Presidential elections followed in November, when Farooq Ahmed Khan Legari was elected with 274 votes against 168 for the acting president, Wasim Sajjad.

The economy is widely diversified and should be able, in principle, to withstand many kinds of external shocks. Yet the occasional droughts and floods in the country appear to inflict disproportionate levels of damage. Islamic law applies to the financial sector, which makes banking difficult.

Sri Lanka

Population ('000)	17,400 (1992)
Urban Population (%)	21.5 (1981)
Land Area (km²)	65,610
Language/s	Sinhala, Tamil, English
Religion/s	Mainly Buddhist (70%)
Currency	Rupee (Rs = 100 cents)
Head of State	President Dingiri Banda Wijetunga (1993)
Head of Government	Ranil Wickremasinghe (1993)
Ruling Party	United National Party forms a coalition with the much smaller Ceylon Workers' Congress.
Main urban areas	**Population**
Colombo (capital)	622,000

(1992 estimate)

The Democratic Socialist Republic of Sri Lanka, which has been independent in its present form since 1978, is a member of the Commonwealth. The country is ruled by an executive President, who is elected by universal suffrage for a six-year term and who appoints the Cabinet in accordance with the 225-seat Parliament - which is itself elected for a five-year term. The country's politics are dominated by ethnic differences which have periodically broken out into civil war: Tamils in the north and east want their own independent republic.In May 1993 President Ranasinghe Premadasa was assassinated in a bomb attack ascribed to Tamils, and a state of emergency was declared.

The last full elections were held in February 1989, when the ruling United National Party won 125 of the 225 seats in Parliament, compared with 67 for the Sri Lanka Freedom Party, 14 for the Independent Tamils, 10 for the Tamil United Liberation Front, and three each for the Sri Lanka Moslem Congress, the United Socialist Alliance and the Mahajana Eksath Peramuna. The elections were marred by widespread political violence.

Sri Lanka's economy has been badly damaged by the civil war, although it is now coming strongly out of recession. The country's foreign investors are still being deterred by the general insecurity. Governmment involvement in industrial policy is strong.

Japan

Japan

Population ('000)	123,360 (1992)
Urban Population (%)	77.4 (1990)
Land Area (km²)	369,700
Language/s	Japanese
Religion/s	Shinto (70%), Buddhist
Currency	Yen (=100 sen)
Head of State	HM Emperor Akihito (1989)

Head of Government	Morihiro Hosokawa (July 1993)
Ruling Party	Japan New Party leads an eight-party coalition

Main urban areas	Population
Tokyo (capital)	8,115,000
Yokohama	3,268,000
Osaka	2,608,000
Nagoya	2,161,000
Sapporo	1,710,000
Kobe	1,488,000
Kyoto	1,457,000
Fukuoka	1,253,000
Kawasaki	1,196,000
Hiroshima	1,094,000
Kitakyushu	1,030,000
Chiba	821,003
Sakai	800,331
Kumamoto	615,154
Okayama	587,348
Hamamatsu	530,905
Kagoshima	529,462
Sagamihara	526,448
Funabashi	524,921

(1992)

Japan is a constitutional monarchy in which the Emperor Akihito plays only a ceremonial role. All political power is vested in a Diet (Parliament), comprising a 512-member House of Representatives elected by universal suffrage for a term of four years, and a 252-member Senate, which serves a six-year term of office with half of its members coming up for election every three years.

The general elections of July 1993 produced a shock result for the ruling LDP, which failed for the first time since 1955 to obtain an absolute majority and which therefore lost power. Racked with internal divisions after a bout of corruption allegations involving senior figures, it saw a large proportion of its votes going instead to the breakaway parties: the Japan New Party of Morihiro Hosokawa, the New Harbinger Party of Asahiko Mihara, and the New Born Party of Tsutomu Hata . Hosokawa therupon formed an eight-party coalition, which excluded the LDP but which included the weakened Social Democrats in an otherwise right-wing administration, and which held 245 seats compared with the LDP's 225.

With one of the world's highest per capita spending levels, Japan's free-enterprise economy has achieved remarkable successes since the collapse at the end of the Second World War. Yet the economy has actually proved irritatingly restrictive for many of Japan's foreign trade partners, and its sometimes aggressively assertive manner in trade negotiations has exacerbated tensions. In the early 1990s the slumping domestic economy forced manufacturers to seek expansion abroad; they have, however, been thwarted by the general stagnation in the USA and Europe. By 1993 a number of massive state investment programmes were needed to boost demand. Yet the uncharacteristically high strength of the Japanese yen was also hampering export growth.

ASEAN/NICs

Brunei

Population ('000)	270	(1992)
Urban Population (%)	63.6	(1982)
Land Area (km^2)	5,765	
Language/s	Malay, Chinese, English	
Religion/s	Muslim (64%), Buddhist (14%), Christian (10%)	
Currency	Brunei dollar (S = 100 sen)	

Head of State	HM Sultan Sir Muda Hassani Bolkiah Mu'izzadin Waddaulah
Head of Government	HM Sultan Sir Muda Hassani Bolkiah Mu'izzadin Waddaulah
Ruling Party	There are no legal political parties.

Main urban areas	Population
Bandar Seri Begawan (capital)	55,000

(1992 estimate)

Brunei achieved full independence from the United Kingdom in 1984, and is ruled by an executive monarch, the Sultan, in whose hands all legal powers are vested. The Sultan is assisted by a Council of Ministers, a Religious Council and a Privy Council. However, part of the Constitution has been revoked since 1962, when massive protests developed, and a state of emergency was declared which has yet to be revoked. The Sultan disbanded the Legislative Council in 1984 and now rules by decree.

There are no elections in Brunei.

The country's economy is one of the most affluent in the developing Far East, with a per capita income in excess of US \$15,000. Its planned diversification away from the stricken world oil markets ought to reinforce this fortunate position; moreover, its central position within (and recent membership of) the ASEAN group ought to be to its advantage. Yet its policy of isolation over the years may leave its neighbours less enthusiastic about future co-operation.

Hong Kong

Population ('000)	5,800	(1992)
Urban Population (%)	93.1	(1986)
Land Area (km^2)	1,062	
Language/s	English, Putonghua (Mandarin), Cantonese	
Religion/s	Mainly Buddhist	
Currency	Hong Kong dollar (HK\$ = 100 cents)	
Head of State	HM Queen Elizabeth II	
Head of Government	Governor: HE Christopher Patten	
Ruling Party	Liberal parties, including the United Democrats of Hong Kong, hold a working majority in the Legislative Council	

Main urban areas	Population
Victoria (capital)	

Hong Kong, which is currently a Crown Colony, is due to be ceded to China in January 1997, and transitional arrangements are being put into place. At present, the British Parliament has an effective veto over the decisions of the Legislative Council (Legco), and the Crown acts through a Governor. The 18 elected Legco members are, however, outweighed by 20 appointed members and seven ex-officio members. An Executive Council of four ex-officio members and 10 nominated members is responsible for policy.

The first full elections to the Legislative Council were held in September 1991, when the United Democrats of Hong Kong won a sweeping victory with 12 of the 18 directly elected seats. Other allied democratic parties won a further three seats, and the remaining three were won by independents. Despite vigorous campaigning, none of the four candidates backed by China won a seat, leading Beijing to complain that the 37% turnout had produced an "insufficiently pluralist" result.

Recent statements from Beijing have reassured Hong Kong about the stability of its capitalist structure after 1997, and foreign investment has accordingly flooded in. Property markets, once afflicted by uncertainties, are now looking more robust.

Indonesia

Population ('000)	191,170 (1992)
Urban Population (%)	30.9 (1990)
Land Area (km²)	1,919,445
Language/s	English, 27 local languages
Religion/s	Mainly Islam (87%)
Currency	Rupiah (Rp = 100 sen)
Head of State	President Suharto
Head of Government	President Suharto
Ruling Party	Sekretariat Bersana Golongan (Golkar)

Main urban areas	Population
Jakarta (capital)	8,200,000
Surabaya	2,545,000
Medan	2,400,000
Bandung	1,800,000
Semarang	1,600,000
Palembang	1,020,000
Ujung Pandang	1,001,000
Padang	730,000
Malang	610,000
Surakarta	505,000

(1992 estimate)

Indonesia's ethnically diverse population is dominated by the Javanese factions around President Suharto which hold most of the power. Suharto succeeded his predecessor President Sukarno, who seized power in the coup of 1967, and exercises almost absolute power through the ruling Golkar coalition, which has strong army backing. The President is elected for a five-year term by the 1,000-member People's Consultative Assembly - of whom 500 are elected by universal franchise and the remainder appointed by the President, often from the armed forces.

The ruling Golkar group was returned to power in the general elections of June 1992, with a slightly reduced majority in the 400-seat House of Representatives. Golkar won 299 seats, and came first in all 27 provinces. The two legal opposition parties, the (Islamic) United Development Party and the (populist) Democratic Party of Indonesia, won 61 and 40 seats respectively. In March 1993 President Suharto was re-elected, unopposed.

Indonesia's economy is growing very rapidly in the 1990s, in line with the objectives of the Fifth and Sixth Economic Plans (1984-1989 and 1990-1994) which envisaged a move away from dependence on oil. However, the country remains very poor and has only a limited potential domestic market for consumer goods.

South Korea

Population ('000)	43,660 (1992)
Urban Population (%)	70.8 (1989)
Land Area (km²)	98,445
Language/s	Hangul (Korean)
Religion/s	Mahayana Buddhist, Christian
Currency	Won (W = 100 jeon)
Head of State	Kim Young Sam (1992)
Head of Government	Hwang In Sung (February 1993)
Ruling Party	Democratic Liberal Party (ruling coalition, incorporating two independents)

Main urban areas	Population
Seoul (capital)	10,627,790
Pusan	3,797,566
Taegu	2,228,834
Inchon	1,818,293
Kwangchu	1,144,695
Taejon	1,062,084
Ulsan	682,978
Suwon	644,968
Songnam	540,764
Chonju	517,104

(1990 census)

Although South Korea has a Prime Minister, in practice real power lies with the executive President. The Constitution grants the National Assembly, whose 299 members are elected by universal suffrage for a four-year term, with most legislative authority. But since the collapse of the Fifth Republic in 1987, amid violent protests, the Parliament has been hampered by the small working majority of the ruling party. Relations are now improving with North Korea, from which South Korea split in 1948 after the Korean War, and also with China.

Elections to the National Assembly were held in March 1992, in which the President's Democratic Liberal Party won only 38.5% of the vote, compared with 29.2% for the Democratic Party and 17.3% for the Unification National Party. After the complex allocation of non-directly elected seats, the DLP emerged with 149 of the 299 seats, the DP with 97 seats and the UNP 31 seats. The Party for New Political Reform won one seat, and there were 21 independents. At presidential elections in December 1992 Kim Young-Sam of the DLP won 41.4% of the vote, to become South Korea's first president without a military background.

South Korea's economic expansion since the 1960s has been achieved very largely through the Government's policy of backing a handful of large and very diversified enterprises, the so-called chaebols, in the hope that their affluence would impact favourably on other businesses. The policy was backed up by protectionist measures against imports which are only now being relaxed. Living standards are high.

Macau

Population ('000)	500 (1991)
Land Area (km²)	16
Language/s	Portuguese (official), Cantonese, English
Religion/s	Buddhist, Roman Catholic
Currency	Pataca (Pt = 100 avos)
Head of State	President Mário A. Nombre Lopes Soares (Portugal)
Head of Government	Gen. Vasco Rocha Vieira
Ruling Party	There are no political parties in Macau

Main urban areas	Population
Macau (capital)	356,000

(1992)

Macau, currently described as a Special Territory of Portugal, is due to return to Chinese rule in 1999, when it will become the Chinese Special Administrative Region (SAR) of Macau. Under the 1976 Constitution, as revised in 1990, the Governor exercises all executive power except in the field of foreign affairs, which are determined by Portugal. He presides over a 23-member Legislative Assembly, of whom only eight members are directly elected, seven are government appointees and eight are nominated by businesses. A Basic Law has been agreed with China for the period after the handover in 1999.

Elections to the Legislative Assembly were held in October 1988, when independent "liberals" were appointed to three of the eight directly elected seats.

Macau's firm commitment to capitalism stands in stark contrast to the collectivism of China, to which it will shortly revert, but like Hong Kong it has received sufficient pledges of good intent to be fairly confident about its future after 1999. Its functions as a port and transshipment centre at the mouth of the Pearl River would appear to give it some degree of natural protection against a major deterioration; it can also look forward to tourism from China.

Malaysia

Population ('000)	18,790 (1992)
Urban Population (%)	37.2 (1980)
Land Area (km²)	332,965
Language/s	Bahasa Malaysia (Malay); also English, dialects of Chinese, Tamil and native languages
Religion/s	Muslim (53%), Buddhist (19%), Christian
Currency	Malaysian dollar/Ringgit (= 100 cents)
Head of State	HM Sultan Azlan Muhibuddin Shah (1989)
Head of Government	Datuk Seri Dr Mahathir Mohamed
Ruling Party	The Barisan Nasional (National Front) coalition, dominated by the United Malays National Organisation (UMNO)

Main urban areas	Population
Kuala Lumpur (capital)	1,115,000

(1992 estimate)

Malaysia is a constitutional monarchy in which, unusually, the monarch (Yang di-Pertuan Agong) is elected every five years from among the tribal elders of Peninsular Malaysia. All effective power is exercised by the Prime Minister and his Cabinet, who report to a bicameral legislature. The House of Representatives (Dewan Rakyat, or Lower House) has 180 members elected for five years, while the 70-member Senate (Dewan Negara) is appointed by the monarch. There are numerous regional assemblies. Constitutional amendments in 1993 reduced the legal immunity of the nine Malay rulers.

IIn recent elections to the House of Representatives, held in October 1990, the UMNO coalition was returned with a substantial majority. Opposition groups were combined in the Angkatan Perpaduan Ummah coalition, but failed to make a significant impact. The Sultan was last elected in March 1989.

Malaysia's economy is still run along the lines of multi-year plans, although these are perceived as guidelines rather than fixed targets. Rapid industrialisation is transforming the economy away from its traditional agricultural base, and in the process it is creating major new opportunities for providers of consumer goods and services.

Philippines

Population ('000)	64,260 (1992)
Urban Population (%)	43.2 (1991)
Land Area (km²)	300,000
Language/s	Filipino, English, also Spanish, Cebuano and other local dialects
Religion/s	Mainly Roman Catholic (84%), Muslim
Currency	Philippine peso (=100 centavos)
Head of State	President Fidel Ramos (June 1992)
Head of Government	President Fidel Ramos
Ruling Party	Lakas ng Edsa-National Union of Christian Democrats leads a coalition

Main urban areas	Population
Quezon City	1,669,766
Manila (capital)	1,601,234
Davao	849,947
Caloocan	763,415
Cebu	610,417

(1990 census)

The Republic of the Philippines has an executive President who is elected by universal mandate and who appoints a Cabinet. It was not until 1986, however, that the first presidential election was held: although the incumbent Ferdinand Marcos claimed to have won, he was overthrown by a "People's Power" movement led by Corazon Aquino. In 1992 Gen. Fidel Ramos succeeded Mrs Aquino as President.

Elections to the legislature and to local government positions were held in May 1992, when the Laban ng Demokratikong of the former President Corazon Aquino won 89 seats in the 200-member House of Representatives and 16 Senate seats. The Nationalist People's Coalition won 42 seats in the House, and the Lakas-NUCD 33 seats (although only two Senate seats), the Liberals won 15 House seats, and the remainder went to independents. On the same day, the presidential elections gave 23.6% of the vote to Ramos, 19.7% to the independent Miriam Defensor Santiago and 18.2% to Eduardo Cojuangco, of the Nationalist Party.

The inability of the Ramos regime to still all of the uncertainties about the Philippine economy is significant. The withdrawal of the US forces simultaneously casts further doubt on the viability of one of the poorest semi-developed economies in Asia; yet the low wage rates and potentially huge domestic consumer market militate in favour of a withholding of judgement in the medium term.

Singapore

Population ('000)	2,810 (1992)
Urban Population (%)	100 (1985)
Land Area (km²)	616
Language/s	Malay, Mandarin, Tamil, English
Religion/s	Buddhist/Daoist (53%), Muslim (16%), Christian (12%)
Currency	Singapore dollar (S$ = 100 cents)
Head of State	President Wee Kim Wee (1985)
Head of Government	Goh Chok Tong (1991)
Ruling Party	People's Action Party (PAP)

Main urban areas	Population
Singapore City (capital)	2,818,200

(1992)

The Republic of Singapore, an independent member of the Commonwealth, achieved its independence from the United Kingdom in 1965 when it separated from Malaya (now Malaysia). Its executive President is elected by the unicameral Parliament for a term of four years; the 81-member Parliament is itself elected every four years, by a complex system of single-member constituencies and by professional constituencies representing professional groups. In January 1991 the Parliament voted to award the President substantially increased powers.

General elections were held prematurely in August 1991, when the PAP saw its support fall from 63% to 61% of the vote, while the opposition Singapore Democratic Party (SDP) and Workers' Party (WP) saw their votes increase accordingly; yet, because of the first-past-the-post electoral system, the PAP carried off 77 of the 81 seats, while the SDP gained three seats and the WP one.

Singapore's economy has boomed since the 1960s, thanks to the Government's policy of encouraging highly skilled and hence high value-added manufacturing facilities. In the early 1980s the country had one of the highest per capita incomes in the Far

East. However, the country keeps a tight rein on imports and engages in extensive regulation of the economy, in manufacturing in particular. Five-year plans are used to co-ordinate development.

Taiwan

Population ('000)	19,900 (1988)
Land Area (km²)	35,990
Language/s	Mandarin
Religion/s	Mainly Buddhist
Currency	New Taiwan dollar (NT$ = 100 cents)
Head of State	President Lee Teng-Hui (1988)
Head of Government	Lien Chan (1993)
Ruling Party	Kuomintang

Main urban areas	Population
Taipei (capital)	2,718,757
Kaohsiung	1,395,816
Taichung	774,484
Tainan	688,958

(1992)

Taiwan, the self-styled Republic of China, has been governed continuously since its foundation in 1947 by the right-wing Kuomintang founded by the nationalist leader Chiang Kai-shek. The executive President has been traditionally elected by an electoral college for a six-year term of office, but demands for a direct electoral system have been growing. Legislative authority is vested in a unicameral National Assembly, the Kuo-Min-Ta-Hui, which considers draft bills from the Legislative Yuan. In 1993 there were growing splits in the Kuomintang which were regarded in some quarters as endangering the authority of the President.

A general election to the Legislative Yuan was held in December 1992. The Kuomintang (KMT) gained 53% of the vote, while the opposition Democratic Progress Party (DPP) gained 31%. The KMT won 73 elected seats and received a further 23 directly allotted seats.

Taiwan's highly diversified and successful economy has been achieved in the face of considerable obstacles, not all of which have yet been addressed. The Government's consistently protectionist stance toward its industries and its financial markets has so far aroused complaints only from the United States; in the 1990s, its fortunes are more likely to depend on China itself.

Thailand

Population ('000)	57,760 (1992)
Urban Population (%)	18.7 (1990)
Land Area (km²)	514,000
Language/s	Thai
Religion/s	Buddhism (95%), Muslim (4%)
Currency	Baht (= 100 satangs)
Head of State	HM King Bhumibol Adulyadej (1946)
Head of Government	Chuan Leekpai (September 1992)
Ruling Party	Democrat Party leads a five-party coalition

Main urban areas	Population
Bangkok (capital)	5,876,000

(1990 census)

Thailand's political system has been heavily dominated for decades by the armed forces, which have nominated even the country's civilian Prime Ministers. In February 1991, however, they initiated a full-scale coup against Gen. Chatichai Choonhavan and dissolved the National Assembly, re-opening it 13 months later after new elections. The new 360-member

elected House acts alongside a 270-member appointed Senate, of whom 154 were from the police or the armed forces in March 1992. The ruling military junta was formally dissolved a month later.

A general election to the House of Representatives was held in September 1992. No party won an overall majority, but the Democrat Party emerged as the biggest group, winning 79 of the 360 seats.

Thailand's economy, although still producing only about $1,400 per capita per annum, is among the fastest growing in the Asia-Pacific region, with up to 8% growth forecast for 1993-1995. The economy has until now been run on a strictly centralist principle, with five-year targets for most product sectors, but policies have now been relaxed to allow foreign companies into the market.

East/SE Asia

Cambodia

Population ('000)	9,050 (1992)
Urban Population (%)	10.8 (1985)
Land Area (km²)	181,000
Language/s	Khmer
Religion/s	Theravada Buddhist
Currency	Riel (R = 100 sen)
Head of State	King Norodom Sihanouk
Head of Government	Prince Norodom Ranariddh
Ruling Party	A four-party coalition of the United National Front, the Cambodian People's Party, the Buddhist Liberal democrats and the National Liberation Movement. The former Khmer Rouge representatives have now left the Government.

Main urban areas	Population
Phnom-Penh (capital)	900,000

(1992 estimate)

The State of Cambodia resumed its traditional title in 1990, having been known since the late 1970s as Kampuchea or Democratic Kampuchea. The country suffered appallingly during the forced collectivist reforms imposed by the Khmer Rouge of Pol Pot in the 1970s; however, when Vietnamese troops invaded the country in 1978 to install a pro-Vietnamese regime, the Khmer Rouge embarked on a civil war. The war ended in 1990 with a UN-sponsored compromise, which effectively left the Khmer Rouge, in collaboration with Prince Norodom Sihanouk, in power.

The first multi-party elections to the 120-member Assembly since 1973 were held in May 1993, when the United National Front won 58 seats, the Cambodian People's Party 51, the Buddhist Liberal Democrats 10 and the National Liberation Movement one seat. The turnout was 90%. The Khmer Rouge, which had dominated the outgoing administration, pulled completely out of the capital Phnom Penh and regrouped in the rural areas. President Sihanouk was also confirmed in office on the same day.

Cambodia's future as a potential market for the 1990s remains on a knife edge as its delicate political balance of left and ultra-left politicians attempt to convince the international community of their good intent. At present the economy is still organised according to five-year plans.

China

Population ('000)	1,188,000 (1992)
Urban Population (%)	26.2 (1990)
Land Area (km²)	9,597,000
Language/s	Putonghua (Mandarin), Cantonese, Hakka, Amoy, Foochow, numerous other dialects
Religion/s	Mainly Buddhism
Currency	Renminbi/Yuan (RMB/Y = 100 fen)
Head of State	President Jiang Shemin (1993)
Head of Government	Li Peng
Ruling Party	Chinese Communist Party

Main urban areas	Population
Shanghai	7,830,000
Tianjin	5,770,000
Shenyang	4,540,000
Beijing (capital)	4,000,000
Wuhan	3,750,000
Guangzhou (Canton)	3,580,000
Chongqing	2,980,000
Harbin	2,830,000
Chengdu	2,810,000
Xian	2,760,000
Nanjing	2,500,000
Zibo	2,430,000
Dalian	2,400,000
Jinan	2,320,000
Changchun	2,110,000
Taiyuan	2,060,000
Zhengzhou	1,960,000
Kunming	1,710,000
Guiyang	1,530,000
Tangshan	1,520,000

(1991)

The People's Republic of China has been run as a communist one-party state since 1949, when Mao Tse-Tung's forces overcame the nationalists and drove them offshore to what is now Taiwan. Despite various economic reforms, there are few signs that the political commitment to pluralism is keeping pace: the 1982 Constitution still vests all legislative authority in the 3,000-member National People's Congress, which is elected every five years; but since it meets only once a year, the Communist Party undertakes most political decisions. In 1993 the illness of Premier Li Peng raised doubts about future developments; however, a hard-line crackdown on political dissidence suggested that conservative forces were still strong.

In the absence of true multi-party elections, the National People's Congress elections of September 1987 and March 1988 were a foregone conclusion: the vast majority of the elected delegates were from the Chinese Communist Party.

It is easy to overstate the scale of the conversion from communist collectivism to free-market capitalism; the Communist Party leadership has made it clear that it intends to keep a tight rein on the changes, and the harsh crackdown on economic crimes in 1993 gave notice that the authorities are anxious about the disruptive power of the changes going on. However, the vast potential consumer market means that even small shifts in policy will yield potentially large rewards. Inflation was becoming serious by the autumn of 1993.

North Korea

Population ('000)	22,920 (1992)
Urban Population (%)	63.8 (1985)
Land Area (km²)	122,310
Language/s	Korean
Religion/s	Buddhist, Christian, Chundo Kyo
Currency	Won (= 100 chon)
Head of State	President Kim Il Sung
Head of Government	Kang Song San
Ruling Party	The Korean Workers' Party is the only legal political party.

Main urban areas	Population
Pyongyang (capital)	2,000,000
Hamhung	670,000
Chongjin	530,000

(1986, estimate)

The Democratic People's Republic of Korea has been a communist one-party state since 1948. The 1972 Constitution provides for an executive President who is elected by the Supreme People's Assembly, or Parliament. Yet although the Assembly's members are elected every four years by universal suffrage, from a single list, they meet only occasionally; in effect, power is exercised by the Central People's Committee, in which the Korean Workers' Party dominates. President Kim Il Sung appears to be preparing his son, Kim Jong Il, to take over.

Elections to the Supreme People's Assembly were held in April 1990, when the Korean Workers' Party won all of the 687 seats. Voter turnout was officially reported to have been 99.78%.

The North Korean economy remains rigidly centralised, and is organised according to five-year plans which are seldom debated at popular level. However, with the withdrawal of Soviet assistance the trend is toward liberalisation. The country's debts to the former USSR are vast.

Laos

Population ('000)	4,470 (1992)
Urban Population (%)	15.9 (1985)
Land Area (km²)	236,725
Language/s	Laotian, French, tribal languages including Meo
Religion/s	Mainly Buddhist
Currency	Kip (= 100 at)
Head of State	President Nouhak Phoumsavanh
Head of Government	Gen. Khamtay Siphandone (1991)
Ruling Party	Lao People's Revolutionary Party

Main urban areas	Population
Vientiane (capital)	449,000

(1992 estimate)

The Lao Constitution, approved in August 1991, provides in principle for the creation of a National Assembly to be elected by universal suffrage and to serve for five years. The Assembly elects the executive President, who also serves for five years.

The last full elections to the new National Assembly took place in December 1992, following the death of President Phomvihane, in which 154 LPRP approved candidates contested the 85 seats. Nouhak Phoumsavanh was elected President by the Supreme People's Assembly in November 1992, itself made up of LPRP members.

The country's economy remains seriously affected by the lack of investment with which to repair the terrible damage inflicted by the wars of the 1960s. However, the Government hopes that the economy, which is run on the basis of a five-year plan scheme, will recover with the aid of its mineral revenues; with the stabilisation of the political situation, foreign investment might also be forthcoming.

Mongolia

Population ('000)	2,310 (1992)
Urban Population (%)	57.1 (1989)
Land Area (km²)	1,565,000
Language/s	Khalkha Mongolian, Kazakh
Religion/s	Buddhist

Currency	Tugruk (= 100 möngö)
Head of State	President Punsalmaagiyn Ochirbat (1990)
Head of Government	Puntsagiyn Jasray
Ruling Party	Mongolian People's Revolutionary Party

Main urban areas	**Population**
Ulan Bator (capital)	600,900

(1992 estimate)

Mongolia has achieved a significant transition from the single-party communist administration which characterised the country from 1945 to July 1990. Its semi-executive President and its Prime Minister answer to a Parliament comprising a 430-member People's Great Hural (Lower House) and a 169-seat Little Hural (meeting more frequently). Since the end of 1990 a concerted policy of democratisation has been in progress, and political reforms have been echoed by a radical economic restructuring.

Elections to the Great Hural were held in June 1992, when the ruling Mongolian People's Revolutionary Party, only recently converted from its former allegiance to communism, won 70 of the 76 seats on offer, despite winning only 56.9% of the vote - largely thanks to the first-past-the-post constituency system. The Mongolian Democratic Party, the Mongolian Party of National Progress and the Mongolian United Party put up an opposing coalition which won 17.5% of the vote but which secured only four seats: the remaining two seats went to the Social Democratic Party and to an independent MPRP member. Presidential elections were held in June 1993, when the incumbent Punsalmaagiyn Ochirbat won 57.8% of the vote, against 38.7% for Lodongiyn Tudev.

The opening of the economy in the wake of political reform has the capacity to transform the essentially undeveloped, commodity-based character of the country in the 1990s. However, transport links still need to be improved. A foreign investment law was passed in May 1993, and the tugruk was allowed to float freely for the first time.

Myanmar

Population ('000)	42,330 (1992)
Urban Population (%)	23.9 (1983)
Land Area (km²)	678,030
Language/s	Burmese; also Shan, Karen, Chin, Kayeh, Kachin, English
Religion/s	Mainly Buddhist (87%)
Currency	Kyat (= 100 pyas)
Head of State	President Suchinda Kraprayoon (April 1992)
Head of Government	Prime Minister Gen. Than Shwe
Ruling Party	Burmese Socialist Programme Party leads a five-party coalition

Main urban areas	**Population**
Rangoon (capital)	3,150,000
Mandalay	600,000

(1993 estimate)

Myanmar, or Burma as it was known until 1988, was run as a one-party socialist state until September 1988, when a military coup overthrew the administraton and declared martial law. A 485-member Constituent Assembly was formed in May 1990, but has been banned from meeting, although there were signs of a softening by late 1993. Serious guerrilla activities have been taking place along the Thai border, where ethnic insurgency remains a problem.

Multi-party elections were held in May 1990 to the newly created Constituent Assembly, and they were contested by some 93 different parties as well as 87 independents. The election produced a crushing defeat for the ruling junta, the State Law and Order Restoration Council, whose own favoured party, the

National Unity Party, polled less than 20% of the vote, compared with more than 50% for the opposition National League for Democracy; indeed, the NLD took 95% of the Rangoon seats. Shortly afterwards, the junta banned the new Assembly from meeting.

Myanmar's growing openness to the world has met with much scepticism from its neighbours, and its chances of escaping the UN's classification as one of the world's poorest countries - an ignominy in view of its natural resources - appear slim at present.

Vietnam

Population ('000)	69,480 (1992)
Urban Population (%)	19.9 (1988)
Land Area (km²)	329,565
Language/s	Vietnamese
Religion/s	Buddhist
Currency	New dông (= 10 hào = 100 xu)
Head of State	President Vo Chi Cong
Head of Government	Senior Gen. Vo Van Vliet
Ruling Party	Vietnamese Communist Party (VCP)

Main urban areas	**Population**
Hanoi (capital)	3,924,435
Ho Chi Minh City	3,056,146
Haiphong	1,447,523

(1989 census)

Vietnam's conversion to a capitalist economy has not, so far, been reflected in any abandonment of the Communist Party's hold on power. The country has a semi-executive President who has until recently been elected from single-candidate lists, and a 496-member National Assembly (now reduced to 395) which is formally vested with all legislative power. In practice, the VCP controls the armed forces and the judiciary.

The ninth National Assembly election was held in July 1992, when the VCP won all but two of the 395 seats: although non-communists had been allowed to stand, and although some 165 candidates did so, the system remained effectively stacked against them.

Vietnam's transition to the free market principle has come as a complete reversal of the centrally planned and interventionist, collectivist strategies of the last 50 years. In early 1993 it remained uncertain how much could be achieved without a serious upset to the continuing single-party state, however. There is substantial self-sufficiency, and as such all per capita income figures are inevitably no more than nominal under the circumstances. Yet many foreign observers expect to see massive growth in the national economy during the later 1990s.

Australasia

Australia

Population ('000)	17,530 (1992)
Urban Population (%)	85.4 (1986)
Land Area (km²)	7,682,300
Language/s	English
Religion/s	Mainly Christian
Currency	Australian dollar (A$ = 100 cents)
Head of State	HM Queen Elizabeth II
Head of Government	Paul Keating (1991)
Ruling Party	Australian Labor Party

Main urban areas	Population
Sydney	3,656,500
Melbourne	3,080,900
Brisbane	1,301,700
Perth/Fremantle	1,193,100
Adelaide	1,049,900
Newcastle	428,800
Canberra (capital)	310,100

(1990)

Australia is a federation of six states and two territories (Northern Territory and Capital Territory of Canberra), each of which exercises considerable autonomy over its own affairs. The country's central affairs are run by a Cabinet which answers to a 148-member House of Representatives, elected for a term of three years, and a 76-member Senate drawn from the various parliaments of the states and territories. The question of Australia's status in the Commonwealth, and the possibility of it becoming a republic, has recently been revived.

The ALP was narrowly returned to power in the last general elections to the House of Representatives, in March 1993; it won only 78 of the 146 seats, compared with 69 for a coalition of Liberals and Nationals.

Despite the apparently healthy spread of Australia's economy, it remains in deep recession in the early 1990s. Since the mid 1970s it has suffered a number of setbacks. First came the loss of its almost guaranteed markets in Britain, after that country's accession to the EC, then came the slump in world mineral prices, which was exacerbated by the government's failure to reduce public spending. By the mid-1980s, Finance Minister Paul Keating had to jolt the country out of complacency with talk of becoming a "banana republic"; since then, steep spending cuts and rising unemployment have characterised the economy.

New Zealand

Population ('000)	3,410 (1992)
Urban Population (%)	83.7 (1986)
Land Area (km^2)	265,150
Language/s	English
Religion/s	Mainly Christian (75%)
Currency	New Zealand dollar (NZ$ = 100 cents)
Head of State	HM Queen Elizabeth II
Head of Government	Jim Bolger (1990)
Ruling Party	New Zealand National Party

Main urban areas	Population
Auckland	855,377
Wellington (capital)	325,682

(1991 census)

New Zealand, an independent member of the Commonwealth, is ruled by the Crown acting through a Governor-General. Executive power is exercised by the Prime Minister, who is appointed by the unicameral House of Representatives (Parliament). The 97 members of the House are elected by universal suffrage for a term of three years.

In the general elections of October 1990 the NZ National Party won a landslide victory, winning 67 of the 97 seats even though it had obtained only 48% of the vote. The ruling Labour Party won only 29 seats, despite obtaining 35% of the vote, and the left-wing New Labour Party retained its single seat. New parliamentary elections were due to be held in November 1993.

The economy has had to withstand two major crises in 20 years: first the loss of a large part of the UK market in the 1970s and 1980s, and secondly the curtailment of government overspending in the early 1980s, which effectively enforced a 10-year austerity plan. As social spending has been squeezed, unemployment has reached high levels and consumer confidence is currently at a low ebb.

Pacific

American Samoa

Population ('000)	40 (1991)
Urban Population (%)	17.5 (1980)
Land Area (km^2)	197
Language/s	English, Samoan
Religion/s	Mainly Christian
Currency	US dollar (US$ = 100 cents)
Head of State	President Bill Clinton (1993)
Head of Government	Governor: A P Lutali (November 1992)
Ruling Party	None

Main urban areas	Population
Pago Pago (capital)	3,200

(1992 estimate)

American Samoa is an unincorporated territory of the United States, whose executive authority rests in the Governor, appointed for a four-year term. Legislative authority lies with the House of Representatives, part of which is elected every two years, as in the USA; however, the Senate (Upper House) is directly appointed by the island's tribal elders (Matai). One observer is sent to the US Congress in Washington. The US voted in 1986 to revise the country's Constitution, but the moves had not been ratified by Congress at mid-1993.

The last gubernatorial elections were held in November 1992, when A P Lutali ousted Peter Coleman, gaining 52.4% of the vote against the latter's 35.7%.

American Samoa remains, naturally, highly dependent on the United States, with which it enjoys tax advantages and some immunity from that country's often restrictive import regimes. A government scheme is in place to encourage further foreign investment. Yet the heavy dependence on US aid is a problem in a period when Washington is withdrawing its defence activities in the Pacific region.

Fiji

Population ('000)	740 (1992)
Urban Population (%)	38.7 (1987)
Land Area (km^2)	18,330
Language/s	Fijian, Hindi, English
Religion/s	Christian (53%), Hindu (38%), Muslim (8%)
Currency	Fiji dollar (F$ = 100 cents)
Head of State	President Ratu Sir Penaia Ganilau (1987)
Head of Government	Maj.-Gen. Sitiveni Rabuka
Ruling Party	Sokosoko ni Vakavulewa ni Taukei (Fijian Political Party) leads a coalition with the Fijian Nationalist Party.

Main urban areas	Population
Suva (capital)	75,000

(1992 estimate)

Fiji left the Commonwealth in 1987 after two successive coups in which ethnic Fijians asserted their precedence over the ethnic Chinese and Indians who were effectively running the country at the time. The new Constitution, approved in July 1990, reserves an automatic majority in the House of Representatives (Lower House of Parliament) for ethnic Fijians.

The first elections since the military coups of 1987 were held in May 1992, when the Fijian Political Party, led by the coup leader Maj.-Gen. Sitiveni Rabuka, won 30 of the 37 Fijian seats in the new 70-member House of Representatives. The Fijian Nationalist United Front, a more moderate party advocating the same policies as the FPP, won another five seats, and the Fijian Labour Party won two. The FLP also won 13 of the 27 Indian seats in the House, compared with 14 for the National Federation Party. The General Voters' Party won all five of the seats reserved for Chinese, Europeans and others.

Fiji remains to some extent on trial in the aftermath of the racially motivated coup of the mid-1980s, and as such the country has received only modest international help. However, its domestic economy is in fair shape, and its central role at the hub of the Pacific Islands communications network has inevitably ensured that it remains a country to be courted by its neighbours.

French Polynesia

Population ('000)	210 (1992)
Land Area (km²)	3,940
Language/s	French
Religion/s	Mainly Christian (55%)
Currency	Franc CFP (= 100 centimes)
Head of State	President François Mitterrand (France)
Head of Government	Gaston Flosse (1991)
Ruling Party	Tahoeraa Huiraatira/Rassemblement pour la République leads a coalition with Pupu Here Ai'a Te Nunaa Ia Ora.

Main urban areas	Population
Papeete (capital)	26,000

(1992 estimate)

French Polynesia is one of the four French Overseas Territories, which do not enjoy full département status but which are regarded as an integral part of France. As such, most important decisions are taken in France rather than locally. The 41-member Territorial Assembly is elected by universal suffrage for a term of four or sometimes five years, and it elects its own representatives to the National Assembly in Paris. Executive power is wielded locally by the President of the Territorial Government, who approximates to a Prime Minister.

In the legislative elections of March 1991, the Tahoeraa Huiraatira of Gaston Flosse won 18 of the 41 parliamentary seats and formed a coalition with the small Ai'a Api. But after violent protests over economic reforms Ai'a Api quit the government, whereupon Flosse joined up with the Ai'a Te Nunaa La Ora, giving him 23 seats in all. The incumbent Government of Alexandre Lentieff, Te Tiamara, secured only 14 seats, while the hardline independence party Tavini Huiraatira held four.

Although the economy remains centred on its foreign activities, the Government is trying to promote the domestic economy with a range of incentives aimed at making the country more self-sufficient in the medium term.

Guam

Population ('000)	140 (1992)
Urban Population (%)	39.5 (1980)
Land Area (km²)	450
Language/s	Chamorro, English
Religion/s	Mainly Roman Catholic (89%)
Currency	US dollar (US$ = 100 cents)
Head of State	President Bill Clinton (USA)
Head of Government	Joseph F. Ada (Governor)
Ruling Party	Democratic Party

Main urban areas	Population
Agaña (capital)	4,000

(1992 census)

Guam's status as a US unincorporated territory is currently under review in the light of the general US withdrawal from the Pacific region. A referendum in 1982 produced a majority in favour of commonwealth status, but since then opinion has shifted back toward the status quo. The Guam authorities are particularly anxious to acquire a right of veto over the extraterritorial application of US law. The Governor is elected every four years and the Legislature for two years. Guam also elects one non-voting delegate to the US Congress.

Elections to the Guam Legislature are held every two years, and the election system mirrors that in the United States. In the November 1992 elections the Democrats won 14 of the 21 seats while the Republicans won 7. In the same month Governor Joseph F. Ada was re-elected to the Governorship.

Guam's economy remains basically dependent on the United States, despite the tourism inflows from Japan and other parts of the region. The Government is attempting to encourage foreign investment with a range of incentives aimed at widening the economic base.

Kiribati

Population ('000)	70 (1992)
Land Area (km²)	684
Language/s	I-Kiribati, English
Religion/s	Mainly Christian
Currency	Australian dollar (A$ = 100 cents)
Head of State	President Teatao Teannaki (1991)
Head of Government	President Teatao Teannaki
Ruling Party	National Progressive Party

Main urban areas	Population
Bairiki (capital)	25,300
	(1992)

Kiribati (pronounced Kiribass) is an independent republic within the Commonwealth, whose executive President (Beretitenti) is popularly elected from among the members of the House of Assembly (Maneaba). The House, a unicameral parliament, has 40 members of whom one is an appointed representative of the Banaban community: the others are all elected by universal suffrage for a period of up to four years - although the President may dissolve Parliament at any time and order fresh elections.

Elections to the 39 elected seats in the House of Assembly were held in May 1991, when the National Progressive Party scored a substantial win over the Christian Democratic Party and the Kiribati United Party. Afterwards one Cabinet minister was stripped of his seat for vote buying.

With its domestic economy slumping and with little sense of political direction which might effect a turnaround, Kiribati's economy is likely to remain heavily dependent on aid from the United Kingdom and New Zealand, and on investment from Australia. An approach has been made by Japan to use Christmas Island as a launch site for space projects.

Nauru

Population ('000)	9 (1989)
Land Area (km²)	21
Language/s	Nauruan, English
Religion/s	Nauruan Protestant Church
Currency	Australian dollar (A$=100 cents)
Head of State	President Bernard Dowiyogo (1989)
Head of Government	President Bernard Dowiyogo
Ruling Party	The Democratic Party of Nauru is the only legal political party.

Main urban areas	Population
Yaren District (capital)	6,000

The Republic of Nauru is an associate member of the Commonwealth, in which the executive President governs with the aid of a Cabinet whose number may not exceed six people. The President is elected for a period of three years from the 18-member unicameral Parliament, which is also elected, by universal suffrage, for a period of three years. Voting is compulsory in all elections.

General elections were held in December 1989, in the course of which the Democratic Party was opposed only by independents. Bernard Dowiyogo was chosen as President shortly afterwards, to be replaced the following year by Kenas Aroi.

Nauru's economy remains extremely weak at present, and its dependence on Australia is still growing. It has started to establish itself as an offshore financial centre, but a major financial scandal in 1993 has set the economy back.

New Caledonia

Population ('000)	170 (1992)
Urban Population (%)	59.4 (1989)
Land Area (km²)	19,105
Language/s	French
Religion/s	Mainly Roman Catholic (60%)
Currency	Franc CFP (= 100 centimes)
Head of State	President François Mitterrand (France)
Head of Government	Alain Christnacht
Ruling Party	Rassemblement pour la République

Main urban areas	Population
Nouméa (capital)	65,110

(1989)

New Caledonia is an external department of France and is governed to a considerable degree from Paris. The country sends deputies to the French Assemblée Nationale, and is represented at the European Community. Since being accorded regional status in 1974, however, the country elects its own Regional Council for a term of six years, with responsibility for economic and social planning. A referendum was held in 1987 on whether to declare independence, but the vote was boycotted by the Kanak majority and came out against the move.

The last full elections were to the French Assemblée Nationale in 1988, in which both seats were won by the Rassemblement pour la République.

At present New Caledonia's economy is run as an integral part of the French economy, an arrangement which has not always proved satisfactory to the local population. The fall in revenues, however, has led to demands for more aid from France.

Papua New Guinea

Population ('000)	4,060 (1992)
Urban Population (%)	13.1 (1980)
Land Area (km²)	462,840
Language/s	Pidgin, English, Motu; more than 700 native languages
Religion/s	Mainly Christian (93%)
Currency	Kina (K = 100 toea)
Head of State	HM Queen Elizabeth II
Head of Government	Paias Wingti (July 1992)
Ruling Party	People's Democratic Movement leads a multi-party coalition

Main urban areas	Population
Port Moresby (capital)	147,000

(1992 estimate)

Papua New Guinea, a member of the British Commonwealth, has a Governor-General who represents the Queen; however, executive power is exercised by a Prime Minister and a National Executive Council, who are appointed by the Governor on the advice of the unicameral National Parliament. The 109 members are elected by universal suffrage for a period of not more than five years. Papua New Guinea receives both military support and economic assistance from Australia.

In the parliamentary elections of June 1992, Pangu Pati won 22 of the 109 seats, while the People's Democratic Movement of Paias Wingti won 15, the People's Action Party 13, the People's Progress Party 10, the Melanesian Alliance nine, the League of National Advancement five, the National Party two and the Melanesian United Front one. There were also 31 independent seats, and one remained unoccupied.

Papua New Guinea's economy is broadly based and yet still vulnerable to large external shocks. The country's topography presents structural hurdles in the way of communications, and its considerable level of external debt is a problem. High wage rates for civil servants are a political problem which the Government has yet to deal with effectively.

Solomon Islands

Population ('000)	340 (1992)
Land Area (km²)	29,790
Language/s	English, Pidgin
Religion/s	Mainly Christian (95%)
Currency	Solomon Island dollar (SI$ = 100 cents)
Head of State	HM Queen Elizabeth II
Head of Government	Frances Billy Hilly (June 1993)
Ruling Party	A national coalition of non-National Union parties

Main urban areas	Population
Honiara (capital)	37,000

(1992 estimate)

The Solomon Islands are an independent member of the Commonwealth, in which the Crown is represented by a Governor-General. Legislative authority is vested in the 47-member unicameral Parliament, which is elected by universal adult suffrage for a term of up to four years. The Prime Minister is elected from among the Parliament's members, by secret ballot. Since 1990 the political scene has moved away from party lines and has instead drifted back toward the personal influence of tribal and other figures as the main centres of political opinion.

In the May 1993 elections to the National Parliament, the Group for National Unity and Reconciliation won 21 of the 38 seats while the People's Alliance Party won 7 seats, the National Action Party 5 seats, the Labour Party 4 seats, the United Party 4 seats and independents 6 seats.

The Solomon Islands economy made only slow growth until the 1980s, thanks to the country's relatively remote geograhical location and its limited infrastructure. The traditionalistic political system almost dictated that opportunities for new development would be only slowly taken up, if at all, and in the event the country has shown little inclination to change. Per capita incomes, at around $500 per annum, are nevertheless close to the level in the Philippines or Indonesia.

Tonga

Population ('000)	100 (1992)
Urban Population (%)	30.7 (1986)
Land Area (km²)	699
Language/s	Tongan, English
Religion/s	Mainly Christian (Wesleyan)
Currency	Pa'anga (T$ = 100 seniti)
Head of State	HM King Taufa'ahau Tupou IV
Head of Government	Baron Vaea
Ruling Party	There are no official political parties in Tonga at present, although unofficial groupings exist

Main urban areas	Population
Nuku'alofa (capital)	28,500

(1992 estimate)

The Kingdom of Tonga is a constitutional monarchy and an independent member of the Commonwealth, in which the King exercises full executive powers. He is assisted by a 10-member Privy Council, or Cabinet, and legislative powers are held by a 30-member unicameral Legislative Assembly. Apart from the King, the Privy Council and nine hereditary nobles, the Assembly includes nine members who are elected by universal adult suffrage for a term of only three years. A bitter debate is currently raging about the need for constitutional reform.

Elections to the nine elected seats in the National Assembly were held in February 1993, when members of the pro-democracy movement won six seats. But the dissident politicians Akalisi Pohive and Laki Niu, the leaders of the unofficial People's Party, were effectively outweighed by the heavy parliamentary weighting in favour of hereditary and nominated members,so little change was expected.

Tonga's political uncertainties come at a time when the economy is actually starting to grow, albeit hesitantly. The economy remains primitive and undiversified, however, and there is little likelihood of rapid change.

Tuvalu

Population ('000)	8 (1985)
Land Area (km²)	25
Language/s	Tuvaluan, English
Religion/s	Protestant (98%)
Currency	Australian dollar (A$ = 100 cents)
Head of State	HM Queen Elizabeth II
Head of Government	Bikenibeu Paeniu
Ruling Party	There are no political parties in Tuvalu

Main urban areas	Population
Funafuti (capital)	2,860

(1992 estimate)

Tuvalu, an independent special member of the Commonwealth since 1978, is formally ruled by the British monarch acting through a Governor-General. In practice, all executive power is exercised by a Prime Minister and Cabinet who are elected from among the 12 members of the unicameral Parliament. The Parliament in turn is elected by universal adult suffrage for a term of up to four years.

General elections were held in September 1989, in which the supporters of Tomasi Puapua, the Prime Minister since 1981, were routed by the supporters of Bikenibeu Paeniu, who thereupon became Premier.

Tuvalu's economy remains in a depressed state at present, with little immediate incentive for new growth as the traditional activities lose ground. The country is heavily dependent on foreign assistance.

Vanuatu

Population ('000)	160 (1992)
Urban Population (%)	18.2 (1989)
Land Area (km²)	14,765
Language/s	Bislama (pidgin), English, French
Religion/s	Mainly Christian
Currency	Vatu (V = 100 centimes)
Head of State	President Frederick Karlomuana Timakata (1989)
Head of Government	Maxime Carlot
Ruling Party	Union of Moderate Parties (UMP) rules with the support of the Vanuatu National United Party (VNUP)

Main urban areas	Population
Port Vila (capital)	20,000

(1992 estimate)

The Republic of Vanuatu is an independent member of the Commonwealth, in which the executive President is elected for a five-year term by an electoral college on which not only the Parliament but also the presidents of the numerous Regional Councils serve. These Councils enjoy a considerable degree of regional autonomy.The 46 members of the unicameral national Parliament are elected by universal adult suffrage for a four-year term.

Elections were held in December 1991 to the Parliament, in which the administration of Walter Lini was overturned as the UMP won 19 of the 46 seats. Lini's Vanua'aku Pati, which had governed since independence, had been split in September 1991 after his forced removal from the Premiership, after which he decided to launch his own party, the Vanuatu National United Party; in the event, each won 10 seats. The Melanesian Progressive Party won four seats, the Fren Melanesia won one and independents won two seats. Afterwards, the VNUP agreed to support the UMP.

Although far from poor by the standards of the region, Vanuatu has seen little growth in its economy during recent years and is looking to the services sector for new directions.

Western Samoa

Population ('000)	160 (1992)
Urban Population (%)	21.2 (1981)
Land Area (km²)	2,840
Language/s	Samoan, English
Religion/s	Mainly Christian
Currency	Tala (W$ - 100 sene)
Head of State	HH King Susuga Malietoa Tanumafili II
Head of Government	Tofilau eti Alesana
Ruling Party	Human Rights Protection Party

Main urban areas	Population
Apia (capital)	37,000

(1992 estimate)

Western Samoa, an independent member of the Commonwealth, has a constitutional monarch who may dissolve the 47-member Fono (Parliament) at any time and who appoints the Prime Minister on the recommendation of the Fono. A system of full universal voting was introduced in December 1990, prior to the country's first fully franchised elections.

During the general election of April 1991, the ruling Human Rights Protection Party of Tofilau eti Alesana was returned with 30 of the 47 seats in the Fono, while the Samoan National Development Party obtained 16 and the remaining seat went to an independent. Elections for two additional seats were won by the HRPP in early 1992.

With a per capita income of around $600, Western Samoa

represents only a small consumer market. At present the economy centres firmly on agriculture, but the Government is trying to encourage a diversification into other sectors.

Middle East

Bahrain

Population ('000)	530 (1992)
Urban Population (%)	80.7 (1981)
Land Area (km²)	661
Language/s	Arabic
Religion/s	Islam
Currency	Bahraini dinar (BD = 1000 fils)
Head of State	HH Shaikh Isa bin Sulman Al Khalifa
Head of Government	HE Shaikh Khalifa bin Sulman Al Khalifa
Ruling Party	There are no political parties in Bahrain

Main urban areas	Population
Manama (capital)	142,500
	(1992)

Bahrain is an absolute monarchy in which traditional consultative procedures, involving senior figures in the tribal hierarchy, are preferred to a formal parliamentary system as such. Despite Bahrain's relatively liberal attitudes in other respects, there are no moves at present toward any constitutional change which might affect this situation.

Theoretically, Bahrain's 1973 Constitution provides for a 30-member National Assembly elected by popular mandate; however, there have been no elections in Bahrain since the Assembly was forcibly dissolved in 1975, allegedly for interfering with the system of government. The possibility of restoring a multi-party system remains under discussion.

Bahrain's economy has been broadening in scope since the early 1980s, when the original decision was taken to move away from the country's heavy dependence on oil activities. Yet the diversification has not been without problems, and growing pressure from within the Arab world may put an end to Bahrain's bid to become the liberal society of the Middle East.

Egypt

Population ('000)	55,160 (1992)
Urban Population (%)	43.9 (1991)
Land Area (km²)	997,739
Language/s	Arabic
Religion/s	Mainly Islam (80%)
Currency	Egyptian pound (£E = 100 piastres)
Head of State	President Muhammad Hosni Mubarak (1981)
Head of Government	Dr Atef Mohamed Naguib Sidki
Ruling Party	National Democratic Party

Main urban areas	Population
Cairo (capital)	8,000,000
Alexandria	4,000,000
Giza	2,100,000
Shoubra el-Kheima	900,000
	(1992 estimate)

Egypt's 1972 Constitution provides for an executive President who answers to a unicameral People's Assembly with 454 members, 10 of whom he appoints personally. The People's Assembly, which is elected by universal suffrage for a term of five years, then elects the President for a six-year term. There is also a 210-member Consultative Council (Majlis as-Shoura), 140 of whose members are elected with the other 70 appointed by the President.

The National Democratic Party won a sweeping victory in the last general elections to the People's Assembly, in November-December 1990, with 348 of the 444 elected seats. Independent candidates won 83 seats. However, the validity of the election was compromised by the boycott imposed by the three largest opposition parties. Only about 30% of the electorate voted. President Mubarak personally appointed another 10 delegates to the Assembly.

Egypt's economy has been successfully diversified away from the dependence on oil and agriculture which typifies many of its neighbours. Its strategic position on the Red Sea, and especially its positive relationship with Saudi Arabia, will help to ensure that its economic influence in the region remains impossible to overlook.

Iran

Population ('000)	59,920 (1992)
Urban Population (%)	54.3 (1986)
Land Area (km²)	1,648,000
Language/s	Farsi
Religion/s	Islam
Currency	Iranian rial (R = 100 dinars)
Head of State	President Ali Akhbar Rafsanjani (1989)
Head of Government	President Ali Akhbar Rafsanjani
Ruling Party	There are no officially recognized political parties.

Main urban areas	Population
Tehran (capital)	6,042,584
Meshed	1,463,508
Isfahan	986,753
Tabriz	971,482
Shiraz	848,289
Ahwaz	579,826
Bakhtaran	560,514
Qom	543,139
	(1986 census)

Modern Iran has its foundations in the Islamic revolution of 1979/1980, when the religious supporters of Ayatollah Ruhollah Khomeini overcame and ousted the rule of Shah Reza Pahlavi. The last legal political party, the Islamic Republican Party, was disbanded in 1987, at which point religion became the main political criterion. Under the new system, political power rests loosely in the clerical and religious hierarchy; the religious crackdowns in 1993 have been seen as evidence of armed forces, however, play a much smaller role than in the 1980s.

The last elections to the Majlis (Parliament) took place in April and May 1992, when it was extended to 268 members. Of these, more than 70% represented the Rafsanjani faction, which accounted for all candidates in the Tehran area. The Secretary-General of the Council of Guardians reported afterwards that 80% of those presenting themselves for election had been disqualified in the pre-election religious screening. Presidential elections took place in June 1993, when Rafsanjani was confirmed in office was a smaller majority of 63% of the vote, compared with 23.8% for Ahmed Tavakkoli.

In the early 1990s Iran made vigorous efforts to improve its relations with the pro-Western elements in the Middle East, marking a major change of direction after the Islamic fundamentalism and vigorous anti-US sentiment of the 1980s. Yet a serious deterioration in the economic climate during 1993 was accompanied by a revival of anti-Western sentiment. Inflation has been very high in recent months, and in March 1993 the currency was devalued by 95.6% in an effort to regain the country's export markets.

Iraq

Population ('000)	19,290 (1992)
Urban Population (%)	69.9 (1990)
Land Area (km²)	438,445
Language/s	Arabic, English
Religion/s	Mainly Islam (95%)
Currency	Iraqi dinar (ID = 100 fils)
Head of State	President Saddam Hussein (1979)
Head of Government	Mohammed Hamzah Al-Subaydi
Ruling Party	Arab Ba'ath Socialist Party

Main urban areas	Population
Baghdad (capital)	4,698,600
Basrah	1,540,000
Mosul	570,926
Kirkuk	535,000

(1987 estimates)

The overthrow of the monarchy in 1958 led to the creation of a republic which in turn has been heavily dominated since the late 1970s by Saddam Hussein. Hussein, who has been chief of the armed forces for most of this time, was also Prime Minister from 1979 to March 1991. The President is elected by the Revolutionary Command Council from among its members, and appoints the Cabinet. The RCC shares legislative powers with the 250-member National Assembly, which is elected by universal suffrage for a term of five years.

There have been no national elections in recent years. The Kurdish minority, however, held their own (officially unrecognised) elections to the (equally unrecognised) 105-member Iraqi Kurdistan National Assembly in May 1992, when the Kurdistan Democratic Party and the Patriotic Union of Kurdistan each obtained 50 seats. The remaining five seats were reserved for Christian Assyrians.

The international isolation of the economy has failed to deliver the body blow which many hoped the sanctions would produce. This is largely due to the high degree of self-sufficiency in the agricultural economy, and the developed nature of the construction business; it is also due, however, to the country's continuing ability to buy products in breach of sanctions.

Israel

Population ('000)	5,190 (1992)
Urban Population (%)	90.0 (1990)
Land Area (km²)	20,770
Language/s	Hebrew, Arabic
Religion/s	Jewish (82%)
Currency	New shekel (NIS = 100 agorot)
Head of State	President Ezer Weizmann (May 1993)
Head of Government	Itzhak Rabin
Ruling Party	Labour Party leads a Left Bloc alliance

Main urban areas	Population
Jerusalem (capital)	524,500

(1992 estimate)

The territory of Israel was created in 1948 through the concerted efforts of Western governments to find a homeland for the displaced Jewish people. It was carved out of mainly Palestinian-owned land, and was effectively extended after the 1967 war to include the West Bank territory, including East Jerusalem (formerly in Jordan). Since 1987 the Palestinian residents of the West Bank have been engaged in a campaign of disruption and non-co-operation. Israel has an non-executive President; the Knesset (Parliament) has 120 members. A historic agreement was reached in October 1993 on the creation of an autonomous region within the occupied territories taken from Jordan in the 1967 war. The decision marks a particularly significant departure because hitherto Israel has refused to recognise the Palestinian Liberation Organisation, and the PLO had refused to recognise the state of Israel.

Elections to the 120-member Knesset (Lower House of Parliament) in June 1992 resulted in a win for the Left Bloc, comprising the Labour Party (44 seats), the Meretz (12 seats), Hadash (3 seats) and Arab Democratic Party (2 seats), although the Progressive List for Peace lost its only seat. The Right Bloc led by Itzhak Shamir thus lost its majority - its Likud Party having obtained 43 votes while the Tsomet obtained 8 seats, Moledet 3 and Tehit none. Of the right-wing religious groups the Shas party obtained 6 seats, the National Religious Party 6 and United Tora Judaism 4 seats. Presidential elections were held in March 1993, when Ezer Weizmann was appointed by a large majority.

Despite its general commitment to free trade and free enterprise, Israel's economy actually retains many of the collectivist hallmarks of its Government's historical predecessors, in its nationalised industries and its comprehensive social care systems - excluding the West Bank. However, the country's perennial trade deficit, and its soaring inflation, have created pressures which have worsened since the arrival of thousands of refugees from Eastern Europe in the early 1990s.

Jordan

Population ('000)	4,290 (1992)
Urban Population (%)	59.4 (1979)
Land Area (km²)	90,650
Language/s	Arabic
Religion/s	Mainly Islam (90%)
Currency	Jordanian dinar (JD = 1,000 fils)
Head of State	King Hussein ibn Talal
Head of Government	Abdul Salam Majali (1993)
Ruling Party	The Parliamentary Arab-Islamic Coalition Front, a coalition of Islamic groups and nationalists

Main urban areas	Population
Amman (capital)	1,213,300
Zarqa	514,980

(1990, excluding refugees)

Jordan is a constitutional monarchy in which the King nevertheless plays an active role. The country has an 80-member House of Representatives, reduced substantially from the 142 delegates in the former assembly; but in practice,the country was effectively ruled by the armed forces for many years. Indeed, it was only in April 1992 that the last of the martial law provisions imposed in the aftermath of the 1967 war with Israel were removed - most of them having remained in force until July 1991. Political parties were legalised in July 1992. Jordan will be affected by the agreement of October 1993 where Israel will allow the principle of a Palestinian autonomous region within the former occupied territories taken from Jordan in the 1967 war. The country is expected to play a role in advising the new administration.

The first elections to the House of Representatives for 22 years were held in November 1989, when the Muslim Brotherhood won 20 of the 80 seats, with 14 seats going to related Islamic groups, and with all others going to independents. In August 1993 King Hussein announced changes to the electoral law permitting the country's first multi-party elections to take place in November 1993.

Jordan's economy is in a weak state at present, thanks in part to the loss of some Iraqi business. Although still rooted in collectivism, the Government has attempted to encourage the private sector in recent years.

Kuwait

Population ('000)	1,970 (1992)
Land Area (km²)	24,280
Language/s	Arabic, English
Religion/s	Mainly Islam
Currency	Kuwaiti dinar (= 10 dirhams)
Head of State	Amir: HH Shaikh Jabir Al Ahmad As Sabah
Head of Government	HH Shaikh Saad Al Abdullah
Ruling Party	There are no political parties in Kuwait

Main urban areas	**Population**
Kuwait City (capital)	44,335

(1985 census)

Kuwait became an independent state in 1961, having been a British protectorate since 1899. The Amir exercises almost complete political control: in 1986 he dissolved the National Assembly (Parliament), and ruled by decree for some years thereafter. Yet the growing pressure for political reform was overtaken by the Iraqi invasion of August 1990, and by the ensuing Gulf War in which Iraq was finally driven out by allied forces. In April 1991, after the liberation, the Amir appointed an interim government and announced the October 1992 elections.

The first elections to the 50-seat National Assembly were held in October 1992, when Islamic candidates obtained about 18 seats, with another 12 going to liberal opposition figures. Candidates for the Government won 30 seats, and as such were expected to dominate the new Assembly.

The country's economic reconstruction after the chaos inflicted by Iraq was close to completion by 1993, following massive investment by Kuwait and by Saudi Arabia. The construction industry has been a major beneficiary.

Lebanon

Population ('000)	2,840 (1992)
Urban Population (%)	83.4 (1985)
Land Area (km²)	10,400
Language/s	Arabic, French , English
Religion/s	Muslim, Christian, Jewish
Currency	Lebanese pound (£L = 100 piastres)
Head of State	President Elias Hrawi (1989)
Head of Government	Rafiq al-Hariri
Ruling Party	Parti socialiste progressiste leads a coalition

Main urban areas	**Population**
Beirut (capital)	702,000

(1983)

The electoral system has been only recently restored, having been effectively in abeyance since 1979; in the interim, the National Assembly was kept going by continually voting to extend its term of office, and at present it is due to sit until the end of 1994. It was, however, expanded in 1990 and 1992 from 60 to 128 members. In September 1993 it remained to be seen how the executive President could assimilate the Islamic extremist factions now sitting in the Parliament. Early indications were that the Islamic Hizbollah guerrillas, who attracted a heavy bombardment of southern Lebanon from Israeli forces in the summer of 1993, would remain problematic.

The first parliamentary elections since 1972 started in August 1992, and produced a strong vote for the Parti socialiste progressiste; yet the Islamic militant organisation Hezbollah, which favoured strong links with Syria and which was participating for the first time, also fared well. The results were called into question firstly by the boycott imposed by Maronite Christian groups, and secondly by the non-participation of the powerful Phalangist Party.

As the country attempts to repair the shattering damage of the civil war, it will rely on support from Syria, Iran and other neighbouring states. The restoration of political calm is likely to be a contributory factor; however, the role and the interests of Israel will continue to be vital.

Oman

Population ('000)	1,640 (1992)
Land Area (km²)	271,950
Language/s	Arabic, English
Religion/s	Islam
Currency	Omani rial (OR = 1000 baiza)
Head of State	Sultan Qaboos Bin-Said (1970)
Head of Government	Sultan Qaboos Bin-Said
Ruling Party	There are no legal political parties in Oman

Main urban areas	**Population**
Muscat (capital)	350,000

(1992 estimate)

The Sultanate of Oman is ruled by decree by the Sultan, Qaboos Bin-Said, who deposed his father in the coup of 1970. The Sultan is also Prime Minister, and is advised by a Cabinet which he appoints. Since November 1991 there has also been a State Consultative Council, whose members are chosen by the Sultan from three-candidate lists drawn up by each of the various regions. Although the Council has no powers whatever, its introduction was seen as a move toward greater democratisation. Oman favours tighter co-operation in the Gulf region.

There are no elections in Oman at present, although the prospect of non-party polls has been discussed at some point in the future.

The country's dependence on the oil sector has been reduced to some extent by government action in the 1980s and early 1990s, with encouragement for foreign investment. However, the mood remains quiet in view of the global downturn in oil prices.

Qatar

Population ('000)	450 (1992)
Land Area (km²)	11,435
Language/s	Arabic, English
Religion/s	Islam
Currency	Qatar riyal (QR = 100 dirhams)
Head of State	HH Shaikh Khalifa bin Hamad al Thani (1972)
Head of Government	HH Shaikh Khalifa bin Hamad al Thani
Ruling Party	There are no political parties in Qatar

Main urban areas	**Population**
Doha (capital)	243,000

(1992 stimate)

Under the president system Qatar is ruled exclusively by the Amir and by his immediate family. In recent years, however, there have been growing calls for a democratisation of the country: in January 1992 the Amir rejected a call by 50 leading public figures demanding the establishment of a consultative and legislative assembly of the type already approved in Kuwait. There have been allegations that abuses of power are taking place.

There are no elections in Qatar.

Qatar's economy made enormous strides during the 1970s and 1980s, thanks to the exploitation of its oil and later its gas fields. Yet since the late 1980s the fall-off in world oil prices has forced a reduction in its investment and in its spending power. Qatar is an active member of the Gulf Co-operation Council.

Saudi Arabia

Population ('000)	15,920 (1992)
Urban Population (%)	72.4 (1985)
Land Area (km²)	2,400,900
Language/s	Arabic
Religion/s	Islam
Currency	Saudi riyal (SR = 20 qursh = 100 halalas)
Head of State	HM King Fahd ibn Abdul Aziz (1982)
Head of Government	HM King Fahd ibn Abdul Aziz
Ruling Party	There are no political parties in Saudi Arabia

Main urban areas	Population
Riyadh (capital)	2,000,000
Jeddah	1,500,000
Makkah	800,000

(1992 estimate)

Saudi Arabia is an absolute monarchy in which the majority of senior government posts are filled by members of the royal family. Technically, it has no constitution except for the Koran, reflecting its official role as keeper of the shrines of Makkah and Medina. Saudi Arabia is a Sunni state. Representation takes place primarily through personal petitions to royal figures, but royal audiences are held almost daily. Moves are under way to develop a new constitution, including a 60-member Consultative Council.
There are no general elections in Saudi Arabia.
Saudi Arabia's economy boomed in the 1970s, as rising oil prices produced an opportunity for major expansion. In the process, several new industrial zones were set up at Jeddah, Jebel Ali and elsewhere. Since then, however, the contraction of the oil market has left the Government in perennial deficit, although the country's trade position remains satisfactory.

Syria

Population ('000)	12,960 (1992)
Urban Population (%)	50.2 (1990)
Land Area (km²)	185,680
Language/s	Arabic; also Kurdish, Turkish, Aramaic
Religion/s	Mainly Muslim
Currency	Syrian pound (£Syr = 100 piastres)
Head of State	President Hafez al Assad (1971)
Head of Government	Mahmoud Zubi
Ruling Party	Ba'ath Party leads the National Progressive Front coalition

Main urban areas	Population
Damascus (capital)	1,500,000
Aleppo	1,390,000
Homs	500,000

(1992 estimate)

The Socialist Popular Democracy of Syria, as its 1973 Constitution styles it, has an executive President who is formally re-elected by universal suffrage every seven years. In principle, the President answers to a People's Assembly, whose 250 members are elected for four years. In practice, however, the Alawite group around President Assad has dominated Syrian politics since he seized power in 1970, and most decisions are taken by the ruling Ba'ath Arab Socialist Renaissance party.
The last elections to the Majlis (Parliament) took place in May 1990, when the Ba'ath Party won 134 of the 250 seats and went on to form a coalition with the other parties of the Progressive National Front, which had won 32 seats. Independents won 84 seats. President Assad was sworn in again in March 1992, after being approved in an uncontested national referendum.
Syria's economy does not share the advantages of most other Arab countries: it has only small amounts of oil, and relies mainly on farming for its livelihood. Nevertheless, incomes have been fairly steady in recent years, and should improve following the country's successful withdrawal from Lebanon after its peacemaking efforts in that country.

United Arab Emirates

Population ('000)	1,670 (1992)
Land Area (km²)	75,150
Language/s	Arabic, English
Religion/s	Muslim
Currency	UAE dirham (= 100 fils)
Head of State	Shaikh Zaid bin Sultan al-Nahayyan (President)
Head of Government	Shaikh Maktoum bin Rashid al-Maktoum
Ruling Party	There are no legal political parties in the United Arab Emirates.

Main urban areas	Population
Abu Dhabi	460,000

(1992 estimate)

The United Arab Emirates is a federation of seven Emirates (Abu Dhabi, Dubai, Sharjah, Ras al-Khaimah, Fujairah, Umm al-Qaiwain and Ajman), each of which is a monarchy in its own right. The seven monarchs together comprise the Supreme Council, and elect the President and Vice-President from among their members; the President then appoints his Cabinet. The 40-member Federal National Council is appointed indirectly by the seven Emirates. Different laws apply in the various Emirates: for example, Sharjah but not Dubai has a ban on alcohol.
There have been no elections to any of the UAE's bodies in recent decades.
With a per capita income of more than $20,000, the United Arab Emirates ranks among the richest states in the Middle East. Its access to a variety of sea routes has proved strategically convenient during hostilities in the Gulf region, so that it has proved immune to many setbacks.

Yemen

Population ('000)	12,530 (1992)
Urban Population (%)	52.7 (1980)
Land Area (km²)	527,968
Language/s	Arabic
Religion/s	Islam
Currency	Yemeni riyal (= 100 fils)
Head of State	President Ali Abdullah Saleh (1990)
Head of Government	Haider Abu Bakr al-Attas (May 1993)
Ruling Party	Coalition of the General People's Congress, the Yemeni Islah Party and the Yemen Socialist Party

Main urban areas	Population
Sana'a (capital)	500,000

(1992 estimate)

The Republic of Yemen was formed in May 1990 by the union of the Yemen Arab Republic (North Yemen) with the People's Democratic Republic of Yemen (South Yemen). The North Yemeni President, Lt.-Gen. Ali Abdullah Saleh, became national President, and a transitional government was formed. The unified House of Representatives comprises 301 members, and a 45-member Advisory Council supports the executive President and his Cabinet.
Elections were held for the first time in April 1993, when the General People's Congress won 121 of the 301 seats in the House of Representatives, the Yemen Alliance for Reform won 62 and the Yemen Socialist Party 56 seats. The Arab Socialist Ba'ath Party (the old communist administration) won 7 seats,

independents took 47 seats, and other parties obtained 8 seats. The country has a moderately diversified economy, with oil revenues, farming production and entrepôt and transhipment fees all contributing to the general wealth. However, incomes are still low - about half of the average in Syria, for example.

North Africa

Algeria

Population ('000)	26,350 (1992)
Urban Population (%)	45.3 (1991)
Land Area (km²)	2,381,745
Language/s	Arabic (official), French
Religion/s	Islam
Currency	Algerian dinar (= 100 centimes)
Head of State	President Ali Kafi (June 1992)
Head of Government	Abdesselam Belaid (July 1992)
Ruling Party	A five-member High Council of State (HCE) has replaced the former coalition and rules by decree under an indefinite state of emergency.

Main urban areas	Population
Algiers (capital)	1,690,000
Oran	690,000

(1992 estimate)

Algeria has an executive presidency which is technically answerable to an elected parliament (Majlis). However, considerable unrest has been occurring since the virtual collapse in 1991 of the National Liberation Front, which had been the sole political party since 1962 under President Benjedid Chadli: the cancellation of elections in January 1992 was followed by the assassination in June of his successor, Mohammed Boudiaf, and since then the new President has ruled by decree, with the imposition of an indefinite state of emergency. However, draft proposals for a return to democracy were announced in June 1993, and are expected to take effect over a three to four year period if approved.

In the general elections of December 1991, the militant Islamic Salvation Front gained an unexpectedly large majority over the ruling socialist National Liberation Front, with 47.5% of the vote against 23.5% for the FLN. However, the result aroused such unrest that the second ballot was suspended indefinitely.

Although Algeria's economy is still dominated by the socialised sector, and although all foreign-owned land was expropriated in the 1960s, it still has one of the most developed systems in North Africa. However, the country faces two challenges: firstly the failing health of the five-year plan system, which has seen mass demonstrations calling for its abolition, and secondly the very real possibility that Islamic law may be introduced if the current tide toward militant Islam continues.

Chad

Population ('000)	5,960 (1992)
Urban Population (%)	30.5 (1991)
Land Area (km²)	1,284,000
Language/s	French and Arabic (official); some 25 others
Religion/s	Muslim (50%), Christian (7%), traditional
Currency	CFA franc (= 100 centimes)
Head of State	President Idriss Déby (1991)
Head of Government	Fidèle Moungar (April 1993)
Ruling Party	Patriotic Salvation Movement

Main urban areas	Population
N'Djaména (capital)	615,000

(1992 estimate)

President Déby has survived two abortive coup attempts in recent years, one in October 1991 and another in February 1992. A new and provisional Council of the Republic was formed in February 1992, and included Maldom Bada Abbas, who had been implicated in the 1991 coup attempt. Opposition political parties were legalised in March 1992, and a transitional administration was installed in April 1993; yet the unrest in the country has continued since then.

There have been no multi-party elections in Chad in recent years; indeed, opposition parties such as the Rally for Democracy and Progress, the Union for Democracy and the Republic, or the Chadian Union for Democracy and Progress, have only recently been permitted.

Although the country is continually battling against a dry and frequently drought-ridden climate, and although the prospects for a major consumer upturn remain slim, Chad has generally managed to avoid the worst privations being experienced by its neighbours in recent years. The arrival at a negotiated settlement over the Aozou Strip would greatly enhance its attraction to foreign investors; meanwhile, it remains heavily dependent on France.

Djibouti

Population ('000)	470 (1992)
Land Area (km²)	23,000
Language/s	Arabic, French
Religion/s	Islam
Currency	Djibouti franc (= 100 centimes)
Head of State	President Hassan Gouled Aptidon (1977)
Head of Government	Barkat Gourad Hamadou
Ruling Party	Rassemblement populaire pour le progrès (RPP)

Main urban areas	Population
Djibouti (capital)	310,000

(1992 estimate)

Djibouti, which became independent from France in 1977, has been ruled continuously since then by President Hassan Gouled Aptidon. He was last re-elected in April 1987, for a term of six years, but is not technically entitled to stand for a third term of office when his current term expires in 1993. He answers to a 65-member Chamber of Deputies, which serves a five-year term of office. Since the end of 1990 the President has faced violent clashes with political opponents, especially in the north and west of the country.

The first multiparty congressional election was held in December 1992. The RPP won all 65 seats in the Chamber of Deputies, winning 78% of the vote. Presidential elections followed in May 1993, when President Hassan obtained 60.8% of the vote against 22% for Mohammed Djaba Elabe.

Djibouti would clearly have enough economic problems to tackle even without the crisis in neighbouring Ethiopia and Somalia; as it is, the country is forced to rely on foreign assistance, mainly from France.

Ethiopia

Population ('000)	55,110 (1992)
Urban Population (%)	14.4 (1991)
Land Area (km²)	1,023,050
Language/s	Amharic (official); also English, Tigrigna, Arabic
Religion/s	Islam (45%), Ethiopian Orthodox (40%)

Currency	Birr (= 100 cents)
Head of State	President Meles Zenawi (1991)
Head of Government	Tamirat Layne (1991)
Ruling Party	Ethiopian People's Revolutionary Democratic Front

Main urban areas	Population
Addis Ababa (capital)	1,555,000

(1991 census)

Ethiopia has an executive President and an 87-member Council of Representatives designed to operate in the interim period, while the socialist one-party state which ruled it for many years is dismantled. During the 1980s the country's political and economic life was devastated by the civil war raging between the government and the Eritrean People's Revolutionary Democratic Front, who campaigned, ultimately successfully, for independence. In April 1992 a ceasefire was reached and a timetable was agreed for Eritrea's eventual independence.

There have been no national elections since the overthrow of President Mengistu Haile Mariam in May 1991; however, a tentative date has been set for mid-1993. Elections to the newly created regional councils were held in June 1992, in 11 of the 14 regions (excluding Eritrea); the ruling Ethiopian People's Revolutionary Democratic Front obtained most of the votes. Yet the majority of the opposition parties boycotted the ballot, and afterwards there were widespread allegations of corruption.

In a good year Ethiopia's economy provides an adequate degree of self-sufficiency, but there have been few good years in the last decade. Recurrent droughts and the disruption of war have rendered the whole country very largely dependent on foreign aid, especially from France.

Eritrea

Population ('000)	2,615 (1984)
Land Area (km²)	93,679
Language/s	Amharic (official); also English, Tigrigna, Arabic
Religion/s	Islam (50%), Coptic (50%)
Currency	Birr (= 100 cents)
Head of State	President Issaias Afewerki (May 1993)
Head of Government	President Issaias Afewerki
Ruling Party	Eritrean People's Liberation Front

Main urban areas	Population
Asmara (capital)	1,000,000

(1992 estimate)

Eritrea has an executive President and a unicameral National Assembly which comprises all Central Committee members of the ruling EPLF, together with 60 others, of whom at least 11 must be women. The National Assembly elects the President directly. Executive Power is vested in a State Council chaired by the President.

There have been no elections yet, apart from the regional referendum of April 1993 in which 99.8% of the electorate voted for independence from Ethiopia.

Eritrea's territory contains much of the good arable land in the former Ethiopia, but like Ethiopia it has faced recurrent droughts in recent years.

Libya

Population ('000)	4,810 (1992)
Urban Population (%)	24.1 (1991)
Land Area (km²)	1,759,540
Language/s	Arabic
Religion/s	Islam
Currency	Libyan dinar (LD = 100 dirhams)

Head of State	President Col. Muammar al-Qaddafi
Head of Government	Abu Zayd Umar Durdah
Ruling Party	Technically, there are no parties, with the Arab Socialist Union the sole authorised political group.

Main urban areas	Population
Tripoli	1,100,000
Benghazi	700,000

(1992 estimate)

Strictly speaking, Col. Qaddafi has no formal post and no title except "Leader of the Revolution and Supreme Commander of the Armed Forces"; in practice, however, he is effectively the country's President. Power is nominally vested in the Libyan people, acting through some 1,500 "basic people's congresses" at local level, and influencing the activities of the national General People's Congress and its Secretariat. The GPC meets for about one week every year.

There have been no multi-party elections in recent years.

Libya's economy has been able to endure the strains of political isolation with surprising ease, thanks largely to the weight of its oil industries. However, in the 1980s and early 1990s a falling level of export revenues has forced many major cutbacks in public spending. Meanwhile the Government has announced a limited privatisation programme.

Mali

Population ('000)	9,820 (1992)
Urban Population (%)	22.0 (1991)
Land Area (km²)	1,240,140
Language/s	French
Religion/s	Islam (80%), traditional
Currency	CFA franc (= 100 centimes)
Head of State	President Alpha Oumar Konaré (June 1992)
Head of Government	Abdoulaye Sekou Sow (April 1993)
Ruling Party	Alliance for Democracy in Mali (ADEMA)

Main urban areas	Population
Bamako (capital)	440,000

(1992 estimate)

Mali's political system has been generally confused since the March 1991 overthrow of President Moussa Traoré, who came to power in the 1968 coup. The 25-member Transition Committee for the Salvation of the People which succeeded him was later withdrawn and was replaced in 1992 by an elected Parliament. Traoré was sentenced to death for murder in February 1993.

Alpha Oumar Konaré was elected President in April 1992, after winning 69% of the second-ballot votes in a national election. His party had earlier won the March 1992 elections to the national Parliament, with 76 of the 116 elected seats. The National Committee for Democratic Initiative won nine seats, the Sudanese Union-African Democratic Rally eight, the Popular Movement for the Development of the Republic of West Africa six, and various other 17 seats. 13 seats were reserved for representatives of Malian expatriates. Yet most of the major opposition parties had boycotted the poll, raising doubts as to its validity.

Mali's parched climate and its geographical isolation from the rest of the world have combined to present major obstacles to its economic development. At present the country relies heavily on external assistance, especially from France.

Mauritania

Population ('000)	2,140 (1992)
Urban Population (%)	48.2 (1991)
Land Area (km²)	1,030,700
Language/s	Arabic, French
Religion/s	Islam
Currency	Ouguiya (UM = 5 khous)
Head of State	President Col. Maawiya Ould Sidi Mohamed Taya
Head of Government	Sidi Mohamed Ould Boubakar
Ruling Party	Democratic and Social Republican Party (PRDS)

Main urban areas	Population
Nouakchott (capital)	600,000

(1992 estimate)

Mauritania has been steadily democratising its political institutions since the end of 1990, faced with growing pressure from abroad. Political parties were legalised for the first time only in July 1991, and the first free elections were held the following spring. Mauritania has a non-executive President and a Prime Minister and Cabinet who are answerable to an elected National Assembly, appointed for five years. There is also a Senate, appointed for six years in an indirect election. President Taya came to power in a 1984 coup.

The country's first elections to the National Assembly were held in January and February 1992, when the ruling PRDS won 67 of the 79 elected seats. The Rally for Democracy and National Unity won one seat, the Mauritanian Renewal Party one seat, and various independents 10 seats. However, the poll was boycotted by the leading opposition group, the Union of Democratic Forces, and by five other parties. Only 39% of the electorate voted in the first round of polling, and 33.4% in the second.

The country's heavy overseas debts, which are well in excess of two years' gross domestic product, are a major problem which constrains growth at present. Political uncertainties have only added to the pressures on the Government in recent years.

Morocco

Population ('000)	26,320 (1992)
Urban Population (%)	48.7 (1991)
Land Area (km²)	458,730
Language/s	Arabic, Berber, French, Spanish
Religion/s	Islam
Currency	Moroccan dirham (DH = 100 centimes)
Head of State	HM King Hassan II (1961)
Head of Government	Mohamed Karim Lamrani
Ruling Party	Bloc démocratique: a coalition of the Union socialiste des Forces populaires and Istiqlal

Main urban areas	Population
Casablanca	3,210,000
Marrakesh	1,517,000
Rabat (capital)	1,472,000
Fez	1,012,000
Oujda	962,000
Kénitra	905,000
Tétouan/Larache	856,000
Safi	845,000
Agadir	779,000
Meknès	750,000
Tangier	554,000

(1990 estimate, including suburbs)

Morocco is a constitutional monarchy in which legislative authority is vested in a unicameral Chamber of Representatives, 222 of whose 333 members are elected by universal suffrage for a six-year term while the remainder are chosen by an electoral college. The Prime Minister is appointed accordingly by the monarch.

The first legislative elections in recent years were held in April 1993, when the ruling coalition of the Union constitutionelle, the Rassemblement national des indépendants and the Mouvement populaire were overturned by the Union socialiste des Forces populaires (with 48 of the 222 elected seats) and Istiqlal (a fellow member of the bloc démocratique) , with 43 seats. The Mouvement populaire won 33 seats, the Rassemblement national des indépendants 28, the Union constitutionnelle 27, the Parti Nationale démocratique 14 and the Mouvement Nationale Populaire 14. Other small parties obtained 15 seats.

The highly diversified economy appears well placed to grow in the 1990s, assuming that militant pro-Islamic elements do not gain control in such a way as to inhibit the strong interest being shown by Western Europe. At present, however, this cannot be ruled out. The country is one of the few which is still run on the lines of a five-year plan.

Niger

Population ('000)	8,250 (1992)
Urban Population (%)	20.2 (1991)
Land Area (km²)	1,186,410
Language/s	French, Hausa, Tuareg, Djerma, Fulani
Religion/s	Muslim (85%)
Currency	CFA franc (= 100 centimes)
Head of State	President Mahamane Ousmane
Head of Government	Mahamdou Issoufou (April 1993)
Ruling Party	The Mouvement national pour une société de développement (MNSD), which was formerly the only legal political body, leads a coalition with the Social Democrats

Main urban areas	Population
Niamey (capital)	450,000

(1992 estimate)

From 1974 until the return of parliamentary democracy in 1993, Niger was run by a military administration which had overthrown the previous administration. The holding of elections, which finally took place in January 1993, followed a period of serious deterioration in the political climate, but the situation quietened thereafter.

The first free elections since 1974 were held in February 1993, when the MNSD, which was formerly the only legal political body, won 29 of the 83 seats on the National Assembly and formed a coalition with the Social Democrats (22 seats). The Party for Unity and Democracy won 13 seats. In presidential elections held during 1993, Mahame Ousmane won 54.5% in the second round, despite having been beaten in the first round by Tandja Mamadou. The voter turnout was only 35%.

101

Niger's economy remains highly dependent on France for aid; several years of drought have left the country in a poor condition.

Somalia

Population ('000)	9,200 (1992)
Urban Population (%)	23.5 (1987)
Land Area (km²)	630,000
Language/s	Arabic
Religion/s	Muslim
Currency	Somali shilling (SSh = 100 cents)
Head of State	President Ali Mahdi Mohammed (1991)
Head of Government	Umer Arteh Ghaleb
Ruling Party	The United Somali Congress is the umbrella organisation closest to the President.

Main urban areas	Population
Mogadishu (capital)	1,000,000

(1992 estimate)

The Republic of Somalia was ruled from 1969 until January 1991 by Maj.-Gen. Siyad Barre, who seized power in a coup and who declared a socialist state in 1979, led by the Somali Revolutionary Socialist Party. The Constitution remained suspended from 1969 until 1991, when it was reintroduced in its unaltered form. Barre's removal in January 1991, and the installation of an interim President, failed to stem the ruinous inter-ethnic feuding in virtually all rural areas of the country, and plans for multi-party elections have not materialised. By 1993 the situation had desended into full-scale guerilla war, with an international contingent of some 50,000 United Nations peacekeeping forces attempting to support the government agains the troops of Gen. Mohammed Aideed. Fighting had become severe, and casualties were mounting.

The last full elections were held in 1984, under the single-party regulations of the Siyad Barre regime. The Somali Revolutionary Socialist Party won all the seats.

Somalia's economy has been almost wrecked by the civil war raging through the country in recent years, and in 1993 few of the country's manufacturing plants were able to function fully because of the internal disruption.

Sudan

Population ('000)	26,660 (1992)
Urban Population (%)	20.5 (1983)
Land Area (km²)	2,505,815
Language/s	Arabic, English
Religion/s	Muslim, traditional, Christian
Currency	Sudanese pound (S£ = 100 piastres)
Head of State	President Omar Hassan Ahmad Al-Bashir
Head of Government	President Omar Hassan Ahmad Al-Bashir
Ruling Party	National Movement for Correction

Main urban areas	Population
Khartoum (capital)	2,000,000

(With Omdurman, 1992 estimate)

Sudanese politics have been dominated since 1989 by the aftermath of the military coup which overthrew the elected regime in that year. As allegations about the former regime had continued to mount, the new military rulers led by Gen. Al-Bashir had dissolved the National Assembly and had instituted what amounted to rule by decree, in order to enforce drastic austerity measures. By late 1991, however, public protests were mounting, and a 300-member Transitional National Assembly was formed in February 1992, amid reports of a failed coup attempt.

There have been no elections in Sudan since the suspension of the Constitution in 1989, and at present all political parties are officially banned.

Sudan's economy has suffered since the mid-1980s from drought, combined with the slump in world commodity prices, which have reduced its export potential. However, real incomes have been picking up in recent years, thanks in part to much-needed changes in agriculture.

Tunisia

Population ('000)	8,400 (1992)
Urban Population (%)	59.2 (1989)
Land Area (km²)	164,150
Language/s	Arabic, French
Religion/s	Muslim
Currency	Tunisian dinar (TD = 1,000 millimes)
Head of State	President Gen. Zine el-Abidine Ben-Ali (1987)
Head of Government	Hamed Karoui
Ruling Party	Rassemblement constitutionnel démocratique (RCD)

Main urban areas	Population
Tunis (capital)	1,394,749
Sfax	577,992

(1984, including suburbs)

The Republic of Tunisia became independent from France in 1957, and was ruled until 1981 as a one-party state by the Parti socialiste Destour, now known as the Rassemblement constitutionnel démocratique; the party still rules the country almost without opposition. The executive President is elected for a maximum of three five-year terms by universal suffrage, although in practice he has always stood unopposed. The 141 members of the unicameral National Assembly are also elected by popular vote.

In the general elections to the National Assembly in April 1989, the ruling RCD was declared to have taken all 141 seats. The Government announced its decision in 1991 to allow more opposition parties to win seats - local elections in June 1990 having given the RCD control of 244 out of 245 municipal councils. Yet the six opposition parties voted to boycott the subsequent by-elections in October 1991, so that the RCD was returned unopposed.

Tunisia's oil industry is modest in relation to its neighbours, though it is sufficient to boost the general wealth. Yet even a modest growth of spending power has not prevented the growth of public dissent among consumers dissatisfied with the Government's performance in recent years.

West Africa

Benin

Population ('000)	4,920 (1992)
Urban Population (%)	38.4 (1991)
Land Area (km²)	112,620
Language/s	French
Religion/s	Mainly traditional; some Christian (15%) and Muslim (13%)
Currency	CFA franc (= 100 centimes)
Head of State	President Nicéphore Soglo (1991)
Head of Government	President Nicéphore Soglo
Ruling Party	Union pour le triomphe du renouveau démocratique leads a multi-party coalition

Main urban areas	Population
Cotonou	1,000,500
Porto Novo (capital)	860,000
Borgou	712,000

(1992 estimate)

Benin's transition to multi-party democracy occurred only in 1991, when the first elections were held under the terms of the 1990 Constitution; by late 1993 the political system was still taking shape. In practice, all power rests with the President, who is elected by universal suffrage for a five-year term, and who answers to the 64-seat National Assembly. He organises a multi-party coalition, but even this controls only 21 seats.

In the country's first multi-party elections to the National Assembly, which took place in March 1991, the Union pour le triomphe du renouveau démocratique won the largest number of votes, yet even this was only enough to leave it with 12 seats. The party therefore relies for its support on the goodwill of President Soglo, who was elected President on the same day with some 67% of the votes in the second round of voting.

Benin's severe poverty is in part the result of its inhospitable climate and in part the result of decades of political mismanagement. Since the economic reforms of the early 1990s, however, the prospect of change for the better has been growing.

Burkina Faso

Population ('000)	9,490 (1992)
Urban Population (%)	19.5 (1991)
Land Area (km^2)	274,122
Language/s	French, Mossi
Religion/s	Traditional (more than 50%)
Currency	CFA franc (= 100 centimes)
Head of State	President Youssouf Ouedraogo (1992)
Head of Government	President Youssouf Ouedraogo
Ruling Party	Organisation for Popular Democracy - Labour Movement

Main urban areas	Population
Ouagadougou (capital)	482,000

(1992 estimate)

Burkina Faso, which was known until 1984 as Upper Volta, has an executive President who is elected by universal suffrage for a seven-year term. The 107-member National Assembly is still a novelty; from 1980 until the multi-party elections of 1992, the country was ruled first directly by the President and then by a transitional government. The first President, Thomas Sankara, who had led the 1980 coup, was killed during the 1987 revolt which eventually brought the more moderate Blaise Compaoré to power.

Legislative elections were held in May 1992, when the OPT-MT of President Blaise Compaoré (later replaced) won 78 of the 107 seats. The National Convention of Progressive Patriots -Social Democratic Party (CNPP-PSD) won eight seats, the African Democratic Assembly six, and the African Independent Party three. Four other parties each won one seat, and four results were undeclared. Yet the voter turnout was below 29%, and there were allegations of ballot rigging.

Burkina Faso's low standard of living clearly precludes the prospect of any major economic expansion in the 1990s, and its military history does little to encourage would-be foreign investors. However, the country is a major recipient of international aid, a fact which in turn will open up possibilities for trade activity from abroad.

Cameroon

Population ('000)	12,200 (1992)
Urban Population (%)	42.2 (1985)
Land Area (km^2)	465,500
Language/s	French, English
Religion/s	Christian (53%); traditional (23%); Muslim (22%)
Currency	CFA franc (= 100 centimes)
Head of State	President Paul Biya (1982)
Head of Government	Simon Achidi Achu (1992)
Ruling Party	Cameroon People's Party

Main urban areas	Population
Douala	1,110,000
Yaoundé (capital)	700,000

(1992 estimate)

Cameroon was effectively run as a one-party socialist state from 1964, when all but the ruling party were banned, until 1992. Under the 1990 Constitution the executive President is elected for a five-year term by popular mandate, while the 180-member National Assembly which wields most of the legislative power is similarly elected for a five-year term. However, the losing candidate in the 1992 elections, John Fru Ndi, attempted in April 1993 to set up his own government.

The country's first multi-party elections since 1964 were held in March 1992, when the ruling Cameroon People's Party won 88 of the 180 seats. The National Union for Democracy and Progress won 68 seats, the Union of the Peoples of Cameroon won 18, and the Movement for the Defence of the Republic won six seats in the far north of the country. Voter turnout was officially quoted at 60%, but in the west it fell as low as 10%.

Although one of the poorer economies in Africa, Cameroon's oil production gives it some degree of security. Agricultural reforms now in progress ought to impress upon the international agencies the extent of the political changes now in progress, and aid programmes should be forthcoming.

Cape Verde

Population ('000)	380 (1992)
Urban Population (%)	33.1 (1991)
Land Area (km^2)	4,035
Language/s	Portuguese, Crioulo
Religion/s	Roman Catholic (97%)
Currency	Escudo (Esc = 100 centavos)
Head of State	President Antonio Mascarenhas Monteiro (1991)
Head of Government	M. Carlos Veiga
Ruling Party	Movimento para Democracia

Main urban areas	Population
Praia (capital)	69,000

(1992 estimate)

The Republic of Cape Verde became independent from Portugal in 1985, and quickly established itself as a one-party state with a socialist orientation. An attempt was made to re-forge a political alliance with Guinea-Bissau which had existed until 1879, but this idea was dropped after the 1980 coup in Guinea-Bissau. Under the 1990 Constitution the country has an executive President, elected by popular mandate for a five-year term, who answers to a 79-member National Assembly, also elected for five years.

The country's first multi-party elections were held in January 1991, when the Movimento para Democracia obtained some 65% of the votes and assumed a 56-seat majority in the 79-member National Assembly. The main opposition party is the Partido Africano da Independencia de Cabo Verde, which had ruled until the elections. The first free presidential elections, which followed soon afterwards, saw the MPD's candidate Antonio Monteiro win a convincing victory.

The political difficulties are mirrored to a considerable extent by the economic problems being experienced at present. As much as 80% of the country's gross domestic product comes from abroad, half of it in the form of remittances by expatriate workers. These are effectively the main source of consumer purchasing power.

Côte d'Ivoire

Population ('000)	12,910 (1992)
Urban Population (%)	41.0 (1991)
Land Area (km²)	322,465
Language/s	French
Religion/s	Muslim (23%), Christian (12%), traditional
Currency	CFA franc (= 100 centimes)
Head of State	President Félix Houphouët-Boigny (1960)
Head of Government	Alessane Ouattara (1990)
Ruling Party	Parti démocratique de la Côte d'Ivoire

Main urban areas	Population
Abidjan (seat of government)	2,100,000

(1992 estimate)

Côte d'Ivoire, the former Ivory Coast, became fully independent from France in 1960. The executive President exercises a very large degree of power, and is elected for five years by universal suffrage. Legislative authority is vested in the 175-member National Assembly, which is also elected for five years. Considerable political changes have been taking place since 1990: although Houphouët-Boigny was re-elected in the country's first multi-candidate competition, a power struggle quickly developed with the country's first Prime Minister.

The country's first multi-party elections, in November 1990, gave the PDCI an overwhelming victory, with all except 10 of the 175 seats in the National Assembly. The Front populaire ivorien obtained nine seats, and the Parti ivorien des travailleurs one seat.

The country's continuing dependence on the highly vulnerable commodity markets remains a problem, and at present the Government is still being criticised for taking too long to approve new projects which might speed the diversification into industrial activities.

Equatorial Guinea

Population ('000)	370 (1992)
Urban Population (%)	37.0 (1991)
Land Area (km²)	28,050
Language/s	Spanish
Religion/s	Roman Catholic (94%)
Currency	CFA franc (= 100 centimes)
Head of State	President Teodoro Obiang Nguema Mbasogo
Head of Government	Capt. Silvestre Siale Bileka
Ruling Party	Partido Democratico de Guinea Ecuatorial

Main urban areas	Population
Malabo (capital)	34,890

(1992 estimate)

Until the end of 1991 Equatorial Guinea was, to all intents and purposes, a one-party state in which nearly all power rested with the President and with his military-backed Cabinet. Since then, however, the country has been preparing itself for multi-party politics; a transitional government was formed in January 1992, with a view to multi-party elections later in the year.

There had been no multi-party elections by the autumn of 1993, although a multi-party system was being put into place.

The extreme dependence on foreign aid is if anything worsening at present, and there seems little real prospect of a significant change in the foreseeable future. Consumer marketing options will therefore centre on the availability of bilateral or multilateral aid programmes.

Gabon

Population ('000)	1,240 (1992)
Urban Population (%)	46.6 (1991)
Land Area (km²)	2,667,665
Language/s	French
Religion/s	Mainly Christian (60%), traditional
Currency	CFA franc (= 100 centimes)
Head of State	President El Hadj Omar Bongo (1967)
Head of Government	Casimir Oyé Mba
Ruling Party	Parti démocratique gabonais

Main urban areas	Population
Libreville (capital)	395,000

(1992 estimate)

Gabon, which achieved independence from France in 1960, was run as a single-party socialist system from 1968 until March 1991, when a new multi-party Constitution came into force. The country has an executive President (currently Omar Bongo who has ruled since 1967), who is elected by universal suffrage for a seven-year term. He answers to a 120-member National Assembly (Parliament), which is elected every five years.

At the general election of March 1991 the Parti démocratique gabonais won 66 seats in the 120-member National Assembly.

Gabon's economy, although potentially wealthy and reasonably diversified, remains handicapped by massive past overspending, and austerity plans have been necessary for most of the last ten years.

Gambia

Population ('000)	880 (1992)
Urban Population (%)	23.8 (1991)
Land Area (km²)	10,690
Language/s	English (official); Mandinka, Fula, Wolof
Religion/s	Islam (85%)
Currency	Dalasi (D = 100 butut)
Head of State	President Alhaji Sir Dawda Kairaba Jawara
Head of Government	President Alhaji Sir Dawda Kairaba Jawara
Ruling Party	People's Progressive Party

Main urban areas	Population
Kombo St Mary	105,000
Banjul (capital)	59,000

(1992 estimate)

The Gambia has been independent since 1965, and it became a republic in 1970. The executive President is elected for a five-year term by universal suffrage, and answers to a 50-member unicameral legislative assembly, the House of Representatives. 36 of the House's members are directly elected for a five-year term, while five are tribal chiefs and eight are non-voting nominees. The Attorney General is the other member.

Elections for the 36 House of Representatives seats were held in April 1992, when the PPP obtained 25, the National Convention Party six, and the Gambia People's Party two; Independents took the remaining seats. The presidential elections of April 1992 showed a 58.4% share of the vote for President Dawda Jawara, who began his fifth term of office. sherif Mustapha Dibba, who stood against him, obtained 22%.

Gambia's economy, although fairly diversified, remains highly reliant on foreign aid at present, and is vulnerable to short-term disturbances amid the current political troubles.

Ghana

Population ('000)	15,960 (1992)
Urban Population (%)	33.4 (1991)
Land Area (km²)	238,305
Language/s	English, Akan, several other dialects
Religion/s	Christian 43%, traditional 38%, Muslim 12%
Currency	Cedi (C = 100 pesawas)
Head of State	Flt.-Lt. Jerry Rawlings
Head of Government	P.V. Obeng
Ruling Party	National Democratic Congress

Main urban areas	Population
Accra (capital)	1,420,000

(1992 estimate)

Ghana has an executive President who governs through an essentially benevolent military administration. The current administration seized power in a military coup in 1981, following a period of prolonged instability but has recently held elections (see below). Political dissent has been allowed for some time under the freedom of association laws. The Fourth Republic was pronounced in January 1993, following the 1992 elections.

Parliamentary elections were held in December 1992, at which the National Democratic Congress won an overwhelming majority, largely as a result of a boycott by the four major opposition parties. Presidential elections took place in November 1992, at which Flt-Lt. Rawlings obtained 58% of the vote.

The success of the Government in turning round the country's overspent and often corrupt economy has been reflected in a growing interest from abroad in Ghanaian projects. The country's widely based economy remains a further safeguard against future downturns.

Guinea

Population ('000)	6,120 (1992)
Urban Population (%)	26.3 (1991)
Land Area (km²)	245,855
Language/s	French
Religion/s	Muslim (95%), Christian
Currency	Franc guinéen (= 100 centimes)
Head of State	President Maj.-Gen. Lansana Conté (1984)
Head of Government	President Lansana Conté
Ruling Party	All political parties are banned

Main urban areas	Population
Conakry (capital)	810,000

(1992 estimate)

Guinea's 1982 Constitution was placed in suspense upon the military takeover of 1984 which brought the present Administration to power, but a new draft was approved by a national referendum in December 1990; details had yet to be worked out by the autumn of 1992. At present the country is run by the Transitional Committee for National Recovery, whose membership has been cut from 36 members to 15, and political parties are still banned - although a two-party system is still scheduled for the future.

There have been no elections since 1984, when the armed forces seized power. At that time the sole legal political party was the Democratic Party of Guinea.

Guinea's mineral wealth is thrown into sharp relief by the poverty of its population. A lack of basic infrastructural facilities (especially roads) is currently hampering its development.

Guinea-Bissau

Population ('000)	1,010 (1992)
Urban Population (%)	20.4 (1991)
Land Area (km²)	36,125
Language/s	Portuguese
Religion/s	Traditional (54%), Muslim (38%), Christian (8%)
Currency	Guinea peso (= 100 centavos)
Head of State	President Joao Bernando Vieira
Head of Government	Prime Minister: Carlos Correia
Ruling Party	Partido Africano da Independencia da Guiné e Cabo Verde

Main urban areas	Population
Bissau (capital)	145,000

(1992 estimate)

Democratic systems have been more or less suspended since the military coup of 1980 which brought the Vieira Administration to power: President Vieira's execution of his Vice-President in 1986 has ensured that his position remains unchallenged. Under what the 1984 Constitution calls "a state of revolutionary national democracy", all 150 deputies in the National Assembly are drawn from the ruling party, via elections which are held to the eight directly elected regional councils. The Assembly in turn appoints a 15-member Council of State.

The last direct elections for the National Assembly were held in June 1989, when 95.8% of the 223,592 votes cast went to the sole candidate, the PAIGC - a turnout of less than 50%. President Vieira, who took power in the 1980 coup, was re-elected unopposed for a further five-year term. However, new and multi-party elections were due by the end of 1992; opposition political parties have been legal since mid-1991.

The ongoing crisis in the political sphere has been mirrored in the economy, and confidence from abroad has been sapped to the point of near-collapse. Guinea-Bissau has applied, unsuccessfully, to join the CFA franc zone, the inference being that its currency is not sufficiently stable at present.

Liberia

Population ('000)	2,580 (1992)
Urban Population (%)	47.0 (1991)
Land Area (km²)	111,370
Language/s	English
Religion/s	Christian, Muslim
Currency	Liberian dollar (L$ = 100 cents)
Head of State	President Amos Sawyer (1992)
Head of Government	President Amos Sawyer
Ruling Party	None. At the time of President Doe's removal (see below) the National Democratic Party of Liberia had been in power.

Main urban areas	Population
Monrovia (capital)	490,000

(1992 estimate)

Liberia's political system was thrown into turmoil in the mid-1980s by the revival of bloody rivalries between the three main warring factions: the Government's administration, the National Patriotic Front for Liberia (NPFL), led by Charles Taylor, and the Independent NPFL led by Prince Yormie Johnson. 1992 brought some progress: a ceasefire was signed, and Johnson was offered the Vice-Presidency. Yet the rebels refused the Government's calls to disarm, and they continued to reject its authority.

The last full elections to the Presidency and the National Assembly were held in October 1985, and were quickly overshadowed by the looming civil war. Yet the prospect of new elections improved in January 1992 with the establishment of a new electoral commission. No date had been set by the autumn of 1992.

The severe damage inflicted by the civil war of the late 1980s and early 1990s continues to impair the growth of the economy in 1993, and under current circumstances it appears unlikely that the country will attract much foreign investment.

Nigeria

Population ('000)	115,660 (1992)
Urban Population (%)	36.0 (1991)
Land Area (km^2)	923,850
Language/s	English, Igbo, Yoruba, Hausa
Religion/s	Muslim (47%), Christian, traditional
Currency	Naira (N = 100 kobo)
Head of State	Chief Ernest Shonekan (August 1993)
Head of Government	Chief Ernest Shonekan
Ruling Party	A temporary civilian administration, Transitional Council, was formed in December 1992.

Main urban areas	Population
Lagos (business capital)	3,200,000
Uyo	1,100,000
Ibadan	847,000
Ogbomosho	555,000
Abuja (capital)	300,000

(1992 estimate)

Nigeria, an independent member of the Commonwealth, was ruled from 1985 until 1993 by Maj.-Gen. Ibrahim Babangida, who overthrew his predecessor in a coup. In July 1993, presidential elections produced a clear majority for Aloshood Abiola, but Babangida immediately annulled the election and in August he installed a temporary administration led by Chief Ernest Shonekan; by the end of August he was forced by the new administration to abandon the Presidency, and Abiola returned to the country in September to begin a campaign for his own claim as Head of State. The National Assembly is elected by the people. In practice, Nigerian politics are dominated by the tribal tensions between the Yoruba, the Hausa and the Fulani, and these have been responsible for much of the political disruption of recent years.The capital was moved from Lagos to the new city of Abuja in December 1991.

Elections were held in July 1992 to both Houses of the new National Assembly, which started its work in January 1993. In the 91-seat senate (Upper House), the ruling Social Democratic Party won 52 seats, the National Republican Convention won 37, and two seats were unfilled. In the 593-member House of Representatives, the SDP won 314 seats, the NRC 275, and four seats were unfilled. The SDP is supported mainly by Yoruba voters, the NRC by Hausas and Fulanis. Only 25% of the electorate voted.

Nigeria's broadly spread economy has the potential to become the largest consumer market in Africa; yet the continuing uncertainty about the economic situation, caused by past overspending in the light of the oil price slump of the 1980s, casts a serious shadow over the whole economy.

Sao Tomé e Príncipe

Population ('000)	120 (1992)
Urban Population (%)	37.6 (1991)
Land Area (km^2)	964
Language/s	Portuguese
Religion/s	Mainly Roman Catholic
Currency	Dobra (D = 100 centimes)
Head of State	President Miguel Trovoada (1991)
Head of Government	Norberto José d'Alva Costa Alegre
Ruling Party	Partido de Convergência Democrática

Main urban areas	Population
Sao Tomé (capital)	36,000

(1992 estimate)

The Democratic Republic of Sao Tomé e Príncipe was an overseas territory of Portugal until 1975, and quickly became a single-party state run by the socialist Movimento de Liberaçao de Sao Tomé e Príncipe (MLSTP). Multi-party elections became a possibility only in 1990, when a new Constitution was introduced. The new document provides for a semi-executive President who appoints the Prime Minister on the advice of the 55-member legislature.

The country's first multi-party elections to the 55-member National People's Assembly were held in January 1991, when the ruling MLSTP-PSD was unexpectedly defeated, winning only 21 seats on 30.5% of the vote. The opposition Partido de Convergência Democrática, which won 33 seats and 54.4% of the vote, went on to form a government, while the Coligaçao Democrático da Oposiçao won one seat. Presidential elections in March 1991 produced a landslide for Miguel Trovoada.

As Sao Tomé e Principe moves away from the one-party system, its economy is being decentralised and deregulated. However, the poor performance of the export markets has severely hampered the country's development.

Senegal

Population ('000)	7,740 (1992)
Urban Population (%)	38.9 (1991)
Land Area (km^2)	196,720
Language/s	French
Religion/s	Mainly Muslim (90%)
Currency	CFA franc (= 100 centimes)
Head of State	President Abdou Diouf (1981)
Head of Government	Habib Thiam
Ruling Party	Parti socialiste sénégalais (PS) leads a coalition including the Parti démocratique sénégalais (PDS)

Main urban areas	Population
Dakar (capital)	1,450,000

(estimate)

The Republic of Senegal was proclaimed in September 1960, having seceded from the Federation of Mali, which in turn had left French domination in June 1960. The executive President is also the head of the government, and is elected by direct popular vote for a seven-year term. He answers to a 120-member National Assembly, which is elected by universal suffrage for a term of five years.

The May 1993 elections produced a setback for the ruling Parti socialiste sénégalais, with only 56.6% of the vote and 84 of the 120 seats in the National Assembly, compared with 30.2% and 27 seats for the Parti démocratique sénégalais. Jappoo Liggeyal Senegal won 3 seats, and other minority parties won another 6 seats. President Diouf, the incumbent President, had been re-elected in February 1993 with 58.4% of the vote compared with 32% for Abdoulaye Wade.

Senegal is one of the poorest countries in Africa, with three-quarters of the population dependent on farming although there are significant mineral resources as well.

Sierra Leone

Population ('000)	4,380 (1992)
Urban Population (%)	33.0 (1991)
Land Area (km²)	72,325
Language/s	English, Mende and Temba dialects
Religion/s	Mainly traditional
Currency	Leone (Le = 100 cents)
Head of State	President Valentine E Strasser (1992)
Head of Government	President Valentine E Strasser
Ruling Party	All-People's Congress

Main urban areas	Population
Freetown (capital)	505

(1992 estimate)

Sierra Leone's ruling authority was overthrown by the armed forces in a military coup during April 1992. The House of Representatives was dissolved, and a 23-member National Provisional Ruling Council (NPRC) was appointed to administer the country in the interim period leading to multi-party elections. In July 1992 President Strasser announced the conversion of the NPRC into the Supreme Council of State. Sierra Leone is at war with rebel forces in neighbouring Liberia.
All political activity is currently banned.
Sierra Leone's economy has traditionally relied on farming, but the expansion of the mineral sector has created massive new possibilities since the 1960s. Even so, living standards are low except in Freetown.

Togo

Population ('000)	3,760 (1992)
Urban Population (%)	26.6 (1991)
Land Area (km²)	56,785
Language/s	French
Religion/s	Traditional (50%), Christian (35%), Muslim (15%)
Currency	CFA franc (= 100 centimes)
Head of State	President Gnassingbé Eyadéma (1967)
Head of Government	Joseph Kokou Koffigoh
Ruling Party	There are no legal political parties

Main urban areas	Population
Lomé (capital)	590,000

(1992 estimate)

Although Togo has a non-executive President, he nonetheless retains significant powers during the current period of economic unrest. Recent years have been dominated by the growing split between President Eyadéma and Premier Koffigoh, who appears to have wider public backing but who faces a variety of obstacles. He was effectively debarred from standing for President in 1992 by a new constitutional clause which raised the minimum age from 40 to 45; he was 44. In 1991 he was briefly kidnapped by the President's supporters.
Elections originally promised for April 1992 were postponed repeatedly until August 1993, when President Eyadéma was returned to office.
The slow decline in Togo's economy can only be partly attributed to the poor state of its export markets: political mismanagement is equally important. At present, moreover, there are few signs of any concerted effort to move away from the commodity-dependence of the status quo.

East/Central Africa

Angola

Population ('000)	9,890 (1992)
Urban Population (%)	29.1 (1991)
Land Area (km²)	1,246,700
Language/s	Portuguese (official; Ovimbundu, Kimbundu, Bakongo, Chokwe spoken)
Religion/s	Roman Catholic (majority)
Currency	New kwanza (Kw= 100 lwei)
Head of State	President José Eduardo dos Santos
Head of Government	Marcolino Moco
Ruling Party	People's Movement for the Liberation of Angola

Main urban areas	Population
Luanda (capital)	1,750,000

(1992 estimate)

Angola has an executive President who is answerable to an elected National People's Assembly, although in practice he has the power to rule by decree. The ending of the chronic civil war in 1991, between the Marxist MPLA and South African-backed UNITA guerrilla movement, was welcomed at first as heralding the return of democracy. However, the victory of the MPLA in the elections of October 1992 was immediately contested by the losing UNITA candidates, and by the autumn of 1993 the country was once again locked in conflict.
Elections were held in October 1992, in which the government of the ruling MPLA faced competition for the first time from opposition parties. In the event, however, it obtained more than 60% of the national vote - though much less in many rural areas. The UNITA rebels, who were backing many of the opposition parties, denounced the result as a sham and alleged that election fraud had taken place.
Angola's war-torn economy is struggling with the need to eliminate the aftermath of its centrally planned economy, and to find replacements for the economic aid from Cuba and the former Soviet Union, both of which have now retreated. However, the return of international aid and a probable improvement in relations with South Africa will make up some of the deficit.

Burundi

Population ('000)	5,780 (1992)
Urban Population (%)	5.0 (1990)
Land Area (km²)	27,835
Language/s	Kirundi, French, Kiswahili
Religion/s	Mainly Christian (60%)
Currency	Burundi franc (= 100 centimes)
Head of State	President Melchior Ndadaye (1993) was overthrown in a military coup in October 1993
Head of Government	Adrien Sibomana (1991)
Ruling Party	Front pour la démocratie en Burundi

Main urban areas	Population
Bujumbura (capital)	220,100

(1992 estimate)

Burundi, which was formerly a Belgian trusteeship under United Nations auspices, became fully independent in 1962; the monarchy was deposed in 1966. A military coup in 1976 brought Col. Jean-Baptiste Bagaza to power, but he too was deposed in 1987 by Maj. Pierre Buyoya. Buyoya suspended the Constitution and instituted a system of direct rule through the Military Council for National Salvation. Democracy was resumed in June 1993 with the holding of free elections, but three months later the new President was overthrown and killed in a military coup backed by the minority Tutsi tribes who resented their loss of political dominance to the majority Hutus.

The first multi-party elections since 1970 were held in June 1993, when the Front pour la démocratie en Burundi (Frodebu) of Melchior Ndadaye won 65 of the 81 seats in Parliament, compared with 16 for the incumbent Union pour le progrès national (Uprona) of Buyoya. In presidential elections held on the same day, Ndadaye beat the incumbent Pierre Buyoya by 64.8% to 32.4%. The turnout was extremely high at 97.3%.z

Burundi's modest economy and geographical inaccessibility combine to make it improbable that the country will see a major expansion of its limited industrial base in the 1990s. Moreover, the likelihood of large international aid awards has receded with the recent political problems in the country.

Central African Republic

Population ('000)	3,170 (1992)
Urban Population (%)	47.5 (1991)
Land Area (km²)	624,975
Language/s	Sangho, French
Religion/s	Traditional (60%), Christian (35%), Muslim (5%)
Currency	CFA franc (= 100 centimes)
Head of State	President Ange-Félix Patasse (1993)
Head of Government	Enoch Derant Lakoné (March 1992)
Ruling Party	Rassemblement démocratique centrafricain

Main urban areas	Population
Bangui (capital)	600,000

(1992 estimate)

1993 saw the restarting of talks on the restitution of multi-party democracy, following the collapse of the "Grand National Debate" for much of 1992. Current plans for the constitution envisage that the President would be only semi-executive, with most of the power being vested in the Prime Minister; in the meantime, the President has the authority to rule by decree.

The last elections were held in July 1987, when only the Rassemblement démocratique centrafrican was allowed to stand. Pending the return of a true multi-party electoral system, some 15 organisations have now registered as opposition parties. Ange-Felix Patasse was elected President in September 1993, with 52% of the votes in the second round of balloting.

Comoros

Population ('000)	580 (1992)
Urban Population (%)	28.4 (1991)
Land Area (km²)	1,860
Language/s	Arabic and French (official); Comoran
Religion/s	Islam
Currency	Comoros franc (= 100 centimes)
Head of State	President Ahmen Ben Cheikh (June 1993)
Head of Government	President Ahmen Ben Cheikh (June 1993)
Ruling Party	Union comorienne pour le progrès

Main urban areas	Population
Moroni (capital)	22,000

(1992 estimate)

In June 1992 a referendum returned a 74% vote in favour of a new constitution, which would create a new system with a President elected for a five-year term, renewable once only, and for a 15-member Senate comprising five from each island. Legislative power is exercised by a 42-member Federal Assembly elected for a four-year term.

The first multiparty elections took place in November 1992 for the 42-seat Federal Assembly. Voting was disrupted by violence, and the opposition parties boycotted the election. Consequently the final results, released in early 1993, were considered invalid.

The country remains highly dependent on its trade relationship with France, and its lack of self-sufficiency in food products has caused some concern recently. It was estimated in the late 1980s that French aid comprised 40% of GDP.

Congo

Population ('000)	2,370 (1992)
Urban Population (%)	41.1 (1991)
Land Area (km²)	342,000
Language/s	French
Religion/s	Traditional (50%), Roman Catholic (40%)
Currency	CFA franc (= 100 centimes)
Head of State	President Pascal Lissouba (August 1992)
Head of Government	Claude Antoine Dacosta (1992)
Ruling Party	Pan-African Union for Social Democracy leads a coalition with the Union for Democracy and Republic

Main urban areas	Population
Brazzaville (capital)	690,000

(1992 estimate)

The traditional dominance of the Congolese Labour Party came to an abrupt end in July 1992, with the country's first multi-party elections in many decades. The new system, which replaces the old collectivist system, provides for an executive President elected for a term of five years, and legislative authority is vested in a 125-member National Assembly (Lower House of Parliament) and a 60-member Senate (Upper House).

Elections to the National Assembly were held in June 1993, when the coalition government of President Pascal Lissouba won 69 of the 125 seats in the Assembly and all of the 11 constituencies (UPADS 7, UDR 4). But despite the decisive win, there were still calls for new elections.

At present the country's economy is still run on the lines of a five-year plan system, with most strategic decisions being taken by the Government. There are signs that this will change in the future, however. The slump in world oil prices and the withdrawal of Soviet aid have made it more difficult to finance domestic infrastructure development in recent years.

Kenya

Population ('000)	26,980 (1992)
Urban Population (%)	24.4 (1991)
Land Area (km²)	582,645
Language/s	Swahili, English
Religion/s	Mainly traditional
Currency	Kenya shilling (Ksh = 100 cents)
Head of State	President Daniel arap Moi
Head of Government	President Daniel arap Moi
Ruling Party	Kenya African National Union (KANU)

Main urban areas	Population
Nairobi (capital)	1,310,000
Mombasa	530,000

(1992 estimate)

Kenya has an executive Presidency whose incumbent since independence, President Moi, has exerted an almost unchallenged level of influence over the country's affairs. There is a multi-party system in operation, in which opposition figures are elected to Parliament in the normal way; however, the President has used his extensive personal powers since the late 1980s to imprison and to suspend many of them. By mid-1993 there was mounting public criticism of the regime.

Presidential elections took place in January 1993, at which President Moi won 1.8 million votes, ahead of three opponents. Legislative elections at the same time gave Moi's KANU party 95 seats in the 188-seat parliament, compared with 31 for the FORD-Asili party and 31 for FORD-Kenya, 23 for the Democratic Party and 3 others.

The economy remains depressed in the early 1990s, partly as a result of the need for continuing economic austerity to correct the imbalances of past decades, and partly because of domestic political uncertainties. Much is likely to depend on the attitudes of the country's major trade partners in the 1990s, especially South Africa. The country had a brief standoff against the International Monetary Fund in 1993, over debt payments and economic reforms, but it appeared to be resolved by August 1993.

Madagascar

Population ('000)	12,830 (1992)
Urban Population (%)	24.5 (1985)
Land Area (km²)	594,180
Language/s	Malagasy, French
Religion/s	Traditional (50%), Christian (43%), Muslim
Currency	Franc malgache (franc MG = 100 centimes)
Head of State	President Albert Zafy (1993)
Head of Government	Guy Razanamasy
Ruling Party	Antoky Ny Revolusiona Malagasy (Arema - Vanguard of the Malagasy Revolution)

Main urban areas	Population
Antananarivo (capital)	805,450

(1992 estimate)

Madagascar, which was known until 1975 as the Malagasy Republic, became independent from France in 1960. The President is elected by universal suffrage for a seven-year term, but it is the Prime Minister who directs the country through a 131-member National Committee for Economic and Social Recovery - the National Assembly having been dissolved in October 1991 together with the Supreme Revolutionary Council. There is also a High State Authority for the Transition to the Third Republic, whose functions will cease when a new Constitution is agreed.

The National People's Assembly was last elected in June 1993, when the Comité des Forces Vives won 48 of the 138 seats, compared with 10 for the GRAD party, 10 seats for the Famima Party of the outgoing President Didier Ratsiraka, and 4 seats for the Fihaonana Party of Prime Minister Guy Razanamasy. The Leader Party obtained 8 seats.

Madagascar's economy has been hurt by the long austerity programme of the 1980s, which was imposed in an effort to end the overspending which had plunged the country into insupportable levels of external debt. Although confidence is now returning, the country remains crippled by heavy debt servicing costs.

Maldives

Population ('000)	230 (1992)
Urban Population (%)	25.5 (1985)
Land Area (km²)	298
Language/s	Maldivian (Dhivehi)
Religion/s	Islam
Currency	Rufiyaa (Rf = 100 laris)
Head of State	President Maumoon Abdul Gayoom (1978)
Head of Government	President Maumoon Abdul Gayoom
Ruling Party	There are no political parties in the Maldives

Main urban areas	Population
Malé (capital)	56,700

(1992 estimate)

The Republic of Maldives is an independent member of the Commonwealth in which all executive functions are vested in the President and his Cabinet. The President is elected for a five-year term of office, and reports to a 48-member Citizens' Assembly (Majlis), of which he appoints eight members personally. The remainder are elected by universal adult suffrage for a term of five years.

Elections to the Majlis were held in November 1989, when all candidates were obliged to campaign on independent tickets in the absence of political parties. The President was elected unopposed in September 1988

The Maldives has a diversified and potentially prosperous economy, but still requires additional funds if it is to raise its infrastructural facilities to a level which would facilitate a major expansion of the tourism industry.

Mauritius

Population ('000)	1,080 (1992)
Urban Population (%)	40.5 (1991)
Land Area (km²)	1,865
Language/s	English, French, Creole
Religion/s	Hindu, Christian, Muslim
Currency	Mauritian rupee (Rs = 100 cents)
Head of State	President Cassam Uterem (June 1992)
Head of Government	Aneerood Jugnauth
Ruling Party	Mouvement socialiste mauricien leads a coalition with the Mouvement militant mauricien and the Mouvement des travaillistes démocrates.

Main urban areas	Population
Port Louis (capital)	142,087

(1991)

Mauritius became an independent republic in March 1992, and thereupon left the Commonwealth. A non-executive President is appointed by the Prime Minister and the unicameral Legislative Assembly, 62 of whose members are elected by popular vote for a term of five years while the President appoints a maximum of eight further members.

The last legislative elections took place in September 1991, when Jugnauth's MSM/MMM coalition won 55 of the 62 directly elected seats in the 70-member Legislative Assembly.

The fairly high standard of living and the rapid diversification of the economy appear to indicate a fair degree of insulation from future shocks in the consumer market. Recent economic policies have aimed at encouraging foreign investment and establishing Mauritius as an international centre of financial services.

Réunion

Population ('000)	620 (1992)
Land Area (km²)	2,510
Language/s	French
Religion/s	Mainly Roman Catholic (87%)
Currency	French franc (= 100 centimes)
Head of State	President François Mitterrand (France)
Head of Government	Eric Boyer
Ruling Party	The Gaullist Rassemblement pour la république leads a coalition with the Union pour la démocratie française.

Main urban areas	Population
St Denis (capital)	121,922

(1990 census)

Réunion is an external department of France and is governed to a considerable degree from Paris. The country sends deputies to the French Assemblée Nationale, and is represented at the European Community. Since being accorded regional status in 1974, however, Réunion elects its own 45-member Regional Council for a term of six years, with responsibility for economic and social planning. Other executive powers rest in a 45-member General Council.

The last full elections were to the French Assemblée Nationale in 1988, in which the Communists returned two delegates, the Union pour la démocratie française one, the Rassemblement pour la république one. A right-wing independent secured the remaining seat. In the last General Council elections, in March 1988, the RPR/UDF coalition obtained 18 of the 45 seats and went on to form a coalition.

Réunion's economy is very heavily dependent on aid from France, which supplies as much as half of the country's gross domestic product. Expatriate workers are important to the economy.

Rwanda

Population ('000)	7,530 (1992)
Urban Population (%)	8.0 (1991)
Land Area (km²)	26,330
Language/s	Kinyarwanda, French, Kiswahili
Religion/s	Traditional (50%), Roman Catholic (40%)
Currency	Rwanda franc (RF = 100 centimes)
Head of State	President Juvénal Habyarimana (1973)
Head of Government	Dismas Nsengiyaremye (1992)
Ruling Party	Mouvement républicain national pour la démocratie et le développement (MRND) leads a five-party coalition

Main urban areas	Population
Kigali (capital)	170,000

(1992 estimate)

Rwanda has a non-executive President who at present appoints the Prime Minister, in the absence of multi-party elections through which a conventional government could be appointed. Opposition parties have been allowed since 1991, however, and a multi-party poll is expected shortly. In a deliberate attempt to distance himself from the military administrations of the past, the President has introduced constitutional measures barring members of the armed forces from joining political parties.

Legislative elections were held in December 1988, when all of the 140 candidates for the National Development Council were approved by the ruling MRND.

Rwanda's economy has been hit by the turbulence in surrounding states in recent years, and the country has had to resort in many cases to import substitution, and relies heavily on foreign aid, especially from countries of the EC.

Seychelles

Population ('000)	70 (1992)
Urban Population (%)	49.8 (1990)
Land Area (km²)	404
Language/s	Creole (official), English, French
Religion/s	Roman Catholic (90%)
Currency	Seychelles rupee (SR = 100 cents)
Head of State	President France Albert René (1977)
Head of Government	President France Albert René
Ruling Party	Seychelles People's Progressive Front

Main urban areas	Population
Victoria (capital)	30,000

(1992 estimate)

The rule of Sir James Mancham in the Seychelles was overthrown in 1977 by a coup led by France Albert René, who thereupon suspended all political parties except for his own Seychelles People's Progressive Front and declared himself President. René, having in turn fought off a coup attempt by South African-backed mercenaries in 1981, went on to institute an executive Presidency in which the President, like all but 11 of the 33-member unicameral National Assembly, is elected for a five-year term. Multi-party politics were readmitted in 1992.

The first elections since the 1977 coup were held in July 1992, when President René's Seychelles People's Progressive Front won 14 of the seats on the constitutional commission, compared with eight for the opposition Democratic Party and one for the Parti Seselwa. The voter turnout was over 90%. A constitutional referendum in June 1993 produced a 73.6% majority in favour of a new multi-party Constitution.

The Seychelles have achieved a reasonable standard of living since the 1960s, although the heavy dependence on farming means that the country is still vulnerable to fluctuating world markets. A high trade deficit has encouraged a shift toward self-sufficiency in recent years.

Tanzania

Population ('000)	27,830 (1992)
Urban Population (%)	20.8 (1991)
Land Area (km²)	939,760
Language/s	Kiswahili, English
Religion/s	Muslim (35%), Christian (32%), Roman Catholic (22%)
Currency	Tanzanian shilling (Tsh = 100 cents)
Head of State	President Ali Hassan Mwinyi (1985)
Head of Government	John Samuel Malecela
Ruling Party	Chama Cha Mapinduzi (Revolutionary Party of Tanzania)

Main urban areas	Population
Dar es Salaam (capital)	1,220,000

(1992 estimate)

The Republic of Tanzania is an independent member of the Commonwealth, whose executive President is elected for a maximum of two five-year terms by direct popular vote. Legislative authority is vested in a unicameral National Assembly, which serves for a five-year term: 216 of its members are elected by universal suffrage and another 65 are nominated by the President. Until 1992 the Chama Cha Mapinduzi was the only legal political party; in February 1992, however, the party's leaders met to discuss the legalisation of alternative parties.

At present there are no multi-party elections in Tanzania: constitutional reforms currently planned may make this a possibility, however. The last single-list elections took place in October 1990, when the CCM won convincingly; on the same day President Mwinyi was elected unopposed, having obtained 95.5% of the vote on a turnout of 75%.

Tanzania's economy is emerging from decades of centralist direction only with some difficulty. The poor economic growth of recent decades owes at least as much to economic mismanagement as it does to the poor state of the commodity markets, and infrastructural shortcomings are likely to hamper its progress in the 1990s. Yet the low level of nominal per capita income is probably misleading: there is a high level of self-sufficiency among subsistence farmers.

Uganda

Population ('000)	18,670 (1992)
Urban Population (%)	11.3 (1991)
Land Area (km²)	236,580
Language/s	English, Bantu, Kiswahili
Religion/s	Christian (60%), Muslim (5%)
Currency	New Uganda shilling (Ush = 100 cents)
Head of State	President Yoweri Museveni (1986)
Head of Government	George Adyebo
Ruling Party	The National Resistance Movement is the political wing of the pro-Museveni National Resistance Army

Main urban areas	Population
Kampala (capital)	661,000

(1992 estimate)

An independent member of the Commonwealth, Uganda is ruled by an executive President who is assisted by a Cabinet. The current President, Yoweri Museveni, came to power in the military coup of 1986 and immediately banned all political activity, although political parties remain suspended rather than banned. All authority is exercised by a National Resistance Council, whose 278 members include 210 people elected by universal suffrage and 68 who are nominated by the President. There are plans for a Constituent Assembly, comprising 180 members and with powers to draw up a new Constitution.

The last elections to the National Resistance Council were held in February 1989, when supporters of Museveni obtained a substantial majority. Polling was subdued, in the absence of any effective political parties, and in view of the continuing (but briefly lifted) ban on political activity.

Uganda's economy has been very largely disrupted by internal dissent in recent years, and there are severe shortages of adequate infrastructural facilities. Consequently, nominal gross domestic product is of a very low order, although the high degree of agricultural self-sufficiency should be taken into account. Recently the Government has been reversing some of the forced expropriations and nationalisations conducted in the 1960s and 1970s by the deposed dictator Idi Amin.

Zaire

Population ('000)	39,880 (1992)
Urban Population (%)	40.1 (1991)
Land Area (km²)	2,345,410
Language/s	Bantu, Lingala, Kikongo, French
Religion/s	Mainly Roman Catholic (55%), also traditional
Currency	Zaïre (Z = 100 makuta = 10,000 sengi)
Head of State	President Mobutu Sésé Seko (1965)
Head of Government	Faustin Birindwa (June 1993)
Ruling Party	Mouvement populaire de la révolution (MPR)

Main urban areas	Population
Kinshasa (capital)	3,910,000
Lubumbashi	723,300
Mbuji-Mayi	505,000

(1992 estimate)

Zaire, or the Republic of the Congo as it is shortly to be known once again, has a nominally executive President who is elected for a seven-year term by universal vote, and who is de facto the head of the ruling Mouvement populaire de la révolution. Yet President Mobutu Sésé Seko, who seized power in 1972, has found his role under attack from the 310-member Legislative Council (Parliament), and during 1992 he was reduced almost to a figurehead as plans were laid for the country's first multi-party elections since 1972. Mobuto fought back by appointing his own, unrecognised, government under Faustin Birindwa.

Legislative elections were held in September 1987, when the MPR was the only legal contestant. President Mobutu was last re-elected in July 1984, and should have been up for re-election in December 1991; however, he stopped the ballot.

Zaire's centrally planned economy is now showing signs of coming apart, as declining commodity prices for diamonds, gold and other products have impacted on a Government which was already overspent before the crisis struck. Per capita spending power is of the order of $200 per annum.

Southern Africa

Botswana

Population ('000)	1,390 (1992)
Urban Population (%)	25.3 (1991)
Land Area (km²)	575,000
Language/s	English (official), Setswana (national)
Religion/s	Mainly traditional (70%)
Currency	Pula (P = 100 thebe)
Head of State	President Dr Quett K J Masire
Head of Government	President Dr Quett K J Masire
Ruling Party	Botswana Democratic Party

Main urban areas	Population
Gaborone (capital)	137,522

(1992, estimate)

Botswana is an independent member of the Commonwealth in which an executive President is elected by universal suffrage for a term of five years. Legislative power is vested in the National Assembly, which has 34 members elected in the normal way, as well as four specially elected members and two seats which are held ex officio. Draft legislation is considered by the 15-member House of Chiefs, wherever it pertains to constitutional or chieftaincy matters.

Legislative elections were held in October 1989, when the ruling Botswana Democratic Party was returned to power with 31 of the 34 seats. The remainder went to the Botswana National Front, a group which draws its support from the urban working class. The Botswana People's Party lost its only seat.

Botswana's fast-growing mineral economy offers significant hopes of a major expansion in the consumer economy during the later 1990s, although it appears unlikely that the wealth will be at all evenly shared. The relationship with South Africa will be of crucial importance in future years.

Lesotho

Population ('000)	1,840 (1992)
Urban Population (%)	21.0 (1991)
Land Area (km²)	30,345
Language/s	English, Sesotho
Religion/s	Roman Catholic, Lesotho Evangelical and Anglican
Currency	Loti (= 100 lisente)
Head of State	HM Mohato Seeisha, King Letsie III (1990)
Head of Government	Ntsu Mokhehle (April 1993)
Ruling Party	Basotho Congress Party (1992)

Main urban areas	Population
Maseru (capital)	130,000
	(1992 estimate)

Lesotho's recent political history has been unusually turbulent. The former monarch, King Moshoeshoe, was stripped of his office and exiled in 1990 after the armed forces took from him the executive and legislative powers which had been conferred on him in 1986 by the South African-backed forces which had deposed the Prime Minister, Jonathan Leabua. In April 1991, however, the new leader of the ruling Military Council, Justin Lekhanya, was himself deposed in a bloodless coup by Col. Elias Tutsoane Ramaema.

The first multi-party elections in recent years were held in March 1993, when the BCP won about five times as many votes as the Basotho National Party of the deposed leader Justin Lekhanya.

The generally depressed state of the economy reflects the low level of confidence in the regime and the serious climatic conditions which have prevailed in recent years. The relationship with South Africa will remain a largely determining factor in future years.

Malawi

Population ('000)	8,560 (1991)
Urban Population (%)	15.9 (1991)
Land Area (km²)	94,080
Language/s	Chichewa, English
Religion/s	Christian (50%), Muslim, Hindu
Currency	Kwacha (K = 100 tambala)
Head of State	President Hastings Kamuzu Banda (1966)
Head of Government	President Hastings Kamuzu Banda
Ruling Party	The Malawi Congress Party is the only legal political party

Main urban areas	Population
Blantyre-Limbe	331,588
Lilongwe (capital)	233,973
	(1987 census)

Malawi has an executive President who appoints his own Cabinet. Theoretically, all legislative power is vested in the National Assembly, which comprises 141 elected seats and an unlimited number of delegates who may be directly appointed by the President; in practice, the President and the ruling Malawi Congress Party have continued to control all political activities. In October 1993, however, agreement was reached on the creation of a three-member Presidential Council which will effectively take over from Banda. The Council will be led by Gwanda Chakuamba, the leader of the ruling Malawi Congress Party.

A general election to the National Assembly was held in June 1992, when all 675 candidates were from the ruling Malawi Congress Party. Voter turnout was estimated as low as 40%, although the Government claimed 80%. But in June 1993 a referendum found a 63.2% majority in favour of multi-party elections.

Malawi's economy remains constrained by political and economic uncertainties at present, and by the tensions along its borders. It does, however, have considerable scope for expansion.

Mozambique

Population ('000)	16,080 (1991)
Urban Population (%)	28.3 (1991)
Land Area (km²)	784,755
Language/s	Portuguese (official); Ronga, Shangaan, Muchope spoken
Religion/s	Traditional, Christian, Muslim
Currency	Metical (MT = 100 centavos)
Head of State	President Joaquim Alberto Chissano (1986)
Head of Government	Mario da Graça Machungo
Ruling Party	Frelimo (Mozambique Liberation Front)

Main urban areas	Population
Maputo (capital)	1,200,000
	(1992 estimate)

Mozambique's November 1990 Constitution marks a significant turn away from the single-party collectivist state which had characterised the period since 1975. The executive President, who had hitherto been the de facto chairman of the Front for the Liberation of Mozambique, was henceforth to be elected by universal suffrage for a maximum of two five-year terms. Legislative power is vested in the Assembly of the Republic, with 200-250 members who are elected, also by universal suffrage, for a term of five years.

A treaty signed in March 1992 provided for the holding of free elections to the Assembly of the Republic, based on a system of proportional representation, and for both legislative and presidential elections to be held within one year of a peace treaty being signed. However, the promised elections were still being postponed in mid-1993.

The political reforms of the last five years have been reflected in a reversal of the collectivist trends in the economy and a renewed openness to foreign investment and the profit principle. Yet the severe poverty of the population remains an obstacle to the vigorous development of a consumer economy.

Namibia

Population ('000)	1,530 (1992)
Urban Population (%)	28.4 (1991)
Land Area (km²)	824,295
Language/s	English (official, but most African ethnic groups have their own language), Afrikaans, German
Religion/s	Mainly Christian (90%)
Currency	Namibian dollar (= 100 cents)
Head of State	President Sam Nujoma (1990)
Head of Government	Hage Geingob
Ruling Party	South West Africa People's Organisation (SWAPO)

Main urban areas	Population
Windhoek (capital)	126,000
	(1992 estimate)

The Republic of Namibia became fully independent in March 1990, having been effectively annexed by South Africa in 1966 after the United Nations had ended that country's right to act as administrator to the territory. Namibia has an executive President who is elected by the Constituent Assembly (Parliament) for a maximum of two five-year terms; the Assembly's 72 members are elected in turn by universal adult suffrage for a term of five years. An Upper House of Parliament was created and held its first session in May 1993.

In the country's first elections to the National Assembly, in November 1989, SWAPO delegates won 41 of the 72 seats against 21 for the right-wing Democratic Turnhalle Alliance, four for the United Democratic Front and three for the Action Christian National Party. The Namibia Patriotic Front and the Federal Convention of Namibia each won one seat. A system of proportional representation is planned. Nujoma was unanimously elected as President by the Assembly in February 1990.

With its considerable natural resources and its new-found political respectability, Namibia appears to be poised for substantial growth in the 1990s. However, its indifferent communications, especially with Botswana, and its difficult geographical position are hindering factors. In September 1993 the country launched its first national currency, the Namibian dollar, which was initially fixed at par with the South African rand.

South Africa

Population ('000)	39,820 (1992)
Urban Population (%)	57.1 (1989)
Land Area (km²)	1,184,825
Language/s	Afrikaans, English (official languages); principal African languages are Xhosa, Zulu and Sesotho
Religion/s	Mainly Christian
Currency	Rand (R = 100 cents)
Head of State	President F W de Klerk (1989)
Head of Government	President F W de Klerk
Ruling Party	National Party

Main urban areas	Population
Cape Town (seat of legislature)	1,911,521
Johannesburg	1,609,408
Durban	982,075
Pretoria (seat of government)	822,925
Port Elizabeth	651,993
Bloemfontein (judicial capital)	104,381

(1985 census, including suburbs)

South Africa has an executive President and a three-chamber Parliament: the 166-member House of Assembly, for whites, an 80-member House of Representatives, for coloureds, and a 40-member House of Delegates, for Indians. Blacks, who comprise about five-sixths of the population, have no representation: the Government takes the view that they are represented instead in the allegedly independent "homeland" republics of Venda, Bophuthatswana, Ciskei and Transkei, and in six "self-governing states". The United Nations recognises none of these. However in early 1993 the African National Congress (ANC) reached a power-sharing agreement with the ruling National Party, paving the way for constitutional reform and the eventual transition to majority rule.Non-racial multi-party elections have been provisionally fixed for April 1994.

The last general election took place in September 1989, when members to the three houses of parliament were elected. The House of Assembly was dominated by the National Party, which won 93 seats.The Labour Party won 69 seats in the House of Representatives, while the Solidarity Party gained 16 seats in the House of Delegates.

South Africa's economy has managed to withstand the pressures of international trade sanctions fairly well, thanks to its abundance of domestic resources. Yet the slump in world commodity prices, especially for gold, almost wrecked its economy in the 1980s and the rapid rise in external debt has caused a major crisis. Disruption during the transition to multi-ethnic elections seems likely to worsen the situation in the early 1990s. In October 1993 the United Nations formally approved the lifting of trade sanctions against South Africa, as an expression of its approval for the country's transition to multi-party democracy and power sharing provisions.

Swaziland

Population ('000)	790 (1992)
Urban Population (%)	34.3 (1986)
Land Area (km²)	17,365
Language/s	English, Siswati
Religion/s	Christian (60%), remainder mainly traditional beliefs
Currency	Lilangeni (L = 100 cents)
Head of State	HM King Mswati III (1986)
Head of Government	Obed Dlamini (1990)
Ruling Party	All political parties are banned under the 1978 constitutional amendments

Main urban areas	Population
Mbabane (capital)	42,400

(1992 estimate)

The Kingdom of Swaziland is an independent member of the Commonwealth, in which considerable power still attaches to the King. He appoints the Prime Minister and Cabinet directly, and they answer to him rather than to the 50-member House of Assembly or the 20-member Senate. 40 of the House of Assembly members and 10 Senators are elected by the 40 traditional tribal communities, with the King appointing all the others.

The last elections to the Legislature (Libandla) took place in November 1987, ahead of schedule, in what was widely perceived as an attempt by the King to purge the political structure of people he did not favour. In the absence of political parties, all appointments were made according to tribal considerations.

With a per capita GDP of around $800, Swaziland ranks among the more prosperous countries of the region. With a fairly well-diversified economy, it has proved fairly robust in the face of collapsing commodity prices, though recent instabilities have brought difficulties.

Zambia

Population ('000)	8,640 (1992)
Urban Population (%)	49.3 (1990)
Land Area (km²)	752,615
Language/s	English (official); Nyanja, Bemba, Tonga, Lozi, Lunda and Luvale
Religion/s	Mainly traditional (70%), Christian (20%)
Currency	Zambian kwacha (Kw = 100 ngee)
Head of State	President Frederick Chiluba (1991)
Head of Government	President Frederick Chiluba (1991)
Ruling Party	Movement for Multi-Party Democracy

Main urban areas	Population
Lusaka	982,362
Kitwe	500,000

(1990 census)

From 1972 to 1991 Zambia was run as a single-party state, in which the United National Independence Party (UNIP) stood unopposed at every level; in August 1991, however, a new multi-party Constitution was introduced, leading in October 1991 to multi-party elections in which UNIP was beaten. A week later the 27-year state of emergency was ended. The executive President is elected by universal suffrage for a five-year term, and answers to a 150-member National Assembly which sits also for five years. In March 1993, however, President Chiluba declared an indefinite state of emergency after reports of an attempted coup against him.

The country's first multi-party elections took place in October 1991, when the Movement for Multi-Party Democracy defeated the UNIP of President Kenneth Kaunda, who had ruled since 1964. The MMD gained 125 of the 150 seats in the National Assembly, against UNIP's 25 seats. Only four of the 20 UNIP Cabinet ministers were returned to their parliamentary seats. However, it was reported that over half of the electorate had not voted.

Zambia's economy, although basically dependent on commodity exports, has made a reasonable recovery since the late 1970s, when the share of mining in the Gross National Product fell from 30% to below 10%. In fact, most of the population is engaged in some sort of subsistence activity, which is why an apparent per capita GDP of $200-400 is manageable.

Zimbabwe

Population ('000)	10,580 (1992)
Urban Population (%)	26.7 (1987)
Land Area (km²)	390,310
Language/s	English (official); Chishona, Sindebele
Religion/s	Christian (55%), traditional
Currency	Zimbabwe dollar (Z$ = 100 cents)
Head of State	President Robert G. Mugabe (1987)
Head of Government	President Robert G. Mugabe
Ruling Party	Zimbabwe African National Union-Patriotic Front (ZANU-PF)

Main urban areas	Population
Harare (capital)	810,000
Bulawayo	505,000

(1992 estimate)

Zimbabwe, an independent member of the Commonwealth, has an executive President who is elected by universal suffrage for a six-year term and who presides over a single-chamber House of Assembly. The Assembly's 150 members, who also serve for six years, include 120 elected members, 10 tribal chiefs, eight provincial governors appointed by the President, and 12 other presidential appointees. Since 1991 the Government has sought to break with its colonial past through controversial land appropriations, which remove farm lands from white farmers.

In the March 1990 elections to the House of Assembly, the ZANU-PF coalition won 116 of the 120 elected seats, swamping the white-dominated Zimbabwe United Movement, the Zimbabwe African National Union (Ndonga), the National Democratic Union and the Democratic Party.

Zimbabwe's economy has fared poorly since the mid-1980s, when budget deficits and high external debts forced a clampdown on spending an investment. Several years of drought, accompanied by a period of poor government management, have further complicated the picture, and in early 1993 there appeared to be little likelihood of a rapid upturn.

Section Two
Demographic Trends and Forecasts

TOTAL POPULATION   Table No. 0201

Trends in Total Population 1977-1992: International Estimates at Mid-Year

Units: Millions

	1977	1980	1985	1986	1987	1988	1989	1990	1991	1992	% growth 1977-92
North America											
Canada [a]	23.27	24.04	25.36	25.61	25.62	25.91	26.24	26.60	27.03	27.44	17.92
USA [a]	220.24	227.74	238.47	240.66	242.82	245.05	247.35	249.97	252.69		
Regional total	*243.51*	*251.78*	*263.83*	*266.27*	*268.44*	*270.96*	*273.59*	*276.57*	*279.72*		
South America											
Argentina	26.91	28.24	30.33	30.74	31.14	31.53	31.93	32.32	32.71	33.10	23.01
Bolivia	5.16	5.60	6.43	6.55	6.67	6.83	7.00	7.17	7.35	7.52	45.81
Brazil [b]	110.21	121.29	135.56	138.49	141.45	144.43	147.40	150.37	153.32	156.28	41.80
Chile [c]	10.55	11.14	12.12	12.33	12.54	12.75	12.96	13.17	13.39		
Colombia	24.43	25.89	28.62	29.19	29.73	30.24	32.35	32.99	33.61	34.20	39.98
Ecuador	7.45	8.12	9.38	9.65	9.92	10.20	10.49	10.78	10.85	11.12	49.23
French Guiana [c]	0.06	0.07	0.09	0.09	0.10	0.11	0.11	0.11	0.11	0.11	83.33
Guyana [d,e]	0.81	0.87	0.97	0.97	0.99	1.01	1.02	1.04	1.06	1.07	32.35
Paraguay [c]	2.87	3.15	3.69	3.81	3.92	4.04	4.16	4.28	4.40	4.52	57.49
Peru	15.99	17.30	19.42	19.84	20.26	20.68	21.11	21.55	22.00	22.45	40.43
Suriname	0.36	0.35	0.37	0.38	0.35	0.39	0.40	0.40	0.41	0.42	15.56
Uruguay	2.86	2.91	2.93	2.98	3.06	3.06	3.08	3.10	3.11	3.13	9.48
Venezuela	13.59	15.02	17.32	17.79	18.27	18.75	19.25	19.73	20.23	20.72	52.47
Regional total	*221.25*	*239.95*	*267.23*	*272.81*	*278.40*	*284.02*	*291.26*	*297.01*	*302.54*		
Caribbean											
Anguilla											
Antigua				0.06	0.06	0.06	0.07	0.07	0.07	0.07	
Aruba	0.06	0.06	0.06	0.06	0.06	0.06	0.06	0.06	0.06	0.06	
Bahamas	0.20	0.21	0.23	0.24	0.24	0.24	0.25	0.26	0.26	0.27	33.50
Barbados	0.25	0.25	0.25	0.25	0.25	0.25	0.26	0.26	0.26	0.27	6.00
Bermuda	0.05	0.05	0.06	0.06	0.06	0.06	0.06	0.06	0.06	0.06	20.00
British Virgin Islands											
Cayman Islands											
Cuba	9.55	9.72	10.10	10.19	10.29	10.40	10.52	10.61	10.70	10.81	13.17
Dominica				0.07	0.07	0.07	0.07	0.07	0.07	0.07	
Dominican Republic	5.03	5.44	6.24	6.42	6.72	6.87	7.02	7.17	7.32	7.47	48.53
Grenada	0.10	0.09	0.10	0.10	0.10	0.10	0.10	0.10	0.10	0.11	5.00
Guadeloupe	0.33	0.33	0.33	0.33	0.33	0.34	0.34	0.34	0.34	0.34	3.64
Haiti [f]	4.75	5.01	5.86	5.99	6.11	6.24	6.36	6.51	6.65	6.78	42.82
Jamaica	2.10	2.13	2.31	2.37	2.41	2.45	2.48	2.52	2.56	2.60	23.57
Martinique	0.33	0.31	0.34	0.33	0.33	0.33	0.33	0.33	0.32	0.33	0.91
Netherlands Antilles	0.18	0.19	0.18	0.18	0.19	0.19	0.19	0.19	0.20	0.20	10.56
St Kitts	0.04	0.04	0.05	0.04	0.04	0.04	0.04	0.04	0.04	0.04	5.00
St Lucia	0.12	0.12	0.13	0.13	0.13	0.13	0.14	0.14	0.14	0.14	16.67
St Vincent/Grenadines [c]	0.10	0.10	0.10	0.10	0.10	0.11	0.11	0.11	0.11	0.11	9.00
Trinidad and Tobago	1.04	1.08	1.18	1.18	1.19	1.21	1.22	1.24	1.25	1.27	21.63
Regional total	*24.23*	*25.13*	*27.52*	*28.10*	*28.69*	*29.15*	*29.61*	*30.08*	*30.51*	*30.98*	*27.86*
Central America											
Belize	0.14	0.15	0.17	0.17	0.17	0.17	0.18	0.18	0.19	0.19	35.00
Costa Rica [e,g,h]	2.07	2.25	2.49	2.67	2.78	2.85	2.96	2.99	3.06	3.16	52.71
El Salvador	4.26	4.51	4.82	4.91	5.01	5.11	5.21	5.25	5.38	5.51	29.30
Guatemala	6.36	6.92	7.96	8.19	8.44	8.68	8.94	9.20	9.47	9.74	53.21
Honduras	3.32	3.69	4.37	4.51	4.66	4.80	4.95	5.14	5.30	5.46	64.52
Mexico	63.81	69.39	77.94	79.57	81.20	82.84	84.49	86.15	87.84	89.54	40.32
Nicaragua	2.32	2.73	3.27	3.38	3.50	3.62	3.74	3.87	4.00	4.13	78.06
Panama	1.79	1.96	2.18	2.23	2.27	2.32	2.37	2.42	2.47	2.52	40.50
Puerto Rico [e]	3.08	3.21	3.28	3.31	3.43	3.46	3.49	3.53	3.55	3.58	16.23
Regional total	*87.15*	*94.81*	*106.48*	*108.94*	*111.46*	*113.85*	*116.33*	*118.73*	*121.26*	*123.83*	*42.09*
South Asia											
Afghanistan	12.40	15.95	18.14	18.61	15.22	15.51	15.81	16.12	16.43		
Bangladesh	82.71	88.68	98.66	100.62	102.56	104.53	106.51	113.68	116.44	119.29	44.23
Bhutan	1.21	1.28	1.40	1.41	1.42	1.45	1.48	1.52	1.55	1.61	33.06
India [c]	625.82	675.00	750.90	766.14	781.37	796.60	811.82	827.00	849.64	879.55	40.54
Nepal	13.14	14.01	16.69	17.13	17.56	17.99	18.44	18.90	19.60	20.58	56.62
Pakistan	75.44	82.58	96.18	99.16	102.24	105.41	108.68	112.03	115.52	119.11	57.88
Sri Lanka	13.94	14.75	15.84	16.12	16.36	16.59	16.81	16.99	17.24	17.40	24.82
Regional total	*824.66*	*892.25*	*997.81*	*1019.19*	*1036.73*	*1058.08*	*1079.55*	*1106.24*	*1136.42*		

TOTAL POPULATION

Trends in Total Population 1977-1992: International Estimates at Mid-Year

Units: Millions

	1977	1980	1985	1986	1987	1988	1989	1990	1991	1992	% growth 1977-92
Japan											
Japan	113.90	116.80	120.80	121.50	122.09	122.61	123.12	123.54	123.92	123.36	8.31
Regional total	*113.90*	*116.80*	*120.80*	*121.50*	*122.09*	*122.61*	*123.12*	*123.54*	*123.92*	*123.36*	*8.31*
ASEAN/NICs											
Brunei	0.17	0.19	0.22	0.23	0.24	0.24	0.25	0.27	0.27	0.27	58.82
Hong Kong [c]	4.51	5.06	5.46	5.53	5.56	5.68	5.76	5.80	5.75	5.80	28.60
Indonesia	136.63	147.49	164.05	168.35	172.02	175.59	179.14	179.30	187.76	191.17	39.92
Macau [i]	0.28	0.32	0.39	0.42	0.43	0.44	0.45	0.48	0.50		
Malaysia	12.58	13.70	15.68	16.11	16.53	16.94	17.35	17.76	18.34	18.79	49.36
Philippines	44.58	48.32	54.67	56.00	57.36	58.72	60.10	61.48	62.87	64.26	44.15
Singapore	2.33	2.41	2.56	2.59	2.61	2.65	2.68	2.71	2.76	2.81	20.60
South Korea	36.41	38.12	41.06	41.57	41.80	41.97	42.38	42.87	43.27	43.66	19.91
Taiwan	16.81	17.80	19.26	19.46	19.68	19.90					
Thailand	44.04	46.72	51.68	52.65	53.60	54.54	55.21	56.08	56.92	57.76	31.15
Regional total	*298.34*	*320.13*	*355.03*	*362.91*	*369.83*	*376.67*					
East/SE Asia											
Cambodia	6.79	6.40	7.28	7.49	7.60	7.87	8.06	8.25	8.81	9.05	33.28
China	957.38	996.13	1070.60	1086.60	1102.90	1119.50	1136.40	1153.50	1170.70	1188.00	24.09
Laos	3.53	3.21	3.59	3.69	3.80	3.91	4.02	4.14	4.26	4.47	26.63
Mongolia	1.53	1.66	1.88	1.93	1.97	2.02	2.07	2.20	2.25	2.31	50.98
Myanmar [d,e]	31.50	33.64	37.15	39.41	39.14	39.97	40.81	41.67	42.56	42.33	34.38
North Korea	16.70	18.03	19.89	20.24	20.60	20.98	21.37	21.77	22.19	22.92	37.25
Vietnam	50.48	54.18	59.90	61.20	62.52	63.87	65.25	66.23	68.18	69.48	37.64
Regional total	*1067.91*	*1113.25*	*1200.29*	*1220.56*	*1238.53*	*1258.12*	*1277.97*	*1297.76*	*1318.95*	*1,338.56*	*25.34*
Australasia											
Australia	14.19	14.70	15.79	16.02	16.26	16.54	16.81	17.09	17.34	17.53	23.54
New Zealand	3.12	3.11	3.25	3.25	3.28	3.29	3.31	3.35	3.38	3.41	9.29
Regional total	*17.31*	*17.81*	*19.04*	*19.27*	*19.54*	*19.83*	*20.12*	*20.44*	*20.72*	*20.94*	*20.97*
Pacific											
American Samoa	0.03	0.03	0.04	0.04	0.04	0.04	0.04	0.04	0.04		
Fiji	0.60	0.63	0.70	0.71	0.73	0.74	0.75	0.73	0.74	0.74	23.33
French Polynesia	0.14	0.15	0.16	0.17	0.18	0.19	0.19	0.21	0.21	0.21	50.00
Guam [d]	0.10	0.11	0.11	0.12	0.12	0.12	0.12	0.12	0.14	0.14	40.00
Kiribati	0.06	0.06	0.06	0.06	0.06	0.06	0.07	0.07	0.07	0.07	16.67
Nauru							0.01				
New Caledonia	0.14	0.14	0.15	0.15	0.16	0.16	0.16	0.17	0.17	0.17	21.43
Papua New Guinea [j]	2.81	2.96	3.30	3.37	3.44	3.52	3.59	3.67	3.77	4.06	44.48
Solomon Islands	0.21	0.23	0.27	0.28	0.29	0.30	0.31	0.32	0.33	0.34	61.90
Tonga	0.09	0.09	0.10	0.10	0.10	0.09	0.09	0.09	0.09	0.10	11.11
Tuvalu											
Vanuatu [b]	0.10	0.12	0.14	0.14	0.14	0.15	0.15	0.15	0.16	0.16	60.00
Western Samoa	0.15	0.16	0.16	0.16	0.16	0.16	0.16	0.16	0.16	0.16	6.67
Regional total	*4.43*	*4.68*	*5.19*	*5.30*	*5.42*	*5.53*	*5.64*	*5.73*	*5.88*	*6.15*	*39.73*
Middle East											
Bahrain	0.30	0.34	0.42	0.44	0.46	0.47	0.49	0.50	0.52	0.53	76.67
Egypt	38.79	42.13	46.43	47.70	49.01	50.35	51.73	53.15	54.61	55.16	42.20
Iran [b]	34.69	39.30	47.82	49.44	51.02	52.52	54.20	54.61	57.73	59.92	72.73
Iraq	12.03	13.24	15.58	16.11	16.33	17.25	17.50	18.08	18.68	19.29	60.35
Israel	3.61	3.88	4.23	4.30	4.37	4.44	4.51	4.66	4.95	5.19	43.77
Jordan	2.71	2.92	3.41	3.52	3.63	3.75	3.88	4.01	4.15	4.29	58.30
Kuwait [k]	1.14	1.37	1.71	1.79	1.87	1.96	2.05	2.14	2.09	1.97	72.81
Lebanon	2.76	2.67	2.67	2.67	2.68	2.69	2.71	2.74	2.78	2.84	2.90
Oman [d,e]	0.84	0.98	1.23	1.29	1.34	1.39	1.45	1.50	1.56	1.64	95.24
Qatar [k]	0.19	0.23	0.30	0.31	0.33	0.34	0.42	0.49	0.44	0.45	136.84
Saudi Arabia	8.06	9.37	11.60	12.07	13.61	14.02	14.43	14.87	15.39	15.92	97.52
Syria	7.88	8.70	10.27	10.61	10.97	11.34	11.72	12.12	12.99	12.96	64.47
United Arab Emirates	0.69	0.98	1.33	1.38	1.45	1.50	1.55	1.59	1.63	1.67	142.03
Yemen [l]	7.33	7.88	9.01	9.27	9.59	9.87	10.50	11.28	12.10	12.53	70.94
Regional total	*121.02*	*133.99*	*156.01*	*160.90*	*166.66*	*171.89*	*177.14*	*181.74*	*189.62*	*194.36*	*60.60*

TOTAL POPULATION — Table No. 0201 (cont'd)

Trends in Total Population 1977-1992: International Estimates at Mid-Year

Units: Millions

	1977	1980	1985	1986	1987	1988	1989	1990	1991	1992	% growth 1977-92
North Africa											
Algeria	17.06	18.67	22.52	23.02	23.65	24.29	24.29	25.01	25.64	26.35	54.45
Chad	4.21	4.48	5.02	5.14	5.27	5.40	5.54	5.68	5.82	5.96	41.57
Djibouti c	0.25	0.36	0.43	0.46	0.40	0.42	0.43	0.44	0.45	0.47	88.00
Ethiopia d	35.92	38.52	43.35	44.93	46.18	47.88	49.51	51.69	53.38	55.11	53.42
Libya b,d	2.63	3.04	3.60	3.74	4.08	4.23	4.38	4.54	4.71	4.81	82.89
Mali	6.51	7.10	8.21	7.57	7.70	7.83	7.96	8.16	9.51	9.82	50.84
Mauritania	1.50	1.55	1.77	1.81	1.86	1.92	1.97	2.02	2.04	2.14	42.67
Morocco f	18.36	20.05	22.03	22.61	23.20	23.81	24.43	25.06	25.70	26.32	43.36
Niger	4.86	5.31	6.61	6.82	7.04	7.26	7.49	7.73	7.98	8.25	69.75
Somalia g	3.56	5.35	7.87	8.04	8.18	8.32	8.48	8.68	8.92	9.20	158.43
Sudan	16.95	18.68	21.55	22.18	23.13	23.80	24.49	25.20	25.92	26.66	57.29
Tunisia	5.93	6.39	7.26	7.46	7.63	7.81	8.00	8.18	8.36	8.40	41.65
Regional total	117.74	129.50	150.22	153.78	158.32	162.97	166.97	172.39	178.43	183.49	55.84
West Africa											
Benin m	3.29	3.46	4.04	4.17	4.30	4.45	4.59	4.74	4.89	4.92	49.54
Burkina Faso h	5.84	6.15	7.89	8.10	8.31	8.54	8.77	9.00	9.24	9.49	62.50
Cameroon	7.91	8.50	10.17	10.46	10.82	10.88	11.54	11.52	11.86	12.20	54.24
Cape Verde	0.29	0.30	0.33	0.34	0.34	0.35	0.36	0.37	0.38	0.38	31.03
Côte d'Ivoire	7.30	8.17	9.93	10.32	10.71	11.12	11.55	12.00	12.46	12.91	76.85
Equatorial Guinea	0.33	0.35	0.31	0.32	0.33	0.34	0.34	0.35	0.36	0.37	12.12
Gabon	1.00	0.81	0.98	1.02	1.06	1.10	1.13	1.17	1.21	1.24	24.00
Gambia	0.55	0.60	0.74	0.77	0.79	0.81	0.84	0.86	0.88	0.88	60.00
Ghana	10.45	11.35	12.72	13.05	13.39	14.13	14.57	15.03	15.51	15.96	52.73
Guinea g	5.06	5.41	4.66	4.79	4.93	5.07	5.59	5.75	5.93	6.12	20.95
Guinea-Bissau	0.70	0.78	0.87	0.89	0.91	0.93	0.94	0.96	0.98	1.01	44.29
Liberia	1.67	1.85	2.19	2.22	2.28	2.34	2.40	2.46	2.52	2.58	54.49
Nigeria	72.58	80.56	95.69	98.17	101.41	104.96	105.02	108.54	112.07	115.66	59.36
Sao Tomé e Príncipe	0.08	0.09	0.11	0.11	0.10	0.11	0.12	0.12	0.12	0.12	50.00
Senegal	5.25	5.70	6.44	6.61	6.79	7.11	7.13	7.33	7.53	7.74	47.43
Sierra Leone	3.14	3.30	3.60	3.67	3.85	3.95	4.05	4.15	4.26	4.38	39.49
Togo	2.35	2.55	3.03	3.12	3.22	3.32	3.42	3.53	3.64	3.76	60.00
Regional total	127.79	139.93	163.70	168.13	173.54	179.51	182.36	187.88	193.84	199.72	56.29
East/Central Africa											
Angola	7.00	7.72	7.98	8.19	8.41	8.64	9.74	10.02	9.52	9.89	41.29
Burundi	3.90	4.12	4.72	4.86	4.92	5.15	5.30	5.46	5.62	5.78	48.21
Central African Republic	2.17	2.31	2.61	2.74	2.79	2.87	2.95	3.04	3.13	3.17	46.08
Comoros	0.35	0.38	0.46	0.48	0.50	0.51	0.53	0.55	0.57	0.58	65.71
Congo	1.44	1.53	1.94	2.00	2.06	2.13	2.20	2.27	2.35	2.37	64.58
Kenya	14.35	16.67	20.33	21.16	22.94	23.88	24.87	24.03	25.91	26.98	88.01
Madagascar	8.02	8.78	9.98	10.55	10.90	11.26	11.20	11.20	11.49	12.83	59.98
Maldives	0.14	0.15	0.18	0.19	0.20	0.20	0.21	0.21	0.22	0.23	64.29
Mauritius	0.88	0.94	0.99	0.99	1.00	1.02	1.03	1.07	1.07	1.08	22.73
Réunion	0.49	0.51	0.55	0.56	0.56	0.58	0.59	0.59	0.61	0.62	26.53
Rwanda	4.36	5.16	6.10	6.31	6.53	6.76	6.99	7.18	7.27	7.53	72.71
Seychelles	0.06	0.06	0.07	0.07	0.07	0.07	0.07	0.07	0.07	0.07	16.67
Tanzania	16.92	18.58	21.73	22.46	23.22	24.00	24.80	25.63	26.90	27.83	64.48
Uganda g	12.35	13.11	15.03	15.49	15.97	16.49	17.02	17.56	18.11	18.67	51.17
Zaire j	24.02	26.38	30.98	31.50	32.46	33.46	34.49	35.56	36.67	39.88	66.03
Regional total	96.45	106.40	123.65	127.55	132.53	137.02	141.99	144.44	149.51	157.51	63.31
Southern Africa											
Botswana	0.74	0.82	1.09	1.13	1.17	1.21	1.26	1.30	1.35	1.39	87.84
Lesotho	1.24	1.34	1.53	1.58	1.62	1.68	1.70	1.75	1.79	1.84	48.39
Malawi	5.54	6.05	7.06	7.28	7.50	7.75	8.02	8.29	8.56		
Mozambique b	10.66	12.13	13.81	14.17	14.40	14.93	15.33	15.66	16.08		
Namibia g	0.92	1.01	1.23	1.27	1.31	1.35	1.38	1.44	1.49	1.53	65.58
South Africa	26.68	28.61	33.60	34.44	35.30	36.17	37.06	37.96	38.88	39.82	49.25
Swaziland	0.50	0.55	0.64	0.66	0.71	0.74	0.76	0.77	0.77	0.79	58.00
Zambia	5.30	5.83	6.67	7.28	7.56	7.53	7.80	8.07	8.39	8.64	63.02
Zimbabwe	6.52	7.10	8.38	8.41	8.64	8.88	9.12	9.37	10.27	10.58	62.27
Regional total	58.10	63.44	74.01	76.22	78.21	80.24	82.43	84.61	87.58		53.58

Source: UN, Monthly Bulletin of Statistics/national statistical offices

Notes: see end of section

TOTAL POPULATION — Table No. 0202

Trends in Total Population 1977-1992: National Estimates at Mid-Year

Units: Millions

	1977	1980	1985	1987	1988	1989	1990	1991	1992	% growth 1977-92
North America										
Canada [a]	23.27	24.04	25.36	25.63	25.91	26.22	26.58	26.99	27.41	17.77
USA [a]	220.24	227.72	238.19	242.84	245.06	247.34	249.42	252.16	255.08	15.82
Regional total	*243.51*	*251.77*	*263.55*	*268.46*	*270.97*	*273.56*	*276.00*	*279.15*	*282.49*	
South America										
Argentina [b]	26.91	28.24	30.56	31.50	31.53	31.93	32.32	32.71		
Bolivia [b]	5.16	5.60	6.43	6.55	6.99	7.19	7.40	7.61		
Brazil [c 80,d]	110.21	121.29	135.56	141.45	144.43	147.40	150.37	153.32	156.28	41.80
Chile [e 84]	10.66	11.15	12.12	12.54	12.75	12.96	13.17	13.39	13.60	27.53
Colombia	24.43	25.89	28.62	29.94	30.24	31.72	32.30	32.84		
Ecuador	7.46	8.12	9.38	9.92	10.20	10.49	10.78	11.08		
French Guiana [a]	0.06	0.07	0.09	0.10	0.11	0.11	0.12			
Guyana [e 79-84,88,c 85]	0.81	0.87	0.97	1.00	1.01	1.02	1.04			
Paraguay	2.85	3.15	3.69	3.92	4.04	4.16	4.28	4.40		
Peru [b]	15.99	17.30	19.70	20.27	20.70	21.12	21.55	22.00	22.45	40.43
Suriname [e 83-86,88]	0.36	0.36	0.38	0.38	0.39	0.40	0.40			
Uruguay [e 85]	2.86	2.91	3.01	2.92	3.06	3.08	3.09	3.11		
Venezuela [b]	13.59	15.02	17.32	18.26	18.76	19.25	19.74	20.23		
Regional total	*221.36*	*239.95*	*267.84*	*278.75*	*284.20*	*290.83*	*296.56*	*300.69*	*192.33*	
Caribbean										
Anguilla [f]	0.01	0.01	0.01	0.01	0.01	0.01	0.01			
Antigua					0.06	0.06	0.07	0.06	0.06	
Aruba [a,f]	0.06	0.06	0.07	0.07	0.06	0.06	0.06			
Bahamas	0.20	0.21	0.23	0.24	0.25	0.25	0.26	0.26	0.26	31.47
Barbados [e 86]	0.25	0.25	0.25	0.25	0.25	0.26	0.26	0.26	0.26	5.26
Bermuda [f]	0.05	0.05	0.06	0.06	0.06	0.06	0.06	0.06		
British Virgin Islands [e 85-86]	0.01	0.01	0.01	0.01	0.01	0.01	0.01			
Cayman Islands [a]	0.02	0.02	0.02	0.02	0.03	0.02	0.02	0.02		
Cuba	9.55	9.72	10.10	10.29	10.41	10.51	10.63	10.74		
Dominica			0.07	0.07	0.07	0.07	0.07	0.07		
Dominican Republic	5.03	5.44	6.24	6.56	6.87	7.01	7.17	7.31		
Grenada			0.09	0.10	0.10					
Guadeloupe [a,e 88]			0.34	0.36	0.37	0.38	0.39			
Haiti [a, c 82]	4.75	5.01	5.87	6.11	6.24	6.36	6.49	6.63		
Jamaica [e 83-86,88,c 88]	2.10	2.13	2.31	2.41	2.45	2.38	2.30	2.37		
Martinique [a]	0.33	0.33	0.34	0.35	0.35	0.36	0.36	0.36		
Netherlands Antilles [b]	0.18	0.19	0.18	0.19	0.19	0.19	0.19	0.19		
St Kitts [e 84-86]	0.05	0.04	0.05	0.05	0.05	0.05	0.05			
St Lucia [e 85-86]	0.12	0.12	0.13	0.13	0.15	0.15	0.15			
St Vincent & the Grenadines [c80,88, e85-88]		0.12	0.10	0.10	0.10	0.11	0.11	0.11		
Trinidad and Tobago [e 84-86,88]	1.04	1.08	1.18	1.21	1.21	1.21	1.23	1.25		
Regional total	*23.84*	*24.79*	*27.65*	*28.57*	*29.29*	*29.51*	*29.88*	*29.58*	*0.58*	
Central America										
Belize [e 78-80]	0.14	0.15	0.17	0.18	0.18	0.18	0.18	0.19		
Costa Rica [a,e 83-86]	2.07	2.25	2.49	2.78	2.85	2.92	2.99	3.03	3.10	50.00
El Salvador	4.26	4.51	4.82	5.01	5.03	5.14	5.25			
Guatemala	6.36	6.92	7.96	8.43	8.68	8.94	9.20	9.45		
Honduras [e 86]	3.32	3.69	4.37	4.82	4.80	4.95	5.11			
Mexico [a]	63.81	69.39	78.52	81.21	82.73	84.49	86.15	87.84		
Nicaragua [a]	2.33	2.73	3.27	3.50	3.62	3.75	3.87	4.00		
Panama [g]	1.79	1.96	2.18	2.28	2.32	2.37	2.42	2.47	2.51	40.32
Puerto Rico [c86,88, e86,88]	3.07	3.21	3.28	3.29	3.46	3.49	3.53	3.55		
Regional total	*87.14*	*94.79*	*107.07*	*111.50*	*113.68*	*116.23*	*118.71*	*110.53*	*5.61*	
South Asia										
Afghanistan [b]	12.40	15.95	18.14	15.22	15.51	15.81	16.12	16.43		
Bangladesh [b]	82.71	88.68	98.66	102.56	104.53	106.51	108.48			
Bhutan [f]	1.10	1.17	1.29	1.34	1.38	1.41	1.44			
India [b]	631.00	675.00	750.86	781.37	796.60	811.82	827.00	849.64		
Nepal [a,c 81]	13.14	14.01	16.63	17.63	17.99	18.44	18.92			
Pakistan	75.44	82.58	96.18	102.24	105.41	108.68	112.05	115.52		
Sri Lanka	13.94	14.75	15.84	16.36	16.59	16.81	16.99	17.24		
Regional total	*829.73*	*892.14*	*997.59*	*1036.73*	*1058.01*	*1079.47*	*1101.00*	*998.83*		

TOTAL POPULATION   Table No. 0202 (cont'd)

Trends in Total Population 1977-1992: National Estimates at Mid-Year

Units: Millions

	1977	1980	1985	1987	1988	1989	1990	1991	1992	% growth 1977-92
Japan										
Japan	113.87	116.81	121.05	122.26	122.61	123.12	123.54	123.92		
Regional total	*113.87*	*116.81*	*121.05*	*122.26*	*122.61*	*123.12*	*123.54*	*123.92*		
ASEAN/NICs										
Brunei [b]	0.17	0.19	0.22	0.24	0.24	0.25	0.26			
Hong Kong [b,h]	4.58	5.06	5.46	5.58	5.63	5.69	5.65	5.69	5.76	25.61
Indonesia	136.63	146.36	163.39	170.53	175.59	179.14	179.30			
Macau [a,c 81]	0.28	0.32	0.39	0.43	0.44	0.45	0.46			
Malaysia	12.58	13.70	15.68	16.53	16.94	17.35	17.76	18.18		
Philippines [a]	44.58	48.32	54.38	57.36	58.72	60.10	61.48	62.87		
Singapore	2.33	2.41	2.56	2.61	2.65	2.69	2.72	2.76	2.82	21.20
South Korea [b]	36.41	38.12	41.06	41.98	41.98	42.38	42.87	43.27	43.66	19.91
Taiwan	17.12	17.81	19.26	19.76	19.90	20.05	20.19			
Thailand [c 80]	44.04	46.46	51.30	53.61	54.52	55.45	56.08	56.92		
Regional total	*298.72*	*318.75*	*353.70*	*368.63*	*376.61*	*383.53*	*386.76*	*189.69*	*52.24*	
East/SE Asia										
Cambodia [f]	6.79	6.40	7.29	7.68	7.87	8.06	8.24			
China [f]	957.38	996.13	1059.52	1088.57	1103.98	1119.69	1130.51			
Laos [f]	3.53	3.68	4.12	3.78	3.88	3.97	4.07			
Mongolia [c 88,91]	1.53	1.66	1.89	1.97	2.09	2.16	2.23	2.13	2.18	42.07
Myanmar [f]	31.51	33.64	38.54	39.14	39.97	40.81	41.65	42.43		
North Korea	16.70	18.03	20.39	21.39	21.90	22.42	22.94			
Vietnam [c 88,f]	50.48	54.18	59.71	62.81	64.23	65.68	66.20			
Regional total	*1067.92*	*1113.72*	*1191.45*	*1225.35*	*1243.92*	*1262.79*	*1275.84*	*44.56*	*2.18*	
Australasia										
Australia [a,b]	14.19	14.70	15.76	16.26	16.53	16.83	17.09	17.29		
New Zealand	3.12	3.11	3.25	3.34	3.35	3.36	3.37	3.42	3.46	10.74
Regional total	*17.31*	*17.81*	*19.01*	*19.61*	*19.88*	*20.19*	*20.46*	*20.71*	*3.46*	
Pacific										
American Samoa [a, c 90]	0.03	0.03	0.04	0.04	0.04	0.04	0.05			
Fiji [c 88,e 86,88]	0.60	0.63	0.70	0.71	0.73	0.74	0.74	0.75		
French Polynesia			0.18	0.19	0.19	0.19	0.20	0.20		
Guam [c85,88, e85-88]	0.10	0.11	0.11	0.13	0.12	0.12	0.12			
Kiribati [f]	0.06	0.06	0.06	0.07	0.07	0.07	0.07			
Nauru [f]	0.01	0.01	0.01	0.01	0.01	0.01	0.01			
New Caledonia [c 88,e 88,f]	0.14	0.14	0.15	0.16	0.16	0.16	0.17			
Papua New Guinea	2.81	3.00	3.30	3.44	3.52	3.63	3.70	3.77		
Solomon Islands [e 80-86]	0.21	0.23	0.27	0.29	0.30	0.31	0.32			
Tonga	0.09	0.09	0.11	0.11	0.12	0.12	0.12			
Tuvalu [f]	0.01	0.01	0.01	0.01	0.01	0.01	0.01			
Vanuatu [c 88]			0.14	0.15	0.15	0.16	0.16			
Western Samoa [e 88]	0.15	0.16	0.16	0.17	0.17	0.17	0.17			
Regional total	*4.19*	*4.45*	*5.23*	*5.46*	*5.57*	*5.72*	*5.82*	*4.72*		
Middle East										
Bahrain [e 77-80]	0.30	0.35	0.42	0.43	0.47	0.49	0.50	0.52		
Egypt [a, c 88]	38.79	42.13	48.50	50.74	50.36	51.74	53.15	54.69		
Iran [c 86,e 88]	34.69	38.35	44.21	51.72	52.52	54.20	55.88	57.73		
Iraq [e 83-86]	12.03	13.24	15.59	16.28	17.25	18.28	19.31			
Israel [a]	3.61	3.88	4.23	4.37	4.44	4.52	4.66	4.98		
Jordan [f]	2.71	2.92	3.52	3.80	3.94	4.10	4.26			
Kuwait	1.14	1.37	1.71	1.87	1.96	2.05	2.14			
Lebanon [f]	2.76	2.67	2.67	2.76	2.83	2.90	2.97			
Oman [c85,88,e77-84,88]	0.84	0.98	2.00	1.33	1.38	1.42	1.47			
Qatar [c 88,e 88,f]	0.19	0.23	0.32	0.33	0.34	0.42	0.49			
Saudi Arabia [f]	8.06	9.37	11.54	13.61	14.02	14.44	14.87			
Syria	7.88	8.70	10.27	10.95	11.34	11.72	12.12	12.53		
United Arab Emirates [f]	0.69	0.98	1.33	1.45	1.50	1.55	1.74	1.84	1.91	177.47
Yemen [c 88, f]	7.33	7.95	9.18	9.73	9.87	10.17	11.28			
Regional total	*121.02*	*133.11*	*155.48*	*169.37*	*172.22*	*177.98*	*184.83*	*132.28*	*1.91*	

TOTAL POPULATION

Trends in Total Population 1977-1992: National Estimates at Mid-Year

Units: Millions

	1977	1980	1985	1987	1988	1989	1990	1991	1992	% growth 1977-92
North Africa										
Algeria [a, e 84-86,88]	17.06	18.67	21.72	23.11	23.84	24.60	25.35	25.32		
Chad [e 84-86]	4.21	4.48	5.02	5.26	5.43	5.54	5.68	5.82		
Djibouti [c 88,e 88]	0.30	0.36	0.43	0.37	0.38	0.40	0.41			
Ethiopia	35.92	38.52	43.35	44.18	47.88	50.17	51.69	53.38		
Libya [a,c 85, e 85,88]	2.67	3.04	3.36	3.63	3.77	4.39	4.54			
Mali [c 89]	6.51	7.10	8.21	8.68	8.92	7.96	8.16			
Mauritania [e 86,88]	1.50	1.63	1.89	1.86	1.92	1.92	2.02	2.04		
Morocco [c80, e 82-86,88]	18.36	20.05	21.94	23.38	23.91	24.57	25.21			
Niger [c88,e80-86, 88]	4.86	5.31	6.12	6.47	7.25	6.90	7.10			
Somalia [e 80-85,87-88]	3.56	4.02	6.40	6.87	7.11	7.40	7.69			
Sudan [e 78-86, 88]	16.95	18.68	21.55	22.78	23.80	24.49	25.17			
Tunisia [e 84-86]	5.93	6.39	7.26	7.82	7.77	7.91	8.07			
Regional total	*117.82*	*128.24*	*147.24*	*154.40*	*161.97*	*166.22*	*171.09*			*86.56*
West Africa										
Benin	3.29	3.42	3.93	4.13	4.45	4.59	4.74	4.89		
Burkina Faso	5.84	6.15	6.64	6.86	8.54	8.77	9.00	9.24		
Cameroon [c88,e88,b78-79]	7.91	8.50	10.19	10.82	10.88	11.54	12.41			
Cape Verde [f]	0.29	0.30	0.33	0.35	0.36	0.37	0.38			
Côte d'Ivoire [e 88]	7.30	8.17	9.81	10.58	11.61	12.10	12.58			
Equatorial Guinea [c 88,f]	0.33	0.35	0.39	0.41	0.42	0.34	0.35	0.36		
Gabon [c 88,f]	1.03	1.06	1.15	1.06	1.09	1.11	1.13			
Gambia [c 83,88,b 83-86]	0.55	0.60	0.64	0.79	0.81	0.84	0.86			
Ghana [e 77-79,81,84-88]	10.45	11.54	12.84	13.70	14.13	14.57	15.00			
Guinea			4.71	4.93	5.07					
Guinea-Bissau [f]	0.70	0.81	0.89	0.92	0.93	0.94	0.95			
Liberia	1.67	1.85	2.19	2.30	2.43	2.40	2.46	2.52		
Nigeria [f,i]	72.58	80.56	95.69	101.91	104.96	109.18	113.39	88.52		
Sao Tomé e Príncipe [f]	0.08	0.09	0.11	0.11	0.12	0.12	0.12			
Senegal [c85,88,e82,85-88]	5.25	5.70	6.44	6.71	7.11	7.17	7.23			
Sierra Leone [f]	3.14	3.30	3.60	3.85	3.95	4.05	4.15			
Togo [e 80-86,88]	2.35	2.55	2.96	3.14	3.25	3.30	3.35			
Regional total	*122.75*	*134.95*	*162.52*	*172.57*	*180.10*	*181.37*	*188.10*	*105.52*		
East/Central Africa										
Angola [e 88]	7.00	7.72	8.75	9.23	9.48	9.75	10.02			
Burundi	3.90	4.12	4.72	4.99	5.15	5.30	5.46	5.62		
Central African Republic [c 88,b 81-84,88]		2.17	2.31	2.61	2.83	2.77	2.84	2.91		
Comoros [c88,e77-85,88]	0.35	0.38	0.44	0.47	0.48	0.50	0.52			
Congo [f]	1.44	1.53	1.74	1.84	1.89	1.94	1.99			
Kenya [b]	14.35	16.67	20.33	21.95	23.88	24.87	25.86	25.91		
Madagascar [e77-82,84-85,88]	8.02	8.70	9.99	10.55	11.24	11.60	11.20	11.49		
Maldives [c 85,e 88]	0.14	0.15	0.18	0.20	0.20	0.21	0.22	0.22		
Mauritius	0.91	0.96	1.02	1.04	1.05	1.06	1.07			
Réunion [e77,85-86,88]	0.49	0.51	0.53	0.54	0.58	0.59	0.60			
Rwanda [e84-86,88]	4.36	5.16	6.07	6.46	6.76	6.99	7.15	7.17		
Seychelles	0.06	0.06	0.07	0.07	0.07	0.07	0.07	0.07		
Tanzania	16.92	18.58	21.73	23.13	24.00	24.80	25.64			
Uganda [c 80,88,e 84,88]	12.35	13.11	14.30	15.09	15.51	15.95	16.37	16.82		
Zaire [e 81-82, 86]	24.02	26.38	30.36	31.84	33.46	34.49	35.56	36.67		
Regional total	*96.47*	*106.34*	*122.84*	*130.23*	*136.51*	*140.97*	*144.64*	*103.97*		
Southern Africa										
Botswana	0.74	0.82	1.09	1.17	1.21	1.26	1.29	1.35		
Lesotho [e77-79,82-88]	1.24	1.34	1.53	1.62	1.68	1.70	1.72			
Malawi [c 88]	5.55	6.05	7.06	7.50	7.76	8.02	8.29	8.56		
Mozambique [f]	10.66	12.12	13.96	14.55	14.93	15.33	15.73			
Namibia [f]	1.25	1.35	1.55	1.68	1.76	1.82	1.88	1.40		
South Africa [f]	23.48	25.08	27.90	29.03	29.60	30.19	30.80			
Swaziland [e 88]	0.50	0.55	0.65	0.69	0.74	0.76	0.77			
Zambia [c 81, e 81-86]	5.30	5.83	6.67	7.12	7.53	7.80	8.02			
Zimbabwe	6.52	7.10	8.38	8.64	8.88	9.12	9.37			
Regional total	*55.23*	*60.23*	*68.77*	*71.99*	*74.09*	*76.00*	*77.86*	*11.31*		

Source: UN/national statistical offices

Notes: see end of section

TOTAL POPULATION

Total Population: Latest Official Census Year

Units: '000

	Date	Total	Male	Female	Estimated level of under-enumeration (%)
North America					
Canada [a]	4/6/91	27,297	13,455	13,842	
USA [a,b]	1/4/90	248,710	121,239	127,470	
South America					
Argentina [c]	15/5/91	32,370			1.00
Bolivia	29/9/76	4,613	2,276	2,337	6.99
Brazil [c,d,e]	1/9/91	146,154	72,171	73,983	
Chile	22/4/92	13,232	6,501	6,731	
Colombia	15/10/85	27,876	13,799	14,078	
Ecuador	25/11/90	9,648	4,796	4,852	
French Guiana [a]	15/3/90	115	60	55	
Guyana	12/5/80	759	376	383	
Paraguay	11/7/82	3,030	1,521	1,508	
Peru [c,d,f]	30/6/91	22,006			4.10
Suriname	1/7/80	355	176	179	2.60
Uruguay	23/10/85	2,955	1,439	1,516	
Venezuela [d]	21/10/90	18,105	9,005	9,100	6.85
Caribbean					
Anguilla	1992	9			
Antigua	1991	64			
Aruba [a]	1/2/81	60			
Bahamas	2/5/90	255	124	131	
Barbados	2/5/90	257			
Bermuda	12/5/80	55			
British Virgin Islands	12/5/80	17	9	8	
Cayman Islands [a]	5/10/89	25	12	13	
Cuba	11/9/81	9,724	4,915	4,809	
Dominica	12/5/91	71	36	36	
Dominican Republic	12/12/81	5,648	2,833	2,816	
Grenada	30/4/81	89			
Guadeloupe [a]	15/3/90	387	189	198	
Haiti [a]	30/8/82	5,054	2,448	2,605	
Jamaica [c]	7/4/91	2,374	1,080	1,126	
Martinique [a]	15/3/90	360			
Netherlands Antilles [a]	1/2/81	172	83	89	2.00
St Kitts	12/5/80	43	21	22	
St Lucia	1991	136			
St Vincent/Grenadines	1991	108	54	54	
Trinidad and Tobago	2/5/90	1,234			
Central America					
Belize	1991	191			
Costa Rica [a]	1/6/84	2,417	1,208	1,209	
El Salvador	28/6/71	3,555	1,763	1,792	
Guatemala	26/3/81	6,054	3,016	3,038	
Honduras	5/88	4,249			10.00
Mexico [a]	16/3/90	81,250	39,894	41,356	
Nicaragua [a]	20/4/71	1,878	922	956	
Panama	13/5/90	2,329	1,179	1,151	
Puerto Rico [a]	1/4/90	3,522			
South Asia					
Afghanistan [f,g]	23/6/79	13,051	6,712	6,339	10.00
Bangladesh	11/3/91	104,766	53,918	50,848	1.06
Bhutan	12/80	1,165			
India	1/3/91	843,931	439,230	407,072	1.70
Nepal [a]	22/6/81	15,023	9,221	9,241	
Pakistan	1/3/81	84,254	44,233	40,021	
Sri Lanka	17/3/81	14,847	7,568	7,278	

TOTAL POPULATION   Table No. 0203 (cont'd)

Total Population: Latest Official Census Year

Units: '000

	Date	Total	Male	Female	Estimated level of under-enumeration (%)
Japan					
Japan	1/10/90	123,611	60,697	62,914	
ASEAN/NICs					
Brunei	26/8/81	193			1.06
Hong Kong [c,h]	15/3/91	5,674	2,900	2,774	
Indonesia	31/10/90	179,322			
Macau	16/3/81	248			6.85
Malaysia	10/6/80	13,436	6,748	6,688	
Philippines [a]	1/5/90	60,703			
Singapore	30/6/90	2,705			
South Korea [c,i]	1/11/90	43,411	21,782	21,629	
Taiwan [c]	1991	20,555			
Thailand [a]	1/4/90	54,532	27,031	27,501	3.20
East/SE Asia					
Cambodia	4/81	6,682			
China	1/7/90	1,130,511			
Laos	1/3/85	3,585	1,757	1,828	
Mongolia [c]	5/1/89	2,043			
Myanmar	31/3/83	35,306	17,508	17,798	
North Korea					
Vietnam	1/4/89	64,376			
Australasia					
Australia	6/8/91	16,850	8,364	8,486	1.80
New Zealand [c,j]	5/3/91	3,435	1,693	1,742	
Pacific					
American Samoa [a,k]	1/4/80	32	16	16	
Fiji	31/8/86	715	363	353	
French Polynesia [c]	6/9/88	189	98	91	
Guam [a,k]	1/4/90	133	71	62	1.90
Kiribati	7/11/90	72	36	37	
Nauru	13/5/83	8			
New Caledonia	4/4/89	164	84	80	
Papua New Guinea	22/9/80	3,011	1,576	1,435	
Solomon Islands	23/11/86	285	148	137	
Tonga [a]	28/11/86	95	48	47	
Tuvalu [c]	6/85	8	4	4	
Vanuatu [c]	15/5/89	143	74	69	
Western Samoa	3/11/91	160			
Middle East					
Bahrain	5/4/81	351	205	146	
Egypt [c]	18/11/86	48,254	24,709	23,545	
Iran [a]	8/10/86	49,445	25,281	24,164	
Iraq	17/10/87	16,335	8,396	7,939	
Israel [a,l]	4/6/83	4,038	2,012	2,026	1.50
Jordan [m]	10/11/79	2,100			
Kuwait	21/4/85	1,697	965	732	
Lebanon	15/11/70	2,126			
Oman [n]					
Qatar	16/3/86	369	248	121	
Saudi Arabia [c]	14/9/74	7,013			
Syria	8/9/81	9,053	4,625	4,428	
United Arab Emirates [c]	12/85	1,622	1,052	570	
Yemen [a,c,o]	1/2/86	11,619			

TOTAL POPULATION

Total Population: Latest Official Census Year

Units: '000

	Date	Total	Male	Female	Estimated level of under-enumeration (%)
North Africa					
Algeria [a,c]	20/4/87	22,971			
Chad [a]	1963/64	3,254			
Djibouti	1960/61	81			
Ethiopia [c]	9/5/84	42,185	21,080	21,105	
Libya [a,c]	31/7/84	3,637	1,950	1,687	
Mali [a,c]	30/4/87	7,620	3,733	3,887	
Mauritania	20/4/88	1,864			
Morocco	21/9/82	20,388	10,206	10,182	
Niger	24/5/88	7,250			
Somalia [p]	1986-87	7,114	3,742	3,373	
Sudan	1/2/83	20,594	10,513	10,081	
Tunisia	30/3/84	6,966	3,547	3,419	
West Africa					
Benin	30/3/79	3,331	1,597	1,734	
Burkina Faso	20/12/85	7,965	3,833	4,132	
Cameroon	4/87	10,494			
Cape Verde	2/6/80	289			
Côte d'Ivoire	1988	10,816	5,527	5,288	
Equatorial Guinea	17/7/83	300	144	156	
Gabon	10/5/61	449	211	237	
Gambia	24/4/83	699			
Ghana	11/3/84	12,296	6,064	6,232	
Guinea [c,p]	17/2/83	4,533			
Guinea-Bissau	30/4/79	753	363	391	
Liberia [c]	14/2/84	2,102			
Nigeria [p]	11/91	88,514	44,545	43,970	
Sao Tomé e Príncipe	15/8/81	97	48	49	
Senegal	5/6/88	6,882	3,387	3,495	
Sierra Leone [c]	14/12/85	3,516	1,746	1,770	5.00
Togo [c]	22/11/81	2,705			
East/Central Africa					
Angola	15/12/70	5,646			
Burundi [a]	16/8/79	4,028	1,946	2,082	
Central African Republic	22/12/75	2,088	1,023	1,065	
Comoros	15/9/80	335	167	168	
Congo	22/12/84	1,843			
Kenya	24/8/89	21,400			5.00
Madagascar [c]	1974/75	7,604	3,805	3,798	
Maldives	2/3/90	213	109	104	
Mauritius [q]	1/7/90	1,059			
Réunion [a]	15/3/90	598	294	304	
Rwanda [c]	16/8/90	7,149	3,484	3,665	
Seychelles	17/8/87	69	34	34	
Tanzania	26/8/78	17,513	8,587	8,926	
Uganda [c]	12/1/91	16,583			
Zaire	1/7/84	29,671	14,593	15,078	
Southern Africa					
Botswana [c]	23/8/91	1,325			
Lesotho	12/4/86	1,447			
Malawi [c]	21/9/87	7,983	3,880	4,103	
Mozambique	1/8/80	11,674	5,671	6,003	3.80
Namibia [c]	21/10/91	1,402			
South Africa [r]	1991	26,288	12,834	13,454	
Swaziland	25/8/86	682	322	359	
Zambia	20/8/90	7,818			
Zimbabwe [c]	18/8/92	10,402			

Source: UN

Notes: see end of section

| VITAL STATISTICS | | | | | | | | Table No. 0204 | | |

Number of Live Births 1977-1991

Units: '000

	1977	1980	1983	1984	1985	1986	1987	1988	1989	1990	1991
North America											
Canada [a]	361.4	370.7	373.7	368.5	367.2	364.8	369.4	375.7	391.9	405.5	411.9
USA [a]	3,326.6	3,612.3	3,638.9	3,669.1	3,749.0	3,757.0	3,809.0	3,910.0	4,041.5	4,179.0	4,111.0
South America											
Argentina [a]	661.2	697.5	707.0	635.3	650.8	675.4	662.9	653.6		699.9	
Bolivia [b]	142.3	139.5									
Brazil [b,c]	2,398.5	4,156.2	2,710.4	2,559.0	2,619.6	2,779.3	2,660.9	2,809.7	2,581.0		
Chile [a]	228.3	247.0	260.7	265.0	262.0	273.0	279.8	296.6	303.8	292.1	
Colombia [b]	806.5	821.6	829.3	825.8	835.9	931.9	937.4				
Ecuador [b]	223.7	223.4	206.4	206.2	210.0	205.8	261.3	267.6	200.1	201.7	
French Guiana [a]	1.5	1.9	2.3	2.3	2.5	2.4			3.2		
Guyana					37.0	36.9	37.7				
Paraguay [b]			121.5	124.5	130.5	130.5	133.5	136.5	143.4	142.5	
Peru [b]	436.2	692.5	689.0	698.0	699.0	714.0	721.0	727.0	730.0	734.0	647.0
Suriname [a]		9.8						9.7	9.1		
Uruguay [a]	58.0	53.9	53.4	52.9	53.8	54.1	53.5	54.0	55.3	56.5	
Venezuela [a]	465.3	493.0	514.4	504.0	502.3	504.3	516.8	522.4	529.0	578.0	
Caribbean											
Anguilla [a]					0.2						
Antigua [a]	1.4	1.2	1.2	1.1	1.2	1.1	1.1				
Aruba [b]	1.0	1.1	1.1		1.1	1.0	0.9	0.9	1.1		
Bahamas [a]	4.9	5.0	5.3	5.2	5.4	5.6	4.3	4.9	5.0	4.9	
Barbados [a]	4.3	4.1	4.5	4.2	4.3	4.0	3.8	3.7	4.0	4.3	4.2
Bermuda [a]	0.8	0.8	0.9	0.8	0.9	0.9	0.9	0.9	0.9	0.9	
British Virgin Islands [a]	0.2	0.3	0.3	0.2	0.2	0.2	0.3	0.2	0.2		
Cayman Islands [a]	0.3	0.3	0.4	0.4	0.4	0.4	0.4	0.4	0.4	0.5	0.4
Cuba [a]	169.0	136.9	165.3	166.3	182.1	166.0	179.5	187.9	184.9	186.7	173.9
Dominica [a]	1.7	1.8	1.9	1.7			1.6	1.7	1.7	1.6	
Dominican Republic [b]		192.8		175.9							
Grenada [a]	2.6										
Guadeloupe [a]	6.3	6.4	6.7	6.7	6.8	6.4	6.9				
Haiti											
Jamaica [a]	59.9	57.4	61.4	57.5	56.2	54.1	52.3	53.6	55.5	59.6	
Martinique [a]	5.4	5.4	5.6	5.7	5.7	6.0	6.3	6.4	6.4	6.4	
Netherlands Antilles [a]	3.3	3.3				3.7	3.6	3.5	3.5	3.6	3.5
St Kitts [a]	1.2	1.2	1.1	1.1	1.0	1.0	0.9	1.0	1.0		
St Lucia [a]	4.1	3.8	4.1	4.0	4.2	3.9	3.8	3.6	3.2	3.7	
St Vincent/Grenadines [a]	3.2	3.1	3.3	2.8		2.7			2.5	2.5	
Trinidad and Tobago	27.9	29.9	33.2	31.6				29.2	27.3	25.1	
Central America											
Belize [b]	5.6	6.3	6.0	6.2	5.9	6.1	6.1	6.7	6.8	7.0	6.0
Costa Rica [a]	64.2	66.1	73.0	76.0	84.3		80.3	81.4	81.5	81.9	
El Salvador [d]	177.5	169.9	144.2	142.2	139.5	145.1	148.3	149.3	151.9	147.1	
Guatemala [a]	284.7	303.4	306.8	312.1	323.0	389.3	324.8	341.4	345.2		
Honduras [b]	145.6	155.9	158.4								
Mexico [b]	2,379.4	2,446.2	2,609.0	2,511.9	2,655.6	2,579.3	2,794.4	2,602.6	2,586.7	2,692.9	
Nicaragua [b]	98.4	120.6	135.1			141.0	98.2			93.1	
Panama [a,d]	53.3	52.6	55.2	56.7	58.0	57.7	57.6	57.6	57.8	57.9	
Puerto Rico [a]	75.2	73.1	65.7	63.3	63.6		64.4	64.1	66.7	66.5	
South Asia											
Afghanistan [d]											
Bangladesh [b]		2,947.5			3,442.1	3,489.0	3,414.2	3,476.5			
Bhutan											
India											
Nepal											
Pakistan		3,608.7	3,800.2	4,039.5	4,164.6	4,293.6	4,427.0	4,269.1	4,444.9	5,154.3	
Sri Lanka [a]	389.5	418.4	403.7	386.7	384.6	359.3	358.1	343.7	358.0		

VITAL STATISTICS   Table No. 0204 (cont'd)

Number of Live Births 1977-1991

Units: '000

	1977	1980	1983	1984	1985	1986	1987	1988	1989	1990	1991
Japan											
Japan	1,755.1	1,576.9	1,508.7	1,489.8	1,431.6	1,396.0	1,371.0	1,314.0	1,243.0	1,228.0	1,223.2
ASEAN/NICs											
Brunei [a]	5.4	5.8	6.0	6.3	6.7	6.9	7.1	6.9	6.9		
Hong Kong [a]	80.0	85.3	83.3	77.3	76.4	72.2	70.2	75.6	69.6	67.9	
Indonesia [d]					5,400.6		4,884.1				
Macau [d]	2.5	3.8	6.2	6.7	7.6	7.6	7.6	7.9	7.6	6.9	
Malaysia [b]	390.4	425.4	450.9	475.3	497.4	498.7	488.2	507.6	469.7	497.5	
Philippines [b]	1,344.8	1,456.9	1,506.4	1,478.2	1,437.2	1,494.0	1,582.5	1,462.2	1,260.9	1,829.2	
Singapore [a]	38.4	41.2	40.6	41.6	42.5	38.4	43.6	52.8	47.7	51.1	
South Korea [b]	790.1	892.1	860.0	836.0	643.3	622.0	606.6	620.3	613.2	701.0	
Taiwan [d]		413.0	383.0	370.0	345.0	308.0	313.0	341.0			
Thailand [b]	1,079.3	1,077.3	1,055.8	956.7	973.6	945.8	884.0	870.5	902.8	956.2	
East/SE Asia											
Cambodia							321.2	321.9	317.4	321.4	
China							25,363.7	24,729.2	24,185.3	23,843.4	
Laos							161.4	158.9	184.3	181.9	
Mongolia [d]		63.1		68.1	69.6	71.8	71.4	75.8	73.6	78.6	
Myanmar							1,119.5	1,143.0	1,220.2	1,257.9	
North Korea											
Vietnam							1,713.0	1,697.5	1,973.7	1,986.0	
Australasia											
Australia [a]	226.3	225.5	242.6	238.5	247.3	243.4	244.0	246.1	255.7	262.7	
New Zealand [a]	54.2	50.5	50.5	51.6	51.8	52.8	55.3	57.5	58.1	60.1	60.0
Pacific											
American Samoa [a]	1.0	1.1	1.2	1.4	1.5	1.5	1.6	1.6			
Fiji [a]	16.1	18.8	19.8	19.5	19.5	19.0	19.4		17.6	18.2	
French Polynesia [d]	4.4	4.5	5.0	5.1			5.1	5.7	5.4	5.4	
Guam [a]	3.0	3.0	3.2	3.1	3.2	3.3	3.3				
Kiribati								1,479.0			
Nauru		0.3									
New Caledonia [d]	3.9	3.7	3.8	3.4	3.6	3.8	3.9				
Papua New Guinea [d]					111.0		122.2				
Solomon Islands											
Tonga [d]		2.7	2.8	2.9	2.8	2.8	2.5	2.3	2.2	2.2	
Tuvalu											
Vanuatu									2.0		
Western Samoa [b]	3.3	2.7									
Middle East											
Bahrain [b]	9.1	10.1			12.3	12.9	12.7	12.6	13.6	13.4	
Egypt [a]	1,447.4	1,569.2	1,690.0		1,817.3	1,878.0	1,902.6				
Iran [b,f]	1,409.0	2,450.3	2,203.4	2,067.8		2,033.3	1,832.1	1,944.1	1,784.8	1,729.0	2,309.1
Iraq [b]	289.5	371.0			445.3	468.8	470.4	549.2			
Israel [a]	95.3	94.3	98.7	98.5	99.4	99.3	99.0	99.8	100.5	103.0	
Jordan [a]	79.9		98.4	102.5	102.7	112.5	107.5	116.3	115.7		
Kuwait [a]	46.9	51.1	55.6	56.8	55.1	53.8	50.2				
Lebanon											
Oman											
Qatar [a]		6.8	8.3	8.6	9.2	9.9	9.9	10.8	10.9	11.0	
Saudi Arabia											
Syria [b,e]	395.7	510.4	419.2	433.9	548.6	429.4	478.1	435.8	421.7	359.4	
United Arab Emirates [d]		34.8	43.4	43.7				50.8	51.9	52.3	
Yemen										577.8	

VITAL STATISTICS   Table No. 0204 (cont'd)

Number of Live Births 1977-1991

Units: '000

	1977	1980	1983	1984	1985	1986	1987	1988	1989	1990	1991
North Africa											
Algeria [a]	727.5	818.6	822.6	833.1	845.4		775.0	806.0	755.0	775.0	
Chad											
Djibouti [b,g]	5.0	4.4	5.1	5.2	5.6						
Ethiopia											
Libya [a]	118.7	113.1					167.0	173.5			
Mali							375.1				
Mauritania											
Morocco [b]					377.9	412.3	465.9	488.0			
Niger											
Somalia											
Sudan											
Tunisia [a]	220.5	225.2	216.4	226.3	227.5	231.8	222.1	214.7	199.1	208.3	
West Africa											
Benin											
Burkina Faso											
Cameroon											
Cape Verde [a]	10.0	9.3	11.4	11.7	12.6	12.6	12.8	12.4			
Côte d'Ivoire											
Equatorial Guinea											
Gabon											
Gambia											
Ghana											
Guinea											
Guinea-Bissau											
Liberia											
Nigeria [d]								5,037.9			
Sao Tomé e Príncipe [a]	3.6				3.9	4.0	3.9	4.2	4.0		
Senegal											
Sierra Leone [d]					75.8	84.0					
Togo											
East/Central Africa											
Angola											
Burundi											
Central African Republic											
Comoros [d]		26.2				24.0					
Congo											
Kenya [b]	275.8	365.6	316.9	312.1							
Madagascar [b]											
Maldives						8.3	8.4			8.6	
Mauritius [a]	22.7	24.5	19.8	19.1	18.2	18.2	19.2	20.0	21.0	21.6	22.2
Réunion [a]	12.5	12.3	12.5	13.1	13.2	12.8	12.6	13.6	13.9	13.9	14.1
Rwanda [b]		280.6								409.0	
Seychelles [a]	1.6	1.8	1.7	1.7	1.7	1.7	1.7	1.6	1.6	1.6	1.7
Tanzania											
Uganda											
Zaire											
Southern Africa											
Botswana [b]					16.7	45.6	32.0				
Lesotho											
Malawi	267.8										
Mozambique											
Namibia											
South Africa											
Swaziland											
Zambia											
Zimbabwe											

Source: UN
Notes: see end of section

VITAL STATISTICS — Table No. 0205

Number of Deaths 1977-1991

Units: '000

	1977	1980	1983	1984	1985	1986	1987	1988	1989	1990	1991
North America											
Canada [a]	167.5	171.5	174.5	175.7	181.3	186.4	185.0	190.0	191.0	192.0	196.0
USA [a]	1,899.6	1,989.8	2,019.2	2,039.4	2,086.0	2,105.0	2,123.0	2,168.0	2,151.0	2,162.0	2,165.0
South America											
Argentina [a]	234.4	241.1			241.4	241.0	250.2	263.7		256.0	
Bolivia [b]	35.4	26.8									
Brazil [c]	783.4	809.2	798.4	852.9	853.0	852.5	816.4	844.0	835.1		
Chile [a]	73.4	74.1	74.3	74.7	73.5	72.2	70.6	74.4	75.5	78.4	
Colombia [b]	145.4	125.6	140.3	137.2	153.9	146.3	151.9	153.1	154.7		
Ecuador [b]	59.2	57.0	55.2	52.1	51.1	51.0	51.6	52.7	51.7	50.2	
French Guiana [b]	0.5	0.5	0.5	0.5	0.5	0.5					
Guyana [a]	5.9										
Paraguay [b]	14.9	12.8	12.0	12.0	14.1	11.5	13.2				
Peru [c]	181.2	193.1	199.0	198.0	196.0	196.0	194.0	192.0	189.0	186.0	174.0
Suriname [a]		2.8			2.3						
Uruguay [a]	28.9	29.8	28.5	30.0	28.6	28.8	29.9		29.7	30.6	
Venezuela [a]	74.3	77.0	75.7	78.1	78.9	77.6	80.3	81.4	84.8		
Caribbean											
Anguilla [a]					0.1						
Antigua [a]	0.5	0.4	0.4	0.4	0.4	0.4	0.4				
Aruba [b]	0.3	0.3	0.3		0.3	0.4	0.4	0.3			
Bahamas [a]	1.1	1.3	1.1	1.1	1.3	1.4	1.4	1.3	1.4	1.1	
Barbados [a]	2.1	2.0	2.1	2.0	2.1	2.1	2.2	2.2	2.3	2.2	2.3
Bermuda [a]	0.4	0.4	0.4	0.4	0.4	0.4	0.4	0.4	0.5	0.4	0.4
British Virgin Islands [a]	0.1	0.1	0.1	0.1	0.1	0.1	0.1	0.1	0.1		
Cayman Islands [b]	0.1	0.1	0.1	0.1	0.1	0.1	0.1	0.1	0.1	0.1	0.1
Cuba [a]	56.1	55.7	58.3	59.9	64.4	63.1	54.7	67.9	67.4	72.1	71.0
Dominica [a]	0.5		0.3	0.4			0.4	0.4	0.5	0.6	
Dominican Republic [b]	25.0	26.2			27.8						
Grenada [a]	0.8										
Guadeloupe [a]	2.3	2.1	2.2	2.2	2.3	2.2	2.2				
Haiti											
Jamaica [a]	14.2	12.7	12.6	13.4	13.9	13.3	12.4	12.2		12.2	13.3
Martinique [a]	2.2	2.1	2.2	2.1	2.2	2.1	2.1	2.1	2.2	2.2	
Netherlands Antilles [a]	1.0	1.0				1.0	1.1	1.2	1.2	1.2	1.1
St Kitts [a]	0.7	0.7	0.8	0.7		0.5	0.5	0.5	0.5		
St Lucia [a]	0.5	0.5	0.5	0.5	0.4	0.8	0.9	0.9	0.8		
St Vincent/Grenadines [a]	0.8	0.8	0.8	0.7	0.8	0.7		0.7	0.7		
Trinidad and Tobago [a]	7.3	7.5	7.5	7.8				8.1	8.0	8.2	
Central America											
Belize [b]	0.8	0.7	0.7	0.8	0.7	0.7	0.7	0.7	0.8	0.9	0.7
Costa Rica [a]	8.9	9.3	9.4	9.9	10.5	10.4	10.7	10.9	11.3	11.4	
El Salvador [c]	33.0	39.0	32.7	28.9	27.2	25.7	27.6	27.8	27.8	28.2	
Guatemala [a]	71.8	71.4	74.4	65.8	69.5	69.3	66.7	64.8	64.5		
Honduras [b]	18.6	18.3	19.3								
Mexico [a]	450.5	434.5			414.0	400.1	400.3	423.4	428.7	434.1	
Nicaragua [b]	12.9	28.6	29.0			27.0	11.0			14.3	
Panama [b,d]	8.0	8.0	8.5	8.3	9.0	8.9	9.1	8.7	8.7	8.6	
Puerto Rico [a]	19.9	20.5	21.5	21.7	23.2		24.0	25.1	26.0	26.1	
South Asia											
Afghanistan											
Bangladesh [b]		913.3			1,195.1	1,213.8	1,173.4	1,178.6			
Bhutan											
India											
Nepal											
Pakistan [c]	619.7				839.2	761.0	809.2	852.3			
Sri Lanka [a]	103.3	91.0	94.1	100.7	98.0	96.1	96.5	96.5	104.6		

VITAL STATISTICS

Table No. 0205 (cont'd)

Number of Deaths 1977-1991

Units: '000

	1977	1980	1983	1984	1985	1986	1987	1988	1989	1990	1991
Japan											
Japan	690.1	722.8	740.0	740.2	752.3	767.0	751.0	793.0	791.0	826.0	829.5
ASEAN/NICs											
Brunei [a]	0.7	0.7	0.7	0.8	0.8	0.7	0.8	0.8	0.8		
Hong Kong [a]	23.3	25.0	26.5	25.5	25.3	26.0	27.0	27.6	28.7	28.7	
Indonesia [c]					1,846.4		1,344.4				
Macau [c]	1.4	1.5		1.6	1.5	1.4	1.3	1.4	1.5	1.5	1.3
Malaysia [b]					68.4	66.5	65.3	68.9	81.2	83.2	
Philippines [b]	308.9	298.0	327.3	313.4	334.7	326.7	335.4	305.1	261.8		
Singapore [a]	12.0	12.5	13.3	13.2	13.3	12.8	13.2	13.7	14.7	13.9	13.9
South Korea [c]	227.1	257.0	252.0	254.0	256.0	253.7	239.2		248.0	248.0	
Taiwan		84.0	90.6	89.6	92.0	94.7	96.0	101.8		105.3	105.5
Thailand [b]	236.8	248.0	252.6	225.3	202.6	218.0	233.0	231.2	246.6	252.5	
East/SE Asia											
Cambodia											
China											
Laos											
Mongolia [c]	15.5	17.3		20.4	18.7	16.4	15.9	17.7	17.0		
Myanmar											
North Korea											
Vietnam							415.9	401.5		529.6	
Australasia											
Australia [a]	108.8	108.7	110.1	111.9	118.8	115.0	117.3	118.9	124.2	120.0	
New Zealand [a]	26.0	26.7	26.0	25.4	27.5	27.0	27.4	27.4	27.0	26.5	26.5
Pacific											
American Samoa [a]		0.2	0.1	0.2	0.2	0.2	0.2	0.2			
Fiji [a]	2.3	4.1	3.5	3.2	3.7	3.9	3.2			3.6	
French Polynesia [c]			0.9			0.9	1.0	0.9	1.0	0.8	
Guam [a]	0.4	0.4	0.5		0.4	0.5	0.5				
Kiribati											
Nauru [a]											
New Caledonia [c]	0.9	1.0	0.8	0.8	0.9	0.9	0.9				
Papua New Guinea [c]					40.9		42.5				
Solomon Islands											
Tonga [c]			0.4	0.3	0.3		0.4	0.3	0.4	0.5	
Tuvalu											
Vanuatu											
Western Samoa [c]	0.5	0.5	0.3						0.2		
Middle East											
Bahrain [c]		1.1			1.2	1.4	1.6	1.4	1.6	1.5	
Egypt [a]	457.6	421.2	412.7	400.6	442.3	466.2	466.2	427.0			461.8
Iran [b]	147.0	162.2	207.2	186.4		190.1	204.2	238.4	199.6	217.6	
Iraq	50.6	64.7			72.1	75.3	77.9				
Israel [a]	25.0	26.3	27.8	27.9	29.4	29.4	29.4	29.4	28.6	29.0	
Jordan [b]	5.2	6.3	7.9	8.3	8.7	8.9	8.6	9.4	9.7		
Kuwait [a]	5.4	4.9	4.7	4.5	4.7	4.4	4.1				
Lebanon											
Oman											
Qatar [a]		0.7	0.8	0.6	0.8	0.8	0.8	0.9	0.8	0.9	
Saudi Arabia											
Syria [b]	43.1	46.4	51.1	50.6	61.0	50.7	51.6	44.9	45.5	33.0	
United Arab Emirates [a]			1.5	1.3				3.4	3.6	3.9	
Yemen, Arab Republic										329.0	

Demographic Trends and Forecasts

VITAL STATISTICS

Table No. 0205 (cont'd)

Number of Deaths 1977-1991

Units: '000

	1977	1980	1983	1984	1985	1986	1987	1988	1989	1990	1991
North Africa											
Algeria [b]	156.5	219.7	173.4		138.0		161.0	157.0	153.0	151.0	
Chad											
Djibouti											
Ethiopia											
Libya [b]	15.4	15.1					25.4	26.4			
Mali							96.2				
Mauritania											
Morocco [b]					64.3	65.5	74.7	78.0			
Niger											
Somalia											
Sudan											
Tunisia [b]	36.3	36.4	35.1	33.7	36.0	35.5	34.3	33.8	34.9	37.5	
West Africa											
Benin											
Burkina Faso											
Cameroon											
Cape Verde [a]	2.6	2.3	2.6	2.9	2.7						
Côte d'Ivoire											
Equatorial Guinea											
Gabon											
Gambia											
Ghana [c]		33.9									
Guinea											
Guinea-Bissau [b]											
Liberia											
Nigeria [c]					1,531.0	1,570.7	1,622.5	1,679.3			
Sao Tomé e Príncipe [a]	0.9				1.1	1.3	1.0	1.3	1.2		
Senegal [c]											
Sierra Leone					30.1	36.9					
Togo											
East/Central Africa											
Angola											
Burundi											
Central African Republic											
Comoros [c]		5.4			7.5	7.5					
Congo											
Kenya [b]	47.9	50.8	51.1	58.9							
Madagascar [b]											
Maldives [a]	1.7	1.8	1.8	1.6		1.5	1.5	1.5	1.5	1.4	
Mauritius [a]	7.0	6.7	6.3	6.4	6.7	6.6	6.6	6.7	6.9	7.0	7.0
Réunion [a]	3.1	3.2	3.3	3.0	3.1	3.1	3.1	3.3	3.3	3.2	3.4
Rwanda [b]		27.2	17.9								
Seychelles [a]	0.5	0.4	0.5	0.5	0.5	0.5	0.5	0.5	0.6	0.5	0.5
Tanzania											
Uganda											
Zaire											
Southern Africa											
Botswana					1.7	4.6	3.5				
Lesotho											
Malawi [c]	138.7										
Mozambique											
Namibia											
South Africa											
Swaziland											
Zambia											
Zimbabwe [c]		22.4				23.0					

Source: UN/national statistical offices
Notes: see end of section

VITAL STATISTICS

Birth Rates 1977-1991

Units: Per '000 inhabitants

	1977	1980	1983	1984	1985	1986	1987	1988	1989	1990	1991
North America											
Canada [a]	15.5	15.4	15.0	14.7	14.5	14.2	14.4	14.5	14.9		
USA [a]	15.1	15.9	15.5	15.5	15.7	15.5	15.7	15.9	16.3	16.7	
South America											
Argentina [a]	24.6	24.7	24.0	21.1	21.5	21.8	21.3	20.7		21.4	
Bolivia	27.6	24.9								36.6	
Brazil	21.8	34.3	20.9	19.3	19.3	20.1	18.8	17.9	17.5	28.6	
Chile [a]	21.6	22.2	22.2	22.2	21.6	22.1	22.3	23.3	23.4	23.8	
Colombia	33.0	31.7	30.2	29.4	29.2	27.8				27.4	
Ecuador	30.0	27.5	23.3	22.6	22.4	21.3	26.3	26.7	19.5	32.9	
French Guiana [a]	24.6	27.6	28.9	28.9	27.6	26.6					
Guyana										26.9	
Paraguay			35.0	34.8	35.3	34.3	34.1	33.8	34.5	34.9	
Peru	27.3	40.0	37.1	36.8	36.0	36.0	35.6	35.2	34.6	34.1	29.4
Suriname		28.1						23.3		28.1	
Uruguay	20.3	18.5	18.0	17.7	18.4	18.1	17.5	17.6	18.0	18.2	
Venezuela	34.2	32.8	31.4	29.9	29.0	28.3	28.3	27.9	27.5	30.7	
Caribbean											
Anguilla [a]					25.3						
Antigua [a]	20.4	15.5	14.7	14.1	14.9	14.1	13.7				
Aruba	16.6	18.8	18.9		18.5	16.9	14.0	15.8	14.7		
Bahamas [a]	24.4	24.0	24.0	22.5	23.6	23.2	18.0	20.6	20.1	19.5	
Barbados [a]	17.3	16.6	18.0	16.9	17.1	16.2	15.3	15.0	15.4	16.2	
Bermuda [a]	16.2	16.1	18.3	14.0	15.2	14.8	15.0	15.6	15.2	16.1	
British Virgin Islands											
Cayman Islands [a,b]	24.4	28.9	29.8	31.8	30.6	27.7	16.1	16.1	17.5	18.5	18.7
Cuba [a]	17.7	14.1	16.7	16.6	18.0	16.3	17.4	18.1	17.6	17.4	16.2
Dominica [a]	21.8	26.0	23.3	21.5			21.4	21.0	21.0	20.4	
Dominican Republic		35.4		28.8						31.3	
Grenada [a]	26.3										
Guadeloupe [a]	19.2	19.5	20.4	20.2	20.5	19.3	20.8				
Haiti										31.3	
Jamaica [a]	28.5	26.9	27.4	25.2	24.3	23.1	22.1	22.3	23.4	24.6	
Martinique [a]	16.4	17.3	17.1	13.3	16.8	17.6	18.1	18.2	17.8	17.9	
Netherlands Antilles [a]	18.3	17.5				20.3	18.8	18.2	18.3	18.9	18.3
St Kitts [a]	30.3	29.3	21.9	22.3	20.5	20.1	19.1	19.8	20.0		
St Lucia [a]	34.4	31.6	31.3	31.1	32.5	27.9	27.4	24.3	21.1	24.5	
St Vincent/Grenadines [a]	31.5	30.8	30.0	25.7		27.1	28.4	23.1	22.7		
Trinidad and Tobago [a]	26.8	27.7	29.1	27.0			24.1	22.6	20.7	26.3	
Central America											
Belize [c]	39.8	41.8	37.8	38.4	34.8	36.1	36.0	37.2	36.5	38.1	
Costa Rica [a]	31.0	29.4	29.9	31.4	33.8		28.9	28.6	27.5	27.4	26.5
El Salvador	41.7	37.7	30.5	29.7	28.9	29.6	29.6	29.2	29.1	36.3	
Guatemala [a]	44.8	43.9	40.8	40.3	40.6	47.5	38.5	39.3	38.6	40.8	
Honduras [c]	43.9	42.3	38.7							39.8	
Mexico [c]	37.3	35.3			34.1		34.4	31.4	30.7	31.3	
Nicaragua [c]	42.4	44.2	44.2			41.7				24.1	
Panama [a]	29.8	26.9	26.4	26.6	26.6	25.9	25.4	24.8	24.4	23.9	
Puerto Rico [a]	24.4	22.8	20.1	19.4	19.4		18.8	18.5	19.1	17.9	
South Asia											
Afghanistan							47.5	49.6	47.4	50.7	50.4
Bangladesh [c]		33.2			34.9	34.7	33.3	33.3	33.0	32.8	39.1
Bhutan							38.6	38.3	39.2	38.3	38.2
India							32.2	31.5	30.4	29.9	29.2
Nepal							41.0	39.3	41.0	38.0	37.4
Pakistan		43.7	42.0	43.3	43.3	43.3	43.3	40.5	40.9	44.4	39.1
Sri Lanka [a]	27.9	28.4	26.2	24.8	24.3	22.3	21.9	20.7	21.3	20.2	21.2

VITAL STATISTICS	Table No. 0206 (cont'd)

Birth Rates 1977-1991

Units: Per '000 inhabitants

	1977	1980	1983	1984	1985	1986	1987	1988	1989	1990	1991
Japan											
Japan [a]	15.4	13.5	12.6	12.4	11.9	11.5	11.2	10.7	10.1	10.0	9.9
ASEAN/NICs											
Brunei [a]	31.7	30.4	28.5	28.8	30.4	30.1	29.5	28.7	27.7	26.9	23.6
Hong Kong [a]	17.7	16.9	15.6	14.3	14.0	13.1	12.6	13.4	12.3	12.0	12.0
Indonesia					32.9	29.6	28.4	27.2	27.6	27.6	32.2
Macau	9.0	11.8	18.7	18.5	19.4	18.1	17.6	18.0	16.8	14.3	
Malaysia [c]	31.0	31.1	30.4	31.3	31.7	31.0	29.5	30.0	27.1	28.0	27.7
Philippines [c]	30.2	30.2	28.9	27.7	26.3	26.7	27.6	30.8	29.9	31.8	31.2
Singapore [a]	16.5	17.1	16.2	16.4	16.6	14.8	16.7	19.9	17.5	18.4	17.3
South Korea	21.7	23.4	21.5	20.6	15.7	15.0	16.5	16.5	16.5	15.6	16.3
Taiwan		23.2	20.5	19.5	17.9	15.8	15.9	17.1			
Thailand [c]	24.5	23.1	21.2	18.9	18.8	18.0	16.5	16.0	16.3	17.0	20.3
East/SE Asia											
Cambodia							41.8	40.9	39.4	39.0	40.0
China							23.3	22.4	21.6	21.0	21.1
Laos							42.7	41.0	46.4	44.7	44.1
Mongolia		38.0		37.2	37.0	37.2	35.9	37.0	37.5	35.3	34.9
Myanmar							28.6	28.6	29.9	30.2	29.9
North Korea									29.0	20.1	
Vietnam							33.1	31.7	31.3	30.0	30.6
Australasia											
Australia [a]	15.9	15.3	15.8	15.3	15.7	15.2	15.0	14.9	14.9	14.9	14.0
New Zealand [a]	17.4	16.3	15.8	16.0	15.9	16.3	16.8	17.3	17.4	17.9	17.6
Pacific											
American Samoa [a]	34.3	36.5	39.4	45.6	38.2	37.9	41.0	40.6			
Fiji [a]	26.8	29.9	29.6	28.3	27.8	26.8	28.2	26.8	25.3	24.7	25.3
French Polynesia	31.4	30.3	29.5	30.2			28.5	27.3	28.2		
Guam [a]	30.1	27.3	26.5	25.6	29.1	27.6	26.9	28.1	25.9		24.9
Kiribati							18.2	21.7	34.1	32.5	33.1
Nauru											
New Caledonia	28.1	26.2	25.4	22.4	23.7	25.2	24.3				
Papua New Guinea					33.6	34.6	35.5	35.0	35.3	33.8	33.5
Solomon Islands							44.9	44.5	41.4	43.1	41.5
Tonga		29.6	28.2	29.3	28.1	28.4	24.9	30.4	31.2	30.4	
Tuvalu											
Vanuatu							38.1	40.7	38.3	39.3	
Western Samoa [c]	21.8	16.8					33.2	33.1	33.0	32.5	32.3
Middle East											
Bahrain [c]	30.2	29.8			29.3	29.3	27.6	26.7	27.8		
Egypt [a]	37.3	37.2	38.4		39.1	39.4	38.8				35.0
Iran	40.6	62.3	49.9	45.0		41.1	38.6	42.1	40.2	34.1	35.2
Iraq [c]	24.1	28.0			28.6	29.1	28.8				
Israel [a]	26.4	24.3	24.0	23.7	23.5	23.1	22.7	22.5	22.3	22.1	
Jordan [a]	29.5		30.7	31.1	30.1	31.9	29.6	31.0			
Kuwait [a]	41.1	37.3	35.4	34.6	32.2	30.1	26.8				
Lebanon											
Oman											
Qatar [a]		29.3	30.6	30.8	30.8	32.1	30.1	31.9		22.5	
Saudi Arabia											
Syria [c]	50.2	58.7	43.6	43.7	53.4	40.5	43.6	38.4		29.7	
United Arab Emirates		35.5	35.9	34.4					29.8	28.3	
Yemen										51.2	

VITAL STATISTICS

Table No. 0206 (cont'd)

Birth Rates 1977-1991

Units: Per '000 inhabitants

	1977	1980	1983	1984	1985	1986	1987	1988	1989	1990	1991
North Africa											
Algeria [a]	42.6	43.8	40.1	38.1	37.5					31.0	35.0
Chad											43.5
Djibouti [c]	20.1	12.2	13.4	12.8	13.0						45.9
Ethiopia											48.4
Libya [a]	45.1	37.2						41.0			43.5
Mali							48.7				50.8
Mauritania											46.0
Morocco [c]					17.2	18.2	20.1	20.5			33.2
Niger											51.3
Somalia											47.5
Sudan											43.6
Tunisia [a]	37.2	35.2	31.6	32.2	31.3	31.1	29.1	27.5	24.9		28.0
West Africa											
Benin											49.1
Burkina Faso											47.0
Cameroon											47.3
Cape Verde [a]	34.4	31.0	36.9	36.6	38.3	37.2	37.6	35.6			40.8
Côte d'Ivoire											50.0
Equatorial Guinea											43.6
Gabon											42.6
Gambia											45.4
Ghana											43.7
Guinea											50.8
Guinea-Bissau											42.7
Liberia											46.8
Nigeria								48.0			46.9
Sao Tomé e Príncipe [a]	44.4				35.7	36.6	39.1	38.2	33.7		
Senegal											44.2
Sierra Leone					21.1	22.9					48.1
Togo											44.5
East/Central Africa											
Angola											46.7
Burundi											47.0
Central African Republic											45.2
Comoros		68.9				50.0					47.3
Congo											46.1
Kenya	19.2	21.9	16.9	16.0							47.0
Madagascar											45.1
Maldives		44.6	42.9	47.7	49.4	46.2	43.3	41.3	43.0	41.1	
Mauritius	25.8	26.0	20.4	19.5	18.4	18.4	19.2	19.6	20.3	21.1	17.6
Réunion [a]	25.5	24.1	23.6	24.2	24.0	22.9	22.5	23.4	23.5	23.6	23.1
Rwanda		54.4								57.0	50.2
Seychelles [a]	26.7	30.5	27.7	29.0	24.7	24.6	24.1	23.5	22.9	23.1	24.2
Tanzania											50.3
Uganda											51.6
Zaire											45.4
Southern Africa											
Botswana [c]					15.4	40.3	27.3				43.8
Lesotho											40.3
Malawi	48.3										55.6
Mozambique											44.2
Namibia											42.1
South Africa											
Swaziland											46.7
Zambia											50.5
Zimbabwe											40.3

Source: UN/national statistical offices
Notes: see end of section

VITAL STATISTICS — Table No. 0207

Death Rates 1977-1991

Units: Per '000 inhabitants

	1977	1980	1983	1984	1985	1986	1987	1988	1989	1990	1991
North America											
Canada [a]	7.2	7.1	7.0	7.0	7.1	7.3	7.2	7.3	7.3		
USA [a]	8.6	8.7	8.6	8.6	8.7	8.7	8.8	8.9	8.7	8.6	
South America											
Argentina [a]	8.7	8.5	8.5	8.5	8.0	7.8	8.0	8.4		8.6	
Bolivia	6.9	4.8								10.6	
Brazil	7.1	6.7	6.2	6.4	6.3	6.2	5.8		5.7	7.9	
Chile [a]	7.0	6.7	6.3	6.3	6.1	5.9	5.6	5.8	5.8	6.4	
Colombia	6.0	4.9	5.1	4.9	5.4	5.0			4.8	6.1	
Ecuador [b]	7.9	7.0	6.2	5.7	5.5	5.3	5.2	5.2	4.9	4.0	
French Guiana [a]	7.6	6.5	6.1	6.1	5.6	5.5					
Guyana [a]	7.3									7.8	
Paraguay	5.2	4.1	3.4	3.3	3.8	3.0	3.4			6.6	
Peru	11.3	11.2	10.7	10.4	10.1	9.9	9.6	9.3	9.0	8.6	7.9
Suriname		8.0			6.1					6.2	
Uruguay	10.1	10.3	9.6	10.0	9.7	9.7	9.8		9.6	9.9	
Venezuela	5.5	.5.1	4.6	4.6	4.6	4.4	4.4	4.3	4.4	5.4	
Caribbean											
Anguilla [a]					10.4						
Antigua [a]	7.0	4.8	5.1	4.8	5.1	4.8	4.6				
Aruba	5.3	4.8	5.7		5.6	6.3	5.8	5.6			
Bahamas [a]	5.3	6.4	5.0	5.0	5.8	5.9	5.7	5.5	5.4	4.6	
Barbados [a]	8.6	8.0	8.3	7.9	8.5	8.3	8.8	8.9	8.8	9.0	
Bermuda [a]	7.5	7.9	8.0	6.6	7.0	6.9	7.3	6.7	7.7		
British Virgin Islands [a]	5.8	6.3	5.3	5.6	5.0	6.3	6.4	4.9	4.8		
Cayman Islands [a]	5.2	6.2	5.5	5.6	5.9	5.9	4.7	4.7	4.4	4.1	4.2
Cuba [a]	5.9	5.7	5.9	6.0	6.4	6.2	6.3	6.5	6.4	6.5	
Dominica [a]	6.7		4.4	5.4					7.6		
Dominican Republic	5.0	4.8			4.5					6.8	
Grenada [a]	8.1										
Guadeloupe [a]	6.9	6.4	6.7	6.8	7.0	6.8	6.8				
Haiti										13.1	
Jamaica [a]	6.8	6.0	5.6	5.9	6.0	5.7	5.2	5.1		5.5	
Martinique [a]	6.5	6.9	6.7	4.8	6.3	6.2	6.1	6.0		6.2	
Netherlands Antilles [a]	5.4	5.1			5.8	5.8	6.4	6.3	6.4		5.8
St Kitts [a]	12.6	12.3	9.6	9.6	8.8	9.2			9.7		
St Lucia [a]	6.8	7.0	6.1	5.7	6.3	6.0	6.7	6.0	5.4		
St Vincent/Grenadines [a]	7.3	7.2	7.1	6.4		6.6		6.5	6.3		
Trinidad and Tobago [a]	7.0	7.0	6.6	6.7			6.7	6.6	6.8	6.2	
Central America											
Belize [b]	5.5	4.8	4.5	5.0	4.1	4.0	4.0	4.1	4.2	5.0	
Costa Rica [a]	4.3	4.1	3.9	4.1	4.2	3.9	3.8	3.8	3.8	3.8	3.9
El Salvador	7.7	8.6	6.9	6.0	5.6	5.2			5.3	8.4	
Guatemala [a]	11.3	10.3	9.9	8.5	8.7	8.5	7.9	7.5	7.2	8.9	
Honduras [b]	5.6	5.0	4.7							5.5	
Mexico	7.1	6.3	5.5	5.4	5.3	5.0	5.0	5.2	5.2	5.1	
Nicaragua [b]	5.6	10.5	9.5			8.0				3.7	
Panama [a]	4.5	4.1	4.1	3.9	4.1	4.0	4.0	3.8	3.7	3.5	
Puerto Rico [a]	6.5	6.4	6.6	6.6	7.1		7.0	7.3	7.4		
South Asia											
Afghanistan							22.5	22.8	22.5	22.6	22.2
Bangladesh [b]		10.3			12.1	12.1	11.4	11.3	11.4	11.3	14.1
Bhutan							17.0	16.7	16.7	16.2	15.9
India							10.9	11.0	10.2	9.6	10.3
Nepal							16.0	14.6	14.9	13.9	13.5
Pakistan	8.2				8.7	7.7	10.5	10.8	10.5	11.6	10.7
Sri Lanka [a]	7.4	6.2	6.1	6.5	6.2	6.0	5.9	5.8	6.2	6.0	5.8

VITAL STATISTICS — Table No. 0207 (cont'd)

Death Rates 1977-1991

Units: Per '000 inhabitants

	1977	1980	1983	1984	1985	1986	1987	1988	1989	1990	1991
Japan											
Japan [a]	6.1	6.2	6.2	6.2	6.2	6.3	6.2	6.5	6.4	6.7	6.7
ASEAN/NICs											
Brunei [a]	4.4	3.9	3.4	3.5	3.6	3.2	3.2	3.2	3.3	4.0	3.6
Hong Kong [a]	5.2	4.9	5.0	4.7	4.6	4.7	4.8	4.9	5.1	5.2	4.9
Indonesia					11.3		7.8	11.1	8.8	9.0	11.7
Macau	5.1	4.6		4.4	3.8	3.4	3.1	3.3	3.4	3.1	
Malaysia [b]					4.4	4.1	3.9	4.1	4.7	4.7	4.7
Philippines [b]	6.9	6.2	6.3	5.9	6.1	5.8	7.5	7.5	7.4	7.4	7.3
Singapore [a]	5.1	5.2	5.3	5.2	5.2	5.0	5.0	5.2	5.2	4.8	4.7
South Korea	6.2	6.7	6.3	6.3	6.2	6.1	6.1	5.9	5.8	5.8	5.8
Taiwan		4.7	4.8	4.7	4.8	4.9	4.9	5.1	5.1	5.2	
Thailand [b]	5.4	5.3	5.1	4.4	3.9	4.1	4.3	4.2	4.4	4.5	6.1
East/SE Asia											
Cambodia							16.9	16.4	15.8	15.6	15.0
China							6.7	6.4	6.5	6.7	6.7
Laos							14.1	16.2	16.3	16.0	15.6
Mongolia	10.1	10.4		11.1	9.9	8.5	8.0	8.6	8.7	8.3	8.1
Myanmar							8.4	8.9	9.4	9.2	9.0
North Korea								5.0	5.1		
Vietnam							10.0	9.4	7.3	8.0	8.6
Australasia											
Australia [a]	7.7	7.4	7.2	7.2	7.5	7.2	7.2	7.2	7.1	6.7	6.4
New Zealand [a]	8.3	8.6	8.1	7.9	8.5	8.3	8.3	8.2	8.1	7.9	7.8
Pacific											
American Samoa [a]		5.0	4.8	5.0	3.9	4.3	3.9	4.9			
Fiji [a]	3.8	6.4	5.2	4.6	5.3	5.5	5.3	5.0	4.9	4.9	6.7
French Polynesia			5.4			5.5		4.4	5.4	6.7	
Guam [a]	3.8	3.8	3.8		4.0	3.8	3.9	3.9	4.2	4.3	4.3
Kiribati		5.2	6.9	6.9	8.8	5.9	5.8	4.9	11.5	12.7	11.1
Nauru											
New Caledonia	6.6	7.2	5.5	5.2	5.8	5.8	5.4				
Papua New Guinea					12.4		11.8	13.0	11.5	11.1	10.9
Solomon Islands								9.9	7.5	9.3	7.3
Tonga			4.0	2.7	3.4		3.5	7.3	6.6	7.1	
Tuvalu			9.6							11.0	
Vanuatu				12.0				7.8	7.7	7.3	
Western Samoa [b]	3.5	3.0	7.0			5.0		7.1	7.0	6.9	6.8
Middle East											
Bahrain [b]		3.2			2.9	3.2	3.4	3.0	3.2		
Egypt [a]	11.8	10.0	9.4	8.9	9.5	9.8	9.5				12.2
Iran	4.2	4.1	4.7	4.1		3.8	10.7	7.9	8.2	7.2	
Iraq [b]	4.2	4.9			4.6	4.7	4.8				
Israel [a]	6.9	6.8	6.8	6.7	7.0	6.8	6.7	6.6	6.3	6.2	
Jordan [a]	1.9	2.2	2.5	2.5	2.6	2.5	2.4	2.5			
Kuwait [a]	4.7	3.6	3.0	2.8	2.8	2.5	2.2				
Lebanon											
Oman											
Qatar [a]		2.9	3.0	2.3	2.6	2.5	2.4	2.5		1.8	
Saudi Arabia											
Syria [b]	5.5	5.3	5.3	5.1	5.9	4.8	4.7	4.0		2.7	
United Arab Emirates			1.2	1.0					2.1	2.1	
Yemen										29.2	

VITAL STATISTICS

Death Rates 1977-1991

Units: Per '000 inhabitants

	1977	1980	1983	1984	1985	1986	1987	1988	1989	1990	1991
North Africa											
Algeria [a]	9.2	11.8	8.5		6.1					6.0	9.3
Chad											20.7
Djibouti											18.9
Ethiopia											22.6
Libya [a]	5.9	5.0						6.2			10.4
Mali							12.5				22.0
Mauritania											20.2
Morocco [b]					2.9	2.9	3.2	3.3			11.0
Niger											21.8
Somalia											21.9
Sudan											16.9
Tunisia [a]	6.1	5.7	5.1	4.8	5.0	4.8	4.5	4.3	4.4		8.0
West Africa											
Benin											20.6
Burkina Faso											19.4
Cameroon											16.2
Cape Verde [a]	8.8	7.6	8.5	8.9	8.3						9.3
Côte d'Ivoire											15.5
Equatorial Guinea											20.9
Gabon											17.4
Gambia											22.9
Ghana		3.0									14.1
Guinea											23.4
Guinea-Bissau											24.4
Liberia											17.2
Nigeria					16.0	16.0	16.0	16.0			16.9
Sao Tomé e Príncipe [a]	10.7				9.7	11.4	10.2	11.8	9.8		
Senegal											19.0
Sierra Leone					8.3	10.1					24.8
Togo											15.1
East/Central Africa											
Angola											21.5
Burundi											19.2
Central African Republic											19.0
Comoros		14.2				15.6					14.0
Congo											15.8
Kenya	3.3	3.1	2.7	3.0							12.6
Madagascar											15.1
Maldives	11.8	11.9	10.3	9.6	8.9	8.1	7.6	7.7	7.0	6.4	
Mauritius	7.9	7.1	6.5	6.5	6.8	6.7	6.6	6.6	6.7	6.6	6.5
Réunion [a]	6.3	6.3	6.3	5.6	5.6	5.5	5.5	5.6	5.6	5.4	5.6
Rwanda		5.3	3.1								18.5
Seychelles [a]	8.0	7.4	7.5	8.1	6.7	7.1	7.2	7.2	8.0	7.8	7.7
Tanzania											15.0
Uganda											16.9
Zaire											15.2
Southern Africa											
Botswana [b]					1.6	4.1	3.0				13.3
Lesotho											13.5
Malawi	25.0										21.9
Mozambique											19.7
Namibia											13.3
South Africa											
Swaziland											13.6
Zambia											14.7
Zimbabwe											11.4

Source: UN/national statistical offices
Notes: see end of section

VITAL STATISTICS | Table No. 0208

Infant Mortality Rates 1977-1991

Units: Deaths per '000 live births

	1977	1980	1983	1984	1985	1986	1987	1988	1989	1990	1991
North America											
Canada	12.4	10.4	8.5	8.1	7.9	7.9	7.3	7.2	7.1	6.8	
USA	14.1	12.6	11.2	10.8	10.6	10.4	10.0	9.9	9.5	9.1	8.9
South America											
Argentina	44.6	33.2	35.3		26.2		26.0	25.8		25.1	
Bolivia [a,b,c]	138.2	138.2	124.4	124.4	124.4	110.0	110.0	110.0	110.0	92.0	
Brazil [a,b,c]	78.8	78.8	70.6	70.6	70.6	63.0	63.0	63.0	63.0	57.0	
Chile	50.1	33.0	21.9	19.6	19.5	19.1	18.5	18.9	17.1	16.8	
Colombia [a,b,c]	59.4	59.4	50.0	50.0	50.0	46.0	46.0	46.0	46.0	37.0	
Ecuador	63.0	54.3	50.0	43.4	40.5	40.3	37.4	35.3	44.2	55.0	
French Guiana						22.2					
Guyana [a,b]	48.7	48.7	36.2	36.2	36.2		57.4	56.0			
Paraguay [a,b,c]	48.6	48.6	45.0	45.0	45.0	42.0	42.0	42.0	42.0	32.0	
Peru [a]	104.9	104.9	140.6	135.9	90.8	90.3	122.3	94.6	114.1	109.9	78.1
Suriname [a,b,c]	39.2	39.2	36.2	36.2	36.2	31.0	31.0	31.0	31.0		
Uruguay	48.5	37.6	28.6	30.4	29.4	27.8	24.2	21.0	21.9	20.4	
Venezuela [a]	43.3	43.3	26.3	27.3	26.1	24.7	23.7	21.5	23.3	34.0	
Caribbean											
Anguilla											
Antigua					24.4						
Aruba											
Bahamas	27.7	31.9	21.6	22.2	26.3	36.7	28.4	21.4	22.3	26.3	
Barbados	26.3		14.0				16.2		9.0		
Bermuda											
British Virgin Islands	12.4	10.4									
Cayman Islands							3.0	5.0	9.0	6.0	14.0
Cuba	23.5	19.6	16.8	15.0	16.5	13.6	13.3	11.9	11.1	10.7	10.7
Dominica									18.4		
Dominican Republic [a,b,c]	73.1	73.1	74.5	74.5	74.5	65.0	65.0	65.0	65.0	56.0	
Grenada											
Guadeloupe			16.4	17.2	15.3	15.4		14.0			
Haiti [b,c]			127.8	127.8	127.8	117.0	117.0	117.0	117.0	95.0	
Jamaica	15.2							18.0	17.0	16.0	
Martinique [a,b]	59.8	59.8	14.1	14.1	14.1			8.6		7.1	
Netherlands Antilles								13.9	6.3		
St Kitts							39.7		22.2		
St Lucia		30.1	25.8		23.7				17.7		
St Vincent/Grenadines		60.2	37.0				24.7	21.7			
Trinidad and Tobago	21.0		12.7	13.7			11.4	13.2	10.2	25.0	
Central America											
Belize			23.2	23.4	20.6	23.1	20.7	20.6	19.4	22.5	15.1
Costa Rica	27.9	20.2	18.6	18.4			17.4	14.7	13.9	15.3	13.6
El Salvador [c]	59.3	42.0		35.1	59.0	59.0	59.0	59.0	59.0	53.0	
Guatemala			65.7	55.4	56.0	56.8	51.7	46.6	43.6	62.0	
Honduras [b,c]			81.5	81.5	81.5	69.0	69.0	69.0	69.0	64.0	
Mexico [b,c]			53.0	53.0	53.0	47.0	47.0	47.0	47.0	39.0	
Nicaragua [a,b,c]	36.2	36.2	76.4	76.4	76.4	62.0	62.0	62.0	62.0	55.0	
Panama [b,c]			25.6	25.6	25.6	23.0	23.0	23.0	23.0	21.0	
Puerto Rico			15.6		14.9		14.2	12.6	14.3	13.0	
South Asia											
Afghanistan [b]			193.8	193.8	193.8		172.2	171.0	170.4	167.0	165.0
Bangladesh [a,b]	139.6	139.6	128.2	128.2	128.2	116.0	113.0	116.0	98.0	94.0	110.0
Bhutan [a,b,c]	156.3	156.3	138.7	138.7	128.0	128.0	128.0	128.0	128.0	122.5	121.0
India			104.9		97.2	96.4	95.0	94.0	91.0	80.0	91.0
Nepal [a,b,c]	156.3	156.3	138.7	138.7	138.7	128.0	128.0	128.0	128.0	121.0	121.0
Pakistan [a,b]	131.2	131.2	120.0	120.0	115.9	105.6	103.9	107.7	106.7	104.0	101.0
Sri Lanka	42.4	34.4	28.4	23.1	23.5	22.6	24.0	21.1	20.2	21.1	25.0

VITAL STATISTICS — Table No. 0208 (cont'd)

Infant Mortality Rates 1977-1991

Units: Deaths per '000 live births

	1977	1980	1983	1984	1985	1986	1987	1988	1989	1990	1991
Japan											
Japan	8.9	7.5	6.2	6.0	5.5	5.2	5.0	4.8	4.6	4.6	4.4
ASEAN/NICs											
Brunei							10.0	6.8	9.0	12.0	11.0
Hong Kong	13.5	11.2	9.9	8.8	7.5	7.7	7.4	7.4	6.8	6.2	6.7
Indonesia [a,b,c]	114.8	114.8	84.4	84.4	84.4	84.0	84.0	84.0	84.0	65.0	90.0
Macau								9.4		8.4	
Malaysia	33.3	23.9	20.2	17.5	16.4	15.6	14.5	14.2	13.4	13.3	12.6
Philippines [a]	58.9	58.9	59.2	57.9	56.6	55.3	54.2	52.8	42.7	43.0	42.0
Singapore	12.4	11.7	9.4	8.8	9.3	9.4	7.4	7.0	6.6	6.7	5.5
South Korea [a]	36.7	36.7	29.6	29.2	13.3	28.4	12.5	12.5	12.8	12.8	12.0
Taiwan											
Thailand [a,b,c]	58.9	58.9	47.5	47.5	47.5	39.0	39.0	39.0	39.0	27.0	
East/SE Asia											
Cambodia [a,b]	263.2	263.2	159.9	159.9	159.9	140.0	133.0	129.0	122.5	123.0	120.0
China [a,b,c]	48.7	48.7	39.3	39.3	39.3	32.0	32.0	32.0	33.0	30.0	29.0
Laos [a,b]	135.0	135.0	122.5	122.5	122.5	137.0	111.0	109.0	105.7	104.0	101.0
Mongolia [a,b]	59.1	59.1	53.0	53.0	53.0	70.0	65.9	63.9	64.4	61.8	62.0
Myanmar [a]	107.1	107.1	47.2	47.1	47.2	47.1	44.3	47.0	66.5	65.0	62.0
North Korea [a,b,c]	36.7	36.7	29.7	29.7	29.7	24.0	24.0	28.0	26.8		
Vietnam [a,b]	106.4	106.4	75.8	75.8	75.8	69.0	68.0	63.0	43.4	46.0	57.0
Australasia											
Australia	12.5	11.0	9.6	9.2	9.9	8.8	8.7	8.7	8.9	7.7	7.0
New Zealand	14.2	12.9	12.5	11.6	10.8	11.2	10.0	10.8	10.2	8.3	8.3
Pacific											
American Samoa							10.4	10.5			
Fiji		38.5	21.0	16.4	18.5	20.5	19.0	26.1	25.1	24.2	25.0
French Polynesia			22.7	20.5			20.4		16.4		
Guam		16.3	11.0	11.1	12.2	9.7	7.5	4.5	12.3		
Kiribati								110.0	59.1	59.0	56.0
Nauru											
New Caledonia	28.5						15.2				
Papua New Guinea [a]	110.9	110.9	71.8	69.6	67.4	65.2	63.0	61.2	59.3	57.5	55.0
Solomon Islands		56.8	61.8	59.6	57.4	55.2	53.0	51.1	49.2	47.3	47.0
Tonga					5.0		6.8				
Tuvalu											
Vanuatu			90.2	86.4	82.7	78.9	75.1	73.1	71.2	69.2	
Western Samoa			33.3	50.8	50.8	50.8	50.0	48.8	47.6	46.3	45.6
Middle East											
Bahrain [a,b,c]	57.0	57.0	31.6	31.6	31.6	26.0	26.0	26.0	26.0		
Egypt	85.3						49.4			66.0	
Iran [a,b]	114.8	114.8	115.0	115.0	115.0		63.0	52.0		88.0	
Iraq [a,b,c]	84.0	84.0	77.1	77.1	77.1	69.0	69.0	69.0	69.0	65.0	
Israel	18.2	15.1	13.7	12.8	11.9	11.4	11.1	10.0	10.1	9.7	
Jordan [a,b,c]	75.1	75.1	54.1	54.1	54.1	44.0	44.0	44.0	44.0	51.0	
Kuwait	39.1	27.7	19.0	18.5	18.4	15.6	19.1	18.0			
Lebanon [a,b,c]	43.7	43.7	48.0	48.0	48.0	40.0	40.0	40.0	40.0	46.0	
Oman [a,b,c]	135.2	135.2	117.2	117.2	117.2	100.0	100.0	100.0	100.0		
Qatar [a,b,c]	57.0	57.0	37.8	37.8	37.8	31.0	31.0	31.0	31.0	33.0	
Saudi Arabia [a,b,c]	121.0	121.0	66.1	66.1	66.1	71.0	71.0	71.0	71.0	65.0	
Syria [a,b,c]	67.2	67.2	58.8	58.8	58.8	48.0	48.0	48.0	48.0	43.0	
United Arab Emirates [a,b,c]	57.0	57.0	37.8	37.8	37.8	26.0	26.0	26.0	26.0		
Yemen [a,b,c]	165.0	165.0	134.9	134.9	134.9	116.0	116.0	116.0	116.0	132.0	

VITAL STATISTICS

Table No. 0208 (cont'd)

Infant Mortality Rates 1977-1991

Units: Deaths per '000 live births

	1977	1980	1983	1984	1985	1986	1987	1988	1989	1990	1991
North Africa											
Algeria [a,b,c]	125.3	125.3	88.0	88.0	88.0	74.0	74.0	74.0	74.0	72.0	
Chad [a,b,c]	154.3	154.3	142.8	142.8	142.8	132.0	132.0	132.0	132.0	132.0	
Djibouti [c]					122.0	122.0	122.0	122.0	122.0	117.0	
Ethiopia [a,b,c]	150.0	150.0	154.9	154.9	154.9	154.0	154.0	154.0	154.0	137.0	
Libya [a,b,c]	106.9	106.9	96.5	96.5	96.5	82.0	82.0	82.0	82.0	82.0	
Mali [a,b,d]	160.4	160.4	179.5	179.5	179.5		169.0			169.0	
Mauritania [a,b,c]	148.5	148.5	137.3	137.3	137.3	127.0	127.0	127.0	127.0	127.0	
Morocco [a,b,c]	114.4	114.4	96.5	96.5	96.5	82.0	82.0	82.0	82.0	82.0	
Niger [a,b,c]	151.4	151.4	145.7	145.7	145.7	135.0	135.0	135.0	135.0	135.0	
Somalia [a,b,c]	150.0	150.0	154.9	154.9	154.9	132.0	132.0	132.0	132.0	132.0	
Sudan [a,b,c]	131.1	131.1	117.8	117.8	117.8	108.0	108.0	108.0	108.0	108.0	
Tunisia [a,b,c]	106.5	106.5	85.3	85.3	85.3	59.0	59.0	59.0	59.0	52.0	
West Africa											
Benin [a,b,c]	160.4	160.4	120.1	120.1	120.1	110.0	110.0	110.0	110.0	90.0	
Burkina Faso [a,b,c]	218.8	218.8	150.3	150.3	150.3	138.0	138.0	138.0	138.0	138.0	
Cameroon [a,b,c]	114.5	114.5	103.2	103.2	103.2	94.0	94.0	94.0	94.0	94.0	
Cape Verde [d]			65.3	62.8	68.3		63.0			44.0	
Côte d'Ivoire [a,b,c]	132.0	132.0	109.9	109.9	109.9	96.0	96.0	96.0	96.0	96.0	
Equatorial Guinea [a,b,c]	148.5	148.5	137.3	137.3	137.3	127.0	127.0	127.0	127.0	127.0	
Gabon [a,b,c]	121.6	121.6	111.9	111.9	111.9	103.0	103.0	103.0	103.0	103.0	
Gambia [a,b,c]	203.5	203.5	174.1	174.1	174.1	143.0	143.0	143.0	143.0	143.0	
Ghana [a,b,c]	107.3	107.3	98.3	98.3	98.3	90.0	90.0	90.0	90.0	90.0	
Guinea [a,b,c]	171.5	171.5	159.1	159.1	159.1	147.0	147.0	147.0	147.0	145.0	
Guinea-Bissau [a,b,c]	154.3	154.3	142.8	142.8	142.8	132.0	132.0	132.0	132.0	151.0	
Liberia [a,b,c]	159.8	159.8	132.5	132.5	132.5	87.0	87.0	87.0	87.0	142.0	
Nigeria [a,b,c]	140.5	140.5	114.2	114.2	114.2	105.0	105.0	105.0	105.0	105.0	
Sao Tomé e Príncipe [d]	57.1				65.5	73.5	56.2	70.0	71.9	43.0	
Senegal [a,b,c]	152.6	152.6	142.2	142.2	142.2	128.0	128.0	128.0	128.0	87.0	
Sierra Leone [a,b,c]	215.0	215.0	179.5	179.5	179.5	154.0	154.0	154.0	154.0	154.0	
Togo [a,b,c]	114.7	114.7	102.3	102.3	102.3	94.0	94.0	94.0	94.0	94.0	
East/Central Africa											
Angola [a,b,c]	160.4	160.4	148.5	148.5	148.5	137.0	137.0	137.0	137.0	137.0	
Burundi [a,b,c]	126.6	126.6	124.1	124.1	124.1	112.0	112.0	112.0	112.0	119.0	
Central African Republic [a,b,c]	154.3	154.3	142.0	142.0	142.0	132.0	132.0	132.0	132.0	104.0	
Comoros [a,b,c]	96.9	96.9	88.3	88.3	88.3	80.0	80.0	80.0	80.0	99.0	
Congo [a,b,c]	134.5	134.5	81.1	81.1	81.1	73.0	73.0	73.0	73.0	73.0	
Kenya [a,b,c]	92.0	92.0	80.2	80.2	80.2	72.0	72.0	72.0	72.0	137.0	
Madagascar [a,b,c]	75.7	75.7	67.0	67.0	67.0	120.0	120.0	120.0	120.0	120.0	
Maldives	118.0	94.4	74.6	67.9	60.4	57.7	49.9	48.4	43.0	33.6	
Mauritius [b,d]			28.4	28.4	28.4		23.0			20.4	
Réunion [a,b,c]	20.5	20.5	13.1	13.1	13.1	14.0	9.8	6.6	8.3	6.8	7.3
Rwanda [a,b,c]	111.9	111.9	132.0	132.0	132.0	122.0	122.0	122.0	122.0	122.0	
Seychelles [d]							30.0	17.0	18.1	13.0	12.9
Tanzania [a,b,c]	107.4	107.4	114.8	114.8	114.8	106.0	106.0	106.0	106.0	106.0	
Uganda [a,b,c]	100.5	100.5	111.9	111.9	111.9	103.0	103.0	103.0	103.0	103.0	
Zaire [a,b,c]	116.6	116.6	107.3	107.3	107.3	98.0	98.0	98.0	98.0	83.0	
Southern Africa											
Botswana [a,b,c]	87.5	87.5	76.2	76.2	76.2	67.0	67.0	67.0	67.0	67.0	
Lesotho [a,b,c]	120.0	120.0	111.1	111.1	111.1	100.0	100.0	100.0	100.0	100.0	
Malawi [a,b,d]	178.9	178.9	163.4	163.4	163.4		150.0			150.0	
Mozambique [a,b,c]	119.6	119.6	153.5	153.5	153.5	141.0	141.0	141.0	141.0	141.0	
Namibia [a,b,c]	125.3	125.3	115.6	115.6	115.6	106.0	106.0	106.0	106.0	106.0	
South Africa [a,b,c]	100.6	100.6	83.3	83.3	83.3	72.0	72.0	72.0	72.0		
Swaziland [a,b,c]	140.1	140.1	129.2	129.2	129.2	118.0	118.0	118.0	118.0	118.0	
Zambia [a,b,c]	110.5	110.5	88.3	88.3	88.3	80.0	80.0	80.0	80.0	80.0	
Zimbabwe [a,b,c]	78.8	78.8	80.2	80.2	80.2	72.0	72.0	72.0	72.0	66.0	

Source: UN/national statistical offices

Notes: see end of section

VITAL STATISTICS   Table No. 0209

Marriage Rates 1977-1991

Units: Per '000 inhabitants

	1977	1980	1983	1984	1985	1986	1987	1988	1989	1990	1991
North America											
Canada [a]	8.1	7.9	7.4	7.4	7.3	6.9	7.1	7.2	7.3		
USA [a]	9.9	10.5	10.4	10.5	10.2	10.0	9.9	9.8	9.7	9.8	9.4
South America											
Argentina [a]	6.9	5.9	6.3							5.8	
Bolivia [b]	5.5	4.8									
Brazil [b]	8.0	7.8	6.7	7.1	7.0	7.3	6.6	6.6	5.6		
Chile [a]	7.0	7.7	7.0	7.3	7.5	7.6	7.6	8.1	8.0	7.5	
Colombia [b]	3.5	3.9			3.3	2.4					
Ecuador [b]	6.2	5.9	5.6	5.9	6.0	6.2	6.2	6.5	6.0	6.7	
French Guiana [b]	3.3	2.8	3.1	3.9	3.8	3.9					
Guyana											
Paraguay [b]	6.4	5.4	3.9	4.6	5.0	4.2	4.5	3.9	3.0	1.8	
Peru [a]	2.3	2.8									
Suriname [b]		6.7									
Uruguay [a]	7.8	7.7	6.5	6.8	7.4	7.2	7.5	7.0			
Venezuela [a]	7.1	6.2	5.7	5.5	5.4	5.6	5.8	6.1	5.9		
Caribbean											
Anguilla [a]					13.8						
Antigua [a]	2.5	2.7	2.4	2.6	3.5		4.5				
Aruba [a]			7.3		7.0	5.9	6.3	6.4			
Bahamas [a]	6.6	6.6	6.7	7.3	8.5	7.6	7.9	8.9	8.6	8.6	
Barbados [a]	2.8	4.2	5.0	4.6	4.7	5.8	6.0	8.1	8.0		
Bermuda [a]	8.6	10.2	12.3	11.9	12.4	13.7	13.7	14.5	14.6	15.0	
British Virgin Islands [a]		10.0	12.1	12.7	13.0	11.6	15.5	14.2			
Cayman Islands [c]		10.6	10.6	11.2	8.5	10.1	12.3	10.2	10.3	10.6	10.4
Cuba [a]	6.5	7.1	7.7	7.6	8.0	8.2	7.6	7.9	8.1	9.6	15.0
Dominica										2.7	
Dominican Republic [a]		5.3			3.3						
Grenada											
Guadeloupe [a]	4.4	4.9	4.8	5.0	4.8	5.1					
Haiti											
Jamaica [a]	4.1	3.6	3.7	4.5	5.1	4.6	4.5	4.3	4.7	5.4	
Martinique [a]	3.9	3.6	4.1	4.0	4.0	4.6	4.6	4.6	4.4	4.3	
Netherlands Antilles							5.7	6.7	6.5	6.7	6.4
St Kitts [a]	2.6										
St Lucia [a]	3.5	3.6	3.1	3.3	3.1	3.1	2.9	2.8	2.7		
St Vincent/Grenadines [a]		3.4	4.0	3.6		3.8		4.1			
Trinidad and Tobago [a]	7.3		7.4	7.2	6.7	7.6	6.3	6.0	5.6		
Central America											
Belize [a]			6.5	5.3	6.0	5.9	6.1	6.0	6.2		
Costa Rica [a]	7.5	7.8	7.9	8.5			7.8	8.0	7.9	7.6	
El Salvador [a]	4.2	4.8		3.5	3.8	4.0	4.4	4.2	4.0	4.4	
Guatemala [a]	4.4	4.5	4.0	4.3	4.8	5.6	5.3	5.3	4.7	5.4	
Honduras [a]	4.2		4.9								
Mexico [a]	7.3	7.2	6.8	6.5	6.6		7.4	7.6	7.4	7.4	
Nicaragua [a]	5.3	6.3				3.5	3.3				
Panama [a]	5.0	5.2	5.4	5.7	5.7	5.4	5.8	5.2	5.2	5.2	
Puerto Rico [a]	11.3	10.3	9.1	9.0	9.2		9.7	9.3	9.1	9.2	
South Asia											
Afghanistan											
Bangladesh [c]		9.1			10.2	8.8	11.5	11.3			
Bhutan											
India											
Nepal											
Pakistan											
Sri Lanka [b]	7.6	8.2	7.9	7.9	8.1	7.9	7.9	7.9	8.4		

VITAL STATISTICS   Table No. 0209 (cont'd)

Marriage Rates 1977-1991

Units: Per '000 inhabitants

	1977	1980	1983	1984	1985	1986	1987	1988	1989	1990	1991
Japan											
Japan [a]	7.2	6.6	6.4	6.2	6.1	5.9	5.7	5.8	5.8	5.8	6.0
ASEAN/NICs											
Brunei [a]	6.6		7.3	7.5	8.6	7.4	7.9	7.4	7.2		
Hong Kong [a]	9.0	10.1	8.9	9.9	8.3	7.8	8.6	8.0	7.6	8.1	
Indonesia [c]			7.2	6.7	7.4						
Macau	2.8	3.2		8.2	8.3	6.8	5.8	5.2	3.9	3.7	
Malaysia [b,d]	1.8				3.1	2.8	3.1	3.2			
Philippines [b]	7.3		6.8	7.2	6.9	7.0	7.0	6.7	5.0	5.0	
Singapore [a]	9.0	9.8	8.8	9.9	9.2	7.8	9.0	9.4			
South Korea [b]	8.1	9.7	8.9		9.0	8.9	8.8	8.8	7.3		
Taiwan			8.5	8.2	8.0	7.5	7.5	7.9	7.9	7.1	7.9
Thailand [a]		6.6	7.7	7.8	6.6	6.3		7.2	7.4	8.2	
East/SE Asia											
Cambodia											
China											
Laos											
Mongolia [c]				6.1	6.6	7.8	9.7	10.8	7.5		
Myanmar											
North Korea											
Vietnam											
Australasia											
Australia [a]	7.4	7.4	7.5	7.4	7.3	7.2	7.0	7.1	7.0	6.8	
New Zealand [a]	7.2	7.4	7.7	7.8	7.6	7.4	7.5	7.1	6.9	7.0	6.8
Pacific											
American Samoa [a]		10.6			11.2	10.6	8.6	9.1			
Fiji [b]	9.6	9.8	10.1	9.6	9.5	8.4	8.4	9.3			
French Polynesia [c]			8.0				6.8	6.7	5.7		
Guam [c]	17.2	15.3			13.1	12.3	12.0				
Kiribati											
Nauru											
New Caledonia [c]	5.4	5.6	5.7		5.0	5.1	4.6				
Papua New Guinea											
Solomon Islands											
Tonga [c]			7.3	6.9	6.6		6.0	3.6	6.2	7.3	
Tuvalu											
Vanuatu											
Western Samoa [b]	4.9	5.4	4.4								
Middle East											
Bahrain [c]	5.0	6.8			6.3	6.1	6.4	6.6	6.2	5.8	
Egypt [c]	9.5				9.1						
Iran [b]	5.2	8.8	9.8	8.9		8.3	6.8	6.9	8.5	8.3	
Iraq [c]	11.1						5.8	8.5			
Israel [a]	8.1	7.6	7.5	7.2	6.9	7.0	6.9	6.9	7.0	7.0	
Jordan [a]	5.2	5.3	5.2	5.4	5.7	5.3	6.4	7.5	8.1		
Kuwait [a]	5.0	6.2	6.1	5.9	5.6	5.5	5.3	5.2	5.4		
Lebanon											
Oman											
Qatar [c]			3.8	3.9	3.7	3.8	4.1	3.1	2.9	2.8	
Saudi Arabia											
Syria [c]	9.0	10.1	8.2	8.4	9.4	9.1	9.4	8.8	8.8	7.5	
United Arab Emirates									4.4	4.0	
Yemen											

VITAL STATISTICS   Table No. 0209 (cont'd)

Marriage Rates 1977-1991

Units: Per '000 inhabitants

	1977	1980	1983	1984	1985	1986	1987	1988	1989	1990	1991
North Africa											
Algeria c		6.9			5.7						
Chad											
Djibouti											
Ethiopia											
Libya b	6.8	5.3					4.9	4.5			
Mali											
Mauritania											
Morocco											
Niger											
Somalia											
Sudan											
Tunisia	8.1	7.5	7.6	7.6	6.9	6.4	6.5	6.4	7.0	6.9	
West Africa											
Benin											
Burkina Faso											
Cameroon											
Cape Verde											
Côte d'Ivoire											
Equatorial Guinea											
Gabon											
Gambia											
Ghana											
Guinea											
Guinea-Bissau b											
Liberia											
Nigeria											
Sao Tomé e Príncipe											
Senegal											
Sierra Leone											
Togo											
East/Central Africa											
Angola											
Burundi											
Central African Republic											
Comoros											
Congo											
Kenya											
Madagascar											
Maldives c	24.4										
Mauritius a	9.5	9.3	10.4	10.9	11.3	10.4	11.2	11.1	10.7	10.6	10.6
Réunion c	6.4	6.3	6.1	6.2	5.8	5.7	5.3	5.8	6.0	6.4	
Rwanda c		2.7									
Seychelles a	4.5	5.6	4.8	6.0	8.9	8.6	9.4		11.6	15.4	13.5
Tanzania											
Uganda											
Zaire											
Southern Africa											
Botswana c			3.4	3.4		1.5	1.6				
Lesotho											
Malawi											
Mozambique											
Namibia											
South Africa											
Swaziland								3.2	3.5	4.1		
Zambia											
Zimbabwe											

Source: UN
Notes: see end of section

VITAL STATISTICS

Divorce Rates 1977-1991

Units: Per '000 inhabitants

	1977	1980	1983	1984	1985	1986	1987	1988	1989	1990	1991
North America											
Canada [a]	2.4	2.6	2.8	2.6	2.5		3.1		3.1		
USA [a]	5.0	5.2	4.9	4.9	5.0	4.8	4.8	4.8	4.7	4.7	4.7
South America											
Argentina											
Bolivia											
Brazil [b,c]			0.2	0.2	0.3	0.2	0.2	0.2	0.4		
Chile [b,c]				0.3	0.4	0.4	0.4	0.4	0.4	0.5	
Colombia											
Ecuador [b,c]	0.3	0.3	0.4	0.4	0.4	0.4	0.4	0.4	0.5		
French Guiana											
Guyana											
Paraguay											
Peru											
Suriname [b,c]		1.1									
Uruguay [a]	1.8	1.6	1.0	1.0	1.4	1.4	1.4	2.1			
Venezuela [b,c]	0.4	0.3	0.4		1.4	1.4	1.3	1.3	1.2		
Caribbean											
Anguilla					0.9						
Antigua					0.5						
Aruba [a]			2.4	2.2	2.8	3.2	3.6	3.2			
Bahamas [b]	0.7	0.7	0.8	1.6	1.5	1.6	1.8	1.5	1.1		
Barbados [a]	0.6		1.3	1.2	1.2	1.4	1.4	1.5	1.6		
Bermuda [a]	4.6	5.5	4.9	3.9	3.7	3.0	3.2	3.1	2.9		
British Virgin Islands								0.7			
Cayman Islands									2.9		
Cuba [a]	2.4	2.5	3.0	2.8	2.9	3.2	3.1	3.4	3.6	3.5	4.1
Dominica											
Dominican Republic [a]				1.9	1.2						
Grenada											
Guadeloupe [c]	0.9	1.4	1.4	1.5	1.2	1.5					
Haiti											
Jamaica [a]	0.3		0.3	0.3	0.4	0.4	0.4	0.4	0.3		
Martinique [b]	1.2	1.2	1.0	1.0	1.1	1.1	1.1	1.1	0.8	0.7	
Netherlands Antilles							2.3	2.3	2.2	2.1	
St Kitts											
St Lucia									0.3		
St Vincent/Grenadines											
Trinidad and Tobago [a]	0.6		0.8	0.8	0.8	1.0	0.9	0.9	0.9		
Central America											
Belize									0.6		
Costa Rica [a]	0.5	0.8					1.0	0.9	1.0	1.1	
El Salvador [c]	0.3	0.3		0.3	0.4	0.4	0.5	0.4	0.4		
Guatemala [a]	0.1	0.2	0.2	0.2	0.2	0.2	0.2	0.2			
Honduras [a]	0.2		0.4								
Mexico [a]	0.3	0.3		0.4	0.3		0.6	0.6	0.6	0.6	
Nicaragua [b,c]	0.3	0.3				0.2	0.2	0.4	0.5	0.2	
Panama [a]	0.6	0.6	0.6	0.6	0.7	0.7	0.7	0.7	0.8		
Puerto Rico [a]	4.0	4.8	4.0	4.2	4.5		4.3	4.0	3.9	3.8	
South Asia											
Afghanistan											
Bangladesh											
Bhutan											
India											
Nepal											
Pakistan											
Sri Lanka [d]		0.2		0.2	0.2	0.2	0.2	0.2			

VITAL STATISTICS | Table No. 0210 (cont'd)

Divorce Rates 1977-1991

Units: Per '000 inhabitants

	1977	1980	1983	1984	1985	1986	1987	1988	1989	1990	1991
Japan											
Japan	1.1	1.2	1.5	1.5	1.4	1.4	1.3	1.3	1.3	1.3	
ASEAN/NICs											
Brunei [b,c]			0.7	0.7	0.7	0.9	0.9	0.8	0.8		
Hong Kong [b,c]				0.6	0.8	0.8	0.9		1.0	1.0	
Indonesia [b]				1.1	1.0	0.8					
Macau											
Malaysia											
Philippines											
Singapore [b]		0.7	0.8	0.8	0.8	0.9	1.0	1.0			
South Korea [d]	0.5	0.5	0.7	0.6	0.9	0.9	0.9	0.9	0.8		
Taiwan											
Thailand [b,c]				0.6	0.6	0.7					
East/SE Asia											
Cambodia											
China											
Laos											
Mongolia [b]		0.3		0.3	0.4	0.5	0.5	0.8	0.5		
Myanmar											
North Korea											
Vietnam											
Australasia											
Australia [a]	3.2	2.7	2.8	2.8	2.5	2.5	2.4	2.5	2.5	2.5	
New Zealand [a]	1.7	2.1	3.0	2.8	2.6	2.7	2.7	2.6	2.6	2.7	2.7
Pacific											
American Samoa											
Fiji											
French Polynesia											
Guam [a]	3.1	4.6		4.6	7.7	8.2	10.1				
Kiribati											
Nauru											
New Caledonia [b]	0.8	0.9	1.1		1.1	1.0	1.1				
Papua New Guinea											
Solomon Islands											
Tonga											
Tuvalu											
Vanuatu											
Western Samoa											
Middle East											
Bahrain [b,c]		4.2		1.3	1.1	1.1	1.4	1.3	1.5	1.2	
Egypt [b]	2.0				1.6						
Iran [b]	0.5	0.6	0.9	0.8		0.8	0.7	0.6	0.6	0.7	
Iraq [b]	0.8										
Israel [a]	1.0	1.1	1.2	1.2	1.2	1.2	1.2	1.3	1.3	1.3	
Jordan [a]	1.0	0.9	0.8	0.8	1.1	0.9	1.0	1.2	1.2		
Kuwait [a]	1.5	1.5	1.6	1.6	1.6	1.6	1.4	1.5	1.5		
Lebanon											
Oman											
Qatar [b,c]			1.0	1.1	1.0	1.0	1.0	0.9	0.9	0.7	
Saudi Arabia											
Syria [b,c]	0.6	0.6	0.6	0.6	0.7	0.6	0.7	0.8	0.7	0.7	
United Arab Emirates											
Yemen											

VITAL STATISTICS

Divorce Rates 1977-1991

Units: Per '000 inhabitants

	1977	1980	1983	1984	1985	1986	1987	1988	1989	1990	1991
North Africa											
Algeria											
Chad											
Djibouti											
Ethiopia											
Libya [b]	1.8	1.2						0.6			
Mali											
Mauritania											
Morocco											
Niger											
Somalia											
Sudan											
Tunisia [b,c]	1.1	1.1		1.0	1.0				1.6		
West Africa											
Benin											
Burkina Faso											
Cameroon											
Cape Verde											
Côte d'Ivoire											
Equatorial Guinea											
Gabon											
Gambia											
Ghana											
Guinea											
Guinea-Bissau											
Liberia											
Nigeria											
Sao Tomé e Príncipe											
Senegal											
Sierra Leone											
Togo											
East/Central Africa											
Angola											
Burundi											
Central African Republic											
Comoros											
Congo											
Kenya											
Madagascar											
Maldives [b]										7.9	
Mauritius [a]	0.2	0.4	0.4	0.5	0.5	0.6	0.8	0.7	0.7	0.7	
Réunion [b,c]	0.7	0.8	0.8	1.0	1.2	1.4	1.3	1.1			
Rwanda											
Seychelles									0.7		
Tanzania											
Uganda											
Zaire											
Southern Africa											
Botswana											
Lesotho											
Malawi											
Mozambique											
Namibia											
South Africa											
Swaziland											
Zambia											
Zimbabwe											

Source: UN
Notes: see end of section

VITAL STATISTICS   Table No. 0211

Life Expectancy at Birth: Males and Females, Latest Year

Units: Years

	Year	Male	Female
North America			
Canada	1985-87	73.0	79.8
USA	1990	72.0	78.8
South America			
Argentina	1985-90	70.6	71.4
Bolivia	1985-90	58.8	61.1
Brazil	1985-90	64.9	66.3
Chile	1985-90	71.5	72.0
Colombia	1985-90	68.2	69.2
Ecuador	1985-90	65.4	66.6
French Guiana			
Guyana	1985-90	63.2	65.2
Paraguay	1985-90	66.9	67.3
Peru	1985-90	61.4	64.6
Suriname	1985-90	68.8	70.3
Uruguay	1985-90	72.0	72.4
Venezuela	1985-90	69.7	70.3
Caribbean			
Anguilla			
Antigua			
Aruba	1972-78	68.3	74.4
Bahamas	1985	68.2	74.5
Barbados	1985-90	74.6	75.6
Bermuda	1980	68.8	76.3
British Virgin Islands			
Cayman Islands			
Cuba	1985-90	75.2	75.7
Dominica			
Dominican Republic	1985-90	65.9	67.6
Grenada			
Guadeloupe	1975-79	66.4	72.4
Haiti	1985-90	54.7	56.6
Jamaica	1985-90	72.5	73.6
Martinique	1985	70.6	77.1
Netherlands Antilles			
St Kitts	1988	66.0	71.0
St Lucia	1986	68.0	74.8
St Vincent/Grenadines	1986	67.8	71.3
Trinidad and Tobago	1985-90	70.9	72.2
Central America			
Belize	1984	68.1	74.8
Costa Rica	1985-90	75.3	76.3
El Salvador	1985-90	65.4	66.6
Guatemala	1985-90	62.0	64.8
Honduras	1985-90	64.0	65.8
Mexico	1985-90	68.8	70.8
Nicaragua	1985-90	62.4	66.6
Panama	1985-90	72.1	72.8
Puerto Rico	1986	70.3	78.0
South Asia			
Afghanistan	1990	42.0	43.0
Bangladesh	1990	52.1	51.5
Bhutan	1990	49.6	48.3
India	1990	59.0	59.3
Nepal	1990	55.4	52.6
Pakistan	1990	59.3	60.7
Sri Lanka	1990	68.9	73.2

VITAL STATISTICS

Life Expectancy at Birth: Males and Females, Latest Year

Units: Years

	Year	Male	Female
Japan			
Japan	1990	75.9	81.8
ASEAN/NICs			
Brunei	1990	74.4	74.4
Hong Kong	1990	74.7	80.1
Indonesia	1990	59.7	63.3
Macau	1988	75.0	80.3
Malaysia	1990	68.1	72.3
Philippines	1990	62.8	66.4
Singapore	1990	71.3	76.9
South Korea	1990	67.0	73.1
Taiwan			
Thailand	1990	64.1	68.2
East/SE Asia			
Cambodia	1990	48.3	51.3
China	1990	68.6	71.8
Laos	1990	48.3	51.3
Mongolia	1990	61.2	63.8
Myanmar	1990	59.6	63.1
North Korea	1990	66.2	72.7
Vietnam	1990	60.4	64.8
Australasia			
Australia	1990	73.3	79.9
New Zealand	1990	72.3	78.3
Pacific			
American Samoa			
Fiji	1990	62.8	67.1
French Polynesia	1989	66.1	71.3
Guam	1990	72.1	72.1
Kiribati	1990	53.1	53.1
Nauru			
New Caledonia			
Papua New Guinea	1990	54.2	55.7
Solomon Islands	1989	59.7	64.9
Tonga			
Tuvalu			
Vanuatu			
Western Samoa	1976	61.0	64.3
Middle East			
Bahrain	1986-91	66.8	69.4
Egypt	1985-90	57.8	60.3
Iran	1990	65.8	66.7
Iraq	1985-90	63.0	64.8
Israel	1988	73.9	77.4
Jordan	1985-90	64.2	67.8
Kuwait	1985-90	70.8	75.0
Lebanon	1985-90	65.1	69.0
Oman	1985-90	54.1	56.8
Qatar	1985-90	66.9	71.8
Saudi Arabia	1985-90	61.7	65.2
Syria	1980-85	62.8	67.2
United Arab Emirates	1985-90	68.6	72.9
Yemen	1985-90	49.0	52.0

VITAL STATISTICS   Table No. 0211 (cont'd)

Life Expectancy at Birth: Males and Females, Latest Year

Units: Years

	Year	Male	Female
North Africa			
Algeria	1985	61.6	63.3
Chad	1985-90	43.9	47.1
Djibouti	1985-90	45.4	48.7
Ethiopia	1985-90	42.5	45.6
Libya	1985-90	59.1	62.5
Mali	1980-85	42.0	46.0
Mauritania	1985-90	44.4	47.6
Morocco	1985-90	59.1	62.5
Niger	1985-90	42.9	46.1
Somalia	1985-90	43.4	46.6
Sudan	1985-90	48.6	51.0
Tunisia	1985-90	64.9	66.4
West Africa			
Benin	1985-90	44.4	47.6
Burkina Faso	1985-90	45.6	48.9
Cameroon	1985-90	51.0	54.0
Cape Verde	1979-81	59.0	61.0
Côte d'Ivoire	1985-90	50.8	54.2
Equatorial Guinea	1985-90	44.4	47.6
Gabon	1985-90	49.9	53.2
Gambia	1985-90	41.4	44.6
Ghana	1985-90	52.2	55.8
Guinea	1985-90	42.0	43.0
Guinea-Bissau	1985-90	39.9	43.1
Liberia	1985-90	53.0	56.0
Nigeria	1985-90	48.8	52.2
Sao Tomé e Príncipe	1985	64.3	66.8
Senegal	1985-90	46.3	48.3
Sierra Leone	1985-90	39.5	42.6
Togo	1985-90	51.3	54.8
East/Central Africa			
Angola	1985-90	42.9	46.1
Burundi	1985-90	45.9	49.2
Central African Republic	1985-90	46.0	51.0
Comoros	1985-90	53.5	54.5
Congo	1985-90	50.1	55.3
Kenya	1985-90	56.5	60.5
Madagascar	1985-90	52.0	55.0
Maldives	1990	55.3	55.3
Mauritius	1989-90	65.0	73.0
Réunion	1990	69.0	78.3
Rwanda	1980-85	45.1	47.7
Seychelles	1987	64.4	72.9
Tanzania	1985-90	51.3	54.7
Uganda	1985-90	49.4	52.7
Zaire	1985-90	50.3	53.7
Southern Africa			
Botswana	1981	55.0	58.2
Lesotho	1985-90	51.5	60.5
Malawi	1980-85	46.2	48.0
Mozambique	1985-90	44.9	48.1
Namibia	1985-90	55.0	57.5
South Africa	1985-90	57.5	63.5
Swaziland	1980-85	48.8	52.3
Zambia	1980-85	52.4	55.0
Zimbabwe	1985-90	56.5	60.1

Source: UN/World Health Organisation/national statistical offices
Notes: see end of section

POPULATION DENSITY | Table No. 0212

Population Density 1977-1992

Units: Persons per sq km

	1977	1980	1983	1984	1985	1986	1987	1988	1989	1990	1991	1992
North America												
Canada	2.3	2.4	2.5	2.5	2.6	2.6	2.6	2.6	2.6	2.7	2.7	2.8
USA	23.5	24.3	25.0	25.2	25.4	25.7	25.9	26.2	26.4	26.6	26.9	27.2
South America												
Argentina	9.7	10.2	10.7	10.8	11.0	11.2	11.3	11.4	11.5	11.6	11.8	
Bolivia	4.7	5.1	5.5	5.7	5.9	6.0	6.0	6.4	6.5	6.7	6.9	
Brazil	12.9	14.2	15.2	15.6	15.9	16.3	16.6	17.0	17.3	17.7	18.0	18.4
Chile	14.2	14.8	15.6	15.9	16.1	16.4	16.7	17.0	17.2	17.5	17.8	18.1
Colombia	21.5	22.7	24.1	24.6	25.1	25.6	26.3	26.6	27.8	28.4	28.8	
Ecuador	28.2	30.8	33.6	34.5	35.5	36.5	37.6	38.7	39.7	40.8	42.0	
French Guiana	0.7	0.7	0.9	1.0	1.0	1.1	1.1	1.2	1.2	1.3		
Guyana	3.7	4.0	4.3	4.4	4.5	4.5	4.7	4.7	4.8	4.8		
Paraguay	7.0	7.7	8.5	8.8	9.1	9.4	9.6	9.9	10.2	10.5	10.8	
Peru	12.4	13.5	14.6	14.9	15.3	15.4	15.8	16.1	16.4	16.8	17.1	17.5
Suriname	2.2	2.2	2.2	2.3	2.3	2.3	2.3	2.4	2.4	2.5		
Uruguay	15.3	15.6	15.9	16.0	16.1	16.0	15.6	16.4	16.5	16.6	16.6	
Venezuela	14.9	16.5	18.0	18.5	19.0	19.5	20.0	20.6	21.1	21.6	22.2	
Caribbean												
Anguilla	65.9	76.9	76.9	76.9	76.9	76.9	76.9	87.9	87.9	87.9		
Antigua								142.5	144.8	147.1	144.8	144.8
Aruba	326.4	331.6	347.2	347.2	352.3	357.5	357.5	316.1	316.1	316.1		
Bahamas	14.2	15.1	16.2	16.5	16.7	17.0	17.3	17.7	18.0	18.6	18.6	18.7
Barbados	574.4	579.1	583.7	586.0	588.4	590.7	590.7	590.7	595.3	604.7	593.0	604.7
Bermuda	981.5	1,000.0	1,018.5	1,037.0	1,037.0	1,055.6	1,055.6	1,111.1	1,074.1	1,037.0	1,129.6	
British Virgin Islands	71.9	71.9	78.4	78.4	85.0	85.0	85.0	78.4	85.0	91.5		
Cayman Islands	61.8	65.6	73.4	77.2	81.1	84.9	84.9	96.5	84.9	73.4	73.4	
Cuba	83.4	84.9	86.4	87.3	88.2	89.0	89.8	90.9	91.8	92.8	93.7	
Dominica			97.2	97.2	95.9	95.9	95.9	95.9	95.9	94.5	94.5	
Dominican Republic	103.8	112.4	123.1	126.0	128.9	132.5	135.3	141.8	144.8	148.0	151.0	
Grenada			263.8	269.6	272.5	275.4	278.3	281.2				
Guadeloupe			183.7	188.2	192.1	196.6	200.6	209.0	213.5	217.4		
Haiti	171.1	180.5	204.0	207.6	211.4	215.8	220.3	224.8	229.2	233.7	238.7	
Jamaica	183.5	186.7	196.1	199.6	202.3	204.5	210.9	214.2	207.9	201.6	207.1	
Martinique	303.1	302.1	306.8	309.5	312.3	316.0	319.7	324.4	329.9	335.5	337.3	
Netherlands Antilles	182.3	188.3	176.2	179.3	182.3	184.3	191.3	191.3	192.3	192.3	192.3	
St Kitts	191.6	168.6	176.2	176.2	176.2	180.1	180.1	187.7	191.6	195.4		
St Lucia	189.9	201.3	212.7	217.5	211.0	214.3	214.3	235.4	240.3	245.1		
St Vincent/Grenadines	295.6	264.8	275.1	277.6	267.4	269.9	244.2	277.6	282.8	287.9		
Trinidad and Tobago	201.8	210.9	222.0	228.1	229.6	233.1	236.3	236.3	236.5	239.2	244.2	
Central America												
Belize	5.9	6.3	6.9	7.1	7.2	7.4	7.7	7.8	8.0	8.0	8.4	
Costa Rica	40.6	44.1	47.8	47.5	48.9	52.4	54.6	56.0	57.4	58.8	59.5	60.9
El Salvador	198.9	210.7	220.8	223.4	225.2	229.6	234.1	235.1	240.1	245.4		
Guatemala	58.4	63.5	69.1	71.1	73.1	75.3	77.5	79.7	82.1	84.5	86.8	
Honduras	29.6	32.9	36.5	37.8	39.0	40.3	43.0	42.8	44.2	45.5		
Mexico	32.4	35.2	38.0	38.9	39.8	40.3	41.2	41.9	42.8	43.7	44.5	
Nicaragua	15.7	18.5	20.7	21.4	22.1	22.9	23.6	24.5	25.3	26.2	27.0	
Panama [a]	22.8	24.9	26.6	27.2	27.8	28.4	29.0	29.6	30.2	30.8	31.4	32.0
Puerto Rico	343.1	357.8	364.4	364.8	366.3	365.6	367.6	386.2	390.0	394.0	396.3	
South Asia												
Afghanistan	19.5	25.1	27.1	27.8	28.5	29.3	23.9	24.4	24.9	25.3	25.8	
Bangladesh	574.4	615.8	657.3	671.7	685.1	698.7	712.2	725.9	739.6	753.3		
Bhutan	23.6	25.1	26.7	27.2	27.8	28.2	28.8	29.5	30.1	30.8		
India	199.3	213.1	227.4	232.4	237.1	241.9	246.7	251.5	256.4	261.1	268.3	
Nepal	92.9	99.1	111.3	113.9	117.6	121.1	124.7	127.2	130.4	133.8		
Pakistan	93.8	102.7	112.5	116.0	119.6	123.3	127.2	131.1	135.2	139.4	143.7	
Sri Lanka	212.5	224.8	235.0	237.8	241.4	245.6	249.4	252.8	256.1	259.0	262.8	

POPULATION DENSITY

Population Density 1977-1992

Units: Persons per sq km

	1977	1980	1983	1984	1985	1986	1987	1988	1989	1990	1991	1992
Japan												
Japan	308.0	316.0	323.3	325.4	327.4	329.1	330.7	331.7	333.0	334.2	335.2	
ASEAN/NICs												
Brunei	29.0	32.1	36.1	37.5	38.9	42.3	42.3	41.8	43.2	44.6		
Hong Kong	4,316.4	4,767.4	5,033.0	5,082.9	5,137.5	5,202.4	5,254.2	5,299.4	5,354.0	5,320.2	5,361.6	5,421.8
Indonesia	71.2	76.3	81.5	83.3	85.1	87.0	88.8	91.5	93.3	93.4		
Macau	17,375.0	19,875.0	20,750.0	22,437.5	24,500.0	25,812.5	26,875.0	27,437.5	28,000.0	28,562.5		
Malaysia	37.8	41.1	44.5	45.6	47.1	48.4	49.6	50.9	52.1	53.3	54.6	
Philippines	148.6	161.1	173.2	177.2	181.3	185.3	191.2	195.7	200.3	204.9	209.6	
Singapore	3,774.4	3,918.8	4,061.7	4,105.5	4,152.6	4,198.1	4,241.6	4,297.1	4,358.8	4,420.5	4,485.4	4,574.7
South Korea	369.9	387.3	405.6	411.5	417.0	422.3	426.4	426.4	430.5	435.5	439.5	443.5
Taiwan	475.7	494.9	520.5	528.3	535.1	540.6	549.1	553.0	557.0	560.9		
Thailand	85.7	90.4	96.2	98.0	99.8	102.4	104.3	106.1	107.9	109.1	110.7	
East/SE Asia												
Cambodia	37.5	35.4	37.7	39.0	40.2	41.4	42.5	43.5	44.5	45.5		
China	99.8	103.8	108.2	108.9	110.4	111.7	113.4	115.0	116.7	117.8		
Laos	14.9	15.6	16.6	17.0	17.4	17.8	16.0	16.4	16.8	17.2		
Mongolia	1.0	1.1	1.1	1.2	1.2	1.2	1.3	1.3	1.4	1.4	1.4	1.4
Myanmar	46.5	49.6	54.2	55.5	56.8	58.1	57.7	58.9	60.2	61.4	62.6	
North Korea	136.5	147.4	158.8	162.7	166.7	170.7	174.9	179.1	183.3	187.5		
Vietnam	153.2	164.4	174.4	177.7	181.2	184.8	190.6	194.9	199.3	200.9		
Australasia												
Australia	1.8	1.9	2.0	2.0	2.1	2.1	2.1	2.2	2.2	2.2	2.3	
New Zealand	11.8	11.7	12.1	12.2	12.3	12.5	12.6	12.6	12.7	12.7	12.9	13.0
Pacific												
American Samoa	157.4	162.4	177.7	172.6	177.7	177.7	182.7	187.8	192.9	238.6		
Fiji	32.6	34.6	36.7	37.4	38.0	38.4	38.9	39.7	40.3	40.5	40.7	
French Polynesia			42.4	44.2	44.9	45.9	47.0	48.0	48.5	49.5	50.5	
Guam	224.4	237.8	257.8	266.7	253.3	257.8	280.0	264.4	268.9	273.3		
Kiribati	81.9	84.8	89.2	90.6	93.6	95.0	96.5	98.0	99.4	105.3		
Nauru	333.3	381.0	381.0	381.0	381.0	381.0	381.0	428.6	428.6	428.6		
New Caledonia	7.1	7.3	7.6	7.9	8.0	8.2	8.2	8.4	8.6	8.6		
Papua New Guinea	6.1	6.5	6.8	7.0	7.1	7.3	7.4	7.6	7.8	8.0	8.1	
Solomon Islands	6.9	7.6	8.4	8.7	9.1	9.6	9.9	10.1	10.4	10.7		
Tonga	130.2	130.2	144.5	148.8	153.1	158.8	163.1	166.0	170.2	174.5		
Tuvalu	280.0	320.0	320.0	320.0	320.0	320.0	320.0	360.0	360.0	360.0		
Vanuatu			8.7	8.9	9.2	9.5	9.8	10.2	10.5	10.0		
Western Samoa	53.9	54.9	56.3	57.0	57.4	58.1	58.5	58.8	59.5	60.2		
Middle East												
Bahrain	453.9	525.0	580.9	605.1	630.9	623.3	644.5	715.6	739.8	756.4	780.6	
Egypt	38.9	42.2	46.0	47.3	48.6	49.7	50.9	50.5	51.9	53.3	54.8	
Iran	21.0	23.3	25.5	26.3	26.8	30.3	31.4	31.9	32.9	33.9	35.0	
Iraq	27.4	30.2	33.8	35.0	35.5	36.7	37.1	39.3	41.7	44.0		
Israel	174.0	186.7	196.2	200.2	203.8	207.0	210.4	213.8	217.5	224.4	239.5	
Jordan	29.9	32.2	35.9	37.3	38.8	40.3	42.0	43.5	45.3	47.0		
Kuwait	46.9	56.4	64.5	67.4	70.5	73.8	77.1	80.6	84.3	88.1		
Lebanon	265.2	256.6	253.4	254.2	256.5	260.3	265.4	271.9	278.6	285.2		
Oman	3.1	3.6	4.2	4.4	7.4	7.6	4.9	5.1	5.2	5.4		
Qatar	16.7	19.7	24.1	25.8	27.5	28.4	28.9	29.8	36.9	42.5		
Saudi Arabia	3.4	3.9	4.4	4.6	4.8	5.0	5.7	5.8	6.0	6.2		
Syria	42.5	46.9	51.8	53.5	55.3	57.2	59.0	61.1	63.1	65.3	67.5	
United Arab Emirates	9.2	13.0	16.0	16.9	17.7	18.4	19.2	20.0	20.6	23.1	24.5	25.4
Yemen	13.9	15.1	16.4	16.9	17.4	17.9	18.4	18.7	19.3	21.4		

POPULATION DENSITY

Population Density 1977-1992

Units: Persons per sq km

	1977	1980	1983	1984	1985	1986	1987	1988	1989	1990	1991	1992
North Africa												
Algeria	7.2	7.8	8.6	8.8	9.1	9.4	9.7	10.0	10.3	10.6	10.6	
Chad	3.3	3.5	3.7	3.8	3.9	4.0	4.1	4.2	4.3	4.4	4.5	
Djibouti	13.0	15.4	16.7	17.6	18.7	19.8	16.2	16.7	17.2	17.7		
Ethiopia	35.1	37.7	40.5	41.5	42.4	43.9	43.2	46.8	49.0	50.5	52.2	
Libya	1.5	1.7	1.8	1.8	1.9	2.0	2.1	2.1	2.5	2.6		
Mali	5.2	5.7	6.2	6.4	6.6	6.8	7.0	7.2	6.4	6.6		
Mauritania	1.5	1.6	1.7	1.8	1.8	1.9	1.8	1.9	1.9	2.0	2.0	
Morocco	40.0	43.7	45.5	46.7	47.8	49.0	51.0	52.1	53.6	55.0		
Niger	4.1	4.5	4.9	5.0	5.2	5.3	5.5	6.1	5.8	6.0		
Somalia	5.6	6.4	9.5	9.8	10.2	11.3	10.9	11.3	11.7	12.2		
Sudan	6.8	7.5	8.1	8.4	8.6	8.9	9.1	9.5	9.8	10.0		
Tunisia	36.1	38.9	41.6	42.9	44.2	45.9	47.7	47.3	48.2	49.2		
West Africa												
Benin	29.2	30.4	33.0	34.0	34.9	35.9	36.6	39.5	40.8	42.1	43.4	
Burkina Faso	21.3	22.4	23.4	23.8	24.2	24.6	25.0	31.2	32.0	32.8	33.7	
Cameroon	17.0	18.3	20.6	21.2	21.9	22.5	23.2	23.4	24.8	26.7		
Cape Verde	71.1	73.4	77.3	79.1	82.8	82.5	86.2	88.7	91.4	94.2		
Côte d'Ivoire	22.6	25.3	28.8	29.3	30.4	31.5	32.8	36.0	37.5	39.0		
Equatorial Guinea	11.8	12.5	13.4	13.7	14.0	14.3	14.7	15.0	12.2	12.4	12.7	
Gabon	0.4	0.4	0.4	0.4	0.4	0.4	0.4	0.4	0.4	0.4		
Gambia	51.7	56.2	57.8	58.9	60.1	61.4	73.8	76.0	78.1	80.3		
Ghana	43.9	48.4	53.3	51.2	53.9	56.2	57.5	59.3	61.1	63.0		
Guinea			18.5	18.8	19.2	19.5	20.1	20.6				
Guinea-Bissau	19.4	22.4	23.9	24.2	24.6	25.1	25.3	25.8	26.1	26.4		
Liberia	15.0	16.6	18.3	18.9	19.7	20.0	20.7	21.8	21.5	22.1	22.6	
Nigeria [b]	78.6	87.2	97.8	101.0	103.6	106.6	110.3	113.6	118.2	122.7	95.8	
Sao Tomé e Príncipe	85.1	88.2	95.4	97.5	112.0	112.0	114.1	119.3	120.3	121.4		
Senegal	26.7	29.0	32.1	32.5	32.8	33.9	34.1	36.2	36.5	36.8		
Sierra Leone	43.4	45.6	48.0	48.9	49.8	50.7	53.2	54.6	56.0	57.4		
Togo	41.3	45.0	49.1	50.6	52.1	53.7	55.3	57.2	58.0	58.9		
East/Central Africa												
Angola	5.6	6.2	6.7	6.9	7.0	7.2	7.4	7.6	7.8	8.0		
Burundi	140.2	148.1	158.9	163.0	169.5	174.5	179.2	185.0	190.5	196.1	201.9	
Central African Republic	3.5	3.7	3.9	4.0	4.2	4.4	4.5	4.4	4.5	4.7		
Comoros	185.5	204.8	226.3	231.7	238.7	260.2	254.3	260.2	270.4	280.6		
Congo	4.2	4.5	4.8	5.0	5.1	5.2	5.4	5.5	5.7	5.8		
Kenya	24.6	28.6	32.2	33.5	34.9	36.3	37.7	41.0	42.7	44.4	44.5	
Madagascar	13.5	14.6	15.8	16.4	16.8	17.3	17.8	18.9	19.5	18.8	19.3	
Maldives	469.8	513.4	563.8	580.5	594.0	634.2	654.7	677.9	704.7	731.5	748.3	
Mauritius	486.3	512.1	531.4	542.6	547.5	552.3	557.6	565.1	570.5	575.9		
Réunion	196.0	202.4	210.0	213.9	211.6	213.5	215.1	229.1	233.5	237.8		
Rwanda	165.7	196.1	218.6	223.0	230.5	237.6	245.2	256.6	265.4	271.5	272.1	
Seychelles	153.5	155.9	158.4	160.9	160.9	163.4	168.3	168.3	170.8	170.8	173.3	
Tanzania	18.0	19.8	21.7	22.4	23.1	23.9	24.6	25.5	26.4	27.3		
Uganda	52.2	55.4	58.4	59.4	60.4	62.1	63.8	65.5	67.4	69.2	71.1	
Zaire	10.2	11.2	12.0	12.7	12.9	13.2	13.6	14.3	14.7	15.2	15.6	
Southern Africa												
Botswana	1.3	1.4	1.8	1.8	1.9	2.0	2.0	2.1	2.2	2.2	2.3	
Lesotho	41.0	44.1	48.3	48.4	50.4	51.4	53.4	55.3	56.0	56.7		
Malawi	59.0	64.3	70.3	72.7	75.0	77.4	79.7	82.4	85.3	88.1	90.9	
Mozambique	13.6	15.4	16.9	17.3	17.8	18.3	18.5	19.0	19.5	20.0		
Namibia	1.5	1.6	1.8	1.8	1.9	1.9	2.0	2.1	2.2	2.3	1.7	
South Africa	19.8	21.2	22.6	23.0	23.5	24.0	24.5	25.0	25.5	26.0		
Swaziland	28.6	31.5	34.8	36.0	37.3	38.6	39.7	42.4	43.9	44.2		
Zambia	7.0	7.8	8.3	8.6	8.9	9.2	9.5	10.0	10.4	10.7		
Zimbabwe	16.7	18.2	19.8	20.4	21.5	21.6	22.1	22.7	23.4	24.0		

Source: UN/national statistical offices/Euromonitor
Notes: see end of section

| URBANISATION | | | | | | Table No. 0213 |

Urban Population, City Population, Latest Year: Growth Rates 1975-1985, 1985-1990

	Year	Urban population	Urban population as % of total	% urban population in largest city	% urban population in cities over 500,000	Average annual growth of urban population (%) 1975-85	1985-90
North America							
Canada	1986	19,352.1	76.5	5.1	19.8	1.2	2.0
USA	1990	187,053.0	73.7	4.3	17.6	1.0	
South America							
Argentina [a]	1991	28,165.3	86.1	11.6	15.3	2.1	2.8
Bolivia [b]	1990	3,763.2	50.9	31.0	40.0	4.1	4.0
Brazil [c]	1991	115,794.0	75.5	9.5	30.5	3.9	2.9
Chile [d]	1991	11,363.0	84.9	44.0	44.0	2.2	2.0
Colombia	1988	20,575.0	68.0	20.3	41.0	3.2	2.7
Ecuador [b]	1990	5,345.9	55.4	27.6	47.5	5.0	4.3
French Guiana						4.3	
Guyana	1990	359.8	34.6			2.9	
Paraguay	1982	1,295.3	42.8	35.3		4.5	4.2
Peru [e]	1990	15,599.3	72.4	37.9	48.9	3.6	2.9
Suriname						0.5	
Uruguay [a]	1991	2,772.8	89.1	49.9	49.9	0.8	0.9
Venezuela	1990	16,231.2	84.0	8.0	25.0	3.9	3.0
Caribbean							
Anguilla							
Antigua						1.3	
Aruba							
Bahamas						1.3	
Barbados	1990	116.9	44.8			1.2	
Bermuda						2.3	
British Virgin Islands							
Cayman Islands						3.5	
Cuba [a]	1989	7,694.4	73.1	30.0	30.0	1.8	1.9
Dominica							
Dominican Republic	1982	2,985.6	49.9			4.4	3.7
Grenada							
Guadeloupe						1.1	
Haiti [f]	1991	2,000.5	30.2	34.4		4.5	4.3
Jamaica	1985	1,260.0	52.3	8.3		3.0	
Martinique						1.6	
Netherlands Antilles						1.5	
St Kitts						2.0	
St Lucia							
St Vincent/Grenadines							
Trinidad and Tobago	1990	854.2	69.1			4.4	
Central America							
Belize						2.3	
Costa Rica	1990	1,602.6	53.6			4.5	3.5
El Salvador	1989	2,327.7	44.8			2.9	2.8
Guatemala	1990	3,864.0	42.0	38.1	38.1	3.6	3.1
Honduras [f]	1991	2,331.5	44.3	34.4	34.4	5.8	4.7
Mexico	1990	62,544.9	72.6	19.7	36.3	3.8	3.1
Nicaragua	1991	2,439.9	61.0	41.7	41.7	4.2	4.1
Panama [e]	1990	1,278.6	52.9	39.0		2.9	2.7
Puerto Rico	1980	2,134.4	66.8	19.9		2.6	
South Asia							
Afghanistan [g]	1988	2,752.0	17.7	56.0	56.0	4.1	
Bangladesh [d]	1986	13,987.9	13.8	28.3	44.7	5.4	
Bhutan						4.8	
India [h]	1991	218,527.0	25.7	4.1	21.7	3.7	
Nepal	1986	1,224.0	7.1	19.2		7.0	
Pakistan [b]	1991	32,595.0	28.2	18.4	46.4	4.2	
Sri Lanka	1981	3,192.5	21.5	20.1	20.1	1.3	

URBANISATION   Table No. 0213 (cont'd)

Urban Population, City Population, Latest Year: Growth Rates 1975-1985, 1985-1990

	Year	Urban population	Urban population as % of total	% urban population in largest city	% urban population in cities over 500,000	Average annual growth of urban population (%) 1975-85	1985-90
Japan							
Japan	1990	95,643.5	77.4	20.0	50.3	0.9	
ASEAN/NICs							
Brunei	1982	127.0	63.6	39.3		3.4	
Hong Kong	1986	5,024.0	93.1	12.6	12.6	2.5	
Indonesia	1990	55,433.8	30.9	15.1	33.5	4.7	
Macau						4.2	
Malaysia [i]	1980	4,073.1	37.2	22.6	22.6	4.6	
Philippines [c]	1991	27,186.8	43.2	7.5	21.8	3.6	
Singapore	1985	2,560.0	100.0	100.0	100.0	1.2	
South Korea [c]	1989	29,984.0	70.8	32.9	69.3	4.6	
Taiwan							
Thailand	1990	10,206.9	18.7	61.5	61.5	4.8	
East/SE Asia							
Cambodia	1985	790.0	10.8			0.7	
China	1990	296,958.3	26.2	5.5	53.1	1.5	
Laos	1985	650.0	15.9			5.2	
Mongolia [b]	1989	1,165.9	57.1	50.6	50.6	3.2	
Myanmar	1983	8,455.8	23.9	29.1	35.4	2.0	
North Korea	1985	13,010.0	63.8			4.0	
Vietnam	1988	12,662.4	19.9			3.0	
Australasia							
Australia [j]	1986	13,316.9	85.4	27.2	67.7	1.4	
New Zealand	1986	2,768.4	83.7	5.4		0.8	0.8
Pacific							
American Samoa	1980	5.7	17.5	52.6		2.5	
Fiji	1987	279.1	38.7			3.0	
French Polynesia						2.7	
Guam	1980	41.9	39.5	21.0		5.5	
Kiribati						2.8	
Nauru							
New Caledonia [g]	1989	97.6	59.4	68.2		3.8	
Papua New Guinea	1980	393.1	13.1	30.1		4.4	
Solomon Islands						4.0	
Tonga	1986	29.0	30.7			1.8	
Tuvalu							
Vanuatu	1989	25.9	18.2	49.0		8.0	
Western Samoa	1981	33.2	21.2	96.4		1.3	
Middle East							
Bahrain	1981	283.2	80.7	38.3		4.9	
Egypt [b]	1991	23,983.0	43.9	26.4	49.1	3.2	
Iran [e]	1986	26,844.6	54.3	25.7	47.0	4.2	
Iraq [d]	1990	12,149.9	69.9	20.7	20.7	5.1	
Israel [h]	1990	4,193.4	90.0	12.3		2.5	
Jordan	1979	1,266.7	59.4	64.1	64.1	4.5	
Kuwait						7.0	
Lebanon	1985	2,140.0	83.4			1.2	
Oman						8.5	
Qatar						6.6	
Saudi Arabia	1985	8,360.0	72.4			6.8	
Syria [b]	1990	6,087.0	50.2	23.4	46.3	4.3	
United Arab Emirates						9.4	
Yemen [k]	1980	1,533.5	52.7			8.6	

URBANISATION   Table No. 0213 (cont'd)

Urban Population, City Population, Latest Year: Growth Rates 1975-1985, 1985-1990

	Year	Urban population	Urban population as % of total	% urban population in largest city	% urban population in cities over 500,000	Average annual growth of urban population (%) 1975-85	1985-90
North Africa							
Algeria	1991	11,614.9	45.3	16.4	21.7	3.6	4.0
Chad	1991	1,775.1	30.5			7.9	6.1
Djibouti						6.6	6.4
Ethiopia [f]	1991	7,669.4	14.4	32.7	32.7	4.3	5.1
Libya	1991	3,339.4	24.1	64.0	64.0	7.2	5.5
Mali [f]	1991	1,690.3	22.0	27.6		3.5	4.4
Mauritania	1991	983.3	48.2			8.5	7.0
Morocco	1991	12,515.9	48.7	27.6	43.5	4.1	4.2
Niger	1991	1,612.0	20.2			6.9	7.1
Somalia	1987	1,674.5	23.5			6.1	5.6
Sudan	1983	4,219.8	20.5	13.5	13.5	3.9	4.3
Tunisia	1989	4,685.3	59.2	16.2	16.2	4.1	2.9
West Africa							
Benin	1991	1,877.8	38.4	29.0		7.8	4.9
Burkina Faso	1991	1,800.1	19.5	56.0		4.4	5.6
Cameroon	1985	4,190.0	42.2	24.6	40.2	7.2	6.0
Cape Verde	1991	125.8	33.1			1.7	5.4
Côte d'Ivoire	1991	5,108.6	41.0	36.0	36.0	6.4	5.4
Equatorial Guinea	1991	131.8	37.0			4.5	3.4
Gabon	1991	563.9	46.6			4.3	5.9
Gambia	1991	209.4	23.8	100.0		4.0	5.5
Ghana	1991	5,180.4	33.4			3.8	4.1
Guinea	1991	1,559.6	26.3			5.4	5.9
Guinea-Bissau	1991	199.9	20.4			6.2	3.9
Liberia [b]	1991	1,184.4	47.0	45.0		5.9	6.1
Nigeria [e]	1991	40,345.0	36.0	35.1	63.2	5.8	6.0
Sao Tomé e Príncipe	1991	41.4	37.6			4.9	
Senegal	1991	2,929.2	38.9	34.1	34.1	3.6	4.0
Sierra Leone	1991	1,405.8	33.0	48.7		4.6	5.2
Togo	1991	968.2	26.6			6.1	6.3
East/Central Africa							
Angola	1991	2,770.2	29.1	22.1		6.2	5.7
Burundi [b]	1990	272.9	5.0	32.4		8.6	5.6
Central African Republic	1991	1,486.8	47.5	57.9		4.4	4.8
Comoros	1991	161.9	28.4	22.2		4.9	5.5
Congo	1991	965.9	48.4			3.5	4.6
Kenya	1991	6,322.0	24.4	48.8	60.3	8.3	7.5
Madagascar	1985	2,815.1	24.5			5.6	6.0
Maldives	1985	46.3	25.5			4.4	
Mauritius [f]	1991	433.4	40.5	33.2		1.6	0.7
Réunion						2.8	
Rwanda	1991	581.6	8.0	51.6		7.7	7.9
Seychelles	1990	33.5	49.8	100.0		6.8	
Tanzania	1991	5,333.0	20.8			11.4	10.6
Uganda	1991	1,876.0	11.3			4.7	5.9
Zaire	1991	14,704.7	40.1			4.9	4.8
Southern Africa							
Botswana [b]	1991	341.1	25.3	38.8		8.5	10.0
Lesotho	1991	376.0	21.0			6.9	6.9
Malawi [f]	1991	1,359.0	15.9			7.5	6.3
Mozambique	1991	4,550.6	28.3			11.8	9.5
Namibia	1991	522.6	37.3			5.4	5.4
South Africa [l]	1989	17,547.0	57.1	5.9	19.6	3.4	3.1
Swaziland	1986	226.4	34.3			9.3	8.3
Zambia [m]	1990	3,979.4	49.3	22.1	22.1	6.3	6.0
Zimbabwe	1987	2,318.9	26.7	23.5		5.9	5.6

Source: UN, various publications
Notes: see end of section

DEMOGRAPHIC ANALYSIS   Table No. 0214

Percentage of Population Aged 0-14 Years, Estimates and Projections 1975-2025

Units: % of total population

	1975	1980	1985	1990	1995	2000	2005	2010	2015	2020	2025
North America											
Canada	26.4	22.5	21.5	20.9	20.0	18.7	17.7	17.3	17.0	16.7	16.4
USA	25.2	22.5	21.7	21.4	21.2	20.2	19.2	18.6	18.4	18.1	17.9
South America											
Argentina	29.2	30.1	30.5	29.9	28.3	27.3	26.6	26.0	25.3	24.5	23.6
Bolivia	43.1	43.4	43.8	43.9	43.9	43.5	42.9	41.8	40.3	38.6	36.6
Brazil	40.1	37.7	36.4	35.2	33.7	31.7	29.8	28.2	26.9	25.7	24.6
Chile	36.8	33.4	31.5	30.6	30.4	29.4	27.7	26.3	25.2	24.5	23.9
Colombia	42.6	39.4	37.1	36.1	34.1	32.3	30.6	28.8	27.3	25.9	24.8
Ecuador	44.6	43.3	41.8	39.5	37.7	35.8	33.9	31.9	29.8	27.9	26.3
French Guiana											
Guyana	43.7	39.4	37.0	33.4	31.8	29.3	26.8	24.8	23.6	22.8	22.0
Paraguay	44.3	42.1	41.0	40.4	39.6	38.2	36.6	35.0	33.6	32.4	31.2
Peru	43.2	41.8	40.4	37.6	35.5	33.6	31.8	29.8	27.8	26.0	24.4
Suriname	47.7	39.8	37.3	34.0	33.7	30.9	27.5	25.0	24.0	23.5	22.7
Uruguay	27.7	27.0	26.8	25.8	24.4	23.9	23.4	23.0	22.4	21.7	21.2
Venezuela	43.5	41.1	39.5	38.3	36.6	34.5	32.7	31.2	30.1	29.0	18.3
Caribbean											
Anguilla											
Antigua											
Aruba											
Bahamas											
Barbados	31.5	29.6	27.1	24.5	23.6	22.2	21.1	19.9	18.8	18.0	17.2
Bermuda											
British Virgin Islands											
Cayman Islands											
Cuba	36.9	31.3	27.7	22.7	23.2	23.3	22.2	20.7	19.8	19.6	19.7
Dominica											
Dominican Republic	45.3	42.2	39.7	37.9	36.3	33.9	31.3	29.0	27.0	25.5	24.0
Grenada											
Guadeloupe	41.9	31.5	28.0	27.0	28.8	27.4	25.1	22.7	21.5	21.3	21.1
Haiti	42.0	41.4	40.2	40.2	40.2	39.8	39.1	38.3	37.4	36.5	35.6
Jamaica	45.3	40.6	36.7	33.2	30.9	28.6	26.5	24.7	23.6	22.4	21.8
Martinique	40.2	28.5	24.4	24.1	26.1	25.3	23.2	21.1	20.0	20.0	20.0
Netherlands Antilles											
St Kitts											
St Lucia											
St Vincent/Grenadines											
Trinidad and Tobago	37.4	34.5	32.9	34.0	33.3	30.5	27.7	25.6	24.4	23.6	22.9
Central America											
Belize											
Costa Rica	42.2	38.8	36.8	36.2	34.5	32.3	30.0	28.2	26.7	25.5	24.3
El Salvador	45.9	46.0	46.0	44.5	42.5	41.5	40.4	38.5	36.1	33.8	31.9
Guatemala	45.7	45.9	45.9	45.5	44.3	42.9	41.2	39.6	37.1	34.9	32.6
Honduras	48.2	47.5	46.3	44.6	43.2	41.2	38.7	36.2	33.7	31.7	30.0
Mexico	46.7	44.1	40.9	37.2	35.0	32.8	30.7	28.7	27.1	25.9	24.9
Nicaragua	47.9	47.5	46.8	45.8	44.6	42.7	40.4	37.9	35.6	33.3	31.1
Panama	43.1	40.4	37.6	34.9	33.1	31.5	29.4	27.4	25.7	24.3	23.2
Puerto Rico	33.6	31.6	29.7	26.0	24.8	24.6	23.4	22.4	21.5	20.8	20.4
South Asia											
Afghanistan	43.8	43.0	41.8	42.0	39.8	42.7	42.5	38.1	35.2	32.3	30.3
Bangladesh	45.9	46.2	45.8	43.9	42.1	40.6	39.3	36.7	33.2	29.6	26.8
Bhutan	40.4	40.4	40.0	39.7	39.7	40.0	39.8	39.1	37.4	34.8	31.6
India	39.8	38.5	37.6	36.5	36.0	34.5	32.8	30.4	27.9	25.1	23.3
Nepal	42.9	41.2	42.2	42.2	41.4	39.6	37.3	34.6	31.2	28.4	26.2
Pakistan	45.4	44.4	44.7	45.6	46.4	43.3	39.6	36.4	33.7	31.2	28.4
Sri Lanka	39.4	35.3	34.5	32.6	30.3	27.3	25.3	23.9	23.0	22.4	12.6

DEMOGRAPHIC ANALYSIS   Table No. 0214 (cont'd)

Percentage of Population Aged 0-14 Years, Estimates and Projections 1975-2025

Units: % of total population

	1975	1980	1985	1990	1995	2000	2005	2010	2015	2020	2025
Japan											
Japan	24.3	23.6	21.5	18.4	17.0	16.9	17.4	17.3	16.3	15.2	14.9
ASEAN/NICs											
Brunei											
Hong Kong	30.4	25.5	23.1	20.7	18.8	17.6	16.6	15.7	14.5	13.7	13.0
Indonesia	42.0	41.0	38.7	35.7	33.4	31.3	28.8	26.1	24.1	23.1	22.6
Macau											
Malaysia	42.1	39.4	37.7	38.2	37.6	34.3	30.2	26.4	24.3	23.7	23.6
Philippines	42.8	42.0	41.4	40.1	38.4	36.2	33.7	31.1	29.0	26.6	24.9
Singapore	32.8	27.0	24.5	23.3	23.2	22.2	20.1	18.1	17.1	16.9	16.9
South Korea	37.8	34.0	30.0	25.6	23.0	21.3	20.3	19.4	18.3	17.4	16.7
Taiwan											
Thailand	44.9	40.0	36.5	32.7	29.3	26.5	25.4	24.6	23.5	22.1	21.0
East/SE Asia											
Cambodia	41.6	32.9	32.6	34.9	41.8	38.6	34.4	31.0	29.6	29.3	28.2
China	39.4	35.5	29.7	26.4	26.3	26.6	24.3	21.3	19.0	18.4	18.5
Laos	42.1	42.0	42.7	43.6	44.5	44.0	42.0	38.8	35.3	31.6	28.6
Mongolia	43.8	43.0	41.6	41.3	40.2	39.2	37.8	36.3	34.6	32.9	31.1
Myanmar	40.7	39.6	39.2	37.2	36.0	34.9	33.5	31.3	28.9	26.4	24.5
North Korea	41.7	40.4	38.6	28.6	29.3	30.0	28.4	25.0	22.2	20.7	20.2
Vietnam	43.7	42.5	40.6	39.4	37.6	35.5	33.4	30.6	27.6	25.5	24.1
Australasia											
Australia	27.6	25.3	23.6	22.1	21.6	20.6	19.8	19.2	18.8	18.3	18.0
New Zealand	30.0	26.8	24.3	22.7	22.4	22.0	20.9	19.7	18.8	18.2	18.0
Pacific											
American Samoa											
Fiji	39.9	37.5	37.2	36.9	34.0	30.9	28.7	27.1	25.3	23.8	22.6
French Polynesia											
Guam											
Kiribati											
Nauru											
New Caledonia											
Papua New Guinea	41.9	43.0	41.6	40.5	40.0	39.1	37.5	35.2	32.6	30.3	28.3
Solomon Islands											
Tonga											
Tuvalu											
Vanuatu											
Western Samoa											
Middle East											
Bahrain	43.0	34.6	33.3	32.5	31.9	29.6	27.1	25.4	24.0	22.6	21.6
Egypt	40.0	40.0	40.4	39.4	37.7	34.6	31.7	29.2	27.1	24.8	23.1
Iran	45.4	44.4	43.2	43.9	41.9	38.6	37.6	36.4	34.5	31.6	28.4
Iraq	46.6	47.0	47.0	46.4	45.3	44.1	42.6	40.7	38.6	36.1	33.7
Israel	32.9	33.2	32.5	31.3	29.6	28.1	26.6	25.2	23.7	22.4	21.6
Jordan	47.2	49.4	48.1	44.5	43.4	43.2	41.7	39.0	36.0	33.3	30.6
Kuwait	44.4	40.3	40.0	35.5	33.5	31.2	29.1	27.5	26.0	24.7	23.5
Lebanon	41.2	40.1	37.5	36.0	36.0	35.7	33.0	30.1	27.7	25.9	24.6
Oman	44.6	44.0	44.3	46.5	47.2	47.1	46.3	45.5	44.2	41.7	38.5
Qatar	33.4	32.4	33.9	34.8	35.7	34.4	33.8	33.9	34.2	34.0	33.5
Saudi Arabia	34.3	44.2	44.8	45.3	45.3	45.7	45.8	45.4	43.8	41.2	38.0
Syria	48.5	47.5	48.1	48.3	47.7	46.5	44.7	42.1	39.2	35.9	32.6
United Arab Emirates	28.2	28.6	30.9	30.7	28.6	26.5	26.6	27.1	26.9	25.8	24.1
Yemen	47.0	47.0	47.0	44.7	45.6	45.6	44.6	42.8	40.3	37.4	34.3

DEMOGRAPHIC ANALYSIS — Table No. 0214 (cont'd)

Percentage of Population Aged 0-14 Years, Estimates and Projections 1975-2025

Units: % of total population

	1975	1980	1985	1990	1995	2000	2005	2010	2015	2020	2025
North Africa											
Algeria	47.7	46.8	45.6	43.6	41.6	39.3	38.1	35.7	32.1	28.1	25.4
Chad	41.7	41.9	42.3	42.8	43.3	43.3	42.9	42.3	44.3	39.7	37.3
Djibouti	44.6	45.2	45.7	45.5	45.4	45.5	45.6	45.3	44.3	42.2	39.3
Ethiopia	44.5	44.4	46.3	45.6	46.2	46.3	46.0	45.0	43.6	41.1	38.0
Libya	46.1	46.6	46.4	46.0	45.7	45.6	45.2	43.7	41.1	37.9	34.6
Mali	45.4	46.0	46.3	46.9	47.4	47.8	47.6	46.7	44.8	41.9	38.1
Mauritania	43.3	43.8	44.1	44.6	45.0	45.2	45.2	44.6	43.3	41.0	37.7
Morocco	47.1	43.2	42.2	40.5	38.8	36.9	34.1	31.0	28.2	26.0	24.4
Niger	44.9	45.9	46.7	47.7	48.1	48.4	48.2	47.4	45.5	42.5	38.6
Somalia	44.3	43.5	45.9	47.0	47.7	46.2	45.3	44.8	43.9	41.6	38.2
Sudan	44.4	44.9	45.2	45.2	44.8	44.2	43.4	42.1	39.9	37.1	
Tunisia	43.8	41.7	39.7	38.0	35.8	33.0	29.8	27.2	25.2	24.0	23.0
West Africa											
Benin	44.9	45.9	46.7	46.5	47.0	47.3	47.3	46.6	44.8	42.0	38.3
Burkina Faso	44.0	43.9	43.7	44.0	44.6	45.0	45.1	44.6	43.5	41.4	38.3
Cameroon	41.6	42.3	43.3	46.6	47.4	47.9	47.7	47.2	46.0	43.7	40.3
Cape Verde	48.1	46.7	41.7	45.0	45.3	44.8	42.9	39.8	36.4	33.5	30.9
Côte d'Ivoire	47.8	48.3	48.9	48.1	48.9	49.3	49.4	49.0	47.4	44.6	40.6
Equatorial Guinea	39.9	40.7	41.4	42.3	43.2	43.5	43.5	42.9	41.9	40.1	37.2
Gabon	32.4	32.7	34.3	32.4	36.1	41.0	43.3	42.2	39.8	38.5	36.9
Gambia	42.1	42.6	43.4	44.1	44.2	44.0	43.3	42.3	40.3	37.2	33.5
Ghana	45.4	44.8	45.3	45.4	45.8	45.1	44.1	41.6	38.1	33.9	30.7
Guinea	42.7	42.9	43.1	46.7	47.1	47.3	47.4	46.7	45.1	42.5	38.8
Guinea-Bissau	38.3	40.1	40.7	40.9	41.7	41.8	41.6	40.9	39.5	37.0	33.7
Liberia	43.9	44.5	45.1	45.2	45.9	46.1	45.9	45.1	43.6	41.4	38.3
Nigeria	47.6	48.2	48.2	47.4	47.3	46.7	45.5	43.9	41.7	38.7	35.2
Sao Tomé e Príncipe											
Senegal	43.8	44.1	44.3	45.4	44.8	44.3	43.9	42.8	40.5	37.2	33.5
Sierra Leone	42.5	43.2	43.8	44.5	45.0	45.3	45.3	44.9	43.8	41.6	38.4
Togo	43.9	44.3	44.8	45.4	45.8	45.8	45.7	45.1	43.9	41.5	38.1
East/Central Africa											
Angola	43.9	44.3	44.8	44.9	45.1	45.3	44.9	44.1	42.8	40.6	37.7
Burundi	42.5	43.7	44.8	45.3	46.2	45.8	44.6	42.7	40.3	37.2	33.6
Central African Republic	40.6	41.6	42.6	44.7	45.3	45.5	45.4	44.9	43.7	41.5	38.3
Comoros	45.5	45.7	46.1	47.6	47.9	48.1	48.0	47.2	45.4	42.6	38.8
Congo	42.8	43.2	43.6	46.1	46.6	46.9	46.9	46.2	44.7	42.2	38.9
Kenya	49.1	50.1	51.2	49.9	48.9	48.4	48.3	47.6	45.9	43.3	39.7
Madagascar	44.0	44.1	44.4	45.1	45.6	45.7	45.2	44.4	43.1	41.1	38.3
Maldives											
Mauritius	39.7	34.1	30.7	29.2	25.8	23.4	22.3	21.3	20.2	19.2	18.2
Réunion	42.0	38.0	33.3	31.8	29.9	28.0	25.8	24.2	23.1	22.3	21.4
Rwanda	48.3	48.7	49.0	49.0	48.9	48.5	47.4	45.2	41.6	37.6	34.1
Seychelles											
Tanzania	47.8	48.3	48.5	49.1	49.5	49.4	48.8	47.4	45.5	42.6	39.0
Uganda	47.4	47.8	48.1	49.6	50.3	49.4	47.9	45.5	43.1	40.2	36.6
Zaire	44.6	46.3	46.2	46.2	46.0	46.0	45.8	44.9	43.6	41.4	38.3
Southern Africa											
Botswana	50.3	47.3	48.2	49.3	48.7	46.9	44.3	42.0	39.4	36.2	32.8
Lesotho	41.7	42.0	42.6	43.1	43.5	43.0	42.4	41.4	40.2	38.1	35.2
Malawi	47.2	46.6	46.1	48.6	49.1	48.7	47.5	45.5	43.4	40.7	37.4
Mozambique	43.8	43.4	43.7	44.0	44.2	43.9	43.2	41.9	40.1	37.4	34.2
Namibia	43.7	44.5	45.1	45.8	45.4	45.0	44.1	43.2	41.3	38.4	35.2
South Africa	40.0	38.6	37.8	37.1	36.5	35.6	34.3	32.7	31.0	29.2	27.2
Swaziland	45.4	46.2	46.8	47.4	47.8	47.6	46.8	45.0	42.7	39.6	36.0
Zambia	46.5	49.4	48.6	49.1	49.8	49.6	48.5	46.9	45.0	42.5	39.3
Zimbabwe	49.0	47.8	46.3	44.9	44.1	43.1	41.2	38.8	36.2	33.6	30.5

Source: UN, World Population Prospects
Notes: see end of section

DEMOGRAPHIC ANALYSIS   Table No. 0215

Percentage of Population of Working Age (15-64 Years), Estimates and Projections 1975-2025

Units: % of total population

	1975	1980	1985	1990	1995	2000	2005	2010	2015	2020	2025
North America											
Canada	65.1	67.8	68.1	67.7	67.8	68.6	69.1	68.3	66.5	64.5	62.4
USA	64.3	66.2	66.4	66.0	65.9	67.0	67.9	67.8	66.4	64.4	62.3
South America											
Argentina	63.2	61.7	60.9	61.0	62.1	62.9	63.5	64.0	64.3	64.5	64.9
Bolivia	53.6	53.3	53.0	52.9	52.9	53.3	53.9	55.0	56.3	57.9	59.6
Brazil	56.2	58.3	59.3	60.1	61.2	62.9	64.4	65.5	66.1	66.2	66.1
Chile	57.8	61.0	62.7	63.4	63.2	63.9	65.2	66.0	66.3	65.9	65.2
Colombia	54.2	57.1	59.1	59.8	61.6	63.2	64.6	65.9	66.5	66.6	66.3
Ecuador	51.8	53.1	54.5	56.7	58.4	60.0	61.6	63.2	64.7	65.8	66.5
French Guiana											
Guyana	52.8	56.9	59.1	62.8	64.2	66.4	68.7	70.3	70.7	70.3	69.2
Paraguay	52.2	54.4	55.5	56.0	56.8	58.2	59.7	61.0	62.1	62.4	62.7
Peru	53.3	54.6	56.0	58.6	60.4	61.8	63.2	64.7	66.0	67.0	67.5
Suriname	48.4	55.7	58.4	61.8	61.7	64.0	67.0	69.3	70.0	69.7	68.7
Uruguay	62.7	62.6	62.5	62.6	63.3	63.4	64.0	64.5	65.1	65.5	65.4
Venezuela	53.4	55.7	57.1	58.0	59.4	61.2	62.6	63.7	64.0	64.2	74.0
Caribbean											
Anguilla											
Antigua											
Aruba											
Bahamas											
Barbados	58.6	59.9	62.2	63.7	64.6	66.7	68.5	70.1	70.2	68.9	66.8
Bermuda											
British Virgin Islands											
Cayman Islands											
Cuba	56.6	61.4	64.3	68.9	67.8	67.3	67.4	67.6	67.2	66.2	65.4
Dominica											
Dominican Republic	51.7	54.7	57.1	56.4	57.3	59.2	61.2	62.9	63.9	63.9	63.3
Grenada											
Guadeloupe	52.3	61.1	63.9	64.1	61.9	62.8	64.6	66.2	66.2	65.6	64.2
Haiti	54.3	54.8	56.0	55.7	55.9	56.4	57.1	57.9	58.7	59.4	60.0
Jamaica	48.9	53.6	57.2	60.2	62.7	65.0	67.1	68.7	69.3	69.5	68.3
Martinique	53.6	63.1	66.4	65.9	63.3	63.4	65.2	66.7	66.9	66.1	63.8
Netherlands Antilles											
St Kitts											
St Lucia											
St Vincent/Grenadines											
Trinidad and Tobago	58.5	60.0	61.7	60.6	61.2	64.0	66.5	68.1	68.4	68.0	67.0
Central America											
Belize											
Costa Rica	54.4	57.6	59.3	59.6	60.9	62.6	64.5	65.8	66.5	66.4	66.1
El Salvador	51.2	50.9	50.6	51.8	53.5	54.3	55.2	56.9	59.2	61.3	62.0
Guatemala	51.5	51.3	51.2	51.3	52.2	53.4	55.0	56.5	58.8	60.6	62.5
Honduras	49.1	49.5	50.5	52.1	53.5	55.3	57.7	59.9	62.1	63.6	64.7
Mexico	49.9	52.4	55.5	59.0	60.8	62.6	64.3	65.7	66.7	67.0	66.8
Nicaragua	49.7	50.1	50.7	51.5	52.5	54.2	56.3	58.6	60.5	62.2	63.7
Panama	53.0	55.5	57.9	60.3	61.8	63.1	64.8	66.1	67.0	67.4	67.2
Puerto Rico	60.1	60.5	62.0	63.5	64.4	64.3	65.2	65.4	65.3	65.6	65.4
South Asia											
Afghanistan	53.8	54.5	55.5	55.2	57.6	54.6	54.5	58.6	61.0	63.7	65.1
Bangladesh	50.5	50.4	51.1	53.2	55.1	56.5	57.8	60.2	63.4	66.6	68.5
Bhutan	56.4	56.4	56.7	56.9	56.8	56.5	56.6	57.1	58.6	60.9	63.8
India	56.4	57.5	58.1	59.0	59.2	60.4	61.7	63.7	65.7	67.7	68.5
Nepal	53.8	55.8	54.8	54.7	55.4	57.0	59.0	61.3	64.3	66.6	68.3
Pakistan	51.6	52.7	52.5	51.7	50.8	53.8	57.4	60.4	62.8	64.6	66.5
Sri Lanka	56.5	60.4	60.8	62.2	63.8	66.2	67.6	68.3	68.0	67.3	75.5

DEMOGRAPHIC ANALYSIS — Table No. 0215 (cont'd)

Percentage of Population of Working Age (15-64 Years), Estimates and Projections 1975-2025

Units: % of total population

	1975	1980	1985	1990	1995	2000	2005	2010	2015	2020	2025
Japan											
Japan	67.8	67.4	68.1	69.9	69.2	67.2	65.0	63.1	61.3	61.1	61.2
ASEAN/NICs											
Brunei											
Hong Kong	64.2	68.0	69.3	70.5	71.1	71.2	71.5	72.1	70.7	67.9	63.7
Indonesia	54.8	55.7	57.7	60.4	62.2	63.6	65.4	67.5	69.0	69.1	68.3
Macau											
Malaysia	54.2	56.9	58.5	58.1	58.5	61.5	65.0	68.3	69.5	69.0	67.8
Philippines	54.5	54.6	55.2	56.5	58.1	60.1	62.3	64.5	66.1	67.6	68.2
Singapore	63.1	68.3	70.3	71.1	70.4	70.6	71.4	72.4	70.7	67.7	64.0
South Korea	58.6	62.2	65.7	69.6	71.6	72.3	72.0	71.9	71.8	70.9	68.8
Taiwan											
Thailand	52.1	56.5	59.9	63.4	66.3	68.5	69.0	69.2	69.5	69.5	68.8
East/SE Asia											
Cambodia	55.6	64.6	64.8	62.2	55.0	57.9	61.9	65.0	65.6	64.9	65.0
China	56.2	59.8	65.0	67.8	67.4	66.4	68.2	70.6	71.8	70.3	68.7
Laos	55.2	55.2	54.4	53.4	52.5	53.0	54.9	57.9	61.2	64.5	67.0
Mongolia	53.0	53.8	55.2	55.5	56.5	57.3	58.4	59.5	60.8	62.0	63.3
Myanmar	55.5	56.4	57.0	58.7	59.7	60.4	61.6	63.7	65.9	67.8	68.6
North Korea	54.8	56.1	57.8	67.3	66.1	65.0	66.0	68.8	70.7	71.0	69.4
Vietnam	52.3	52.7	54.9	56.2	58.0	60.0	62.2	65.2	68.1	69.3	69.4
Australasia											
Australia	63.7	65.1	66.3	67.0	66.9	67.7	68.2	68.0	66.9	65.8	64.5
New Zealand	61.3	63.2	65.2	66.4	66.4	66.8	67.6	68.0	67.1	66.2	64.7
Pacific											
American Samoa											
Fiji	57.4	59.4	59.3	60.0	62.5	65.0	66.5	67.3	68.1	68.5	68.1
French Polynesia											
Guam											
Kiribati											
Nauru											
New Caledonia											
Papua New Guinea	55.0	55.4	56.0	57.1	57.4	58.3	59.8	62.1	64.2	66.2	67.8
Solomon Islands											
Tonga											
Tuvalu											
Vanuatu											
Western Samoa											
Middle East											
Bahrain	54.7	63.3	64.8	65.7	66.3	68.5	70.8	72.2	73.1	73.2	72.4
Egypt	55.8	55.9	55.7	56.7	58.2	61.0	63.7	65.9	67.3	68.2	68.5
Iran	51.3	52.2	53.5	52.4	54.0	57.0	58.1	59.5	61.3	63.6	66.0
Iraq	50.9	50.4	50.3	50.9	51.9	52.9	54.3	56.0	57.8	59.9	61.9
Israel	59.3	58.2	58.7	59.9	61.7	63.3	64.9	66.2	66.4	66.2	65.8
Jordan	50.0	47.5	49.2	52.8	53.9	53.9	55.1	57.7	60.6	63.2	65.3
Kuwait	54.0	58.3	58.7	63.2	64.8	66.4	67.4	67.5	66.9	65.6	64.1
Lebanon	53.8	54.5	57.4	59.0	58.7	58.8	61.6	64.8	67.1	68.3	68.6
Oman	52.7	53.4	53.2	50.9	50.1	50.0	50.6	51.1	52.1	54.3	57.3
Qatar	64.6	66.5	64.5	63.4	61.8	62.5	62.1	60.7	58.9	57.7	57.6
Saudi Arabia	62.7	53.0	52.6	52.1	52.1	51.7	51.5	51.7	53.0	55.1	57.9
Syria	47.8	49.3	49.1	49.1	49.7	50.9	52.7	55.3	58.1	61.0	63.7
United Arab Emirates	69.8	70.2	67.6	67.6	69.1	70.4	68.8	66.2	63.3	60.5	60.4
Yemen	50.0	50.0	50.2	52.5	51.5	51.5	52.4	54.2	56.6	59.4	62.3

DEMOGRAPHIC ANALYSIS   Table No. 0215 (cont'd)

Percentage of Population of Working Age (15-64 Years), Estimates and Projections 1975-2025

Units: % of total population

	1975	1980	1985	1990	1995	2000	2005	2010	2015	2020	2025
North Africa											
Algeria	48.1	49.3	50.7	52.8	55.0	57.4	58.3	60.6	64.1	67.5	69.2
Chad	54.7	54.5	54.1	53.6	53.1	53.2	53.6	54.2	52.2	56.7	58.8
Djibouti	53.3	52.6	52.1	51.9	51.9	51.7	51.4	51.6	52.4	54.4	57.2
Ethiopia	52.9	53.0	50.8	51.5	51.0	50.9	51.2	52.1	53.5	55.8	58.7
Libya	51.7	51.2	51.3	51.6	51.7	51.6	51.8	53.0	55.3	58.2	61.2
Mali	51.9	51.2	51.0	50.5	50.1	49.7	49.9	50.9	52.7	55.4	58.9
Mauritania	53.7	53.2	52.8	52.3	51.9	51.7	51.7	52.3	53.5	55.7	58.8
Morocco	49.2	52.7	53.9	55.9	57.3	59.1	61.6	64.7	67.0	68.3	68.6
Niger	52.7	51.7	50.8	49.8	49.5	49.2	49.4	50.2	52.0	54.8	58.5
Somalia	52.6	53.6	51.4	50.3	49.6	51.1	51.9	52.3	53.0	55.0	58.2
Sudan	52.9	52.4	52.0	52.0	52.3	52.8	53.5	54.7	56.7	59.2	
Tunisia	52.7	54.5	56.5	58.0	59.9	62.2	65.0	67.7	69.4	69.5	68.9
West Africa											
Benin	51.6	51.1	50.4	50.7	50.2	50.0	50.0	50.7	52.4	55.1	58.6
Burkina Faso	53.2	53.3	53.4	53.0	52.4	51.9	51.8	52.2	53.3	55.3	58.2
Cameroon	54.9	54.2	53.2	50.0	49.3	48.9	49.2	49.8	51.0	53.2	56.5
Cape Verde	46.5	47.2	53.2	50.8	50.8	51.5	53.6	57.3	61.2	64.0	65.7
Côte d'Ivoire	49.9	49.4	48.6	49.4	48.5	48.0	47.9	48.3	49.9	52.6	56.5
Equatorial Guinea	55.8	55.1	54.4	53.6	52.8	52.6	52.8	53.5	54.6	56.2	58.9
Gabon	61.8	61.4	59.8	61.7	58.2	53.5	51.3	52.6	55.4	57.1	59.0
Gambia	55.0	54.5	53.7	53.0	52.8	52.8	53.3	54.2	56.1	59.0	62.4
Ghana	51.9	52.4	51.9	51.8	51.3	52.0	52.9	55.2	58.4	62.2	64.9
Guinea	54.8	54.5	54.3	50.7	50.3	50.1	50.1	50.8	52.4	54.8	58.2
Guinea-Bissau	58.0	55.9	55.2	55.0	54.2	54.2	54.4	55.1	56.3	58.6	66.3
Liberia	52.4	51.8	51.2	51.1	50.4	50.2	50.4	51.2	52.7	54.8	57.7
Nigeria	50.0	49.3	49.3	50.1	50.1	50.7	51.8	53.3	55.3	58.1	61.3
Sao Tomé e Príncipe											
Senegal	53.4	53.1	52.8	51.7	52.3	52.8	53.1	54.2	56.3	59.3	62.6
Sierra Leone	54.4	53.7	53.1	52.4	51.9	51.6	51.7	52.1	53.2	55.3	58.3
Togo	53.0	52.5	52.0	51.4	51.0	51.1	51.2	51.8	52.9	55.2	58.3
East/Central Africa											
Angola	53.2	52.7	52.2	52.1	51.8	51.6	52.0	52.8	54.1	56.2	58.8
Burundi	54.1	52.9	51.9	51.6	51.0	51.5	52.8	54.7	57.0	59.5	62.5
Central African Republic	55.5	54.5	53.6	51.5	51.0	50.9	51.1	51.8	53.0	55.1	58.1
Comoros	51.9	51.7	51.4	49.9	49.7	49.5	49.6	50.4	52.2	54.8	58.4
Congo	53.9	53.5	53.0	50.6	50.2	50.0	50.1	50.8	52.3	54.7	57.8
Kenya	47.2	46.5	45.7	47.2	48.3	48.9	49.1	50.0	51.7	54.0	57.3
Madagascar	53.0	52.9	52.6	51.9	51.5	51.4	52.0	52.8	54.0	55.9	58.4
Maldives											
Mauritius	57.7	63.2	67.5	66.3	69.0	70.9	71.3	71.7	71.5	70.4	68.9
Réunion	54.2	57.6	62.0	63.0	64.6	66.1	67.9	69.1	70.0	69.9	68.7
Rwanda	49.3	48.9	48.6	48.6	48.7	49.1	50.2	52.3	55.7	59.6	62.8
Seychelles											
Tanzania	49.9	49.4	49.2	48.6	48.2	48.2	48.8	50.1	51.9	54.7	58.1
Uganda	50.1	49.7	49.4	47.9	47.3	48.2	49.8	52.1	54.4	57.0	60.3
Zaire	52.6	51.2	51.3	51.2	51.4	51.3	51.4	52.2	53.4	55.4	58.2
Southern Africa											
Botswana	47.6	47.6	47.9	47.4	48.3	50.2	52.9	55.1	57.6	60.4	63.3
Lesotho	54.7	54.4	53.8	53.2	52.8	53.2	53.7	54.5	55.6	57.6	60.2
Malawi	50.6	51.1	51.3	48.9	48.3	48.7	49.8	51.7	53.7	56.2	59.3
Mozambique	53.1	53.5	53.1	52.8	52.6	52.8	53.5	54.8	56.4	59.0	61.8
Namibia	53.1	52.3	51.6	50.9	51.3	51.6	52.5	53.4	55.1	57.8	60.7
South Africa	56.1	57.4	58.1	58.7	59.2	59.9	60.9	62.2	63.4	64.5	65.6
Swaziland	51.7	50.9	50.2	49.7	49.3	49.5	50.3	52.1	54.2	57.1	60.4
Zambia	50.9	48.2	49.1	48.6	47.9	48.1	49.2	50.7	52.5	54.8	57.7
Zimbabwe	48.4	49.6	51.0	52.4	53.1	54.0	55.8	58.0	60.4	62.5	64.8

Source: UN, World Population Prospects
Notes: see end of section

DEMOGRAPHIC ANALYSIS | Table No. 0216

Percentage of Population Aged 65 Years and Over, Estimates and Projections 1975-2025

Units: % of total population

	1975	1980	1985	1990	1995	2000	2005	2010	2015	2020	2025
North America											
Canada	8.5	9.7	10.4	11.4	12.2	12.7	13.2	14.4	16.5	18.8	21.2
USA	10.5	11.3	11.9	12.6	12.9	12.8	12.9	13.6	15.2	17.5	19.8
South America											
Argentina	7.6	8.2	8.6	9.1	9.6	9.8	9.9	10.0	10.4	11.0	11.5
Bolivia	3.3	3.3	3.2	3.2	3.2	3.2	3.2	3.2	3.4	3.5	3.8
Brazil	3.7	4.0	4.3	4.7	5.1	5.4	5.8	6.3	7.0	8.1	9.3
Chile	5.4	5.6	5.8	6.0	6.4	6.7	7.1	7.7	8.5	9.6	10.9
Colombia	3.2	3.5	3.8	4.1	4.3	4.5	4.8	5.3	6.2	7.5	8.9
Ecuador	3.6	3.6	3.7	3.8	3.9	4.2	4.5	4.9	5.5	6.3	7.2
French Guiana											
Guyana	3.5	3.7	3.9	3.8	4.0	4.3	4.5	4.9	5.7	6.9	8.8
Paraguay	3.5	3.5	3.5	3.6	3.6	3.6	3.7	4.0	4.3	5.2	6.1
Peru	3.5	3.6	3.6	3.8	4.1	4.6	5.0	5.5	6.2	7.0	8.1
Suriname	3.9	4.5	4.3	4.2	4.6	5.1	5.5	5.7	6.0	6.8	8.6
Uruguay	9.6	10.4	10.7	11.6	12.3	12.7	12.6	12.5	12.5	12.8	13.4
Venezuela	3.1	3.2	3.4	3.7	4.0	4.3	4.7	5.1	5.9	6.8	7.7
Caribbean											
Anguilla											
Antigua											
Aruba											
Bahamas											
Barbados	9.9	10.5	10.7	11.8	11.8	11.1	10.4	10.0	11.0	13.1	16.0
Bermuda											
British Virgin Islands											
Cayman Islands											
Cuba	6.5	7.3	8.0	8.4	9.0	9.4	10.4	11.7	13.0	14.2	14.9
Dominica											
Dominican Republic	3.0	3.1	3.2	5.7	6.4	6.9	7.5	8.1	9.1	10.6	12.7
Grenada											
Guadeloupe	5.8	7.4	8.1	8.9	9.3	9.8	10.3	11.1	12.3	13.1	14.7
Haiti	3.7	3.8	3.8	4.1	3.9	3.8	3.8	3.8	3.9	4.1	4.4
Jamaica	5.8	5.8	6.1	6.6	6.4	6.4	6.4	6.6	7.1	8.1	9.9
Martinique	6.2	8.4	9.2	10.0	10.6	11.3	11.6	12.2	13.1	13.9	16.2
Netherlands Antilles											
St Kitts											
St Lucia											
St Vincent/Grenadines											
Trinidad and Tobago	4.1	5.5	5.4	5.4	5.5	5.5	5.8	6.3	7.2	8.4	10.1
Central America											
Belize											
Costa Rica	3.4	3.6	3.9	4.2	4.6	5.1	5.5	6.0	6.8	8.1	9.6
El Salvador	2.9	3.1	3.4	3.7	4.0	4.2	4.4	4.6	4.7	4.9	6.1
Guatemala	2.8	2.8	2.9	3.2	3.5	3.7	3.8	3.9	4.1	4.5	4.9
Honduras	2.7	3.0	3.2	3.3	3.3	3.5	3.6	3.9	4.2	4.7	5.3
Mexico	3.4	3.5	3.6	3.8	4.2	4.6	5.0	5.6	6.2	7.1	8.3
Nicaragua	2.4	2.4	2.5	2.7	2.9	3.1	3.3	3.5	3.9	4.5	5.2
Panama	3.9	4.1	4.5	4.8	5.1	5.4	5.8	6.5	7.3	8.3	9.6
Puerto Rico	6.3	7.9	8.3	10.5	10.8	11.1	11.4	12.2	13.2	13.6	14.2
South Asia											
Afghanistan	2.4	2.5	2.7	2.8	2.6	2.7	3.0	3.3	3.8	4.0	4.6
Bangladesh	3.6	3.4	3.1	2.9	2.8	2.9	2.9	3.1	3.4	3.8	4.7
Bhutan	3.2	3.2	3.3	3.4	3.5	3.5	3.6	3.8	4.0	4.3	4.6
India	3.8	4.0	4.3	4.5	4.8	5.1	5.5	5.9	6.4	7.2	8.2
Nepal	3.3	3.0	3.0	3.1	3.2	3.4	3.7	4.1	4.5	5.0	5.5
Pakistan	3.0	2.9	2.8	2.7	2.8	2.9	3.0	3.2	3.5	4.2	5.1
Sri Lanka	4.1	4.3	4.7	5.2	5.9	6.5	7.1	7.8	9.0	10.3	11.9

DEMOGRAPHIC ANALYSIS Table No. 0216 (cont'd)

Percentage of Population Aged 65 Years and Over, Estimates and Projections 1975-2025

Units: % of total population

	1975	1980	1985	1990	1995	2000	2005	2010	2015	2020	2025
Japan											
Japan	7.9	9.0	10.4	11.7	13.8	15.9	17.6	19.6	22.4	23.7	23.9
ASEAN/NICs											
Brunei											
Hong Kong	5.4	6.5	7.6	8.8	10.1	11.2	11.9	12.2	14.8	18.4	23.3
Indonesia	3.2	3.3	3.6	3.9	4.4	5.1	5.8	6.4	6.9	7.8	9.1
Macau											
Malaysia	3.7	3.7	3.8	3.7	3.9	4.2	4.8	5.3	6.2	7.3	8.6
Philippines	2.7	3.4	3.4	3.4	3.5	3.7	4.0	4.4	4.9	5.8	6.9
Singapore	4.1	4.7	5.2	5.6	6.4	7.2	8.5	9.5	12.2	15.4	19.1
South Korea	3.6	3.8	4.3	4.8	5.4	6.4	7.7	8.7	9.9	11.7	14.5
Taiwan											
Thailand	3.0	3.5	3.6	3.9	4.4	5.0	5.6	6.2	7.0	8.4	10.2
East/SE Asia											
Cambodia	2.8	2.5	2.6	2.9	3.2	3.5	3.7	4.0	4.8	5.8	6.8
China	4.4	4.7	5.3	5.8	6.3	7.0	7.5	8.1	9.2	11.3	12.8
Laos	2.7	2.8	2.9	3.0	3.0	3.0	3.1	3.3	3.5	3.9	4.4
Mongolia	3.2	3.2	3.2	3.2	3.3	3.5	3.8	4.2	4.6	5.1	5.6
Myanmar	3.8	4.0	3.8	4.1	4.3	4.7	4.9	5.0	5.2	5.8	6.9
North Korea	3.5	3.5	3.6	4.1	4.6	5.0	5.6	6.2	7.1	8.3	10.4
Vietnam	4.0	4.8	4.5	4.4	4.4	4.5	4.4	4.2	4.3	5.2	6.5
Australasia											
Australia	8.7	9.6	10.1	10.9	11.5	11.7	12.0	12.8	14.3	15.9	17.5
New Zealand	8.7	10.0	10.5	10.9	11.2	11.2	11.5	12.3	14.1	15.6	17.3
Pacific											
American Samoa											
Fiji	2.7	3.1	3.5	3.1	3.5	4.1	4.8	5.6	6.6	7.7	9.3
French Polynesia											
Guam											
Kiribati											
Nauru											
New Caledonia											
Papua New Guinea	3.1	1.6	2.4	2.4	2.6	2.6	2.7	2.7	3.2	3.5	3.9
Solomon Islands											
Tonga											
Tuvalu											
Vanuatu											
Western Samoa											
Middle East											
Bahrain	2.3	2.1	1.9	1.8	1.8	1.9	2.1	2.4	2.9	4.2	6.0
Egypt	4.2	4.1	3.9	3.9	4.1	4.4	4.6	4.9	5.6	7.0	8.4
Iran	3.3	3.4	3.3	3.7	4.1	4.4	4.3	4.1	4.2	4.8	5.6
Iraq	2.5	2.6	2.7	2.7	2.8	3.0	3.1	3.3	3.6	4.0	4.4
Israel	7.8	8.6	8.8	8.8	8.7	8.6	8.5	8.6	9.9	11.4	12.6
Jordan	2.8	3.1	2.7	2.7	2.7	2.9	3.2	3.3	3.4	3.5	4.1
Kuwait	1.6	1.4	1.3	1.3	1.7	2.4	3.5	5.0	7.1	9.7	12.4
Lebanon	5.0	5.4	5.1	5.0	5.3	5.5	5.4	5.1	5.2	5.8	6.8
Oman	2.7	2.6	2.5	2.6	2.7	2.9	3.1	3.4	3.7	4.0	4.2
Qatar	2.0	1.1	1.6	1.8	2.5	3.1	4.1	5.4	6.9	8.3	8.9
Saudi Arabia	3.0	2.8	2.6	2.6	2.6	2.6	2.7	2.9	3.2	3.7	4.1
Syria	3.7	3.2	2.8	2.6	2.6	2.6	2.6	2.6	2.7	3.1	3.7
United Arab Emirates	2.0	1.2	1.5	1.7	2.3	3.1	4.6	6.7	9.8	13.7	15.5
Yemen	3.0	3.0	2.8	2.8	2.9	2.9	3.0	3.0	3.1	3.2	3.4

DEMOGRAPHIC ANALYSIS

Table No. 0216 (cont'd)

Percentage of Population Aged 65 Years and Over, Estimates and Projections 1975-2025

Units: % of total population

	1975	1980	1985	1990	1995	2000	2005	2010	2015	2020	2025
North Africa											
Algeria	4.2	3.9	3.7	3.6	3.4	3.3	3.6	3.7	3.8	4.4	5.4
Chad	3.6	3.6	3.6	3.6	3.6	3.5	3.5	3.5	3.5	3.6	3.9
Djibouti	2.1	2.2	2.2	2.6	2.7	2.8	3.0	3.1	3.3	3.4	3.5
Ethiopia	2.6	2.6	2.9	2.9	2.8	2.8	2.8	2.9	2.9	3.1	3.3
Libya	2.2	2.2	2.3	2.4	2.6	2.8	3.0	3.3	3.6	3.9	4.2
Mali	2.7	2.8	2.7	2.6	2.5	2.5	2.5	2.4	2.5	2.7	3.0
Mauritania	3.0	3.0	3.1	3.1	3.1	3.1	3.1	3.1	3.2	3.3	3.5
Morocco	3.7	4.1	3.9	3.6	3.9	4.0	4.3	4.3	4.8	5.7	7.0
Niger	2.4	2.4	2.5	2.5	2.4	2.4	2.4	2.4	2.5	2.7	2.9
Somalia	3.1	2.9	2.7	2.7	2.7	2.7	2.8	2.9	3.1	3.4	3.6
Sudan	2.7	2.7	2.8	2.8	2.9	3.0	3.1	3.2	3.4	3.7	4.1
Tunisia	3.5	3.8	3.8	4.0	4.3	4.8	5.2	5.1	5.4	6.5	8.1
West Africa											
Benin	3.5	3.0	2.9	2.8	2.8	2.7	2.7	2.7	2.8	2.9	3.1
Burkina Faso	2.8	2.8	2.9	3.0	3.0	3.1	3.1	3.2	3.2	3.3	3.5
Cameroon	3.5	3.5	3.5	3.4	3.3	3.2	3.1	3.0	3.0	3.1	3.2
Cape Verde	5.4	6.1	5.1	4.2	3.9	3.7	3.5	2.9	2.4	2.5	3.4
Côte d'Ivoire	2.3	2.3	2.5	2.5	2.6	2.7	2.7	2.7	2.7	2.8	2.9
Equatorial Guinea	4.3	4.2	4.2	4.1	4.0	3.9	3.7	3.6	3.5	3.7	3.9
Gabon	5.8	5.9	5.9	5.9	5.7	5.5	5.4	5.2	4.8	4.4	4.1
Gambia	2.9	2.9	2.9	2.9	3.0	3.2	3.4	3.5	3.6	3.8	4.1
Ghana	2.7	2.8	2.8	2.8	2.9	2.9	3.0	3.2	3.5	3.9	4.4
Guinea	2.5	2.6	2.6	2.6	2.6	2.6	2.5	2.5	2.5	2.7	3.0
Guinea-Bissau	3.7	4.0	4.1	4.1	4.1	4.0	4.0	4.0	4.2	4.4	
Liberia	3.7	3.7	3.7	3.7	3.7	3.7	3.7	3.7	3.7	3.8	4.0
Nigeria	2.4	2.5	2.5	2.5	2.6	2.6	2.7	2.8	3.0	3.2	3.5
Sao Tomé e Príncipe											
Senegal	2.8	2.8	2.9	2.9	2.9	2.9	3.0	3.0	3.2	3.5	3.9
Sierra Leone	3.1	3.1	3.1	3.1	3.1	3.1	3.0	3.0	3.0	3.1	3.3
Togo	3.1	3.2	3.2	3.2	3.2	3.1	3.1	3.1	3.2	3.3	3.6
East/Central Africa											
Angola	2.9	3.0	3.0	3.0	3.1	3.1	3.1	3.1	3.1	3.2	3.5
Burundi	3.4	3.4	3.3	3.1	2.8	2.7	2.6	2.6	2.7	3.3	3.9
Central African Republic	3.9	3.9	3.8	3.8	3.7	3.6	3.5	3.3	3.3	3.4	3.6
Comoros	2.6	2.6	2.5	2.5	2.4	2.4	2.4	2.4	2.4	2.6	2.8
Congo	3.3	3.3	3.4	3.3	3.2	3.1	3.0	3.0	3.0	3.1	3.3
Kenya	3.7	3.4	3.1	2.9	2.8	2.7	2.6	2.4	2.4	2.7	3.0
Madagascar	3.0	3.0	3.0	3.0	2.9	2.9	2.8	2.8	2.9	3.0	3.3
Maldives											
Mauritius	2.6	2.7	1.8	4.5	5.2	5.7	6.4	7.0	8.3	10.4	12.9
Réunion	3.8	4.4	4.7	5.2	5.5	5.9	6.3	6.7	6.9	7.8	9.9
Rwanda	2.4	2.4	2.4	2.4	2.4	2.4	2.4	2.5	2.7	2.8	3.1
Seychelles											
Tanzania	2.3	2.3	2.3	2.3	2.3	2.4	2.4	2.5	2.6	2.7	2.9
Uganda	2.5	2.5	2.5	2.5	2.4	2.4	2.3	2.4	2.5	2.8	3.1
Zaire	2.8	2.5	2.5	2.6	2.6	2.7	2.8	2.9	3.0	3.2	3.5
Southern Africa											
Botswana	2.1	5.1	3.9	3.3	3.0	2.9	2.8	2.9	3.0	3.4	3.9
Lesotho	3.6	3.6	3.6	3.7	3.7	3.8	3.9	4.1	4.2	4.3	4.6
Malawi	2.2	2.3	2.6	2.5	2.6	2.6	2.7	2.8	2.9	3.1	3.3
Mozambique	3.1	3.1	3.2	3.2	3.2	3.3	3.3	3.3	3.5	3.6	4.0
Namibia	3.2	3.2	3.3	3.3	3.3	3.4	3.4	3.4	3.6	3.8	4.1
South Africa	3.9	4.0	4.1	4.2	4.3	4.5	4.8	5.1	5.6	6.3	7.2
Swaziland	2.9	2.9	3.0	2.9	2.9	2.9	2.9	2.9	3.1	3.3	3.6
Zambia	2.6	2.4	2.3	2.3	2.3	2.3	2.3	2.4	2.5	2.7	3.0
Zimbabwe	2.6	2.6	2.7	2.7	2.8	2.9	3.0	3.2	3.4	3.9	4.7

Source: UN, World Population Prospects
Notes: see end of section

DEMOGRAPHIC ANALYSIS   Table No. 0217

Population by Age and Sex: Latest Official Estimates

Units: '000

		Total all ages, both sexes	Males				Females			
	Year		Total	0-14	15-64	65+	Total	0-14	15-64	65+
North America										
Canada	1989	26,218.3	12,924.4	2,818.1	8,864.6	1,241.7	13,293.9	2,682.0	8,882.6	1,729.3
USA	1989	248,240.0	120,982.0	27,607.0	80,737.0	12,638.0	127,258.0	26,305.0	82,605.0	18,348.0
Regional total		*274,458.3*	*133,906.4*	*30,425.1*	*89,601.6*	*13,879.7*	*140,551.9*	*28,987.0*	*91,487.6*	*20,077.3*
South America										
Argentina	1988	31,534.3	15,622.7	4,845.1	9,581.1	1,196.5	15,911.6	4,697.9	9,601.2	1,612.5
Bolivia	1988	6,020.1	2,994.3	1,267.6	1,604.7	122.0	3,025.8	1,205.9	1,688.3	131.6
Brazil	1990	150,367.0	74,992.0	26,648.0	45,039.0	3,305.0	75,375.0	26,330.0	45,353.0	3,692.0
Chile	1990	13,173.3	6,505.6	2,050.7	4,130.5	324.4	6,667.7	1,982.6	4,216.6	468.5
Colombia	1985	27,837.9	13,777.7	5,107.3	8,149.5	520.9	14,060.2	4,933.7	8,608.7	517.8
Ecuador	1989	10,490.2	5,276.8	2,193.9	2,693.6	389.3	5,213.4	2,108.4	2,923.4	181.6
French Guiana	1982	73.0	38.3	12.1	24.6	1.6	34.7	11.7	21.1	1.9
Guyana	1980	758.6	375.8	155.4	206.5	13.9	382.8	154.0	213.0	15.8
Paraguay	1988	4,039.2	2,045.1	830.7	1,149.7	64.7	1,994.1	800.3	1,114.3	79.5
Peru	1989	21,791.0	10,977.0	4,370.0	6,245.0	362.0	10,814.0	4,224.0	6,158.0	432.0
Suriname	1980	354.9	175.6	70.4	97.8	7.4	179.3	68.9	102.1	8.3
Uruguay	1985	2,955.4	1,439.1	402.6	898.0	138.5	1,516.3	387.3	937.7	191.3
Venezuela	1990	19,735.0	9,954.3	3,847.5	5,777.2	329.6	9,780.7	3,703.4	5,682.4	394.9
Regional total		*289,129.9*	*144,174.3*	*51,801.3*	*85,597.2*	*6,775.8*	*144,955.6*	*50,608.1*	*86,619.8*	*7,727.7*
Caribbean										
Anguilla										
Antigua										
Aruba	1981	60.3	29.3	7.7	19.9	1.7	31.0	7.6	21.1	2.3
Bahamas	1990	253.3	123.0	38.8	79.4	4.8	130.3	38.2	84.7	7.4
Barbados	1992	258.8	123.7	32.7	78.8	12.2	135.1	32.2	85.7	17.2
Bermuda	1990	60.7	29.6	6.1	21.2	2.3	31.1	6.0	21.7	3.4
British Virgin Islands	1988	12.4	6.1	1.8	3.9	0.4	6.3	1.8	4.1	0.4
Cayman Islands	1989	25.4	12.4	2.9	8.8	0.7	13.0	2.9	9.2	0.9
Cuba	1988	10,468.6	5,270.8	1,250.0	3,577.1	443.7	5,197.8	1,191.3	3,555.0	451.5
Dominica	1981	73.8	36.8	15.1	19.5	2.2	37.0	14.3	19.6	3.1
Dominican Republic	1980	5,430.9	2,710.0	1,300.6	1,324.5	84.9	2,720.9	1,284.9	1,352.4	83.6
Grenada	1981	89.1	42.9	17.4	23.0	2.5	46.2	17.0	25.2	4.0
Guadeloupe	1985	333.4	163.1	51.9	100.7	10.5	170.3	50.5	105.9	13.9
Haiti	1988	5,525.9	2,678.7	1,066.8	1,457.5	154.4	2,847.2	1,100.1	1,575.3	171.8
Jamaica	1989	2,392.0	1,191.0	409.9	697.0	84.1	1,201.0	397.5	708.3	95.2
Martinique	1985	330.9	162.1	50.0	101.9	10.2	168.8	48.7	106.5	13.6
Netherlands Antilles	1989	190.1	92.9	24.9	62.7	5.3	97.2	24.5	64.9	7.8
St Kitts	1988	44.4	22.7	7.5	13.5	1.7	21.7	7.3	12.0	2.4
St Lucia	1989	148.2	72.0	33.2	35.5	3.3	76.2	32.7	38.5	5.0
St Vincent/Grenadines	1980	97.8	47.4	21.7	23.4	2.3	50.4	21.1	25.9	3.4
Trinidad and Tobago	1987	1,211.7	631.2	143.2	455.6	32.4	580.5	139.6	406.5	34.4
Regional total		*27,007.7*	*13,445.7*	*4,482.2*	*8,103.9*	*859.6*	*13,562.0*	*4,418.2*	*8,222.5*	*921.3*
Central America										
Belize	1990	1,627.3	93.9	41.8	47.2	4.9	1,533.4	550.4	912.0	71.0
Costa Rica	1992	2,488.7	1,244.1	464.1	726.4	53.6	1,244.6	446.7	740.3	57.6
El Salvador	1986	4,845.2	2,388.9	1,130.7	1,183.8	74.4	2,456.3	1,089.4	1,275.0	91.9
Guatemala	1990	9,197.3	4,646.7	2,129.0	2,376.3	141.4	4,550.6	2,050.6	2,349.3	150.7
Honduras	1985	4,372.5	2,192.0	1,030.3	1,101.2	60.5	2,180.5	1,021.0	1,093.9	65.6
Mexico	1985	78,524.2	39,314.9	16,724.4	21,335.2	1,255.3	39,209.3	16,134.9	21,533.2	1,541.2
Nicaragua	1980	2,732.6	1,338.1	662.3	638.3	37.5	1,394.5	647.2	701.6	45.7
Panama	1990	2,417.9	1,230.0	431.7	740.7	57.6	1,187.9	413.6	716.3	58.0
Puerto Rico	1988	3,293.0	1,576.9	488.4	939.5	149.0	1,716.1	459.4	1,088.3	168.4
Regional total		*109,498.7*	*54,025.5*	*23,102.7*	*29,088.6*	*1,834.2*	*55,473.2*	*22,813.2*	*30,409.9*	*2,250.1*
South Asia										
Afghanistan	1988	15,513.3	7,962.4	3,610.6	4,015.0	336.8	7,550.9	3,535.9	3,776.6	238.4
Bangladesh	1990	109,291.0	56,381.0	24,366.0	26,000.0	6,015.0	52,910.0	23,488.0	24,554.0	4,868.0
Bhutan										
India	1990	827,050.0	426,153.0	152,165.0	257,090.0	16,898.0	400,897.0	144,355.0	239,549.0	16,993.0
Nepal	1986	17,143.5	8,819.7	3,775.5	4,774.0	270.2	8,323.8	3,468.4	4,610.5	244.9
Pakistan	1981	84,253.7	44,232.7	19,392.2	22,794.2	2,046.3	40,021.0	18,124.5	20,381.7	1,514.8
Sri Lanka	1990	16,993.0	8,661.0	3,056.0	5,217.0	388.0	8,332.0	2,936.0	5,047.0	349.0
Regional total		*1,070,244.5*	*552,209.8*	*206,365.3*	*319,890.2*	*25,954.3*	*518,034.7*	*195,907.8*	*297,918.8*	*24,208.1*

DEMOGRAPHIC ANALYSIS   Table No. 0217 (cont'd)

Population by Age and Sex: Latest Official Estimates

Units: '000

	Year	Total all ages, both sexes	Males Total	0-14	15-64	65+	Females Total	0-14	15-64	65+
Japan										
Japan	1989	123,254.7	60,581.2	11,893.2	42,950.8	5,737.2	62,673.5	11,307.5	42,794.0	8,572.0
Regional total		*123,254.7*	*60,581.2*	*11,893.2*	*42,950.8*	*5,737.2*	*62,673.5*	*11,307.5*	*42,794.0*	*8,572.0*
ASEAN/NICs										
Brunei	1989	249.0	128.6	46.0	79.1	3.5	120.4	44.0	73.3	3.1
Hong Kong	1990	5,800.6	2,963.8	646.7	2,095.4	221.7	2,836.8	598.2	1,949.7	288.9
Indonesia	1985	164,047.0	81,644.0	33,169.0	45,852.0	2,623.0	82,403.0	31,395.0	48,052.0	2,956.0
Macau	1988	443.5	228.4	49.5	168.1	10.8	215.1	47.1	152.5	15.5
Malaysia [a]	1990	17,860.6	8,992.5	3,381.4	5,310.3	300.8	8,868.1	3,219.3	5,285.7	363.1
Philippines	1990	61,480.1	30,882.6	12,148.5	17,756.1	978.0	30,597.5	11,606.7	17,841.4	1,149.4
Singapore	1989	2,685.4	1,366.4	321.7	976.5	68.2	1,319.0	298.0	937.7	83.3
South Korea	1989	42,792.5	21,563.5	5,744.1	15,078.2	741.2	21,229.0	5,325.5	14,619.1	1,284.4
Taiwan										
Thailand	1989	55,448.0	27,754.0	9,551.0	17,283.0	920.0	27,694.0	9,297.0	17,248.0	1,149.0
Regional total		*350,806.7*	*175,523.8*	*65,057.9*	*104,598.7*	*5,867.2*	*175,282.9*	*61,830.8*	*106,159.4*	*7,292.7*
East/SE Asia										
Cambodia										
China	1987	1,067,930.6	544,147.1	159,281.6	358,553.9	26,311.6	523,783.5	147,885.9	343,660.9	32,236.7
Laos										
Mongolia										
Myanmar	1987	38,541.2	19,107.7	7,178.2	11,207.0	722.5	19,433.5	7,202.2	11,462.8	768.5
North Korea										
Vietnam	1989	64,411.7	31,336.6	12,926.2	17,189.7	1,220.7	33,075.1	12,191.9	19,042.5	1,840.7
Regional total										
Australasia										
Australia	1990	17,086.2	8,531.2	1,917.5	5,801.6	812.1	8,555.0	1,824.2	5,635.3	1,095.5
New Zealand	1992	3,454.9	1,703.9	278.2	1,145.2	280.5	1,751.0	263.2	1,138.7	349.1
Regional total		*20,541.1*	*10,235.1*	*2,195.7*	*6,946.8*	*1,092.6*	*10,306.0*	*2,087.4*	*6,774.0*	*1,444.6*
Pacific										
American Samoa	1990	38.9	19.6	8.4	10.5	0.7	19.3	7.6	10.9	0.8
Fiji	1986	716.7	363.2	140.5	211.0	11.7	353.5	133.5	208.3	11.7
French Polynesia	1988	188.9	98.4	34.8	60.8	2.8	90.5	33.1	54.3	3.1
Guam	1980	106.0	55.3	18.9	35.0	1.4	50.7	18.1	31.0	1.6
Kiribati	1978	56.2	27.7	11.8	15.0	0.9	28.5	11.3	16.0	1.2
Nauru										
New Caledonia	1989	164.2	84.0	27.4	53.2	3.4	80.2	26.3	50.1	3.8
Papua New Guinea	1987	3,479.4	1,803.3	734.8	1,029.8	38.7	1,676.1	695.4	944.1	36.6
Solomon Islands	1986	284.8	147.8	70.3	71.9	5.6	137.0	64.5	68.8	3.7
Tonga	1986	93.0	46.7	19.8	25.0	1.9	46.3	18.4	25.9	2.0
Tuvalu										
Vanuatu	1989	150.1	78.2	35.6	40.7	1.9	71.9	32.8	37.1	2.0
Western Samoa	1981	156.3	81.0	36.5	42.3	2.2	75.3	32.7	40.1	2.5
Regional total		*5,434.5*	*2,805.2*	*1,138.8*	*1,595.2*	*71.2*	*2,629.3*	*1,073.7*	*1,486.6*	*69.0*
Middle East										
Bahrain	1990	503.0	290.0	90.6	193.1	6.3	213.0	87.4	120.3	5.3
Egypt	1988	50,355.0	25,754.0	10,499.0	14,535.0	720.0	24,601.0	9,905.0	13,974.0	722.0
Iran	1986	49,445.0	25,281.0	11,493.2	13,005.9	781.9	24,164.0	10,980.8	12,439.7	743.5
Iraq	1988	17,249.9	8,863.9	3,942.7	4,639.3	281.9	8,386.0	3,735.2	4,344.6	306.2
Israel	1989	4,518.2	2,253.2	736.1	1,332.0	185.1	2,265.0	698.1	1,346.6	220.3
Jordan	1989	3,111.0	1,627.0	779.4	807.1	40.5	1,484.0	717.2	726.4	40.4
Kuwait	1989	2,048.5	1,158.8	379.4	766.8	12.6	889.7	371.2	506.2	12.3
Lebanon										
Oman										
Qatar	1986	369.1	247.9	52.6	193.1	2.2	121.2	49.8	69.8	1.6
Saudi Arabia										
Syria	1990	12,116.0	6,189.0	3,090.0	2,830.0	269.0	5,927.0	2,878.0	2,788.0	261.0
United Arab Emirates	1977	862.0	613.7	119.1	486.9	7.7	248.3	108.0	134.5	5.8
Yemen	1987	2,278.0	1,127.0	565.0	504.0	58.0	1,151.0	516.0	579.0	56.0
Regional total										

DEMOGRAPHIC ANALYSIS　　　　　　　　　　　　　　　　Table No. 0217 (cont'd)

Population by Age and Sex: Latest Official Estimates

Units: '000

	Year	Total all ages, both sexes	Males Total	Males 0-14	Males 15-64	Males 65+	Females Total	Females 0-14	Females 15-64	Females 65+
North Africa										
Algeria	1984	20,841.0	10,348.0	4,888.0	5,091.0	369.0	10,493.0	4,700.0	5,344.0	449.0
Chad [b]	1978	4,308.1	2,218.7	812.0	1,349.0	57.7	2,089.4	800.3	1,232.7	56.4
Djibouti										
Ethiopia	1989	49,513.2	24,893.1	12,406.3	11,232.7	1,254.1	24,620.1	11,467.2	12,080.7	1,072.2
Libya	1984	3,237.1	1,653.3	814.9	801.5	36.9	1,583.8	793.3	452.2	338.3
Mali [b]	1987	7,696.3	3,760.7	1,801.0	1,813.1	146.6	3,935.6	1,734.2	2,055.4	146.0
Mauritania	1977	1,338.8	658.4	305.2	332.1	21.1	680.4	283.4	367.3	29.7
Morocco	1982	20,449.6	10,236.1	4,393.2	5,418.1	424.8	10,213.5	4,228.1	5,610.2	375.2
Niger										
Somalia										
Sudan	1983	20,594.2	10,512.9	4,686.3	5,468.6	358.0	10,081.3	4,378.5	5,443.9	258.9
Tunisia	1989	7,909.5	4,013.8	1,537.6	2,267.7	208.5	3,895.7	1,462.4	2,254.8	178.5
Regional total		*135,887.8*	*68,295.0*	*31,644.5*	*33,773.8*	*2,876.7*	*67,592.8*	*29,847.4*	*34,841.2*	*2,904.2*
West Africa										
Benin	1987	4,304.0	2,086.0	992.0	1,045.0	49.0	2,218.0	1,013.0	1,148.0	57.0
Burkina Faso	1985	7,964.7	3,833.2	1,945.0	1,734.9	153.3	4,131.5	1,900.0	2,055.8	175.7
Cameroon	1986	10,446.4	5,212.5	2,365.7	2,667.3	179.5	5,233.9	2,351.1	2,674.9	207.9
Cape Verde	1987	347.0	162.2	77.0	77.7	7.5	184.8	76.8	97.6	10.4
Côte d'Ivoire	1978	7,540.1	3,761.4	1,584.1	2,087.6	89.7	3,778.7	1,712.1	1,968.3	98.3
Equatorial Guinea	1990	348.2	168.9	74.7	88.0	6.2	179.3	73.6	98.0	7.7
Gabon										
Gambia	1983	687.8	342.1	151.6	176.7	13.8	345.7	149.4	184.6	11.7
Ghana										
Guinea										
Guinea-Bissau	1989	943.0	456.0	205.0	236.0	15.0	487.0	203.0	270.0	14.0
Liberia	1977	1,684.0	850.3	355.5	458.2	36.6	833.7	333.3	474.9	25.5
Nigeria										
Sao Tomé e Príncipe	1981	96.6	48.0	23.2	22.8	2.0	48.6	21.9	24.0	2.7
Senegal										
Sierra Leone										
Togo										
Regional total										
East/Central Africa										
Angola										
Burundi	1988	5,068.9	2,468.3	1,135.6	1,257.2	75.5	2,600.6	1,137.2	1,375.7	87.7
Central African Republic	1985	2,607.8	1,263.5	552.2	668.3	43.0	1,344.3	559.4	726.9	58.0
Comoros	1980	335.2	167.1	81.1	78.6	7.4	168.1	77.0	84.0	7.1
Congo	1985	1,924.3	934.0	429.8	442.4	61.8	990.3	430.0	526.6	33.7
Kenya	1985	20,333.2	10,126.1	5,272.2	4,657.3	196.6	10,207.1	5,160.1	4,815.8	231.2
Madagascar										
Maldives	1985	180.1	93.5	41.6	49.1	2.8	86.6	39.7	45.2	1.7
Mauritius	1989	1,026.8	510.6	156.4	332.6	21.6	516.2	150.7	335.1	30.4
Réunion	1988	569.5	278.9	90.9	176.8	11.2	290.6	89.1	183.9	17.6
Rwanda	1978	4,800.4	2,331.1	1,090.9	1,172.0	68.2	2,469.3	1,099.3	1,302.7	67.3
Seychelles	1989	67.1	33.5	12.0	20.0	1.5	33.6	11.5	19.3	2.8
Tanzania	1985	21,733.0	10,637.0	5,208.0	5,099.0	330.0	11,096.0	5,190.0	5,540.0	366.0
Uganda										
Zaire	1985	30,981.3	15,326.7	7,313.6	7,662.4	350.7	15,654.6	7,120.8	8,087.3	446.5
Regional total		*89,627.6*	*44,170.3*	*21,384.3*	*21,615.7*	*1,170.3*	*45,457.3*	*21,064.8*	*23,042.5*	*1,350.0*
Southern Africa										
Botswana	1990	1,301.0	624.0	315.6	291.5	16.9	677.0	316.0	336.8	24.2
Lesotho										
Malawi	1987	7,554.2	3,673.6	1,802.4	1,785.9	85.3	3,880.6	1,814.3	1,959.8	106.5
Mozambique [b]	1987	14,548.4	7,095.4	3,174.8	3,761.2	159.4	7,453.0	3,271.6	3,969.9	211.5
Namibia										
South Africa [c]	1985	31,231.0	16,211.0	5,721.0	10,004.0	486.0	15,020.0	6,672.0	7,710.0	638.0
Swaziland	1986	681.0	321.7	159.5	151.2	11.0	359.3	163.0	181.3	15.0
Zambia	1980	5,661.8	2,770.0	1,383.2	1,301.6	85.2	2,891.8	1,389.6	1,429.9	72.3
Zimbabwe	1987	8,639.7	4,239.3	1,220.6	2,212.2	806.5	4,400.4	1,265.1	2,312.1	823.2
Regional total		*69,617.1*	*34,935.0*	*13,777.1*	*19,507.6*	*1,650.3*	*34,682.1*	*14,891.6*	*17,899.8*	*1,890.7*

Source: UN

Notes: see end of section

DEMOGRAPHIC ANALYSIS   Table No. 0218

Population by Age and Sex (% Analysis): Latest Official Estimates

Units: % of total population

	Year	Total all ages, both sexes	Males Total	Males 0-14	Males 15-64	Males 65+	Females Total	Females 0-14	Females 15-64	Females 65+
North America										
Canada	1989	100.0	49.3	10.7	33.8	4.7	50.7	10.2	33.9	6.6
USA	1989	100.0	48.7	11.1	32.5	5.1	51.3	10.6	33.3	7.4
South America										
Argentina	1988	100.0	49.5	15.4	30.4	3.8	50.5	14.9	30.4	5.1
Bolivia	1988	100.0	49.7	21.1	26.7	2.0	50.3	20.0	28.0	2.2
Brazil	1990	100.0	49.9	17.7	30.0	2.2	50.1	17.5	30.2	2.5
Chile	1990	100.0	49.4	15.6	31.4	2.5	50.6	15.1	32.0	3.6
Colombia	1985	100.0	49.5	18.3	29.3	1.9	50.5	17.7	30.9	1.9
Ecuador	1989	100.0	50.3	20.9	25.7	3.7	49.7	20.1	27.9	1.7
French Guiana	1982	100.0	52.5	16.6	33.7	2.2	47.5	16.0	28.9	2.6
Guyana	1980	100.0	49.5	20.5	27.2	1.8	50.5	20.3	28.1	2.1
Paraguay	1988	100.0	50.6	20.6	28.5	1.6	49.4	19.8	27.6	2.0
Peru	1989	100.0	50.4	20.1	28.7	1.7	49.6	19.4	28.3	2.0
Suriname	1980	100.0	49.5	19.8	27.6	2.1	50.5	19.4	28.8	2.3
Uruguay	1985	100.0	48.7	13.6	30.4	4.7	51.3	13.1	31.7	6.5
Venezuela	1990	100.0	50.4	19.5	29.3	1.7	49.6	18.8	28.8	2.0
Caribbean										
Anguilla										
Antigua										
Aruba	1981	100.0	48.6	12.8	33.0	2.8	51.4	12.6	35.0	3.8
Bahamas	1990	100.0	48.6	15.3	31.3	1.9	51.4	15.1	33.4	2.9
Barbados	1987	100.0	47.3	12.5	30.2	4.6	52.7	12.6	33.5	6.7
Bermuda	1990	100.0	48.8	10.0	34.9	3.8	51.2	9.9	35.7	5.6
British Virgin Islands	1988	100.0	49.2	14.5	31.5	3.2	50.8	14.5	33.1	3.2
Cayman Islands	1989	100.0	48.8	11.4	34.6	2.8	51.2	11.4	36.2	3.5
Cuba	1988	100.0	50.3	11.9	34.2	4.2	49.7	11.4	34.0	4.3
Dominica	1981	100.0	49.9	20.5	26.4	3.0	50.1	19.4	26.6	4.2
Dominican Republic	1980	100.0	49.9	23.9	24.4	1.6	50.1	23.7	24.9	1.5
Grenada	1981	100.0	48.1	19.5	25.8	2.8	51.9	19.1	28.3	4.5
Guadeloupe	1985	100.0	48.9	15.6	30.2	3.1	51.1	15.2	31.8	4.2
Haiti	1988	100.0	48.5	19.3	26.4	2.8	51.5	19.9	28.5	3.1
Jamaica	1989	100.0	49.8	17.1	29.1	3.5	50.2	16.6	29.6	4.0
Martinique	1985	100.0	49.0	15.1	30.8	3.1	51.0	14.7	32.2	4.1
Netherlands Antilles	1981	100.0	48.3	15.2	30.3	2.7	51.7	14.7	33.1	3.9
St Kitts	1988	100.0	51.1	16.9	30.4	3.8	48.9	16.4	27.0	5.4
St Lucia	1989	100.0	48.6	22.4	24.0	2.2	51.4	22.1	26.0	3.4
St Vincent/Grenadines	1980	100.0	48.5	22.2	23.9	2.4	51.5	21.6	26.5	3.5
Trinidad and Tobago	1985	100.0	49.8	17.0	30.3	2.5	50.2	16.6	30.5	3.1
Central America										
Belize	1989	100.0	50.7	22.5	25.4	2.7	49.3	22.1	24.3	2.9
Costa Rica	1985	100.0	50.0	18.6	29.2	2.2	50.0	17.9	29.7	2.3
El Salvador	1986	100.0	49.3	23.3	24.4	1.5	50.7	22.5	26.3	1.9
Guatemala	1990	100.0	50.5	23.1	25.8	1.5	49.5	22.3	25.5	1.6
Honduras	1985	100.0	50.1	23.6	25.2	1.4	49.9	23.4	25.0	1.5
Mexico	1985	100.0	50.1	21.3	27.2	1.6	49.9	20.5	27.4	2.0
Nicaragua	1980	100.0	49.0	24.2	23.4	1.4	51.0	23.7	25.7	1.7
Panama	1990	100.0	50.9	17.9	30.6	2.4	49.1	17.1	29.6	2.4
Puerto Rico	1988	100.0	47.9	14.8	28.5	4.5	52.1	14.0	33.0	5.1
South Asia										
Afghanistan	1988	100.0	51.3	23.3	25.9	2.2	48.7	22.8	24.3	1.5
Bangladesh	1990	100.0	51.6	22.3	23.8	5.5	48.4	21.5	22.5	4.5
Bhutan										
India	1990	100.0	51.5	18.4	31.1	2.0	48.5	17.5	29.0	2.1
Nepal	1986	100.0	51.4	22.0	27.8	1.6	48.6	20.2	26.9	1.4
Pakistan	1981	100.0	52.5	23.0	27.1	2.4	47.5	21.5	24.2	1.8
Sri Lanka	1990	100.0	51.0	18.0	30.7	2.3	49.0	17.3	29.7	2.1

DEMOGRAPHIC ANALYSIS | Table No. 0218 (cont'd)

Population by Age and Sex (% Analysis): Latest Official Estimates

Units: % of total population

	Year	Total all ages, both sexes	Males Total	Males 0-14	Males 15-64	Males 65+	Females Total	Females 0-14	Females 15-64	Females 65+
Japan										
Japan	1989	100.0	49.2	9.6	34.8	4.7	50.8	9.2	34.7	7.0
ASEAN/NICs										
Brunei	1989	100.0	51.6	18.5	31.8	1.4	48.4	17.7	29.4	1.2
Hong Kong	1990	100.0	51.1	11.1	36.1	3.8	48.9	10.3	33.6	5.0
Indonesia	1985	100.0	49.8	20.2	28.0	1.6	50.2	19.1	29.3	1.8
Macau	1988	100.0	51.5	11.2	37.9	2.4	48.5	10.6	34.4	3.5
Malaysia [a]	1990	100.0	50.3	18.9	29.7	1.7	49.7	18.0	29.6	2.0
Philippines	1990	100.0	50.2	19.8	28.9	1.6	49.8	18.9	29.0	1.9
Singapore	1989	100.0	50.9	12.0	36.4	2.5	49.1	11.1	34.9	3.1
South Korea	1989	100.0	50.4	13.4	35.2	1.7	49.6	12.4	34.2	3.0
Taiwan										
Thailand	1989	100.0	50.1	17.2	31.2	1.7	49.9	16.8	31.1	2.1
East/SE Asia										
Cambodia										
China	1987	100.0	51.0	14.9	33.6	2.5	49.0	13.8	32.2	3.0
Laos										
Mongolia										
Myanmar	1987	100.0	49.6	18.6	29.1	1.9	50.4	18.7	29.7	2.0
North Korea										
Vietnam	1989	100.0	48.7	20.1	26.7	1.9	51.3	18.9	29.6	2.9
Australasia										
Australia	1990	100.0	49.9	11.2	34.0	4.8	50.1	10.7	33.0	6.4
New Zealand	1988	100.0	49.5	11.9	33.1	4.4	50.5	11.4	32.8	6.2
Pacific										
American Samoa	1990	100.0	50.4	21.6	27.0	1.8	49.6	19.5	28.0	2.1
Fiji	1986	100.0	50.7	19.6	29.4	1.6	49.3	18.6	29.1	1.6
French Polynesia										
Guam	1980	100.0	52.2	17.8	33.0	1.3	47.8	17.1	29.2	1.5
Kiribati	1978	100.0	49.3	21.0	26.7	1.6	50.7	20.1	28.5	2.1
Nauru										
New Caledonia	1989	100.0	51.2	16.7	32.4	2.1	48.8	16.0	30.5	2.3
Papua New Guinea	1987	100.0	51.8	21.1	29.6	1.1	48.2	20.0	27.1	1.1
Solomon Islands	1986	100.0	51.9	24.7	25.2	2.0	48.1	22.7	24.2	1.3
Tonga	1986	100.0	50.2	21.3	26.9	2.0	49.8	19.8	27.8	2.2
Tuvalu										
Vanuatu	1989	100.0	52.1	23.7	27.1	1.3	47.9	21.9	24.7	1.3
Western Samoa	1981	100.0	51.8	23.4	27.1	1.4	48.2	20.9	25.7	1.6
Middle East										
Bahrain	1990	100.0	57.7	18.0	38.4	1.3	42.3	17.4	23.9	1.1
Egypt	1988	100.0	51.1	20.8	28.9	1.4	48.9	19.7	27.8	1.4
Iran	1986	100.0	51.1	23.2	26.3	1.6	48.9	22.2	25.2	1.5
Iraq	1988	100.0	51.4	22.9	26.9	1.6	48.6	21.7	25.2	1.8
Israel	1989	100.0	49.9	16.3	29.5	4.1	50.1	15.5	29.8	4.9
Jordan	1989	100.0	52.3	25.1	25.9	1.3	47.7	23.1	23.3	1.3
Kuwait	1989	100.0	56.6	18.5	37.4	0.6	43.4	18.1	24.7	0.6
Lebanon										
Oman										
Qatar	1986	100.0	67.2	14.3	52.3	0.6	32.8	13.5	18.9	0.4
Saudi Arabia										
Syria	1990	100.0	51.1	25.5	23.4	2.2	48.9	23.8	23.0	2.2
United Arab Emirates	1977	100.0	71.2	13.8	56.5	0.9	28.8	12.5	15.6	0.7
Yemen	1987	100.0	49.5	24.8	22.1	2.5	50.5	22.7	25.4	2.5

DEMOGRAPHIC ANALYSIS   Table No. 0218 (cont'd)

Population by Age and Sex (% Analysis): Latest Official Estimates

Units: % of total population

	Year	Total all ages, both sexes	Males Total	Males 0-14	Males 15-64	Males 65+	Females Total	Females 0-14	Females 15-64	Females 65+
North Africa										
Algeria	1984	100.0	49.7	23.5	24.4	1.8	50.3	22.6	25.6	2.2
Chad	1978	100.0	51.5	18.8	31.3	1.3	48.5	18.6	28.6	1.3
Djibouti										
Ethiopia	1989	100.0	50.3	25.1	22.7	2.5	49.7	23.2	24.4	2.2
Libya	1984	100.0	51.1	25.2	24.8	1.1	48.9	24.5	14.0	10.5
Mali	1987	100.0	48.9	23.4	23.6	1.9	51.1	22.5	26.7	1.9
Mauritania	1977	100.0	49.2	22.8	24.8	1.6	50.8	21.2	27.4	2.2
Morocco	1982	100.0	50.1	21.5	26.5	2.1	49.9	20.7	27.4	1.8
Niger										
Somalia										
Sudan	1983	100.0	51.0	22.8	26.6	1.7	49.0	21.3	26.4	1.3
Tunisia	1989	100.0	50.7	19.4	28.7	2.6	49.3	18.5	28.5	2.3
West Africa										
Benin	1987	100.0	48.5	23.0	24.3	1.1	51.5	23.5	26.7	1.3
Burkina Faso	1985	100.0	48.1	24.4	21.8	1.9	51.9	23.9	25.8	2.2
Cameroon	1986	100.0	49.9	22.6	25.5	1.7	50.1	22.5	25.6	2.0
Cape Verde	1987	100.0	46.7	22.2	22.4	2.2	53.2	22.1	28.1	3.0
Côte d'Ivoire	1978	100.0	49.9	21.0	27.7	1.2	50.1	22.7	26.1	1.3
Equatorial Guinea	1990	100.0	48.5	21.5	25.3	1.8	51.5	21.1	28.1	2.2
Gabon										
Gambia	1983	100.0	49.7	22.0	25.7	2.0	50.3	21.7	26.8	1.7
Ghana										
Guinea										
Guinea-Bissau	1989	100.0	48.4	21.7	25.0	1.6	51.6	21.5	28.6	1.5
Liberia	1977	100.0	50.5	21.1	27.2	2.2	49.5	19.8	28.2	1.5
Nigeria										
Sao Tomé e Príncipe	1981	100.0	49.7	24.0	23.6	2.1	50.3	22.7	24.8	2.8
Senegal										
Sierra Leone										
Togo										
East/Central Africa										
Angola										
Burundi	1988	100.0	48.7	22.4	24.8	1.5	51.3	22.4	27.1	1.7
Central African Republic	1985	100.0	48.5	21.2	25.6	1.6	51.5	21.5	27.9	2.2
Comoros	1980	100.0	49.9	24.2	23.4	2.2	50.1	23.0	25.1	2.1
Congo	1985	100.0	48.5	22.3	23.0	3.2	51.5	22.3	27.4	1.8
Kenya	1985	100.0	49.8	25.9	22.9	1.0	50.2	25.4	23.7	1.1
Madagascar										
Maldives	1985	100.0	51.9	23.1	27.3	1.6	48.1	22.0	25.1	0.9
Mauritius	1989	100.0	49.7	15.2	32.4	2.1	50.3	14.7	32.6	3.0
Réunion	1988	100.0	49.0	16.0	31.0	2.0	51.0	15.6	32.3	3.1
Rwanda	1978	100.0	48.6	22.7	24.4	1.4	51.4	22.9	27.1	1.4
Seychelles	1989	100.1	50.0	17.9	29.9	2.2	50.1	17.2	28.8	4.2
Tanzania	1985	100.0	48.9	24.0	23.5	1.5	51.1	23.9	25.5	1.7
Uganda										
Zaire	1985	100.0	49.5	23.6	24.7	1.1	50.5	23.0	26.1	1.4
Southern Africa										
Botswana	1990	100.0	48.0	24.3	22.4	1.3	52.0	24.3	25.9	1.9
Lesotho										
Malawi	1987	100.0	48.6	23.9	23.6	1.1	51.4	24.0	25.9	1.4
Mozambique	1987	100.0	48.8	21.8	25.9	1.1	51.2	22.5	27.3	1.5
Namibia										
South Africa	1985	100.0	49.4	17.6	28.8	3.0	50.6	17.5	29.1	4.1
Swaziland	1986	100.0	47.2	23.4	22.2	1.6	52.8	23.9	26.6	2.2
Zambia	1980	100.0	48.9	24.4	23.0	1.5	51.1	24.5	25.3	1.3
Zimbabwe	1987	100.0	49.1	14.1	25.6	9.3	50.9	14.6	26.8	9.5

Source: UN/Euromonitor

Notes: see end of section

POPULATION FORECASTS	Table No. 0219

Population Projections 1990-2025: UN Estimates

Units: '000

	Actual 1990	1995	2000	2005	2010	2015	2020	2025	% growth 1990-2025
North America									
Canada	26,521	27,557	28,488	29,332	30,149	30,885	31,491	31,923	20.4
USA	249,224	258,162	266,096	273,482	280,919	288,247	294,750	299,884	20.3
Regional total	*275,745*	*285,719*	*294,584*	*302,814*	*311,068*	*319,132*	*326,241*	*331,807*	*20.3*
South America									
Argentina	32,322	34,264	36,238	38,235	40,193	42,063	43,837	45,505	40.8
Bolivia	7,314	8,421	9,724	11,195	12,820	14,565	16,401	18,294	150.1
Brazil	150,368	165,083	179,487	193,603	207,454	220,960	233,817	245,809	63.5
Chile	13,173	14,237	15,272	16,246	17,182	18,100	18,973	19,774	50.1
Colombia	32,978	36,182	39,397	42,556	45,645	48,647	51,520	54,196	64.3
Ecuador	10,587	11,934	13,319	14,712	16,083	17,421	18,706	19,923	88.2
French Guiana	98	114	130		160	172	182	188	91.8
Guyana	796	829	891	948	1,005	1,060	1,111	1,156	45.2
Paraguay	4,277	4,893	5,538	6,215	6,928	7,667	8,423	9,182	114.7
Peru	21,550	23,854	26,276	28,702	31,047	33,283	35,390	37,350	73.3
Suriname	422	460	497	530	564	599	633	664	57.3
Uruguay	3,094	3,186	3,274	3,365	3,453	3,535	3,615	3,691	19.3
Venezuela	19,735	22,212	24,715	27,321	30,006	32,712	35,394	37,999	92.5
Regional total	*296,714*	*325,669*	*354,758*	*383,628*	*412,540*	*440,784*	*468,002*	*493,731*	*66.4*
Caribbean									
Anguilla	7	8	8		9	10	10	10	42.9
Antigua	76	77	79		82	85	87	91	19.7
Aruba	60	58	58		58	59	61	63	5.0
Bahamas	253	275	295		334	352	367	381	50.6
Barbados	255	259	265	272	280	287	293	298	16.9
Bermuda	58	60	62		67	69	72	74	27.6
British Virgin Islands	13	14	15		16	17	18	18	38.5
Cayman Islands	25	30	35		44	48	51	53	112.0
Cuba	10,608	11,091	11,504	11,848	12,155	12,467	12,756	12,993	22.5
Dominica	82	85	87		93	97	100	104	26.8
Dominican Republic	7,170	7,915	8,621	9,282	9,902	10,480	11,001	11,447	59.7
Grenada	85	83	83		83	85	87	91	7.1
Guadeloupe	343	354	365	373	380	386	393	397	15.7
Haiti	6,513	7,215	8,003	8,876	9,835	10,882	12,017	13,232	103.2
Jamaica	2,456	2,603	2,735	2,873	3,011	3,146	3,304	3,452	40.6
Martinique	341	352	362	371	378	385	392	398	16.7
Netherlands Antilles	188	195	203		218	226	235	243	29.3
St Kitts	44	44	44		46	47	48	50	13.6
St Lucia	150	164	177		201	212	222	230	53.3
St Vincent/Grenadines	116	122	128		140	146	152	158	36.2
Trinidad and Tobago	1,281	1,376	1,484	1,588	1,687	1,791	1,891	1,983	54.8
Regional total	*30,124*	*32,380*	*34,613*		*39,019*	*41,277*	*43,557*	*45,766*	*51.9*
Central America									
Belize	187	209	230		268	285	299	310	65.8
Costa Rica	3,015	3,374	3,711	4,041	4,366	4,681	4,977	5,250	74.1
El Salvador	5,252	5,943	6,739	7,600	8,491	9,409	10,348	11,299	115.1
Guatemala	9,197	10,621	12,222	13,971	15,827	17,752	19,706	21,668	135.6
Honduras	5,138	5,968	6,846	7,748	8,668	9,606	10,558	11,510	124.0
Mexico	88,598	97,967	107,233	116,302	125,166	133,799	142,135	150,062	69.4
Nicaragua	3,871	4,540	5,261	6,029	6,824	7,631	8,435	9,219	138.2
Panama	2,418	2,659	2,893	3,116	3,325	3,521	3,702	3,864	59.8
Puerto Rico	3,480	3,659	3,836	4,001	4,156	4,304	4,447	4,579	31.6
Regional total	*121,156*	*134,940*	*148,971*	*162,808*	*177,091*	*190,988*	*204,607*	*217,761*	*79.7*
South Asia									
Afghanistan	16,557	23,122	26,511	29,589	32,422	35,221	37,934	40,475	144.5
Bangladesh	115,593	132,219	150,589	170,138	188,196	204,631	220,119	234,987	103.3
Bhutan	1,516	1,698	1,906	2,137	2,388	2,634	2,861	3,070	102.5
India	853,094	946,716	1,041,543	1,134,690	1,223,483	1,304,001	1,371,767	1,442,386	69.1
Nepal	19,143	21,521	24,084	26,575	28,900	31,055	33,080	34,973	82.7
Pakistan	122,626	141,522	162,409	183,640	205,496	227,324	248,116	267,112	117.8
Sri Lanka	17,217	18,338	19,416	20,434	21,520	22,625	23,656	24,572	42.7
Regional total	*1,145,746*	*1,285,136*	*1,426,458*	*1,567,203*	*1,702,405*	*1,827,491*	*1,937,533*	*2,047,575*	*78.7*

POPULATION FORECASTS

Table No. 0219 (cont'd)

Population Projections 1990-2025: UN Estimates

Units: '000

	Actual 1990	1995	2000	2005	2010	2015	2020	2025	% growth 1990-2025
Japan									
Japan	123,460	125,904	128,470	130,468	131,035	130,348	129,029	127,496	3.3
Regional total	*123,460*	*125,904*	*128,470*	*130,468*	*131,035*	*130,348*	*129,029*	*127,496*	*3.3*
ASEAN/NICs									
Brunei	266	301	333		377	390	399	405	52.3
Hong Kong	5,851	6,108	6,336	6,443	6,505	6,526	6,510	6,456	10.3
Indonesia	184,283	201,797	218,661	233,389	246,680	260,089	273,349	285,913	55.1
Macau	479	571	656		780	810	820	820	71.2
Malaysia	17,891	20,037	21,983	23,674	25,169	26,813	28,503	30,116	68.3
Philippines	62,413	69,935	77,473	84,922	92,095	99,301	105,384	111,509	78.7
Singapore	2,723	2,874	2,997	3,094	3,170	3,237	3,290	3,319	21.9
South Korea	42,793	44,655	46,403	48,106	49,459	50,480	51,178	51,631	20.7
Taiwan									
Thailand	55,702	59,605	63,670	67,724	71,594	75,065	78,118	80,911	45.3
Regional total	*372,401*	*405,883*	*438,512*	*467,352*	*495,829*	*522,711*	*547,551*	*571,080*	*53.4*
East/SE Asia									
Cambodia	8,246	9,205	10,046	10,784	11,539	12,405	13,266	13,989	69.6
China	1,139,060	1,222,562	1,299,180	1,354,235	1,395,328	1,435,683	1,476,852	1,512,585	32.8
Laos	4,139	4,788	5,463	6,163	6,838	7,462	8,046	8,600	107.8
Mongolia	2,190	2,503	2,847	3,215	3,606	4,012	4,423	4,829	120.5
Myanmar	41,675	46,275	51,129	55,950	60,567	64,864	68,743	72,619	74.3
North Korea	21,773	23,966	26,117	27,896	29,325	30,640	31,929	33,063	51.9
Vietnam	66,693	74,475	82,427	90,171	97,396	103,906	110,638	117,491	76.2
Regional total	*1,283,776*	*1,383,774*	*1,477,209*	*1,548,414*	*1,604,599*	*1,658,972*	*1,713,897*	*1,763,176*	*37.3*
Australasia									
Australia [a]	16,873	17,901	18,855	19,769	20,649	21,506	22,309	23,038	36.5
New Zealand	3,392	3,534	3,662	3,775	3,874	3,967	4,051	4,117	21.4
Regional total	*20,265*	*21,435*	*22,517*	*23,544*	*24,523*	*25,473*	*26,360*	*27,155*	*34.0*
Pacific									
American Samoa	38	38	39		39	39	39	39	2.6
Fiji	764	824	883	942	994	1,040	1,083	1,121	46.7
French Polynesia	206	237	268		323	346	365	378	83.5
Guam	118	123	128		135	136	137	137	16.1
Kiribati	66	69	72		78	80	80	80	21.2
Nauru	9	10	10		12	12	12	13	44.4
New Caledonia	167	182	195		217	226	233	238	42.5
Papua New Guinea	3,874	4,341	4,845	5,346	5,846	6,342	6,828	7,291	88.2
Solomon Islands	320	374	429		551	615	680	743	132.2
Tonga	95	94	92		91	90	89	89	-6.3
Tuvalu	9	10	11		12	12	12	12	33.3
Vanuatu	158	182	206		257	282	307	331	109.5
Western Samoa	168	171	171		172	172	172	172	2.4
Regional total	*5,992*	*6,655*	*7,349*		*8,727*	*9,392*	*10,037*	*10,644*	*77.6*
Middle East									
Bahrain	516	602	683	759	827	888	943	998	93.4
Egypt	52,426	58,388	64,210	70,099	75,746	81,050	85,768	90,355	72.3
Iran	54,607	60,390	68,759	78,064	87,776	97,194	105,966	113,831	108.5
Iraq	18,920	22,411	26,339	30,677	35,323	40,175	45,080	49,992	164.2
Israel	4,600	4,958	5,321	5,676	6,011	6,318	6,620	6,908	50.2
Jordan	4,009	4,738	5,558	6,412	7,284	8,160	9,042	9,879	146.4
Kuwait	2,039	2,347	2,639	2,907	3,153	3,384	3,593	3,775	85.1
Lebanon	2,701	3,014	3,327	3,620	3,898	4,176	4,446	4,703	74.1
Oman	1,502	1,811	2,176	2,608	3,106	3,649	4,202	4,754	216.5
Qatar	368	436	499	564	631	704	781	860	133.7
Saudi Arabia	14,134	17,124	20,697	24,868	29,557	34,562	39,650	44,752	216.6
Syria	12,530	15,001	17,826	20,988	24,320	27,668	30,924	34,082	172.0
United Arab Emirates	1,589	1,771	1,951	2,114	2,283	2,435	2,559	2,651	66.8
Yemen	9,196	11,065	13,219		18,522	21,677	24,953	28,171	206.3
Regional total	*179,137*	*204,056*	*233,204*	*249,356*	*298,437*	*332,040*	*364,527*	*395,711*	*120.9*

POPULATION FORECASTS

Table No. 0219 (cont'd)

Population Projections 1990-2025: UN Estimates

Units: '000

	Actual 1990	1995	2000	2005	2010	2015	2020	2025	% growth 1990-2025
North Africa									
Algeria	24,960	28,704	32,904	37,286	41,510	45,279	48,484	51,950	108.1
Chad	5,678	6,447	7,337	8,352	9,491	10,728	12,013	13,245	133.3
Djibouti	409	474	552	644	748	862	979	1,094	167.5
Ethiopia	49,240	57,140	66,364	76,961	88,889	101,753	114,313	126,618	157.1
Libya	4,545	5,446	6,500	7,695	8,977	10,276	11,567	12,841	182.5
Mali	9,214	10,799	12,685	14,885	17,350	19,918	22,439	24,774	168.9
Mauritania	2,024	2,335	2,702	3,129	3,612	4,129	4,642	5,119	152.9
Morocco	25,061	28,301	31,559	34,648	37,586	40,408	43,022	45,647	82.1
Niger	7,731	9,104	10,752	12,694	14,884	17,167	19,406	21,482	177.9
Somalia	7,497	8,441	9,736	11,312	13,114	15,035	16,905	18,701	149.4
Sudan	25,203	29,128	33,625	38,647	44,017	49,416	54,627	59,605	136.5
Tunisia	8,180	9,076	9,924	10,702	11,464	12,188	12,925	13,630	66.6
Regional total	*169,742*	*195,395*	*224,640*	*256,955*	*291,642*	*327,159*	*361,322*	*394,706*	*132.5*
West Africa									
Benin	4,630	5,421	6,369	7,486	8,745	10,065	11,369	12,587	171.9
Burkina Faso	8,996	10,396	12,092	14,080	16,349	18,822	21,327	23,710	163.6
Cameroon	11,833	14,037	16,701	19,897	23,665	27,893	32,264	36,547	208.9
Cape Verde	370	438	515	595	676	757	841	922	149.2
Côte d'Ivoire	11,997	14,535	17,600	21,218	25,503	30,069	34,776	39,334	227.9
Equatorial Guinea	352	400	455	519	592	671	752	828	135.2
Gabon	1,172	1,382	1,612	1,827	2,052	2,309	2,594	2,875	145.3
Gambia	861	984	1,119	1,271	1,434	1,593	1,736	1,864	116.5
Ghana	15,028	17,608	20,564	23,845	26,931	29,884	32,708	35,442	135.8
Guinea	5,755	6,700	7,830	9,162	10,667	12,252	13,820	15,273	165.4
Guinea-Bissau	964	1,073	1,197	1,338	1,491	1,649	1,791	1,918	99.0
Liberia	2,575	3,032	3,575	4,207	4,921	5,689	6,477	7,245	181.4
Nigeria	108,542	127,694	149,621	174,307	201,266	228,753	255,393	280,890	158.8
Sao Tomé e Príncipe	121	135	151		184	201	219	235	94.2
Senegal	7,327	8,423	9,716	11,172	12,730	14,269	15,685	16,988	131.9
Sierra Leone	4,151	4,740	5,437	6,250	7,172	8,161	9,139	10,045	142.0
Togo	3,531	4,138	4,861	5,711	6,687	7,750	8,821	9,842	178.7
Regional total	*188,205*	*221,136*	*259,415*	*302,885*	*351,065*	*400,787*	*449,712*	*496,545*	*163.8*
East/Central Africa									
Angola	10,020	11,531	13,295	15,317	17,561	20,004	22,438	24,731	146.8
Burundi	5,472	6,362	7,358	8,469	9,657	10,841	11,950	12,976	137.1
Central African Republic	3,039	3,511	4,074	4,740	5,497	6,325	7,154	7,947	161.5
Comoros	550	658	789	945	1,123	1,315	1,510	1,697	208.5
Congo	2,271	2,678	3,167	3,746	4,406	5,130	5,860	6,568	189.2
Kenya	24,031	28,978	35,060	42,389	50,905	60,071	69,799	79,113	229.2
Madagascar	12,004	14,113	16,627	19,529	22,827	26,476	30,272	34,014	183.4
Maldives	215	248	283		350	382	409	432	100.9
Mauritius	1,082	1,142	1,201	1,258	1,309	1,354	1,391	1,419	31.1
Réunion	598	647	692	735	777	817	855	889	48.7
Rwanda	7,237	8,602	10,200	11,973	13,791	15,511	17,196	18,847	160.4
Seychelles	69	72	75		80	82	83	84	21.7
Tanzania	27,318	32,971	39,639	47,460	56,333	65,845	75,485	84,917	210.8
Uganda	18,794	22,666	26,958	31,730	36,982	42,561	48,101	53,144	182.8
Zaire	35,568	41,813	49,190	57,780	67,509	78,135	88,972	99,366	179.4
Regional total	*148,268*	*175,992*	*208,608*	*246,071*	*289,107*	*334,849*	*381,475*	*426,144*	*187.4*
Southern Africa									
Botswana	1,304	1,549	1,822	2,124	2,451	2,779	3,095	3,397	160.5
Lesotho	1,774	2,053	2,370	2,731	3,138	3,579	4,013	4,427	149.5
Malawi	8,754	10,494	12,458	14,654	17,104	19,701	22,278	24,730	182.5
Mozambique	15,656	17,922	20,493	23,365	26,456	29,592	32,593	35,416	126.2
Namibia	1,781	2,079	2,437	2,847	3,303	3,776	4,245	4,698	163.8
South Africa	35,282	39,348	43,666	48,139	52,662	57,150	61,446	65,363	85.3
Swaziland	788	943	1,121	1,326	1,554	1,790	2,023	2,249	185.4
Zambia	8,452	10,222	12,267	14,632	17,328	20,264	23,286	26,260	210.7
Zimbabwe	9,709	11,340	13,123	15,012	16,974	18,951	20,870	22,616	132.9
Regional total	*83,500*	*95,950*	*109,757*	*124,830*	*140,970*	*157,582*	*173,849*	*189,156*	*126.5*

Source: UN, World Population Prospects
Notes: see end of section

POPULATION FORECASTS

Population Projections by Age and Sex 2000: National and UN Estimates

Units: '000

	Total	Male	Female	% 0-14	% 15-64	% 65+
North America						
Canada	28,488	14,094	14,394	18.7	68.6	12.7
USA	266,096	129,992	136,104	20.2	67.0	12.8
Regional total	*294,584*	*144,086*	*150,498*			
South America						
Argentina	36,238	17,904	18,334	27.3	62.9	9.8
Bolivia	9,724	4,800	4,924	43.5	53.3	3.2
Brazil	179,487	89,323	90,164	31.7	62.9	5.4
Chile	15,272	7,544	7,728	29.4	63.9	6.7
Colombia	39,397	19,516	19,881	32.3	63.2	4.5
Ecuador	13,319	6,697	6,622	35.8	60.0	4.2
French Guiana						
Guyana	891	441	450	29.3	66.4	4.3
Paraguay	5,538	2,802	2,736	38.2	58.2	3.6
Peru	26,276	13,220	13,055	33.6	61.8	4.6
Suriname	497	247	250	30.9	64.0	5.1
Uruguay	3,274	1,595	1,679	23.9	63.4	12.7
Venezuela	24,715	12,426	12,289	34.5	61.2	4.3
Regional total	*354,628*	*176,515*	*178,112*			
Caribbean						
Anguilla						
Antigua						
Aruba						
Bahamas						
Barbados	265	128	137	22.2	66.7	11.1
Bermuda						
British Virgin Islands						
Cayman Islands						
Cuba	11,504	5,769	5,735	23.3	67.3	9.4
Dominica [a]	481	237	244			
Dominican Republic	8,621	4,382	4,239	33.9	59.2	6.9
Grenada [a]						
Guadeloupe	365	178	187	27.4	62.8	9.8
Haiti	8,003	3,937	4,066	39.8	56.4	3.8
Jamaica	2,735	1,368	1,368	28.6	65.0	6.4
Martinique	362	176	186	25.3	63.4	11.3
Netherlands Antilles						
St Kitts						
St Lucia [a]						
St Vincent/Grenadines [a]						
Trinidad and Tobago	1,484	737	746	30.5	64.0	5.5
Regional total	*33,820*	*16,912*	*16,908*			
Central America						
Belize						
Costa Rica	3,711	1,875	1,836	32.3	62.6	5.1
El Salvador	6,739	3,309	3,430	41.5	54.3	4.2
Guatemala	12,222	6,167	6,055	42.9	53.4	3.7
Honduras	6,845	3,451	3,396	41.2	55.3	3.5
Mexico	107,233	53,341	53,892	32.8	62.6	4.6
Nicaragua	5,261	2,646	2,615	42.7	54.2	3.1
Panama	2,893	1,466	1,427	31.5	63.1	5.4
Puerto Rico	3,836	1,860	1,976	24.6	64.3	11.1
Regional total	*148,740*	*74,115*	*74,627*			
South Asia						
Afghanistan	26,511	13,561	12,950	42.7	54.6	2.7
Bangladesh	150,589	77,523	73,066	40.6	56.5	2.9
Bhutan	1,906	988	918	40.0	56.5	3.5
India	1,041,543	536,864	504,679	34.5	60.4	5.1
Nepal	24,084	12,383	11,701	39.6	57.0	3.4
Pakistan	162,409	84,272	78,137	43.3	53.8	2.9
Sri Lanka	19,416	9,645	9,771	27.3	66.2	6.5
Regional total	*1,426,458*	*735,236*	*691,222*			

POPULATION FORECASTS — Table No. 0220 (cont'd)

Population Projections by Age and Sex 2000: National and UN Estimates

Units: '000

	Total	Male	Female	% 0-14	% 15-64	% 65+
Japan						
Japan	128,470	63,238	65,232	16.9	67.2	15.9
Regional total	*128,470*	*63,238*	*65,232*			
ASEAN/NICs						
Brunei						
Hong Kong	6,336	3,271	3,066	17.6	71.2	11.2
Indonesia	218,661	109,073	109,588	31.3	63.6	5.1
Macau						
Malaysia	21,983	11,096	10,887	34.3	61.5	4.2
Philippines	77,473	38,978	38,494	36.2	60.1	3.7
Singapore	2,997	1,520	1,477	22.2	70.6	7.2
South Korea	46,403	23,375	23,028	21.3	72.3	6.4
Taiwan						
Thailand	63,670	31,944	31,726	26.5	68.5	5.0
Regional total	*437,523*	*219,257*	*218,266*			
East/SE Asia						
Cambodia	10,046	5,019	5,027	38.6	57.9	3.5
China	1,299,180	666,624	632,556	26.6	66.4	7.0
Laos	5,463	2,747	2,716	44.0	53.0	3.0
Mongolia	2,847	1,438	1,409	39.2	57.3	3.5
Myanmar	51,129	25,505	25,624	34.9	60.4	4.7
North Korea	26,117	12,903	13,214	30.0	65.0	5.0
Vietnam	82,427	40,698	41,729	35.5	60.0	4.5
Regional total	*1,477,209*	*754,934*	*722,275*			
Australasia						
Australia	18,855	9,421	9,434	20.6	67.7	11.7
New Zealand	3,820	1,894	1,926	22.0	66.8	11.2
Regional total	*22,675*	*11,315*	*11,360*			
Pacific						
American Samoa						
Fiji	883	445	438	30.9	65.0	4.1
French Polynesia						
Guam						
Kiribati						
Nauru						
New Caledonia						
Papua New Guinea	4,845	2,500	2,345	39.1	58.3	2.6
Solomon Islands						
Tonga						
Tuvalu						
Vanuatu						
Western Samoa						
Regional total	*5,728*	*2,945*	*2,783*			
Middle East						
Bahrain	683	404	279	29.6	68.5	1.9
Egypt	64,210	32,660	31,550	34.6	61.0	4.4
Iran	68,759	35,150	33,609	38.6	57.0	4.4
Iraq	26,339	13,413	12,926	44.1	52.9	3.0
Israel	5,321	2,668	2,653	28.1	63.3	8.6
Jordan	5,558	2,840	2,718	43.2	53.9	2.9
Kuwait	2,639	1,453	1,186	31.2	66.4	2.4
Lebanon	3,327	1,630	1,697	35.7	58.8	5.5
Oman	2,176	1,127	1,049	47.1	50.0	2.9
Qatar	499	302	197	34.4	62.5	3.1
Saudi Arabia	20,697	11,084	9,612	45.7	51.7	2.6
Syria	17,826	9,002	8,824	46.5	50.9	2.6
United Arab Emirates	1,951	1,261	690	26.5	70.4	3.1
Yemen	13,219	6,594	6,626	45.6	51.5	2.9
Regional total	*233,204*	*119,588*	*113,616*			

POPULATION FORECASTS   Table No. 0220 (cont'd)

Population Projections by Age and Sex 2000: National and UN Estimates

Units: '000

	Total	Male	Female	% 0-14	% 15-64	% 65+
North Africa						
Algeria	32,904	16,508	16,396	39.3	57.4	3.3
Chad	7,337	3,628	3,709	43.3	53.2	3.5
Djibouti	552	277	275	45.5	51.7	2.8
Ethiopia	66,364	33,100	33,264	46.3	50.9	2.8
Libya	6,500	3,365	3,135	45.6	51.6	2.8
Mali	12,685	6,256	6,429	47.8	49.7	2.5
Mauritania	2,702	1,337	1,365	45.2	51.7	3.1
Morocco	31,559	15,814	15,746	36.9	59.1	4.0
Niger	10,752	5,319	5,433	48.4	49.2	2.4
Somalia	9,736	4,746	4,990	46.2	51.1	2.7
Sudan	33,625	16,921	16,704	44.2	52.8	3.0
Tunisia	9,924	5,015	4,909	33.0	62.2	4.8
Regional total	*224,640.0*	*112,286*	*112,355*			
West Africa						
Benin	6,369	3,154	3,216	47.3	50.0	2.7
Burkina Faso	12,092	5,997	6,094	45.0	51.9	3.1
Cameroon	16,701	8,311	8,390	47.9	48.9	3.2
Cape Verde	515	247	268	44.8	51.5	3.7
Côte d'Ivoire	17,600	8,907	8,693	49.3	48.0	2.7
Equatorial Guinea	455	225	230	43.5	52.6	3.9
Gabon	1,612	799	813	41.0	53.5	5.5
Gambia	1,119	552	567	44.0	52.8	3.2
Ghana	20,564	10,222	10,342	45.1	52.0	2.9
Guinea	7,830	3,940	3,890	47.3	50.1	2.6
Guinea-Bissau	1,197	590	607	41.8	54.2	4.0
Liberia	3,575	1,805	1,770	46.1	50.2	3.7
Nigeria	149,621	74,243	75,378	46.7	50.7	2.6
Sao Tomé e Príncipe						
Senegal	9,716	4,866	4,850	44.3	52.8	2.9
Sierra Leone	5,437	2,679	2,758	45.3	51.6	3.1
Togo	4,861	2,411	2,450	45.8	51.1	3.1
Regional total	*259,264.0*	*128,948*	*130,316*			
East/Central Africa						
Angola	13,295	6,570	6,725	45.3	51.6	3.1
Burundi	7,358	3,617	3,741	45.8	51.5	2.7
Central African Republic	4,074	1,983	2,091	45.5	50.9	3.6
Comoros	789	401	388	48.1	49.5	2.4
Congo	3,167	1,553	1,614	46.9	50.0	3.1
Kenya	35,060	17,554	17,506	48.4	48.9	2.7
Madagascar	16,627	8,264	8,363	45.7	51.4	2.9
Maldives						
Mauritius	1,201	600	601	23.4	70.9	5.7
Réunion	692	336	356	28.0	66.1	5.9
Rwanda	10,200	5,047	5,153	48.5	49.1	2.4
Seychelles						
Tanzania	39,639	19,676	19,963	49.4	48.2	2.4
Uganda	26,958	13,404	13,554	49.4	48.2	2.4
Zaire	49,190	24,420	24,770	46.0	51.3	2.7
Regional total	*208,250.0*	*103,425*	*104,825*			
Southern Africa						
Botswana	1,822	883	939	46.9	50.2	2.9
Lesotho	2,370	1,141	1,229	43.0	53.2	3.8
Malawi	12,458	6,119	6,339	48.7	48.7	2.6
Mozambique	20,493	10,133	10,360	43.9	52.8	3.3
Namibia	2,437	1,217	1,220	45.0	51.6	3.4
South Africa	43,666	21,694	21,972	35.6	59.9	4.5
Swaziland	1,121	556	566	47.6	49.5	2.9
Zambia	12,267	6,091	6,176	49.6	48.1	2.3
Zimbabwe	13,123	6,508	6,615	43.1	54.0	2.9
Regional total	*109,757.0*	*54,342*	*55,416*			

Source: UN, World Population Prospects (1990 estimates)
Notes: see end of section

| POPULATION FORECASTS | | | | | | | Table No. 0221 |

Projected Population Density 1990-2025: UN Estimates

Units: Persons per sq km

	1990	1995	2000	2010	2015	2020	2025	% growth 1990-2025
North America								
Canada	3	3	3	3	3	3	3	20.4
USA	27	28	28	30	31	31	32	20.3
South America								
Argentina	12	12	13	14	15	16	16	40.8
Bolivia	7	8	9	12	13	15	17	150.1
Brazil	18	19	21	24	26	27	29	63.5
Chile	18	19	20	23	24	25	26	50.1
Colombia	29	32	35	40	43	45	48	64.3
Ecuador	40	45	50	61	66	71	75	88.2
French Guiana	1	1	1	2	2	2	2	91.8
Guyana	4	4	4	5	5	5	5	45.2
Paraguay	11	12	14	17	19	21	23	114.7
Peru	17	19	20	24	26	28	29	73.3
Suriname	3	3	3	3	4	4	4	57.3
Uruguay	17	17	18	18	19	19	20	19.3
Venezuela	22	24	27	33	36	39	42	92.5
Caribbean								
Anguilla	77	88	88	99	110	110	110	42.9
Antigua	172	174	179	186	192	197	206	19.7
Aruba	311	301	301	301	306	316	326	5.0
Bahamas	18	20	21	24	25	26	27	50.6
Barbados	593	602	616	651	667	681	693	16.9
Bermuda	1,074	1,111	1,148	1,241	1,278	1,333	1,370	27.6
British Virgin Islands	85	92	98	105	111	118	118	38.5
Cayman Islands	97	116	135	170	185	197	205	112.0
Cuba	93	97	100	106	109	111	113	22.5
Dominica	109	113	116	124	129	133	138	26.8
Dominican Republic	148	163	178	204	216	227	236	59.7
Grenada	246	241	241	241	246	252	264	7.1
Guadeloupe	193	199	205	213	217	221	223	15.7
Haiti	235	260	288	354	392	433	477	103.2
Jamaica	215	228	239	264	275	289	302	40.6
Martinique	316	326	335	350	357	363	369	16.7
Netherlands Antilles	189	196	204	220	228	237	245	29.3
St Kitts	169	169	169	176	180	184	192	13.6
St Lucia	244	266	287	326	344	360	373	53.3
St Vincent/Grenadines	298	314	329	360	375	391	406	36.2
Trinidad and Tobago	250	268	289	329	349	369	387	54.8
Central America								
Belize	8	9	10	12	12	13	13	65.8
Costa Rica	59	66	73	86	92	98	103	74.1
El Salvador	245	278	315	397	440	484	528	115.1
Guatemala	84	98	112	145	163	181	199	135.6
Honduras	46	53	61	77	86	94	103	124.0
Mexico	45	50	54	63	68	72	76	69.4
Nicaragua	26	31	36	46	52	57	62	138.2
Panama	31	34	37	42	45	47	49	59.8
Puerto Rico	388	408	428	464	480	496	511	31.6
South Asia								
Afghanistan	26	36	42	51	55	60	64	144.5
Bangladesh	803	918	1,046	1,307	1,421	1,529	1,632	103.3
Bhutan	33	36	41	51	56	61	66	102.5
India	269	299	329	386	412	433	455	69.1
Nepal	135	152	170	204	220	234	247	82.7
Pakistan	153	176	202	256	283	309	332	117.8
Sri Lanka	262	280	296	328	345	361	375	42.7

POPULATION FORECASTS

Projected Population Density 1990-2025: UN Estimates

Units: Persons per sq km

	1990	1995	2000	2010	2015	2020	2025	% growth 1990-2025
Japan								
Japan	334	341	347	354	353	349	345	3.3
ASEAN/NICs								
Brunei	46	52	58	65	68	69	70	52.3
Hong Kong	5,509	5,751	5,966	6,125	6,145	6,130	6,079	10.3
Indonesia	96	105	114	129	136	142	149	55.1
Macau	29,938	35,688	41,000	48,750	50,625	51,250	51,250	71.2
Malaysia	54	60	66	76	81	86	90	68.3
Philippines	208	233	258	307	331	351	372	78.7
Singapore	4,420	4,666	4,865	5,146	5,255	5,341	5,388	21.9
South Korea	435	454	471	502	513	520	524	20.7
Taiwan								
Thailand	108	116	124	139	146	152	157	45.3
East/SE Asia								
Cambodia	46	51	56	64	69	73	77	69.6
China	119	127	135	145	150	154	158	32.8
Laos	17	20	23	29	32	34	36	107.8
Mongolia	1	2	2	2	3	3	3	120.5
Myanmar	61	68	75	89	96	101	107	74.3
North Korea	178	196	214	240	251	261	270	51.9
Vietnam	202	226	250	296	315	336	357	76.2
Australasia								
Australia [a]	2	2	2	3	3	3	3	36.5
New Zealand	13	13	14	15	15	15	16	21.4
Pacific								
American Samoa	193	193	198	198	198	198	198	2.6
Fiji	42	45	48	54	57	59	61	46.7
French Polynesia	52	60	68	82	88	93	96	83.5
Guam	262	273	284	300	302	304	304	16.1
Kiribati	96	101	105	114	117	117	117	21.2
Nauru	429	476	476	571	571	571	619	44.4
New Caledonia	9	10	10	11	12	12	12	42.5
Papua New Guinea	8	9	10	13	14	15	16	88.2
Solomon Islands	11	13	14	18	21	23	25	132.2
Tonga	136	134	132	130	129	127	127	-6.3
Tuvalu	360	400	440	480	480	480	480	33.3
Vanuatu	11	12	14	17	19	21	22	109.5
Western Samoa	59	60	60	61	61	61	61	2.4
Middle East								
Bahrain	781	911	1,033	1,251	1,343	1,427	1,510	93.4
Egypt	53	59	64	76	81	86	91	72.3
Iran	33	37	42	53	59	64	69	108.5
Iraq	43	51	60	81	92	103	114	164.2
Israel	221	239	256	289	304	319	333	50.2
Jordan	44	52	61	80	90	100	109	146.4
Kuwait	84	97	109	130	139	148	155	85.1
Lebanon	260	290	320	375	402	428	452	74.1
Oman	6	7	8	11	13	15	17	216.5
Qatar	32	38	44	55	62	68	75	133.7
Saudi Arabia	6	7	9	12	14	17	19	216.6
Syria	67	81	96	131	149	167	184	172.0
United Arab Emirates	21	24	26	30	32	34	35	66.8
Yemen	17	21	25	35	41	47	53	206.3

POPULATION FORECASTS

Table No. 0221 (cont'd)

Projected Population Density 1990-2025: UN Estimates

Units: Persons per sq km

	1990	1995	2000	2010	2015	2020	2025	% growth 1990-2025
North Africa								
Algeria	10	12	14	17	19	20	22	108.1
Chad	4	5	6	7	8	9	10	133.3
Djibouti	18	21	24	33	37	43	48	167.5
Ethiopia	48	56	65	87	99	112	124	157.1
Libya	3	3	4	5	6	7	7	182.5
Mali	7	9	10	14	16	18	20	168.9
Mauritania	2	2	3	4	4	5	5	152.9
Morocco	55	62	69	82	88	94	100	82.1
Niger	7	8	9	13	14	16	18	177.9
Somalia	12	13	15	21	24	27	30	149.4
Sudan	10	12	13	18	20	22	24	136.5
Tunisia	50	55	60	70	74	79	83	66.6
West Africa								
Benin	41	48	57	78	89	101	112	171.9
Burkina Faso	33	38	44	60	69	78	86	163.6
Cameroon	25	30	36	51	60	69	79	208.9
Cape Verde	92	109	128	168	188	208	229	149.2
Côte d'Ivoire	37	45	55	79	93	108	122	227.9
Equatorial Guinea	13	14	16	21	24	27	30	135.2
Gabon		1	1	1	1	1	1	145.3
Gambia	81	92	105	134	149	162	174	116.5
Ghana	63	74	86	113	125	137	149	135.8
Guinea	23	27	32	43	50	56	62	165.4
Guinea-Bissau	27	30	33	41	46	50	53	99.0
Liberia	23	27	32	44	51	58	65	181.4
Nigeria	117	138	162	218	248	276	304	158.8
Sao Tomé e Príncipe	126	140	157	191	209	227	244	94.2
Senegal	37	43	49	65	73	80	86	131.9
Sierra Leone	57	66	75	99	113	126	139	142.0
Togo	62	73	86	118	136	155	173	178.7
East/Central Africa								
Angola	8	9	11	14	16	18	20	146.8
Burundi	197	229	264	347	389	429	466	137.1
Central African Republic	5	6	7	9	10	11	13	161.5
Comoros	296	354	424	604	707	812	912	208.5
Congo	7	8	9	13	15	17	19	189.2
Kenya	41	50	60	87	103	120	136	229.2
Madagascar	20	24	28	38	45	51	57	183.4
Maldives	721	832	950	1,174	1,282	1,372	1,450	100.9
Mauritius	580	612	644	702	726	746	761	31.1
Réunion	238	258	276	310	325	341	354	48.7
Rwanda	275	327	387	524	589	653	716	160.4
Seychelles	171	178	186	198	203	205	208	21.7
Tanzania	29	35	42	60	70	80	90	210.8
Uganda	79	96	114	156	180	203	225	182.8
Zaire	15	18	21	29	33	38	42	179.4
Southern Africa								
Botswana	2	3	3	4	5	5	6	160.5
Lesotho	58	68	78	103	118	132	146	149.5
Malawi	93	112	132	182	209	237	263	182.5
Mozambique	20	23	26	34	38	42	45	126.2
Namibia	2	3	3	4	5	5	6	163.8
South Africa	30	33	37	44	48	52	55	85.3
Swaziland	45	54	65	89	103	116	130	185.4
Zambia	11	14	16	23	27	31	35	210.7
Zimbabwe	25	29	34	43	49	53	58	132.9

Source: UN, World Population Prospects/Euromonitor
Notes: see end of section

Notes to Tables in Section Two

Table 0201
a De jure
b New series starting 1980
c New series starting 1978
d New series starting 1985
e New series starting 1986
f New series starting 1982
g New series starting 1983
h New series starting 1984
i New series starting 1981
j New series starting 1992
k New series starting 1991
l From reunification in 1990, Yemen Arab Republic includes the former Yemen PDR
m New series starting 1979

Table 0202
a De jure
b Data adjusted for underenumeration at latest census
c New series starting in year(s) specified
d Excludes Indian jungle population
e UN estimates for year(s) specified
f All figures are UN estimates
g Estimates not revised to take account of 1990 census
h Excludes Vietnamese immigrants
i Estimates not revised to take account of 1991 census

Table 0203 Estimated level of underenumeration given where appropriate
a De jure
b Data exclude armed forces overseas
c Provisional
d Excludes Indian jungle population
e Excludes adjustment for underenumeration
f Excludes nomadic Indians
g Rural underenumeration figure (urban estimate: 5%)
h Includes transients and Vietnamese refugees
i Includes foreign residents
j Includes islands of Huon, Chesterfield, Loyalty and Walpole
k Includes US armed forces
l Includes Jerusalem and Israeli residents of occupied territories
m Excludes Jordanian territory occupied by Israeli forces
n No census has been held in Oman
o Yemen Arab Republic - 9,274,000 at 1/2/86; Yemen PDR - 2,345,000 at 29/3/88
p Excludes underenumeration at unspecified rate
q Excludes Agalega and St Brandon
r Excludes Bophuthatswana, Transkei and Venda

Table 0204
a Figures include 90% or more of occurrences
b Figures include less than 90% of occurrences
c New series starting 1983
d Figures of unknown completeness

e 1991 data are provisional
f New series starting 1986
g New series starting 1979

Table 0205
a Figures include 90% or more of occurrences
b Figures include less than 90% of occurrences
c Figures of unknown quality
d Excluding canal zone prior to 1980

Table 0206
a Figures include more than 90% of occurrences
b New series starting 1987
c Figures include less than 90% of occurrences

Table 0207
a Figures include 90% or more of occurrences
b Figures include under 90% of occurrences

Table 0208 Deaths of infants of under one year of age only. Foetal deaths are excluded
a UN estimates 1975-1980
b UN estimates 1980-1985
c UN estimates 1985-1990
d Data for 1987 are from UN African population study

Table 0209
a Figures include more than 90% of occurrences
b Figures include less than 90% of occurrences
c Figures of unknown quality
d Peninsular Malaysia only

Table 0210
a Figures include 90% or more of occurrences
b Figures of unknown quality
c Civil registered divorces only
d Figures include less than 90% of occurrences

Table 0212
a Estimates not revised to take account of 1990 census
b Estimates not revised to take account of 1991 census

Table 0213
a Columns b and c refer to 1983
b Columns b and c refer to 1986
c Columns b and c refer to 1988
d Columns b and c refer to 1982
e Columns b and c refer to 1984
f Columns b and c refer to 1985
g Columns b and c refer to 1979
h Columns b and c refer to 1987
i Peninsular Malaysia only (except urban population figures)
j Columns b and c refer to 1981
k YAR only

l Census data, not adjusted for
underenumeration; data exclude the tribal
homelands

m Columns b and c refer to 1980

Table 0217 Because of rounding by census-taking
agencies totals are not always the sum of the
parts

a Peninsular Malaysia only

b "15 to 64 years" gives data for 15 to 59
years, "65 years and over" gives data for 60
years and over

c Excluding tribal homelands

Table 0218 Because of rounding by census-taking
agencies totals are not always the sum of the
parts

a Peninsular Malaysia only

b "15 to 64 years" gives data for 15 to 59
years, "65 years and over" gives data for 60
years and over

c Excluding tribal homelands

Table 0219 a Includes Christmas Isles,
Cocos (Keeling) Islands and Norfolk Island

Table 0220 a Data for Dominica include Grenada, St
Lucia and St Vincent and the Grenadines

Table 0221 a Includes Christmas Isles,
Cocos (Keeling) Islands and Norfolk Island

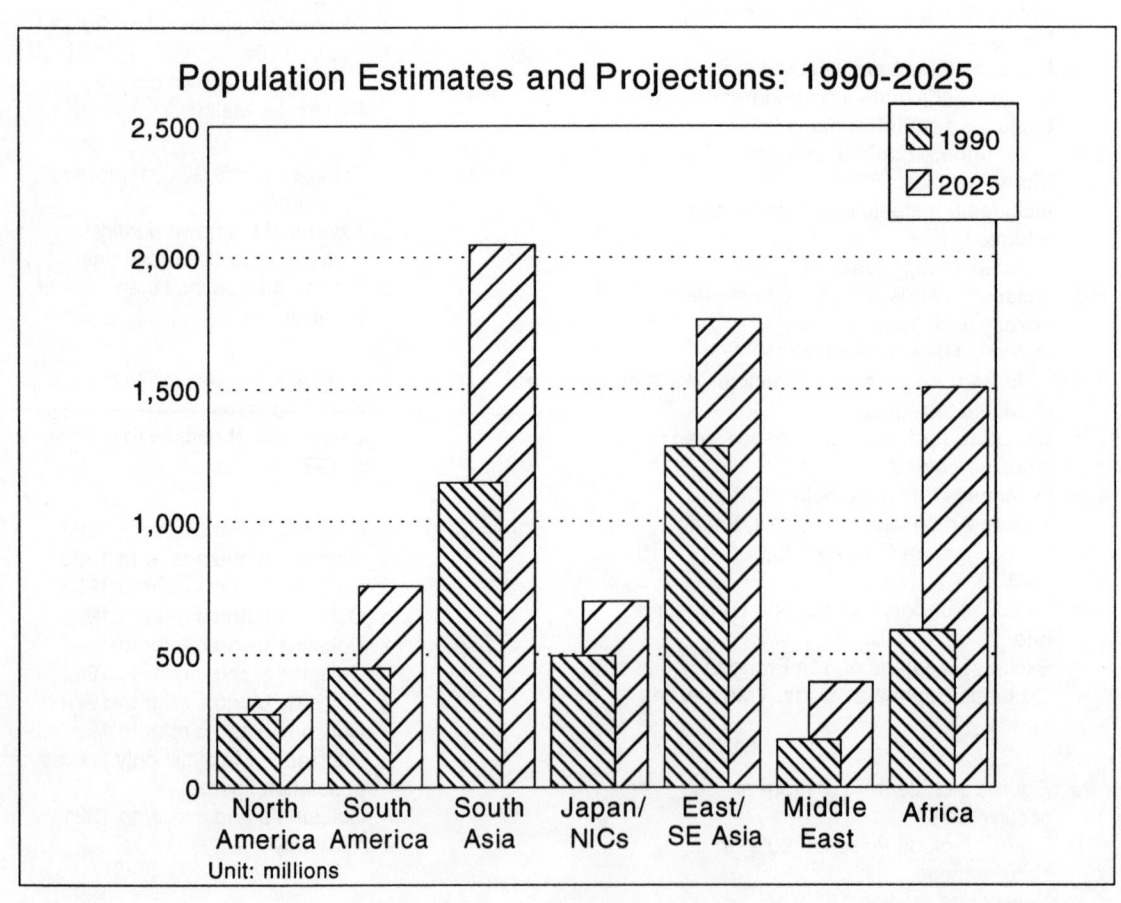

Section Three
Economic Indicators

GROSS DOMESTIC PRODUCT   Table No. 0301

Trends in Total Gross Domestic Product 1977-1992 (national currencies)

Units: Million units of national currency

	1977	1980	1985	1986	1987	1988	1989	1990	1991	1992
North America										
Canada	217,880	309,891	477,988	505,666	551,597	605,906	649,916	667,843	674,388	687,334
USA	1,974,100	2,708,000	4,038,700	4,268,600	4,539,900	4,900,400	5,250,800	5,522,200	5,677,500	5,950,700
South America										
Argentina [a]		2,834	3,959	9,984	23,332	111	3,244	68,922	180,898	226,638
Bolivia			2,867	8,924	10,179	12,301	14,749	17,542	21,690	
Brazil [b]	3	13	1,383	3,673	11,574	86,551	1,272	32,731	164,991	1,778,961
Chile	287,800	1,075,300	2,576,600	3,246,100	4,159,800	5,411,000	6,778,400	8,477,900	10,939,200	13,739,600
Colombia	716,000	1,579,100	4,965,900	6,788,000	8,824,400	11,731,600	15,126,700	20,234,100	26,393,300	
Ecuador	166,380	293,340	1,109,940	1,383,230	1,794,500	3,019,700	5,171,000	8,204,000	12,201,000	19,452,000
French Guiana										
Guyana	1,125	1,508	1,964	2,219	3,382	4,138	10,330	15,665	38,385	46,796
Paraguay	263,610	560,460	1,393,890	1,833,800	2,493,600	3,319,100	4,608,400	6,474,400	7,545,300	
Peru [c,d]	1	5	189	360	722	4,383	110	6,849	33,912	60,284
Suriname	1,283	1,590	1,747	1,803	1,974	2,321	2,707	3,060		
Uruguay	19,915	92,204	478,600	890,500	1,661,500	2,725,500	4,839,300	9,784,000	19,793,000	34,523,000
Venezuela	155,710	254,200	449,030	492,130	679,440	875,500	1,485,500	2,279,300	3,036,300	4,180,300
Caribbean										
Anguilla			45	57	69	76	104	120	135	
Antigua [e]	174	281	465	552	648	771	874	919	947	
Aruba					886	1,034	1,168			
Bahamas	955	1,320	1,868	2,098	2,324	2,458				
Barbados	890	1,731	2,410	2,646	2,914	3,099	3,427	3,440	3,393	
Bermuda		752	1,174	1,297	1,415	1,502	1,594	1,649		
British Virgin Islands		54	90	98	117	131				
Cayman Islands			255	285	349	429	497	596		
Cuba [f]		9,853	13,952	12,857	12,284	12,764	12,791			
Dominica	97	159	266	303	339	393	423	452	479	
Dominican Republic	4,587	6,631	13,972	15,780	19,536	28,354	42,393	60,555	91,402	99,811
Grenada	134	202	311	350	406	449	491	541	567	
Guadeloupe		5,860	9,650	10,569						
Haiti [g]	4,897	7,183	10,047	11,179	10,042	9,907	10,595	12,510	12,861	
Jamaica	2,960	4,773	11,203	13,389	16,002	18,748	22,315	29,823	42,367	
Martinique		6,102	12,577	13,846						
Netherlands Antilles		1,559	1,966							
St Kitts	69	121	172	256	288	338	385	412	396	
St Lucia	176	305	441	602	647	729	821	876	938	
St Vincent/Grenadines	96	159	303	344	384	434	469	525	481	
Trinidad and Tobago	7,533	14,966	17,801	17,260	17,272	17,285	18,373	21,766	22,434	23,129
Central America										
Belize [d]	212	342	381	417	503	571	665	733	791	835
Costa Rica	26,331	41,406	197,920	246,579	284,039	346,558	421,807	519,535	674,622	835,802
El Salvador	7,167	8,917	14,331	19,763	23,141	27,366	32,230	41,057	47,792	54,762
Guatemala	5,481	7,879	11,180	15,838	17,711	20,545	23,685	34,317	47,034	54,298
Honduras	3,339	5,088	7,279	7,617	8,305	9,251	10,334	12,540	16,072	18,166
Mexico [h]	1,849	4,277	45,588	79,191	192,802	389,259	503,668	678,924	865,166	1,033,224
Nicaragua [i]	3	4	23	87	538	62,200	3,038	232,733	6,628,806	
Panama	2,070	3,559	4,901	5,791	5,363	4,605	4,639	5,009	5,491	
Puerto Rico		15,956	21,969	23,878	26,178	28,156	30,497			
South Asia										
Afghanistan	80,160	171,900	250,400							
Bangladesh [d]	105,360	197,990	405,410	465,610	539,200	597,140	659,600	737,570	802,220	826,287
Bhutan [d]		1,113	2,391	2,802	3,608	3,934	4,382	4,961	5,135	5,340
India [d,j]	960,700	1,360,100	2,619,200	2,929,500	3,332,000	3,965,900	4,539,900	5,308,700	6,095,000	6,357,085
Nepal [k]	17,280	23,351	44,417	50,428	59,246	68,858	77,534	90,825	105,300	130,685
Pakistan [d,l]	149,750	234,180	472,160	514,530	572,480	675,390	769,750	862,450	1,016,730	1,084,851
Sri Lanka [d]	36,407	66,527	162,375	179,474	196,723	221,982	251,891	321,751	375,339	397,484

GROSS DOMESTIC PRODUCT   Table No. 0301 (cont'd)

Trends in Total Gross Domestic Product 1977-1992 (national currencies)

Units: Million units of national currency

	1977	1980	1985	1986	1987	1988	1989	1990	1991	1992
Japan										
Japan [h]	185,443	240,176	320,419	334,609	348,425	371,429	396,197	424,537	450,795	464,842
ASEAN/NICs										
Brunei	4,227	10,554	7,752	5,190	6,021	5,771	6,443	7,527		
Hong Kong [d]	68,905	137,081	261,195	300,818	369,275	434,023	499,157	559,623	643,728	732,998
Indonesia [d,h]	19,011	45,446	96,997	102,683	124,817	142,105	167,185	196,919	227,163	242,383
Macau			12,683	14,597	18,440	21,561	25,270	29,608		
Malaysia [d]	32,340	53,308	77,547	71,594	79,625	90,861	101,463	114,616	128,352	139,262
Philippines	154,230	264,650	571,700	609,300	685,900	803,000	925,200	1,070,900	1,244,000	1,342,500
Singapore [d]	16,039	25,091	38,924	38,664	42,636	49,998	56,844	63,673	69,076	73,290
South Korea [d,h]	18,074	38,041	80,847	93,426	108,428	127,963	143,001	172,724	207,517	222,666
Taiwan [d]	820,473	1,470,175	2,473,786	2,855,180	3,222,993	3,497,000	3,879,000	4,222,004	4,704,137	5,197,268
Thailand [d]	403,500	658,500	1,041,400	1,095,400	1,253,200	1,507,000	1,776,000	2,051,200	2,205,040	2,381,432
East/SE Asia										
Cambodia										
China [d,f,h]	264	369	703	789	932	1,177	1,323	1,438	1,592	1,716
Laos [d]		6,264	84,406	124,304	160,878	228,604	431,322	612,848	724,975	776,448
Mongolia [d,f]		7,244	10,310	10,653	10,056	10,330	11,113	8,328	11,599	10,903
Myanmar [d,j]	29,619	38,609	55,989	59,028	68,698	76,243	119,281	138,136	149,256	155,226
North Korea										
Vietnam [d,f,h]		3	76	395	1,899	9,751	17,414	27,514	45,551	47,829
Australasia										
Australia	91,300	131,621	229,632	250,917	281,455	317,927	356,837	378,056	381,008	392,245
New Zealand [j]	14,879	22,947	45,435	55,088	61,867	66,403	71,505	73,343	73,213	
Pacific										
American Samoa										
Fiji [d]	660	984	1,316	1,462	1,465	1,588	1,861	2,090	2,199	2,280
French Polynesia		96,832	226,772	266,935						
Guam										
Kiribati		25	33	36	37	45				
Nauru										
New Caledonia		90,800	139,650	151,281	162,627	224,498				
Papua New Guinea [d]	1,410	1,855	2,403	2,572	2,854	3,170	3,046	3,076	3,606	4,080
Solomon Islands [d]	74	119	237	253	293	367	393	410	425	440
Tonga [d]	31	53	80	100	99	97	99	102	106	111
Tuvalu										
Vanuatu [d]			12,534	12,179	13,404	15,006	16,351	17,899	18,633	19,173
Western Samoa			191	201	211	246	248	238	236	
Middle East										
Bahrain	770	1,230	1,393	1,198	1,192	1,263	1,348	1,468		
Egypt [m]	8,210	15,470	32,516	42,563	52,142	61,109	71,786	87,741	110,444	136,190
Iran [h,n]	5,948	6,622	16,556	16,227	19,949	2,304	27,787	36,645	47,882	62,825
Iraq	6,042	15,825	15,369	13,938	15,201	17,898				
Israel	15	111	28,396	44,369	56,466	69,385	85,015	104,745	134,756	159,589
Jordan	625	1,196	1,898	2,080	2,136	2,235	2,403	2,618	2,806	
Kuwait	4,052	7,755	6,450	5,203	6,233	5,704	7,128	5,247	3,184	6,367
Lebanon		14,000								
Oman	947	2,047	3,454	2,800	3,003	2,926	3,231	4,051	3,936	
Qatar	14,322	28,631	22,398	18,393	19,825	21,979	23,616	26,792	24,289	
Saudi Arabia [o]	205,060	490,940	313,940	271,090	275,450	285,150	310,820		297,895	327,068
Syria	27,013	51,270	83,225	99,933	127,712	186,047	208,892	268,328	305,605	
United Arab Emirates	63,400	109,800	99,400	79,500	87,300	87,100	101,000	125,300	126,000	129,300
Yemen [p]	8,220	12,681	30,969	38,389	43,559					

GROSS DOMESTIC PRODUCT   Table No. 0301 (cont'd)

Trends in Total Gross Domestic Product 1977-1992 (national currencies)

Units: Million units of national currency

	1977	1980	1985	1986	1987	1988	1989	1990	1991	1992
North Africa										
Algeria	87,200	162,500	291,600	296,600	312,706	334,607	403,460			
Chad			298,700	283,000	246,100	310,800	325,000	332,000	363,600	
Djibouti	34,800	60,313								
Ethiopia [q]	6,826	8,499	9,923	10,906	11,399	11,851	12,421	12,533	13,331	13,384
Libya	5,763	10,535	7,203	6,473						
Mali		300,600	479,360	585,100	540,000	533,500	599,800	612,500	620,000	
Mauritania	24,998	31,728	53,230	62,699	69,171	72,053	81,517	84,615	93,050	
Morocco	49,760	70,160	129,510	154,730	156,690	181,580	193,930	213,990	240,760	
Niger	288,800	536,200	647,100	685,200	649,900	694,200	651,800	648,800	700,000	
Somalia		17,341	87,290	118,781	169,608					
Sudan [l]	2,883	4,951	13,913	22,009	31,157					
Tunisia	2,199	3,510	6,910	7,021	7,997	8,685	9,661	10,990	12,172	13,994
West Africa										
Benin	148,500	245,600	469,778	462,535	469,554	482,434	487,525	516,000	547,000	
Burkina Faso	184,900	272,000	461,400	503,500	711,700	755,400	752,600	762,400	839,000	
Cameroon [l]	789,900	1,410,100	3,838,900	4,135,100	3,969,000	3,697,000	3,496,000	3,347,000	3,179,700	
Cape Verde	3,172	5,919	12,625	15,286	17,884	20,640				
Côte d'Ivoire	1,590,400	2,234,200	3,134,800	3,171,700	3,133,000	3,150,000	2,950,000	2,639,000	2,615,000	
Equatorial Guinea			38,756	37,736	35,900	38,500	39,500	41,100	40,600	
Gabon	690,200	904,500	1,645,800	1,201,100	1,043,600	965,900	1,269,000	1,374,000	1,372,000	
Gambia [l]	355	425	870	1,085	1,486	1,636	1,942	2,345	2,689	
Ghana	11,163	42,853	344,182	511,373	746,000	1,051,200	1,389,000	1,995,000		
Guinea			44,924							
Guinea-Bissau				46,973	92,375	171,949				
Liberia	706	917	1,057	1,034	1,100	1,174	1,182			
Nigeria	32,747	50,849	72,355	73,062	108,885	145,243	224,797	260,637	288,560	
Sao Tomé e Príncipe		1,625		2,478	3,003	4,221				
Senegal	487,500	627,600	1,152,000	1,307,000	1,382,000	1,483,000	1,478,000	1,588,000	1,643,000	
Sierra Leone [l]	744	1,156	4,785	7,481	19,705	29,080	43,947	82,837	151,345	
Togo	168,800	238,400	338,200	365,300	375,000	411,000	430,000	446,000	469,000	
East/Central Africa										
Angola			144,747							
Burundi	49,578	85,607	141,347	140,842	143,590	152,907	173,295	189,142	210,259	
Central African Republic	106,900	188,300	316,200	330,900	315,700	327,500	340,600	353,000	362,100	
Comoros		26,700	48,750	56,500	59,700	61,700	63,900	67,100	70,500	
Congo [h]	182	360	971	640	691	659	763	773	821	
Kenya	37,197	52,649	100,663	117,687	131,170	151,193	172,859	198,786	227,243	
Madagascar	468,100	698,800	1,553,400	2,203,800	2,743,100	3,436,700	4,005,300	4,601,600	4,906,400	
Maldives	142	321	600	691	845	949	1,045	1,164		
Mauritius	5,442	8,697	16,618	19,700	23,576	27,803	32,265	37,990	42,750	47,000
Réunion		8,449	17,315	19,520	21,856	23,861				
Rwanda	71,600	108,000	173,600	170,300	171,400	175,600	190,200	190,400	209,000	
Seychelles	493	942	1,205	1,290	1,396	1,528	1,741	1,991		
Tanzania	28,868	42,118	120,621	159,648	226,950	331,217	406,542	494,999	690,421	
Uganda	486	1,352	24,072	59,126	211,384	593,128	1,112,414	495,258	2,103,892	
Zaire [r]	3,956	17,183	359,000	483,000	861,000	1,657,000	3,441,000	6,277,000	133,011	
Southern Africa										
Botswana [s]	320	710	1,829	2,421	2,810	3,796	5,472	6,130	6,995	
Lesotho [j]	168	286	551	631	753	1,026	1,287	1,506	1,644	
Malawi	728	1,005	1,945	2,198	2,614	3,418	4,388	5,070	6,144	6,631
Mozambique			76,894	167,000	423,000	657,000	966,000	1,388,000	1,871,000	
Namibia										
South Africa [d]	34,120	63,237	123,126	142,135	164,524	197,910	233,134	263,812	296,667	321,864
Swaziland [l]	263	422	743	956	1,133	1,384				
Zambia	1,986	3,064	7,072	12,963	19,632	22,495				
Zimbabwe	2,198	3,441	7,019	7,902	8,928					

Source: International Monetary Fund (IMF)/UN/Asian Development Bank (ADB)/national statistical offices

Notes: see end of section

GROSS NATIONAL PRODUCT | Table No. 0302

Trends in Total Gross National Product 1977-1992 (national currencies)

Units: Million units of national currency

	1977	1980	1985	1986	1987	1988	1989	1990	1991	1992
North America										
Canada	213,310	302,060	463,660	489,260	535,150	587,190	628,410	643,590	652,000	662,440
USA	1,990,500	2,732,000	4,053,600	4,277,800	4,544,500	4,908,200	5,248,200	5,524,600	5,694,900	5,962,000
South America										
Argentina [a]		2,800	3,613	7,014	16,737	74	2,332			
Bolivia			2,598	9,963						
Brazil [b]	2	13	1,309	3,510	11,138	83,132	1,233	31,887	160,584	1,736,795
Chile	280,000	1,039,000	2,270,800	2,882,000	3,786,900	4,940,700	6,264,300	7,937,400	10,307,200	13,065,300
Colombia [c]	708,000	1,573,000	4,824,000	6,486,200	8,394,900	11,247,500	14,360,400	19,157,000	25,043,300	
Ecuador	162,000	279,000	1,030,000	1,271,600	1,672,200	2,812,900	4,786,000	7,575,000	11,462,000	18,453,000
French Guiana										
Guyana	1,058	1,425	1,719	1,936	2,551	3,269	7,540	11,426	26,446	34,222
Paraguay	264,000	566,000	1,381,000	1,812,700	2,425,400	3,310,300	4,700,900	6,618,000	7,660,100	
Peru [d]	1	5	153							
Suriname	1,221	1,559	1,746	1,797	1,966	2,306	2,696	3,044		
Uruguay [e]	20	91	443	846	1,593	2,613	4,628	9,407	19,324	33,956
Venezuela	155,340	255,400	438,420	489,180	679,200	873,350	1,423,100	2,237,100	2,992,300	4,125,300
Caribbean										
Anguilla										
Antigua										
Aruba										
Bahamas										
Barbados	986	1,680	2,372							
Bermuda										
British Virgin Islands										
Cayman Islands										
Cuba										
Dominica										
Dominican Republic	4,464	6,421	13,273	15,056	18,727	27,532	42,133	60,895	91,761	100,382
Grenada										
Guadeloupe										
Haiti [c,f]	4,834	7,111	9,946	11,081	9,937	9,773	10,467	12,401	12,736	
Jamaica [g]	2,862	4,455	9,736	11,836	14,104	16,864	20,015	26,823		
Martinique										
Netherlands Antilles										
St Kitts										
St Lucia										
St Vincent/Grenadines										
Trinidad and Tobago [c,g]	6,340	14,485	16,942	16,349	16,298	16,158	16,802	19,741	19,919	
Central America										
Belize										
Costa Rica	25,705	39,417	183,805	231,480	265,423	320,897	391,068	496,545	670,641	853,875
El Salvador	7,095	8,789	13,977	19,292	22,616	26,857	31,662	40,282	46,970	54,264
Guatemala	5,448	7,809	10,849	15,402	17,239	20,074	23,141	33,489	46,169	53,365
Honduras	3,215	4,813	6,945	7,245	7,916	8,824	9,808	11,672	15,356	17,649
Mexico [c]	1,806	4,159	45,181	74,936	184,462	375,864	490,107	666,037	845,189	
Nicaragua	14,140	20,970								
Panama	2,007	3,449	4,855	5,147	5,322	4,370	4,366	4,756	5,260	
Puerto Rico										
South Asia										
Afghanistan										
Bangladesh [h]	105,780	201,460	414,050	477,540	554,750	617,600	682,130	759,840	859,470	
Bhutan		913	1,942	2,335	3,258	3,571	4,210	4,665		
India [i]	896,200	1,363,600	2,604,900	2,911,400	3,305,800	3,921,000	4,482,600	5,240,300	6,026,700	
Nepal [j]	17,599	23,845	45,078	51,137	60,450	70,433	79,973	89,941	102,028	
Pakistan [h]	155,230	252,460	510,470	555,890	608,860	704,480	797,750	894,710	1,053,090	1,225,390
Sri Lanka	31,256	66,095	158,975	175,613	192,387	216,716	246,152	315,066	368,023	415,595

GROSS NATIONAL PRODUCT

Trends in Total Gross National Product 1977-1992 (national currencies)

Units: Million units of national currency

	1977	1980	1985	1986	1987	1988	1989	1990	1991	1992
Japan										
Japan [e]	185,351	239,718	321,556	335,838	350,479	373,731	399,046	427,469	453,985	469,186
ASEAN/NICs										
Brunei										
Hong Kong										
Indonesia [e]	18,332	43,435	93,056	98,490	118,795	135,183	159,111	187,305	216,403	
Macau										
Malaysia	31,064	51,390	71,962	66,814	74,679	85,777	96,631	110,505	125,530	
Philippines	153,260	264,530	555,900	596,600	673,900	795,700	913,800	1,076,200	1,261,700	1,370,000
Singapore	15,852	24,189	40,330	39,613	42,257	49,862	57,278	64,467	70,657	76,172
South Korea [e]	17,807	36,750	78,088	90,599	106,024	126,231	141,794	171,488	206,027	229,939
Taiwan [k]	815,349	1,468,069	2,515,049	2,925,772	3,288,973	3,585,294	3,968,975	4,326,956	4,821,233	5,296,962
Thailand	402,300	653,100	996,800	1,072,900	1,230,800	1,482,200	1,752,600	2,030,100		
East/SE Asia										
Cambodia										
China [e]		447	856	970	1,130	1,402	1,592	1,769	1,976	2,399
Laos										
Mongolia										
Myanmar [i]	29,577	38,449	55,408	58,370	68,178	75,982	118,977	137,900	149,063	
North Korea										
Vietnam										
Australasia										
Australia	92,190	133,520	222,080	242,200	272,380	307,050	341,390	358,330	362,170	376,180
New Zealand [i]	14,543	22,436	42,915	52,321	58,661	63,174	67,245	69,534	69,700	
Pacific										
American Samoa										
Fiji	662	1,011	1,280	1,427	1,417	1,553	1,825	2,048	2,159	
French Polynesia										
Guam										
Kiribati										
Nauru										
New Caledonia										
Papua New Guinea	1,437	1,914	2,491	2,645	2,985	3,292	3,161	3,332	3,962	4,137
Solomon Islands										
Tonga	31	55								
Tuvalu										
Vanuatu			12,936	12,690	12,541	14,581	16,904	19,182		
Western Samoa										
Middle East										
Bahrain		1,112	1,283	1,085	1,084	1,095	1,249	1,339		
Egypt [l]	8,643	17,231	35,892	39,397	46,818					
Iran [d,m]	5,850	6,628	16,522	16,208	19,910	22,188	27,575	36,381	47,696	
Iraq		16,299								
Israel [c,i]	15	107	27,265	42,846	54,674	67,599	82,823	100,801	132,056	
Jordan	663	1,195	1,893	2,063	2,086	2,146	2,280	2,347	2,586	
Kuwait	4,558	9,065	7,837	7,323	7,658	7,564	9,154	7,407	4,657	7,385
Lebanon										
Oman	817	1,835	3,055	2,464	2,722	2,520	2,825	3,621	3,528	
Qatar										
Saudi Arabia [n]	207,720	478,780	327,530	289,670	292,840	304,660	322,500			
Syria										
United Arab Emirates										
Yemen [o]	8,577	13,672	37,239	45,644	50,429					

GROSS NATIONAL PRODUCT

Trends in Total Gross National Product 1977-1992 (national currencies)

Units: Million units of national currency

	1977	1980	1985	1986	1987	1988	1989	1990	1991	1992
North Africa										
Algeria										
Chad										
Djibouti										
Ethiopia k,p	6,820	8,514	9,855	10,846	11,322	11,712	12,265	12,336	13,549	13,424
Libya	5,304									
Mali										
Mauritania										
Morocco	51,150	75,720	132,070	162,330	164,730	185,960	197,450	224,440	250,030	
Niger										
Somalia										
Sudan h	2,868									
Tunisia	2,217	3,488	6,842	6,971	7,995	8,737	9,727	11,203	12,226	14,064
West Africa										
Benin	151,300	245,800	479,700	494,600			471,700	462,000	486,700	519,500
Burkina Faso	184,100	273,100	454,100							
Cameroon h	627,900									
Cape Verde										
Côte d'Ivoire	1,488,800									
Equatorial Guinea										
Gabon	651,400									
Gambia										
Ghana	11,123	42,671	337,280	498,800	725,500	1,024,700	1,389,000	1,995,000		
Guinea										
Guinea-Bissau										
Liberia	626	833	986	924	924	981	984			
Nigeria	32,272	49,759	70,732	68,682	97,225	132,503	207,173	238,624	264,616	
Sao Tomé e Príncipe										
Senegal										
Sierra Leone h	733	1,111	4,704	7,542	21,567	29,610	44,337	82,964	143,774	
Togo	167,500									
East/Central Africa										
Angola										
Burundi										
Central African Republic										
Comoros										
Congo										
Kenya	35,623	50,969	96,998	113,504	126,197	144,782	165,762	188,605	213,829	253,839
Madagascar	467,500									
Maldives										
Mauritius	5,425	8,519	15,918	18,971	23,038	27,210	31,962	37,651	42,840	47,330
Réunion										
Rwanda										
Seychelles	463	908	1,163	1,238	1,318	1,434	1,657	1,887		
Tanzania	28,780	42,006	119,917	156,367	216,418	312,675	377,499	454,513	648,736	
Uganda										
Zaire	3,152	13,087	105,000	132,000	220,000	438,000	827,000			
Southern Africa										
Botswana	291									
Lesotho	308	491	1,063	1,197	1,452	1,822	2,082	2,465		
Malawi	705	924	1,854	2,085	2,488	3,280	4,251	4,914	6,014	6,448
Mozambique										
Namibia										
South Africa	32,683	60,501	116,608	135,125	157,831	190,491	224,118	252,674	288,386	317,923
Swaziland h	261	416	820	993	1,140	1,449				
Zambia	2,055	3,202	6,986	12,802	19,985	22,608				
Zimbabwe	2,150	3,394	6,735	7,518	8,573					

Source: IMF/UN/national statistical offices
Notes: see end of section

GROSS DOMESTIC PRODUCT   Table No. 0303

Trends in Total Gross Domestic Product 1977-1992 (US $)

Units: Million current US dollars

	1977	1980	1985	1987	1988	1989	1990	1991	1992	% growth 1977-91
North America										
Canada	204,871	265,045	351,462	417,877	492,607	548,916	575,727	588,625	568,656	187.3
USA	1,974,100	2,708,000	4,038,700	4,539,900	4,900,400	5,250,800	5,522,200	5,677,500	5,950,700	187.6
South America										
Argentina			65,983	109,028	126,857	76,629	141,352	189,710	228,779	
Bolivia	2,999	4,894	6,516	4,965	5,234	5,479	5,529	6,058		102.0
Brazil	176,803	250,427	223,065	295,105	330,095	448,836	479,224	405,772	394,184	129.5
Chile	13,374	27,572	15,996	18,948	22,081	25,372	27,791	31,311	37,893	134.1
Colombia	19,472	33,399	34,895	36,373	39,214	39,540	40,286	41,692		114.1
Ecuador	6,655	11,734	15,959	10,527	10,012	9,824	10,686	11,662	12,741	75.2
French Guiana										
Guyana	441	591	462	347	414	380	396	343	374	-22.2
Paraguay	2,092	4,448	4,545	4,534	6,035	4,363	5,265	5,694		172.1
Peru	12,500	17,241	17,229	42,900	34,022	41,257	36,450	43,899	48,390	251.2
Suriname	721	893	981	1,109	1,304	1,517	1,709			
Uruguay	4,264	10,143	4,719	7,330	7,583	7,991	8,355	9,804	11,405	129.9
Venezuela	36,296	59,254	59,871	46,858	60,379	42,830	48,599	53,441	61,137	47.2
Caribbean										
Anguilla			17	26	28	39	44	50		
Antigua	64	104	172	240	286	324	340	351		444.3
Aruba				495	578	653				
Bahamas	955	1,320	1,868	2,324	2,458					
Barbados	445	866	1,205	1,457	1,550	1,704	1,710	1,687		279.1
Bermuda		752	1,174	1,415	1,502	1,594	1,649			
British Virgin Islands		54	90	117	131					
Cayman Islands			319	420	517	599	718			
Cuba [a]		13,877	15,855	15,749	15,955	15,989				
Dominica	36	59	99	126	146	157	167	177		393.8
Dominican Republic	4,587	6,631	4,507	5,088	4,625	6,687	7,103	7,202	7,814	57.0
Grenada	50	75	115	150	166	182	200	210		323.1
Guadeloupe		1,389	1,075							
Haiti [b]	979	1,437	2,009	2,008	1,981	2,119	2,502	2,572		162.6
Jamaica	3,289	2,681	2,019	2,920	3,421	3,885	4,154	3,497		6.3
Martinique		1,446	1,401							
Netherlands Antilles		866	1,092							
St Kitts	26	45	64	107	125	143	153	147		473.9
St Lucia	65	113	163	240	270	304	324	347		433.0
St Vincent/Grenadines	36	59	112	142	161	174	194	178		401.0
Trinidad and Tobago	3,139	6,236	7,266	4,798	4,501	4,323	5,121	5,279	5,442	68.2
Central America										
Belize	106	171	191	252	286	333	367	396	418	273.1
Costa Rica	3,072	4,832	3,923	4,525	4,572	5,175	5,673	5,510	6,214	79.3
El Salvador	2,867	3,567	5,732	4,628	5,473	6,446	5,113	5,915	5,972	106.3
Guatemala	5,481	7,879	11,180	7,084	7,872	8,411	7,660	9,353	10,501	70.6
Honduras	1,670	2,544	3,640	4,153	4,626	5,167	6,270	2,976	3,116	78.3
Mexico	81,936	186,362	177,454	139,894	171,246	204,618	241,387	286,631	333,847	249.8
Nicaragua						1,013	1,824	1,552		
Panama	2,070	3,559	4,901	5,363	4,605	4,639	5,009	5,491		165.3
Puerto Rico		15,956	21,969	26,178	28,156	30,497				
South Asia										
Afghanistan	1,781	3,896	4,949							
Bangladesh	6,855	12,815	14,484	17,422	18,819	20,440	21,337	21,921	21,213	219.8
Bhutan		142	193	278	283	270	283	226	206	
India [c]	110,046	173,041	211,909	257,099	285,111	279,792	303,285	268,006	245,277	143.5
Nepal [d]	1,382	1,946	2,435	2,716	2,958	2,852	3,093	2,826	3,059	104.5
Pakistan [e]	15,126	23,655	29,658	32,920	37,522	37,474	39,731	42,718	43,250	182.4
Sri Lanka	4,105	4,025	5,978	6,682	6,981	6,988	8,031	9,072	9,069	121.0

GROSS DOMESTIC PRODUCT

Table No. 0303 (cont'd)

Trends in Total Gross Domestic Product 1977-1992 (US $)

Units: Million current US dollars

	1977	1980	1985	1987	1988	1989	1990	1991	1992	% growth 1977-91
Japan										
Japan	690,637	1,059,257	1,343,251	2,408,912	2,898,393	2,871,825	2,932,088	3,346,411	3,670,288	384.5
ASEAN/NICs										
Brunei	1,740	4,932	3,650	2,995	2,950	3,379	4,199			
Hong Kong	14,786	27,582	33,530	47,404	55,573	63,994	71,747	82,731	94,690	459.5
Indonesia	45,810	72,483	87,337	75,932	85,673	94,449	106,859	116,476	119,406	154.3
Macau			1,587	2,305	2,685	3,145	3,690			
Malaysia	13,146	24,566	31,269	31,723	34,813	37,457	42,373	46,672	54,668	255.0
Philippines	20,842	35,240	30,737	33,361	38,075	42,563	44,050	45,271	52,622	117.2
Singapore	6,600	11,725	17,693	20,303	24,875	29,146	35,130	39,984	44,991	505.8
South Korea	37,343	62,626	92,925	131,816	174,940	212,970	244,043	282,971	285,232	657.8
Taiwan	21,591	40,827	62,093	112,889	124,139	148,223	155,736	182,685	204,054	746.1
Thailand	19,779	32,169	38,357	48,725	59,589	69,108	80,172	86,415	93,757	336.9
East/SE Asia										
Cambodia										
China [a]	142,919	247,517	239,966	250,565	316,398	351,341	300,698	299,113	311,264	109.3
Laos		626	2,412	894	570	735	864	1,033		
Mongolia		2,456	3,041	3,480	3,574	3,704	1,783	449		
Myanmar [c]	4,166	5,859	6,610	10,331	11,465	17,790	21,793	23,753	25,428	470.2
North Korea										
Vietnam [a]		1,442	5,241	8,440	10,834	4,050	4,046	4,141		
Australasia										
Australia	101,444	151,289	161,713	198,208	249,315	282,800	295,379	296,851	288,415	192.6
New Zealand [c]	14,446	22,497	22,718	36,826	43,560	42,797	43,787	42,405		193.6
Pacific										
American Samoa										
Fiji	725	1,215	1,144	1,201	1,110	1,255	1,411	1,490	1,517	105.5
French Polynesia		1,260	1,388							
Guam										
Kiribati		29	23	26	35					
Nauru										
New Caledonia		1,182	855	1,488						
Papua New Guinea	1,785	2,769	2,403	3,171	3,658	3,559	3,220	3,750	4,230	110.1
Solomon Islands	82	145	160	147	176	172	162	157	150	90.4
Tonga	34	61	56	70	76	78	80	82	82	137.4
Tuvalu										
Vanuatu			118	122	144	141	154	167	169	
Western Samoa			85	100	118	109	103	98		
Middle East										
Bahrain	1,974	3,324	3,765	3,222	3,414	3,585	3,904			
Egypt [f]	21,051	22,100	46,451	74,489	87,299	65,260	43,871	33,166	40,894	57.6
Iran [g]	84,964	94,600	181,834	279,163	33,547	385,850	538,137	709,310	958,399	734.8
Iraq	20,834	54,569	49,577	49,035	57,735					
Israel			24,270	35,513	43,638	44,362	51,952	59,127	64,897	
Jordan	1,953	4,124	4,867	6,473	6,016	4,213	3,945	4,122		111.0
Kuwait [e]	14,471	28,722	21,500	23,085	20,371	24,361	17,932	11,199	21,701	-22.6
Lebanon		4,082								
Oman	2,785	6,021	10,159	7,903	7,610	8,403	10,536	10,237		267.5
Qatar	3,626	7,844	6,170	5,461	6,038	6,488	7,360	6,673		84.0
Saudi Arabia [h]	58,589	148,770	87,206	73,650	76,243	82,996		79,545	87,335	35.8
Syria	6,926	13,146	21,340	11,383	16,582	18,610	23,904	27,225		293.1
United Arab Emirates	16,256	29,676	27,084	23,787	23,733	27,513	34,132	34,323	35,222	111.1
Yemen [i]	1,803	2,781	4,208	4,213						

GROSS DOMESTIC PRODUCT   Table No. 0303 (cont'd)

Trends in Total Gross Domestic Product 1977-1992 (US $)

Units: Million current US dollars

	1977	1980	1985	1987	1988	1989	1990	1991	1992	% growth 1977-91
North Africa										
Algeria	21,063	42,428	58,320	65,147	56,617	53,027				
Chad			665	819	1,043	1,019	1,219	1,289		
Djibouti	196	339								
Ethiopia [j]	3,298	4,106	4,794	5,507	5,725	6,000	6,055	6,440	2,677	95.3
Libya	19,210	35,117	24,010							
Mali		1,423	1,067	1,797	1,791	1,880	2,250	2,198		
Mauritania	548	691	691	936	957	982	1,050	1,136		107.0
Morocco	11,058	17,852	12,874	18,745	22,144	22,848	25,963	27,651		150.1
Niger	1,176	2,538	1,440	2,162	2,331	2,043	2,383	2,481		111.1
Somalia		2,757	2,211	1,613						
Sudan [e]	8,479	9,902	6,102	11,088						
Tunisia	5,236	8,775	8,325	9,752	10,218	10,177	12,513	13,165	15,823	151.4
West Africa										
Benin	604	1,162	1,046	1,562	1,620	1,528	1,895	1,939		220.8
Burkina Faso	753	1,287	1,027	2,368	2,536	2,359	2,800	2,974		295.2
Cameroon [e]	3,215	6,674	8,545	13,206	12,412	10,959	12,293	11,271		250.6
Cape Verde	94	139	138	247	286					
Côte d'Ivoire	6,473	10,575	6,978	10,425	10,576	9,247	9,693	9,269		43.2
Equatorial Guinea			86	119	129	124	151	144		
Gabon	2,809	4,281	3,663	3,472	3,243	3,978	5,047	4,863		73.1
Gambia [e]	155	237	226	210	244	256	297	305		97.0
Ghana	9,707	15,583	6,368	5,073	5,195	5,144	6,113			
Guinea			1,999							
Guinea-Bissau				165	155					
Liberia	706	917	1,057	1,100	1,174	1,182				
Nigeria	51,167	94,165	81,298	27,221	32,013	30,543	32,426	29,121		-43.1
Sao Tomé e Príncipe		46								
Senegal	1,984	2,970	2,564	4,598	4,979	4,633	5,833	5,824		193.5
Sierra Leone [e]	511	1,112	940	579	894	735	547	512		0.4
Togo	687	1,128	753	1,248	1,380	1,348	1,638	1,662		142.0
East/Central Africa										
Angola			4,841							
Burundi	551	951	1,171	1,162	1,089	1,092	1,104	1,158		110.3
Central African Republic	435	891	704	1,050	1,100	1,068	1,297	1,284		195.0
Comoros		126	109	199	207	200	246	250		
Congo	1	2	2	2	2	2	3	3		292.8
Kenya	4,498	7,096	6,127	7,972	8,523	8,403	8,675	8,261		83.7
Madagascar	1,905	3,307	2,345	2,566	2,442	2,498	3,080	2,673		40.3
Maldives	16	43	85	92	108	116	122			
Mauritius	825	1,132	1,076	1,832	2,070	2,116	2,556	2,731	3,020	231.2
Réunion		2,002	1,946	3,637	3,977					
Rwanda	771	1,163	1,714	2,151	2,297	2,378	2,305	1,670		116.6
Seychelles	65	147	169	249	284	308	373			
Tanzania	3,483	5,143	6,904	3,532	3,336	2,835	2,538	3,150		-9.5
Uganda	5,884	18,221	3,883	4,934	5,588	4,986	1,155	2,866		-51.3
Zaire	4,654	6,137	7,199	7,660	8,858	9,021	8,735	9		-99.8
Southern Africa										
Botswana [e]	381	922	973	1,683	2,090	2,719	3,296	3,468		810.2
Lesotho [c]	195	371	252	371	454	492	582	596		205.3
Malawi	809	1,241	1,137	1,188	1,335	1,590	1,858	2,192	1,840	171.0
Mozambique			1,849							
Namibia										
South Africa	39,674	82,126	56,222	81,046	87,528	89,098	102,004	107,632	112,949	171.3
Swaziland [e]	306	548	339	558	612					
Zambia	2,546	3,928	2,607	2,211	2,735					
Zimbabwe	3,545	5,377	4,360	5,378						

Source: Euromonitor from IMF/UN/Asian Development Bank (ADB)/national statistical offices

Notes: see end of section

GROSS NATIONAL PRODUCT	Table No. 0304

Trends in Total Gross National Product 1977-1992 (US $)

Units: Million current US dollars

	1977	1980	1985	1987	1988	1989	1990	1991	1992	% growth 1977-91
North America										
Canada	200,574	258,348	340,926	405,417	477,390	530,752	554,819	569,084	548,060	183.7
USA	1,990,500	2,732,000	4,053,600	4,544,500	4,908,200	5,248,200	5,524,600	5,694,900	5,962,000	186.1
South America										
Argentina			60,217	78,210	84,571	55,086				
Bolivia	2,999	4,078	5,905							
Brazil	169,731	246,633	211,129	283,988	317,056	435,074	466,867	394,934	384,841	132.7
Chile	13,011	26,641	14,097	17,249	20,162	23,448	26,019	29,502	36,033	126.7
Colombia	19,255	33,270	33,898	34,602	37,596	37,537	38,142	39,560		105.5
Ecuador	6,480	11,160	14,809	9,810	9,326	9,093	9,866	10,955	12,087	69.1
French Guiana										
Guyana	415	559	404	262	327	278	289	237	274	-43.0
Paraguay	2,095	4,492	4,503	4,410	6,019	4,451	5,381	5,780		175.9
Peru	12,938	16,655	13,953							
Suriname	686	876	981	1,104	1,296	1,510	1,701			
Uruguay	4	10	4	7	7	8	8	10	11	123.5
Venezuela	36,210	59,534	58,456	46,841	60,231	41,031	47,699	52,667	60,333	45.4
Caribbean										
Anguilla										
Antigua										
Aruba										
Bahamas										
Barbados	493	840	1,186							
Bermuda										
British Virgin Islands										
Cayman Islands										
Cuba										
Dominica										
Dominican Republic	4,464	6,421	4,282	4,877	4,491	6,646	7,143	7,230	7,858	62.0
Grenada										
Guadeloupe										
Haiti [a]	967	1,422	1,989	1,987	1,955	2,093	2,480	2,547		163.5
Jamaica	3,180	2,503	1,754	2,574	3,077	3,484	3,736			
Martinique										
Netherlands Antilles										
St Kitts										
St Lucia										
St Vincent/Grenadines										
Trinidad and Tobago	2,642	6,035	6,915	4,527	4,208	3,953	4,645	4,687		77.4
Central America										
Belize										
Costa Rica	2,999	4,599	3,643	4,229	4,233	4,798	5,422	5,478	6,348	82.6
El Salvador	2,838	3,516	5,591	4,523	5,371	6,332	5,016	5,813	5,918	104.8
Guatemala	5,448	7,809	10,849	6,896	7,691	8,217	7,475	9,181	10,321	68.5
Honduras	1,608	2,407	3,473	3,958	4,412	4,904	5,836	2,844	3,027	76.9
Mexico	80,018	181,220	175,870	133,843	165,353	199,109	236,805	280,012		249.9
Nicaragua										
Panama	2,007	3,449	4,855	5,322	4,370	4,366	4,756	5,260		162.1
Puerto Rico										
South Asia										
Afghanistan										
Bangladesh [b]	6,882	13,039	14,793	17,924	19,464	21,138	21,982	23,485		241.2
Bhutan		116	157	251	257	259	267			
India [c]	102,658	173,486	210,752	255,077	281,884	276,260	299,377	265,003		158.1
Nepal [d]	1,408	1,987	2,471	2,772	3,025	2,941	3,062	2,739		94.5
Pakistan [b]	15,680	25,501	32,065	35,012	39,138	38,837	41,218	44,246	48,853	182.2
Sri Lanka	3,524	3,998	5,853	6,535	6,815	6,829	7,864	8,895	9,482	152.4

GROSS NATIONAL PRODUCT

Table No. 0304 (cont'd)

Trends in Total Gross National Product 1977-1992 (US $)

Units: Million current US dollars

	1977	1980	1985	1987	1988	1989	1990	1991	1992	% growth 1977-91
Japan										
Japan	690,295	1,057,237	1,348,017	2,423,113	2,916,356	2,892,476	2,952,338	3,370,091	3,704,587	388.2
ASEAN/NICs										
Brunei										
Hong Kong										
Indonesia	44,173	69,275	83,789	72,269	81,499	89,888	101,642	110,959		151.2
Macau										
Malaysia	12,628	23,682	29,017	29,753	32,865	35,673	40,854	45,646		261.5
Philippines	20,711	35,224	29,887	32,777	37,729	42,039	44,268	45,915	53,700	121.7
Singapore	6,523	11,303	18,332	20,122	24,807	29,369	35,568	40,899	46,760	527.0
South Korea	36,791	60,501	89,754	128,894	172,572	211,173	242,297	280,940	294,548	663.6
Taiwan	21,457	40,768	63,129	115,200	127,273	151,661	159,607	187,232	207,969	772.6
Thailand	19,721	31,905	36,715	47,854	58,608	68,197	79,347			
East/SE Asia										
Cambodia										
China		300,000	292,150	303,763	376,747	422,842	369,836	371,191	434,991	
Laos										
Mongolia										
Myanmar [c]	4,160	5,834	6,542	10,252	11,426	17,745	21,756	23,722		470.3
North Korea										
Vietnam										
Australasia										
Australia [c]	102,433	153,471	156,394	191,817	240,786	270,558	279,967	282,174	276,603	175.5
New Zealand	14,119	21,996	21,458	34,917	41,442	40,247	41,513	40,371		185.9
Pacific										
American Samoa										
Fiji	727	1,248	1,113	1,161	1,086	1,230	1,383	1,463		101.1
French Polynesia										
Guam										
Kiribati										
Nauru										
New Caledonia										
Papua New Guinea	1,819	2,857	2,491	3,317	3,798	3,694	3,488	4,120	4,289	126.5
Solomon Islands										
Tonga	34	63								
Tuvalu										
Vanuatu			122	114	140	146	165			
Western Samoa										
Middle East										
Bahrain		3,005	3,468	2,930	2,959	3,322	3,561			
Egypt [e]	22,162	24,616	51,274	66,883						
Iran [f]	83,571	94,686	181,461	278,617	323,063	382,906	534,260	706,555		745.5
Iraq [c]		56,203								
Israel [c]			23,303	34,386	42,515	43,218	49,996	57,942		
Jordan	2,072	4,121	4,854	6,321	5,777	3,997	3,537	3,798		83.3
Kuwait	16,279	33,574	26,123	28,363	27,014	31,285	25,314	16,381	25,170	0.6
Lebanon										
Oman	2,403	5,397	8,985	7,163	6,554	7,347	9,417	9,176		281.8
Qatar										
Saudi Arabia [g]	59,349	145,085	90,981	78,299	81,460	86,115				
Syria										
United Arab Emirates										
Yemen [h]	1,881	2,998	5,060	4,877						

GROSS NATIONAL PRODUCT

Trends in Total Gross National Product 1977-1992 (US $)

Units: Million current US dollars

	1977	1980	1985	1987	1988	1989	1990	1991	1992	% growth 1977-91
North Africa										
Algeria										
Chad										
Djibouti										
Ethiopia [i]	3,295	4,113	4,761	5,470	5,658	5,925	5,959	6,545	2,685	98.7
Libya	17,680									
Mali										
Mauritania										
Morocco	11,367	19,267	13,128	19,707	22,678	23,262	27,231	28,716		152.6
Niger										
Somalia										
Sudan [b]	8,435									
Tunisia	5,279	8,720	8,243	9,750	10,279	10,246	12,755	13,223	15,902	150.5
West Africa										
Benin	616	1,163	1,068		1,584	1,448	1,788	1,841		199.0
Burkina Faso	749	1,293	1,011							
Cameroon [b]	2,556									
Cape Verde										
Côte d'Ivoire	6,060									
Equatorial Guinea										
Gabon	2,651									
Gambia										
Ghana	9,672	15,517	6,240	4,934	5,064	5,144	6,113			
Guinea										
Guinea-Bissau										
Liberia	626	833	986	924	981	984				
Nigeria	50,425	92,146	79,474	24,306	29,205	28,149	29,687	26,705		-47.0
Sao Tomé e Príncipe										
Senegal [b]										
Sierra Leone	503	1,068	924	634	911	741	548	487		-3.2
Togo	682									
East/Central Africa										
Angola										
Burundi										
Central African Republic										
Comoros										
Congo										
Kenya	4,307	6,869	5,904	7,670	8,161	8,058	8,231	7,773	7,879	80.5
Madagascar	1,903									
Maldives										
Mauritius	822	1,109	1,031	1,790	2,026	2,096	2,533	2,737	3,041	233.0
Réunion										
Rwanda										
Seychelles	61	142	163	235	267	293	354			
Tanzania	3,472	5,129	6,864	3,368	3,149	2,633	2,330	2,960		-14.7
Uganda										
Zaire	3,708	4,674	2,105	1,957	2,341	2,168				
Southern Africa										
Botswana	346									
Lesotho	358	638	485	715	806	796	953			
Malawi	783	1,141	1,084	1,131	1,281	1,540	1,801	2,145	1,789	173.9
Mozambique										
Namibia										
South Africa	38,003	78,573	53,246	77,749	84,247	85,652	97,697	104,628	111,566	175.3
Swaziland [b]	303	540	374	562	641					
Zambia	2,635	4,105	2,575	2,251	2,749					
Zimbabwe	3,468	5,303	4,183	5,164						

Source: Euromonitor from IMF/UN/national statistical offices

Notes: see end of section

MONEY SUPPLY

Trends in Money Supply 1977-1992

Units: Million units of national currency

	1977	1980	1985	1987	1988	1989	1990	1991	1992	% nominal change 1977-92
North America										
Canada [a,b]	29	35	69	85	90	95	96	100	106	264
USA [a]	344	424	641	767	812	824	854	923	1,059	208
South America										
Argentina [c]				1	6	231	2,706	4,397		
Bolivia [d]			198	516	698	715	997	1,447	1,697	
Brazil [e,f]	319	1,288	106,149	1,440,000						
Chile [a]	18	79	148	229	386	442	518	784	689	3,665
Colombia [a,g]	104	212	545	1,019	1,282		2,116	2,786	4,015	3,779
Ecuador	29,876	53,584	158,100	246,200	372,600	539,800	852,900	1,333,600		
French Guiana										
Guyana [b]	285	328	740	1,333	2,095	2,923	4,262	7,466	6,618	2,223
Paraguay [c,h]	28,574	62,364	125,202	243,667	328,488	438,044	840,091	835,029		
Peru [c,i]		1	23	96	593	10,403	570	664		
Suriname [b]	220	294	880	1,562	1,945	2,165	2,251	2,886	3,141	1,330
Uruguay [a]	4	27	46	135	222	383	770	1,527	2,544	65,131
Venezuela [j]	34,027	50,209	105,220	122,560	145,450	169,950	269,260	347,590	375,450	1,003
Caribbean										
Anguilla										
Antigua	31	39	68	111	128	141	157	168	183	492
Aruba [k]				158	190	243	264	314	331	
Bahamas	90	136	208	278	297	298	328	355	365	308
Barbados	135	245	354	467	525	459	526	495	502	271
Bermuda										
British Virgin Islands										
Cayman Islands										
Cuba										
Dominica	12	27	31	59	57	56	70	74	86	646
Dominican Republic	460	580	1,355	2,773	4,324	5,374	7,587	9,448	11,047	2,302
Grenada	30	48	54	74	83	88	91	90	110	273
Guadeloupe										
Haiti [l]	629	945	1,076	2,098	1,635	2,634	2,083		2,582	310
Jamaica [b]	474	717	1,520	2,252	3,445	3,153	4,016	7,818	10,469	2,107
Martinique										
Netherlands Antilles [b]	310	387	528	569	578	569	643	679	709	129
St Kitts		8	33	55	48	61	60	60	65	
St Lucia	33	53	71	123	140	158	168	168	212	542
St Vincent/Grenadines	17	28	53	53	63	70	73	61	91	448
Trinidad and Tobago	725	1,337	2,261	2,170	1,893	2,144	2,576	2,922	2,696	272
Central America										
Belize	25	42	59	84	82	100	106	118	126	410
Costa Rica	4,504	7,271	32,439	42,611	65,267	63,975	66,500	79,800		
El Salvador [m]	988	1,429	2,306	2,762	2,996	3,370	4,153	4,872	6,284	536
Guatemala	594	753	1,347	1,766	2,019	2,438	3,242	3,843	4,193	606
Honduras	411	610	856	1,119	1,253	1,524	1,970	2,277	2,582	528
Mexico	208	477	3,462	12,627	21,191	29,087	47,439	106,227	122,020	58,563
Nicaragua [n]	1,699	4,102	55	1,422						
Panama [b]	213	335	410	442	304	307	433	557	531	149
Puerto Rico										
South Asia										
Afghanistan [c]	23,752	39,779	76,359	131,419	179,414	251,062	351,025	371,479		
Bangladesh	11,667	20,171	45,955	51,000	53,165	60,004	65,735	70,804	80,442	589
Bhutan [b]		40	262	317	412	546	540	750	728	
India [a]	179	205	412	543	633	747	854	1,046	1,175	558
Nepal [b]	1,933	2,864	5,616	8,682	9,826	11,720	14,205	17,614	19,164	892
Pakistan	39,966	60,671	123,060	173,016	189,834	217,027	254,620	305,978	371,796	830
Sri Lanka [o]	5,332	9,333	18,662	24,901	32,155	35,088	39,596	46,600	50,057	839

MONEY SUPPLY

Table No. 0305 (cont'd)

Trends in Money Supply 1977-1992

Units: Million units of national currency

	1977	1980	1985	1987	1988	1989	1990	1991	1992	% nominal change 1977-92
Japan										
Japan [a]	60,786	69,572	88,980	102,973	111,844	114,474	119,628	131,040	136,140	124
ASEAN/NICs										
Brunei										
Hong Kong	18,081	24,198	45,266	81,902	88,834	94,858	107,509	128,497	155,557	760
Indonesia [a]	2,006	5,011	10,124	12,705	14,392	20,559	23,819	26,693	28,801	1,336
Macau [b]							8,979	16,229	20,106	
Malaysia [b]	6,127	9,757	14,132	16,375	18,730	21,978	25,405	27,928	29,292	378
Philippines [a]	15	23	36	54	61	81	93	108	118	690
Singapore	4,412	6,135	8,785	11,031	11,958	13,745	15,261	16,430	18,515	320
South Korea [a]	2,173	3,807	7,558	10,107	12,152	14,328	15,905	21,752	24,586	1,031
Taiwan [b]	219,188	396,862	751,469	1,568,225	1,950,473	2,068,759	1,931,897	2,165,291	2,291,627	946
Thailand [a]	45	71	86	132	149	175	195	222	250	451
East/SE Asia										
Cambodia										
China [a,d]	58	92	302	457	549	583	701	899	1,171	1,919
Laos [p]	111	768	2,226	6,888	12,104	25,126	28,252	29,729		
Mongolia		2,114	3,032	2,835	3,022	3,510	4,659	7,285		
Myanmar	5,619	7,916	11,613	9,713	15,937	21,536	32,334	36,409		
North Korea										
Vietnam				442	2,327	4,857	7,494	11,361		
Australasia										
Australia [q]	11,390	17,220	23,298	31,218	40,470	43,514	46,699	49,983	60,292	429
New Zealand [b,q]	1,946	2,535	4,104	6,667	14,673	21,382	23,684	23,481	25,066	1,188
Pacific										
American Samoa										
Fiji	87	105	138	168	273	264	265	274	314	259
French Polynesia										
Guam										
Kiribati			4							
Nauru										
New Caledonia										
Papua New Guinea	169	202	244	281	322	345	344	417	438	159
Solomon Islands		15	28	37	49	51	64	80	109	
Tonga	4	5	11	15	16	17	22	26	22	435
Tuvalu										
Vanuatu [b]	1,770	1,882	2,643	4,219	3,516	4,369	3,894	4,377	4,735	168
Western Samoa	5	9	20	29	30	33	47	43	38	707
Middle East										
Bahrain [b]	152	192	243	247	239	235	259	305	339	122
Egypt	2,943	6,775	14,696	18,241	20,579	22,471	26,205	28,337	30,832	948
Iran [a,c]	822	2,258		6,462	7,118	8,238	9,729	11,274		
Iraq										
Israel	2	8	1,051	3,346	3,723	5,376	7,022	7,988	10,336	516,700
Jordan [b]	329	581	848	980	1,167	1,302	1,425	1,647	1,821	453
Kuwait [l]	491	721	944	1,036	958	939	995	1,230	1,076	119
Lebanon	5,062	7,667	20,200	68,900	182,900	287,200	449,900	689,400	1,199,400	23,594
Oman	111	155	329	335	315	345	391	406	433	289
Qatar	2,087	2,274	4,017	4,778	3,399	3,403	4,055	3,629	3,868	85
Saudi Arabia [a]	38	59	82	91	93	91	102	112		
Syria [l]	10,924	21,854	54,976	67,163	79,814	95,030	107,925			
United Arab Emirates	5,215	7,355	9,505	10,096	10,753	11,056	10,762	13,012	14,981	187
Yemen [l]	4,479	7,569	18,823	26,641	27,342	29,086	30,973			

MONEY SUPPLY
Table No. 0305 (cont'd)

Trends in Money Supply 1977-1992

Units: Million units of national currency

	1977	1980	1985	1987	1988	1989	1990	1991	1992	% nominal change 1977-92
North Africa										
Algeria [b]	48,555	84,434	202,230	223,910	252,210	250,010	270,040	324,470	347,870	616
Chad [a,b,q]	23	26	68	71	62	66	66	69	54	140
Djibouti			20,533	25,331	27,066	25,184	27,362	31,649	34,981	
Ethiopia	1,179	1,568	2,702	3,341	3,722	4,322	5,273	6,199	7,142	506
Libya [b]	1,444	2,899	3,492	3,439	3,012	3,521	4,452	4,293	4,939	242
Mali [a,b]	41	60	114	109	114	110	98	107	101	148
Mauritania [r]	4,095	5,677	12,173	13,516	14,150	17,028	17,621	19,376	20,202	393
Morocco [b]	15,102	23,352	42,820	54,489	62,032	68,395	80,914	92,080	92,353	512
Niger [a,b]	32	65	81	73	82	88	78	80	70	117
Somalia [l]	1,325	2,783	9,773	30,046	45,436	139,830	143,000			
Sudan [d,s]	497	1,097	4,145	7,768	11,218	18,899	27,659	44,305	93,006	18,613
Tunisia	576	951	2,059	2,126	2,494	2,524	2,678	2,697	2,892	402
West Africa										
Benin [a,b,d]	29	45	87	62	72	84	105	117	123	320
Burkina Faso [a,b]	31	42	70	91	101	105	104	109	113	267
Cameroon [a,b,q]	127	208	427	387	422	452	419	430	416	229
Cape Verde [b]	1,411	2,302	4,843	5,710	6,038	6,411	6,926	7,538	9,782	593
Côte d'Ivoire [a,b]	260	434	620	599	578	511	526	510	444	71
Equatorial Guinea [a,b,q]			8	9	5	7	3	3	2	
Gabon [a,b,q]	96	94	177	133	163	171	181	195	169	76
Gambia [a]	40	61	162	198	214	260	296	394	435	993
Ghana [a,b]	2	6	38	84	122	186	206	236	254	10,514
Guinea										
Guinea-Bissau										
Liberia										
Nigeria [b]	5,558	9,227	13,227	14,906	21,446	25,813	34,540	48,708	62,378	1,022
Sao Tomé e Príncipe										
Senegal [a,b]	109	138	193	214	215	231	204	213	189	73
Sierra Leone	85	153	900	2,889	4,637	8,675	14,253	25,092	31,387	37,044
Togo [a,b]	36	55	83	91	64	63	75	78	65	78
East/Central Africa										
Angola										
Burundi	6,155	9,643	18,453	19,786	20,507	21,112	23,233			
Central African Republic [a,b,q]	18	35	52	54	50	57	55	53	51	180
Comoros [b]			7,177	7,812	8,879	10,256	10,888	9,932	10,679	
Congo [a,b,q]	31	54	112	102	98	97	121	112	118	285
Kenya [b]	7,333	8,434	12,923	18,917	19,160	21,647	27,529	31,667	42,156	475
Madagascar [a,b]	100	151	239	372	455	598	575	753	849	749
Maldives [a,b]	46	81	172	204	230	270	318	404	460	896
Mauritius	1,219	1,720	2,039	3,304	3,820	4,511	5,578	6,677	7,505	516
Réunion										
Rwanda [b]	8,035	12,026	14,699	17,791	18,332	16,053	16,846	18,145	21,611	169
Seychelles	84	159	155	155	188	220	217	266	293	250
Tanzania [h]	6,383	13,346	25,514	47,131	64,126	65,350				
Uganda [n]	5,772	13,959	2,256							
Zaire [a,b]	1	3	22	68	150	263	746	18,056	342,803	33,378,965
Southern Africa										
Botswana	58	91	188	312	407	507	586	614	607	943
Lesotho		49	133	157	220	245	264	313	351	
Malawi	100	97	167	298	436	453	482	634	793	693
Mozambique [l]					244	365	485			
Namibia										
South Africa [c]	4,648	8,398	21,332	32,026	39,934	43,343	49,858	51,499		
Swaziland	34	50	77	125	143	169	198	212	254	644
Zambia [b,q]	393	519	1,231	3,225	5,244	7,947	12,543	22,360	21,707	5,426
Zimbabwe [b]	375	633	1,016	1,225	1,603	1,905	2,418	2,978	2,886	671

Source: IMF/UN/national statistical offices

Notes: see end of section

INFLATION RATES   Table No. 0306

Annual Rates of Inflation 1977-1992

Units: % growth

	1977	1980	1984	1985	1986	1987	1988	1989	1990	1991	1992
North America											
Canada [a]	8.0	10.2	4.3	4.0	4.2	4.4	4.0	5.0	4.8	5.6	1.5
USA	6.5	13.5	4.3	3.6	1.9	3.7	4.0	4.8	5.4	4.3	3.0
South America											
Argentina [b,c,d]	176.1	100.8	626.7	672.1	90.1	131.3	343.0	3,079.8	2,311.3	171.7	24.9
Bolivia [e]	8.1	47.2	1,281.0	11,750.0	276.0	15.0	16.0	15.0	17.0	21.4	
Brazil [f,g]	43.7	82.8	197.0	226.9	145.2	229.7	682.3	1,287.0	2,937.8	440.8	1,066.7
Chile [d]	91.9	35.4	19.9	30.7	19.5	19.9	14.7	17.0	26.0	21.9	15.6
Colombia [d]	33.1	26.5	16.1	24.0	18.9	23.3	28.1	25.8	29.1	30.4	27.0
Ecuador [a,e]	13.0	13.0	31.2	28.0	23.0	29.5	58.2	75.6	48.5	48.7	54.6
French Guiana											
Guyana [h]	8.3	14.1	25.2	15.0	7.9	28.7	39.9	61.1			
Paraguay	9.3	22.4	20.3	25.2	31.7	21.8	22.8	26.2	38.2	24.3	
Peru [i,j]	38.1	59.2	110.2	163.4	77.9	85.8	667.0	3,398.6	7,458.4	409.5	73.5
Suriname [e,k]	9.7	14.1	3.7		18.6	53.3					
Uruguay [l]	58.2	63.5	55.3	72.2	76.4	63.6	62.2	80.4	112.5	102.0	68.5
Venezuela [c]	7.8	21.5	12.2	11.4	11.5	28.1	29.5	84.2	40.8	34.2	31.4
Caribbean											
Anguilla											
Antigua	13.8	19.0	3.9	1.0							
Aruba					1.1	3.7	3.1	4.0	5.9	5.6	3.9
Bahamas	3.2	12.1	3.9	4.6	5.4	6.0	4.1	5.4	4.7	7.1	5.7
Barbados [i]	8.3	14.5	4.6	3.9	1.3	3.3	4.9	6.2	3.1	6.3	6.1
Bermuda											
British Virgin Islands											
Cayman Islands											
Cuba											
Dominica [j]	9.5	30.6	2.2	2.1	3.0	5.3	1.8	6.3	1.4	5.2	
Dominican Republic [f,k]	12.8	16.8	27.0	37.5	9.7	15.9	44.4	45.4	59.4	53.9	2.0
Grenada [f,k]	18.5	21.2	5.6	2.5	0.5	-0.9	4.0	5.6	2.7	2.6	4.0
Guadeloupe											
Haiti [a,e,j]	6.5	17.8	6.4	10.6	3.3	-11.4	4.1	6.9	21.5	11.8	
Jamaica [d,f]	11.2	27.3	27.8	25.7	15.1	6.7	8.3	14.3	21.9	51.1	99.6
Martinique											
Netherlands Antilles [o,f]	5.5	14.6	2.1	0.5	1.3	3.8	2.6	3.9	3.7	4.0	1.5
St Kitts [f]						0.8	0.5	4.9	4.2	4.2	4.3
St Lucia [f]	8.9	19.5	1.2	1.3	2.3	7.0	0.8	4.1	4.7	5.7	5.0
St Vincent/Grenadines [a]	10.2	17.2	2.7	2.1	1.2	2.9	0.2	2.8	7.6	5.6	
Trinidad and Tobago [n]	11.8	17.5	13.3	7.6	7.7	10.8	7.8	11.4	11.0	3.9	6.5
Central America											
Belize			3.7	3.7	1.0	2.0	3.2	2.1	3.0	5.6	2.8
Costa Rica	4.2	18.1	12.0	15.1	11.8	16.8	20.8	16.5	19.0	28.7	21.8
El Salvador [f]	11.8	17.4	11.5	22.3	31.9	24.9	19.8	17.6	24.0	14.4	7.3
Guatemala	12.3	10.8	3.4	18.7	36.9	12.3	10.8	11.4	41.2	33.2	10.0
Honduras [l]	8.4	18.1	4.7	3.4	4.4	2.5	4.5	9.9	23.3	34.0	8.8
Mexico	29.0	26.4	65.5	57.7	86.2	131.8	114.2	20.0	26.7	22.7	15.5
Nicaragua [d,e,h,k]	11.4	35.3	35.4	219.5	747.7	912.9	10,087.5	3,414.0			
Panama	4.5	13.8	1.6	1.0	-0.1	1.0	0.3	0.1	0.8	1.3	1.8
Puerto Rico											
South Asia											
Afghanistan	7.7	0.9	7.7	9.2	-2.1	19.7	19.7	75.1	47.2	56.7	
Bangladesh [f]	8.6	13.4	10.5	10.7	11.0	9.5	9.3	10.0	8.1	7.2	4.7
Bhutan [f]		4.4	8.4	3.9	0.6	6.4	10.1	8.8	10.0	11.8	14.5
India [d]	8.4	11.4	8.3	5.6	8.7	8.8	9.4	6.2	9.0	13.9	11.8
Nepal [d]	9.9	14.7	2.8	8.1	19.0	10.8	9.0	8.8	8.2	15.6	17.1
Pakistan [b]	10.1	11.9	6.6	5.8	3.7	4.8	8.8	7.8	9.1	11.8	9.5
Sri Lanka	1.2	26.2	16.6	1.5	8.0	7.7	14.0	11.6	21.5	12.2	11.4

INFLATION RATES

Annual Rates of Inflation 1977-1992

Units: % growth

	1977	1980	1984	1985	1986	1987	1988	1989	1990	1991	1992
Japan											
Japan	8.2	7.7	2.2	2.0	0.6	0.1	0.7	2.3	3.1	3.3	1.7
ASEAN/NICs											
Brunei											
Hong Kong	5.6	14.8	8.5	3.4	3.2	5.3	7.4	9.7	9.7	11.0	9.6
Indonesia [i]	11.0	18.5	10.5	4.7	5.8	9.3	8.0	6.4	7.4	9.2	7.5
Macau [f]								8.8	8.0	8.9	8.2
Malaysia [e,f,q]	4.8	6.7	3.9	0.3	0.7	1.1	2.0	2.8	2.6	4.4	4.5
Philippines [a]	9.9	18.2	50.3	23.1	0.8	3.8	8.8	10.6	12.7	18.7	8.9
Singapore [g]	3.2	8.5	2.6	0.5	-1.4	0.5	1.5	2.4	3.4	3.4	2.3
South Korea	10.2	28.7	2.3	2.5	2.8	3.0	7.1	5.7	8.6	9.7	6.2
Taiwan	7.0	19.0		-0.2	0.7	0.5	1.3	4.4	4.1	3.6	4.1
Thailand [f]	7.6	19.7	0.9	2.4	1.8	2.5	3.9	5.4	6.0	5.7	4.7
East/SE Asia											
Cambodia											
China	2.5	7.4	2.7	11.5	6.0	7.3	20.7	16.3	1.3		
Laos [k]		61.9	52.7	65.3			5.0	62.9	35.1	13.4	
Mongolia		0.1		0.6	-1.0						
Myanmar [f]	-1.1	0.6	4.8	6.8	9.3	24.8	16.0	27.2	17.6	32.3	23.5
North Korea											
Vietnam					490.0	349.2	317.0	76.9	29.0	83.0	
Australasia											
Australia [i]	12.3	10.1	4.0	6.7	9.1	8.5	7.2	7.6	7.3	3.2	1.0
New Zealand [b]	14.4	17.2	6.2	15.4	13.2	15.7	6.4	5.7	6.1	2.6	1.0
Pacific											
American Samoa											
Fiji [i]	7.5	14.5	5.3	4.4	4.4	5.7	11.8	6.2	8.2	6.5	4.9
French Polynesia											
Guam											
Kiribati	8.9	16.1	5.5	4.5	6.0	6.5	3.1				
Nauru											
New Caledonia											
Papua New Guinea [f]	4.5	12.1	7.4	3.7	5.5	3.3	5.4	4.5	7.0	7.0	3.6
Solomon Islands	8.6	13.1	11.0	9.6	13.6	11.0	16.7	14.9	8.7	15.1	10.8
Tonga	17.6	22.4	0.1	19.6	21.7	4.7	9.9	-22.4	9.7	10.6	7.9
Tuvalu											
Vanuatu [f]	5.7	11.2	5.5	1.0	4.8	14.8	8.7	7.7	4.8	6.5	2.0
Western Samoa	14.4	33.0	11.9	9.1	5.7	4.6	8.5	6.5	15.2	-1.4	8.5
Middle East											
Bahrain [c]	17.7	3.8	0.3	-2.6	-2.3	-1.7	0.3	1.5	1.0	0.8	-0.2
Egypt	12.7	20.7	17.1	13.3	22.6	19.7	17.7	21.3	16.8	19.8	13.6
Iran	27.2	20.7	12.5	4.4	18.4	28.6	28.7	22.3	7.6	17.1	22.9
Iraq											
Israel [e,m,o]	34.6	131.0	373.8	304.6	48.1	19.8	16.3	20.2	17.2	19.0	11.9
Jordan [d,i,f]	14.6	11.1	3.8	3.0		-0.3	3.2	25.7	16.2	8.2	2.9
Kuwait [l,n]	9.9	6.9	1.2	1.5	1.0	0.7	1.5	3.3	1.3		
Lebanon											
Oman											
Qatar		6.8	1.1	1.9	1.6	2.7	4.6	3.3	3.0		
Saudi Arabia [a,i,l]	11.4	3.8	-1.2	-3.3	-3.0	-1.0	1.1	1.0	2.1	4.9	-0.1
Syria [f]	11.8	18.9	9.2	17.3	36.1	59.5	34.6	11.4	19.4	7.7	8.1
United Arab Emirates											
Yemen [i]	24.9	5.3	12.8								

INFLATION RATES

Annual Rates of Inflation 1977-1992

Units: % growth

	1977	1980	1984	1985	1986	1987	1988	1989	1990	1991	1992
North Africa											
Algeria [j]	12.1	9.5	6.3	10.5	12.4	7.5	5.9	9.3	16.6	21.3	
Chad			20.3	5.1	-13.1	-6.0	15.5	-4.9	0.6		
Djibouti											
Ethiopia	16.7	4.5	8.4	19.1	-9.8	-2.4	7.1	7.8	5.2	35.7	10.5
Libya											
Mali	25.7	21.9							0.6	2.1	-6.1
Mauritania	10.3	10.7	7.0	13.5	7.4	8.2	1.3	13.0	6.5	5.6	
Morocco	12.6	9.4	12.4	7.7	8.7	2.7	2.4	3.1	7.0	8.0	4.9
Niger	23.3	10.3	8.4	-0.9	-3.2	-6.7	-1.4	-2.8	-0.8	-7.8	
Somalia [h]	10.6	58.8	91.2	37.8	35.8	28.2	81.9	83.9			
Sudan [f]	17.1	25.4	34.1	45.4	24.5		64.7	63.5	65.2	123.6	112.6
Tunisia	6.7	10.0	8.4	8.0	5.8	7.2	6.4	7.4	6.8	8.2	5.4
West Africa											
Benin											
Burkina Faso	30.0	12.3	4.8	6.9	-2.6	-2.8	4.4	-0.5	-0.5	1.9	-1.4
Cameroon [n]	14.7	9.6	11.4	1.3	7.7	6.0	8.6	-2.3	-0.1		
Cape Verde			11.2	5.4	10.9	3.9	4.3	4.2	11.2	9.4	
Côte d'Ivoire	27.4	14.7	4.3	1.8	7.3	0.4	7.0	1.3	-0.7	1.5	3.5
Equatorial Guinea [f]					-17.8	-12.9	2.3	5.9	1.1	-3.2	-8.1
Gabon	13.9	12.3	5.8	7.3	6.3	-1.0	-9.8	7.0	8.6		
Gambia	12.4	6.7	22.1	18.3	56.6	23.5	11.7	8.3	12.2	8.6	9.5
Ghana [f]	116.5	50.1	39.7	10.3	24.6	39.8	31.4	25.2	37.2	18.0	11.1
Guinea											
Guinea-Bissau											
Liberia [n]	6.2	14.7	1.2	-0.6	3.6	5.0	9.6	9.1	8.1		
Nigeria [d,f]	21.4	10.0	39.6	5.5	5.4	10.2	38.3	50.8	7.5	13.0	52.6
Sao Tomé e Príncipe											
Senegal	11.3	8.7	11.8	13.0	6.4	-4.3	-1.8	0.4	0.3	-1.8	
Sierra Leone [i]	8.3	12.9	66.6	76.6	80.9	178.7	34.3	60.8	111.0	102.7	65.5
Togo	22.5	12.3	-3.5	-1.8	4.1	0.1	-0.1	-0.8	1.0	0.4	
East/Central Africa											
Angola											
Burundi [e]	6.9	9.4	14.4	3.6	1.9	7.1	4.5	11.6	7.0	8.8	4.7
Central African Republic [a,i,f]	11.1	17.1	2.6	10.4	2.2	-7.0	-4.0	0.7		-3.1	0.4
Comoros											
Congo [n]	14.4	7.3	12.7	6.1	2.5	2.3	3.7	4.1	1.9		
Kenya [o,f]	14.9	13.8	10.2	13.0	4.0	7.7	11.2	12.9	15.6	19.8	35.6
Madagascar	3.1	18.2	9.9	10.6	14.5	15.0	26.8	9.0	11.8	8.6	14.5
Maldives		23.8									
Mauritius [a]	9.2	42.0	7.4	6.7	1.9	0.5	9.2	12.7	13.5	7.0	4.6
Réunion											
Rwanda	13.7	7.2	5.4	1.7	-1.1	4.1	3.0	1.0	4.2	19.6	9.5
Seychelles [a]	14.9	13.5	4.1	0.8	0.3	2.6	1.8	1.5	4.0	1.9	3.3
Tanzania [a]	11.6	30.3	35.3	34.1	32.4	30.0	31.2	25.8	19.7	22.3	22.1
Uganda				132.4	168.5	200.0	196.2	61.4	33.1	28.1	52.4
Zaire [d,f]	69.0	42.1	52.2	23.8	46.7	90.4	82.7	104.1	81.3	2,154.4	3,023.8
Southern Africa											
Botswana [a,r]	12.2	13.7	8.6	8.1	10.0	9.8	8.4	11.6	11.4	11.8	16.2
Lesotho [e,l]	16.7	15.7	11.0	13.3	18.0	11.8	11.4	14.7	11.6	17.7	
Malawi [e,f]	4.1	19.0	20.0	10.5	14.0	25.2	33.9	12.5	11.8	12.6	12.4
Mozambique											
Namibia											
South Africa [e,k]	11.1	13.8	11.7	16.2	18.6	16.1	12.8	14.7	14.3	15.3	13.9
Swaziland [e,f]	20.8	18.7	13.0	19.8	11.8	13.5	12.5	9.0	15.9	12.1	5.5
Zambia	19.8	11.7	20.0	37.4	51.6	43.0	55.6	128.7	111.0	92.6	
Zimbabwe [l]	10.3	5.4	20.2	8.5	14.3	12.5	7.4	12.9	17.4	24.3	46.3

Source: IMF/national statistical offices
Notes: see end of section

PUBLIC AND PRIVATE CONSUMPTION — Table No. 0307

Government and Private Consumption: Growth Rates for Selected Periods

Units: Average annual growth rate (%)

	Government 1965-80	Government 1980-86	Private 1965-80	Private 1980-86
North America				
Canada	4.8	1.9	5.1	2.8
USA	1.9	3.6	3.5	3.7
South America				
Argentina	3.2	-1.2	2.7	0.1
Bolivia	8.0	2.4	4.0	-2.0
Brazil	6.5	1.7	9.1	2.6
Chile	4.0	-0.7	1.0	-1.4
Colombia	6.7	2.6	5.9	2.0
Ecuador	12.2	-2.6	6.8	1.7
French Guiana		1.4		0.8
Guyana		-6.3		-3.8
Paraguay	5.1	2.6	6.3	3.1
Peru	5.6	2.3	4.2	0.4
Suriname		1.0		-4.8
Uruguay	3.2	1.2	2.4	-4.1
Venezuela	7.4	0.8	8.5	-1.7
Caribbean				
Anguilla				
Antigua		6.4		4.8
Aruba				
Bahamas		1.4		0.8
Barbados		-1.5		0.1
Bermuda		1.4		0.8
British Virgin Islands		16.1		2.6
Cayman Islands				
Cuba		10.2		2.9
Dominica		3.5		3.4
Dominican Republic	0.3	4.4	7.3	0.3
Grenada		1.0		2.8
Guadeloupe		1.4		0.8
Haiti	1.9	1.4	2.4	-1.5
Jamaica	9.8	-1.3	1.5	2.8
Martinique		1.4		0.8
Netherlands Antilles [a]		1.4		0.8
St Kitts		1.4		0.8
St Lucia		10.8		4.6
St Vincent/Grenadines		5.1		6.3
Trinidad and Tobago		-0.7	7.5	-6.7
Central America				
Belize	6.7	3.3	5.9	-1.0
Costa Rica	6.8	-0.4	5.1	1.3
El Salvador	12.2	3.1	6.8	-1.1
Guatemala	7.0	0.9	4.1	-0.4
Honduras	7.3	2.2	4.3	0.7
Mexico	6.2	3.8	5.3	0.1
Nicaragua	8.5	17.3	5.9	-3.4
Panama	6.6	3.5	2.0	4.3
Puerto Rico	7.4	4.5	4.7	3.3
South Asia				
Afghanistan				
Bangladesh		6.4	2.7	6.0
Bhutan		4.0		3.5
India [b]	6.3	8.2	3.1	4.2
Nepal		4.0		3.5
Pakistan [c]	4.7	7.1	5.5	6.4
Sri Lanka	1.1	7.1	3.2	5.1

PUBLIC AND PRIVATE CONSUMPTION — Table No. 0307 (cont'd)

Government and Private Consumption: Growth Rates for Selected Periods

Units: Average annual growth rate (%)

	Government 1965-80	Government 1980-86	Private 1965-80	Private 1980-86
Japan				
Japan	5.1	3.1	6.1	3.0
ASEAN/NICs				
Brunei		4.0		3.5
Hong Kong	7.7	5.9	9.0	6.5
Indonesia	11.4	4.4	6.3	5.7
Macau				
Malaysia	8.5	2.7	6.0	2.1
Philippines	7.7	-0.4	4.5	1.1
Singapore	10.1	10.2	7.8	3.6
South Korea	6.7	4.2	7.9	5.6
Taiwan				
Thailand	9.3	4.0	6.8	4.4
East/SE Asia				
Cambodia		4.0		3.5
China	6.0	6.3	5.3	7.7
Laos		4.0		3.5
Mongolia				
Myanmar		5.9	3.7	5.9
North Korea				
Vietnam				
Australasia				
Australia [c]	5.4	3.8	4.1	2.6
New Zealand	2.9	1.7	3.2	1.6
Pacific				
American Samoa				
Fiji		4.4		1.7
French Polynesia		8.0		7.3
Guam				
Kiribati		3.7		2.5
Nauru				
New Caledonia		3.7		2.5
Papua New Guinea	0.1	-1.7	3.7	1.7
Solomon Islands		3.7		2.5
Tonga		3.7		2.5
Tuvalu				
Vanuatu		6.0		5.0
Western Samoa		3.7		2.5
Middle East				
Bahrain		4.4		6.4
Egypt		14.3	5.7	3.1
Iran [c]	14.9	-0.8	8.4	5.4
Iraq		-3.6		-8.4
Israel	8.4	-1.1	6.1	3.9
Jordan		6.3		4.4
Kuwait		3.9	8.4	-3.3
Lebanon		-4.9		-9.5
Oman		11.8		18.7
Qatar		0.9		-1.7
Saudi Arabia		7.1	15.4	3.9
Syria	15.0	4.2	10.1	3.2
United Arab Emirates		4.1		6.8
Yemen		9.2		1.3

PUBLIC AND PRIVATE CONSUMPTION

Table No. 0307 (cont'd)

Government and Private Consumption: Growth Rates for Selected Periods

Units: Average annual growth rate (%)

	Government 1965-80	Government 1980-86	Private 1965-80	Private 1980-86
North Africa				
Algeria	8.6	3.6	9.0	4.6
Chad		-5.2		-2.8
Djibouti		3.3		4.4
Ethiopia ^d	6.4	-0.9	3.6	-1.9
Libya	19.2	-1.4		-0.2
Mali	5.1	5.8	5.0	0.7
Mauritania	10.0	-2.5	1.8	1.7
Morocco	11.0	1.4	4.6	2.4
Niger	2.9	1.7	-0.6	2.1
Somalia	12.7	-6.5	3.1	5.6
Sudan	0.2	-1.6	4.5	-1.7
Tunisia	7.2	5.5	7.9	4.6
West Africa				
Benin	0.7	2.5	1.7	1.2
Burkina Faso	8.7	3.0	2.1	-0.4
Cameroon ^c	5.0	8.4	3.8	4.1
Cape Verde		6.0		3.8
Côte d'Ivoire	12.7	-3.7	7.9	2.1
Equatorial Guinea		2.7		2.6
Gabon		7.3		3.5
Gambia		7.1		3.8
Ghana ^c	3.8	-4.2	1.2	1.2
Guinea		-15.3		-3.1
Guinea-Bissau		2.1		2.5
Liberia ^c	3.4	-8.3	3.1	-1.6
Nigeria	13.5	-1.1	7.0	-1.1
Sao Tomé e Príncipe		4.2		-8.1
Senegal ^c	2.9	2.9	1.8	2.0
Sierra Leone ^c	-0.2	-0.7	4.0	-6.8
Togo	9.5	-0.5	5.4	1.2
East/Central Africa				
Angola		2.8		2.8
Burundi	7.3	5.7	3.9	2.5
Central African Republic	-1.1	-2.5	4.2	0.5
Comoros		3.0		3.1
Congo	5.5	10.5	2.8	8.1
Kenya ^c	10.4	-0.3	5.3	2.9
Madagascar	2.0	0.7	1.5	-0.4
Maldives		11.8		-0.4
Mauritius ^c	7.1	2.3	6.2	3.1
Réunion		6.7		5.1
Rwanda	6.2	4.5	4.0	2.7
Seychelles		0.1		4.4
Tanzania ^c		5.7	4.6	2.7
Uganda ^c		9.6	1.1	8.9
Zaire	0.7	-6.6	-0.2	1.1
Southern Africa				
Botswana	12.0	9.9	9.2	5.4
Lesotho	12.3	6.7	8.5	5.3
Malawi	5.7	3.9	3.9	2.3
Mozambique		-2.2		-8.3
Namibia		2.9		
South Africa	5.7	3.7	4.3	1.5
Swaziland		3.5		6.4
Zambia	5.1	-3.3	0.1	0.5
Zimbabwe	10.6	8.4	5.4	-1.5

Source: IMF/UN/national statistical offices

Notes: see end of section

GOVERNMENT FINANCE   Table No. 0308

Government Finance and International Liquidity: Latest Year

Units: Million units of national currency

	Year	Budget revenue	Budget expenditure	Budget surplus/ deficit	Foreign debt	Exchange reserves (million US dollars, 1992)	Gold reserves (million troy oz, 1992)
North America							
Canada [a,b,c]	1992	135.6	167.1	-34.8	62.1	9,382.0	9.94
USA [a,d,e]	1992	1,128.0	1,468.2	-335.3	455.0	40,010.0	261.84
South America							
Argentina [e]	1989	319.4	305.6	-12.4	339.1	6,422.0	4.12
Bolivia	1991	2,842.0	3,221.0	-13.0	465.0	169.5	0.89
Brazil [a,f]	1990	24,179.3	11,075.4	-1,847.2	3.1	22,520.0	2.23
Chile [a,g]	1988	1,550.3	1,620.4	-12.2	1,338.0	9,167.0	1.87
Colombia [a,h]	1991	3,221.6	3,196.4	25.2	3,740.2	7,236.0	0.54
Ecuador [a]	1991	1,820.1	1,634.1	186.0		829.6	0.44
French Guiana							
Guyana	1992	17,192.0	21,332.0	-3,975.0	136,523.0	191.1	
Paraguay [a,g,i]	1990	792.7	600.9	190.7	43.5	452.8	0.04
Peru	1992	5,651.7	6,533.6	-870.9		2,849.0	1.82
Suriname [j]	1986	494.9	925.7	-445.7	124.2	3.9	0.05
Uruguay [a,k]	1991	3,714.4	3,573.3	141.1	2,634.0	509.0	2.03
Venezuela [f,i]	1992	723,730.0	856,800.0	-133,070.0	191,454.0	9,288.0	11.46
Caribbean							
Anguilla							
Antigua						50.5	
Aruba						142.0	0.10
Bahamas [l]	1991	475.6	549.7	-101.3	121.8	144.2	
Barbados [b,i]	1991	1,016.7	1,079.7	-69.3	712.8	139.6	
Bermuda							
British Virgin Islands							
Cayman Islands							
Cuba							
Dominica						20.3	
Dominican Republic [m]	1991	16,499.2	13,220.2	3,318.5	1,113.5	499.7	0.02
Grenada	1980	59.1	91.0	-4.6	4.2	25.9	
Guadeloupe							
Haiti [n]	1990	1,198.3	1,854.5	-628.6		17.5	0.02
Jamaica [j]	1986	3,700.5	4,869.3	-1,300.8	2,702.9	106.0	
Martinique							
Netherlands Antilles	1991	458.3	560.1	-31.3	233.9	183.0	0.55
St Kitts [i]	1990	104.4	144.3	0.2		26.2	
St Lucia [b,i]	1991	299.8	280.2	19.6		53.7	
St Vincent/Grenadines [k]	1990	137.2	155.4	-18.2	145.3	32.6	
Trinidad and Tobago	1989	4,965.2	5,854.9	-709.6	4,932.5	171.9	0.05
Central America							
Belize [b,e]	1992	233.8	316.8	-49.0	177.1	48.7	
Costa Rica [n]	1991	162,520.0	171,100.0	-9,200.0	162,117.0	1,006.4	0.04
El Salvador	1992	3,715.6	7,253.7	-1,839.3	15,647.5	422.1	0.47
Guatemala [o]	1992	5,575.0	5,168.0	407.0	711.4	749.6	0.12
Honduras [n]	1992	3,200.0	3,053.8	146.2	14,083.2	197.3	0.02
Mexico	1991	177,618.0	148,403.0	29,213.0		18,577.0	0.69
Nicaragua [p,q]	1990	39.9	80.5	-36.2	18.0	174.7	0.12
Panama [l]	1990	1,469.4	368.7	160.1	2,624.9	483.5	
Puerto Rico							
South Asia							
Afghanistan [r]	1984	37,615.0	43,177.0	-13,562.0	68,310.0	214.1	0.97
Bangladesh [s,t]	1991	80,505.0	73,000.0	7,505.0	179,644.0	1,783.2	0.09
Bhutan [t]	1991	1,001.8	2,220.7	-135.0	3,266.2	95.8	
India [a,b]	1990	755.2	916.3	-368.6	318.5	5,461.0	11.35
Nepal	1991	9,847.0	18,989.0	-6,428.0	43,926.0	461.7	0.15
Pakistan [e,t]	1992	222,874.0	281,154.0	-77,181.0	197,018.0	850.0	2.02
Sri Lanka [e]	1992	85,000.0	118,802.0	-30,290.0	214,579.0	899.0	0.16

GOVERNMENT FINANCE   Table No. 0308 (cont'd)

Government Finance and International Liquidity: Latest Year

Units: Million units of national currency

	Year	Budget revenue	Budget expenditure	Budget surplus/ deficit	Foreign debt	Exchange reserves (million US dollars, 1992)	Gold reserves (million troy oz, 1992)
Japan							
Japan [a]	1990	62,146.0	67,533.0	-6,781.0		61,888.0	24.23
ASEAN/NICs							
Brunei							
Hong Kong [b,f]	1991	89,523.0	85,556.0	3,967.0	1,958.0		
Indonesia [a,b]	1990	39,566.0	38,720.0	798.0	85,891.0	10,181.0	3.10
Macau							
Malaysia [c,u]	1991	33,607.0	30,835.0	2,772.0	24,192.0	8,991.0	2.35
Philippines [e]	1992	240,571.0	265,620.0	-15,966.0	289,858.0	4,283.0	2.80
Singapore [b,k]	1992	25,355.0	14,804.0	9,537.0	61.0	39,661.0	
South Korea [a,e]	1992	42,756.0	40,364.0	-2,008.0	5,700.0	16,639.9	0.32
Taiwan [f]	1991	617,900.0	608,500.0	9,400.0	518.5	82,405.0	
Thailand [e]	1992	88,600.0	426,800.0	62,000.0	99,653.0	20,012.0	2.47
East/SE Asia							
Cambodia	1984				14,730.0		
China [a]	1991	358.3	379.4	-21.1		45,229.0	12.70
Laos [s,j]	1991	79,022.0	81,922.0	-2,900.0	18,410.0	53.4	
Mongolia [v]	1991	6,022.2	8,101.4	-2,079.2		75.9	0.28
Myanmar [b]	1991	9,713.0	11,676.0	-1,963.0		280.1	0.25
North Korea							
Vietnam [a,m]	1991	8,210.0	9,180.0	-970.0	392,000.0		
Australasia							
Australia [t]	1991	102,913.0	102,128.0	2,400.0	4,957.0	10,526.0	7.93
New Zealand [e,t]	1992	27,727.0	29,466.0	-1,317.0	22,950.0	2,929.0	
Pacific							
American Samoa							
Fiji [e]	1992	574.3	599.4	-2.6	206.0	294.3	
French Polynesia							
Guam							
Kiribati [w]	1990	25.1	22.1	3.0		94.0	
Nauru							
New Caledonia							
Papua New Guinea [o]	1990	766.7	1,058.7	-100.3	1,034.8	238.4	0.06
Solomon Islands [m]	1991	132.3	231.7		29.6	22.6	
Tonga [f,t]	1991	51.7	99.2	-10.1	38.7	29.6	
Tuvalu							
Vanuatu	1989	4,154.6	7,287.3	-1,323.8	1,714.8	8.7	
Western Samoa [m]	1990	121.1	64.8	56.4	122.2	57.7	
Middle East							
Bahrain	1991	469.9	502.2	105.7	50.8	1,330.0	0.15
Egypt [t]	1989	22,601.0	23,913.0	-4,126.0		10,677.0	2.43
Iran [a,t,x]	1992	10,505.0	11,257.0	-752.0		5,287.0	5.92
Iraq							
Israel [b,k]	1991	40,867.0	50,818.0	-8,051.0	41,362.0	5,127.1	0.10
Jordan [y]	1988	746.1	1,001.2	-95.0	1,410.7	750.2	0.79
Kuwait [t]	1989	3,025.0	2,901.0	124.0		4,834.8	2.54
Lebanon						1,457.5	9.22
Oman	1991	1,261.4	1,575.1	-284.3	932.1	1,549.1	0.29
Qatar [z]	1982	13,434.0	12,619.0	815.0		594.0	0.86
Saudi Arabia [a,m]	1987	57.0	114.6	-34.8	29.6	4,561.0	4.60
Syria [aa]	1990	58,639.0	58,481.0	921.0		193.0	0.83
United Arab Emirates	1991	1,629.0	13,264.0			5,404.9	0.80
Yemen [bb]	1990	19,631.0	23,596.0	-5,123.0		226.8	

GOVERNMENT FINANCE

Table No. 0308 (cont'd)

Government Finance and International Liquidity: Latest Year

Units: Million units of national currency

	Year	Budget revenue	Budget expenditure	Budget surplus/ deficit	Foreign debt	Exchange reserves (million US dollars, 1992)	Gold reserves (million troy oz, 1992)
North Africa							
Algeria						1,456.0	5.58
Chad	1991	32,241.0	113,771.0	-26,502.0		74.4	0.01
Djibouti	1988	20,101.0	22,234.0	-733.0		80.3	
Ethiopia [cc,dd]	1990	3,104.5	5,163.2	-1,798.0	4,439.5	222.8	0.11
Libya						5,361.0	3.60
Mali [a]	1988	114.3	174.8	-27.6	726.8	295.9	0.02
Mauritania						61.1	0.01
Morocco [s]	1987	37,089.0	44,163.0	-7,025.0	84,835.0	3,465.0	0.70
Niger	1980	77,436.0	98,727.0	-25,241.0		213.2	0.01
Somalia [bb]						11.4	0.02
Sudan [t]	1982	839.5	1,198.2	-326.4		3.0	
Tunisia [e]	1992	3,956.4	4,391.7	-349.0	4,435.0	839.9	0.22
West Africa							
Benin						242.4	0.01
Burkina Faso [i]	1987	89,852.0	85,377.0	1,976.0		323.7	0.01
Cameroon [a,t,o]	1989	601.7	707.5	-110.2	546.9	32.1	0.03
Cape Verde						67.3	
Côte d'Ivoire [ee]	1984	815,699.0	903,847.0	-90,033.0	611,435.0	6.7	0.05
Equatorial Guinea						5.7	
Gabon [a]	1991	441.7	465.5	-25.2		167.2	0.01
Gambia [g,t,j]	1987	294.6	381.4		144.8	66.8	
Ghana [o,t]	1988	142,238.0	143,897.0	3,911.0	16,633.0	398.1	0.28
Guinea							
Guinea-Bissau							
Liberia [i,t,dd,ff]	1988	212.8	283.4	-91.9	1,427.1	7.8	
Nigeria [b,g]	1987	17,376.0	26,081.0	-9,702.0	2,594.7	966.0	0.69
Sao Tomé e Príncipe							
Senegal [a,t]	1984	192.5	298.5	-82.4	520.7	10.9	0.03
Sierra Leone [t]	1990	5,499.0	8,191.0	-2,413.0	87,566.0	18.9	
Togo [dd]	1987	99,492.0	117,144.0	-9,380.0	308,066.0	271.9	0.01
East/Central Africa							
Angola							
Burundi [n]	1990	36,921.0	34,436.3	2,484.7	194,212.0	164.6	0.02
Central African Republic	1981	30,365.0	41,538.0	-6,671.0		103.2	0.01
Comoros [o]	1987	6,820.0	21,037.0	-7,395.0	80,823.0	29.0	
Congo	1983	280,510.0	310,450.0	-26,650.0		3.5	0.01
Kenya [t]	1991	49,474.0	65,753.0	-11,171.0		35.4	0.08
Madagascar						89.7	
Maldives	1990	466.3	699.5	-64.8	432.2	27.0	
Mauritius [e,t]	1992	11,562.5	11,629.7	-93.5	5,964.0	787.3	0.06
Réunion							
Rwanda	1980	13,805.0	15,458.0	-1,875.0	14,979.0	61.1	
Seychelles [dd]	1989	963.1	977.5	-119.8	618.3	30.1	
Tanzania [j]	1991	137,092.9	207,292.4			203.9	
Uganda [g,t]	1991	51,686.0	99,175.0	-10,051.0	540.3	53.5	
Zaire [g]	1988	161,613.0	317,378.0	-116,759.0	8,078.0	56.7	0.03
Southern Africa							
Botswana [b]	1990	3,596.5	2,368.3	793.4	801.9	3,816.0	
Lesotho [b]	1991	820.0	970.0	-9.9	1,070.6	152.0	
Malawi [b]	1989	1,021.8	1,243.2	-80.5	2,740.3	36.9	0.01
Mozambique							
Namibia							
South Africa	1992	76,867.0	106,402.0	-29,535.0	2,367.0	1,568.0	6.65
Swaziland [b,k]	1991	791.4	781.4	-6.7	561.2	296.9	
Zambia [o,v]	1989	6,553.0	11,985.0	-2,757.0	20,459.0	184.6	0.01
Zimbabwe [k,t]	1991	6,521.0	7,419.0	-1,430.0	4,037.0	221.7	0.55

Source: IMF/UN/national statistical offices

Notes: see end of section

GOVERNMENT EXPENDITURE | Table No. 0309

Government Expenditure by Object: Latest Year

Units: Million units of national currency

	Year	A	B	C	D	E	F	G	H	I	Total
North America											
Canada [a]	1989	14,802	11,055	4,344	7,783	52,328	1,914	901	16,748	39,087	148,962
USA [b]	1991	105,460	308,860	24,720	196,540	373,490	36,550	3,720	144,070	235,640	1,429,050
South America											
Argentina	1989	25	30	30	9	119	1	3	49	39	306
Bolivia	1991	375	422	601	106	599	6	5	544	563	3,221
Brazil [c,d]	1990	1,465	391	348	742	2,799	22	11	356	4,941	11,075
Chile	1988	117,340	136,050	163,370	94,830	483,520	65,230	13,500	142,010	404,590	1,620,440
Colombia	1984	116,081	38,391	114,694	26,348	114,810	18,963	3,474	111,629	32,909	577,299
Ecuador [c]	1990	85	156	219	133	23	7	5	142	520	1,290
French Guiana											
Guyana	1985		144	128	74	86	9	4	365		810
Paraguay [c]	1990	132	80	76	26	71	18		77	121	601
Peru	1990	38	8	12	4					13	75
Suriname	1986	283	41	162	34	58	11	20	234	83	926
Uruguay [c]	1990	175	233	187	114	1,274	2	14	222	318	2,539
Venezuela	1986	2,777	6,099	20,573	10,539	7,273	5,006	937	18,228	29,128	100,560
Caribbean											
Anguilla											
Antigua											
Aruba											
Bahamas	1991	116	19	106	85	22	2	4	125	71	550
Barbados [a]	1989	104	21	212	136	246	42	42	177	158	1,138
Bermuda											
British Virgin Islands											
Cayman Islands	1990	31		18	16	4	1	1	22	18	111
Cuba											
Dominica [e]	1979	13		5	5	1	2		12	16	53
Dominican Republic [f]	1990	1,176	341	715	986	329	1,094	80	2,565	-257	7,029
Grenada	1977	2	5	6	5	2			12	1	35
Guadeloupe											
Haiti											
Jamaica [a]	1977	132	28	196	83	35	62	31	243	255	1,065
Martinique											
Netherlands Antilles	1991	83		31	39	199	6	4	41	157	560
St Kitts	1987	11		15	10	8	8		12	17	81
St Lucia											
St Vincent/Grenadines [e]	1990	38	9	28	24	4	4		38	10	155
Trinidad and Tobago	1981	1,380	103	568	299	324	577	62	1,573	180	5,066
Central America											
Belize [a]	1992	42	10	51	33	10	19	11	100	41	317
Costa Rica [g]	1991			32,750	54,730	21,450	1,290	1,070	14,740	45,070	171,100
El Salvador	1990	532	1,011	707	378	146	71	64	937	1,060	4,906
Guatemala [f]	1989	801	368	542	275	144	73		602	-30	2,775
Honduras	1979	121	99	155	70	39	18	6	225	136	869
Mexico [c]	1990	3,423	2,815	16,527	2,279	14,776	722	346	15,930	62,434	119,252
Nicaragua	1980	1,589	695	734	923	281	185		1,304	621	6,332
Panama	1990	164	73	233	281	277	49	7	84	201	1,369
Puerto Rico											
South Asia											
Afghanistan											
Bangladesh [e]	1989	25,880	9,932	11,053	4,718	7,410	442	377	33,810	4,719	98,341
Bhutan [e]	1991	352		237	106	12	170	61	1,071	212	2,221
India [a,c]	1990	57	156	23	15		63		190	412	916
Nepal [h]	1991	1,525	1,114	2,078	885		1,284		8,161	3,942	18,989
Pakistan [e]	1986	8,154	35,404	3,108	1,058	6,710	3,718	1,658	41,470	18,834	120,114
Sri Lanka	1991	7,292	10,317	9,129	5,230	19,281	919		26,967	30,589	109,724

GOVERNMENT EXPENDITURE

Government Expenditure by Object: Latest Year

Units: Million units of national currency

	Year	A	B	C	D	E	F	G	H	I	Total
Japan											
Japan c	1989	4,478	3,920	4,937	1,142	2,231	1,719			41,987	60,414
ASEAN/NICs											
Brunei											
Hong Kong a	1992	14,245	14,577	18,895	11,164	6,913	6,762	12,577	5,869	17,420	108,422
Indonesia a,c	1990	13,998	3,158	3,512	938		685	281	10,505	5,643	38,720
Macau											
Malaysia	1989	2,623	2,540	5,557	1,450		1,150		6,253	6,898	26,471
Philippines	1991	21,221	26,010	38,643	10,158	5,885	3,035	1,514	59,158	81,512	247,136
Singapore a	1990	897	3,409	2,828	652	300	870	174	2,389	2,704	14,223
South Korea c	1992	4,271	8,924	6,538	469	3,958	1,102	264	6,675	8,163	40,364
Taiwan c,e,i,j	1992	430		292		260			283	651	1,916
Thailand b	1991	22,409	62,214	73,503	26,794	12,919	8,732	1,865	88,344	67,239	364,019
East/SE Asia											
Cambodia											
China	1985	13,100	19,150	10,400					62,300	79,530	184,480
Laos											
Mongolia											
Myanmar a	1990	5,035	5,436	3,875	1,588	1,075	2,031	378	4,772	159	24,349
North Korea											
Vietnam											
Australasia											
Australia e	1991	8,907	8,738	7,182	12,967	30,526	1,386	1,026	8,432	22,964	102,128
New Zealand e	1992	1,337	1,141	3,822	3,505	10,300	551	240	2,838	5,732	29,466
Pacific											
American Samoa											
Fiji	1992	155	35	134	49	30	13	1	111	71	599
French Polynesia											
Guam											
Kiribati											
Nauru											
New Caledonia											
Papua New Guinea	1988	122	41	134	82	4	23	16	182	271	875
Solomon Islands	1988	11		31	9	1	4	1	48	24	128
Tonga e	1991	26		13	7	1	2		50		99
Tuvalu											
Vanuatu	1989	999		920	479		3	10	4,254	622	7,287
Western Samoa	1984	15		8	5			1	24	5	58
Middle East											
Bahrain	1991	154	89	78	46	12	10	10	92	11	502
Egypt e	1989	699	3,027	3,201	664	2,869	1,377	1,913	1,951	8,212	23,913
Iran c,k	1992	317	969	2,392	938	1,406	601	179	1,560	2,895	11,257
Iraq											
Israel a	1991	881	11,377	5,279	1,888	11,358	4,127	472	5,154	10,282	50,818
Jordan	1990	45	205	142	48	151	19	15	100	239	964
Kuwait e	1989	282	577	406	216	365	229	64	420	342	2,901
Lebanon											
Oman	1991	171	557	180	85	53	154	37	162	176	1,575
Qatar											
Saudi Arabia											
Syria	1990	2,275	18,429	4,335	1,117	1,306	609	963	17,930	11,517	58,481
United Arab Emirates	1989	613	5,827	1,985	916	420	54	357	572	2,520	13,264
Zimbabwe	1992	9,810	11,220	11,615	2,540			1,686	8,061	9,613	54,545

GOVERNMENT EXPENDITURE

Table No. 0309 (cont'd)

Government Expenditure by Object: Latest Year

Units: Million units of national currency

	Year	A	B	C	D	E	F	G	H	I	Total
North Africa											
Algeria											
Chad	1976	5,191	5,977	3,128	979	439	95	157	6,134	1,069	23,169
Djibouti	1981	5,658	1,942	1,431	1,337	1,014			884	4,130	16,396
Ethiopia [i,l]	1988	1,521		438	142	194	242	47	1,066	492	4,142
Libya											
Mali	1988	36,200	14,000	15,800	3,600	5,500		800	9,300	89,600	174,800
Mauritania	1979	2,490	3,238	1,147	310	423	12	160	1,485	1,748	11,013
Morocco	1987	4,715	6,687	7,515	1,342	3,061	183	266	9,455	10,939	44,163
Niger [b]	1980	19,337	3,719	17,792	4,003	1,646	2,073	2,184	32,027	15,946	98,727
Somalia	1978	476	512	167	66	34			236	559	2,050
Sudan [e]	1982	216	114	73	16	27	1	17	281	465	1,210
Tunisia	1992	852	237	771	291	627	192	115	989	318	4,392
West Africa											
Benin	1979	5,507	190	3,680	1,753	3,659	1,072	193	8,765	17,246	42,065
Burkina Faso	1987	8,479	15,241	11,931	4,455		192	1,123	5,979	37,977	85,377
Cameroon [c]	1989	66	47	85	24	46	16	10	340	73	707
Cape Verde											
Côte d'Ivoire	1985	75,712	35,353	195,485	36,613	35,899	16,233	12,758	44,470		452,523
Equatorial Guinea											
Gabon											
Gambia [e]	1982	57		28	13	6	5	4	40	7	160
Ghana [e]	1988	28,055	4,603	36,995	12,880	9,904	7,197		27,563	16,700	143,897
Guinea											
Guinea-Bissau	1987	12,456	2,168	2,541	2,638	4,273	4,067	198	19,524	957	48,822
Liberia [e]	1988	68	27	31	15	3	2	4	80	53	283
Nigeria	1987	1,209	723	733	204	2	392	9	9,359	13,450	26,081
Sao Tomé e Príncipe											
Senegal [e]	1984	53,560	25,830	43,910	11,850	16,360	5,760	11,190	63,410	60,910	292,780
Sierra Leone	1990	896	808	1,088	786	185	68	4	2,373	1,983	8,191
Togo	1987	22,817	13,047	23,311	6,088	8,253	1,672	3,072	36,503	2,381	117,144
East/Central Africa											
Angola											
Burundi	1977	1,722	1,195	2,190	496	363		295	3,279	1,098	10,638
Central African Republic	1981	9,542	4,029	7,319	2,112	2,555	75	490	8,140	7,276	41,538
Comoros	1987	2,600	911	5,288	1,527			1,036	9,180	495	21,037
Congo	1983			34,930		13,620	2,810		109,980	149,110	310,450
Kenya [e]	1990	6,292	5,385	10,680	2,886	52	2,037	1,220	11,134	14,015	53,701
Madagascar [c]	1991	148	56	128	49	11		2	266	80	740
Maldives	1990	251		79	68	14	83		166	39	700
Mauritius [e]	1992	1,416	167	1,654	970	1,854	628	185	1,965	2,791	11,630
Réunion											
Rwanda	1980	2,399	2,027	2,910	703	445	183	144	6,406	241	15,458
Seychelles	1977	55		22	21	11	10		39		159
Tanzania [e]	1985	7,884	3,658	1,919	1,312	125	258	589	6,367	4,442	26,554
Uganda	1986	991	1,204	686	109	97	35	58	675	718	4,573
Yemen	1988	78,413	44,283	19,388	13,752	7,726	6,962		82,192	64,662	317,378
Southern Africa											
Botswana [a]	1990	324	316	486	120	16	368	32	397	309	2,368
Lesotho [a]	1991	91	63	213	111	15	40	7	307	123	970
Malawi [a]	1989	233	67	110	92		39		435	267	1,243
Mozambique											
Namibia	1991	460	184	628	275	193	225	84	491	290	2,830
South Africa [a,m]	1984	265	178	243	45	3	93	16	733	1,648	3,224
Swaziland [a]	1991	143	34	199	66	8	42	5	188	96	781
Zaire [l]	1988	3,050		738	636	130	41	135	2,122	1,707	8,559
Zambia [e]	1989	554	818	1,163	379	169	23	57	1,111	742	5,016

Source: IMF/national statistical offices
Notes: see end of section

GOVERNMENT EXPENDITURE | Table No. 0310

Government Expenditure by Object (% Analysis): Latest Year

Units: % of total expenditure

	Year	A	B	C	D	E	F	G	H	I	Total
North America											
Canada [a]	1989	9.9	7.4	2.9	5.2	35.1	1.3	0.6	11.2	26.2	100.0
USA [b]	1991	7.4	21.6	1.7	13.8	26.1	2.6	0.3	10.1	16.5	100.0
South America											
Argentina	1989	8.3	9.9	9.9	3.0	39.1	0.3	0.8	16.0	12.6	100.0
Bolivia	1991	11.6	13.1	18.7	3.3	18.6	0.2	0.2	16.9	17.5	100.0
Brazil	1990	13.2	3.5	3.1	6.7	25.3	0.2	0.1	3.2	44.6	100.0
Chile	1988	7.2	8.4	10.1	5.9	29.8	4.0	0.8	8.8	25.0	100.0
Colombia	1984	20.1	6.7	19.9	4.6	19.9	3.3	0.6	19.3	5.7	100.0
Ecuador	1990	6.6	12.1	17.0	10.3	1.8	0.5	0.4	11.0	40.3	100.0
French Guiana											
Guyana	1985		17.8	15.8	9.1	10.6	1.1	0.5	45.1		100.0
Paraguay	1990	22.0	13.3	12.6	4.3	11.8	3.0		12.8	20.1	100.0
Peru	1990	50.7	10.7	16.0	5.3					17.3	100.0
Suriname	1986	30.6	4.4	17.5	3.7	6.3	1.2	2.2	25.3	9.0	100.0
Uruguay	1990	6.9	9.2	7.4	4.5	50.2	0.1	0.6	8.7	12.5	100.0
Venezuela	1986	2.8	6.1	20.5	10.5	7.2	5.0	0.9	18.1	29.0	100.0
Caribbean											
Anguilla											
Antigua											
Aruba											
Bahamas	1991	21.1	3.5	19.3	15.5	4.0	0.4	0.7	22.7	12.9	100.0
Barbados	1989	9.1	1.8	18.6	12.0	21.6	3.7	3.7	15.6	13.9	100.0
Bermuda											
British Virgin Islands											
Cayman Islands	1990	27.9		16.2	14.4	3.6	0.9	0.9	19.8	16.2	100.0
Cuba											
Dominica [c]	1979	23.6	0.2	10.1	8.8	1.5	3.2	0.8	21.6	30.2	100.0
Dominican Republic [d]	1990	16.7	4.9	10.2	14.0	4.7	15.6	1.1	36.5	-3.7	100.0
Grenada	1977	6.1	15.6	18.3	15.6	5.0	1.2	0.7	34.0	3.5	100.0
Guadeloupe											
Haiti											
Jamaica [a]	1977	12.4	2.6	18.4	7.8	3.3	5.8	2.9	22.8	23.9	100.0
Martinique											
Netherlands Antilles	1991	14.8		5.5	7.0	35.5	1.1	0.7	7.3	28.0	100.0
St Kitts	1987	13.6		18.5	12.3	9.9	9.9		14.8	21.0	100.0
St Lucia											
St Vincent/Grenadines [c]	1990	24.5	5.8	18.1	15.5	2.6	2.6		24.5	6.5	100.0
Trinidad and Tobago	1981	27.2	2.0	11.2	5.9	6.4	11.4	1.2	31.1	3.6	100.0
Central America											
Belize [a]	1992	13.2	3.2	16.1	10.4	3.2	6.0	3.5	31.5	12.9	100.0
Costa Rica [e]	1991			19.1	32.0	12.5	0.8	0.6	8.6	26.3	100.0
El Salvador	1990	10.8	20.6	14.4	7.7	3.0	1.4	1.3	19.1	21.6	100.0
Guatemala [c]	1989	28.9	13.3	19.5	9.9	5.2	2.6		21.7	-1.1	100.0
Honduras	1979	13.9	11.4	17.8	8.1	4.5	2.1	0.7	25.9	15.7	100.0
Mexico	1990	2.9	2.4	13.9	1.9	12.4	0.6	0.3	13.4	52.4	100.0
Nicaragua	1980	25.1	11.0	11.6	14.6	4.4	2.9		20.6	9.8	100.0
Panama	1990	12.0	5.3	17.0	20.5	20.2	3.6	0.5	6.1	14.7	100.0
Puerto Rico											
South Asia											
Afghanistan											
Bangladesh	1989	26.3	10.1	11.2	4.8	7.5	0.4	0.4	34.4	4.8	100.0
Bhutan	1991	15.8		10.7	4.8	0.5	7.7	2.7	48.2	9.5	100.0
India [a]	1990	6.2	17.0	2.5	1.6		6.9		20.7	45.0	100.0
Nepal [f]	1991	8.0	5.9	10.9	4.7		6.8		43.0	20.8	100.0
Pakistan [c]	1986	6.8	29.5	2.6	0.9	5.6	3.1	1.4	34.5	15.7	100.0
Sri Lanka	1991	6.6	9.4	8.3	4.8	17.6	0.8		24.6	27.9	100.0

209

GOVERNMENT EXPENDITURE

Government Expenditure by Object (% Analysis): Latest Year

Units: % of total expenditure

	Year	A	B	C	D	E	F	G	H	I	Total
Japan											
Japan	1989	7.4	6.5	8.2	1.9	3.7	2.8			69.5	100.0
ASEAN/NICs											
Brunei											
Hong Kong [a]	1992	13.1	13.4	17.4	10.3	6.4	6.2	11.6	5.4	16.1	100.0
Indonesia [a]	1990	36.2	8.2	9.1	2.4		1.8	0.7	27.1	14.6	100.0
Macau											
Malaysia	1989	9.9	9.6	21.0	5.5		4.3		23.6	26.1	100.0
Philippines	1991	8.6	10.5	15.6	4.1	2.4	1.2	0.6	23.9	33.0	100.0
Singapore [a]	1990	6.3	24.0	19.9	4.6	2.1	6.1	1.2	16.8	19.0	100.0
South Korea	1992	10.6	22.1	16.2	1.2	9.8	2.7	0.7	16.5	20.2	100.0
Taiwan [c,g,h]	1992	22.4		15.2		13.6			14.8	34.0	100.0
Thailand [b]	1991	6.2	17.1	20.2	7.4	3.5	2.4	0.5	24.3	18.5	100.0
East/SE Asia											
Cambodia											
China	1985	7.1	10.4	5.6					33.8	43.1	100.0
Laos											
Mongolia											
Myanmar [a]	1990	20.7	22.3	15.9	6.5	4.4	8.3	1.6	19.6	0.7	100.0
North Korea											
Vietnam											
Australasia											
Australia [c]	1991	8.7	8.6	7.0	12.7	29.9	1.4	1.0	8.3	22.5	100.0
New Zealand [c]	1992	4.5	3.9	13.0	11.9	35.0	1.9	0.8	9.6	19.5	100.0
Pacific											
American Samoa											
Fiji	1992	25.9	5.8	22.4	8.2	5.0	2.2	0.2	18.5	11.9	100.0
French Polynesia											
Guam											
Kiribati											
Nauru											
New Caledonia											
Papua New Guinea	1988	13.9	4.7	15.3	9.4	0.5	2.6	1.8	20.8	31.0	100.0
Solomon Islands	1988	8.9		24.1	6.7	0.9	2.9	0.7	37.4	18.5	100.0
Tonga [c]	1991	26.4		13.2	7.1	0.6	2.0		50.7		100.0
Tuvalu											
Vanuatu	1989	13.7		12.6	6.6			0.1	58.4	8.5	100.0
Western Samoa	1984	25.8		13.8	9.3		0.3	1.6	40.8	8.4	100.0
Middle East											
Bahrain	1991	30.7	17.7	15.5	9.2	2.4	2.0	2.0	18.3	2.2	100.0
Egypt [c]	1989	2.9	12.7	13.4	2.8	12.0	5.8	8.0	8.2	34.3	100.0
Iran [i]	1992	2.8	8.6	21.2	8.3	12.5	5.3	1.6	13.9	25.7	100.0
Iraq											
Israel [a]	1991	1.7	22.4	10.4	3.7	22.4	8.1	0.9	10.1	20.2	100.0
Jordan	1990	4.7	21.3	14.7	5.0	15.7	2.0	1.6	10.4	24.8	100.0
Kuwait [c]	1989	9.7	19.9	14.0	7.4	12.6	7.9	2.2	14.5	11.8	100.0
Lebanon											
Oman	1991	10.9	35.4	11.4	5.4	3.4	9.8	2.3	10.3	11.2	100.0
Qatar											
Saudi Arabia											
Syria	1990	3.9	31.5	7.4	1.9	2.2	1.0	1.6	30.7	19.7	100.0
United Arab Emirates	1989	4.6	43.9	15.0	6.9	3.2	0.4	2.7	4.3	19.0	100.0
Zimbabwe	1992	18.0	20.6	21.3	4.7			3.1	14.8	17.6	100.0

GOVERNMENT EXPENDITURE   Table No. 0310 (cont'd)

Government Expenditure by Object (% Analysis): Latest Year

Units: % of total expenditure

	Year	A	B	C	D	E	F	G	H	I	Total
North Africa											
Algeria											
Chad	1976	22.4	25.8	13.5	4.2	1.9	0.4	0.7	26.5	4.6	100.0
Djibouti	1981	34.5	11.8	8.7	8.2	6.2			5.4	25.2	100.0
Ethiopia g,j	1988	36.7		10.6	3.4	4.7	5.8	1.1	25.7	11.9	100.0
Libya											
Mali	1988	20.7	8.0	9.0	2.1	3.1		0.5	5.3	51.3	100.0
Mauritania	1979	22.6	29.4	10.4	2.8	3.8	0.1	1.5	13.5	15.9	100.0
Morocco	1987	10.7	15.1	17.0	3.0	6.9	0.4	0.6	21.4	24.8	100.0
Niger b	1980	19.6	3.8	18.0	4.1	1.7	2.1	2.2	32.4	16.2	100.0
Somalia	1978	23.2	25.0	8.1	3.2	1.7			11.5	27.3	100.0
Sudan c	1982	17.9	9.4	6.0	1.3	2.2	0.1	1.4	23.2	38.4	100.0
Tunisia	1992	19.4	5.4	17.6	6.6	14.3	4.4	2.6	22.5	7.2	100.0
West Africa											
Benin	1979	13.1	0.5	8.7	4.2	8.7	2.5	0.5	20.8	41.0	100.0
Burkina Faso	1987	9.9	17.9	14.0	5.2		0.2	1.3	7.0	44.5	100.0
Cameroon	1989	9.3	6.6	12.0	3.4	6.5	2.3	1.4	48.1	10.3	100.0
Cape Verde											
Côte d'Ivoire	1985	16.7	7.8	43.2	8.1	7.9	3.6	2.8	9.8		100.0
Equatorial Guinea											
Gabon											
Gambia	1982	36.0		17.4	8.0	3.6	3.3	2.3	25.0	4.4	100.0
Ghana	1988	19.5	3.2	25.7	9.0	6.9	5.0		19.2	11.6	100.0
Guinea											
Guinea-Bissau	1987	25.5	4.4	5.2	5.4	8.8	8.3	0.4	40.0	2.0	100.0
Liberia	1988	24.1	9.6	11.0	5.3	0.9	0.7	1.4	28.3	18.8	100.0
Nigeria	1987	4.6	2.8	2.8	0.8		1.5		35.9	51.6	100.0
Sao Tomé e Príncipe											
Senegal	1984	18.3	8.8	15.0	4.0	5.6	2.0	3.8	21.7	20.8	100.0
Sierra Leone	1990	10.9	9.9	13.3	9.6	2.3	0.8		29.0	24.2	100.0
Togo	1987	19.5	11.1	19.9	5.2	7.0	1.4	2.6	31.2	2.0	100.0
East/Central Africa											
Angola											
Burundi	1977	16.2	11.2	20.6	4.7	3.4		2.8	30.8	10.3	100.0
Central African Republic	1981	23.0	9.7	17.6	5.1	6.2	0.2	1.2	19.6	17.5	100.0
Comoros	1987	12.4	4.3	25.1	7.3			4.9	43.6	2.4	100.0
Congo	1983			11.3		4.4	0.9		35.4	48.0	100.0
Kenya	1990	11.7	10.0	19.9	5.4	0.1	3.8	2.3	20.7	26.1	100.0
Madagascar	1991	20.0	7.6	17.3	6.6	1.5		0.3	35.9	10.8	100.0
Maldives	1990	35.9		11.3	9.7	2.0	11.9		23.7	5.6	100.0
Mauritius	1992	12.2	1.4	14.2	8.3	15.9	5.4	1.6	16.9	24.0	100.0
Réunion											
Rwanda	1980	15.5	13.1	18.8	4.5	2.9	1.2	0.9	41.4	1.6	100.0
Seychelles	1977	34.8		14.1	12.9	6.7	6.5	0.1	24.7	0.2	100.0
Tanzania	1985	29.7	13.8	7.2	4.9	0.5	1.0	2.2	24.0	16.7	100.0
Uganda	1986	21.7	26.3	15.0	2.4	2.1	0.8	1.3	14.8	15.7	100.0
Yemen	1988	24.7	14.0	6.1	4.3	2.4	2.2		25.9	20.4	100.0
Southern Africa											
Botswana a	1990	13.7	13.3	20.5	5.1	0.7	15.5	1.4	16.8	13.0	100.0
Lesotho a	1991	9.4	6.5	22.0	11.4	1.5	4.1	0.7	31.6	12.7	100.0
Malawi a	1989	18.7	5.4	8.8	7.4		3.1		35.0	21.5	100.0
Mozambique											
Namibia	1991	16.3	6.5	22.2	9.7	6.8	8.0	3.0	17.3	10.2	100.0
South Africa a,k	1984	8.2	5.5	7.5	1.4	0.1	2.9	0.5	22.7	51.1	100.0
Swaziland a	1991	18.3	4.4	25.5	8.5	1.0	5.4	0.6	24.1	12.3	100.0
Zaire g	1988	35.6		8.6	7.4	1.5	0.5	1.6	24.8	19.9	100.0
Zambia c	1989	11.0	16.3	23.2	7.6	3.4	0.5	1.1	22.1	14.8	100.0

Source: Euromonitor from IMF/national statistical offices

Notes: see end of section

GROSS DOMESTIC PRODUCT

Table No. 0311

Origin of Gross Domestic Product: Latest Year

Units: Million units of national currency

	Year	A	B	C	D	E	F	G	H	Total
North America										
Canada	1989	23,825	42,453	14,431		58,546	94,394	61,063	356,904	651,616
USA [a]	1988	100	80	949		233	1,653	441	1,391	4,847
South America										
Argentina	1983	86	27	210	17	42	113	39	148	683
Bolivia	1986	2,450	890	1,184	96	255	970	1,056	2,022	8,924
Brazil	1989	98,799	18,086	342,465	28,083	106,250	90,176	63,983	518,506	1,266,348
Chile [a]	1985	205	282	602	81	113	441	149	869	2,742
Colombia [a]	1990	3,454	1,563	4,332	586	1,169	2,910	1,910	4,730	20,654
Ecuador [a]	1990	1,101	1,257	1,904	-2	308	1,729	695	1,358	8,350
French Guiana										
Guyana [b,c]	1990	2,204	1,314	917		522	610	582	3,982	10,131
Paraguay [a,c]	1989	1,362	21	786	112	259	1,263	174	632	4,608
Peru [a]	1990	508	168	2,039	66	538	1,724	537	2,094	7,673
Suriname	1990	308	91	304	136	213	573	178	1,257	3,060
Uruguay [a]	1990	1,046	19	2,678	276	342	1,141	572	3,551	9,624
Venezuela [a]	1990	125	533	457	37	102	388	106	515	2,264
Caribbean										
Anguilla	1989	5	1	1	2	20	31	13	42	114
Antigua	1988	32	17	24	31	99	184	111	279	776
Aruba										
Bahamas										
Barbados	1990	160	20	238	92	194	928	245	1,566	3,440
Bermuda										
British Virgin Islands [d]	1988	4		3	5	7	34	14	45	114
Cayman Islands	1990	1	3	9	18	56	142	67	300	596
Cuba [e,f]	1989	1,555	4,656			1,172	4,295	1,038	76	12,791
Dominica	1990	97	3	27	12	28	50	62	183	462
Dominican Republic	1984	1,916	244	1,708	94	882	1,782	523	3,559	10,706
Grenada	1990	71	2	23	13	45	82	60	246	541
Guadeloupe [g]	1986	1,095	548		-12	538	1,806	652	6,332	10,958
Haiti										
Jamaica	1990	1,502	2,840	5,883	960	3,587	6,808	1,994	5,118	28,692
Martinique	1986	1,092	937		537	550	2,245	723	7,738	13,824
Netherlands Antilles [h]	1985	19		139	66	156	454	213	920	1,966
St Kitts	1989	28	1	47	3	36	62	44	82	302
St Lucia	1987	64	3	35	19	36	104	43	142	446
St Vincent/Grenadines	1989	68	1	36	26	35	52	76	176	470
Trinidad and Tobago	1990	497	4,851	2,675	349	1,902	3,643	1,874	5,859	21,650
Central America										
Belize	1990	140	4	74	16	53	108	73	267	733
Costa Rica [g]	1990	83,295	99,999		16,227	16,486	104,607	25,756	176,358	522,728
El Salvador	1990	4,599	65	7,647	793	1,072	14,187	1,897	10,797	41,057
Guatemala										
Honduras [c]	1989	1,779	134	1,369	255	395	1,093	599	4,158	9,782
Mexico [a]	1990	54,444	17,515	156,621	9,383	27,124	180,470	56,478	176,888	678,923
Nicaragua										
Panama	1990	490	5	407	229	82	627	635	2,476	4,949
Puerto Rico	1990	470	32	12,672	981	732	5,169	1,691	10,721	32,469
South Asia										
Afghanistan [f]	1985	143,200	59,400			16,400	20,300	7,400	3,700	250,400
Bangladesh [c,g]	1991	300,600	72,910		11,200	47,260	68,280	97,700	235,020	832,970
Bhutan	1989	1,924	36	303	391	358	269	236	765	4,281
India [a]	1990	1,531	94	858	97	253	598	341	955	4,726
Nepal	1991	56,012	100	5,430	821	6,837	4,427	4,364	22,637	100,628
Pakistan [a,c]	1991	230	6	154	29	37	152	73	335	1,017
Sri Lanka	1990	72,788	4,570	54,943	5,635	21,592	61,784	29,614	66,978	317,904

GROSS DOMESTIC PRODUCT

Table No. 0311 (cont'd)

Origin of Gross Domestic Product: Latest Year

Units: Million units of national currency

	Year	A	B	C	D	E	F	G	H	Total
Japan										
Japan [a,c]	1990	10,667	1,129	122,973	12,095	41,739	54,566	27,627	154,939	425,735
ASEAN/NICs										
Brunei [g]	1990	159	3,128		30	215	790	556	2,650	7,527
Hong Kong	1991	1,441	222	94,491	13,463	32,106	154,423	58,970	253,444	608,560
Indonesia [a,c]	1990	43,062	28,748	38,602	1,258	10,828	32,154	11,041	32,029	197,721
Macau										
Malaysia	1989	14,437	7,343	18,251	1,322	2,314	7,547	4,747	15,333	71,294
Philippines [a]	1991	262	18	316	31	62	172	74	305	1,239
Singapore	1991	165	128	19,988	1,304	4,728	11,535	9,294	21,934	69,076
South Korea [a]	1991	16,715	897	57,070	4,257	32,056	22,039	14,650	59,833	207,517
Taiwan	1992	184,280	26,779	1,710,711	148,181	267,323	842,745	332,003	1,692,027	5,204,049
Thailand [a]	1990	255	74	535	47	147	313	139	542	2,051
East/SE Asia										
Cambodia										
China [e]	1991	520,500		767,700		97,500	121,600	85,000		1,592,300
Laos [e]	1991	386,503	995	97,723	12,451	27,029	56,838	40,521	102,915	724,975
Mongolia [e,g]	1991	2,944	4,792			530	2,022	1,105	206	11,599
Myanmar	1991	84,509	952	12,095	464	2,350	34,093	4,178	10,615	149,256
North Korea										
Vietnam [a,e,f]	1991	21,685	10,371			2,015	8,148	878	2,454	45,551
Australasia										
Australia [c]	1990	12,406	18,679	56,925	12,631	30,037	65,813	27,835	152,788	377,114
New Zealand	1989	6,157	897	12,662	2,095	3,419	10,992	5,768	29,560	71,550
Pacific										
American Samoa										
Fiji	1989	326	56	175	55	66	379	169	636	1,861
French Polynesia	1990	13,849		21,648	4,957	18,294	67,632		171,374	297,754
Guam										
Kiribati	1988	13		1	1	2	6	6	12	41
Nauru										
New Caledonia	1988	3,575	51,796	11,222	5,723	10,712	46,794	8,806	85,870	224,498
Papua New Guinea [c]	1991	939	527	343	57	216	299	237	848	3,465
Solomon Islands	1987	112	-2	8	3	11	36	14	112	293
Tonga	1983	36		4		3	13	5	11	73
Tuvalu										
Vanuatu	1990	3,582		1,050	339	1,033	5,771	1,517	4,607	17,899
Western Samoa										
Middle East										
Bahrain	1990	14	324	253	29	94	148	140	466	1,468
Egypt [g]	1986	8,640	8,623		518	1,989	10,865	3,756	9,659	44,050
Iran [a]	1989	5,699	1,224	2,252	241	1,335	7,834	1,768	7,934	28,288
Iraq	1989	3,358	4,713	2,288	382	1,520	2,369	1,411	3,969	20,010
Israel [g]	1990	2,521	16,402		1,899	4,418	8,292	6,989	34,604	75,125
Jordan	1987	125	63	200	49	124	272	231	684	1,746
Kuwait	1989	46	2,773	974	-43	155	555	272	2,047	6,779
Lebanon [g]	1982	1,076	1,644		683	431	3,565	471	4,730	12,600
Oman [c]	1990	127	2,068	151	51	125	467	132	963	4,084
Qatar	1988	243	5,644	2,462	366	1,015	1,374	518	9,188	20,810
Saudi Arabia	1988	20,695	63,466	24,740	722	31,594	26,654	22,709	91,391	281,971
Syria	1990	76,261	39,872	16,173	-216	9,836	68,681	25,490	41,941	278,038
United Arab Emirates	1990	2,012	57,939	9,242	2,313	9,987	11,285	5,931	25,299	124,008
Yemen	1989	15,081	3,676	8,713	1,155	2,771	10,986	9,600	22,086	74,068

GROSS DOMESTIC PRODUCT   Table No. 0311 (cont'd)

Origin of Gross Domestic Product: Latest Year

Units: Million units of national currency

	Year	A	B	C	D	E	F	G	H	Total
North Africa										
Algeria	1987	24,460	52,330	29,460	4,730	44,750	30,980	14,130	47,260	248,100
Chad	1989	133,458	1,073	52,712	2,223	5,214	90,970	7,027	35,238	327,915
Djibouti	1989	1,745		3,055	3,552	3,515	11,780	8,165	26,763	58,575
Ethiopia [c]	1989	4,666	14	1,230	159	440	1,121	783	4,078	12,491
Libya	1987	353	1,579	465	126	783	531	416	1,934	6,187
Mali [a,i]	1990	313	10	53	25		123	32	127	683
Mauritania [b]	1989	25,818	7,887	7,782		4,815		3,729	33,489	83,520
Morocco [a]	1990	33	5	38	14	12	27	13	66	208
Niger	1987	219,070	49,386	56,642	17,900	33,375	88,859	26,942	157,672	649,846
Somalia	1989	337,973	1,692	9,544	500	18,076	47,364	32,610	37,138	484,897
Sudan	1987	5,456	18	1,684	433	995	4,495	1,892	3,961	18,934
Tunisia	1989	1,153	758	1,375	152	446	1,936	626	3,051	9,497
West Africa										
Benin	1989	177,129	4,406	42,882	4,107	15,225	82,110	36,475	125,191	487,525
Burkina Faso	1987	200,479	89	63,216	6,645	2,800	53,801	19,349	79,352	425,731
Cameroon [a]	1989	740	428	406	36	168	369	196	733	3,076
Cape Verde	1987	2,466	32	637	327	2,345	2,868	1,438	1,578	11,691
Côte d'Ivoire [a]	1987	1,382	35	302	36	104	366	207	490	2,922
Equatorial Guinea	1989	22,991		545	1,277	2,402	3,594	823	11,291	42,923
Gabon	1989	117,200	364,100	64,300	27,700	62,300	140,000	92,600	299,866	1,168,066
Gambia	1990	640	1	161	19	131	1,062	247	429	2,689
Ghana	1987	271,601	13,489	76,250	3,535	20,786	65,435	22,139	130,839	604,074
Guinea [a]	1987	274	87	51	7	49	184	26	130	808
Guinea-Bissau	1988	78,470	57	11,763	1,809	10,947	41,075	6,375	21,453	171,949
Liberia	1989	411	122	82	19	26	63	79	391	1,194
Nigeria	1987	37,577	10,749	4,645	453	1,314	21,845	3,980	10,125	90,688
Sao Tomé e Príncipe	1989	928	4	364	93	333	377	455	1,211	3,764
Senegal [a]	1987	241	16	217	21	83	159	102	294	1,133
Sierra Leone	1987	11,198	2,822	1,722	99	501	5,878	2,576	4,398	29,193
Togo	1987	103,664	35,667	24,334	6,641	12,172	38,903	21,990	53,385	296,756
East/Central Africa										
Angola	1989	77,000	22,333	5,330	948	3,423	12,153	12,265	35,514	168,966
Burundi	1989	71,967	718	17,243	813	6,257	14,777	4,233	25,738	141,746
Central African Republic	1989	139,900	8,960	23,990	1,500	8,830	76,603	15,307	52,720	327,810
Comoros	1989	28,370		2,590	620	5,010	11,020	2,930	14,460	65,000
Congo	1989	100,839	216,192	54,483	14,014	13,955	111,321	70,075	192,645	773,524
Kenya	1989	2,271	19	855	111	477	829	486	3,472	8,521
Madagascar [a]	1989	838	6	253	22	80	211	171	509	2,089
Maldives	1986	213	12	38		53	104	159	119	697
Mauritius	1989	3,386	30	6,052	577	1,720	4,605	2,920	12,356	31,646
Réunion	1989	1,940		840	450	2,580	5,280	970	13,940	26,000
Rwanda [a]	1989	56		15		9	22	9	18	130
Seychelles [g]	1989	74	160		33	87	181	265	543	1,343
Tanzania	1989	207,059	1,129	30,353	4,831	5,904	53,572	23,345	77,962	404,155
Uganda	1989	666,217	37	40,840	1,459	29,210	122,680	39,919	95,217	995,579
Zaire [a]	1989	200	154	9		35	114	5	122	639
Southern Africa										
Botswana	1989	149	2,542	209	93	166	432	82	928	4,601
Lesotho	1989	179	4	148	8	168	101	46	495	1,149
Malawi	1989	1,426		471	85	150	443	235	1,227	4,037
Mozambique [a]	1989	102	1	56	10	16	11	23	9	228
Namibia	1989	486	1,426	184	45	82	517	310	1,448	4,498
South Africa	1990	12,272	25,079	59,945	10,710	7,446	31,620	19,376	97,364	263,812
Swaziland	1988	183	16	265	35	37	142	82	341	1,101
Zambia	1989	10,562	7,720	21,933	398	884	5,109	2,881	7,432	56,919
Zimbabwe	1989	1,390	1,001	2,932	367	253	1,273	858	4,528	12,602

Source: UN/national statistical offices
Notes: see end of section

GROSS DOMESTIC PRODUCT

Usage of Gross Domestic Product: Latest Year

Units: Million units of national currency

	Year	A	B	C	D	E	F	Total incl. others
North America								
Canada	1992	146,205.0	419,852.0	-2,363.0	129,886.0	182,200.0	186,108.0	687,334.0
USA [a]	1992	1,114.9	4,095.8	4.4	766.0	636.3	666.7	5,950.7
South America								
Argentina [b]	1989	201.0	1,850.0	1.0	240.0	503.0	242.0	2,551.0
Bolivia	1991	2,491.0	15,500.0	274.0	2,594.0	5,875.0	5,042.0	21,690.0
Brazil [a]	1991	23,812.0	106,711.0		31,175.0	14,042.0	10,750.0	164,991.0
Chile [a]	1992	1,251.7	9,273.3	265.0	2,665.9	4,588.1	4,304.5	13,739.6
Colombia [a]	1991	2,805.9	17,433.2	137.7	3,889.2	5,568.3	3,441.0	26,393.3
Ecuador [a]	1991	973.0	8,562.0	437.0	2,205.0	3,753.0	3,780.0	12,149.0
French Guiana								
Guyana	1991	4,610.0	21,504.0		1,674.0		28,196.0	38,385.0
Paraguay [a]	1991	543.3	6,038.4	77.0	1,810.9	1,500.3	2,424.6	7,545.3
Peru	1991	1,902.0	29,865.0	765.0	5,203.0	3,169.0	3,993.0	33,912.0
Suriname [c]	1990	777.0	1,622.1		636.2	868.6	844.4	3,059.5
Uruguay [a]	1991	2,551.9	13,385.9	197.1	2,283.0	4,498.7	3,781.1	19,135.5
Venezuela [a]	1992	372.7	2,974.9	152.6	804.1	1,065.4	1,189.5	4,180.3
Caribbean								
Anguilla	1987	12.0	28.4		19.7	38.6	29.8	68.9
Antigua	1986	121.2	447.6		231.9	482.7	641.5	641.9
Aruba								
Bahamas	1988	370.1	1,132.8	27.4	510.7	1,763.8	1,346.9	2,457.9
Barbados [c]	1991	642.0	2,282.0		571.0	1,527.0	1,629.0	3,393.0
Bermuda [c]	1990	207.7	1,157.2		237.0	1,006.8	959.6	1,649.1
British Virgin Islands	1988	26.4	90.5	3.5	45.1	141.3	175.4	131.3
Cayman Islands	1989	69.0	296.0		110.0	315.0	313.0	477.0
Cuba [d,e]	1989	1,213.0	10,658.8	137.1	2,233.0	-2,681.2		12,790.9
Dominica	1989	86.7	312.8		148.6	173.4	298.7	422.7
Dominican Republic	1992	6,011.0	82,523.0	150.0	23,242.0	22,733.0	34,848.0	99,811.0
Grenada	1991	106.8	392.6	20.9	226.8	257.3	437.2	567.2
Guadeloupe	1986	3,659.4	9,718.8	-140.9	2,387.6	817.6	5,873.7	10,568.8
Haiti	1991		12,344.0		1,678.0	1,912.0	3,073.0	12,861.0
Jamaica	1990	4,178.0	17,311.0	72.0	8,362.0	15,132.0	16,549.0	29,823.0
Martinique	1986	4,440.3	11,558.5	-107.2	2,594.5	1,502.7	6,143.4	13,845.5
Netherlands Antilles	1985	626.5	1,375.5	15.4	294.8	1,308.4	1,655.0	1,965.6
St Kitts	1984	37.5	129.6		53.3	92.8	146.0	167.2
St Lucia	1984	102.7	266.7	21.0	105.0	261.4	348.6	408.2
St Vincent/Grenadines	1990	93.6	352.9			370.5	458.2	524.9
Trinidad and Tobago [c]	1991	3,391.0	14,129.0		3,024.0	9,264.0	7,388.0	22,419.0
Central America								
Belize	1991	175.5	511.1	23.8	265.5	431.7	616.4	791.2
Costa Rica	1992	131,086.0	518,700.0	60,193.0	168,510.0	333,855.0	376,542.0	835,802.0
El Salvador	1992	5,789.0	49,019.0	324.0	8,540.0	7,374.0	16,284.0	54,762.0
Guatemala	1991	2,833.0	40,161.0	316.0	5,613.0	8,461.0	10,396.0	46,988.0
Honduras	1992	1,961.0	13,082.0	1,100.0	3,921.0	5,250.0	7,148.0	18,166.0
Mexico [a]	1990	54,151.0	483,232.0	20,093.0	127,918.0	108,898.0	115,368.0	678,924.0
Nicaragua [a]	1991	1,412.9	6,205.6	-17.7	699.0	1,367.8	3,038.7	6,628.8
Panama	1991	962.0	3,458.4	75.9	925.8	2,054.4	1,985.4	5,491.1
Puerto Rico	1989	4,414.9	19,671.6	438.9	4,782.8	23,416.0	22,228.3	30,496.7
South Asia								
Afghanistan								
Bangladesh	1991	88,110.0	719,520.0	8,760.0	78,070.0	73,630.0	135,130.0	832,960.0
Bhutan	1990	1,223.0	2,695.8	-33.7	1,690.9	1,484.9	2,099.9	4,961.0
India [a]	1991	695.7	3,894.2	103.4	1,360.9			6,095.0
Nepal	1992	11,756.0	106,876.0	4,048.0	23,745.0	24,592.0	40,332.0	130,685.0
Pakistan [a]	1991	137.5	731.3	15.8	170.7	157.0	195.6	1,016.7
Sri Lanka	1991	37,750.0	289,528.0	950.0	85,426.0	106,386.0	144,701.0	375,339.0

GROSS DOMESTIC PRODUCT   Table No. 0312 (cont'd)

Usage of Gross Domestic Product: Latest Year

Units: Million units of national currency

	Year	A	B	C	D	E	F	Total incl. others
Japan								
Japan [a]	1992	43,737.0	264,988.8	2,419.3	142,450.8	47,401.8	36,156.0	464,841.5
ASEAN/NICs								
Brunei	1984	2,512.1		2.1	524.5			8,068.5
Hong Kong	1992	63,955.0	452,252.0	7,445.0	206,156.0	1,067,706.0	1,054,932.0	742,582.0
Indonesia [a,c]	1991	20,861.0	125,143.0		7,655.0	62,322.0	60,819.0	227,163.0
Macau	1990	2,336.5	10,189.5	-560.0	6,176.3	24,862.9	13,396.8	29,608.3
Malaysia	1990	15,593.0	62,030.0	-417.0	37,490.0	89,393.0	89,473.0	114,616.0
Philippines [a]	1992	129.8	1,017.0	3.0	280.3	394.2	448.8	1,342.5
Singapore [d]	1991	7,263.0	29,949.0	-1,691.0	27,529.0	6,518.0		69,076.0
South Korea [a]	1991	22,478.0	109,450.0	2,321.0	78,765.0	60,801.0	66,167.0	207,517.0
Taiwan	1992	911,440.0	2,903,603.0	58,552.0	1,208,573.0	2,302,419.0	180,538.0	5,204,049.0
Thailand [a]	1990	200.7	1,214.3	24.9	729.1	755.4	892.1	2,051.2
East/SE Asia								
Cambodia								
China [e]	1991	165.0	917.8	136.5	371.5			1,590.8
Laos								
Mongolia [e]	1990	2,040.3	5,746.1	1,477.3	806.6			8,328.0
Myanmar [e,f]	1991	131,907.0		1,103.0	18,731.0	4,151.0	6,636.0	149,256.0
North Korea								
Vietnam								
Australasia								
Australia	1992	73,758.0	243,351.0	-505.0	75,856.0	71,969.0	72,749.0	392,245.0
New Zealand	1991	12,138.0	46,960.0	313.0	12,042.0	21,470.0	20,108.0	73,213.0
Pacific								
American Samoa								
Fiji	1990	322.0	1,355.0	25.0	379.0	1,338.0	1,329.0	2,089.9
French Polynesia [a,c]	1986	104.7	143.9	1.1	88.3	21.6	92.7	266.9
Guam								
Kiribati	1988	20.8	32.7	0.5	12.0	11.4	34.0	44.9
Nauru								
New Caledonia	1988	69,654.0	101,420.0	1,006.0	45,584.0	71,209.0	64,645.0	224,498.0
Papua New Guinea	1992	932.0	2,378.0		875.0	1,936.0	2,040.0	4,080.0
Solomon Islands	1988	115.3	251.7	10.0	110.0	192.2	311.9	367.3
Tonga	1983	10.3	91.5	0.7	20.4	14.3	50.9	72.7
Tuvalu								
Vanuatu	1990	5,054.0	11,267.0	488.0	7,311.0	8,301.0	13,714.0	17,899.0
Western Samoa [c]	1988	45.8	212.7		77.7	74.8	164.5	246.4
Middle East								
Bahrain	1990	378.7			400.8			1,467.5
Egypt	1992	12,130.0	110,026.0	200.0	24,417.0	40,122.0	50,705.0	136,190.0
Iran [a]	1990	4,054.0	24,071.0	4,827.0	5,663.0	5,395.0	6,792.0	36,645.0
Iraq	1985	4,609.5	8,098.7	-337.1	3,699.4	3,774.7	4,476.0	15,369.4
Israel	1992	45,757.0	98,570.0	2,561.0	36,685.0	49,407.0	73,391.0	159,589.0
Jordan	1991	713.0	2,580.0		595.7	1,190.3	2,273.5	2,805.5
Kuwait	1989	1,603.0	3,162.0	44.0	1,292.0	3,725.0	3,047.0	6,779.0
Lebanon [c]	1982	4,850.0	15,840.0		1,179.0	5,255.0	14,525.0	12,599.0
Oman [c]	1991	1,394.7	1,505.7		659.4	1,891.0	1,515.0	3,935.8
Qatar	1987	8,776.0	6,362.0	-126.0	2,984.0	8,188.0	6,359.0	19,825.0
Saudi Arabia [a]	1989	96.6	145.0	6.8	60.4	118.2	116.2	310.8
Syria [c]	1991	42,779.0	237,488.0		49,231.0	76,038.0	99,931.0	305,605.0
United Arab Emirates [a]	1991	21.0	51.5	1.5	24.9	81.8	57.1	123.6
Yemen	1989	16,159.0	61,019.0	153.0	11,103.0	10,148.0	24,514.0	74,068.0

GROSS DOMESTIC PRODUCT — Table No. 0312 (cont'd)

Usage of Gross Domestic Product: Latest Year

Units: Million units of national currency

	Year	A	B	C	D	E	F	Total incl. others
North Africa								
Algeria	1988	60,000.0	158,800.0	1,000.0	97,300.0	48,900.0	46,000.0	320,000.0
Chad [c]	1989	88,499.0	293,007.0		43,070.0	66,430.0	145,436.0	345,570.0
Djibouti	1989	23,294.0	45,935.0	1,779.0	16,196.0	29,911.0	59,952.0	57,163.0
Ethiopia [c]	1992	2,165.0	11,582.0		1,215.0	1,039.0	2,617.0	13,385.0
Libya [c]	1987	2,251.0	2,669.0		1,660.0	2,401.0	2,144.0	6,837.0
Mali [a]	1989	109.8	471.4	8.3	126.5	103.3	175.3	644.0
Mauritania	1987	9,137.0	55,544.0	1,114.0	13,975.0	32,487.0	45,041.0	67,216.0
Morocco	1991	36,800.0	168,020.0	1,270.0	53,790.0	44,340.0	63,460.0	240,760.0
Niger [a]	1989	104.5	557.9	-15.5	86.5	129.1	185.0	676.9
Somalia [c]	1989	58,533.0	403,983.0		134,146.0	8,885.0	57,660.0	547,887.0
Sudan [c]	1987	3,672.0	15,558.0		3,442.0	1,700.0	3,900.0	20,472.0
Tunisia	1992	2,180.0	8,835.0	261.0	3,532.0	5,300.0	6,114.0	13,994.0
West Africa								
Benin	1989	58,313.0	409,359.0	-12,500.0	70,123.0	99,738.0	137,507.0	487,525.0
Burkina Faso	1987	76,604.0	436,330.0		11,856.0	137,592.0	203,113.0	459,269.0
Cameroon [a]	1989	364.0	2,348.0	19.0	935.0	547.0	654.0	3,568.0
Cape Verde	1988	3,968.0	17,848.0	-434.0	7,721.0	3,190.0	11,653.0	20,640.0
Côte d'Ivoire [a]	1987	471.0	2,198.0	8.0	335.0	1,668.0	1,074.0	3,606.0
Equatorial Guinea	1989	9,297.0	27,465.0	-7.0	8,959.0	11,267.0	14,058.0	42,923.0
Gabon [a,g]	1989	215.4	565.2		271.7	587.0	471.0	1,168.1
Gambia	1989	292.9			128.2	1,122.1	1,256.0	2,534.4
Ghana [a]	1990	222.0	1,736.1	1.4	247.7	312.6	488.0	2,031.7
Guinea	1987	80,300.0	694,700.0	2,200.0	161,500.0	299,900.0	321,800.0	916,800.0
Guinea-Bissau	1988	20,134.0	160,420.0	192.0	49,672.0	22,666.0	81,134.0	171,949.0
Liberia	1989	160.0	656.8	4.0	96.8	521.4	275.2	1,181.6
Nigeria [c]	1991	12,690.0	128,230.0		36,560.0	181,030.0	69,950.0	288,560.0
Sao Tomé e Príncipe [c]	1989	2,653.7	3,753.7		1,208.1	1,880.9	3,756.4	5,740.0
Senegal [a]	1988	247.7	1,069.7	93.7	216.4	397.1	466.5	1,558.1
Sierra Leone	1991	15,676.0	119,647.0	1,287.6	15,185.4	38,123.7	38,574.4	151,345.3
Togo [a]	1987	53.4	262.5	1.2	92.8	128.6	166.6	371.9
East/Central Africa								
Angola [c]	1989	63,020.0	136,760.0		19,150.0	64,160.0	61,190.0	221,900.0
Burundi [c]	1991	32,845.0	179,405.0		35,926.0	21,229.0	59,146.0	210,259.0
Central African Republic [c]	1989	38,210.0	294,730.0		45,890.0	51,180.0	88,340.0	341,670.0
Comoros	1989	19,640.0	52,800.0	1,510.0	13,130.0	11,030.0	25,000.0	73,110.0
Congo	1989	144,600.0	408,500.0	-3,776.0	126,700.0	368,100.0	270,600.0	773,524.0
Kenya	1991	39,407.0	144,070.0	4,351.0	42,760.0	60,436.0	63,781.0	227,243.0
Madagascar [a,c]	1989	493.4	2,777.9		489.6	501.4	511.3	3,751.0
Maldives	1990	351.4	517.5		629.0	418.9	1,096.2	970.3
Mauritius	1992	5,360.0	30,015.0	-326.0	14,125.0	29,784.0	31,958.0	47,000.0
Réunion	1989	5,040.0	27,220.0	700.0	4,925.0	1,420.0	10,010.0	29,295.0
Rwanda [a]	1991	46.2	167.5	-2.9	25.6	21.0	48.3	209.0
Seychelles	1990	544.4	1,004.9	32.0	451.9	1,056.2	1,098.2	1,990.7
Tanzania	1991	92,920.0	526,831.0	19,998.0	262,376.0	122,002.0	333,709.0	690,421.0
Uganda [a,c]	1989	124.5	879.5		116.4	12.5	27.9	1,105.1
Zaire [a]	1991	18,846.0	109,244.0	-3.0	6,000.0	30,970.0	31,314.0	133,011.0
Southern Africa								
Botswana [c]	1989	1,362.0	1,926.0		1,000.0	3,162.0	2,462.0	4,988.0
Lesotho	1991	278.6	2,175.9		1,228.8	224.5	2,264.0	1,643.8
Malawi	1992	1,240.9	5,314.4	180.0	1,077.0	1,591.8	2,773.6	6,630.5
Mozambique [a,c]	1989	73.6	291.4		27.2	17.7	118.7	291.2
Namibia [c]	1989	1,179.0	2,570.0		797.0	2,483.0	2,423.0	4,606.0
South Africa	1991	61,988.0	179,000.0	-5,731.0	53,957.0	74,589.0	59,180.0	296,667.0
Swaziland	1989	348.0	718.0	26.0	452.0	1,329.0	1,397.0	1,477.0
Zambia	1989	7,574.0	50,360.0	2,321.0	3,643.0	14,792.0	18,665.0	60,025.0
Zimbabwe [c]	1989	3,876.0	6,384.0		2,185.0	4,407.0	3,890.0	12,962.0

Source: UN/IMF/national statistical offices
Notes: see end of section

EXCHANGE RATES
Table No. 0313

Exchange Rates Against US Dollar 1977-1993

Units: National currency units per US dollar

	1977	1980	1985	1988	1989	1990	1991	1992	Nov 93	Units of currency
North America										
Canada	1.06	1.17	1.32	1.23	1.18	1.16	1.15	1.21	1.32	Canadian dollar
USA	1.00	1.00	1.00	1.00	1.00	1.00	1.00	1.00	1.00	US dollar
South America										
Argentina			2.14	8.75	423.34	4,875.90	9,535.50	9,906.40	9,984.00	Peso argentino
Bolivia [a]	20.00	24.51	2.05	2.35	2.69	3.17	3.58	3.90	4.42	Boliviano
Brazil [b]	14.14	52.71	39.22	0.26	2.83	68.30	406.61	4,513.02	37.60	Cruzeiro
Chile [c]	21.52	39.00	219.54	245.05	267.16	305.06	349.37	362.59	412.83	Chilean peso
Colombia	36.77	47.28	242.61	299.17	382.57	502.26	633.05	759.28	818.26	Colombian peso
Ecuador	25.00	25.00	170.46	301.61	526.35	767.75	1,046.25	1,526.70	1,988.21	Sucre
French Guiana	4.91	4.22	6.01	6.00	6.40	5.45	5.64	5.29	5.95	French franc
Guyana	2.55	2.55	9.75	10.00	27.16	39.53	111.80	125.00	126.30	Guyana dollar
Paraguay [c]	126.00	126.00	550.00	550.00	1,056.22	1,229.80	1,325.20	1,500.30	1,802.28	Guaraní
Peru [d]	.08	0.29	16.83	128.83	2,666.19	187.90	772.50	1,245.80	2,165.10	New sol
Suriname	1.78	1.78	1.78	1.78	1.79	1.79	1.79	1.79	1.79	Suriname guilder
Uruguay	4.67	9.09	226.67	359.44	605.62	1,171.00	2,018.80	3,027.00	4,360.30	New Uruguayan peso
Venezuela	4.29	4.29	14.50	14.50	34.68	46.90	56.82	68.38	102.56	Bólivar
Caribbean										
Anguilla	2.70	2.70	2.70	2.70	2.70	2.70	2.70	2.70	2.70	East Caribbean dollar
Antigua	2.70	2.70	2.70	2.70	2.70	2.70	2.70	2.70	2.70	East Caribbean dollar
Aruba	1.80	1.80	1.79	1.79	1.79	1.79	1.79	1.79	1.79	Aruban guilder
Bahamas [c]	1.00	1.00	1.00	1.00	1.00	1.00	1.00	1.00	1.00	Bahamian dollar
Barbados [c]	2.00	2.00	2.00	2.00	2.01	2.01	2.01	2.01	2.02	Barbados dollar
Bermuda	1.00	1.00	1.00	1.00	1.00	1.00	1.00	1.00	1.00	Bermudan dollar
British Virgin Islands	1.00	1.00	1.00	1.00	1.00	1.00	1.00	1.00	1.00	US dollar
Cayman Islands	0.80	0.80	0.83	0.83	0.83	0.83	0.84	0.84	0.85	Cayman Islands dollar
Cuba [e,f]	0.71	0.71	0.78	0.80	0.80	0.80	0.80	0.80	0.76	Cuban peso
Dominica	2.70	2.70	2.70	2.70	2.70	2.70	2.70	2.70	2.71	East Caribbean dollar
Dominican Republic [c]	1.00	1.00	3.84	6.13	6.34	8.53	12.69	12.77	12.53	Dominican Republic peso
Grenada	2.70	2.70	2.70	2.70	2.70	2.70	2.70	2.70	2.71	East Caribbean dollar
Guadeloupe	4.90	4.22	6.01	6.00	6.40	5.45	5.64	5.29	5.95	French franc
Haiti	5.00	5.00	5.00	5.00	5.00	5.00	5.00	5.00	12.03	Gourde
Jamaica	0.90	1.78	5.48	5.48	5.74	7.18	12.12	22.96	27.57	Jamaican dollar
Martinique	4.91	4.22	6.01	6.00	6.40	5.45	5.64	5.29	5.95	French franc
Netherlands Antilles	1.80	1.80	1.80	1.80	1.79	1.79	1.79	1.79	1.79	Netherlands Antilles guilder
St Kitts	2.70	2.70	2.70	2.70	2.70	2.70	2.70	2.70	2.71	East Caribbean dollar
St Lucia	2.70	2.70	2.70	2.70	2.70	2.70	2.70	2.70	2.71	East Caribbean dollar
St Vincent/Grenadines	2.70	2.70	2.70	2.70	2.70	2.70	2.70	2.70	2.71	East Caribbean dollar
Trinidad and Tobago	2.40	2.40	3.60	3.84	4.25	4.25	4.25	4.25	5.53	Trinidad and Tobago dollar
Central America										
Belize [c]	2.00	2.00	2.00	2.00	2.00	2.00	2.00	2.00	2.00	Belize dollar
Costa Rica	8.57	8.57	62.77	75.80	81.50	91.58	122.43	134.51	149.36	Colón
El Salvador [c]	2.50	2.50	5.00	5.00	5.00	8.03	8.08	9.17	8.73	Salvadorean colón
Guatemala [g]	1.00	1.00	2.50	2.61	2.82	4.48	5.03	5.17	5.90	Quetzal
Honduras	2.00	2.00	2.00	2.00	2.00	2.00	5.40	5.83	6.98	Lempira
Mexico	22.57	22.95	1,378.20	2,273.10	2,461.50	2,812.60	3,018.40	3,094.90	3,120.00	Mexican peso
Nicaragua [h]	.01	.02	0.10	270.00	3,000.00	0.13	4.27	5.00	6.28	Córdoba oro (gold córdoba)
Panama	1.00	1.00	1.00	1.00	1.00	1.00	1.00	1.00	1.00	Balboa
Puerto Rico	1.00	1.00	1.00	1.00	1.00	1.00	1.00	1.00	1.00	US dollar
South Asia										
Afghanistan	45.00	44.12	50.60	50.60	50.60	50.60	50.60	50.60	1,555.18	Afghani
Bangladesh [c]	15.37	15.45	30.95	31.73	32.27	34.57	36.60	38.95	39.33	Taka
Bhutan	8.73	7.86	12.96	13.91	16.23	17.50	22.74	25.92	31.44	Ngultrum
India	8.73	7.86	12.96	13.91	16.23	17.50	22.74	25.92	31.44	Indian rupee
Nepal [c]	12.50	12.00	21.81	23.28	27.19	29.37	37.26	42.72	46.49	Nepalese rupee
Pakistan	9.90	9.90	17.39	18.00	20.54	21.71	23.80	25.08	30.09	Pakistani rupee
Sri Lanka	8.87	16.53	29.44	31.80	36.05	40.06	41.37	43.83	49.10	Rupee

EXCHANGE RATES

Exchange Rates Against US Dollar 1977-1993

Units: National currency units per US dollar

	1977	1980	1985	1988	1989	1990	1991	1992	Nov 93	Units of currency
Japan										
Japan	268.51	226.74	144.64	128.15	137.96	144.79	134.71	126.65	108.36	Yen
ASEAN/NICs										
Brunei	2.43	2.14	2.01	1.96	1.91	1.79			1.60	Brunei dollar
Hong Kong	4.66	4.97	7.79	7.81	7.80	7.80	7.78	7.74	7.73	Hong Kong dollar
Indonesia	415.00	626.99	1,643.80	1,658.70	1,770.10	1,842.80	1,950.30	2,029.90	2,113.69	Rupiah
Macau [e,i]		5.33		8.03	8.03	8.02	8.01	7.96	8.00	Pataca
Malaysia	2.46	2.17	2.51	2.61	2.71	2.70	2.75	2.55	2.55	Malaysian dollar (ringgit)
Philippines	7.40	7.51	20.56	21.09	21.74	24.31	27.48	25.51	28.72	Philippine peso
Singapore	2.43	2.14	2.10	2.01	1.95	1.81	1.73	1.63	1.60	Singapore dollar
South Korea	484.00	607.43	822.57	731.47	671.46	707.76	733.35	780.65	806.45	Won
Taiwan [e]	38.00	36.01	28.55	28.17	26.17	27.11	25.75	25.47	26.89	New Taiwan dollar
Thailand	20.40	20.47	25.72	25.29	25.70	25.59	25.52	25.40	25.41	Baht
East/SE Asia										
Cambodia [j]		4.00	30.00						3,508.32	Riel
China [c]	1.85	1.49	3.72	3.72	3.77	4.78	5.32	5.51	5.87	Renminbi/Yuan
Laos [k]	1.90	10.00	180.00	401.00	587.00	709.00	702.00		721.74	Kip
Mongolia	3.27	2.95	2.90	2.89	3.00	4.67	25.86		400.95	Tugruk
Myanmar	7.11	6.59	6.65	6.65	6.70	6.34	6.28	6.10	6.44	Kyat
North Korea [e]	0.90	0.76							2.16	Won
Vietnam [l]	1.75	2.08	225.00	900.00	4,300.00	6,800.00	11,000.00		10,875.80	New dồng
Australasia										
Australia	0.90	0.87	1.42	1.28	1.26	1.28	1.28	1.36	1.52	Australian dollar
New Zealand	1.03	1.02	1.68	1.52	1.67	1.68	1.73	1.86	1.82	New Zealand dollar
Pacific										
American Samoa	1.00	1.00	1.00	1.00	1.00	1.00	1.00	1.00	1.00	US dollar
Fiji	0.91	0.81	1.22	1.43	1.48	1.48	1.48	1.50	1.55	Fiji dollar
French Polynesia	89.34	76.83	109.29						106.66	Franc CFP
Guam	1.00	1.00	1.00	1.00	1.00	1.00	1.00	1.00	1.00	US dollar
Kiribati	0.90	0.87	1.42	1.28	1.26	1.28	1.30	1.35	1.52	Australian dollar
Nauru	0.90	0.87	1.42	1.28	1.26	1.28	1.30	1.35	1.52	Australian dollar
New Caledonia	89.34	76.83	109.29						106.66	Franc CFP
Papua New Guinea	0.79	0.67	0.90	0.87	0.86	0.96	0.96	0.96	1.02	Kina
Solomon Islands	0.90	0.82	2.00	2.08	2.29	2.53	2.71	2.93	3.21	Solomon Islands dollar
Tonga	0.90	0.87	1.42	1.28	1.26	1.28	1.30	1.35	1.52	Pa'anga (Tongan dollar)
Tuvalu	0.90	0.87	1.42	1.28	1.26	1.28	1.30	1.35	1.52	Australian dollar
Vanuatu	79.41	68.29	109.85	104.43	116.04	116.57	111.68	113.39	120.89	Vatu
Western Samoa	0.78	0.91	2.12	2.08	2.27	2.31	2.40	2.47	2.60	Tala
Middle East										
Bahrain	0.39	0.37	0.37	0.37	0.38	0.38	0.38	0.38	0.38	Bahraini dinar
Egypt [c]	0.39	0.70	0.70	0.70	1.10	2.00	3.33	3.33	3.38	Egyptian pound
Iran [c]	70.61	70.61	71.46	68.68	72.02	68.10	67.51	65.55	1,706.52	Iranian rial
Iraq	0.29	0.29	0.31	0.31	0.31	0.31	0.31	0.31	0.31	Iraqi dinar
Israel			1.59	1.59	1.92	2.02	2.28	2.46	2.96	New shekel
Jordan	0.32	0.29	0.33	0.37	0.57	0.66	0.68	0.68	0.70	Jordanian dinar
Kuwait	0.28	0.27			0.29	0.29	0.28	0.29	0.30	Kuwaiti dinar
Lebanon	3.06	3.43	224.60	409.23	496.69	695.09	928.20	1,712.80	1,722.59	Lebanese pound
Oman [c,e]	0.34	0.34	0.38	0.38	0.38	0.38	0.38	0.38	0.39	Omani rial
Qatar	3.95	3.65	3.63	3.64	3.64	3.64	3.64	3.64	3.65	Qatar riyal
Saudi Arabia	3.50	3.30	3.74	3.74	3.75	3.75	3.75	3.75	3.75	Saudi riyal
Syria [c]	3.90	3.90	11.22	11.22	11.23	11.23	11.23	11.23	21.05	Syrian pound
United Arab Emirates	3.90	3.70	3.67	3.67	3.67	3.67	3.67	3.67	3.67	UAE dirham
Yemen	4.56	4.56	10.34	9.77	9.76	11.26			16.54	Yemeni riyal

EXCHANGE RATES

Exchange Rates Against US Dollar 1977-1993

Units: National currency units per US dollar

	1977	1980	1985	1988	1989	1990	1991	1992	Nov 93	Units of currency
North Africa										
Algeria	4.14	3.83	4.80	5.91	7.61	8.96	18.47	21.84	24.09	Algerian dinar
Chad	245.68	211.28	300.54	297.85	319.01	272.26	282.11	264.69	297.47	CFA franc
Djibouti	177.72	177.72	177.72	177.72	177.72	177.72	177.72	177.72	176.63	Djibouti franc
Ethiopia	2.07	2.07	2.07	2.07	2.07	2.07	2.07	5.00	4.94	Birr
Libya [e]	0.30	0.30	0.29	0.29	0.29	0.27	0.27	0.30	0.30	Libyan dinar
Mali	245.68	211.28	300.54	297.85	319.01	272.26	282.11	264.69	297.47	CFA franc
Mauritania	45.58	45.91	73.87	75.26	83.05	80.61	81.95	87.03	123.49	Ouguiya
Morocco	4.50	3.93	8.36	8.20	8.49	8.24	8.71	8.54	9.55	Moroccan dirham
Niger	245.68	211.28	300.54	297.85	319.01	272.26	282.11	264.69	297.47	CFA franc
Somalia [c,m]	6.29	6.29	105.17	170.45	490.68	1,055.90			2,626.22	Somali shilling
Sudan	0.34	0.50	2.81	4.50	4.50	4.50	5.00	70.42	13.03	Sudanese pound
Tunisia	0.42	0.40	0.82	0.85	0.95	0.88	0.92	0.88	1.04	Tunisian dinar
West Africa										
Benin	245.68	211.28	300.54	297.85	319.01	272.26	282.11	264.69	297.47	CFA franc
Burkina Faso	245.68	211.28	300.54	297.85	319.01	272.26	282.11	264.69	297.47	CFA franc
Cameroon	245.68	211.28	300.54	297.85	319.01	272.26	282.11	264.69	297.47	CFA franc
Cape Verde	33.90	42.49	72.47	72.07	77.98	70.03	71.41	68.02	74.38	Escudo
Côte d'Ivoire	245.68	211.28	300.54	297.85	319.01	272.26	282.11	264.69	297.47	CFA franc
Equatorial Guinea [n]	75.96	110.63	300.54	297.85	319.01	272.26	282.11	264.69	297.47	CFA franc
Gabon	245.68	211.28	300.54	297.85	319.01	272.26	282.11	264.69	297.47	CFA franc
Gambia	2.29	1.79	7.06	6.71	7.59	7.88	8.80	8.89	8.42	Dalasi
Ghana	1.15	2.75	147.05	202.35	270.00	326.33	367.83	437.09	718.70	Cedi
Guinea [e,o]	20.32	19.35							814.20	Franc guinéen
Guinea-Bissau [e]	34.26	34.49	559.33	1,111.06					5,011.89	Guinea peso
Liberia	1.00	1.00	1.00	1.00	1.00	1.00	1.00	1.00	1.00	Liberian dollar
Nigeria	0.64	0.54	4.00	4.54	7.36	8.04	9.91	17.30	21.94	Naira
Sao Tomé e Príncipe [e]	37.25	35.47							240.57	Dobra
Senegal	245.68	211.28	300.54	297.85	319.01	272.26	282.11	264.69	297.47	CFA franc
Sierra Leone	1.46	1.04	34.04	32.51	59.81	151.45	295.34	499.44	551.31	Leone
Togo	245.68	211.28	300.54	297.85	319.01	272.26	282.11	264.69	297.47	CFA franc
East/Central Africa										
Angola [p]	29.92	29.90	29.90	29.90	29.90	29.90	550.00	60.00	6,708.39	New kwanza
Burundi	90.00	90.00	123.56	140.40	158.67	171.26	181.51	208.30	262.84	Burundi franc
Central African Republic	245.68	211.28	300.54	297.85	319.01	272.26	282.11	264.69	297.47	CFA franc
Comoros	245.68	211.28	300.54	297.85	319.01	272.26	282.11	264.69	297.47	Comoros franc
Congo	245.68	211.28	300.54	297.85	319.01	272.26	282.11	264.69	297.47	CFA franc
Kenya	8.27	7.42	16.45	17.74	20.57	22.92	27.51	32.22	69.12	Kenya shilling
Madagascar [q]	245.68	211.28	1,069.21	1,407.10	1,603.40	1,494.10	1,835.40	1,788.50	1,922.50	Franc malgache
Maldives	8.76	7.55	9.22	8.78	9.04	9.51	10.25	10.57	12.00	Rufiyaa
Mauritius	6.60	7.68	12.87	13.43	15.25	14.86	15.65	15.56	18.59	Mauritian rupee
Réunion	4.91	4.22	6.01	6.00	6.40	5.45	5.64	5.29	5.95	French franc
Rwanda	92.84	92.84	79.67	76.45	79.98	82.60	125.14	133.35	144.77	Rwanda franc
Seychelles	7.60	6.39	5.60	5.38	5.65	5.34	5.29	5.12	5.25	Seychelles rupee
Tanzania	8.29	8.19	64.26	99.29	143.38	195.06	219.16	297.71	445.05	Tanzanian shilling
Uganda	.08	.07	42.84	106.14	223.09	428.85	734.00	1,133.80	1,152.72	New Uganda shilling
Zaire [r]	0.85	2.80	112.40	187.07	381.45	718.60	15,587.00	645.55	4,008.10	Zaïre
Southern Africa										
Botswana	0.84	0.77	1.67	1.82	2.01	1.86	2.02	2.13	2.55	Pula
Lesotho	0.86	0.77	2.03	2.26	2.62	2.59	2.76	2.85	3.37	Loti
Malawi	0.90	0.81	2.20	2.56	2.76	2.73	2.80	3.60	4.45	Malawi kwacha
Mozambique [s]	32.20	33.08							5,174.25	Metical
Namibia	0.87	0.77	2.03	2.26	2.62	2.59	2.76	2.85	3.37	Namibian dollar
South Africa	0.86	0.77	2.03	2.26	2.62	2.59	2.76	2.85	3.37	Rand
Swaziland	0.86	0.77	2.03	2.26	2.62	2.59	2.76	2.85	3.37	Lilangeni
Zambia [t]	0.78	0.78	8.88	8.22	12.90	28.99	61.73	144.93	374.76	Zambian kwacha
Zimbabwe	0.62	0.64	1.66	1.80	2.11	2.45	3.43	5.10	6.87	Zimbabwe dollar

Source: IMF/UN/national statistical offices

Notes: see end of section

Notes to Tables in Section Three

Table 0301   0 = less than 0.5 million
- a Currency changes in 1984 and 1988; pesos from 1977 to 1984, '000 pesos from 1985 to 1987; million pesos from 1988
- b Billion novo cruzados from 1989
- c Thousand new soles to 1988; millions from 1989
- d Data for 1992 are estimated
- e Data for 1991 are estimated
- f Net material product/national income
- g Year ending 30 September
- h Billion units of national currency
- i Billion crdobas beginning 1988; trillions beginning 1990
- j Year beginning 1 April
- k Year ending 15 July
- l Year ending 30 June
- m From 1980, year ending 30 June
- n Year beginning 21 March
- o Islamic lunar year
- p Until 1980, year ending 30 June
- q Year ending 7 July
- r Billion units from 1991
- s New series starting 1985

Table 0302   0 = less than 0.5 million
- a Currency changes in 1984 and 1988; pesos from 1977 to 1984, '000 pesos from 1985 to 1987; million pesos from 1988
- b Billion novo cruzados from 1989
- c Data for 1991 are estimated
- d Thousand new soles
- e Billion units of national currency
- f Year ending 30 September
- g Data for 1990 are estimated
- h Year ending 30 June
- i Year beginning 1 April
- j Year ending 15 July
- k Data for 1992 are estimated
- l Until 1980, year ending 30 June
- m Year beginning 21 March
- n Islamic lunar year
- o From 1980, year ending 30 June
- p Year ending 7 July

Table 0303   0 = less than 0.5 million
- a Net material product/national income
- b Year ending 30 September
- c Year beginning 1 April
- d Year ending 15 July
- e Year ending 30 June
- f From 1980, year ending 30 June
- g Year beginning 21 March
- h Islamic lunar year
- i Until 1980, year ending 30 June
- j Year ending 7 July
- k New series starting 1985

Table 0304   0 = less than 0.5 million
- a Year ending 30 September
- b Year ending 30 June
- c Year beginning 1 April
- d Year ending 15 July
- e Until 1980, year ending 30 June
- f Year beginning 21 March
- g Islamic lunar year
- h From 1980, year ending 30 June
- i Year ending 7 July

Table 0305
- a Billion units of national currency
- b Data for 1992 are estimated
- c Data for 1991 are estimated
- d New series starting 1985
- e Thousand units of national currency
- f New series starting 1986
- g New series starting 1990
- h Data for 1989 are estimated
- i Currency reform 1991; thousands of new soles
- j New series starting 1987
- k Included in Netherlands Antilles
- l Data for 1990 are estimated
- m New series starting 1982
- n Currency reform occurred in 1984
- o New series starting 1991
- p New series starting 1980
- q New series starting 1988
- r New series starting 1989
- s New series starting 1992

Table 0306
- a New series starting 1981
- b New series starting 1982
- c New series starting 1984
- d New series starting 1988
- e New series starting 1980
- f Data for 1992 are estimated
- g New series starting 1989
- h Data for 1989 are estimated
- i New series starting 1979
- j Data for 1991 are estimated
- k New series starting 1987
- l New series starting 1978
- m New series starting 1985
- n Data for 1990 are estimated
- o New series starting 1986
- p New series starting 1983
- q New series starting 1990
- r New series starting 1991

Table 0307
- a Includes Aruba
- b Year beginning 1 April
- c Year ending 30 June
- d Year ending 7 July

Table 0308   0 = less than 0.5 million
- * Budget surplus/deficit includes grants received and lending minus repayments which may not be covered by revenue/expenditure columns
- a Budget revenue, expenditure, surplus/deficit and foreign debt in billion units national currency
- b Year beginning 1 April
- c Foreign debt refers to 1989
- d Year ending 30 September
- e Foreign debt refers to 1991
- f Foreign debt refers to 1986
- g Foreign debt refers to 1982
- h Foreign debt refers to foreign currency debt for 1983

i   Data not comparable with earlier years
j   Exchange reserves refer to 1991
k   Foreign debt refers to 1990
l   Foreign debt refers to 1992
m   Foreign debt refers to 1984
n   Foreign debt referts to foreign currency debt for 1992
o   Foreign debt refers to 1987
p   Exchange and gold reserves refer to 1983
q   Foreign debt refers to 1983
r   Data are estimated
s   Foreign debt refers to 1985
t   Year ending 30 June
u   Foreign debt refers to foreign currency debt for 1989
v   Exchange and gold reserves refer to 1991
w   Exchange reserves refer to 1985
x   Exchange and gold reserves refer to 1982
y   Foreign debt refers to foreign currency debt for 1988
z   Islamic lunar year
aa   Exchange reserves refer to 1988
bb   Exchange and gold reserves refer to 1990
cc   Year ending 7 July
dd   Foreign debt refers to 1988
ee   Foreign debt refers to 1980
ff   Exchange reserves refer to 1989

Table 0309

A   General public services
B   Defence
C   Education
D   Health
E   Social security and welfare
F   Housing and community amenities
G   Other community/social services
H   Economic services
I   Other purposes

a   Year beginning 1 April
b   Year ending 30 September
c   Billion units of national currency
d   Currency revaluation occurred in March 1990
e   Year ending 30 June
f   Floating debt adjustment
g   Other purposes includes general public services
h   Year ending 14/15 July
i   General public spending includes defence
j   Other purposes includes health
k   Year beginning 21 March
l   Year ending 7 July
m   Data refer to capital expenditure only

Table 0310

A   General public services
B   Defence
C   Education
D   Health
E   Social security and welfare
F   Housing and community amenities
G   Other community/social services

H   Economic services
I   Other purposes

a   Year beginning 1 April
b   Year ending 30 September
c   Year ending 30 June
d   Floating debt adjustment
e   Other purposes includes general public services
f   Year ending 14/15 July
g   General public spending includes defence
h   Other purposes includes health
i   Year beginning 21 March
j   Year ending 7 July
k   Data refer to capital expenditure only

Table 0311

A   Agriculture/forestry/fishing
B   Mining and quarrying
C   Manufacturing
D   Electricity, gas and water
E   Construction
F   Wholesale and retail trade, restaurants and hotels
G   Transport, storage and communications
H   Others

a   Billion units of national currency
b   Manufacturing includes electricity, gas & water
c   Restaurants and hotels are included in others
d   Transport, storage etc. includes finance, insurance etc.
e   Data refer to origin of Net Material Product
f   Mining and quarrying includes the two following columns
g   Mining and quarrying includes manufacturing
h   Agriculture etc. includes mining and quarrying
i   Electricity, gas and water includes construction

Table 0312

A   Government final consumption expenditure
B   Private final consumption expenditure
C   Increase in stocks
D   Gross fixed capital formation
E   Exports of goods and services
F   Imports of goods and services

a   Billion units of national currency
b   Data not comparable with previous years due to introduction of new currency
c   Gross fixed capital formation includes increase in stocks
d   Exports (net) ie include import component
e   Data derived from net material product
f   Government consumption includes private consumption
g   Trillion units of national currency

Table 0313   Data refer to the period averages of
              market exchange rates
          a   Currency devaluation Feb. 1985; new
              currency from Jan. 1987
          b   Units of currency per million US dollars
              to 1982, per thousand dollars 1983-
              1987; per single dollar 1988-1992;
              '000 units per
              dollar in 1993. Figure quoted as
              November 1993 refers instead to
              average rate during second quarter
              of that year
          c   Official rate
          d   New soles per million US dollars to 1989;
              new soles per thousand US dollars from 1990
          e   End of year exchange rate
          f   1987 rate on 30 September
          g   Official rate up to May 1986
          h   Official rate to January 1985 then
              principal rate; gold crdobas per billion
              US dollars to 1987, per million
              US dollars to 1988, per thousand US
              dollars thereafter
          i   Figure quoted as November 1993
              refers instead to average rate during
              second quarter of that year

          j   General internal use of currency
              suspended 1975 to March 1980
          k   Devaluation in March 1990
          l   Separate north and south currencies
              to 3 May 1978, replaced by Dong
          m   Data for 1990 and 1991 are estimated
          n   Up to 1980: end of year exchange rate
          o   Syli up to 1985; replaced by Guinean
              franc
          p   1991 figure refers to official rate set after
              October 1990 devaluation; 1992
              figure refers to official rate set after April
              1992 devaluation
          q   Figure quoted as average for 1992
              refers instead to average rate during
              third quarter of that year
          r   Figure quoted as November 1993
              refers instead to average rate during
              third quarter of that year. From 1992
              data is in thousand units per US dollar
          s   Mozambique escudo replaced by
              Metical 16 June 1980
          t   Figure quoted as average for 1992
              refers instead to average rate during
              second quarter of that year

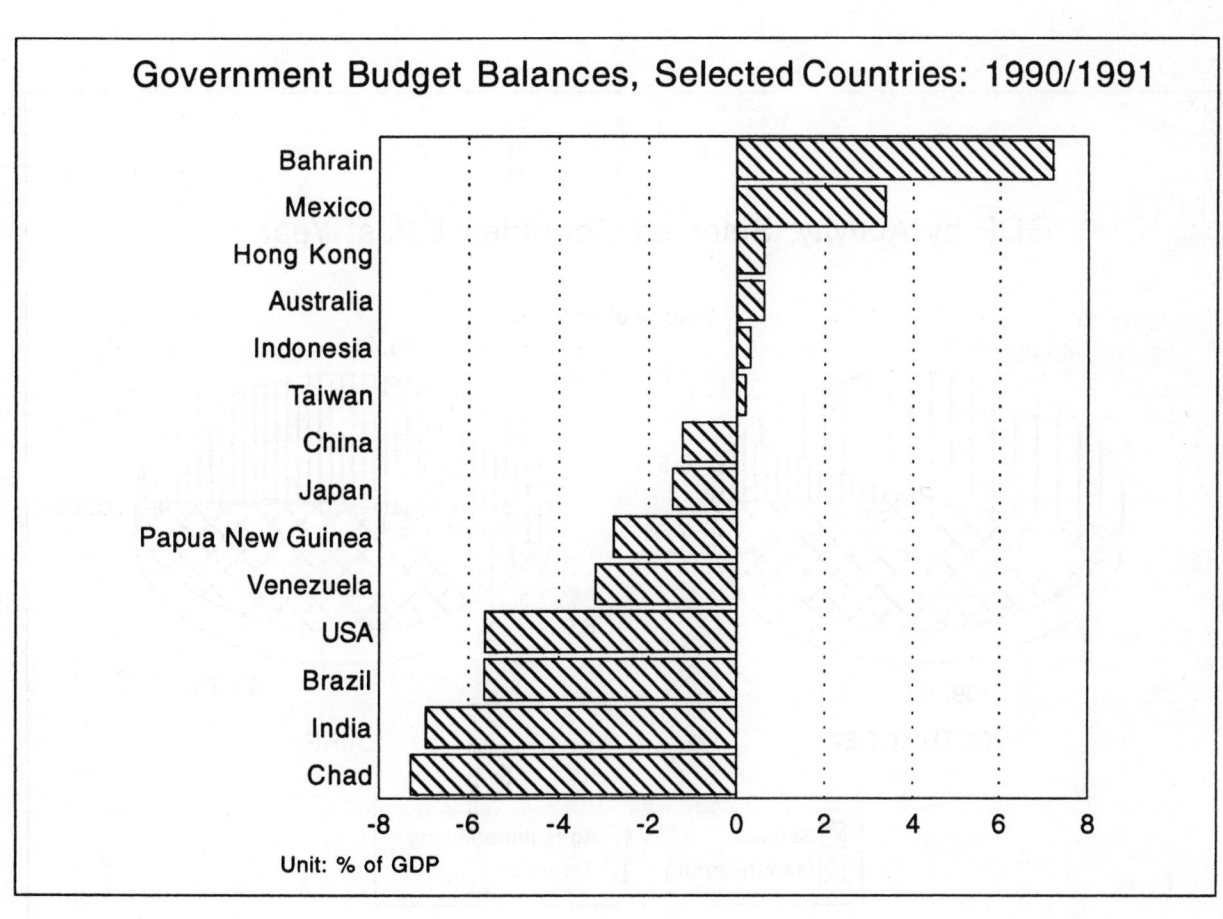

Government Budget Balances, Selected Countries: 1990/1991

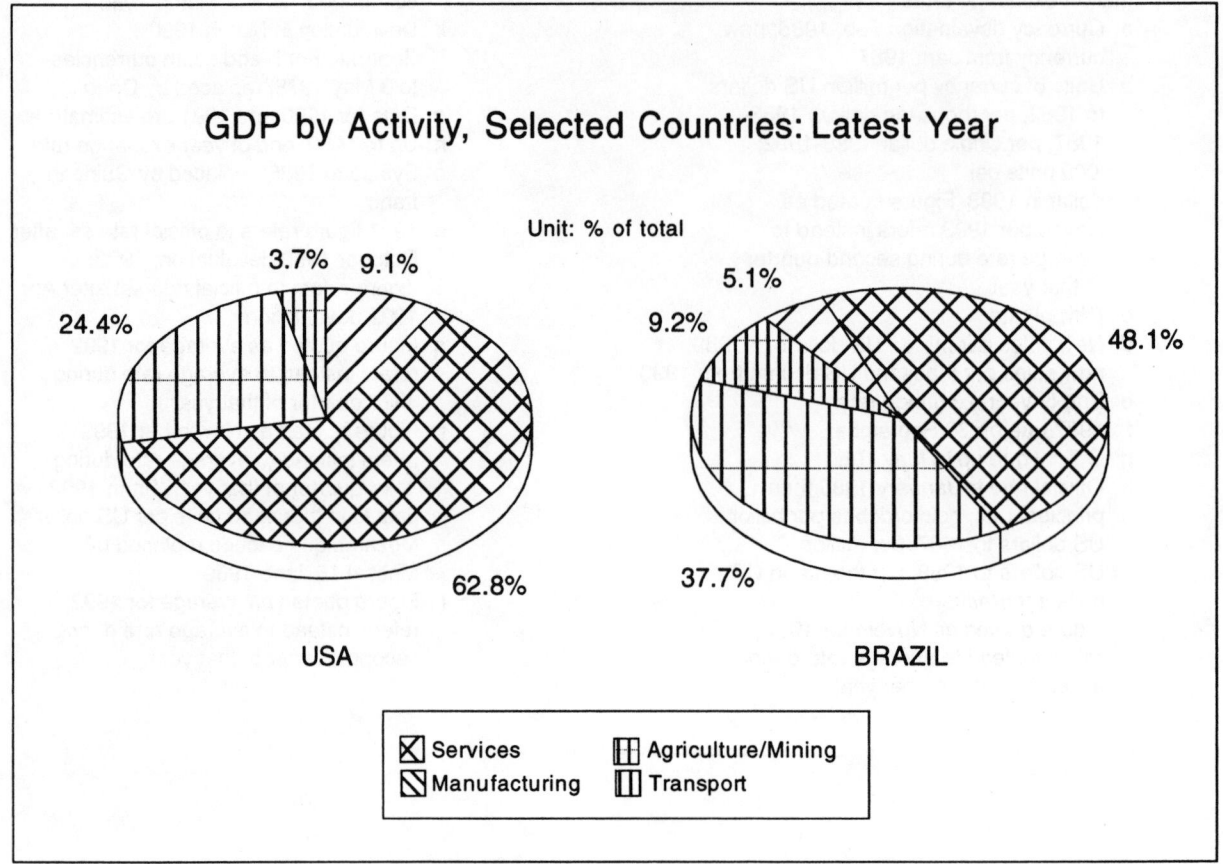

GDP by Activity, Selected Countries: Latest Year

Unit: % of total

USA

9.1%
3.7%
24.4%
62.8%

BRAZIL

5.1%
9.2%
48.1%
37.7%

Legend:
- ☒ Services
- ⊞ Agriculture/Mining
- ◩ Manufacturing
- ⫼ Transport

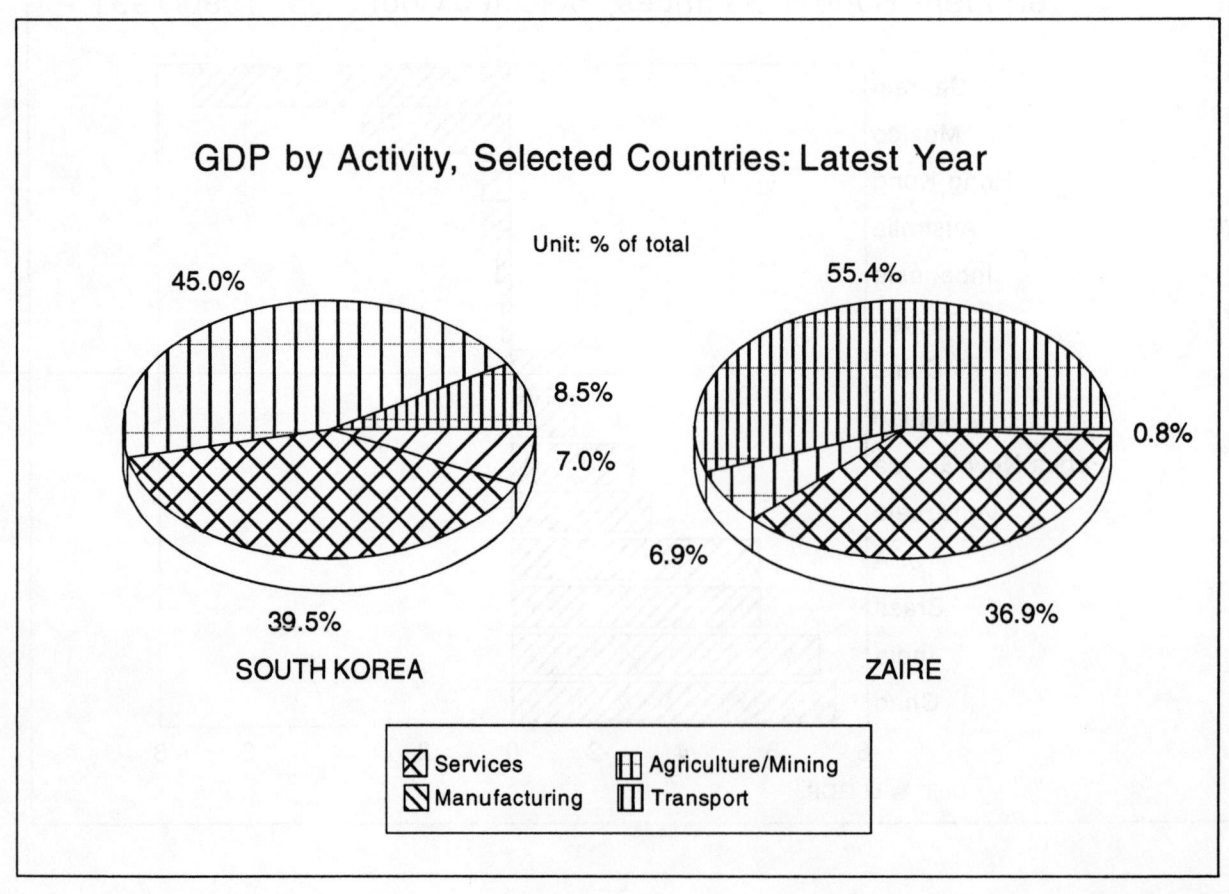

GDP by Activity, Selected Countries: Latest Year

Unit: % of total

SOUTH KOREA

45.0%
8.5%
7.0%
39.5%

ZAIRE

55.4%
0.8%
6.9%
36.9%

Legend:
- ☒ Services
- ⊞ Agriculture/Mining
- ◩ Manufacturing
- ⫼ Transport

Section Four
Finance and Banking

INTEREST RATES — Table No. 0401

Lending Rates 1980-1992

Units: % per annum

	1980	1981	1983	1985	1987	1988	1989	1990	1991	1992
Argentina		122.70	407.80	1,160.00	243.00	430.00	796,725.00	315.33	113.00	19.00
Australia	10.58	12.92	14.04	15.96	19.83	18.52	21.69	20.33	16.38	12.02
Brazil [a]		49.00	197.00	385.00	401.00	2,282.00	38,341.00	1,083.00	2,494.00	1,489.00
Canada	18.25	17.25	11.00	10.00	9.52	10.83	13.33	14.06	9.94	7.48
Chile	47.14	52.02	42.82	40.81	32.80	21.17	35.92	48.83	28.55	23.92
China	5.04	5.04	7.20	7.74	7.92	8.28	11.15			
Colombia		31.30	28.00	29.10	41.10	42.69	43.04	45.25	47.13	37.28
Ecuador	9.00	9.00	12.33	18.00	18.42	23.00	30.08	37.50	46.67	60.17
Hong Kong [b]					7.00	5.50	10.00	10.00	10.00	8.50
India	16.50	16.50	16.50	16.50	16.50	16.50	16.50	16.50	17.88	18.92
Indonesia	9.00	9.00	9.00	12.00	22.00	27.13	21.70	20.61	26.21	24.03
Israel		170.60	186.20	503.40	61.40	41.70	31.60	26.10	26.60	20.00
Japan	7.00	7.00	7.05	6.52	5.09	4.93	5.29	6.95	7.53	6.15
Malaysia [c]		8.50	11.08	11.54	8.19	7.25	7.00	7.17	8.13	9.25
Mexico [d]		36.60	63.03	62.40	96.00	69.01	47.43	37.36	23.58	18.87
New Zealand [c,e]	12.63	13.50	13.83	16.00	20.84	16.96	14.71	14.36	12.06	10.60
Nigeria	8.43	8.92	9.98	9.43	13.96				20.04	24.76
Pakistan [a]	10.00	10.00	10.00	10.00	10.00	10.00	10.00	10.00	10.00	10.00
Peru			60.00		35.70	174.30	1,515.90	4,774.50	751.50	173.80
Philippines		15.34	19.24	28.61	13.34	15.92	19.27	24.12	23.07	19.52
Singapore		13.65	9.05	7.93	6.10	5.96	6.21	7.36	7.58	5.95
South Africa	9.50	17.00	16.67	21.50	12.50	15.33	19.83	21.00	20.31	18.91
South Korea	18.00	17.38	10.00	10.00	10.00	10.13	11.25	10.00	10.00	10.00
Taiwan [f]	14.58	16.78	7.32	5.09	4.00	5.13	6.86			
Thailand [g]	18.00	19.00	17.63	19.00	15.00	15.00	15.00			
USA	15.27	18.87	10.79	9.93	8.21	9.32	10.92	10.01	8.46	6.25
Venezuela				9.33	8.48	8.50	22.57	28.23	29.78	33.91
Vietnam										

Source: IMF

Notes: see end of section

BANK RESERVES — Table No. 0402

Deposit Bank Reserves 1981-1992

Units: Million units of national currency

	1981	1983	1984	1985	1986	1987	1988	1989	1990	1991	1992
Argentina [a,b]							3	189	1,342	2,289	
Australia	2,910	3,451	3,648	4,280	4,472	4,813	5,111	4,447	4,281	4,083	4,265
Brazil [c]		2	5	16	112	967	1,500				
Canada	7,280	6,000	5,760	5,570	6,140	6,650	6,610	6,140	6,430	7,010	5,760
Chile	40,000	39,400	66,800	96,000	102,200	127,500	160,300	153,100	178,100	337,000	528,600
China				96,070	111,560	113,990	128,860	178,150	263,810	359,320	367,800
Colombia [d]	134,490	169,490	202,250	268,840		483,900	560,780		1,000,600	1,323,100	1,791,600
Ecuador	12,700	17,400	31,600	36,400	47,800	56,300	104,200	152,100	241,400	397,200	
Hong Kong											
India	54,760	76,650	81,940	131,700	164,320	194,790	239,100	268,100	287,400	352,000	375,600
Indonesia [e]	1,430	1,815	2,273	2,940	2,935	3,433	5,151	5,615	4,893	12,300	15,879
Israel [f]	96	836	4,601	11,107	11,227	13,026	13,314	14,224	15,910	17,053	17,753
Japan [e]	4,985	5,810	6,513	6,298	5,921	6,337	7,941	7,887	10,610	9,220	7,290
Malaysia [g]	1,834	2,451	2,816	2,552	2,440	2,472	2,598	4,204	6,205	7,807	9,277
Mexico	746	2,514	3,801	3,927	5,310	7,075	7,390	5,710	6,637	7,436	7,690
New Zealand [g,h]	109	140	87	182	97	316	280	437	1,745	1,679	1,496
Nigeria [g]	1,396	1,285	1,051	824	1,506	2,202	2,355	2,741	4,777	13,736	22,041
Pakistan	7,451	10,101	13,809	13,871	15,103	21,994	23,661	29,874	28,931	50,592	51,207
Peru [g,i]	1	2	6	19	23	37	260	3,391	267	852	1,273
Philippines	6,170	8,120	11,870	14,420	21,770	22,370	26,650	40,050	46,800	59,970	70,540
Singapore	1,428	1,900	2,060	2,219	2,318	2,476	2,932	3,709	3,951	4,750	5,301
South Africa [j]	1,826	1,394	1,621	1,860	1,580	1,748	3,006	4,468	4,704	3,352	
South Korea [e]	738	1,129	856	1,016	1,307	3,017	4,535	6,613	6,717	8,304	9,399
Taiwan	91,045	113,892	140,446	177,132	235,026	303,167	427,350	654,085	649,634		
Thailand	11,810	14,960	14,610	21,170	22,110	25,750	32,400	33,800	51,600	60,400	60,900
USA	42,500	39,000	40,300	47,600	67,800	65,900	66,800	67,800	70,500	61,700	72,300
Venezuela	15,392	23,244	19,867	22,040	23,620	25,150	32,620	52,710	171,730	294,740	294,060
Vietnam											

Source: IMF

Notes: see end of section

FOREIGN ASSETS — Table No. 0403

Foreign Assets of Deposit Banks 1981-1992

Units: Million units of national currency

	1981	1983	1984	1985	1986	1987	1988	1989	1990	1991	1992
Argentina [a,b]							2	280	1,249	2,767	
Australia	351	198	1,103	2,178	5,462	7,473	7,491	9,456	14,827	15,458	17,863
Brazil [c]		2	7	21	50	255	3,639	77,577	1,254,600	6,192,000	72,293
Canada	44,240	49,230	52,100	59,910	68,410	63,920	52,880	53,090	57,130	50,810	57,440
Chile	31,000	62,600	79,500	63,800	96,600	81,000	98,700	107,000	179,400	197,300	207,800
China				29,670	31,400	45,830	52,760	54,170	64,810	113,860	147,050
Colombia [d]	10,270	28,300	50,950	44,690		83,730	166,700		148,000	265,600	313,600
Ecuador	3,400	4,300	4,900	6,100	9,600	14,900	27,300	42,900	68,700	109,700	
Hong Kong											
India											
Indonesia [e]	3,233	4,520	5,107	6,239	8,193	7,807	8,397	10,731	11,681	11,076	13,011
Israel [f]	99	738	4,239	9,567	9,744	9,919	12,241	14,580	17,033	20,311	28,898
Japan [e]	12,826	17,085	17,917	25,329	36,022	48,346	63,787	81,620	96,678	86,510	77,990
Malaysia [g]	2,003	5,390	2,451	2,995	3,821	4,863	7,267	6,841	6,672	5,500	4,732
Mexico [e]	26	313	367	781	1,833	6,241	5,873	6,947	10,402	13,617	14,798
New Zealand [d,g]	503	699	707	950	1,107	1,392	2,078	1,345	3,169	2,358	2,330
Nigeria [g]	259	344	413	415	1,740	3,128	5,077	7,489	6,634	10,663	18,160
Pakistan	3,190	6,243	8,426	8,988	11,848	13,903	15,391	20,008	31,872	38,974	35,563
Peru [h]		1	2	3	4	10	200	2,927	273,000	1,011,000	1,269,000
Philippines		24,080	42,900	41,080	44,310	54,920	69,540	79,420	109,490	105,180	117,730
Singapore	11,530	12,387	17,139	20,197	26,214	29,499	34,570	48,769	43,860	42,089	51,644
South Africa [i]	445	750	938	1,876	1,822	2,101	1,801	1,721	1,192	1,320	
South Korea [e]	1,987	2,836	4,126	5,558	5,023	4,474	5,824	5,400	6,829	8,145	10,174
Taiwan	130,337	211,359	242,093	338,301	221,573	125,129	150,126	208,846	272,718		
Thailand	25,730	24,580	30,790	33,700	41,950	38,600	45,000	70,200	56,400	72,600	74,500
USA	221,700	258,100	189,300	189,600	198,600	229,800	243,000	290,700	263,400	292,000	281,500
Venezuela	2,632	5,158	8,390	6,950	9,220	15,390	19,150	43,260	64,810	86,190	113,220
Vietnam											

Source: IMF

Notes: see end of section

FOREIGN LIABILITIES — Table No. 0404

Foreign Liabilities of Deposit Banks 1980-1992

Units: Billion current US dollars

	1980	1981	1983	1984	1985	1986	1987	1988	1989	1990	1991	1992
Argentina		7.2	7.8	7.2	6.7	6.6	7.9	9.3	6.1	7.0	6.2	
Australia [a,b]	0.7	0.7	0.7	1.3	2.9	18.3	21.8	32.1	41.1	45.8	53.1	60.0
Brazil	16.6	22.1	24.0	23.9	20.6	20.4	19.4					
Canada	43.0	61.0	61.3	61.6	64.6	68.9	71.7	69.5	70.8	78.0	76.7	73.6
Chile	3.5	6.2	6.3	6.7	6.6	6.2	5.1	4.2	3.3	3.0	2.3	3.5
China	5.7	3.9	3.3	3.7	6.6	8.4	10.2	11.7	10.9	12.9	19.9	19.4
Colombia	1.5	1.6	1.7	1.8						2.2	2.1	2.8
Ecuador	0.1	0.1	0.1	0.1	0.1	0.2	0.3	0.3	0.3	0.3	0.3	
Hong Kong	32.6	45.3	59.6	65.9	83.3	125.8	229.4	269.6	310.1	402.7	431.6	427.8
India	0.3	0.4	0.5	0.5	0.6	0.8	1.3	1.6	1.6	1.9	1.7	
Indonesia	0.6	0.7	1.0	0.7	0.5	0.3	0.5	0.7	1.8	6.7	6.0	7.9
Israel	3.4	8.7	10.6	10.3	10.0	10.3	10.3	10.7	10.0	11.0	11.5	11.6
Japan	80.2	100.4	106.7	127.1	179.3	346.0	592.0	772.4	879.7	958.5	845.7	708.6
Malaysia	1.3	1.6	3.0	2.5	2.7	2.4	2.0	1.9				
Mexico	20.9	31.4	33.9	34.0	34.8	36.0	36.7	36.6	36.4	34.9	41.7	44.9
New Zealand	0.2	0.2	0.4	0.3	0.5	0.8						
Nigeria	0.2	0.2	0.4	0.1	0.3	0.3	0.2	0.1	0.2	0.1	0.1	0.1
Pakistan	0.2	0.3	0.4	0.8	1.1	1.5	1.8	2.0	2.4	2.7	3.6	4.4
Peru	0.8	1.0	0.7	0.6	0.4	0.4	0.4	0.4	0.4	0.4	0.4	0.4
Philippines	8.8	9.7	9.0	8.6	7.5	5.3	4.9	4.6	4.3	4.4	3.8	4.9
Singapore	43.5	69.6	92.6	108.4	129.7	171.2	216.8	252.4	308.4	354.9	329.0	328.0
South Africa	0.8	1.5	1.6	1.3	1.8	2.1	2.3	2.1	2.4	2.6	2.8	
South Korea	10.0	12.9	17.9	20.5	24.3	23.1	16.8	14.1	13.2	14.8	21.4	24.4
Taiwan												
Thailand	1.8	1.9	2.4	2.7	2.5	2.1	2.3	3.3	4.3	5.9	6.8	7.0
USA	151.5	189.9	305.8	338.1	381.3	477.2	573.0	645.3	713.6	733.3	718.5	755.2
Venezuela	2.7	3.2	4.4	3.0								
Vietnam												

Source: IMF

Notes: see end of section

PRIVATE LENDING — Table No. 0405

Bank Claims on the Private Sector 1981-1992

Units: Million units of national currency

	1981	1983	1984	1985	1986	1987	1988	1989	1990	1991	1992
Argentina [a]				1	2	5	22	1,279	10,702	17,442	
Australia		55,334	64,627	86,991	105,049	122,489	151,623	225,978	255,585	261,094	274,929
Brazil [b]		16	53	186	787	2,609	8,400				
Canada	189,240	184,930	199,780	216,850	223,580	244,670	272,640	307,060	334,870	349,050	372,510
Chile	583,300	891,800	1,149,400	1,448,400	1,696,300	2,122,200	2,606,700	3,531,500	4,152,100	5,155,600	6,892,800
China				554,440	718,680	850,260	1,001,680	1,181,110	1,445,090	1,718,700	2,050,080
Colombia [c]	298,100	479,220	584,830	747,830			1,229,290	1,680,300	3,142,100	3,481,200	4,902,700
Ecuador	54,800	131,900	177,800	223,600	264,000	343,200	418,000	568,200	894,100	1,493,000	
Hong Kong											
India	366,720	515,260	612,380	705,610	818,480	918,500	1,085,200	1,263,100	435,500	1,577,600	1,757,600
Indonesia [d]	5,942	10,490	14,086	17,281	21,731	28,034	38,809	58,404	97,145	114,453	123,553
Israel [e]	165	1,097	6,237	17,053	23,267	31,698	40,720	49,464	60,957	75,468	93,160
Japan [d]	221,837	262,696	287,365	318,501	348,729	387,695	430,125	480,168	524,378	552,110	564,980
Malaysia [f]	24,976	35,403	41,976	47,849	51,275	51,308	55,763	68,219	82,657	99,668	107,616
Mexico [g]	1,015	1,822	3,376	5,167	8,742	22,571	41,275	81,598	141,596	228,627	337,402
New Zealand [c,f]	5,305	6,569	7,843	10,020	14,230	18,315	19,293	29,321	49,823	51,739	56,379
Nigeria [f]	8,236	10,283	10,820	11,723	15,390	16,560	19,514	21,675	25,410	29,458	34,949
Pakistan	61,313	88,431	103,071	132,590	155,298	160,908	181,571	195,274	210,491	232,651	290,851
Peru [f,h]	1	4	7	16	26	46	340	7,451	437,000	1,857,000	2,720,000
Philippines [i]	97,000	139,900	128,350	115,030	90,450	109,080	128,850	159,870	206,560	221,640	276,300
Singapore	22,867	32,578	35,602	35,790	34,484	36,693	40,789	48,757	55,798	62,725	68,851
South Africa [j]	21,419	30,298	39,529	46,273	49,413	56,765	76,660	103,299	118,655	128,578	
South Korea [d]	20,114	29,693	33,946	40,376	46,474	53,016	59,724	75,118	92,604	114,969	130,056
Taiwan											
Thailand	237,320	371,650	433,480	481,230	501,500	614,760	795,980	1,045,200	1,409,000	1,696,900	2,047,700
USA	1,058,400	1,234,000	1,396,100	1,539,200	1,752,700	1,930,200	2,153,500	2,360,700	2,499,500	2,548,300	2,590,100
Venezuela	75,648	89,045	103,643	115,386	149,751	201,250	261,920	300,880	379,380	570,160	769,550
Vietnam											

Source: IMF

Notes: see end of section

Notes to Tables in Section Four

Table 0401   a Bank rate
    b End of period
    c Data for 1992 are estimated
    d Money market rates 1985-1990
    e New series starting 1987 and 1988
    f Money market rates (182 days)
    g Data for 1991 are estimated

Table 0402   No data available for Hong Kong
    a Million pesos (currency reform 1992: 1 peso argentino = 10,000 australes)
    b New series starting 1989
    c Million novo cruzados (currency reform 1988: 1 novo cruzado = 1,000 cruzados = 1,000,000 old cruzeiros; in second reform of March 1990, the cruzeiro again replaced the novo cruzado: 1 cruzeiro = 1,000 novo cruzados
    d New series starting 1990
    e Billion units of national currency
    f Million new shekels (currency reform 1985: 1 new shekel = 1,000 shekels)
    g Data for 1992 are estimated
    h New series starting 1988
    i Thousand new soles from 1988; million new soles from 1990
    j Data for 1991 are estimated

Table 0403   No data available for Hong Kong or India
    a Million pesos (currency reform 1992: 1 peso argentino = 10,000 australes)
    b New series starting 1989
    c Million novo cruzados (currency reform 1988: 1 novo cruzado = 1,000 cruzados = 1,000,000 old cruzeiros; in a second reform of March 1990, the cruzeiro again replaced the novo cruzado: 1 cruzeiro = 1,000 novo cruzados); from 1992 billion novo cruzados
    d New series starting 1988
    e Billion units of national currency
    f Million new shekels (currency reform 1985: 1 new shekel = 1,000 shekels)
    g Data for 1992 are estimated
    h From 1990 thousand new soles
    i Data for 1991 are estimated

Table 0404   a New series starting 1984
    b New series starting 1986

Table 0405   No data available for Hong Kong or Taiwan
    a Million pesos (currency reform 1992: 1 peso argentino = 10,000 australes)
    b Million novo cruzados (currency reform 1988: 1 novo cruzado = 1,000 cruzados = 1,000,000 old cruzeiros; in a second reform of March 1990, the cruzeiro again replaced the novo cruzado: 1 cruzeiro = 1,000 novo cruzados
    c New series starting 1988
    d Billion units of national currency
    e Million new shekels (currency reform 1985: 1 new shekel = 1,000 shekels)
    f Data for 1992 are estimated
    g Millions of new pesos
    h From 1990 thousand new soles
    i New series starting 1984
    j Data for 1991 are estimated

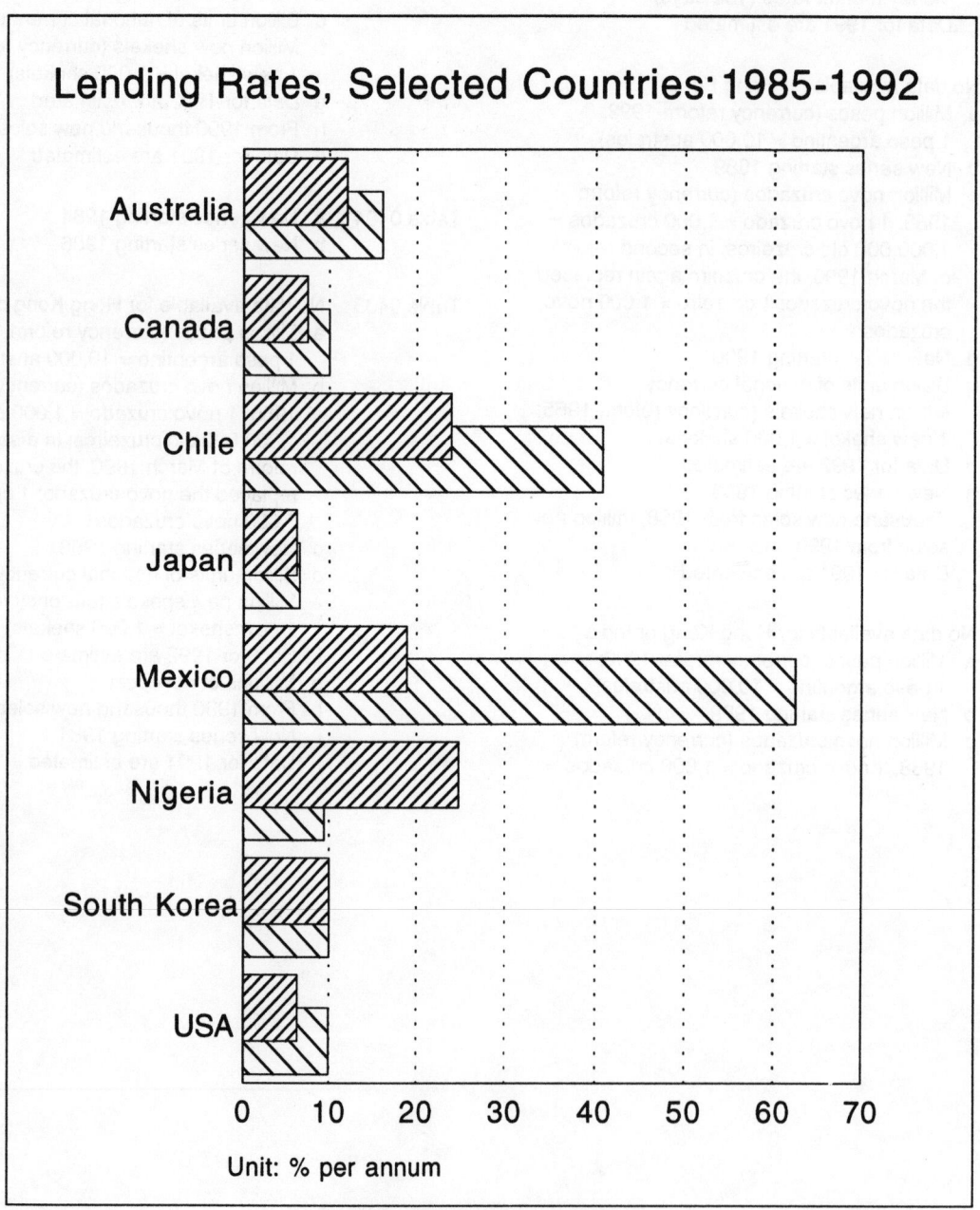

Lending Rates, Selected Countries: 1985-1992

Unit: % per annum

☒ 1992 ☒ 1985

Section Five
External Trade

TOTAL IMPORTS

Table No. 0501

Trends in Total Imports (cif) 1977-1992

Units: Million units of national currency

	1977	1980	1983	1985	1987	1988	1989	1990	1991	1992
North America										
Canada	44,758.0	73,150.0	79,857.0	110,130.0	122,719.0	138,154.0	141,866.0	143,837.0	142,913.0	156,111.0
USA [a]	160.4	257.0	269.9	352.5	424.4	459.5	492.9	517.0	508.4	553.7
South America										
Argentina [b]	4,161.5	10,540.6	4,504.2	3,814.2	5,817.8	5,321.6	4,203.2	4,076.7	8,275.3	
Bolivia [b,c]	591.2	678.4	589.1	551.9	766.3	590.5	619.9	715.7	941.7	1,086.2
Brazil [b]	13,257.0	24,961.0	16,801.0	14,332.0	16,581.0	16,055.0	20,016.0	22,524.0	22,959.0	23,068.0
Chile [b,d]	2,259.0	5,124.0	2,754.0	2,743.0	3,994.0	4,833.0	6,502.0	7,037.0	7,354.0	9,237.0
Colombia [b,c]	2,028.3	4,662.6	4,968.1	4,140.9	4,321.9	5,001.8	5,004.1	5,589.5	4,967.0	6,285.1
Ecuador [b]	1,188.5	2,253.3	1,487.4	1,766.6	2,251.5	1,713.5	1,854.8	1,861.9	2,397.4	2,500.5
French Guiana	706.0	1,078.0	2,137.0	2,287.0	2,372.0					
Guyana	804.3	1,009.6	737.3	1,053.5			11,599.5	20,219.0		
Paraguay	38,830.0	77,453.0	79,532.0	195,727.0	373,407.0	427,935.0	840,437.0	1,052,942.0		
Peru [b,e]	271.0	1,329.0	3,761.0	1,835.0	3,562.3	3,348.0	2,749.2	3,469.8	4,193.3	4,861.0
Suriname	709.9	900.3	808.5	532.9	525.4	626.4	790.7	842.4		
Uruguay [b,c]	721.0	1,680.3	787.5	707.7	1,141.9	1,157.2	1,173.8	1,317.7	1,623.4	2,032.4
Venezuela [c,f]	46,952.0	50,766.0	37,428.0	8,106.0	9,659.0	12,726.0	7,803.0	7,335.0	11,049.0	14,589.0
Caribbean										
Anguilla										
Antigua	109.4	284.9	294.1	301.8	600.1	608.8				
Aruba						422.6	602.1			
Bahamas	2,871.0	5,507.0	3,252.0	3,078.0	3,037.0	2,264.0	3,001.0	2,920.0		
Barbados	545.1	1,049.1	1,249.0	1,210.7	1,035.9	1,170.4	1,354.0	1,407.9	1,394.0	
Bermuda		311.5	378.0	402.5	419.9	488.3	534.6	540.6	463.7	
British Virgin Islands		40.5								
Cayman Islands		85.8	110.0	122.7						
Cuba	3,462.0	4,509.0	6,218.0	7,905.0	7,611.5	7,579.4				
Dominica	59.1	128.7	121.7	149.4	179.2	236.3	289.1	318.4	296.0	300.0
Dominican Republic	975.0	1,639.6	1,470.9	4,628.3	7,036.8	11,303.3	14,455.9	17,533.6	25,120.2	31,958.8
Grenada	87.3	135.6	154.5	187.0	239.2	249.0				
Guadeloupe	1,844.0	3,074.0	5,039.0	5,745.0	6,228.7					
Haiti [c]	1,063.3	1,876.7	2,202.6	2,207.8	1,871.8	1,721.3	1,455.0	1,477.5	1,868.1	2,025.6
Jamaica	781.6	2,086.6	2,841.0	6,146.7	6,790.5	7,983.0	10,403.0	13,427.0	20,237.0	36,969.5
Martinique	2,099.0	3,564.0	5,578.0	6,050.0	6,708.0					
Netherlands Antilles [g]	5,631.0	10,216.0	9,335.0	4,061.0	2,703.0	2,526.0	2,900.0	3,843.0		
St Kitts	59.1	121.1								
St Lucia	160.2	334.3	288.4	337.5	483.9	595.0	739.1	731.6	802.0	
St Vincent/Grenadines	81.9	154.2	190.0	213.9	266.4	330.1	344.2	367.4		
Trinidad and Tobago [c]	4,365.2	7,626.4	6,196.7	3,739.0	4,387.5	4,310.3	5,190.4	5,361.8	7,067.0	6,143.3
Central America										
Belize	180.2	299.5	223.6	256.3	287.2	352.2	431.4	422.5	501.5	545.4
Costa Rica [b]	1,021.4	1,540.4	987.8	1,098.2	1,382.5	1,409.8	1,717.4	1,989.7	1,876.6	2,457.8
El Salvador	2,322.7	2,404.3	2,228.7	2,403.4	4,970.3	5,034.9	5,757.8	10,137.9	11,359.7	15,575.2
Guatemala [b]	1,052.5	1,598.2	1,126.1	1,174.9	1,447.2	1,557.0	1,653.8	1,648.8	1,851.3	2,462.8
Honduras [h]	1,158.8	2,079.0	1,605.2	1,776.2	1,797.3	1,865.8	1,962.2	2,056.8	4,750.9	
Mexico [a]	133.0	447.0	972.4	3,597.5	17,951.0	44,573.9	60,341.7	88,058.0	115,436.0	
Nicaragua [b]	762.0	887.2	825.6	964.3	922.6					
Panama	861.2	1,448.6	1,411.9	1,391.8	1,306.2	751.0	985.9	1,538.6	1,695.0	2,023.6
Puerto Rico										
South Asia										
Afghanistan [b,c]	328.0	551.8	846.0	1,194.2	995.9	900.3	821.7	936.4	812.4	
Bangladesh	17,831.0	40,121.0	53,305.0	70,867.0	84,087.0	96,558.0	117,797.0	126,039.0	122,701.0	152,222.0
Bhutan [i]		394.5	823.3	1,041.6	1,194.6	1,874.5	1,770.2	1,243.9		
India	57,937.0	116,771.0	142,012.0	198,588.0	216,134.0	266,059.0	334,850.0	413,603.0	458,957.0	610,504.0
Nepal [c]	2,104.1	4,107.3	6,746.4	8,267.1	12,444.0	15,850.0	15,780.0	20,157.0	28,235.0	33,059.0
Pakistan	24,216.0	52,968.0	69,855.0	93,793.0	101,310.0	118,681.0	146,444.0	160,134.0	201,409.0	235,296.0
Sri Lanka	6,061.0	33,942.0	45,558.0	54,049.0	60,528.0	71,200.0	79,225.0	107,729.0	126,643.0	152,407.0

TOTAL IMPORTS

Trends in Total Imports (cif) 1977-1992

Units: Million units of national currency

	1977	1980	1983	1985	1987	1988	1989	1990	1991	1992
Japan										
Japan [a]	19,132.0	31,995.0	30,015.0	31,076.0	21,739.0	24,007.0	28,981.0	33,854.0	31,900.0	29,527.0
ASEAN/NICs										
Brunei	680.0	1,233.0	1,542.0	1,348.0	1,350.4	1,451.0	1,722.7	1,847.8		
Hong Kong	48,701.0	111,651.0	175,442.0	231,420.0	377,948.0	498,798.0	562,781.3	642,530.4	778,982.0	955,295.0
Indonesia	6,230.0	10,834.0	16,352.0	10,262.0	12,891.0	13,249.0	16,444.0	21,837.0	25,869.0	27,311.0
Macau [c]	1,102.0	2,780.0	5,423.0	6,179.0	9,017.2	10,375.5	11,879.2	12,343.1	14,832.4	16,235.9
Malaysia [c]	11,165.0	23,451.0	30,795.0	30,438.0	31,934.0	43,293.0	60,858.0	79,119.0	100,831.0	101,321.0
Philippines [c]	31,606.0	62,308.0	88,657.0	101,518.0	147,875.0	184,246.0	243,013.0	317,977.0	353,189.0	372,228.0
Singapore	25,522.0	51,345.0	59,504.0	57,819.0	68,416.0	88,228.0	96,864.0	109,800.0	114,191.0	117,524.0
South Korea [a]	5,233.0	13,541.0	20,318.0	27,089.0	33,742.0	37,898.0	41,271.0	49,433.0	59,787.0	63,782.0
Taiwan [a]	323.8	711.4	813.9	801.8	1,113.9	1,423.1	1,385.7	1,471.8	1,690.8	1,816.0
Thailand	94,177.0	188,686.0	236,609.0	251,169.0	334,209.0	513,114.0	662,679.0	844,448.0	958,832.0	1,033,244.0
East/SE Asia										
Cambodia [b]		72.4	102.4	117.7						
China [a]	13.3	29.1	42.2	126.0	161.5	205.8	220.0	251.2	333.1	421.1
Laos [b]		92.0	150.0	193.0	216.0	193.0	197.0	276.0	292.0	
Mongolia	804.0	1,999.0	3,259.0	3,730.0	3,925.0	4,214.0	3,824.0	3,517.0		
Myanmar [c]	1,946.5	2,337.3	2,150.8	2,401.5	1,785.6	1,538.0	1,348.7	1,709.4	4,058.8	3,866.2
North Korea [b]		1,200.0	1,600.0							
Vietnam [b]		1,296.0	1,310.0	1,550.0	2,455.0	2,757.0	2,566.0	2,752.0	2,194.0	
Australasia										
Australia	12,186.0	19,632.0	23,839.0	37,054.0	41,816.0	45,925.0	56,801.0	53,785.0	53,361.0	59,673.0
New Zealand	3,464.0	5,615.9	7,991.9	12,075.5	12,242.5	11,216.9	14,710.1	15,895.5	14,526.8	17,131.0
Pacific										
American Samoa	55.0	95.0	227.0	105.0						
Fiji	281.0	459.0	493.0	508.0	465.1	658.8	864.3	1,097.0	947.8	929.1
French Polynesia	29,187.0	42,030.0	74,242.0	89,037.0	90,587.0					
Guam	318.0	400.0	320.0							
Kiribati	11.7	18.3	19.6	21.6	25.1	28.2	28.6	34.4		
Nauru				350.0						
New Caledonia	26,032.0	35,041.0	42,201.0	55,931.0	68,533.0					
Papua New Guinea	507.4	786.8	944.9	1,006.0	1,144.9	1,378.9	1,324.8	1,138.6	1,537.0	1,467.9
Solomon Islands	29.6	73.9	84.8	123.2	161.9	244.0	262.5	233.2		
Tonga	17.7	30.1	41.7	58.9	68.5	70.7	68.3	79.0	76.8	84.3
Tuvalu										
Vanuatu [c]	4,155.0	4,993.0	6,260.0	7,462.0	7,450.0	7,066.0	7,882.0	10,768.0	9,174.0	9,018.0
Western Samoa	32.3	57.4	75.1	115.1	131.0	157.3	174.6	173.4	230.1	278.4
Middle East										
Bahrain [c]	802.7	1,251.3	1,256.6	1,187.6	1,020.3	975.1	1,178.2	1,395.4	1,531.3	1,644.2
Egypt [c]	1,884.3	3,401.9	7,192.7	6,973.0	11,357.8	16,308.6	16,623.7	24,823.2	25,216.2	27,968.3
Iran [a]	1,034.2	863.3	1,582.7	1,038.7	669.5	561.2	917.9	1,075.2	1,450.9	1,528.9
Iraq	1,323.2	3,709.1	3,086.2	3,276.3	2,241.2	2,867.2	3,059.2	2,022.6	115.5	133.1
Israel [c]	6.0	49.6	540.4	11,920.3	22,889.5	24,032.3	27,574.7	33,282.4	42,497.0	48,199.0
Jordan	454.4	716.0	1,103.3	1,074.5	916.4	1,022.5	1,230.0	1,725.8	1,710.5	2,214.1
Kuwait	1,387.1	1,764.9	2,149.2	1,965.1	1,561.8	1,706.5	1,849.4	1,145.7	1,353.3	1,585.8
Lebanon	4,373.0	11,614.0	16,300.0	33,194.0	406,919.0	957,946.0	1,115,620.0	756,000.0	3,426,000.0	7,213,000.0
Oman [c]	302.1	598.2	860.9	1,088.9	700.7	846.5	867.9	1,031.0	1,228.0	1,385.8
Qatar	4,850.0	5,265.0	5,299.0	4,147.0	4,226.0	4,613.0	4,827.0	6,169.0	6,261.0	
Saudi Arabia [a]	51.7	100.4	135.4	85.6	75.3	81.6	79.2	90.1		
Syria [c]	10,497.0	16,165.0	17,829.0	15,570.0	9,761.0	24,951.0	23,544.0	26,936.0	30,237.0	44,934.0
United Arab Emirates [c]	19,733.0	32,425.0	30,447.0	24,040.0	26,526.0	31,283.0	36,746.0	41,111.0	50,462.0	61,432.0
Yemen	4,932.0	15,527.7	15,354.2	9,573.0	9,132.0	13,524.0				

TOTAL IMPORTS

Trends in Total Imports (cif) 1977-1992

Units: Million units of national currency

	1977	1980	1983	1985	1987	1988	1989	1990	1991	1992
North Africa										
Algeria	29,534.0	41,545.0	49,782.0	49,491.0	34,153.0	48,002.0	67,781.0	92,908.0	167,040.0	184,334.0
Chad	46,465.0	15,533.0	59,707.0	107,985.0	110,026.0	124,893.0	137,161.0			
Djibouti		37,890.0	39,307.0	35,670.0	36,487.0	35,771.0	34,920.0	38,174.0	38,103.0	
Ethiopia [c]	727.8	1,494.7	1,813.3	2,056.4	2,205.9	2,336.2	1,967.7	2,238.5	976.8	1,465.8
Libya	1,117.1	2,006.2	2,287.4	1,637.9	1,278.3	1,223.6	1,314.4	1,573.4	1,667.8	1,536.6
Mali [a]	39.0	93.1	134.6	134.5	112.4	152.8	159.8			
Mauritania	9,458.0	13,199.0	12,445.0	17,958.0	17,392.0	18,029.0	18,462.0			
Morocco [c]	14,400.0	16,793.0	25,542.0	38,675.0	35,271.0	39,133.0	46,594.0	57,021.0	59,720.0	62,949.0
Niger	48,221.0	125,426.0	123,288.0	154,787.0	80,745.0					
Somalia	1,432.7	2,190.6	5,509.2	4,425.4	13,914.0	31,362.0	76,055.0			
Sudan	376.5	788.2	1,760.8	1,739.1	2,612.9	4,772.1				
Tunisia	782.5	1,427.4	2,109.8	2,287.0	2,509.2	3,167.0	4,150.6	4,852.1	4,789.1	5,673.9
West Africa										
Benin [a]	65.8	70.0	112.0	152.8	105.0	168.7	134.0	148.3	2,715.7	1,553.1
Burkina Faso [a,j]	51.4	75.6	109.6	146.2	130.5	134.9	125.4	161.5	169.6	
Cameroon [a,j]	192.4	337.6	463.9	508.7	526.2	378.7	449.1	403.1	410.0	
Cape Verde	1,284.7	2,742.3	5,720.3	7,445.3	7,281.0	7,652.0	8,706.0			
Côte d'Ivoire [a]	429.6	631.9	704.3	773.0	673.9	619.9	673.5			
Equatorial Guinea		3,454.0	7,406.0	12,040.0	14,576.0	11,255.0	17,544.0			
Gabon [a]	176.0	142.3	261.2	430.0	237.9	276.0	266.7	234.0	302.8	286.2
Gambia [c]	177.7	285.4	304.6	362.3	897.2	919.4	1,221.1	1,573.9	1,932.7	2,087.0
Ghana	1,193.3	3,104.0	11,022.0	39,826.0	149,319.0	185,605.0	346,983.0			
Guinea [b]	167.0	270.0	260.1	376.9	414.0	451.8				
Guinea-Bissau [b]	31.0	55.0	67.4	60.4	83.8	98.8				
Liberia	463.5	534.6	411.6	284.4	307.6	272.3				
Nigeria	7,160.0	9,096.0	8,904.0	5,537.0	15,694.0	21,446.0	30,860.0	45,718.0	89,488.0	143,151.0
Sao Tomé e Príncipe	524.0	656.0	780.0	496.0	655.0	831.0	1,399.0			
Senegal [a]	187.6	222.3	396.1	418.3	353.4	321.6	390.3	389.1	378.5	366.0
Sierra Leone	206.2	447.5	286.9	788.7	4,423.7	5,215.0	10,901.8	23,606.8	45,487.9	65,176.1
Togo	69,834.0	116,357.0	108,141.0	129,406.0	127,308.0	145,170.0	150,533.0			
East/Central Africa										
Angola		39,720.0	20,197.0	19,694.0	30,411.0	21,539.0	44,877.0			
Burundi [c]	6,678.0	15,114.0	17,075.0	22,360.0	25,465.0	28,885.0	29,910.0	40,179.0	46,154.0	45,584.0
Central African Republic	15,540.0	17,010.8	74,995.0	50,686.0	61,370.0	59,760.0	47,994.0		40,853.0	
Comoros		6,147.0	13,099.0	16,481.0	15,560.0	15,647.0	13,576.0			
Congo [a]	50.5	122.5	262.1	268.7	159.1	168.0	172.2	169.1		
Kenya	10,626.0	19,181.0	18,398.0	24,023.0	28,904.0	35,072.0	44,235.0	48,661.0	49,147.0	
Madagascar [a]	85.2	126.8	166.8	265.9	323.1	512.1	545.4			
Maldives [b]		26.0	56.9	52.7	81.0	90.1	105.2	128.9	150.9	
Mauritius [c]	2,950.8	4,721.4	5,254.9	8,119.0	13,037.0	17,242.0	20,217.0	24,019.0	24,650.0	26,159.0
Réunion		3,748.9	6,404.0	7,457.0	8,571.0	7,302.0	10,693.0			
Rwanda	11,406.0	22,568.0	25,453.0	30,244.0	28,018.0	28,280.0	26,642.0	23,059.0	38,454.0	9,555.0
Seychelles [c]	349.7	631.4	594.1	704.7	633.9	856.6	930.2	993.8	910.4	976.4
Tanzania	6,161.0	10,308.0	8,877.0	17,962.0	59,340.0	80,828.0	146,705.0	199,260.0	256,393.0	
Uganda		22.0	473.5	1,886.0	21,511.0	48,975.0	102,051.0	200,017.0	336,219.0	471,101.0
Zaire [c]	522.7	2,327.8	6,818.0	39,478.0	84,998.0	142,698.0	324,154.0	637,899.0	11,076,500.0	318,259,400.0
Southern Africa										
Botswana	231.9	536.9	806.5	1,101.0	1,572.5	2,172.2	3,019.6	3,659.2	3,975.7	
Lesotho	199.4	372.3	539.7	751.0	954.8	1,328.4	1,614.8	1,808.3	2,259.7	
Malawi	209.8	357.3	362.9	506.2	653.9	1,080.2	1,398.8	1,572.5	1,975.8	2,653.8
Mozambique	10,658.0	23,200.0	25,571.0	18,295.0	180,900.0	377,935.0	610,283.0			
Namibia										
South Africa [k]	5,452.0	14,919.0	17,545.0	25,303.0	31,175.0	42,733.0	48,421.0	47,221.0	51,908.0	60,836.0
Swaziland	194.8	468.5	612.8	707.1	885.8	1,167.6	1,524.5	1,760.2	2,057.6	
Zambia [c]	620.8	1,052.0	1,071.8	1,932.1	7,423.9	6,861.2	12,600.5	36,553.6	59,988.0	137,790.0
Zimbabwe [h]	446.3	930.8	1,067.0	1,663.5	2,003.0	2,349.7	3,438.1	4,528.4	7,171.6	

Source: IMF/UN/national statistical offices
Notes: see end of section

TOTAL EXPORTS

Trends in Total Exports 1977-1992

Units: Million units of national currency

	1977	1980	1983	1985	1987	1988	1989	1990	1991	1992
North America										
Canada	46,337.0	79,208.0	94,603.0	124,249.0	130,089.0	143,406.0	142,376.0	147,713.0	145,658.0	162,119.0
USA [a]	121.2	225.6	205.6	218.8	254.1	322.4	363.8	393.6	421.7	447.5
South America										
Argentina [b]	5,651.8	8,021.4	7,836.1	8,396.1	6,360.2	9,134.8	9,579.3	12,352.5	11,971.8	
Bolivia [b]	631.7	942.2	755.2	623.4	565.8	600.2	821.8	926.1	848.6	710.1
Brazil [b]	12,120.0	20,132.0	21,899.0	25,639.0	26,225.0	33,783.0	34,383.0	31,414.0	31,620.0	36,103.0
Chile [b]	2,190.0	4,671.0	3,836.0	3,823.0	5,224.0	7,052.0	8,080.0	8,310.0	8,929.0	9,986.0
Colombia [b,c]	2,443.2	3,945.0	3,080.9	3,551.6	4,642.2	5,037.0	5,716.5	6,765.8	7,244.2	7,166.0
Ecuador [b]	1,436.3	2,480.8	2,347.7	2,904.7	1,927.8	2,192.4	2,353.8	2,714.3	2,851.5	3,007.4
French Guiana	36.0	105.0	294.0	331.0	324.0					
Guyana	661.2	992.4	566.5	875.4	2,367.2	2,295.6	6,123.2	10,207.7	28,107.2	36,125.8
Paraguay	34,564.0	39,089.0	43,161.0	96,708.0	208,614.0	237,026.0	361,399.0	1,237,026.0		
Peru [b]	1,725.6	3,898.3	3,015.2	2,978.5	2,660.8	2,701.0	3,488.0	3,230.9	3,329.1	3,484.4
Suriname	552.8	918.2	654.7	587.0	546.3	730.6	966.6	843.4		
Uruguay [b,c]	607.5	1,058.5	1,045.1	909.0	1,189.2	1,404.5	1,593.6	1,692.7	1,593.9	1,688.1
Venezuela [b]	9,551.0	19,221.0	13,937.0	14,438.0	10,577.0	10,244.0	13,313.0	17,497.0	15,053.0	13,348.0
Caribbean										
Anguilla										
Antigua	17.8	82.1	53.3	35.6	46.5	60.0				
Aruba					46.7	54.6				
Bahamas	2,409.0	4,906.0	2,561.0	2,728.0	2,728.0	2,164.0	2,786.0			
Barbados	193.0	455.4	646.0	698.5	313.5	348.9	374.5	421.1	411.5	
Bermuda		36.7	22.8	23.1	29.2	30.8	50.0	59.7	48.7	
British Virgin Islands		1.2								
Cayman Islands [b]		2.2	1.0	1.5						
Cuba	2,918.0	3,967.0	5,523.0	5,983.0	5,401.0	5,518.3				
Dominica	32.3	26.3	74.0	76.8	129.6	146.4	121.8	148.6	146.6	150.8
Dominican Republic	780.5	961.9	785.2	2,288.3	2,734.6	5,438.3	5,860.6	6,262.2	8,355.7	6,965.3
Grenada	38.8	47.0	51.1	60.3	90.6					
Guadeloupe	388.0	446.0	627.0	669.0	564.0					
Haiti [c]	742.8	1,131.0	830.0	842.0	1,067.7	896.4	720.3	791.5	514.8	606.5
Jamaica	698.6	1,715.0	1,391.9	3,128.3	3,873.6	4,830.0	5,841.0	8,046.0	13,074.0	26,615.2
Martinique	630.0	492.0	867.0	1,300.0	1,163.0					
Netherlands Antilles [d]	4,764.0	9,292.0	8,319.0	3,023.0	2,354.0	2,041.0	2,608.0	3,204.0		
St Kitts	40.5	65.1	47.1	58.9						
St Lucia	61.0	124.3	128.2	140.5						
St Vincent/Grenadines	26.8	42.9	110.8	170.8	141.3	230.2	201.4	223.3		
Trinidad and Tobago [c]	5,231.5	9,784.8	5,646.3	5,247.1	5,264.6	5,424.2	6,706.9	8,842.0	8,425.9	7,939.5
Central America										
Belize	124.2	205.2	155.5	181.2	198.7	232.5	249.1	258.1	252.0	282.2
Costa Rica [b]	828.2	1,001.7	870.4	976.0	1,158.3	1,245.7	1,414.6	1,448.2	1,597.7	1,833.8
El Salvador	2,430.9	2,864.0	1,838.3	1,697.5	2,954.7	3,043.8	2,485.8	4,669.4	4,751.0	5,479.1
Guatemala [b]	1,160.0	1,557.1	1,158.8	1,057.0	981.4	1,033.8	1,126.2	1,200.0	1,202.2	1,071.1
Honduras [c]	1,037.1	1,700.5	1,343.6	1,529.2	1,616.1	1,737.4	1,824.2	1,831.6	4,363.7	4,873.9
Mexico [a]	102.0	357.9	2,632.0	5,705.1	28,939.2	47,201.7	56,769.1	76,611.0	82,508.0	
Nicaragua [b]	636.8	450.6	428.8	301.5	299.9	235.7				
Panama	251.0	360.5	320.6	336.2	357.7	306.9	317.9	340.1	358.4	501.5
Puerto Rico										
South Asia										
Afghanistan [b,e]	306.1	670.2	728.6	556.8	511.9	394.7	235.9	235.1	245.5	
Bangladesh	7,314.0	11,728.0	17,837.0	27,997.0	33,030.0	40,967.0	42,108.0	57,885.0	61,866.0	81,724.0
Bhutan		131.5	160.7	272.0	711.9	1,041.3	1,190.7	1,387.6		
India	55,734.0	67,517.0	92,430.0	113,192.0	146,417.0	184,099.0	257,726.0	314,451.0	401,230.0	506,784.0
Nepal [c]	1,007.2	964.2	1,360.9	2,914.7	3,290.0	4,433.0	4,303.0	6,160.0	9,831.0	16,036.0
Pakistan	11,766.0	25,923.0	40,320.0	43,645.0	72,583.0	81,348.0	96,646.0	121,345.0	155,398.0	183,599.0
Sri Lanka	6,570.0	17,595.0	25,096.0	36,207.0	41,133.0	46,928.0	56,175.0	79,481.0	84,378.0	110,052.0

TOTAL EXPORTS

Trends in Total Exports 1977-1992

Units: Million units of national currency

	1977	1980	1983	1985	1987	1988	1989	1990	1991	1992
Japan										
Japan [a]	21,648.0	29,382.0	34,910.0	41,959.0	33,316.0	33,928.0	37,823.0	41,457.0	42,359.0	43,011.0
ASEAN/NICs										
Brunei	4,000.0	9,853.0	7,171.0	6,533.0	4,005.6	3,463.4	3,693.5			
Hong Kong	44,833.0	98,242.0	160,699.0	235,152.0	378,034.0	493,069.0	570,509.5	639,874.1	765,886.1	924,952.7
Indonesia [b]	10,853.0	21,909.0	21,152.0	18,590.0	17,135.0	19,465.0	22,160.0	25,674.0	29,543.0	29,322.0
Macau [c]	1,222.0	2,742.0	5,673.0	7,181.0	11,233.5	12,003.2	13,193.9	13,638.2	13,326.1	15,934.3
Malaysia [c]	14,959.0	28,172.0	32,771.0	38,328.0	45,138.0	55,260.0	67,824.0	79,647.0	94,497.0	103,018.0
Philippines [c]	23,148.0	43,142.0	54,641.0	85,283.0	116,237.0	148,151.0	168,928.0	211,052.0	241,612.0	242,710.0
Singapore	20,091.0	41,452.0	46,155.0	50,179.0	60,266.0	79,051.0	87,117.0	95,205.0	101,879.0	103,349.0
South Korea [a]	4,863.0	10,633.0	18,963.0	26,347.0	38,892.0	44,398.0	41,883.0	46,016.0	52,706.0	59,940.0
Taiwan [a]	355.2	712.2	1,005.4	1,222.9	1,705.6	1,731.8	1,747.8	1,802.8	2,040.8	2,048.0
Thailand	71,198.0	133,197.0	146,472.0	193,366.0	301,453.0	403,570.0	516,315.0	589,813.0	725,630.0	824,139.0
East/SE Asia										
Cambodia										
China [a]	14.0	27.1	43.8	80.9	147.2	177.0	195.3	293.1	375.0	444.0
Laos [b]		28.0	41.0	54.0	62.0	63.0	63.0	146.0	113.0	
Mongolia		1,198.0	1,814.0	2,050.0	2,136.0	2,199.0	2,148.0	1,966.0		
Myanmar	516.7	3,122.6	3,039.4	2,803.5	1,449.8	936.3	1,439.4	2,039.0	2,634.4	3,271.9
North Korea [b]		900.0	1,200.0							
Vietnam [b]		537.0	588.0	750.0	854.0	1,038.0	1,946.0	2,404.0	1,970.0	
Australasia										
Australia	12,050.0	19,341.0	21,417.0	32,601.0	37,798.0	42,176.0	47,643.0	50,995.0	53,806.0	57,966.0
New Zealand	3,294.9	5,568.5	8,110.0	11,603.2	12,149.7	13,388.2	14,819.5	15,917.4	16,618.6	18,284.0
Pacific										
American Samoa	82.0	127.0	177.0	136.0						
Fiji	164.0	306.0	244.9	271.4	408.6	531.5	631.3	785.9	575.1	
French Polynesia	1,464.0	2,340.0	5,762.0	6,564.0	9,095.0					
Guam	22.0	33.0	60.0	58.0						
Kiribati	18.2	2.6	4.0	6.1	2.9	6.7	6.4	3.7		
Nauru										
New Caledonia	27,799.0	31,340.0	21,272.0	43,938.0	24,479.0					
Papua New Guinea	539.8	691.7	687.5	926.2	1,283.8	1,751.6	1,111.6	1,122.4	1,283.8	1,751.6
Solomon Islands [e]	29.6	60.8	71.2	103.8	128.3	170.6	172.8	176.0	222.1	
Tonga	6.5	7.2	6.5	7.8	8.1	8.4	12.3	15.3	18.0	17.4
Tuvalu										
Vanuatu	2,536.0	2,449.0	2,940.0	3,205.0	1,942.0	2,066.0	2,563.0	2,202.0	1,810.0	
Western Samoa	11.6	15.8	27.4	66.7	25.0	31.4	29.2	20.5	15.5	14.8
Middle East										
Bahrain [c]	730.1	1,294.3	1,202.8	1,089.2	913.5	906.7	1,064.5	1,414.0	1,304.3	12,964.0
Egypt [c]	668.5	2,132.8	2,250.1	2,600.0	3,046.0	3,994.4	5,734.7	6,953.8	11,764.6	10,929.6
Iran [a]	1,713.1	994.4	1,684.7	1,218.6						
Iraq	2,849.6	7,760.4	3,041.8							
Israel	3.2	28.4	287.1	7,380.1	13,515.2	15,592.2	20,577.5	23,598.1	26,743.0	31,888.0
Jordan	82.1	171.5	210.6	310.9	315.7	381.5	637.6	706.1	770.7	829.3
Kuwait	2,792.6	5,368.9	3,373.6	3,185.0	2,304.4	2,166.2	3,378.0	2,031.4		
Lebanon	2,120.0	2,983.0	2,533.0	6,124.0	107,345.0	246,911.0	249,483.0	354,566.0	491,000.0	931,000.0
Oman	543.3	1,138.2	1,463.7	1,548.0	1,319.8	1,256.9				
Qatar	8,205.0	20,741.0	17,592.0							
Saudi Arabia [a]	153.2	362.9	158.4	99.5	86.9	91.3	106.3	166.3		
Syria [c]	4,199.0	8,273.0	7,547.0	6,427.0	5,312.0	15,093.0	33,740.0	47,373.0	40,613.0	34,897.0
United Arab Emirates	37,891.0	76,627.0	55,378.0	48,180.0						
Yemen	51.0	103.0	123.0	97.0	491.8					

TOTAL EXPORTS

Trends in Total Exports 1977-1992

Units: Million units of national currency

	1977	1980	1983	1985	1987	1988	1989	1990	1991	1992
North Africa										
Algeria	24,650.0	53,229.0	60,256.0	64,564.0	39,891.0	48,113.0				
Chad	26,177.0	14,999.0	39,824.0	39,381.0	33,224.0	41,867.0	47,528.0			
Djibouti	3,364.0	2,221.0	1,919.0	2,488.0	4,976.0	4,116.0	4,423.0	4,420.0	3,083.0	
Ethiopia [c]	689.0	878.8	833.3	689.4	735.2	888.6	911.5	615.8	390.5	280.8
Libya	3,378.2	6,489.2	3,616.6	3,645.6	2,372.0	1,907.0				
Mali [a]	30.6	43.3	62.9	55.6	53.8	74.9	86.5			
Mauritania	7,156.0	8,916.0	15,982.0	28,887.0	31,608.0	26,655.0	36,332.0			
Morocco [c]	5,858.0	9,645.0	14,324.0	21,740.0	23,390.0	29,751.0	28,271.0	35,135.0	37,283.0	35,389.0
Niger	39,335.0	119,523.0	113,896.0	93,901.0	93,863.0	85,941.0	77,710.0	76,939.0		
Somalia	396.5	835.0	1,717.1	3,576.5	10,900.0	10,994.0	41,708.0			
Sudan	230.2	271.3	810.6	844.7	1,497.1	2,290.9	3,023.0			
Tunisia	398.3	904.8	1,263.9	1,443.0	1,770.7	2,056.0	2,782.0	3,086.5	3,429.9	3,566.7
West Africa										
Benin [a]	7.6	13.3	25.4	68.5	34.3	24.8	36.5	31.3	35.2	30.8
Burkina Faso [a]	13.6	19.1	21.7	31.2	46.6	42.0	30.3			
Cameroon [a]	172.9	290.6	358.9	321.7	248.8	275.1	406.0	549.8		
Cape Verde		170.5	238.0	463.0	561.0	241.0	527.0			
Côte d'Ivoire [a]	529.2	663.9	796.8	1,318.1	929.1	826.5	895.6			
Equatorial Guinea	1,136.0	2,399.0	5,908.0	11,289.0	12,745.0	10,169.0	13,078.0			
Gabon [a]	330.0	459.1	762.2	876.7	387.0	356.1	509.6	670.8		
Gambia [c]	110.2	54.9	126.9	172.9	281.4	388.7	198.1	316.7	364.8	559.1
Ghana	1,166.1	3,458.9	10,225.0	33,185.0	147,275.0	205,705.0	275,290.0			
Guinea	5,498.0	8,090.8	8,282.0	10,317.0	210,204.0					
Guinea-Bissau	427.6	382.3	1,043.0	1,362.1	4,766.1					
Liberia	447.4	600.4	427.6	435.6	382.2	396.3	460.1			
Nigeria	7,631.0	14,187.0	7,963.0	11,215.0	29,578.0	31,193.0	57,971.0	109,886.0	121,534.0	205,613.0
Sao Tomé e Príncipe	864.0	591.0	366.0	335.0	387.0	704.0	674.0			
Senegal [a]	152.9	100.8	235.5	240.9	182.3	176.1	212.3	195.4	212.5	178.0
Sierra Leone	140.3	217.3	201.9	649.0	4,661.7	3,329.5	8,269.5	20,915.3	43,946.0	74,873.0
Togo	39,115.0	71,285.0	61,921.0	85,380.0	73,212.0	72,209.0	78,188.0			
East/Central Africa										
Angola	25,000.0	56,329.0	54,501.0	66,968.0	69,574.0	58,168.0	75,000.0			
Burundi [c]	8,011.0	5,884.0	7,494.0	13,462.0	11,117.0	18,589.0	12,304.0	12,784.0	16,645.0	15,831.0
Central African Republic	20,033.0	24,384.0	28,405.0	41,217.0	39,180.0	38,750.0	42,866.0		20,938.0	
Comoros	2,203.0	1,961.0	7,419.0	7,048.0	3,485.0	6,399.0	5,758.0			
Congo [a]	65.5	192.4	406.3	514.3	155.4	223.9	291.0	267.2		
Kenya	9,824.0	10,314.0	13,044.0	16,047.0	15,790.0	19,012.0	19,904.0	23,677.0	30,376.0	
Madagascar [a,c]	82.9	84.8	113.4	181.6	354.0	385.1	506.2	460.3	559.1	526.9
Maldives [b]	3.4	7.8	13.4	23.0	30.8	40.2	44.7	52.1	53.7	
Mauritius [c]	2,041.5	3,341.3	4,396.0	6,729.0	11,336.0	13,455.0	15,049.0	17,677.0	18,672.0	19,633.0
Réunion	561.0	552.9	667.0	868.0	887.0	1,063.0	922.0			
Rwanda	8,511.0	10,354.0	11,405.0	13,221.0	8,949.0	8,291.0	7,635.0	9,224.0	11,598.0	2,280.0
Seychelles [c]	84.8	135.2	137.3	199.7	124.1	171.3	193.5	301.5	258.3	248.4
Tanzania	4,198.0	4,192.0	4,138.0	4,960.0	18,512.0	27,041.0	51,463.0	80,999.0	78,986.0	
Uganda [c]	48.6	25.6	593.0		13,684.0	29,070.0	55,674.0	64,653.0	146,661.0	162,379.0
Zaire [c]	846.9	4,553.8	13,921.0	47,372.0	109,532.0	209,598.0	478,409.0	717,942.0	12,934,000.0	309,661,200.0
Southern Africa										
Botswana [c]	151.6	390.7	697.2	1,405.7	2,782.9	2,678.3	3,742.6	3,342.7	3,743.2	3,850.4
Lesotho	12.2	45.3	41.8	50.0	94.7	144.9	172.6	156.4	186.2	
Malawi	180.3	228.0	270.6	428.1	614.8	753.4	743.2	1,123.5	1,326.4	1,488.9
Mozambique	4,923.0	9,097.0	5,287.0	3,309.0	28,076.0	54,444.0	75,318.0			
Namibia										
South Africa [f]	8,685.0	19,981.0	20,708.0	36,737.0	43,849.0	49,170.0	58,406.0	61,068.0	68,815.0	68,075.0
Swaziland	143.1	286.9	338.5	385.2	826.2	1,025.0	1,159.1			
Zambia [c]	708.0	1,023.3	1,052.3	2,451.4	8,058.4	9,791.3	18,477.4	39,143.2	47,851.0	196,655.0
Zimbabwe [e]	550.9	909.2	1,025.7	1,795.5	2,371.4	2,539.5	2,832.1	3,659.5	4,094.0	

Source: IMF/UN/national statistical offices
Notes: see end of section

EXTERNAL TRADE BY DESTINATION AND ORIGIN

Table No. 0503

Imports (cif) by Country of Origin 1991

Units: Million current US dollars

	USA	Japan	EC	Former USSR	Africa	Asia	Middle East	South America/ Caribbean	Australia	Total (inc. others)
North America										
Canada [a]	75,025.0	8,891.0	12,650.0	185.0	912.0	8,259.0	689.0	4,419.0	582.0	120,410.0
USA		95,010.0	89,433.0	915.0	14,940.0	108,595.0	17,485.0	65,755.0	4,317.0	509,300.0
South America										
Argentina	2,253.9	494.6	2,304.3	13.6	23.6	597.1	44.0	1,718.9	100.3	7,994.0
Bolivia	208.8	55.0	172.0	2.1	0.7	16.0	1.3	378.0	0.1	877.7
Brazil	5,536.0	1,336.0	5,128.0	131.0	868.0	800.0	3,067.0	4,425.0	139.0	23,420.0
Chile	1,581.9	645.7	1,405.0		455.8	631.5	41.2	2,079.2	47.0	7,683.0
Colombia	2,141.4	544.0	1,192.9	10.6	3.3	124.5	13.7	1,158.4	8.1	5,683.9
Ecuador	1,042.4	212.8	654.4	4.1	12.5	122.9	12.8	555.6	4.3	2,759.2
French Guiana	164.5	11.7	1,691.2	0.3	0.2	0.8		79.4	0.1	1,963.9
Guyana	94.5	16.6	74.8	0.2	0.2	10.7		51.2		278.1
Paraguay [a]	194.9	161.2	173.5			37.2	8.6		406.8	1,335.4
Peru [a]	617.7	140.9	441.7	2.4	9.0	111.6	3.2	972.0	13.7	2,475.9
Suriname	148.1	21.4	125.8			24.1		110.2		434.2
Uruguay	228.4	77.6	335.9	48.0	13.8	96.2	52.6	685.8	1.9	1,628.3
Venezuela [a]	4,668.0	529.0	2,257.0	4.0	38.0	353.0	33.0	883.0	13.0	9,456.0
Caribbean										
Anguilla										
Antigua										
Aruba										
Bahamas	793.1	423.6	346.7	5.5	335.8	143.5	27.3	126.5	0.6	2,519.7
Barbados	208.5	31.7	112.1	0.2	0.2	21.2	0.1	192.5	1.7	624.9
Bermuda	304.5	24.1	62.8	0.1	0.1	9.7	0.3	34.0	0.2	463.7
British Virgin Islands										
Cayman Islands										
Cuba	1.4	39.3	858.2		11.5	290.7		1,100.9	0.3	2,646.9
Dominica	46.8	5.1	52.8		0.1	69.9	0.3	27.4	0.1	205.2
Dominican Republic [a]	908.6	104.0	283.2	0.1	5.0	121.1	0.6	494.9		1,995.5
Grenada	34.7	7.0	21.8			13.2		39.8		131.3
Guadeloupe	92.0		1,365.4	0.7	4.5	10.6	0.6	114.0		1,605.1
Haiti	431.3	22.7	66.8		0.3	55.9	1.9	58.2		662.7
Jamaica	1,059.0	76.3	264.5	6.5	0.9	92.3	0.4	355.3	0.7	2,014.8
Martinique	40.0		1,310.6	0.1	1.6	2.2	72.4	85.9		1,575.0
Netherlands Antilles	691.9	85.3	381.3		37.9	175.4		371.9	1.0	1,799.4
St Kitts										
St Lucia										
St Vincent/Grenadines	47.7	6.9	57.8			20.4		9.4		153.9
Trinidad and Tobago	656.0	93.2	247.4	4.7	19.7	73.4	1.3	413.9	9.7	1,647.1
Central America										
Belize	125.7	9.5	48.5			14.3		31.0		233.6
Costa Rica	805.2	110.8	199.3		0.5	89.6	5.4	556.3	0.2	1,849.8
El Salvador	587.3	68.2	235.0		0.6	44.3	0.7	468.4		1,498.4
Guatemala	783.5	121.9	229.1			45.7		516.6		1,851.3
Honduras	356.6	78.9	133.2					254.8		879.8
Mexico [a]	33,276.0	2,822.0	5,935.0	20.0	154.0	1,781.0	43.0	1,428.0	67.0	47,033.0
Nicaragua	161.5	33.8	105.9	77.3		14.0	0.8	237.5	0.3	759.2
Panama	607.0	114.7	124.0		4.8	91.9	1.5	677.1	0.1	1,695.0
Puerto Rico										
South Asia										
Afghanistan	3.2	127.7	72.3	964.7		265.2	1.5	2.6	0.5	1,669.6
Bangladesh	174.5	302.9	445.5	21.2	4.6	1,134.0	200.7	64.4	68.5	3,381.4
Bhutan										
India	2,234.0	1,634.0	6,896.0	1,478.0	703.0	2,962.0	3,138.0	492.0	472.0	21,687.0
Nepal	6.6	107.7	49.6			227.6	2.5	3.1	1.8	455.3
Pakistan	942.9	1,245.5	2,159.8	129.2	156.5	1,580.4	1,255.7	175.4	147.3	8,431.5
Sri Lanka	132.9	321.3	574.0	3.8	128.3	1,521.8	273.0	40.5	37.4	3,162.7

EXTERNAL TRADE BY DESTINATION AND ORIGIN

Table No. 0503 (cont'd)

Imports (cif) by Country of Origin 1991

Units: Million current US dollars

	USA	Japan	EC	Former USSR	Africa	Asia	Middle East	South America/ Carib- bean	Aus- tralia	Total (inc. others)
Japan										
Japan	53,634.0		31,971.0	3,318.0	3,633.0	74,533.0	29,252.0	9,335.0	12,965.0	236,633.0
ASEAN/NICs										
Brunei	178.5	141.7	529.0		10.2	828.7	0.9	1.0	14.5	1,780.7
Hong Kong	7,576.0	16,397.0	9,253.0	55.0	557.0	61,281.0	719.0	756.0	949.0	100,274.0
Indonesia	3,397.0	6,327.0	4,704.0	47.0	189.0	6,729.0	1,069.0	597.0	1,378.0	25,869.0
Macau	78.8	293.9	140.3	4.5	12.1	1,267.6	5.5	2.1	24.1	1,855.8
Malaysia	5,626.0	9,582.0	5,001.0	75.0	183.0	12,380.0	318.0	510.0	1,175.0	36,749.0
Philippines	2,609.6	2,517.0	1,318.0	37.8	67.7	3,843.6	1,331.8	293.4	420.1	12,944.5
Singapore	10,501.0	14,115.0	7,978.0	193.0	404.0	22,665.0	6,066.0	796.0	1,247.0	66,257.0
South Korea	19,183.0	21,334.0	12,298.0		245.0	10,035.0	6,021.0	2,178.0	2,742.0	81,114.0
Taiwan [b]	12,611.8	15,998.4	9,585.8		1,220.5	11,157.3			1,659.7	54,716.0
Thailand	3,996.5	10,802.8	5,200.4	238.2	402.3	11,578.4	1,282.1	778.1	576.6	37,518.0
East/SE Asia										
Cambodia										
China	8,003.0	10,079.0	8,500.0	2,109.0	376.0	26,508.0	809.0	1,358.0	1,555.0	63,957.0
Laos	0.9	23.5	14.5		0.1	108.7	0.1	0.3	0.4	150.3
Mongolia										
Myanmar	26.2	90.8	87.0	7.0	3.0	766.1	0.2	0.7	3.4	1,073.2
North Korea		246.3	143.6		2.7	823.8	11.0	18.9	24.7	1,457.3
Vietnam	4.0	239.4	251.9		0.2	994.6	2.1	1.9	35.4	1,620.5
Australasia										
Australia [a]	9,455.0	6,799.0	8,054.0	28.0	118.0	8,457.0	1,120.0	455.0		38,625.0
New Zealand	1,406.2	1,310.7	1,510.6	2.2	34.2	1,082.1	453.0	107.6	1,848.8	8,391.7
Pacific										
American Samoa										
Fiji	28.3	74.1	32.1			140.1			205.1	652.1
French Polynesia										
Guam										
Kiribati										
Nauru										
New Caledonia	60.3	50.0	526.6	0.2	7.6	66.1	0.2	0.4	83.9	865.6
Papua New Guinea [a]	95.9	163.4	65.2	0.2	1.3	264.4	0.2	6.2	676.8	1,344.3
Solomon Islands [a]	4.5	23.1	5.7		0.3	30.4		0.3	34.9	107.6
Tonga	5.9	5.3	1.3			13.7		0.4	15.1	59.3
Tuvalu										
Vanuatu	1.2	29.7	35.8			7.1	0.1	12.0	29.7	124.4
Western Samoa	10.3	9.4	4.5			14.2		0.9	19.8	99.0
Middle East										
Bahrain	551.2	182.2	895.2		4.7	276.8	1,762.8	15.1	107.6	3,992.8
Egypt	1,323.5	334.7	2,267.4	149.5	61.0	390.4	261.5	262.4		8,226.7
Iran	580.0	2,724.0	10,061.0	220.0	94.0	1,830.0	1,314.0	1,045.0	338.0	21,688.0
Iraq			68.0			2.0	116.0		28.0	284.0
Israel	3,250.7	733.4	7,995.2	48.6	286.2	622.5	12.6	230.3	53.1	16,819.1
Jordan	261.7	89.8	752.2	27.4	59.5	331.8	524.3	46.7	37.2	2,512.1
Kuwait	1,351.0	481.0	962.0		1.0	292.0	24.0		20.0	3,882.0
Lebanon	181.8	118.3	1,753.6		19.3	452.5	549.7	31.1	2.6	3,748.4
Oman	223.5	673.9	1,039.6		11.9	415.1	723.6	10.0	57.5	3,309.7
Qatar	161.9	230.4	822.9		4.5	208.3	199.2	36.2	21.2	1,862.1
Saudi Arabia	7,229.0	4,292.0	13,315.0	53.0	433.0	4,845.0	831.0	435.0	409.0	34,587.0
Syria	240.3	125.3	1,107.9	69.7	18.0	157.0	118.0	63.3	0.1	2,857.3
United Arab Emirates	1,601.0	2,374.0	5,016.0	19.0	69.0	4,441.0	1,037.0	117.0	271.0	16,049.0
Yemen [c]	211.0	141.2	549.7	12.6	55.6	449.4	299.4	12.7	62.4	1,951.3

EXTERNAL TRADE BY DESTINATION AND ORIGIN — Table No. 0503 (cont'd)

Imports (cif) by Country of Origin 1991

Units: Million current US dollars

	USA	Japan	EC	Former USSR	Africa	Asia	Middle East	South America/ Carib- bean	Aus- tralia	Total (inc. others)
North Africa										
Algeria	800.0	402.0	5,845.0	37.0	254.0	209.0	77.0	253.0	44.0	9,104.0
Chad	15.1	5.0	114.2		16.2	3.7	0.4	0.2		158.2
Djibouti	11.0	27.2	171.5		28.4	92.0	23.5	0.5	0.2	376.0
Ethiopia	231.3	61.0	404.5	181.2	17.1	51.8	48.0	1.5	0.6	1,114.3
Libya		152.0	3,712.0		367.0	428.0	211.0	78.0	9.0	6,001.0
Mali	20.4	10.0	244.9	30.6	184.9	43.8	20.4	3.4	0.2	569.6
Mauritania	23.5	6.8	331.9		24.3	38.4	1.3	4.3	2.0	471.7
Morocco	442.9	140.2	4,896.9	277.0	220.2	290.3	238.3	179.1	2.8	7,458.2
Niger	11.7	14.8	183.2		56.4	23.6		4.8	0.2	407.2
Somalia	7.9	2.5	59.7	0.2	40.8	14.3	52.1	3.1		196.9
Sudan	101.5	57.9	558.2	0.5	44.5	222.4	328.0	4.2	2.2	1,419.1
Tunisia	243.7	120.9	3,719.3	117.6	202.4	169.3	151.3	149.9	0.5	5,444.6
West Africa										
Benin	28.8	15.2	275.4	3.0	53.4	224.1		2.1		636.6
Burkina Faso	26.0	21.4	251.3	0.6	180.6	54.4		4.5		552.5
Cameroon	78.9	72.1	866.3	13.1	99.7	71.3	2.8	40.6	0.3	1,345.0
Cape Verde	4.7		109.0	2.0	4.3	0.2		6.3		144.4
Côte d'Ivoire	89.7	74.2	1,179.4	14.7	377.3	261.8	3.3	60.7	0.1	2,240.4
Equatorial Guinea	13.3	0.1	41.4		31.6	0.9		0.3		91.1
Gabon	93.3	66.1	627.2	0.7	101.9	48.6	0.4	8.3	0.1	961.9
Gambia	11.7	11.7	133.2	8.5	7.3	95.5	0.2	2.1		287.4
Ghana	156.1	84.3	740.9	2.4	192.1	160.5	5.3	35.6	14.5	1,481.7
Guinea	97.6	25.8	354.0		18.9	71.5	4.6	19.4	0.1	604.6
Guinea-Bissau	1.7	6.9	62.8	4.4	9.9	16.1		0.2	24.2	134.0
Liberia	50.6	878.5	637.2		4.3	1,645.8	5.2	20.3	0.1	4,081.2
Nigeria	916.0	453.0	3,975.0	119.0	151.0	1,165.0	297.0	132.0	3.0	7,781.0
Sao Tomé e Príncipe	4.8	1.5	26.4		0.3	0.4		0.1		35.0
Senegal	83.9	29.1	753.1	2.3	210.9	135.9	24.6	13.0	0.1	1,358.9
Sierra Leone	27.2	8.9	111.4	0.2	61.5	25.2	0.1	1.1	0.2	246.1
Togo	26.4	33.2	385.4	3.1	104.6	276.4		5.3	2.2	863.7
East/Central Africa										
Angola	207.0	153.0	1,283.2		20.2	57.2		174.4	1.1	1,971.0
Burundi	2.7	21.3	98.7	0.1	35.5	25.0	29.0	1.4		247.3
Central African Republic	1.2	11.1	104.0	0.2	28.3	6.5	0.3	58.5	0.1	292.7
Comoros		3.6	95.5		7.6	6.8	4.7	0.1		119.6
Congo	47.4	23.1	450.4	7.5	41.6	86.5	1.0	4.0		681.6
Kenya	101.2	227.1	1,008.3	1.9	80.2	332.5	343.6	11.5	9.0	2,228.8
Madagascar	15.6	26.6	224.3	3.2	37.7	84.5	53.8	12.4	0.9	556.0
Maldives	1.2	6.5	15.1		0.1	132.3	3.3	0.2	1.1	161.2
Mauritius	16.9	86.1	489.6	0.8	227.8	446.2	68.8	17.2	44.0	1,444.9
Réunion	2.1	43.7	1,723.4		130.3	65.2	129.5	7.2	4.2	2,177.0
Rwanda	2.1	10.5	96.4	2.1	52.3	15.0	13.7	2.1		212.9
Seychelles	2.1	7.9	55.3		6.5	37.7	7.3	0.6	1.7	124.0
Tanzania	38.1	107.8	466.9		42.3	180.7	152.0	7.8	7.4	1,089.6
Uganda	14.6	43.0	184.7		110.2	75.9	10.5	2.1	0.8	464.1
Zaire	67.9	42.9	601.9		102.3	135.9	2.0	4.5		992.5
Southern Africa										
Botswana										
Lesotho										
Malawi	60.2	44.3	162.6		232.7	26.8	0.3		1.1	544.6
Mozambique	111.1	42.8	296.4		100.6	175.5	105.9	7.1	8.7	899.1
Namibia										
South Africa [a]	2,113.0	1,639.0	7,185.0		403.0	1,144.0	100.0	334.0	123.0	16,981.0
Swaziland										
Zambia [a]	23.5	69.6	224.2		417.8	56.5	36.7	2.9	1.3	888.2
Zimbabwe [a]	53.3	79.4	585.4	0.5	157.6	69.4	10.3	17.8	6.9	1,294.2

Source: IMF, Direction of Trade Statistics
Notes: see end of section

EXTERNAL TRADE BY DESTINATION AND ORIGIN — Table No. 0504

Imports (cif) by Country of Origin 1991 (% Analysis)

Units: % of total imports

	USA	Japan	EC	Former USSR	Africa	Asia	Middle East	South America/ Caribbean	Australia	Total (inc. others)
North America										
Canada [a]	62.3	7.4	10.5	0.2	0.8	6.9	0.6	3.7	0.5	100.0
USA		18.7	17.6	0.2	2.9	21.3	3.4	12.9	0.8	100.0
South America										
Argentina	28.2	6.2	28.8	0.2	0.3	7.5	0.6	21.5	1.3	100.0
Bolivia	23.8	6.3	19.6	0.2	0.1	1.8	0.1	43.1		100.0
Brazil	23.6	5.7	21.9	0.6	3.7	3.4	13.1	18.9	0.6	100.0
Chile	20.6	8.4	18.3		5.9	8.2	0.5	27.1	0.6	100.0
Colombia	37.7	9.6	21.0	0.2	0.1	2.2	0.2	20.4	0.1	100.0
Ecuador	37.8	7.7	23.7	0.1	0.5	4.5	0.5	20.1	0.2	100.0
French Guiana	8.4	0.6	86.1					4.0		100.0
Guyana	34.0	6.0	26.9	0.1	0.1	3.8		18.4		100.0
Paraguay [a]	14.6	12.1	13.0		2.8	0.6		30.5		100.0
Peru [a]	24.9	5.7	17.8	0.1	0.4	4.5	0.1	39.3	0.6	100.0
Suriname	34.1	4.9	29.0			5.6		25.4		100.0
Uruguay	14.0	4.8	20.6	2.9	0.8	5.9	3.2	42.1	0.1	100.0
Venezuela [a]	49.4	5.6	23.9		0.4	3.7	0.3	9.3	0.1	100.0
Caribbean										
Anguilla										
Antigua										
Aruba										
Bahamas	31.5	16.8	13.8	0.2	13.3	5.7	1.1	5.0		100.0
Barbados	33.4	5.1	17.9			3.4		30.8	0.3	100.0
Bermuda	65.7	5.2	13.5			2.1	0.1	7.3		100.0
British Virgin Islands										
Cayman Islands										
Cuba	0.1	1.5	32.4		0.4	11.0		41.6		100.0
Dominica	22.8	2.5	25.7			34.1	0.1	13.4		100.0
Dominican Republic [a]	45.5	5.2	14.2		0.3	6.1		24.8		100.0
Grenada	26.4	5.3	16.6			10.1		30.3		100.0
Guadeloupe	5.7		85.1		0.3	0.7		7.1		100.0
Haiti	65.1	3.4	10.1			8.4	0.3	8.8		100.0
Jamaica	52.6	3.8	13.1	0.3		4.6		17.6		100.0
Martinique	2.5		83.2		0.1	0.1	4.6	5.5		100.0
Netherlands Antilles	38.5	4.7	21.2		2.1	9.7		20.7	0.1	100.0
St Kitts										
St Lucia										
St Vincent/Grenadines	31.0	4.5	37.6			13.3		6.1		100.0
Trinidad and Tobago	39.8	5.7	15.0	0.3	1.2	4.5	0.1	25.1	0.6	100.0
Central America										
Belize	53.8	4.1	20.8			6.1		13.3		100.0
Costa Rica	43.5	6.0	10.8			4.8	0.3	30.1		100.0
El Salvador	39.2	4.6	15.7			3.0		31.3		100.0
Guatemala	42.3	6.6	12.4			2.5		27.9		100.0
Honduras	40.5	9.0	15.1					29.0		100.0
Mexico [a]	70.8	6.0	12.6		0.3	3.8	0.1	3.0	0.1	100.0
Nicaragua	21.3	4.5	13.9	10.2		1.8	0.1	31.3		100.0
Panama	35.8	6.8	7.3		0.3	5.4	0.1	39.9		100.0
Puerto Rico										
South Asia										
Afghanistan	0.2	7.6	4.3	57.8		15.9	0.1	0.2		100.0
Bangladesh	5.2	9.0	13.2	0.6	0.1	33.5	5.9	1.9	2.0	100.0
Bhutan										
India	10.3	7.5	31.8	6.8	3.2	13.7	14.5	2.3	2.2	100.0
Nepal	1.4	23.7	10.9			50.0	0.5	0.7	0.4	100.0
Pakistan	11.2	14.8	25.6	1.5	1.9	18.7	14.9	2.1	1.7	100.0
Sri Lanka	4.2	10.2	18.1	0.1	4.1	48.1	8.6	1.3	1.2	100.0

EXTERNAL TRADE BY DESTINATION AND ORIGIN · Table No. 0504 (cont'd)

Imports (cif) by Country of Origin 1991 (% Analysis)

Units: % of total imports

	USA	Japan	EC	Former USSR	Africa	Asia	Middle East	South America/ Caribbean	Aus- tralia	Total (inc. others)
Japan										
Japan	22.7		13.5	1.4	1.5	31.5	12.4	3.9	5.5	100.0
ASEAN/NICs										
Brunei	10.0	8.0	29.7		0.6	46.5	0.1	0.1	0.8	100.0
Hong Kong	7.6	16.4	9.2	0.1	0.6	61.1	0.7	0.8	0.9	100.0
Indonesia	13.1	24.5	18.2	0.2	0.7	26.0	4.1	2.3	5.3	100.0
Macau	4.2	15.8	7.6	0.2	0.7	68.3	0.3	0.1	1.3	100.0
Malaysia	15.3	26.1	13.6	0.2	0.5	33.7	0.9	1.4	3.2	100.0
Philippines	20.2	19.4	10.2	0.3	0.5	29.7	10.3	2.3	3.2	100.0
Singapore	15.8	21.3	12.0	0.3	0.6	34.2	9.2	1.2	1.9	100.0
South Korea	23.6	26.3	15.2		0.3	12.4	7.4	2.7	3.4	100.0
Taiwan [b]	23.0	29.2	17.5		2.2	20.4			3.0	100.0
Thailand	10.7	28.8	13.9	0.6	1.1	30.9	3.4	2.1	1.5	100.0
East/SE Asia										
Cambodia										
China	12.5	15.8	13.3	3.3	0.6	41.4	1.3	2.1	2.4	100.0
Laos	0.6	15.6	9.6		0.1	72.3	0.1	0.2	0.3	100.0
Mongolia										
Myanmar	2.4	8.5	8.1	0.7	0.3	71.4		0.1	0.3	100.0
North Korea		16.9	9.9		0.2	56.5	0.8	1.3	1.7	100.0
Vietnam	0.2	14.8	15.5			61.4	0.1	0.1	2.2	100.0
Australasia										
Australia [a]	24.5	17.6	20.9	0.1	0.3	21.9	2.9	1.2		100.0
New Zealand	16.8	15.6	18.0		0.4	12.9	5.4	1.3	22.0	100.0
Pacific [c]										
American Samoa										
Fiji	4.3	11.4	4.9			21.5			31.5	100.0
French Polynesia										
Guam										
Kiribati										
Nauru										
New Caledonia	7.0	5.8	60.8		0.9	7.6			9.7	100.0
Papua New Guinea [a]	7.1	12.2	4.9		0.1	19.7		0.5	50.3	100.0
Solomon Islands [a]	4.2	21.5	5.3		0.3	28.3		0.3	32.4	100.0
Tonga	9.9	8.9	2.2			23.1		0.7	25.5	100.0
Tuvalu										
Vanuatu	1.0	23.9	28.8			5.7	0.1	9.6	23.9	100.0
Western Samoa	10.4	9.5	4.5			14.3		0.9	20.0	100.0
Middle East										
Bahrain	13.8	4.6	22.4		0.1	6.9	44.1	0.4	2.7	100.0
Egypt	16.1	4.1	27.6	1.8	0.7	4.7	3.2	3.2		100.0
Iran	2.7	12.6	46.4	1.0	0.4	8.4	6.1	4.8	1.6	100.0
Iraq			23.9			0.7	40.8		9.9	
Israel	19.3	4.4	47.5	0.3	1.7	3.7	0.1	1.4	0.3	100.0
Jordan	10.4	3.6	29.9	1.1	2.4	13.2	20.9	1.9	1.5	100.0
Kuwait	34.8	12.4	24.8			7.5	0.6		0.5	100.0
Lebanon	4.9	3.2	46.8		0.5	12.1	14.7	0.8	0.1	100.0
Oman	6.8	20.4	31.4		0.4	12.5	21.9	0.3	1.7	100.0
Qatar	8.7	12.4	44.2		0.2	11.2	10.7	1.9	1.1	100.0
Saudi Arabia	20.9	12.4	38.5	0.2	1.3	14.0	2.4	1.3	1.2	100.0
Syria	8.4	4.4	38.8	2.4	0.6	5.5	4.1	2.2		100.0
United Arab Emirates	10.0	14.8	31.3	0.1	0.4	27.7	6.5	0.7	1.7	100.0
Yemen [c]	10.8	7.2	28.2	0.6	2.8	23.0	15.3	0.7	3.2	100.0

EXTERNAL TRADE BY DESTINATION AND ORIGIN   Table No. 0504 (cont'd)

Imports (cif) by Country of Origin 1991 (% Analysis)

Units: % of total imports

	USA	Japan	EC	Former USSR	Africa	Asia	Middle East	South America/ Carib- bean	Aus- tralia	Total (inc. others)
North Africa										
Algeria	8.8	4.4	64.2	0.4	2.8	2.3	0.8	2.8	0.5	100.0
Chad	9.5	3.2	72.2		10.2	2.3	0.3	0.1		100.0
Djibouti	2.9	7.2	45.6		7.6	24.5	6.3	0.1	0.1	100.0
Ethiopia	20.8	5.5	36.3	16.3	1.5	4.6	4.3	0.1	0.1	100.0
Libya		2.5	61.9		6.1	7.1	3.5	1.3	0.1	100.0
Mali	3.6	1.8	43.0	5.4	32.5	7.7	3.6	0.6		100.0
Mauritania	5.0	1.4	70.4		5.2	8.1	0.3	0.9	0.4	100.0
Morocco	5.9	1.9	65.7	3.7	3.0	3.9	3.2	2.4		100.0
Niger	2.9	3.6	45.0		13.9	5.8		1.2		100.0
Somalia	4.0	1.3	30.3	0.1	20.7	7.3	26.5	1.6		100.0
Sudan	7.2	4.1	39.3		3.1	15.7	23.1	0.3	0.2	100.0
Tunisia	4.5	2.2	68.3	2.2	3.7	3.1	2.8	2.8		100.0
West Africa										
Benin	4.5	2.4	43.3	0.5	8.4	35.2		0.3		100.0
Burkina Faso	4.7	3.9	45.5	0.1	32.7	9.8		0.8		100.0
Cameroon	5.9	5.4	64.4	1.0	7.4	5.3	0.2	3.0		100.0
Cape Verde	3.3		75.5	1.4	3.0	0.1		4.4		100.0
Côte d'Ivoire	4.0	3.3	52.6	0.7	16.8	11.7	0.1	2.7		100.0
Equatorial Guinea	14.6	0.1	45.4		34.7	1.0		0.3		100.0
Gabon	9.7	6.9	65.2	0.1	10.6	5.1		0.9		100.0
Gambia	4.1	4.1	46.3	3.0	2.5	33.2	0.1	0.7		100.0
Ghana	10.5	5.7	50.0	0.2	13.0	10.8	0.4	2.4	1.0	100.0
Guinea	16.1	4.3	58.6		3.1	11.8	0.8	3.2		100.0
Guinea-Bissau	1.3	5.1	46.9	3.3	7.4	12.0		0.1	18.1	100.0
Liberia	1.2	21.5	15.6		0.1	40.3	0.1	0.5		100.0
Nigeria	11.8	5.8	51.1	1.5	1.9	15.0	3.8	1.7		100.0
Sao Tomé e Príncipe	13.7	4.3	75.4		0.9	1.1		0.3		100.0
Senegal	6.2	2.1	55.4	0.2	15.5	10.0	1.8	1.0		100.0
Sierra Leone	11.1	3.6	45.3	0.1	25.0	10.2		0.4	0.1	100.0
Togo	3.1	3.8	44.6	0.4	12.1	32.0		0.6	0.3	100.0
East/Central Africa										
Angola	10.5	7.8	65.1		1.0	2.9		8.8	0.1	100.0
Burundi	1.1	8.6	39.9		14.4	10.1	11.7	0.6		100.0
Central African Republic	0.4	3.8	35.5	0.1	9.7	2.2	0.1	20.0		100.0
Comoros		3.0	79.8		6.4	5.7	3.9	0.1		100.0
Congo	7.0	3.4	66.1	1.1	6.1	12.7	0.1	0.6		100.0
Kenya	4.5	10.2	45.2	0.1	3.6	14.9	15.4	0.5	0.4	100.0
Madagascar	2.8	4.8	40.3	0.6	6.8	15.2	9.7	2.2	0.2	100.0
Maldives	0.7	4.0	9.4		0.1	82.1	2.0	0.1	0.7	100.0
Mauritius	1.2	6.0	33.9	0.1	15.8	30.9	4.8	1.2	3.0	100.0
Réunion	0.1	2.0	79.2		6.0	3.0	5.9	0.3	0.2	100.0
Rwanda	1.0	4.9	45.3	1.0	24.6	7.0	6.4	1.0		100.0
Seychelles	1.7	6.4	44.6		5.2	30.4	5.9	0.5	1.4	100.0
Tanzania	3.5	9.9	42.9		3.9	16.6	14.0	0.7	0.7	100.0
Uganda	3.1	9.3	39.8		23.7	16.4	2.3	0.5	0.2	100.0
Zaire	6.8	4.3	60.6		10.3	13.7	0.2	0.5		100.0
Southern Africa										
Botswana										
Lesotho										
Malawi	11.1	8.1	29.9		42.7	4.9	0.1		0.2	100.0
Mozambique	12.4	4.8	33.0		11.2	19.5	11.8	0.8	1.0	100.0
Namibia										
South Africa [a]	12.4	9.7	42.3		2.4	6.7	0.6	2.0	0.7	100.0
Swaziland										
Zambia [a]	2.6	7.8	25.2		47.0	6.4	4.1	0.3	0.1	100.0
Zimbabwe [a]	4.1	6.1	45.2		12.2	5.4	0.8	1.4	0.5	100.0

Source: IMF, Direction of Trade Statistics/Euromonitor
Notes: see end of section

EXTERNAL TRADE BY DESTINATION AND ORIGIN — Table No. 0505

Exports by Country of Destination 1991

Units: Million current US dollars

	USA	Japan	EC	Former USSR	Africa	Asia	Middle East	South America/ Carib- bean	Aus- tralia	Total (inc. others)
North America										
Canada	95,574.0	6,190.0	9,913.0	1,282.0	757.0	6,600.0	1,162.0	2,107.0	582.0	126,160.0
USA		48,147.0	103,120.0	3,578.0	6,103.0	67,616.0	17,995.0	63,471.0	8,415.0	421,755.0
South America										
Argentina	1,281.7	549.7	4,227.0	548.6	263.7	1,059.6	773.0	3,628.0	51.5	13,222.0
Bolivia	122.5	1.0	178.7			5.7	0.4	333.6	0.2	652.0
Brazil	6,575.0	2,899.0	10,476.0	345.0	809.0	3,830.0	1,015.0	3,815.0	250.0	32,424.0
Chile	1,596.3	1,644.0	2,883.8		79.0	1,008.9	107.1	1,303.0	27.4	9,028.3
Colombia	2,698.6	250.0	1,878.1	15.9	5.3	47.4	41.9	1,045.9	6.6	6,661.7
Ecuador	1,375.8	97.5	608.5	2.2	12.2	351.4	1.9	850.8	2.5	3,579.6
French Guiana	0.5	0.2	49.5		0.7	2.2		14.8		68.8
Guyana	91.2	16.8	127.6	5.2	1.0	2.4		24.2	0.4	302.5
Paraguay	34.2	3.8	220.9					259.4		737.3
Peru	857.2	322.1	841.1	40.3	24.2	507.1	27.9	575.8	6.5	3,422.9
Suriname	50.6	17.9	151.9		0.1	1.5		43.9		382.8
Uruguay	164.8	19.9	384.2	50.2	8.7	153.3	67.7	637.7	4.2	1,577.0
Venezuela	7,979.0	428.0	1,615.0	6.0	46.0	245.0	19.0	4,211.0	14.0	15,727.0
Caribbean										
Anguilla										
Antigua										
Aruba										
Bahamas	443.8	16.0	223.7		0.4	7.9	0.4	30.9	3.0	873.6
Barbados	29.6	0.9	46.1		0.1	0.3		76.1	0.1	231.3
Bermuda	36.0		10.9					0.4		54.5
British Virgin Islands										
Cayman Islands										
Cuba		129.1	338.8		16.2	193.3	30.5	182.3	0.4	1,090.1
Dominica	5.6	3.1	52.6	0.1		4.4		17.7		84.2
Dominican Republic	539.7	19.7	146.0		64.0	67.2		29.8	0.2	925.4
Grenada	7.7	1.3	11.3			0.1		6.4		29.4
Guadeloupe	1.6		127.4		0.5	0.1		32.5		162.2
Haiti	270.1	1.2	29.4			0.2		2.7	0.2	317.3
Jamaica	561.9	15.1	388.9	28.7	33.6	1.8	0.8	108.2	0.5	1,408.6
Martinique	0.6		180.2			0.4		51.4		233.4
Netherlands Antilles	642.3	15.2	242.7		27.5	68.3	0.1	487.5	1.4	1,584.0
St Kitts										
St Lucia										
St Vincent/Grenadines	7.1	6.5	54.8			12.2		7.6	4.2	95.1
Trinidad and Tobago	992.4	23.9	183.4		16.1	38.4	6.9	652.8	0.3	1,981.9
Central America										
Belize	43.9	0.8	36.4			2.5		20.5		111.0
Costa Rica	768.7	20.9	440.5	0.1	1.3	21.0	8.2	271.2	0.7	1,613.3
El Salvador	293.1	15.9	193.2		0.4	1.6	0.5	185.5	0.6	722.5
Guatemala	454.4	34.1	128.6			15.7	46.3	438.2		1,202.2
Honduras	419.6	41.3	174.0					57.2		779.9
Mexico	28,969.0	1,583.0	3,332.0	22.0	58.0	748.0	48.0	1,601.0	67.0	38,868.0
Nicaragua	59.6	40.0	111.0	10.1	4.6	5.2		46.2	0.4	363.4
Panama	138.7	2.8	91.9			1.9	0.3	90.5		341.8
Puerto Rico										
South Asia										
Afghanistan	4.2	2.8	65.6	650.8		106.3	4.2	0.7	0.2	932.8
Bangladesh	449.5	53.4	676.5	27.7	29.6	177.3	99.1	18.4	20.3	1,687.5
Bhutan										
India	3,126.0	1,960.0	5,111.0	2,957.0	377.0	3,675.0	1,099.0	78.0	199.0	20,492.0
Nepal	60.6	1.5	141.8			28.8		0.1	0.4	256.1
Pakistan	742.0	520.5	1,910.7	70.0	275.8	1,474.4	790.1	43.9	73.1	6,494.2
Sri Lanka	595.3	119.9	674.7	44.6	28.1	203.5	246.9	34.8	28.1	2,199.8

244

EXTERNAL TRADE BY DESTINATION AND ORIGIN   Table No. 0505 (cont'd)

Exports by Country of Destination 1991

Units: Million current US dollars

	USA	Japan	EC	Former USSR	Africa	Asia	Middle East	South America/ Caribbean	Aus- tralia	Total (inc. others)
Japan										
Japan	92,200.0		59,606.0	2,117.0	4,960.0	105,902.0	11,841.0	12,221.0	6,504.0	314,892.0
ASEAN/NICs										
Brunei	25.9	1,364.5	247.7		3.7	811.2		0.7	55.9	2,597.4
Hong Kong	22,391.0	5,307.0	17,184.0	198.0	1,670.0	41,324.0	1,612.0	2,286.0	1,386.0	98,579.0
Indonesia	3,509.0	10,767.0	3,743.0	40.0	234.0	8,500.0	1,068.0	184.0	628.0	29,142.0
Macau	523.8	26.5	612.8	0.5	4.7	373.4	3.5	4.4	13.0	1,637.3
Malaysia	5,808.0	5,458.0	5,082.0	81.0	159.0	15,258.0	776.0	373.0	587.0	34,405.0
Philippines	3,151.4	1,771.3	1,645.4	15.5	17.5	1,649.1	149.6	94.9	103.9	8,839.6
Singapore	11,674.0	5,133.0	8,278.0	324.0	1,182.0	26,039.0	1,818.0	965.0	1,458.0	59,188.0
South Korea	18,311.0	12,195.0	9,858.0		1,686.0	15,362.0	2,790.0	2,378.0	1,006.0'	69,489.0
Taiwan [a]	21,745.9	8,337.7	12,233.4		1,257.1	18,754.5			1,279.2	67,214.4
Thailand	6,020.7	5,037.8	5,733.9	83.2	541.2	6,128.6	1,329.0	282.8	463.0	27,562.0
East/SE Asia										
Cambodia										
China	6,192.0	10,265.0	6,826.0	1,860.0	784.0	41,008.0	1,568.0	567.0	555.0	71,986.0
Laos	2.0	4.0	21.2		0.7	54.2			0.1	84.2
Mongolia										
Myanmar	26.6	44.9	30.9	9.9	56.0	377.1	7.4	16.1	2.8	588.1
North Korea		250.2	104.3		14.8	232.0	5.1	40.7	0.3	692.6
Vietnam		602.1	194.1		16.6	614.5	1.5	56.9	23.6	1,598.2
Australasia										
Australia	4,271.0	11,661.0	4,947.0	376.0	174.0	14,270.0	1,458.0	430.0		42,044.0
New Zealand	1,228.2	1,523.0	1,394.2	127.1	157.7	2,114.7	282.0	278.1	1,812.1	9,584.5
Pacific										
American Samoa										
Fiji	50.9	25.7	118.3			21.2			70.9	450.6
French Polynesia										
Guam										
Kiribati										
Nauru										
New Caledonia	21.6	132.1	210.6			48.1			19.4	447.6
Papua New Guinea	34.3	344.4	227.1		0.2	219.8		0.3	631.1	1,496.6
Solomon Islands	0.2	36.8	19.2			20.9			1.2	80.2
Tonga	2.6	9.5	0.2			0.8			1.4	15.9
Tuvalu										
Vanuatu	1.6	4.8	13.4		0.1	1.5	0.1	0.1	0.9	22.6
Western Samoa	0.6					1.5			2.1	7.6
Middle East										
Bahrain	90.8	409.2	136.1		314.4	904.9	613.4	0.1	10.8	3,160.9
Egypt	291.9	53.9	1,085.8	243.3	76.0	68.7	387.8	1.5		3,838.2
Iran	237.0	2,538.0	7,253.0		109.0	2,667.0	193.0	1,020.0	11.0	15,916.0
Iraq			30.0			1.0	262.0	1.0		297.0
Israel	3,441.9	713.4	3,984.7	17.5	165.9	1,015.6	4.8	271.8	101.7	11,598.3
Jordan	3.3	15.6	27.2	24.6	34.9	333.7	280.5	3.3	1.1	879.2
Kuwait	35.0	52.0	232.0			47.0	43.0		7.0	422.0
Lebanon	25.9	1.4	111.3		25.4	5.5	212.5	0.6	2.3	490.2
Oman	119.3	1,965.7	151.0		169.3	1,881.0	2,822.9	24.3	24.7	7,236.2
Qatar	29.3	1,962.5	76.2		1.0	617.2	200.3	178.2	1.6	3,197.8
Saudi Arabia	11,049.0	9,174.0	12,217.0		988.0	10,887.0	3,008.0	1,375.0	596.0	51,719.0
Syria	18.6	3.6	1,689.4	698.5	83.9	6.7	786.0	1.8		3,699.8
United Arab Emirates	699.0	9,557.0	2,061.0		382.0	4,756.0	1,799.0	237.0	301.0	24,261.0
Yemen [b]	115.5	151.6	528.8		4.9	123.9	65.7	0.1	45.7	1,110.4

EXTERNAL TRADE BY DESTINATION AND ORIGIN　　　Table No. 0505 (cont'd)

Exports by Country of Destination 1991

Units: Million current US dollars

	USA	Japan	EC	Former USSR	Africa	Asia	Middle East	South America/ Carib-bean	Aus-tralia	Total (inc. others)
North Africa										
Algeria	2,068.0	110.0	8,338.0	37.0	151.0	187.0	128.0	345.0		12,314.0
Chad	0.2	9.2	55.5		5.2	17.8		0.3		89.8
Djibouti		0.1	5.6		25.8	0.2	21.9			54.5
Ethiopia	14.1	44.8	119.8	23.9	29.6	4.9	53.0	0.7	0.5	307.3
Libya	2.0	1.0	9,030.0		80.0	100.0	39.0	26.0		10,775.0
Mali	1.7	5.4	86.0	38.8	61.4	92.5		0.3		294.0
Mauritania	11.7	114.3	291.3		32.3	2.3	1.2			515.2
Morocco	148.0	274.0	3,488.4	13.2	230.3	264.4	206.6	73.9	4.3	5,148.8
Niger	4.8	0.2	200.1		25.8	2.3		0.1		240.7
Somalia	2.5		17.5	0.2	1.0	2.3	81.7			106.5
Sudan	14.9	27.9	113.4	39.0	2.1	87.2	54.6	0.3	0.2	358.1
Tunisia	24.2	10.2	2,824.9	40.9	150.7	154.1	330.5	33.1		3,826.7
West Africa										
Benin	22.6	0.5	42.2	0.2	18.1	21.5		2.6		121.2
Burkina Faso	0.5	2.1	68.0		42.6	79.9				197.3
Cameroon	44.1	6.4	1,544.8	2.4	206.1	55.3	2.6	10.7		1,909.5
Cape Verde			4.5		4.1			0.1		8.9
Côte d'Ivoire	220.5	18.7	1,769.6	186.6	756.3	242.5	12.2	10.5	1.7	3,505.5
Equatorial Guinea	0.3		35.1			0.1				36.9
Gabon	696.7	138.7	1,245.3	8.8	88.8	119.6	28.4	210.2		2,573.2
Gambia	1.9	37.8	107.8		9.1	4.7		0.1		166.2
Ghana	145.8	64.1	723.3	51.7	26.1	57.4	12.5	22.1	0.5	1,194.3
Guinea	151.7	1.7	351.2		45.1	8.9		26.4		637.8
Guinea-Bissau	0.1	0.1	7.3		0.3	11.3				19.7
Liberia	7.6	5.1	263.9		1.3	95.0	2.3	9.1		556.5
Nigeria	5,168.0	7.0	5,335.0	11.0	473.0	72.0	1.0	687.0		12,710.0
Sao Tomé e Príncipe			2.9			0.2				3.3
Senegal	11.6	12.0	404.1		123.3	118.6	0.2	0.6		736.8
Sierra Leone	48.7		78.1		1.9					145.4
Togo	2.9	0.6	91.0	27.8	43.5	63.7		12.1	1.1	302.1
East/Central Africa										
Angola	1,750.9	3.0	1,012.5		27.3	0.7		187.1		3,090.9
Burundi	8.2	1.7	77.5		2.6	5.0	0.2			100.6
Central African Republic	0.6	0.3	99.8		3.6	20.3	7.2	0.3		133.3
Comoros	8.8	0.1	17.6		0.3	0.7		0.2		27.8
Congo	405.4	1.6	637.3	7.3	22.3	4.9	0.3	0.3		1,098.0
Kenya	66.8	16.1	610.3	2.3	284.7	132.2	69.4	0.8	6.6	1,324.2
Madagascar	44.2	33.9	191.1	2.5	40.7	26.3	0.1	0.2	0.3	356.7
Maldives	12.4	2.1	18.1			20.1				53.7
Mauritius	129.0	2.9	882.9	1.1	57.0	19.9		0.5	3.4	1,120.0
Réunion	1.0	0.5	112.2		12.9	7.8		1.5	0.1	136.6
Rwanda	7.0	0.6	84.8		94.2	10.7		4.3		202.7
Seychelles	0.9	0.4	61.5		0.1	32.7				118.4
Tanzania	14.6	20.5	192.5		21.5	104.0	16.6	0.1	0.6	385.3
Uganda	18.6	2.5	130.4		4.3	6.4	2.1	0.1	0.3	171.5
Zaire	287.7	86.5	1,048.1		31.4	53.0		3.0	0.6	1,572.0
Southern Africa										
Botswana										
Lesotho										
Malawi	70.6	70.6	187.7		68.0	14.5	2.4	0.1	9.0	443.4
Mozambique	22.1	20.2	77.6		12.4	222.6	5.2	2.5	0.8	389.6
Namibia										
South Africa	1,618.0	1,666.0	7,493.0		1,346.0	1,330.0	213.0	222.0	74.0	26,576.0
Swaziland										
Zambia	39.0	304.8	314.4		52.5	303.2	32.2		1.5	1,061.1
Zimbabwe	85.7	147.5	660.7		333.5	102.1	68.2	51.4	10.1	1,541.3

Source: IMF, Direction of Trade Statistics

Notes: see end of section

EXTERNAL TRADE BY DESTINATION AND ORIGIN　　Table No. 0506

Exports by Country of Destination 1991 (% Analysis)

Units: % of total exports

	USA	Japan	EC	Former USSR	Africa	Asia	Middle East	South America/ Carib-bean	Aus-tralia	Total (inc. others)
North America										
Canada	75.8	4.9	7.9	1.0	0.6	5.2	0.9	1.7	0.5	100.0
USA		11.4	24.5	0.8	1.4	16.0	4.3	15.0	2.0	100.0
South America										
Argentina	9.7	4.2	32.0	4.1	2.0	8.0	5.8	27.4	0.4	100.0
Bolivia	18.8	0.2	27.4			0.9	0.1	51.2		100.0
Brazil	20.3	8.9	32.3	1.1	2.5	11.8	3.1	11.8	0.8	100.0
Chile	17.7	18.2	31.9		0.9	11.2	1.2	14.4	0.3	100.0
Colombia	40.5	3.8	28.2	0.2	0.1	0.7	0.6	15.7	0.1	100.0
Ecuador	38.4	2.7	17.0	0.1	0.3	9.8	0.1	23.8	0.1	100.0
French Guiana	0.7	0.3	71.9		1.0	3.2		21.5		100.0
Guyana	30.1	5.6	42.2	1.7	0.3	0.8		8.0	0.1	100.0
Paraguay	4.6	0.5	30.0					35.2		100.0
Peru	25.0	9.4	24.6	1.2	0.7	14.8	0.8	16.8	0.2	100.0
Suriname	13.2	4.7	39.7			0.4		11.5		100.0
Uruguay	10.5	1.3	24.4	3.2	0.6	9.7	4.3	40.4	0.3	100.0
Venezuela	50.7	2.7	10.3		0.3	1.6	0.1	26.8	0.1	100.0
Caribbean										
Anguilla										
Antigua										
Aruba										
Bahamas	50.8	1.8	25.6			0.9		3.5	0.3	100.0
Barbados	12.8	0.4	19.9			0.1		32.9		100.0
Bermuda	66.1		20.0					0.7		100.0
British Virgin Islands										
Cayman Islands										
Cuba		11.8	31.1		1.5	17.7	2.8	16.7		100.0
Dominica	6.7	3.7	62.5	0.1		5.2		21.0		100.0
Dominican Republic	58.3	2.1	15.8		6.9	7.3		3.2		100.0
Grenada	26.2	4.4	38.4			0.3		21.8		100.0
Guadeloupe	1.0		78.5		0.3	0.1		20.0		100.0
Haiti	85.1	0.4	9.3			0.1		0.9	0.1	100.0
Jamaica	39.9	1.1	27.6	2.0	2.4	0.1	0.1	7.7		100.0
Martinique	0.3		77.2			0.2		22.0		100.0
Netherlands Antilles	40.5	1.0	15.3		1.7	4.3		30.8	0.1	100.0
St Kitts										
St Lucia										
St Vincent/Grenadines	7.5	6.8	57.6			12.8		8.0	4.4	100.0
Trinidad and Tobago	50.1	1.2	9.3		0.8	1.9	0.3	32.9		100.0
Central America										
Belize	39.5	0.7	32.8			2.3		18.5		100.0
Costa Rica	47.6	1.3	27.3		0.1	1.3	0.5	16.8		100.0
El Salvador	40.6	2.2	26.7		0.1	0.2	0.1	25.7	0.1	100.0
Guatemala	37.8	2.8	10.7			1.3	3.9	36.4		100.0
Honduras	53.8	5.3	22.3					7.3		100.0
Mexico	74.5	4.1	8.6	0.1	0.1	1.9	0.1	4.1	0.2	100.0
Nicaragua	16.4	11.0	30.5	2.8	1.3	1.4		12.7	0.1	100.0
Panama	40.6	0.8	26.9			0.6	0.1	26.5		100.0
Puerto Rico										
South Asia										
Afghanistan	0.5	0.3	7.0	69.8		11.4	0.5	0.1		100.0
Bangladesh	26.6	3.2	40.1	1.6	1.8	10.5	5.9	1.1	1.2	100.0
Bhutan										
India	15.3	9.6	24.9	14.4	1.8	17.9	5.4	0.4	1.0	100.0
Nepal	23.7	0.6	55.4			11.2			0.2	100.0
Pakistan	11.4	8.0	29.4	1.1	4.2	22.7	12.2	0.7	1.1	100.0
Sri Lanka	27.1	5.5	30.7	2.0	1.3	9.3	11.2	1.6	1.3	100.0

EXTERNAL TRADE BY DESTINATION AND ORIGIN　　Table No. 0506 (cont'd)

Exports by Country of Destination 1991 (% Analysis)

Units: % of total exports

	USA	Japan	EC	Former USSR	Africa	Asia	Middle East	South America/ Carib-bean	Aus-tralia	Total (inc. others)
Japan										
Japan	29.3		18.9	0.7	1.6	33.6	3.8	3.9	2.1	100.0
ASEAN/NICs										
Brunei	1.0	52.5	9.5		0.1	31.2			2.2	100.0
Hong Kong	22.7	5.4	17.4	0.2	1.7	41.9	1.6	2.3	1.4	100.0
Indonesia	12.0	36.9	12.8	0.1	0.8	29.2	3.7	0.6	2.2	100.0
Macau	32.0	1.6	37.4		0.3	22.8	0.2	0.3	0.8	100.0
Malaysia	16.9	15.9	14.8	0.2	0.5	44.3	2.3	1.1	1.7	100.0
Philippines	35.7	20.0	18.6	0.2	0.2	18.7	1.7	1.1	1.2	100.0
Singapore	19.7	8.7	14.0	0.5	2.0	44.0	3.1	1.6	2.5	100.0
South Korea	26.4	17.5	14.2		2.4	22.1	4.0	3.4	1.4	100.0
Taiwan [a]	32.4	12.4	18.2		1.9	27.9			1.9	100.0
Thailand	21.8	18.3	20.8	0.3	2.0	22.2	4.8	1.0	1.7	100.0
East/SE Asia										
Cambodia										
China	8.6	14.3	9.5	2.6	1.1	57.0	2.2	0.8	0.8	100.0
Laos	2.4	4.8	25.2		0.8	64.4			0.1	100.0
Mongolia										
Myanmar	4.5	7.6	5.3	1.7	9.5	64.1	1.3	2.7	0.5	100.0
North Korea		36.1	15.1		2.1	33.5	0.7	5.9		100.0
Vietnam		37.7	12.1		1.0	38.4	0.1	3.6	1.5	100.0
Australasia										
Australia	10.2	27.7	11.8	0.9	0.4	33.9	3.5	1.0		100.0
New Zealand	12.8	15.9	14.5	1.3	1.6	22.1	2.9	2.9	18.9	100.0
Pacific										
American Samoa										
Fiji	11.3	5.7	26.3			4.7			15.7	100.0
French Polynesia										
Guam										
Kiribati										
Nauru										
New Caledonia	4.8	29.5	47.1			10.7			4.3	100.0
Papua New Guinea	2.3	23.0	15.2			14.7			42.2	100.0
Solomon Islands	0.2	45.9	23.9			26.1			1.5	100.0
Tonga	16.4	59.7	1.3			5.0			8.8	100.0
Tuvalu										
Vanuatu	7.1	21.2	59.3		0.4	6.6	0.4	0.4	4.0	100.0
Western Samoa	7.9					19.7			27.6	100.0
Middle East										
Bahrain	2.9	12.9	4.3		9.9	28.6	19.4		0.3	100.0
Egypt	7.6	1.4	28.3	6.3	2.0	1.8	10.1			100.0
Iran	1.5	15.9	45.6		0.7	16.8	1.2	6.4	0.1	100.0
Iraq			10.1			0.3	88.2	0.3		
Israel	29.7	6.2	34.4	0.2	1.4	8.8		2.3	0.9	100.0
Jordan	0.4	1.8	3.1	2.8	4.0	38.0	31.9	0.4	0.1	100.0
Kuwait	8.3	12.3	55.0			11.1	10.2		1.7	100.0
Lebanon	5.3	0.3	22.7		5.2	1.1	43.3	0.1	0.5	100.0
Oman	1.6	27.2	2.1		2.3	26.0	39.0	0.3	0.3	100.0
Qatar	0.9	61.4	2.4			19.3	6.3	5.6	0.1	100.0
Saudi Arabia	21.4	17.7	23.6		1.9	21.1	5.8	2.7	1.2	100.0
Syria	0.5	0.1	45.7	18.9	2.3	0.2	21.2			100.0
United Arab Emirates	2.9	39.4	8.5		1.6	19.6	7.4	1.0	1.2	100.0
Yemen [b]	10.4	13.7	47.6		0.4	11.2	5.9		4.1	100.0

EXTERNAL TRADE BY DESTINATION AND ORIGIN
Table No. 0506 (cont'd)

Exports by Country of Destination 1991 (% Analysis)

Units: % of total exports

	USA	Japan	EC	Former USSR	Africa	Asia	Middle East	South America/ Caribbean	Australia	Total (inc. others)
North Africa										
Algeria	16.8	0.9	67.7	0.3	1.2	1.5	1.0	2.8		100.0
Chad	0.2	10.2	61.8		5.8	19.8		0.3		100.0
Djibouti		0.2	10.3		47.3	0.4	40.2			100.0
Ethiopia	4.6	14.6	39.0	7.8	9.6	1.6	17.2	0.2	0.2	100.0
Libya			83.8		0.7	0.9	0.4	0.2		100.0
Mali	0.6	1.8	29.3	13.2	20.9	31.5		0.1		100.0
Mauritania	2.3	22.2	56.5		6.3	0.4	0.2			100.0
Morocco	2.9	5.3	67.8	0.3	4.5	5.1	4.0	1.4	0.1	100.0
Niger	2.0	0.1	83.1		10.7	1.0				100.0
Somalia	2.3		16.4	0.2	0.9	2.2	76.7			100.0
Sudan	4.2	7.8	31.7	10.9	0.6	24.4	15.2	0.1	0.1	100.0
Tunisia	0.6	0.3	73.8	1.1	3.9	4.0	8.6	0.9		100.0
West Africa										
Benin	18.6	0.4	34.8	0.2	14.9	17.7		2.1		100.0
Burkina Faso	0.3	1.1	34.5		21.6	40.5				100.0
Cameroon	2.3	0.3	80.9	0.1	10.8	2.9	0.1	0.6		100.0
Cape Verde			50.6		46.1			1.1		
Côte d'Ivoire	6.3	0.5	50.5	5.3	21.6	6.9	0.3	0.3		100.0
Equatorial Guinea	0.8		95.1			0.3				100.0
Gabon	27.1	5.4	48.4	0.3	3.5	4.6	1.1	8.2		100.0
Gambia	1.1	22.7	64.9		5.5	2.8		0.1		100.0
Ghana	12.2	5.4	60.6	4.3	2.2	4.8	1.0	1.9		100.0
Guinea	23.8	0.3	55.1		7.1	1.4		4.1		100.0
Guinea-Bissau	0.5	0.5	37.1		1.5	57.4				100.0
Liberia	1.4	0.9	47.4		0.2	17.1	0.4	1.6		100.0
Nigeria	40.7	0.1	42.0	0.1	3.7	0.6		5.4		100.0
Sao Tomé e Príncipe			87.9			6.1				
Senegal	1.6	1.6	54.8		16.7	16.1		0.1		100.0
Sierra Leone	33.5		53.7		1.3					100.0
Togo	1.0	0.2	30.1	9.2	14.4	21.1		4.0	0.4	100.0
East/Central Africa										
Angola	56.6	0.1	32.8		0.9			6.1		100.0
Burundi	8.2	1.7	77.0		2.6	5.0	0.2			100.0
Central African Republic	0.5	0.2	74.9		2.7	15.2	5.4	0.2		100.0
Comoros	31.7	0.4	63.3		1.1	2.5		0.7		100.0
Congo	36.9	0.1	58.0	0.7	2.0	0.4				100.0
Kenya	5.0	1.2	46.1	0.2	21.5	10.0	5.2	0.1	0.5	100.0
Madagascar	12.4	9.5	53.6	0.7	11.4	7.4		0.1	0.1	100.0
Maldives	23.1	3.9	33.7			37.4				100.0
Mauritius	11.5	0.3	78.8	0.1	5.1	1.8			0.3	100.0
Réunion	0.7	0.4	82.1		9.4	5.7		1.1	0.1	100.0
Rwanda	3.5	0.3	41.8		46.5	5.3		2.1		100.0
Seychelles	0.8	0.3	51.9		0.1	27.6				100.0
Tanzania	3.8	5.3	50.0		5.6	27.0	4.3		0.2	100.0
Uganda	10.8	1.5	76.0		2.5	3.7	1.2	0.1	0.2	100.0
Zaire	18.3	5.5	66.7		2.0	3.4		0.2		100.0
Southern Africa										
Botswana										
Lesotho										
Malawi	15.9	15.9	42.3		15.3	3.3	0.5		2.0	100.0
Mozambique	5.7	5.2	19.9		3.2	57.1	1.3	0.6	0.2	100.0
Namibia										
South Africa	6.1	6.3	28.2		5.1	5.0	0.8	0.8	0.3	100.0
Swaziland										
Zambia	3.7	28.7	29.6		4.9	28.6	3.0		0.1	100.0
Zimbabwe	5.6	9.6	42.9		21.6	6.6	4.4	3.3	0.7	100.0

Source: IMF, Direction of Trade Statistics/Euromonitor
Notes: see end of section

EXTERNAL TRADE BY COMMODITY   Table No. 0507

Imports by Commodity: SITC Classification, Latest Year

Units: Million current US dollars

	Year	0	1	2	3	4	5	6	7	8	9	Total
North America												
Canada	1991	6,664	616	3,704	5,747	117	8,143	14,782	60,365	14,264	3,304	117,706
USA	1991	23,924	5,132	14,317	58,557	927	25,289	60,362	215,950	87,375	15,422	507,255
South America												
Argentina	1989	139		448	375		1,090	547	1,384	196	22	4,201
Bolivia	1990	92	4	12	5	7	66	126	258	48	2	620
Brazil	1989	1,610		1,456	4,320	117	2,929	2,271	5,342	1,070	61	19,176
Chile	1989	179	18	212	806	34	842	994	2,874	411	126	6,496
Colombia	1989	270	11	281	244	50	1,174	865	1,784	214	117	5,010
Ecuador	1989	133	4	89	81	25	428	373	627	98	2	1,860
French Guiana	1990	83	28	3	57	2	38	141	299	81	10	743
Guyana	1979	42	2	3	63	8	32	66	57	16	2	290
Paraguay	1988	12	54	6	132		65	81	174	49	1	574
Peru	1988	523	2	130	135	49	537	338	677	108	609	3,109
Suriname												
Uruguay	1990	70	18	73	256	8	289	199	427	74	1	1,415
Venezuela	1990	541	55	445	195	128	1,004	943	2,541	466	46	6,364
Caribbean												
Anguilla												
Antigua	1984	25	4	3	33		8	17	29	12	1	132
Aruba												
Bahamas	1989	202	30	20	1,919		149	220	259	199	3	3,001
Barbados	1990	97	16	21	100	7	71	126	169	74	17	698
Bermuda	1989	83	28	5	34		51	73	140	120	1	535
British Virgin Islands	1982	12	3	1	6		2	7	19	5	3	59
Cayman Islands	1989	38	14	5	19		17	44	71	41	5	254
Cuba	1989	925		307		78	530	838	2,531	276		8,124
Dominica	1990	20	4	2	7	3	13	29	31	8		118
Dominican Republic	1985	80	3	44	440	48	146	170	289	29		1,248
Grenada	1987	21	2	4	5		8	17	21	9		89
Guadeloupe	1990	248	66	36	92	8	130	286	522	252	40	1,681
Haiti	1984	87	9	13	61	34	43	93	92	38	3	472
Jamaica	1989	257	23	46	275	15	208	379	391	183	33	1,809
Martinique	1990	258	44	25	173	7	158	252	551	235	37	1,740
Netherlands Antilles [a]	1987	154	13	7	1,050		65	110	154	128		1,682
St Kitts	1988	15	2	2	5	1	7	19	30	12	1	93
St Lucia	1986	31	5	4	12		19	33	31	20		155
St Vincent/Grenadines	1980	17	3	2	5		6	11	9	5		57
Trinidad and Tobago	1990	202	6	104	144	6	176	246	286	87	4	1,262
Central America												
Belize	1988	37	5	1	19		16	28	47	25	2	181
Costa Rica	1987	81	8	56	141	3	285	311	387	90	14	1,377
El Salvador	1987	116	3	37	113	20	190	199	261	48		987
Guatemala	1987	99	4	101	185	49	282	263	385	79		1,449
Honduras	1989	97	3	24	138	3	190	161	216	41	1	876
Mexico	1990	3,653	163	1,853	1,163	367	3,150	4,166	10,144	2,998	405	28,063
Nicaragua	1986	73		12	138	20	142	141	211	37		774
Panama	1989	127	6	15	160	12	183	196	170	93		964
Puerto Rico												
South Asia												
Afghanistan [b]	1990	44,622	5,748		1,765	14,705	9,157	20,160	208,997	6,082	114,355	433,591
Bangladesh	1987	567		145	354	163	214	596	442	76	11	2,573
Bhutan [b]	1986											1,125
India	1988	1,022		1,825	3,277	523	2,571	4,743	3,547	674	1,162	19,351
Nepal [b]	1987	939	74	645	933	180	1,315	3,337	2,943	646	8	11,020
Pakistan	1989	847		468	1,216	470	1,107	884	1,903	208		7,119
Sri Lanka	1987	297	7	50	309	11	198	592	445	96	17	2,021

EXTERNAL TRADE BY COMMODITY

Table No. 0507 (cont'd)

Imports by Commodity: SITC Classification, Latest Year

Units: Million current US dollars

	Year	0	1	2	3	4	5	6	7	8	9	Total
Japan												
Japan	1991	30,707	3,733	28,450	55,189	424	16,864	30,254	37,573	28,257	2,652	234,103
ASEAN/NICs												
Brunei	1986	94	38	8	7	2	46	138	248	69	4	653
Hong Kong	1990	4,569	1,747	2,016	2,010		6,137	20,323	23,031	22,131	373	82,497
Indonesia	1990	851		1,879	1,960	26	3,350	3,652	9,305	725	36	21,837
Macau	1989	102	54	90	62		80	764	193	99	29	1,476
Malaysia	1990	1,695	108	946	1,421	80	2,489	4,635	14,739	1,669	1,478	29,261
Philippines	1988	788	97	456	1,161		1,128	1,331	1,726	201	1,823	8,731
Singapore	1990	2,385	789	1,313	9,649	417	4,557	7,856	27,163	5,872	790	60,790
South Korea	1990	3,240	188	8,551	11,096	184	7,298	10,796	23,928	3,994	569	69,844
Taiwan [b]	1987	49	8	131	118	2	149	161	385	68	28	1,099
Thailand	1988	1,026	104	1,479	1,566		2,537	3,901	7,957	808	885	20,285
East/SE Asia												
Cambodia												
China	1990	3,458	157	4,107	1,272	982	6,670	11,583	21,513	3,319	285	53,345
Laos												
Mongolia												
Myanmar [b]	1989	27	2	18	114	73	374	371	1,208	138	1,070	3,395
North Korea												
Vietnam [b]	1991	676	14	266	702	8	14	89	1	183	18	2,194
Australasia												
Australia	1991	1,534	302	922	2,278	108	3,551	5,779	16,713	5,632	1,086	37,906
New Zealand	1991	514	99	331	645	33	1,088	1,439	3,188	1,156		8,494
Pacific												
American Samoa	1983	11	1	1	9		4	11	12	3		53
Fiji	1988	78	4	3	62	8	46	109	97	40	15	461
French Polynesia	1988	130	19	14	44	3	52	141	290	115		808
Guam	1983											636
Kiribati [b]	1990	9	2	1	4		2	4	7	6		34
Nauru [c]	1982	2,693	1,203	204	277	24	662	1,124	986	201	5,701	13,078
New Caledonia	1986	70	17	5	63	2	28	64	146	60	3	458
Papua New Guinea	1988	212	18	10	113	4	98	241	533	117		1,347
Solomon Islands	1987	10	2		10		5	14	20	6		68
Tonga	1988	14	3	2	5		4	11	12	5		55
Tuvalu	1986	1										3
Vanuatu	1988	12	4	1	6		4	14	17	8	2	68
Western Samoa [b]	1983	15	2	1	13		4	15	15	5		71
Middle East												
Bahrain	1988	218	43	31	1,086		171	298	529	204	7	2,714
Egypt	1989	2,015	82	642	173	246	938	1,361	1,723	266		7,448
Iran	1984	189	8	48	28	33	170	321	501	32	2	1,332
Iraq												
Israel	1990	943	73	605	1,363	37	1,470	5,362	4,044	1,096	333	15,324
Jordan	1988	468	19	102	431	35	276	483	628	201	143	2,786
Kuwait	1989	1,092	85	86	61	35	474	1,386	1,861	1,096	123	6,302
Lebanon												
Oman	1990	421	51	33	110	9	168	435	970	236	249	2,681
Qatar	1988	218	20	39	9	7	82	239	500	147	6	1,267
Saudi Arabia	1989	2,861	280	401		45	1,553	4,132	7,935	2,759	1,120	21,153
Syria	1989	492		74	123	28	351	579	370	55	21	2,097
United Arab Emirates	1986	1,086	101	120	322	33	454	1,475	2,079	1,092	13	6,777
Yemen	1985	368	30	30	87	26	118	283	300	64	5	1,290

EXTERNAL TRADE BY COMMODITY   Table No. 0507 (cont'd)

Imports by Commodity: SITC Classification, Latest Year

Units: Million current US dollars

	Year	0	1	2	3	4	5	6	7	8	9	Total
North Africa												
Algeria	1988	1,789	33	419	173	212	967	1,522	2,032	249	1	7,397
Chad	1987	32	5	6	38	2	44	50	78	15	1	366
Djibouti	1987	39	21	6	29	1	6	25	33	4	37	201
Ethiopia	1988	150	14	25	108	22	96	148	481	41		1,085
Libya	1988	755	25	68	19	114	464	1,059	2,287	1,022	67	5,879
Mali	1987	61	13	5	55	4	56	94	83		2	374
Mauritania	1987	33	2	3	33	3	6	32	122	2		382
Morocco	1989	525	63	511	846	113	577	1,111	1,535	203		5,492
Niger	1987	86	4	11	30	7	25	43	55	5	2	269
Somalia	1987	27	1	7	2	5	4	21	58	5	1	132
Sudan	1987	145	5	5	172	2	88	175	304	33		929
Tunisia	1990	473	33	421	494	71	476	1,495	1,551	453	8	5,476
West Africa												
Benin	1987	42	53	5	20	1	20	95	79	53	2	370
Burkina Faso	1988	95	9	12	33	5	54	121	128			455
Cameroon	1989	180	21	48	18	6	194	293	392	109	13	1,273
Cape Verde	1989	28	5	4	7	3	7	22	28	7		112
Côte d'Ivoire	1987	453	53	27	336		310	562	478		19	2,241
Equatorial Guinea	1987	11	2	3	9		3	7	9	4		48
Gabon ^d	1987	101	23	10	9	7	62	189	305	73	1	779
Gambia	1987	43	8	3	17	1	8	38	26	9	4	157
Ghana	1987	91	4	10	327	3	101	99	191	44	48	919
Guinea	1987	23	7	5	46	2	39	65	136		112	435
Guinea-Bissau	1987	17	2	2	6	5	5	23	35	4	2	97
Liberia	1987	61	6	4	73	3	17	43	83	15	2	308
Nigeria	1987	731	7	155	36	63	522	844	1,386	159	15	3,917
Sao Tomé e Príncipe	1987	2	1		3		2	2	4			13
Senegal	1990	403	29	59	259	33	158	260	344	75		1,620
Sierra Leone	1987	39	3	2	22	2	9	20	33	5	1	164
Togo	1989	88	25	9	29	7	43	120	119	29	2	472
East/Central Africa												
Angola	1987	259	15	17	7	42	109	204	257	83	34	1,027
Burundi	1989	13	1	7	22	1	28	41	58	10	5	188
Central African Republic	1989	23	6	3	11	2	22	28	53	12		159
Comoros	1989											43
Congo ^d	1987	84	10	3	20	4	45	138	174	39		516
Kenya	1988	47		57	291	71	355	321	764	75		1,987
Madagascar	1987	29	1	9	84	6	35	44	78	15	1	302
Maldives	1985	11	3		7		3	12	9		3	48
Mauritius	1989	154	5	49	99	14	87	497	304	110	6	1,326
Réunion	1990	314	54	37	130	10	191	318	635	334	50	2,074
Rwanda	1988	18	4	19	48		10	86	111	4	69	369
Seychelles	1989	27	3	3	30	1	10	28	45	16		163
Tanzania	1988	81		56	152	48	132	244	682	96		1,495
Uganda	1986	22	2	8	62	3	43	90	142	26	1	398
Zaire	1987	148	8	22	57		78	159	240	38	6	756
Southern Africa												
Botswana	1987	131	20	43	68	8	58	170	300	58	81	937
Lesotho	1987	77	18	5	30	3	27	75	64	83	18	518
Malawi	1987	14	2	10	40	7	60	66	89	14	2	298
Mozambique	1987	129	46	44	95	2	47	31	120	104	9	625
Namibia												
South Africa ^e	1985	373	94	405	59	157	1,258	1,137	4,123	755	1,937	10,297
Swaziland	1987	50	7	6	65	2	33	50	67	49	102	431
Zambia ^f	1987	27	2	12	167	1	113	124	248	25	21	739
Zimbabwe ^f	1987	15	2	64	143	13	185	168	379	68	4	1,043

Source: UN, Trade Statistics/national statistical offices
Notes: see end of section

EXTERNAL TRADE BY COMMODITY

Table No. 0508

Imports by Commodity: SITC Classification, Latest Year (% Analysis)

Units: % of total imports

	Year	0	1	2	3	4	5	6	7	8	9	Total
North America												
Canada	1991	5.7	0.5	3.1	4.9	0.1	6.9	12.6	51.3	12.1	2.8	100.0
USA	1991	4.7	1.0	2.8	11.5	0.2	5.0	11.9	42.6	17.2	3.0	100.0
South America												
Argentina	1989	3.3		10.7	8.9		25.9	13.0	32.9	4.7	0.3	100.0
Bolivia	1990	14.8	0.6	1.9	0.8	1.1	10.6	20.3	41.6	7.7	0.3	100.0
Brazil	1989	8.4		7.6	22.5	0.6	15.3	11.8	27.9	5.6		100.0
Chile	1989	2.8	0.3	3.3	12.4	0.5	13.0	15.3	44.2	6.3	2.0	100.0
Colombia	1989	5.4	0.2	5.6	4.9	1.0	23.4	17.3	35.6	4.3	2.3	100.0
Ecuador	1989	7.2	0.2	4.8	4.4	1.3	23.0	20.1	33.7	5.3		100.0
French Guiana	1990	11.2	3.8	0.4	7.7	0.3	5.1	19.0	40.2	10.9	1.3	100.0
Guyana	1979	14.5	0.6	0.9	21.8	2.7	11.1	22.8	19.7	5.4	0.5	100.0
Paraguay	1988	2.1	9.4	1.0	23.0		11.3	14.1	30.3	8.5		100.0
Peru	1988	16.8	0.1	4.2	4.3	1.6	17.3	10.9	21.8	3.5	19.6	100.0
Suriname												
Uruguay	1990	4.9	1.3	5.2	18.1	0.6	20.4	14.1	30.2	5.2		100.0
Venezuela	1990	8.5	0.9	7.0	3.1	2.0	15.8	14.8	39.9	7.3	0.7	100.0
Caribbean												
Anguilla												
Antigua	1984	19.0	3.3	1.9	24.9		6.4	12.6	21.8	9.0		100.0
Aruba												
Bahamas	1989	6.7	1.0	0.7	63.9		5.0	7.3	8.6	6.6		100.0
Barbados	1990	13.9	2.3	3.0	14.3	1.0	10.2	18.1	24.2	10.6	2.4	100.0
Bermuda	1989	15.5	5.2	0.9	6.4		9.5	13.6	26.2	22.4		100.0
British Virgin Islands	1982	20.8	5.3	1.9	10.5		3.4	11.2	32.7	8.5	3.4	100.0
Cayman Islands	1989	15.0	5.5	2.0	7.5		6.7	17.3	28.0	16.1	1.6	100.0
Cuba	1989	11.4		3.8		1.0	6.5	10.3	31.2	3.4		100.0
Dominica	1990	16.9	3.4	1.7	5.9	2.5	11.0	24.6	26.3	6.8		100.0
Dominican Republic	1985	6.4	0.2	3.5	35.3	3.8	11.7	13.6	23.2	2.3		100.0
Grenada	1987	23.6	1.7	4.5	5.6		9.0	19.1	23.6	10.1		100.0
Guadeloupe	1990	14.8	3.9	2.1	5.5	0.5	7.7	17.0	31.1	15.0	2.4	100.0
Haiti	1984	18.4	1.9	2.8	12.9	7.1	9.1	19.6	19.5	8.0	0.6	100.0
Jamaica	1989	14.2	1.3	2.5	15.2	0.8	11.5	21.0	21.6	10.1	1.8	100.0
Martinique	1990	14.8	2.5	1.4	9.9	0.4	9.1	14.5	31.7	13.5	2.1	100.0
Netherlands Antilles [a]	1987	9.2	0.8	0.4	62.4		3.9	6.5	9.2	7.6		100.0
St Kitts	1988	16.1	2.2	2.2	5.4	0.8	7.5	20.4	32.3	12.9	1.1	100.0
St Lucia	1986	20.0	3.2	2.6	7.7		12.3	21.5	20.0	12.9		100.0
St Vincent/Grenadines	1980	29.8	5.3	3.5	8.8		9.6	19.3	15.8	8.8		100.0
Trinidad and Tobago	1990	16.0	0.5	8.2	11.4	0.5	13.9	19.5	22.7	6.9	0.3	100.0
Central America												
Belize	1988	20.4	2.8	0.6	10.5		8.8	15.5	26.0	13.8	1.1	100.0
Costa Rica	1987	5.9	0.6	4.1	10.2	0.2	20.7	22.6	28.1	6.5	1.0	100.0
El Salvador	1987	11.8	0.3	3.7	11.4	2.0	19.3	20.2	26.4	4.9		100.0
Guatemala	1987	6.8	0.3	7.0	12.8	3.4	19.5	18.2	26.6	5.5		100.0
Honduras	1989	11.1	0.3	2.7	15.8	0.3	21.7	18.4	24.7	4.7	0.1	100.0
Mexico	1990	13.0	0.6	6.6	4.1	1.3	11.2	14.8	36.1	10.7	1.4	100.0
Nicaragua	1986	9.4		1.6	17.8	2.6	18.3	18.2	27.3	4.8		100.0
Panama	1989	13.2	0.6	1.6	16.6	1.2	19.0	20.3	17.6	9.6		100.0
Puerto Rico												
South Asia												
Afghanistan	1990	10.3	1.3		0.4	3.4	2.1	4.6	48.2	1.4	26.4	100.0
Bangladesh	1987	22.0		5.6	13.8	6.3	8.3	23.2	17.2	3.0	0.4	100.0
Bhutan	1986											100.0
India	1988	5.3		9.4	16.9	2.7	13.3	24.5	18.3	3.5	6.0	100.0
Nepal	1987	8.5	0.7	5.9	8.5	1.6	11.9	30.3	26.7	5.9	0.1	100.0
Pakistan	1989	11.9		6.6	17.1	6.6	15.5	12.4	26.7	2.9		100.0
Sri Lanka	1987	14.7	0.3	2.5	15.3	0.5	9.8	29.3	22.0	4.8	0.8	100.0

EXTERNAL TRADE BY COMMODITY

Imports by Commodity: SITC Classification, Latest Year (% Analysis)

Units: % of total imports

	Year	0	1	2	3	4	5	6	7	8	9	Total
Japan												
Japan	1991	13.1	1.6	12.2	23.6	0.2	7.2	12.9	16.0	12.1	1.1	100.0
ASEAN/NICs												
Brunei	1986	14.4	5.8	1.2	1.1	0.3	7.0	21.1	38.0	10.6	0.6	100.0
Hong Kong	1990	5.5	2.1	2.4	2.4		7.4	24.6	27.9	26.8	0.5	100.0
Indonesia	1990	3.9		8.6	9.0	0.1	15.3	16.7	42.6	3.3	0.2	100.0
Macau	1989	6.9	3.7	6.1	4.2		5.4	51.8	13.1	6.7	2.0	100.0
Malaysia	1990	5.8	0.4	3.2	4.9	0.3	8.5	15.8	50.4	5.7	5.1	100.0
Philippines	1988	9.0	1.1	5.2	13.3		12.9	15.2	19.8	2.3	20.9	100.0
Singapore	1990	3.9	1.3	2.2	15.9	0.7	7.5	12.9	44.7	9.7	1.3	100.0
South Korea	1990	4.6	0.3	12.2	15.9	0.3	10.4	15.5	34.3	5.7	0.8	100.0
Taiwan	1987	4.5	0.7	11.9	10.7	0.2	13.6	14.6	35.0	6.2	2.5	100.0
Thailand	1988	5.1	0.5	7.3	7.7		12.5	19.2	39.2	4.0	4.4	100.0
East/SE Asia												
Cambodia												
China	1990	6.5	0.3	7.7	2.4	1.8	12.5	21.7	40.3	6.2	0.5	100.0
Laos												
Mongolia												
Myanmar	1989	0.8	0.1	0.5	3.4	2.2	11.0	10.9	35.6	4.1	31.5	100.0
North Korea												
Vietnam	1991	30.8	0.6	12.1	32.0	0.4	0.6	4.1		8.3	0.8	100.0
Australasia												
Australia	1991	4.0	0.8	2.4	6.0	0.3	9.4	15.2	44.1	14.9	2.9	100.0
New Zealand	1991	6.1	1.2	3.9	7.6	0.4	12.8	16.9	37.5	13.6		100.0
Pacific												
American Samoa	1983	20.8	1.9	1.9	17.0		7.5	20.8	22.6	5.7		100.0
Fiji	1988	16.9	0.9	0.7	13.4	1.7	10.0	23.6	21.0	8.7	3.3	100.0
French Polynesia	1988	16.1	2.4	1.7	5.4	0.4	6.4	17.5	35.9	14.2		100.0
Guam	1983											100.0
Kiribati	1990	26.5	5.9	2.9	11.8		5.9	11.8	20.6	17.6		100.0
Nauru	1982	20.6	9.2	1.6	2.1	0.2	5.1	8.6	7.5	1.5	43.6	100.0
New Caledonia	1986	15.3	3.7	1.1	13.8	0.4	6.1	14.0	31.9	13.1	0.7	100.0
Papua New Guinea	1988	15.7	1.3	0.7	8.4	0.3	7.3	17.9	39.6	8.7		100.0
Solomon Islands	1987	14.7	2.9		14.7		7.4	20.6	29.4	8.8		100.0
Tonga	1988	25.5	5.5	3.6	9.1		7.3	20.0	21.8	9.1		100.0
Tuvalu	1986	33.3										100.0
Vanuatu	1988	17.6	5.9	1.5	8.8		5.9	20.6	25.0	11.8	2.9	100.0
Western Samoa	1983	21.3	2.7	1.1	18.4	0.6	5.9	21.3	21.1	7.4	0.1	100.0
Middle East												
Bahrain	1988	8.0	1.6	1.1	40.0		6.3	11.0	19.5	7.5	0.3	100.0
Egypt	1989	27.1	1.1	8.6	2.3	3.3	12.6	18.3	23.1	3.6		100.0
Iran	1984	14.2	0.6	3.6	2.1	2.5	12.8	24.1	37.6	2.4	0.2	100.0
Iraq												
Israel	1990	6.2	0.5	3.9	8.9	0.2	9.6	35.0	26.4	7.2	2.2	100.0
Jordan	1988	16.8	0.7	3.7	15.5	1.3	9.9	17.3	22.5	7.2	5.1	100.0
Kuwait	1989	17.3	1.3	1.4	1.0	0.6	7.5	22.0	29.5	17.4	2.0	100.0
Lebanon												
Oman	1990	15.7	1.9	1.2	4.1	0.3	6.3	16.2	36.2	8.8	9.3	100.0
Qatar	1988	17.2	1.6	3.1	0.7	0.6	6.5	18.9	39.5	11.6	0.5	100.0
Saudi Arabia	1989	13.5	1.3	1.9		0.2	7.3	19.5	37.5	13.0	5.3	100.0
Syria	1989	23.5		3.5	5.9	1.3	16.7	27.6	17.6	2.6	1.0	100.0
United Arab Emirates	1986	16.0	1.5	1.8	4.8	0.5	6.7	21.8	30.7	16.1	0.2	100.0
Yemen	1985	28.5	2.3	2.3	6.7	2.0	9.1	21.9	23.3	4.9	0.4	100.0

EXTERNAL TRADE BY COMMODITY

Table No. 0508 (cont'd)

Imports by Commodity: SITC Classification, Latest Year (% Analysis)

Units: % of total imports

	Year	0	1	2	3	4	5	6	7	8	9	Total
North Africa												
Algeria	1988	24.2	0.4	5.7	2.3	2.9	13.1	20.6	27.5	3.4		100.0
Chad	1987	8.7	1.4	1.6	10.4	0.5	12.0	13.7	21.3	4.1	0.3	100.0
Djibouti	1987	19.4	10.4	3.0	14.4	0.5	3.0	12.4	16.4	2.0	18.4	100.0
Ethiopia	1988	13.8	1.3	2.3	10.0	2.0	8.8	13.6	44.3	3.8		100.0
Libya	1988	12.8	0.4	1.2	0.3	1.9	7.9	18.0	38.9	17.4	1.1	100.0
Mali	1987	16.3	3.5	1.4	14.7	1.1	15.0	25.1	22.2		0.5	100.0
Mauritania	1987	8.6	0.5	0.8	8.6	0.8	1.6	8.4	31.9	0.5		100.0
Morocco	1989	9.6	1.1	9.3	15.4	2.1	10.5	20.2	27.9	3.7		100.0
Niger	1987	32.0	1.5	4.1	11.2	2.6	9.3	16.0	20.4	1.9	0.7	100.0
Somalia	1987	20.5	0.8	5.3	1.5	3.8	3.0	15.9	43.9	3.8	0.8	100.0
Sudan	1987	15.6	0.5	0.5	18.5	0.2	9.5	18.8	32.7	3.6		100.0
Tunisia	1990	8.6	0.6	7.7	9.0	1.3	8.7	27.3	28.3	8.3	0.1	100.0
West Africa												
Benin	1987	11.4	14.3	1.4	5.4	0.3	5.4	25.7	21.4	14.3	0.5	100.0
Burkina Faso	1988	20.9	2.0	2.6	7.3	1.1	11.9	26.6	28.1			100.0
Cameroon	1989	14.1	1.6	3.8	1.4	0.5	15.2	23.0	30.8	8.6	1.0	100.0
Cape Verde	1989	25.0	4.5	3.6	6.3	2.7	6.3	19.6	25.0	6.3		100.0
Côte d'Ivoire	1987	20.2	2.4	1.2	15.0		13.8	25.1	21.3		0.8	100.0
Equatorial Guinea	1987	22.9	4.2	6.3	18.8		6.3	14.6	18.8	8.3		100.0
Gabon [b]	1987	13.0	3.0	1.3	1.2	0.9	8.0	24.3	39.2	9.4	0.1	100.0
Gambia	1987	27.4	5.1	1.9	10.8	0.6	5.1	24.2	16.6	5.7	2.5	100.0
Ghana	1987	9.9	0.4	1.1	35.6	0.3	11.0	10.8	20.8	4.8	5.2	100.0
Guinea	1987	5.3	1.6	1.1	10.6	0.5	9.0	14.9	31.3		25.7	100.0
Guinea-Bissau	1987	17.5	2.1	2.1	6.2	5.2	5.2	23.7	36.1	4.1	2.1	100.0
Liberia	1987	19.8	1.9	1.3	23.7	1.0	5.5	14.0	26.9	4.9	0.6	100.0
Nigeria	1987	18.7	0.2	4.0	0.9	1.6	13.3	21.5	35.4	4.1	0.4	100.0
Sao Tomé e Príncipe	1987	15.4	7.7		23.1		15.4	15.4	30.8			100.0
Senegal	1990	24.9	1.8	3.6	16.0	2.0	9.8	16.0	21.2	4.6		100.0
Sierra Leone	1987	23.8	1.8	1.2	13.4	1.2	5.5	12.2	20.1	3.0	0.6	100.0
Togo	1989	18.6	5.3	1.9	6.1	1.5	9.1	25.4	25.2	6.1	0.4	100.0
East/Central Africa												
Angola	1987	25.2	1.5	1.7	0.7	4.1	10.6	19.9	25.0	8.1	3.3	100.0
Burundi	1989	6.9	0.5	3.7	11.7	0.5	14.9	21.8	30.9	5.3	2.7	100.0
Central African Republic	1989	14.5	3.8	1.9	6.9	1.3	13.8	17.6	33.3	7.5		100.0
Comoros	1989											100.0
Congo [b]	1987	16.3	1.9	0.6	3.9	0.8	8.7	26.7	33.7	7.6		100.0
Kenya	1988	2.4		2.9	14.6	3.6	17.9	16.2	38.4	3.8		100.0
Madagascar	1987	9.6	0.3	3.0	27.8	2.0	11.6	14.6	25.8	5.0	0.3	100.0
Maldives	1985	22.1	6.5	0.6	15.4		6.3	25.3	17.7		6.1	100.0
Mauritius	1989	11.6	0.4	3.7	7.5	1.1	6.6	37.5	22.9	8.3	0.5	100.0
Réunion	1990	15.1	2.6	1.8	6.3	0.5	9.2	15.3	30.6	16.1	2.4	100.0
Rwanda	1988	4.9	1.1	5.1	13.0		2.7	23.3	30.1	1.1	18.7	100.0
Seychelles	1989	16.6	1.8	1.8	18.4	0.6	6.1	17.2	27.6	9.8		100.0
Tanzania	1988	5.4		3.7	10.2	3.2	8.8	16.3	45.6	6.4		100.0
Uganda	1986	5.5	0.5	2.0	15.6	0.8	10.8	22.6	35.7	6.5	0.3	100.0
Zaire	1987	19.6	1.1	2.9	7.5		10.3	21.0	31.7	5.0	0.8	100.0
Southern Africa												
Botswana	1987	14.0	2.1	4.6	7.3	0.9	6.2	18.1	32.0	6.2	8.6	100.0
Lesotho	1987	14.9	3.5	1.0	5.8	0.6	5.2	14.5	12.4	16.0	3.5	100.0
Malawi	1987	4.7	0.7	3.4	13.4	2.3	20.1	22.1	29.9	4.7	0.7	100.0
Mozambique	1987	20.6	7.4	7.0	15.2	0.3	7.5	5.0	19.2	16.6	1.4	100.0
Namibia												
South Africa [c]	1985	3.6	0.9	3.9	0.6	1.5	12.2	11.0	40.0	7.3	18.8	100.0
Swaziland	1987	11.6	1.6	1.4	15.1	0.5	7.7	11.6	15.5	11.4	23.7	100.0
Zambia [d]	1987	3.7	0.3	1.6	22.6	0.1	15.3	16.8	33.6	3.4	2.8	100.0
Zimbabwe [d]	1987	1.4	0.2	6.1	13.7	1.2	17.7	16.1	36.3	6.5	0.4	100.0

Source: UN, Trade Statistics/national statistical offices/Euromonitor

Notes: see end of section

EXTERNAL TRADE BY COMMODITY | Table No. 0509

Exports by Commodity: SITC Classification, Latest Year

Units: Million current US dollars

	Year	0	1	2	3	4	5	6	7	8	9	Total
North America												
Canada	1991	9,591	852	15,214	13,823	215	6,685	20,260	45,469	4,421	2,235	118,765
USA	1991	29,555	6,750	25,462	12,033	1,147	42,965	35,566	187,360	43,162	13,448	397,448
South America												
Argentina	1989	4,098	81	566	334	874	681	2,035	622	265		9,565
Bolivia	1990	151		351	227	7	5	167		11		923
Brazil	1990	6,618	673	4,803	683	493	1,850	8,126	5,798	1,985	384	31,413
Chile	1988	1,532	34	1,869	12	25	206	2,917	53	98	49	6,794
Colombia	1989	2,127	21	283	1,858		198	592	69	564	29	5,739
Ecuador	1989	1,101		40	1,147		8	35	8	8	3	2,354
French Guiana	1990	57		4			2	2	17	3	5	90
Guyana	1979	131	6	135			5	3	5	4	1	290
Paraguay	1990	210	7	634		13	31	41		22		959
Peru	1988	640		808	167	2	58	696	39	96		2,506
Suriname												
Uruguay	1990	655	3	365		7	131	302	34	194	9	1,708
Venezuela	1988	72	15	75	24		146	1,220	89	32	219	1,892
Caribbean												
Anguilla												
Antigua	1984	1			2		1	1	5	7		18
Aruba												
Bahamas	1989	34	20	18	2,149		529	16	13			2,786
Barbados	1990	44	14		59		25	26	26	15	4	213
Bermuda	1985						13		2	2	4	23
British Virgin Islands	1982		1	1								1
Cayman Islands	1989						1				1	2
Cuba	1989	4,318	103	522			65	47	43	24		5,392
Dominica	1990	35		1			13	3	1	3		55
Dominican Republic	1985											739
Grenada	1987	29								1	2	32
Guadeloupe	1990	84	10	1			4	3	15	3		122
Haiti	1984	64					6	28		67		179
Jamaica	1989	143	36	627	16		25	22	32	129		1,029
Martinique	1990	134	33	2	44		9	16	31	5		276
Netherlands Antilles [a]	1987			6	1,218		16	4	12	7	8	1,274
St Kitts	1988	10	1						9	5		26
St Lucia	1986	58	2	1		2		7	4	9		83
St Vincent/Grenadines	1980	12							1	1		16
Trinidad and Tobago	1990	86	25	12	1,396		294	189	40	32		2,080
Central America												
Belize	1988	72		4			1			19	21	116
Costa Rica	1987	762	6	47	12		53	99	36	83	16	1,114
El Salvador	1987	427		27	8		38	76	9	25		613
Guatemala	1987	587	9	72	16		94	79	9	31		899
Honduras	1989	941	13	57	4	10	14	141		13		
Mexico	1990	2,762	304	1,112	9,876		1,820	3,095	6,649	1,070		26,714
Nicaragua	1986	169	2	49			6	5		3		234
Panama	1989	223	5	7		2	15	20		24		297
Puerto Rico												
South Asia												
Afghanistan [b]	1990	60,423		28,206			26,803			25,266	140,698	
Bangladesh	1987	202	1	4	15			432	17	424	3	1,194
Bhutan [b]	1986											323
India	1988	2,173	88	1,117	356	8	828	5,947	998	2,067	291	13,872
Nepal [b]	1987	694	1	508		118	2	1,055	3	678		3,059
Pakistan	1989	536	6	829	44		26	2,326	43	922	18	4,751
Sri Lanka	1987	471		152	80	9	13	145	22	451		1,346

EXTERNAL TRADE BY COMMODITY

Table No. 0509 (cont'd)

Exports by Commodity: SITC Classification, Latest Year

Units: Million current US dollars

	Year	0	1	2	3	4	5	6	7	8	9	Total
Japan												
Japan	1991	1,575	215	2,011	1,302	76	17,396	37,030	223,087	26,830	4,874	314,395
ASEAN/NICs												
Brunei	1986	8			1,747		6	25		6		1,798
Hong Kong	1990	1,767	1,479	1,555	536		4,343	14,681	21,176	36,011	556	82,185
Indonesia	1990	2,291	136	1,970	11,239	420	618	5,675	367	2,835	124	25,675
Macau	1989	11	6	17			17	217	34	1,341		1,643
Malaysia	1990	1,277		4,247	5,247	2,101	489	2,343	10,625	2,938	117	29,419
Philippines	1988	1,057	32	709	153	425	257	690	694	953	2,103	7,074
Singapore	1990	1,511	769	1,614	9,587	421	3,265	3,692	26,437	4,733	701	52,730
South Korea	1990	2,015		991	699		2,469	14,523	25,542	18,438	216	65,016
Taiwan [b]	1987	94		25	14		45	343	550	633		1,704
Thailand	1987	4,228	56	1,040	85	14	193	1,921	1,389	2,626	106	11,659
East/SE Asia												
Cambodia												
China	1990	6,735	342	3,537	5,237		3,750	12,796	10,833	17,529	1,171	62,091
Laos												
Mongolia												
Myanmar [b]	1989	551		1,060	46		37	134		15	907	2,762
North Korea												
Vietnam [b]	1991	117	11	73	503	5	358	484	572	55	18	1,970
Australasia												
Australia	1991	6,501	194	7,262	7,317	26	981	4,568	2,758	882	6,964	37,453
New Zealand	1991	4,345	35	1,686	308	62	571	1,384	422	296	160	9,269
Pacific												
American Samoa	1983	6	1	2		8			1			19
Fiji	1988	194		16		3	2	12	1	15	61	363
French Polynesia	1988	1		1		3	1	24	29	7	8	75
Guam	1983											39
Kiribati [b]	1990	2				1						4
Nauru												
New Caledonia	1986	2		43				107				189
Papua New Guinea	1989	243		956	1	63		13	50	3	78	1,412
Solomon Islands	1987	32		25		3					4	64
Tonga	1988	4				1		1		1	1	8
Tuvalu												
Vanuatu	1988											15
Western Samoa [b]	1983	5	2	7		11					2	27
Middle East												
Bahrain	1988			7	1,831		95	361	88	22		2,418
Egypt	1989	227		311	807		118	971	11	196		2,648
Iran												
Iraq												
Israel	1990	975		437	80		1,648	4,399	2,928	1,544		12,052
Jordan	1988	89	4	414		2	257	112	60	46	50	1,036
Kuwait	1989	63		27	31		276	216	288	125	34	1,064
Lebanon												
Oman	1990	73	5	11	11	2	15	76	190	47	28	458
Qatar	1981				5,059		211	118				5,389
Saudi Arabia	1989	359		211	24,094		2,593	362			633	28,369
Syria	1989	343		159	1,177		356	647	16	305		3,006
United Arab Emirates	1986	283	20	34	48		85	461	389	222	107	1,651
Yemen	1985											13

EXTERNAL TRADE BY COMMODITY　　　　　　　Table No. 0509 (cont'd)

Exports by Commodity: SITC Classification, Latest Year

Units: Million current US dollars

	Year	0	1	2	3	4	5	6	7	8	9	Total
North Africa												
Algeria	1988		16	46	7,743		69	133	129			8,164
Chad	1987	20		75	11		1	2	1		1	111
Djibouti	1987										6	7
Ethiopia	1988	315		79	13	2	5			5		421
Libya	1988				6,274		408					6,683
Mali	1987	15		109				55				179
Mauritania	1987	213		210		1		3				428
Morocco	1989	865		761	86		535	321	148	611		3,337
Niger	1987	66	1	356	6		1	4	6	1	1	443
Somalia	1987	47		3	2							104
Sudan	1987	154		338	14	9		4	7		6	532
Tunisia	1990	234	29	82	604	121	507	407	273	1,240	1	3,498
West Africa												
Benin	1987	23		27	22	22	1	2	2	11	3	113
Burkina Faso	1988	10		75		1		6	9			142
Cameroon	1989	435	10	246	231	10	21	244	67	8	11	1,282
Cape Verde	1989	8			17			1	2			28
Côte d'Ivoire	1987	1,956	10	378	339	60	72	229	47			3,110
Equatorial Guinea	1987	28		11								42
Gabon ᶜ	1987	6		161	1,198		19	29	2	1		1,416
Gambia	1987	11		31		18				2	1	64
Ghana	1987	456		41	53		1	67	21	4	265	909
Guinea	1987	31		402							55	488
Guinea-Bissau	1987	3		4				1				8
Liberia	1987	27		339	2	3		1	3		6	382
Nigeria	1987	361		46	6,875	1	1	2			97	7,383
Sao Tomé e Príncipe	1987	4		1								7
Senegal	1990	271	3	106	97	130	117	29	18	12		783
Sierra Leone	1987	58	2	53	5			10		1	2	144
Togo	1989	48		173		4		12	3	2	3	245
East/Central Africa												
Angola	1987	164		8	1,880			291			6	2,349
Burundi	1989	66		3				3			5	78
Central African Republic	1989	40	2	35				59			2	140
Comoros	1980											18
Congo ᶜ	1987	15	1	33	977		1	35	2	1		1,065
Kenya	1988	655	8	122	137		32	79	21	19		1,073
Madagascar	1987	274		18	8		8	18	3	2		317
Maldives	1985	11	3		7		3	12	9		3	48
Mauritius	1987	364		3			5	34	5	488		901
Réunion	1990	148	5	1			5	6	16	5		186
Rwanda	1988	89		6							1	96
Seychelles	1989	12			17				2	1		32
Tanzania	1988	153	15	93	10		3	40	2	4	16	337
Uganda	1986	339	3	39	2			12				398
Zaire	1987	271		109	14	10	2	540	6	1	18	970
Southern Africa												
Botswana	1987	50	2	45	1	7	9	1,413	35	13	12	1,588
Lesotho	1987	2	1	3			1	11	1	6	1	47
Malawi	1987	116	142	4			1	6	5	1	1	276
Mozambique	1987	58	1	12	5			9	1		10	96
Namibia												
South Africa ᵈ	1985	765		1,459	1,458		460	3,222	413	146	8,419	16,419
Swaziland	1987	155		64	3		36	28	11	5	8	391
Zambia	1987	4	2	6	11		2	838	3	2	7	873
Zimbabwe	1987	210	259	174	4	2	17	392	18	52		1,156

Source: UN, Trade Statistics/national statistical offices

Notes: see end of section

EXTERNAL TRADE BY COMMODITY   Table No. 0510

Exports by Commodity: SITC Classification, Latest Year (% Analysis)

Units: % of total exports

	Year	0	1	2	3	4	5	6	7	8	9	Total
North America												
Canada	1991	8.1	0.7	12.8	11.6	0.2	5.6	17.1	38.3	3.7	1.9	100.0
USA	1991	7.4	1.7	6.4	3.0	0.3	10.8	8.9	47.1	10.9	3.4	100.0
South America												
Argentina	1989	42.8	0.8	5.9	3.5	9.1	7.1	21.3	6.5	2.8		100.0
Bolivia	1990	16.4		38.0	24.6	0.8	0.5	18.1		1.2		100.0
Brazil	1990	21.1	2.1	15.3	2.2	1.6	5.9	25.9	18.5	6.3	1.2	100.0
Chile	1988	22.5	0.5	27.5	0.2	0.4	3.0	42.9	0.8	1.4	0.7	100.0
Colombia	1989	37.1	0.4	4.9	32.4		3.5	10.3	1.2	9.8	0.5	100.0
Ecuador	1989	46.8		1.7	48.7		0.3	1.5	0.3	0.3	0.1	100.0
French Guiana	1990	63.3		4.4			2.2	2.2	18.9	3.3	5.6	100.0
Guyana	1979	45.2	2.1	46.7			1.6	0.9	1.7	1.2	0.3	100.0
Paraguay	1990	21.9	0.7	66.1		1.4	3.2	4.3		2.3		100.0
Peru	1988	25.5		32.2	6.7	0.1	2.3	27.8	1.6	3.8		100.0
Suriname												
Uruguay	1990	38.3	0.2	21.4		0.4	7.7	17.7	2.0	11.4	0.5	100.0
Venezuela	1988	3.8	0.8	4.0	1.3		7.7	64.5	4.7	1.7	11.6	100.0
Caribbean												
Anguilla												
Antigua	1984	3.3			11.4		5.7	5.7	28.4	37.8		100.0
Aruba												
Bahamas	1989	1.2	0.7	0.6	77.1		19.0	0.6	0.5			100.0
Barbados	1990	20.7	6.6		27.7		11.7	12.2	12.2	7.0	1.9	100.0
Bermuda	1985						56.5		8.7	7.0	17.4	100.0
British Virgin Islands	1982	30.0	70.0	110.0								100.0
Cayman Islands	1989						50.0				50.0	100.0
Cuba	1989	80.1	1.9	9.7			1.2	0.9	0.8	0.4		100.0
Dominica	1990	63.6		1.8			23.6	5.5	1.8	5.5		100.0
Dominican Republic	1985											100.0
Grenada	1987	90.6								3.1	6.3	100.0
Guadeloupe	1990	68.9	8.2	0.8			3.3	2.5	12.3	2.5		100.0
Haiti	1984	35.8					3.1	15.5		37.6		100.0
Jamaica	1989	13.9	3.5	60.9	1.6		2.4	2.1	3.1	12.5		100.0
Martinique	1990	48.6	12.0	0.7	15.9		3.3	5.8	11.2	1.8		100.0
Netherlands Antilles [a]	1987			0.5	95.6		1.3	0.3	0.9	0.5	0.6	100.0
St Kitts	1988	38.5	3.8						34.6	19.2		100.0
St Lucia	1986	69.9	2.4	1.2		2.4		8.4	4.8	10.8		100.0
St Vincent/Grenadines	1980	79.0							4.5	6.4		100.0
Trinidad and Tobago	1990	4.1	1.2	0.6	67.1		14.1	9.1	1.9	1.5		100.0
Central America												
Belize	1988	62.1		3.4			0.9			16.4	18.1	100.0
Costa Rica	1987	68.4	0.5	4.2	1.1		4.8	8.9	3.2	7.5	1.4	100.0
El Salvador	1987	69.7		4.4	1.3		6.2	12.4	1.5	4.1		100.0
Guatemala	1987	65.3	1.0	8.0	1.8		10.5	8.8	1.0	3.4		100.0
Honduras	1989											100.0
Mexico	1990	10.3	1.1	4.2	37.0		6.8	11.6	24.9	4.0		100.0
Nicaragua	1986	72.2	0.9	20.9			2.6	2.1		1.3		100.0
Panama	1989	75.1	1.7	2.4		0.7	5.1	6.7		8.1		100.0
Puerto Rico												
South Asia												
Afghanistan	1990	42.9		20.0			19.1				18.0	100.0
Bangladesh	1987	16.9	0.1	0.3	1.3			36.2	1.4	35.5	0.3	100.0
Bhutan	1986											100.0
India	1988	15.7	0.6	8.1	2.6	0.1	6.0	42.9	7.2	14.9	2.1	100.0
Nepal	1987	22.7		16.6		3.9	0.1	34.5	0.1	22.2		100.0
Pakistan	1989	11.3	0.1	17.4	0.9		0.5	49.0	0.9	19.4	0.4	100.0
Sri Lanka	1987	35.0		11.3	5.9	0.7	1.0	10.8	1.6	33.5		100.0

EXTERNAL TRADE BY COMMODITY   Table No. 0510 (cont'd)

Exports by Commodity: SITC Classification, Latest Year (% Analysis)

Units: % of total exports

	Year	0	1	2	3	4	5	6	7	8	9	Total
Japan												
Japan	1991	0.5	0.1	0.6	0.4		5.5	11.8	71.0	8.5	1.6	100.0
ASEAN/NICs												
Brunei	1986	0.4			97.2			0.3	1.4	0.3		100.0
Hong Kong	1990	2.2	1.8	1.9	0.7		5.3	17.9	25.8	43.8	0.7	100.0
Indonesia	1990	8.9	0.5	7.7	43.8	1.6	2.4	22.1	1.4	11.0	0.5	100.0
Macau	1989	0.7	0.4	1.0			1.0	13.2	2.1	81.6		100.0
Malaysia	1990	4.3		14.4	17.8	7.1	1.7	8.0	36.1	10.0	0.4	100.0
Philippines	1988	14.9	0.5	10.0	2.2	6.0	3.6	9.8	9.8	13.5	29.7	100.0
Singapore	1990	2.9	1.5	3.1	18.2	0.8	6.2	7.0	50.1	9.0	1.3	100.0
South Korea	1990	3.1		1.5	1.1		3.8	22.3	39.3	28.4	0.3	100.0
Taiwan	1987	5.5		1.5	0.8		2.6	20.1	32.3	37.1		100.0
Thailand	1987	36.3	0.5	8.9	0.7	0.1	1.7	16.5	11.9	22.5	0.9	100.0
East/SE Asia												
Cambodia												
China	1990	10.8	0.6	5.7	8.4		6.0	20.6	17.4	28.2	1.9	100.0
Laos												
Mongolia												
Myanmar	1989	19.9		38.4	1.7		1.3	4.9		0.5	32.8	100.0
North Korea												
Vietnam	1991	5.9	0.6	3.7	25.5	0.3	18.2	24.6	29.0	2.8	0.9	100.0
Australasia												
Australia	1991	17.4	0.5	19.4	19.5	0.1	2.6	12.2	7.4	2.4	18.6	100.0
New Zealand	1991	46.9	0.4	18.2	3.3	0.7	6.2	14.9	4.6	3.2	1.7	100.0
Pacific												
American Samoa	1983	31.6	5.3	10.5		42.1			5.3			100.0
Fiji	1988	53.4		4.4	0.8		0.6	3.3	0.3	4.1	16.8	100.0
French Polynesia	1988	1.3		1.3		4.0	1.3	32.0	38.7	9.3	10.7	100.0
Guam	1983											100.0
Kiribati	1990	50.0				25.0						100.0
Nauru												
New Caledonia	1986	1.1		22.8				56.6				100.0
Papua New Guinea	1989	17.2		67.7	0.1	4.5		0.9	3.5	0.2	5.5	100.0
Solomon Islands	1987	50.0		39.1		4.7					6.3	100.0
Tonga	1988	50.0				12.5		12.5		12.5	12.5	100.0
Tuvalu												
Vanuatu	1988											100.0
Western Samoa	1983	18.5	7.4	25.9		40.7					7.4	100.0
Middle East												
Bahrain	1988			0.3	75.7		3.9	14.9	3.6	0.9		100.0
Egypt	1989	8.6		11.7	30.5		4.5	36.7	0.4	7.4		100.0
Iran												
Iraq												
Israel	1990	8.1		3.6	0.7		13.7	36.5	24.3	12.8		100.0
Jordan	1988	8.6	0.4	40.0		0.2	24.8	10.8	5.8	4.4	4.8	100.0
Kuwait	1989	5.9		2.5	2.9		25.9	20.3	27.1	11.7	3.2	100.0
Lebanon												
Oman	1990	15.9	1.1	2.4	2.4	0.4	3.3	16.6	41.5	10.3	6.1	100.0
Qatar	1981				93.9		3.9	2.2				100.0
Saudi Arabia	1989	1.3		0.7	84.9		9.1	1.3			2.2	100.0
Syria	1989	11.4		5.3	39.2		11.8	21.5	0.5	10.1		100.0
United Arab Emirates	1986	17.1	1.2	2.1	2.9		5.1	27.9	23.6	13.4	6.5	100.0
Yemen	1985											100.0

EXTERNAL TRADE BY COMMODITY

Table No. 0510 (cont'd)

Exports by Commodity: SITC Classification, Latest Year (% Analysis)

Units: % of total exports

	Year	0	1	2	3	4	5	6	7	8	9	Total
North Africa												
Algeria	1988		0.2	0.6	94.8		0.8	1.6	1.6			100.0
Chad	1987	18.0		67.6	9.9		0.9	1.8	0.9		0.9	100.0
Djibouti	1987										85.7	100.0
Ethiopia	1988	74.8		18.8	3.1	0.5	1.2			1.2		100.0
Libya	1988				93.9		6.1					100.0
Mali	1987	8.4		60.9				30.7				100.0
Mauritania	1987	49.8		49.1		0.2		0.7				100.0
Morocco	1989	25.9		22.8	2.6		16.0	9.6	4.4	18.3		100.0
Niger	1987	14.9	0.2	80.4	1.4		0.2	0.9	1.4	0.2	0.2	100.0
Somalia	1987	45.2		2.8	1.9							100.0
Sudan	1987	28.9		63.5	2.6	1.7		0.8	1.3		1.1	100.0
Tunisia	1990	6.7	0.8	2.3	17.3	3.5	14.5	11.6	7.8	35.4		100.0
West Africa												
Benin	1987	20.4		23.9	19.5	19.5	0.9	1.8	1.4	9.7	2.7	100.0
Burkina Faso	1988	7.0		52.8		0.7		4.2	6.3			100.0
Cameroon	1989	33.9	0.8	19.2	18.0	0.8	1.6	19.0	5.2	0.6	0.9	100.0
Cape Verde	1989	28.6		0.9	60.7			3.6	7.1			100.0
Côte d'Ivoire	1987	62.9	0.3	12.2	10.9	1.9	2.3	7.4	1.5			100.0
Equatorial Guinea	1987	66.7		26.2								100.0
Gabon [b]	1987	0.4		11.4	84.6		1.3	2.0	0.1	0.1		100.0
Gambia	1987	17.2		48.4		28.1				3.1	1.6	100.0
Ghana	1987	50.2		4.5	5.8		0.1	7.4	2.3	0.4	29.2	100.0
Guinea	1987	6.4		82.4							11.3	100.0
Guinea-Bissau	1987	37.5		50.0				10.0				100.0
Liberia	1987	7.1		88.7	0.5	0.8		0.3	0.8		1.6	100.0
Nigeria	1987	4.9		0.6	93.1						1.3	100.0
Sao Tomé e Príncipe	1987	57.1		14.3								100.0
Senegal	1990	34.6	0.4	13.5	12.4	16.6	14.9	3.7	2.3	1.5		100.0
Sierra Leone	1987	40.3	1.4	36.8	3.5			6.9		0.7	1.4	100.0
Togo	1989	19.6		70.6		1.6		4.9	1.2	0.8	1.2	100.0
East/Central Africa												
Angola	1987	7.0		0.3	80.0			12.4			0.3	100.0
Burundi	1989	84.6		3.8				3.8			6.4	100.0
Central African Republic	1989	28.6	1.7	25.0				42.1			1.4	100.0
Comoros	1980											100.0
Congo [b]	1987	1.4	0.1	3.1	91.7		0.1	3.3	0.2	0.1		100.0
Kenya	1988	61.0	0.7	11.4	12.8		3.0	7.4	2.0	1.8		100.0
Madagascar	1987	86.4		5.7	2.5		2.5	5.7	0.9	0.8		100.0
Maldives	1985	22.1	6.5	0.6	15.4		6.3	25.3	17.7		6.1	100.0
Mauritius	1987	40.4		0.3			0.6	3.8	0.6	54.2		100.0
Réunion	1990	79.6	2.7	0.5			2.7	3.2	8.6	2.7		100.0
Rwanda	1988	92.7		6.3							1.0	100.0
Seychelles	1989	37.5			53.1				6.3	3.1		100.0
Tanzania	1988	45.4	4.5	27.6	3.0		0.9	11.9	0.6	1.2	4.7	100.0
Uganda	1986	85.2	0.8	9.8	0.5			3.0				100.0
Zaire	1987	27.9		11.2	1.4	1.0	0.2	55.7	0.6	0.1	1.9	100.0
Southern Africa												
Botswana	1987	3.1	0.1	2.8	0.1	0.4	0.6	89.0	2.2	0.8	0.8	100.0
Lesotho	1987	4.3	2.1	6.4			2.1	23.4	2.1	12.8	2.1	100.0
Malawi	1987	42.0	51.4	1.4			0.5	2.2	1.8	0.4	0.4	100.0
Mozambique	1987	60.4	1.0	12.5	5.2			9.4	1.0		10.4	100.0
Namibia												
South Africa [c]	1985	4.7		8.9	8.9		2.8	19.6	2.5	0.9	51.3	100.0
Swaziland	1987	39.6		16.4	0.8		9.2	7.2	2.8	1.3	2.0	100.0
Zambia	1987	0.5	0.2	0.7	1.3		0.2	96.0	0.3	0.2	0.8	100.0
Zimbabwe	1987	18.2	22.4	15.1	0.3	0.2	1.5	33.9	1.6	4.5		100.0

Source: UN, Trade Statistics/national statistical offices/Euromonitor

Notes: see end of section

Notes to Tables in Section Five

Table 0501   a Billion units of national currency
                b Million US dollars
                c Data for 1992 are estimated
                d Imports (fob)
                e Data for 1990 are estimated
                f Data are US dollar equivalents from July 1987 onwards
                g Data from 1986 not comparable (exclude Aruba)
                h Data for 1991 are estimated
                i Imports from India only (approx. 95% of total)
                j Imports (fob) 1990 and 1991
                k Southern Africa Customs Union (SACU). Includes Botswana, Lesotho, Namibia, South Africa and Swaziland

Table 0502   a Billion units of national currency
                b Million US dollars
                c Data for 1992 are estimated
                d Data from 1986 not comparable (exclude Aruba).
                e Data for 1991 are estimated
                f South Africa Customs Union (SACU). Includes Botswana, Lesotho, Namibia, South Africa and Swaziland. Separate data are given for individual countries where available

Table 0503   Entries showing 0.0 denote values of less than $0.05 million
Data for Asia do not include Japan
                a Imports are fob
                b Data refer to 1990
                c Data refer to YAR only

Table 0504   Entries showing 0.0 denote values of less than 0.05 per cent
Data for Asia do not include Japan
                a Imports are fob
                b Data refer to 1990
                c Data refer to YAR only

Table 0505   Entries showing 0.0 denote values of less than $0.05 million
Data for Asia do not include Japan
                a Data refer to 1990
                b Data refer to YAR only

Table 0506   Entries showing 0.0 denote values of less than 0.05 per cent
Data for Asia do not include Japan
                a Data refer to 1990
                b Data refer to YAR only

Table 0507   Entries showing 0 denote values of less than $0.5 million
                a Data refer to Aruba and Curaçao only
                b Million units of national currency
                c Thousand Australian dollars
                d Data exclude trade with other countries comprising the customs and economic union of Central Africa

e Southern Africa Customs Union (SACU). Includes Botswana, Lesotho, Namibia, South Africa and Swaziland
f Imports (fob)

Table 0508   a Data refer to Aruba and Curaçao only
                b Data exclude trade with other countries comprising the customs and economic union of Central Africa
                c Southern Africa Customs Union (SACU). Includes Botswana, Lesotho, Namibia South Africa and Swaziland
                d Imports (fob)

Table 0509   Entries showing 0 denote values of less than $0.5 million
                a Data refer to Aruba and Curaçao only
                b Million units of national currency
                c Data exclude trade with other countries comprising the customs and economic union of Central Africa
                d Southern Africa Customs Union (SACU). Includes Botswana, Lesotho, Namibia, South Africa and Swaziland

Table 0510   Entries showing 0.0 denote values of less than 0.05 per cent
                a Data refer to Aruba and Curaçao only
                b Data exclude trade with other countries comprising the customs and economic union of Central Africa
                c Southern Africa Customs Union (SACU). Includes Botswana, Lesotho, Namibia, South Africa and Swaziland

Tables 0507-0510:
        SITC Classification:
        0 Food and live animals
        1 Beverages and tobacco
        2 Crude materials, excluding fuels
        3 Mineral fuels, etc
        4 Oils and fats
        5 Chemicals
        6 Basic manufactures
        7 Machinery and transport equipment
        8 Miscellaneous and manufactured goods
        9 Other

Section Six
Labour Force Indicators

EMPLOYMENT	Table No. 0601

General Level of Employment 1977-1991

Units: '000

	1977	1980	1983	1985	1986	1987	1988	1989	1990	1991	% change 1977-91
North America											
Canada [a]	9,651	10,708	10,675	11,221	11,531	11,861	12,245	12,486	12,572	12,340	27.9
USA [a]	92,017	99,303	100,834	107,150	109,597	112,440	114,968	117,342	117,914	116,877	27.0
Regional total	*101,668*	*110,011*	*111,509*	*118,371*	*121,128*	*124,301*	*127,213*	*129,828*	*130,486*	*129,217*	*27.1*
South America											
Argentina [b]			3,663								
Bolivia [c]	1,589	1,720	1,679	1,686	1,661	1,670	1,769	1,662	1,843		
Brazil [a,d]	40,179		48,466	53,237	55,436	57,410	58,729				
Chile [e,f]	2,821	3,257	3,216	3,721	3,896	4,011	4,266	4,425	4,460	4,540	61.0
Colombia [b]	2,530	3,202	3,221	3,100	3,248	3,443	3,572	3,668	4,325	4,611	82.2
Ecuador											
French Guiana	13	14									
Guyana											
Paraguay [a,g]			334	407	412	426	448	490	486	495	
Peru [a]	4,827	5,195	5,586	5,782	6,214						
Suriname	98	99	102								
Uruguay [h]	478	476	491	519	500	577	577	594	597		
Venezuela [a,i]	3,781	4,245	4,908	5,106	5,396	5,694	5,954	6,115	6,402		
Regional total	*56,316*		*71,666*	*73,558*	*76,762*	*73,231*	*75,314*				
Caribbean											
Anguilla											
Antigua											
Aruba											
Bahamas [j]	71				97						
Barbados [a]	87	99	96	92	96	98	100	107	105	101	16.3
Bermuda		30	32	32	33	35	36	36		35	
British Virgin Islands			5	5	6	7					
Cayman Islands											
Cuba [a,k]	2,487	2,607	2,961	3,164	3,294	3,347	3,445				
Dominica											
Dominican Republic											
Grenada		39									
Guadeloupe											
Haiti [a]	1,894	1,954	1,878				1,789				
Jamaica [a]	676	699	742	782	809	845	872	881			
Martinique											
Netherlands Antilles [c,k,l]	78	76	84	60	59	54					
St Kitts	22		15								
St Lucia											
St Vincent/Grenadines		33									
Trinidad and Tobago [e]	371	388	399	400	391	372	372	366	374		
Regional total	*5,686*	*5,923*	*6,212*				*6,614*				
Central America											
Belize		46									
Costa Rica [a,m]	659	725	768	827	854	923	951	987	1,017	1,007	52.8
El Salvador [n]					299		717	790	885	890	
Guatemala	709	756	584	632	660	679	780	788	786		
Honduras	971	996	956	1,304			1,354	1,394	1,213	1,494	54.0
Mexico [k]	3,868	5,166	5,935	6,700	6,884	7,355	7,765	8,291	8,899		
Nicaragua [b,k]	134	146	243	290	303	312	296	261	258	229	70.4
Panama [a]	471		597	627	644	678	654	686		722	53.5
Puerto Rico [a]	700	760	722	758	809	848	900	907	920	926	32.3
Regional total	*7,511*	*8,595*	*9,805*	*11,138*			*13,417*	*14,104*	*13,978*		
South Asia											
Afghanistan											
Bangladesh [o]	1,097		27,976	30,585							
Bhutan											
India [p]	20,634	22,305	24,008	24,578	25,056	25,388	25,712	25,986			
Nepal		6,754		7,540							
Pakistan [a]	21,930	24,341	25,856	26,961	27,033	28,703	28,995	29,895	30,822	29,828	36.0
Sri Lanka [q]	1,039	1,078	762	781	799		542	537	763		
Regional total	*44,700*		*78,602*	*90,445*							

EMPLOYMENT

General Level of Employment 1977-1991

Units: '000

	1977	1980	1983	1985	1986	1987	1988	1989	1990	1991	% change 1977-91
Japan											
Japan [r]	53,420	55,360	57,330	58,070	58,530	59,110	60,110	61,280	62,490	63,690	19.2
Regional total	*53,420*	*55,360*	*57,330*	*58,070*	*58,530*	*59,110*	*60,110*	*61,280*	*62,490*	*63,690*	*19.2*
ASEAN/NICs											
Brunei [s]	22	27	32	33	30						
Hong Kong [a,f,t]		2,238	2,427	2,543	2,625	2,689	2,741	2,749	2,741	2,749	
Indonesia [a]	48,315			62,457	68,338	70,402	72,518	73,908	73,425	75,851	57.0
Macau											
Malaysia [c]	3,734	4,787	5,457	5,653	5,760	5,984	6,176	6,391	6,685		
Philippines	14,323	17,154	19,366	20,327	20,926	20,795	21,497	21,849	22,532		
Singapore [a,u]	904	1,069	1,168	1,154	1,149	1,193	1,239	1,277	1,325	1,321	46.1
South Korea [a,t]	12,929	13,683	14,505	14,970	15,505	16,354	16,870	17,511	18,036	18,576	43.7
Taiwan	7,040	7,797	8,586	9,026	9,187	9,444	9,667	10,045	10,066		
Thailand [a]	18,138	22,524	22,911	24,227	26,691	27,639	29,464				
Regional total	*105,405*			*140,390*	*150,211*	*154,500*	*160,172*				
East/SE Asia											
Cambodia											
China [c]	393,770	418,960	464,360	498,730	512,820	527,830	543,340	553,290	567,400	583,640	48.2
Laos		1,839		2,014							
Mongolia		623		714							
Myanmar [a]		13,208	14,185	14,792	15,130	15,505	15,813	16,086	15,221		
North Korea		8,007		8,234							
Vietnam	22,187										
Regional total											
Australasia											
Australia [a,v]	5,995	6,284	6,300	6,697	6,975	7,129	7,398	7,728	7,872	7,713	28.7
New Zealand [r,t]	1,248	1,275	1,278	1,341	1,544	1,554	1,502	1,461	1,472	1,451	16.3
Regional total	*7,243*	*7,559*	*7,578*	*8,038*	*8,519*	*8,683*	*8,900*	*9,189*	*9,344*	*9,164*	*26.5*
Pacific											
American Samoa [a]	8	8	9	10	10						
Fiji [k]	72	80	80	81	80	78	78	88	89	92	26.4
French Polynesia [k]	25		36	40	41	42	38	42			
Guam [a]	32	32	32	32	34	35	36	38			
Kiribati											
Nauru											
New Caledonia				33	34	38	40	44			
Papua New Guinea [w]	101	68									
Solomon Islands		20	21	24	24	25	22	25	26	27	
Tonga											
Tuvalu											
Vanuatu											
Western Samoa											
Regional total	*239*	*209*	*178*	*220*	*223*	*218*	*214*	*237*			
Middle East											
Bahrain [a]	128	133	101	112		86	86	92	92	93	-27.8
Egypt [c]	9,198	9,799	11,526								
Iran											
Iraq											
Israel [a,f]	1,159	1,254	1,339	1,349	1,368	1,404	1,453	1,461	1,492	1,583	36.6
Jordan											
Kuwait											
Lebanon											
Oman		169	286	342	316						
Qatar											
Saudi Arabia											
Syria [a]	1,894		2,126								
United Arab Emirates											
Yemen		497		565							
Regional total											

EMPLOYMENT

General Level of Employment 1977-1991

Units: '000

	1977	1980	1983	1985	1986	1987	1988	1989	1990	1991	% change 1977-91
North Africa											
Algeria	2,337	3,145	3,633	3,884		4,138		4,418			
Chad					9	9	11	11			
Djibouti											
Ethiopia											
Libya	765										
Mali											
Mauritania											
Morocco											
Niger [k]	31	26	20	23	26	28	26	28			
Somalia											
Sudan	5,012	6,086		6,991							
Tunisia	1,480	1,609			1,874						
Regional total											
West Africa											
Benin [k]	39	66	81	81	77	78	78				
Burkina Faso											
Cameroon	213	282	349								
Cape Verde											
Côte d'Ivoire		470	433	406	410	406	405	400	385		
Equatorial Guinea		102		111							
Gabon	139	502		518							
Gambia [r,x]	27		29	24	21	26					
Ghana [k]			312	464	414	394	307				
Guinea											
Guinea-Bissau											
Liberia	40										
Nigeria		32,087		36,568							
Sao Tomé e Príncipe											
Senegal [c]	107			85	86						
Sierra Leone [y]	61	70	74	69	74	67					
Togo		46	67	61	62	64					
Regional total											
East/Central Africa											
Angola [k]			356	377	368						
Burundi [b,k]	34	38	41	45	47	50	54	58			
Central African Republic		24	18	20	16						
Comoros											
Congo		649		710							
Kenya [k,z]	903	1,006	1,093	1,174	1,221	1,265	1,311	1,356	1,409		
Madagascar	99										
Maldives											
Mauritius [k]	194	197	192	210	231	252	267	270	278		
Rwanda		2,671									
Réunion											
Seychelles	16	18	18	18	18	19	21	22	24		
Tanzania	484	636	633								
Uganda		6,163		7,054							
Zaire		11,745		13,006							
Regional total											
Southern Africa											
Botswana [c,f,i]	63	83	101	117	130	150	170	176	209	223	255.3
Lesotho											
Malawi	322	370	391	415	432	407	432	441			
Mozambique [k]						193	202				
Namibia											
South Africa											
Swaziland [k]	66	75	79	73	76	83					
Zambia [z]	370	379	364	362	361	362	361	360			
Zimbabwe [r,z]	1,012	1,010	1,033	1,061							
Regional total											

Source: International Labour Office (ILO)/national statistical offices
Notes: see end of section

UNEMPLOYMENT Table No. 0602

Trends in Total Unemployed 1977-1991

Units: '000

	1977	1980	1983	1985	1986	1987	1988	1989	1990	1991	% change 1977-91
North America											
Canada	849.0	865.0	1,434.0	1,311.0	1,215.0	1,150.0	1,031.0	1,018.0	1,109.0	1,417.0	66.9
USA	6,991.0	7,637.0	10,717.0	8,312.0	8,237.0	7,425.0	6,701.0	6,528.0	6,874.0	8,426.0	20.5
Regional total	*7,840.0*	*8,502.0*	*12,151.0*	*9,623.0*	*9,452.0*	*8,575.0*	*7,732.0*	*7,546.0*	*7,983.0*	*9,843.0*	*25.5*
South America											
Argentina [a]	103.3	82.2	159.4	216.2	177.8	230.5	251.2	322.6			
Bolivia	88.9	105.9	277.6	370.9	415.4	430.7	388.4	443.2	433.4		
Brazil [b]	953.0		2,474.0	1,875.0	1,380.0	2,133.0	2,319.0				
Chile [c,d]	378.5	378.4	551.9	516.5	374.2	343.5	286.1	249.8	268.9	253.6	-33.0
Colombia [a]	261.0	320.8	377.0	499.9	482.8	429.0	403.0	356.5	491.6	501.6	92.2
Ecuador						89.5	155.3	187.0			
French Guiana [a]	0.8	1.1	2.4	4.2	3.7	3.4	3.3	3.8	4.4	4.7	459.5
Guyana [a]	2.4	15.6	7.2	13.3	10.6	9.2					
Paraguay											
Peru	298.2	391.1	565.9	773.2	554.1						
Suriname [e,f]	3.0	2.4	10.7	17.0	13.4	2.8	3.0	2.4			
Uruguay [a,g]	64.1	40.0	89.7	77.9	64.2	48.4	57.1	98.4	105.7		
Venezuela [g]	192.6	272.4	552.0	767.1	668.1	573.5	478.2	621.1	741.7		
Regional total	*2,345.8*		*5,067.8*	*5,131.2*	*4,144.3*						
Caribbean											
Anguilla											
Antigua											
Aruba											
Bahamas [h]	19.4				13.5		13.7	14.9			
Barbados	17.7	14.5	16.9	21.2	20.7	21.4	21.2	17.1	18.6	20.9	18.1
Bermuda											
British Virgin Islands											
Cayman Islands											
Cuba											
Dominica											
Dominican Republic											
Grenada											
Guadeloupe	1.4	14.3	18.6	24.2	27.2	27.8	29.5	30.8	29.4	34.3	2,385.5
Haiti											
Jamaica	215.1	261.8	266.0	260.8	250.4	224.3	203.3	177.4	166.6		
Martinique		32.0	24.6	29.5	33.9	30.7	31.4	30.8	30.2		
Netherlands Antilles [i]		17.8	20.1	17.2	17.9	17.6	13.3	11.7	11.2	9.4	
St Kitts											
St Lucia											
St Vincent/Grenadines											
Trinidad and Tobago [j]	57.5	42.4	50.0	72.8	81.2	106.6	104.7	103.4			
Regional total											
Central America											
Belize											
Costa Rica [f]	31.8	45.6	76.2	60.8	56.7	54.5	54.9	62.1	49.5	59.1	85.8
El Salvador											
Guatemala	0.3	0.3	3.6	2.7	2.7	2.2	1.9	1.7	1.8		
Honduras	104.8	117.0	254.2								
Mexico [a]	472.1										
Nicaragua				34.6	51.8	66.6	71.8	107.2	145.6	193.4	
Panama	45.0		64.2	88.3	75.8	91.1	127.8	133.7		134.0	197.8
Puerto Rico [k]	174.0	156.0	220.0	211.0	188.0	171.0	158.0	155.0	152.0	176.0	1.1
Regional total											
South Asia											
Afghanistan											
Bangladesh											
Bhutan											
India	10,513.0	15,317.0	20,802.0	24,861.0	28,261.0	30,542.0	30,050.0	32,776.0	34,632.0	36,300.0	245.3
Nepal											
Pakistan	155.3	144.3	152.3	212.3	224.6	247.6	265.5	251.8			
Sri Lanka											
Regional total											

UNEMPLOYMENT

Trends in Total Unemployed 1977-1991

Units: '000

	1977	1980	1983	1985	1986	1987	1988	1989	1990	1991	% change 1977-91
Japan											
Japan	1,100.0	1,140.0	1,560.0	1,560.0	1,670.0	1,730.0	1,550.0	1,420.0	1,340.0	1,360.0	23.6
Regional total	*1,100.0*	*1,140.0*	*1,560.0*	*1,560.0*	*1,670.0*	*1,730.0*	*1,550.0*	*1,420.0*	*1,340.0*	*1,360.0*	*23.6*
ASEAN/NICs											
Brunei	1.9	2.3	2.1								
Hong Kong [d,j]	83.0	87.5	113.8	83.6	76.1	47.5	38.0	30.0	37.0	50.3	-39.4
Indonesia	153.5	232.8	353.5	785.2	855.0	1,017.2	1,352.4	1,518.5	1,238.7		
Macau											
Malaysia	122.7	86.2	67.5	80.7	86.9	78.6	78.8	70.8			
Philippines	671.0	856.0	1,003.0	1,316.0	1,438.0	2,085.0	1,954.0	2,009.0	1,993.0		
Singapore [l]	36.9	33.5	38.8	49.8	79.6	58.8	42.9	28.1	22.7	30.0	-18.6
South Korea [h]	511.0	748.0	613.0	622.0	611.0	519.0	435.0	459.0	451.0	436.0	-14.7
Taiwan	107.0	82.0	197.0	222.0	212.0	160.9					
Thailand [m]	190.6	204.2	1,146.8	1,337.0	968.7	1,721.6	929.2				
Regional total	*1,877.5*	*2,332.5*	*3,535.5*	*4,496.3*	*4,327.2*	*5,688.6*					
East/SE Asia											
Cambodia											
China [a]		5,415.0	2,714.0	2,385.0	2,644.0	2,766.0	2,960.0	3,779.0	3,832.0	3,522.0	
Laos											
Mongolia											
Myanmar	296.8	486.0	430.4	338.0	354.4	331.4	312.7	485.8	555.3		
North Korea											
Vietnam											
Regional total											
Australasia											
Australia [l]	359.3	394.5	697.0	602.9	613.1	628.9	576.2	509.1	587.1	821.0	128.5
New Zealand	7.4	36.5	76.5	53.2	67.2	88.1	120.9	153.6	164.0	196.0	2,555.8
Regional total	*366.7*	*431.0*	*773.5*	*656.1*	*680.3*	*717.0*	*697.1*	*662.7*	*751.1*	*1,017.0*	*177.3*
Pacific											
American Samoa	1.4	1.1	1.4	1.5	1.6						
Fiji	0.3										
French Polynesia		0.1	0.9	0.9	1.0	0.5	0.7	0.6	0.6		
Guam	2.0	3.5	3.3	2.7	2.2	1.6	1.6	1.1	1.3		
Kiribati	2.0										
Nauru											
New Caledonia [f,n]	0.8	1.0	1.5	1.5	1.6	4.5	5.0	5.2	5.7		
Papua New Guinea											
Solomon Islands											
Tonga											
Tuvalu											
Vanuatu											
Western Samoa											
Regional total											
Middle East											
Bahrain			3.5	6.3	6.7	4.0	4.5	3.4	3.0	3.3	
Egypt	296.1	535.9	812.7								
Iran											
Iraq	9.6										
Israel [d]	47.4	64.0	63.2	97.0	104.2	90.1	100.0	142.5	158.0	187.2	294.9
Jordan											
Kuwait											
Lebanon											
Oman											
Qatar											
Saudi Arabia											
Syria	100.3		92.1								
United Arab Emirates											
Yemen											
Regional total											

UNEMPLOYMENT

Table No. 0602 (cont'd)

Trends in Total Unemployed 1977-1991

Units: '000

	1977	1980	1983	1985	1986	1987	1988	1989	1990	1991	% change 1977-91
North Africa											
Algeria											
Chad			4.5		4.5	3.7	5.0	10.7			
Djibouti											
Ethiopia		86.1	57.2	56.4	52.6	58.2	55.3	51.3	44.2	44.3	
Libya											
Mali											
Mauritania											
Morocco	22.4	16.4	23.3	30.2							
Niger	9.5	24.4	19.5	29.0	27.7	27.2	26.1	24.6			
Somalia											
Sudan		78.3	38.8	48.8	63.1			25.4	70.1	19.9	
Tunisia	79.2	66.6	72.1	84.0	80.2	83.7	91.5	105.9			
Regional total											
West Africa											
Benin											
Burkina Faso [a]	5.0	2.7									
Cameroon [a]	38.4	41.7	44.8	14.3	25.5	19.2					
Cape Verde											
Côte d'Ivoire	6.5		59.1								
Equatorial Guinea											
Gabon											
Gambia											
Ghana	31.9	40.0	23.7	24.2	25.8	26.3	28.7	27.4	30.0		
Guinea											
Guinea-Bissau											
Liberia											
Nigeria	15.8	16.9	31.0	28.3	32.5	57.3	60.5	57.6	57.1		
Sao Tomé e Príncipe											
Senegal [a]	4.6	12.2	11.8	10.8	10.2	8.1	17.3				
Sierra Leone	9.2	8.9	2.8	0.3	0.3						
Togo			4.8	4.1							
Regional total											
East/Central Africa											
Angola				56.1	69.4						
Burundi			3.4	1.9	6.8	8.2	9.3	11.1	14.5		
Central African Republic	7.3	8.8	11.0	8.2	9.1	8.7	8.2				
Comoros											
Congo											
Kenya											
Madagascar [a]	46.5	40.6	29.5								
Maldives											
Mauritius	17.1	32.0	73.0	64.8	54.6	46.8	27.7	18.1	12.8	10.6	-37.9
Rwanda											
Réunion	17.3	31.0	33.8	45.0	51.6	52.8	56.7	59.5	56.5		
Seychelles		0.6	4.0	5.7							
Tanzania											
Uganda											
Zaire											
Regional total											
Southern Africa											
Botswana											
Lesotho											
Malawi											
Mozambique											
Namibia											
South Africa [f]		533.0	483.0	495.0	519.0	1,018.0	874.0	755.0			
Swaziland											
Zambia											
Zimbabwe											
Regional total											

Source: ILO/national statistical offices
Notes: see end of section

EMPLOYMENT	Table No. 0603

Level of Paid Employment in Manufacturing 1977-1991

Units: '000

	1977	1980	1983	1985	1986	1987	1988	1989	1990	1991	% change 1977-91
North America											
Canada [a]	1,888.0	1,613.7	1,738.6	1,703.9	1,739.2	1,892.1	1,903.7	1,878.4	1,794.5		
USA	20,889.0	20,285.0	18,434.0	19,260.0	18,965.0	19,024.0	19,350.0	19,442.0	19,111.0	18,426.0	-11.8
Regional total	*22,777.0*	*21,898.7*	*20,172.6*	*20,963.9*	*20,704.2*	*20,916.1*	*21,253.7*	*21,320.4*	*20,905.5*		
South America											
Argentina [b]		180.6	149.3	151.2							
Bolivia	160.5	177.1	33.9	28.0	43.7	25.5	23.3				
Brazil [c,d]	6,510.0		6,775.0	5,080.0	5,851.0	5,710.0	5,736.0				
Chile [e,f]	472.2	524.1	405.9	494.7	531.3	606.9			725.7		
Colombia	647.1	821.0	465.1	439.9	456.1	469.7	475.3				
Ecuador		111.7	94.3	96.9	101.7	108.1		110.0			
French Guiana	1.0	0.7									
Guyana											
Paraguay [g]	124.0	139.5									
Peru [h]	741.2	812.5	71.7	71.5	75.8	82.2	80.3	72.2			
Suriname			5.5	5.2	6.5	5.0	4.9	5.0	4.9		
Uruguay [b,i]	139.6		110.5	123.0	111.3	142.3	135.5	142.0	140.5		
Venezuela [j]	628.6		453.5	790.4	878.1	978.0					
Regional total			*8,564.6*	*7,280.8*							
Caribbean											
Anguilla											
Antigua											
Aruba											
Bahamas [k]	3.2				4.9						
Barbados	14.8		11.5	9.6	9.9	9.2	10.8	11.3			
Bermuda		1.1	1.1	1.2	1.1	0.9				1.1	
British Virgin Islands			0.2	0.2	0.3	0.4					
Cayman Islands											
Cuba [l]	550.5	565.7	639.2	695.1	711.9	722.5					
Dominica											
Dominican Republic			149.8	140.8							
Grenada											
Guadeloupe											
Haiti	116.6	132.1	121.7								
Jamaica	73.6	73.0	90.8	98.6	115.3	131.4	131.1	136.4	136.1		
Martinique											
Netherlands Antilles [m]	11.1	10.1	7.8	5.6	5.3	4.7					
St Kitts	1.5		2.2								
St Lucia			2.1								
St Vincent/Grenadines											
Trinidad and Tobago [c,j]	72.4		67.5	59.1	53.7	51.4					
Regional total			*1,093.9*								
Central America											
Belize											
Costa Rica [b,n]	104.1	95.9	98.3	100.0	112.5	122.4			137.4	138.1	32.7
El Salvador [o]		54.3	50.6	49.0	47.2	47.1					
Guatemala	84.5	80.7	77.8	78.2	78.3	78.4	103.4	101.3	103.3		
Honduras	111.6	127.8	125.5								
Mexico		2,066.0	2,089.0	2,387.0	2,371.0	2,546.0			3,021.0		
Nicaragua [b]	30.5	30.1	53.8	57.0	59.7	61.6			45.4		
Panama	48.5		49.6	51.0	48.8	55.6					
Puerto Rico	139.0	154.6	143.7	147.5	148.8	151.0			154.9		
Regional total		*2,609.4*	*2,688.3*	*2,869.7*	*2,866.3*	*3,062.1*					
South Asia											
Afghanistan											
Bangladesh [a]	368.4	418.0	448.9	468.6							
Bhutan											
India [p]	5,391.0	5,862.0	6,289.0	6,183.0	6,263.0	6,272.0					
Nepal											
Pakistan	2,989.0	3,264.0	3,582.0		3,560.0						
Sri Lanka [o]	194.7	180.0	162.4	169.0	179.1		140.9	109.0	236.8		
Regional total											

EMPLOYMENT

Table No. 0603 (cont'd)

Level of Paid Employment in Manufacturing 1977-1991

Units: '000

	1977	1980	1983	1985	1986	1987	1988	1989	1990	1991	% change 1977-91
Japan											
Japan	13,400.0	11,350.0	11,750.0	12,350.0	12,290.0	12,150.0			13,060.0	13,570.0	1.3
Regional total	*13,400.0*	*11,350.0*	*11,750.0*	*12,350.0*	*12,290.0*	*12,150.0*			*13,060.0*	*13,570.0*	*1.3*
ASEAN/NICs											
Brunei		2.2	2.8	2.9	2.7						
Hong Kong [f,q]		907.5	855.4	847.6	865.5	867.9			715.6	629.2	
Indonesia [q]	4,171.0	969.1	1,119.8	1,684.7	1,691.4						
Macau											
Malaysia			489.8								
Philippines	1,561.0	2,207.8	1,169.0	1,303.0	1,267.0	1,412.0	1,552.0	1,610.0	2,188.0		
Singapore	245.5	292.0	301.6	274.3	270.0	298.7				408.6	66.4
South Korea	1,702.0	2,341.0	2,703.0	2,997.0	3,164.0	3,675.0			4,198.0	4,215.0	147.6
Taiwan	1,767.0	2,138.0	2,305.0	2,488.0	2,614.0	2,810.0					
Thailand [a,i]	1,329.2	1,788.7	2,189.6	2,280.0	2,068.8	2,437.8					
Regional total			*11,136.0*								
East/SE Asia											
Cambodia											
China			51,260.0	55,561.0	57,811.0	59,715.0			53,040.0	54,428.0	
Laos											
Mongolia											
Myanmar		1,009.0	1,150.0	1,234.0							
North Korea											
Vietnam	-										
Sub total											
Australasia											
Australia [o,r]	1,276.8	1,240.0	1,132.0	1,028.7	1,038.7	1,060.4		1,062.7	1,056.6	935.5	-26.7
New Zealand [q]	316.0	267.1	254.6	271.7	287.0	277.7	251.0	233.6	225.6	220.1	-30.3
Regional total	*1,592.8*	*1,507.1*	*1,386.6*	*1,300.4*	*1,325.7*	*1,338.1*		*1,296.3*	*1,282.2*	*1,155.6*	*-27.4*
Pacific											
American Samoa											
Fiji	11.3	15.4	14.7	14.1	14.0	13.7			21.1	23.4	108.0
French Polynesia	2.9		1.7	1.8	2.0	2.1					
Guam [s]	1.0	1.2	1.2	1.1	1.3	1.8			1.9		
Kiribati											
Nauru											
New Caledonia		4.7	4.2	4.3	4.4	4.5					
Papua New Guinea	12.6	6.9	21.6								
Solomon Islands		2.1	1.8	1.8	1.9	2.3	2.3	2.3	2.3	2.1	
Tonga											
Tuvalu											
Vanuatu											
Western Samoa											
Regional total											
Middle East											
Bahrain			16.5	17.6		17.0					
Egypt	1,353.4	1,146.4	1,296.7								
Iran											
Iraq											
Israel [a,i]	277.6	280.4	297.2	301.2	304.9	322.7	311.2	292.0	315.0	330.8	19.2
Jordan [o]	12.5	13.2	19.1	26.3	23.1	23.8	28.6	34.6			
Kuwait											
Lebanon											
Oman											
Qatar											
Saudi Arabia											
Syria	256.3		281.3								
United Arab Emirates											
Yemen											
Regional total											

EMPLOYMENT

Level of Paid Employment in Manufacturing 1977-1991

Units: '000

	1977	1980	1983	1985	1986	1987	1988	1989	1990	1991	% change 1977-91
North Africa											
Algeria											
Chad					0.5	1.7	3.4	2.0			
Djibouti											
Ethiopia		76.6	83.4	88.1	90.8	95.0					
Libya	41.7										
Mali											
Mauritania											
Morocco											
Niger	1.5	2.7	1.5	2.4	2.5	2.5	3.0	2.9			
Somalia											
Sudan											
Tunisia	289.0	339.7									
Regional total											
West Africa											
Benin	1.6	6.5	5.6	8.3							
Burkina Faso											
Cameroon	49.9	88.6									
Cape Verde											
Côte d'Ivoire		73.5	68.6								
Equatorial Guinea											
Gabon	17.1										
Gambia ᵒ	3.9		4.0	1.4	2.4	2.4					
Ghana			43.0	51.7	53.6	78.6	43.6				
Guinea											
Guinea-Bissau											
Liberia	1.5	13.2									
Nigeria											
Sao Tomé e Príncipe											
Senegal	30.5										
Sierra Leone	6.0	7.4	8.0	8.1	8.3	7.5					
Togo		6.7	6.6	5.2	5.0	5.1					
Regional total											
East/Central Africa											
Angola			57.8	62.0	66.1						
Burundi ᵇ	2.8	3.9	3.4	5.6	5.9	6.2	6.5	7.4	7.0		
Central African Republic		3.3	5.5	7.8	5.3						
Comoros											
Congo											
Kenya ᵗ	117.9	141.3	148.8	158.8	164.8	169.8	170.3	178.7			
Madagascar											
Maldives											
Mauritius	33.2	36.4	38.3	62.9	83.9	99.9	106.3	107.8	107.8	108.5	226.5
Rwanda											
Réunion											
Seychelles ᵘ		1.1	1.0	1.1	1.8	2.1	2.5	2.5			
Tanzania		109.1	83.2								
Uganda											
Zaire											
Regional total											
Southern Africa											
Botswana ᶠʲ	4.2	5.6	9.8	9.9	12.2	14.8	16.5	18.1	24.3	26.0	526.5
Lesotho											
Malawi	33.7	39.7	38.5	46.2	52.9	49.6	52.4	51.4			
Mozambique											
Namibia											
South Africa ᵛ		1,421.4	1,465.8	1,429.0	1,415.5	1,427.8	1,448.5	1,458.8	1,462.1		
Swaziland	8.4	9.3	11.3	10.6	10.9	11.4	13.6				
Zambia	45.8	47.8	48.8	48.5	48.9	50.0	50.4	50.9			
Zimbabwe ᵗ	145.1	159.4	173.4	169.6	176.9	177.4	183.7	195.3	197.0		
Regional total											

Source: ILO/national statistical offices

Notes: see end of section

HOURS OF WORK — Table No. 0604

Average Working Week in Non-Agricultural Activities 1977-1991

Units: Hours

	1977	1980	1983	1985	1986	1987	1988	1989	1990	1991	% change 1977-91
Argentina											
Australia [a]	35.0	34.5	39.6	40.1	34.1	34.5	34.9	34.6	34.8	34.4	-1.7
Brazil											
Canada			32.4	32.5	32.3	32.0	32.1	31.8	31.5	31.0	
Chile			42.4	43.0	44.4	44.4	45.3	44.3	44.9	45.2	
China											
Colombia											
Ecuador											
Hong Kong		53.1	47.8	47.6	47.6	47.0	47.9	46.7	46.0	46.5	
India											
Indonesia											
Israel	36.5	35.8	35.2	35.3	35.7	35.6	35.6	36.1	35.9	35.9	-1.6
Japan	40.3	40.6	40.4	40.6	40.4	40.6	40.6	40.2	39.5	38.8	-3.7
Malaysia		45.0	43.9								
Mexico											
New Zealand [b]	39.4	38.9	38.9	39.6	38.9	38.8	38.6	38.8	38.7		
Nigeria											
Pakistan											
Peru		46.0	49.6	46.5	47.9	47.8	49.5	48.5	48.5		
Philippines											
Singapore [c]	48.3	48.6	49.1	48.0	48.5	49.0	45.6	46.6	46.5	46.7	-3.3
South Africa											
South Korea	51.4	51.6	52.5	51.9	52.5	51.9	51.1	49.2	48.2	47.9	-6.8
Taiwan											
Thailand [d]			216.2	220.5	212.7	220.8	222.4	225.8			
USA	36.0	35.3	35.0	34.9	34.8	34.8	34.7	34.6	34.5	34.3	-4.7
Venezuela	42.9	43.8	41.9	40.7	41.3	40.5					
Vietnam											

Source: ILO

Notes: see end of section

HOURS OF WORK — Table No. 0605

Average Working Week in Manufacturing 1977-1991

Units: Hours

	1977	1980	1983	1985	1986	1987	1988	1989	1990	1991	% change 1977-91
Argentina [a]		186.7	177.9	179.7	188.4						
Australia [b]	37.6	37.4	35.5	36.9	37.0	37.3	37.9	37.7	38.1	37.4	-0.5
Brazil											
Canada	38.7	38.5	38.4	38.8	38.7	38.8	38.8	38.6	38.2	37.8	-2.3
Chile [c]			43.2	43.1	44.3	44.1	44.0	43.2	44.9	45.3	
China											
Colombia											
Ecuador		45.0	44.0								
Hong Kong		49.1	45.5	44.8	45.2	44.5	45.9	44.8	44.0	45.2	
India			46.2		45.7	46.1	46.4	46.4			
Indonesia											
Israel		38.6	38.2	38.6	38.8	38.3	38.3	39.3	38.9	39.1	
Japan		46.0	46.2	46.2	46.0	46.3	46.8	46.3	45.7		
Malaysia		47.0	45.2								
Mexico	45.5	46.6	43.0	46.4	46.4	44.2	44.9	45.1	45.4	45.5	
New Zealand [d]	40.3	39.6	39.5	40.7	39.6	40.2	39.9	40.5	40.7	40.4	0.2
Nigeria											
Pakistan											
Peru		45.6	47.8	44.8	48.5	47.4	48.5	46.7	47.5	44.9	
Philippines		46.2	46.5	47.0	48.1	49.4					
Singapore [e]	48.8	48.6	48.9	47.0	48.5	49.2	47.4	48.6	48.5	48.7	-0.2
South Africa	46.5	48.4	46.2	46.2	46.6	46.8	47.3	46.9	45.9	41.4	-11.0
South Korea	52.9	53.1	54.4	53.8	54.7	54.0	52.6	50.7	49.8	49.3	-6.8
Taiwan						48.4					
Thailand [a]			215.0	211.5	216.6	211.6	218.0	219.4			
USA		39.7	40.1	40.5	40.7	41.0	41.1	41.0	40.8	40.7	
Venezuela	43.7	44.1	43.3	40.6	40.7	40.2					
Vietnam											

Source: ILO

Notes: see end of section

ECONOMICALLY ACTIVE POPULATION — Table No. 0606

Economically Active Population by Sex: Latest Year

Units: '000

	Year	Total ('000)	Males ('000)	% Total EAP	Females ('000)	% Total EAP
North America						
Canada [a,b]	1991	13,757.0	7,569	55.0	6,188	45.0
USA	1991	126,867.0	69,810	55.0	57,057	45.0
South America						
Argentina	1990	12,305.3	8,871	72.1	3,434	27.9
Bolivia	1991	924.9	538	58.2	387	41.8
Brazil [a]	1991	61,048.0	39,632	64.9	21,416	35.1
Chile	1991	4,794.1	3,323	69.3	1,471	30.7
Colombia	1991	5,112.2	2,933	57.4	2,179	42.6
Ecuador	1990	3,359.7	2,471	73.6	888	26.4
French Guiana	1990	48.7	30	61.8	19	38.2
Guyana	1987	270.1	189	70.1	81	29.9
Paraguay	1990	520.2	302	58.0	218	42.0
Peru [a]	1991	2,523.2	1,533	60.7	991	39.3
Suriname	1989	98.4	58	59.1	40	40.9
Uruguay	1990	1,241.9	738	59.4	504	40.6
Venezuela	1990	7,245.7	4,963	68.5	2,283	31.5
Caribbean						
Anguilla						
Antigua						
Aruba						
Bahamas	1989	127.4	67	52.7	60	47.3
Barbados	1991	122.3	64	52.2	59	47.8
Bermuda	1987	35.2	19	52.8	17	47.2
British Virgin Islands	1987	6.5	4	56.9	3	43.1
Cayman Islands	1989	15.8	8	52.5	8	47.5
Cuba	1988	4,570.2	2,921	63.9	1,650	36.1
Dominica	1989	30.6	18	58.2	13	41.8
Dominican Republic	1981	1,915.4	1,361	71.1	554	28.9
Grenada	1988	38.9	20	51.4	19	48.6
Guadeloupe	1990	172.4	94	54.5	79	45.5
Haiti	1990	2,679.1	1,607	60.0	1,072	40.0
Jamaica	1990	1,060.1	567	53.5	493	46.5
Martinique	1982	130.5	72	55.3	58	44.7
Netherlands Antilles	1990	56.6	34	59.2	23	40.8
St Kitts	1984	14.8	9	60.1	6	39.9
St Lucia	1980	49.5	22	44.6	27	55.2
St Vincent/Grenadines	1980	34.7	22	64.0	13	36.0
Trinidad and Tobago [c]	1990	467.8	308	65.9	159	34.0
Central America						
Belize	1980	47.3	37	77.3	11	22.6
Costa Rica	1991	1,065.7	747	70.1	319	29.9
El Salvador [b]	1991	962.8	529	54.9	434	45.1
Guatemala	1989	2,898.3	2,158	74.5	740	25.5
Honduras	1991	1,566.6	1,099	70.2	468	29.8
Mexico	1990	24,063.3	18,419	76.5	5,645	23.5
Nicaragua	1991	1,386.3	926	66.8	461	33.2
Panama [a]	1989	820.0	548	66.9	272	33.2
Puerto Rico [b]	1992	1,096.0	683	62.3	413	37.7
South Asia						
Afghanistan	1982	3,829.0	3,511	91.7	318	8.3
Bangladesh	1986	30,920.0	27,690	89.6	3,230	10.4
Bhutan	1981	638.0				
India	1981	244,605.0	181,080	74.0	63,525	26.0
Nepal [a]	1981	6,850.9	4,480	65.4	2,371	34.6
Pakistan [a]	1992	32,814.0	28,154	85.8	4,660	14.2
Sri Lanka	1990	6,968.8	4,372	62.7	2,596	37.3

ECONOMICALLY ACTIVE POPULATION

Table No. 0606 (cont'd)

Economically Active Population by Sex: Latest Year

Units: '000

	Year	Total ('000)	Males ('000)	% Total EAP	Females ('000)	% Total EAP
Japan						
Japan	1991	65,050.0	38,540	59.2	26,510	40.8
ASEAN/NICs						
Brunei	1981	70.7	54	76.2	17	23.8
Hong Kong [b]	1991	2,798.8	1,753	62.6	1,046	37.4
Indonesia	1989	75,508.1	45,360	60.1	30,148	39.9
Macau	1990	228.5	134	58.6	94	41.3
Malaysia [a]	1990	6,685.0	4,311	64.5	2,374	35.5
Philippines [b]	1990	25,311.0	15,946	63.0	9,364	37.0
Singapore [b]	1990	1,347.4	822	61.0	526	39.0
South Korea [b]	1991	19,012.0	11,355	59.7	7,657	40.3
Taiwan	1984	7,308.0	4,619	63.2	2,689	36.8
Thailand	1988	30,393.2	16,138	53.1	14,255	46.9
East/SE Asia						
Cambodia	1985	4,095.0	2,505	61.2	1,590	38.8
China [b]	1982	524,907.0	295,252	56.2	229,656	43.8
Laos	1980	1,839.0	990	53.8	849	46.2
Mongolia	1985	714.0	475	66.5	239	33.5
Myanmar	1988	15,847.0				
North Korea	1985	9,234.0	4,979	53.9	4,255	46.1
Vietnam	1985	24,241.0	14,137	58.3	10,104	41.7
Australasia						
Australia [b]	1990	8,459.1	4,953	58.6	3,506	41.4
New Zealand [b]	1991	1,607.7	909	56.5	699	43.5
Pacific						
American Samoa	1980	8.5	5	61.0	3	39.2
Fiji [d]	1990	250.0	190	76.0	51	20.5
French Polynesia	1988	75.4	47	62.9	28	37.1
Guam [b]	1988	37.4	22	58.6	15	41.2
Kiribati	1985	25.4	16	63.8	9	36.2
Nauru						
New Caledonia	1989	65.9	41	62.5	25	37.5
Papua New Guinea	1985	1,694.0	1,006	59.4	688	40.6
Solomon Islands [e]	1986	24.0	20	84.6	4	15.4
Tonga	1986	24.3	19	78.6	5	21.4
Tuvalu						
Vanuatu	1989	67.0	36	53.7	31	46.3
Western Samoa	1985	41.5	35	84.8	6	14.9
Middle East						
Bahrain [a]	1987	74.0	60	80.7	14	19.3
Egypt	1986	13,349.2	11,890	89.1	1,459	10.9
Iran [a]	1986	12,854.7	11,535	89.7	1,320	10.3
Iraq	1987	3,956.3	3,496	88.4	460	11.6
Israel [b]	1991	1,770.4	1,043	58.9	728	41.1
Jordan	1979	446.3	413	92.5	33	7.5
Kuwait	1988	730.0	553	75.7	177	24.3
Lebanon						
Oman						
Qatar	1982	112.4	103	91.7	9	8.3
Saudi Arabia	1980	2,751.0	2,579	93.7	172	6.3
Syria [a,b]	1989	3,068.8	2,596	84.6	473	15.4
United Arab Emirates	1980	560.0	532	94.9	28	5.1
Yemen [f]	1975	1,127.6	996	88.3	132	11.7

ECONOMICALLY ACTIVE POPULATION   Table No. 0606 (cont'd)

Economically Active Population by Sex: Latest Year

Units: '000

	Year	Total ('000)	Males ('000)	% Total EAP	Females ('000)	% Total EAP
North Africa						
Algeria	1987	5,341.1	4,849	90.8	492	9.2
Chad	1988	2,032.4	1,548	76.1	485	23.9
Djibouti	1985	161.0	98	60.9	63	39.1
Ethiopia	1991	22,343.3	13,404	60.0	8,939	40.0
Libya	1985	939.0	863	91.9	76	8.1
Mali	1985	2,599.0	2,162	83.2	437	16.8
Mauritania	1985	546.0	431	78.9	115	21.1
Morocco	1985	6,702.0	5,382	80.3	1,320	19.7
Niger	1985	3,405.0	1,791	52.6	1,614	47.4
Somalia	1985	2,569.0	1,550	60.3	1,019	39.7
Sudan	1985	7,037.0	5,576	79.2	1,461	20.8
Tunisia	1989	2,360.6	1,866	79.1	494	20.9
West Africa						
Benin	1986	1,446.6	932	64.4	515	35.6
Burkina Faso	1985	4,067.1	2,078	51.1	1,989	48.9
Cameroon	1987	4,269.0	2,627	61.5	1,643	38.5
Cape Verde	1985	125.0	89	71.2	36	28.8
Côte d'Ivoire [a]	1988	4,262.8	2,886	67.7	1,376	32.3
Equatorial Guinea	1985	177.0	105	59.3	72	40.7
Gabon	1985	597.0	368	61.6	229	38.4
Gambia	1985	346.0	209	60.4	137	39.6
Ghana	1985	4,632.0	2,752	59.4	1,880	40.6
Guinea	1985	2,708.0	1,604	59.2	1,104	40.8
Guinea-Bissau	1988	279.1	270	96.7	9	3.3
Liberia	1985	805.0	554	68.8	251	31.2
Nigeria	1986	30,765.5	20,514	66.7	10,252	33.3
Sao Tomé e Príncipe	1985	46.0	29	63.0	17	37.0
Senegal	1990	2,433.1	1,801	74.0	633	26.0
Sierra Leone	1985	1,374.0	911	66.3	463	33.7
Togo	1985	1,254.0	784	62.5	470	37.5
East/Central Africa						
Angola	1985	3,693.0	2,228	60.3	1,465	39.7
Burundi	1991	2,779.8	1,317	47.4	1,463	52.6
Central African Republic	1985	1,337.0	709	53.0	628	47.0
Comoros	1985	190.0	111	58.4	79	41.6
Congo	1985	807.0	490	60.7	317	39.3
Kenya	1985	8,242.0	4,871	59.1	3,371	40.9
Madagascar	1985	4,496.0	2,682	59.7	1,814	40.3
Maldives	1990	56.4	45	80.1	11	19.9
Mauritius	1991	462.6	300	64.8	163	35.2
Réunion	1990	233.6	138	58.9	96	41.1
Rwanda	1989	3,143.1	1,462	46.5	1,681	53.5
Seychelles	1989	29.5	17	57.6	13	42.4
Tanzania	1985	10,272.0	5,247	51.1	5,025	48.9
Uganda	1985	7,147.0	4,149	58.1	2,998	41.9
Zaire [a]	1985	11,926.0	7,564	63.4	4,362	36.6
Southern Africa						
Botswana	1985	368.0	173	47.0	195	53.0
Lesotho	1985	722.0	400	55.4	322	44.6
Malawi	1987	3,300.2	1,599	48.5	1,701	51.5
Mozambique	1985	7,565.0	3,884	51.3	3,681	48.7
Namibia						
South Africa [a]	1991	10,215.3	6,027	59.0	4,189	41.0
Swaziland	1985	312.0	187	59.9	125	40.1
Zambia	1985	2,221.0	1,595	71.8	626	28.2
Zimbabwe	1987	3,260.0	1,701	52.2	1,559	47.8

Source: ILO/national statistical offices

Notes: see end of section

EMPLOYMENT

Table No. 0607

Employment by Activity: Latest Year

Units: % of total workforce

	Year	A	B	C	D	E	F	G	H	I	J	Total
North America												
Canada	1991	4.5	1.4	15.1	1.1	5.2	23.8	6.3	11.9	30.2	0.5	100.0
USA	1991	2.9	0.6	17.5	1.3	6.1	20.6	5.7	11.3	34.0		100.0
South America												
Argentina [a,b,c]	1980	12.0	0.6	19.9	1.0	10.0	17.0	4.6	4.0	24.0	6.9	100.0
Bolivia	1991	1.2	2.1	15.6	0.6	6.5	25.7	7.6	3.0	37.3	0.4	100.0
Brazil [b,c]	1991	23.3		14.7	1.7	6.1	11.1	3.6	5.7	30.0	3.8	100.0
Chile	1991	19.1	2.2	16.6	0.5	7.0	17.1	6.8	5.0	25.7		100.0
Colombia	1991	1.2	0.4	23.4	0.8	5.5	26.0	6.0	7.7	28.8	0.2	100.0
Ecuador [b]	1990	30.8	0.6	11.0	0.4	5.9	14.2	3.9	2.4	24.9	5.9	100.0
French Guiana [b,c]	1982	11.4	0.5	4.2	1.2	8.7	6.3	4.2	11.3	27.6	24.6	100.0
Guyana	1980	25.0	4.8	14.4	1.4	3.4	7.5	4.7	1.5	29.5	7.8	100.0
Paraguay	1991	1.2	0.2	15.8	1.1	9.2	26.6	5.7	6.8	33.4		100.0
Peru [b]	1991	0.9	0.4	19.3	0.3	4.9	31.8	6.3	5.7	24.0	6.4	100.0
Suriname	1990		4.0	7.3	1.9	3.6	5.0	5.0	2.7	70.5		100.0
Uruguay	1990		5.1	21.3		6.6	17.9	6.1	4.8	38.2		100.0
Venezuela	1990	12.7	1.0	15.5	1.0	7.5	20.9	6.1	6.0	29.1	0.2	100.0
Caribbean												
Anguilla												
Antigua												
Aruba												
Bahamas [b,c]	1989	3.9	0.3	3.3	1.2	7.8	28.5	7.0	6.7	28.1	13.2	100.0
Barbados	1991	5.5		10.1	1.7	8.4	15.8	4.7	3.8	41.2	8.8	100.0
Bermuda	1989	1.1	0.3	3.0	1.4	8.0	32.6	6.9	13.8	32.9		100.0
British Virgin Islands	1987	1.5		6.1	3.0	7.6	9.1	6.1	4.5	62.1		100.0
Cayman Islands [b,c]	1991	1.4		1.3	1.9	16.0	30.2	7.3	16.6	24.2	1.1	100.0
Cuba	1988	19.2	1.0	19.8	1.1	9.4	12.7	7.0	1.8	27.9		100.0
Dominica [b,c]	1989	25.2		10.8	1.0	8.5	9.5	5.2	2.3	18.6	18.9	100.0
Dominican Republic [a,b,c]	1981	23.6	0.3	12.6	0.8	4.5	10.7	2.2	1.3	20.4	23.6	100.0
Grenada [b,c]	1988	14.3	0.3	7.3	1.0	9.1	13.9	4.4	2.0	15.3	32.4	100.0
Guadeloupe [b,c,d]	1982	13.1		2.8	0.5	8.1	8.1	3.9	12.2	21.1	30.2	100.0
Haiti [b,c]	1990	57.3	0.9	5.7	0.1	1.0	13.2	0.8	0.2	5.8	15.0	100.0
Jamaica	1990	26.1	0.8	15.2		6.6		4.7	16.2	29.9	0.5	100.0
Martinique	1982	10.4	2.0	4.2	1.1	8.3	10.4	5.5	18.9	31.1	8.1	100.0
Netherlands Antilles	1989		0.8	9.6	2.1	9.0	24.4	8.7	9.9	35.5		100.0
St Kitts	1984	29.6		14.7	7.0	2.7	6.4	3.0	1.9	31.8	2.9	100.0
St Lucia	1970	38.0	19.3			13.1	3.9	3.9	20.6		1.2	100.0
St Vincent/Grenadines [b,c]	1980	25.7	0.3	5.1	1.2	10.2	7.4	5.4	1.0	21.8	21.9	100.0
Trinidad and Tobago [b,c]	1990	10.8	4.5	10.0	1.8	13.9	17.3	6.6	6.0	28.5	0.6	100.0
Central America												
Belize [a]	1980	31.2	0.1	8.8	1.3	3.7	11.9	3.6	0.8	18.9	19.7	100.0
Costa Rica	1991	25.4	0.1	18.7	1.1	6.3	15.6	4.3	3.7	23.7	1.1	100.0
El Salvador [b,c,d,e]	1991	10.4	0.1	22.1	0.8	5.5	24.6	5.3	2.9	26.0	2.3	100.0
Guatemala	1990	35.5	0.4	13.1	1.6	2.3	10.7	2.7		33.5	0.2	100.0
Honduras	1991	38.0	0.4	14.9	2.4	5.5	14.2	3.0	1.7	19.8	0.1	100.0
Mexico [b,c]	1990	22.0	1.1	18.7	0.6	6.6	16.1	4.5	3.3	21.1	6.0	100.0
Nicaragua	1991	13.3	0.6	16.1	2.4	3.9	9.1	4.1	6.2	41.4	2.5	100.0
Panama	1991	26.6	0.2	9.4	1.3	3.2	20.0	6.8	4.3	27.7	0.5	100.0
Puerto Rico [b,c,d]	1992	3.6	0.2	17.2	1.3	7.4	19.7	3.5	2.5	43.8	0.8	100.0
South Asia												
Afghanistan [b]	1979	61.3	1.5	10.9	0.3	1.3	3.6	1.7	19.4			100.0
Bangladesh [b,c]	1985	56.6		10.4	0.3	1.9	12.2	4.0	3.1	6.7	4.8	100.0
Bhutan												
India [a]	1989	5.5	4.1	24.0	3.5	4.8	1.7	11.8	5.2	39.4		100.0
Nepal [b]	1981	89.7		0.5			1.6	0.1	0.1	4.5	3.5	100.0
Pakistan	1991	46.4	0.2	12.2	0.8	6.6	13.2	5.3	0.9	13.3	1.1	100.0
Sri Lanka	1990	42.0	0.6	31.1	1.5	3.1	9.3	3.0	5.9	3.5		100.0

EMPLOYMENT   Table No. 0607 (cont'd)

Employment by Activity: Latest Year

Units: % of total workforce

	Year	A	B	C	D	E	F	G	H	I	J	Total
Japan												
Japan	1991	6.7	0.1	24.4	0.5	9.5	22.5	6.0	8.4	21.5	0.4	100.0
ASEAN/NICs												
Brunei [e]	1986	2.3	16.0	9.0		30.7	21.3	4.7	6.7	9.3		100.0
Hong Kong [b,c,d]	1991	0.8		25.5	0.7	8.0	26.1	9.8	8.2	19.1	1.8	100.0
Indonesia [b,c]	1989	54.7	0.6	9.8	0.2	2.4	14.4	2.9	0.5	11.7	2.8	100.0
Macau [b,c]	1990	0.2		31.4	1.1	8.5	20.9	4.5	3.3	26.7	3.4	100.0
Malaysia [b]	1988	30.6	0.5	16.0	0.7	5.5	18.1	4.3	3.7	20.6		100.0
Philippines [b,c,d]	1990	41.5	0.5	9.0	0.4	4.0	12.8	4.6	1.8	17.2	8.2	100.0
Singapore [b,c,d]	1991	0.3		27.6	0.5	6.4	22.2	9.8	10.5	20.8	1.9	100.0
South Korea [b,c,d]	1991	16.3	0.4	26.0	0.4	8.1	21.5	5.2	5.3	14.6	2.2	100.0
Taiwan	1987	15.3	0.4	35.0	0.3	6.9	17.9	5.4	2.9	15.9		100.0
Thailand [b,c,d]	1988	64.4	0.1	8.1	0.4	2.3	9.5	2.2		9.9	3.1	100.0
East/SE Asia												
Cambodia												
China [b,c,d]	1989	7.9	7.7	33.1	1.5	5.7	9.7	6.3	1.3	25.8	1.0	100.0
Laos												
Mongolia	1984	14.5	31.0			9.8	14.5	15.6			14.6	100.0
Myanmar [b,c]	1990	67.6	0.5	7.2	0.1	1.1	8.9	2.5	6.1		6.0	100.0
North Korea												
Vietnam												
Australasia												
Australia [b,d]	1990	5.3	1.2	15.1	1.3	7.5	20.1	6.7	11.1	28.8	2.9	100.0
New Zealand [b,c,d]	1991	8.9	0.3	14.6	0.7	5.3	17.9	5.3	10.1	23.1	13.8	100.0
Pacific												
American Samoa	1980	1.2		20.6	7.6	6.6	10.1	2.3	2.3	39.3	10.0	100.0
Fiji	1990	2.6	1.6	23.7	2.9	6.4	16.7	10.7	6.3	29.1		100.0
French Polynesia	1989	1.9	0.2	4.8	0.9	11.5	20.6	21.0	6.1	33.1		100.0
Guam	1987	0.5		4.1	3.6	10.2	18.3	5.2	4.5	17.7	36.0	100.0
Kiribati												
Nauru												
New Caledonia [b]	1989	11.8	1.4	7.1	0.9	6.7	14.3	4.7	3.8	33.4	15.9	100.0
Papua New Guinea [b,c]	1980	77.0	0.6	1.9	0.4	2.9	3.4	2.4	0.7	10.5	0.2	100.0
Solomon Islands	1990	28.8		8.7	1.1	5.4	10.1	5.2	3.3	37.4		100.0
Tonga [b,c]	1986	42.9	0.1	2.5	1.4	7.1	6.7	4.8	1.9	22.6	10.0	100.0
Tuvalu												
Vanuatu [b,c]	1989	61.4		1.3	0.2	2.0	4.1	1.5	1.0	11.8	16.7	100.0
Western Samoa [b]	1986	63.6	3.5		1.9	0.1	3.7	3.3	1.8	20.7	1.4	100.0
Middle East												
Bahrain	1990	0.8	1.0	18.6	3.0	32.4	16.8	9.8	6.3	10.1	1.2	100.0
Egypt [b,c,f]	1986	35.7	0.3	11.3	0.7	6.5	6.4	5.0	1.8	19.7	12.6	100.0
Iran [b]	1986	25.0	0.3	11.4	0.7	9.4	6.8	4.9	0.9	23.7	16.9	100.0
Iraq [b,c]	1987	12.5	1.1	6.7	0.9	8.6	5.4	5.7	0.8	49.4	8.9	100.0
Israel [b,c,e]	1991	3.1	19.2		1.0	5.4	12.7	5.5	9.1	32.8	11.2	100.0
Jordan [g]	1989		3.0	15.4	2.0	2.2	4.8	5.3	4.9	62.4		100.0
Kuwait [b,c]	1988	1.3	0.9	7.2	1.2	15.7	11.4	5.2	3.0	52.6	1.5	100.0
Lebanon	1985	22.8		9.9	2.3	5.5	17.2	4.5	37.8			100.0
Oman												
Qatar												
Saudi Arabia [f]	1985	0.2	4.4	12.4	2.5	23.6	19.9	5.9	4.5	6.7	19.9	100.0
Syria [b,c,e]	1989	22.0	0.3	14.8	1.0	11.7	12.2	6.0	1.3	26.9	3.8	100.0
United Arab Emirates	1980	6.4	1.4	9.3	3.0	17.1	14.9	10.6	2.8	34.5		100.0
Yemen [b]	1975	73.6	0.1	3.0	0.1	4.7	6.1	2.2	0.2	7.6	2.4	100.0

EMPLOYMENT

Employment by Activity: Latest Year

Units: % of total workforce

	Year	A	B	C	D	E	F	G	H	I	J	Total
North Africa												
Algeria [b,c,e]	1987	13.6	1.3	9.6	0.8	12.9	7.3	4.1	2.7	22.1	25.6	100.0
Chad	1989	7.9	3.5	17.5	0.9	14.9	30.7	1.8	3.5	19.3		100.0
Djibouti [g]	1982		3.8		2.1	21.7	9.4	3.0	21.7	14.5	23.8	100.0
Ethiopia [b,c]	1984	88.2	0.1	1.6	0.1	0.3	3.8	0.4	0.1	5.1	0.3	100.0
Libya	1978	19.1	2.6	6.1	2.0	21.2	6.1	8.7	1.2	24.7	8.3	100.0
Mali [b]	1980	85.5		0.1		12.4					2.0	100.0
Mauritania												
Morocco [b]	1982	39.2	1.1	15.5	0.4	7.3	8.3	2.3	16.8		9.1	100.0
Niger	1989	3.4	14.5	10.2	12.4	12.7	11.0	8.1	4.2	20.5	3.0	100.0
Somalia	1978	6.4	13.5				24.0	7.1	1.4	23.6	24.0	100.0
Sudan [b,c]	1983	63.5	0.1	4.2	0.7	2.2	4.6	3.4	0.3	8.7	12.3	100.0
Tunisia [b,c]	1989	21.6		16.2	1.5	10.5	13.9			18.8	17.5	100.0
West Africa												
Benin	1985	7.5	0.5	10.3	1.4	6.7	11.2	11.1	3.1	48.2		100.0
Burkina Faso												
Cameroon [b,c]	1985	74.0	0.1	4.4	0.1	1.7	4.0	1.3	0.2	7.5	6.7	100.0
Cape Verde [b]	1980	33.2	0.8	2.9	0.5	28.3	5.9	5.1	0.4	22.9		100.0
Côte d'Ivoire	1983	17.3	15.9			5.2	7.9	14.2		39.5		100.0
Equatorial Guinea [b,c]	1983	57.9	0.1	1.5	0.2	1.8	3.0	1.7	0.4	8.2	25.2	100.0
Gabon	1985	11.7	3.7	41.8			9.3	10.5	13.7		9.3	100.0
Gambia [h]	1987	7.7		9.2	3.5	11.5	16.9	11.9	3.8	35.4		100.0
Ghana [i]	1987	8.1	7.1	19.9	1.7	4.6	4.6	4.6	4.6	44.8		100.0
Guinea [b]	1983	78.1	0.7	0.6	0.2	0.6	2.0	1.6	0.2	7.5	8.5	100.0
Guinea-Bissau [b]	1979	70.2	0.1	1.3	0.1	0.8	2.3	1.1	0.1	12.0	12.0	100.0
Liberia	1980	71.6	5.1	1.3	0.9		3.8	1.5	10.0		5.8	100.0
Nigeria [b,c]	1986	43.1		4.1	0.4	1.8	24.2	3.6	0.4	15.9	6.5	100.0
Sao Tomé e Príncipe [b]	1981	52.9	5.2		0.9	5.8	6.4	3.3	0.5	18.7	6.3	100.0
Senegal	1982	8.1	1.5	23.4	2.5	6.4	11.2	18.9	6.0	10.9	11.1	100.0
Sierra Leone [a]	1987	10.5	10.2	11.1	3.3	10.8	7.4	11.1	2.7	32.9		100.0
Togo [b,c]	1981	64.3	0.3	6.0	0.3	2.3	11.6	2.3	0.3	7.0	5.6	100.0
East/Central Africa												
Angola	1986	20.3		18.0		5.9	8.7	7.5	0.4	36.9	2.3	100.0
Burundi [a]	1989	14.1	0.7	11.5	1.9	18.4	7.9	5.2	3.3	34.3	2.7	100.0
Central African Republic [b,c]	1986	18.0		32.9	5.6	5.0	22.4	5.0	2.5		8.7	100.0
Comoros	1980	52.4	0.1	3.9	0.1	3.2	1.8	2.1	0.2	7.0	29.2	100.0
Congo												
Kenya [a]	1989	19.0	0.3	13.2	1.6	5.0	8.1	5.1	4.7	43.0		100.0
Madagascar												
Maldives [b,c]	1990	25.2	0.9	15.1	0.8	5.6	15.9	9.5	1.9	21.2	3.9	100.0
Mauritius [b,c]	1991	17.5		30.7	0.7	5.2	13.2	6.9	2.4	20.3	3.1	100.0
Réunion	1982	13.2	6.1			8.5	10.8	4.5	12.3	33.8	10.8	100.0
Rwanda [b]	1989	90.1	0.1	1.4	0.3	1.2	2.5	0.2	0.1	3.8	0.3	100.0
Seychelles	1989	9.9		11.2		7.7	19.7	13.9	3.1	20.6	13.9	100.0
Tanzania [b]	1984	15.0	0.9	16.4	3.7	4.0	7.0	9.9	2.9	40.1		100.0
Uganda												
Zaire												
Southern Africa												
Botswana [d]	1989	3.8	4.3	10.3	1.3	13.6	16.3	4.2	6.6	39.6		100.0
Lesotho [b,c]	1976	23.3	30.5	2.6	0.2	2.9	2.0	1.0	0.1	17.5	19.9	100.0
Malawi	1988	46.3	0.1	12.7	1.2	7.5	7.7	5.9	3.0	15.6		100.0
Mozambique [b,j]	1980	80.6	5.9			0.7	1.9	0.8	4.1	4.1	1.9	100.0
Namibia												
South Africa [a]	1990		13.2	27.8	1.0	7.9	15.4	6.9	3.6	24.2		100.0
Swaziland	1987	25.4	3.0	13.8	1.8	5.8	12.1	5.3	11.2	21.6		100.0
Zambia	1989	10.4	15.1	14.2	2.4	5.8	7.4	7.3	6.9	30.7		100.0
Zimbabwe [b,c]	1987	64.7	0.5	5.1	0.4	1.6	4.0	2.3	0.8	12.2	8.4	100.0

Source: ILO/national statistical offices

Notes: see end of section

ECONOMICALLY ACTIVE POPULATION

Table No. 0608

Economically Active Population by Age Group: Latest Year (% Analysis)

Units: % of total

	Year	0-14	15-19	20-24	25-29	30-34	35-39	40-44	45-49	50-54	55-59	60-64	64+
North America													
Canada	1991		7.2	11.0	14.0	14.6	13.6	13.0	9.7	7.2	5.3	3.0	1.4
USA	1991		5.5	10.9	13.5	14.7	13.8	12.6	9.5	7.3	5.6	3.8	2.8
South America													
Argentina	1990	1.7	9.3	13.6	13.3	12.7	11.8	10.4	8.6	7.1	5.5	3.3	2.8
Bolivia	1991	2.6	8.8	13.9	14.5	14.6	13.7	10.7	8.1	4.9	3.3	2.4	2.5
Brazil	1988	4.9	13.4	15.4	13.8	23.3		15.6		9.0	4.6		
Chile	1991		4.9	13.2	15.9	14.3	12.2	10.7	9.2	7.5	5.2	3.6	3.3
Colombia	1991	0.8	7.5	34.5		28.6		16.4		8.2	4.0		
Ecuador	1990	4.2	11.0	14.6	14.5	12.9	10.9	8.5	6.5	5.3	3.9	3.1	4.6
French Guiana	1990		3.7	13.8	17.8	17.2	15.2	11.9	8.4	5.8	3.6	1.9	0.7
Guyana	1987		14.8	19.8	16.8	13.3	10.1	7.8	6.1	5.0	3.9	2.4	
Paraguay	1990	2.1	9.6	16.5	14.4	12.4	11.3	10.4	7.2	6.1	4.3	2.8	3.0
Peru	1991	0.4	8.8	16.4	14.7	13.9	13.5	10.2	7.1	6.3	3.8	2.6	2.3
Suriname	1989		5.7	18.2	20.5	26.2		16.7		11.1	1.6		
Uruguay	1990		8.3	11.4	11.5	23.8		20.8		16.4	7.8		
Venezuela	1990		23.9		54.6				18.7			2.8	
Caribbean													
Anguilla													
Antigua													
Aruba													
Bahamas	1980		12.2	19.1	15.3	12.3	11.2	9.0	6.8	5.2	3.6	2.7	2.6
Barbados	1991		6.9	13.9	16.2	16.5	14.0	10.7	6.6	6.0	4.3	2.9	2.0
Bermuda	1986		5.0	11.9	16.3	14.6	12.3	10.1	7.8	7.4	5.8	4.4	4.4
British Virgin Islands	1980		9.1	17.8	18.5	15.4	11.3	7.4	4.9	4.9	3.9	2.9	3.9
Cayman Islands	1991		16.5	30.3		27.0		26.2					
Cuba	1988		6.8	32.1		57.4				3.7			
Dominica	1989		13.4	19.3	12.4	11.1	9.2	8.5	5.5	3.9	5.5	3.6	7.6
Dominican Republic	1981	6.0	11.6	15.2	13.9	11.3	8.7	7.6	6.3	5.8	4.6	3.2	5.8
Grenada	1988		12.0	18.7	18.4	14.2	8.5	7.2	5.6	5.7	4.6	5.1	
Guadeloupe	1990		66.0					31.2		2.8			
Haiti	1990	6.8	10.2	14.6	14.2	11.6	8.3	8.1	7.0	5.7	4.7	3.4	5.4
Jamaica	1990		10.8	18.7	25.5		17.3		13.3	8.7			5.7
Martinique	1982		7.2	19.4	14.4	12.7	10.9	9.3	9.0	7.3	5.9	2.9	1.0
Netherlands Antilles	1986		8.7	19.0	17.3	15.2	11.6	8.9	7.0	5.3	3.8	1.8	1.4
St Kitts	1980		16.1	23.5	14.2	8.0	5.7	5.0	5.2	5.5	5.0	5.0	6.8
St Lucia													
St Vincent/Grenadines	1980		25.7	26.9	22.3		7.0		8.0	6.4			3.7
Trinidad and Tobago	1990		8.4	15.8	16.7	14.5	12.4	9.7	8.7	6.0	3.6	2.2	2.0
Central America													
Belize	1980		24.2	18.5	12.2	9.2	6.8	6.6	5.8	5.4	3.7	3.0	4.6
Costa Rica	1991	2.0	11.1	16.4	14.0	26.3		16.1		8.5	5.6		
El Salvador	1991	2.5	9.5	14.9	14.0	12.3	11.4	9.4	7.7	6.2	4.5	3.0	4.6
Guatemala	1989	7.3	15.1	13.8	12.2	11.0	10.0	7.8	6.1	4.9	4.4	7.4	
Honduras	1991	3.9	14.1	27.5		31.3			16.1	7.1			
Mexico	1990	1.9	13.0	17.0	15.3	13.0	10.9	8.1	6.6	4.8	3.6	2.5	3.4
Nicaragua	1991	6.2	11.8	14.5	67.5								
Panama	1989		9.8	16.2	15.5	24.7		18.1		9.7	5.8		
Puerto Rico	1992		3.3	12.0	14.7	13.9	12.7	12.5	11.2	8.5	5.7	3.0	2.5
South Asia													
Afghanistan	1979	10.9	13.2	14.7	13.2	10.9	9.3	7.5	6.1	4.8	3.7	2.6	3.1
Bangladesh	1986	9.0	15.1	12.8	10.9	11.6	8.5	8.0	6.5	5.2	4.4	2.6	5.1
Bhutan													
India	1981	5.6	10.6	12.8	13.0	11.5	10.8	17.8		10.9	7.0		
Nepal	1981	14.2	11.8	12.9	11.6	9.7	9.2	7.8	6.5	5.6	3.5	3.4	3.8
Pakistan	1992	5.7	12.4	13.6	12.7	10.2	10.2	8.7	8.0	6.6	4.0	3.8	4.1
Sri Lanka	1990	1.3	7.9	17.6	14.5	12.8	11.6	9.6	7.6	6.1	4.7	6.3	

ECONOMICALLY ACTIVE POPULATION — Table No. 0608 (cont'd)

Economically Active Population by Age Group: Latest Year (% Analysis)

Units: % of total

	Year	0-14	15-19	20-24	25-29	30-34	35-39	40-44	45-49	50-54	55-59	60-64	64+
Japan													
Japan	1991		2.7	10.6	10.0	9.0	10.7	14.5	11.3	10.3	8.9	6.0	6.0
ASEAN/NICs													
Brunei	1981		8.1	22.0	20.8	14.2	9.6	7.6	5.8	4.5	3.0	2.1	2.3
Hong Kong	1991		4.1	13.0	17.3	16.7	13.7	11.8	6.9	6.2	4.9	3.1	2.3
Indonesia	1989	3.6	10.4	11.3	12.2	12.1	11.9	9.2	9.1	7.5	5.4	3.7	3.5
Macau													
Malaysia [a]	1990		9.4	17.8	17.0	14.5	12.0	9.8	7.4	6.2	3.5	2.4	
Philippines	1990	3.1	10.9	13.4	23.4		20.7		15.1		9.0		4.3
Singapore	1990		3.8	14.8	18.1	17.1	14.3	12.0	6.9	6.2	3.4	3.3	
South Korea	1991		3.3	11.1	13.9	15.1	12.9	11.3	9.6	9.0	6.7	3.6	3.5
Taiwan	1987		6.9	12.9	17.3	16.4	13.2	8.4	8.1	6.4	5.6	3.4	1.4
Thailand	1988	4.0	14.1	16.5	14.6	12.6	10.1	14.3		9.6		4.1	
East/SE Asia													
Cambodia													
China	1982		18.2	13.3	16.6	13.1	9.7	8.4	7.7	5.6	3.8	2.1	1.5
Laos [b]	1985	4.1	16.7	15.0	13.0	11.3	9.9	8.5	7.0	5.5	4.3	2.5	2.2
Mongolia [b]	1985	3.2	13.4	16.1	44.9				13.1		6.9		2.4
Myanmar													
North Korea [b]	1985	0.7	11.1	16.7	48.2				13.5		7.3		2.5
Vietnam													
Australasia													
Australia	1990		9.9	13.4	26.4		25.3		16.2		4.7	2.9	1.2
New Zealand	1991		8.9	12.9	13.0	13.0	12.6	12.7	9.8	7.8	5.4	2.4	1.5
Pacific													
American Samoa	1980		4.1	15.3	15.3	15.6	24.8		15.9		4.1	3.0	1.9
Fiji	1986		12.1	18.3	16.1	13.0	10.7	8.8	7.0	5.3	3.6	2.2	2.9
French Polynesia	1988	0.5	9.2	17.6	17.1	15.3	12.1	9.8	7.7	5.6	3.3	1.2	0.7
Guam	1988		6.7	13.9	26.5		24.6		21.4			6.9	
Kiribati	1978		17.3	16.3	13.7	10.7	9.7	7.5	7.8	5.9	4.5	3.4	3.2
Nauru													
New Caledonia	1989		8.2	17.1	15.9	14.1	12.6	11.2	8.9	6.2	3.5	1.4	0.9
Papua New Guinea													
Solomon Islands													
Tonga	1986		10.6	20.7	13.9	11.1	8.6	7.8	7.3	6.2	5.0	3.5	5.3
Tuvalu													
Vanuatu	1989		14.8	16.0	15.0	11.7	10.5	7.8	7.2	4.6	3.9	3.1	5.4
Western Samoa	1981	0.9	11.5	22.2	14.0	9.8	8.6	8.3	7.0	6.4	5.2	3.1	3.0
Middle East													
Bahrain	1987		6.3	24.1	19.5	12.5	8.3	7.3	6.6	5.6	4.3	2.9	2.6
Egypt	1986	4.1	9.1	16.0	15.2	12.8	12.0	8.3	7.4	5.9	4.7	2.8	1.7
Iran	1986	4.0	12.4	16.1	15.0	12.3	8.6	6.8	6.3	6.3	4.9	4.0	3.3
Iraq	1987	2.4	11.3	19.0	15.2	14.7	10.1	8.0	6.0	3.6	3.4	6.3	
Israel	1991		1.8	13.5	28.2		28.1		16.1		5.9	3.6	2.8
Jordan	1979		10.9	17.7	14.6	12.5	11.8	9.9	7.7	5.9	3.8	2.5	2.7
Kuwait	1988		1.7	12.7	19.3	20.5	16.6	11.6	8.5	5.0	2.8	1.0	0.3
Lebanon	1975	2.9	10.8	15.8	44.5				26.0				
Oman													
Qatar	1984		4.2	15.3	21.0	18.8	14.4	10.4	6.2	4.7	2.0	1.7	1.3
Saudi Arabia													
Syria	1984	3.0	13.9	14.5	44.0				5.1	19.5			
United Arab Emirates	1980		2.8	16.3	26.9	21.1	13.8	8.9	5.1	2.8	1.2	0.7	0.4
Yemen [c]	1985	3.9	11.8	15.5	46.1				12.9		7.1		2.7

ECONOMICALLY ACTIVE POPULATION

Table No. 0608 (cont'd)

Economically Active Population by Age Group: Latest Year (% Analysis)

Units: % of total

	Year	0-14	15-19	20-24	25-29	30-34	35-39	40-44	45-49	50-54	55-59	60-64	64+
North Africa													
Algeria	1987	0.2	10.1	20.2	17.0	14.2	10.3	6.9	6.5	5.8	4.5	2.3	2.3
Chad	1988	11.8	11.8	14.3	13.3	11.3	9.5	7.9	6.2	5.0	3.8	5.1	
Djibouti													
Ethiopia	1991	14.2	15.3	12.3	10.4	8.8	8.3	7.8	6.7	4.9	4.1	2.9	4.3
Libya	1973	0.9	4.8	12.7	15.7	38.5			9.4	6.4	4.2	3.0	4.4
Mali	1976	17.4	13.9	10.8	10.7	9.7	8.3	7.1	5.5	5.2	3.7	3.5	4.2
Mauritania													
Morocco	1982	6.9	13.9	15.8	14.4	10.7	7.6	7.6	6.4	6.1	4.1	3.2	3.3
Niger	1977	4.2	15.0	13.3	13.6	13.0	9.7	9.4	5.1	6.1	2.7	3.7	4.2
Somalia													
Sudan	1983	12.5	13.0	11.1	12.2	9.3	10.8	7.7	7.1	5.5	3.1	3.1	4.6
Tunisia	1989		12.0	16.4	16.6	13.7	10.4	7.4	6.4	6.3	5.1	2.7	3.1
West Africa													
Benin	1986	12.8	14.0	12.8	11.4	10.5	9.3	7.5	6.0	4.8	3.2	2.6	5.1
Burkina Faso	1985	16.1	15.4	11.9	11.0	8.6	8.1	6.5	6.0	4.9	3.9	3.2	4.4
Cameroon	1985	6.3	10.1	12.3	12.2	39.9				19.2			
Cape Verde	1980	1.0	13.1	17.3	11.2	5.9	5.8	8.3	7.9	7.2	4.2	4.0	7.8
Côte d'Ivoire	1988	11.0	11.6	15.1	14.8	11.9	9.5	7.0	6.0	4.6	3.5	2.3	2.7
Equatorial Guinea	1985	3.6	12.6	14.4	43.2				13.5	8.2			4.5
Gabon	1985	4.8	7.7	11.8	12.4	11.4	10.8	9.8	8.5	7.3	6.0	4.1	5.4
Gambia	1983	8.4	11.2	13.6	15.2	11.6	8.7	7.9	5.4	5.2	2.7	3.5	6.6
Ghana													
Guinea	1983	8.6	11.7	10.5	13.2	11.0	9.9	8.6	7.3	6.3	4.3	3.6	5.0
Guinea-Bissau	1979	15.6	9.2	10.6	12.2	8.7	8.8	6.7	6.2	4.8	3.8	4.4	9.0
Liberia	1974	2.4	5.0	8.8	13.3	46.4				7.5	5.0	4.8	6.8
Nigeria	1986	1.2	6.6	8.4	14.2	13.3	12.7	11.6	11.0	8.6	4.9	3.7	3.8
Sao Tomé e Príncipe	1981	0.9	11.8	17.7	13.0	9.2	7.8	9.6	8.5	7.3	5.6	3.7	4.9
Senegal	1990	32.6		23.7		18.1		11.1		7.8	6.6		
Sierra Leone													
Togo	1981	4.4	10.8	12.8	15.9	22.3		15.3		8.3	10.2		
East/Central Africa													
Angola	1980	2.5	13.6	16.5	45.5				12.3	6.7			2.9
Burundi	1986	12.6	12.2	15.3	14.7	11.3	8.1	6.2	5.1	4.3	3.5	2.7	4.0
Central African Republic	1985	4.0	7.7	9.1	9.5	9.8	9.7	9.7	9.6	9.2	8.7	7.6	5.4
Comoros	1980	4.9	10.4	12.1	12.2	11.5	9.6	10.2	6.2	7.1	3.3	5.1	7.4
Congo	1985	5.6	10.9	12.9	12.8	30.4			7.7	6.5	5.2	3.8	4.2
Kenya													
Madagascar	1975	9.8	14.1	13.4	11.3	8.5	8.8	7.7	7.0	6.1	4.8	3.7	4.8
Maldives	1990	0.7	11.8	17.8	15.2	11.8	8.7	6.2	7.7	6.8	5.3	4.3	3.7
Mauritius	1991		8.7	15.9	17.2	15.4	13.7	10.7	6.7	5.1	4.2	1.3	1.1
Réunion	1990		4.6	17.7	19.8	15.5	13.5	10.3	7.8	6.1	3.5	1.0	0.2
Rwanda	1978	8.5	19.0	17.1	12.2	8.1	7.3	6.8	5.7	5.0	3.9	3.1	3.3
Seychelles	1989		8.3	20.8	20.4	16.0	9.5	6.5	5.3	5.0	4.0	2.9	1.3
Tanzania	1978	0.9	9.5	14.5	15.6	11.6	10.9	8.3	7.8	5.6	4.6	4.0	6.7
Uganda	1985	11.2	16.1	14.4	12.5	10.6	8.6	7.1	5.3	4.7	3.7	2.6	3.2
Zaire	1985	4.2	12.1	15.3	45.9				13.0	6.9			2.6
Southern Africa													
Botswana	1985	2.5	11.2	17.1	24.8		16.5		13.1	8.2			6.6
Lesotho	1976	3.7	9.7	14.2	12.4	10.0	9.1	9.3	6.9	5.6	5.7	3.6	6.5
Malawi	1987	10.2	12.2	13.1	12.6	11.1	9.0	7.1	6.3	5.7	4.1	3.4	5.2
Mozambique	1980		4.0	11.9	14.3	34.1		26.2		9.5			
Namibia													
South Africa	1985	6.8		17.2	31.4		35.9			6.7			2.0
Swaziland	1976	1.5	30.4		16.8	12.8	10.8	8.2	7.4	4.7	5.8	1.6	
Zambia	1984		18.1	16.6	14.3	27.5			6.5	5.8	11.2		
Zimbabwe	1987		14.5	13.8	13.6	12.5	18.8		18.3	8.5			

Source: ILO/national statistical offices

Notes: see end of section

ECONOMICALLY ACTIVE POPULATION

Economically Active Population by Status: Latest Year (% Analysis)

Units: % of total

	Year	AB	C	D	E	F	G	HIJ	K	Total
North America										
Canada	1991	17.2	12.7	16.2	9.4	13.5	4.9	25.4	0.7	100.0
USA	1991	16.1	12.2	15.2	11.7	13.6	3.0	26.4	1.8	100.0
South America										
Argentina										
Bolivia [a]	1991	12.2	2.4	6.7	20.0	14.7	1.3	34.5	8.2	100.0
Brazil	1988	7.4	13.3		9.4	9.9	21.8	23.1	15.1	100.0
Chile	1991	8.2	3.4	11.9	10.2	12.2	18.1	29.8	6.2	100.0
Colombia	1991	10.0	1.8	11.3	18.2	17.0	1.3	30.5	9.9	100.0
Ecuador	1990	8.5	0.7	5.7	12.1	8.5	30.3	24.3	9.9	100.0
French Guiana [a]	1982	12.1	2.6	15.1	7.4	11.9	14.4	34.6	1.9	100.0
Guyana	1980	9.0	0.7	8.2	4.6	8.5	16.7	31.8	20.5	100.0
Paraguay	1991	8.8	3.1	11.3	20.8	20.3	1.2	29.5	5.0	100.0
Peru [b]	1991	16.3	4.4	10.1	25.5	7.3	1.0	29.6	5.8	100.0
Suriname	1987	11.4	0.6	14.6	5.4	13.6	4.5	26.7	23.2	100.0
Uruguay [c]	1990	11.1	3.8	16.4	12.6	16.8	2.8	34.1	2.4	100.0
Venezuela	1990	11.9	3.7	10.4	15.0	14.1	11.7	31.6	1.6	100.0
Caribbean										
Anguilla										
Antigua										
Aruba										
Bahamas	1989	10.2	3.0	15.0	8.5	22.3	5.0	23.3	12.7	100.0
Barbados	1991	7.2	3.8	15.0	7.8	19.1	4.0	26.0	17.1	100.0
Bermuda	1989	13.8	10.2	23.2	7.2	22.7	2.5	20.4		100.0
British Virgin Islands [d]	1980	11.3	4.0	9.5	6.7	24.7	5.5	31.1	3.0	100.0
Cayman Islands	1991	7.8	22.2	17.6	5.3	11.1	1.8	33.1	1.1	100.0
Cuba										
Dominica	1989	7.4	4.5	6.8		8.4	17.6	19.0	36.3	100.0
Dominican Republic	1981	4.3	1.1	5.4	7.5	11.7	24.0	19.4	26.6	100.0
Grenada	1988	6.9	1.4	8.1	8.1	8.1	13.8	23.6	30.0	100.0
Guadeloupe										
Haiti	1990	2.0	0.5	0.4	9.1	2.2	49.9	6.7	29.2	100.0
Jamaica	1990	6.8		11.7		15.5	32.4	26.0	7.6	100.0
Martinique										
Netherlands Antilles	1983	11.7	2.4	20.6	10.3	19.4	0.9	34.7		100.0
St Kitts	1980	7.8	1.4	8.0	6.7	10.0	25.2	29.2	11.7	100.0
St Lucia										
St Vincent/Grenadines	1980	7.9	0.7	7.0	5.6	9.0	20.4	28.2	21.2	100.0
Trinidad and Tobago	1990	8.9	1.9	11.8	10.5	15.4	10.0	41.2	0.3	100.0
Central America										
Belize [c]	1980	9.0	0.6	7.0	6.8	8.8	33.8	23.8	10.2	100.0
Costa Rica [c]	1991	9.1	3.6	7.3	10.0	14.5	23.7	29.9	1.9	100.0
El Salvador	1991	8.9	0.9	9.2	19.2	14.1	10.2	35.0	2.5	100.0
Guatemala	1989	5.1	2.6	3.2	9.6	7.1	47.7	22.7	2.0	100.0
Honduras	1991	7.2	1.5	3.5	11.6	6.9	35.0	17.0	17.3	100.0
Mexico	1990	10.3	2.4	9.1	11.2	9.4	21.5	31.3	4.8	100.0
Nicaragua										
Panama	1989	10.3	4.4	9.9	8.0	15.6	24.1	21.8	5.9	100.0
Puerto Rico	1992	15.6	10.5	14.5	6.8	13.4	3.5	34.9	0.8	100.0
South Asia										
Afghanistan	1979	2.6	0.2	2.2	3.8	2.0	60.7	28.5		100.0
Bangladesh	1986	3.2	0.9	3.0	11.6	6.5	57.2	16.6	1.0	100.0
Bhutan										
India	1981	2.9	0.9	3.0	4.2	2.8	62.5	13.9	9.8	100.0
Nepal	1981	3.7	0.1	0.9	1.1	0.3	88.6	5.3		100.0
Pakistan	1992	4.5	0.9	4.2	11.5	4.6	43.7	24.3	6.3	100.0
Sri Lanka [d]	1986	3.7	2.0	12.1	3.0	4.1	40.8	23.8	10.5	100.0

ECONOMICALLY ACTIVE POPULATION · Table No. 0609 (cont'd)

Economically Active Population by Status: Latest Year (% Analysis)

Units: % of total

	Year	AB	C	D	E	F	G	HIJ	K	Total
Japan										
Japan	1991	11.3	3.9	18.5	14.5	8.5	6.5	34.3	2.5	100.0
ASEAN/NICs										
Brunei [e]	1986	11.0	15.3		16.3		2.7	54.7		100.0
Hong Kong	1991	8.2	5.0	19.4	12.3	18.0	0.9	34.4	1.8	100.0
Indonesia [b]	1985	3.4	0.1	3.8	14.4	3.6	53.6	17.9	3.2	100.0
Macau	1990		5.2	23.3		14.0	0.1	54.3	3.1	100.0
Malaysia [b]	1988	7.4	2.1	9.4	11.8	11.8	30.6	26.9		100.0
Philippines	1990	5.7	1.1	4.0	12.3	8.5	41.0	18.9	8.5	100.0
Singapore	1991	16.9	8.8	14.5		13.9	0.2	39.7	6.0	100.0
South Korea	1991	7.4	1.6	13.0	14.3	11.2	16.2	34.0	2.3	100.0
Taiwan	1987	3.6	0.8	14.4	13.3	8.6	15.2	41.2	2.9	100.0
Thailand	1988	3.2	1.3	2.8	9.0	3.3	64.4	12.9	3.1	100.0
East/SE Asia										
Cambodia										
China [a]	1982	5.1	1.5	1.3	1.8	2.2	72.0	16.0	0.1	100.0
Laos										
Mongolia										
Myanmar										
North Korea										
Vietnam										
Australasia										
Australia	1990	10.4	12.2	5.7	15.1	16.3	14.5	22.9	2.9	100.0
New Zealand	1991	20.0	10.2	12.6	4.9	5.8	8.6	24.0	13.9	100.0
Pacific										
American Samoa	1980	17.6	9.4	13.2	5.6	12.9	2.6	38.7		100.0
Fiji [f]	1986	7.4	1.1	6.5	6.1	6.4	44.0	19.8	8.7	100.0
French Polynesia	1988	7.0	2.7	24.7	6.6	6.8	12.4	25.2	14.6	100.0
Guam										
Kiribati										
Nauru										
New Caledonia	1989	13.2	1.5	18.6	8.6	9.1	13.6	35.4		100.0
Papua New Guinea	1980	27.6	6.0	10.0	0.1	6.5	15.0	34.8		100.0
Solomon Islands										
Tonga	1986	8.8	1.5	8.7	4.2	5.5	40.8	17.5	13.0	100.0
Tuvalu										
Vanuatu	1979	4.8	0.5	3.0	2.0	4.4	76.5	8.4	0.4	100.0
Western Samoa	1981	11.5	1.2	6.9	3.1	4.2	55.8	16.8	0.5	100.0
Middle East										
Bahrain [g]	1990	8.9	7.0	8.3	3.1	11.2	0.7	57.7	3.1	100.0
Egypt [g]	1986	11.7	0.7	7.8	4.8	6.3	33.6	21.7	13.4	100.0
Iran	1986	8.2	0.3	3.0	5.9	3.6	25.4	28.4	25.2	100.0
Iraq	1987	10.1	0.4	38.9	3.1	4.6	12.6	28.2	2.1	100.0
Israel	1991	22.8	4.5	14.6	7.7	11.7	2.9	24.3	11.5	100.0
Jordan	1979	15.0	1.4	5.8	9.1	6.3	6.0	56.4		100.0
Kuwait	1988	16.8	1.6	12.1	5.4	30.6	1.2	30.9	1.4	100.0
Lebanon										
Oman										
Qatar										
Saudi Arabia										
Syria	1989	13.0	0.5	8.8	11.2	4.9	22.0	35.8	3.8	100.0
United Arab Emirates	1980	9.5	2.0	12.5	5.7	15.9	4.4	50.0		100.0
Yemen	1975	5.5	0.7	1.5	6.4	6.6	60.4	16.9	2.0	100.0

ECONOMICALLY ACTIVE POPULATION

Economically Active Population by Status: Latest Year (% Analysis)

Units: % of total

	Year	AB	C	D	E	F	G	HIJ	K	Total
North Africa										
Algeria	1987	14.3	1.4	10.0	6.7	8.2	16.2	34.4	8.8	100.0
Chad										
Djibouti										
Ethiopia	1984	1.3	0.1	0.6	3.3	1.9	88.2	3.7	0.9	100.0
Libya	1973	10.1	0.8	7.2	5.8	15.1	21.1	35.9	4.0	100.0
Mali	1976	1.5		0.6	2.0	1.0	84.8	7.1	3.0	100.0
Mauritania										
Morocco [b]	1982	10.1	8.6		13.2	13.8	3.5	43.5	7.3	100.0
Niger	1989	10.5	6.2	19.3			1.4	62.6		100.0
Somalia										
Sudan	1983	2.6	0.2	2.0	4.3	4.8	62.5	10.1	13.5	100.0
Tunisia	1984	3.1	1.4	11.9	2.4	9.8	26.2	38.6	6.6	100.0
West Africa										
Benin										
Burkina Faso	1985	0.7		0.3	2.8	0.9	91.3	2.4	1.6	100.0
Cameroon	1982	2.5	0.1	2.0	3.4	2.1	77.1	11.8	1.0	100.0
Cape Verde										
Côte d'Ivoire										
Equatorial Guinea	1983	2.3	0.2	2.9	2.3	3.7	57.6	6.7	24.3	100.0
Gabon										
Gambia	1987	18.7	3.8	16.4	26.3				34.7	100.0
Ghana	1984	4.0	0.3	2.3	13.4	2.3	59.0	15.9		100.0
Guinea	1983	2.0	0.7		1.5	1.2	77.0	15.9	1.7	100.0
Guinea-Bissau	1979	2.5	0.1	1.9	1.8	3.8	72.6	7.5	9.8	100.0
Liberia										
Nigeria	1986	6.6	0.2	3.8	24.1	3.3	42.8	12.9	6.3	100.0
Sao Tomé e Príncipe	1981	5.5	0.6	8.9	5.3	5.5	49.7	24.5		100.0
Senegal										
Sierra Leone										
Togo	1981	3.5	0.1	1.9	7.2	1.5	66.6	19.2		100.0
East/Central Africa										
Angola										
Burundi	1979	0.9		0.4	0.7	2.0	92.8	2.9	0.3	100.0
Central African Republic	1975	1.9		1.4	3.1	2.3	84.1	5.5	1.7	100.0
Comoros	1980	3.0	0.2	1.5	1.8	2.5	50.0	10.4	30.6	100.0
Congo										
Kenya										
Madagascar										
Maldives	1990	7.0	1.3	9.7	5.8	12.5	25.4	31.9	5.5	100.0
Mauritius [g]	1987	7.1	0.9	9.2	8.2	10.4	17.9	46.3		100.0
Réunion										
Rwanda	1989	1.1		0.6	1.6	2.4	89.8	4.3	0.2	100.0
Seychelles	1985	11.1	1.6	10.1	4.9	24.6	7.5	40.2		100.0
Tanzania										
Uganda										
Zaire										
Southern Africa										
Botswana [a]	1986	13.6	2.3	14.8	6.2	14.4	3.4	44.6	0.7	100.0
Lesotho [g]	1976	1.8	0.2	0.9	1.9	14.8	23.2	37.4	19.8	100.0
Malawi	1987	1.0	0.1	1.3	3.1	2.7	85.8	6.0		100.0
Mozambique										
Namibia										
South Africa [g]	1985	8.2	3.0	13.4		16.8	13.9	34.9	9.8	100.0
Swaziland	1987	12.8	4.1	12.9					70.3	100.0
Zambia	1984	6.7	1.1	3.7	6.8	7.9	51.2	16.3	6.3	100.0
Zimbabwe	1987	4.3	0.8	3.5	2.8	7.1	63.9	9.2	8.4	100.0

Source: ILO/national statistical offices

Notes: see end of section

Notes to Tables in Section Six

Table 0601
a Civilian labour force employed
b Capital city and/or major urban area only
c Excludes armed forces
d Figure for 1977 excludes rural areas
e New series starting 1982
f New series starting 1985
g Metropolitan area only
h New series starting 1981 and 1983; data refer to Montevideo only
i New series starting 1981
j 1977 data refer to persons aged 14 and over
k Data refer to employees
l Includes Aruba until 1983
m New series starting 1987
n Data refer to metropolitan population to 1987 and to urban population from 1988
o Prior to 1983 data refer to establishments with five or more employees only
p Data refer to public sector and establishments with 10 or more employees only
q Data refer to establishments with seven or more employees only
r Includes armed forces
s Excludes government services
t New series starting 1980 and 1981
u New series starting 1978
v New series starting 1986
w Excludes public sector
x Excludes mining and quarrying
y Data refer to establishments with six or more employees only
z Excludes small rural establishments

Table 0602
a Capital city and/or major urban area only
b Data for 1986 exclude rural north
c New series starting 1982
d New series starting 1985
e Capital city only until 1981
f New series starting 1987
g New series starting 1981
h New series starting 1986
i Includes Aruba until 1983
j New series starting 1989
k Excludes workers temporarily laid off
l New series starting 1978
m New series starting 1983
n Whole territory

Table 0603
a New series starting 1987
b Capital city and/or major urban area only
c Includes mining and quarrying
d Data for 1985 exclude rural north
e New series starting 1982
f New series starting 1985
g Includes repair and installation
h New series starting 1982 referring to capital city only
i New series starting 1983
j New series starting 1981
k New series starting 1986
l Prior to 1988, includes mining, fishing, quarrying, water and gas
m Includes Aruba until 1983

n Prior to 1987, includes mining and quarrying
o Data refer to establishments with five or more employees only
p Data refer to public sector and establishments with 10 or more employees
q New series starting 1980
r New series starting 1984
s Includes multiple job holders
t Excludes small rural establishments
u Prior to 1986, excludes electricity and water
v Excludes tribal homelands

Table 0604
a New series starting 1984
b New series starting 1982
c New series starting 1988
d Per month

Table 0605
a Per month
b New series starting 1984
c New series starting 1985
d New series starting 1980 and 1982
e New series starting 1988

Table 0606
a Not whole country coverage
b Excluding armed forces
c Sample surveys
d Male/female breakdown refers to 1986
e Wage-earners only
f Excludes the former Yemen PDR

Table 0607
A blank entry in the table means that information for that division has been incorporated in the preceding figure (unless otherwise noted)
A Agriculture/forestry/fishing
B Mining and quarrying
C Manufacturing
D Electricity, gas and water
E Construction
F Wholesale/retail trade, restaurants and hotels
G Transport, storage and communications
H Financing, insurance, real estate and business services
I Community, social and personal services
J Not adequately defined

a Not whole country coverage
b Data refer to economically active population
c Column J includes unemployed
d Excludes armed forces
e Excludes government employees
f Excludes foreigners
g Excludes agricultural activities
h Excludes mining and quarrying
i Estimated employment

j   Data for electricity, gas and water are
    not available

Table 0608   A blank entry in the table means that
             information for that division has been
             incorporated in the preceding figure
             a   Peninsular Malaysia only
             b   ILO estimate
             c   Data for Yemen PDR only

Table 0609   A blank entry in the table means that
             relevant information is incorporated
             in the preceding figure
             AB Professional, technical and related
                 workers
             C   Administrative and managerial workers
             D   Clerical and related workers
             E   Sales workers

F   Service workers
G   Agricultural, animal husbandry
     and forestry workers, fishermen
     and hunters
HIJ Production/related workers, transport
     equipment operators and labourers
K   Workers not classifiable by occupation,
     armed forces and unemployed
a   Excludes armed forces
b   Not whole country coverage
c   Capital city and/or major urban areas
     only
d   Data refers to establishments with five
     or more employees only
e   Excludes government services
f   Includes statistical office estimates
g   Excludes foreigners

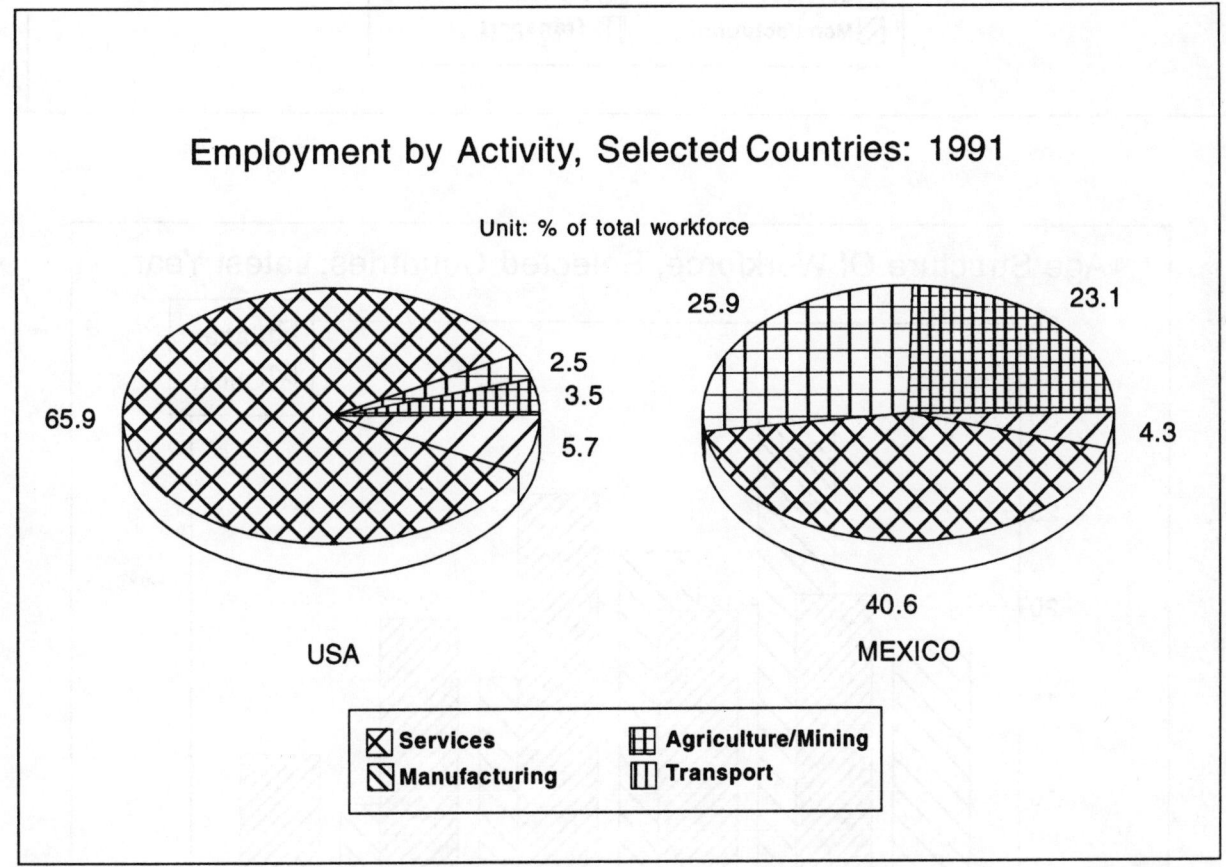

Employment by Activity, Selected Countries: 1991

Unit: % of total workforce

USA: 65.9, 2.5, 3.5, 5.7

MEXICO: 25.9, 23.1, 4.3, 40.6

Legend:
- Services
- Manufacturing
- Agriculture/Mining
- Transport

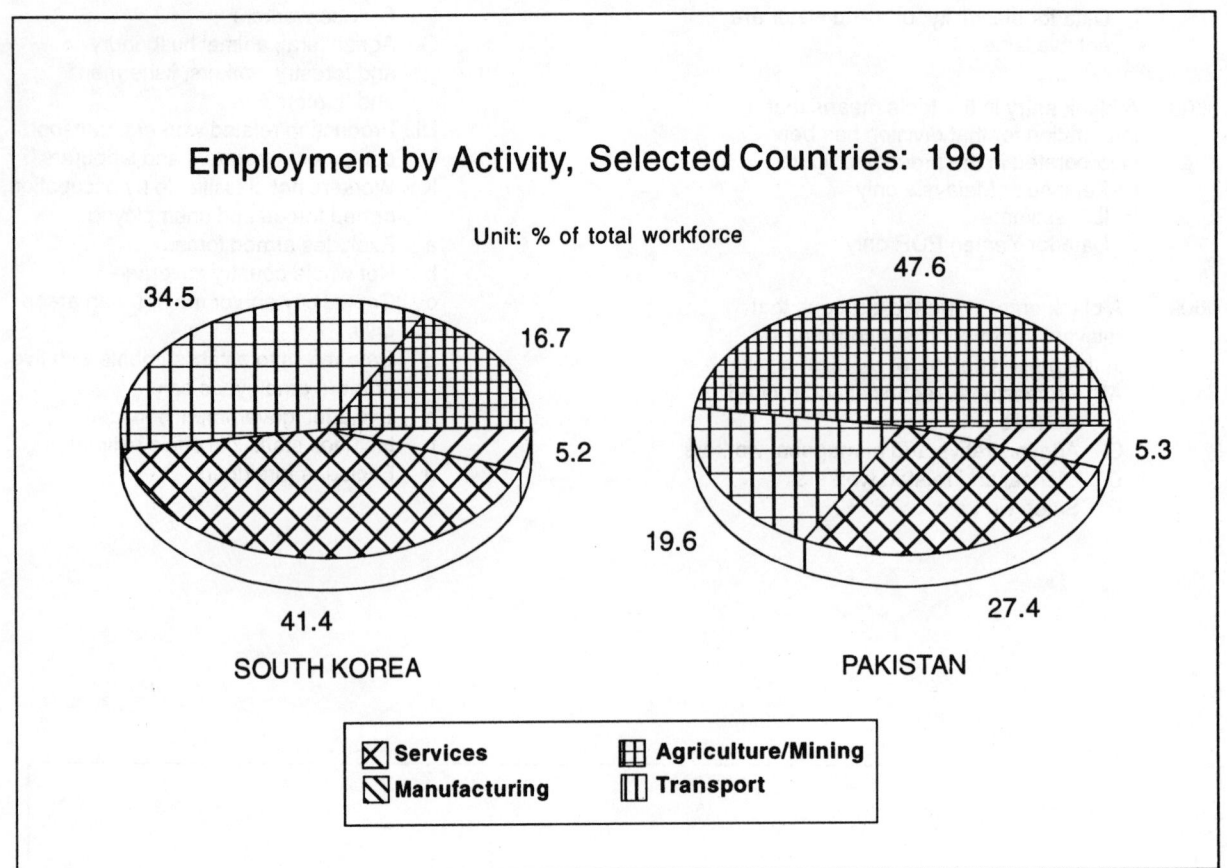

Employment by Activity, Selected Countries: 1991

Unit: % of total workforce

SOUTH KOREA

34.5
16.7
5.2
41.4

PAKISTAN

47.6
5.3
19.6
27.4

⊠ Services   ⊞ Agriculture/Mining
⊠ Manufacturing   ⊞ Transport

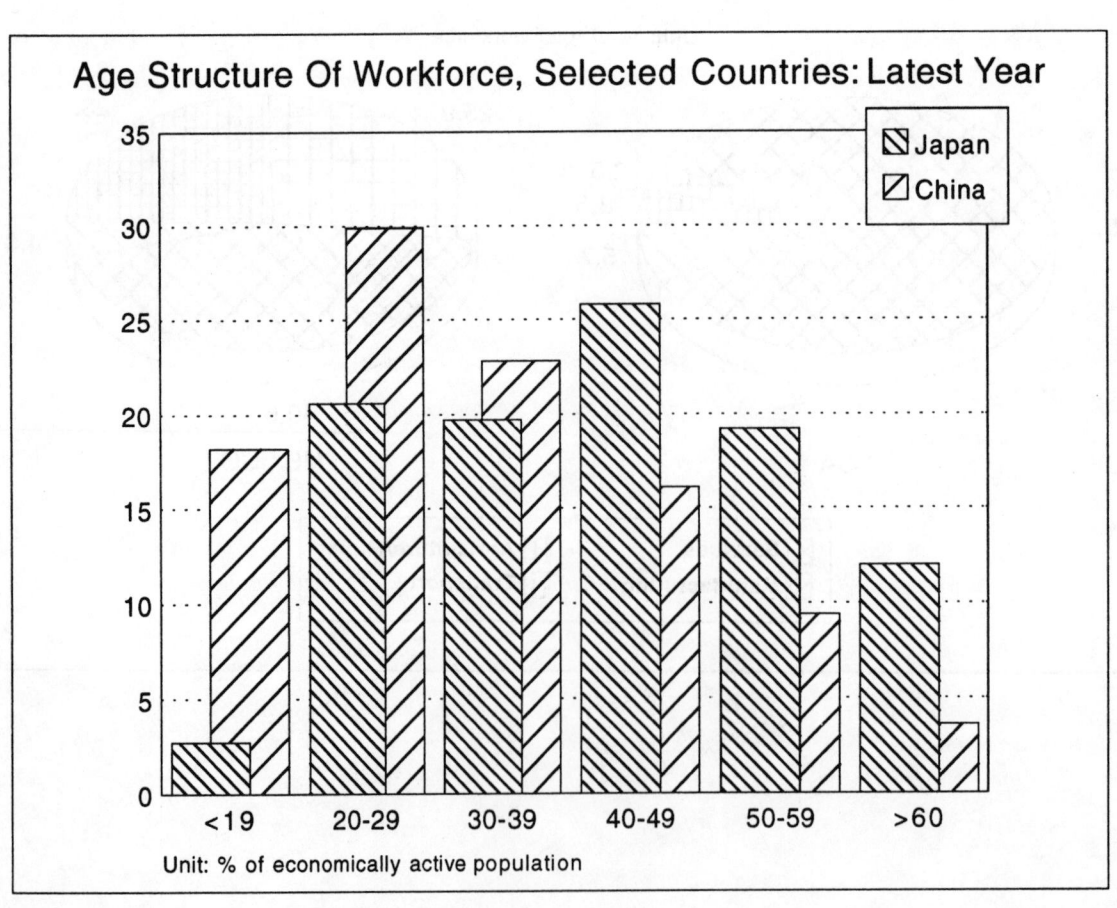

Age Structure Of Workforce, Selected Countries: Latest Year

⊠ Japan
⊠ China

Unit: % of economically active population

Industrial Resources and Output

INDUSTRIAL OUTPUT — Table No. 0701

Indices of General Industrial Production 1977-1991

Units: 1980 = 100

	1977	1979	1980	1981	1982	1983	1984	1985	1986	1987	1988	1989	1990	1991
North America														
Canada	93	102	100	101	91	97	109	115	115	121	126	128	128	126
USA	94	104	100	102	95	101	110	112	113	119	125	125	130	127
South America														
Argentina	104	103	100	85	81	90	94	86	96	95	85	79		
Bolivia	99	98	100	99	88	85	74	67						
Brazil	81	93	100	90	90	85	91	99	110	111	107	110	100	100
Chile														
Colombia	86	94	100	100	100	101	108	110	127	139	141			
Ecuador														
French Guiana														
Guyana														
Paraguay	78	90	100	107	104	101	104	108	108					
Peru														
Suriname														
Uruguay					81	76	78	77	86	96	94	91	109	
Venezuela					122	123	156	181	217	310	392			
Caribbean														
Anguilla														
Antigua														
Aruba														
Bahamas														
Barbados	93	97	100	97	93	97	100	97	102	97	102	107	109	105
Bermuda														
British Virgin Islands														
Cayman Islands														
Cuba	88	98	100											
Dominica														
Dominican Republic														
Grenada														
Guadeloupe														
Haiti														
Jamaica														
Martinique														
Netherlands Antilles														
St Kitts														
St Lucia														
St Vincent/Grenadines														
Trinidad and Tobago [a]		95	101	90	93	85	104	100	122	126	121	121	125	
Central America														
Belize														
Costa Rica	88	97	100	97	90	93	102	104	113	119	122	127		
El Salvador	113	110	100	86	84	86	87	91						
Guatemala	83	94	100	97	92	90	91	91						
Honduras	77	104	100	102	96	101	110	109						
Mexico [b]	74	91	100	109	107	97	102	108	103	107	109	114	120	124
Nicaragua	126	86	100	102										
Panama														
Puerto Rico														
South Asia														
Afghanistan [c]	49	82	100	102	97									
Bangladesh [a]	94	87	91	98	93	94	99	100	98	108	108	113	113	122
Bhutan														
India	92	99	100	109	113	117	128	140	149	165	178	188	210	212
Nepal														
Pakistan	76	90	100	113										
Sri Lanka														

INDUSTRIAL OUTPUT

Indices of General Industrial Production 1977-1991

Units: 1980 = 100

	1977	1979	1980	1981	1982	1983	1984	1985	1986	1987	1988	1989	1990	1991
Japan														
Japan	84	96	100	101	101	104	114	118	118	122	134	142	149	152
ASEAN/NICs														
Brunei														
Hong Kong [d]	47	76	100	116	120	150	145							
Indonesia														
Macau														
Malaysia [e]	79	94	100	103	109	122	142	138	152	164	186	205	231	255
Philippines [f]	83	96	100	113	128	142	193	231	258	296	358	329	466	508
Singapore														
South Korea	74	102	100	113	118	137	158	164	199	237	269	277	302	327
Taiwan	72	94	100	104	103	117	132	134	153	169	176	182	180	193
Thailand														
East/SE Asia														
Cambodia														
China [a]	42	52	57	59	64	71	82	100	112	131	159	172	186	
Laos														
Mongolia	75	91	100	110	122	133								
Myanmar														
North Korea														
Vietnam														
Australasia														
Australia	91	99	100	100	92	101	108	114	113	121	126	133	130	129
New Zealand														
Pacific														
American Samoa														
Fiji	88	108	100	110	109	97	116	103	123	110	117	128	138	155
French Polynesia														
Guam														
Kiribati														
Nauru														
New Caledonia														
Papua New Guinea														
Solomon Islands														
Tonga														
Tuvalu														
Vanuatu														
Western Samoa														
Middle East														
Bahrain														
Egypt	53	79	100	131	138	163	169							
Iran														
Iraq														
Israel	93	103	100	106	107	111	116	120	124	130	126	124	132	141
Jordan	57	84	100	116	120	126	152	155	157	171	158	165	166	162
Kuwait														
Lebanon														
Oman														
Qatar														
Saudi Arabia														
Syria	82	89	100	109	112	137	139	136	141	146	150	169	186	
United Arab Emirates														
Yemen														

INDUSTRIAL OUTPUT

Table No. 0701 (cont'd)

Indices of General Industrial Production 1977-1991

Units: 1980 = 100

	1977	1979	1980	1981	1982	1983	1984	1985	1986	1987	1988	1989	1990	1991
North Africa														
Algeria	75	99	100	108	125	140	152	157	164	161	165	162	166	
Chad														
Djibouti														
Ethiopia														
Libya														
Mali														
Mauritania														
Morocco	86	98	100	103	108	111	113	117	121	124	136	131	144	143
Niger														
Somalia														
Sudan														
Tunisia	76	94	100	104	103	112	109	109	110	110				
West Africa														
Benin														
Burkina Faso														
Cameroon														
Cape Verde														
Côte d'Ivoire	70	87	100	101	97	83	90	106	115	115	111	109		
Equatorial Guinea														
Gabon														
Gambia														
Ghana	141	98	100	92	75	53	50	52	50					
Guinea														
Guinea-Bissau														
Liberia														
Nigeria	74	101	100	97	98	87	82	94	92	108	113	135	151	163
Sao Tomé e Príncipe														
Senegal	120	121	100	109	113	118	115	118	106	118	124	112	118	
Sierra Leone														
Togo														
East/Central Africa														
Angola														
Burundi														
Central African Republic														
Comoros														
Congo														
Kenya	78	95	100	105	106	111	115	121	128	135	143	152	160	
Madagascar														
Maldives														
Mauritius														
Réunion														
Rwanda														
Seychelles	39	73	100	144	140	159	156							
Tanzania														
Uganda														
Zaire														
Southern Africa														
Botswana			100	89	105	97	94							
Lesotho														
Malawi														
Mozambique														
Namibia														
South Africa	88	96	100	104	98	102	99	105	108	103	107			
Swaziland	64	75	100	89	88	71								
Zambia	105	97	100	98	100	97	92	88	90	121	96	100	101	
Zimbabwe	85	88	100	106	105	102	109	113	118	122	129	134		

Source: UN/national statistical offices/IMF
Notes: see end of section

INDUSTRIAL OUTPUT — Table No. 0702

Indices of Manufacturing Production 1977-1991

Units: 1980 = 100

	1977	1979	1980	1981	1982	1983	1984	1985	1986	1987	1988	1989	1990	1991
North America														
Canada	93	103	100	101	88	94	106	112	113	118	123	125	118	111
USA	89	105	100	102	94	102	113	116	120	127	134	138	139	136
South America														
Argentina	87	104	100	84	80	89	93	84	95	88	82	76		
Bolivia	117	99	100	96	87	84	71	64	67	69	72	74	76	
Brazil [a]	76	93	100	90	89	84	89	97	108	109	105	108	98	97
Chile [a]	94	94	100	101	85	89	98	98	106	110	119	129	128	136
Colombia	90	98	100	99	93	93	102	104	112	120	122	125	132	
Ecuador	88	94	100	102	105	101	107	113	117	120	126	131		
French Guiana														
Guyana	109		100											
Paraguay		89	100	107	100	97	98	102	101	106	114	148	135	
Peru		95	100	100	96	78	84	89	105	120	104	84	81	
Suriname	49		100											
Uruguay [b]		96	100	95	79	70	76	75	84	93	91	89	98	
Venezuela [c]	87	87	100	111	119	119	152	176	218	311	393			
Caribbean														
Anguilla														
Antigua														
Aruba														
Bahamas														
Barbados	74	98	100	95	89	91	92	87	92	87	91	99	99	95
Bermuda														
British Virgin Islands														
Cayman Islands														
Cuba	95	98	100											
Dominica														
Dominican Republic [a]	113	96	100	103	110									
Grenada														
Guadeloupe														
Haiti	148		100											
Jamaica	95		100	100	102	110	109	112	122	133				
Martinique														
Netherlands Antilles														
St Kitts														
St Lucia														
St Vincent/Grenadines														
Trinidad and Tobago		94	100	89	104	109	103	99	121	125	120	121	124	
Central America														
Belize														
Costa Rica	88	98	100	95	88	90	99	101	108	114	117			
El Salvador	95	118	100	84	82	85	88							
Guatemala	21	95	100	98	92	90	91	90						
Honduras	75	103	100	102	94	99	107	105						
Mexico [a]	62	93	100	107	104	96	101	108	105	109	112	119	125	129
Nicaragua	94	85	100	103	103									
Panama		100	100	96	110	109	105	110	113	121	92			
Puerto Rico														
South Asia														
Afghanistan [d]	20	122	100	87	72									
Bangladesh [e]	77	93	100	100	95	99	103	126	144	145	148	167	171	177
Bhutan														
India	97	99	100	108	109	113	122	135	143	160	174	181	205	204
Nepal	87	94	100	100	112	134	145	143	170	220	229	219	230	273
Pakistan [e]	81	90	100	116	123	133	143	154	165	179	183	192	203	181
Sri Lanka [a]		92	100	107	110									

| **INDUSTRIAL OUTPUT** | **Table No. 0702** (cont'd) |

Indices of Manufacturing Production 1977-1991

Units: 1980 = 100

	1977	1979	1980	1981	1982	1983	1984	1985	1986	1987	1988	1989	1990	1991
Japan														
Japan [a]	105	96	100	101	101	104	114	119	118	122	134	142	149	152
ASEAN/NICs														
Brunei														
Hong Kong [f]	63	76	100	115	117	144	138	132	153	177	188			
Indonesia	106	81	100	109	110	113	121	130	145	162	185	208	236	261
Macau														
Malaysia [a]	95	94	100	103	109	116	130	122	133	150	177	197	232	262
Philippines [a,e]	83	97	100	116	131	153	207	241	291	333	406		506	560
Singapore		89	100	110	104	106	116	107	116	136	161	178	196	206
South Korea	99	102	100	113	119	139	161	167	204	244	278	286	312	338
Taiwan	107	94	100	104	105	121	137	138	161	182	195	201	197	212
Thailand	76	96	100	107	112	120	128	131	138	149	175	202	232	253
East/SE Asia														
Cambodia														
China	83	100	100	92	106	125	149	177	138	233	244	259		
Laos														
Mongolia														
Myanmar	83	93	100	107	112	116	124	133	131	135	133			
North Korea														
Vietnam														
Australasia														
Australia	65	99	100	100	88	96	100	104	104	111	117	121	114	112
New Zealand [d]			100	115	144	157	166	197	216					
Pacific														
American Samoa														
Fiji	98	109	100	111	108	95	113	98	118	102	103	114	126	152
French Polynesia														
Guam														
Kiribati														
Nauru														
New Caledonia														
Papua New Guinea [f]		73	100	99	91	87								
Solomon Islands														
Tonga [d]		70	100	101										
Tuvalu														
Vanuatu														
Western Samoa														
Middle East														
Bahrain														
Egypt	22	92	100											
Iran [a]		88	100	106	119	140								
Iraq														
Israel	78	103	100	106	107	111	116	120	124	130	126	124	132	141
Jordan [f]	53	74	100	118	126	131	131							
Kuwait [f]	43		100	86	85	78	64							
Lebanon														
Oman														
Qatar														
Saudi Arabia														
Syria	102	85	100	111	117	167	166	163	163					
United Arab Emirates														
Yemen														

INDUSTRIAL OUTPUT Table No. 0702 (cont'd)

Indices of Manufacturing Production 1977-1991

Units: 1980 = 100

	1977	1979	1980	1981	1982	1983	1984	1985	1986	1987	1988	1989	1990	1991
North Africa														
Algeria	79	88	100	114	142	150	174	179	189	186	182	172	174	
Chad														
Djibouti														
Ethiopia [f]			100	97	107	113	126							
Libya														
Mali														
Mauritania														
Morocco [a]	77	96	100	100	103	110	110	116	121	124	135	137	149	152
Niger														
Somalia														
Sudan														
Tunisia	76	91	100	108	109	116	119	123	123	126				
West Africa														
Benin														
Burkina Faso														
Cameroon														
Cape Verde														
Côte d'Ivoire			100	76	88									
Equatorial Guinea														
Gabon														
Gambia [f]			100		421	354								
Ghana	136	98	100	92	73	51	57	71	79	82	90			
Guinea														
Guinea-Bissau														
Liberia														
Nigeria	102	95	100	106	101	79	70	84	81	109	124	131	153	165
Sao Tomé e Príncipe														
Senegal	120	124	100	108	120	134	113	133	127	117	119	105	115	
Sierra Leone														
Togo														
East/Central Africa														
Angola														
Burundi														
Central African Republic [f]			100	93	61	112								
Comoros														
Congo														
Kenya	96	95	100	105	106	111	115	109	116	125	132	138	143	
Madagascar														
Maldives														
Mauritius [f]		99	100	93	99	90	105							
Réunion														
Rwanda														
Seychelles	112	67	100	131	126	143	134							
Tanzania														
Uganda														
Zaire	104	102	100	102	93									
Southern Africa														
Botswana [f]	65		100	118	156	128	99							
Lesotho														
Malawi [e]		99	100	110	88	98	94	97	99	92	98	107	121	147
Mozambique														
Namibia														
South Africa	95	91	100	106	103	97	100	99	98	101	108	108	106	103
Swaziland [f]	20	72	100	88	88	69								
Zambia [a]	108	98	100	111	106	100	100	115	111	112	119	118	125	111
Zimbabwe [a]	108	87	100	109	109	106	101	112	115	118	124	131	139	143

Source: UN/national statistical offices/IMF

Notes: see end of section

MINERAL PRODUCTION	Table No. 0703

Production of Selected Minerals 1992

Units: '000 metric tonnes, unless otherwise stated

	Gold (tonnes)	Silver (tonnes)	Iron Ore (1991)	Bauxite	Copper Ore	Lead Ore	Tin Ore	Zinc Ore
North America								
Canada [a]	156.1	1,128.3	35,460.0		764.2	342.5	4.5	1,311.9
USA	296.0	1,741.0	55,512.0	50.0	1,760.5	418.7	0.1	550.6
South America								
Argentina [b]	1.5	69.6	636.0		0.3	18.0	0.4	41.0
Bolivia	4.7	282.4			0.1	20.0	16.5	143.9
Brazil [c]	88.8	48.0	153,696.0	10,800.0	39.8	8.6	23.2	103.2
Chile [d]	30.0	1,042.9	8,460.0		1,932.7	1.1		29.7
Colombia	32.1	8.3	600.0		2.2			0.2
Ecuador	4.5							
French Guiana [e]	0.5							
Guyana [f]	0.6			2,204.0				
Paraguay								
Peru	6.2	1,595.2	2,724.0		367.7	195.4	9.7	607.4
Suriname				3,159.5				
Uruguay								
Venezuela	7.6		21,216.0	952.7				
Caribbean								
Anguilla								
Antigua								
Aruba								
Bahamas								
Barbados								
Bermuda								
British Virgin Islands								
Cayman Islands								
Cuba [g]					2.0			
Dominica								
Dominican Republic [h]	2.6	16.9		6.5				
Grenada								
Guadeloupe								
Haiti								
Jamaica				11,359.5				
Martinique								
Netherlands Antilles								
St Kitts								
St Lucia								
St Vincent/Grenadines								
Trinidad and Tobago								
Central America								
Belize								
Costa Rica [f]	0.3							
El Salvador								
Guatemala								
Honduras [f]	0.1	44.0				10.4		32.1
Mexico [i]	10.9	2,325.0	6,192.0		277.1	173.0	0.2	340.7
Nicaragua	1.2	1.0						
Panama								
Puerto Rico								
South Asia								
Afghanistan								
Bangladesh								
Bhutan								
India [j]	1.6	44.7	46,776.0	5,402.4	49.0	35.6		153.9
Nepal								
Pakistan								
Sri Lanka								

MINERAL PRODUCTION Table No. 0703 (cont'd)

Production of Selected Minerals 1992

Units: '000 metric tonnes, unless otherwise stated

	Gold (tonnes)	Silver (tonnes)	Iron Ore (1991)	Bauxite	Copper Ore	Lead Ore	Tin Ore	Zinc Ore
Japan								
Japan	8.9	178.3	36.0		12.1	18.8		134.5
ASEAN/NICs								
Brunei								
Hong Kong								
Indonesia	17.0	80.0	168.0	766.9	292.0		29.4	
Macau								
Malaysia	3.5	15.3	384.0	330.6	28.6		14.3	
Philippines [k]	23.9	30.8			123.5			0.1
Singapore								
South Korea	23.3	80.4	564.0			17.5		21.9
Taiwan [l,m]	0.2	3.9						
Thailand			228.0			16.7	11.5	69.0
East/SE Asia								
Cambodia								
China [n]	110.0	180.0	175,296.0	3,000.0	309.0	319.7	33.7	710.0
Laos							0.3	
Mongolia [a]					105.1		0.3	
Myanmar		6.5					0.5	1.7
North Korea [j,o]	5.0	300.0	9,000.0			80.0		215.0
Vietnam [p]							0.8	15.0
Australasia								
Australia	240.0	1,248.0	9,285.0	39,964.0	342.0	579.0	6.3	1,019.0
New Zealand [l]	2.4							
Pacific								
American Samoa								
Fiji [m]	3.7	1.0						
French Polynesia								
Guam								
Kiribati								
Nauru								
New Caledonia								
Papua New Guinea	71.2	95.5			193.4			
Solomon Islands [f]	0.1							
Tonga								
Tuvalu								
Vanuatu								
Western Samoa								
Middle East								
Bahrain								
Egypt [b]			2,580.0					
Iran [q]		30.0			105.0	12.4		65.0
Iraq								
Israel								
Jordan								
Kuwait								
Lebanon								
Oman					13.4			
Qatar								
Saudi Arabia								
Syria								
United Arab Emirates								
Yemen								

MINERAL PRODUCTION

Production of Selected Minerals 1992

Units: '000 metric tonnes, unless otherwise stated

	Gold (tonnes)	Silver (tonnes)	Iron Ore (1991)	Bauxite	Copper Ore	Lead Ore	Tin Ore	Zinc Ore
North Africa								
Algeria [b,r]		3.0	2,124.0			0.9		3.9
Chad								
Djibouti								
Ethiopia [f]	0.7							
Libya								
Mali [f]	0.6							
Mauritania			10,248.0					
Morocco		234.0	96.0		12.4	71.6		23.6
Niger [b]							0.1	
Somalia								
Sudan								
Tunisia			288.0			0.8		3.6
West Africa								
Benin								
Burkina Faso [f]	2.8							
Cameroon [f]								
Cape Verde								
Côte d'Ivoire								
Equatorial Guinea								
Gabon [f]	0.1							
Gambia								
Ghana [r]	26.4	0.1		309.8				
Guinea				17,054.0				
Guinea-Bissau								
Liberia [e]			12,924.0					
Nigeria							0.2	
Sao Tomé e Príncipe								
Senegal								
Sierra Leone [f]	0.4			1,262.2				
Togo								
East/Central Africa								
Angola								
Burundi [f]								
Central African Republic [f]	0.4							
Comoros								
Congo [f]								
Kenya [f]								
Madagascar								
Maldives								
Mauritius								
Réunion								
Rwanda [e]							0.7	
Seychelles								
Tanzania [f]	0.2							
Uganda								
Zaire [b]	6.1	50.0			144.0		1.6	44.8
Southern Africa								
Botswana [f]					20.4			
Lesotho								
Malawi								
Mozambique [s]				8.8	0.1			
Namibia [f]	0.2	72.0			35.0	21.0	0.9	36.1
South Africa	608.5	178.2	28,944.0		198.0	76.7	0.6	69.8
Swaziland								
Zambia	0.2	18.3			432.6	9.7		24.6
Zimbabwe [b]	18.5	20.4	1,258.6		10.5		0.7	

Source: Metallstatistik/World Metal Statistics/UN/national statistical offices

Notes: see end of section

METAL PRODUCTION   Table No. 0704

Production of Selected Metals 1992

Units: '000 metric tonnes

	Pig Iron (1991)	Crude Steel (1991)	Aluminium	Refined Copper	Refined Lead	Refined Tin	Zinc
North America							
Canada	8,268.0	23,844.0	1,971.8	539.3	255.2	0.1	671.7
USA	48,504.0	87,444.0	4,042.1	2,153.8	1,150.4	0.2	393.9
South America							
Argentina [a]	2,100.0	2,964.0	153.2	15.0	29.7	0.1	37.3
Bolivia						14.4	
Brazil	23,424.0	22,608.0	1,195.2	157.1	67.2	20.7	164.4
Chile [a]	732.0	804.0		1,242.3			
Colombia [b]	313.0	336.0					
Ecuador							
French Guiana							
Guyana							
Paraguay							
Peru [a,c]	120.0	490.0		250.2	80.4		128.5
Suriname			32.4				
Uruguay							
Venezuela [c]	314.0	3,108.0	566.2		12.0		
Caribbean							
Anguilla							
Antigua							
Aruba							
Bahamas							
Barbados							
Bermuda							
British Virgin Islands							
Cayman Islands							
Cuba [a]		312.0					
Dominica							
Dominican Republic							
Grenada							
Guadeloupe							
Haiti							
Jamaica							
Martinique							
Netherlands Antilles							
St Kitts							
St Lucia							
St Vincent/Grenadines							
Trinidad and Tobago [d]		301.2					
Central America							
Belize							
Costa Rica							
El Salvador							
Guatemala							
Honduras							
Mexico	3,228.0	7,716.0	24.8	154.3	253.6	4.0	151.4
Nicaragua							
Panama							
Puerto Rico							
South Asia							
Afghanistan							
Bangladesh							
Bhutan							
India [c]	12,204.0	16,392.0	496.2	45.1	56.8	0.3	126.0
Nepal							
Pakistan [d]	910.0						
Sri Lanka							

METAL PRODUCTION

Table No. 0704 (cont'd)

Production of Selected Metals 1992

Units: '000 metric tonnes

	Pig Iron (1991)	Crude Steel (1991)	Aluminium	Refined Copper	Refined Lead	Refined Tin	Zinc
Japan							
Japan	81,144.0	109,644.0	18.9	1,160.9	331.1	0.7	729.5
ASEAN/NICs							
Brunei							
Hong Kong							
Indonesia [e]		1,850.0	187.0			28.2	
Macau							
Malaysia [e]		550.0			16.0	45.6	
Philippines [e]		300.0		145.7	16.8		
Singapore [e]		425.0				0.6	
South Korea [f]	18,744.0	26,808.0	13.3	209.8	73.2	2.4	255.5
Taiwan [b,e]	5,491.0	8,288.0			19.9		
Thailand [e]		535.0			15.9	10.9	70.3
East/SE Asia							
Cambodia							
China [g]	69,480.0	70,560.0	1,080.0	622.0	296.1	26.6	576.7
Laos							
Mongolia							
Myanmar							
North Korea [h]	5,900.0	6,830.0	10.0	40.0	65.0		227.0
Vietnam [i]						0.5	10.0
Australasia							
Australia	5,592.0	6,216.0	1,236.0	327.0	243.7	0.6	336.5
New Zealand [a]		538.0	247.0		5.0		
Pacific							
American Samoa							
Fiji							
French Polynesia							
Guam							
Kiribati							
Nauru							
New Caledonia							
Papua New Guinea							
Solomon Islands							
Tonga							
Tuvalu							
Vanuatu							
Western Samoa							
Middle East							
Bahrain			292.5				
Egypt [b,e]	1,100.0	2,025.0	175.4	4.0			
Iran [e,j]	250.0	978.0	70.3	101.8	7.8		
Iraq							
Israel [e]		99.0					
Jordan [e]		218.0					
Kuwait							
Lebanon							
Oman				14.2			
Qatar [e]		527.0					
Saudi Arabia [e]		1,614.0					
Syria [e]		70.0					
United Arab Emirates			244.6				
Yemen							

METAL PRODUCTION

Table No. 0704 (cont'd)

Production of Selected Metals 1992

Units: '000 metric tonnes

	Pig Iron (1991)	Crude Steel (1991)	Aluminium	Refined Copper	Refined Lead	Refined Tin	Zinc
North Africa							
Algeria [b,e]	1,100.0	1,400.0			3.6		29.6
Chad							
Djibouti							
Ethiopia							
Libya							
Mali							
Mauritania							
Morocco					72.0		
Niger							
Somalia							
Sudan							
Tunisia	168.0	192.0					
West Africa							
Benin							
Burkina Faso							
Cameroon			82.5				
Cape Verde							
Côte d'Ivoire							
Equatorial Guinea							
Gabon							
Gambia							
Ghana			179.9				
Guinea							
Guinea-Bissau							
Liberia							
Nigeria [e]		139.3			4.8	0.2	
Sao Tomé e Príncipe							
Senegal							
Sierra Leone							
Togo							
East/Central Africa							
Angola [e]		10.0					
Burundi							
Central African Republic							
Comoros							
Congo							
Kenya							
Madagascar							
Maldives							
Mauritius							
Réunion							
Rwanda							
Seychelles							
Tanzania							
Uganda							
Zaire				57.0			24.0
Southern Africa							
Botswana							
Lesotho							
Malawi							
Mozambique							
Namibia					30.7		
South Africa	1,764.0	8,940.0	174.0	115.8	30.0	1.6	83.2
Swaziland							
Zambia				458.8	2.9		7.3
Zimbabwe [b,e]	484.0	602.0		24.0		0.7	

Source: UN, Monthly Bulletin of Statistics/British Geological Survey/World Bureau of Metal Statistics
Notes: see end of section

TEXTILE PRODUCTION · Table No. 0705

Production of Selected Textiles 1992

Units: '000 metric tonnes

	Cotton Yarn	Woven Cotton Fabric	Wool Yarn	Woven Woollen Fabric	Chemical Fibre Yarn
North America					
Canada	31.6				157.3
USA [a,b]	1,600.8	876.3	611.7	36.5	3,190.0
South America					
Argentina [a]	103.7	86.5	1.3		32.9
Bolivia	3.4				
Brazil	599.2				307.6
Chile	16.5	126.0			15.7
Colombia	94.4	44.4			66.9
Ecuador	35.3	31.8			2.3
French Guiana					
Guyana					
Paraguay	0.7	2.8			
Peru	16.2	19.4			41.8
Suriname					
Uruguay [b,c]				8.2	5.2
Venezuela [a]					49.9
Caribbean					
Anguilla					
Antigua					
Aruba					
Bahamas					
Barbados					
Bermuda					
British Virgin Islands					
Cayman Islands					
Cuba [b,c]	23.1	16.9		0.1	8.9
Dominica					
Dominican Republic	1.2	2.8			
Grenada					
Guadeloupe					
Haiti					
Jamaica					
Martinique					
Netherlands Antilles					
St Kitts					
St Lucia					
St Vincent/Grenadines					
Trinidad and Tobago					
Central America					
Belize					
Costa Rica					4.4
El Salvador	6.4				
Guatemala					
Honduras	1.4	2.3			
Mexico [b,d]	145.0	87.9	2.8	3.5	397.2
Nicaragua					
Panama					
Puerto Rico					
South Asia					
Afghanistan	0.6	6.3			
Bangladesh	71.0	10.9			17.7
Bhutan					
India [a,b]	1,505.7	1,384.3	60.1	31.4	644.0
Nepal					
Pakistan [b,c,d]	1,030.0	711.6	55.4	1.8	47.3
Sri Lanka	8.1	4.4			2.3

TEXTILE PRODUCTION

Table No. 0705 (cont'd)

Production of Selected Textiles 1992

Units: '000 metric tonnes

	Cotton Yarn	Woven Cotton Fabric	Wool Yarn	Woven Woollen Fabric	Chemical Fibre Yarn
Japan					
Japan [e]	378.9	286.7	106.9	344.9	1,692.4
ASEAN/NICs					
Brunei					
Hong Kong [d]	192.0	110.7	7.0		
Indonesia	665.9	639.3			514.8
Macau					
Malaysia	42.0				57.1
Philippines	55.4	62.6			121.6
Singapore					
South Korea [e]	483.6	78.9	30.1	19.8	1,591.6
Taiwan	354.7	241.6	15.1		1,836.6
Thailand	292.7	275.1			482.2
East/SE Asia					
Cambodia					
China [a,f]	4,572.3	2,144.4	238.0	295.1	1,846.7
Laos					
Mongolia [b,c,d]			6.3	3.1	
Myanmar	9.9	4.1			
North Korea					
Vietnam	35.9				
Australasia					
Australia [e,g]	26.0	6.0	19.0	7.7	14.4
New Zealand [a,b,c]			18.3	2.1	
Pacific					
American Samoa					
Fiji					
French Polynesia					
Guam					
Kiribati					
Nauru					
New Caledonia					
Papua New Guinea					
Solomon Islands					
Tonga					
Tuvalu					
Vanuatu					
Western Samoa					
Middle East					
Bahrain					
Egypt [e]	277.9	76.3	16.3	22.7	67.5
Iran	150.3	87.2			54.3
Iraq					3.5
Israel [b,d]	24.5		4.9	0.5	12.7
Jordan					
Kuwait					
Lebanon					
Oman					
Qatar					
Saudi Arabia					
Syria [b,d]	43.6	21.8	2.0	0.5	
United Arab Emirates					
Yemen					

TEXTILE PRODUCTION   Table No. 0705 (cont'd)

Production of Selected Textiles 1992

Units: '000 metric tonnes

	Cotton Yarn	Woven Cotton Fabric	Wool Yarn	Woven Woollen Fabric	Chemical Fibre Yarn
North Africa					
Algeria	32.6	10.4			7.8
Chad					
Djibouti					
Ethiopia	8.7	13.9			
Libya					
Mali					
Mauritania					
Morocco	67.8	38.6			
Niger					
Somalia					
Sudan					
Tunisia					
West Africa					
Benin					
Burkina Faso	0.6	0.1			
Cameroon	4.3	3.7			
Cape Verde					
Côte d'Ivoire	14.4				
Equatorial Guinea					
Gabon					
Gambia					
Ghana					
Guinea					
Guinea-Bissau					
Liberia					
Nigeria					8.3
Sao Tomé e Príncipe					
Senegal	0.6	1.4			
Sierra Leone					
Togo					
East/Central Africa					
Angola					
Burundi					
Central African Republic					
Comoros					
Congo					
Kenya	4.2	10.6			6.1
Madagascar	12.2	6.2			
Maldives					
Mauritius					
Réunion					
Rwanda					
Seychelles					
Tanzania [h]	9.2	34.0			3.0
Uganda	2.3	1.7			
Zaire	4.1	6.7			
Southern Africa					
Botswana					
Lesotho					
Malawi	5.4	3.2			
Mozambique					
Namibia					
South Africa [a,b]	43.2	32.6	1.2	13.4	71.3
Swaziland					
Zambia	7.3	34.4			
Zimbabwe					

Source: International Cotton Advisory Committee/Commonwealth Secretariat/UN/Textile Economics Bureau/national statistical offices

Notes: see end of section

Notes to Tables in Section Seven

Table 0701   Indices relate to the value at constant prices of census value added, or to the contributions to the gross or net domestic product, except where noted
   a   1985 = 100
   b   Figure calculated including construction
   c   Index calculated from value of output in US dollars
   d   Index calculated from value added in US dollars
   e   Peninsular Malaysia only
   f   Figure for 1991 is estimated

Table 0702   Indices based on constant prices
   a   Index covers only selected manufacturing industries
   b   Includes mining industries
   c   Excludes footwear industries
   d   Index calculated from value of output in US dollars
   e   Figure for 1991 is estimated
   f   Index calculated from value added in US dollars

Table 0703   a   Figure for tin refers to 1991
   b   Figure for tin refers to 1990
   c   Production of gold in Brazil is known to be significantly higher than reported
   d   Figure for iron ore refers to 1989
   e   Data refer to 1988
   f   Figure for gold refers to 1988
   g   Figure for copper ore refers to 1991
   h   Figure for bauxite refers to 1991
   i   Figure for tin refers to 1989

   j   Figure for iron ore refers to 1990
   k   Figure for zinc refers to 1990
   l   Figure for gold refers to 1989
   m   Figure for silver refers to 1990
   n   Figure for copper ore refers to 1991
   o   Data refer to 1991 except iron ore
   p   Data for tin and zinc refer to 1991
   q   Figure for silver refers to 1988
   r   Figure for silver refers to 1989

Table 0704   a   Figure for crude steel refers to 1989
   b   Figure for pig iron refers to 1990
   c   Figure for pig iron refers to 1989
   d   Data refer to 1990
   e   Figure for crude steel refers to 1988
   f   Figure for aluminium refers to 1990
   g   Data refer to 1991 except for aluminium and refined copper
   h   Data refer to 1990 except for lead and zinc (1991)
   i   Data refer to 1991
   j   Figure for pig iron refers to 1988

Table 0705   a   Figure for wool yarn refers to 1989
   b   Figure for woven wool fabric refers to 1990
   c   Figure for woven wool fabric is in '000 square metres
   d   Figure for wool yarn refers to 1989
   e   Figure for woven wool fabric is in million square metres
   f   Figure for woven wool fabric is in million metres
   g   Includes New Zealand
   h   Figure for chemical fibre yarn refers to 1988

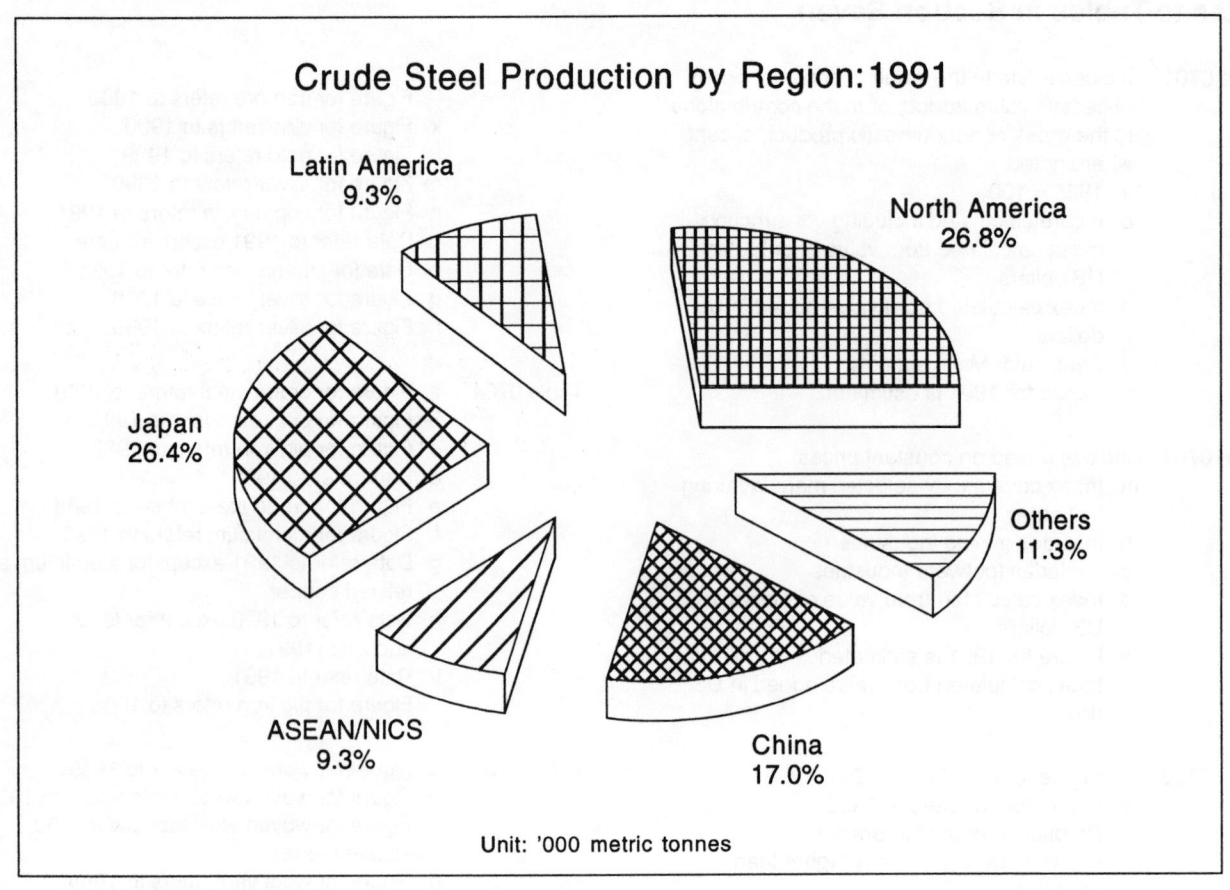

Crude Steel Production by Region: 1991

Latin America
9.3%

North America
26.8%

Japan
26.4%

Others
11.3%

ASEAN/NICS
9.3%

China
17.0%

Unit: '000 metric tonnes

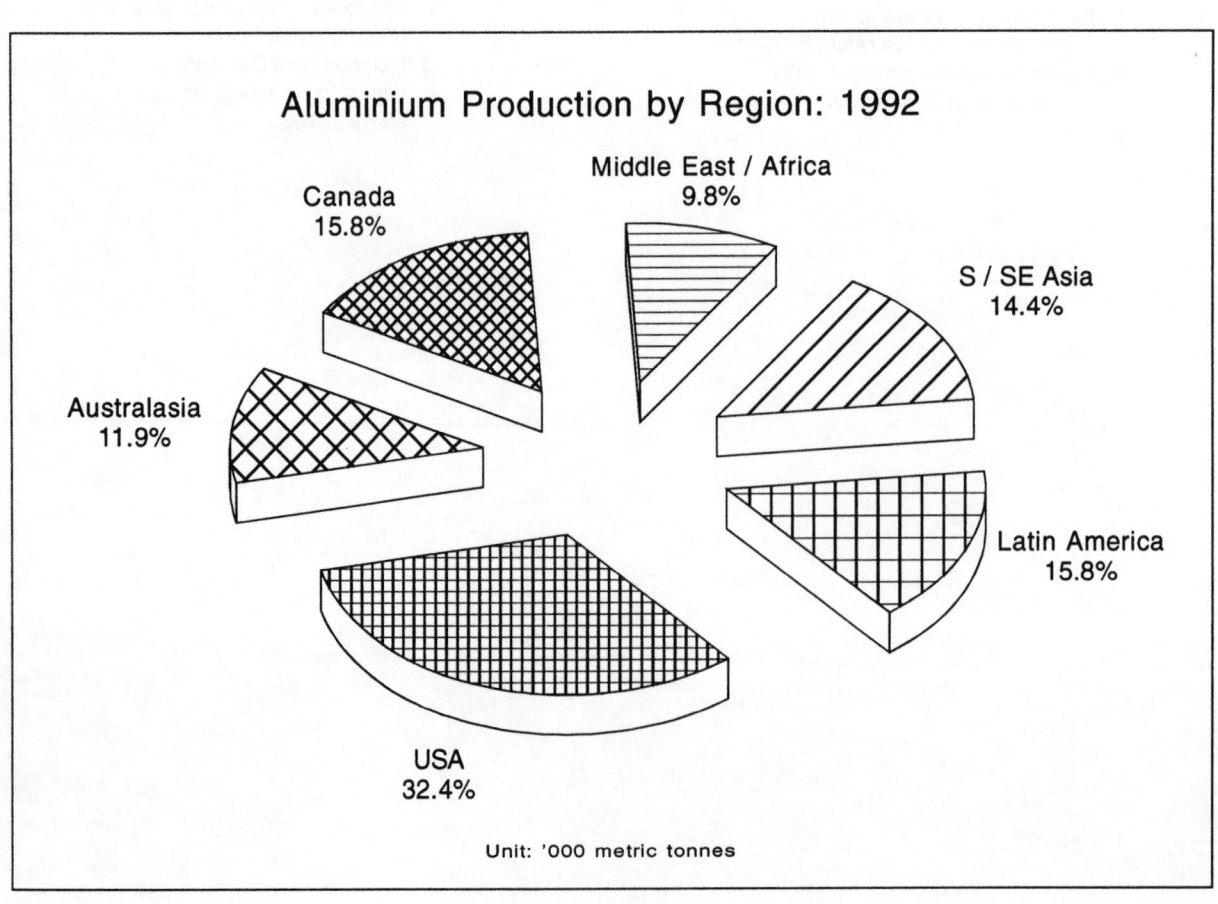

Aluminium Production by Region: 1992

Middle East / Africa
9.8%

Canada
15.8%

S / SE Asia
14.4%

Australasia
11.9%

Latin America
15.8%

USA
32.4%

Unit: '000 metric tonnes

Section Eight
Energy Resources and Output

ENERGY PRODUCTION

Primary Energy Production: Selected Materials 1990

Units: Million tonnes of oil equivalent

	Solid Fuels	Oil and NGL	Natural Gas	Electricity	Total
North America					
Canada	52.8	130.2	136.2	45.4	364.5
USA	788.8	605.9	598.5	108.8	2,102.0
Regional total				*154.2*	*2,466.5*
South America					
Argentina	0.2	37.1	27.1	3.1	67.5
Bolivia		1.6	3.9	0.2	5.7
Brazil	3.0	46.3	5.0	25.7	80.1
Chile	2.2	1.9	2.4	1.1	7.7
Colombia	17.6	31.9	5.6	3.3	58.5
Ecuador		21.5	0.2	0.6	22.3
French Guiana					
Guyana				0.0	
Paraguay				0.3	0.3
Peru	0.1	10.0	0.7	1.3	12.1
Suriname		0.4		0.1	0.5
Uruguay				0.8	0.8
Venezuela	1.9	165.2	26.8	4.6	198.4
Regional total				*41.1*	*453.9*
Caribbean					
Anguilla					
Antigua					
Aruba					
Bahamas					
Barbados		0.0	0.0		0.1
Bermuda					
British Virgin Islands					
Cayman Islands					
Cuba		1.2	0.0	0.0	1.2
Dominica				0.0	
Dominican Republic				0.1	0.1
Grenada					
Guadeloupe					
Haiti				0.0	
Jamaica				0.0	
Martinique					
Netherlands Antilles					
St Kitts					
St Lucia					
St Vincent/Grenadines				0.0	
Trinidad and Tobago		11.2	7.3		18.6
Regional total				*0.1*	*20.0*
Central America					
Belize					
Costa Rica				0.4	0.4
El Salvador				0.3	0.3
Guatemala		0.2		0.3	0.5
Honduras				0.1	0.1
Mexico	7.1	211.2	34.5	4.0	256.9
Nicaragua				0.0	
Panama				0.3	0.3
Puerto Rico				0.0	
Regional total				*5.4*	*258.5*
South Asia					
Afghanistan	0.1	0.0	3.9	0.1	4.1
Bangladesh		0.2	5.3	0.1	5.5
Bhutan				0.2	0.2
India	170.4	47.7	13.2	8.9	240.2
Nepal				0.0	
Pakistan	1.9	3.7	14.6	2.1	22.3
Sri Lanka				0.4	0.4
Regional total				*11.8*	*272.7*

ENERGY PRODUCTION

Table No. 0801 (cont'd)

Primary Energy Production: Selected Materials 1990

Units: Million tonnes of oil equivalent

	Solid Fuels	Oil and NGL	Natural Gas	Electricity	Total
Japan					
Japan	7.3	0.8	2.8	36.8	47.6
Regional total	*7.3*	*0.8*	*2.8*	*36.8*	*47.6*
ASEAN/NICs					
Brunei		11.3	13.9		25.3
Hong Kong					
Indonesia	7.3	100.6	53.9	1.1	162.9
Macau					
Malaysia	0.1	43.5	17.0	0.9	61.5
Philippines	0.8	0.4		1.4	2.6
Singapore					
South Korea	11.1			7.3	18.3
Taiwan					
Thailand	4.6	4.0	7.0	0.6	16.3
Regional total					*286.9*
East/SE Asia					
Cambodia	0.0				
China	770.7	197.3	20.3	13.6	1,001.8
Laos	0.0			0.1	0.1
Mongolia	3.1				3.1
Myanmar	0.0	1.3	1.4	0.2	3.0
North Korea	48.5			3.9	52.4
Vietnam	5.0	3.9	0.0	0.7	9.5
Regional total	*827.3*			*18.5*	*1,069.9*
Australasia					
Australia	143.4	40.3	26.7	1.8	212.2
New Zealand	1.9	2.7	6.1	2.9	13.6
Regional total	*145.3*	*43.0*	*32.8*	*4.7*	*225.8*
Pacific					
American Samoa					
Fiji					
French Polynesia					
Guam					
Kiribati					
Nauru					
New Caledonia				0.1	0.1
Papua New Guinea				0.1	0.1
Solomon Islands					
Tonga					
Tuvalu					
Vanuatu					
Western Samoa					
Regional total				*0.2*	*0.2*
Middle East					
Bahrain		3.5	6.9		10.4
Egypt		69.8	8.7	1.0	79.5
Iran	1.3	227.6	31.9	0.8	261.6
Iraq		145.9	4.3		150.3
Israel		0.0	0.0		0.1
Jordan			0.0		
Kuwait [a]		89.7	7.0		96.7
Lebanon				0.1	0.1
Oman		48.8	3.6		52.4
Qatar		29.5	7.2		36.7
Saudi Arabia [a]		484.2	37.6		521.8
Syria		32.8	0.4	0.6	33.7
United Arab Emirates		153.4	26.9		180.3
Yemen		12.1			12.1
Regional total		*1,297.3*	*134.5*		*1,435.7*

ENERGY PRODUCTION   Table No. 0801 (cont'd)

Primary Energy Production: Selected Materials 1990

Units: Million tonnes of oil equivalent

	Solid Fuels	Oil and NGL	Natural Gas	Electricity	Total
North Africa					
Algeria	0.0	89.3	67.4	0.0	156.7
Chad					
Djibouti					
Ethiopia				0.1	0.1
Libya		97.9	12.7		110.5
Mali				0.0	
Mauritania				0.0	
Morocco	0.5	0.0	0.1	0.2	0.8
Niger	0.2				0.2
Somalia					
Sudan				0.1	0.1
Tunisia		6.7	0.5	0.0	7.1
Regional total					*275.5*
West Africa					
Benin		0.4			0.4
Burkina Faso					
Cameroon	0.0	12.1		0.3	12.4
Cape Verde					
Côte d'Ivoire		0.4		0.2	0.6
Equatorial Guinea				0.0	
Gabon		19.3	0.1	0.1	19.5
Gambia					
Ghana		0.0		0.7	0.7
Guinea				0.0	
Guinea-Bissau					
Liberia				0.0	
Nigeria	0.1	123.6	4.9	0.3	128.9
Sao Tomé e Príncipe				0.0	
Senegal					
Sierra Leone					
Togo					
Regional total					*162.5*
East/Central Africa					
Angola		33.6	0.2	0.2	34.0
Burundi	0.0				
Central African Republic				0.0	
Comoros					
Congo		11.5	0.0	0.0	11.6
Kenya				0.4	0.4
Madagascar				0.0	
Maldives					
Mauritius				0.0	
Réunion				0.1	0.1
Rwanda			0.0	0.0	
Seychelles					
Tanzania	0.0			0.1	0.1
Uganda				0.1	0.1
Zaire	0.1	2.0		0.7	2.9
Regional total					*49.2*
Southern Africa					
Botswana					
Lesotho					
Malawi				0.1	0.1
Mozambique	0.0			0.0	
Namibia					
South Africa [b]	133.1			0.6	133.7
Swaziland					
Zambia	0.3			1.0	1.3
Zimbabwe	5.0			0.4	5.4
Regional total					*140.5*

Source: UN/OECD/International Energy Authority (IEA)/national statistical offices

Notes: see end of section

ENERGY PRODUCTION	Table No. 0802

Refinery Capacities and Utilisation 1990

Units: '000 metric tonnes

	Capacity (1990)	Output (1990)	Utilisation Rate (%, 1989)
North America			
Canada	92,506	78,446.00	87.3
USA	787,859	720,270.00	92.1
Regional total	*880,365*	*798,716*	
South America			
Argentina	32,350	22,321.00	64.5
Bolivia	3,000	972.00	39.3
Brazil	70,771	59,258.00	80.2
Chile	6,000	5,946.00	94.2
Colombia	12,470	10,879.00	99.8
Ecuador	6,719	6,075.00	82.2
French Guiana			
Guyana			
Paraguay	375	342.00	57.3
Peru	9,440	7,443.00	89.9
Suriname			
Uruguay	2,408	1,164.00	50.0
Venezuela	61,220	47,681.00	82.6
Regional total	*204,753*	*162,081*	
Caribbean			
Anguilla			
Antigua	900		
Aruba	7,480		
Bahamas			
Barbados	300	275.00	95.7
Bermuda			
British Virgin Islands			
Cayman Islands			
Cuba	8,826	7,604.00	89.7
Dominica			
Dominican Republic	2,350	1,258.00	63.0
Grenada			
Guadeloupe			
Haiti			
Jamaica	1,850	875.00	50.0
Martinique	580	578.00	96.0
Netherlands Antilles	16,675	10,965.00	61.8
St Kitts			
St Lucia			
St Vincent/Grenadines			
Trinidad and Tobago	18,680	4,557.00	26.8
Regional total			
Central America			
Belize			
Costa Rica	680	381.00	89.7
El Salvador	812	649.00	78.7
Guatemala	1,250	598.00	51.2
Honduras	700	245.00	38.6
Mexico	84,000	61,431.00	82.5
Nicaragua	750	465.00	69.3
Panama	5,000	1,161.00	25.0
Puerto Rico	12,225	7,210.00	46.6
Regional total	*105,417*	*72,140*	
South Asia			
Afghanistan			
Bangladesh	1,500	821.00	86.5
Bhutan			
India	51,850	49,262.00	99.7
Nepal			
Pakistan	6,700	6,254.00	88.5
Sri Lanka	2,350	1,810.00	68.0
Regional total	*62,400*	*58,147*	

ENERGY PRODUCTION   Table No. 0802 (cont'd)

Refinery Capacities and Utilisation 1990

Units: '000 metric tonnes

	Capacity (1990)	Output (1990)	Utilisation Rate (%, 1989)
Japan			
Japan	225,000	172,273	73.2
Sub total	*225,000*	*172,273*	
ASEAN/NICs			
Brunei	500	298	50.0
Hong Kong			
Indonesia	46,000	35,129	75.0
Macau			
Malaysia	10,250	9,284	75.6
Philippines	14,775	10,471	68.9
Singapore	43,820	39,401	83.9
South Korea	42,000	41,919	96.1
Taiwan			
Thailand	12,987	11,575	115.9
Sub total	*170,332*	*148,077*	
East/SE Asia			
Cambodia			
China	112,000	91,627	92.4
Laos [a]			
Mongolia			
Myanmar	2,500	677	35.6
North Korea	3,000	2,770	83.3
Vietnam	40	30	
Sub total	*117,540*	*95,104*	
Australasia			
Australia	36,093	30,641	81.3
New Zealand	4,500	4,360	98.4
Sub total	*40,593*	*35,001*	
Pacific			
American Samoa			
Fiji			
French Polynesia			
Guam			
Kiribati			
Nauru			
New Caledonia			
Papua New Guinea			
Solomon Islands			
Tonga			
Tuvalu			
Vanuatu			
Western Samoa			
Regional total			
Middle East			
Bahrain	12,500	12,067	98.7
Egypt	27,000	22,700	94.3
Iran	35,927	35,170	122.8
Iraq	26,970	17,320	89.4
Israel	11,000	7,997	67.3
Jordan	4,000	2,672	50.3
Kuwait	41,319	27,835	96.7
Lebanon	1,850	1,192	47.7
Oman	3,820	3,100	68.8
Qatar	3,040	2,649	62.8
Saudi Arabia	87,600	73,410	98.6
Syria	12,870	11,438	93.2
United Arab Emirates	9,249	9,070	99.9
Yemen	9,400	4,026	120.4
Sub total	*286,545*	*230,646*	

ENERGY PRODUCTION

Table No. 0802 (cont'd)

Refinery Capacities and Utilisation 1990

Units: '000 metric tonnes

	Capacity (1990)	Output (1990)	Utilisation Rate (%, 1989)
North Africa			
Algeria	22,278	21,980	92.1
Chad			
Djibouti			
Ethiopia	804	601	90.2
Libya	16,720	14,130	71.0
Mali			
Mauritania	1,150	815	85.7
Morocco	7,000	5,378	75.0
Niger			
Somalia	500	214	49.6
Sudan	1,290	951	78.4
Tunisia	1,690	1,631	98.2
Sub total	*51,432*	*45,700*	
West Africa			
Benin			
Burkina Faso			
Cameroon	3,500	1,943	57.3
Cape Verde			
Côte d'Ivoire	3,000	1,457	60.4
Equatorial Guinea			
Gabon	2,300	653	47.6
Gambia			
Ghana	1,320	549	74.6
Guinea			
Guinea-Bissau			
Liberia	750		
Nigeria	21,458	8,993	50.0
Sao Tomé e Príncipe			
Senegal [a]	900	699	88.6
Sierra Leone	700	280	40.3
Togo	1,000		
Sub total	*34,928*	*14,574*	
East/Central Africa			
Angola	2,250	1,332	66.7
Burundi			
Central African Republic			
Comoros			
Congo	1,100	570	47.0
Kenya	4,750	2,124	42.3
Madagascar	810	159	24.1
Maldives			
Mauritius			
Réunion			
Rwanda			
Seychelles			
Tanzania	850	526	64.7
Uganda			
Zaire	850	260	39.4
Sub total	*10,610*	*4,971*	
Southern Africa			
Botswana			
Lesotho			
Malawi			
Mozambique	800		
Namibia			
South Africa	21,090	15,481	77.3
Swaziland			
Zambia	1,220	510	48.4
Zimbabwe	1,000		
Sub total	*24,110*	*15,991*	

Source: UN, Energy Statistics Yearbook/OECD/IEA
Notes: see end of section

ENERGY CONSUMPTION

Table No. 0803

Commercial Energy Consumption 1990

Units: Million tonnes of coal equivalent

	Solid Fuels	Oil and NGL	Natural Gas	Primary Electricity	Total
North America					
Canada	33.7	110.4	82.5	45.3	272.0
USA	693.6	1,049.0	630.1	109.0	2,481.7
Regional total	*727.3*	*1,159.4*	*712.6*	*154.3*	*2,753.7*
South America					
Argentina	1.2	24.6	30.0	3.2	59.0
Bolivia		1.5	0.9	0.2	2.6
Brazil	12.8	68.6	4.9	28.8	115.1
Chile	3.7	9.3	2.3	1.1	16.5
Colombia	4.9	11.6	5.6	3.4	25.4
Ecuador		6.9	0.2	0.6	7.7
French Guiana		0.3			0.3
Guyana		0.3			0.3
Paraguay		0.7		0.2	0.9
Peru	0.2	8.4	0.7	1.3	10.6
Suriname	0.0	0.6		0.1	0.8
Uruguay		1.7		0.6	2.3
Venezuela	0.2	24.4	26.8	4.6	56.0
Regional total	*23.0*	*158.9*	*71.4*	*44.1*	*297.5*
Caribbean					
Anguilla					
Antigua		0.1			0.1
Aruba		0.2			0.2
Bahamas		0.6			0.6
Barbados		0.4	0.0		0.4
Bermuda		0.3			0.3
British Virgin Islands		0.0			
Cayman Islands		0.1	0.0		0.1
Cuba	0.3	15.0	0.0		15.3
Dominica		0.0			
Dominican Republic		2.5		0.1	2.6
Grenada		0.0			
Guadeloupe		0.5			0.5
Haiti		0.3			0.3
Jamaica		2.0			2.0
Martinique		0.6			0.6
Netherlands Antilles		1.8			1.8
St Kitts		0.0			
St Lucia		0.1			0.1
St Vincent/Grenadines		0.0			
Trinidad and Tobago		1.4	7.3		8.8
Regional total	*0.3*	*25.9*	*7.3*	*0.1*	*33.7*
Central America					
Belize		0.1			0.1
Costa Rica		1.3		0.5	1.8
El Salvador		1.0		0.3	1.3
Guatemala		1.5		0.3	1.7
Honduras		0.7		0.1	0.9
Mexico	7.5	108.9	35.0	3.9	155.3
Nicaragua		0.9		0.1	1.0
Panama	0.0	1.1	0.1	0.3	1.5
Puerto Rico	0.2	10.2			10.5
Regional total	*7.7*	*125.7*	*35.1*	*5.5*	*174.1*
South Asia					
Afghanistan	0.1	0.9	2.5	0.1	3.6
Bangladesh	0.4	2.7	5.3	0.1	8.4
Bhutan	0.0	0.0			0.1
India	177.6	65.2	13.2	9.0	264.9
Nepal	0.0	0.3		0.1	0.4
Pakistan	2.7	14.7	14.6	2.1	34.0
Sri Lanka	0.0	1.8		0.4	2.2
Regional total	*180.8*	*85.6*	*35.6*	*11.8*	*313.6*

ENERGY CONSUMPTION

Table No. 0803 (cont'd)

Commercial Energy Consumption 1990

Units: Million tonnes of coal equivalent

	Solid Fuels	Oil and NGL	Natural Gas	Primary Electricity	Total
Japan					
Japan	114.8	292.1	68.4	36.8	512.10
Regional total	*114.8*	*292.1*	*68.4*	*36.8*	*512.1*
ASEAN/NICs					
Brunei		0.8	3.2		4.00
Hong Kong	6.8	3.8		-0.2	10.40
Indonesia	3.5	34.5	10.6	1.1	49.70
Macau		0.5			0.50
Malaysia	1.9	19.6	4.5	0.9	27.00
Philippines	2.1	15.2		1.4	18.80
Singapore	0.0	15.0			15.10
South Korea	35.4	58.9	4.3	7.3	105.90
Taiwan					
Thailand	4.9	28.5	7.0	0.7	41.10
Regional total	*54.6*	*176.8*	*29.6*	*11.2*	*272.5*
East/SE Asia					
Cambodia		0.2			0.20
China	759.4	128.8	20.3	13.8	922.20
Laos		0.1			0.20
Mongolia	2.9	1.0			3.90
Myanmar	0.1	0.8	1.4	0.2	2.50
North Korea	51.2	5.0		3.9	60.10
Vietnam	4.4	4.3		0.7	9.40
Regional total	*818.0*	*140.2*	*21.7*	*18.6*	*998.5*
Australasia					
Australia	54.1	48.2	23.1	1.8	127.10
New Zealand	1.6	6.3	6.1	2.9	16.90
Regional total	*55.7*	*54.5*	*29.2*	*4.7*	*144.0*
Pacific					
American Samoa		0.1			0.10
Fiji	0.0	0.3			0.40
French Polynesia		0.3			0.30
Guam		0.7			0.70
Kiribati		0.0			
Nauru		0.1			0.10
New Caledonia	0.2	0.5		0.1	0.70
Papua New Guinea	0.0	1.1		0.1	1.10
Solomon Islands		0.1			0.10
Tonga		0.0			
Tuvalu					
Vanuatu		0.0			
Western Samoa		0.1			0.10
Regional total	*0.2*	*3.3*		*0.2*	*3.6*
Middle East					
Bahrain		1.2	6.9		8.00
Egypt	0.7	19.5	6.1	0.7	27.00
Iran	1.8	57.7	30.1	0.8	90.30
Iraq	0.0	14.9	1.5	0.1	16.50
Israel	3.7	11.0	0.1		14.70
Jordan		4.3			4.30
Kuwait [a]		4.6	9.7		14.30
Lebanon		4.0		0.1	4.10
Oman		2.3	3.6		5.90
Qatar		1.5	7.2		8.70
Saudi Arabia [a]		52.8	37.6		90.40
Syria		12.4	0.4	0.6	13.30
United Arab Emirates		9.4	22.6		32.10
Yemen		3.9			3.90
Regional total	*6.2*	*199.5*	*125.8*	*2.3*	*333.5*

315

ENERGY CONSUMPTION

Table No. 0803 (cont'd)

Commercial Energy Consumption 1990

Units: Million tonnes of coal equivalent

	Solid Fuels	Oil and NGL	Natural Gas	Primary Electricity	Total
North Africa					
Algeria	0.9	7.0	18.0		25.9
Chad		0.1			0.1
Djibouti		0.1			0.1
Ethiopia		0.8		0.1	0.9
Libya	0.0	7.3	7.7		15.0
Mali		0.1			0.2
Mauritania	0.0	0.8			0.8
Morocco	1.2	5.0	0.0	0.1	6.4
Niger	0.1	0.2			0.3
Somalia		0.3			0.3
Sudan		1.0		0.1	1.1
Tunisia	0.1	3.0	1.5		4.7
Regional total	*2.3*	*25.7*	*27.2*	*0.3*	*55.8*
West Africa					
Benin		0.1			0.1
Burkina Faso		0.2			0.2
Cameroon	0.0	1.8		0.2	2.0
Cape Verde		0.0			
Côte d'Ivoire		1.5		0.1	1.6
Equatorial Guinea		0.0			
Gabon		0.4	0.1	0.1	0.6
Gambia		0.1			0.1
Ghana	0.0	0.6		0.4	1.0
Guinea		0.3			0.3
Guinea-Bissau		0.1			0.1
Liberia		0.1			0.2
Nigeria	0.0	10.6	3.5	0.2	14.3
Sao Tomé e Príncipe		0.0			
Senegal		0.7			0.7
Sierra Leone		0.2			0.2
Togo		0.1			0.2
Regional total	*16.8*	*3.6*	*1.0*	*21.6*	
East/Central Africa					
Angola		0.4	0.2	0.1	0.6
Burundi	0.0	0.1			0.1
Central African Republic		0.1			0.1
Comoros		0.0			
Congo		0.6	0.0		0.6
Kenya	0.1	1.5		0.3	1.9
Madagascar	0.0	0.3			0.3
Maldives		0.0			
Mauritius	0.1	0.3			0.4
Réunion		0.3			0.3
Rwanda		0.1	0.0		0.1
Seychelles		0.1			0.1
Tanzania	0.0	0.6		0.1	0.7
Uganda		0.3			0.3
Zaire	0.2	0.9		0.5	1.6
Regional total	*0.4*	*5.6*	*0.2*	*1.0*	*7.1*
Southern Africa					
Botswana					
Lesotho					
Malawi	0.0	0.1			0.2
Mozambique	0.0	0.3			0.3
Namibia					
South Africa [b]	63.4	10.8		0.2	74.4
Swaziland					
Zambia	0.2	0.4		0.5	1.2
Zimbabwe	3.5	0.6		0.4	4.4
Regional total	*67.1*	*12.2*		*1.1*	*80.5*

Source: UN/OECD/IEA/national statistical offices

Notes: see end of section

ENERGY CONSUMPTION

Table No. 0804

Consumption of Motor Gasoline 1977-1991

Units: '000 metric tonnes

	1977	1980	1983	1985	1986	1987	1988	1989	1990	1991
North America										
Canada	26,072	28,290	23,814	24,078	24,174	24,423	25,090	25,581	24,951	24,211
USA	308,188	285,052	284,370	289,922	296,996	307,129	315,690	315,901	312,705	307,658
Regional total	*334,260*	*313,342*	*308,184*	*314,000*	*321,170*	*331,552*	*340,780*	*341,482*	*337,656*	*331,869*
South America										
Argentina	4,490	5,445	5,288	4,383	4,531	4,549	4,039	4,025	4,003	
Bolivia	481	413	335	340	321	356	363	376	362	
Brazil	9,902	7,928	9,925	11,712	14,590	13,990	14,323	15,813	16,119	
Chile	1,018	1,100	1,181	997	1,039	1,094	1,220	1,330	1,374	
Colombia	2,879	3,145	3,435	3,639	3,764	3,932	4,485	4,474	4,501	
Ecuador	768	1,264	1,113	1,089	1,237	1,197	1,347	1,273	1,367	
French Guiana	28	25	25	22	17	27	28	28	30	
Guyana	40	37	48	49	30	28	25	25	25	
Paraguay	96	126	70	112	117	116	117	116	116	
Peru	1,299	1,168	1,196	1,129	1,116	1,309	1,307	1,135	1,185	
Suriname	37	42	35	48	45	43	35	35		
Uruguay	227	221	171	166	169	179	191	203	190	
Venezuela	5,510	6,966	7,100	6,652	6,510	4,060	5,100	4,657	7,042	
Regional total	*26,775*	*27,880*	*29,922*	*30,338*	*33,486*	*30,880*	*32,580*	*33,490*	*36,314*	
Caribbean										
Anguilla										
Antigua	5	8	56	111	112	112	113	113	114	
Aruba					8	20	22	20	20	
Bahamas	89	83	65	50	50	50	50	60	55	
Barbados	55	51	48	47	47	51	53	57	58	
Bermuda	39	22	23	21	20	26	27	33	22	
British Virgin Islands	3	3	4	4	4	5	5	5	5	
Cayman Islands	6	10	11	10	17	19	19	19	20	
Cuba	978	1,088	1,160	1,156	1,198	1,172	1,208	1,261	1,165	
Dominica	5	5	6	6	8	8	9	10	10	
Dominican Republic	322	289	274	297	346	361	360	362	365	
Grenada	7	7	6	5	6	7	10	11	14	
Guadeloupe	64	45	58	59	91	97	104	108	110	
Haiti	30	45	42	42	41	40	41	40	40	
Jamaica	286	205	180	170	188	193	174	214	205	
Martinique	81	77	86	62	67	70	69	71	72	
Netherlands Antilles [a]	108	150	77	100	100	99	100	100	100	
St Kitts	3	5	5	5	5	5	6	6	6	
St Lucia	9	20	11	15	17	18	20	20	20	
St Vincent/Grenadines	4	5	5	5	7	9	8	10	10	
Trinidad and Tobago	243	765	684	402	469	440	460	432	432	
Regional total	*2,337*	*2,883*	*2,801*	*2,567*	*2,801*	*2,802*	*2,858*	*2,952*	*2,843*	
Central America										
Belize	21	22	20	24	18	20	21	20	21	
Costa Rica	136	129	136	163	179	165	167	172	218	
El Salvador	140	133	130	135	133	148	158	161	162	
Guatemala	241	254	235	250	234	263	284	290	282	
Honduras	119	93	120	130	123	115	115	115	112	
Mexico	8,395	13,764	13,604	13,971	14,183	14,823	14,903	15,800	18,200	
Nicaragua	185	130	126	121	130	128	131	130	120	
Panama	254	218	182	186	180	175	180	170	160	
Puerto Rico	1,860	1,940	1,847	1,700	1,930	2,145	1,900	1,900	2,000	
Regional total	*11,351*	*16,683*	*16,400*	*16,680*	*17,110*	*17,982*	*17,859*	*18,758*	*21,275*	
South Asia										
Afghanistan	68	102	98	95	55	123	108	110	113	
Bangladesh	57	58	35	40	53	53	53	60	72	
Bhutan		1	1	1	1	1	1	1	2	
India	1,370	1,459	1,928	2,238	2,449	2,658	2,683	3,238	3,527	
Nepal	18	13	11	13	14	14	16	14	11	
Pakistan	522	578	552	784	823	872	940	1,010	1,117	
Sri Lanka	110	102	113	123	131	141	159	150	169	
Regional total	*2,145*	*2,313*	*2,738*	*3,294*	*3,526*	*3,862*	*3,960*	*4,583*	*5,011*	

ENERGY CONSUMPTION   Table No. 0804 (cont'd)

Consumption of Motor Gasoline 1977-1991

Units: '000 metric tonnes

	1977	1980	1983	1985	1986	1987	1988	1989	1990	1991
Japan										
Japan	23,127	25,432	26,474	26,878	27,506	27,987	29,023	30,782	32,624	33,683
Regional total	*23,127*	*25,432*	*26,474*	*26,878*	*27,506*	*27,987*	*29,023*	*30,782*	*32,624*	*33,683*
ASEAN/NICs										
Brunei	54	72	65	110	148	162	169	173	180	
Hong Kong	133	190	220	195	186	197	196	222	293	
Indonesia	2,112	2,892	3,670	3,011	3,376	3,580	3,789	3,801	3,668	
Macau	10	12	13	14	15	15	19	19	18	
Malaysia	543	1,254	1,616	1,955	2,000	2,169	2,265	2,429	2,682	
Philippines	1,720	1,552	1,077	992	1,074	1,193	1,294	1,447	1,508	
Singapore	293	349	615	695	700	695	759	681	760	
South Korea	818	769	544	814	1,007	1,218	1,597	2,159	2,787	
Taiwan										
Thailand	1,608	1,706	1,530	1,547	1,680	1,899	2,177	2,463	2,728	
Regional total	*7,291*	*8,796*	*9,350*	*9,333*	*10,186*	*11,128*	*12,265*	*13,394*	*14,624*	
East/SE Asia										
Cambodia	15	12	11	25	39	30	33	32	32	
China	10,305	9,920	9,497	13,996	15,002	16,273	17,553	19,431	19,790	
Laos			10	14	14	14	14	15	15	
Mongolia	170	220	250	260	329	358	375	339	310	
Myanmar	219	247	243	234	210	176	134	126	124	
North Korea	504	700	850	950	1,000	1,020	1,020	1,070	1,065	
Vietnam	160	250	250	270	280	280	280	471	703	
Regional total	*11,373*	*11,349*	*11,111*	*15,749*	*16,874*	*18,151*	*19,409*	*21,484*	*22,039*	
Australasia										
Australia	10,479	10,915	11,082	11,540	11,755	11,742	12,157	12,534	12,735	12,389
New Zealand	1,700	1,645	1,676	1,624	1,680	1,712	1,793	1,872	1,929	1,794
Regional total	*12,179*	*12,560*	*12,758*	*13,164*	*13,435*	*13,454*	*13,950*	*14,406*	*14,664*	*14,183*
Pacific										
American Samoa	6	9	8	8	12	5	17	12	16	
Fiji	39	43	37	45	41	48	50	52	52	
French Polynesia	30	31	35	36	37	38	38	38	40	
Guam	97	90	85	85	85	85	85	90	90	
Kiribati	1	1	1	1	1	1	1	1	1	
Nauru	5	6	6	6	6	6	6	6	6	
New Caledonia	54	93	77	47	50	49	52	53	55	
Papua New Guinea	95	86	80	84	76	83	85	85	87	
Solomon Islands	4	4	6	6	7	7	8	8	8	
Tonga	3	3	4	4	4	6	8	8	8	
Tuvalu										
Vanuatu				5	4	3	4	4	4	
Western Samoa	8	10	14	14	14	14	14	15	15	
Regional total	*342*	*376*	*353*	*341*	*337*	*345*	*368*	*372*	*382*	
Middle East										
Bahrain	75	110	150	170	179	186	198	200	200	
Egypt	1,531	1,325	1,583	1,958	2,025	2,105	2,109	2,140	2,210	
Iran	3,102	3,596	3,854	4,457	4,300	4,310	4,575	4,810	5,000	
Iraq	580	1,150	1,340	1,450	1,550	2,079	2,303	2,300	2,300	
Israel	702	750	1,010	1,014	1,101	1,265	1,363	1,368	1,682	
Jordan	215	270	319	332	347	338	338	339	400	
Kuwait	605	892	1,063	1,127	1,120	1,152	1,200	1,250	1,080	
Lebanon	400	500	320	739	666	680	650	690	710	
Oman	139	200	300	397	411	347	394	438	483	
Qatar	110	170	223	247	249	339	343	346	455	
Saudi Arabia	1,958	3,240	5,502	6,100	6,070	6,111	5,845	6,200	6,400	
Syria	482	600	693	845	1,135	943	960	950	1,200	
United Arab Emirates	371	585	684	770	890	840	929	900	850	
Yemen	196	256	415	379	359	444	456	466	495	
Regional total	*10,466*	*13,644*	*17,456*	*19,985*	*20,402*	*21,139*	*21,663*	*22,397*	*23,465*	

ENERGY CONSUMPTION

Table No. 0804 (cont'd)

Consumption of Motor Gasoline 1977-1991

Units: '000 metric tonnes

	1977	1980	1983	1985	1986	1987	1988	1989	1990	1991
North Africa										
Algeria	798	1,214	1,294	1,680	1,789	1,716	1,740	1,744	1,780	
Chad	23	24	25	25	23	24	24	24	25	
Djibouti	10	14	11	11	14	14	15	15	16	
Ethiopia	75	160	123	116	123	124	119	119	123	
Libya	575	818	1,080	983	742	1,128	1,000	1,350	1,400	
Mali	45	54	60	51	52	51	55	57	55	
Mauritania	26	31	32	32	29	31	31	31	23	
Morocco	366	378	346	332	338	382	366	383	393	
Niger	25	35	33	42	39	41	43	43	44	
Somalia	73	45	70	68	77	82	83	85	82	
Sudan	225	152	187	194	190	184	187	189	200	
Tunisia	141	154	189	220	220	218	240	246	251	
Regional total	*2,382*	*3,079*	*3,450*	*3,754*	*3,636*	*3,995*	*3,903*	*4,286*	*4,392*	
West Africa										
Benin	31	34	27	59	56	59	58	59	59	
Burkina Faso	31	53	57	51	47	51	53	54	55	
Cameroon	138	320	429	413	408	400	394	396	379	
Cape Verde	1	2	3	3	2	3	4	4	4	
Côte d'Ivoire	216	317	223	272	407	436	407	307	339	
Equatorial Guinea	5	2	4	5	1	3	3	4	5	
Gabon	15	30	80	38	40	39	41	50	53	
Gambia	18	22	22	22	23	24	25	25	25	
Ghana	225	246	253	280	281	232	224	231	183	
Guinea	42	46	47	65	67	66	69	67	64	
Guinea-Bissau	6	7	6	7	7	9	8	9	10	12
Liberia	67	69	72	49	50	49	54	54	29	
Nigeria	982	2,955	4,183	2,979	3,655	3,618	4,327	4,180	4,540	
Sao Tomé e Príncipe	3	5	5	5	5	5	5	5	5	
Senegal	86	130	122	108	144	84	93	201	182	
Sierra Leone	42	20	25	30	30	32	34	35	35	
Togo	39	50	36	34	36	34	36	38	40	
Regional total	*1,947*	*4,308*	*5,594*	*4,420*	*5,261*	*5,143*	*5,836*	*5,720*	*6,009*	
East/Central Africa										
Angola	86	80	80	84	75	75	70	70	71	
Burundi	13	16	13	17	15	16	18	20	24	
Central African Republic	15	22	23	15	15	19	14	19	12	
Comoros	3	3	3	3	3	3	3	3	4	
Congo	30	35	41	42	45	41	41	55	44	
Kenya	280	313	223	239	254	252	250	333	298	
Madagascar	100	95	13	48	47	75	58	52	60	
Maldives		1	1	1	1	1	1	1	1	
Mauritius	56	33	35	32	39	44	47	53	56	
Rwanda	18	23	28	21	23	22	23	23	24	
Réunion	72	98	91	69	77	77	76	74	76	
Seychelles	6	6	5	5	5	6	6	6	6	
Tanzania	99	87	82	87	85	90	92	85	92	
Uganda	95	88	79	79	74	74	82	85	86	
Zaire	154	198	190	175	176	182	185	185	204	
Regional total	*1,027*	*1,098*	*907*	*917*	*934*	*977*	*966*	*1,064*	*1,058*	
Southern Africa										
Botswana										
Lesotho										
Malawi	36	55	48	46	46	43	47	47	48	
Mozambique	79	93	90	40	33	35	36	38	39	
Namibia										
South Africa [b]	3,559	3,680	4,500	4,400	4,400	4,350	4,355	4,360	4,350	
Swaziland										
Zambia	174	170	150	110	105	107	109	110	106	
Zimbabwe	200	180	211	184	198	165	170	175	171	
Regional total	*4,048*	*4,178*	*4,999*	*4,780*	*4,782*	*4,700*	*4,717*	*4,730*	*4,714*	

Source: UN/national statistical offices/OECD-IEA

Notes: see end of section

ENERGY PRODUCTION   Table No. 0805

Electricity Production 1990

Units: Million kWh

	Thermal	Hydro	Nuclear	Other	Total	Public Supply	Self-producer Supply
North America							
Canada	112,194	296,685	72,886	26	481,791	440,317	41,474
USA	2,145,603	290,964	576,862	17,629	3,031,058	2,807,058	224,000
Regional total	*2,257,797*	*587,649*	*649,748*	*17,655*	*3,512,849*	*3,247,375*	*265,474*
South America							
Argentina	25,493	18,133	7,281		50,907	47,007	3,900
Bolivia	670	1,285			1,955	1,645	310
Brazil	12,728	207,230	2,237		222,195	211,324	10,871
Chile	9,298	9,074			18,372	13,822	4,550
Colombia	8,800	27,200			36,000	33,555	2,445
Ecuador	1,355	4,972			6,327	6,327	
French Guiana	335				335	335	
Guyana	215	5			220	106	114
Paraguay	4	2,430			2,434	2,434	
Peru	3,344	10,473			13,817	9,557	4,260
Suriname	255	1,095			1,350	125	1,225
Uruguay	1,000	6,372			7,372	7,285	87
Venezuela	23,755	37,245			61,000	55,850	5,150
Regional total	*87,252*	*325,514*	*9,518*		*422,284*	*389,372*	*32,912*
Caribbean							
Anguilla							
Antigua	95				95	95	
Aruba	375				375	375	
Bahamas	950				950	900	50
Barbados	468				468	468	
Bermuda	490				490	490	
British Virgin Islands	45				45	45	
Cayman Islands	225				225	225	
Cuba	16,160	85			16,245	14,545	1,700
Dominica	14	16			30	30	
Dominican Republic	4,475	850			5,325	3,325	2,000
Grenada	51				51	51	
Guadeloupe	684				684	684	
Haiti	150	325			475	450	25
Jamaica	2,600	130			2,730	1,880	850
Martinique	615				615	615	
Netherlands Antilles	735				735	335	400
St Kitts	37				37	30	7
St Lucia	104				104	104	
St Vincent/Grenadines	12	36			48	48	
Trinidad and Tobago	3,480				3,480	3,365	115
Regional total	*31,765*	*1,442*			*33,207*	*28,060*	*5,147*
Central America							
Belize	105				105	105	
Costa Rica	95	3,514			3,609	3,544	65
El Salvador	204	1,673		419	2,296	2,243	53
Guatemala	235	2,090			2,325	2,225	100
Honduras	220	885			1,105	1,045	60
Mexico	89,672	25,205	2,900	4,700	122,477	114,277	8,200
Nicaragua	485	263		290	1,038	965	73
Panama	688	2,213			2,901	2,661	240
Puerto Rico	15,048	280			15,328	14,948	380
Regional total	*106,752*	*36,123*	*2,900*	*5,409*	*151,184*	*142,013*	*9,171*
South Asia							
Afghanistan	364	764			1,128	814	314
Bangladesh	7,173	884			8,057	7,732	325
Bhutan	7	1,557			1,564	1,557	7
India	213,860	66,094	6,075	6	286,035	264,300	21,735
Nepal	27	712			739	714	25
Pakistan	26,659	16,947	293		43,899	37,999	5,900
Sri Lanka	5	3,145			3,150	3,150	
Regional total	*248,095*	*90,103*	*6,368*	*6*	*344,572*	*316,266*	*28,306*

ENERGY PRODUCTION

Electricity Production 1990

Units: Million kWh

	Thermal	Hydro	Nuclear	Other	Total	Public Supply	Self-producer Supply
Japan							
Japan	557,424	95,836	202,272	1,741	857,273	757,594	99,679
Regional total	*557,424*	*95,836*	*202,272*	*1,741*	*857,273*	*757,594*	*99,679*
ASEAN/NICs							
Brunei	1,215				1,215	1,150	65
Hong Kong	28,938				28,938	28,938	
Indonesia	35,100	8,950		210	44,260	29,810	14,450
Macau	790				790	753	37
Malaysia	17,615	7,108			24,723	23,523	1,200
Philippines	14,783	6,078		5,466	26,327	25,249	1,078
Singapore	15,618				15,618	15,618	
South Korea	59,490	6,361	52,887		118,738	107,670	11,068
Taiwan							
Thailand	41,199	4,976			46,175	44,175	2,000
Regional total	*214,748*	*33,473*	*52,887*	*5,676*	*306,784*	*276,886*	*29,898*
East/SE Asia							
Cambodia	40	30			70	70	
China	507,500	110,500			618,000	618,000	
Laos	45	825			870	870	
Mongolia	3,600				3,600	3,275	325
Myanmar	1,357	1,244			2,601	2,540	61
North Korea	21,750	31,750			53,500	53,500	
Vietnam	3,351	5,371			8,722	8,722	
Regional total	*537,643*	*149,720*			*687,363*	*686,977*	*386*
Australasia							
Australia	139,786	14,785			154,571	143,261	11,310
New Zealand	6,404	21,944		1,810	30,158	30,158	
Regional total	*146,190*	*36,729*		*1,810*	*184,729*	*173,419*	*11,310*
Pacific							
American Samoa	90				90	90	
Fiji	100	335			435	395	40
French Polynesia	205	70			275	275	
Guam	800				800	800	
Kiribati	7				7	7	
Nauru	29				29	29	
New Caledonia	683	461			1,144	1,144	
Papua New Guinea	1,330	460			1,790	535	1,255
Solomon Islands	30				30	25	5
Tonga	22				22	22	
Tuvalu							
Vanuatu	26				26	20	6
Western Samoa	30	20			50	42	8
Regional total	*3,352*	*1,346*			*4,698*	*3,384*	*1,314*
Middle East							
Bahrain	3,490				3,490	3,180	310
Egypt	31,450	8,100			39,550	37,100	2,450
Iran	49,400	6,600			56,000	53,200	2,800
Iraq	28,550	610			29,160	28,410	750
Israel	20,730				20,730	20,250	480
Jordan	3,670	18			3,688	3,308	380
Kuwait	20,610				20,610	20,200	410
Lebanon	4,185	550			4,735	4,600	135
Oman	5,345				5,345	4,504	841
Qatar	4,624				4,624	4,600	24
Saudi Arabia	47,400				47,400	46,000	1,400
Syria	5,820	4,780			10,600	9,680	920
United Arab Emirates	13,590				13,590	1,290	12,300
Yemen	1,740				1,740	1,600	140
Regional total	*240,604*	*20,658*			*261,262*	*237,922*	*23,340*

ENERGY PRODUCTION

Electricity Production 1990

Units: Million kWh

	Thermal	Hydro	Nuclear	Other	Total	Public Supply	Self-producer Supply
North Africa							
Algeria	15,859	135			15,994	15,442	552
Chad	82				82	82	
Djibouti	175				175	175	
Ethiopia	118	722		66	906	790	116
Libya	19,000				19,000	19,000	
Mali	42	172			214	201	13
Mauritania	115	25			140	140	
Morocco	8,408	1,220			9,628	8,618	1,010
Niger	163				163	163	
Somalia	230				230	230	
Sudan	390	937			1,327	1,201	126
Tunisia	5,500	36			5,536	4,936	600
Regional total	*50,082*	*3,247*		*66*	*53,395*	*50,978*	*2,417*
West Africa							
Benin	5				5	5	
Burkina Faso	155				155	155	
Cameroon	70	2,635			2,705	2,705	
Cape Verde	36				36	35	1
Côte d'Ivoire	775	1,590			2,365	2,365	
Equatorial Guinea	16	2			18	18	
Gabon	210	705			915	915	
Gambia	67				67	56	11
Ghana	53	5,235			5,288	5,284	4
Guinea	343	175			518	213	305
Guinea-Bissau	17				17	13	4
Liberia	320	245			565	297	268
Nigeria	7,730	2,215			9,945	9,870	75
Sao Tomé e Príncipe	7	8			15	15	
Senegal	684				684	672	12
Sierra Leone	224				224	137	87
Togo	36	5			41	40	1
Regional total	*10,748*	*12,815*			*23,563*	*22,795*	*768*
East/Central Africa							
Angola	480	1,360			1,840	1,685	155
Burundi	2	104			106	106	
Central African Republic	18	77			95	95	
Comoros	14	2			16	16	
Congo		398			398	398	
Kenya	171	2,537		336	3,044	2,974	70
Madagascar	248	318			566	450	116
Maldives	29				29	29	
Mauritius	685	85			770	570	200
Réunion	316	501			817	788	29
Rwanda	4	172			176	64	112
Seychelles	85				85	85	
Tanzania	273	612			885	787	98
Uganda	7	596			603	566	37
Zaire	155	6,000			6,155	4,029	2,126
Regional total	*2,487*	*12,762*		*336*	*15,585*	*12,642*	*2,943*
Southern Africa							
Botswana [a]							
Lesotho [a]							
Malawi	14	573			587	571	16
Mozambique	435	50			485	335	150
Namibia [a]							
South Africa	159,824	764	3,930		164,518	157,480	7,038
Swaziland [a]							
Zambia	40	7,731			7,771	7,546	225
Zimbabwe	6,036	3,523			9,559	9,401	158
Regional total	*166,349*	*12,641*	*3,930*		*182,920*	*175,333*	*7,587*

Source: UN/OECD/IEA/national statistical offices

Notes: see end of section

ENERGY CONSUMPTION	Table No. 0806

Household Consumption of Electricity 1977-1990

Units: Terajoules

	1977	1980	1983	1985	1986	1987	1988	1989	1990	% growth 1977-90
North America										
Canada	276,167	305,811	345,589	373,946	393,190	402,340	434,853	468,128	468,957	69.8
USA	2,326,108	2,586,593	2,707,192	2,861,776	2,947,702	3,062,883	3,216,140	3,260,748	3,331,115	43.2
Regional total	*2,602,275*	*2,892,404*	*3,052,781*	*3,235,722*	*3,340,892*	*3,465,223*	*3,650,993*	*3,728,876*	*3,800,072*	*46.0*
South America										
Argentina	24,641	29,199	32,566	35,086	37,642	44,003	44,640	38,084	38,513	56.3
Bolivia	942	1,303	1,478	1,447	1,512	2,066	2,336	2,513	2,538	169.4
Brazil	61,762	84,029	107,193	117,486	127,440	138,164	145,922	157,421	172,796	179.8
Chile	5,249	6,507	7,321	7,186	8,388	8,460	8,640	8,899	9,000	71.5
Colombia	18,820	26,801	35,111	33,581	35,100	38,077	40,122	43,128	45,238	140.4
Ecuador	2,629	3,775	4,834	5,634	6,444	5,879	6,048	6,156	6,707	155.1
French Guiana [a]	108	144	162	209	223	245	288	306	328	203.7
Guyana										
Paraguay										
Peru		9,319	10,260	10,800	11,574	8,777	9,572	9,518	9,583	
Suriname										
Uruguay	3,605	4,196	5,047	5,080	5,224	5,677	6,160	5,605	7,150	98.3
Venezuela	14,037	20,879	26,741	26,474	27,806	30,586	32,854	32,551	30,586	117.9
Regional total	*131,793*	*186,152*	*230,713*	*242,983*	*261,353*	*281,934*	*296,582*	*304,181*	*322,439*	
Caribbean										
Anguilla										
Antigua										
Aruba										
Bahamas										
Barbados	249	328	342	360	360	432	457	486	518	108.0
Bermuda										
British Virgin Islands										
Cayman Islands				9,655	10,436	10,483	11,030	11,707	14,040	
Cuba										
Dominica										
Dominican Republic [a]	3,966	5,414	5,277	6,078	6,233	7,138	7,102	7,120	7,120	79.5
Grenada [a]		68	66	68	68	79	83	123	144	
Guadeloupe										
Haiti [a]	495	573	540	577	631	613	703	703	703	42.0
Jamaica	1,251	1,146	1,316	1,224	1,260	1,501	1,465	1,685	1,692	35.3
Martinique										
Netherlands Antilles										
St Kitts										
St Lucia										
St Vincent/Grenadines										
Trinidad and Tobago		1,752	2,163	2,851	2,963	3,132	3,132	3,132	3,150	
Regional total										
Central America										
Belize [a]	122	141	155	187	198	209	234	260	292	139.3
Costa Rica	2,426	3,082	3,533	4,043	4,475	4,892	5,062	5,249	5,152	112.4
El Salvador	1,194	1,389	1,568	1,706	1,728	1,987	2,131	2,232	2,344	96.3
Guatemala [a]	2,473	2,433	2,653	3,043	3,587	3,764	4,193	4,405	4,452	80.0
Honduras	538	779	1,017	1,080	1,080	1,062	1,080	1,080	1,062	97.4
Mexico [b]	27,025	35,472	43,471	109,521	114,932	120,844	126,151	130,949	136,865	406.4
Nicaragua	1,434	1,329	1,557	1,368	1,368	1,350	1,368	1,368	1,350	-5.9
Panama [a]	3,893	5,400								
Puerto Rico [a]	23,086	25,206	24,785	25,257	26,775	28,606	29,940	29,742	31,868	38.0
Regional total	*62,191*	*75,231*	*78,739*	*146,205*	*154,143*	*162,714*	*170,159*	*175,285*	*183,385*	*194.9*
South Asia										
Afghanistan										
Bangladesh [a]	567	1,045	1,583	3,078	3,427	3,791	4,165	5,112	4,756	738.8
Bhutan										
India	24,589	33,539	47,681	61,596	80,640	9,632	89,165	101,462	102,294	316.0
Nepal	266	310	451	450	605	677	666	684	839	215.4
Pakistan	6,340	8,771	13,525	18,274	23,285	24,502	28,440	31,255	33,894	434.6
Sri Lanka	550	721	1,099	1,246	1,328	1,375	1,458	1,512	1,850	236.4
Regional total	*32,312*	*44,386*	*64,339*	*84,644*	*109,285*	*39,977*	*123,894*	*140,025*	*143,633*	*344.5*

ENERGY CONSUMPTION Table No. 0806 (cont'd)

Household Consumption of Electricity 1977-1990

Units: Terajoules

	1977	1980	1983	1985	1986	1987	1988	1989	1990	% growth 1977-90
Japan										
Japan	365,734	418,512	479,408	515,804	525,992	558,329	582,851	618,288	666,372	82.2
Regional total	*365,734*	*418,512*	*479,408*	*515,804*	*525,992*	*558,329*	*582,851*	*618,288*	*666,372*	*82.0*
ASEAN/NICs										
Brunei [a]	541	779	1,208	1,370	1,575	1,712	1,976	2,069	2,167	300.6
Hong Kong	6,957	8,424	10,699	11,520	12,809	14,022	15,710	17,075	19,037	173.6
Indonesia	5,674	7,426	13,702	18,576	23,400	24,480	25,560	27,288	28,926	409.8
Macau [a]	443	570								
Malaysia	3,675	5,433	7,909	9,648	10,620	11,520	12,654	13,392	14,670	299.2
Philippines	10,616	13,518	13,922	10,397	10,915	9,090	10,138	10,768	10,800	1.7
Singapore	2,808	3,655	4,733	5,263	5,634	6,372	7,020	7,585	8,446	200.8
South Korea	10,486	19,167	27,912	48,366	52,438	60,052	71,392	90,630	102,272	875.3
Taiwan										
Thailand	7,231	10,148	15,097	18,594	20,862	22,090	22,514	25,290	29,117	302.7
Regional total	*48,431*	*69,120*	*95,182*	*123,734*	*138,253*	*149,338*	*166,964*	*194,097*	*215,435*	*344.8*
East/SE Asia										
Cambodia										
China										
Laos										
Mongolia										
Myanmar	1,274	1,579	1,586	577	624	676	690	756	830	-34.9
North Korea										
Vietnam										
Regional total										
Australasia										
Australia	91,272	104,438	116,572	117,438	124,258	128,188	130,369	132,038	138,945	52.2
New Zealand	29,972	28,966	32,377	32,734	33,974	33,970	35,210	34,291	37,002	23.5
Regional total	*121,244*	*133,404*	*148,949*	*150,172*	*158,232*	*162,158*	*165,579*	*166,329*	*175,947*	*45.1*
Pacific										
American Samoa										
Fiji		185	198	209	223	223	227	241		
French Polynesia										
Guam										
Kiribati										
Nauru										
New Caledonia										
Papua New Guinea		431	469	504	540	464	450	450	450	
Solomon Islands		17	18	25	25	25	25	25	25	
Tonga										
Tuvalu										
Vanuatu										
Western Samoa										
Regional total										
Middle East										
Bahrain										
Egypt	16,782	13,108	13,662	10,649	10,800	10,476	10,476	10,440	10,800	-35.6
Iran										
Iraq										
Israel	9,564	10,760	12,256	12,582	13,612	14,580	17,420	18,684	19,188	100.6
Jordan	469	1,081	2,163	2,358	2,534	2,711	2,956	3,028	2,930	524.7
Kuwait	10,508	15,372	22,170	27,522	28,440	28,800	32,400	34,200	33,840	222.0
Lebanon										
Oman										
Qatar [c]		5,177	3,618	4,810	5,382	5,400	5,436	5,472	5,508	
Saudi Arabia [a]	14,856	43,503	75,341	79,560	79,920					
Syria										
United Arab Emirates										
Yemen										
Regional total										

ENERGY CONSUMPTION

Household Consumption of Electricity 1977-1990

Units: Terajoules

	1977	1980	1983	1985	1986	1987	1988	1989	1990	% growth 1977-90
North Africa										
Algeria [a]	4,821	7,657	12,582	14,564	15,141	13,735	13,555	14,096	14,240	195.4
Chad [a]	88	110	112	79	79	83	83	87	87	-1.1
Djibouti				916	908	465	469	469	469	
Ethiopia [a]	1,282	1,420	1,590							
Libya										
Mali [a]	202	234	288							
Mauritania										
Morocco	2,631	3,449	4,600	5,267	5,364	6,282	6,815	7,582	7,596	188.7
Niger			428	428	436	439	428	428	432	
Somalia										
Sudan [a]	1,428	1,586	1,586	1,586	1,283	1,305	1,424			
Tunisia	1,619	2,325	2,956	3,787	3,949	4,237	4,457	4,464	4,536	180.2
Regional total										
West Africa										
Benin [a]	70	126	292	317	324	317	317	303	303	332.9
Burkina Faso										
Cameroon [a]	451	505								
Cape Verde										
Côte d'Ivoire	937	1,081	1,074	1,868	1,861	1,530	1,566	1,613	1,656	76.7
Equatorial Guinea										
Gabon	613	649	685	1,404	1,368	1,408	1,415	1,422	1,433	133.8
Gambia										
Ghana [a]	13,430	14,399	5,220	1,662	1,590	1,485	1,496	1,507	1,424	-89.4
Guinea										
Guinea-Bissau										
Liberia										
Nigeria	5,393	11,788	11,910	11,200	11,160	11,178	11,160	11,160	11,196	107.6
Sao Tomé e Príncipe										
Senegal [a]	454	653	588	606	595	642	653	663		
Sierra Leone										
Togo										
Regional total										
East/Central Africa										
Angola										
Burundi [a]	72	105	133	78	191	202	220	234	234	225.0
Central African Republic [a]	155	163	166	126	133	144	144	144	148	-4.5
Comoros										
Congo										
Kenya	1,096	1,449	1,745	1,505	1,530	2,282	2,552	2,624	2,808	156.2
Madagascar		786	844	681	710	638	432			
Maldives										
Mauritius [a]	826	919	934	616	721	804	995	793	1,244	50.6
Réunion										
Rwanda [a]	150	209	270	314	324	328	328	328	332	121.3
Seychelles [a]	47	54	55	61	65	65	65	65	68	44.7
Tanzania										
Uganda										
Zaire [a]	3,454	3,255	4,503	5,693	6,125	6,165	6,093	6,111	6,132	77.5
Regional total										
Southern Africa										
Botswana [a]				346	526	490	667	703	703	
Lesotho										
Malawi	162	180	216	263	270	270	270	270	270	66.7
Mozambique										
Namibia										
South Africa [a]	118,392	143,711	166,971	176,668	238,711	247,922	261,347	269,638	269,783	127.9
Swaziland										
Zambia		3,152	3,389	3,456	3,492	3,600	3,240	2,016	2,880	
Zimbabwe		3,352	3,342	4,399	4,601	4,676	4,907	5,209	5,501	
Regional total										

Source: UN, Energy Balances and Electricity Profiles 1992/OECD
Notes: see end of section

ENERGY PRODUCTION — Table No. 0807

Solid Fuels: Production and Consumption 1988-1992

Units: Million tonnes of oil equivalent

	Production					Consumption			
	1988	1989	1990	1991	1992	1988	1989	1990	1991
Argentina						1.30	1.40	1.40	1.40
Australia	90.40	98.90	106.60	110.70	117.80	36.10	38.30	39.50	39.90
Brazil	3.70	3.70	2.60	2.90	2.60	9.30	9.10	9.30	9.70
Canada	39.40	39.40	37.10	38.10	33.90	30.50	27.50	24.40	25.30
Chile									
China	481.40	517.70	530.10	520.30	543.70	466.00	495.90	518.90	543.80
Colombia	10.90	13.60	14.80	15.30	17.30				
Ecuador									
Hong Kong									
India	91.90	97.00	103.30	105.40	105.60	96.20	99.30	102.40	106.00
Indonesia						2.40	3.60	3.50	3.90
Israel									
Japan	7.40	6.80	5.50	5.30	5.00	76.20	75.60	76.00	78.70
Malaysia						0.30	0.60	0.50	0.50
Mexico	5.10	5.40	6.20	6.20	6.20	6.20	6.40	6.50	6.60
New Zealand	1.60	1.60	1.60	0.90	0.80	1.20	1.40	1.30	1.30
Nigeria									
Pakistan	1.30	1.30	1.30	1.40	1.40				
Peru									
Philippines						1.10	0.90	1.00	1.20
Singapore									
South Africa									
South Korea	12.60	11.10	9.10	8.00	6.40	25.20	24.50	24.40	24.10
Taiwan						10.20	10.50	12.80	14.00
Thailand						2.30	2.80	3.70	4.70
USA	518.50	533.70	561.50	539.90	538.90	474.90	477.40	480.90	477.90
Venezuela						0.20	0.30	0.30	0.30
Vietnam									

Source: BP, Statistical Review of World Energy

ENERGY PRODUCTION AND CONSUMPTION — Table No. 0808

Gas: Production and Consumption 1988-1992

Units: Million tonnes of oil equivalent

	Production					Consumption			
	1988	1989	1990	1991	1992	1988	1989	1990	1991
Argentina	19.30	21.80	20.70	19.80	20.70	17.80	19.00	18.10	19.00
Australia [a]	18.00	20.10	22.80	23.50	25.30	14.30	15.70	16.50	16.50
Brazil						3.10	3.20	3.60	3.70
Canada	81.70	87.00	89.40	94.80	103.80	52.80	57.50	55.60	57.20
Chile									
China	12.60	12.90	13.20	13.40	13.60	12.70	12.90	13.20	13.40
Colombia	4.40	4.30	4.70	4.80	4.70				
Ecuador									
Hong Kong									
India									
Indonesia	34.20	39.90	42.70	45.70	48.10	6.60	9.60	11.20	12.80
Israel									
Japan	1.90	1.90	1.80	1.90	1.90	39.60	42.40	45.40	49.50
Malaysia	14.80	16.80	17.30	19.30	23.70	5.60	6.70	6.80	8.10
Mexico	23.50	24.10	25.50	25.40	25.10	24.10	25.10	30.60	33.40
New Zealand									
Nigeria	3.40	3.90	3.80	4.00	4.40				
Pakistan	11.30	11.20	12.90	13.60	14.80				
Peru									
Philippines									
Singapore									
South Africa									
South Korea						2.70	2.60	2.90	3.50
Taiwan						1.00	1.00	1.30	1.90
Thailand						5.20	4.60	5.60	6.80
USA	436.10	441.40	454.20	452.70	452.30	467.50	488.80	486.30	507.70
Venezuela	16.90	16.80	19.50	22.90	22.90	17.00	17.10	17.60	18.60

Source: BP, Statistical Review of World Energy/UN/Euromonitor

ENERGY RESERVES — Table No. 0809

Proven Oil Reserves at End-1992

Units: As stated

	Reserves ('000 MTOE)	R/P Ratio (years)
North America		
USA	4.1	9.8
Canada	0.9	9.6
Regional total	*5.0*	*9.8*
Latin America		
Argentina	0.2	8.0
Brazil	0.4	12.2
Ecuador	0.2	12.8
Mexico	7.2	46.2
Venezuela	9.0	69.7
Other Latin America	0.5	13.1
Regional total	*17.5*	*44.1*
Middle East		
United Arab Emirates [a]	12.9	
Iran	12.7	73.6
Iraq [a]	13.4	
Kuwait [a]	12.9	
Oman	0.6	17.1
Qatar	0.5	21.6
Saudi Arabia	35.1	82.0
Syria	0.2	9.7
Yemen	0.5	60.9
Other Middle East		
Regional total	*88.8*	*129.1*
Africa		
Algeria	1.2	21.0
Angola	0.2	7.9
Egypt	0.9	18.6
Gabon	0.1	6.8
Libya	3.0	41.2
Nigeria	2.4	26.6
Tunisia	0.2	42.7
Other Africa	0.3	14.1
Regional total	*8.3*	*24.8*
Asia/Australia		
Brunei	0.2	20.3
China	3.2	22.2
India	0.8	28.1
Indonesia	0.8	10.5
Japan [b]		9.0
Malaysia	0.5	14.9
Other Asia	0.2	14.0
Australia	0.2	9.4
New Zealand [b]		11.6
Regional total	*5.9*	*18.0*
Western Europe		
Western Europe (total)	2.2	9.2
Regional total	*2.2*	*9.2*
USSR/Eastern Europe		
USSR	7.8	17.3
Eastern Europe	0.3	24.5
Regional total	*8.1*	*17.5*
World total	*136.5*	*43.1*

Source: BP, Statistical Review of World Energy
Notes: see end of section

ENERGY RESERVES

Coal Reserves at End-1992

Units: As stated

	Coal reserves (million tonnes)	Coal reserves ('000 MTOE)	R/P Ratio (years)
North America			
USA	240,560.0	160.4	
Canada	8,623.0	5.7	
Regional total	*249,183.0*	*166.1*	259
Latin America			
Brazil	2,359.0	1.6	
Colombia	4,539.0	3.0	
Mexico	1,720.0	1.1	
Venezuela	417.0	0.3	
Other Latin America	2,395.0	1.6	
Regional total	*11,430.0*	*7.6*	248
Africa			
South Africa	55,333.0	36.9	
Zimbabwe	734.0	0.5	
Other Africa	6,011.0	4.0	
Regional total	*62,078.0*	*41.4*	349
Middle East			
Middle East (total)	193.0	0.1	
Regional total	*193.0*	*0.1*	
Asia/Australia			
China	114,500.0	76.3	
India	62,548.0	41.7	
Indonesia	32,063.0	21.4	
Japan	844.0	0.6	
South Korea	203.0	0.1	
Taiwan	100.0	0.1	
Other Asia	2,610.0	1.5	
Australia	90,940.0	60.6	
New Zealand	117.0	0.1	
Regional total	*303,925.0*	*202.4*	179
Western Europe			
Western Europe (total)	98,571.0	65.7	177
Regional total	*98,571.0*	*65.7*	
USSR/Eastern Europe			
USSR	241,000.0	160.7	
Poland	41,200.0	27.5	
Other Eastern Europe	33,249.0	22.2	
Regional total	*315,449.0*	*210.4*	301
World total	*1,040,829.0*	*693.6*	232

Source: BP, Statistical Review of World Energy
Notes: see end of section

ENERGY RESERVES

Proven Natural Gas Reserves at End-1992

Units: As stated

	Gas reserves (trillion cu ft)	Gas reserves ('000 MTOE)	R/P Ratio (years)
North America			
USA	167.1	4.3	9
Canada	95.7	2.5	24
Regional total	*262.8*	*6.8*	*12*
Latin America			
Argentina	22.7	0.5	28
Ecuador [a]	3.9	0.1	
Mexico	70.9	1.8	8
Trinidad	8.7	0.2	45
Venezuela [a]	126.5	2.8	
Other Latin America	26.8	0.6	51
Regional total	*259.5*	*6.0*	*69*
Middle East			
United Arab Emirates [a]	204.6	5.1	
Bahrain	5.8	0.2	23
Iran [a]	699.2	15.3	
Iraq [a]	109.5	2.4	
Kuwait [a]	52.4	1.2	
Qatar [a]	227.0	4.1	
Saudi Arabia [a]	182.6	4.7	
Other Middle East [a]	39.0	0.6	
Regional total	*1,520.1*	*33.7*	
Africa			
Algeria	128.0	3.0	70
Egypt	15.4	0.3	45
Gabon [a]	0.4		
Libya [a]	46.2	1.1	
Nigeria [a]	120.0	2.7	
Others Africa [a]	36.9	0.8	
Regional total	*346.9*	*7.9*	
Asia/Australasia			
Bangladesh	25.4	0.7	
Brunei	14.0	0.3	40
China	49.4	0.9	93
India	25.9	0.7	50
Indonesia	64.4	1.7	34
Japan	1.0		13
Malaysia	67.8	1.5	73
Pakistan	31.0	0.6	54
Other Asia [a]	40.5	0.9	
Australia	18.2	0.4	22
New Zealand	3.4	0.1	21
Regional total	*341.0*	*7.8*	*53*
Western Europe			
Western Europe (total)	191.8	4.5	28
Regional total	*191.8*	*4.5*	
USSR/Eastern Europe			
USSR	1,942.3	44.6	68
Eastern Europe	21.0	0.4	16
Regional total	*1,963.3*	*45.0*	*66*
World total	*4,885.4*	*111.7*	*65*

Source: BP, Statistical Review of World Energy
Notes: see end of section

ENERGY CONSUMPTION   Table No. 0812

Crude Oil Consumption: Selected Countries, 1983-1992

Units: Million tonnes

	1983	**1984**	**1985**	**1986**	**1987**	**1988**	**1989**	**1990**	**1991**	**1992**
North America										
USA	704.9	723.3	720.2	749.3	764.8	796.7	795.3	781.8	765.6	781.0
Canada	68.2	66.7	68.5	71.0	73.1	76.8	80.3	77.7	74.8	76.4
Regional total	*773.1*	*790.0*	*788.7*	*820.3*	*837.9*	*873.5*	*875.6*	*859.5*	*840.4*	*857.4*
Australasia										
Australia	27.3	28.5	27.0	28.2	28.7	29.9	31.1	31.6	30.8	31.1
New Zealand	3.8	3.9	3.8	4.0	4.3	4.4	4.5	4.8	5.1	5.2
Regional total	*31.1*	*32.4*	*30.8*	*32.2*	*33.0*	*34.3*	*35.6*	*36.4*	*35.9*	*36.3*
Asia										
China	84.7	86.5	90.3	100.0	105.3	110.2	112.3	110.3	117.9	128.1
India	37.2	39.9	43.3	45.5	47.0	51.5	55.8	57.9	58.9	62.0
Korea	25.2	25.2	24.7	27.4	29.0	34.7	39.8	48.5	58.7	71.2
Taiwan	14.6	15.2	15.9	18.1	19.0	22.9	25.0	26.2	27.9	28.6
Other Asia	84.8	86.5	87.0	90.2	95.7	103.4	112.9	123.1	127.9	140.6
Regional total	*246.5*	*253.3*	*261.2*	*281.2*	*296.0*	*322.7*	*345.8*	*366.0*	*391.3*	*430.5*
Rest of Non-OECD										
USSR	416.6	417.0	415.7	416.5	418.5	413.2	411.4	406.3	390.6	333.4
Europe	87.7	88.2	89.3	94.2	93.5	94.1	94.6	87.3	67.1	58.1
Latin America	209.8	208.1	208.9	216.9	223.2	228.2	233.1	233.4	238.7	242.0
Middle East	132.2	140.3	144.7	143.6	149.1	147.5	152.7	162.8	162.5	168.4
Africa	78.9	78.9	82.7	81.8	85.4	87.6	91.8	95.1	96.3	97.0
Regional total	*925.2*	*932.5*	*941.3*	*953.0*	*969.7*	*970.6*	*983.6*	*984.9*	*955.2*	*898.9*
Overall total	*1,975.9*	*2,008.2*	*2,022.0*	*2,086.7*	*2,136.6*	*2,201.1*	*2,240.6*	*2,246.8*	*2,222.8*	*2,223.1*

Source: BP, Statistical Review of World Energy

ENERGY CONSUMPTION   Table No. 0813

Coal Consumption: Selected Countries, 1983-1992

Units: Million tonnes of oil equivalent

	1983	**1984**	**1985**	**1986**	**1987**	**1988**	**1989**	**1990**	**1991**	**1992**
North America										
USA	397.4	430.2	440.5	435.0	453.8	475.0	476.9	481.4	473.0	476.7
Canada	28.2	32.3	29.3	32.6	33.4	30.5	27.5	24.4	25.5	25.2
Regional total	*425.6*	*462.5*	*469.8*	*467.6*	*487.2*	*505.5*	*504.4*	*505.8*	*498.5*	*501.9*
Australasia										
Australia	31.2	32.6	35.3	38.3	41.4	36.1	38.3	39.5	37.4	39.9
New Zealand	1.5	1.3	0.9	0.9	1.1	1.2	1.4	1.3	0.9	0.8
Regional total	*32.7*	*33.9*	*36.2*	*39.2*	*42.5*	*37.3*	*39.7*	*40.8*	*38.3*	*40.7*
Asia										
China	352.4	388.5	417.0	434.1	449.1	468.4	504.9	516.1	504.0	527.1
India	68.1	69.3	76.4	81.7	88.6	96.2	99.3	102.4	106.1	111.5
Korea	16.7	19.9	22.0	23.3	23.6	25.2	24.5	24.4	24.5	23.3
Taiwan	5.3	5.9	7.4	7.6	9.7	10.2	10.5	12.8	14.0	16.5
Other Asia	40.3	40.2	43.9	46.4	49.5	52.2	55.8	58.5	62.0	66.6
Regional total	*482.8*	*523.8*	*566.7*	*593.1*	*620.5*	*652.2*	*695.0*	*714.2*	*710.6*	*745.0*
Rest of Non-OECD										
USSR	328.1	322.6	322.6	330.2	335.6	327.0	312.7	307.9	277.6	270.7
Europe	193.6	193.8	197.1	201.7	204.0	200.9	189.5	160.9	152.4	143.8
Latin America	14.8	16.4	18.3	19.1	19.2	19.3	20.2	20.5	21.2	21.4
Middle East	1.6	2.5	2.7	2.9	3.1	3.0	3.2	3.4	3.7	4.4
Africa	73.9	73.7	74.0	74.4	76.3	81.8	77.2	80.5	78.5	79.0
Regional total	*612.0*	*609.0*	*614.7*	*628.3*	*638.2*	*632.0*	*602.8*	*573.2*	*533.4*	*519.3*
Overall total	*1,553.1*	*1,629.2*	*1,687.4*	*1,728.2*	*1,788.4*	*1,827.0*	*1,841.9*	*1,834.0*	*1,780.8*	*1,806.9*

Source: BP, Statistical Review of World Energy

ENERGY CONSUMPTION   Table No. 0814

Natural Gas Consumption: Selected Countries, 1983-1992

Units: Million tonnes of oil equivalent

	1983	1984	1985	1986	1987	1988	1989	1990	1991	1992
North America										
USA	433.9	466.4	449.4	421.1	447.2	467.5	488.4	486.3	494.7	512.2
Canada	47.3	47.8	44.8	40.9	41.2	52.8	57.5	55.6	56.7	58.9
Sub total	*481.2*	*514.2*	*494.2*	*462.0*	*488.4*	*520.3*	*545.9*	*541.9*	*551.4*	*571.1*
Australasia										
Australia	11.2	11.7	12.4	13.8	14.0	14.3	15.7	16.5	15.3	15.3
New Zealand	2.1	2.6	3.3	4.2	3.8	4.2	4.0	4.0	4.0	4.2
Sub total	*13.3*	*14.3*	*15.7*	*18.0*	*17.8*	*18.5*	*19.7*	*20.5*	*19.3*	*19.5*
Rest of Non-OECD										
USSR	409.6	447.0	489.7	505.0	529.7	558.6	570.4	608.9	599.0	573.2
Europe	61.9	65.6	67.6	70.7	71.3	67.9	72.2	67.7	59.9	51.8
Latin America	63.7	65.1	65.6	65.7	66.5	68.5	71.2	73.0	76.4	77.9
Middle East	35.5	40.9	45.3	51.4	56.8	66.0	73.5	74.0	71.6	80.0
Africa	25.2	24.9	26.2	27.4	27.6	28.8	30.7	32.0	31.4	32.6
Sub total	*595.9*	*643.5*	*694.4*	*720.2*	*751.9*	*789.8*	*818.0*	*855.6*	*838.3*	*815.5*
Asia										
China	10.7	10.8	11.5	12.1	12.8	12.7	12.9	13.2	13.4	13.6
India	2.4	2.9	3.5	5.5	5.7	6.6	9.6	11.2	12.7	14.4
Korea				0.1	2.1	2.7	2.6	2.9	3.5	4.6
Taiwan	1.1	1.1	1.0	0.9	0.9	1.0	1.0	1.3	1.9	2.0
Other Asia	17.1	19.5	21.9	23.9	27.2	30.7	33.6	36.4	40.8	44.5
Sub total	*31.3*	*34.3*	*37.9*	*42.5*	*48.7*	*53.7*	*59.7*	*65.0*	*72.3*	*79.1*
Overall total	*1,121.7*	*1,206.3*	*1,242.2*	*1,242.7*	*1,306.8*	*1,382.3*	*1,443.3*	*1,483.0*	*1,481.3*	*1,485.2*

Source: BP, Statistical Review of World Energy

Notes to Tables in Section Eight

Table 0801   Entries of 0.0 denote values of less than 50,000 tonnes
Totals affected by rounding
Yemeni states merged in 1990
a   Includes share of Neutral Zone production
b   Southern African Customs Union (SACU). Includes Botswana, Lesotho, Namibia, South Africa and Swaziland

Table 0802   Utilisation rate = throughput divided by capacity x 100
a   Includes share of Neutral Zone

Table 0803   Entries of 0.0 denote values of less than 50,000 tonnes
Totals affected by rounding
a   Includes share of Neutral Zone
b   Southern African Customs Union (SACU). Includes Botswana, Lesotho, Namibia, South Africa and Swaziland

Table 0804   a   Until 1986, includes Aruba
b   Southern African Customs Union (SACU). Includes Botswana, Lesotho, Namibia, South Africa and Swaziland

Table 0805   a   Southern African Customs Union (SACU). Includes Botswana, Lesotho, Namibia, South Africa and Swaziland

Table 0806   a   Includes agricultural and public sector use
b   From 1985, includes agricultural and public sector use
c   Prior to 1983, includes agricultural and public sector use

Table 0807   Commercial solid fuels only (hard coal; lignite; sub-bituminous)

Table 0808   a   Data for production include New Zealand

Table 0809   R/P ratio refers to Reserves/Production ratio
a   R/P ratio more than 100 years
b   Reserves of less than 0.05 TMTOE

Table 0810   R/P ratio refers to ratio, in years, of Reserves/Production
Western Europe includes former East Germany

Table 0811   R/P Ratio refers to ratio, in years, of Reserves/Production
a   R/P ratio more than 100 years

Table 0812   Totals affected by rounding

Table 0813   Totals affected by rounding

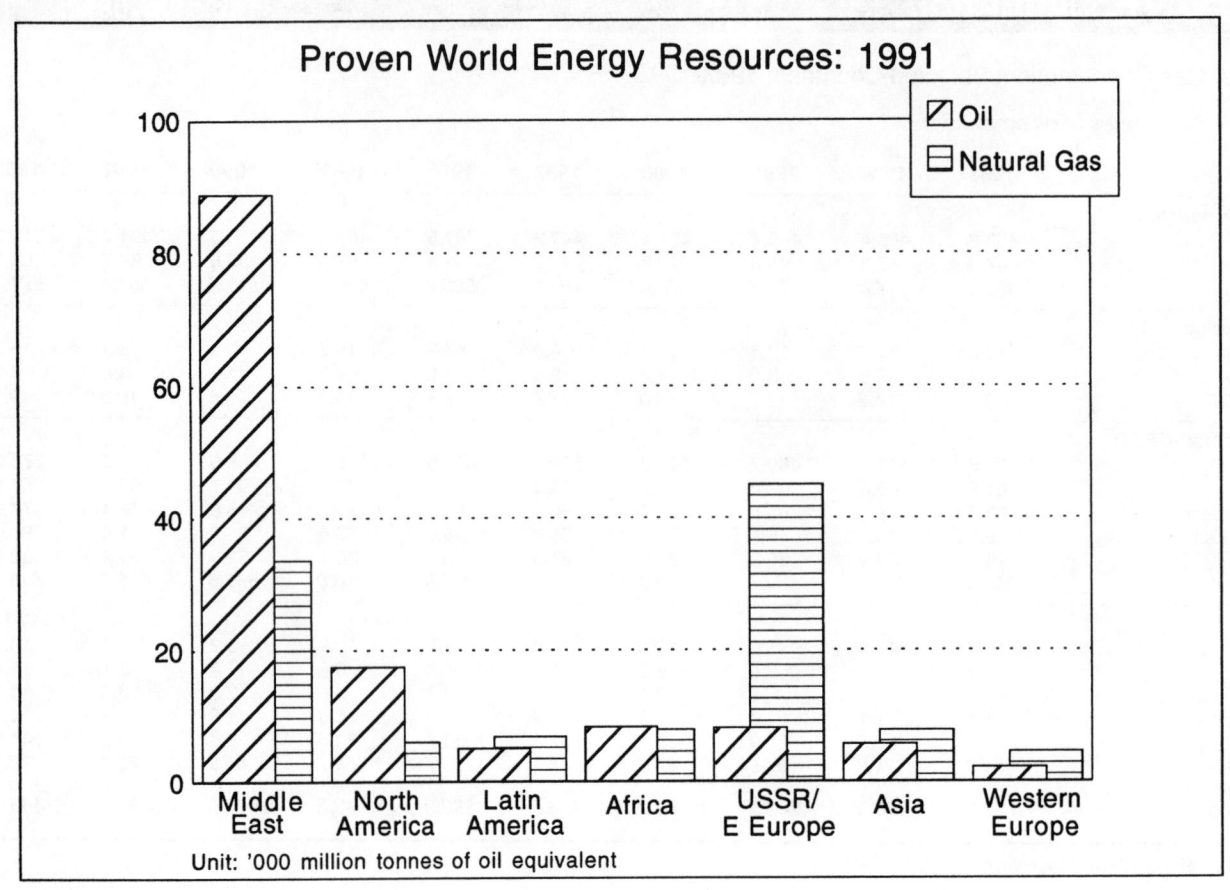

Proven World Energy Resources: 1991

Unit: '000 million tonnes of oil equivalent

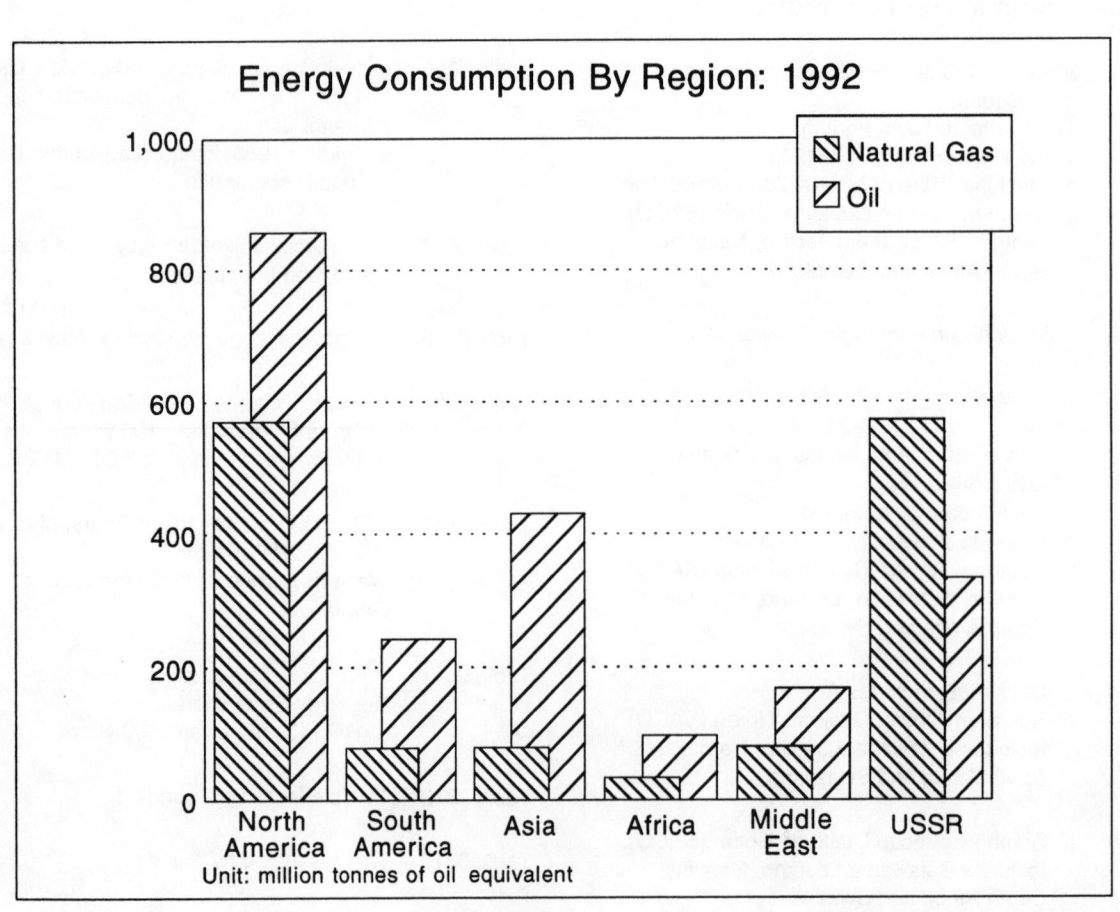

Energy Consumption By Region: 1992

Unit: million tonnes of oil equivalent

Section Nine
Defence

DEFENCE

Defence Spending and Personnel 1992

Units: Million current US dollars/'000 persons

	Defence Spending	Defence spending: % of GDP	Regular Forces	Reserve Forces	Army Personnel	Naval Personnel	Air Force Personnel	Conscripts as % of regular Forces
North America								
Canada [a]	10,310.0	1.8	84.0	29.7	22.0	17.0	22.4	
USA [a]	286,890.0	4.8	1,913.7	1,784.0	674.8	546.6	499.3	
South America								
Argentina	2,020.0		65.0	377.0	35.0	20.0	10.0	19.7
Bolivia	117.4	1.9	31.5		23.0	4.5	4.0	60.3
Brazil	2,120.0	0.5	296.7	1,115.0	196.0	50.0	50.7	43.3
Chile	1,020.0	2.7	91.8	45.0	54.0	25.0	12.8	33.6
Colombia	1,090.0	2.6	139.0	116.9	120.0	12.0	7.0	29.1
Ecuador [b]	260.9	2.2	57.5	100.0	50.0	4.5	3.5	
French Guiana								
Guyana [c]	14.4	3.8	2.0	2.0	1.7	0.1	0.2	
Paraguay	115.9	2.0	16.5	45.0	12.5	3.0	1.0	66.7
Peru	782.6	1.6	112.0	188.0	75.0	22.0	15.0	61.6
Suriname	61.6		1.8		1.4	0.3	0.2	
Uruguay [b]	240.8	2.5	24.7		17.2	4.5	3.0	
Venezuela	772.2	1.3	75.0		34.0	11.0	7.0	24.0
Caribbean								
Anguilla								
Antigua								
Aruba								
Bahamas [d]	66.9		0.7			0.8		
Barbados								
Bermuda								
British Virgin Islands								
Cayman Islands								
Cuba [b]	1.2		175.0	135.0	145.0	13.5	17.0	45.4
Dominica								
Dominican Republic [e]	108.8	1.4	22.2		15.0	3.0	4.2	
Grenada								
Guadeloupe								
Haiti	55.0	2.1	7.4		7.0	0.3	0.2	
Jamaica	19.4	0.6	3.3	0.8	3.0	0.2	0.2	
Martinique								
Netherlands Antilles								
St Kitts								
St Lucia								
St Vincent/Grenadines								
Trinidad and Tobago	74.0	1.4	2.7		2.0	0.6	0.1	
Central America								
Belize [f]	9.7	2.3	0.7	0.5	0.6	0.1		
Costa Rica								
El Salvador	100.0	1.7	43.7		40.0	1.3	2.4	
Guatemala	109.2	1.2	44.6	5.0	42.0	1.2	1.4	
Honduras	42.5	1.4	16.8	60.0	14.4	1.1	1.8	66.7
Mexico	1,520.0	0.5	175.0	300.0	130.0	37.0	8.0	34.3
Nicaragua	214.5	0.1	14.7		13.5	0.5	1.2	
Panama	75.0	1.4	11.7		11.0	0.3	0.3	
Puerto Rico								
South Asia								
Afghanistan [g]	286.6		45.0		40.0		5.0	
Bangladesh [f]	326.9	1.5	107.0		93.0	7.5	6.5	
Bhutan								
India	6,750.0	2.8	1,265.0	1,155.0	1,100.0	55.0	110.0	
Nepal	35.0	1.1	35.0		34.8		0.2	
Pakistan	3,550.0	8.2	580.0	513.0	515.0	20.0	45.0	
Sri Lanka	547.2	6.0	105.9	12.0	89.0	8.9	8.0	

DEFENCE

Defence Spending and Personnel 1992

Units: Million current US dollars/'000 persons

	Defence Spending	Defence spending: % of GDP	Regular Forces	Reserve Forces	Army Personnel	Naval Personnel	Air Force Personnel	Conscripts as % of regular Forces
Japan								
Japan	39,710.0	1.1	246.0	48.4	156.0	44.0	46.0	
ASEAN/NICs								
Brunei	395.6		4.4	0.9	3.6	0.5	0.3	
Hong Kong								
Indonesia	1,840.0	1.5	283.0	400.0	215.0	44.0	24.0	
Macau								
Malaysia	2,670.0	4.9	127.5	44.3	105.0	10.5	12.0	
Philippines	764.4	1.5	106.5	131.0	68.0	23.0	15.5	
Singapore [b]	2,130.0	4.7	55.5	250.0	45.0	4.5	6.0	62.7
South Korea	11,190.0	3.9	633.0	4,500.0	520.0	60.0	53.0	
Taiwan	10,030.0	4.9	360.0	1,657.5	260.0	30.0	70.0	
Thailand	2,710.0	3.0	283.0	500.0	190.0	50.0	43.0	31.8
East/SE Asia								
Cambodia [h]			135.0		80.0	4.0	1.0	
China	21,760.0	7.0	3,030.0	1,200.0	2,300.0	260.0	470.0	35.5
Laos	102.2	9.2	37.0		33.0	0.5	3.5	
Mongolia	20.5	4.9	15.5	200.0	14.0		1.5	71.0
Myanmar	1,257.1	4.9	286.0		265.0	13.5	9.0	
North Korea	5,540.0		1,132.0	540.0	1,000.0	40.0	92.0	
Vietnam [i]	1,750.0	10.9	857.0	3,500.0	700.0	42.0	15.0	
Australasia								
Australia	6,890.0	2.4	67.9	29.2	30.3	15.3	22.3	
New Zealand	656.6	1.5	10.9	8.5	4.8	2.4	3.7	
Pacific								
American Samoa								
Fiji	23.1	1.5	5.0	5.0	4.7	0.3		
French Polynesia								
Guam								
Kiribati								
Nauru								
New Caledonia								
Papua New Guinea	58.6	1.5	3.8		3.2	0.5	0.1	
Solomon Islands								
Tonga								
Tuvalu								
Vanuatu								
Western Samoa								
Middle East								
Bahrain	237.6		6.1		5.0	0.5	0.7	
Egypt [i]	2,470.0	6.0	410.0	604.0	290.0	20.0	30.0	61.5
Iran [j]	1,800.0		528.0	350.0	305.0	18.0	35.0	47.3
Iraq [f]	8,610.0		382.5	650.0	350.0	1.0	30.0	
Israel	7,370.0	11.4	175.0	430.0	134.0	10.0	32.0	79.7
Jordan	525.2	12.7	99.4	35.0	85.0	0.4	14.0	
Kuwait	9,300.0		11.7	19.0	8.0	1.2	2.5	
Lebanon [b]	141.1		36.8		35.7	0.4	0.8	
Oman [k]	1,730.0	16.9	35.7		20.0	3.0	3.5	
Qatar [b]	934.1	14.0	7.5		6.0	0.7	0.8	
Saudi Arabia [b,i]	35.0		102.0		73.0	11.0	18.0	
Syria [b,i]	2,730.0	10.0	408.0	400.0	300.0	8.0	40.0	31.9
United Arab Emirates [b]	4,900.0	14.6	54.5		50.0	2.0	2.5	
Yemen	935.0		63.5	40.0	60.0	1.5	2.0	70.9

DEFENCE

Defence Spending and Personnel 1992

Units: Million current US dollars/'000 persons

	Defence Spending	Defence spending: % of GDP	Regular Forces	Reserve Forces	Army Personnel	Naval Personnel	Air Force Personnel	Conscripts as % of regular Forces
North Africa								
Algeria	1,050.0		139.0	150.0	120.0	7.0	12.0	60.4
Chad	35.3	2.7	17.2		17.0		0.2	
Djibouti [l]	37.9		3.8		3.0	0.1	0.1	
Ethiopia [f]	1.3		100.0					
Libya [f]	1,820.0		85.0	40.0	55.0	8.0	22.0	
Mali	65.6	3.0	7.3		6.9	0.1	0.4	
Mauritania	37.0	3.3	9.6		9.0	0.4	0.2	
Morocco	1,140.0	4.1	195.5	100.0	175.0	7.0	13.5	
Niger	23.3	0.9	3.3		3.2		0.1	
Somalia [m,n]	18.0							
Sudan	1,010.0		82.5		75.0	1.5	6.0	
Tunisia	529.1	3.3	35.0		27.0	4.5	3.5	75.4
West Africa								
Benin	27.2	1.4	4.3		3.8	0.1	0.3	
Burkina Faso [l]	139.0	4.7	8.7		7.0		0.2	
Cameroon [l]	134.1	1.2	11.7		6.6	0.8	0.3	
Cape Verde			1.3		1.0	0.2	0.1	
Côte d'Ivoire	80.8	0.9	7.1	12.0	5.5	0.7	0.9	
Equatorial Guinea			1.3		1.1	0.1	0.1	
Gabon [n]	145.8	3.0	4.7		3.2	0.5	1.0	
Gambia [c]	88.0	28.8	0.8					
Ghana	42.4		7.2		5.0	1.0	1.2	
Guinea [n]	27.0		9.7		8.5	0.4	0.8	77.3
Guinea-Bissau [l,n]	4.4		9.2		6.8	0.3	0.1	
Liberia [e,o]	14.4							
Nigeria	176.9	0.6	76.0		62.0	4.5	9.5	
Sao Tomé e Príncipe								
Senegal	126.7	2.2	9.7		8.5	0.7	0.5	
Sierra Leone [n]	5.2	1.0	6.1		6.0	0.2		
Togo [b]	47.4	2.9	5.2		4.8	0.2	0.2	
East/Central Africa								
Angola [n]	2.7		127.5		120.0	1.5	6.0	
Burundi [c,l]	32.1	2.8	7.2		5.5	0.1	0.2	
Central African Republic [l]	28.0	2.2	6.5		3.5		0.3	
Comoros								
Congo	125.6	4.3	10.8		10.0	0.4	0.5	
Kenya	256.2	3.1	24.2		20.5	1.2	2.5	
Madagascar	31.0	1.2	21.0		20.0	0.5	0.5	
Maldives								
Mauritius								
Réunion								
Rwanda	112.5	6.7	5.2		5.0		0.2	
Seychelles	15.2		1.3		1.0	0.2	0.1	
Tanzania	107.7	3.4	46.8	10.0	45.0	0.8	1.0	42.7
Uganda	86.8	3.0	70.0		70.0			
Zaire [e,l]	234.7	27.5	54.1		26.0	1.3	1.8	
Southern Africa								
Botswana [f]	130.9	3.8	6.1		6.0		0.1	
Lesotho	37.8	6.3	2.0		2.0			
Malawi	19.4	1.1	10.7	1.0	10.5	0.1	0.1	
Mozambique [p]	100.7	0.2	50.0		45.0	1.2	4.0	
Namibia	64.6		7.5		7.4	0.1		
South Africa [q]	3.3		72.4	360.0	49.9	4.5	10.0	50.3
Swaziland								
Zambia	95.0		24.0		20.0		4.0	
Zimbabwe	224.8		48.5		46.0		2.5	

Source: International institute for Strategic Studies (IISS)

Notes: see end of section

DEFENCE

Defence Equipment 1992

Units: Numbers

	No. of Combat Aircraft	No. of Tanks	No. of Submarines	No. of Aircraft Carriers	Other Combat Vessels
North America					
Canada	198	114	3		149
USA	3,784	15,629	110	12	265
South America					
Argentina	174	266	4	1	34
Bolivia	50	36			20
Brazil	307	520	5	1	56
Chile	106	171	4		20
Colombia	68	12	2		82
Ecuador	85	153	2		14
French Guiana					
Guyana					1
Paraguay	17	23			7
Peru	107	300	9		28
Suriname	5				5
Uruguay	37	67			13
Venezuela	120	70	2		46
Caribbean					
Anguilla					
Antigua					
Aruba					
Bahamas					15
Barbados					
Bermuda					
British Virgin Islands					
Cayman Islands					
Cuba	162	1,700	3		132
Dominica					
Dominican Republic	10	14			18
Grenada					
Guadeloupe					
Haiti	2				15
Jamaica					5
Martinique					
Netherlands Antilles					
St Kitts					
St Lucia					
St Vincent/Grenadines					
Trinidad and Tobago					9
Central America					
Belize	2				2
Costa Rica					6
El Salvador	30	5			30
Guatemala	22	10			20
Honduras	46	15			11
Mexico	113	50			125
Nicaragua	16	130			32
Panama					
Puerto Rico					
South Asia					
Afghanistan	233	1,200			80
Bangladesh	85	50			39
Bhutan					
India	674	3,800	15	2	101
Nepal					
Pakistan	352	1,980	6		38
Sri Lanka	30	25			56

DEFENCE   Table No. 0902 (cont'd)

Defence Equipment 1992

Units: Numbers

	No. of Combat Aircraft	No. of Tanks	No. of Submarines	No. of Aircraft Carriers	Other Combat Vessels
Japan					
Japan	440	1,210	17		82
ASEAN/NICs					
Brunei	4	16			13
Hong Kong					
Indonesia	81	125	2		60
Macau					
Malaysia	69	26			42
Philippines	49	41			140
Singapore	192	350			38
South Korea	403	1,800	4		119
Taiwan	486	459	4		131
Thailand	166	150			73
East/SE Asia					
Cambodia	17	150			12
China	4,970	7,750	46		1,300
Laos	31	30			42
Mongolia	15	650			10
Myanmar	37	26			70
North Korea	732	3,000	26		432
Vietnam	185	1,300			91
Australasia					
Australia	157	103	5		40
New Zealand	41	26			8
Pacific					
American Samoa					
Fiji					8
French Polynesia					
Guam					
Kiribati					
Nauru					
New Caledonia					
Papua New Guinea	3				5
Solomon Islands					
Tonga					
Tuvalu					
Vanuatu					
Western Samoa					
Middle East					
Bahrain	24	81			22
Egypt	492	3,090	4		108
Iran	262	700	1		41
Iraq	216	2,300			11
Israel	662	3,890	3		154
Jordan	113	1,131			27
Kuwait	73	200			22
Lebanon	3	140			9
Oman	52	88			12
Qatar	18	24			29
Saudi Arabia	293	700			21
Syria	639	4,600	3		132
United Arab Emirates	105	131			38
Yemen	101	1,275			27

Defence Equipment 1992

Units: Numbers

	No. of Combat Aircraft	No. of Tanks	No. of Submarines	No. of Aircraft Carriers	Other Combat Vessels
North Africa					
Algeria	242	960	2		26
Chad	4				
Djibouti					9
Ethiopia	58	350			29
Libya	409	2,150	6		90
Mali	16	21			3
Mauritania	7				5
Morocco	90	284			51
Niger					
Somalia [a]					
Sudan	51	320			4
Tunisia	38	84			39
West Africa					
Benin		20			2
Burkina Faso	18				
Cameroon	16				6
Cape Verde					5
Côte d'Ivoire	6	5			4
Equatorial Guinea					3
Gabon	20				10
Gambia					3
Ghana	18				4
Guinea	12	38			9
Guinea-Bissau	3	30			8
Liberia [b]					
Nigeria	95	157			65
Sao Tomé e Príncipe					
Senegal	9				10
Sierra Leone					3
Togo	10	11			2
East/Central Africa					
Angola	146	240			59
Burundi	3				3
Central African Republic		4			
Comoros					
Congo	22	45			12
Kenya	40	80			45
Madagascar	12	12			1
Maldives					
Mauritius					
Réunion					
Rwanda	2				
Seychelles	1				6
Tanzania	24	60			21
Uganda					
Zaire	28	60			2
Southern Africa					
Botswana	13				
Lesotho					
Malawi					5
Mozambique	43	100			18
Namibia					
South Africa	259	250	3		9
Swaziland					
Zambia	67	30			
Zimbabwe	36	40			

Source: IISS

Notes: see end of section

Notes to Tables in Section Nine

Table 0901 a Data exclude NATO spending
b Defence spending refers to 1991
c Defence spending refers to 1988
d Defence spending includes spending on police services
e Defence spending refers to 1993
f Defence spending refers to 1990
g Defence spending refers to 1985
h Total forces includes provincial forces
i Total forces includes air defence command
j Total forces includes revolutionary guard
k Total forces includes royal household forces
l Total forces includes gendarmerie
m Figures for personel are not yet available in the wake of the 1991 revolution
n Defence spending refers to 1989
o The former national armed forces have ceased to exist as a result of the civil war
p Total forces includes border guards
q Total forces includes medical services

Table 0902 a Figures are not yet available in the wake of the 1991 revolution
b The former national armed forces have ceased to exist as a result of the civil war

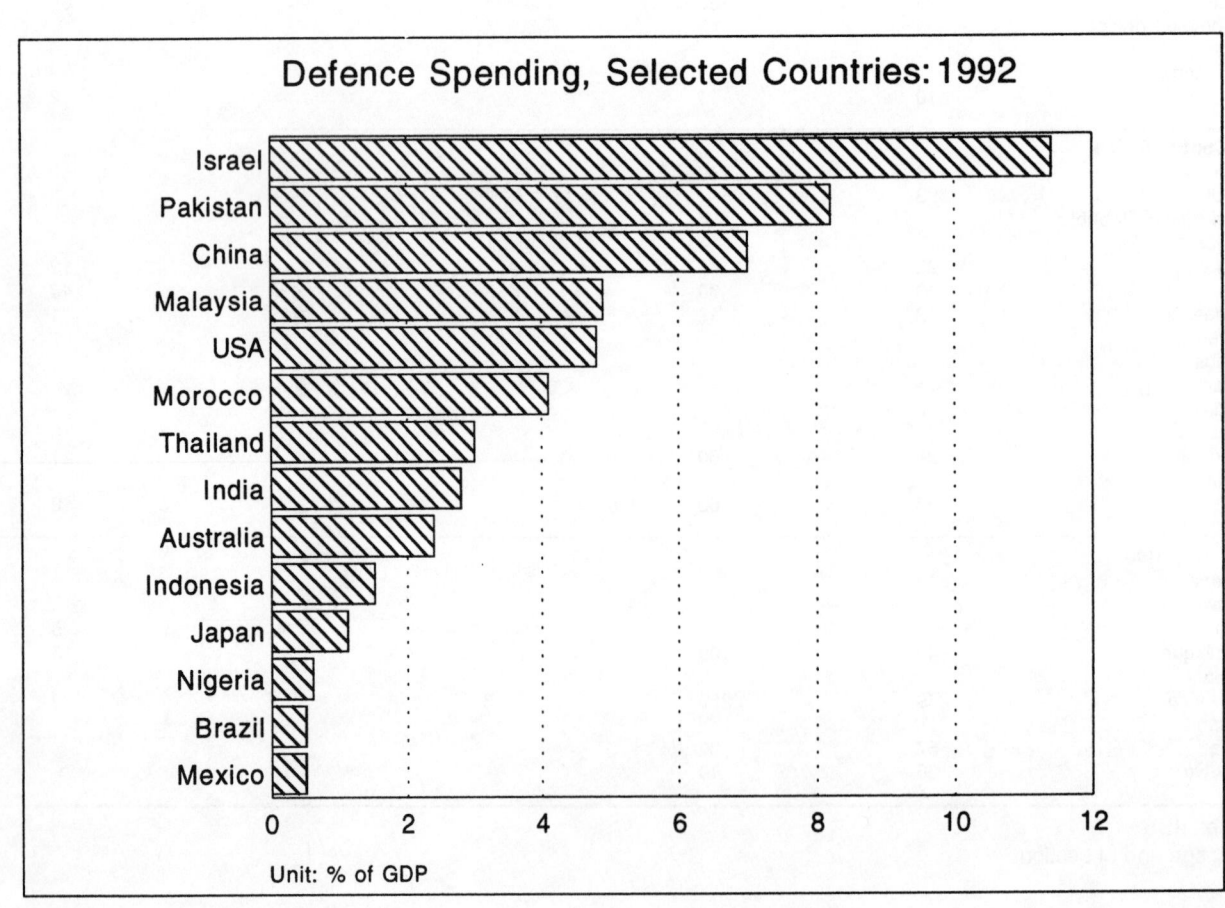

Defence Spending, Selected Countries: 1992

Unit: % of GDP

Section Ten
Environmental Data

CONSERVATION   Table No. 1001

Forest Resources

Units: 100,000 ha unless otherwise stated

	Forest and woodland 1985	Forest and woodland 1990	% of total land area	Deforestation, annual average ('000)	Deforestation % per year	Reforestation, latest year ('000)
North America						
Canada [a]	3,500	3,590	38.9	55	3.1	720
USA [b]	2,952	2,936	32.0	159	0.1	1,775
South America						
Argentina [c]	597	592	21.6	105		40
Bolivia	559	556	51.3	117	0.2	1
Brazil [d]	5,057	4,930	58.3	1,380		449
Chile	88	88	11.8	50	0.7	74
Colombia	518	503	48.4	890	1.7	8
Ecuador	124	109	39.4	340	2.3	4
French Guiana	73	73	82.8			
Guyana	164	164	83.2	3		
Paraguay [d]	178	138	34.7	450		1
Peru [e]	697	684	53.4	300	0.4	6
Suriname	149	149	95.2	3		
Uruguay	7	7	3.8			5
Venezuela	316	302	34.2	245	0.7	19
Caribbean						
Anguilla						
Antigua			11.4			
Aruba						
Bahamas	3	3	32.4			
Barbados						
Bermuda			20.0			
British Virgin Islands			6.7			
Cayman Islands			23.1			
Cuba	27	28	25.1	2	0.1	11
Dominica			41.3			
Dominican Republic	6	6	12.8	4	0.6	1
Grenada			8.8			
Guadeloupe	1	1	42.0			
Haiti	1		1.5	2	3.7	
Jamaica	2	2	17.3	2	3.0	1
Martinique		1	47.2			
Netherlands Antilles						
St Kitts			16.7			
St Lucia			13.1			
St Vincent/Grenadines			35.9			
Trinidad and Tobago	2	2	43.3	1	0.4	1
Central America						
Belize	10	10	44.4	9	0.6	
Costa Rica	16	16	32.1	65	3.6	
El Salvador	1	1	5.0	5	3.2	
Guatemala	42	38	34.6	90	2.0	8
Honduras	37	33	29.1	90	2.3	
Mexico	452	425	22.2	615	1.3	22
Nicaragua	39	34	28.5	121	2.7	1
Panama	37	33	43.4	36	0.9	
Puerto Rico	2	2	20.0			
South Asia						
Afghanistan	19	19	2.9			
Bangladesh	21	19	14.3	8	0.9	17
Bhutan	26	26	55.5	1	0.1	1
India	672	667	22.4	147	0.3	138
Nepal	25	25	18.1	84	4.0	4
Pakistan	32	36	4.6	9	0.4	7
Sri Lanka	18	21	32.3	58	3.5	13

CONSERVATION

Forest Resources

Units: 100,000 ha unless otherwise stated

	Forest and woodland 1985	Forest and woodland 1990	% of total land area	Deforestation, annual average ('000)	Deforestation % per year	Reforestation, latest year ('000)
Japan						
Japan	251	251	66.7			3
ASEAN/NICs						
Brunei	3	2	43.6			
Hong Kong			12.1			
Indonesia [f]	1,134	1,134	62.6	1,000		131
Macau						
Malaysia [g]	206	193	58.8	270		20
Philippines [h]	114	104	34.7	150		50
Singapore						
South Korea	65	65	65.6			67
Taiwan						
Thailand [i]	149	141	27.6	235	2.6	24
East/SE Asia						
Cambodia	134	134	75.8	30	0.2	
China	1,298	1,265	13.6			378
Laos	132	127	55.0	130	1.0	1
Mongolia	152	139	8.9			
Myanmar	322	324	49.3	105	0.3	
North Korea	90	90	74.5			200
Vietnam	85	99	30.3	65	0.6	29
Australasia						
Australia	1,060	1,060	13.9			62
New Zealand	72	74	27.4			43
Pacific						
American Samoa			70.0			
Fiji	12	12	64.9	2	0.2	7
French Polynesia	1	1	31.4			
Guam			18.2			
Kiribati			2.8			
Nauru						
New Caledonia	7	7	38.7			
Papua New Guinea	383	382	84.4	23	0.1	2
Solomon Islands	26	26	91.5	1		
Tonga			11.1			
Tuvalu						
Vanuatu	1	1	7.4			
Western Samoa	1	1	47.3			
Middle East						
Bahrain						
Egypt						
Iran	180	180	11.0	20	0.5	
Iraq	19	19	4.3			2
Israel	1	1	5.3			2
Jordan	1	1	0.8			3
Kuwait			0.1			
Lebanon	1	1	7.8			
Oman	10	10	4.7			
Qatar	1	1	4.5			
Saudi Arabia	12	12	0.6			
Syria	5	7	3.9			10
United Arab Emirates						
Yemen	41	41	7.7			

CONSERVATION   Table No. 1001 (cont'd)

Forest Resources

Units: 100,000 ha unless otherwise stated

	Forest and woodland 1985	Forest and woodland 1990	% of total land area	Deforestation, annual average ('000)	Deforestation % per year	Reforestation, latest year ('000)
North Africa						
Algeria	44	47	2.0	40	2.3	52
Chad	131	127	10.1	80	0.6	
Djibouti			0.3			
Ethiopia	276	271	24.6	88	0.3	10
Libya	7	7	0.4			32
Mali	71	70	5.7	36	0.5	1
Mauritania	45	44	4.3	13	2.4	
Morocco	79	90	20.2	13	0.4	13
Niger	23	20	1.6	67	2.6	2
Somalia	91	91	14.5	14	0.1	2
Sudan	451	451	19.0	504	1.1	13
Tunisia	6	7	4.5	5	1.7	3
West Africa						
Benin	37	35	31.4	67	1.7	
Burkina Faso	69	66	24.1	80	1.7	2
Cameroon	251	245	52.7	110	0.4	1
Cape Verde			0.2			
Côte d'Ivoire	86	74	23.2	510	5.2	6
Equatorial Guinea	13	13	46.3	3	0.2	
Gabon	200	200	77.6	15	0.1	1
Gambia	2	2	16.0	5	2.4	
Ghana	84	81	35.1	72	0.8	2
Guinea	149	146	59.3	86	0.8	
Guinea-Bissau	11	11	38.1	57	2.7	
Liberia	18	17	18.1	46	2.3	2
Nigeria	134	119	13.1	400	2.7	26
Sao Tomé e Príncipe						
Senegal	108	106	54.8	50	0.5	3
Sierra Leone	21	21	28.8	6	0.3	
Togo	17	16	29.4	12	0.7	
East/Central Africa						
Angola	533	520	41.7	94	0.2	3
Burundi	1	1	2.5	1	2.7	3
Central African Republic	359	358	57.5	55	0.2	
Comoros			15.7			
Congo	213	212	62.0	22	0.1	
Kenya	24	23	4.1	39	1.7	
Madagascar	163	155	26.7	156	1.2	12
Maldives			3.3			
Mauritius	1	1	30.8			
Réunion	1	1	35.2			
Rwanda	6	6	22.0	5	2.2	3
Seychelles			18.5			
Tanzania	415	409	46.2	130	0.3	9
Uganda	58	56	27.9	50	0.8	2
Zaire	1,760	1,743	76.9	370	0.2	
Southern Africa						
Botswana	110	109	19.3	20	0.1	
Lesotho						
Malawi	42	36	38.6	150	3.5	1
Mozambique	149	143	18.2	120	0.8	4
Namibia	183	181	22.0	30	0.2	
South Africa	45	45	3.7			
Swaziland	1	1	5.8			
Zambia	292	289	38.8	70	0.2	2
Zimbabwe	195	191	49.5	80	0.4	4

Source: FAO Production Yearbook/World Resources Institute
Notes: see end of section

CONSERVATION

Coastal Areas and Fresh Water Availability

Units: As stated

	Length of marine coastline (km)	Extent of territorial sea (nautical miles)	Availability of fresh water (km³ per annum)	Fresh water per capita ('000 m³ per annum)	Availability of safe drinking water 1988 (%)	Availability of sanitation services 1988 (%)
North America						
Canada [a]	58,808	12	2,901	109		
USA	19,924	3	2,478	10		
South America						
Argentina	4,989	200	694	22	45	64
Bolivia			300	41	46	34
Brazil	7,491	200	5,190	35	93	65
Chile	6,435	12	468	36	60	53
Colombia	2,414	12	1,070	34	87	51
Ecuador	2,237	200	314	29	56	54
French Guiana	378	12				
Guyana	459	12	241	232	84	85
Paraguay			94	22	36	57
Peru	2,414	200	40	2	50	44
Suriname	386	12	200	496	69	50
Uruguay	660	200	59	19	45	62
Venezuela	2,800	12	856	43	89	83
Caribbean						
Anguilla						
Antigua	153	12				
Aruba						
Bahamas	3,542	3				
Barbados	97	12				
Bermuda	103	3				
British Virgin Islands						
Cayman Islands	160	3				
Cuba	3,735	12	35	3		
Dominica	148	12				
Dominican Republic	1,288	6	20	3	57	56
Grenada	121	12				
Guadeloupe	306	12				
Haiti	1,771	12	11	2	45	
Jamaica	1,022	12	8	3	70	
Martinique	290	12				
Netherlands Antilles						
St Kitts						
St Lucia						
St Vincent/Grenadines						
Trinidad and Tobago	362	12	5	4	93	98
Central America						
Belize	386	3	16		69	61
Costa Rica	1,290	12	95	32	92	96
El Salvador	307	200	19	4	43	62
Guatemala	400	12	116	13	66	60
Honduras	820	12	102	20	74	66
Mexico	9,330	12	357	4	64	56
Nicaragua	910	200	175	45	48	
Panama	2,490	200	144	60	83	84
Puerto Rico						
South Asia						
Afghanistan			50	3	28	
Bangladesh	580	12	1,357	12	63	20
Bhutan			95	63	97	99
India	7,000	12	1,850	2	76	21
Nepal			170	9	49	
Pakistan	1,046	12	298	2	67	24
Sri Lanka	1,340	12	43	3	87	65

| CONSERVATION | Table No. 1002 (cont'd) |

Coastal Areas and Fresh Water Availability

Units: As stated

	Length of marine coastline (km)	Extent of territorial sea (nautical miles)	Availability of fresh water (km³ per annum)	Fresh water per capita ('000 m³ per annum)	Availability of safe drinking water 1988 (%)	Availability of sanitation services 1988 (%)
Japan						
Japan	13,685	12	547	4		
ASEAN/NICs						
Brunei						
Hong Kong	733	3			85	75
Indonesia	54,716	12	2,530	14	50	42
Macau	40	6				
Malaysia	4,675	12	456	26	80	
Philippines	22,540		323	5	87	91
Singapore	193	3	1			
South Korea	2,413	12	63	1	70	99
Taiwan						
Thailand	3,219	12	110	2	71	
East/SE Asia						
Cambodia	443	12	88	11		
China	14,500	12	2,800	3	76	97
Laos			270	66	39	
Mongolia			25	11	64	71
Myanmar	3,060	12	1,082	26	33	31
North Korea	2,495	12	67	3		
Vietnam [a]	3,444	12	376	6	46	51
Australasia						
Australia	25,760	3	343	21		
New Zealand	15,134	12	397	118		
Pacific						
American Samoa						
Fiji	1,129	12	29	38		77
French Polynesia	2,525	12				
Guam					100	95
Kiribati	1,143	12			71	63
Nauru						
New Caledonia	2,254	12				
Papua New Guinea	5,152	12	801	200	58	55
Solomon Islands	5,313	12	45	149	75	30
Tonga	419	12			94	82
Tuvalu	24	12			99	78
Vanuatu	2,528	12			82	57
Western Samoa					76	93
Middle East						
Bahrain	161	3			78	97
Egypt	2,450	12	2		89	67
Iran	3,180	12	118	2	87	67
Iraq	58	12	34	2	86	55
Israel	273	6	2			
Jordan	26	3	1		99	100
Kuwait	499	12				
Lebanon	225	12	5	2		
Oman	2,092	12	2	1	64	67
Qatar	563	3			74	92
Saudi Arabia	2,510	12	2		87	65
Syria	193	35	8	1		
United Arab Emirates [b]	1,448	3				
Yemen	1,906	24	3		74	

CONSERVATION

Coastal Areas and Fresh Water Availability

Units: As stated

	Length of marine coastline (km)	Extent of territorial sea (nautical miles)	Availability of fresh water (km³ per annum)	Fresh water per capita ('000 m³ per annum)	Availability of safe drinking water 1988 (%)	Availability of sanitation services 1988 (%)
North Africa						
Algeria	1,183	12	19	1		
Chad			38	7		
Djibouti	314	12		1		
Ethiopia	1,094	12	110	2	40	52
Libya	1,770	12	1		90	92
Mali			62	7	68	49
Mauritania	754	70			66	
Morocco	1,835	12	30	1	62	59
Niger			14	2	76	21
Somalia	3,025	200	12	2	39	23
Sudan	853	12	30	1		
Tunisia			4		65	43
West Africa						
Benin	121	200	26	6	56	36
Burkina Faso			28	3	58	20
Cameroon	402	50	208	19	98	
Cape Verde	965	12		1	76	
Côte d'Ivoire	515	12	74	6	87	44
Equatorial Guinea	296	12	30	68		
Gabon	885	12	164	140	70	
Gambia	80	12	3	4	82	
Ghana	539	12	53	4	66	39
Guinea	346	12	226	33	39	
Guinea-Bissau	274	12	31	31	22	24
Liberia	579	200	232	90	57	
Nigeria	853	30	261	2	60	
Sao Tomé e Príncipe					32	10
Senegal	531	12	23	3		
Sierra Leone	402	200	160	39		
Togo	56	30	12	3	80	29
East/Central Africa						
Angola	1,600	20	158	16	47	22
Burundi			4	1	67	42
Central African Republic			141	48	12	
Comoros	340	12	1	2		
Congo	169	200	181	91	47	
Kenya	536	12	15	1		
Madagascar	4,828	12	40	3	36	
Maldives	644	12				
Mauritius	177	12	2	2	96	94
Réunion	201	12				
Rwanda			6	1	55	53
Seychelles	491	12			99	58
Tanzania	1,424	50	76	3	60	76
Uganda			66	4		
Zaire	37	12	1,019	28	38	14
Southern Africa						
Botswana			1	1		59
Lesotho			4	2	52	18
Malawi			9	1		
Mozambique	2,470	12	58	4	30	36
Namibia	1,489	6	9			
South Africa	2,881	12	50	1		
Swaziland			7	9		
Zambia			96	11	59	55
Zimbabwe			23	2	55	58

Source: UN/World Resources Institute
Notes: see end of section

CONSERVATION

Table No. 1003

Protection of Natural Areas 1990

'000 hectares

	National systems, sites	area	% of total land area	Biosphere reserves, sites	area	Natural world sites	Wetlands, sites	area	Threat-ened species
North America									
Canada	426	49,452	5.4	6	1,050	6	30	12,938	23
USA	968	98,342	10.7	43	19,108	10	8	1,116	2,379
South America									
Argentina	113	12,639	4.6	5	2,410	2			240
Bolivia	23	6,774	6.2	3	435		1	5	88
Brazil	162	20,525	2.4			1			392
Chile	65	13,650	18.2	7	2,407		1	5	311
Colombia	42	9,302	9.0	3	2,514				431
Ecuador	14	10,686	38.6	2	1,446	2			349
French Guiana									64
Guyana	1	12	0.1						92
Paraguay	12	1,186	3.0						67
Peru	24	5,518	4.3	3	2,507	3			471
Suriname	14	763	4.9				1	12	86
Uruguay	8	32	0.2	1	200		1	200	32
Venezuela	74	20,265	23.0				1	10	162
Caribbean									
Anguilla									3
Antigua							1		
Aruba									33
Bahamas	5	123	12.3						3
Barbados									13
Bermuda	2	12	244.0						5
British Virgin Islands									4
Cayman Islands	2	5	19.2						
Cuba	29	714	6.5	4	324				890
Dominica	1	7	9.1						65
Dominican Republic	14	552	11.4						60
Grenada									6
Guadeloupe	2	21	12.5						15
Haiti	2	8	0.3						22
Jamaica									20
Martinique	1	70	66.2						5
Netherlands Antilles	4	15							5
St Kitts									1
St Lucia									8
St Vincent/Grenadines									3
Trinidad and Tobago	6	15	3.0						9
Central America									
Belize	8	74	3.3						51
Costa Rica	28	606	11.9	2	729	1			445
El Salvador	9	26	1.3						35
Guatemala	9	88	0.8			1	1		306
Honduras	34	709	6.3	1	500	1			64
Mexico	61	9,420	4.9	6	1,289	1	1	48	963
Nicaragua	6	43	0.4						85
Panama	16	1,326	17.5	1	597	1			578
Puerto Rico				2	15				
South Asia									
Afghanistan	4	142	0.2						32
Bangladesh	8	97	0.7						89
Bhutan	7	924	19.7						41
India	359	13,481	4.5			5	6	193	1,467
Nepal	11	959	7.0			2	1	18	84
Pakistan	53	3,655	4.7	1	31		9	21	60
Sri Lanka	43	784	12.1	2	9	1	1	6	238

CONSERVATION

Protection of Natural Areas 1990

'000 hectares

	National systems,		% of total	Biosphere reserves,		Natural world	Wetlands,		Threat-ened
	sites	area	land area	sites	area	sites	sites	area	species
Japan									
Japan	65	2,402	6.4	4	116		3	10	78
ASEAN/NICs									
Brunei	4	122	23.2						62
Hong Kong	12	38	38.2						17
Indonesia	169	17,800	9.8	6	1,482				267
Macau									
Malaysia	45	1,162	3.5						592
Philippines	28	584	2.0	2	1,174				216
Singapore	1	3							29
South Korea	17	578	5.9	1	37				61
Taiwan									
Thailand	83	5,106	10.0	3	26				137
East/SE Asia									
Cambodia									51
China	394	22,236	2.4	7	1,819				481
Laos									49
Mongolia	14	5,618	3.6						22
Myanmar	2	173	0.3						75
North Korea	2	58	0.5	1	132				30
Vietnam	58	892	2.7				1	12	409
Australasia									
Australia	728	46,654	6.1	12	4,743	8	39	4,478	2,113
New Zealand	152	2,839	10.6			2	5	38	263
Pacific									
American Samoa									2
Fiji	2	5	0.3						36
French Polynesia	4	11	2.9	1	2				85
Guam									18
Kiribati	3	27	37.5						2
Nauru									2
New Caledonia	12	64	3.5						174
Papua New Guinea	5	29	0.1						119
Solomon Islands									53
Tonga									3
Tuvalu									1
Vanuatu									13
Western Samoa									15
Middle East									
Bahrain									5
Egypt	9	685	0.7	1	1		2	106	118
Iran	60	7,529	4.6	9	2,610		18	1,088	340
Iraq									27
Israel	18	226	11.0						28
Jordan	2	34	0.4				1	7	768
Kuwait									13
Lebanon	1	4	0.3						25
Oman	2	54	0.3						16
Qatar									3
Saudi Arabia	7	5,619	2.6						23
Syria									31
United Arab Emirates									11
Yemen									149

CONSERVATION

Protection of Natural Areas 1990

'000 hectares

	National systems, sites	area	% of total land area	Biosphere reserves, sites	area	Natural world sites	Wetlands, sites	area	Threat-ened species
North Africa									
Algeria	19	11,898	5.0	1	7,200	1	2	5	172
Chad	1	114	0.1				1	195	38
Djibouti	1	10	0.4						12
Ethiopia	24	6,223	5.7			1			84
Libya	3	155	0.1						80
Mali	7	889	0.7	1	771				37
Mauritania	3	1,733	1.7				1	1,173	23
Morocco	11	368	0.8				4	11	217
Niger	4	1,654	1.3				1	220	18
Somalia	1	334	0.5						77
Sudan	13	7,732	3.3	2	1,901				35
Tunisia	7	45	0.3	4	32	1	1	13	47
West Africa									
Benin	2	844	7.6	1	880				17
Burkina Faso	7	739	2.7	1	16		3		13
Cameroon	13	2,100	4.5	3	850	1			121
Cape Verde									5
Côte d'Ivoire	12	2,020	6.4	2	1,480	3			99
Equatorial Guinea									29
Gabon	5	1,790	6.9	1	15		3	1,080	103
Gambia	2	12	1.2						10
Ghana	8	1,075	4.7	1	8		1	7	57
Guinea	2	129	0.5	2	133	1			61
Guinea-Bissau							1	39	9
Liberia	1	131	1.4						31
Nigeria	15	1,547	1.7	1	1				46
Sao Tomé e Príncipe									9
Senegal	10	2,181	11.3	3	1,094	2	4	100	50
Sierra Leone	3	101	1.4						34
Togo	11	647	11.9						12
East/Central Africa									
Angola	6	2,692	2.2						47
Burundi	1	38	1.5						10
Central African Republic	7	3,904	6.3	2	1,640				16
Comoros									11
Congo	10	1,333	3.9	2	172				21
Kenya	36	3,347	5.9	4	851		1	19	181
Madagascar	36	1,078	1.9	1	140				282
Maldives									
Mauritius	3	4	2.2	1	4				288
Réunion	2	5	2.2						97
Rwanda	2	327	13.1	1	15				20
Seychelles	4	39	143.0			2			90
Tanzania	20	11,913	13.4	2	2,338	4			217
Uganda	19	1,756	8.8	1	220		1	15	40
Zaire	9	8,827	3.9	3	298	4			63
Southern Africa									
Botswana	9	10,025	17.7						20
Lesotho	1	7							16
Malawi	9	1,067	11.3	1		1			79
Mozambique	1	2							106
Namibia	9	10,346	12.6						37
South Africa	178	6,310	5.2				7	208	1,058
Swaziland	3	40	2.3						31
Zambia	20	6,361	8.6			1			23
Zimbabwe	21	2,831	7.3			2			112

Source: UN/World Resources Institute

AIR POLLUTION

Table No. 1004

Carbon Dioxide and Methane Emissions 1989

Units: '000 metric tonnes

	CO$_2$ from industrial processes, total	CO$_2$ from industrial processes per capita (kg)	CO$_2$ from land use changes, total	Methane
North America				
Canada	455.5	17.8		4.1
USA	4,869.0	20.2	22.0	37.0
South America				
Argentina	118.2	3.8		3.8
Bolivia	5.1	0.8	37.0	0.4
Brazil	207.0	1.5	950.0	8.8
Chile	31.8	2.6		0.3
Colombia	53.8	1.8	420.0	1.5
Ecuador	15.3	1.6	160.0	0.3
French Guiana				
Guyana	0.7	0.7	1.1	
Paraguay	1.7	0.4	67.0	0.3
Peru	21.2	1.1	140.0	0.3
Suriname	1.4	3.7	1.1	
Uruguay	4.7	1.6		0.5
Venezuela	95.9	5.4	59.0	1.4
Caribbean				
Anguilla				
Antigua				
Aruba				
Bahamas				
Barbados	1.0	4.0		
Bermuda				
British Virgin Islands				
Cayman Islands				
Cuba	36.3	3.6	0.9	0.3
Dominica				
Dominican Republic	6.7	1.0	1.3	0.2
Grenada				
Guadeloupe				
Haiti	0.7	0.1	0.9	0.1
Jamaica	4.9	2.1	0.8	
Martinique				
Netherlands Antilles				
St Kitts				
St Lucia				
St Vincent/Grenadines				
Trinidad and Tobago	18.6	15.8	0.3	0.5
Central America				
Belize	0.2	1.2		
Costa Rica	2.6	1.0	26.0	0.1
El Salvador	2.4	0.5	1.6	0.1
Guatemala	4.1	0.5	41.0	0.1
Honduras				
Mexico	319.7	4.0	200.0	2.3
Nicaragua	2.2	0.7	59.0	0.1
Panama	2.7	1.2	19.0	0.1
Puerto Rico				
South Asia				
Afghanistan	6.3	0.3		0.5
Bangladesh	14.1	0.1	8.7	6.9
Bhutan			0.9	
India	651.9	0.9	120.0	36.0
Nepal	0.9	0.1	32.0	1.0
Pakistan	61.0	0.6	4.0	3.4
Sri Lanka	4.0	0.2	22.0	0.6

351

AIR POLLUTION

Carbon Dioxide and Methane Emissions 1989

Units: '000 metric tonnes

	CO$_2$ from industrial processes, total	CO$_2$ from industrial processes per capita (kg)	CO$_2$ from land use changes, total	Methane
Japan				
Japan	1,040.6	8.6		4.1
ASEAN/NICs				
Brunei				
Hong Kong				
Indonesia	137.7	0.8	870.0	6.5
Macau				
Malaysia	49.1	3.0	280.0	0.9
Philippines	41.1	0.7	190.0	2.4
Singapore	35.9	13.9		
South Korea	221.1	5.3		1.2
Taiwan				
Thailand	77.7	1.5	290.0	6.3
East/SE Asia				
Cambodia	0.5	0.1	11.0	1.1
China	2,388.6	2.2		40.0
Laos	0.2	0.1	240.0	0.4
Mongolia	10.3	5.3		0.3
Myanmar	5.0	0.1	380.0	3.2
North Korea	151.5	7.5		1.2
Vietnam	18.2	0.3	150.0	3.6
Australasia				
Australia	257.5	16.1		5.0
New Zealand	26.2	8.1		1.1
Pacific				
American Samoa				
Fiji	0.7	1.0		
French Polynesia				
Guam				
Kiribati				
Nauru				
New Caledonia				
Papua New Guinea	2.3	0.7	12.0	
Solomon Islands	0.2	0.7		
Tonga				
Tuvalu				
Vanuatu				
Western Samoa				
Middle East				
Bahrain	12.2	27.7		0.1
Egypt	79.5	1.7		0.7
Iran	166.1	3.4		1.5
Iraq	68.9	4.3		1.0
Israel	32.9	7.7		0.1
Jordan	9.4	2.7		
Kuwait	31.2	17.4		0.3
Lebanon	8.7	3.3		0.2
Oman	10.3	8.0		0.1
Qatar	13.3	42.9		1.1
Saudi Arabia	173.8	14.4		
Syria	28.2	2.7		0.2
United Arab Emirates	50.9	36.9		0.5
Yemen	3.5	0.4		0.1

AIR POLLUTION

Carbon Dioxide and Methane Emissions 1989

Units: '000 metric tonnes

	CO$_2$ from industrial processes, total	CO$_2$ from industrial processes per capita (kg)	CO$_2$ from land use changes, total	Methane
North Africa				
Algeria	46.5	2.0		1.0
Chad	0.2		15.0	0.2
Djibouti	0.3	0.7		
Ethiopia	2.6	0.1	30.0	1.4
Libya	37.8	10.1		0.3
Mali	0.4	0.1	7.7	0.3
Mauritania	3.0	1.7		0.1
Morocco	22.1	1.0		0.3
Niger	1.0	0.1	7.4	0.2
Somalia	1.0	0.2	5.2	0.8
Sudan	3.3	0.1	98.0	1.2
Tunisia	13.9	1.9		0.1
West Africa				
Benin	0.7	0.2	9.5	0.1
Burkina Faso	0.5	0.1	17.0	0.2
Cameroon	5.8	0.6	60.0	0.2
Cape Verde	0.1	0.3		
Côte d'Ivoire	7.6	0.7	350.0	0.2
Equatorial Guinea	0.1	0.3	1.8	
Gabon	7.8	7.6	9.3	0.2
Gambia	0.2	0.3	1.9	
Ghana	3.5	0.3	31.0	0.1
Guinea	1.0	0.2	37.0	0.3
Guinea-Bissau	0.1	0.1	18.0	0.1
Liberia	0.8	0.4	39.0	0.1
Nigeria	79.3	0.8	270.0	3.7
Sao Tomé e Príncipe				
Senegal	3.2	0.5	11.0	0.2
Sierra Leone	0.7	0.2	4.6	0.1
Togo	0.6	0.2	2.9	
East/Central Africa				
Angola	5.0	0.6	33.0	0.3
Burundi	0.2		0.5	
Central African Republic	0.3	0.1	13.0	0.1
Comoros	0.1	0.2		
Congo	1.8	0.9	12.0	
Kenya	5.2	0.2	13.0	0.6
Madagascar	1.0	0.1	120.0	0.9
Maldives				
Mauritius	1.0	1.0		
Réunion				
Rwanda	0.4	0.1	2.1	
Seychelles				
Tanzania	2.1	0.1	21.0	0.7
Uganda	0.9	0.1	10.0	0.2
Zaire	3.8	0.1	130.0	0.3
Southern Africa				
Botswana	1.7	1.5	2.6	0.1
Lesotho				
Malawi	0.6	0.1	58.0	0.1
Mozambique	1.2	0.1	30.0	0.1
Namibia				
South Africa	278.5	8.6		3.4
Swaziland	0.4	0.6		
Zambia	2.6	0.4	27.0	0.1
Zimbabwe	16.1	1.9	16.0	0.3

Source: World Resources Institute

AIR POLLUTION

Consumption of CFCs and Halons 1986

Units: Metric tonnes

	Consumption of CFCs and halons, total	Consumption per capita (kg)	% of world consumption
North America			
Canada	21,171	0.83	1.81
USA	330,094	1.37	28.19
South America			
Argentina	6,091	0.20	0.52
Bolivia	650	0.10	0.06
Brazil	11,244	0.08	0.96
Chile	741	0.06	0.06
Colombia	2,900	0.10	0.25
Ecuador	618	0.06	0.05
French Guiana			
Guyana			
Paraguay	320	0.08	0.03
Peru	832	0.04	0.07
Suriname			
Uruguay	330	0.11	0.03
Venezuela	3,940	0.22	0.34
Caribbean			
Anguilla			
Antigua			
Aruba			
Bahamas			
Barbados			
Bermuda			
British Virgin Islands			
Cayman Islands			
Cuba	620	0.06	0.05
Dominica	2	0.03	
Dominican Republic	620	0.10	0.05
Grenada			
Guadeloupe			
Haiti	160	0.03	0.01
Jamaica	1,098	0.46	0.09
Martinique			
Netherlands Antilles			
St Kitts			
St Lucia			
St Vincent/Grenadines			
Trinidad and Tobago			
Central America			
Belize	16	0.10	
Costa Rica			
El Salvador	480	0.10	0.04
Guatemala	1,880	0.23	0.16
Honduras	160	0.04	0.01
Mexico	8,363	0.11	0.71
Nicaragua	300	0.09	0.03
Panama	304	0.14	0.03
Puerto Rico			
South Asia			
Afghanistan			
Bangladesh			
Bhutan			
India	5,300	0.01	0.45
Nepal			
Pakistan	10,000	0.10	0.85
Sri Lanka	258	0.02	0.02

AIR POLLUTION

Consumption of CFCs and Halons 1986

Units: Metric tonnes

	Consumption of CFCs and halons, total	Consumption per capita (kg)	% of world consumption
Japan			
Japan	132,320	0.01	0.11
ASEAN/NICs			
Brunei			
Hong Kong			
Indonesia	2,494		
Macau			
Malaysia	2,597		
Philippines	2,439		
Singapore	4,823	0.02	
South Korea	9,394		0.01
Taiwan			
Thailand	2,520		
East/SE Asia			
Cambodia			
China	18,000		0.02
Laos			
Mongolia			
Myanmar			
North Korea			
Vietnam			
Australasia			
Australia	13,900	0.01	0.01
New Zealand	2,240	0.01	
Pacific			
American Samoa			
Fiji	70		
French Polynesia			
Guam			
Kiribati			
Nauru			
New Caledonia			
Papua New Guinea			
Solomon Islands			
Tonga			
Tuvalu			
Vanuatu			
Western Samoa			
Middle East			
Bahrain	108		
Egypt	5,042		
Iran	4,400		
Iraq	1,590		
Israel	5,000	0.01	
Jordan	315		
Kuwait	1,065	0.01	
Lebanon			
Oman			
Qatar			
Saudi Arabia	5,181		
Syria	1,409		
United Arab Emirates	1,630	0.01	
Yemen			

AIR POLLUTION

Consumption of CFCs and Halons 1986

Units: Metric tonnes

	Consumption of CFCs and halons, total	Consumption per capita (kg)	% of world consumption
North Africa			
Algeria	2,200		
Chad			
Djibouti			
Ethiopia			
Libya			
Mali			
Mauritania			
Morocco	2,200		
Niger			
Somalia			
Sudan			
Tunisia	800		
West Africa			
Benin			
Burkina Faso			
Cameroon			
Cape Verde			
Côte d'Ivoire	980		
Equatorial Guinea			
Gabon	115		
Gambia			
Ghana			
Guinea			
Guinea-Bissau			
Liberia			
Nigeria			
Sao Tomé e Príncipe			
Senegal	600		
Sierra Leone			
Togo	300		
East/Central Africa			
Angola			
Burundi			
Central African Republic			
Comoros			
Congo			
Kenya	137		
Madagascar	49		
Maldives			
Mauritius			
Réunion			
Rwanda	8		
Seychelles			
Tanzania			
Uganda			
Zaire			
Southern Africa			
Botswana			
Lesotho			
Malawi			
Mozambique			
Namibia			
South Africa	13,195		0.01
Swaziland			
Zambia			
Zimbabwe	830		

Source: UN, Environmental Data Report 1991-1992/Annual Bulletin of Statistics

Notes to Tables in Section Ten

Table 1001   a Deforestation refers to 1986
                b Deforestation refers to 1977-87
                c Deforestation refers to 1980-89
                d Deforestation refers to 1989-90
                e Deforestation refers to 1989
                f   Deforestation refers to 1982-90
                g Deforestation refers to 1979-89
                h Deforestation refers to 1980-87
                i   Deforestation refers to 1985-88

Table 1002   a Length of marine coastline
                    excludes islands
                b Extent of territorial sea for
                    UAE except Sharjah which
                    claims 12 nautical miles

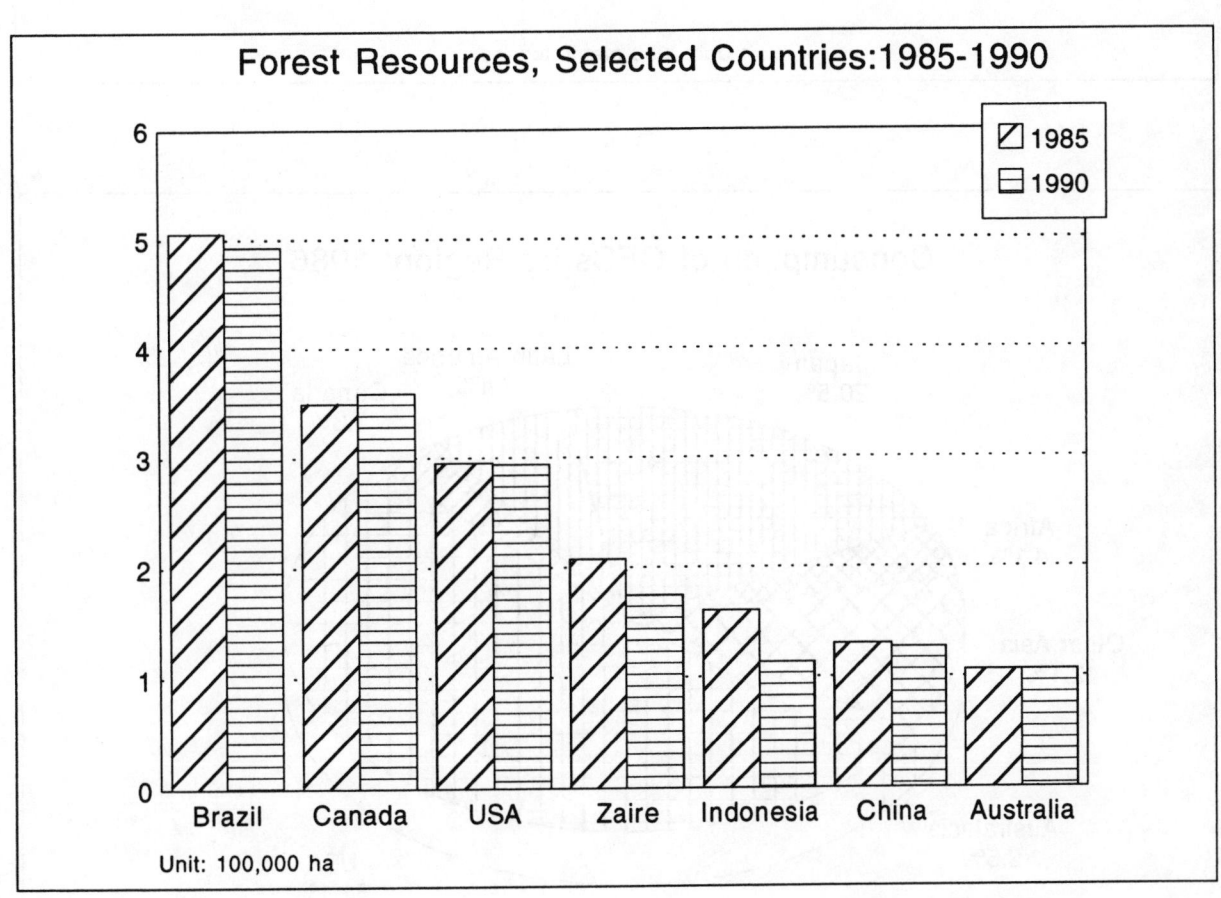

Forest Resources, Selected Countries:1985-1990

Unit: 100,000 ha

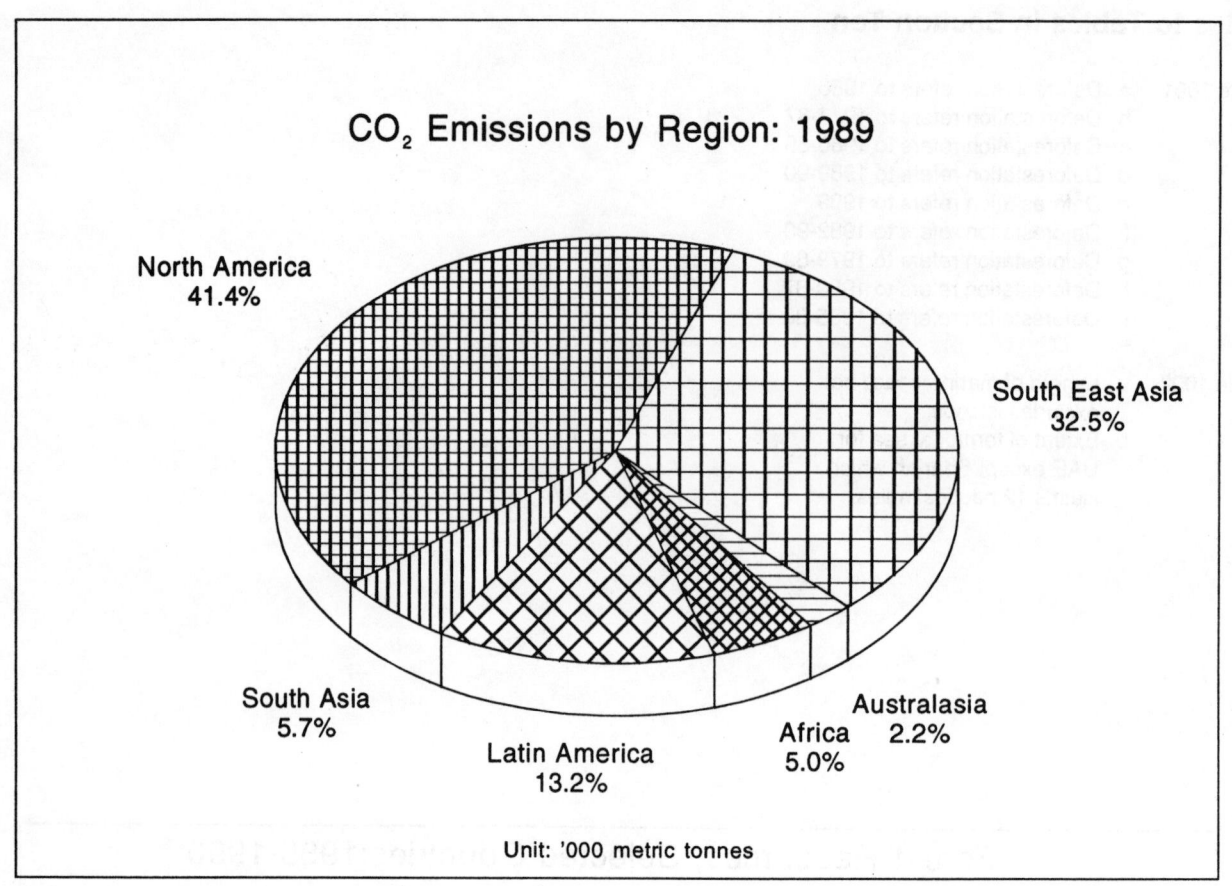

CO₂ Emissions by Region: 1989

North America
41.4%

South East Asia
32.5%

South Asia
5.7%

Latin America
13.2%

Africa
5.0%

Australasia
2.2%

Unit: '000 metric tonnes

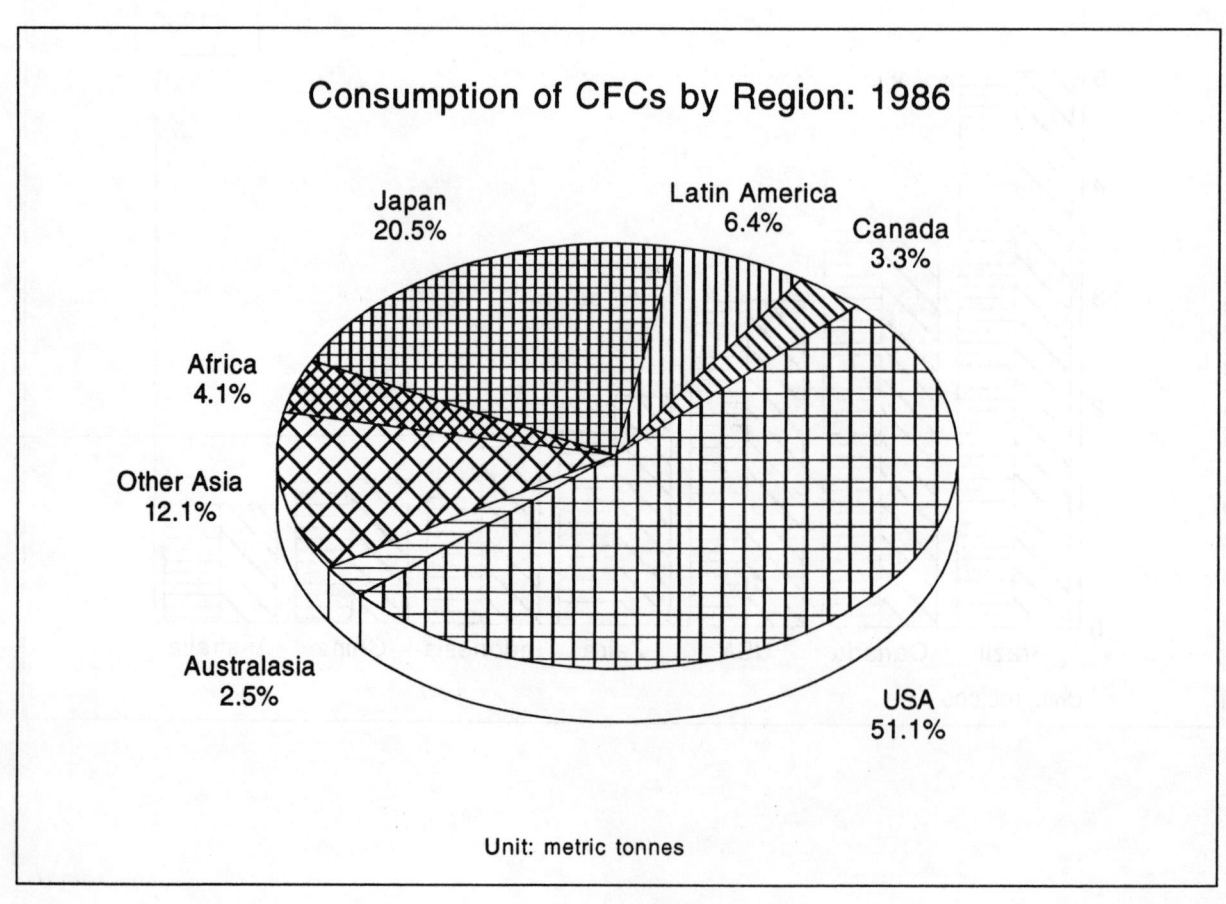

Consumption of CFCs by Region: 1986

Japan
20.5%

Latin America
6.4%

Canada
3.3%

Africa
4.1%

Other Asia
12.1%

Australasia
2.5%

USA
51.1%

Unit: metric tonnes

Section Eleven
Consumer Expenditure Patterns

TRENDS IN TOTAL CONSUMER EXPENDITURE

Table No. 1101

Total Consumer Expenditure 1977-1992

Units: Million units of national currency

	1977	1980	1985	1987	1988	1989	1990	1991	1992
North America									
Canada	123,560	172,420	274,503	322,770	349,937	378,933	398,208	410,413	419,852
USA	1,271,500	1,748,100	2,667,400	3,052,200	3,296,100	3,523,100	3,748,400	3,887,700	4,095,800
South America									
Argentina [a]	1	17	28,230	139,000	583,000	18,496,000			
Bolivia			1,793	7,440	8,803	10,392	12,366	15,498	
Brazil [b]	2	9	913	7,220	51,522	734,942	20,093,559	106,711,485	
Chile	209,500	760,500	1,785,300	2,811,000	3,534,800	4,487,200	5,691,500	7,301,309	9,273,341
Colombia	498,435	1,104,816	3,445,593	5,919,495	7,734,390	9,862,300	13,233,600		
Ecuador	102,600	174,900	715,660	1,269,420	2,086,900	3,706,000	5,703,000	8,562,000	
French Guiana									
Guyana	683	796	1,035	1,715	2,279	3,054	5,307		
Paraguay	190,100	399,400	1,066,900	1,882,600	2,586,700	3,497,000	4,841,800	6,038,400	
Peru [c]	780	3,470	123,490	504,120	3,327,500	79	5,202	30,460	
Suriname	609	916	961	622	971	846			
Uruguay	15,020	69,890	327,975	1,163,700	1,880,400	3,342,603	6,758,358	13,935,277	25,291,268
Venezuela	80,100	135,400	287,320	450,350	597,740	977,281	1,415,400	2,040,100	
Caribbean									
Anguilla									
Antigua		198							
Aruba									
Bahamas	521	666							
Barbados	742	1,081	1,392	1,934	2,004	2,158	2,189	2,261	1,717
Bermuda			781	927	1,018	1,094	1,157		
British Virgin Islands	9								
Cayman Islands									
Cuba		7,651							
Dominica	63	148							
Dominican Republic	3,590	5,109	10,833	15,361	21,808	33,869	51,121	80,542	
Grenada	97	161	249	281					
Guadeloupe	3,344	5,098							
Haiti	4,590	6,840	9,471	9,403	9,436	9,861	11,618	12,344	
Jamaica	2,020	3,147	7,772	9,801	11,458	13,849	17,481		
Martinique	4,633	5,493							
Netherlands Antilles									
St Kitts	47	93							
St Lucia	110	177							
St Vincent/Grenadines	80	140	174						
Trinidad and Tobago	3,605	6,365	9,494	9,883	10,101	10,232	10,924		
Central America									
Belize	154	243	281	321	372	433	465	511	
Costa Rica	17,170	27,100	118,974	176,475	215,794	256,923	321,143	416,899	
El Salvador	4,634	6,405	11,640	18,744	22,153	26,729	36,132	41,821	
Guatemala	4,130	6,217	9,300	14,989	17,289	19,837	28,785	40,161	
Honduras	2,314	3,612	5,446	6,002	6,413	7,219	8,879	11,393	
Mexico [d]	1,230	2,650	30,575	126,873	270,908	355,036	483,232		
Nicaragua [e]	2	3	11	281	5,240	2,421	170	6,206	
Panama	1,240	2,010	3,080	3,055	2,683	3,087	3,168		
Puerto Rico	9,100	12,000							
South Asia									
Afghanistan									
Bangladesh	118,600	173,200	414,335	533,292	584,233	646,614	720,977		
Bhutan			1,506	2,321	2,558	2,582	2,696		
India	631,890	909,390	1,743,800	2,225,300	2,564,950	2,917,300	3,358,400	3,894,200	
Nepal	13,689	19,195	33,807	45,355	52,743	60,639	74,871	87,950	
Pakistan	117,000	193,000	385,350	415,670	486,570	543,300	611,710	701,629	875,010
Sri Lanka	26,700	53,400	126,500	151,949	173,457	194,680	244,288	288,214	318,530

TRENDS IN TOTAL CONSUMER EXPENDITURE

Table No. 1101 (cont'd)

Total Consumer Expenditure 1977-1992

Units: Million units of national currency

	1977	1980	1985	1987	1988	1989	1990	1991	1992
Japan									
Japan [d]	105,870	139,506	188,661	204,585	215,122	228,483	243,628	255,341	264,992
ASEAN/NICs									
Brunei									
Hong Kong	40,779	80,109	162,799	217,711	251,803	284,581	329,103	388,777	
Indonesia [d]	11,214	20,957	57,201	71,989	81,045	88,752	106,312	125,143	
Macau			5,255	8,585	7,869	8,966	10,189		
Malaysia	16,810	26,950	40,360	37,685	44,856	52,930	62,030	72,065	
Philippines	102,626	156,824	420,832	482,330	558,765	649,300	767,100	916,300	1,017,000
Singapore	9,269	12,979	17,553	20,249	23,398	25,781	28,199	30,361	32,289
South Korea [d]	11,273	24,543	47,875	57,989	66,468	77,017	91,882	109,654	123,746
Taiwan [f]	426,802	767,742	1,261,580	1,537,782	1,765,247	2,070,811	2,302,009	2,554,494	2,903,603
Thailand [f]	260,506	437,960	662,665	794,600	964,100	1,134,100	1,307,700	1,543,200	
East/SE Asia									
Cambodia									
China	150,200	222,300	424,000	550,200	699,500	776,100	820,200	924,400	
Laos									
Mongolia									
Myanmar	26,100	31,800	49,532	63,168	67,754	113,726	132,007		
North Korea									
Vietnam									
Australasia									
Australia	56,078	80,744	136,890	166,260	184,590	206,570	216,487	228,778	240,006
New Zealand	9,180	14,260	27,712	37,225	40,733	43,876	46,250	46,960	
Pacific									
American Samoa									
Fiji	415	575	838	960	1,094	1,210			
French Polynesia		61,300							
Guam									
Kiribati		22,711	28,966	31,500	32,700				
Nauru									
New Caledonia		50							
Papua New Guinea	693	1,051	1,600	1,815	1,919	1,962	1,816	2,166	
Solomon Islands			159	252					
Tonga		50							
Tuvalu									
Vanuatu					8,198	9,562	10,546	11,267	
Western Samoa			7,091						
Middle East									
Bahrain		370	438	389	441	505	526		
Egypt	4,920	11,080	22,509	36,372	43,915	56,518	69,592	83,479	110,026
Iran [d]	2,900	3,510	9,627	12,226	14,906	18,448	23,711		
Iraq									
Israel [g]	9	62	16,555	36,223	43,863	53,139	64,955	82,423	98,570
Jordan	471	829	1,579	1,680	1,672	1,766	2,381	2,539	3,023
Kuwait	1,363	2,403	2,357	2,805	3,014	3,193	2,834	2,132	2,517
Lebanon									
Oman	246	577	1,126	930	1,180	1,262	1,081	1,506	
Qatar									
Saudi Arabia	34,400	102,400	158,590	135,540	139,400	145,030			
Syria	18,150	34,110	54,155	98,496	152,683	142,213	187,433	237,488	
United Arab Emirates	11,600	19,000	29,900	33,800	38,700	41,900	47,900	51,500	
Yemen	11,372	18,522	29,457	40,115					

TRENDS IN TOTAL CONSUMER EXPENDITURE   Table No. 1101 (cont'd)

Total Consumer Expenditure 1977-1992

Units: Million units of national currency

	1977	1980	1985	1987	1988	1989	1990	1991	1992
North Africa									
Algeria	38,900	69,900	134,800	154,900	158,800				
Chad	134,300								
Djibouti		38,600							
Ethiopia	5,460	6,800	7,259	8,623	8,421	8,768	8,856	9,321	11,582
Libya	4,500	2,330							
Mali		493,000							
Mauritania	14,210	28,500							
Morocco	31,800	47,100	89,830	111,828	123,265	134,668	147,936	168,022	
Niger	207,000	371,000	510,200	514,000	446,700	505,300			
Somalia									
Sudan	1,830								
Tunisia	1,410	2,170	4,356	5,124	5,582	6,220	7,086	7,905	8,840
West Africa									
Benin [f]	139,000	220,000	404,300	384,500	398,700	390,100	404,100	442,200	
Burkina Faso	162,000	242,000	411,900						
Cameroon	545,000	941,000	2,466,300						
Cape Verde				15,134	17,848				
Côte d'Ivoire	839,000	1,353,200	1,891,700						
Equatorial Guinea									
Gabon	162,000								
Gambia									
Ghana	8,640	34,230	284,600	610,400	834,300	1,186,700	1,736,100		
Guinea									
Guinea-Bissau									
Liberia	493	600	625	714	733	657			
Nigeria	19,061	31,695	54,066	78,329	113,073	138,828	146,420	128,230	294,520
Sao Tomé e Príncipe									
Senegal	364,000	504,000	925,500	1,072,100	1,163,800	1,151,900			
Sierra Leone	631	1,048	3,616	16,271	25,295	38,117	70,140	117,036	
Togo	106,000	152,000	235,400	262,500					
East/Central Africa									
Angola									
Burundi	38,227	70,133	109,478	107,015	114,298	143,025	163,124	179,405	
Central African Republic									
Comoros									
Congo	123,200	147,900	403,600						
Kenya	20,680	32,178	58,405	81,668	93,231	106,627	122,254		
Madagascar	343,100	526,100							
Maldives									
Mauritius	3,025	6,562	11,118	14,395	17,215	20,850	24,890	27,950	30,765
Réunion			14,157	18,039	19,260	21,163	22,974		
Rwanda	51,200	90,000	139,800	137,900	143,500	157,600	159,900	174,900	185,500
Seychelles	199	416	701	870	910	988	1,005		
Tanzania	17,979	32,486	93,130	175,555	311,325	329,592	66,437	526,831	
Uganda									
Zaire					678,000	1,246,000	2,580,000	5,092,000	109,244,000
Southern Africa									
Botswana	194	358	785	987	1,116	1,236			
Lesotho	287	395	838	1,109	1,495	1,667	1,745	2,176	
Malawi	483	631	1,430	1,933	2,771	2,764	4,381	4,809	5,063
Mozambique			23,200	67,500	115,100	194,900	270,800	378,400	
Namibia									
South Africa	19,268	30,922	66,167	93,186	111,057	130,658	154,675	179,000	
Swaziland			592	721	901				
Zambia	1,023	1,692	4,295	11,725	15,103				
Zimbabwe	1,312	2,184	4,142	4,387	5,542	6,807			

Source: IMF/OECD/national statistical offices
Notes: see end of section

ANALYSIS OF CONSUMER EXPENDITURE BY OBJECT — Table No. 1102

Consumer Expenditure by Object 1992

Units: Million current US dollars

	Food/drink/ tobacco	Clo- thing/ footwear	Housing	Fuels	Household goods & services	Health	Leisure & edu- cation	Trans- sport & comms.	Others	Total
Argentina [a]	16,952	2,332	5,031	2,752	2,224	1,835	2,311	2,097	8,156	43,691
Australia	38,530	10,359	33,455	4,054	11,824	13,703	28,075	8,585	27,889	176,475
Brazil [b]	81,934	12,799	72,696	15,484	12,799	13,322	23,378	12,930	17,098	262,442
Canada	57,103	17,601	68,985	12,748	22,849	14,857	34,250	25,823	93,143	347,358
Chile	7,473	1,273	7,228	1,215	992	1,324	2,321	1,283	2,467	25,575
China [b,c]	82,136	25,353	10,975		17,712	4,480	3,456	16,636	12,902	173,648
Colombia [d]	9,264	1,597	2,232	574	1,578	1,626	4,295	1,637	3,546	26,348
Ecuador [b,c]	2,553	786	1,088		333	401	1,092	400	1,531	8,184
Hong Kong [b]	8,236	9,983	6,610	743	5,952	1,827	4,447	3,946	8,221	49,965
India [b,c]	80,866	18,673	14,572		4,461	3,740	12,654	4,721	31,546	171,234
Indonesia [b,c,e]	34,274	3,580	9,766		5,153		2,207	1,240	7,946	64,166
Israel	10,382	2,245	8,418	1,603	4,409	5,612	3,808	3,608		40,084
Japan	410,727	127,420	98,519	105,997	124,702	219,149	207,914	204,691	593,199	2,092,317
Malaysia [b]	10,244	1,811	1,940	1,139	2,949	542	3,880	1,656	2,044	26,205
Mexico [c,d]	57,900	12,066	10,095		14,035	5,910	14,273	5,800	51,730	171,810
New Zealand [b]	3,319	1,390	5,401	680	1,871	1,814	4,632	2,018	6,075	27,200
Nigeria [c,e,f]	8,547	914	2,222		619		525		4,198	17,026
Pakistan	16,435	2,724	4,383	2,019	694	1,701	1,552	692	4,684	34,885
Peru [b,c]	18,927	2,957	4,101		1,814	1,814	3,391	2,721	3,706	39,430
Philippines	22,523	2,990	4,345	2,073	4,186	478	1,427	1,794	48	39,864
Singapore [c]	5,216	1,637	2,374		2,069	1,070	3,374	3,376	704	19,821
South Africa [b]	21,376	4,604	6,312	1,803	5,988	1,880	5,679	2,833	14,467	64,942
South Korea	54,455	6,642	17,849	6,539	9,226	11,615	17,950	17,953	16,288	158,517
Taiwan [c]	27,698	5,267	18,726		5,096	6,031	15,088	19,490	16,606	114,001
Thailand [b]	20,335	7,690	3,961	929	4,862	4,585	6,829	8,628	2,659	60,477
USA	741,340	221,800	600,444	104,689	180,899	635,177	463,604	242,308	905,540	4,095,800
Venezuela [b,c]	15,501	3,679	3,056		1,853	1,116	3,708	1,557	5,438	35,907

Source: Euromonitor/national statistical offices   Notes: see end of section

ANALYSIS OF CONSUMER EXPENDITURE BY OBJECT — Table No. 1103

Consumer Expenditure by Object 1992 (% analysis)

Units: % of total

	Food/drink/ tobacco	Clo- thing/ footwear	Housing	Fuels	Household goods & services	Health	Leisure & edu- cation	Trans- sport & comms.	Others	Total
Argentina [a]	38.8	5.3	11.5	6.3	5.1	4.2	5.3	4.8	18.7	100.0
Australia	21.8	5.9	19.0	2.3	6.7	7.8	15.9	4.9	15.8	100.0
Brazil [b]	31.2	4.9	27.7	5.9	4.9	5.1	8.9	4.9	6.5	100.0
Canada	16.4	5.1	19.9	3.7	6.6	4.3	9.9	7.4	26.8	100.0
Chile	29.2	5.0	28.3	4.8	3.9	5.2	9.1	5.0	9.6	100.0
China [b,c]	47.3	14.6	6.3		10.2	2.6	2.0	9.6	7.4	100.0
Colombia [d]	35.2	6.1	8.5	2.2	6.0	6.2	16.3	6.2	13.5	100.0
Ecuador [b,c]	31.2	9.6	13.3		4.1	4.9	13.3	4.9	18.7	100.0
Hong Kong [b]	16.5	20.0	13.2	1.5	11.9	3.7	8.9	7.9	16.5	100.0
India [b,c]	47.2	10.9	8.5		2.6	2.2	7.4	2.8	18.4	100.0
Indonesia [b,c,e]	53.4	5.6	15.2		8.0		3.4	1.9	12.4	100.0
Israel	25.9	5.6	21.0	4.0	11.0	14.0	9.5	9.0		100.0
Japan	19.6	6.1	4.7	5.1	6.0	10.5	9.9	9.8	28.4	100.0
Malaysia [b]	39.1	6.9	7.4	4.3	11.3	2.1	14.8	6.3	7.8	100.0
Mexico [c,d]	33.7	7.0	5.9		8.2	3.4	8.3	3.4	30.1	100.0
New Zealand [b]	12.2	5.1	19.9	2.5	6.9	6.7	17.0	7.4	22.3	100.0
Nigeria [c,e,f]	50.2	5.4	13.1		3.6		3.1		24.7	100.0
Pakistan	47.1	7.8	12.6	5.8	2.0	4.9	4.5	2.0	13.4	100.0
Peru [b,c]	48.0	7.5	10.4		4.6	4.6	8.6	6.9	9.4	100.0
Philippines	56.5	7.5	10.9	5.2	10.5	1.2	3.6	4.5	0.1	100.0
Singapore [c]	26.3	8.3	12.0		10.4	5.4	17.0	17.0	3.6	100.0
South Africa [b]	32.9	7.1	9.7	2.8	9.2	2.9	8.7	4.4	22.3	100.0
South Korea	34.4	4.2	11.3	4.1	5.8	7.3	11.3	11.3	10.3	100.0
Taiwan [c]	24.3	4.6	16.4		4.5	5.3	13.2	17.1	14.6	100.0
Thailand [b]	33.6	12.7	6.6	1.5	8.0	7.6	11.3	14.3	4.4	100.0
USA	18.1	5.4	14.7	2.6	4.4	15.5	11.3	5.9	22.1	100.0
Venezuela [b,c]	43.2	10.2	8.5		5.2	3.1	10.3	4.3	15.1	100.0

Source: Euromonitor/national statistical offices   Notes: see end of section

TRENDS IN CONSUMER SPENDING BY SECTOR — Table No. 1104

Consumer Expenditure on Food 1977-1992

Units: Million units of national currency

	1977	1980	1984	1985	1986	1987	1988	1989	1990	1991	1992
Argentina a,b,c		0	1	9	19	47	213	6,769	81,916		
Australia d	9,339	13,841	20,101	22,740	24,693	26,482	29,102	32,130	33,857	36,295	
Brazil e		0	0	0	0	2	14	204	5,530		
Canada d	18,068	24,945	31,324	32,806	34,942	37,148	38,543	40,220	42,145	43,390	43,403
Chile c	54,470	196,209	357,717	471,451	609,664	788,648	991,711	1,258,914	1,596,788		
China					194,055	234,300	285,800	316,650	336,282	380,853	
Colombia	177,316	353,089	831,702	1,064,966	1,371,057	1,739,148	2,237,929	2,875,229	3,858,090		
Ecuador f		61,939		237,473	308,371	423,971	651,112	1,182,823	1,779,336		
Hong Kong b,d	10,717	19,461	32,690	32,625	34,405	37,618	41,401	45,620	51,326	57,814	
India f,g	399,060	567,000	856,130	936,300	992,430	1,102,030	1,228,700	1,422,650	1,586,030		
Indonesia b,h	7,154	13,296	25,573	28,965	32,323	36,600	39,604	43,370	51,951		
Israel i,j	2	17	1,131	4,448	7,688	9,940	11,575	14,472	16,856	17,180	20,317
Japan f,h	28,710	34,580	41,069	41,537	42,043	42,825	43,888	46,090	49,180	50,124	
Malaysia b					14,215	14,445	16,858	19,232	21,710	23,478	
Mexico b,f,h	516	989	6,404	10,425	17,828	41,618	65,408	89,198	114,173		
New Zealand f,g		2,447	3,929	4,648	3,932	4,561	4,846	5,276	5,646	5,730	
Nigeria b		14,727			27,018	32,999	46,198	65,555	68,448		
Pakistan f							226,595	253,014	288,189		
Peru f						290,462	1,650,500	50,505,000			
Philippines b,k	55,784	88,974	209,234	238,184	255,026	263,433	292,574	336,335	397,357		
Singapore	2,348	3,107	3,914	3,793	3,778	3,962	4,628	5,597	6,389	6,739	7,059
South Africa	4,606	7,742	14,910	16,956	20,268	24,297	28,495	33,610	39,809		
South Korea c,h	5,846	11,766	17,481	18,850	20,362	22,296	25,139	28,513	33,176	38,004	41,565
Taiwan f	172,924	260,842	369,458	77,440	403,370	433,331	469,450	562,560	574,935	615,230	705,463
Thailand	117,837	183,080	197,453	202,705	211,809	222,667	255,727	283,295	311,607	336,537	
USA	255,900	349,100	448,500	471,600	500,000	530,700	562,600	595,300	624,900	617,700	630,900
Venezuela f	35,534	59,004	103,455	127,395	148,354	205,392	273,425	447,039	611,004		
Vietnam											

Source: Euromonitor/national statistical offices

Notes: see end of section

TRENDS IN CONSUMER SPENDING BY SECTOR — Table No. 1105

Consumer Expenditure on Alcoholic Drinks 1977-1992

Units: Million units of national currency

	1977	1980	1984	1985	1986	1987	1988	1989	1990	1991	1992
Argentina											
Australia	3,236	4,517	6,268	6,857	7,314	8,015	8,353	9,129	9,345	9,028	
Brazil											
Canada a	4,090	5,576	9,175	10,189	11,535	12,919	13,431	14,652	15,466	16,035	
Chile											
China b	4,506	6,669	10,185	12,720	14,319	16,506	20,985	23,283	24,606	27,732	
Colombia	16,180	41,435	131,000	145,780	183,107	238,843	299,884	385,282	516,986		
Ecuador											
Hong Kong	752	1,040	1,564	1,688	2,041	2,518	2,910	2,575	2,892	3,292	
India											
Indonesia a,c	13	30	82	80	68	76	85	93	128		
Israel									545	664	
Japan c									2,892	2,818	
Malaysia					743	763	946	1,079	1,240	1,494	
Mexico .											
New Zealand					1,188	1,144	1,257	1,375	1,648	1,593	
Nigeria											
Pakistan											
Peru											
Philippines d,e	2,309	4,466	9,801	11,812	11,901	12,363	14,477	16,918	19,987		
Singapore	143	206	240	220	219	229	231	251	257	271	
South Africa	1,109	1,462	2,821	2,878	3,238	3,957	4,702	5,546	6,440		
South Korea											
Taiwan d	17,277	34,857	48,281	49,986	52,612	59,256	63,877	71,558	79,382	85,745	89,252
Thailand							68,047	81,476	103,926		
USA											
Venezuela											
Vietnam											

Source: Euromonitor/national statistical offices

Notes: see end of section

TRENDS IN CONSUMER SPENDING BY SECTOR — Table No. 1106

Consumer Expenditure on Non-Alcoholic Drinks 1977-1992

Units: Million units of national currency

	1977	1980	1984	1985	1986	1987	1988	1989	1990	1991	1992
Argentina											
Australia											
Brazil											
Canada											
Chile											
China											
Colombia	5,316	12,821	41,000	46,702	46,567	67,864	85,175	109,430	146,837		
Ecuador											
Hong Kong											
India											
Indonesia											
Israel									1,839	2,064	
Japan [a]									2,159	2,122	
Malaysia					595	649	946	1,079	992	1,209	
Mexico											
New Zealand											
Nigeria [b]		1,490			2,140	2,567	3,594	4,923	5,140		
Pakistan											
Peru											
Philippines											
Singapore	215	343	498	465	463	486	536	540	560	580	
South Africa	264	408	782	880	1,048	1,307	1,500	1,769	2,054		
South Korea											
Taiwan											
Thailand	6,164	9,682	14,716	15,757	16,721	17,987	20,650	24,050	27,839	30,067	
USA											
Venezuela											
Vietnam											

Source: Euromonitor/national statistical offices

Notes: see end of section

TRENDS IN CONSUMER SPENDING BY SECTOR — Table No. 1107

Consumer Expenditure on Tobacco 1977-1992

Units: Million units of national currency

	1977	1980	1984	1985	1986	1987	1988	1989	1990	1991	1992
Argentina [a,b]	0	0	0	0	1	2	12	406	5,020		
Australia	1,185	1,581	2,389	2,657	3,000	3,247	3,555	3,984	4,377	4,626	
Brazil [c]	0	0	0	0	0	0	0	10	29		
Canada [b]	2,557	3,863	5,778	6,368	7,284	8,074	8,150	8,230	8,686	9,006	
Chile	4,190	13,841	20,812	27,937	34,614	42,244	53,121	67,434	85,532		
China											
Colombia	7,914	12,968	34,562	42,222	49,023	56,155	76,182	97,876	131,334		
Ecuador											
Hong Kong	549	907	1,570	1,762	1,658	1,597	1,974	2,486	2,726	2,984	
India											
Indonesia [b,d]	560	1,195	2,251	2,560	2,896	3,188	3,587	3,929	4,706		
Israel									1,301	1,656	
Japan											
Malaysia					1,115	1,184	1,464	1,671	1,860	1,992	
Mexico											
New Zealand					687	869	931	1,086	1,163	1,164	
Nigeria											
Pakistan											
Peru							2,097	13,310	424,800		
Philippines [e]	2,288	3,582	8,454	9,808	10,001	10,694	11,734	13,635	17,067		
Singapore	128	197	240	290	289	304	347	368	402	500	
South Africa	493	765	1,031	1,160	1,349	1,611	1,903	2,245	2,607		
South Korea [d]									830	838	
Taiwan	14,848	21,961	30,433	32,085	32,483	38,028	38,973	41,240	43,310	46,370	45,896
Thailand	8,127	11,803	17,483	17,472	18,069	18,841	20,724	23,338	25,310	29,643	
USA											
Venezuela											
Vietnam											

Source: Euromonitor/national statistical offices

Notes: see end of section

TRENDS IN CONSUMER SPENDING BY SECTOR — Table No. 1108

Consumer Expenditure on Clothing and Footwear 1977-1992

Units: Million units of national currency

	1977	1980	1984	1985	1986	1987	1988	1989	1990	1991	1992
Argentina a,b	0	0	0	1	3	6	26	832	9,874		
Australia	4,394	5,794	8,539	9,635	10,522	11,542	12,198	12,482	12,742	13,434	
Brazil c	0	0	0	0	0	0	2	36	98		
Canada	8,787	11,593	15,225	16,592	18,011	19,210	20,155	21,069	21,420	21,345	21,276
Chile	14,455	47,151	68,941	89,051	111,660	139,880	175,898	223,292	283,220		
China					69,686	80,329	102,127	113,311	109,907	134,962	
Colombia	38,779	76,332	171,590	219,183	272,447	364,368	465,444	597,989	802,404		
Ecuador		19,592		76,483	96,989	129,192	200,342	363,945	547,488		
Hong Kong	7,569	14,646	26,629	28,810	35,565	44,467	54,303	60,054	68,754	77,681	
India d	63,034	107,486	157,670	174,870	205,560	228,350	259,380	312,300	366,243		
Indonesia b,f	516	1,077	2,024	2,359	2,736	3,098	3,485	4,000	5,932		
Israel e	0	3	182	800	1,426	1,944	3,244	3,382	3,752	4,442	5,537
Japan f	9,553	9,350	10,699	12,490	12,873	13,374	13,549	14,289	15,309	15,550	
Malaysia						2,379	2,437	3,155	3,599	4,342	4,980
Mexico f	131	304	1,843	2,851	4,763	12,372	19,443	26,515	33,940		
New Zealand d		972	1,383	1,717	2,239	2,383	2,255	2,407	2,371	2,401	
Nigeria		1,842			2,782	3,933	5,506	7,314	7,868		
Pakistan							37,563	41,942	47,773		
Peru						39,322	249,562	7,965,000			
Philippines g	6,201	11,078	25,213	31,466	33,003	35,994	41,986	49,095	58,003		
Singapore	877	1,275	1,718	1,569	1,656	1,870	2,078	2,225	2,603	2,579	2,669
South Africa	1,878	2,786	4,518	4,734	5,599	6,902	8,173	9,640	10,970		
South Korea f	1,057	1,917	2,612	2,432	2,665	2,956	3,325	3,666	4,238	4,811	5,186
Taiwan	22,305	40,583	59,764	62,297	65,425	72,886	83,671	95,795	107,307	119,218	134,254
Thailand	23,485	47,247	73,168	89,663	99,038	114,185	131,394	153,413	181,693	196,228	
USA	84,100	109,000	146,700	156,400	166,800	178,400	191,100	204,600	213,300	209,000	221,800
Venezuela	5,447	7,467	9,302	10,345	11,800	19,185	25,540	41,757	60,077		
Vietnam											

Source: Euromonitor/national statistical offices

Notes: see end of section

TRENDS IN CONSUMER SPENDING BY SECTOR — Table No. 1109

Consumer Expenditure on Housing 1977-1992

Units: Million units of national currency

	1977	1980	1984	1985	1986	1987	1988	1989	1990	1991	1992
Argentina a,b	0	0	1	8	15	38	67	2,129	25,263		
Australia	8,924	13,704	21,854	24,593	27,594	31,079	35,157	38,810	41,685	43,371	
Brazil c	0	0	0	0	0	2	14	206	557		
Canada	17,402	28,251	45,309	48,674	52,683	57,088	62,547	69,438	75,242	79,735	83,374
Chile	62,850	206,856	387,635	534,311	692,293	794,523	999,104	1,268,298	1,608,692		
China d				30,791	31,074	35,821	45,541	52,904	55,859	58,445	
Colombia	52,522	123,624	278,300	354,704	429,486	528,141	650,609	835,884	1,121,620		
Ecuador d		19,589		79,438	106,436	147,253	253,906	471,892	758,500		
Hong Kong	5,599	10,022	20,148	22,351	25,037	28,277	33,126	38,350	44,095	51,433	
India d,e	96,000	100,000	167,380	186,550	205,920	229,750	252,760	278,710	331,324		
Indonesia b,d,f	1,357	2,550	7,412	8,584	9,919	10,965	12,336	13,510	17,201		
Israel g	1	12	843	3,312	4,578	6,872	7,474	10,209	13,594	17,971	21,011
Japan f,h	5,910	5,902	7,578	35,082	36,113	37,919	40,036	47,251	46,010	12,023	
Malaysia						2,974	3,082	3,493	3,985	4,590	5,336
Mexico d,f	119	236	1,467	2,375	3,985	10,350	16,266	22,182	28,393		
New Zealand e		2,433	4,655	5,282	5,494	6,460	7,750	8,392	9,065	9,325	
Nigeria d		3,408			7,651	9,554	13,375	17,765	19,111		
Pakistan							60,431	67,477	76,858		
Peru d						54,527	346,060	1,044,800			
Philippines b,i	10,732	19,702	38,500	47,619	50,005	53,730	60,931	71,080	83,977		
Singapore d	1,067	1,390	1,976	2,184	2,299	2,430	2,619	2,786	3,137	3,485	3,868
South Africa	1,524	2,134	4,951	6,306	7,484	9,111	10,759	12,691	15,032		
South Korea f	953	2,468	4,752	5,322	5,804	6,232	6,868	7,609	9,644	12,213	13,935
Taiwan d	50,776	91,802	154,924	170,557	189,966	217,189	251,246	292,346	340,573	401,846	476,960
Thailand			44,000	53,214	58,429	64,516	70,301	77,643	86,587	101,128	
USA	182,400	261,500	371,300	403,000	434,300	468,900	502,617	533,992	569,500	574,700	600,500
Venezuela d	5,950	11,178	18,345	20,222	24,678	38,464	51,205	83,718	120,446		
Vietnam											

Source: Euromonitor/national statistical offices

Notes: see end of section

TRENDS IN CONSUMER SPENDING BY SECTOR | Table No. 1110

Consumer Expenditure on Fuel 1977-1992

Units: Million units of national currency

	1977	1980	1984	1985	1986	1987	1988	1989	1990	1991	1992
Argentina [a,b]	0	0	0	1	3	8	36	1,165	13,823		
Australia	1,208	1,756	3,074	3,377	3,681	3,926	4,216	4,659	5,047	5,255	
Brazil [c]	0	0	0	0	0	0	3	44	120		
Canada	4,480	6,340	9,643	10,679	10,680	10,450	11,617	12,233	13,183	14,608	15,426
Chile	11,522	52,474	75,445	104,766	136,225	171,214	215,300	273,309	346,661		
China [d]											
Colombia	5,652	15,085	48,343	70,603	98,463	125,732	167,701	215,457	289,109		
Ecuador [d]											
Hong Kong	883	2,031	3,362	3,215	3,387	3,718	3,950	4,511	5,180	5,781	
India [d]											
Indonesia [d]											
Israel [e]		1	168	410	565	1,095	1,370	1,895	2,444	3,135	4,003
Japan [f]					9,734	11,917	12,057	11,686	12,590	12,936	
Malaysia						1,708	2,028	2,314	2,729	3,130	
Mexico [d]											
New Zealand [g]		360	610	713	716	838	923	1,011	1,087	1,176	
Nigeria [d]											
Pakistan								27,831	31,076	35,397	
Peru [d]											
Philippines	5,644	9,796	22,258	25,241	27,502	28,934	29,057	33,763	39,889		
Singapore [d]											
South Africa	546	870	1,598	1,822	2,141	2,595	3,135	3,697	4,293		
South Korea [f]									4,127	4,523	
Taiwan [d]											
Thailand	7,637	14,337	16,500	16,880	17,225	18,032	18,480	19,694	21,941	23,696	
USA	37,600	56,400	84,800	88,900	87,300	88,600	93,600	97,700	95,600	103,600	104,700
Venezuela [d]											
Vietnam											

Source: Euromonitor/national statistical offices

Notes: see end of section

TRENDS IN CONSUMER SPENDING BY SECTOR | Table No. 1111

Consumer Expenditure on Household Goods and Services 1977-1992

Units: Million units of national currency

	1977	1980	1984	1985	1986	1987	1988	1989	1990	1991	1992
Argentina [a,b]	0	0	0	1	3	8	29	943	11,190		
Australia	4,770	6,418	8,609	10,716	11,417	12,835	13,980	14,845	14,514	15,330	
Brazil [c]	0	0	0	0	0	0	2	36	98		
Canada	12,006	15,509	20,334	22,085	23,784	25,030	26,200	26,500	26,800	27,000	
Chile	14,665	51,714	75,445	90,798	111,660	139,880	175,898	223,292	283,220		
China [d]							87,950	70,220	62,796	94,288	
Colombia	26,717	62,046	123,056	191,057	253,653	348,805	460,102	591,126	793,195		
Ecuador		12,921		13,691	20,989	30,010	42,939	227,466	348,396		
Hong Kong	4,019	8,883	17,534	18,084	21,436	27,061	32,466	34,468	36,554	46,315	
India [e]	25,300	29,082	43,590	45,810	50,860	50,110	62,740	74,900	87,502		
Indonesia [b,f]	762	1,540	3,493	4,067	5,016	5,785	6,509	7,128	8,538		
Israel [g]	0	6	441	1,668	2,652	3,711	4,842	4,729	6,020	8,204	10,878
Japan [f]				11,478	11,819	12,329	12,939	13,591	14,670	15,224	
Malaysia					3,048	3,796	4,732	5,399	6,823	8,110	
Mexico [f]	154	355	2,141	3,382	5,660	14,390	22,615	30,841	39,476		
New Zealand [g]		1,692	2,642	2,932	2,739	2,949	3,020	3,135	3,131	3,230	
Nigeria [e]		1,159			2,140	2,715	3,801	5,049	5,325		
Pakistan							9,585	10,703	12,190		
Peru						24,117	153,065	4,885,200			
Philippines [h]	7,460	13,146	40,470	47,135	48,805	51,122	60,328	70,656	83,475		
Singapore	926	1,322	1,853	2,015	2,051	2,157	2,539	2,736	2,997	3,185	3,371
South Africa	2,361	3,728	6,363	6,697	7,828	9,203	10,412	12,282	14,261		
South Korea [f]	612	1,197	2,200	2,434	2,904	3,426	4,091	4,668	5,526	6,561	7,206
Taiwan	16,823	34,362	48,537	49,657	60,805	66,273	62,350	63,540	105,729	114,188	
Thailand	14,444	14,100	13,550	13,736	14,479	16,558	71,907	89,601	105,136	124,069	
USA	67,100	86,200	118,800	129,900	139,700	148,800	161,800	171,400	176,800	170,400	180,900
Venezuela	7,542	9,660	11,050	12,670	14,200	23,340	31,071	50,799	73,086		
Vietnam											

Source: Euromonitor/national statistical offices

Notes: see end of section

TRENDS IN CONSUMER SPENDING BY SECTOR — Table No. 1112

Consumer Expenditure on Health Goods and Medical Services 1977-1992

Units: Million units of national currency

	1977	1980	1984	1985	1986	1987	1988	1989	1990	1991	1992
Argentina [a,b]	0	0	0	1	2	7	24	776	9,215		
Australia	3,525	5,084	8,328	9,250	10,631	12,065	13,558	15,019	16,629	17,765	
Brazil [c]	0	0	0	0	0	0	2	37	102		
Canada [b]	4,267	5,455	9,051	10,298	11,654	12,919	14,652	16,040	16,931	17,554	
Chile	10,684	44,869	66,340	87,305	116,126	145,476	182,934	232,223	294,549		
China	0	0	6,150	6,494	7,564	9,491	12,758	17,477	21,690	23,859	
Colombia	24,441	60,935	141,900	203,686	280,243	376,744	473,915	608,873	817,008		
Ecuador		6,412		11,588	16,824	23,598	35,067	185,763	279,447		
Hong Kong	1,734	3,060	6,160	6,766	7,607	8,625	9,456	9,902	11,973	14,219	
India [d]	14,580	29,146	46,660	48,280	50,890	53,550	59,230	63,900	73,362		
Indonesia											
Israel [e]	0	5	210	725	1,671	3,075	4,152	4,966	7,000	11,558	
Japan [f]				19,549	20,737	22,053	23,126	24,056	25,518	26,745	
Malaysia					595	607	874	997	1,240	1,494	
Mexico [f]	45	107	899	1,481	2,358	6,067	9,535	13,003	16,644		
New Zealand [e,g]		500	1,000	1,351	1,728	2,100	2,390	2,591	2,936	3,132	
Nigeria											
Pakistan							23,452	26,187	29,827		
Peru						24,117	153,065	4,885,200			
Philippines [h]	2,907	5,059	5,450	5,555	5,501	5,999	6,937	8,103	9,573		
Singapore	298	411	627	702	898	962	1,107	1,265	1,459	1,661	1,757
South Africa	514	792	1,683	1,935	2,204	2,752	3,269	3,856	4,477		
South Korea [f]	324	930	2,509	2,968	3,371	3,963	4,675	5,530	6,710	8,050	9,067
Taiwan	19,218	35,118	60,532	65,284	70,604	76,786	85,325	95,445	108,333	129,191	153,683
Thailand	20,000	30,000	48,222	54,603	66,720	75,551	81,755	95,484	110,521	117,000	
USA	111,500	164,200	265,300	291,500	318,400	357,300	398,400	434,300	483,400	580,200	635,200
Venezuela	3,436	4,917	6,692	7,449	10,603	14,050	18,704	30,581	43,998		
Vietnam											

Source: Euromonitor/national statistical offices

Notes: see end of section

TRENDS IN CONSUMER SPENDING BY SECTOR — Table No. 1113

Consumer Expenditure on Transport and Communications 1977-1992

Units: Million units of national currency

	1977	1980	1984	1985	1986	1987	1988	1989	1990	1991	1992
Argentina [a,b]		0	0	1	3	9	30	980	11,978		
Australia [b]	7,884	12,745	19,031	21,185	22,303	25,285	28,261	32,199	34,679	36,397	
Brazil [c]	0	0	0	0	0	0	4	66	178		
Canada [b]	17,068	24,848	35,832	36,000	36,350	36,100	35,780	35,565	34,591	40,471	
Chile	12,570	61,600	115,770	157,150	203,221	255,142	320,839	407,284	516,594		
China			7,444	7,619	9,125	10,615	10,227	13,107	16,770	18,448	
Colombia	63,118	159,617	343,000	483,357	636,561	883,337	1,251,580	1,607,995	2,157,668		
Ecuador		17,541		28,788	42,154	59,870	93,751	496,634	760,664		
Hong Kong	2,928	6,341	11,579	12,648	13,850	16,558	20,553	22,723	27,063	34,610	
India [d]	40,910	41,757	96,450	112,400	132,000	157,160	187,490	215,700	248,300		
Indonesia [b,e]	336	660	1,497	1,806	2,137	2,480	2,791	3,056	3,661		
Israel [f]	0	6	499	1,906	3,141	3,535	4,712	5,000	6,200	8,200	
Japan [e]	7,920	10,551	15,157	18,120	18,620	19,351	20,904	22,560	24,450	25,375	
Malaysia					5,576	5,865	6,851	7,816	9,304	10,672	
Mexico [e]	110	273	2,227	3,354	5,754	14,633	22,997	31,361	40,143		
New Zealand [d]		2,533	4,518	7,449	5,980	6,787	7,338	8,062	8,117	7,998	
Nigeria	852	1,432	2,158	1,903	1,881	2,304	3,225	4,284	4,518		
Pakistan							21,409	23,905	27,228		
Peru						45,089	286,165	9,133,200			
Philippines [g]	2,728	5,839	13,345	15,227	16,502	17,475	19,908	23,245	27,463		
Singapore	1,325	2,231	2,942	2,678	2,609	2,997	3,696	4,320	4,776	4,966	5,497
South Africa	1,742	3,407	5,896	5,904	6,556	7,547	9,405	11,093	13,525		
South Korea [e]	765	2,137	4,280	4,821	5,319	6,119	6,984	8,022	9,479	11,928	14,013
Taiwan	23,905	59,646	110,284	112,858	144,342	176,991	222,360	283,216	308,554	347,496	384,306
Thailand	22,714	45,296	62,223	68,192	70,979	79,981	101,665	121,912	147,665	174,260	
USA [h]	181,500	242,100	329,500	359,500	365,500	378,900	421,000	425,700	443,600	438,200	463,600
Venezuela	12,990	14,413	24,597	29,676	34,898	46,680	62,142	101,599	146,173		
Vietnam											

Source: Euromonitor/national statistical offices

Notes: see end of section

TRENDS IN CONSUMER SPENDING BY SECTOR | Table No. 1114

Consumer Expenditure on Leisure and Education 1977-1992

Units: Million units of national currency

	1977	1980	1984	1985	1986	1987	1988	1989	1990	1991	1992
Argentina a,b	0	0	0	1	2	7	27	887	10,532		
Australia b	4,432	4,370	7,792	8,673	9,629	10,816	12,242	13,653	14,928	15,708	
Brazil c	0	0	0	0	0	0	2	36	98		
Canada b	9,266	12,750	17,730	19,240	21,109	22,931	25,468	27,880	29,428	30,511	
Chile	13,617	47,151	62,438	87,305	116,126	141,000	177,305	225,078	285,486		
China			24,060	56,455	57,221	56,276	70,881	80,831	80,500	88,550	
Colombia	24,705	58,208	130,000	190,997	258,113	351,194	476,904	612,713	822,161		
Ecuador		7,809		11,858	16,924	24,018	34,351	181,972	278,716		
Hong Kong	3,354	6,497	13,158	15,006	16,493	19,651	22,926	25,778	28,167	30,702	
India d	10,520	17,502	43,050	48,820	55,359	67,550	73,350	80,450	92,600		
Indonesia b,e	269	452	1,151	1,203	1,311	1,392	1,566	1,715	2,055		
Israel f	0	4	358	1,515	2,315	2,651	4,712	5,000	7,100	8,000	
Japan e				18,259	19,303	20,069	21,115	22,351	23,833	24,979	
Malaysia					2,044	2,353	2,884	3,291	3,969	4,553	
Mexico e	62	149	873	1,425	2,320	5,948	9,348	12,748	16,317		
New Zealand d	1,450	1,710	2,005	2,249	2,673	3,009	3,285	3,378	3,369	3,484	
Nigeria											
Pakistan							9,536	10,648	12,129		
Peru						36,176	229,597	7,327,800			
Philippines g	4,376	7,663	16,188	20,409	20,752	21,909	25,337	29,602	34,972		
Singapore	1,144	1,802	2,472	2,453	2,817	3,258	3,979	4,479	5,270	5,353	5,500
South Africa	857	1,395	2,700	3,021	3,461	4,141	4,926	5,810	6,747		
South Korea e	705	1,812	4,524	5,152	5,883	6,711	7,791	8,966	10,501	12,269	14,015
Taiwan	38,264	94,912	164,675	179,931	195,056	223,517	271,277	318,475	374,448	428,490	496,395
Thailand	11,302	38,900	71,100	82,201	91,266	109,436	129,740	158,987	186,558	220,155	
USA	76,689	107,100	168,300	185,700	201,700	223,300	261,471	282,422	295,555	230,000	
Venezuela	7,961	12,763	11,253	13,183	14,867	19,605	26,099	42,671	61,392		
Vietnam											

Source: Euromonitor/national statistical offices | Notes: see end of section

Notes to Tables in Section Eleven

Table 1101   Entries of 0 denote values of less than 0.5 million
   a   Million australes (currency reform 1985: 1 austral = 1,000 pesos); in a second reform of 1992, 1 peso argentino = 10,000 australes
   b   Million novo cruzados (currency reform 1988: 1 novo cruzado = 1,000 cruzados = 1,000,000 old cruzeiros); in a second reform of March 1990, the cruzeiro again replaced the novo cruzado: 1 cruzeiro = 1,000 novo cruzados
   c   Thousand new soles to 1988; million from 1989
   d   Billion units of national currency
   e   Gold crdobas to 1989, millions from 1990
   f   New series starting 1988
   g   Million new shekels (currency reform 1985; 1 new shekel - 1,000 shekels)

Table 1102   a   Data refer to 1989
   b   Data refer to 1991
   c   Household fuels included under "housing"
   d   Data refer to 1990
   e   Health included under "household goods"
   f   Leisure included under "household goods"

Table 1103   a   Data refer to 1989
   b   Data refer to 1991

   c   Household fuels included under "housing"
   d   Data refer to 1990
   e   Health included under "household goods"
   f   Leisure included under "household goods"

Table 1104   a   Million pesos (currency reform 1992: 1 peso argentino = 10,000 australes)
   b   Includes Euromonitor estimates
   c   Includes all beverages
   d   Includes non-alcoholic beverages
   e   Million cruzeiros (currency reform March 1990: 1 cruzeiro = 1,000 novo cruzados = 1,000,000 old cruzados = 1,000 million old cruzeiros)
   f   Includes all beverages and tobacco
   g   Year beginning April 1
   h   Billion units of national currency
   i   Million new shekels (currency reform 1985: 1 new shekel = 1,000 shekels)
   j   Includes all beverages and tobacco until 1990
   k   New series starting 1988

Table 1105   a   Includes Euromonitor estimates
   b   Includes non-alcoholic beverages and tea
   c   Billion units of national currency
   d   Includes non-alcoholic beverages
   e   New series starting 1988

Table 1106   a   Billion units of national currency
            b   Includes all drinks and tobacco

Table 1107   Entries of 0 denote values of less than 0.5 million
     a   Million pesos (currency reform 1992: 1 peso argentino = 10,000 australes)
     b   Includes Euromonitor estimates
     c   Million cruzeiros (currency reform March 1990: 1 cruzeiro = 1,000 novo cruzados = 1,000,000 old cruzados = 1,000 million old cruzeiros)
     d   Billion units of national currency
     e   New series starting 1988

Table 1108   Entries of 0 denote values of less than 0.5 million
     a   Million pesos (currency reform 1992: 1 peso argentino = 10,000 australes)
     b   Includes Euromonitor estimates
     c   Million cruzeiros (currency reform March 1990: 1 cruzeiro = 1,000 novo cruzados = 1,000,000 old cruzados = 1,000 million old cruzeiros)
     d   Year beginning April 1
     e   Million new shekels (currency reform 1985: 1 new shekel = 1,000 shekels)
     f   Billion units of national currency
     g   New series starting 1988

Table 1109   Entries of 0 denote values of less than 0.5 million
     a   Million pesos (currency reform 1992: 1 peso argentino = 10,000 australes)
     b   Includes Euromonitor estimates
     c   Million cruzeiros (currency reform March 1990: 1 cruzeiro = 1,000 novo cruzados = 1,000,000 old cruzados = 1,000 million old cruzeiros)
     d   Includes fuels etc.
     e   Year beginning April 1
     f   Billion units of national currency
     g   Million new shekels (currency reform 1985: 1 new shekel = 1,000 shekels)
     h   Includes fuels and power from 1985
     i   New series starting 1988

Table 1110   Entries of 0 denote values of less than 0.5 million
     a   Million pesos (currency reform 1992: 1 peso argentino = 10,000 australes)
     b   Includes Euromonitor estimates
     c   Million cruzeiros (currency reform March 1990: 1 cruzeiro = 1,000 novo cruzados = 1,000,000 old cruzados = 1,000 million old cruzeiros)
     d   Included with housing
     e   Million new shekels (currency reform 1985: 1 new shekel = 1,000 shekels)
     f   Billion units of national currency
     g   Year beginning April 1

Table 1111   Entries of 0 denote values of less than 0.5 million
     a   Million pesos (currency reform 1992: 1 peso argentino = 10,000 australes)
     b   Includes Euromonitor estimates
     c   Million cruzeiros (currency reform March 1990: 1 cruzeiro = 1,000 novo cruzados = 1,000,000 old cruzados = 1,000 million old cruzeiros)
     d   Itemised in national accounts as "articles for daily use"
     e   Year beginning April 1
     f   Billion units of national currency
     g   Million new shekels (currency reform 1985: 1 new shekel = 1,000 shekels)
     h   New series starting 1988

Table 1112   Entries of 0 denote values of less than 0.5 million
     a   Million pesos (currency reform 1992: 1 peso argentino = 10,000 australes)
     b   Includes Euromonitor estimates
     c   Million cruzeiros (currency reform March 1990: 1 cruzeiro = 1,000 novo cruzados = 1,000,000 old cruzados = 1,000 million old cruzeiros)
     d   Million new shekels (currency reform 1985: 1 new shekel = 1,000 shekels)
     e   Year beginning April 1
     f   Billion units of national currency
     g   Medical services only
     h   New series starting 1988

Table 1113   Entries of 0 denote values of less than 0.5 million
     a   Million pesos (currency reform 1992: 1 peso argentino = 10,000 australes)
     b   Includes Euromonitor estimates
     c   Million cruzeiros (currency reform March 1990: 1 cruzeiro = 1,000 novo cruzados = 1,000,000 old cruzados = 1,000 million old cruzeiros)
     d   Year beginning April 1
     e   Billion units of national currency
     f   Million new shekels (currency reform 1985: 1 new shekel = 1,000 shekels)
     g   New series starting 1988
     h   Excludes communications

Table 1114   Entries of 0 denote values of less than 0.5 million
     a   Million pesos (currency reform 1992: 1 peso argentino = 10,000 australes)
     b   Includes Euromonitor estimates
     c   Million cruzeiros (currency reform March 1990: 1 cruzeiro = 1,000 novo cruzados = 1,000,000 old cruzados = 1,000 million old cruzeiros)
     d   Year beginning April 1
     e   Billion units of national currency
     f   Million new shekels (currency reform 1985: 1 new shekel = 1,000 shekels)
     g   New series starting 1988

Section Twelve
Retailing and Retail Distribution

RETAIL STRUCTURES

Table No. 1201

Retail Outlets, Employment and Sales: Latest Year

Units: As stated

	Year	Retail outlets ('000)	Population per outlet	Retail staff ('000)	Per outlet	Total sales (Mn national currencies 1990)	Total (US $mn 1990)	Total per head US$ 1990
North America								
Canada [a]	1990	134.5	185	1,259	9	233,300	192,810	8,502
USA [b,c]	1990	1,872.5	228	20,042	11	1,821,825	1,821,825	7,210
South America								
Argentina [d,f]	1985	787.0	40	2,183	3			
Bolivia [e]						2,950	930	126
Brazil	1992	806.0	194	3,525	4	6,500,000	95,168	633
Chile [d,e]	1986			650		1,707,000	5,596	425
Colombia [g]	1973	0.5		30	55	4,500,000	8,960	272
Ecuador	1976	1.8	294	17	9	1,650,000	2,149	199
French Guiana								
Guyana	1970			3				
Paraguay [e]	1977			92		635,000	516	121
Peru [d,e]	1987			1,081		90,000	479	22
Suriname [e]	1977			13		200	112	267
Uruguay								
Venezuela [d,h]	1987			1,210		1,100,000	23,454	1,189
Caribbean								
Anguilla								
Antigua [e]	1975	0.3	294	2	6	72	27	333
Aruba								
Bahamas [e]						460	460	1,840
Barbados	1979	1.9	136	2	1			
Bermuda	1981	0.3	197	5	17			
British Virgin Islands								
Cayman Islands								
Cuba [d,e]	1989	30.0		413	14	6,754	8,443	794
Dominica [d,e]	1986	0.2		3	15	2,450	907	11,343
Dominican Republic								
Grenada								
Guadeloupe								
Haiti [d,e]	1979	1.1	410	8	7	2,500	500	77
Jamaica [e]	1980	10.2				5,075	707	292
Martinique								
Netherlands Antilles								
St Kitts								
St Lucia								
St Vincent/Grenadines								
Trinidad and Tobago [e]	1977	0.3	284	70	233	6,000	1,412	1,148
Central America								
Belize [e]						65	33	171
Costa Rica	1975	10.0	201	42	4	1,920,000	20,965	7,012
El Salvador [e,i]	1984	0.8	1,771	7	9	860	107	20
Guatemala [e]	1982	88.2	84			1,200	268	29
Honduras [d,e]	1988			149		1,075	538	105
Mexico [f,j]	1992	825.0	109	2,200	3	225,500	80,175	931
Nicaragua [e]	1982	20.6	150	90	4	46,500	66	17
Panama [e,k]	1987	8.0		59	7	827	827	342
Puerto Rico								
South Asia								
Afghanistan								
Bangladesh [e,l]	1985	271.0	390	2,936	11	159,000	4,600	40
Bhutan								
India [m]	1989	3,140.0	259			235,000	16,894	21
Nepal								
Pakistan [n]	1985	277.4	325	337	1	240,500	11,079	99
Sri Lanka [f,o]	1980	10.0	1,475	50	5	13,005	325	19

RETAIL STRUCTURES

Retail Outlets, Employment and Sales: Latest Year

Units: As stated

	Year	Retail outlets ('000)	Population per outlet	Retail staff ('000)	Per outlet	Total sales (Mn national currencies 1990)	Total (US $mn 1990)	Total per head US$ 1990
Japan								
Japan [a,f,o]	1991	1,821.0	68	5,857	3	139,156	1,098,745	8,961
ASEAN/NICs								
Brunei [d]	1986			5				
Hong Kong [a]	1991	54.8	105	136	2	161,125	20,817	3,589
Indonesia [a,f]	1991	856.2	219	11,204	13	93,605	46,113	241
Macau								
Malaysia [a]	1991	148.3	124	1,314	9	34,101	13,373	712
Philippines [a,q]	1991	118.5	531	3,400	29	688,515	10,698	420
Singapore [a]	1991	19.9	137	84	4	17,438	11,215	3,807
South Korea [a,f]	1991	716.8	60	1,424	2	55,594	35,536	814
Taiwan [a]	1991	409.6	52	969	2	905,100		
Thailand [a,d]	1991	721.5	79	1,108	2	735,000	28,937	501
East/SE Asia								
Cambodia								
China [a]	1992	9,100.0	129	20,330	2	835,700	151,670	128
Laos								
Mongolia								
Myanmar								
North Korea								
Vietnam								
Australasia								
Australia [c]	1986	160.2	100	929	6	89,095	69,606	4,014
New Zealand [c]	1990	42.0		203	5	28,678	16,577	4,904
Pacific								
American Samoa								
Fiji [e]	1982	6.3	108			115	78	106
French Polynesia								
Guam								
Kiribati								
Nauru								
New Caledonia								
Papua New Guinea								
Solomon Islands								
Tonga								
Tuvalu								
Vanuatu								
Western Samoa								
Middle East								
Bahrain								
Egypt [e]	1981	2.1	20,000	48	23	20,800	10,400	196
Iran [e]	1971	214.0	175	328	2	2,990,000	43,909	804
Iraq	1977	77.7	164	107	1			
Israel [a]	1990	45.8		106	2	42,000	17,073	3,290
Jordan [d,e,r]	1987	0.5		10	21	785	1,183	295
Kuwait [e]	1985	14.6	116	60	4	2,070	7,075	3,306
Lebanon								
Oman [e,m]	1978	0.3	2,866	5	17	433	1,126	751
Qatar	1982	1.7	163	4	2			
Saudi Arabia [n]	1981	80.3	130	174	2	101,000	26,969	1,814
Syria [d,e,n]	1981	100.6	111	243	2	48,900	4,356	359
United Arab Emirates [d]	1985	25.0				21,700	5,911	3,718
Yemen [e,s]	1988					12,300	1,092	97

RETAIL STRUCTURES

Table No. 1201 (cont'd)

Retail Outlets, Employment and Sales: Latest Year

Units: As stated

	Year	Retail outlets ('000)	Population per outlet	Retail staff ('000)	Per outlet	Total sales (Mn national currencies 1990)	Total (US $mn 1990)	Total per head US$ 1990
North Africa								
Algeria [e]	1971	3.6	5,146	18	5	81,000	9,042	362
Chad	1975	101.8	427	36				
Djibouti								
Ethiopia								
Libya								
Mali								
Mauritania								
Morocco [e]	1988			575		51,900	6,297	251
Niger								
Somalia								
Sudan								
Tunisia [e,n]	1973	2.2	2,905	5	2	1,850	2,106	257
West Africa								
Benin [e]	1979	0.2	18,825	2	10	66,200	243	51
Burkina Faso								
Cameroon [e]	1980	1.3	6,737	14	11	5,000,000	18,365	1,552
Cape Verde								
Côte d'Ivoire [e]	1981	2.0	4,367	17	8	720,000	2,645	220
Equatorial Guinea								
Gabon								
Gambia								
Ghana [e]	1983	1.5	8,693	16	11	22,500	69	5
Guinea								
Guinea-Bissau								
Liberia [e]	1981			32		175	175	67
Nigeria [a]	1982	22.2	4,045	266	12	16,000	16,000	138
Sao Tomé e Príncipe								
Senegal	1982	0.5	11,760	6	11			
Sierra Leone [t]	1986			2				
Togo	1980	0.2	14,445	2	9			
East/Central Africa								
Angola								
Burundi [e]						24,000	140	26
Central African Republic								
Comoros								
Congo								
Kenya [d,u]	1990	2.9		34	12	1,190	52	2
Madagascar								
Maldives [e]						35	4	18
Mauritius [e,v]	1987			12		150	10	9
Réunion [d,e]	1989			7				
Rwanda [e]						30,000	363	51
Seychelles								
Tanzania [e]	1983	1.6	12,963	17	10	130,000	666	26
Uganda								
Zaire	1981	3.0	10,210	34	11			
Southern Africa								
Botswana	1982	0.1	12,510	3	26			
Lesotho								
Malawi [e,v]	1987			40		170	62	8
Mozambique								
Namibia								
South Africa [a,w]	1990	60.4		421	7	90,000	31,579	793
Swaziland								
Zambia [e]	1982	0.8	7,500	36	45	760	26	3
Zimbabwe [e]	1990	10.3	5,843	41	4	875	357	38

Source: Euromonitor from retail censuses/UN

Notes: see end of section

RETAIL SALES — Table No. 1202

Trends in Retail Sales 1979-1992

Units: Million units of national currency

	1979	1981	1985	1986	1987	1988	1989	1990	1991	1992
Argentina			134	300	750	3,500	120,000	3,000,000		
Australia [a,b]	29,098	37,158	52,445	56,610	60,249	78,092	82,944	86,660	89,095	
Brazil					2,750	20,000	350,000	6,500,000		
Canada [c]	76,993	94,293	129,446	140,009	153,785	165,123	172,745	191,500	214,000	233,300
Chile				1,707,000						
China	117,400	200,200	339,140	391,200	456,200	653,460	707,420	725,030	765,000	835,700
Colombia [d]					2,098	2,850	3,750	4,500		
Ecuador [d]			222	310	462	800	1,500	1,650		
Hong Kong		48,735	67,901	71,996	84,003	101,896	107,524	115,365	135,400	161,125
India	58,900	79,700	130,000	167,000	200,000	235,000				
Indonesia [d]			12,530	13,878		50,020	58,774	70,000	82,110	93,605
Israel				11,843	17,086	21,203	25,541	31,315	36,000	42,000
Japan	64,179	73,390	78,467	79,722	112,252	118,192	125,074	135,279	141,374	139,156
Malaysia			12,530	15,878	16,917	19,439	23,385	27,631	31,575	34,101
Mexico [d]			11,180	19,000	65,215	143,925	175,500	225,500		
New Zealand [b]		8,801	21,269	24,041	26,469	28,236	27,857	29,336	28,678	
Nigeria					13,600	14,060	14,590	14,975	15,500	16,000
Pakistan [d]			186	200	215	228	241			
Peru										
Philippines	53,970	62,000		90,000		348,325	404,505	481,575	590,493	688,515
Singapore	6,659	8,436	9,462	9,581	11,430	14,529	16,532	16,929	17,047	17,438
South Africa	10,691	17,698	30,695	34,780	41,000	50,184	59,978	70,995	80,000	90,000
South Korea [d]	7,187		17,265	21,674	25,000	29,036	34,207	41,108	52,178	55,594
Taiwan	280,200	283,400	572,649	610,000	670,000	770,000	823,000	788,155	855,747	905,100
Thailand	173,100	260,900	350,000	362,500	381,000	464,000	555,000	659,000	692,000	735,000
USA [b]			1,071,730	1,115,900	1,542,100	1,651,400	1,733,700	1,797,900	1,821,825	
Venezuela [d]					265	335	750	1,100		
Vietnam										

Source: Euromonitor from national statistical offices

Notes: see end of section

RETAIL SALES — Table No. 1203

Index of Retail Sales Volume 1981-1991

Units: 1985 = 100

	1981	1982	1983	1984	1985	1986	1987	1988	1989	1990	1991
Argentina											
Australia					100	101	101	102	103	103	103
Brazil											
Canada					100	105	110	115	115	112	100
Chile											
China [a]	55	60	67	79	100	115	136	174			
Colombia	98	100	99	101	100	112					
Ecuador					100	139	208	360	674	742	
Hong Kong				99	100	103	113	123	122	123	135
India											
Indonesia											
Israel [b]	80	91	99	94	100	114	125				
Japan					100	106	114	123	116	122	123
Malaysia [c]						100	105	115	127	145	158
Mexico											
New Zealand					100	100	100	101	102	99	97
Nigeria											
Pakistan				95	100	108	116	123	130		
Peru											
Philippines											
Singapore [c,d]						100	124	155	172	176	179
South Africa	99	100	99	104	100	93	93	100	103		
South Korea	71	73	84	93	100	117	130	143	165	185	206
Taiwan [c]						100	110	111	112	101	105
Thailand											
USA					100	106	108	112	115	114	112
Venezuela											
Vietnam											

Source: Euromonitor from OECD/national statistical offices

Notes: see end of section

RETAIL TRADE   Table No. 1204

Analysis of Retail Sales by Form of Organisation: Latest Year

Units: % of total retail sales

	Year	LMRs	Mult	Co-op	VCBG	IND	Other	Total
Argentina	1986	2	6	2		65	25	100
Australia	1990	14	27		16	35	8	100
Brazil	1990	12	23				65	100
Canada [a]	1990	10	23			67		100
Chile								
China	1986				16	80	4	100
Colombia								
Ecuador								
Hong Kong	1990	7	23	5		57	8	100
India								
Indonesia								
Israel	1990	8	27	9		56		100
Japan	1990	24		3	13		60	100
Malaysia	1989		35	1	19	45		100
Mexico	1989	11	23			55	11	100
New Zealand	1990	12	48		10	27	3	100
Nigeria	1987		5	1	10	84		100
Pakistan								
Peru								
Philippines								
Singapore								
South Africa	1990	14	25	5		43	13	100
South Korea	1986		77			20	3	100
Taiwan	1990		30	2	18	43	7	100
Thailand								
USA	1989	16	38			44	2	100
Venezuela								
Vietnam								

Source: Euromonitor from national statistical offices   Notes: see end of section

RETAIL TRADE   Table No. 1205

Number of Selected Retail Outlets: Latest Year

Units: Number

	Year	Food	Super	DS	VS	Cloth	Appl	Drug
Argentina	1974	24,500				71,000	16,000	12,000
Australia	1986	51,652		250	405	25,817	15,122	
Brazil	1985	538,638		19,553		117,595	63,510	33,631
Canada	1990					12,167		
Chile								
China [a,b]	1989	350,000		159,000	619,000	38,000	71,000	27,000
Colombia								
Ecuador								
Hong Kong [c]	1990	20,510	808	215		11,797	20,863	
India								
Indonesia								
Israel	1982	11,256		200	304	6,855	5,408	
Japan	1990	872,051		2,473	1,704	168,822		106,131
Malaysia	1980	62,157				7,195	6,774	4,852
Mexico	1988	415,943		905		53,896	11,284	11,263
New Zealand	1990	6,396	381	223	314	4,375	2,196	6,030
Nigeria [d]	1974	200				77	212	64
Pakistan								
Peru								
Philippines								
Singapore	1988	931	141		3,896	2,617	1,686	770
South Africa [e]	1977	22,567		303	7,997	9,873	4,125	2,190
South Korea	1986	304,404	2,123	97	5,129	102,570	48,310	38,897
Taiwan								
Thailand	1980	1,169		55	157	768	5,540	779
USA	1990	204,225	21,040	2,794	10,500	134,137	93,934	49,527
Venezuela								
Vietnam								

Source: National statistical offices   Notes: see end of section

RETAIL TRADE — Table No. 1206

Analysis of Retail Sales by Form of Outlet 1990

Units: % of total retail sales

	Department stores	Variety stores	Both	Superstores/ hypermarkets	Super-markets	Mail order	Direct sales
Argentina							
Australia			14	3		3	
Brazil [a]			5		16		
Canada [b]	12	1	13		22		2
Chile							
China							
Colombia							
Ecuador							
Hong Kong	7				12	1	
India							
Indonesia							
Israel			8		20		
Japan	13				11		
Malaysia							
Mexico	7		10		17		
New Zealand [b]			9		30		
Nigeria							
Pakistan							
Peru							
Philippines							
Singapore [b]	18	8	26		5		
South Africa [b]	8	8	16		13		
South Korea [b]	7				4		
Taiwan							
Thailand							
USA	10	1	11		15	2	
Venezuela							

Source: Euromonitor from national statistical offices

Notes: see end of section

LARGE MIXED RETAILERS — Table No. 1207

Retail Sales through Department and Variety Stores: Latest Year

Units: As stated; values in million units of national currency

	Year	Dept. stores (no.)	Variety stores (no.)	Total (no.)	Dept. stores sales	Variety stores sales	Total sales
Argentina							
Australia	1986	231	424	655	7,249	807	8,056
Brazil							
Canada	1990	987		987	15,520		
Chile							
China	1988	169,000	662,000	831,000			
Colombia							
Ecuador							
Hong Kong	1990			7,499			
India							
Indonesia							
Israel	1988	705		705			12
Japan	1990	377	1,450	1,827	11,456,000		
Malaysia							
Mexico	1988	905		905	4,377,000		
New Zealand	1990	537		537	878	118	996
Nigeria							
Pakistan							
Peru							
Philippines	1973			2,980			174
Singapore	1984	141		141	2,591		
South Africa	1990	330		330	4,287		
South Korea	1990	63		63	2,610,000		
Taiwan							
Thailand	1984	542	123	665	628	460	1,088
USA	1990	2,794	10,939	13,733	175,100	7,100	182,200
Venezuela							

Source: Euromonitor from national statistical offices

FOOD RETAILING   Table No. 1208

Food Distribution by Form of Outlet: Latest Year

Units: % of total food sales

	Specialists	Dept./Variety stores	Super-markets	Grocery	Other
Argentina					
Australia	24	2			74
Brazil		10	16	18	56
Canada	8	2	60	27	3
Chile					
China					
Colombia					
Ecuador					
Hong Kong			46		54
India					
Indonesia					
Israel [a]	24	6	21	36	13
Japan [a]		6	11		83
Malaysia					
Mexico					
New Zealand [a]	15	5	45	22	13
Nigeria					
Pakistan					
Peru					
Philippines					
Singapore	53	21	16	10	
South Africa [a]	10	6	40	27	17
South Korea [a]	46	7	20	27	
Taiwan					
Thailand					
USA	2		92	4	2
Venezuela					

Source: Euromonitor from national statistical offices   Notes: see end of section

FOOD RETAILING   Table No. 1209

Numbers of Food Outlets by Type: Latest Year

Units: Number

	Year	General	Fruit/veg	Dairy	Meat	Fish	Bakery	Confect-ionery	Drinks	Tob-acco	Other	Total
Argentina												
Australia	1986	17,058	3,820		6,944		2,118					51,652
Brazil	1985											538,638
Canada												
Chile												
China	1989	167,000									183,000	350,000
Colombia												
Ecuador												
Hong Kong	1990											24,774
India												
Indonesia												
Israel	1982											11,256
Japan [a]	1990	107,168	59,809		38,381	51,831	172,869		187,919		254,074	872,051
Malaysia	1980		7,998		3,158	4,074	781	1,564	487	310	43,785	62,157
Mexico [b]	1975	193,081	46,638		33,647	2,501			5,410	507	22,495	304,279
New Zealand [b]	1990	1,693	658	2,787	1,062	196						6,396
Nigeria												
Pakistan												
Peru												
Philippines [c]	1988	13,844	2,108		2,650		766			204	18,305	37,877
Singapore [c]	1983		298		173				97	53	278	
South Africa	1977	15,607		365	4,208				2,387			22,567
South Korea	1986		32,825			26,231	21,778			19,653	203,917	304,404
Taiwan												
Thailand [d]	1984	731	10		8	20					228	997
USA [c]	1990	145,000			11,845		25,937				21,443	204,225
Venezuela												

Source: Euromonitor from national statistical offices   Notes: see end of section

NON-FOOD RETAILING   Table No. 1210

Numbers of Non-Food Specialist Outlets by Type: Latest Year

Units: Number

	Year	Pharma-cists	Drug-gists	Opti-cians	Photo-graphic	Book-sellers	Stat-ioners
Argentina							
Australia [a]	1986	5,786			673		
Brazil [b,c]	1980	33,631				20,192	
Canada	1990	6,955					
Chile							
China [c,d,e]	1989	27,000				26,000	
Colombia							
Ecuador							
Hong Kong [f,g]	1989						
India							
Indonesia							
Israel [d,f]	1983						
Japan [g,h]	1990	10,631				96,711	
Malaysia [d,i,j]	1980	2,426				2,232	
Mexico [b,k]	1975	11,263				1,099	
New Zealand [b,k,l,m]	1990	1,289		160	134	1,276	669
Nigeria							
Pakistan							
Peru [j,m,n,o]							
Philippines	1988	6,381		543			5,662
Singapore [j,p]	1989	828		498		863	
South Africa [i,q]	1977	2,190				854	
South Korea [m,n]	1986	24,915	6,921	1,064		10,731	23,888
Taiwan							
Thailand [r]	1980	591	188				238
USA	1990	64,597					
Venezuela							
Vietnam							

Source: Euromonitor from national statistical offices   Notes: see end of section

NON-FOOD RETAILING   Table No. 1210 (cont'd)

Numbers of Non-Food Specialist Outlets by Type: Latest Year

Units: Number

	Year	News-agents	Clothing	Footwear	Hardware/Housewares	Furnishings	Furniture
Argentina							
Australia [a]	1986		14,917	2,978	14,968	2,838	
Brazil [b,c]	1980		117,595		37,394		
Canada	1990						
Chile							
China [c,d,e]	1989		38,000		136,000		
Colombia							
Ecuador							
Hong Kong [f,g]	1989		10,196		18,739		
India							
Indonesia							
Israel [d,f]	1983		6,855				
Japan [g,h]	1990		141,161	27,661	232,137		
Malaysia [d,i,j]	1980		5,538	711		1,975	
Mexico [b,k]	1975	1,249	23,471	12,229			
New Zealand [b,k,l,m]	1990	291	4,375	593	1,125	423	
Nigeria							
Pakistan							
Peru [j,m,n,o]							
Philippines	1988		17,036	3,115	7,027	4,391	
Singapore [j,p]	1989		2,792			1,818	
South Africa [i,q]	1977		8,657	1,216	1,049		
South Korea [m,n]	1986		58,920	14,395	13,184		
Taiwan							
Thailand [r]	1980		1,121	137	235		
USA	1990		182,396			89,493	29,700
Venezuela							
Vietnam							

Source: Euromonitor from national statistical offices   Notes: see end of section

NON-FOOD RETAILING   Table No. 1210 (cont'd)

Numbers of Non-Food Specialist Outlets by Type: Latest Year

Units: Number

	Year	Electrical Appliances	TV/video/ audio	Records	Clocks/ jewellery	Toys/ Sports	Florists
Argentina							
Australia [a]	1986					4,330	4,035
Brazil [b,c]	1980						
Canada	1990						
Chile							
China [c,d,e]	1989						
Colombia							
Ecuador							
Hong Kong [f,g]	1989						
India							
Indonesia							
Israel [d,f]	1983						
Japan [g,h]	1990		74,386				
Malaysia [d,i,j]	1980		3,184		2,319	1,316	
Mexico [b,k]	1975	5,545	1,452	1,307	3,673	1,404	3,875
New Zealand [b,k,l,m]	1990	605	2,196				
Nigeria							
Pakistan							
Peru [j,m,n,o]							
Philippines	1988	855			866	269	
Singapore [j,p]	1989		470			688	
South Africa [i,q]	1977	4,125			984	1,153	
South Korea [m,n]	1986	7,165			10,737	8,506	
Taiwan							
Thailand [r]	1980	48	2,174		560		
USA	1990	10,100	24,000		24,500		
Venezuela							
Vietnam							

Source: Euromonitor from national statistical offices   Notes: see end of section

FOOD RETAILING   Table No. 1211

Turnover of Food Outlets by Type: Latest Year

Units: Million units of national currency

	Year	General	Fruit/ veg	Dairy	Meat	Fish	Bakery	Confect- ionery	Drinks	Tob- acco	Total
Argentina											
Australia	1991	25,468			2,237						33,644
Brazil [a]	1986										122,499
Canada	1990										1,052,511
Chile											
China	1988										354,000
Colombia											
Ecuador											
Hong Kong	1990										24,803
India											
Indonesia											
Israel											
Japan [b]	1985	12,846	1,701		1,354	1,509		2,478	12,846		
Malaysia	1980		216		320	173	18	29	54	8	
Mexico											
New Zealand	1990	6,086			480						
Nigeria											
Pakistan											
Peru											
Philippines [c]	1988	2,643									
Singapore	1988	416	62		55				21	6	
South Africa	1990	27,079		597	3,389				2,718		
South Korea	1986		618,000		861,000	548,000				133,000	6,107,000
Taiwan											
Thailand [d]	1980	1,783									2,077
USA [d]	1990	368,500			6,767		5,909				
Venezuela											
Vietnam											

Source: Euromonitor from national statistical offices   Notes: see end of section

NON-FOOD RETAILING   Table No. 1212

Turnover of Non-Food Outlets by Type: Latest Year

Units: Million units of national currency

	Year	Pharma-cists	Drug-gists	Opti-cians	Photo-graphic	Book-sellers	Stat-ioners
Argentina							
Australia [a,b,c]	1991	3,689					
Brazil [d,e,f]	1986					9,368	
Canada [e,g]	1989	8,086				1,082	
Chile							
China [h]	1989	24,000				10,000	
Colombia							
Ecuador							
Hong Kong [i]	1990						
India							
Indonesia							
Israel							
Japan [b,e,g,j,k,l]	1985	2,578,000				3,458,000	
Malaysia [b,e,f,j,m,n]	1980	309				201	
Mexico							
New Zealand [b,f,o]	1990	821					
Nigeria							
Pakistan							
Peru							
Philippines [j,o,p,q]	1988		5,552		947	2,230	
Singapore [e,h,j]	1989	301		335		243	
South Africa [e,f,i,r]	1990	2,835				1,429	
South Korea [b,s]	1986	995,000	309,000	67,000		148,000	439,000
Taiwan							
Thailand [h,t]	1984	549				65	904
USA [u]	1990		60,451		8,285	5,854	10,122
Venezuela							
Vietnam							

Source: Euromonitor from national statistical offices   Notes: see end of section

NON-FOOD RETAILING   Table No. 1212 (cont'd)

Turnover of Non-Food Outlets by Type: Latest Year

Units: Million units of national currency

	Year	News-agents	Clothing	Footwear	Hardware/Housewares	Furnishings	Furniture
Argentina							
Australia [a,b,c]	1991	3,080	6,496	1,200	2,592	746	1,828
Brazil [d,e,f]	1986		60,168				
Canada [e,g]	1989		5,240		1,982		2,166
Chile							
China [h]	1989		111,000				
Colombia							
Ecuador							
Hong Kong [i]	1990		10,614				
India							
Indonesia							
Israel							
Japan [b,e,g,j,k,l]	1985		5,495,000		1,667,000	2,390,000	
Malaysia [b,e,f,j,m,n]	1980		782	104	134	284	
Mexico							
New Zealand [b,f,o]	1990		1,383	270	554		860
Nigeria							
Pakistan							
Peru							
Philippines [j,o,p,q]	1988		1,759	1,166	3,410	423	
Singapore [e,h,j]	1989		1,147		266	1,687	
South Africa [e,f,i,r]	1990		11,795		7,120		
South Korea [b,s]	1986		510,000	333,000			381,000
Taiwan							
Thailand [h,t]	1984		427	35	2,815	323	
USA [u]	1990		67,165	15,703	24,903	19,066	28,266
Venezuela							
Vietnam							

Source: Euromonitor from national statistical offices   Notes: see end of section

NON-FOOD RETAILING

Table No. 1212 (cont'd)

Turnover of Non-Food Outlets by Type: Latest Year

Units: Million units of national currency

	Year	Electrical Appliances	TV/video/ audio	Records	Clocks/ jewellery	Toys/ Sports	Florists
Argentina							
Australia [a,b,c]	1991	5,217					
Brazil [d,e,f]	1986						
Canada [e,g]	1989	714	1,815		1,229	2,912	666
Chile							
China [h]	1989						
Colombia							
Ecuador							
Hong Kong [i]	1990						
India							
Indonesia							
Israel							
Japan [b,e,g,j,k,l]	1985	4,611,000				2,051,000	2,494,000
Malaysia [b,e,f,j,m,n]	1980	1,020			482	53	
Mexico							
New Zealand [b,f,o]	1990	1,350					
Nigeria							
Pakistan							
Peru							
Philippines [j,o,p,q]	1988	4,450			80	210	
Singapore [e,h,j]	1989					363	
South Africa [e,f,i,r]	1990				514	691	
South Korea [b,s]	1986	116,000			331,000	190,000	
Taiwan							
Thailand [h,t]	1984	2,841	1,084		538		
USA [u]	1990	9,945	34,838		19,395	13,767	
Venezuela							
Vietnam							

Source: Euromonitor from national statistical offices

Notes: see end of section

RETAIL TECHNOLOGY

Table No. 1213

Number of Scanning Stores 1988-1992

Units: Number

	1988	1989	1990	1991	1992	% change 1988-92
Argentina	44	62	90	153	232	427.3
Australia	1,098	1,665	2,168	2,587	3,661	233.4
Brazil	2	2	12	25	81	3,950.0
Canada						
Chile				7	53	
China				2	11	
Colombia			7	2	8	
Ecuador					14	
Hong Kong				133	537	
India						
Indonesia						
Israel	10	41	109	130	187	1,770.0
Japan	40,000	100,000		92,461	122,141	205.4
Malaysia	4	3	4	6	9	125.0
Mexico	43	66	99	152	372	765.1
New Zealand	330	486		862	1,241	276.1
Nigeria						
Pakistan						
Peru				8	16	
Philippines						
Singapore		6	5	8	81	
South Africa	100	126	170	323	481	381.0
South Korea	17	25	172	511	2,737	16,000.0
Taiwan	111	191	260	1,367	1,290	1,062.2
Thailand	3	4	4			
USA						
Venezuela	5	7	7	7	11	120.0
Vietnam						

Source: European Article Numbering Association/Euromonitor

RETAIL TECHNOLOGY   Table No. 1214

Scanning Stores by Type 1992

Units: Number

	No.of scanning stores	of which: Self-service grocery	of which: Dept. stores	of which: General stores	of which: Others
Argentina	232	229		3	
Australia	3,661	206	585	75	
Brazil	81	43	12	25	1
Canada					
Chile	53	35	10	8	
China	11	11			
Colombia	8	5	1	2	
Ecuador	14	2	6	6	
Hong Kong	537	353	23	161	
India					
Indonesia					
Israel	187	147		40	
Japan	122,141				
Malaysia	9	6	3		
Mexico	372	260	60	52	
New Zealand	1,241	481	16	744	
Nigeria					
Pakistan					
Peru	16	16			
Philippines					
Singapore	81	52	7		22
South Africa	481	280		161	40
South Korea	2,737	795	74	1,868	
Taiwan	1,290	990	45	25	230
Thailand					
USA					
Venezuela	11	3	6		2
Vietnam					

Source: European Article Numbering Association/Euromonitor

SERVICE STATIONS   Table No. 1215

Service Stations: Outlets and Sales, Latest Year

Units: As stated

	Year	Number	Sales (million units of national currency)
Argentina	1991	7,385	
Australia [a,b]	1992	8,900	26,963
Brazil [c,d]	1991	18,181	
Canada [e]	1992	17,638	13,519
Chile			
China			
Colombia			
Ecuador			
Hong Kong			
India			
Indonesia			
Israel			
Japan [f,g]	1991	54,223	2,494,000
Malaysia [c,d]	1991	1,600	1,382
Mexico	1991	3,800	
New Zealand [h]	1989	1,500	8,800
Nigeria			
Pakistan			
Peru			
Philippines	1973	3,944	1,345
Singapore	1983	230	720
South Africa			
South Korea [b]	1991	5,260	1,752
Taiwan			
Thailand [i]	1980	988	16,151
USA [j]	1992	103,500	131,700
Venezuela			
Vietnam			

Source: Euromonitor/national statistical offices   Notes: see end of section

Notes to Tables in Section Twelve

Table 1201 a Data for sales refer to 1992
    b Data for outlets refer to 1987
    c Data for sales refer to 1991
    d Outlets and staff include wholesaling
    e Data for sales refer to 1986
    f Sales are in billion
    g Establishments with sales of 3 million pesos or more per annum
    h Total sales: GDP arising in commerce
    i Outlets, staff and turnover refer to businesses with a capital of 20,000 colones or more
    j Staff includes wholesaling and catering; outlets 1975
    k Panama and San Miguelito districts only
    l Data for outlets refer to 1989
    m Data for sales refer to 1988
    n Data for sales refer to 1989
    o Totals are 1985 data
    p Staff includes wholesale and retail/catering
    q Data refer to establishments with 10 or more employees
    r Establishments with 5 or more employees
    s Sales include wholesaling in 1988
    t Establishments with 6 employees or more
    u Data for outlets and staff refer to 1989
    v Including wholesaling, catering and hotels
    w Data for staff refer to 1992

Table 1202 a Year beginning July
    b Excluding automotive sector
    c Including fuels and car sales
    d Billion units of national currency

Table 1203 a Value index
    b Sales in large stores only
    c 1986=100
    d Including motor vehicles

Table 1204 LMR (large mixed retailers), Mult (multiples), Coop (co-operatives), VCBG (voluntary chains and buying groups), IND (independents)
    a Multiples includes cooperatives

Table 1205 Food (food outlets), Super (supermarkets), DS (department stores), VS (variety stores), Cloth (clothing, textile and footwear retailers), Appl (hardware, appliance retailers), Drug (drugstores, perfumeries, etc).
    a Appliances includes hardware, communications and chemical stores
    b Includes only a small proportion of total shops, namely those not individually run
    c Appliances = durables
    d Establishments with 10 or more employees
    e Appliances includes furniture

Table 1206 a Supermarkets include hypermarkets
    b Data refer to 1988

Table 1208 a Data refer to 1990

Table 1209 a Bakery includes confectionery; drinks includes seasonings
    b Includes supermarkets
    c Meat includes fish
    d Data refer to establishments with 5 or more employees

Table 1210 a Clothing includes fabrics and furnishings
    b Pharmacy includes cosmetics
    c Data for housewares/hardware refer to all household goods
    d Clothing includes all textiles
    e Excluding individually-run shops
    f Clothing includes footwear
    g Data for housewares/hardware to all durables
    h Pharmacy includes toiletries
    i Books includes toiletries
    j Furnishings include furniture
    k Electrical goods include TV, video and audio
    l Newsagents includes stationers
    m Optical includes photographic
    n Housewares include electricals, TV, video and audio
    o Druggists includes pharmacy
    p Books include stationery and newsagents
    q Furniture includes household appliances
    r Businesses with 5 or more employees

Table 1211 a Meat includes fish; drinks includes tobacco
    b Confectionery includes bakery
    c Businesses with 10 employees or more
    d Meat includes fish

Table 1212 a Clothing includes drapery
    b Appliances include TV, video and audio
    c Furnishings include floor coverings only
    d New cruzados
    e Books includes stationery
    f Clothing includes textiles
    g Pharmacy includes cosmetics and perfumes
    h Books includes newsagents
    i Clothing includes footwear
    j Furnishings include furniture
    k Toys/sports includes instruments
    l Florists includes garden and farm supply
    m Pharmacy includes druggists
    n Toys/sports refer to bicycles only
    o Pharmacy includes all chemist goods
    p Optical includes photographic
    q Newsagents includes lottery stands
    r All household goods and furniture
    s Ambiguous classification system
    t Businesses with 5 employees or more
    u Druggists includes pharmacy

Table 1215 a Includes vehicle and tyre dealers
    b Sales data refer to 1986
    c All fuels and lubricants
    d Sales data refer to 1980
    e Sales data refer to 1989
    f All fuels
    g Sales data refer to 1985
    h Sales includes automotive repairs
    i Businesses with 5 employees or more
    j Sales data refer to 1990

Section Thirteen
Advertising Patterns and Media Access

ADVERTISING EXPENDITURE — Table No. 1301

Trends in Advertising Expenditure 1982-1992

Units: Million units of national currency

	1982	1985	1986	1987	1988	1989	1990	1991	1992
Argentina		276	824	1,901	8,261	232,512	4,045,645		
Australia	2,298	3,314	3,543	3,881	4,432	5,026	4,925	4,703	4,973
Brazil [a]	381	10,667	25,498	81,367	734	7,750	217,638		
Canada	4,622	6,233	6,800	7,267	7,457	8,304			7,429
Chile	9,569	19,133	26,340	34,970	46,200	61,800			
China	150	605	844	1,112	1,579	1,770	2,134	2,526	6,783
Colombia	24,370	45,639	65,524	97,408	125,982	167,342	239,265		436,920
Ecuador						26,800	35,100		
Hong Kong	1,268	2,870	3,376	3,899	4,712	5,541	6,719	7,569	9,265
India	2,990	4,870	6,240	7,610	9,210	12,660	15,510	17,750	18,844
Indonesia	130,000	192,150	225,500	271,000	295,400	340,700	563,000	841,000	
Israel		243	460	716	839	939	1,185		
Japan	2,462,000	2,760,000	2,922,000	3,177,000	3,587,000	3,924,000	4,201,000	4,309,000	4,184,643
Malaysia	291	421	391	405	516	712	815	1,017	
Mexico	22,104	142,709	217,496	402,710	786,000	1,280,000		6,785,166	7,384,431
New Zealand	345	560	674	771	918	954	1,067	1,048	
Nigeria									
Pakistan		1,019	1,211	1,419	1,620	1,841	2,063	2,310	
Peru									
Philippines	1,193	1,639	1,794	2,098	2,766	3,886	4,527	5,704	
Singapore	259	295	296	331	408	468	582	648	
South Africa		1,268	1,557	1,854	2,445	2,933			2,736
South Korea	368,000	724,000	801,000	950,000	1,279,000	1,506,000	2,050,000	2,330,000	2,872,011
Taiwan	13,451	20,436	22,858	29,361	37,469	48,009	49,838	54,658	43,100
Thailand	2,712	5,348	5,378	6,174	7,698	9,623	13,514	15,455	20,371
USA	66,805	95,135	102,675	110,272	118,050	126,318	128,640		83,005
Venezuela	2,523	4,140	4,770	6,406	7,026	10,376	20,600		
Vietnam									

Source: Euromonitor from trade sources/IAA

Notes: see end of section

ADVERTISING EXPENDITURE — Table No. 1302

Advertising Expenditure by Medium 1991/1992

Units: Million units of national currency

	TV	Print	Radio	Cinema	Outdoor/Transit	Total
Argentina	1,464,524	1,533,300	424,792	161,826	461,203	4,045,645
Australia	1,614	2,320	420	83	266	4,703
Brazil	125,577	77,261	10,447		4,353	217,638
Canada [a]	2,217	4,169	980		938	8,304
Chile [a]	26,700	26,600	6,750	150	1,600	61,800
China	471	854	102	97	1,002	2,526
Colombia	142,363	51,920	44,982			239,265
Ecuador	23,236	7,968	3,300	70	526	35,100
Hong Kong	3,777	3,103	356	91	242	7,569
India	3,050	12,500	400	100	1,700	17,750
Indonesia	212,000	451,000	101,000	9,000	68,000	841,000
Israel	38	768	56	11	66	939
Japan	1,676,000	1,735,000	241,000		657,000	4,309,000
Malaysia	420	533	21	5	38	1,017
Mexico	4,639,425	884,585	661,890			6,185,900
New Zealand	352	471	140	14	69	1,046
Nigeria						
Pakistan	1,030	1,120	72	4	84	2,310
Peru						
Philippines	3,468	1,290	891		55	5,704
Singapore	193	404	16	5	30	648
South Africa [a]	833	1,710	299	29	62	2,933
South Korea [b]	646,000	1,145,000	121,000		418,000	2,330,000
Taiwan [b]	17,900	24,800	2,641		9,292	54,633
Thailand	6,100	5,306	1,302	11	522	13,241
USA	45,410	67,536	14,022		1,672	128,640
Venezuela	13,412	6,408	390		390	20,600
Vietnam						

Source: National advertising associations/trade sources/IAA

Notes: see end of section

ADVERTISING EXPENDITURE
Table No. 1303

Advertising Expenditure by Medium 1991/1992 (% analysis)

Units: % of total advertising expenditure

	TV	Print	Radio	Cinema	Outdoor/ Transit	Total
Argentina	36.2	37.9	10.5	4.0	11.4	100
Australia	34.3	49.3	8.9	1.8	5.7	100
Brazil	57.7	35.5	4.8		2.0	100
Canada [a]	26.7	50.2	11.8		11.3	100
Chile [a]	43.2	43.0	10.9	0.2	2.6	100
China	18.6	33.8	4.0	3.8	39.7	100
Colombia	59.5	21.7	18.8			100
Ecuador	66.2	22.7	9.4	0.2	1.5	100
Hong Kong	49.9	41.0	4.7	1.2	3.2	100
India	17.2	70.4	2.3	0.6	9.6	100
Indonesia	25.2	53.6	12.0	1.1	8.1	100
Israel	4.0	81.8	6.0	1.2	7.0	100
Japan	38.9	40.3	5.6		15.2	100
Malaysia	41.3	52.4	2.1	0.5	3.7	100
Mexico	75.0	14.3	10.7			100
New Zealand	33.7	45.0	13.4	1.3	6.6	100
Nigeria						100
Pakistan	44.6	48.5	3.1	0.2	3.6	100
Peru						100
Philippines	60.8	22.6	15.6		1.0	100
Singapore	29.8	62.3	2.5	0.8	4.6	100
South Africa [a]	28.4	58.3	10.2	1.0	2.1	100
South Korea [b]	27.7	49.1	5.2		17.9	100
Taiwan [b]	32.8	45.4	4.8		17.0	100
Thailand	46.1	40.1	9.8	0.1	3.9	100
USA	35.3	52.5	10.9		1.3	100
Venezuela	65.1	31.1	1.9		1.9	100
Vietnam						100

Source: National advertising associations/trade sources/IAA/Euromonitor

Notes: see end of section

ADVERTISING EXPENDITURE
Table No. 1304

Broadcasters' Advertising Revenues: Selected Countries, Latest Year

Units: Million units of national currency

	Year	Government	Public	Commercial	Radio	TV	Total
Bangladesh [a,b]	1989	83.0				83.0	83.0
Benin [a,b]	1987	126.4					126.4
Brunei [a,b]	1989	83.0				83.0	83.0
Canada	1989		292.0		755.0	1,276.0	2,323.0
Chad	1987	21.5			19.5	2.0	21.5
Chile	1987	379.0	114.0	3,053.0			3,546.0
Ethiopia [a,b]	1989	262.0				262.0	262.0
French Guiana [a]	1985		1.0				1.0
French Polynesia [a]	1985		3.8				3.8
Ghana [a,b]	1987	68.1			17.1	51.0	68.1
Guyana	1989			11.7	11.7		11.7
Honduras	1985			50.2	31.7	18.5	50.2
India [a,b]	1989	1,159.0				1,159.0	1,159.0
Iran	1987		266.0				266.0
Japan [c]	1985			1,279.6			1,279.6
Malawi	1989		1.0		1.0		1.0
Malaysia [b]	1989	130.0		130.3		130.3	130.3
Maldives [a,b]	1983	0.8			0.1	0.7	0.8
Mauritius [d]	1983		8.4				8.4
Mexico	1987			53,431.0	53,431.0		53,431.0
Pakistan [a,b]	1989	615.0			51.6	563.4	615.0
Senegal [d]	1986		192.7				192.7
Singapore [a,b]	1983	63.1					63.1
South Korea	1989		371,283.0				371,283.0
Sri Lanka [a,b,d]	1987	59.0				59.0	59.0
Thailand [a,b]	1985	52.0				52.0	52.0
United Arab Emirates [a,b,e]	1987	15.0			1.0	14.0	15.0
Zimbabwe	1989			14.0	5.0	9.0	14.0

Source: UNESCO/national statistical offices

Notes: see end of section

PRESS TRENDS · Table No. 1305

Number and Circulation of Newspapers and Periodicals: Latest Year

Units: As stated

	Dailies		Non-Dailies		Periodicals	
	Number	Sales	Number	Sales	Number	Sales
North America						
Canada [a]	107	5,993	1,425	19,719	1,503	39,510
USA [b]	1,611	62,328	7,000	51,000	11,593	
South America						
Argentina [b]	159	4,000	7	320		
Bolivia [b]	17	400	8	16		
Brazil [b]	356	8,100	1,450	5,000	3,782	980
Chile [c]	45	6,000	37	118	255	909
Colombia [b]	45	2,000	4	336	262	1,015
Ecuador	25	920				
French Guiana [b]	1	1	2	7		
Guyana [b]	2	80				
Paraguay [b]	5	165	2	16		
Peru [b]	66	1,700	12	374	45	90
Suriname [b]	2	40	2	10	22	44
Uruguay [b]	30	720	95		465	
Venezuela [b]	54	2,800	45	450	160	4,649
Caribbean						
Anguilla						
Antigua [b]	1	6	5	10		
Aruba						
Bahamas [b]	3	35	2	13		
Barbados [a]	2	30	4	95	52	
Bermuda [a]	1	18	3	35		
British Virgin Islands [a]			2	4	20	23
Cayman Islands [b]	1	6	1	4		
Cuba [c]	17	1,315	4	21	108	2,894
Dominica [a]			2	7		
Dominican Republic [b]	12	230	39		277	
Grenada [a]			3			
Guadeloupe [b]	1	20	9	28		142
Haiti [b]	4	45	4	16		
Jamaica	3	155				
Martinique [b]	1	32	7	28		17
Netherlands Antilles [b]	6	55	1	3		
St Kitts [a]			2	5	10	43
St Lucia [a]	1	8	3	18		
St Vincent/Grenadines [b]			2	11		
Trinidad and Tobago [a]	4	134	5	125		
Central America						
Belize [a]	1	3	7	37		
Costa Rica [d]	4	280	12	106	274	163
El Salvador [b]	5	243	3	12		
Guatemala	5	190				
Honduras [b]	5	199	1	5		
Mexico [a]	285	11,237	56	1,593	178	28,388
Nicaragua [b]	6	250	8	140		
Panama [b]	8	170	3	50	8	18
Puerto Rico [b]	3	456	4	106		
South Asia						
Afghanistan [b]	14	180	37	223	105	
Bangladesh [b]	52	700	490	916	41	163
Bhutan [b]			3	24		
India [b]	1,978	21,857	8,000	13,000	19,937	50,094
Nepal [b]	28	150	9	43		
Pakistan [a]	237	1,817	724	1,720	282	7,674
Sri Lanka [a]	18	550	81		170	1,770

PRESS TRENDS — Table No. 1305 (cont'd)

Number and Circulation of Newspapers and Periodicals: Latest Year

Units: As stated

	Dailies		Non-Dailies		Periodicals	
	Number	Sales	Number	Sales	Number	Sales
Japan						
Japan [b]	125	72,524	14	7,963	2,877	
ASEAN/NICs						
Brunei [a]	1	10	3	87	4	363
Hong Kong [b]	38	3,700	17		617	
Indonesia [a]	64	5,144	94	4,521	117	4,281
Macau [c]	8	240	3	1	11	
Malaysia [b]	45	2,500	19	4,500		
Philippines [a]	47	3,400	306	610	1,570	9,468
Singapore [b]	8	763	7	470		
South Korea	39	12,000	2	2		
Taiwan						
Thailand [a]	34	4,000	302		1,293	
East/SE Asia						
Cambodia	10					
China [b]	44	39,000	224	46,089	3,100	138,852
Laos [b]	3	14	4	20		
Mongolia [a]	1	162	55	1,133	45	6,361
Myanmar [b]	2	200	4	246		
North Korea [b]	11	5,000	2	2		
Vietnam	5	600				
Australasia						
Australia [b]	62	4,200	460	17,204		
New Zealand [b]	35	1,100	139	1,100		
Pacific						
American Samoa [a]	3	9	2	5		
Fiji [b]	1	27	7	99		
French Polynesia [b]	2	21	1	4		
Guam [b]	1	22	4	26		
Kiribati [b]			2	4		
Nauru						
New Caledonia [b]	1	19	1	5		27
Papua New Guinea [b]	2	49	4	78		
Solomon Islands [b]			4	12		
Tonga [b]	1	7	2	9		
Tuvalu						
Vanuatu [a]			1	2		
Western Samoa						
Middle East						
Bahrain [b]	2	29				
Egypt [b]	14	3,000	33	2,037	265	2,017
Iran [a]	21	1,500	50		318	6,166
Iraq [b]	6	650	12	465		
Israel [b]	30	1,200	80	48	807	
Jordan [a]	4	225	6	122	31	43
Kuwait [b]	9	450	59	420	73	257
Lebanon [b]	14	320	15	240		
Oman [c]	4	62	5	64	11	90
Qatar [a]	5	80	5	64	11	90
Saudi Arabia [a]	12	600	6		58	
Syria	10	280				
United Arab Emirates [a]	10	250	1	30	80	922
Yemen [b]	5	135	12	83		

PRESS TRENDS   Table No. 1305 (cont'd)

Number and Circulation of Newspapers and Periodicals: Latest Year

Units: As stated

	Dailies		Non-Dailies		Periodicals	
	Number	Sales	Number	Sales	Number	Sales
North Africa						
Algeria [a]	10	1,274	37	1,409	48	803
Chad [b]	1	1	1	1	10	
Djibouti [b]			2	7	7	6
Ethiopia [b]	3	42	4	40	3	14
Libya [b]	3	70	1	15		
Mali	2	10				
Mauritania	1	1				
Morocco [b]	13	320	5	35		
Niger [b]	1	4	1	5		
Somalia [b]	1	9	4	13		
Sudan [b]	5	610	10	135		
Tunisia [b]	6	300	9	244		
West Africa						
Benin [b]	1	12	3	20		
Burkina Faso [a]	1	3	10	14	37	24
Cameroon [b]	2	80	25	315	58	127
Cape Verde [b]			3	7		
Côte d'Ivoire [b]	1	90	5	172	12	325
Equatorial Guinea	2	2				
Gabon [b]	1	20	1	20		
Gambia [a]	2	2	6	7		
Ghana [a]	4	200	87	1,111	121	774
Guinea [a]	1	13	1	1	3	5
Guinea-Bissau [b]	1	6	1	2		
Liberia [b]	8	35	8	25		
Nigeria [b]	31	1,700	11	45	92	495
Sao Tomé e Príncipe [b]			2	2		
Senegal [b]	3	50	10	63		
Sierra Leone [b]	1	10	6	65		
Togo [b]	1	10	1	5		
East/Central Africa						
Angola [b]	4	115	2	7		
Burundi [b]	1	20	3	22		
Central African Republic [b]	1	2	2	3		
Comoros						
Congo [a]	5	17	3	139	3	34
Kenya [b]	5	350	8	300		
Madagascar [a]	5	50	27	105	121	261
Maldives [b]	2	2	4	5	64	70
Mauritius [a]	7	80	24	75	48	
Rwanda [a]	1	1	15	155	15	101
Réunion [b]	3	65	4	20		
Seychelles [b]	1	3	4	9	2	2
Tanzania [b]	3	200	9	450		
Uganda [b]	2	30	5	70		
Zaire [a]	5	50	77		68	
Southern Africa						
Botswana [b]	1	18	4	45	20	153
Lesotho [b]	4	20	3	45	2	11
Malawi [b]	1	25	1	45	14	124
Mozambique [b]	2	81	2	85	5	2,263
Namibia [a]	6	220	18	71		
South Africa	22	1,340				
Swaziland [b]	3	10	1	7		
Zambia [b]	2	99	1	72		
Zimbabwe [a]	2	206	16	428	28	680

Source: UNESCO/national statistical offices
Notes: see end of section

| TV AND RADIO | Table No. 1306 |

Televisions in Use 1977-1990

Units: '000

	1977	1980	1983	1985	1986	1987	1988	1989	1990
North America									
Canada [a]	10,000	10,617	11,976	13,128	14,000	14,895	15,250	16,459	17,000
USA	135,000	155,800	185,300	190,000	195,000	197,000	199,000	201,000	203,000
South America									
Argentina	4,600	5,140	5,910	6,500	6,650	6,750	6,850	7,000	7,165
Bolivia	49	300	386	420	500	520	535	700	750
Brazil	11,000	15,000	16,500	25,000	26,000	27,000	28,000	30,000	32,000
Chile [b]	710	1,225	1,350	1,750	2,000	2,050	2,330	2,600	2,700
Colombia	1,850	2,250	2,700	2,750	3,000	3,250	3,350	3,500	3,800
Ecuador	340	500	570	600	700	800	825	850	880
French Guiana [b,c]	5	10	12	13	14	14	15	20	21
Guyana						15	16	25	30
Paraguay	55	68	82	85	88	92	95	100	250
Peru	825	850	950	1,500	1,701	1,750	1,800	2,000	2,080
Suriname	39	40	43	44	48	50	51	55	55
Uruguay	360	363	370	500	520	530	535	700	720
Venezuela	1,530	1,710	2,100	2,250	2,500	2,600	2,760	3,000	3,300
Caribbean									
Anguilla									
Antigua [a]	15	16	19	19	20	20	21	22	23
Aruba									
Bahamas		31	36	51	52	53	54	56	57
Barbados [a]	50	50	55	65	66	68	66	67	68
Bermuda [a]	21	30	39	50	50	50	52	55	55
British Virgin Islands [a]	1	2	3	3	3	3	3	3	3
Cayman Islands		2	4	4	4	4	5	5	5
Cuba	800	1,273	1,658	1,977	2,050	1,957	2,069	2,140	2,200
Dominica								4	5
Dominican Republic [b]	160	400	550	500	515	530	556	575	600
Grenada									30
Guadeloupe [c (1980, 1983)]	20	33	38	70	71	72	72	75	110
Haiti	14	16	19	20	25	26	27	29	30
Jamaica	120	167	200	215	250	260	270	300	320
Martinique [c]	20	38	42	43	45	45	46	47	48
Netherlands Antilles	38	43	57	58	59	60	61	62	63
St Kitts		4	5	5	7	8	8	8	9
St Lucia [a,b]	2	2	2	2	2	3	3	3	4
St Vincent/Grenadines				6	8	8	9	9	15
Trinidad and Tobago	125	210	310	320	345	355	370	380	387
Central America									
Belize						25	26	30	31
Costa Rica [a]	160	162	181	200	210	220	230	250	450
El Salvador	148	300	340	350	400	410	425	450	475
Guatemala	150	175	203	207	300	315	325	400	475
Honduras	48	49	52	280	300	315	330	350	370
Mexico	5,480	5,820	8,100	8,500	9,490	10,000	10,500	11,000	12,350
Nicaragua	100	175	205	190	200	210	220	230	240
Panama	206	220	255	350	360	370	381	390	400
Puerto Rico	535	800	980	850	856	880	900	915	930
South Asia									
Afghanistan		45	51	100	115	120	125	130	135
Bangladesh	36	80	84	300	320	350	470	500	530
Bhutan									
India [c]	627	1,548	2,780	3,500	5,000	5,500	6,000	7,000	8,000
Nepal				20	22	24	27	30	35
Pakistan	625	938	1,116	1,300	1,500	1,504	1,509	1,527	2,080
Sri Lanka		35	50	450	460	520	530	550	600

TV AND RADIO
Table No. 1306 (cont'd)

Televisions in Use 1977-1990

Units: '000

	1977	1980	1983	1985	1986	1987	1988	1989	1990
Japan									
Japan [c (1977)]	27,595	62,976	67,200	70,000	71,000	71,500	72,000	75,000	76,500
ASEAN/NICs									
Brunei	26	26	29	35	38	40	42	45	62
Hong Kong	871	1,114	1,210	1,310	1,312	1,350	1,400	1,500	1,600
Indonesia [a]	1,000	3,000	3,600	6,438	6,600	6,800	7,112	8,000	11,000
Macau						2	3	3	3
Malaysia [c]	658	1,119	1,673	1,565	1,800	2,270	2,350	2,500	2,640
Philippines	850	1,000	1,350	1,500	2,000	2,100	2,200	2,500	3,000
Singapore [c]	329	397	472	500	550	560	950	1,000	1,025
South Korea [c (1977-1983)]	3,505	6,280	7,000	7,721	7,900	8,200	8,643	8,800	9,000
Taiwan									
Thailand	765	810	840	5,000	5,200	5,500	5,600	6,000	6,250
East/SE Asia									
Cambodia [a]	35	35	60	52	55	57	60	65	70
China [c,d (1977)]	913	4,000	7,000	10,000	10,500	18,000	27,000	30,000	35,000
Laos						6	10	20	30
Mongolia [a]	4	5	11	60	60	63	66	80	90
Myanmar		1	6	20	30	50	68	70	80
North Korea				200	250	260	270	300	330
Vietnam				2,000	2,050	2,150	2,200	2,500	2,600
Australasia									
Australia	5,020	5,600	6,600	7,000	7,500	7,800	7,900	8,050	8,200
New Zealand [a]	817	862	922	962	1,200	1,220	1,240	1,250	1,500
Pacific									
American Samoa [a]	6	6	6	7	8	9	9	9	9
Fiji						10	10	11	11
French Polynesia [a]	15	16	26	27	28	29	31	32	33
Guam	57	75	78	80	83	83	84	86	87
Kiribati									
Nauru									
New Caledonia [a]	20	25	30	40	41	41	42	44	45
Papua New Guinea						7	7	8	9
Solomon Islands									
Tonga									
Tuvalu									
Vanuatu							1	1	1
Western Samoa		3	4	5	6	6	6	6	6
Middle East									
Bahrain [a]	62	90	130	170	173	181	189	200	208
Egypt [a]	1,000	1,400	2,000	3,860	4,000	4,150	4,300	5,000	5,700
Iran	1,900	2,000	2,300	2,500	2,600	2,700	2,800	3,500	3,800
Iraq [b]	475	650	800	900	1,000	1,100	1,200	1,250	1,300
Israel [b]	475	900	1,050	1,100	1,125	1,150	1,175	1,200	1,225
Jordan [a]	165	171	220	240	250	260	275	300	325
Kuwait [a]	540	353	431	426	450	480	502	550	580
Lebanon	450	750	780	800	820	840	859	880	890
Oman		350	490	900	940	980	1,015	1,100	1,150
Qatar [a,b]	40	80	143	120	128	134	142	180	190
Saudi Arabia	300	2,100	2,750	3,100	3,210	3,350	3,500	3,750	4,000
Syria [a]	250	385	423	600	625	650	682	710	740
United Arab Emirates	80	93	112	130	145	150	156	165	175
Yemen	32	40	56	67	94	103	122	150	160

TV AND RADIO

Table No. 1306 (cont'd)

Televisions in Use 1977-1990

Units: '000

	1977	1980	1983	1985	1986	1987	1988	1989	1990
North Africa									
Algeria	560	975	1,325	1,557	1,610	1,607	1,700	1,770	1,840
Chad						5	5	6	7
Djibouti [a]	4	5	6	10	14	18	20	22	23
Ethiopia [a]	25	30	40	70	74	70	75	100	115
Libya		165	220	235	245	255	295	400	450
Mali				1	1	2	2	4	10
Mauritania				1	1	2	2	45	47
Morocco [c]	597	749	860	1,150	1,206	1,300	1,320	1,700	1,850
Niger		5	11	12	15	17	25	30	35
Somalia				1	2	3	3	100	105
Sudan	100	800	1,000	1,000	1,150	1,200	1,250	1,500	1,800
Tunisia [a]	213	300	370	400	500	520	540	600	650
West Africa									
Benin		5	13	15	16	17	18	20	23
Burkina Faso [a]			35	36	38	40	42	45	48
Cameroon						120	124	250	270
Cape Verde									
Côte d'Ivoire	300	300	380	500	550	600	625	675	728
Equatorial Guinea	1	1	2	2	2	2	3	3	3
Gabon	9	9	20	22	23	24	25	40	43
Gambia									
Ghana [a]	40	57	76	140	146	171	178	211	225
Guinea		6	8	8	10	10	17	30	40
Guinea-Bissau									
Liberia	10	21	24	35	40	42	43	45	47
Nigeria [a]	450	450	457	500	550	600	650	700	750
Sao Tomé e Príncipe									
Senegal	2	4	6		220	220	234	250	265
Sierra Leone [a]	15	20	22	30	31	33	34	40	42
Togo	7	10	13	15	16	17	18	20	22
East/Central Africa									
Angola		30	33	40	40	50	52	55	57
Burundi						1	1	3	5
Central African Republic		1	1	5	5	6	7	10	13
Comoros									
Congo [a]	4	4	5	5	6	6	7	10	13
Kenya [a]	60	65	75	100	115	125	135	200	225
Madagascar [a]	12	45	71	50	55	60	65	70	75
Maldives		1		3					5
Mauritius [b,c]	41	83	95	107	110	200	203	230	233
Réunion [a]	39	80	91	88	90	92	94	96	98
Rwanda									
Seychelles			1	2	3	3	3	5	6
Tanzania [a]	5	7	9	11	13	15	16	25	40
Uganda [a]	81	74	81	90	100	105	110	150	180
Zaire	8	10	12	13	15	20	22	30	40
Southern Africa									
Botswana						8	8	15	20
Lesotho				1	1	1	1	5	10
Malawi									
Mozambique	1	2	2	7	10	13	21	35	40
Namibia						18	19	27	30
South Africa		2,000	2,300	3,000	3,100	3,200	3,300	3,500	3,700
Swaziland		1	3	8	8	9	9	13	16
Zambia [d]	23	60	76	90	100	110	120	200	250
Zimbabwe [a]	80	73	97	120	130	193	200	250	300

Source: UNESCO/national statistical offices
Notes: see end of section

TV AND RADIO	Table No. 1307

Radios in Use 1977-1990

Units: '000

	1977	1980	1983	1985	1986	1987	1988	1989	1990
North America									
Canada	24,270	17,734	20,551	21,931	22,500	24,624	25,000	27,878	28,000
USA	444,000	453,000	479,000	500,000	510,000	515,000	519,450	524,200	529,000
South America									
Argentina	10,000	12,000	16,000	20,000	20,000	20,500	21,000	21,500	22,000
Bolivia	440	2,800	3,500	3,700	3,850	3,550	3,970	4,250	4,380
Brazil [a]	16,980	35,000	50,000	53,000	50,540	52,000	53,500	55,000	57,000
Chile	2,000	3,250	3,550	4,000	4,100	4,200	4,308	4,400	4,500
Colombia	2,930	3,250	3,650	4,000	4,500	5,000	5,200	5,400	5,600
Ecuador		2,350	2,950	2,750	2,850	2,900	2,987	3,240	3,300
French Guiana		30	60	65	60	65	69	71	74
Guyana	300	303	350		355	360	365	386	387
Paraguay	187	224	260	600	624	645	668	700	730
Peru	2,200	2,750	3,100	4,000	5,000	5,000	5,130	5,300	5,450
Suriname	182	189	220	230	246	250	255	262	268
Uruguay	1,625	1,630	1,700	1,800	1,800	1,820	1,835	1,850	1,865
Venezuela	5,273	5,600	6,800	7,300	7,550	7,200	8,026	8,300	8,600
Caribbean									
Anguilla						2	2	2	2
Antigua	16	17	20	21	22	25	24	26	26
Aruba									
Bahamas	97	108	117	116	120	125	125	134	137
Barbados	100	135	191	220	220	225	223	224	225
Bermuda	51	60	67	70	70	75	72	80	81
British Virgin Islands			6	7	7	7	7	8	8
Cayman Islands	7	16	18	19	20	21	21	22	24
Cuba	1,895	2,914	3,121	3,282	3,400	3,378	3,435	3,608	3,660
Dominica	18	35	44	35	37	36	37	41	42
Dominican Republic	210	900	1,200	1,000	1,050	1,100	1,141	1,180	1,220
Grenada	30	35	38	50	50	50	51	53	54
Guadeloupe				80	82	85	84	85	86
Haiti	98	101	120	140	200	250	250	270	300
Jamaica [b]	555	800	890	900	950	965	980	995	1,010
Martinique	40	49	55	57	58	59	59	60	72
Netherlands Antilles	175		180	190	200	200	203	206	208
St Kitts		20	21	21	23	24	25	26	27
St Lucia	84	91	96	92	93	93	96	98	100
St Vincent/Grenadines				55	66	69	72	73	74
Trinidad and Tobago	275	300	360	380	550	560	570	580	600
Central America									
Belize	85	71	79	88	100	100	103	106	109
Costa Rica	156	180	205	220	700	720	740	760	782
El Salvador	1,415	1,550	1,900	1,900	2,000	2,000	2,040	2,080	2,120
Guatemala	275	310	340	350	500	550	550	570	600
Honduras	163	176	200	350	1,700	1,760	1,847	1,910	1,980
Mexico		9,000	13,020	15,000	16,000	20,000	20,500	21,000	21,500
Nicaragua	600	700	850	800	870	830	890	925	962
Panama	275	300	335	400	410	500	515	527	540
Puerto Rico [b]	1,765	2,000	2,450	2,300	2,350	2,400	2,450	2,480	2,510
South Asia									
Afghanistan	823	1,200	1,350	1,500	1,500	1,550	1,600	1,670	1,745
Bangladesh	500			4,000	4,120	4,250	4,449	4,650	4,855
Bhutan [b]	10	7	12	20	20	21	22	23	24
India			40,000	50,000	60,000	62,000	63,500	65,000	
Nepal	200	300	390	500	500	550	600	625	650
Pakistan	5,000	5,500	7,000	9,000	10,000	10,500	9,775	10,200	10,650
Sri Lanka	1,000	1,454	1,800	2,250	2,750	3,100	3,200	3,300	3,400

TV AND RADIO

Radios in Use 1977-1990

Units: '000

	1977	1980	1983	1985	1986	1987	1988	1989	1990
Japan									
Japan	64,979	79,200	85,000	95,000	100,000	105,000	105,500	110,000	112,000
ASEAN/NICs									
Brunei	30		49	50	55	55	57	60	69
Hong Kong	2,510	2,550	2,750	3,250	3,500	3,550	3,600	3,700	3,800
Indonesia	5,250	15,000	22,000	19,454	20,000	25,000	25,500	26,000	27,000
Macau	70	76	100	100	100	102	108	113	125
Malaysia	1,500	5,760	6,100	6,600	6,850	7,050	7,250	7,460	7,680
Philippines	936	2,100	2,342	3,550	7,500	7,800	8,000	8,300	8,600
Singapore [c]	387	459	681	720	775	800	810	822	850
South Korea	14,574	15,000	18,000	28,000	40,000	41,575	42,070	42,570	43,060
Taiwan									
Thailand	5,700	5,910	7,350	9,000	9,300	9,500	9,567	10,000	10,300
East/SE Asia									
Cambodia [a]	110	600	900	800	800	825	834	860	930
China		55,000	70,000	120,000	150,000	200,000	203,000	206,000	209,500
Laos	200	350	430	430	450	465	480	500	520
Mongolia	125	166	182	250	250	260	271	280	289
Myanmar	693	774	864	3,000	3,000	3,100	3,174	3,300	3,425
North Korea				3,500	2,250	2,350	2,420	2,500	2,600
Vietnam				6,000	6,200	6,200	6,600	7,000	7,200
Australasia									
Australia	14,600	15,000	20,000	20,000	20,000	20,500	20,800	21,000	21,600
New Zealand	2,725	2,755	2,850	3,000	3,000	3,050	3,053	3,100	3,150
Pacific									
American Samoa	28	32	43	40	43	45	46	47	47
Fiji	308	300	330	400	400	410	420	430	440
French Polynesia [a]	70	80	84	90	94	87	94	105	110
Guam	89	100	140	160	160	180	183	185	187
Kiribati	8	12	13	13	14	14	14	15	15
Nauru	4	4	6	5	5	5	5	6	6
New Caledonia	64	76	82	80	85	88	90	92	94
Papua New Guinea	125	200	215	220	225	235	244	260	280
Solomon Islands	10	20	24	25	30	32	34	36	38
Tonga		70	75	80	81	85	51	52	53
Tuvalu						2	2	3	3
Vanuatu						31	38	41	44
Western Samoa		32	70	70	70	73	72	73	74
Middle East									
Bahrain	100	125	175	225	225	235	248	260	274
Egypt	5,275	6,000	8,000	12,000	15,000	15,500	16,000	16,450	17,000
Iran	2,125	6,400	7,500	10,000	11,000	12,000	12,500	13,000	13,500
Iraq	2,000	2,000	2,750	3,000	3,250	3,400	3,530	3,700	2,880
Israel	750	950	1,107	2,000	2,000	2,050	2,074	2,115	2,165
Jordan	532	536	620	791	850	900	940	980	1,020
Kuwait	550	365	480	497	500	600	630	660	700
Lebanon [b]	1,600	2,000	2,100	2,100	2,100	2,150	2,198	2,247	2,270
Oman			700	800	850	860	890	932	970
Qatar		110	131	150	158	165	170	179	189
Saudi Arabia [a]	950	2,500	3,300	3,700	3,850	3,400	3,640	3,800	4,500
Syria		1,720	1,970	2,500	2,500	2,600	2,848	3,000	3,150
United Arab Emirates [b]	55	240	310	350	434	450	470	490	515
Yemen	102	118	132	150	300	350	362	374	400

TV AND RADIO — Table No. 1307 (cont'd)

Radios in Use 1977-1990

Units: '000

	1977	1980	1983	1985	1986	1987	1988	1989	1990
North Africa									
Algeria [b]	3,000	3,700	4,400	4,800	5,000	5,250	5,456	5,645	5,820
Chad [a]	500	750	1,050	1,100	1,200	1,250	1,268	1,310	1,350
Djibouti	16	21	23	30	32	33	34	35	37
Ethiopia [a]	1,000	3,000	3,000	8,000	8,300	8,500	8,700	9,000	9,400
Libya	125	646	750	800	850	900	940	980	1,020
Mali [b]	82	105	121	130	300	320	335	350	400
Mauritania [b]	95	150	180	250	260	260	273	282	291
Morocco	1,600	3,000	3,600	3,850	4,600	4,800	4,950	5,100	5,250
Niger		250	280	300	350	400	420	440	460
Somalia	75	112	134	200	250	260	280	300	320
Sudan	1,400	3,500	5,000	5,400	5,600	5,300	5,550	5,755	6,295
Tunisia	866	1,000	1,124	1,550	1,200	1,300	1,400	1,500	1,600
West Africa									
Benin	150	230	290	300	310	325	340	400	415
Burkina Faso	110	110	123	145	170	200	215	225	235
Cameroon	240	760	830	940	1,250	1,300	1,345	1,500	1,650
Cape Verde	40	41	47	50	52	53	55	57	59
Côte d'Ivoire	800	1,000	1,200	1,300	1,350	1,450	1,478	1,600	1,700
Equatorial Guinea	82	100	115	100	103	103	107	128	149
Gabon	95	96	102	110	117	125	147	155	165
Gambia	63	73	77	105	110	115	134	140	146
Ghana	1,095	1,700	2,200	2,500	2,650	3,000	4,140	4,300	4,500
Guinea	120	135	160	180	200	210	220	230	240
Guinea-Bissau	15	25	28	30	33	35	36	37	38
Liberia	274	335	380	500	510	520	540	560	580
Nigeria	5,250	6,100	7,000	8,100	16,000	16,600	17,260	18,000	18,700
Sao Tomé e Príncipe	21	23	25	26	28	28	29	31	32
Senegal	295	340	440	700	720	700	775	802	830
Sierra Leone	315	450	700	800	820	830	860	890	925
Togo	450	550	590	610	680	560	580	719	745
East/Central Africa									
Angola	118	125	163	230	400	450	470	520	540
Burundi	107	150	178	250	270	280	290	300	320
Central African Republic	80	120	140	150	158	163	171	180	200
Comoros [b]	36	39	56	50	54	53	55	61	69
Congo	88	93		200	210	220	229	240	250
Kenya	525	540	640	1,600	1,800	2,000	2,100	2,200	2,500
Madagascar	1,020	1,700	2,000		2,000	2,100	2,200	2,300	2,400
Maldives	3	7	15	19				24	25
Mauritius [b,c]	200	201	235	250	275	280	285	380	385
Réunion	100	100	120	122	123	130	135	140	145
Rwanda	80	150	300	350	360	350	385	415	450
Seychelles	18	21	23	30	30	30	30	31	32
Tanzania	310	500	591	540	549	549	500	565	600
Uganda	250	295	320	340	1,500	1,600	1,700	1,800	1,900
Zaire	1,250	1,500	3,000	3,000	3,000	3,200	3,349	3,480	3,650
Southern Africa									
Botswana	63		120	140	140	150	160	140	150
Lesotho	25	30	40	43	100	110	114	118	125
Malawi [b]	130	275		1,700	1,800	2,000	1,907	2,000	2,080
Mozambique	230	255	275	450	500	550	580	620	650
Namibia						210	220	230	240
South Africa	2,500	8,000	8,800	10,000	10,300	10,550	10,900	11,200	11,500
Swaziland	70	81	93	100	105	110	112	117	122
Zambia	125	135	170	200	528	550	576	603	650
Zimbabwe	270	240	350	375	480	750	775	801	830

Source: UNESCO/national statistical offices

Notes: see end of section

CINEMA STATISTICS   Table No. 1308

Cinema Screens, Attendances and Revenues: Latest Year

Units: As stated

	Year	No.of fixed cinemas	Seating capacity ('000)	Mobile cinemas	Drive-in cinemas	Total attendance (million)	Gross receipts[a]
North America							
Canada [b]	1988	658	485	0	132	78.8	375
USA	1989	22,029		0	1,103	1,132.5	5,033
South America							
Argentina [c]	1989	531			4	25.3	7,129,404
Bolivia [c]	1989	79				4.6	9,905
Brazil [d]	1985	1,397	708	13	18	91.3	453
Chile	1989	177	98	0			
Colombia	1988	515	325	0		41.0	12,078
Ecuador	1987	118	110			10.1	1,174
French Guiana							
Guyana	1981	50	40	0	1	13.3	29
Paraguay							
Peru	1980	425		0		33.0	5,500
Suriname							
Uruguay	1981	120	80	0		6.2	87
Venezuela [c]	1989	351	136	0	15	25.6	679
Caribbean							
Anguilla							
Antigua							
Aruba							
Bahamas	1979	13	6	0			
Barbados	1975	6		2		1.1	
Bermuda	1981	4	2	0		0.2	1
British Virgin Islands	1977	1					
Cayman Islands	1979	4	1	0		0.2	
Cuba	1989	500	235	680		44.8	17
Dominica							
Dominican Republic	1975	83				6.8	
Grenada							
Guadeloupe							
Haiti	1981	28	14	0	4	2.1	8
Jamaica	1974	44		0			
Martinique	1987	14	4			1.1	3
Netherlands Antilles							
St Kitts							
St Lucia							
St Vincent/Grenadines	1974	3		1			
Trinidad and Tobago	1979	72	57	19		3.7	
Central America							
Belize							
Costa Rica	1985	104		0	1	0.2	11
El Salvador	1985	79	52	0			
Guatemala [c]	1988	110	59			7.7	13
Honduras							
Mexico	1987	2,226		158	5		
Nicaragua	1981	127	74		1	5.2	30
Panama							
Puerto Rico	1974	105				6.8	
South Asia							
Afghanistan	1979	34	19	13			
Bangladesh	1987	781	294	8			2,942
Bhutan	1979	12	5	0			
India	1989	13,021	6,430	150	3	4,297.5	13,200
Nepal							
Pakistan	1989	650		50	2		
Sri Lanka	1987	313	131	0		37.2	

CINEMA STATISTICS   Table No. 1308 (cont'd)

Cinema Screens, Attendances and Revenues: Latest Year

Units: As stated

	Year	No.of fixed cinemas	Seating capacity ('000)	Mobile cinemas	Drive-in cinemas	Total attendance (million)	Gross receipts[a]
Japan							
Japan [c,e]	1989	1,912				143.6	166,681
ASEAN/NICs							
Brunei [c]	1981	7	6	12		2.3	
Hong Kong	1989	153				58.3	1,367
Indonesia	1985	1,833	959	68	1		
Macau							
Malaysia	1989	169	152			41.6	119
Philippines	1975	716		84		318.0	
Singapore	1983	57	63	0	1	31.2	28
South Korea [d]	1989	772				55.3	125,588
Taiwan	1985	602	516			128.0	
Thailand	1989	668					
East/SE Asia							
Cambodia							
China	1989	4,500		140,000		16,000.0	1,950
Laos							
Mongolia	1989	65				20.1	
Myanmar	1987	162	126				
North Korea	1985	1,778	653	3,515		187.4	49
Vietnam [c]	1988	450		1,001		239.9	
Australasia							
Australia	1989	772				39.8	258
New Zealand	1979	172	1,030	0			
Pacific							
American Samoa							
Fiji							
French Polynesia	1987	10	2	0		0.4	80
Guam	1974	7		0		1.0	
Kiribati	1974	6		4		0.4	
Nauru							
New Caledonia	1987	7	2	0	1	0.2	5
Papua New Guinea							
Solomon Islands	1977	2				0.1	
Tonga	1979	3		5		0.1	
Tuvalu							
Vanuatu	1987	1	1				
Western Samoa	1979	6	6	0		0.5	0
Middle East							
Bahrain	1989	6	3			0.6	
Egypt	1987	169	161			30.3	19
Iran	1989	269	166			80.5	8,552
Iraq	1977	84		1			
Israel	1978	214	152	0		24.2	550
Jordan	1989	46	92			0.9	
Kuwait	1987	12	15	0	2	0.9	1
Lebanon							
Oman	1976	12		0		0.9	
Qatar	1989	4	4			0.3	5
Saudi Arabia							
Syria	1989	77	40			6.9	
United Arab Emirates	1989	31	30	1			
Yemen	1980	59	52	0		18.9	

CINEMA STATISTICS

Cinema Screens, Attendances and Revenues: Latest Year

Units: As stated

	Year	No.of fixed cinemas	Seating capacity ('000)	Mobile cinemas	Drive-in cinemas	Total attendance (million)	Gross receipts[a]
North Africa							
Algeria	1988	249				21.0	
Chad	1977	13		3		24.2	
Djibouti	1975	4		3		0.5	
Ethiopia	1985	46		0		38.0	1,228
Libya	1979	49	22	100		11.3	
Mali							
Mauritania	1980	19	8	0			
Morocco [c]	1989	252	166			30.2	143
Niger							
Somalia							
Sudan	1983	56	97	30		13.0	
Tunisia	1987	81	18	25			
West Africa							
Benin	1986	7					196
Burkina Faso	1987	29	34	1		6.0	911
Cameroon	1987	69	41	163			
Cape Verde	1989	20		2			
Côte d'Ivoire	1979	72	42	4		7.0	2,500
Equatorial Guinea	1977	10		0		0.5	
Gabon	1987	14	5	0		0.1	105
Gambia							
Ghana	1981	7	9	0		3.9	2
Guinea	1985	29	61	0		2.6	
Guinea-Bissau							
Liberia	1979	13	9	0		1.5	
Nigeria	1981	240		20		4.6	
Sao Tomé e Príncipe							
Senegal	1976	60				3.8	
Sierra Leone							
Togo							
East/Central Africa							
Angola	1985	44	33	0		3.2	171
Burundi	1981	7	3	0		0.1	18
Central African Republic							
Comoros							
Congo							
Kenya	1977	40		8		6.0	
Madagascar	1987	37	12	8		2.5	441
Maldives	1983	7	3	0			
Mauritius	1989	25	23			0.9	13
Réunion							
Rwanda	1985	34	9	0			
Seychelles	1975	2		4		0.5	
Tanzania	1989	30	14		1	1.7	183
Uganda	1977	17				1.6	
Zaire	1974	91		0		1.6	
Southern Africa							
Botswana	1976	1		0		0.1	
Lesotho							
Malawi	1975	4		13		0.3	
Mozambique	1987	60	30	0		4.1	406
Namibia							
South Africa							
Swaziland	1981	4		0	2		
Zambia	1988	17			1	1.7	
Zimbabwe [f]	1985	32		23	9	5.6	

Source: UNESCO/national statistical offices

Notes: see end of section

MEDIA ACCESS							Table No. 1309

Home Ownership of Media Equipment and Cable TV 1991

Units: % homes equipped with

	Colour TV	Multiset	VCR	Teletext	Remote control	Cable TV Sets ('000)	Cable TV % connected
Argentina [a,b]	70.0	28.2	9.0		48.0	160.0	3.9
Australia	98.0	47.0	73.0	2.0	60.0		
Brazil [a]	48.0	32.0	11.4				
Canada [a]	69.0	49.0	62.0		60.0	6,627.0	71.0
Chile [a]	70.0	24.0	9.4		46.0		0.1
China	57.0						
Colombia [a]	55.1	30.7	15.3		21.2	220.0	4.0
Ecuador [a]	38.0		17.0			11.0	2.1
Hong Kong	97.0	22.0	68.0		60.0		
India	34.0	2.0	8.0			2,000.0	7.7
Indonesia	51.0	9.0	12.0				
Israel							
Japan	99.0	85.0	76.0			6,767.5	16.5
Malaysia	84.0	8.0	37.0	2.0	9.0		
Mexico [a,c]	56.0	37.0	8.0		28.0	100.0	0.9
New Zealand	98.0	43.0	75.0	20.0	61.0		
Nigeria							
Pakistan [a]	3.0		2.0				
Peru	80.0	20.0	5.0		20.0		
Philippines	20.0		14.0			20.0	0.3
Singapore	100.0	40.0	84.0	29.0	66.0		
South Africa							
South Korea	98.0	29.0	54.0		50.0	3,339.0	29.4
Taiwan	99.0		84.0		79.0		
Thailand	51.0	5.0	14.0				
USA [a]	98.0	65.0	66.0	1.0	77.0	51,900.0	56.0
Venezuela [a]	62.0		23.5			76.0	2.2
Vietnam							

Source: Industry sources/Euromonitor   Notes: see end of section

Notes to Tables in Section Thirteen

Table 1301   Includes print, TV, radio, cinema, outdoor, transit
a Figures are expressed in reformed currency from 1988

Table 1302   a Data refer to 1989
b Outdoor/transit includes cinema advertising

Table 1303   a Data refer to 1989
b Outdoor/transit includes cinema advertising

Table 1304   a Commercial revenues not applicable
b Public revenues not applicable
c Government revenues not applicable
d TV only
e Abu Dhabi only

Table 1305   Data for daily newspapers all refer to 1990
Data for non-dailies and periodicals refer to year as follows:
a 1990
b 1988
c 1989
d 1991

Table 1306   Entries of 0 denote less than 500 sets
a National estimates
b Data given for 1977 are actually for 1976

c Number of licences issued ('000)
d Data given for 1977 are actually for 1975

Table 1307   a Data given for 1977 are actually for 1975
b Data given for 1977 are actually for 1976
c Number of licences issued ('000)

Table 1308   a Million units of national currency
b Excludes taxes
c Attendances at fixed cinemas only
d Billion units of national currency
e Mobile units refer to video cinemas
f Excludes attendance at drive-in movies

Table 1309   a Data refer to 1989
b Cable TV figures refer to Buenos Aires area only
c Data for colour TVs, multiset and remote control refer to urban areas only

Consumer Market Sizes

MEAT AND FISH — Table No. 1401

Per Capita Consumption of Meat and Fish 1991

Units: Kg per inhabitant

	Poultry	Beef	Pork	Lamb	Fish	Fresh Fish 1989	Dried Fish 1989
Argentina	11.7	69.0	5.3	2.4	8.5	3.0	5.0
Australia [a]	26.2	37.4	18.0	21.5	7.5		
Brazil	15.2	18.0	7.1	0.5	6.0	5.6	3.0
Canada [a]	29.0	35.8	27.1	0.8	6.2		
Chile	9.6	17.6	8.7	0.7	13.7		
China [b]	2.1	1.1	11.1		3.0		
Colombia	7.5	18.5	4.2	0.4	3.1		
Ecuador [a]	6.1	8.8	4.8	0.6	8.5		
Hong Kong	29.5	16.2	44.3	1.7	58.2		
India [b]	0.4	2.1	0.1	0.7			
Indonesia	1.4	0.9	0.7	0.1	13.2		
Israel [b]	40.0	16.5		0.9	11.0		
Japan [c]	13.3	9.4	16.5	0.9	26.3	18.0	21.0
Malaysia	11.2	2.2	5.2		9.3		
Mexico	10.0	19.0	9.8	1.0			
New Zealand [a,c]	15.7	36.0	14.4	38.8	8.5	8.0	0.5
Nigeria [b]	3.6	3.9	1.0				
Pakistan	1.4	6.3			5.9		
Peru [a]	11.2	5.0	4.1	1.4	20.1		
Philippines	4.1	3.2	1.0		36.6		
Singapore	4.3	6.2	9.4	2.2			
South Africa	14.6	18.2	3.5	5.5			
South Korea	4.2	4.2	12.1	0.6	60.3		
Taiwan		5.0			58.0		
Thailand	5.8	4.6	5.7	0.1	36.9		
USA [a]	43.3	44.0	29.5	0.8	6.2	6.0	0.2
Venezuela [c]	11.6	18.5	5.2	0.3	14.2		
Vietnam							

Source: Euromonitor from national statistical offices/OECD/GATT/trade associations

Notes: see end of section

FRESH PRODUCE — Table No. 1402

Per Capita Consumption of Cereals: Latest Year

Units: Kg per inhabitant

	Total Cereals 1989	Wheat 1989	Barley 1989	Oats 1989	Maize 1989	Rice 1991	Flour 1989
Argentina	47.3	47.3					85.0
Australia [a]	57.8	54.0	0.1	1.2	2.5	3.6	69.0
Brazil	15.0	13.5	0.1	0.4	1.0	48.3	50.0
Canada	68.5	61.0	0.1	4.4	3.0	6.8	60.0
Chile							
China	25.3	25.3				111.6	55.0
Colombia	7.7	7.7					10.5
Ecuador							
Hong Kong							33.5
India	17.9	17.9				86.3	4.0
Indonesia	2.8	2.8				166.7	6.0
Israel [a]	53.0	51.0	0.2	0.8	1.0	7.0	95.0
Japan	35.3	33.0	0.4	1.2	0.7	77.6	36.5
Malaysia							22.5
Mexico	17.0	17.0					52.0
New Zealand [a]	80.4	77.0	0.1	2.0	1.3	2.7	70.0
Nigeria							14.0
Pakistan							
Peru							
Philippines							13.0
Singapore							30.0
South Africa	23.2	21.3	0.1	1.0	0.8		38.0
South Korea	23.5	22.0	0.2	0.8	0.5	126.9	37.0
Taiwan			0.1	0.8			29.0
Thailand							4.0
USA	69.8	58.5	0.5	6.5	4.3	11.9	52.0
Venezuela	19.7	19.7					36.0
Vietnam							

Source: Euromonitor from national statistical offices/OECD/GATT

Notes: see end of section

FRESH PRODUCE Table No. 1403

Per Capita Consumption of Fruit and Vegetables 1991

Units: Kg per inhabitant

	Potatoes	Other Vegetables	Total Fruit	Citrus Fruit	Non-Citrus Fruit
Argentina [a]	64.5	80.0	160.4		
Australia	62.0	89.6	109.2	57.1	52.1
Brazil [a]	20.0		159.7		
Canada	69.0	101.1	144.7	31.4	133.4
Chile			240.7		
China	28.9	102.8	22.4		
Colombia			142.4		
Ecuador					
Hong Kong [a]	3.2		92.1		
India	17.6	59.5	29.1		
Indonesia [a]	1.3	11.0	29.3	3.1	26.4
Israel [a]	38.0	118.0	131.0	39.0	92.0
Japan	19.1	105.8	51.4	18.6	32.8
Malaysia			54.4		
Mexico [a]	15.0		132.0		
New Zealand [a]	51.0	67.0			
Nigeria					
Pakistan			32.0		
Peru					
Philippines [a]	1.5	47.0	70.0	28.3	41.7
Singapore			135.7		
South Africa [a]	15.5				
South Korea [a]	17.0		42.3		
Taiwan [a]	0.3		91.6		
Thailand			84.3		
USA	21.6	65.0	41.8		
Venezuela	15.0		163.7		
Vietnam					

Source: Euromonitor from OECD/GATT/national statistical offices   Notes: see end of section

DAIRY PRODUCTS Table No. 1404

Per Capita Consumption of Dairy Products and Eggs 1991

Units: Kg per inhabitant

	Milk	Butter	Cheese	Eggs
Argentina	45.9	1.3	8.7	105.2
Australia [a]	101.9	2.7	8.3	164.6
Brazil	47.6	0.5	1.4	89.1
Canada [a]	105.0	3.2	10.6	163.1
Chile	23.4	0.5	1.9	140.4
China [a]	5.6	0.2	0.2	48.9
Colombia [a]	42.5	0.7	1.5	126.3
Ecuador [b]	85.7		1.2	64.5
Hong Kong [a]	47.8	0.2	0.4	223.0
India [a]	63.0	0.2	1.1	21.6
Indonesia [a]	3.8	0.1	0.1	40.0
Israel [a]	75.0	0.8	16.1	313.8
Japan	41.5	0.8	1.3	316.1
Malaysia [a]	18.2	0.2	0.1	145.0
Mexico	51.3	0.4	4.7	225.9
New Zealand	135.9	9.2	6.7	195.4
Nigeria [a]	5.0	0.1	0.1	47.7
Pakistan	99.5			26.0
Peru [a]	9.0		0.8	13.0
Philippines [a]	5.1	0.3	0.1	53.0
Singapore [a]	68.8		0.8	229.2
South Africa [a]	39.9	0.5	1.4	121.5
South Korea [a]	20.5	0.3	0.2	146.4
Taiwan	39.6			206.3
Thailand [a]	13.2	0.2	0.1	58.0
USA	50.2	1.2	11.1	207.7
Venezuela	11.4	0.1	4.4	61.5
Vietnam				

Source: Euromonitor from OECD/GATT/trade associations/national statistical offices   Notes: see end of section

MISCELLANEOUS FOODS   Table No. 1405

Per Capita Consumption of Miscellaneous Foods: Latest Year

Units: Kg per inhabitant

	Sugar 1991	Honey 1989	Margarine 1991
Argentina	36.1		
Australia [a]	48.5	2.0	9.1
Brazil	47.0	0.8	2.5
Canada [a]	40.7	0.7	6.1
Chile	38.5		2.2
China [a]	6.3	0.1	6.6
Colombia	40.5	0.1	1.5
Ecuador	33.5		1.0
Hong Kong	26.9	0.1	
India [a]	14.2	0.1	0.5
Indonesia	14.7	0.1	
Israel [a]	57.3		7.3
Japan	23.0		1.4
Malaysia	41.2		
Mexico	50.1	0.9	0.3
New Zealand [a]	47.8	2.4	4.2
Nigeria	5.3		
Pakistan	23.0		
Peru	33.6		0.8
Philippines	24.0		
Singapore	68.8	0.2	
South Africa [a]	36.4	0.1	3.6
South Korea [a]	18.0	0.1	8.5
Taiwan	26.7	0.1	
Thailand [a]	20.9		1.1
USA [a]	31.6	0.6	6.0
Venezuela	37.6	0.1	
Vietnam	7.6		

Source: Euromonitor from International Sugar Organisation/OECD/GATT   Notes: see end of section

HOT DRINKS   Table No. 1406

Per Capita Consumption of Hot Drinks 1992

Units: Kg per inhabitant

	Coffee	Tea	Cocoa
Argentina	1.0		0.3
Australia [a]		1.0	1.9
Brazil	3.6	0.1	0.6
Canada [a]	4.2	0.5	1.9
Chile	0.6	0.9	0.1
China		0.4	
Colombia	2.5		1.2
Ecuador	0.6	0.1	0.5
Hong Kong	0.9	1.7	
India	0.1	0.6	
Indonesia	0.5	0.2	0.1
Israel	3.2	0.6	1.2
Japan	1.7	1.3	1.0
Malaysia	0.8	0.2	0.4
Mexico	0.9		0.4
New Zealand [a]		1.5	0.7
Nigeria			
Pakistan	0.3	0.9	
Peru	0.5	0.1	0.2
Philippines	0.7	0.3	
Singapore	1.4	0.7	
South Africa [b]	0.5	0.7	
South Korea	1.5	0.2	0.2
Taiwan	0.1	0.8	
Thailand	0.2	0.2	
USA [a]	5.2	0.3	2.0
Venezuela	2.6		0.3
Vietnam			

Source: Euromonitor from trade associations/national statistical offices   Notes: see end of section

DRINKS/TOBACCO · Table No. 1407

Per Capita Consumption of Drinks and Tobacco: Latest Year

Units: Litres/units (for cigarettes), per inhabitant	Beer 1991	Wine 1992	Whisky 1992	Gin 1992	Vodka 1992	Rum 1992	Brandy 1992	Soft Drinks 1992	Cigar- ettes 1991
Argentina	24.6	35.6							1,055
Australia [a]	108.2	18.3	1.4	0.1	0.1	0.3	0.3	165.7	2,140
Brazil [a]	46.2	0.6	0.2		0.2	0.1	0.4	36.0	1,076
Canada	75.4	8.4	1.6	0.3	0.8	0.9	0.2	146.9	1,439
Chile	21.9	19.0							799
China	7.9	0.3							1,486
Colombia	51.0	2.5							788
Ecuador									415
Hong Kong	28.3	2.9						85.2	1,043
India	4.1	0.2							100
Indonesia	1.1	0.2						6.4	769
Israel [b,c]	11.5	2.0							1,450
Japan	55.6	1.0	1.5	0.1	0.1	0.1	0.4	38.2	2,649
Malaysia	9.1	0.1						12.8	1,123
Mexico	47.0	2.8						135.9	603
New Zealand [c]	104.8	16.2							1,450
Nigeria [c]	6.6	0.1							210
Pakistan		0.1							261
Peru	27.0	5.6							
Philippines	30.9	0.2						44.0	1,134
Singapore	21.4	0.8						59.5	1,158
South Africa	58.8	8.8	0.5	0.2	0.4	0.1	1.0		1,396
South Korea	36.3	13.4						45.8	2,173
Taiwan	22.5	3.6						62.2	1,703
Thailand	5.0							27.2	711
USA	87.4	6.9	1.7	0.4	1.1	0.4	0.2	259.8	2,015
Venezuela [a]	74.5	1.2						50.0	737

Source: Euromonitor from World Tobacco and various other sources   Notes: see end of section

HOUSEHOLD MATERIALS/FOOTWEAR · Table No. 1408

Per Capita Sales of Selected Household Materials and Footwear: Latest Year

Units: Kg per inhabitant, except shoes (pairs/inhabitant)

	Washing products 1990	Cotton 1991	Paper/board 1991	Tissue paper 1990	Shoes 1991
Argentina		4.1	26.2	1.2	2.4
Australia [a]	15.4	1.7	165.0	10.4	4.7
Brazil	4.1	4.7	27.8	2.7	1.9
Canada [a]	16.0	1.5	215.0	16.6	4.4
Chile		1.9	31.6	4.3	1.2
China		3.6	12.6		1.7
Colombia	1.9	2.9	18.7	2.2	1.9
Ecuador		1.8	30.1		0.2
Hong Kong	0.4	34.4	109.0	5.6	5.9
India	0.4	2.1	2.7		0.4
Indonesia	12.1	2.0	7.5		0.5
Israel [a]		4.2	95.8	8.3	3.2
Japan	11.2	3.7	228.3	11.1	
Malaysia	6.5	2.8	44.5	3.5	1.7
Mexico		2.0	36.4	4.0	1.6
New Zealand [a]			169.1	21.0	3.3
Nigeria		0.8	3.0		
Pakistan		10.4	2.9		1.1
Peru		2.2	5.0		
Philippines	2.7	0.9	9.7		0.9
Singapore	7.9	8.7	190.7		6.9
South Africa [a]		1.8	44.3	3.0	2.5
South Korea	2.1	8.9	101.1	4.6	2.7
Taiwan		18.8	166.0	8.0	3.1
Thailand	1.6	6.4	20.0	0.7	0.7
USA [a]		7.8	309.0	21.4	6.0
Venezuela	3.5	2.3	36.2	5.9	0.9
Vietnam		0.6	1.0		

Source: Euromonitor from International Cotton Advisory Committee/International Wool Secretariat/Shoe and Allied Trades
Research Association   Notes: see end of section

ELECTRICAL APPLIANCES   Table No. 1409

Total Retail Sales of White Goods 1991

Units: '000

	Washing machines	Fridges	Dishwashers	Freezers	Cookers	Microwaves
Argentina	125	178				
Australia						
Brazil	370	2,117	282		2,840	340
Canada	486	527	272	230		700
Chile	125	140				
China [a]	9,000	4,000	600	2,000	9,750	
Colombia [a]	105					
Ecuador	41					
Hong Kong	185	260	8	45		
India	1,500	750	55	160	1,000	55
Indonesia						
Israel						
Japan [b]	5,010	4,700	150		11,050	3,200
Malaysia	150	254	6	30	160	20
Mexico	480	700				
New Zealand						
Nigeria						
Pakistan		100	7			
Peru [c]	33	45				
Philippines	155	210	20	55	310	30
Singapore	128	65	5	16		
South Africa						
South Korea	1,450	2,600	55	800	3,100	800
Taiwan	360	525	40	130	2,000	165
Thailand	105	165	11	30	520	16
USA	5,563	6,724	3,508	1,251	4,888	8,108
Venezuela	110	155				
Vietnam						

Source: Euromonitor   Notes: see end of section

CONSUMER ELECTRONICS   Table No. 1410

Total Retail Sales of Consumer Electronics: Latest Year

Units: '000

	Mono TVs 1991	Colour TVs 1991	VCRs 1991	Radios/ Radio rec- orders 1991	Record players & decks 1991	Tape recorders & decks 1991	CD players 1991
Argentina [a,b]	161	340	103	1,090	115		79
Australia [c,d]	40	810	650	4,770	110	580	280
Brazil [b]	590	2,420	640	6,800	505		350
Canada [c,d,e]	160	1,650	1,400	4,850	4,850	1,950	480
Chile [a]	39	156	45	465		55	30
China		19,800	2,350	18,150			1,700
Colombia [b,f]		160	49		65		4
Ecuador [b,f]		80	23		8		
Hong Kong [c]	61	355	480	5,135	35	2,700	380
India [c]	3,600	1,100	300	10,000	5,600		
Indonesia [c,g]	187	985	127	2,250		1,050	
Israel [h]	20	110	130				
Japan [c,d,i]		9,010	5,200	15,500	1,300	16,100	1,400
Malaysia [b,c]	20	415	250	3,485	2,900		175
Mexico	245	480	165	1,290		340	180
New Zealand		825					
Nigeria							
Pakistan		157	35	1,125			
Peru [j]		90	37				
Philippines [c]	100	144	68	1,000		300	
Singapore [c,k]	105	410	495	5,400	27	1,300	285
South Africa [d,l]	100	185	130	3,110			30
South Korea [c,m]	11	2,090	1,080	4,380	900		3,310
Taiwan	175	550	530	2,100			260
Thailand [c]	377	1,270	220	4,400	270		
USA [c]	1,488	19,343	10,670	27,487			3,388
Venezuela	102	260	75	1,130	505		47

Source: Euromonitor   Notes: see end of section

PERSONAL AND LEISURE GOODS — Table No. 1411

Total Retail Sales of Selected Personal and Leisure Goods 1992

Units: As stated

	Singles and EPs (mn units)	LPs (mn units)	Audio Tapes (mn units)	Compact Discs (mn units)	Toys & Games (US$ mn)	Recorded Music Value (mn units national currency)
Argentina [a]		0.2	8.8	6.7	90.0	184.2
Australia	7.8		11.6	22.9	754.0	684.4
Brazil [a]		16.6	5.6	9.8	600.0	262.4
Canada	2.2		29.5	32.9	1,033.0	1,051.3
Chile			7.0	1.0	35.0	18,869.2
China [a]		30.0	150.0	2.0	140.0	320.8
Colombia [a]	1.3	4.7	2.4	0.9	40.0	35.8
Ecuador	0.2	0.3	0.4	0.1		5,144.7
Hong Kong			3.6	8.6	200.0	934.0
India			240.0	0.5	260.0	6,945.0
Indonesia			47.0	1.0	28.0	216,000.0
Israel			2.9		85.0	85.0
Japan	90.3	0.8	31.7	181.8	7,884.0	542,230.0
Malaysia			11.6	1.3	20.0	168.6
Mexico [a]		2.0	48.7	14.5	220.0	571.2
New Zealand	0.9		2.9	2.4	145.0	103.8
Nigeria [b]		0.6	6.7		10.0	99.0
Pakistan					55.0	
Peru			0.8	0.2	60.0	10.5
Philippines	0.9	0.2	5.9	0.3	32.0	690.0
Singapore			6.3	2.9	55.0	113.7
South Africa		0.7	7.1	4.2	84.0	549.1
South Korea		25.2	45.6	6.9	425.0	363,823.5
Taiwan			32.7	10.4	375.0	8,352.0
Thailand			55.8	0.7	110.0	3,910.0
USA	111.7	2.3	366.4	407.5	20,684.0	8,866.6
Venezuela		2.0	2.2	1.4	60.0	3,138.2
Vietnam						

Source: Euromonitor/International Federation of the Phonographic Industry

Notes: see end of section

Notes to Tables in Section Fourteen

Table 1401 a Some data refer to 1989
b Beef includes lamb
c Some data refer to 1990

Table 1402 a Data for rice refer to 1989

Table 1403 a Some data refer to 1989

Table 1404 a Some data refer to 1989
b Some data refer to 1990

Table 1405 a Data for margarine refer to 1989

Table 1406 a Data for cocoa refer to 1990
b Coffee refers to instant coffee only

Table 1407 a Data for soft drinks refer to 1990
b Beer refers to 1990
c Cigarettes refers to 1990

Table 1408 Paper and board, newsprint, tissue paper and cotton data are for 1990
a Data for shoes refer to 1988

Table 1409 a Data for washing machines refer to 1990
b Fridges include freezers
c Fridges refer to 1990

Table 1410 a Data for mono TVs refer to 1989
b Record players include tape recorders
c Data for record players and/or tape recorders refer to 1989
d Data for CDs refer to 1989
e Record players include radio combinations
f Data for colour TVs refer to 1989
g Tape recorders include radio recorders
h Data refer to 1989
i Colour TVs include monochrome
j Data refer to 1990
k Radio figure includes sales to tourists
l Radios include record players and tape recorders
m Radios include tape recorders

Table 1411 a Recorded music value is in million US dollars
b Data refer to 1990

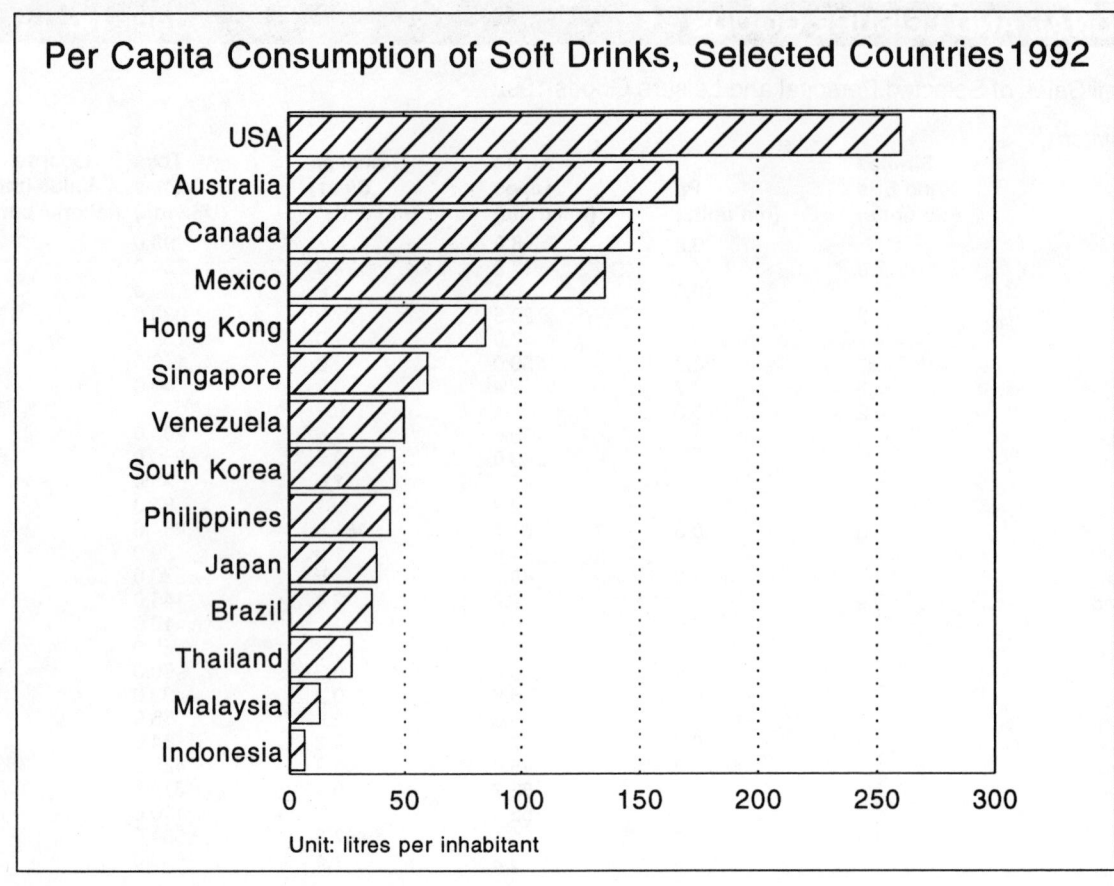

Per Capita Consumption of Soft Drinks, Selected Countries 1992

Unit: litres per inhabitant

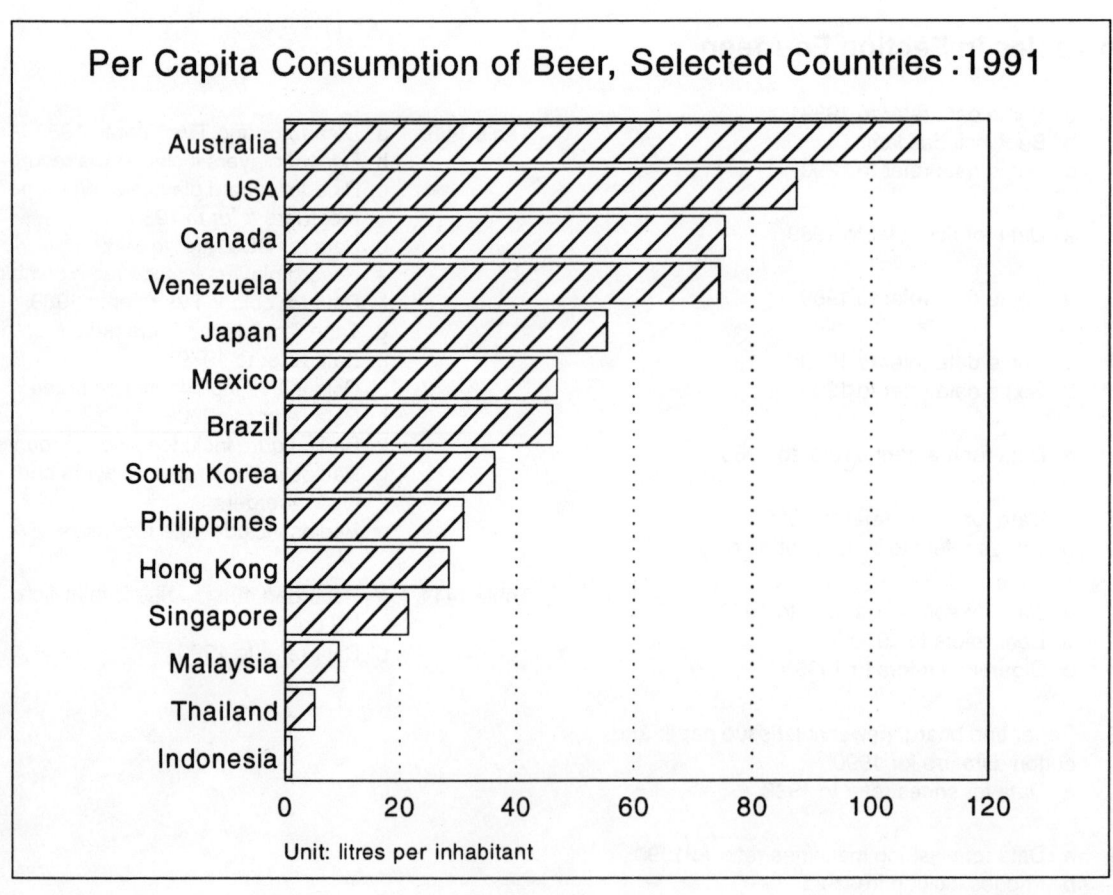

Per Capita Consumption of Beer, Selected Countries : 1991

Unit: litres per inhabitant

Consumer Prices and Costs

CONSUMER PRICES

Table No. 1501

Trends in Consumer Prices 1980-1992

Units: 1980 = 100

	1980	1983	1985	1986	1987	1988	1989	1990	1991	1992
North America										
Canada	100.0	131.8	143.0	148.9	155.5	161.8	169.9	177.8	187.9	190.6
USA	100.0	120.9	130.5	133.1	137.9	143.6	150.5	158.6	165.3	170.3
South America										
Argentina [a,b]		2.0	100.0	190.0	440.0	1,948.0	62.0	1,495.0	4,062.0	5,073.0
Bolivia [a]		0.1	100.0	376.3	431.2	500.2	576.1	674.7	819.4	
Brazil [a,b,c]		10.0	100.0	245.0	808.0	6,325.0	88.0	2,665.0	14,412.0	156,657.5
Chile	100.0	167.5	262.3	313.4	375.7	430.9	504.3	635.6	774.0	893.4
Colombia	100.0	190.2	273.9	325.7	403.7	525.6	525.1	835.7	1,089.8	1,384.5
Ecuador [d]	100.0	200.9	337.4	415.1	461.9	730.8	1,283.7	1,906.4	2,835.2	4,383.5
French Guiana [c]	100.0	145.4	170.4	174.1	181.2	185.3	192.7	199.8	204.4	209.5
Guyana	100.0	169.9	244.7	263.9	339.9	475.7				
Paraguay	100.0	138.0	207.9	273.9	333.8	410.6	517.0	714.6	888.2	
Peru [a,b]	3.0	18.0	100.0	178.0	331.0	2,536.0	89.0	6,727.0	34,274.0	59,476.0
Suriname	100.0	121.8	140.0	166.2	254.8	273.5	275.6	335.5	422.6	
Uruguay	100.0	238.0	636.5	1,122.7	1,836.4	2,978.4	5,374.0	11,422.0	23,069.0	38,862.1
Venezuela [a]	59.1	80.0	100.0	111.5	142.9	185.0	340.9	480.1	644.3	846.8
Caribbean										
Anguilla [a]			100.0	102.3	104.9	109.7	115.1	121.2		
Antigua	100.0	118.8	124.7	125.4	130.0	138.2	143.9	154.0	162.8	
Aruba [a]			100.0	101.1	104.8	108.0	112.2	118.9	125.5	130.4
Bahamas	100.0	122.6	133.2	142.8	148.4	155.3	163.7	171.4	183.8	194.1
Barbados	100.0	133.0	144.7	146.6	151.5	158.8	168.7	173.8	184.7	195.9
Bermuda [c]	100.0	127.9	139.2	144.9	151.2	158.9	167.5	177.5	185.3	190.1
British Virgin Islands	100.0	125.5	128.2	130.5	131.8					
Cayman Islands	100.0	126.0	133.0	136.5	142.2	150.0	159.1	171.3	185.1	190.5
Cuba										
Dominica	100.0	123.2	133.1	132.2	138.6	141.6	156.4	158.7	166.9	
Dominican Republic [c]	100.0	121.3	211.8	232.5	269.4	389.1	565.7	902.1	1,387.9	1,410.1
Grenada [c]	100.0	135.9	147.2	148.0	146.8	152.6	161.0	165.4	169.8	175.7
Guadeloupe [c]	100.0	139.0	160.9	165.4	170.3	173.7	177.8	183.0	188.4	194.1
Haiti	100.0	131.2	154.5	159.6	141.3	147.1	158.1	191.1	220.1	250.7
Jamaica [c]	100.0	134.0	215.3	247.8	264.3	283.9	322.1	399.0	602.8	982.9
Martinique [c]	100.0	143.4	167.2	172.8	179.1	183.4	188.8	196.1	202.4	209.6
Netherlands Antilles [c]	100.0	122.4	125.6	127.2	131.9	135.3	140.6	145.8	151.6	153.6
St Kitts [c]	100.0	120.2	125.7	125.7	127.0	127.2	134.2	139.8	145.7	150.0
St Lucia	100.0	122.2	125.3	128.1	137.0	138.2	144.2	150.4	159.3	168.2
St Vincent/Grenadines [a]	74.8	95.4	100.0	101.0	104.6	104.6	107.6	115.8	122.2	126.8
Trinidad and Tobago	100.0	146.8	179.0	195.4	216.4	233.2	259.8	288.5	299.6	319.0
Central America										
Belize	100.0	124.8	134.1	135.2	137.9	142.2	145.3	149.6	158.0	162.4
Costa Rica	100.0	345.6	445.1	497.8	581.7	702.8	818.8	974.7	1,254.6	1,527.9
El Salvador	100.0	145.3	198.2	261.6	326.6	391.1	460.1	570.5	652.7	726.0
Guatemala	100.0	116.9	143.4	196.3	220.5	244.5	272.3	384.5	512.1	547.8
Honduras	100.0	129.1	139.1	144.0	148.2	156.1	171.5	211.5	283.3	308.2
Mexico	100.0	410.2	1,071.2	1,994.9	4,624.7	9,907.1	11,888.0	15,054.6	18,470.0	21,335.0
Nicaragua [e]	100.0	202.6	877.0	7,432.0	69,347.0	100.0	4,870.2	369,420.0	10,499,800.0	
Panama	100.0	114.2	117.2	117.2	118.3	118.7	118.6	119.3	121.7	123.8
Puerto Rico	100.0	114.6	117.3	117.0	120.2	123.7	128.3	135.6	139.5	143.0
South Asia										
Afghanistan	100.0	107.7	126.6	122.5	146.5	175.6	307.5	436.4	683.6	
Bangladesh	100.0	143.0	163.3	182.4	212.8	232.6	256.1	276.7	296.4	309.2
Bhutan	100.0	136.5	153.7	169.1	179.8	197.8	215.2	236.9	264.8	
India	100.0	136.3	155.9	169.5	184.4	201.8	216.2	235.1	268.0	299.6
Nepal	100.0	139.5	155.0	184.5	204.3	222.7	241.8	264.4	305.5	358.0
Pakistan	100.0	125.8	141.9	147.1	154.3	167.9	181.0	196.8	209.7	229.7
Sri Lanka	100.0	149.0	176.3	190.4	205.1	233.8	260.9	317.0	355.6	396.1

CONSUMER PRICES

Trends in Consumer Prices 1980-1992

Units: 1980 = 100

	1980	1983	1985	1986	1987	1988	1989	1990	1991	1992
Japan										
Japan	100.0	109.9	114.6	115.3	115.4	116.2	118.7	122.4	126.4	128.5
ASEAN/NICs										
Brunei	100.0	117.4	123.9	126.1	127.7	129.2	130.9	133.7		
Hong Kong	100.0	140.1	154.7	159.2	168.7	180.2	198.5	217.8	243.3	266.0
Indonesia	100.0	137.4	158.9	168.2	183.8	198.6	211.3	227.1	248.0	266.6
Macau c			102.1	104.0	108.9	117.3	127.6	137.8	151.0	161.1
Malaysia	100.0	120.4	125.5	125.8	126.8	130.0	133.7	137.8	143.9	150.6
Philippines	100.0	137.1	253.8	255.7	265.4	288.7	319.3	359.8	415.3	452.5
Singapore	100.0	113.8	117.3	115.7	116.3	118.1	120.9	124.9	129.3	132.2
South Korea	100.0	134.5	141.0	145.0	148.8	159.9	169.1	183.6	201.4	213.2
Taiwan	100.0	121.4	121.2	122.0	122.6	124.2	129.7	135.0	139.9	146.1
Thailand	100.0	123.0	127.1	129.4	134.1	139.1	147.9	157.7	162.7	169.4
East/SE Asia										
Cambodia										
China	100.0	106.7	122.6	131.2	142.8	172.3	200.4	203.0	213.3	
Laos f	170.0	389.0	982.0		100.0	105.0	171.0	231.0	262.0	
Mongolia g	100.1	102.5	103.1	102.1	102.1	102.1	102.1	102.1		
Myanmar c	100.0	111.6	125.0	135.0	166.7	198.7	248.7	296.0	386.8	468.3
North Korea										
Vietnam			100.0	590.0	2,650.0	11,050.0	19,550.0	25,220.0	46,150.0	
Australasia										
Australia	100.0	134.3	149.0	162.4	176.3	189.0	203.3	218.1	225.1	227.3
New Zealand	100.0	143.9	176.3	199.5	230.9	245.6	259.6	275.6	282.8	285.5
Pacific										
American Samoa	100.0	100.8	103.7	105.0		115.3	120.3	129.6		
Fiji	100.0	127.0	139.6	145.7	150.2	167.9	177.4	192.8	205.4	215.5
French Polynesia	100.0	147.7	183.5	185.8	187.4	192.3	197.3	200.3	201.6	205.1
Guam	100.0	131.0	148.0	152.0	158.7	167.0	185.2	199.7	233.2	256.9
Kiribati	100.0	120.8	130.9	139.5	148.5	153.1	158.3	165.8		
Nauru										
New Caledonia	100.0	147.3	169.0	171.6	173.2	177.6	184.7	189.4	196.3	201.8
Papua New Guinea c	100.0	123.1	137.1	144.6	149.4	157.5	164.6	176.0	188.3	195.0
Solomon Islands	100.0	139.7	170.0	193.1	215.7	251.8	289.3	318.0	362.0	400.8
Tonga	100.0	139.8	167.4	203.9	213.2	234.7	244.4	267.6	296.0	319.5
Tuvalu	100.0	131.8	142.2	154.3		180.5	185.6	192.7		
Vanuatu	100.0	102.7	112.4	118.5	137.3	148.6	159.8	167.7	178.0	185.4
Western Samoa	100.0	166.0	202.6	214.2	224.1	243.0	256.5	298.2	294.1	319.2
Middle East										
Bahrain	100.0	124.8	121.9	119.1	117.2	118.4	119.7	120.2	121.2	120.8
Egypt	100.0	147.2	195.2	239.3	286.4	337.1	408.8	477.3	571.5	649.3
Iran	100.0	176.5	207.4	245.6	315.9	406.3	497.1	535.1	626.8	770.5
Iraq e	100.0	136.8	199.0	201.6	229.8	278.9	296.0	161.2	461.9	
Israel	100.0	1,174.0	22,498.0	33,330.0	39,937.0	46,447.0	55,833.0	65,418.0	77,838.0	87,144.0
Jordan	100.0	121.5	130.0	130.0	129.6	138.4	174.0	202.1	218.6	233.4
Kuwait h	100.0	121.2	124.4	125.6	126.4	128.3	132.6	135.0		
Lebanon										
Oman										
Qatar	100.0	117.9	121.4	123.4	126.6	132.4	136.8	140.9		
Saudi Arabia	100.0	101.5	99.1	96.0	94.4	95.3	95.7	95.7	102.5	102.4
Syria c	100.0	143.6	183.9	250.3	399.6	537.9	599.2	715.4	770.2	838.4
United Arab Emirates										
Yemen	100.0	125.9	134.2	135.5	139.2	139.2				

CONSUMER PRICES

Table No. 1501 (cont'd)

Trends in Consumer Prices 1980-1992

Units: 1980 = 100

	1980	1983	1985	1986	1987	1988	1989	1990	1991	1992
North Africa										
Algeria c	100.0	131.8	154.7	173.9	186.7	197.9	216.3	252.0	309.6	371.2
Chad	100.0	111.6	141.0	122.6	115.2	133.1	126.6	127.3		
Djibouti i	100.0	104.1	103.4	120.4	125.4	133.4				
Ethiopia	100.0	111.6	144.1	130.0	126.8	135.8	146.2	153.9	209.0	231.1
Libya										
Mali j					100.0	108.7	108.6	109.2	111.2	104.3
Mauritania c	100.0	135.4	164.6	177.4	191.3	193.7	218.9	233.2	246.4	262.1
Morocco	100.0	132.1	160.0	174.0	178.8	182.9	188.6	201.6	217.7	228.4
Niger k	100.0	133.8	143.7	139.1	129.7	127.9	124.3	123.3	96.1	94.5
Somalia	100.0	242.8	639.5	868.2	1,112.1	2,024.7				
Sudan c,e	100.0	204.5	398.8	516.1	649.9	965.2	1,603.7	385.0	790.1	1,461.5
Tunisia	100.0	134.9	158.0	167.1	179.1	190.5	204.5	218.4	236.5	249.3
West Africa										
Benin										
Burkina Faso	100.0	130.6	146.3	142.5	138.4	144.5	143.8	143.1	148.4	
Cameroon	100.0	146.3	165.0	177.7	188.4	204.6	204.6			
Cape Verde i		100.0	117.0	130.0	135.0	140.4	147.9	163.6	179.2	
Côte d'Ivoire	100.0	123.7	131.4	144.2	154.1	164.8	166.5	165.2	168.0	175.2
Equatorial Guinea			185.0	151.7	133.2	135.1	144.3	144.3	139.7	
Gabon	100.0	140.0	159.3	169.1	167.6	152.8	163.7	175.5	176.2	159.4
Gambia	100.0	130.1	188.0	294.3	363.6	406.2	439.7	493.2	535.8	586.7
Ghana	100.0	590.1	909.1	1,132.4	1,583.3	2,079.7	2,605.0	3,574.6	4,219.1	4,643.6
Guinea						100.0	127.3	163.3	194.2	233.1
Guinea-Bissau										
Liberia	100.0	117.2	117.9	122.1	129.4	141.8	150.2	162.4		
Nigeria c	100.0	160.3	236.1	248.8	274.2	379.2	534.1	693.4	783.6	904.4
Sao Tomé e Príncipe										
Senegal	100.0	138.7	175.2	186.5	178.4	175.2	176.0	176.4	173.4	173.4
Sierra Leone	100.0	263.8	776.0	1,403.5	3,951.6	5,189.1	8,446.8	17,818.5	36,115.0	59,770.6
Togo	100.0	145.5	137.8	143.5	143.6	143.9	142.2	143.6	144.3	
East/Central Africa										
Angola								100.0	183.6	693.1
Burundi	100.0	128.3	152.3	155.1	166.1	173.6	193.8	207.4	225.6	236.2
Central African Republic c	100.0	144.3	171.3	184.3	199.1	190.7	192.2	191.8	186.3	185.0
Comoros										
Congo	100.0	142.3	170.1	173.8	176.6	185.0	192.4	196.8	199.8	204.1
Kenya	100.0	150.2	187.0	194.3	204.4	221.4	243.1	271.7	311.9	403.9
Madagascar	100.0	205.3	249.3	285.5	329.6	416.4	454.0	507.5	551.0	631.1
Maldives										
Mauritius	100.0	134.7	154.3	156.8	157.7	172.0	193.8	220.0	235.4	246.2
Réunion	100.0	136.9	158.1	162.2	166.9	169.1	175.7	182.6	190.1	195.9
Rwanda	100.0	127.7	137.0	135.5	141.0	145.2	146.7	152.9	182.9	200.3
Seychelles	100.0	116.3	122.0	122.3	125.4	127.8	129.7	134.8	137.5	142.0
Tanzania	100.0	205.8	373.5	494.6	642.7	843.4	1,061.4	1,342.4	1,553.8	1,896.7
Uganda k		248.9	825.9	2,217.8	7,498.8	21,275.2	100.0	135.3	178.4	
Zaire	100.0	325.5	613.6	900.3	1,714.6	3,134.0	6,395.0	11,592.9	261,370.4	
Southern Africa										
Botswana	100.0	143.0	144.1	158.6	174.1	188.6	210.6	234.4	262.0	304.4
Lesotho	100.0	147.1	192.6	229.4	257.1	287.4	324.7	362.5	426.6	
Malawi	100.0	139.4	184.9	210.8	264.0	353.5	397.4	444.4	492.2	616.1
Mozambique	100.0	155.0	261.0		365.0	548.0	768.0	1,129.0	1,526.0	
Namibia										
South Africa	100.0	148.4	192.6	228.5	265.2	299.3	343.2	392.5	452.2	515.1
Swaziland	100.0	148.8	201.2	224.9	252.8	282.6	311.4	338.2	379.2	
Zambia c	100.0	153.4	253.0	383.6	548.6	853.5	1,918.1	4,239.0	8,163.3	21,400.7
Zimbabwe	100.0	154.1	200.9	229.7	258.3	277.5	313.3	367.6	457.0	668.3

Source: IMF/UN/national statistical offices/ILO

Notes: see end of section

CONSUMER PRICES

Trends in Food Prices 1980-1992

Units: 1980 = 100

	1980	1983	1985	1987	1988	1989	1990	1991	1992
North America									
Canada	100.0	123.8	134.5	147.4	151.3	156.9	163.4	171.2	170.6
USA	100.0	114.8	121.8	130.9	136.3	144.1	152.4	157.8	160.0
South America									
Argentina [a]		0.1	5.0	22.8	100.0	3,187.0	62,808.0	185,492.0	241,460.0
Bolivia [b]	100.0	1,220.0	1,968,800.0	8,176,200.0	9,111,700.0	10,419,300.0	12,372,800.0	15,045,600.0	16,451,000.0
Brazil [c]	100.0	955.0	5,000.0	35,100.0	264,600.0	3,823,300.0	103,994,000.0	510,110,000.0	
Chile	100.0	148.9	231.2	355.6	402.7	486.3	612.5	770.7	909.1
Colombia	100.0	194.5	295.6	447.2	592.9	736.0	936.1	1,215.8	1,576.5
Ecuador	100.0	231.6	414.6	591.8	972.5	1,827.8	2,696.5	4,007.2	6,172.2
French Guiana	100.0	142.6	167.6	177.5	180.3	187.7	195.3	196.7	200.0
Guyana	100.0	199.5	319.8	452.0					
Paraguay	100.0	133.9	220.1	391.2	484.2	582.9	853.4	1,025.5	
Peru [b,d]	100.0	609.0	3,126.0	9,600.0	61,100.0	1.4	100.0	448.2	730.2
Suriname	100.0	116.7	130.1	293.0	306.5	311.3	404.2	479.7	
Uruguay	100.0	216.0	595.0	1,821.4	2,876.8	5,194.0	11,456.0	21,245.0	33,996.0
Venezuela [e]	100.0	140.1	122.4	206.4	288.8	652.1	960.8	1,278.7	
Caribbean									
Anguilla [f]			100.0	104.4	110.3	121.1	127.5		
Antigua [g]		160.8	173.8	181.7	192.3	207.1	220.1	233.8	
Aruba [h]			99.8	110.1	118.2	127.7	138.5	145.3	
Bahamas	100.0	124.3	133.2	157.4	167.5	176.5	190.1	206.5	210.8
Barbados	100.0	126.6	138.4	148.3	157.9	172.3	179.2	187.8	188.2
Bermuda [b]	100.0	123.2	129.1	139.5	146.3	156.8	165.8	170.6	171.4
British Virgin Islands	100.0	121.0	126.9	128.1					
Cayman Islands [f]			100.0	104.2	106.2	111.4	120.6	124.6	123.8
Cuba									
Dominica	100.0	117.5	121.2	132.6	136.8	147.8	145.0	151.6	
Dominican Republic [i]	100.0	115.4	202.0	272.7	418.2	619.6	789.7		
Grenada [b,j]	100.0			100.0	105.1	113.9	118.4	120.6	121.1
Guadeloupe [b]	100.0	137.9	159.6	170.4	172.0	173.6	179.2	182.3	184.7
Haiti	100.0	126.8	150.3	125.9	134.0	144.4	177.3	203.2	223.9
Jamaica [b,k]	100.0	131.1	211.3	267.1	292.3	120.0	146.7	227.1	373.7
Martinique [b]	100.0	140.7	164.3	176.6	178.4	181.0	188.0	193.6	200.2
Netherlands Antilles [b]	100.0	121.9	123.6	131.8	141.9	151.4	163.0	174.7	178.9
St Kitts [b]	100.0	117.7	120.7	121.6	121.6	127.7	130.9	138.3	144.9
St Lucia [f]	100.0	123.1	100.0	115.0	113.8	119.1	123.9	133.9	140.6
St Vincent/Grenadines [l]			103.7	104.3	103.9	112.3	122.5	127.1	
Trinidad and Tobago	100.0	163.3	194.7	256.9	289.7	354.9	415.7	441.1	479.6
Central America									
Belize	100.0	118.9	122.9	125.3	125.9	134.9	137.8	146.2	150.3
Costa Rica [b]	100.0	386.0	471.5	605.0	727.3	857.5	1,013.9	1,277.1	1,576.7
El Salvador	100.0	147.6	200.3	331.1	428.4	543.7	684.4	806.7	909.6
Guatemala [h]	100.0	99.9	120.6	193.8	220.8	247.7	368.8	482.9	507.3
Honduras	100.0	120.6	122.9	127.1	137.7	154.8	195.9	281.6	299.2
Mexico	100.0	370.0	1,035.0	4,440.3	9,304.0	11,192.0	14,034.0	16,855.0	18,748.0
Nicaragua [a]	100.0	235.6	1,156.3	124,481.0	100.0	4,047.8	299,401.0	8,536,400.0	
Panama	100.0	118.3	120.4	124.0	124.3	122.6	123.2	129.4	134.0
Puerto Rico	100.0	113.3	116.7	120.6	125.0	131.4	142.5	149.1	157.0
South Asia									
Afghanistan	100.0	116.5	175.5	289.3	354.2	596.4	1,063.1	1,463.6	
Bangladesh	100.0	133.3	168.9	213.6	227.6	247.5	262.1	278.1	290.3
Bhutan									
India	100.0	138.9	154.2	184.7	198.8	214.7	234.3	272.3	307.9
Nepal [b]	100.0	141.9	153.7	210.0	224.1	249.8	267.9	316.7	347.2
Pakistan	100.0	129.0	146.4	165.9	185.1	201.2	206.1	226.7	251.2
Sri Lanka	100.0	149.0	176.2	205.2	236.1	260.4	321.1	359.2	402.1

CONSUMER PRICES — Table No. 1502 (cont'd)

Trends in Food Prices 1980-1992

Units: 1980 = 100

	1980	1983	1985	1987	1988	1989	1990	1991	1992
Japan									
Japan	100.0	109.4	114.4	113.7	114.4	116.9	121.7	127.5	128.2
ASEAN/NICs									
Brunei	100.0	123.6	128.8	130.7	132.9	134.5	138.3		
Hong Kong	100.0	141.1	151.2	160.3	175.7	197.6	217.2	241.7	262.9
Indonesia [b,j]	100.0	132.6	149.3	180.0	203.2	219.5	109.5	118.3	126.9
Macau [b,h]			100.3	105.8	115.4	127.1	138.3	148.1	188.0
Malaysia	100.0	121.7	123.1	121.8	126.4	131.1	136.6	143.0	152.6
Philippines	100.0	132.8	249.8	258.1	286.2	323.2	356.8	405.5	433.3
Singapore	100.0	115.4	115.7	113.9	115.4	117.1	118.1	119.8	121.4
South Korea	100.0	132.4	139.4	144.6	162.3	173.5	190.9	211.4	227.8
Taiwan [m]			86.0	89.1	90.4	96.0	99.2	100.0	108.7
Thailand	100.0	120.3	116.6	119.1	124.6	137.3	150.5	160.1	166.0
East/SE Asia									
Cambodia									
China	100.0	103.2	126.3	147.8	178.4	208.8	211.1	216.4	
Laos									
Mongolia [b]									
Myanmar [b]	100.0	108.1	120.5	157.0	201.0	251.6	300.0	412.5	501.6
North Korea									
Vietnam [n]			100.0	2,850.0	12,410.0	22,750.0	29,840.0	54,290.0	
Australasia									
Australia	100.0	129.5	145.1	166.8	180.0	195.8	204.2	211.1	214.0
New Zealand	100.0	136.4	165.7	209.3	241.6	241.6	259.1	261.4	261.6
Pacific									
American Samoa	100.0	99.8	100.9		111.0	116.3	124.3		
Fiji [b,n]	100.0	130.6	148.0	104.2	123.4	135.8	146.9	149.3	148.8
French Polynesia [b]	100.0	132.0	162.8	153.6	156.8	163.4	166.6	165.5	166.5
Guam [b]	100.0	142.0	164.9	195.8	216.5	239.2	282.7	334.1	379.7
Kiribati	100.0	114.7	125.1	142.2	148.1	152.4	156.9		
Nauru									
New Caledonia	100.0	153.5	175.8	172.6	178.4	186.4	186.8	192.7	197.9
Papua New Guinea [b]	100.0	119.7	133.2	139.8	145.3	150.9	165.3	178.2	182.8
Solomon Islands	100.0	143.8	175.8	211.6	255.6	300.3	325.6	380.2	423.8
Tonga [b]	100.0	152.4	170.9	222.7	253.4	250.1	254.3	269.5	302.2
Tuvalu	100.0	125.1	137.2		177.2	175.3	179.1		
Vanuatu [c]	74.9	98.6	98.1	125.3	133.8	147.9	154.6	158.8	160.3
Western Samoa	100.0	167.6	200.2	219.0	239.4	246.5	296.3	271.4	
Middle East									
Bahrain	100.0	99.5	100.3	95.7	94.7	95.5	95.6	97.6	97.7
Egypt	100.0	154.9	204.1	313.1	377.6	473.3	548.3	639.0	692.4
Iran	100.0	179.5	205.8		140.5	169.2	174.4	212.9	285.1
Iraq [b,o,p]		186.5	201.9	250.2	309.0	330.9	176.0	640.4	792.5
Israel	100.0	1,104.0	21,640.0	38,909.0	46,029.0	55,484.0	60,231.0	68,518.0	82,681.0
Jordan	100.0	116.1	121.0	119.5	127.6	154.2	185.7	206.3	211.8
Kuwait [i]	100.0	112.4	112.1	110.3	110.7	115.0	117.1		
Lebanon									
Oman			95.9	104.6	106.3	107.8	107.3		
Qatar [c]		110.2	115.8	118.4	120.9	126.0			
Saudi Arabia	100.0	108.1	105.3	100.0	100.0	102.2	103.6	113.7	117.8
Syria [b]	100.0	142.6	180.6	419.4	583.2	632.6	795.5	823.9	842.2
United Arab Emirates									
Yemen	100.0	118.8	120.4	125.5	125.1				

CONSUMER PRICES

Table No. 1502 (cont'd)

Trends in Food Prices 1980-1992

Units: 1980 = 100

	1980	1983	1985	1987	1988	1989	1990	1991	1992
North Africa									
Algeria [b]	100.0	101.9	123.3	155.2	161.1	175.7	208.2	249.0	291.4
Chad [q]		100.0	135.8	85.8	100.0	91.6	91.3		
Djibouti [h]	100.0	97.3	100.6	127.3	137.7				
Ethiopia [b]	100.0	111.6	155.3	123.6	133.4	142.1	149.5	211.2	218.9
Libya									
Mali [a]	100.0	126.1	152.9	125.9	100.0	96.9	98.4	101.8	92.0
Mauritania [r]		108.0							
Morocco [b]	100.0	136.1	165.5	182.3	183.1	186.8	200.3	217.3	226.0
Niger [s]	100.0	129.7	138.5	115.7	113.2	106.0	104.7	94.2	91.6
Somalia	100.0	211.6	511.3	823.8					
Sudan [b,k]	100.0	212.4		679.3	1,107.2	1,602.2	392.1	804.3	1,396.3
Tunisia [b]	100.0	133.4	159.8	180.2	194.4	210.8	225.4	244.6	254.5
West Africa									
Benin									
Burkina Faso [q]		100.0	113.2	92.7	103.3	99.0	97.6	108.5	97.3
Cameroon [i]	100.0	154.4	160.4	171.7	172.5	160.4	144.0		
Cape Verde [q]		100.0	110.0	132.0	134.7	146.9	165.7	184.9	
Côte d'Ivoire	100.0	114.4	122.0	156.1	175.2	176.7	174.5		
Equatorial Guinea									
Gabon	100.0		157.2	165.2	143.2	156.2	174.3	172.1	143.7
Gambia [b]	100.0	130.4	185.5	366.5	413.0	441.6	503.8	533.3	590.9
Ghana [b]	100.0	701.8	692.4	1,153.4	1,546.8	1,935.0	2,711.0	2,955.0	3,217.1
Guinea [b,j]				100.0	132.5	168.6	198.5	231.1	244.9
Guinea-Bissau [j]				100.0	160.3	289.9	385.5	607.6	
Liberia	100.0	111.5	109.3	108.0	128.8	141.2	160.7		
Nigeria [b,k]	100.0	169.2	251.3	273.1	413.6	578.0	158.3	177.1	202.7
Sao Tomé e Príncipe									
Senegal	100.0	135.3	164.6	161.9	160.8	162.1	163.0	157.9	156.3
Sierra Leone	100.0	268.0	736.0	3,625.2	4,859.0	8,069.0	17,231.0	30,323.8	
Togo	100.0	158.8	130.7	134.8	154.6	127.3	129.7	124.2	
East/Central Africa									
Angola								194.1	
Burundi	100.0	127.7	156.5	144.1	155.0	183.8	197.5	210.8	209.2
Central African Republic [b,c]		132.8	147.0	132.5	127.1	128.4	129.3	124.0	122.8
Comoros									
Congo	100.0	152.8	174.4	178.2	184.0	191.1	197.4	198.2	201.2
Kenya [d]	100.0	148.1	184.3	196.4	214.4	245.5	100.0	123.5	166.9
Madagascar	100.0	201.3	251.4	321.1	384.9	420.2	479.1	523.2	610.2
Maldives									
Mauritius [j]	100.0	107.2	125.3	100.0	111.7	127.3	141.1	147.0	
Réunion	100.0	134.5	152.3	158.3	154.2	160.0	162.8	170.3	174.1
Rwanda [c]		147.1	161.3	157.8	171.1	176.1	185.0	210.2	225.0
Seychelles [b]	100.0	115.0	120.2	124.6	125.9	128.2	135.4	138.5	142.0
Tanzania	100.0	208.6	371.6	654.0	881.4	1,094.9	1,209.4	1,481.7	1,798.1
Uganda [r,s]		138.5	539.7	3,660.3	10,875.0	100.0	120.8	146.5	236.5
Zaire	100.0								
Southern Africa									
Botswana [c]	100.0	156.3	152.1	184.2	199.9	218.6	244.2	273.2	324.2
Lesotho [p,t]	100.0	150.1	184.5	255.5	285.6	103.3	114.3	132.7	
Malawi	100.0	132.8	167.1	245.2	323.7	374.7	422.5	477.8	613.3
Mozambique	100.0	155.0	290.0						
Namibia									
South Africa [b]	100.0	151.7	188.4	278.5	322.0	357.7	414.9	496.3	611.1
Swaziland	100.0	152.2	196.6	253.6	286.2	315.4			
Zambia [b]	100.0	158.1	255.8	554.3	877.0	2,027.1	4,261.6	8,138.9	22,628.4
Zimbabwe [b]	100.0	159.1	212.3	276.0	300.2	343.0	406.3	509.0	732.0

Source: ILO
Notes: see end of section

COSTS OF GOODS AND SERVICES | Table No. 1503

Costs of Selected Food and Drink Items 1991

Units: Units of national currency

	Flour kg	Milk litre	Chicken fresh kg	Butter 250g	Pota-toes kg	Apples kg	Sugar kg	Instant coffee 250g	Tea 100g	Beer 0.33cl	Red table wine litre	Soft drink cola or orange 0.33cl
North America												
Canada	1.4	1.3	4.1	1.6	0.5		0.8	6.6	1.4			0.4
USA	0.5	0.7	1.9	1.1	0.6	1.9	0.9					0.3
South America												
Argentina	2,997.0	4,330.0	27,423.0	10,887.0	3,553.0	16,212.0	5,417.0	49,175.0	8,996.0	12,246.0	2,323.0	2,868.0
Bolivia [a]	1.6	1.2		4.4	1.7	4.1	1.8		2.4	6.3	1.1	
Brazil	235.7	295.4	737.7		200.1	1,224.5	259.4		223.9	1,168.7	151.2	
Chile	221.9	165.8	1,133.6	355.9	124.9	212.0	215.5	1,472.7	86.2	572.1	106.8	97.2
Colombia	295.0	237.4	1,236.2	771.0	182.6	1,169.6	255.9	1,570.0	528.0	1,220.0	143.0	168.3
Ecuador	897.5	350.0	2,166.4		273.4	1,194.8	449.1	3,648.9		1,226.5		
French Guiana	9.1	6.8	19.3	11.9	7.1	24.6	8.4		26.0	14.6	4.2	4.1
Guyana [b]	17.6		123.5	24.8	52.9		13.7			70.3		
Paraguay	763.0	724.0	1,790.0		380.0	2,346.0	561.0	5,023.0	2,981.0	1,196.0	417.0	187.0
Peru [c]	0.7	0.7	1.9	1.7	0.4	1.3	0.5	4.8	0.4	4.3	0.4	
Suriname [a]	3.1	0.5	10.4	6.4	2.3		6.7	51.6	10.8	55.0	1.9	0.9
Uruguay	760.3	750.0	5,118.4	2,855.3	1,018.8	1,700.5	1,704.8	13,235.3	6,800.0	1,983.9	729.5	712.5
Venezuela [a]	27.1	25.9	74.7	34.6	29.4	120.0	23.8				14.5	
Caribbean												
Anguilla	3.6	5.2	7.7	3.1	3.3	9.0	3.1	35.7		13.2	2.2	1.6
Antigua [a]	2.7	3.6	9.4	3.5	2.8	6.5	2.9	16.3	13.6	13.7	2.0	1.3
Aruba												
Bahamas	1.0	1.1	3.5	0.8	1.1	2.8	1.0	11.8	4.4	30.5	8.0	0.5
Barbados	1.4	3.1	6.4	2.3	1.7		2.0	15.4	3.3		1.3	0.6
Bermuda	0.9	1.7		1.0	1.4	2.5	0.9	7.0		6.7	3.2	0.6
British Virgin Islands												
Cayman Islands	0.6	0.9	2.2	1.0	1.2	3.3	0.9	4.8	1.9	10.7	2.4	1.1
Cuba [b]	0.2		1.5	1.3	0.3	2.8	0.3	12.5	0.7	9.3	0.6	0.2
Dominica	1.9		6.2	3.8			2.1	32.5			2.8	1.0
Dominican Republic												
Grenada												
Guadeloupe	6.5	6.2	18.0	12.5	6.3	19.3	8.3			13.4	4.5	2.9
Haiti	5.6	5.0	19.6	2.2			5.4	6.9				1.5
Jamaica	5.9	10.6	32.5		21.8			120.5	19.0			
Martinique [a]				12.1								
Netherlands Antilles [a]	2.2	2.0	7.0	1.8	1.5	5.0	1.4	11.4	4.1	18.5	1.7	0.5
St Kitts												
St Lucia	1.8	3.0	6.5	2.3	2.3	7.6	2.4	17.5		11.3	3.0	0.8
St Vincent/Grenadines [a]	1.3		9.2	3.3	2.9		2.4	37.7	3.6	13.7		
Trinidad and Tobago [a]	1.6	3.7	6.5	3.5	2.4		3.4	28.8	3.5	15.2	2.7	1.3
Central America												
Belize	2.6	1.7	4.1	0.9	1.7	4.5	0.8	10.5	9.6	9.3	2.2	0.8
Costa Rica		74.0	230.6	170.5	67.6		50.3				49.4	32.2
El Salvador		3.9	15.6		2.3		3.0	21.3			4.8	
Guatemala [a]		1.6	8.1		1.8	2.6	1.3	13.1			0.8	0.4
Honduras		2.4	9.4		2.7		1.9					
Mexico	1,390.0	1,525.0	6,750.0	2,570.0	3,675.0	6,000.0	1,830.0	8,313.0		11,907.0	1,218.0	372.0
Nicaragua [b]		2.8	10.8	9.9	2.3		3.2				2.9	
Panama		0.6	2.0	1.0	0.7	1.3	0.7		4.9		0.3	0.2
Puerto Rico												
South Asia												
Afghanistan		236.5		553.0	188.0	340.1	573.0		291.0			
Bangladesh [a]	10.8	21.1	67.1	40.0	7.6	52.9	30.5		8.9			
Bhutan												
India	5.2	6.5	29.1		3.8	13.9	6.2		6.5			
Nepal [a]	8.0	10.0	61.8		7.6	24.9	13.5	120.0	13.0		14.2	5.5
Pakistan	4.3	7.8	31.1	16.2	8.9	21.2	12.1	215.0	8.0			
Sri Lanka	12.3	12.5	85.0	36.3	28.7	166.7	25.1	495.6	14.8	394.0	24.0	5.2

COSTS OF GOODS AND SERVICES   Table No. 1503 (cont'd)

Costs of Selected Food and Drink Items 1991

Units: Units of national currency

	Flour kg	Milk litre	Chicken fresh kg	Butter 250g	Pota- toes kg	Apples kg	Sugar kg	Instant coffee 250g	Tea 100g	Beer 0.33cl	Red table wine litre	Soft drink cola or orange 0.33cl
Japan												
Japan	202.0	206.0		418.0	300.0	541.0	235.0	1,868.0	710.0	1,389.0	167.0	93.0
ASEAN/NICs												
Brunei												
Hong Kong	6.3	16.3	16.0	6.1	6.5	18.4	10.5	51.4	20.8	90.7	3.9	3.4
Indonesia	750.0		2,600.3		782.8	2,389.2	1,194.4		200.0		1,000.1	
Macau [a]	4.6	8.1	15.9	6.6	5.1	15.4	5.2	59.0	17.8	34.6	2.8	3.0
Malaysia	1.0	3.1	5.1	3.6	2.0	4.1	1.3	14.9	1.6		2.9	0.7
Philippines	25.9	26.9	69.2	27.0	15.8	55.0	18.0	86.7	30.4		6.2	4.4
Singapore	0.8	3.2	4.4	2.0	1.1	2.3	1.0	8.5	2.4		2.5	0.6
South Korea	336.0	1,165.0	2,254.0	1,593.0	1,189.0	1,636.0	688.0	3,082.0			481.0	228.0
Taiwan												
Thailand		24.0	39.8	26.1			13.0	140.8	37.3		24.0	5.7
East/SE Asia												
Cambodia												
China	0.7	1.4	8.2		0.9	5.4	3.4	7.7	3.2			
Laos												
Mongolia												
Myanmar	22.0	12.2	91.7	28.6	11.0	131.3	30.6	225.0	7.0	233.1	51.3	15.4
North Korea												
Vietnam												
Australasia												
Australia	1.4	1.0	4.1	0.9	0.8	2.7	0.9	7.5	0.7	8.3	1.3	0.8
New Zealand	1.2	1.2	5.2	0.9	0.9	2.6	1.3	8.0	0.9	12.2	2.2	0.4
Pacific												
American Samoa												
Fiji [b]	0.7		3.9	1.3	0.9	2.8	0.5	17.2	0.6		0.6	0.7
French Polynesia	94.0	150.0	867.0	86.0	140.0	331.0	55.0	565.0	452.0	357.0	147.0	78.0
Guam	1.0	1.2	1.8	1.9	1.5	2.3	1.1		2.8	0.9	0.5	0.4
Kiribati												
Nauru												
New Caledonia [a]	172.0		850.0	93.0	101.0	233.0	98.0	944.0	98.0	267.0	85.0	80.0
Papua New Guinea [a]	63.7		364.6	90.9	120.4		126.1		40.6		84.5	
Solomon Islands [a]				3.3			2.8	22.2	2.4			
Tonga [a]	0.7	1.2		1.1	1.6	3.2	1.5	15.3	1.8		1.4	0.6
Tuvalu												
Vanuatu												
Western Samoa												
Middle East												
Bahrain	0.3	0.6	0.9	0.4	0.3	0.6	0.2	3.6	0.3			0.1
Egypt	0.8	0.8	5.7	2.1	1.2	11.3	1.6		0.1			0.6
Iran	235.6	184.0	1,564.3	990.3	192.5	408.0	111.0		156.5			96.3
Iraq												
Israel	1.1	2.1	9.8	2.6	2.0	3.4	1.6	10.3	2.4		1.0	
Jordan	0.1	0.4	1.2	0.3	0.3	0.7	0.3		0.3			
Kuwait [b]	92.0		545.0	213.0	204.0	359.0	90.0	1,499.0	278.0			
Lebanon												
Oman												
Qatar [b]	2.0		11.0	3.7	3.8	5.8	2.8	21.3	6.3			
Saudi Arabia	1.9	3.7	5.3	3.6	3.4	4.5	2.7	25.5	6.5			1.1
Syria [a]	15.0	11.8	54.8	24.2	10.0	20.2	25.0		4.0	36.5		
United Arab Emirates	1.8	5.1	11.6	2.9	2.9	4.9	2.0	19.0	2.1			1.0
Yemen												

417

COSTS OF GOODS AND SERVICES — Table No. 1503 (cont'd)

Costs of Selected Food and Drink Items 1991

Units: Units of national currency

	Flour kg	Milk litre	Chicken fresh kg	Butter 250g	Pota- toes kg	Apples kg	Sugar kg	Instant coffee 250g	Tea 100g	Beer 0.33cl	Red table wine litre	Soft drink cola or orange 0.33cl
North Africa												
Algeria	6.0	2.0	68.0	21.0	11.0	30.0	6.0		80.0			4.6
Chad	900.0	350.0	1,900.0	850.0	1,125.0		500.0	6,300.0	175.0	1,100.0	360.0	220.0
Djibouti												
Ethiopia [a]	1.5	1.2	6.0	3.9	1.0		4.1				1.3	0.6
Libya												
Mali [a]	250.0	380.0	816.0		300.0	1,000.0	314.0	361.0	3,964.0		300.0	121.0
Mauritania												
Morocco [b]	3.4		12.8	5.9	5.5	9.7			6.4			
Niger	290.0	325.0	1,467.0	344.0	200.0	1,600.0	300.0	1,875.0		1,373.0	325.0	225.0
Somalia												
Sudan	30.0	32.0	56.7		35.0		13.8		22.1			
Tunisia	0.3	0.4	1.9	0.9	0.3	1.1	0.4	0.9	0.4	2.7	0.6	0.1
West Africa												
Benin	200.0	280.0	1,200.0	310.0	250.0	750.0	275.0	2,125.0	900.0	2,813.0	85.0	95.0
Burkina Faso		484.0					370.0	1,906.0			122.0	
Cameroon	410.0	370.0	1,490.0	380.0	250.0	975.0	413.0			640.0	180.0	100.0
Cape Verde	27.8	100.0	290.0	85.0	150.0		50.0	318.2	175.0	160.0	60.0	70.0
Côte d'Ivoire	185.0	255.0	1,300.0	413.0	1,000.0	980.0	300.0	300.0		986.0		110.0
Equatorial Guinea	229.0	875.0	758.0	771.0	667.0		450.0	400.0	2,250.0	450.0	250.0	225.0
Gabon	342.0		4,485.0	393.0	1,007.0	1,675.0	530.0		804.0	660.0	110.0	330.0
Gambia												
Ghana [b]			1,122.8				425.8	2,750.0	340.0		118.2	
Guinea	200.0	1,100.0	2,000.0	1,250.0	450.0	3,000.0	700.0	600.0	1,250.0	2,800.0	700.0	250.0
Guinea-Bissau [a]			5,591.0	1,458.3	3,000.0		5,326.0			5,000.0	1,239.8	
Liberia												
Nigeria			31.7				12.4	74.6	14.4		3.0	1.7
Sao Tomé e Príncipe												
Senegal	275.0	340.0	1,495.0		228.0	738.0	340.0	1,938.0	615.0	700.0	170.0	125.0
Sierra Leone												
Togo [a]	559.0	278.0	637.0	373.0	326.0	965.0	285.0	465.0	642.0	441.0	120.0	
East/Central Africa												
Angola												
Burundi	150.0	120.0	700.0	855.0	58.0				40.0	1,066.7	55.0	38.5
Central African Republic	315.0	1,016.9	1,900.0	875.0	1,500.0	3,200.0	450.0			5,146.7	140.0	2,574.0
Comoros												
Congo												
Kenya [a]	8.7	7.8	68.5	11.5	5.6	135.8	12.4	162.0	5.4		8.8	4.3
Madagascar												
Maldives												
Mauritius	2.8	8.0	31.4	12.2	5.0	28.1	3.1	132.0	7.0	36.0	5.4	2.3
Réunion	8.1	5.8	24.7	9.2	9.9	14.1	8.1	13.3		11.1	3.3	
Rwanda	110.0	130.0	550.0	217.0	16.0	1,300.0	160.0	137.0	31.0	1,467.0	46.0	30.0
Seychelles	4.7	1.8	22.5	1.8	8.7	21.6	6.0	9.9	9.7	47.2	6.5	2.2
Tanzania	155.3	150.3		250.0	48.0		213.1	1,008.3			177.5	64.9
Uganda												
Zaire												
Southern Africa												
Botswana	1.3	1.6	6.9	2.9	1.7	2.9	1.3	3.4	1.6		1.2	0.9
Lesotho [a]	1.5	1.3	6.8	3.5	1.5	3.4	1.7	4.1	6.2	6.7	1.5	1.1
Malawi	3.5	1.4	7.3	4.3	1.0	2.5	1.1	12.4	0.8	19.5	1.2	0.7
Mozambique	900.0		6,500.0	1,800.0	800.0	2,000.0	1,400.0	8,750.0		6,500.0	457.0	
Namibia												
South Africa [a]	1.7	1.8	5.7	1.8	1.4	2.6	1.8	3.5	2.2	5.9	1.1	0.7
Swaziland												
Zambia	104.1	71.5	245.4	122.8	50.5		61.4	311.8	32.5		38.8	38.7
Zimbabwe	1.7	1.2	6.3	1.2	1.4	5.5	1.1	8.4	1.1		1.0	0.6

Source: ILO/Executive Living Costs

Notes: see end of section

Notes to Section Fifteen

Table 1501   a 1985=100
                 b New series from 1989; 1985=0.1
                 c Data for 1992 are estimated
                 d 1981=100
                 e New series from 1988
                 f   June 1979=100; Dec 1987=100
                 g 1978=100
                 h Data for 1990 are estimated
                 i   New series from 1984; 1984=100
                 j   1987=100
                 k New series from 1989; 1989=100
                 l   1983=100

Table 1502   a 1988=100
                 b Data for 1992 are estimated
                 c 1981=100
                 d New series from 1990
                 e 1985 onwards based on 1984=100
                 f   1984 onwards based on 1985=100
                 g 1978=100
                 h 1984=100
                 i   Data for 1990 are estimated
                 j   1987=100
                 k New series from 1988 based on 1988=100
                 l   1987 onwards based on 1986=100
                 m 1990 onwards based on 1989=100
                 n 1991=1001
                 o 1986 onwards based on 1985=100
                 p 1979=100
                 q Rebased during 1989
                 r   1983=100
                 s 1982=100
                 t   Data for 1991 are estimated

Table 1503   a Data refer to 1990
                 b Data refer to 1988
                 c New Soles (equivalent to one million intis)

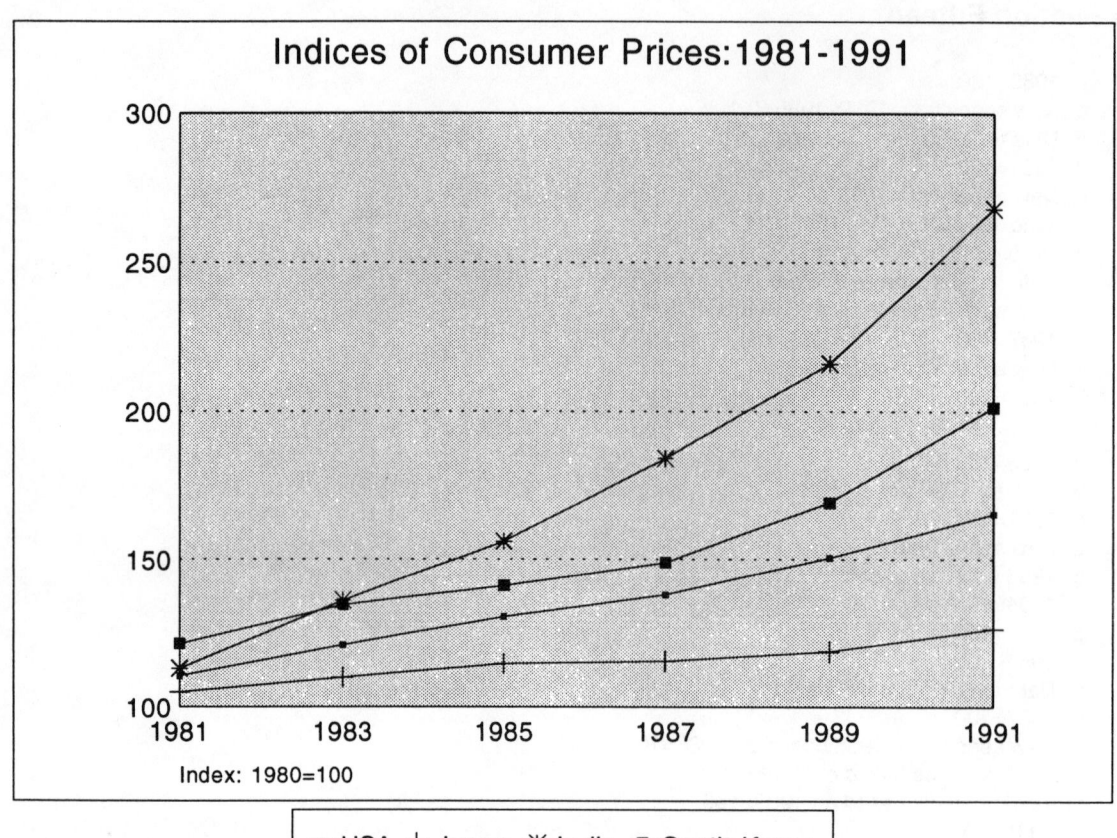

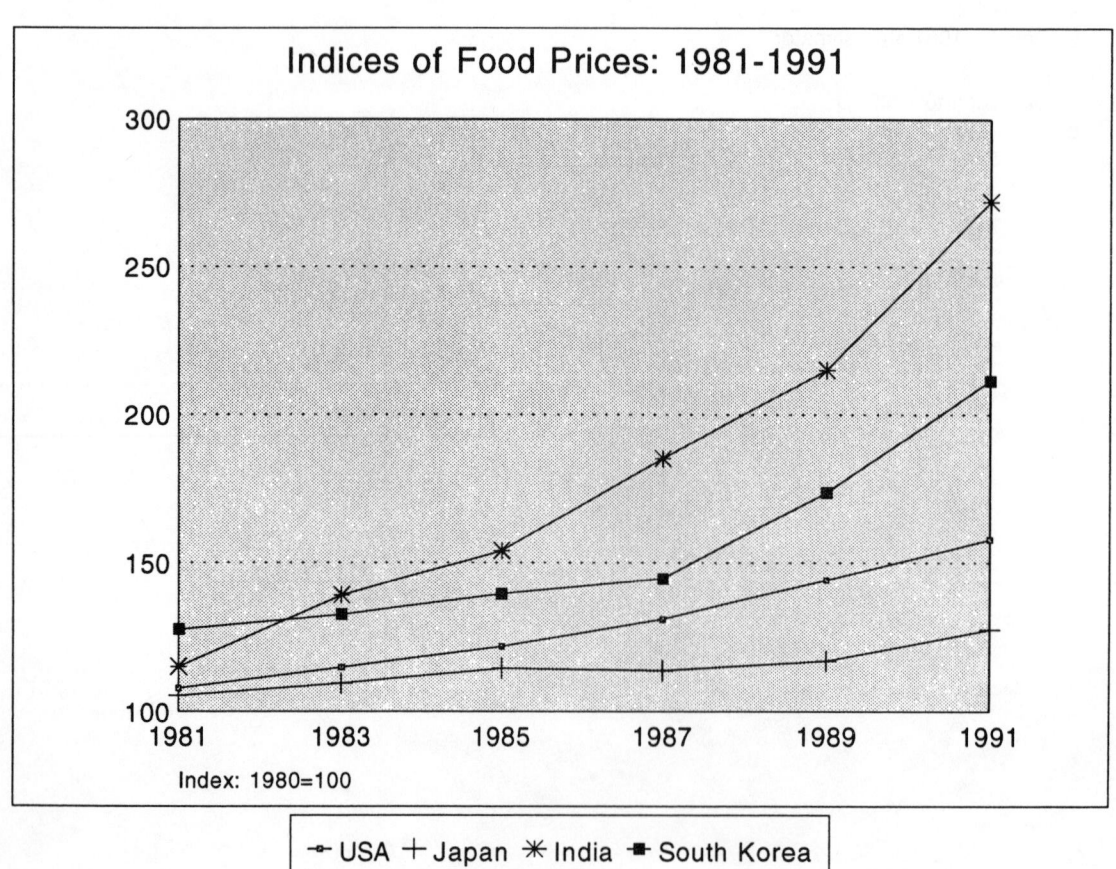

Section Sixteen
Housing and Household Facilities

HOUSING STOCK

Table No. 1601

Total Housing Stock 1977-1992

Units: '000

	1977	1980	1983	1984	1985	1986	1987	1988	1989	1990	1991	1992
Argentina	7,623	8,310	8,533	8,670	8,820	8,890	8,910	9,000	8,890	9,000	9,110	9,221
Australia	3,930	5,066	5,557	5,610	5,690	5,731	5,826	5,914	6,042	6,162	6,250	6,339
Brazil	21,453	25,211	29,656	30,340	31,056	31,100	31,263	31,305	31,650	31,900	32,300	32,705
Canada	7,278	8,063	8,565	8,780	8,906	8,992	9,010	9,244	9,456	9,619	9,632	9,645
Chile											3,261	
China	180,000	205,000	240,000	242,000	260,100	267,000	271,330	274,400	274,800	275,100	275,800	276,502
Colombia	5,258	5,397	5,555	5,710	5,898	6,005	6,150	6,300	6,400	6,500	6,700	6,906
Ecuador												
Hong Kong	979	1,195	1,366	1,280	1,348	1,410	1,493	1,562	1,629	1,710	1,759	1,826
India	106,790	110,100	113,600	114,500	115,100	116,500	117,110	118,130	118,200	119,000	119,870	120,746
Indonesia	29,978	36,700	39,890	40,255	40,920	41,222	42,555	43,500	43,800	43,950	44,400	44,855
Israel	1,030	1,150	1,270	1,300	1,323	1,331	1,352	1,371	1,393	1,410	1,448	1,488
Japan	33,825	36,007	38,607	39,300	40,125	40,400	42,074	43,758	45,549	46,796	47,200	47,607
Malaysia	2,460	2,540	2,700	2,810	2,850	2,904	3,020	3,100	3,150	3,200	3,300	3,403
Mexico	11,896	12,216	13,353	13,888	14,197	14,423	14,822	15,010	15,020	15,040	15,070	15,100
New Zealand	1,018	1,101	1,139	1,190	1,250	1,290	1,310	1,330	1,353	1,370	1,293	1,220
Nigeria	16,567	20,134	23,000	23,155	24,100	24,666	25,050	25,300	25,350	25,420	25,540	25,661
Pakistan												
Peru					4,906							
Philippines	7,389	8,501	9,322	9,651	9,872	10,023	10,123	10,400	10,250	10,450	10,500	10,550
Singapore	297	373	430	506	552	585	618	651	671	686	721	758
South Africa	5,250	6,258	7,100	7,729	8,100	8,300	8,422	8,577	8,577	8,596	8,615	8,633
South Korea	2,890	5,463	5,820	5,999	6,104	6,423	6,672	6,992	7,000	7,270	7,570	7,882
Taiwan	2,997	3,677	4,105	4,432	4,500	4,727	4,822	4,911	4,911	5,088	4,911	4,740
Thailand	6,399	8,311	8,827	9,010	9,016	9,410	9,947	10,417	10,600	10,950	11,050	11,151
USA	87,006	87,550	95,833	97,555	99,931	102,400	105,453	108,506	111,559	112,626	113,539	114,459
Venezuela	2,510	2,650	2,800	2,860	3,050	3,103	3,220	3,303	3,310	3,330	3,357	3,384
Vietnam												

Source: National statistical offices/Euromonitor

HOUSING STOCK

Table No. 1602

New Dwellings Completed 1977-1992

Units: '000 units

	1977	1980	1983	1984	1985	1986	1987	1988	1989	1990	1991	1992
Argentina [a]	54	33						135				
Australia	45	79	98	118	112	141	121	135	159	160	134	132
Brazil	106	148	192	145	136	200	163	130	120	110		
Canada	254	176	163	153	139	185	218	216	216	184	152	166
Chile					61	61	60	77	84	79	88	106
China [b]					911	797	775	697	400	400		
Colombia	43	40	47	47	49	41	51	50				
Ecuador												
Hong Kong	35	57	59	62	69	66	25	32	46	33	26	11
India [a,c]	75	98	121	111		134	149					
Indonesia [d]	12	26	51	40	61	182	187	195	203	210		
Israel			31	27	20	19	20	17	17	17		
Japan	1,702	1,483	1,137	1,187	1,236	1,364	1,674	1,685	1,663	1,708	1,370	1,403
Malaysia				11	12	14						
Mexico												
New Zealand	24	14	18	20	22	23	20	20	20	23	21	18
Nigeria		25										
Pakistan												
Peru												
Philippines	23	22	33	28	26	28						
Singapore	36	24	19	78	60	39	33	33	20	32	14	22
South Africa [e]	22	24	16	13	20	31	27	25	25	36	32	
South Korea	118	77	89	66	61	63	69	89	99	123	91	69
Taiwan												
Thailand												
USA [a]	1,602	1,137	1,390	1,652	1,703	1,756	1,669	1,530	1,423	1,308	1,091	1,157
Venezuela		83			45			126	110	38		
Vietnam												

Source: National statistical offices/OECD

Notes: see end of section

HOUSING STOCK

Dwellings by Number of Rooms: Latest Year

Units: % of total dwellings

	Year	1 Room	2 Rooms	3 Rooms	4 Rooms	5+ Rooms	Total
Argentina							
Australia [a]	1988	5.7	24.4	52.2	15.2	2.5	100.0
Brazil	1986	3.0	7.9	13.5	18.7	56.9	100.0
Canada	1990	0.8	2.2	9.5	15.6	71.9	100.0
Chile							
China							
Colombia							
Ecuador	1982	22.9	33.6	17.9	12.2	13.3	100.0
Hong Kong							
India	1971	49.0	25.0	11.0	9.0	6.0	100.0
Indonesia	1986	37.5	41.1	16.8	3.5	1.1	100.0
Israel [b]	1990	2.5	15.1	43.7	21.0	17.7	100.0
Japan	1988	4.9	10.1	15.4	18.7	49.7	100.0
Malaysia							
Mexico	1990	10.5	23.5	23.2	18.7	24.1	100.0
New Zealand							
Nigeria							
Pakistan							
Peru							
Philippines							
Singapore	1988	8.0	7.4	40.3	29.4	14.9	100.0
South Africa							
South Korea							
Taiwan							
Thailand							
USA [c]	1987	1.0	1.6	10.4	21.1	65.9	100.0
Venezuela [a]	1989	14.6	25.8	39.2	14.8	5.6	100.0
Vietnam							

Source: National statistical offices
Notes: see end of section

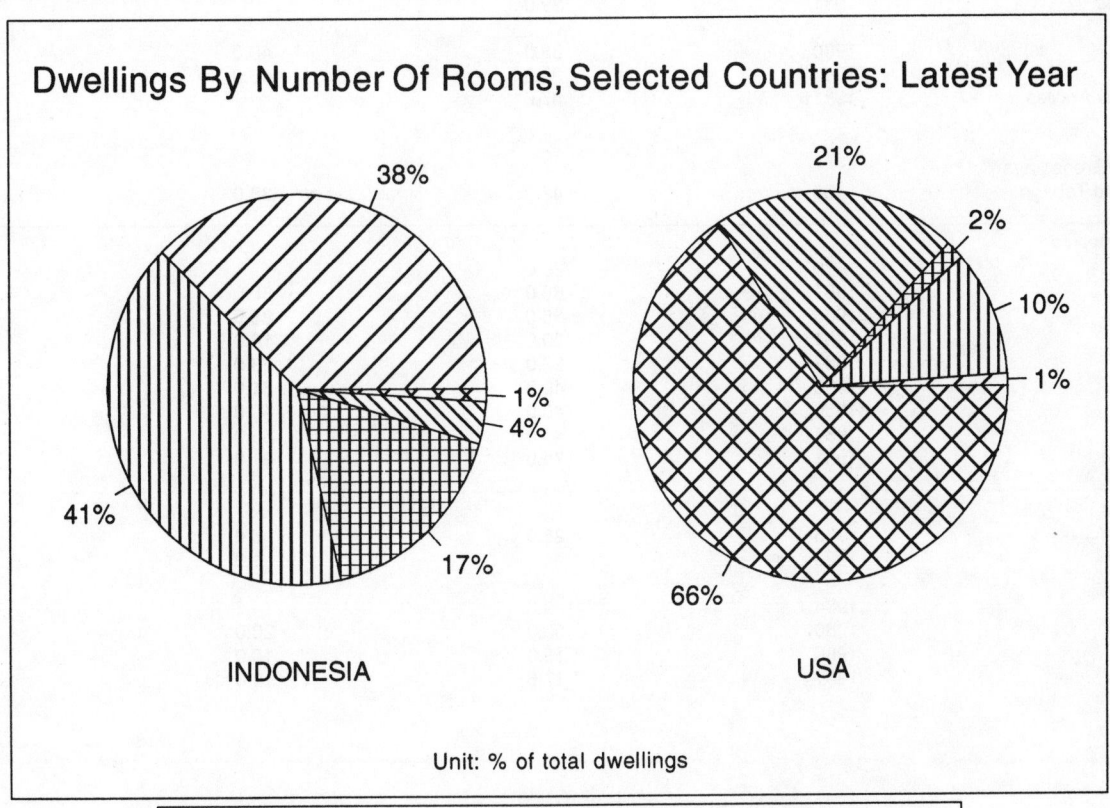

Dwellings By Number Of Rooms, Selected Countries: Latest Year

38%
1%
4%
41%
17%
INDONESIA

21%
2%
10%
1%
66%
USA

Unit: % of total dwellings

⊘1 Room ⊞2 Rooms ⊞3 Rooms ⊠4 Rooms ⊠5+ Rooms

HOUSING STOCK

Table No. 1604

Housing Amenities: Latest Year

Units: % of total households

	Year	Piped Water	Flush Toilet	Electric Lighting
North America				
Canada	1988	99.7	99.2	
USA	1985	99.0	99.0	99.0
South America				
Argentina	1985	75.0	73.0	85.0
Bolivia	1981	35.0	25.0	44.0
Brazil	1990	73.4		
Chile	1981	70.0	59.0	88.0
Colombia	1985	54.0	54.0	60.0
Ecuador	1982	51.8	32.7	62.1
French Guiana				
Guyana				
Paraguay	1981	24.0	80.0	44.0
Peru	1985	48.9	43.0	48.0
Suriname	1980	28.0		51.0
Uruguay	1985	72.0	69.0	93.0
Venezuela	1985	38.0	39.0	89.0
Caribbean				
Anguilla				
Antigua				
Aruba				
Bahamas	1981	60.0		75.0
Barbados				
Bermuda				
British Virgin Islands				
Cayman Islands				
Cuba	1983	59.0	50.0	83.0
Dominica				
Dominican Republic	1981	30.0	28.0	44.0
Grenada				
Guadeloupe	1981	29.0		48.0
Haiti				
Jamaica	1980	35.0	48.0	
Martinique	1981	35.0	48.0	
Netherlands Antilles	1981	87.0		94.0
St Kitts				
St Lucia				
St Vincent/Grenadines				
Trinidad and Tobago	1983	42.0	38.0	84.0
Central America				
Belize	1980	28.0		65.0
Costa Rica	1981	88.0	60.0	73.0
El Salvador	1983	35.0	28.0	39.0
Guatemala	1981	30.0	18.0	40.0
Honduras	1981	26.0	23.0	38.0
Mexico	1990	49.9	51.0	87.5
Nicaragua	1980	45.0	40.0	53.0
Panama	1981	40.0	38.0	65.0
Puerto Rico	1981	75.0	61.0	93.0
South Asia				
Afghanistan	1975	25.0	5.0	67.0
Bangladesh	1983		1.6	6.6
Bhutan				
India	1984	9.8	4.6	16.4
Nepal	1980	66.0	20.0	54.0
Pakistan	1980	15.0	16.0	33.0
Sri Lanka	1981	17.6	10.0	14.9

HOUSING STOCK

Table No. 1604 (cont'd)

Housing Amenities: Latest Year

Units: % of total households

	Year	Piped Water	Flush Toilet	Electric Lighting
Japan				
Japan	1988		65.0	
ASEAN/NICs				
Brunei				
Hong Kong [a]	1986	99.0	80.0	93.0
Indonesia [b]	1989	12.9	17.5	43.8
Macau	1985	51.2	18.4	
Malaysia	1985	96.0		99.0
Philippines	1985	47.5	25.8	64.4
Singapore	1985	48.0	41.9	37.4
South Korea	1980	95.0	86.0	98.3
Taiwan [a]	1981	42.0	18.0	68.0
Thailand [b]	1990	29.6	20.0	89.3
East/SE Asia				
Cambodia				
China [c]	1991	90.6		
Laos				
Mongolia				
Myanmar	1981	13.0	19.0	28.0
North Korea				
Vietnam [b]	1990	34.0	22.0	47.0
Australasia				
Australia	1983	53.5	76.0	94.9
New Zealand	1991	99.0	99.0	99.0
Pacific				
American Samoa				
Fiji				
French Polynesia	1982	90.0		75.0
Guam				
Kiribati				
Nauru				
New Caledonia				
Papua New Guinea				
Solomon Islands				
Tonga				
Tuvalu				
Vanuatu				
Western Samoa				
Middle East				
Bahrain	1985	94.0	79.0	98.0
Egypt	1983	60.0	33.0	65.0
Iran	1979	49.0	47.0	69.0
Iraq	1983	40.0	29.0	38.0
Israel	1986	94.0	58.2	99.0
Jordan	1983	34.0	32.0	51.0
Kuwait	1985	58.0	40.0	57.0
Lebanon				
Oman				
Qatar				
Saudi Arabia	1983	47.0	26.0	61.0
Syria	1985	53.0	25.0	49.0
United Arab Emirates	1980	54.0		
Yemen				

HOUSING STOCK

Table No. 1604 (cont'd)

Housing Amenities: Latest Year

Units: % of total households

	Year	Piped Water	Flush Toilet	Electric Lighting
North Africa				
Algeria	1982	35.0	20.0	47.0
Chad				
Djibouti				
Ethiopia	1981	85.0		62.0
Libya				
Mali				
Mauritania				
Morocco	1981	72.0	24.0	85.0
Niger	1981	17.0	13.0	86.0
Somalia				
Sudan	1981	65.0		30.0
Tunisia	1981	33.0	19.0	50.0
West Africa				
Benin				
Burkina Faso	1981	24.0		
Cameroon	1983	30.0	12.0	45.0
Cape Verde				
Côte d'Ivoire				
Equatorial Guinea				
Gabon				
Gambia				
Ghana				
Guinea				
Guinea-Bissau				
Liberia				
Nigeria	1980	17.0	13.0	86.0
Sao Tomé e Príncipe				
Senegal	1981	88.0		96.0
Sierra Leone	1981	40.0	15.0	40.0
Togo				
East/Central Africa				
Angola	1982	35.0	20.0	47.0
Burundi				
Central African Republic				
Comoros				
Congo				
Kenya	1983	32.0	17.0	53.0
Madagascar				
Maldives				
Mauritius	1981	33.0		
Réunion	1983	33.0		34.0
Rwanda				
Seychelles				
Tanzania				
Uganda				
Zaire	1981	43.0	22.0	55.0
Southern Africa				
Botswana	1984	99.0	39.0	27.0
Lesotho				
Malawi	1982	26.0		25.0
Mozambique				
Namibia				
South Africa	1983	90.0	35.0	90.0
Swaziland				
Zambia	1983	63.0	31.0	77.0
Zimbabwe	1983	80.0	26.0	89.0

Source: National statistical offices/UN
Notes: see end of section

HOUSEHOLD CHARACTERISTICS — Table No. 1605

Number of Households 1977-1992

Units: '000

	1977	1980	1983	1984	1985	1986	1987	1988	1989	1990	1991	1992
Argentina	6,987	7,078	7,013	7,082	7,107	7,126	7,146	7,165	7,169	7,254	7,350	7,450
Australia	4,087	4,455	4,783	4,832	4,907	4,969	5,031	5,316	5,426	5,500	5,578	5,657
Brazil	26,588	27,967	29,248	29,594	30,354	31,110	31,875	32,635	33,395	34,155	34,914	35,690
Canada	7,052	7,608	8,063	8,366	8,650	8,992	9,123	9,244	9,310	9,700	9,700	9,700
Chile	2,739	2,800	2,770	2,805	2,823	2,839	2,856	2,874	2,887	2,933	2,983	3,034
China	176,792	191,765	224,223	233,787	241,336	249,270	253,444	257,618	272,000	276,912	277,390	277,869
Colombia	5,505	5,884	5,304	5,345	5,300	5,319	5,338	5,356	5,377	5,425	5,591	5,763
Ecuador	2,358	2,389	2,367	2,390	2,399	2,405	2,412	2,418	2,419	2,680	2,521	2,371
Hong Kong	1,062	1,200	1,329	1,371	1,412	1,453	1,479	1,505	1,530	1,556	1,582	1,608
India	121,622	130,255	145,500	149,000	150,000	152,000	155,233	158,466	162,300	170,182	171,426	172,680
Indonesia	31,724	30,372	33,222	34,172	35,121	36,071	37,021	37,971	38,921	39,695	39,856	40,018
Israel	941	1,026	1,107	1,133	1,152	1,131	1,149	1,165	1,190	1,228	1,261	1,295
Japan	33,000	34,824	36,504	37,338	37,226	37,544	38,064	39,028	39,417	40,273	40,506	40,740
Malaysia	2,540	2,796	2,960	2,980	3,112	3,200	3,288	3,376	3,458	3,571	3,683	3,798
Mexico	11,043	12,074	13,262	13,658	14,054	14,450	14,846	15,242	15,638	16,035	16,067	16,100
New Zealand	967	997	1,026	1,040	1,048	1,089	1,107	1,125	1,142	1,160	1,178	1,196
Nigeria	11,833	13,890	15,482	16,007	16,557	17,163	17,769	18,376	18,997	19,578	19,671	19,765
Pakistan	14,661	15,677	16,270	16,304	16,337	16,370	16,400	16,438	16,470	17,465	17,800	18,141
Peru	4,152	4,247	4,339	4,416	4,472	4,523	4,575	4,625	4,664	4,758	4,859	4,962
Philippines	8,273	9,117	9,700	9,800	9,847	10,310	10,789	11,248	11,512	12,000	12,058	12,116
Singapore	414	510	568	573	595	612	628	645	652	699	734	771
South Africa	5,824	6,488	7,346	7,590	8,000	8,500	9,000	9,500	9,705	9,885	9,906	9,927
South Korea	6,992	7,981	8,453	9,022	9,582	10,193	10,804	11,357	11,526	11,984	12,479	12,994
Taiwan	3,340	3,872	4,144	4,247	4,361	4,489	4,645	4,808	4,954	5,093	5,217	5,345
Thailand	8,200	8,431	9,300	9,730	10,152	10,578	11,000	11,430	11,854	12,279	12,391	12,504
USA	74,142	80,776	83,918	85,407	86,789	88,458	89,479	91,061	92,830	94,771	95,539	96,313
Venezuela	2,518	2,834	3,079	3,161	3,243	3,325	3,407	3,488	3,570	3,652	3,734	3,818
Vietnam									12,958			

Source: National statistical offices/Euromonitor

HOUSEHOLD CHARACTERISTICS — Table No. 1606

Average Number of Occupants per Household 1977-1992

Units: Persons

	1977	1980	1983	1984	1985	1986	1987	1988	1989	1990	1991	1992
Argentina	3.85	3.99	4.21	4.22	4.27	4.31	4.36	4.40	4.45	4.46	4.45	4.44
Australia	3.47	3.30	3.22	3.22	3.22	3.22	3.23	3.11	3.10	3.11	3.11	3.10
Brazil	4.15	4.34	4.44	4.48	4.47	4.45	4.44	4.43	4.41	4.40	4.39	4.38
Canada	3.30	3.16	3.09	3.00	2.93	2.85	2.81	2.80	2.82	2.74	2.79	2.83
Chile	3.85	3.98	4.23	4.25	4.29	4.34	4.39	4.44	4.49	4.49	4.49	
China	5.42	5.19	4.64	4.51	4.44	4.36	4.35	4.35	4.18	4.17	4.22	4.28
Colombia	4.44	4.40	5.18	5.25	5.40	5.49	5.57	5.65	6.02	6.08	6.01	5.93
Ecuador	3.16	3.40	3.74	3.81	3.91	4.01	4.11	4.22	4.34	4.02	4.30	4.69
Hong Kong	4.25	4.22	4.03	3.94	3.87	3.81	3.76	3.77	3.76	3.73	3.63	3.61
India	5.15	5.18	4.95	4.94	5.01	5.04	5.03	5.03	5.00	4.86	4.96	5.09
Indonesia	4.31	4.86	4.76	4.73	4.67	4.67	4.65	4.62	4.60	4.52	4.71	4.78
Israel	3.84	3.78	3.71	3.67	3.67	3.80	3.80	3.81	3.79	3.80	3.93	4.01
Japan	3.45	3.35	3.27	3.21	3.25	3.24	3.21	3.14	3.12	3.07	3.06	3.03
Malaysia	4.95	4.90	5.01	5.10	5.04	5.03	5.03	5.02	5.02	4.97	4.98	4.95
Mexico	5.78	5.75	5.63	5.59	5.55	5.51	5.47	5.43	5.40	5.37	5.47	5.56
New Zealand	3.23	3.12	3.12	3.11	3.10	2.98	2.96	2.92	2.90	2.89	2.87	2.85
Nigeria	6.13	5.80	5.75	5.83	5.78	5.72	5.71	5.71	5.53	5.54	5.70	5.85
Pakistan	5.15	5.27	5.56	5.72	5.89	6.06	6.23	6.41	6.60	6.41	6.49	6.57
Peru	3.85	4.07	4.28	4.30	4.34	4.39	4.43	4.47	4.53	4.53	4.53	4.53
Philippines	5.39	5.30	5.37	5.44	5.55	5.43	5.32	5.22	5.22	5.12	5.21	5.30
Singapore	5.62	4.73	4.40	4.42	4.30	4.23	4.15	4.11	4.11	3.88	3.76	3.64
South Africa	4.58	4.41	4.35	4.32	4.20	4.05	3.92	3.81	3.82	3.84	3.92	4.01
South Korea	5.21	4.78	4.72	4.49	4.29	4.08	3.87	3.70	3.68	3.58	3.47	3.36
Taiwan	5.03	4.60	4.51	4.48	4.42	4.34	4.24	4.14				
Thailand	5.37	5.54	5.35	5.21	5.09	4.98	4.87	4.77	4.66	4.57	4.59	4.62
USA	2.97	2.82	2.79	2.77	2.75	2.72	2.71	2.69	2.66	2.64	2.64	
Venezuela	5.40	5.30	5.32	5.33	5.34	5.35	5.36	5.38	5.39	5.40	5.42	5.43
Vietnam									5.04			

Source: National statistical offices/Euromonitor

Notes to Tables in Section Sixteen

Table 1602   a   Construction permits
               b   All residential buildings
               c   Major towns only
               d   Public sector construction
                     to 1985; private sector only from 1986
               e   Private sector construction only
               f   Number of dwellings authorised and started

Table 1603   a   By number of bedrooms
               b   New dwellings only
               c   State-owned housing only

Table 1604   a   New dwellings only
               b   Public sector only
               c   Urban areas only

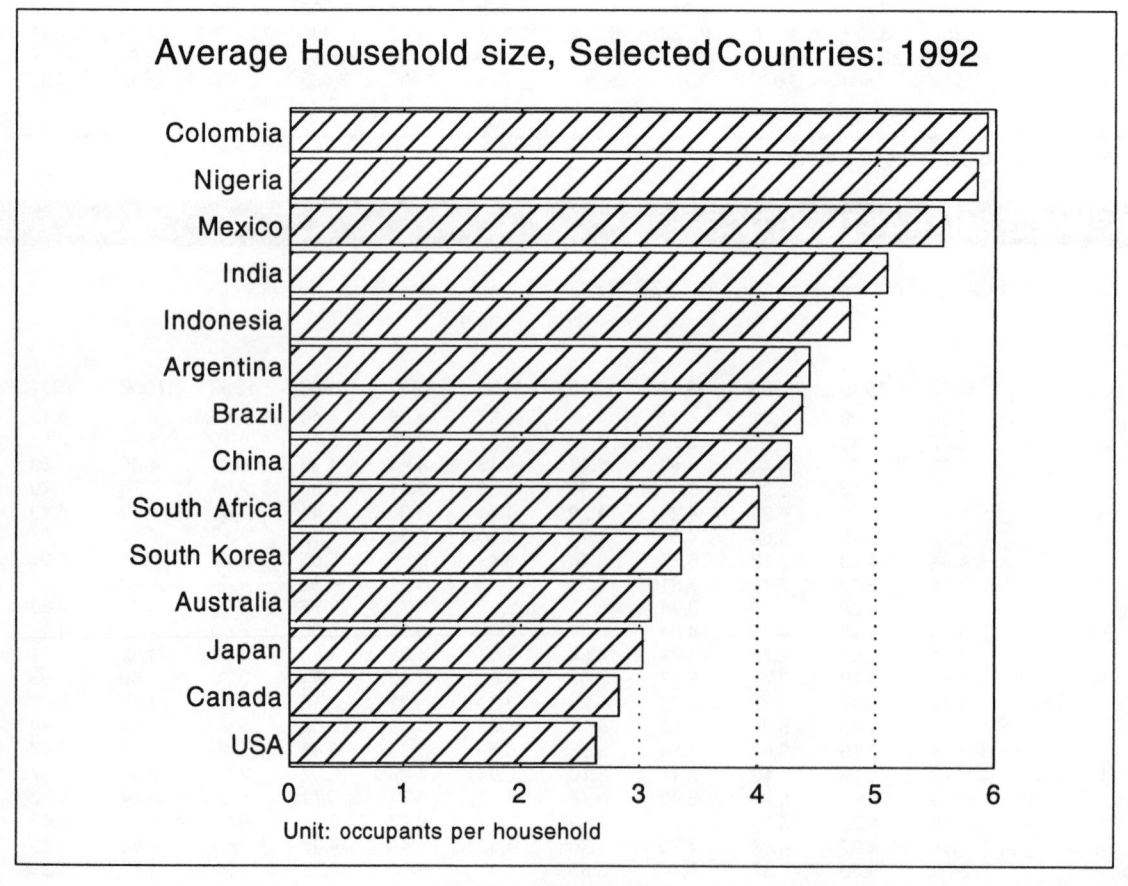

Average Household size, Selected Countries: 1992

Unit: occupants per household

Section Seventeen

Health and Living Standards

MEDICAL SERVICES	Table No. 1701

Access to Health Amenities and Medical Services: Latest Year

Units: % of population with access to:

	Year	Safe water	Adequate sanitary facilities	Polio immunis-ation	Health services 1985-1987
North America					
Canada	1987	100.0	60.0	85.0	99.0
USA [a]	1987	100.0	98.2	97.0	100.0
South America					
Argentina	1988	57.0	70.0	64.0	72.0
Bolivia	1988	47.0	35.0	56.0	64.6
Brazil	1988	96.0	24.0	99.0	
Chile	1988	89.0	83.0	86.0	97.0
Colombia	1988	93.0	71.0	60.0	60.0
Ecuador	1988	58.0	57.0	36.0	64.0
French Guiana					
Guyana	1985	76.1	87.2	59.0	96.0
Paraguay	1988	35.0	84.0	59.0	63.0
Peru	1988	61.0	51.0	26.0	75.0
Suriname [a]	1988	68.0	49.0	79.0	100.0
Uruguay	1988	85.0	59.0	83.0	82.0
Venezuela	1988	89.0	94.0	59.0	
Caribbean					
Anguilla					
Antigua [a]	1988	100.0	100.0	92.0	100.0
Aruba					
Bahamas [a]	1983	59.0	64.0	62.0	100.0
Barbados	1988	100.0	100.0	77.0	100.0
Bermuda					
British Virgin Islands					
Cayman Islands					
Cuba	1982	61.2	31.0	99.0	
Dominica [a]	1983	77.0	86.0	82.0	100.0
Dominican Republic	1988	63.0	61.0	99.0	80.0
Grenada	1983	85.0		75.0	100.0
Guadeloupe					
Haiti	1988	41.0	23.0	12.0	73.0
Jamaica	1988	72.0	91.0	56.0	90.0
Martinique					
Netherlands Antilles					
St Kitts	1988	100.0	100.0	97.0	100.0
St Lucia [a]	1988	67.0	62.0	84.0	100.0
St Vincent/Grenadines [a]	1981	75.0	88.0	90.0	80.0
Trinidad and Tobago	1988	96.0	99.0	66.0	99.0
Central America					
Belize	1988	75.0	94.0		75.0
Costa Rica	1988	91.0	60.0	81.0	80.0
El Salvador	1988	39.0	57.0	44.0	58.0
Guatemala	1988	61.0	76.0	53.0	34.0
Honduras	1988	50.0	44.0	84.0	74.0
Mexico	1988	71.0	27.0	91.0	50.7
Nicaragua	1988	54.0	49.0	73.0	84.0
Panama	1988	84.0	66.0	70.0	
Puerto Rico					
South Asia					
Afghanistan	1988	21.0	2.0	16.0	28.0
Bangladesh	1988	40.0	6.0	1.2	45.0
Bhutan [a]	1987	15.1	11.5	26.0	65.0
India [b]	1988	57.0	8.0	36.9	75.0
Nepal	1988	36.0	2.0	5.3	
Pakistan	1988	45.0	20.0	44.0	55.0
Sri Lanka	1988	41.0	50.0	65.4	93.0

MEDICAL SERVICES   Table No. 1701 (cont'd)

Access to Health Amenities and Medical Services: Latest Year

Units: % of population with access to:

	Year	Safe water	Adequate sanitary facilities	Polio immunis- ation	Health services 1985-1987
Japan					
Japan					
ASEAN/NICs					
Brunei	1984	90.0	80.0		96.0
Hong Kong	1988	98.0	94.0		
Indonesia [c]	1988	46.0	39.0	6.7	80.0
Macau					
Malaysia	1988	51.0	25.0	54.6	
Philippines	1985	64.5	56.5		
Singapore	1988	100.0	85.0	86.0	100.0
South Korea	1988	78.0	100.0	62.4	94.0
Taiwan					
Thailand	1988	66.0	78.0	52.7	70.0
East/SE Asia					
Cambodia					53.0
China	1988	72.0			
Laos	1988		10.0		67.0
Mongolia	1988	65.0	73.0	75.7	100.0
Myanmar	1988	30.0	29.0	1.5	33.0
North Korea [a]	1987	100.0	100.0	90.8	100.0
Vietnam	1988	46.0	30.0		80.0
Australasia					
Australia	1982	98.6	98.6		98.6
New Zealand [a]	1983	100.0	88.0	71.9	100.0
Pacific					
American Samoa					
Fiji	1987	80.4	74.5	82.0	99.9
French Polynesia					
Guam					
Kiribati	1984				95.0
Nauru					
New Caledonia					
Papua New Guinea [a]	1988	34.0	63.0	27.4	93.0
Solomon Islands [d]	1988	82.0	56.0		58.2
Tonga	1984	95.0	40.0		80.0
Tuvalu					
Vanuatu	1988	100.0	82.0		
Western Samoa	1988	83.0	95.0	84.2	100.0
Middle East					
Bahrain	1988	100.0	100.0	78.0	100.0
Egypt	1988	73.0	70.0	67.0	99.0
Iran	1988	78.0	65.0	65.0	80.0
Iraq	1988	87.0	74.0	63.0	89.0
Israel	1984	98.0	95.0	95.0	100.0
Jordan	1988	96.0	98.0	41.0	97.0
Kuwait	1988	100.0	100.0	91.0	100.0
Lebanon	1985	98.0	75.0	50.0	95.0
Oman	1988	53.0	32.0	40.0	91.0
Qatar	1987	100.0	98.2	72.0	100.0
Saudi Arabia	1988	97.0	86.0	81.0	97.0
Syria	1988	76.0	70.0	41.0	76.0
United Arab Emirates	1987	94.9	86.0	65.0	100.0
Yemen	1988	46.0	12.0	8.0	35.0

MEDICAL SERVICES

Access to Health Amenities and Medical Services: Latest Year

Units: % of population with access to:

	Year	Safe water	Adequate sanitary facilities	Polio immunis- ation	Health services 1985-1987
North Africa					
Algeria	1988	71.0	61.0	30.0	90.0
Chad	1984	31.0	14.5	1.1	30.0
Djibouti	1988	45.0	65.0	20.0	78.0
Ethiopia	1988	19.0	19.0	6.0	46.0
Libya	1988	97.0	70.0	75.0	100.0
Mali	1988	38.0	21.0	9.9	15.0
Mauritania	1988	66.0	7.0	21.3	30.0
Morocco	1988	61.0	46.0	44.0	74.0
Niger	1987	48.8	9.2	6.0	48.0
Somalia	1988	35.0	19.0	10.0	28.0
Sudan	1988	21.0	5.0	4.0	51.0
Tunisia	1988	64.0	45.0	61.0	91.0
West Africa					
Benin	1988	35.0	34.0	16.8	18.0
Burkina Faso	1988	67.0	8.0	2.0	49.0
Cameroon	1988	32.0	36.0	6.0	41.0
Cape Verde	1988	69.0	20.0	92.6	
Côte d'Ivoire	1988	18.0	40.0	34.0	31.0
Equatorial Guinea	1983	47.0	28.0		
Gabon	1988	68.0	50.0	47.5	90.0
Gambia [a]	1987	77.1	82.0	70.3	90.0
Ghana	1988	57.0	31.0		61.0
Guinea [e]	1988	32.0	11.6	44.0	32.0
Guinea-Bissau [a]	1988	21.0	20.0	14.0	64.0
Liberia	1988	58.0	21.4	22.6	39.0
Nigeria	1988	48.0	30.0	24.0	46.0
Sao Tomé e Príncipe	1983	52.0	15.0	28.0	80.0
Senegal	1988	54.0	87.0	57.0	40.0
Sierra Leone	1988	42.0	43.0	8.6	36.2
Togo	1988	71.0	23.0		61.0
East/Central Africa					
Angola	1988	35.6	21.0	46.0	30.0
Burundi [d]	1988	38.0	57.0	6.0	61.0
Central African Republic	1988	12.0	19.0	21.0	45.0
Comoros	1987	58.1	82.6	48.5	82.4
Congo	1988	21.0	40.0	42.0	81.0
Kenya	1988	30.0	44.4		
Madagascar	1988	32.0	8.0	7.0	56.0
Maldives	1988	95.0	27.0	9.0	97.0
Mauritius	1988	95.0	98.0	88.0	100.0
Réunion					
Rwanda	1988	64.6	57.0	26.0	28.0
Seychelles	1988	100.0	99.0	99.0	100.0
Tanzania	1988	56.0	77.0	56.0	81.0
Uganda	1988	20.0	30.0	2.0	60.0
Zaire	1988	34.0	14.0	66.0	26.0
Southern Africa					
Botswana	1988	58.0	40.0	77.0	89.0
Lesotho [a]	1988	48.0	14.0	64.0	80.0
Malawi	1988	56.0	55.0	68.0	54.0
Mozambique	1988	24.0	24.0	38.0	49.0
Namibia					
South Africa					
Swaziland	1988	50.0	47.0		80.0
Zambia	1988	59.0	55.0	44.0	75.0
Zimbabwe	1987	35.5	41.9	79.5	77.0

Source: World Health Organisation (WHO), World Health Statistics/national statistical offices/UN

Notes: see end of section

MEDICAL SERVICES   Table No. 1702

Hospitals and Beds: Latest Year

Units: As stated

	Year	Hospitals and clinics	Beds ('000)	Beds per '000 population
North America				
Canada [a]	1988	1,048	176.2	6.8
USA	1988	6,780	1,248.0	5.1
South America				
Argentina	1987	3,186	150.0	5.3
Bolivia	1987	144	8.7	1.3
Brazil [b]	1987	5,761	501.7	3.5
Chile	1987	204	41.8	3.3
Colombia	1987	910	45.8	1.5
Ecuador	1987	380	16.4	1.7
French Guiana	1982	5	0.9	13.4
Guyana	1979	55	4.0	4.7
Paraguay	1987	42	5.5	1.4
Peru	1987	338	30.6	1.5
Suriname	1980	17	3.2	9.1
Uruguay [c]	1987	48	14.2	4.9
Venezuela	1987	541	47.2	2.6
Caribbean				
Anguilla				
Antigua	1978	6	0.6	8.9
Aruba				
Bahamas	1986	2	1.0	4.2
Barbados	1982	11	2.2	8.6
Bermuda	1978	3	0.5	9.6
British Virgin Islands	1980	1		
Cayman Islands	1989	2	0.1	
Cuba	1987	273	50.3	4.9
Dominica	1978	6	0.3	3.9
Dominican Republic [d]	1987	46	13.2	2.0
Grenada	1980	6	0.5	4.7
Guadeloupe	1982	25	3.9	11.7
Haiti	1987	41	5.0	0.8
Jamaica [e]	1990	23	5.1	2.1
Martinique	1982	17	4.3	13.0
Netherlands Antilles	1968	8	2.0	16.4
St Kitts	1980	7	0.4	9.5
St Lucia	1977	7	0.6	4.6
St Vincent/Grenadines	1974		0.5	5.3
Trinidad and Tobago [f]	1988	38	4.5	3.7
Central America				
Belize [g]	1989	12	0.5	2.9
Costa Rica	1987	29	7.2	2.6
El Salvador	1987	38	7.4	1.5
Guatemala [h]	1987	107	13.7	1.6
Honduras [h]	1987	35	5.3	1.1
Mexico	1987	806	60.1	0.7
Nicaragua	1987	30	4.9	1.4
Panama [f]	1987	55	7.2	3.2
Puerto Rico	1980	111	14.0	4.4
South Asia				
Afghanistan	1982	83	6.9	0.4
Bangladesh	1988	875	33.3	0.3
Bhutan [i]	1989	26	0.9	0.6
India	1989	38,500	758.0	0.9
Nepal	1990	123	4.7	0.3
Pakistan	1990	4,447	71.9	0.7
Sri Lanka	1989	419	45.7	2.7

MEDICAL SERVICES   Table No. 1702 (cont'd)

Hospitals and Beds: Latest Year

Units: As stated

	Year	Hospitals and clinics	Beds ('000)	Beds per '000 population
Japan				
Japan	1989	10,081	1,662.0	15.7
ASEAN/NICs				
Brunei	1989	5	0.9	3.8
Hong Kong	1990	88	25.3	4.4
Indonesia	1990	1,552	120.7	0.7
Macau	1981	4	1.7	6.1
Malaysia	1990	276	38.1	2.2
Philippines	1989	1,696	85.0	1.4
Singapore	1991	22	9.8	3.5
South Korea	1989	10,740	126.5	3.0
Taiwan	1989	12,191	86.3	4.4
Thailand	1988	984	102.4	1.9
East/SE Asia				
Cambodia	1988	188	13.0	0.2
China	1989	190,041	2,867.0	2.3
Laos	1985	134	11.7	2.8
Mongolia [j]	1989	1,659	24.2	11.2
Myanmar	1991	711	27.5	0.6
North Korea	1983	2,510		
Vietnam	1989	12,300	217.6	3.3
Australasia				
Australia [e]	1989	1,080	164.7	9.8
New Zealand [k]	1991	326	26.6	7.7
Pacific				
American Samoa	1982	1	0.2	5.0
Fiji	1991	25	1.7	2.3
French Polynesia	1982	31	1.0	6.5
Guam	1982	4	0.2	2.0
Kiribati	1982	34	0.3	4.5
Nauru	1971	2	0.2	
New Caledonia	1981	38	1.5	11.0
Papua New Guinea	1989	492	15.3	4.3
Solomon Islands	1986	136	1.5	5.3
Tonga	1989	15	0.4	3.4
Tuvalu	1982	8	0.1	
Vanuatu	1990	5	0.4	2.7
Western Samoa	1981		0.7	4.3
Middle East				
Bahrain	1982	12	1.3	3.8
Egypt	1986	330	24.8	0.5
Iran	1988	609	77.8	1.5
Iraq	1982	198	24.6	1.7
Israel	1988	161	27.8	6.2
Jordan	1986	47	5.2	1.4
Kuwait	1987	87	6.2	3.3
Lebanon	1979	130	10.8	4.0
Oman	1988	47	3.3	2.4
Qatar	1986	6	0.9	2.7
Saudi Arabia	1986	181	28.0	2.3
Syria	1981	151	10.3	1.1
United Arab Emirates	1984	147	4.9	3.7
Yemen	1986	69	8.0	1.0

MEDICAL SERVICES

Hospitals and Beds: Latest Year

Units: As stated

	Year	Hospitals and clinics	Beds ('000)	Beds per '000 population
North Africa				
Algeria	1988	264	63.5	2.7
Chad [l]	1988	9	3.4	0.8
Djibouti	1988	18	1.9	5.0
Ethiopia [i]	1989	88	11.7	0.3
Libya	1982	64	16.1	4.8
Mali	1984	12	2.7	0.3
Mauritania	1977	12	0.6	0.4
Morocco	1982	141	24.9	1.2
Niger	1978		3.2	0.6
Somalia	1982	76	5.7	1.4
Sudan	1981	160	17.3	0.9
Tunisia	1981	98	13.6	2.1
West Africa				
Benin	1980	131	5.1	1.5
Burkina Faso	1984	7	5.0	0.8
Cameroon	1986	251	26.9	2.6
Cape Verde	1980	21	0.6	2.1
Côte d'Ivoire	1975		8.4	1.2
Equatorial Guinea	1977	65	3.6	10.8
Gabon	1977	41	4.1	4.1
Gambia	1978	16	0.7	1.3
Ghana	1981	329	17.0	1.5
Guinea	1981	314	7.7	1.4
Guinea-Bissau	1981		1.5	1.8
Liberia	1975	41	2.5	1.5
Nigeria	1987	12,391	93.8	0.9
Sao Tomé e Príncipe	1981	16	0.7	7.4
Senegal	1981	44	5.8	1.0
Sierra Leone	1986	53	4.2	1.1
Togo	1980	65	3.4	1.3
East/Central Africa				
Angola	1985	347	14.5	1.7
Burundi	1985	30	6.3	1.3
Central African Republic	1988	22	4.2	1.5
Comoros	1978	6	0.7	1.9
Congo [m]	1988	938	7.6	4.0
Kenya	1989	268	32.5	1.4
Madagascar [m]	1990	791	16.4	1.8
Maldives	1981	1	0.2	0.9
Mauritius	1988	13	2.9	2.8
Réunion	1982	11	2.6	5.2
Rwanda	1987	312	10.4	1.6
Seychelles	1988	5	0.4	5.7
Tanzania	1986	152	22.8	1.0
Uganda [n]	1989	89	14.0	0.9
Zaire	1979	942	79.2	3.1
Southern Africa				
Botswana	1984	15	2.1	2.0
Lesotho	1986	155	2.3	1.5
Malawi [o]	1988	51	7.5	1.0
Mozambique	1987	38	15.9	1.1
Namibia	1987	62	7.1	4.3
South Africa	1983	640	140.7	4.6
Swaziland	1986	24	1.6	2.6
Zambia	1988	82	16.7	2.2
Zimbabwe [n]	1988	1,221	20.2	2.3

Source: Euromonitor from UN, Statistical Yearbook/national statistical offices
Notes: see end of section

| **MEDICAL SERVICES** | **Table No. 1703** |

Health Personnel: Latest Year

Units: Number

	Year	Doctors	Dentists	Pharmacists	Nursing personnel	Midwives
North America						
Canada	1987	55,275	13,503	16,348	241,955	
USA	1988	560,300	140,300	156,300	1,527,000	
South America						
Argentina [a]	1988	96,000	22,500	681	17,118	
Bolivia	1987	1,730	206		891	
Brazil [a]	1988	169,488	97,675	5,846	42,347	
Chile	1984	9,684	3,900		3,355	1,962
Colombia	1988	29,353	13,815		11,940	
Ecuador	1987	9,901	1,269		2,771	
French Guiana	1984	111	24	23	688	16
Guyana	1984	125	11	21	288	546
Paraguay [a,b]	1988	2,536	1,017	860	3,059	783
Peru	1987	20,198	4,826	4,995	15,464	3,468
Suriname [b]	1984	306	22	13	1,400	88
Uruguay [b]	1986	6,529	2,799	560	3,750	1,282
Venezuela [c]	1987	28,400	7,403	3,187	14,398	
Caribbean						
Anguilla	1984	5	1		19	
Antigua	1984	32	4	10	145	163
Aruba						
Bahamas	1984	216	31	37	944	120
Barbados	1984	225	25		744	36
Bermuda	1984	42	30	2	562	
British Virgin Islands	1984	9	24	2	59	1
Cayman Islands	1989	21	9		137	16
Cuba [a]	1988	31,229	6,134	711	57,773	
Dominica	1984	25	2	15	204	47
Dominican Republic [a]	1988	7,332	689	54	723	
Grenada	1984	44	4	20	162	107
Guadeloupe	1984	459	102	115	997	99
Haiti	1988	887	85		691	
Jamaica	1984	1,115	114	102	3,594	485
Martinique	1984	467	113	145	1,091	106
Netherlands Antilles	1968	120	29	18		28
St Kitts	1984	20	5	7	140	123
St Lucia	1984	35	5	13	229	66
St Vincent/Grenadines	1984	27	2	15	327	2
Trinidad and Tobago	1984	1,213	104	115	3,346	
Central America						
Belize	1986	72	12	17	229	164
Costa Rica	1988	2,539	790	702	5,400	
El Salvador [a]	1988	3,200	800	597	4,898	
Guatemala	1988	2,171	251	411	1,225	
Honduras [a]	1988	2,666	416	392	5,557	3,791
Mexico [a,d]	1987	130,000	4,925	116	44,046	634
Nicaragua	1988	1,942	340		1,120	
Panama	1984	2,167	410		2,172	
Puerto Rico	1980	4,057	741	1,436	14,392	199
South Asia						
Afghanistan [a,e]	1987	2,957	329	206	2,135	529
Bangladesh [a]	1990	20,006	619	2,500	9,274	7,485
Bhutan [a]	1989	157		18	317	
India	1987	331,600	9,598	155,621	219,300	181,300
Nepal	1990	951	17	29	601	2,379
Pakistan	1990	51,883	2,077	3,153	16,948	10,650
Sri Lanka	1989	2,456	301	441	9,486	3,255

MEDICAL SERVICES   Table No. 1703 (cont'd)

Health Personnel: Latest Year

Units: Number

	Year	Doctors	Dentists	Pharmacists	Nursing personnel	Midwives
Japan						
Japan	1988	199,958	69,499	122,380	365,298	24,056
ASEAN/NICs						
Brunei	1989	171	30	8	870	173
Hong Kong	1991	6,545	1,526	720	30,043	
Indonesia ^{c,f}	1989	25,752	2,630	3,587	98,842	
Macau ^f	1987	518	105	5	989	
Malaysia ^{f,g,h}	1990	7,012	1,472	626	36,942	
Philippines	1989	9,546	1,163	539	12,170	10,367
Singapore	1991	3,779	682	629	10,233	529
South Korea	1989	39,769	8,630	35,756	211,524	7,397
Taiwan	1989	20,590	4,624	17,641	33,879	2,381
Thailand	1989	12,713	2,107	3,825	74,167	11,354
East/SE Asia						
Cambodia	1988	425	71	79	7,271	2,332
China	1990	1,058,000		104,000	1,102,000	58,000
Laos ^f	1985	551	15	16	6,753	
Mongolia	1988	5,485	179	1,243	9,809	963
Myanmar ^b	1991	12,243	1,029	80	8,811	14,281
North Korea	1982	45,470				
Vietnam	1989	22,300	803	6,400	76,300	14,100
Australasia						
Australia	1986	36,610	6,200	9,800	139,434	5,900
New Zealand ^f	1991	10,179	1,875	3,423	44,780	
Pacific						
American Samoa ^f	1984	25	7	1	18	
Fiji ^f	1991	352	48	44	1,607	
French Polynesia ^f	1985	214	51	24	394	
Guam ^f	1986	147	23	30	594	
Kiribati ^f	1985	15	2	1	125	
Nauru	1971	10	2	1	61	
New Caledonia ^f	1983	95	49		350	
Papua New Guinea ^f	1989	361	16	9	3,241	
Solomon Islands ^f	1986	38			301	
Tonga	1989	43	9	3	162	
Tuvalu ^f	1986	3	2	1	26	
Vanuatu ^f	1990	20			321	
Western Samoa	1981	63	7	4	344	42
Middle East						
Bahrain ^f	1985	518	19	68	1,148	
Egypt	1985	9,495	8,218	18,860	12,458	9,004
Iran	1988	18,350	3,600	2,650	43,291	2,202
Iraq	1987	9,442	1,465	2,132	9,931	2,267
Israel	1982	10,700	2,200	2,800	27,300	115
Jordan ^f	1984	2,958	623	677	2,596	
Kuwait ^f	1987	2,799	329	843	8,690	
Lebanon	1983	3,953	730	1,002	3,681	614
Oman	1988	1,371	96	235	3,810	
Qatar	1986	646	95	17	1,672	70
Saudi Arabia	1986	17,544	1,291	265	37,670	
Syria	1987	8,593	2,487	1,886	12,550	1,776
United Arab Emirates ^f	1984	1,278	97	89	3,328	
Yemen ^f	1985	1,726	70	136	4,987	

MEDICAL SERVICES   Table No. 1703 (cont'd)

Health Personnel: Latest Year

Units: Number

	Year	Doctors	Dentists	Pharmacists	Nursing personnel	Midwives
Japan						
Japan	1988	199,958	69,499	122,380	365,298	24,056
ASEAN/NICs						
Brunei	1989	171	30	8	870	173
Hong Kong	1991	6,545	1,526	720	30,043	
Indonesia ^{c,f}	1989	25,752	2,630	3,587	98,842	
Macau ^f	1987	518	105	5	989	
Malaysia ^{f,g,h}	1990	7,012	1,472	626	36,942	
Philippines	1989	9,546	1,163	539	12,170	10,367
Singapore	1991	3,779	682	629	10,233	529
South Korea	1989	39,769	8,630	35,756	211,524	7,397
Taiwan	1989	20,590	4,624	17,641	33,879	2,381
Thailand	1989	12,713	2,107	3,825	74,167	11,354
East/SE Asia						
Cambodia	1988	425	71	79	7,271	2,332
China	1990	1,058,000		104,000	1,102,000	58,000
Laos ^f	1985	551	15	16	6,753	
Mongolia	1988	5,485	179	1,243	9,809	963
Myanmar ^b	1991	12,243	1,029	80	8,811	14,281
North Korea	1982	45,470				
Vietnam	1989	22,300	803	6,400	76,300	14,100
Australasia						
Australia	1986	36,610	6,200	9,800	139,434	5,900
New Zealand ^f	1991	10,179	1,875	3,423	44,780	
Pacific						
American Samoa ^f	1984	25	7	1	18	
Fiji ^f	1991	352	48	44	1,607	
French Polynesia ^f	1985	214	51	24	394	
Guam ^f	1986	147	23	30	594	
Kiribati ^f	1985	15	2	1	125	
Nauru	1971	10	2	1	61	
New Caledonia ^f	1983	95	49		350	
Papua New Guinea ^f	1989	361	16	9	3,241	
Solomon Islands ^f	1986	38			301	
Tonga	1989	43	9	3	162	
Tuvalu ^f	1986	3	2	1	26	
Vanuatu ^f	1990	20			321	
Western Samoa	1981	63	7	4	344	42
Middle East						
Bahrain ^f	1985	518	19	68	1,148	
Egypt	1985	9,495	8,218	18,860	12,458	9,004
Iran	1988	18,350	3,600	2,650	43,291	2,202
Iraq	1987	9,442	1,465	2,132	9,931	2,267
Israel	1982	10,700	2,200	2,800	27,300	115
Jordan ^f	1984	2,958	623	677	2,596	
Kuwait ^f	1987	2,799	329	843	8,690	
Lebanon	1983	3,953	730	1,002	3,681	614
Oman	1988	1,371	96	235	3,810	
Qatar	1986	646	95	17	1,672	70
Saudi Arabia	1986	17,544	1,291	265	37,670	
Syria	1987	8,593	2,487	1,886	12,550	1,776
United Arab Emirates ^f	1984	1,278	97	89	3,328	
Yemen ^f	1985	1,726	70	136	4,987	

Source: Euromonitor from UN, Statistical Yearbook/national statistical offices
Notes: see end of section

ILLNESS

Major Causes of Death: Latest Year

Units: Death rate per 100,000 inhabitants

	Year	A	B	C	D	E	F	G	H	I
North America										
Canada [a,b]	1989	4.6	223.7	313.9	33.9	19.1	412.4	16.1	19.9	16.7
USA [a,c,d]	1988	12.8	225.4	417.1	41.4	22.7	598.8	19.6	20.0	22.6
South America										
Argentina [d]	1987	26.7	125.3	382.3	27.9	28.4	1,539.5	9.8	24.3	18.7
Bolivia										
Brazil [a,c,d]	1986	37.3	63.6	176.3	31.8	15.9	1,875.3	21.3	18.6	29.3
Chile [d]	1987	19.2	92.3	168.1	55.4	27.4	789.4	7.0	17.2	42.7
Colombia [d]	1986	28.9	62.8	141.9			982.3		44.1	59.5
Ecuador [d]	1988	61.1	45.0	111.6	44.7	19.8	130.5	20.0	28.7	15.0
French Guiana										
Guyana	1984	18.6	29.7	257.3	28.3	25.4	166.6	0.3	28.9	25.3
Paraguay [d]	1986	36.4	25.2	109.4	20.3	7.9	1,904.7	6.3	11.2	6.5
Peru [a,c,d,e]	1983	102.0	39.0	81.2	97.1	15.0	1,120.5	6.7	17.6	6.5
Suriname [d]	1985	35.5	41.7	187.0	40.0	22.4	1,365.7	17.8	20.4	31.3
Uruguay [d]	1989	18.1	201.6	400.4	35.8	23.2	1,166.4	15.5	32.7	16.0
Venezuela [a,c,d,e]	1987	30.9	66.5	132.1	24.2	13.9	1,287.7	24.3	21.3	15.2
Caribbean										
Anguilla										
Antigua										
Aruba										
Bahamas [d]	1987	17.5	100.6	192.5	26.6	27.0	1,844.3	19.6	24.1	32.8
Barbados [a]	1988	20.1	205.1	419.6	30.6	32.2	1,329.4	11.0	17.3	16.1
Bermuda										
British Virgin Islands										
Cayman Islands										
Cuba										
Dominica										
Dominican Republic	1985	51.3	24.2	127.2	24.7	17.7	106.7	8.7	13.8	11.2
Grenada										
Guadeloupe										
Haiti										
Jamaica										
Martinique [d]	1987	20.8	101.5	186.7	26.9	24.4	704.6	12.5	24.6	17.0
Netherlands Antilles										
St Kitts										
St Lucia										
St Vincent/Grenadines										
Trinidad and Tobago [c,d]	1988	15.6	117.5	341.9	33.6	19.6	968.8	10.2	17.4	24.9
Central America										
Belize										
Costa Rica [d]	1988	11.9	73.7	123.9	21.0	14.1	763.6	12.3	19.3	24.0
El Salvador [d]	1984	59.9	26.3	82.0	30.4	11.8	2,321.4	14.4	30.6	79.1
Guatemala [d]	1984	211.6	27.6	116.9	132.1	17.4	3,346.7	1.4	16.9	33.7
Honduras										
Mexico [d]	1986	71.6	38.3	136.4	39.0	34.2	887.0	15.4	39.2	24.1
Nicaragua										
Panama [d]	1987	22.7	51.0	127.5	22.7	12.1	1,043.1	17.1	17.3	16.6
Puerto Rico [d]	1990	47.2	105.1	299.4	43.2	31.5	891.6	15.2	16.4	32.6
South Asia										
Afghanistan										
Bangladesh										
Bhutan										
India										
Nepal										
Pakistan										
Sri Lanka										

ILLNESS

Major Causes of Death: Latest Year

Units: Death rate per 100,000 inhabitants

	Year	A	B	C	D	E	F	G	H	I
Japan										
Japan [a,c,d]	1990	9.7	184.7	256.0	67.7	30.5	234.0	11.7	14.3	19.1
ASEAN/NICs										
Brunei										
Hong Kong [a,c,d,f]	1989	17.5	160.5	143.9	43.8	26.8	426.5	5.4	9.0	14.3
Indonesia										
Macau [d]	1990	9.6	54.7	122.0	23.1	11.0	504.2	2.3	8.6	14.8
Malaysia										
Philippines [d]	1991	122.9	32.4	111.3	121.5	23.2	1,760.2	4.1	8.3	20.0
Singapore [a,c,d,g]	1989	16.3	129.2	206.4	48.3	17.7	360.7	8.4	6.2	19.3
South Korea [a,c,d]	1989	13.1	90.0	141.5	13.9	29.8	133.9	24.4	28.7	13.2
Taiwan										
Thailand										
East/SE Asia										
Cambodia										
China [d]	1987	24.4	108.8	208.1	98.3	23.6	888.0	8.5	5.8	39.8
Laos										
Mongolia										
Myanmar										
North Korea										
Vietnam										
Australasia										
Australia [a,c,d]	1988	4.3	204.0	347.2	24.4	19.9	464.7	18.6	16.2	16.5
New Zealand [a,c,d]	1988	4.4	229.1	386.4	62.2	16.8	402.3	22.0	19.0	17.3
Pacific										
American Samoa										
Fiji [c,d]	1985	31.3	53.3	228.6	43.1	26.2	880.5	12.8	14.9	20.8
French Polynesia										
Guam										
Kiribati										
Nauru										
New Caledonia										
Papua New Guinea										
Solomon Islands										
Tonga										
Tuvalu										
Vanuatu										
Western Samoa										
Middle East										
Bahrain [a]	1988	2.3	42.0	159.7	14.3	3.6	1,594.1	8.0	2.5	12.1
Egypt [d]	1987	98.9	20.1	325.8	82.8	15.6	1,043.8	6.6	11.6	20.9
Iran										
Iraq										
Israel [a,c,d,h]	1989	11.5	145.7	286.2	18.7	21.7	572.6	9.7	20.1	13.9
Jordan										
Kuwait [a,c,d]	1987	6.8	31.0	81.0	13.7	6.5	830.9	18.3	10.2	2.8
Lebanon										
Oman										
Qatar										
Saudi Arabia										
Syria										
United Arab Emirates										
Yemen										

ILLNESS

Table No. 1704 (cont'd)

Major Causes of Death: Latest Year

Units: Death rate per 100,000 inhabitants

	Year	A	B	C	D	E	F	G	H	I
North Africa										
Algeria										
Chad										
Djibouti										
Ethiopia										
Libya										
Mali										
Mauritania										
Morocco										
Niger										
Somalia										
Sudan										
Tunisia										
West Africa										
Benin										
Burkina Faso										
Cameroon										
Cape Verde [c,d]	1980	157.4	50.8	111.8	104.7	10.0	1,378.6	2.8	23.9	4.1
Côte d'Ivoire										
Equatorial Guinea										
Gabon										
Gambia										
Ghana										
Guinea										
Guinea-Bissau										
Liberia										
Nigeria										
Sao Tomé e Príncipe [d]	1987	240.9	14.3	215.9	86.5	17.9	1,065.2	5.4	5.4	3.6
Senegal										
Sierra Leone										
Togo										
East/Central Africa										
Angola										
Burundi										
Central African Republic										
Comoros										
Congo										
Kenya										
Madagascar										
Maldives [d]	1988	26.5		171.0	66.5		781.6		1.5	8.5
Mauritius [d]	1987	14.7	64.4	344.1	43.0	38.4	1,946.1	9.1	22.5	18.5
Réunion										
Rwanda										
Seychelles										
Tanzania										
Uganda										
Zaire										
Southern Africa										
Botswana	1985	38.1	5.4	35.9	9.9	8.2	2.6	0.2	8.2	3.7
Lesotho										
Malawi										
Mozambique										
Namibia										
South Africa										
Swaziland										
Zambia										
Zimbabwe	1986	32.4	22.7	48.9	21.9	8.0	59.5	10.8	15.2	15.2

Source: UN, Demographic Yearbook

Notes: see end of section

ILLNESS

Reported AIDS Cases by Date of Report 1986-1991

Units: Number

	1986	1987	1988	1989	1990	1991
North America						
Canada	1,236	865	961	1,026	1,050	788
USA	39,125	26,551	31,787	34,601	39,249	35,696
South America						
Argentina	72	73	169	229	383	373
Bolivia	3	3	10	2	7	16
Brazil	1,571	2,117	3,432	4,079	6,177	5,914
Chile	22	41	55	60	117	147
Colombia	66	151	213	254	620	669
Ecuador	15	19	25	15	42	51
French Guiana	78	25	34	54	41	
Guyana		10	34	40	61	85
Paraguay	1	6	2	4	12	10
Peru	37	60	68	117	141	155
Suriname	4	5	4	35	35	16
Uruguay	8	9	28	38	76	86
Venezuela	91	132	268	326	426	251
Caribbean						
Anguilla			1	2	1	
Antigua	2	1			3	
Aruba						
Bahamas	86	90	93	168	162	235
Barbados	32	24	15	40	61	78
Bermuda	51	21	28	35	33	23
British Virgin Islands			1		2	1
Cayman Islands	2	1	1	1	2	3
Cuba		27	24	20	10	30
Dominica		6	1	3	2	
Dominican Republic	116	294	292	499	238	162
Grenada	3	5	3	5	5	7
Guadeloupe	47	41	47	54	6	10
Haiti	795	477	731	453	630	
Jamaica	11	33	30	66	62	133
Martinique	25	22	28	50	45	28
Netherlands Antilles						
St Kitts	1		17		8	1
St Lucia	3	7	2	4	15	7
St Vincent/Grenadines	3	5	8	6	4	14
Trinidad and Tobago	151	85	160	167	173	235
Central America						
Belize	1	6	4		1	
Costa Rica	20	23	52	56	69	83
El Salvador	7	16	48	94	54	107
Guatemala	18	16	13	18	78	94
Honduras	15	66	130	301	586	453
Mexico	793	1,027	1,411	900	2,403	950
Nicaragua			2	2	7	13
Panama	25	28	60	67	73	70
Puerto Rico						
Middle East						
Bahrain						
Egypt	2	3	6	9	7	12
Iran		1	3	5	10	25
Iraq						7
Israel	45	5	21	27	32	24
Jordan	1	3	1	5	1	6
Kuwait	1				1	3
Lebanon		2	9	3	8	5
Oman	1	5	6	4	7	1
Qatar	8	8	5	2	7	1
Saudi Arabia		14	4	7	7	8
Syria		3	2	4	1	7
United Arab Emirates					8	
Yemen						

ILLNESS

Table No. 1705 (cont'd)

Reported AIDS Cases by Date of Report 1986-1991

Units: Number

	1986	1987	1988	1989	1990	1991
Japan						
Japan	25	34	31	92	189	82
ASEAN/NICs						
Brunei			1		1	
Hong Kong	4	5	7	6	12	15
Indonesia		1	2	3	6	9
Macau						
Malaysia	1	1	2	8	12	23
Philippines	3	9	8	8	15	11
Singapore	2	2	6	5	8	12
South Korea		1		1	2	1
Taiwan						
Thailand	2	6	4	20	54	82
East/SE Asia						
Cambodia						
China	1	2			2	3
Laos						1
Mongolia						
Myanmar						10
North Korea						
Vietnam						
Australasia						
Australia	390	368	508	532	631	651
New Zealand	33	30	37	60	73	78
Pacific						
American Samoa						
Fiji				1	2	1
French Polynesia		1	6	6	9	5
Guam					2	2
Kiribati						
Nauru						
New Caledonia			2	12	3	2
Papua New Guinea		3	10	6	13	13
Solomon Islands						
Tonga		1	1			
Tuvalu						
Vanuatu						
Western Samoa						
Middle East						
Bahrain						
Egypt	2	3	6	9	7	12
Iran		1	3	5	10	25
Iraq						7
Israel	45	5	21	27	32	24
Jordan	1	3	1	5	1	6
Kuwait	1				1	3
Lebanon		2	9	3	8	5
Oman	1	5	6	4	7	1
Qatar	8	8	5	2	7	1
Saudi Arabia		14	4	7	7	8
Syria		3	2	4	1	7
United Arab Emirates					8	
Yemen						

ILLNESS

Reported AIDS Cases by Date of Report 1986-1991

Units: Number

	1986	1987	1988	1989	1990	1991
North Africa						
Algeria	3	5	5	32	47	
Chad	2	2	7	10	38	165
Djibouti			3	4	51	107
Ethiopia	2	17	62	283	448	889
Libya					4	2
Mali	6	23	99	106	104	
Mauritania			5	6	5	10
Morocco	1	9	13	20	26	28
Niger		18	24	38	213	204
Somalia		1	4	9	5	
Sudan	1	1	64	122	130	182
Tunisia	5	14	17	14	27	5
West Africa						
Benin	3	6	18	57	50	51
Burkina Faso	10	21	394	481	72	
Cameroon	21	20	33	4	61	234
Cape Verde	2	16		10	4	
Côte d'Ivoire	120	404	1,193	1,930	3,189	3,894
Equatorial Guinea		1	1	1	2	2
Gabon	13	4	10	24	66	98
Gambia	11	16	30	24	46	56
Ghana	26	35	266	899	1,011	903
Guinea		4	29	49	138	118
Guinea-Bissau				123	34	
Liberia	2			3		19
Nigeria					36	100
Sao Tomé e Príncipe					2	4
Senegal					118	127
Sierra Leone					7	6
Togo		2	15	39	458	628
East/Central Africa						
Angola	9	32	63		93	130
Burundi	269	652	1,054	809	521	
Central African Republic	254	178	230		702	
Comoros			1		1	1
Congo	250	1,000	346	344	465	1,077
Kenya	274	1,223	2,817	4,825		
Madagascar				2		
Maldives						
Mauritius		1	1	2	1	5
Réunion						
Rwanda						
Seychelles						
Tanzania	699	909	2,550	2,093	7,948	5,341
Uganda	147	3,477	3,625	6,029	8,441	8,471
Zaire	440	1,983	3,121	6,188	2,425	
Southern Africa						
Botswana	11	25	22	29	91	72
Lesotho	1	1	3	6	10	21
Malawi	144	858	3,034	3,124	4,226	
Mozambique	1	3	23	37	98	178
Namibia	4	15	43	127	122	
South Africa						
Swaziland	1	6	7		20	41
Zambia	241	468	985	1,113	1,393	1,601
Zimbabwe		119	202	1,311	4,362	4,587

Source: WHO/UN, Annual Abstract of Statistics
Notes: see end of section

NUTRITION

Food Supply: Calories and Protein Consumed Per Day 1980-1990

Units: Calories/grams per inhabitant

	Calories				Protein (grams)			
	1980	**1986**	**1989**	**1990**	**1980**	**1986**	**1989**	**1990**
North America								
Canada	3,286	3,462	3,483	3,222	96	99	102	101
USA	3,501	3,615	3,671	3,680	103	108	111	111
South America								
Argentina	3,197	3,114	3,113	3,075	106	100	101	98
Bolivia	2,079	2,027	1,916	1,982	55	54	53	51
Brazil	2,736	2,689	2,751	2,723	61	60	62	62
Chile	2,674	2,530	2,581	2,481	72	67	72	70
Colombia	2,509	2,542	2,598	2,492	54	56	59	57
Ecuador	2,299	2,449	2,531	2,410	48	49	54	50
French Guiana	2,517	2,709	2,858	2,823	78	90	96	101
Guyana	2,451	2,599	2,712	2,393	62	65	70	65
Paraguay	2,815	2,765	2,758	2,644	79	72	72	68
Peru	2,187	2,231	2,186	1,890	58	60	57	51
Suriname	2,490	2,812	2,957	2,431	63	67	72	60
Uruguay	2,782	2,711	2,653	2,678	85	81	79	83
Venezuela	2,671	2,388	2,582	2,383	68	60	62	58
Caribbean								
Anguilla	2,106	2,223	2,384	2,381	66	73	81	80
Antigua								
Aruba								
Bahamas	2,639	2,720	2,764	2,782	76	81	80	79
Barbados	3,117	3,192	3,279	3,222	84	102	106	99
Bermuda	3,066	3,014	3,030	2,975	119	115	116	106
British Virgin Islands								
Cayman Islands								
Cuba	2,984	3,148	3,141	3,153	73	75	74	72
Dominica	2,594	2,820	2,810	2,917	64	68	70	75
Dominican Republic	2,280	2,353	2,359	2,297	50	49	48	50
Grenada	2,453	2,556	2,696	2,378	66	72	69	62
Guadeloupe	2,466	2,653	2,715	2,816	81	87	89	91
Haiti	2,026	2,088	2,013	1,987	48	50	49	47
Jamaica	2,638	2,601	2,609	2,527	62	64	63	62
Martinique	2,615	2,734	2,741	2,772	79	81	82	88
Netherlands Antilles	2,876	2,827	2,920	2,651	91	84	91	81
St Kitts	2,247	2,539	2,639	2,424	62	73	77	70
St Lucia	2,220	2,508	2,588	2,429	57	69	73	70
St Vincent/Grenadines	2,391	2,556	2,613	2,470	52	57	57	57
Trinidad and Tobago	2,962	2,986	2,853	2,721	80	80	65	65
Central America								
Belize	2,673	2,576	2,660	2,579	68	67	75	68
Costa Rica	2,564	2,765	2,808	2,712	64	62	66	64
El Salvador	2,269	2,371	2,318	2,306	56	56	56	55
Guatemala	2,118	2,234	2,235	2,254	53	55	56	55
Honduras	2,194	2,178	2,247	2,259	55	51	56	55
Mexico	3,029	3,090	3,052	2,986	79	80	79	82
Nicaragua	2,210	2,166	2,265	2,214	56	51	55	53
Panama	2,203	2,572	2,539	2,291	58	65	65	59
Puerto Rico								
South Asia								
Afghanistan	2,238	2,098	2,022	1,710	63	57	55	48
Bangladesh	1,951	1,956	2,021	2,100	43	42	43	44
Bhutan								
India	2,079	2,129	2,229	2,243	50	53	55	56
Nepal	1,920	1,974	2,077	2,246	50	52	52	58
Pakistan	2,224	2,167	2,219	2,377	62	59	62	65
Sri Lanka	2,170	2,383	2,277	2,286	43	46	46	48

Food Supply: Calories and Protein Consumed Per Day 1980-1990

Units: Calories/grams per inhabitant

	Calories				Protein (grams)			
	1980	1986	1989	1990	1980	1986	1989	1990
Japan								
Japan	2,819	2,883	2,956	2,926	88	92	96	96
ASEAN/NICs								
Brunei	2,699	2,786	2,837	2,869	72	82	79	75
Hong Kong	2,680	2,770	2,853	2,857	84	87	85	85
Indonesia	2,397	2,649	2,750	2,631	51	59	61	57
Macau	2,307	2,247	2,162	2,322	67	63	57	61
Malaysia	2,716	2,738	2,774	2,697	58	58	58	54
Philippines	2,421	2,309	2,375	2,452	54	52	54	57
Singapore	3,340	3,485	3,198	3,114	91	97	89	87
South Korea	2,828	2,870	2,852	2,840	77	77	78	79
Taiwan								
Thailand	2,230	2,303	2,316	2,271	48	50	49	48
East/SE Asia								
Cambodia	1,746	2,131	2,166	2,114	41	50	51	51
China	2,331	2,610	2,639	2,703	55	62	63	66
Laos	2,418	2,411	2,630	2,475	65	67	71	67
Mongolia	2,476	2,539	2,480	2,303	92	92	89	85
Myanmar	2,343	2,485	2,441	2,448	60	65	63	62
North Korea	2,696	2,743	2,823	2,860	76	78	81	82
Vietnam	2,045	2,233	2,233	2,215	46	51	51	51
Australasia								
Australia	3,061	3,182	3,216	3,385	96	100	98	101
New Zealand	3,385	3,314	3,362	3,504	107	103	99	107
Pacific								
American Samoa	2,753	2,819	2,887	2,738	67	67	70	64
Fiji	2,749	2,781	2,786	2,735	75	79	80	76
French Polynesia								
Guam								
Kiribati	2,819	2,890	2,959	2,498	61	67	67	66
Nauru								
New Caledonia	2,859	2,866	2,862	2,943	74	75	75	80
Papua New Guinea	2,307	2,371	2,403	2,609	47	49	49	52
Solomon Islands	2,189	2,185	2,191	2,235	55	54	53	53
Tonga	2,868	2,959	2,984	2,978	66	71	71	78
Tuvalu								
Vanuatu	2,516	2,521	2,567	2,941	70	64	65	64
Western Samoa	2,515	2,502	2,509	2,695	61	63	63	66
Middle East								
Bahrain								
Egypt	3,108	3,332	3,336	3,318	76	84	84	85
Iran	2,406	3,194	3,181	3,038	75	83	84	81
Iraq	2,741	3,027	2,887	2,836	73	78	72	71
Israel	2,963	3,110	3,174	3,204	98	100	105	103
Jordan	2,570	2,678	2,634	2,704	68	73	71	68
Kuwait	2,880	3,106	3,274	3,160	82	83	86	82
Lebanon								
Oman								
Qatar								
Saudi Arabia	2,783	2,774	2,874	3,023	78	84	87	89
Syria	2,920	3,137	3,003	3,107	78	84	79	82
United Arab Emirates	3,190	3,254	3,309	3,331	101	99	102	106
Yemen	2,078	2,086	2,142	2,280	61	59	60	65

NUTRITION

Food Supply: Calories and Protein Consumed Per Day 1980-1990

Units: Calories/grams per inhabitant

	Calories				Protein (grams)			
	1980	1986	1989	1990	1980	1986	1989	1990
North Africa								
Algeria	2,639	2,743	2,866	2,969	67	73	77	76
Chad	1,730	1,808	1,743	1,641	56	56	52	50
Djibouti								
Ethiopia	1,809	1,760	1,667	1,694	60	56	52	53
Libya	3,577	3,412	3,324	3,353	87	82	81	80
Mali	1,769	2,120	2,314	2,233	54	60	64	62
Mauritania	2,102	2,427	2,685	2,469	71	75	79	72
Morocco	2,671	2,921	3,020	3,052	71	80	81	82
Niger	2,196	2,291	2,308	2,263	64	63	65	64
Somalia	1,913	2,002	1,906	1,830	60	62	59	60
Sudan	2,364	2,036	1,974	1,964	67	57	57	57
Tunisia	2,757	3,001	3,121		77	82	83	83
West Africa								
Benin	2,066	2,234	2,305	2,386	50	52	56	56
Burkina Faso	1,870	2,224	2,288	2,137	58	68	69	66
Cameroon	2,227	2,173	2,217	2,201	54	53	53	55
Cape Verde	2,554	2,719	2,706	2,872	64	64	61	67
Côte d'Ivoire	2,595	2,610	2,577	2,411	57	55	54	50
Equatorial Guinea								
Gabon	2,377	2,517	2,383	2,420	63	66	59	61
Gambia	2,024	2,353	2,370	2,249	47	50	55	56
Ghana	1,944	2,154	2,248	1,974	44	46	48	44
Guinea	2,224	2,246	2,132	2,229	50	51	50	51
Guinea-Bissau	1,943	2,314	2,506	2,230	41	49	51	43
Liberia	2,385	2,389	2,382	2,067	47	45	43	37
Nigeria	2,317	2,299	2,312	2,147	52	52	48	43
Sao Tomé e Príncipe	2,303	2,315	2,419	2,171	52	51	51	46
Senegal	2,398	2,440	2,369	2,328	68	72	65	65
Sierra Leone	2,062	1,850	1,799	1,940	44	39	38	40
Togo	2,231	2,125	2,214	2,279	47	49	53	51
East/Central Africa								
Angola	2,169	1,849	1,807	1,877	48	44	46	44
Burundi	2,043	2,054	1,932	1,923	69	66	55	53
Central African Republic	2,085	1,985	2,036	1,867	42	46	50	47
Comoros	1,825	1,850	1,960	1,758	40	41	43	38
Congo	2,441	2,595	2,590	2,321	43	51	51	47
Kenya	2,241	2,204	2,163	2,048	58	60	59	56
Madagascar	2,470	2,344	2,158	2,162	57	55	51	52
Maldives	2,075	2,343	2,386	2,416	69	89	89	88
Mauritius	2,707	2,715	2,887	2,896	62	64	67	72
Réunion	2,860	3,005	3,075	3,112	76	80	81	87
Rwanda	2,041	1,917	1,971	1,961	50	50	52	49
Seychelles	2,278	2,309	2,335	2,344	62	67	59	59
Tanzania	2,267	2,231	2,206	2,181	47	48	49	54
Uganda	2,115	2,012	2,153	2,213	51	47	49	53
Zaire	2,109	2,156	1,991	2,094	34	35	32	34
Southern Africa								
Botswana	2,111	2,273	2,375	2,272	68	70	74	69
Lesotho	2,413	2,359	2,299	2,100	70	68	66	59
Malawi	2,246	2,188	2,139	2,042	65	63	62	58
Mozambique	1,809	1,643	1,680	1,803	30	27	28	30
Namibia	1,922	1,936	1,946	1,945	64	64	62	62
South Africa	2,979	3,058	3,122	3,158	78	77	79	79
Swaziland	2,470	2,618	2,591	2,648	63	63	62	62
Zambia	2,227	2,085	2,078	2,019	58	54	53	54
Zimbabwe	2,200	2,247	2,299	2,247	55	52	53	54

Source: UN

Notes: see end of section

HEALTH EXPENDITURE   Table No. 1707

Government Expenditure on Health 1987-1992

Units: % of total central government expenditure

	1987	1988	1989	1990	1991	1992
North America						
Canada	5.9	5.8	5.2			
USA	12.2	12.5	12.9	13.5	13.8	
South America						
Argentina	2.1	2.0	3.0			
Bolivia	9.0	7.7	6.6	2.3	3.3	
Brazil	9.5	6.1	7.2	6.7		
Chile	6.3	5.9				
Colombia						
Ecuador	11.1	9.8	11.4	11.0		
French Guiana						
Guyana						
Paraguay	3.0		4.5	4.3		
Peru						
Suriname						
Uruguay	4.3	4.5	4.8	4.5		
Venezuela						
Caribbean						
Anguilla						
Antigua						
Aruba						
Bahamas						
Barbados	11.6	11.0	11.9			
Bermuda						
British Virgin Islands						
Cayman Islands	11.3	12.2	12.6	14.1		
Cuba						
Dominica						
Dominican Republic	9.6	10.2	11.3	14.0		
Grenada						
Guadeloupe						
Haiti						
Jamaica						
Martinique						
Netherlands Antilles	5.1	5.6	5.7	6.4	6.9	
St Kitts	12.4					
St Lucia						
St Vincent/Grenadines	12.9	13.4	12.2	15.1		
Trinidad and Tobago						
Central America						
Belize		9.1	7.6	7.9	6.8	10.6
Costa Rica	20.2	24.7	27.2	26.3	32.0	
El Salvador	7.4	7.1	7.4	7.8	7.7	
Guatemala	8.4	9.9	9.9			
Honduras						
Mexico	1.2	1.3	1.5	1.9		
Nicaragua						
Panama	16.8	19.9	17.9	20.5		
Puerto Rico						
South Asia						
Afghanistan						
Bangladesh						
Bhutan	5.7	5.7	5.5	4.8		
India	1.8	1.6	1.6			
Nepal	4.4	4.3	5.0	4.8	4.7	
Pakistan						
Sri Lanka	5.4	5.7	6.0	5.4	4.8	

HEALTH EXPENDITURE   Table No. 1707 (cont'd)

Government Expenditure on Health 1987-1992

Units: % of total central government expenditure

	1987	1988	1989	1990	1991	1992
Japan						
Japan						
ASEAN/NICs						
Brunei						
Hong Kong						
Indonesia	1.5	1.7	2.0	2.4		
Macau						
Malaysia	4.7	4.9	5.0	5.2	5.3	5.3
Philippines	4.6	4.3	4.4	4.1	4.2	
Singapore	3.6	5.2	4.7	4.6		
South Korea						
Taiwan						
Thailand	6.1	6.3	6.3	6.8	7.4	
East/SE Asia						
Cambodia						
China						
Laos						
Mongolia						
Myanmar	5.0	5.0	4.7	6.5		
North Korea						
Vietnam						
Australasia						
Australia	9.4	9.8	12.8	12.7	12.7	
New Zealand	12.1	12.7			12.0	11.9
Pacific						
American Samoa						
Fiji	8.3	7.3	7.2	7.7	7.9	8.1
French Polynesia						
Guam						
Kiribati						
Nauru						
New Caledonia						
Papua New Guinea	9.6	9.4				
Solomon Islands	6.7	6.2				
Tonga	8.7	9.0	8.4	7.0	6.6	
Tuvalu						
Vanuatu	9.6	8.7	6.6			
Western Samoa						
Middle East						
Bahrain	7.7	7.7	7.7	7.6	9.2	
Egypt	2.5	2.4	2.8			
Iran	6.0	7.1	8.3	7.6	7.9	8.3
Iraq						
Israel	3.2	3.8	3.8	4.0	3.7	
Jordan	5.4	4.1	5.8	5.0		
Kuwait						
Lebanon						
Oman	4.8	4.8	5.1	4.6	5.4	
Qatar						
Saudi Arabia						
Syria	1.6	1.3	1.3	1.9		
United Arab Emirates	6.9	7.0	6.9			
Yemen	3.5	3.6	3.9	3.7	4.7	4.7

HEALTH EXPENDITURE   Table No. 1707 (cont'd)

Government Expenditure on Health 1987-1992

Units: % of total central government expenditure

	1987	1988	1989	1990	1991	1992
North Africa						
Algeria						
Chad						
Djibouti						
Ethiopia	3.9	3.4				
Libya						
Mali	2.6	2.1				
Mauritania						
Morocco	3.0					
Niger						
Somalia						
Sudan						
Tunisia	5.9	6.3	6.1	6.1	6.3	6.6
West Africa						
Benin						
Burkina Faso	5.2					
Cameroon						
Cape Verde			3.4			
Côte d'Ivoire						
Equatorial Guinea						
Gabon						
Gambia						
Ghana	8.3	9.0				
Guinea						
Guinea-Bissau	5.4		1.4			
Liberia	7.1	5.1				
Nigeria						
Sao Tomé e Príncipe						
Senegal						
Sierra Leone				9.6		
Togo	5.2					
East/Central Africa						
Angola						
Burundi						
Central African Republic						
Comoros	7.3					
Congo						
Kenya	6.0	5.9	5.4	5.4		
Madagascar		4.3	6.2	7.0	6.6	
Maldives						
Mauritius	7.6	7.7	9.2	8.7	8.7	
Réunion						
Rwanda						
Seychelles						
Tanzania						
Uganda						
Zaire						
Southern Africa						
Botswana	7.4	5.5	4.8	5.1		
Lesotho	7.4	8.8	8.8	10.7	11.5	
Malawi	5.9	7.3	7.4			
Mozambique						
Namibia				11.1	9.7	
South Africa						
Swaziland	9.4	8.6	8.8	8.9	8.5	
Zambia	5.1	7.4				
Zimbabwe	6.8	7.6	7.6			

Source: International Monetary Fund
Notes: see end of section

Notes to Table in Section Seventeen

Table 1701 Immunisation data refer to % of infants
vaccinated, 1983/84
a Health services: data for 1984/85
b Immunisation: infants under 24 months
c Immunisation: infants under 15 months
d Health services: data for 1981 or earlier
e Immunisation: measles only

Table 1702 a Hospitals and clinics: 1987
b Hospitals and clinics refers to hospitals only
c Hospitals and clinics: 1986
d Hospitals and clinics: 1983
e Hospitals and clinics: 1988
f Hospitals and clinics: 1984
g Hospitals and clinics: 1979
h Hospitals and clinics: 1980
i Beds: 1987
j Beds: 1988
k Hospitals and clinics: 1991
l Beds: 1978
m Beds: 1981
n Beds: 1986
o Beds: 1985

Table 1703 a Pharmacists data are not for year stated,
but for latest available previous year
b Nursing personnel includes nursing auxiliaries
c Dentists: 1988
d Dentists and nursing personnel: 1986
e Midwives: 1982
f Nursing personnel includes midwives
g Nursing personnel: government
establishments only
h Peninsular Malaysia only
i Dentists: 1981
j Doctors: 1987
k Nursing personnel and midwives: 1982
l Nursing personnel: 1988
m Nursing personnel: 1981
n Nursing personnel: 1987

Table 1704 A Infectious and parasitic diseases
B Malignant neoplasms
C Diseases of the circulatory system
D Diseases of the respiratory system
E Diseases of the digestive system
F All other diseases
G Motor traffic accidents
H Other accidents
I Violent deaths (including suicide, homicide)

a Column B is made up of some figures relating
only to deaths per 100,000 females over 15
b Includes Canadian citizens temporarily in
the USA
c Column F includes some rates that relate only
to deaths per 100,000 males over 50
d Column F includes some rates per 100,000 live born
e Excludes Indian jungle population
f Excludes Vietnamese refugees
g Excludes transients afloat and non-locally
domiciled military and civilian services personnel
and their dependents

h Includes Israeli residents in certain
other territories under occupation by
Israeli military since June 1967

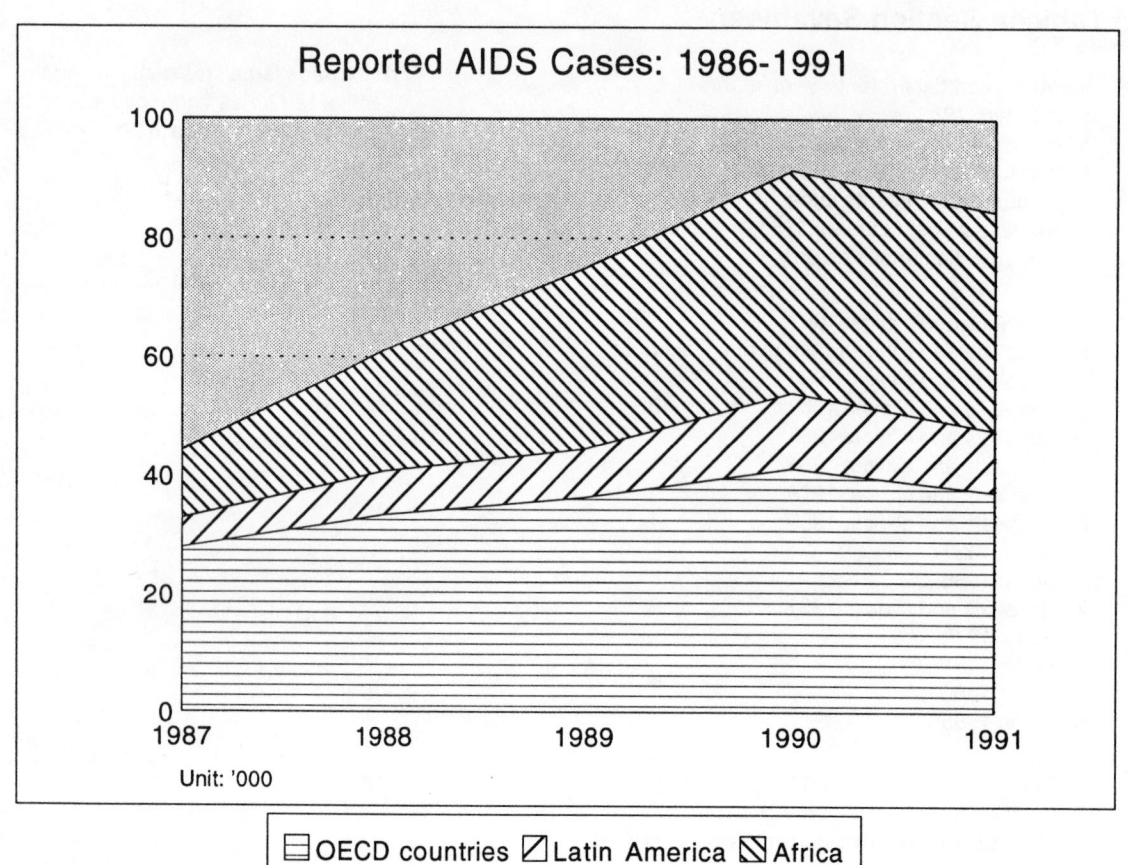

Reported AIDS Cases: 1986-1991

Unit: '000

☐ OECD countries ☑ Latin America ◺ Africa

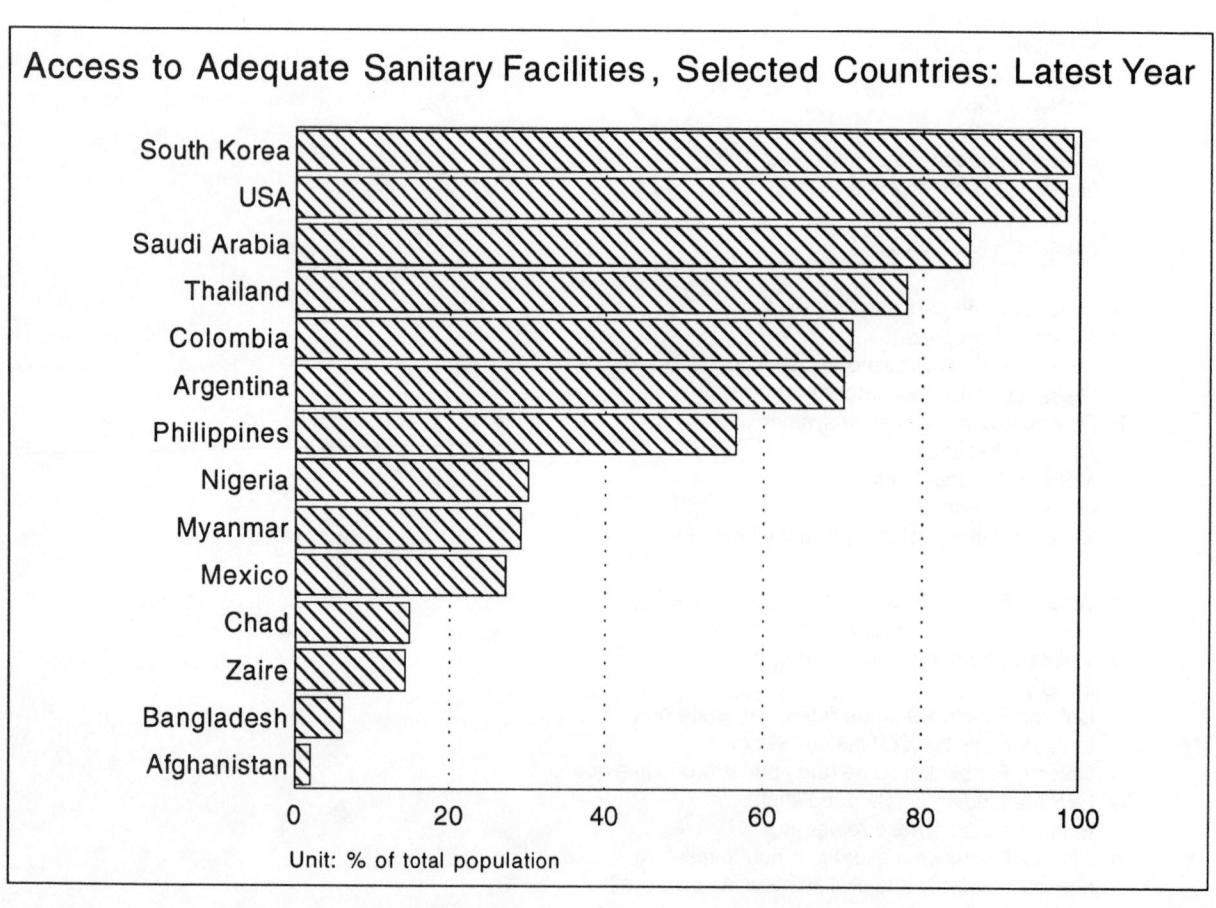

Access to Adequate Sanitary Facilities, Selected Countries: Latest Year

Unit: % of total population

Literacy and Education

BASIC EDUCATION INDICATORS   Table No. 1801

Adult Literacy Rates and School Leaving Age: Latest Year

Units: As stated

	Year	Age group	Literacy rate %	UNESCO estimate 1990	Compulsory education: Commencement age	Leaving age
North America						
Canada	1986	15+	96.6		6	16
USA	1985	14+	99.5		6	16
South America						
Argentina	1980	15+	93.9	95.3	6	14
Bolivia	1976	15+	63.2	77.5	6	13
Brazil	1985	15+	77.8	81.1	7	14
Chile	1982	15+	91.1	93.4	6	13
Colombia	1981	15+	85.2	86.7	6	14
Ecuador	1982	15+	80.2	85.8	6	14
French Guiana	1982	15+	83.0		6	16
Guyana [a]	1970	15+	91.6	96.4	6	14
Paraguay	1982	15+	87.5	90.1	7	13
Peru	1981	15+	81.9	85.1	6	12
Suriname	1985	15+	90.0	94.9	6	12
Uruguay	1985	15+	95.0	96.2	6	14
Venezuela	1981	15+	84.7	88.1	5	14
Caribbean						
Anguilla						
Antigua					5	16
Aruba						
Bahamas					5	14
Barbados [a]	1970	15+	99.3		5	16
Bermuda [a]	1970	15+	98.4		5	16
British Virgin Islands [a]	1970	15+	98.3		5	15
Cayman Islands [a]	1970	15+	97.5		5	15
Cuba	1981	15-49	97.8	94.0	6	11
Dominica [a]	1970	15+	94.1		5	15
Dominican Republic	1981	15+	68.6	83.3	7	14
Grenada [a]	1970	15+	97.8		5	16
Guadeloupe	1982	15+	90.0		6	16
Haiti	1982	15+	34.8	53.0	6	12
Jamaica [a]	1970	15+	96.1	98.4	6	12
Martinique	1982	15+	92.8		6	16
Netherlands Antilles [b]	1981	15+	93.8			
St Kitts [a]	1970	15+	97.6		5	17
St Lucia [a]	1970	15+	81.7		5	15
St Vincent/Grenadines [a,b]	1970	15+	95.6			
Trinidad and Tobago	1980	15+	94.9	96.1	5	11
Central America						
Belize [a]	1970	15+	91.2		5	14
Costa Rica	1984	15+	92.6	92.8	6	15
El Salvador	1980	10+	69.8	73.0	7	15
Guatemala	1985	15+	55.0	55.1	7	14
Honduras	1985	15+	59.5	73.1	7	13
Mexico	1990	15+	87.6	87.3	6	14
Nicaragua	1980	15+	87.0		7	12
Panama	1985	15+	88.2	88.1	6	15
Puerto Rico	1980	15+	89.1		8	14
South Asia						
Afghanistan	1979	15+	18.2	29.4	7	15
Bangladesh	1981	15+	29.2	35.3	6	10
Bhutan [b]						
India	1981	15+	40.8	48.2	6	14
Nepal	1981	15+	20.6	25.6	6	11
Pakistan [b]	1981	15+	26.2	34.8		
Sri Lanka	1981	15+	86.8	88.4	5	15

BASIC EDUCATION INDICATORS

Table No. 1801 (cont'd)

Adult Literacy Rates and School Leaving Age: Latest Year

Units: As stated

	Year	Age group	Literacy rate %	UNESCO estimate 1990	Compulsory education: Commencement age	Leaving age
Japan						
Japan					6	15
ASEAN/NICs						
Brunei	1981	15+	77.8		5	16
Hong Kong [a]	1971	15+	77.3	88.1	6	15
Indonesia	1990	15+	81.6	77.0	7	13
Macau	1970	15+	79.4		6	12
Malaysia	1980	15+	69.6	78.4	6	14
Philippines	1980	15+	83.3	89.7	7	13
Singapore [b]	1980	15+	82.9	86.1		
South Korea	1970	15+	87.6	96.3	6	12
Taiwan	1980	15+	88.0			
Thailand	1980	15+	88.0	93.0	7	15
East/SE Asia						
Cambodia					6	12
China	1987	15+	71.4	73.3	7	16
Laos	1985	15-45	83.9		7	15
Mongolia					8	16
Myanmar	1983	15+	78.6	80.6	5	10
North Korea					5	15
Vietnam	1979	15+	84.0	87.6	6	11
Australasia						
Australia	1985	15+	99.0		6	16
New Zealand	1985	15+	98.5		5	15
Pacific						
American Samoa	1980	15+	97.3		6	18
Fiji [b]	1985	15+	85.5			
French Polynesia					6	14
Guam	1980	15+	96.4		5	16
Kiribati					6	14
Nauru					6	16
New Caledonia	1976	15+	91.3		6	16
Papua New Guinea [b]	1971	10+	32.1	52.0		
Solomon Islands [b]						
Tonga	1976	15+	99.6		6	14
Tuvalu					7	15
Vanuatu [b]	1979	15+	52.9			
Western Samoa [b]	1971	15+	87.9			
Middle East						
Bahrain [b]	1981	15+	69.8	77.4		
Egypt	1986	15+	44.5	48.4	6	15
Iran	1986	15+	52.0	54.0	6	10
Iraq	1985	15-45	89.3	59.7	6	12
Israel [a]	1983	15+	91.8		5	16
Jordan	1979	15+	65.4	80.1	6	15
Kuwait	1985	15+	74.5	73.0	6	14
Lebanon [b]	1970	10+		77.0		
Oman [b]						
Qatar [b]	1986	10+	75.7			
Saudi Arabia [b]	1982	15+	51.1	62.4		
Syria	1981	15+	55.6	64.5	6	11
United Arab Emirates	1975	15+	53.5		6	12
Yemen	1990	15+		38.5	6	12

455

BASIC EDUCATION INDICATORS   Table No. 1801 (cont'd)

Adult Literacy Rates and School Leaving Age: Latest Year

Units: As stated

	Year	Age group	Literacy rate %	UNESCO estimate 1990	Compulsory education: Commence-ment age	Leaving age
North Africa						
Algeria	1987	15+	49.6	57.4	6	15
Chad		15+		29.8	6	14
Djibouti					6	15
Ethiopia	1984	15+	24.3		7	13
Libya	1973	15+	50.1	63.8	6	15
Mali	1976	15+	9.4	32.0	8	15
Mauritania	1976	6+	17.4	34.0		
Morocco	1982	15+	30.3	49.5	7	14
Niger		15+		28.4	7	15
Somalia	1975	10+	54.8	24.1	6	14
Sudan [b]	1973	10-49	31.4	27.1		
Tunisia [b]	1984	15+	50.7	65.3		
West Africa						
Benin	1979	15+	16.5	23.4	6	11
Burkina Faso	1975	15+	8.8	18.2	7	14
Cameroon	1976	15+	41.2	54.1	6	12
Cape Verde	1989	15+	66.5		7	13
Côte d'Ivoire		15+		53.8	7	13
Equatorial Guinea	1983	15+	62.0	50.2	6	14
Gabon		15+		60.7	6	16
Gambia [b]		15+		27.2		
Ghana	1970	15+	30.2	60.3	6	16
Guinea		15+		24.0	7	13
Guinea-Bissau	1979	15+	20.0	36.5	7	13
Liberia	1974	15+	19.6	39.5	7	16
Nigeria		15+		50.7	6	12
Sao Tomé e Príncipe	1981	15+	57.4		6	14
Senegal		15+		38.3	7	13
Sierra Leone [b]		15+		20.7		
Togo	1981	15+	31.4	43.3	6	12
East/Central Africa						
Angola	1985	15+	41.0	41.7	7	15
Burundi	1990	10+	50.0		7	13
Central African Republic	1975	15+	18.2	37.7	6	14
Comoros	1980	15+	47.9		7	16
Congo	1985	15+	62.9	56.6	6	16
Kenya [b]		15+		69.0		
Madagascar		15+		80.2	6	13
Maldives [b]	1985	15+	91.3			
Mauritius [b]		15+		82.6		
Réunion	1982	15+	78.6		6	16
Rwanda	1978	15+	38.2	50.2	7	15
Seychelles	1971	15+	57.7		6	15
Tanzania	1986	15+	90.4		7	14
Uganda [b]		15+		48.3		
Zaire		15+		71.8	6	12
Southern Africa						
Botswana [b]	1971	15+	41.0	73.6		
Lesotho		15+		73.6	6	13
Malawi		15+		41.2	6	14
Mozambique	1980	15+	27.2	32.9	7	14
Namibia		15+		72.5	7	16
South Africa	1986	15+	78.2			
Swaziland [b]	1986	15+	67.3	67.9		
Zambia		15+		72.8	7	14
Zimbabwe	1982	15+	46.3	66.9	7	15

Source: UNESCO/national statistical offices
Notes: see end of section

PRE-PRIMARY EDUCATION   Table No. 1802

Pre-Primary Education: Schools, Staff and Pupils, Latest Year

Units: As stated

	Year	Number of institutions	Number of teaching staff ('000)	Number of pupils ('000)	Pupil/ teacher ratio
North America					
Canada	1990		15	485	31
USA	1989			6,745	
South America					
Argentina	1988	9,137	44	798	18
Bolivia [a]	1990	2,125	3	121	42
Brazil	1990	50,957	155	3,741	24
Chile [b]	1990	4,180	9	220	24
Colombia	1991	7,269	14	343	24
Ecuador	1987	1,235	5	108	23
French Guiana [c]	1990	18		7	48
Guyana	1988	350	1	26	18
Paraguay [a]	1990	94		34	
Peru [a]	1990	8,611	22	604	27
Suriname	1988	286	1	18	27
Uruguay [d]	1988	1,141	1	61	44
Venezuela [e]	1989	1,407	25	571	23
Caribbean					
Anguilla					
Antigua	1983	21		1	29
Aruba					
Bahamas					
Barbados [f]	1982	126		3	23
Bermuda [f]	1984	32		1	35
British Virgin Islands	1984	6			15
Cayman Islands	1979	5			32
Cuba	1989		7	145	20
Dominica	1990	65		2	22
Dominican Republic	1989			22	
Grenada	1987	70		4	24
Guadeloupe	1990	119	1	20	26
Haiti	1984	360	1	21	22
Jamaica	1989	1,673	4	137	35
Martinique	1991	84		20	
Netherlands Antilles	1982	93		9	25
St Kitts	1988	50		2	17
St Lucia	1989	125		5	20
St Vincent/Grenadines	1986	66		2	13
Trinidad and Tobago	1990	43		1	12
Central America					
Belize	1986	72		2	16
Costa Rica	1990	791	2	47	23
El Salvador	1988	1,054	2	72	41
Guatemala	1987	2,992	5	144	29
Honduras	1986	766	1	53	37
Mexico	1990	46,736	105	2,734	26
Nicaragua	1990	978	2	63	33
Panama	1989	797	1	32	23
Puerto Rico	1975			20	
South Asia					
Afghanistan	1988	263	2	20	13
Bangladesh	1988	51,495	63	2,317	37
Bhutan					
India	1990	15,427		1,510	
Nepal	1984	176	1	17	23
Pakistan					
Sri Lanka					

PRE-PRIMARY EDUCATION   Table No. 1802 (cont'd)

Pre-Primary Education: Schools, Staff and Pupils, Latest Year

Units: As stated

	Year	Number of institutions	Number of teaching staff ('000)	Number of pupils ('000)	Pupil/ teacher ratio
Japan					
Japan	1990	15,076	101	2,008	20
ASEAN/NICs					
Brunei [a]	1991	155		8	
Hong Kong	1988	814	8	215	28
Indonesia	1989	37,756	92	1,545	17
Macau	1976	51		7	39
Malaysia	1990	6,046	11	329	31
Philippines	1989	3,827	11	321	29
Singapore	1989	104	1	18	23
South Korea	1991	8,421	20	426	22
Taiwan	1986	2,396	13	238	19
Thailand [g]	1989	25,705	57	224	4
East/SE Asia					
Cambodia	1984	598	1	35	25
China	1990	172,322	750	19,722	26
Laos	1989	638	2	28	19
Mongolia	1986	696	2	62	26
Myanmar					
North Korea	1987	16,964	35	728	21
Vietnam	1985	6,446	66	1,702	26
Australasia					
Australia	1990			180	
New Zealand [a,b]	1990	1,410	2	72	43
Pacific					
American Samoa	1989	95		3	28
Fiji	1986	214		5	17
French Polynesia	1990	75	1	16	25
Guam	1983			3	29
Kiribati					
Nauru	1985	4			19
New Caledonia	1990	73		11	25
Papua New Guinea	1990			1	
Solomon Islands					
Tonga	1975	11		1	23
Tuvalu					
Vanuatu	1981			1	
Western Samoa	1977	40		2	18
Middle East					
Bahrain [h]	1990	71		9	26
Egypt	1990	1,076	8	199	25
Iran	1990	3,586	9	227	27
Iraq	1988	614	5	85	18
Israel	1989			318	
Jordan	1990	546	2	45	23
Kuwait	1988	190	3	52	18
Lebanon	1986	1,776	5	130	25
Oman	1990	8		4	20
Qatar	1990	53		5	18
Saudi Arabia	1989	662	5	70	15
Syria [a]	1990	904	3	84	27
United Arab Emirates	1989		2	47	22
Yemen	1989	39		12	24

PRE-PRIMARY EDUCATION

Table No. 1802 (cont'd)

Pre-Primary Education: Schools, Staff and Pupils, Latest Year

Units: As stated

	Year	Number of institutions	Number of teaching staff ('000)	Number of pupils ('000)	Pupil/ teacher ratio
North Africa					
Algeria					
Chad					
Djibouti [b,i]	1991	2			60
Ethiopia	1988	848	2	87	46
Libya	1985	78	1	15	14
Mali					
Mauritania					
Morocco	1989	32,988	38	787	21
Niger	1990	71		11	40
Somalia	1985	16		1	10
Sudan	1985	4,003	6	236	42
Tunisia	1989	649	2	44	25
West Africa					
Benin	1988	308	1	13	21
Burkina Faso	1989	95		8	30
Cameroon	1989	745	3	93	27
Cape Verde	1986	58		5	33
Côte d'Ivoire	1985			9	
Equatorial Guinea					
Gabon					
Gambia					
Ghana	1989	4,735	15	323	21
Guinea					
Guinea-Bissau	1988	5		1	18
Liberia	1984			71	
Nigeria					
Sao Tomé e Príncipe	1989	13		3	30
Senegal	1989	144	1	16	25
Sierra Leone					
Togo	1988	203		10	29
East/Central Africa					
Angola	1989			182	
Burundi	1988			2	49
Central African Republic	1987	173	1	12	20
Comoros	1980		1	18	30
Congo	1990	56	1	6	10
Kenya	1987	12,466	17	661	38
Madagascar					
Maldives	1986	1		2	
Mauritius	1982	340	1	11	20
Réunion [j]	1988	148	1	40	30
Rwanda	1987	150		8	52
Seychelles	1991	35		3	19
Tanzania					
Uganda					
Zaire					
Southern Africa					
Botswana					
Lesotho					
Malawi					
Mozambique	1986			45	
Namibia [b]	1990			6	226
South Africa	1985		7	109	15
Swaziland	1978	50		2	59
Zambia	1979			6	
Zimbabwe					

Source: UNESCO/national statistical offices
Notes: see end of section

PRIMARY EDUCATION

Table No. 1803

Primary Education: Schools, Staff and Pupils, Latest Year

Units: As stated

	Year	Number of institutions	Number of teaching staff ('000)	Number of pupils ('000)	Pupil/ teacher ratio
North America					
Canada	1990	12,220	155	2,372	15
USA [a]	1989		1,398	28,973	21
South America					
Argentina	1988	21,207	260	4,999	19
Bolivia [b]	1990	12,639	52	1,279	25
Brazil	1990	208,934	1,261	28,944	23
Chile	1990	8,101	55	1,991	36
Colombia	1991	41,044	143	4,311	30
Ecuador	1987		58	1,822	31
French Guiana [c]	1990	51		14	34
Guyana	1988	414	4	118	29
Paraguay	1990	4,602	28	686	25
Peru	1990	24,327	143	4,019	28
Suriname	1988	301	3	66	23
Uruguay	1988	2,381	15	352	23
Venezuela [b,d]	1989	14,661	166	3,871	23
Caribbean					
Anguilla					
Antigua	1983	48		10	23
Aruba					
Bahamas [a,e,f]	1988	90	1	31	22
Barbados [g]	1989	115	2	29	18
Bermuda	1984	22		5	17
British Virgin Islands	1984	19		2	
Cayman Islands [f]	1980	15		2	33
Cuba	1989	9,417	71	886	12
Dominica	1990	65		13	29
Dominican Republic	1989	4,854	22	1,032	47
Grenada	1987	63	1	21	26
Guadeloupe	1990	222	2	39	19
Haiti	1987	4,799	22	781	35
Jamaica [h]	1989	873	10	339	34
Martinique [i]	1991	210		33	
Netherlands Antilles	1982	122		32	
St Kitts	1989	33		8	22
St Lucia	1989	88	1	33	29
St Vincent/Grenadines	1989	61	1	26	18
Trinidad and Tobago [j]	1990	476	7	194	26
Central America					
Belize [d]	1989	235	2	44	25
Costa Rica	1990	3,268	14	435	32
El Salvador	1989	4,160	25	1,149	45
Guatemala [b,k]	1988	8,481	31	1,098	35
Honduras	1988	8,319	21	863	42
Mexico	1990	82,280	472	14,508	31
Nicaragua	1990	4,030	19	633	33
Panama	1989	2,619	18	350	20
Puerto Rico [h]	1981			493	
South Asia					
Afghanistan	1989			726	
Bangladesh	1989	45,383	187	11,285	60
Bhutan	1988	150	2	55	37
India [f]	1989	550,700	1,602	97,318	61
Nepal	1988	13,514	57	2,109	37
Pakistan [l]	1989	118,607	210	8,615	41
Sri Lanka	1987	9,370	143	2,037	14

PRIMARY EDUCATION

Primary Education: Schools, Staff and Pupils, Latest Year

Units: As stated

	Year	Number of institutions	Number of teaching staff ('000)	Number of pupils ('000)	Pupil/ teacher ratio
Japan					
Japan	1990	24,827	444	9,373	21
ASEAN/NICs					
Brunei [i,m]	1991	146	3	36	13
Hong Kong [k]	1989	803	20	536	27
Indonesia	1989	168,625	1,286	29,934	23
Macau	1978	66	1	24	30
Malaysia	1990	6,884	121	2,456	20
Philippines	1989	34,377	315	10,285	33
Singapore	1989	203	10	258	26
South Korea	1991	6,245	138	4,759	34
Taiwan	1986	2,486	75	2,364	32
Thailand	1990	31,349	338	6,676	20
East/SE Asia					
Cambodia	1984		37	1,505	41
China	1990	766,072	5,582	122,414	22
Laos	1989	6,435	20	564	28
Mongolia	1990	638	6	166	28
Myanmar	1989	33,499	193	6,483	34
North Korea	1987	4,813	59	1,543	26
Vietnam [n]	1987	12,511	236	8,666	37
Australasia					
Australia	1990	7,927	96	1,583	17
New Zealand [i,m]	1990	2,310	16	314	19
Pacific					
American Samoa	1989	26		9	19
Fiji	1990	681	4	144	34
French Polynesia	1990	180	2	28	14
Guam [o]	1988	39	1	16	22
Kiribati	1991	102	1	16	29
Nauru	1985	7		1	20
New Caledonia	1990	205	1	23	20
Papua New Guinea	1990	2,606	13	415	32
Solomon Islands [e]	1988	430	2	53	23
Tonga	1990	115	1	17	24
Tuvalu [b]	1990	11		1	21
Vanuatu [h]	1991	267	1	25	29
Western Samoa	1989		2	38	25
Middle East					
Bahrain	1990	112	3	67	22
Egypt	1990	15,082	279	6,402	23
Iran	1990	59,280	339	940	3
Iraq	1988	8,052	131	3,023	23
Israel	1989	1,513	38	702	19
Jordan [b,m]	1990	1,387	21	618	29
Kuwait	1988	297	10	185	18
Lebanon	1986	2,130		399	
Oman	1990	431	10	263	28
Qatar [c]	1990	153	4	49	11
Saudi Arabia	1989	8,808	116	1,801	16
Syria	1990	9,683	98	2,452	25
United Arab Emirates	1989		12	216	18
Yemen [f]	1990	8,237	354	1,291	4

PRIMARY EDUCATION

Table No. 1803 (cont'd)

Primary Education: Schools, Staff and Pupils, Latest Year

Units: As stated

	Year	Number of institutions	Number of teaching staff ('000)	Number of pupils ('000)	Pupil/ teacher ratio
North Africa					
Algeria	1990	13,135	151	4,189	28
Chad	1989	1,868	7	492	67
Djibouti [p]	1991	69	1	33	45
Ethiopia	1988	8,584	66	2,856	43
Libya	1985		42	789	19
Mali [j]	1990	1,428	8	341	42
Mauritania	1983	1,121	3	159	49
Morocco	1989	3,903	84	2,163	26
Niger	1990	2,807	9	369	42
Somalia	1985	1,224	10	194	20
Sudan	1986	7,009	50	1,767	35
Tunisia	1990	3,866	51	1,406	28
West Africa					
Benin	1990	2,808	13	457	35
Burkina Faso	1990	2,486	9	504	57
Cameroon	1989	6,549	38	1,946	51
Cape Verde	1989	545	2	68	34
Côte d'Ivoire [h]	1985	5,796	34	1,215	36
Equatorial Guinea	1983			62	
Gabon	1987	992	4	195	46
Gambia	1989	232	2	75	31
Ghana [f]	1989	9,831	63	1,703	27
Guinea	1990	2,476	9	347	40
Guinea-Bissau [b,k]	1988	632	3	79	26
Liberia	1986			80	
Nigeria	1991	35,446	354	13,777	39
Sao Tomé e Príncipe	1989	64	1	20	35
Senegal	1989	2,422	12	683	58
Sierra Leone	1990	1,795	11	367	34
Togo	1988	2,429	10	569	55
East/Central Africa					
Angola [d]	1989		32	1,041	33
Burundi	1989	1,335	9	596	66
Central African Republic	1989	986	4	324	90
Comoros	1987	257	2	65	36
Congo	1990	1,655	8	503	66
Kenya	1988	14,288	156	5,124	33
Madagascar	1989	13,555	38	1,512	40
Maldives	1982			34	
Mauritius	1990	289	7	137	21
Réunion [a,e]	1988	351	4	74	19
Rwanda	1989	1,671	19	1,059	57
Seychelles [i,m]	1991	25	1	15	19
Tanzania	1990	10,417	97	3,379	35
Uganda	1988	7,905	76	2,633	35
Zaire	1987	10,819	113	4,357	38
Southern Africa					
Botswana	1990	602	9	284	32
Lesotho	1990	1,190	6	352	55
Malawi	1989	2,693	21	1,325	64
Mozambique [i,m]	1990	3,496	21	1,206	57
Namibia [i]	1990	1,134		314	
South Africa [q]	1985	2,452	55	573	10
Swaziland	1989	490	5	157	32
Zambia [d,g]	1989	3,493	32	1,447	45
Zimbabwe	1990	4,534	59	2,116	36

Source: UNESCO/national statistical offices

Notes: see end of section

SECONDARY EDUCATION

Table No. 1804

Secondary Education: Staff and Pupils, Latest Year

Units: As stated

	Year	Number of teaching staff ('000)	Number of pupils ('000)	Pupil/ teacher ratio
North America				
Canada	1990	164	2,293	14
USA [a]	1989	1,042	12,583	12
South America				
Argentina	1987	248	1,862	8
Bolivia	1990	12	219	18
Brazil	1990	243	3,499	14
Chile [b]	1990	42	720	17
Colombia	1991	120	2,378	20
Ecuador	1987	54	772	14
French Guiana [c]	1990	1	11	14
Guyana	1985	2	77	33
Paraguay	1990		164	
Peru	1990	83	1,746	21
Suriname [b]	1988	24	34	1
Uruguay	1988		243	
Venezuela	1989	30	280	9
Caribbean				
Anguilla				
Antigua	1983		4	13
Aruba				
Bahamas	1986	2	30	19
Barbados	1989	1	24	20
Bermuda	1984		5	11
British Virgin Islands	1983		1	13
Cayman Islands	1980		2	10
Cuba	1989	109	1,073	10
Dominica	1986		6	
Dominican Republic	1985	12	439	37
Grenada	1987		6	20
Guadeloupe	1990	3	50	15
Haiti	1985		144	
Jamaica	1989	9	237	26
Martinique [d]	1991	3	46	17
Netherlands Antilles	1981	1	21	15
St Kitts	1984		4	15
St Lucia [a]	1988		6	18
St Vincent/Grenadines	1987		7	16
Trinidad and Tobago	1987		100	
Central America				
Belize	1986	1	8	13
Costa Rica	1990	7	131	19
El Salvador [e]	1989	4	95	26
Guatemala	1987	16	241	15
Honduras	1986	7	179	26
Mexico	1990	402	6,704	17
Nicaragua [e]	1990	7	169	25
Panama	1989	10	190	19
Puerto Rico [f]	1981		191	
South Asia				
Afghanistan	1985	6	105	18
Bangladesh	1988	125	3,340	27
Bhutan	1984	1	6	10
India	1988	2,265	49,441	22
Nepal	1988	21	613	29
Pakistan	1990	209	3,983	19
Sri Lanka	1985		1,463	

SECONDARY EDUCATION

Secondary Education: Staff and Pupils, Latest Year

Units: As stated

	Year	Number of teaching staff ('000)	Number of pupils ('000)	Pupil/ teacher ratio
Japan				
Japan	1989	651	11,144	17
ASEAN/NICs				
Brunei	1987	2	18	12
Hong Kong	1987	20	458	23
Indonesia [g]	1989	870	11,243	13
Macau	1976	1	14	19
Malaysia	1990	74	1,420	19
Philippines [e]	1989	112	3,962	35
Singapore	1989	9	199	22
South Korea	1991	189	4,458	24
Taiwan	1986	78	1,692	22
Thailand	1990	134	2,397	18
East/SE Asia				
Cambodia	1984	5	153	32
China	1990	3,491	51,054	15
Laos	1989	12	138	12
Mongolia	1986		293	
Myanmar	1987	61	1,359	22
North Korea	1987	111	2,468	22
Vietnam	1985	177	4,023	23
Australasia				
Australia	1990	103	1,278	12
New Zealand [c]	1990	17	335	19
Pacific				
American Samoa	1989		3	15
Fiji	1988	3	48	17
French Polynesia	1990	1	20	14
Guam	1988	1	16	24
Kiribati	1990		3	12
Nauru	1985			12
New Caledonia	1989	2	20	13
Papua New Guinea [c]	1990	3	66	21
Solomon Islands	1986		7	
Tonga	1990	1	15	18
Tuvalu	1990			11
Vanuatu [h]	1990		4	22
Western Samoa	1986	1	21	36
Middle East				
Bahrain	1990	3	47	17
Egypt	1990	289	5,261	18
Iran	1990	216	5,085	24
Iraq	1988	54	1,167	22
Israel	1989	43	292	7
Jordan [b]	1990	22	409	19
Kuwait	1988	21	265	13
Lebanon	1980	21	287	13
Oman	1989	6	85	15
Qatar	1990	4	30	8
Saudi Arabia	1989	72	846	12
Syria	1990	52	914	18
United Arab Emirates	1990	9	108	13
Yemen	1990	13	421	32

SECONDARY EDUCATION

Table No. 1804 (cont'd)

Secondary Education: Staff and Pupils, Latest Year

Units: As stated

	Year	Number of teaching staff ('000)	Number of pupils ('000)	Pupil/ teacher ratio
North Africa				
Algeria	1990	127	2,176	17
Chad [e]	1989	1	59	43
Djibouti	1991		10	25
Ethiopia	1988	22	882	40
Libya	1985	36	431	12
Mali	1987		66	
Mauritania	1988	2	39	20
Morocco	1989	72	1,337	18
Niger [c,g]	1990	3	77	30
Somalia	1985	3	44	15
Sudan	1985	23	557	24
Tunisia	1990	33	565	17
West Africa				
Benin	1986	4	102	28
Burkina Faso [b]	1989	1	91	63
Cameroon	1989	18	457	26
Cape Verde [b]	1989		8	29
Côte d'Ivoire	1986		273	
Equatorial Guinea	1982		4	28
Gabon	1987	2	48	21
Gambia [i]	1987	1	16	17
Ghana	1989	46	830	18
Guinea	1990	6	86	14
Guinea-Bissau	1988	1	6	8
Liberia	1980		55	
Nigeria	1991	141	3,123	22
Sao Tomé e Príncipe	1989		6	
Senegal	1989	5	173	34
Sierra Leone	1990	6	102	17
Togo	1988	4	110	25
East/Central Africa				
Angola	1989		171	
Burundi	1989	2	38	18
Central African Republic [c]	1989	1	49	37
Comoros	1989		21	42
Congo [e]	1990	8	183	22
Kenya [b]	1988	26	563	22
Madagascar [f,g]	1989	16	349	22
Maldives	1983		3	
Mauritius [c,g]	1990	4	79	22
Réunion	1986	4	70	17
Rwanda [b]	1989	4	65	18
Seychelles [j]	1991		4	14
Tanzania	1989	8	146	19
Uganda [k]	1988	15	260	17
Zaire [d]	1987	49	1,066	22
Southern Africa				
Botswana	1989	4	62	17
Lesotho	1989	2	47	20
Malawi [d]	1989	1	30	23
Mozambique	1990	5	160	34
Namibia	1990		63	
South Africa [l]	1985	55	433	8
Swaziland [i]	1987	2	34	22
Zambia [f]	1988	6	161	28
Zimbabwe	1988	20	652	33

Source: UNESCO/national statistical offices

Notes: see end of section

HIGHER EDUCATION   Table No. 1805

Higher and University Education: Staff and Students, Latest Year

Units: As stated

	Year	Number of teaching staff ('000)	Number of students ('000)	Student/ staff ratio	Number of students at university ('000)	% of students at university
North America						
Canada	1990	62	1,359	22	841	62
USA [a]	1990	701	13,975	20	7,860	56
South America						
Argentina	1987	75	959	13	755	79
Bolivia	1989		141		106	75
Brazil	1990	132	1,540	12	1,540	100
Chile [b]	1988	15	235	16	158	67
Colombia	1989	52	475	9	410	86
Ecuador [c]	1990	13	207	16	186	90
French Guiana	1983					100
Guyana	1989		5	10	2	48
Paraguay	1990		33		29	90
Peru	1990	58	744	13	505	68
Suriname	1990		4	9	2	55
Uruguay	1988	6	62	10	62	100
Venezuela [d]	1989	39	528	13	348	66
Caribbean						
Anguilla						
Antigua	1986		1			
Aruba						
Bahamas	1987		5	21		
Barbados [b]	1989	1	4	8	2	45
Bermuda	1982		3	24	3	100
British Virgin Islands						
Cayman Islands						
Cuba	1989	24	242	10	242	100
Dominica	1990			13		
Dominican Republic	1985	7	124	19		
Grenada	1983		1	10		
Guadeloupe	1985		2		2	100
Haiti [e]	1985	1	6	10	4	71
Jamaica [f,g]	1989	1	12	12	6	46
Martinique						
Netherlands Antilles						
St Kitts	1987			5		
St Lucia	1987			6		
St Vincent/Grenadines	1989		1	7		
Trinidad and Tobago [g]	1989		7		4	64
Central America						
Belize	1985		1	11		
Costa Rica	1990		75		58	77
El Salvador	1989	3	81	24	71	87
Guatemala [b]	1986	3	52	17	52	100
Honduras [a,h]	1990	3	45	14	39	88
Mexico	1990	134	1,311	10	1,252	96
Nicaragua	1987	2	27	14	24	89
Panama [i]	1989	3	50	15	50	100
Puerto Rico	1981		137			
South Asia						
Afghanistan	1987	1	18	12	13	75
Bangladesh [c]	1990	19	358	19	49	14
Bhutan	1983			3		69
India [j]	1986	320	4,806	15	853	18
Nepal	1989	5	102	22	102	100
Pakistan [f]	1989	8	305	38	244	80
Sri Lanka	1986	4	62	17	35	57

HIGHER EDUCATION

Higher and University Education: Staff and Students, Latest Year

Units: As stated

	Year	Number of teaching staff ('000)	Number of students ('000)	Student/ staff ratio	Number of students at university ('000)	% of students at university
Japan						
Japan	1989	271	2,683	10	2,157	80
ASEAN/NICs						
Brunei	1987		1	5	1	79
Hong Kong	1984	6	77	13	14	19
Indonesia	1984	76	980	13	852	87
Macau						
Malaysia [a]	1990	11	115	11	58	51
Philippines	1989	53	1,516	28	1,225	81
Singapore	1983	3	35	11	14	40
South Korea	1991	77	1,762	23	1,159	66
Taiwan	1986	22	443	20		
Thailand	1989	52	952	18	198	21
East/SE Asia						
Cambodia						
China	1990	395	2,147	5		
Laos	1989	1	5	7	3	72
Mongolia	1986	3	39	14	17	44
Myanmar	1987	9	202	22		
North Korea	1987	27	390	14	325	83
Vietnam	1980	17	115	7	115	100
Australasia						
Australia	1990	28	485	17	485	100
New Zealand	1989	10	121	12	63	52
Pacific						
American Samoa	1988		1			
Fiji [c]	1991		8	29	3	34
French Polynesia	1983			15		
Guam [k,l]	1988		7	27	4	60
Kiribati						
Nauru						
New Caledonia	1985		1	12	1	100
Papua New Guinea	1986	1	6	7	3	53
Solomon Islands						
Tonga	1985		1			12
Tuvalu						
Vanuatu						
Western Samoa	1983		1	15		24
Middle East						
Bahrain	1990	1	7	12	6	90
Egypt [k,m]	1990	32	765	24	520	68
Iran	1988	21	316	15	216	68
Iraq	1988	11	210	19		
Israel [m]	1989		117		68	58
Jordan [a]	1990	3	80	23	40	49
Kuwait [n]	1988	2	26	16	18	69
Lebanon	1984	7	71	9	71	100
Oman	1990	1	6	8	3	51
Qatar	1989		6	14	6	98
Saudi Arabia	1990	13	154	12	129	83
Syria	1989		175		152	87
United Arab Emirates	1990	1	10	12	8	83
Yemen	1988		23	50	23	100

HIGHER EDUCATION
Table No. 1805 (cont'd)

Higher and University Education: Staff and Students, Latest Year

Units: As stated

	Year	Number of teaching staff ('000)	Number of students ('000)	Student/ staff ratio	Number of students at university ('000)	% of students at university
North Africa						
Algeria [a]	1990	21	286	14	212	74
Chad	1988		3	9	3	98
Djibouti	1991					
Ethiopia	1989	2	33	20	26	76
Libya	1985		30		30	100
Mali	1986	1	6	8	6	100
Mauritania	1988		6	22	5	91
Morocco [n]	1990	8	221	26	207	93
Niger	1989		5	13	4	92
Somalia	1986	1	16	19	16	100
Sudan	1989	3	60	24	55	91
Tunisia	1990	5	69	15	69	100
West Africa						
Benin	1990	1	11	11		
Burkina Faso	1986		4	16	4	98
Cameroon	1988	1	27	29	25	92
Cape Verde						
Côte d'Ivoire [o]	1984	1	20	16	11	57
Equatorial Guinea	1981		1	17		
Gabon	1988		4		3	71
Gambia	1983		1	9		
Ghana	1981	2	16	8	8	49
Guinea [n,p]	1988	1	6	7	6	105
Guinea-Bissau	1988					
Liberia	1987		5	11	5	95
Nigeria	1989	20	307	16	181	59
Sao Tomé e Príncipe						
Senegal [o]	1984	1	13	14	12	95
Sierra Leone	1990	1	5	8	3	54
Togo [m]	1989		7		8	104
East/Central Africa						
Angola	1990		7	15	7	100
Burundi	1990		4	8	3	70
Central African Republic [i]	1989		3	9	3	81
Comoros	1989			8		
Congo	1990	1	11	10	11	100
Kenya	1989		31		23	73
Madagascar	1990	1	36	38	36	100
Maldives						
Mauritius [h]	1990		2	5	2	76
Réunion						
Rwanda	1989	1	3	5	2	73
Seychelles	1980			5		100
Tanzania	1989	1	5	4	3	63
Uganda	1989	1	15	11	7	44
Zaire	1988	4	61	16	27	44
Southern Africa						
Botswana [n,p]	1989		3	11	2	87
Lesotho [n,p]	1989		6	19	4	77
Malawi	1988		5	12	2	47
Mozambique	1987		2	6	2	100
Namibia	1991		3	12	1	60
South Africa	1985	12	196	16	196	100
Swaziland [q]	1988		3		1	45
Zambia	1989	1	14	15	6	43
Zimbabwe	1991	3	44	17	10	22

Source: UNESCO/national statistical offices
Notes: see end of section

Notes to Tables in Section Eighteen

Table 1801   Compulsory education is not related only to the specific year quoted
Where two or more patterns of compulsory education are possible in a country, the most common is given
   a   Persons with no schooling are defined as illiterates
   b   No age limits for compulsory education are specified

Table 1802   a   Schools refer to 1989
   b   Staff refers to 1989
   c   Schools and staff refer to 1983
   d   Schools refer to 1987
   e   Schools refer to 1985
   f   Staff refers to teachers in public education only
   g   Staff refer to 1987
   h   Schools refer to 1988
   i   Four teachers only
   j   Schools and staff refer to 1986

Table 1803   a   Staff refers to 1986
   b   Schools refer to 1987
   c   Schools and staff refer to 1983
   d   Staff refers to 1988
   e   Schools refer to 1986
   f   Staff refers to public education only
   g   Schools refer to 1988
   h   Public education only
   i   Schools refer to 1989
   j   Government-aided and -maintained schools only
   k   Staff refers to 1987
   l   Includes pre-primary education
   m   Staff refers to 1989
   n   Schools and staff refer to 1985
   o   Schools refer to 1983
   p   Schools and staff refer to 1990
   q   Staff includes secondary education

Table 1804   a   Staff refers to 1985
   b   Staff refers to 1987
   c   Staff refers to 1989
   d   Staff refers to 1986
   e   Staff refers to 1988
   f   Public education only
   g   Excluding teacher training or vocational education
   h   Staff refers to 1983
   i   Staff refers to 1984
   j   Staff refers to 1990
   k   Government-aided and -maintained schools only
   l   Includes primary education

Table 1805   a   Staff refers to 1989
   b   Staff refers to 1984
   c   University students refers to 1989
   d   University students refers to 1985
   e   Staff refers to 1982
   f   Staff refers to 1986
   g   Students refers to 1986
   h   Students refers to 1989
   i   Staff refers to 1988

j   University students refers to 1987
k   Staff refers to 1985
l   Students refers to 1985
m   Students refers to 1988
n   Staff refers to 1987
o   Staff refers to 1981
p   Students refers to 1987
q   Includes students studying abroad

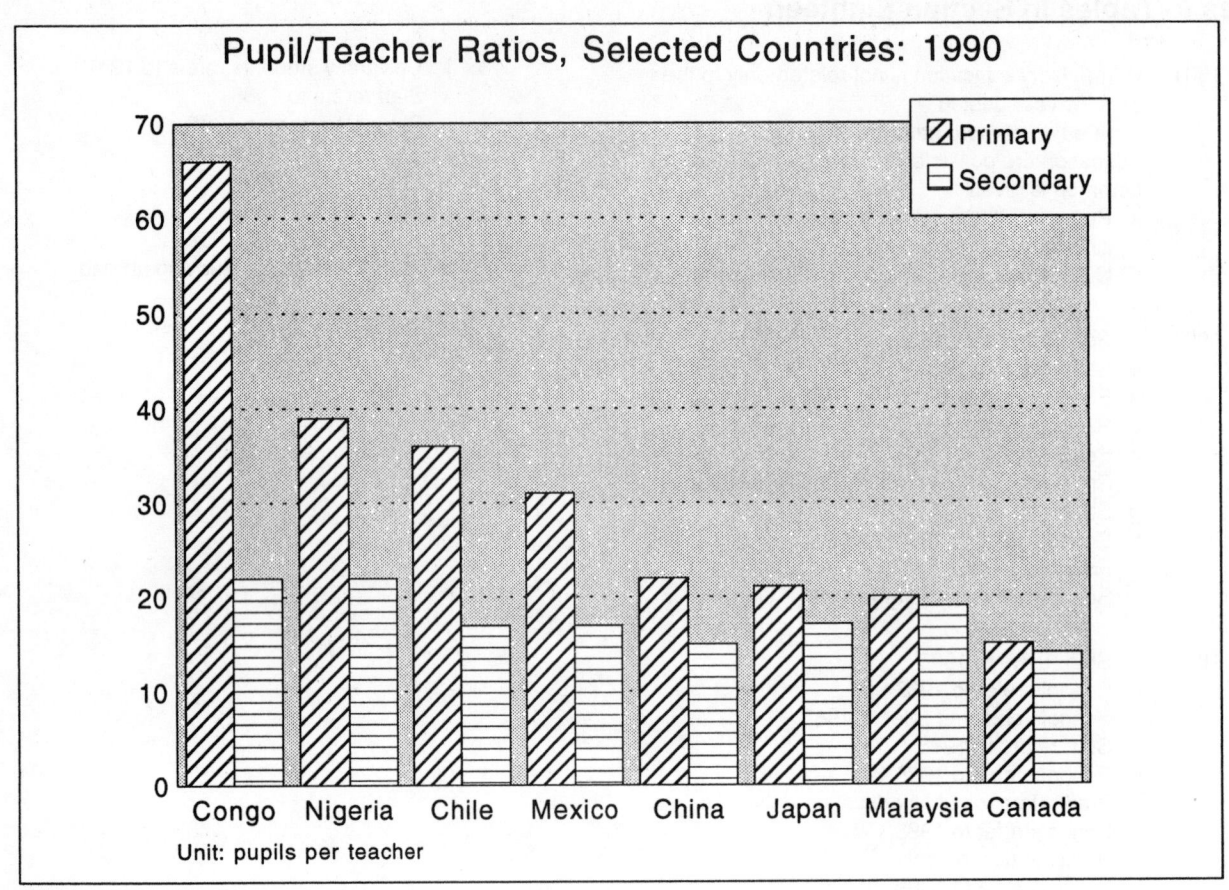

Pupil/Teacher Ratios, Selected Countries: 1990

Legend: Primary, Secondary

Unit: pupils per teacher

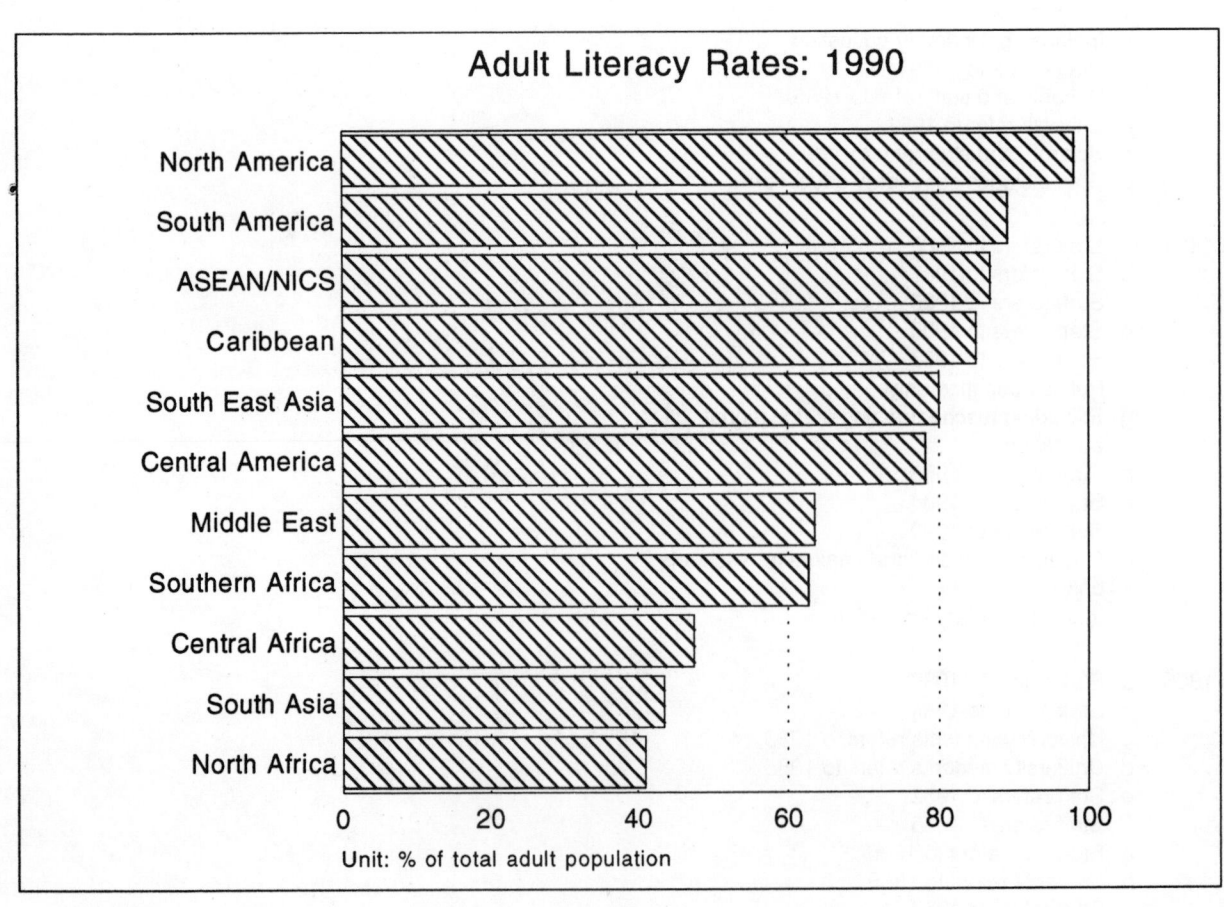

Adult Literacy Rates: 1990

Unit: % of total adult population

Section Nineteen
Agricultural Resources

AGRICULTURAL OUTPUT									Table No. 1901	

Indices of Agricultural Output 1977-1991

Index: 1979-1981 = 100

	1977	1980	1983	1985	1986	1987	1988	1989	1990	1991
North America										
Canada	99.3	99.3	109.7	113.4	124.5	115.9	103.0	113.7	125.6	124.9
USA	97.7	95.8	91.2	107.5	103.9	102.2	97.2	104.9	108.9	108.0
South America										
Argentina	93.0	95.8	104.5	106.8	106.0	106.2	113.3	102.1	109.8	111.3
Bolivia	93.4	99.5	81.5	113.5	110.0	119.8	124.4	125.4	131.0	156.0
Brazil	94.4	100.6	133.7	154.3	146.4	166.2	162.4	162.4	163.8	165.1
Chile	93.7	97.8	99.1	106.3	111.9	115.2	121.8	129.7	135.6	137.3
Colombia	88.9	99.2	100.4	102.3	109.8	111.0	119.3	126.5	135.7	138.1
Ecuador	95.4	100.4	91.5	116.9	121.7	119.7	131.8	137.1	142.5	146.3
French Guiana										
Guyana	87.5	94.1	88.4	84.5	86.7	79.7	72.7	65.9	61.6	66.6
Paraguay	88.6	96.8	113.5	137.2	122.9	134.8	137.8	167.5	170.7	168.2
Peru	106.1	93.3	99.7	109.0	109.3	113.5	124.0	122.4	110.1	110.3
Suriname	75.1	93.4	106.3	125.6	109.2	104.0	98.7	101.8	92.0	100.4
Uruguay	92.3	96.9	117.9	105.4	107.7	107.3	116.0	128.9	123.9	123.2
Venezuela	89.5	100.6	109.3	113.3	123.7	118.1	121.3	129.5	134.1	135.5
Caribbean										
Anguilla										
Antigua										
Aruba										
Bahamas										
Barbados	93.1	109.3	80.2	76.7	83.5	76.3	77.1	80.2	79.0	83.0
Bermuda										
British Virgin Islands										
Cayman Islands										
Cuba	89.3	92.7	105.2	110.5	112.0	106.4	110.4	111.8	107.3	107.3
Dominica										
Dominican Republic	98.2	99.5	110.8	108.7	109.2	111.6	114.4	119.6	119.8	116.6
Grenada										
Guadeloupe	109.0	95.1	114.8	118.2	126.7	116.8	130.1	116.0	97.4	104.7
Haiti	91.9	100.1	104.0	108.8	110.7	110.7	110.6	112.8	107.4	103.0
Jamaica	97.8	97.3	100.2	103.6	110.5	110.0	103.7	105.1	114.8	112.3
Martinique	151.0	74.5	123.6	122.7	134.2	120.2	120.8	122.0	134.2	137.9
Netherlands Antilles										
St Kitts										
St Lucia										
St Vincent/Grenadines										
Trinidad and Tobago	147.0	100.9	88.2	83.7	82.2	81.8	92.1	87.8	98.2	108.3
Central America										
Belize										
Costa Rica	97.0	99.0	102.5	107.7	111.7	114.2	117.0	126.0	131.6	129.0
El Salvador	91.8	101.6	84.7	86.6	83.2	85.0	82.2	81.0	92.8	92.0
Guatemala	95.4	99.7	101.8	105.0	105.0	103.8	107.1	104.3	109.9	108.5
Honduras	87.8	98.0	102.2	101.2	101.3	111.3	120.7	124.7	132.9	139.3
Mexico	89.0	100.1	108.8	112.5	113.7	112.4	117.4	116.1	122.7	121.7
Nicaragua	108.5	83.0	92.0	80.6	77.3	74.0	72.6	74.1	74.6	71.4
Panama	94.0	98.4	107.1	108.5	107.6	112.1	102.3	109.2	111.8	111.7
Puerto Rico	100.4	98.2	93.7	89.4	92.5	102.7	100.8	103.1	97.3	101.5
South Asia										
Afghanistan	92.5	99.6	103.6	103.1	102.3	103.6				
Bangladesh	94.6	100.7	106.7	112.8	114.5	112.5	112.5	122.4	123.2	123.4
Bhutan	93.0	100.3	107.3	109.1	110.1	122.4	97.3	99.2	104.6	107.4
India	97.7	97.7	117.5	123.3	122.5	121.5	137.6	146.2	148.6	150.7
Nepal	95.2	101.2	115.8	117.1	114.8	125.8	147.5	151.5	154.5	163.4
Pakistan	89.0	98.7	108.4	123.6	133.2	135.5	140.9	149.7	155.1	164.6
Sri Lanka	79.7	100.7	107.7	109.3	108.5	97.0	100.5	97.1	106.1	103.5

AGRICULTURAL OUTPUT   Table No. 1901 (cont'd)

Indices of Agricultural Output 1977-1991

Index: 1979-1981 = 100

	1977	1980	1983	1985	1986	1987	1988	1989	1990	1991
Japan										
Japan	112.2	94.9	100.4	107.0	106.0	101.4	97.3	98.0	98.3	93.1
ASEAN/NICs										
Brunei										
Hong Kong	94.1	88.6	60.3	57.0	29.9	48.2				
Indonesia	83.2	100.8	114.5	125.6	135.6	136.5	144.3	149.6	156.9	162.6
Macau										
Malaysia	83.8	100.5	107.3	132.2	144.9	152.6	63.3	171.5	175.1	174.1
Philippines	88.2	99.9	101.3	99.4	107.0	106.4	108.8	114.9	117.1	118.2
Singapore	118.3	96.2	95.8	105.9	104.8	106.9	75.8	91.7	93.2	79.8
South Korea	103.4	90.5	101.2	110.6	109.5	104.9	109.9	107.4	106.2	102.0
Taiwan										
Thailand	87.4	100.0	111.3	122.3	116.2	113.2	124.9	131.8	124.0	129.3
East/SE Asia										
Cambodia	146.6	113.9	141.4	146.8	162.5	156.5	181.8	189.3	193.6	191.2
China	83.2	98.8	122.1	131.4	134.6	141.4	142.8	145.8	158.8	165.5
Laos	70.4	101.2	114.2	134.4	135.4	126.6	119.3	139.6	148.4	146.7
Mongolia	91.3	97.7	108.0	106.9	111.8	108.5	106.7	110.5	113.3	105.0
Myanmar	86.3	99.3	122.6	138.4	140.2	140.2	130.1	117.3	118.6	123.5
North Korea	92.0	99.2	109.0	116.1	119.1	122.5	127.2	125.3	127.3	127.4
Vietnam	83.6	101.6	114.1	120.0	129.7	136.6	141.2	149.3	156.8	161.7
Australasia										
Australia	93.0	92.8	111.2	116.2	111.6	108.8	115.2	115.6	116.6	113.7
New Zealand	99.1	99.9	106.2	113.3	108.7	108.3	110.6	108.5	101.0	106.6
Pacific										
American Samoa										
Fiji	81.0	93.2	78.5	94.5	112.8	87.9	92.8	110.0	115.1	105.8
French Polynesia										
Guam										
Kiribati										
Nauru										
New Caledonia										
Papua New Guinea	93.5	101.0	106.7	114.1	110.2	116.4	121.7	129.3	128.5	127.2
Solomon Islands	78.5	95.3	110.4	118.4	108.9	107.0	114.6	126.8	131.9	134.5
Tonga	95.0	101.5	91.0	92.2	95.7	89.9	86.7	88.7	88.6	88.2
Tuvalu										
Vanuatu	98.6	89.7	104.0	107.1	113.8	113.6	105.2	96.7	125.2	115.5
Western Samoa										
Middle East										
Bahrain										
Egypt	93.4	99.8	112.5	125.9	132.3	136.9	136.6	137.8	142.8	142.4
Iran	88.8	96.3	118.6	133.5	145.3	146.8	141.8	143.7	160.8	169.4
Iraq	101.3	99.9	106.6	143.3	138.9	125.1	121.5	137.8	144.7	113.2
Israel	108.2	96.8	118.0	128.1	112.9	119.2	114.7	112.8	129.8	108.8
Jordan	76.6	116.1	132.6	148.5	134.8	156.0	166.1	119.8	155.2	111.1
Kuwait										
Lebanon	49.5	112.5	108.2	119.0	112.7	120.1				
Oman										
Qatar										
Saudi Arabia	112.4	101.0	157.7	172.7	197.1	198.8				
Syria	71.5	106.6	116.4	111.2	122.7	105.1	137.0	93.8	116.8	117.9
United Arab Emirates										
Yemen	99.9	105.1	81.3	92.6	103.5	97.3	110.0	109.1	105.0	101.1

AGRICULTURAL OUTPUT   Table No. 1901 (cont'd)

Indices of Agricultural Output 1977-1991

Index: 1979-1981 = 100

	1977	1980	1983	1985	1986	1987	1988	1989	1990	1991
North Africa										
Algeria	84.9	106.5	106.2	126.2	118.9	130.4	125.9	144.4	140.7	167.6
Chad	93.2	101.8	111.1	110.5	114.0	115.7	131.9	127.0	125.5	134.5
Djibouti										
Ethiopia	84.1	98.8	99.3	96.6	107.2	102.6	105.1	108.1	111.5	111.0
Libya	78.8	99.9	137.2	118.4	115.3	109.2	113.8	121.9	117.6	129.1
Mali	88.4	97.3	112.3	108.7	117.9	115.3	127.6	128.9	128.3	138.0
Mauritania	89.1	99.8	96.0	96.5	101.4	105.1	110.5	113.8	108.0	106.9
Morocco	84.0	106.9	108.5	129.4	157.3	135.2	164.8	166.2	159.0	178.8
Niger	88.0	101.2	101.1	82.9	90.4	86.5	107.6	95.2	90.3	110.8
Somalia	96.4	98.6	103.5	114.2	114.3	118.8	123.8	126.8	123.9	112.5
Sudan	91.9	99.7	99.4	111.5	103.4	93.3	117.3	93.5	85.1	109.9
Tunisia	97.0	105.9	111.0	138.0	117.5	142.0	104.3	120.7	143.2	158.1
West Africa										
Benin	89.7	98.0	104.7	135.4	145.9	130.9	156.4	162.6	165.8	180.7
Burkina Faso	90.4	95.5	107.4	128.3	145.4	134.4	150.5	147.5	138.0	161.4
Cameroon	102.4	99.3	104.5	109.3	118.7	110.4	113.3	111.4	111.9	107.0
Cape Verde										
Côte d'Ivoire	83.9	97.2	99.2	117.6	119.3	125.2	134.5	133.7	140.1	138.0
Equatorial Guinea										
Gabon	88.7	102.0	99.2	102.2	105.8	107.9	112.3	114.5	122.6	124.1
Gambia	96.7	93.6	107.7	117.1	124.4	124.1	126.8	135.2	112.7	123.5
Ghana	95.5	99.7	89.4	123.2	130.6	136.5	148.9	149.1	128.4	160.3
Guinea	98.8	102.2	100.0	106.8	109.6	110.8	114.9	122.2	129.6	132.7
Guinea-Bissau	81.6	98.2	110.7	118.9	123.7	124.8	122.4	122.6	131.4	131.6
Liberia	95.4	100.5	106.8	115.2	117.0	117.9	118.8	115.6	78.6	69.7
Nigeria	89.1	100.9	102.6	118.0	124.3	121.7	141.2	146.1	162.7	171.2
Sao Tomé e Príncipe										
Senegal	79.4	83.1	87.2	125.7	129.4	143.1	125.6	142.1	134.9	132.4
Sierra Leone	100.2	100.3	105.4	110.7	121.7	119.1	121.8	125.2	125.4	113.3
Togo	86.0	99.7	92.1	108.1	114.6	115.5	127.5	136.7	139.6	137.6
East/Central Africa										
Angola	98.1	103.3	97.9	97.7	100.1	100.2	100.1	98.8	100.0	102.3
Burundi	96.8	94.7	106.4	114.8	120.4	127.1	127.4	120.9	120.2	125.2
Central African Republic	94.7	100.1	105.2	102.4	111.4	112.8	120.5	120.0	120.9	124.5
Comoros										
Congo	91.9	99.7	107.1	113.7	113.7	119.2	122.6	118.1	126.9	129.4
Kenya	105.0	98.7	116.4	122.8	134.7	132.5	146.1	148.1	152.3	151.6
Madagascar	96.0	101.2	107.8	112.0	116.2	114.5	116.4	119.6	121.9	
Maldives										
Mauritius	108.0	88.0	102.7	111.6	119.3	120.1	112.3	112.7	117.1	119.4
Rwanda	87.3	97.3	109.7	120.6	111.2	111.4	111.8	112.3	117.4	123.3
Réunion	98.9	93.1	82.1	85.6	83.2	86.3	95.4	73.5	85.4	87.5
Seychelles										
Tanzania	89.7	97.9	105.0	110.5	115.0	113.8	127.5	136.7	139.6	137.6
Uganda	109.7	98.1	121.2	115.0	115.7	120.4	126.6	136.4	155.7	141.0
Zaire	97.4	100.9	110.6	116.6	118.9	121.6	125.2	127.7	128.9	132.3
Southern Africa										
Botswana	113.5	91.1	97.2	94.4	92.7	87.0	113.5	118.3	109.4	102.2
Lesotho	112.0	97.7	89.9	98.7	91.5	100.0	118.8	115.6	78.6	69.7
Malawi	96.3	98.2	100.4	106.2	109.6	106.9	113.6	111.3	109.6	121.0
Mozambique	97.2	100.1	99.2	100.6	104.7	102.8	104.6	105.5	108.8	101.8
Namibia	94.1	102.0	78.3	82.9	88.5	95.6	94.1	98.6	97.8	101.9
South Africa	90.9	97.1	79.9	95.4	96.9	101.3	105.3	111.3	103.8	104.9
Swaziland	80.2	102.0	107.4	113.7	129.7	121.8	125.3	120.2	119.5	122.3
Zambia	117.0	102.5	104.3	114.6	120.2	118.1	147.0	146.1	126.8	131.5
Zimbabwe	106.9	97.4	84.5	133.9	131.8	108.5	138.9	130.4	127.4	127.7

Source: UN Food and Agriculture Organisation (FAO)

LAND USE   Table No. 1902

Land Use and Irrigation 1990

Units: '000 hectares

	Total area	Land area	Arable land	Perma- nent crops	Perma- nent pasture	Forest & Wood- land	Other land	Irrigated land	As % of land area
North America									
Canada	997,614	922,097	45,870	80	28,100	359,000	489,047	860	0.1
USA	2,240,675	2,137,681	267,050	6,873	364,382	716,030	783,346	26,641	1.2
South America									
Argentina	276,689	273,669	25,000	2,200	142,200	59,200	45,069	1,680	0.6
Bolivia	109,858	108,438	2,100	208	26,600	55,590	23,940	165	0.2
Brazil	851,197	845,651	50,400	9,600	184,200	493,030	108,421	2,760	0.3
Chile	75,695	74,880	4,276	250	13,500	8,800	48,054	1,265	1.7
Colombia	113,891	103,870	3,900	1,520	40,400	50,300	7,750	520	0.5
Ecuador	28,356	27,684	1,700	1,025	5,150	10,900	8,909	552	1.9
French Guiana	9,000	8,815	10	2	9	7,300	1,494	2	
Guyana	21,497	19,685	480	15	1,230	16,369	1,591	130	0.6
Paraguay	40,675	39,730	2,100	116	21,100	13,800	2,614	67	0.2
Peru	128,522	128,000	3,400	330	27,120	68,400	28,750	1,260	1.0
Suriname	16,327	15,600	57	11	20	14,855	657	59	0.4
Uruguay	17,741	17,481	1,260	44	13,515	669	1,993	110	0.6
Venezuela	91,205	88,205	3,200	695	17,700	30,175	36,435	265	0.3
Caribbean									
Anguilla									
Antigua	44	44	8		4	5	27		
Aruba	19	19	2				17		
Bahamas	1,388	1,001	8	2	2	324	665		
Barbados	43	43	33		4		6		
Bermuda	5	5				1	4		
British Virgin Islands	15	15	3	4	5	1	5		
Cayman Islands	26	26			2	6	18		
Cuba	11,086	10,982	2,608	722	2,970	2,760	1,922	900	8.1
Dominica	75	75	7	10	2	31	25		
Dominican Republic	4,873	4,838	1,000	446	2,092	615	685	225	4.6
Grenada	34	34	5	8	1	3	17		
Guadeloupe	171	169	22	8	24	66	49	3	1.8
Haiti	2,775	2,756	555	350	497	38	1,316	75	2.7
Jamaica	1,099	1,083	207	62	190	185	439	35	3.2
Martinique	110	106	10	10	19	47	20	4	3.6
Netherlands Antilles	80	80	8				72		
St Kitts	36	36	8	6	1	6	15		
St Lucia	62	61	5	13	3	8	32	1	1.6
St Vincent/Grenadines	39	39	4	7	2	14	12	1	2.6
Trinidad and Tobago	513	513	74	46	11	220	162	22	4.3
Central America									
Belize	2,296	2,280	44	12	48	1,012	1,164	2	0.1
Costa Rica	5,110	5,106	285	244	2,330	1,640	607	118	2.3
El Salvador	2,104	2,072	565	168	610	104	625	120	5.7
Guatemala	10,889	10,843	1,400	485	1,400	3,750	3,808	78	0.7
Honduras	11,209	11,189	1,610	210	2,560	3,260	3,549	90	0.8
Mexico	195,820	190,869	23,150	1,560	74,499	42,460	49,200	5,180	2.6
Nicaragua	13,000	11,875	1,100	173	5,400	3,380	1,822	85	0.7
Panama	7,708	7,599	499	155	1,560	3,300	2,085	32	0.4
Puerto Rico	890	886	68	59	334	177	248	39	4.4
South Asia									
Afghanistan	65,209	65,209	7,910	144	30,000	1,900	25,255	2,760	4.2
Bangladesh	14,400	13,017	8,853	273	600	1,860	1,431	2,933	20.4
Bhutan	4,700	4,700	113	19	271	2,610	1,687	34	0.7
India	328,759	297,319	165,400	3,680	12,050	66,700	49,489	43,050	13.1
Nepal	14,080	13,680	2,624	29	2,000	2,480	6,547	1,000	7.1
Pakistan	79,610	77,088	20,300	450	5,000	3,550	47,788	16,500	20.7
Sri Lanka	6,561	6,463	925	975	439	2,082	2,042	520	7.9

LAND USE

Land Use and Irrigation 1990

Units: '000 hectares

	Total area	Land area	Arable land	Perma-nent crops	Perma-nent pasture	Forest & Wood-land	Other land	Irrigated land	As % of land area
Japan									
Japan	37,780	37,652	4,121	475	647	25,105	7,304	2,847	7.5
ASEAN/NICs									
Brunei	577	527	3	4	6	225	289	1	0.2
Hong Kong	104	99	7	6	1	12	79	2	1.9
Indonesia	190,457	181,157	16,000	6,000	11,800	113,433	33,924	7,600	4.0
Macau	2	2					2		
Malaysia	32,975	32,855	1,040	3,840	27	19,330	8,618	342	1.0
Philippines	30,000	29,817	4,550	3,420	1,260	10,350	10,237	1,560	5.2
Singapore	62	61	1			3	57		
South Korea	9,902	9,873	1,953	156	80	6,476	1,208	1,355	13.7
Taiwan									
Thailand	51,312	51,089	19,000	3,140	780	14,100	14,069	4,300	8.4
East/SE Asia									
Cambodia	18,104	17,652	2,910	146	580	13,372	644	92	0.5
China	959,696	932,641	93,283	3,280	400,000	126,515	359,583	47,837	5.0
Laos	23,680	23,080	890	21	800	12,700	8,669	122	0.5
Mongolia	156,650	156,650	1,385	1	124,400	13,915	16,949	77	
Myanmar	67,655	65,754	9,567	502	359	32,399	22,927	1,008	1.5
North Korea	12,054	12,041	1,700	300	50	8,970	1,021	1,420	11.8
Vietnam	33,169	32,549	5,690	910	340	9,850	15,759	1,840	5.5
Australasia									
Australia	771,336	764,444	48,741	178	417,642	106,000	191,883	1,900	0.2
New Zealand	27,099	26,799	391	21	13,490	7,350	5,547	280	1.0
Pacific									
American Samoa	20	20	2	2		14	2		
Fiji	1,827	1,827	152	88	60	1,185	342	1	0.1
French Polynesia	400	366	5	22	20	115	204		
Guam	55	55	6	6	8	10	25		
Kiribati	71	71		37		2	32		
Nauru	2	2					2		
New Caledonia	1,858	1,828	10	10	282	708	818		
Papua New Guinea	46,284	45,286	35	360	83	38,230	6,578		
Solomon Islands	2,890	2,799	40	17	39	2,560	143		
Tonga	75	72	17	31	4	8	12		
Tuvalu	3	3					3		
Vanuatu	1,219	1,219	20	124	25	914	136		
Western Samoa	284	283	55	67	1	134	26		
Middle East									
Bahrain	68	68	1	1	4		62	1	1.5
Egypt	100,145	99,545	2,330	100		31	96,907	2,607	2.6
Iran	164,800	163,600	14,100	950	44,000	18,020	86,530	5,750	3.5
Iraq	43,832	43,737	5,250	200	4,000	1,890	32,397	2,550	5.8
Israel	2,077	2,033	351	86	147	112	1,338	206	9.9
Jordan	8,921	8,893	310	90	791	70	7,632	63	0.7
Kuwait	1,782	1,782	4		134	2	1,642	2	0.1
Lebanon	1,040	1,023	208	93	10	80	632	86	8.3
Oman	21,246	21,246	16	45	1,000		20,185	58	0.3
Qatar	1,100	1,100	5		50		1,045		
Saudi Arabia	214,969	214,969	2,290	75	85,000	1,200	126,404	900	0.4
Syria	18,518	18,392	4,877	749	7,869	723	4,174	693	3.7
United Arab Emirates	8,360	8,360	29	10	200	3	8,118	5	0.1
Yemen	52,797	52,797	1,376	105	16,065	4,060	31,191	310	0.6

LAND USE

Land Use and Irrigation 1990

Units: '000 hectares

	Total area	Land area	Arable land	Perma-nent crops	Perma-nent pasture	Forest & Wood-land	Other land	Irrigated land	As % of land area
North Africa									
Algeria	238,174	238,174	7,070	533	31,175	4,699	194,697	336	0.1
Chad	128,400	125,920	3,200	5	45,000	12,730	64,985	10	
Djibouti	2,320	2,318			200	6	2,112		
Ethiopia	122,190	110,100	13,200	730	44,900	27,100	24,170	162	0.1
Libya	175,954	175,954	1,805	350	13,300	690	159,809	244	0.1
Mali	124,019	122,019	2,090	3	30,000	6,950	82,976	205	0.2
Mauritania	102,552	102,522	202	3	39,250	4,430	58,637	12	
Morocco	44,655	44,630	8,713	614	20,900	9,000	5,403	1,270	2.8
Niger	126,700	126,670	3,610		8,900	2,000	112,160	40	
Somalia	63,766	62,734	1,022	17	43,000	9,060	9,635	118	0.2
Sudan	250,581	237,600	12,830	70	110,000	44,840	69,860	1,900	0.8
Tunisia	16,361	15,536	2,909	1,667	3,360	655	6,945	280	1.7
West Africa									
Benin	11,262	11,062	1,410	450	442	3,470	5,290	6	0.1
Burkina Faso	27,420	27,380	3,550	13	10,000	6,600	7,217	20	0.1
Cameroon	47,544	46,540	5,940	1,068	8,300	24,540	6,692	30	0.1
Cape Verde	403	403	37	2	25	1	338	2	0.5
Côte d'Ivoire	32,246	31,800	2,430	1,260	13,000	7,380	7,730	64	0.2
Equatorial Guinea	2,805	2,805	130	100	104	1,295	1,176		
Gabon	26,767	25,767	295	162	4,700	20,000	610		
Gambia	1,130	1,000	178		90	156	576	12	1.1
Ghana	23,854	23,002	1,140	1,580	5,000	8,070	7,212	8	
Guinea	24,586	24,586	610	118	6,150	14,580	3,128	25	0.1
Guinea-Bissau	3,612	2,812	300	35	1,080	1,070	327		
Liberia	9,775	9,675	128	245	5,700	1,740	1,862	2	
Nigeria	92,377	91,077	29,765	2,535	40,000	11,900	6,877	870	0.9
Sao Tomé e Príncipe	96	96	2	35	1		58		
Senegal	19,672	19,253	2,335	15	3,100	10,550	3,253	180	0.9
Sierra Leone	7,174	7,162	500	150	2,204	2,060	2,248	34	0.5
Togo	5,679	5,439	660	69	1,790	1,600	1,380	7	0.1
East/Central Africa									
Angola	124,670	124,670	2,900	500	29,000	52,000	40,270		
Burundi	2,783	2,565	1,120	218	914	66	247	72	2.6
Central African Republic	62,298	62,298	1,920	86	3,000	35,800	21,492		
Comoros	223	223	78	22	15	35	73		
Congo	34,200	34,150	144	24	10,000	21,160	2,822	4	
Kenya	58,037	56,969	1,930	500	38,100	2,340	14,099	54	0.1
Madagascar	58,704	58,154	2,580	522	34,000	15,530	5,522	920	1.6
Maldives	30	30	3		1	1	25		
Mauritius	186	185	100	6	7	57	15	17	9.1
Réunion	251	250	47	5	12	88	98	6	2.4
Rwanda	2,634	2,467	850	305	462	554	296	4	0.2
Seychelles	28	27	1	5		5	16		
Tanzania	94,509	88,604	2,731	636	35,000	40,940	9,297	150	0.2
Uganda	23,588	19,955	5,000	1,710	1,800	5,560	5,885	9	
Zaire	234,541	226,760	7,250	610	15,000	174,310	29,590	10	
Southern Africa									
Botswana	58,173	56,673	1,380		33,000	10,910	11,383	2	
Lesotho	3,035	3,035	320		2,000		715		
Malawi	11,848	9,408	2,390	29	1,840	3,630	1,519	20	0.2
Mozambique	80,159	78,409	2,900	230	44,000	14,260	17,019	115	0.1
Namibia	82,429	82,329	660	2	38,000	18,120	25,547	4	
South Africa	122,104	122,104	12,360	814	81,378	4,515	23,037	1,128	0.9
Swaziland	1,736	1,720	200	4	1,185	104	227	62	3.6
Zambia	75,261	74,339	5,260	8	30,000	28,850	10,221	32	
Zimbabwe	39,058	38,667	2,720	92	4,856	19,130	11,869	220	0.6

Source: FAO, Production Yearbook

| LIVESTOCK | | | | | Table No. 1903 |

Circulation of Livestock 1991

Units: '000 head

	Horses	Asses	Cattle	Pigs	Sheep	Goats
North America						
Canada	415		12,369	10,516	780	28
USA	5,650	52	98,896	54,427	11,200	1,780
South America						
Argentina	3,400	90	50,080	4,464	27,552	3,320
Bolivia	320	630	5,600	2,340	12,300	2,450
Brazil	6,200	1,340	152,000	35,000	20,300	12,500
Chile	520	28	3,300	1,300	6,650	600
Colombia	1,980	705	24,875	2,700	2,745	1,055
Ecuador	512	255	4,200	2,125	1,250	300
French Guiana			19	11	4	1
Guyana	2		230	80	130	77
Paraguay	335	31	8,260	2,450	460	150
Peru	660	490	3,630	2,250	11,250	1,600
Suriname			98	30	10	11
Uruguay	470	1	8,889	215	25,986	14
Venezuela	495	440	13,368	1,971	525	1,530
Caribbean						
Anguilla						
Antigua	1	2	16	4	13	12
Aruba						
Bahamas			5	20	40	19
Barbados	1	2	21	45	56	34
Bermuda			1	2		1
British Virgin Islands			2	2	6	10
Cayman Islands			2			
Cuba	629	5	4,920	1,900	385	110
Dominica			9	5	8	10
Dominican Republic	320	143	2,250	435	120	555
Grenada		1	4	7	11	11
Guadeloupe	1	1	65	36	5	64
Haiti	435	218	1,400	930	92	1,200
Jamaica	4	23	300	250	2	440
Martinique	2		35	49	63	38
Netherlands Antilles		3	1	3	4	14
St Kitts			5	2	15	10
St Lucia	1	1	12	12	16	12
St Vincent/Grenadines		1	8	9	15	5
Trinidad and Tobago	1	2	60	50	14	52
Central America						
Belize	5		51	26	4	1
Costa Rica	114	7	1,741	224	3	2
El Salvador	93	2	1,243	320	5	15
Guatemala	114	9	1,695	1,110	675	77
Honduras	170	22	2,388	740	8	27
Mexico	6,175	3,188	29,847	15,902	6,003	10,772
Nicaragua	250	8	1,680	709	4	6
Panama	156		1,399	256		5
Puerto Rico	23	2	599	209	7	20
South Asia						
Afghanistan	400	1,300	1,650		13,500	2,150
Bangladesh	45		23,500		900	22,000
Bhutan	27	18	413	73	59	38
India	965	1,500	198,400	10,450	55,700	112,000
Nepal			6,350	575	925	5,355
Pakistan	461	3,279	17,785		30,160	36,673
Sri Lanka	2		1,814	102	31	526

LIVESTOCK   **Table No. 1903** (cont'd)

Circulation of Livestock 1991

Units: '000 head

	Horses	Asses	Cattle	Pigs	Sheep	Goats
Japan						
Japan	24		4,863	11,335	32	34
ASEAN/NICs						
Brunei			1	14		
Hong Kong	1		2	304		
Indonesia	750		10,350	6,800	5,750	11,300
Macau				1		
Malaysia	5		658	2,400	200	315
Philippines	200		1,677	8,007	30	2,107
Singapore			1	380		2
South Korea	5		2,126	4,528	5	184
Taiwan						
Thailand	18		6,052	5,000	178	140
East/SE Asia						
Cambodia	18		2,150	1,610		
China	10,174	11,198	81,407	363,975	112,820	97,378
Laos	45		865	1,390		143
Mongolia	2,255		2,849	185	15,083	5,126
Myanmar	121		9,310	2,250	280	1,040
North Korea	45	3	1,350	3,300	390	300
Vietnam	145		3,282	12,583		451
Australasia						
Australia	310	2	23,430	2,530	162,774	730
New Zealand	100		8,200	400	57,000	910
Pacific						
American Samoa				11		
Fiji	43		158	15		123
French Polynesia	2		7	32	2	12
Guam				15		2
Kiribati				11		
Nauru				3		
New Caledonia	9		122	38	3	18
Papua New Guinea	2		105	1,000	4	2
Solomon Islands			13	53		
Tonga	6		10	60		9
Tuvalu				12		
Vanuatu	4		123	60		11
Western Samoa	3	7	31	57		
Middle East						
Bahrain			15		9	16
Egypt	10	2,000	3,500	110	4,900	4,500
Iran	270	1,937	6,800		45,000	23,500
Iraq	48	350	1,400		7,800	1,350
Israel	4	5	331	100	375	115
Jordan	3	19	29		1,400	500
Kuwait						
Lebanon	2	12	57	45	205	400
Oman		26	138		280	725
Qatar	1		10		132	80
Saudi Arabia	3	103	176		5,692	3,350
Syria	45	175	786	1	15,321	1,018
United Arab Emirates			53		270	590
Yemen	3	690	1,180		3,800	3,400

LIVESTOCK   Table No. 1903 (cont'd)

Circulation of Livestock 1991

Units: '000 head

	Horses	Asses	Cattle	Pigs	Sheep	Goats
North Africa						
Algeria	202	340	1,443	5	13,350	3,800
Chad	182	269	4,400	15	1,983	2,923
Djibouti		8	170		420	504
Ethiopia	2,700	5,100	30,000	20	23,000	18,006
Libya	25	62	150		5,500	1,200
Mali	62	550	5,000	61	5,850	5,850
Mauritania	18	153	1,360		4,200	3,310
Morocco	190	942	3,500	9	14,000	5,300
Niger	305	415	2,200	38	6,700	4,860
Somalia	1	25	4,900	10	13,800	20,500
Sudan	22	680	21,028		20,700	15,277
Tunisia	56	229	631	6	6,290	3,306
West Africa						
Benin	6	1	955	730	970	1,080
Burkina Faso	70	476	2,900	520	3,339	6,137
Cameroon	15	36	4,700	1,414	3,550	3,550
Cape Verde	1	11	19	86	6	110
Côte d'Ivoire	1	1	1,064	369	1,150	905
Equatorial Guinea			5	5	36	8
Gabon			28	162	165	81
Gambia	18	41	410	11	170	205
Ghana	1	10	1,300	620	2,500	2,600
Guinea	2	1	1,800	33	518	464
Guinea-Bissau	1	3	410	293	245	208
Liberia			38	120	220	220
Nigeria	206	960	14,500	4,000	24,000	36,000
Sao Tomé e Príncipe			4	3	2	4
Senegal	400	325	2,813	547	4,000	1,200
Sierra Leone			330	52	330	184
Togo	2	3	250	500	1,220	1,741
East/Central Africa						
Angola	1	5	3,100	495	280	990
Burundi			435	103	365	930
Central African Republic			2,677	426	135	1,270
Comoros		5	47		14	125
Congo			68	52	108	272
Kenya	2		13,700	105	6,550	8,100
Madagascar	1		10,265	1,461	753	1,283
Maldives						
Mauritius			34	10	7	96
Réunion			19	87	2	31
Rwanda			630	139	394	1,150
Seychelles			2	18		5
Tanzania		175	13,138	282	3,556	8,814
Uganda		17	5,000	850	1,950	3,300
Zaire			1,600	830	910	3,070
Southern Africa						
Botswana	34	153	2,500	16	320	2,090
Lesotho	122	129	540	75	1,470	1,060
Malawi		2	1,150	280	230	1,100
Mozambique		20	1,370	165	118	380
Namibia	53	68	2,131	51	6,700	1,900
South Africa	230	210	13,512	1,490	32,580	5,900
Swaziland	2	14	750	24	35	320
Zambia		2	3,045	230	65	540
Zimbabwe	24	104	5,950	340	550	2,450

Source: FAO, Production Yearbook

FOOD PRODUCTION

Table No. 1904

Production of Dairy Products 1991

Units: '000 tonnes

	Cow Milk Fresh	Cow Milk Dried	Evaporated Milk	Cheese	Butter and Ghee	Hen Eggs	Honey
North America							
Canada	7,340	9		291	101	320	35
USA	67,373	58		3,090	63	4,005	91
South America							
Argentina	6,200	75		28	38	324	44
Bolivia	118	1		7	1	34	
Brazil	15,300	150		60	70	1,400	17
Chile	1,490	48		31	7	91	5
Colombia	3,600	15		51	15	267	5
Ecuador	1,505	3		13	5	57	1
French Guiana							
Guyana	56					4	
Paraguay	230					36	1
Peru	786			17	2	117	
Suriname	18					3	
Uruguay	900	3		17	14	22	4
Venezuela	1,591	67		92	3	107	1
Caribbean							
Anguilla							
Antigua	6						
Aruba							
Bahamas	3						
Barbados	13					2	
Bermuda	1						
British Virgin Islands							
Cayman Islands							
Cuba	1,070	2		16	9	110	10
Dominica	5						
Dominican Republic	420			3	2	33	2
Grenada	1					1	
Guadeloupe	2					1	
Haiti	20					4	
Jamaica	49					17	1
Martinique	3						
Netherlands Antilles	2						
St Kitts							
St Lucia	1					1	
St Vincent/Grenadines	2					1	
Trinidad and Tobago	12					8	
Central America							
Belize	7					1	
Costa Rica	430	3		6	4	18	1
El Salvador	327			2		39	3
Guatemala	150			11	1	64	4
Honduras	310			8	4	25	1
Mexico	6,925	49		115	34	1,141	69
Nicaragua	161			6	1	26	
Panama	126	1		3		12	
Puerto Rico	388					15	
South Asia							
Afghanistan	340			18	11	14	3
Bangladesh	750			1	13	40	
Bhutan	29			2			
India	27,000				1,040	1,357	51
Nepal	260				16	18	
Pakistan	3,449				298	238	1
Sri Lanka	147	3				48	

FOOD PRODUCTION — Table No. 1904 (cont'd)

Production of Dairy Products 1991

Units: '000 tonnes

	Cow Milk Fresh	Cow Milk Dried	Evaporated Milk	Cheese	Butter and Ghee	Hen Eggs	Honey
Japan							
Japan	8,180	91		85	70	2,466	4
ASEAN/NICs							
Brunei						3	
Hong Kong	2					2	
Indonesia	329					400	
Macau						1	
Malaysia	30					212	
Philippines	15					267	
Singapore						16	
South Korea	1,848	23			48	489	8
Taiwan							
Thailand	178					128	2
East/SE Asia							
Cambodia	17					14	
China	4,816			143	67	6,845	196
Laos	10					34	
Mongolia	203			1	4	1	
Myanmar	456			29	10	35	
North Korea	90					148	
Vietnam	40					100	1
Australasia							
Australia	6,578	60		176	104	187	24
New Zealand	7,973	235		129	292	46	8
Pacific							
American Samoa							
Fiji	62				1	2	
French Polynesia	2					1	
Guam						1	
Kiribati							
Nauru							
New Caledonia	4					2	
Papua New Guinea						3	
Solomon Islands	1						
Tonga							
Tuvalu							
Vanuatu	3						
Western Samoa	1						
Middle East							
Bahrain	19					3	
Egypt	1,140			319	80	128	11
Iran	1,428			184	67	278	8
Iraq	225			27	6	35	
Israel	965			76	7	11	2
Jordan	35			3		22	
Kuwait							
Lebanon	60			7		53	1
Oman	18					6	
Qatar	3					3	
Saudi Arabia	225				1	164	
Syria	775			67	13	65	1
United Arab Emirates	6					9	
Yemen	98			23	5	18	

FOOD PRODUCTION — Table No. 1904 (cont'd)

Production of Dairy Products 1991

Units: '000 tonnes

	Cow Milk Fresh	Cow Milk Dried	Evaporated Milk	Cheese	Butter and Ghee	Hen Eggs	Honey
North Africa							
Algeria	596			1	1	175	2
Chad	113					4	1
Djibouti	6						
Ethiopia	752			5	10	79	23
Libya	140					35	1
Mali	122					12	
Mauritania	98			2	1	4	
Morocco	990			8	16	93	3
Niger	125			1	3	9	
Somalia	497				10	3	
Sudan	2,299			69	14	3	1
Tunisia	396			6		54	1
West Africa							
Benin	16					18	
Burkina Faso	83				1	15	
Cameroon	117					12	3
Cape Verde	1						
Côte d'Ivoire	20					17	
Equatorial Guinea							
Gabon	1					2	
Gambia	7					1	
Ghana	25					13	
Guinea	42					14	
Guinea-Bissau	12					1	
Liberia	1					4	
Nigeria	360			6	8	225	
Sao Tomé e Príncipe							
Senegal	101					12	
Sierra Leone	17					7	1
Togo	7					6	
East/Central Africa							
Angola	148			3	1	4	15
Burundi	26					3	1
Central African Republic	36					1	9
Comoros	4					1	
Congo	3					1	
Kenya	2,189	1			4	42	18
Madagascar	472					17	4
Maldives							
Mauritius	25					4	
Réunion	6					2	
Rwanda	88				1	3	
Seychelles						2	
Tanzania	463			1	4	40	15
Uganda	437					15	
Zaire	7					8	
Southern Africa							
Botswana	105			1	1	1	
Lesotho	24					1	
Malawi	49					11	
Mozambique	68					13	
Namibia	71						
South Africa	2,515	9		40	18	191	1
Swaziland	42						
Zambia	82			1		35	
Zimbabwe	248	1		7	4	14	

Source: FAO, Production Yearbook

FOOD PRODUCTION   Table No. 1905

Production of Meat 1991

Units: '000 tonnes

	Beef and Veal	Mutton and Lamb	Pig Meat	Horse Meat	Goat Meat	Poultry	Total (inc. others)
North America							
Canada	879	9		1,110	25	744	2,769
USA	10,531	165		7,258	63	11,503	29,720
South America							
Argentina	2,640	92	7	216	44	391	3,432
Bolivia	152	29	6	70		33	299
Brazil	2,800	43	35	1,160	5	2,614	6,663
Chile	240	16	5	142	11	129	549
Colombia	823	10	4	112	1	257	1,212
Ecuador	110	5	2	65		75	287
French Guiana				1			2
Guyana	2	1		1		15	19
Paraguay	160	3	1	118		29	334
Peru	112	19	7	84		280	547
Suriname	2			2		11	15
Uruguay	350	64		15	5	29	465
Venezuela	370	2	7	99		340	820
Caribbean							
Anguilla							
Antigua	1						1
Aruba							
Bahamas						7	8
Barbados				5		11	16
Bermuda							
British Virgin Islands							
Cayman Islands							
Cuba	140			90	2	92	325
Dominica							
Dominican Republic	67		2	21		138	228
Grenada							
Guadeloupe	3			2		1	7
Haiti	32	1	4	17	5	16	79
Jamaica	13		2	7		53	76
Martinique	3			2		1	6
Netherlands Antilles							1
St Kitts							
St Lucia	1			1		1	2
St Vincent/Grenadines							1
Trinidad and Tobago	1			3		26	30
Central America							
Belize	1			1		4	6
Costa Rica	91			15		5	112
El Salvador	29			16		37	82
Guatemala	53	3		15	2	18	92
Honduras	45			13	1	21	80
Mexico	1,550	26	39	812	74	897	3,403
Nicaragua	38			13	2	11	64
Panama	60			11		29	100
Puerto Rico	22			29		57	108
South Asia							
Afghanistan	65	115	23			13	227
Bangladesh	142	2	42			58	254
Bhutan	5			1			7
India	857	166	420	364		368	3,282
Nepal	4	3	35	10		9	156
Pakistan	326	229	325			182	1,412
Sri Lanka	20		2	2		12	40

FOOD PRODUCTION

Table No. 1905 (cont'd)

Production of Meat 1991

Units: '000 tonnes

	Beef and Veal	Mutton and Lamb	Pig Meat	Horse Meat	Goat Meat	Poultry	Total (inc. others)
Japan							
Japan	573			1,490	5	1,417	3,486
ASEAN/NICs							
Brunei						5	7
Hong Kong	40			190		65	301
Indonesia	192	44	54	275	1	458	1,091
Macau				8		4	13
Malaysia	12			195		352	563
Philippines	78		26	710	1	237	1,115
Singapore		1		78		67	146
South Korea	130		1	530		203	868
Taiwan							
Thailand	179	1	1	340		717	1,301
East/SE Asia							
Cambodia	19			38		25	91
China	1,302	572	550	25,460	55	3,463	31,907
Laos	9			54		25	113
Mongolia	63	106	19	7	37		243
Myanmar	86	2	5	82		83	281
North Korea [a]	53	2	2	161		48	265
Vietnam	110		3	850	2	168	1,235
Australasia							
Australia	1,760	675		312	8	416	3,200
New Zealand	535	550	2	43	1	58	1,199
Pacific							
American Samoa							
Fiji	2			1		6	9
French Polynesia				1			2
Guam							1
Kiribati							
Nauru							
New Caledonia	2			1		1	4
Papua New Guinea	2			27		5	51
Solomon Islands	1			2			3
Tonga				2			2
Tuvalu							
Vanuatu	3			2			6
Western Samoa	1			1			3
Middle East							
Bahrain	1	5	2			3	11
Egypt	229	69	32	3		219	825
Iran	250	240	100			275	892
Iraq	39	17	8			156	222
Israel	38	5	1	8		186	238
Jordan	1	6	2			56	66
Kuwait							
Lebanon	15	11	4	1		59	90
Oman	3	5	5			3	20
Qatar	1	5	1			3	9
Saudi Arabia	30	78	19			275	434
Syria	28	91	8			62	189
United Arab Emirates	3	22	6			14	52
Yemen	29	38	31			55	156

FOOD PRODUCTION

Production of Meat 1991

Units: '000 tonnes

	Beef and Veal	Mutton and Lamb	Pig Meat	Horse Meat	Goat Meat	Poultry	Total (inc. others)
North Africa							
Algeria	60	71	16		3	69	227
Chad	65	3	10			4	87
Djibouti	2	2	2				7
Ethiopia	245	82	67	1		77	605
Libya	23	60	8			70	171
Mali	75	20	22	2		24	166
Mauritania	14	6	5			4	42
Morocco	145	55	17	1	2	130	351
Niger	21	13	19	1	2	22	93
Somalia	57	37	57			4	175
Sudan	231	72	35			22	428
Tunisia	40	40	8			56	152
West Africa							
Benin	14	3	3	8		30	64
Burkina Faso	29	6	15	12	1	30	101
Cameroon	70	15	13	17		19	145
Cape Verde				3		1	6
Côte d'Ivoire	45	5	4	15		48	145
Equatorial Guinea							
Gabon	1	1		2		3	27
Gambia	6	1	1			1	9
Ghana	22	7	7	14		14	154
Guinea	18	1	1	1		18	43
Guinea-Bissau	3	1	1	9		1	14
Liberia	1	1	1	4		5	17
Nigeria	288	81	184	150		176	979
Sao Tomé e Príncipe							
Senegal	48	13	7	20	5	24	123
Sierra Leone	5	1		2		9	20
Togo	6	3	4	7		7	30
East/Central Africa							
Angola	57	1	3	18		7	92
Burundi	7	1	3	6		4	21
Central African Republic	46	1	4	15		2	76
Comoros	1						2
Congo	2		1	2		5	22
Kenya	326	26	31	5		47	464
Madagascar	142	3	6	39		88	281
Maldives							
Mauritius	2			1		12	15
Réunion	1			7		4	14
Rwanda	14	1	4	3		1	31
Seychelles				1		1	2
Tanzania	197	10	22	8		25	275
Uganda	79	11	14	38		29	188
Zaire	28	3	8	30		17	208
Southern Africa							
Botswana	32	1	6			2	46
Lesotho	13	4	3	3		1	28
Malawi	21	1	4	11		9	46
Mozambique	41	1	2	11		21	76
Namibia	66	50	6	4			130
South Africa	678	133	35	126	1	394	1,377
Swaziland	15		3	1		1	20
Zambia	39		2	8		19	97
Zimbabwe	77		9	11		10	126

Source: FAO, Production Yearbook
Notes: see end of section

FOOD PRODUCTION   Table No. 1906

Production of Cereals 1991

Units: '000 tonnes

	Wheat	Barley	Maize	Millet	Rice	Sorghum	Total (inc. others)
North America							
Canada	32,822	12,463	7,319				55,969
USA	53,915	10,113	189,867	150	7,006	14,720	279,923
South America							
Argentina	9,000	320	7,768	65	347	2,251	20,351
Bolivia	103	62	510		257	47	1,010
Brazil	3,077	188	22,604		9,503	272	35,991
Chile	1,589	109	836		117		2,866
Colombia	94	102	1,274		1,739	738	3,948
Ecuador	28	42	665		841	5	1,583
French Guiana					29		29
Guyana			3		250		253
Paraguay	400		980		99	29	1,508
Peru	128	100	669		814	31	1,757
Suriname					190		190
Uruguay	136	156	124		540	90	1,098
Venezuela			1,100		608	616	2,324
Caribbean							
Anguilla							
Antigua							
Aruba							
Bahamas			1				1
Barbados			2				2
Bermuda							
British Virgin Islands							
Cayman Islands							
Cuba			95		430	1	526
Dominica							
Dominican Republic			43		303	17	363
Grenada							
Guadeloupe							
Haiti			145		120	70	335
Jamaica			3				3
Martinique							
Netherlands Antilles							
St Kitts							
St Lucia							
St Vincent/Grenadines			1				1
Trinidad and Tobago			3		14		17
Central America							
Belize			20		4		24
Costa Rica			60		193	3	256
El Salvador			504		61	163	729
Guatemala	28	1	1,150		42	80	1,301
Honduras	1		584		56	93	734
Mexico	4,115	584	13,527		354	4,367	23,056
Nicaragua			245		140	70	455
Panama			94		180	25	299
Puerto Rico							
South Asia							
Afghanistan	1,726	217	420	26	335		2,724
Bangladesh	1,004	12	3	60	28,575	1	29,655
Bhutan	5	4	40	7	43		105
India	54,522	1,642	8,200	9,000	110,945	10,800	195,109
Nepal	836	28	1,235	220	3,600		5,919
Pakistan	14,505	140	1,190	200	4,903	260	21,198
Sri Lanka			34	9	2,397		2,440

FOOD PRODUCTION   Table No. 1906 (cont'd)

Production of Cereals 1991

Units: '000 tonnes

	Wheat	Barley	Maize	Millet	Rice	Sorghum	Total (inc. others)
Japan							
Japan	860	268	1	1	12,005		13,165
ASEAN/NICs							
Brunei							1
Hong Kong							
Indonesia			6,409		44,321	2	50,732
Macau							
Malaysia			36		1,550		1,586
Philippines			4,655		9,670		14,325
Singapore							
South Korea	1	340	75	2	7,478	2	7,905
Taiwan [a]	5		307		1,900		2,212
Thailand			3,990		20,040	233	24,279
East/SE Asia							
Cambodia			50		2,400		2,450
China	95,003	3,000	93,350	4,501	187,450	5,615	392,919
Laos			60		1,400		1,460
Mongolia	536	45					591
Myanmar	123		190	138	13,201		13,667
North Korea	195	145	4,500	62	5,100	16	10,080
Vietnam [b]			652		19,428	5	20,084
Australasia							
Australia	9,633	4,025	159	43	726	893	17,212
New Zealand	176	440	195				906
Pacific							
American Samoa							
Fiji			2		33		35
French Polynesia							
Guam							
Kiribati							
Nauru							
New Caledonia			1				1
Papua New Guinea			2		1	1	4
Solomon Islands							13
Tonga							
Tuvalu							
Vanuatu			1				1
Western Samoa							
Middle East							
Bahrain							
Egypt	4,483	110	5,270		3,152		13,670
Iran	8,900	3,600	7	19	2,100		14,626
Iraq	525	520	74	1	125	2	1,248
Israel	160	4	3				167
Jordan	40	25				2	68
Kuwait							
Lebanon	50	16	3				71
Oman	1						5
Qatar		3					3
Saudi Arabia	4,000	375	4	12		85	4,476
Syria	2,135	950	185	4		1	3,275
United Arab Emirates	1	2	4				7
Yemen	77	22	46	20		132	298

FOOD PRODUCTION   Table No. 1906 (cont'd)

Production of Cereals 1991

Units: '000 tonnes

	Wheat	Barley	Maize	Millet	Rice	Sorghum	Total (inc. others)
North Africa							
Algeria	1,741	1,751	2		2	1	3,623
Chad	4		49	302	86	365	891
Djibouti							
Ethiopia	890	965	1,590	260		805	6,420
Libya	150	145	1	2			298
Mali	2		226	792	445	729	2,232
Mauritania	1		1	4	52	59	117
Morocco	4,939	3,252	335	5	33	14	8,648
Niger	12		6	1,853	71	472	2,415
Somalia	1		100		5	145	251
Sudan	680		63	308	1	2,941	3,993
Tunisia	1,786	721				2	2,554
West Africa							
Benin			390	26	8	106	534
Burkina Faso			296	757	50	1,113	2,234
Cameroon			450	63	90	400	1,003
Cape Verde			4				4
Côte d'Ivoire			510	52	690	29	1,292
Equatorial Guinea							
Gabon			20		1		21
Gambia			25	51	21	10	108
Ghana			932	112	151	241	1,436
Guinea			79	60	628	35	888
Guinea-Bissau			13	20	118	11	165
Liberia					110		110
Nigeria	85		1,900	4,200	3,185	4,800	14,200
Sao Tomé e Príncipe			1				1
Senegal			106	560	160	85	914
Sierra Leone			11	22	386	22	442
Togo			236	70	34	106	447
East/Central Africa							
Angola	3		299	61	18		381
Burundi [b]	14		190	12	39	88	342
Central African Republic			100	10	15	40	165
Comoros			4		15		19
Congo			25		1		26
Kenya	210		2,250	63	60	140	2,747
Madagascar	1		150		2,200	1	2,352
Maldives							
Mauritius			2				2
Réunion			13				13
Rwanda	10		104	3	8	205	330
Seychelles							
Tanzania	75	5	2,332	270	664	480	3,826
Uganda	8		600	600	64	380	1,652
Zaire	7		906	31	365	49	1,359
Southern Africa							
Botswana	2		4	1		38	45
Lesotho	10	1	95			18	125
Malawi [b]	2		1,590	8	61	19	1,679
Mozambique	3		327	5	56	155	546
Namibia	6		50	50		8	114
South Africa	2,245	183	8,200	15	3	251	10,945
Swaziland			153		3	3	159
Zambia	68	2	1,448	31	14	40	1,603
Zimbabwe	253	24	1,586	122	1	68	2,054

Source: FAO, Production Yearbook
Notes: see end of section

FORESTRY PRODUCTS — Table No. 1907

Production of Forestry Products 1991

Units: '000 cu m

	Roundwood	Fuelwood and charcoal	Sawnwood and sleepers	Wood based panels
North America				
Canada	170,849	6,834	52,040	5,555
USA	495,800	85,900	103,893	30,409
South America				
Argentina	10,819	4,332	1,446	386
Bolivia	1,632	1,376	93	4
Brazil	264,621	190,143	17,179	2,892
Chile	18,817	6,757	3,218	370
Colombia	19,702	17,029	889	165
Ecuador	7,762	6,726	1,641	145
French Guiana	254	66	19	
Guyana	175	14	7	
Paraguay	8,466	5,360	313	112
Peru	7,912	6,868	479	25
Suriname	140	18	40	6
Uruguay	3,829	2,972	205	8
Venezuela	1,290	778	235	183
Caribbean				
Anguilla				
Antigua				
Aruba				
Bahamas	115		1	
Barbados				
Bermuda				
British Virgin Islands				
Cayman Islands				
Cuba	3,140	2,529	130	149
Dominica				
Dominican Republic	982	976		
Grenada				
Guadeloupe	17	15	1	
Haiti	5,957	5,718	14	
Jamaica	180	13	32	
Martinique	12	10	1	
Netherlands Antilles				
St Kitts				
St Lucia				
St Vincent/Grenadines				
Trinidad and Tobago	72	22	53	
Central America				
Belize	188	126	14	
Costa Rica	4,201	3,031	412	70
El Salvador	4,666	4,520	70	
Guatemala	8,049	7,935	83	6
Honduras	6,288	5,501	302	10
Mexico	23,617	15,854	2,696	645
Nicaragua	4,182	3,302	222	9
Panama	1,872	1,708	48	8
Puerto Rico				
South Asia				
Afghanistan	6,759	5,185	400	1
Bangladesh	31,757	30,865	79	8
Bhutan	1,560	1,282	40	13
India	279,801	255,279	17,460	442
Nepal	18,704	18,084	620	
Pakistan	27,174	24,740	1,520	82
Sri Lanka	9,096	34,265	5	10

FORESTRY PRODUCTS

Production of Forestry Products 1991

Units: '000 cu m

	Roundwood	Fuelwood and charcoal	Sawnwood and sleepers	Wood based panels
Japan				
Japan	28,272	327	28,264	8,387
ASEAN/NICs				
Brunei	295	79	90	
Hong Kong	193	193	421	12
Indonesia	172,984	143,669	9,145	9,594
Macau				
Malaysia	49,327	8,939	8,929	2,630
Philippines	38,738	34,265	723	408
Singapore			206	489
South Korea	6,485	4,491	4,041	1,582
Taiwan				
Thailand	37,940	35,065	939	398
East/SE Asia				
Cambodia	6,387	5,512	122	2
China	282,334	192,235	20,521	3,325
Laos	6,485	3,944	71	10
Mongolia	2,390	1,350	470	4
Myanmar	23,182	18,159	466	15
North Korea	4,737	4,137	280	
Vietnam	23,585	24,679	885	39
Australasia				
Australia	19,315	2,892	2,751	865
New Zealand	13,987	50	2,198	687
Pacific				
American Samoa				
Fiji	307	37	91	16
French Polynesia				
Guam				
Kiribati				
Nauru				
New Caledonia	12		5	
Papua New Guinea	8,188	5,533	117	46
Solomon Islands	449	138	16	
Tonga	5		1	
Tuvalu				
Vanuatu	63	24	7	
Western Samoa	131	70	21	
Middle East				
Bahrain				
Egypt	2,300	2,193		59
Iran	6,792	2,465	173	317
Iraq	155	105	8	3
Israel	113	13		177
Jordan	9	5		
Kuwait				
Lebanon	481	463	18	46
Oman				
Qatar				
Saudi Arabia				
Syria	58	15	9	27
United Arab Emirates				
Yemen	324	324		

FORESTRY PRODUCTS

Table No. 1907 (cont'd)

Production of Forestry Products 1991

Units: '000 cu m

	Roundwood	Fuelwood and charcoal	Sawnwood and sleepers	Wood based panels
North Africa				
Algeria	2,221	1,953	13	50
Chad	4,141	3,553	2	
Djibouti				
Ethiopia	43,686	41,973	12	10
Libya	645	536	31	
Mali	5,768	5,400	13	
Mauritania	13	8		
Morocco	2,549	1,405	83	160
Niger	5,116	4,800		
Somalia	7,326	7,233	14	
Sudan	23,449	21,279	4	2
Tunisia	3,320	3,152	16	97
West Africa				
Benin	5,203	4,924	14	
Burkina Faso	8,995	8,588	2	
Cameroon	14,637	11,523	574	80
Cape Verde				
Côte d'Ivoire	13,061	10,129	753	248
Equatorial Guinea	607	447	52	10
Gabon	4,286	2,653	126	228
Gambia	940	919	1	
Ghana	17,122	15,512	400	88
Guinea	3,988	3,560	70	
Guinea-Bissau	569	422	16	
Liberia	6,134	4,962	411	5
Nigeria	111,059	103,191	2,706	233
Sao Tomé e Príncipe	9		5	
Senegal	5,098	4,479	22	
Sierra Leone	3,146	3,024	10	
Togo	1,234	1,047	2	
East/Central Africa				
Angola	6,593	5,661	5	11
Burundi	4,343	4,291	3	
Central African Republic	3,444	3,055	60	1
Comoros				
Congo	3,760	2,147	49	55
Kenya	36,861	35,063	185	52
Madagascar	8,335	7,528	233	5
Maldives				
Mauritius	17	3	5	
Réunion	36	31	2	
Rwanda	5,620	5,392	8	2
Seychelles				
Tanzania	35,545	33,458	156	15
Uganda	15,715	13,689	28	3
Zaire	40,079	37,147	105	28
Southern Africa				
Botswana	1,440	1,351		
Lesotho	631	631		
Malawi	8,515	8,103	43	14
Mozambique	16,065	15,022	16	3
Namibia				
South Africa	19,679	7,078	1,792	350
Swaziland	2,223	560	103	8
Zambia	13,719	12,952	101	41
Zimbabwe	7,925	6,269	190	26

Source: FAO, Yearbook of Forest Products

FISHERY PRODUCTS

Production of Fishery Products 1991

Units: '000 tonnes

	A	B	C	D	E	F	G
North America							
Canada	232,560	83,180	42,930	58,086	980	9,070	67,920
USA	692,769	10,499	281,882	380,510	53,715	128,357	354,222
South America							
Argentina	226,500	9,534	30,486	16,500	1,130	4,100	17,400
Bolivia							
Brazil	174,250	21,870	14,300	52,400		2,900	27,000
Chile	104,813	3,138	10,433	69,151	9,992	188,270	1,073,207
Colombia		14,333	10,010	505		90	85
Ecuador	47,572	152	64,720	36,250	4	7,200	59,152
French Guiana	500		3,606				
Guyana		105	2,308				
Paraguay							
Peru	166,608	14,013	10,222	38,654	938	191,726	1,204,210
Suriname		500	310				
Uruguay	35,805	2	348	15	3	136	4,179
Venezuela	8,260	71,947	3,500	36,350	3,500		4,500
Caribbean							
Anguilla							
Antigua							
Aruba							
Bahamas	5		2,000				
Barbados							
Bermuda							
British Virgin Islands							
Cayman Islands							
Cuba	88,143		7,893	6,455			5,637
Dominica							
Dominican Republic							
Grenada							
Guadeloupe							
Haiti							
Jamaica							
Martinique							
Netherlands Antilles							
St Kitts							
St Lucia							
St Vincent/Grenadines							
Trinidad and Tobago							
Central America							
Belize	46	16	588				
Costa Rica				4,800			
El Salvador			2,335				
Guatemala		30	2,500				
Honduras			2,700				
Mexico	79,690	1,166	42,766	65,715	3,966	12,941	82,846
Nicaragua			857				
Panama			1,582			8,125	22,922
Puerto Rico							
South Asia							
Afghanistan							
Bangladesh	3,066	17,809	17,505				
Bhutan							
India	291,175	189,012	128,105			7,263	57,907
Nepal							
Pakistan	7,614	13,164	15,864				34,571
Sri Lanka		14,302	2,020				

FISHERY PRODUCTS

Production of Fishery Products 1991

Units: '000 tonnes

	A	B	C	D	E	F	G
Japan							
Japan	3,092,464	984,162	507,333	1,625,370	61,687	418,063	976,552
ASEAN/NICs							
Brunei							
Hong Kong	4,347	1,433	5,152	395	452		6,400
Indonesia	28,680	750,945	100,679	29,000	4,332	7,000	1,550
Macau	325	13	2,315				
Malaysia	4,600	12,222	6,049	16,877	4,595		43,019
Philippines	13,323	244,238	5,324	71,288	102,115		
Singapore	16,930		4,505	1,557			895
South Korea	1,368,000	31,900	41,200	183,500	20,000	6,300	50,000
Taiwan							
Thailand	223,300	70,400	187,000	267,000	100,600		264,700
East/SE Asia							
Cambodia							
China	1,290,974	180,655	163,596	72,018	16,283		78,936
Laos							
Mongolia							
Myanmar	4,200	60,361	4,121	114,948			
North Korea	630,144	138,880	8,690	1,973	500		
Vietnam							
Australasia							
Australia	9,506		19,299	7,580	1,878		1,000
New Zealand	129,290	7,943	34,480	2,325	734		937
Pacific							
American Samoa							
Fiji	607	78	324	15,617			1,285
French Polynesia							
Guam							
Kiribati							
Nauru							
New Caledonia							
Papua New Guinea							
Solomon Islands	17,090	463		6,062			
Tonga							
Tuvalu							
Vanuatu							
Western Samoa							
Middle East							
Bahrain							
Egypt			10				
Iran				10,290			11,450
Iraq							
Israel				8,300			
Jordan							
Kuwait			1,300				
Lebanon							
Oman							
Qatar							
Saudi Arabia							
Syria							
United Arab Emirates		21,500					
Yemen	3,000	6,342					2,300

FISHERY PRODUCTS

Production of Fishery Products 1991

Units: '000 tonnes

	A	B	C	D	E	F	G
North Africa							
Algeria		250		6,500			
Chad		19,200					
Djibouti							
Ethiopia		10					
Libya				800			300
Mali		3,500					
Mauritania	34,000	1,167	33,685				
Morocco	58,930	100	59,500	87,120		5,400	31,700
Niger		1,162					
Somalia		1,200					
Sudan		3,257					
Tunisia			13,067	6,500			236
West Africa							
Benin		2,100	140				
Burkina Faso							
Cameroon		1,500	1,050				
Cape Verde	3,700		40	200			40
Côte d'Ivoire		15,200		41,382			3,000
Equatorial Guinea							
Gabon		4,500					
Gambia		654					
Ghana		58,000		3,800			
Guinea		10,000					
Guinea-Bissau							
Liberia							
Nigeria		70,077					
Sao Tomé e Príncipe							
Senegal	78,800	25,005	11,847	17,699		23	3,958
Sierra Leone		19,000					
Togo		3,580					
East/Central Africa							
Angola	14,039	17,957		4,966		1,400	228
Burundi							
Central African Republic							
Comoros							
Congo		4,000					
Kenya	1,114	11,966					
Madagascar		2,000	7,612				
Maldives		3,084				22	
Mauritius	7,542	808	10	6,400			1,648
Réunion	860		370				
Rwanda	25	85					
Seychelles	920	200		4,076			950
Tanzania		65,000					
Uganda							
Zaire							
Southern Africa							
Botswana							
Lesotho							
Malawi							
Mozambique		3,100	6,020	200			
Namibia							
South Africa	142,650	7,800	3,480	10,000	110	4,253	54,354
Swaziland							
Zambia		18,056					
Zimbabwe	1,900	5,100		230			

Source: FAO, Yearbook of Fishery Statistics
Notes: see end of section

Notes to Tables in Section Nineteen

Table 1905   Totals may be affected by rounding

Table 1906   Totals may be affected by rounding
Rice is paddy rice, not coarse grain primary
Total also includes coarse grain primary rice
a   Data refers to 1990

Table 1907   Wood-based panels includes veneer sheets,
plywood, particle board and fibreboard

Table 1908   A Fish; fresh,chilled or frozen
B Fish; dried,salted or smoked
C Crustaceans and molluscs
D Fish products and preparations
E Crustacean and mollusc products
F Oils and fats of aquatic animal origin
G Meals, solubles etc. of aquatic animal origin

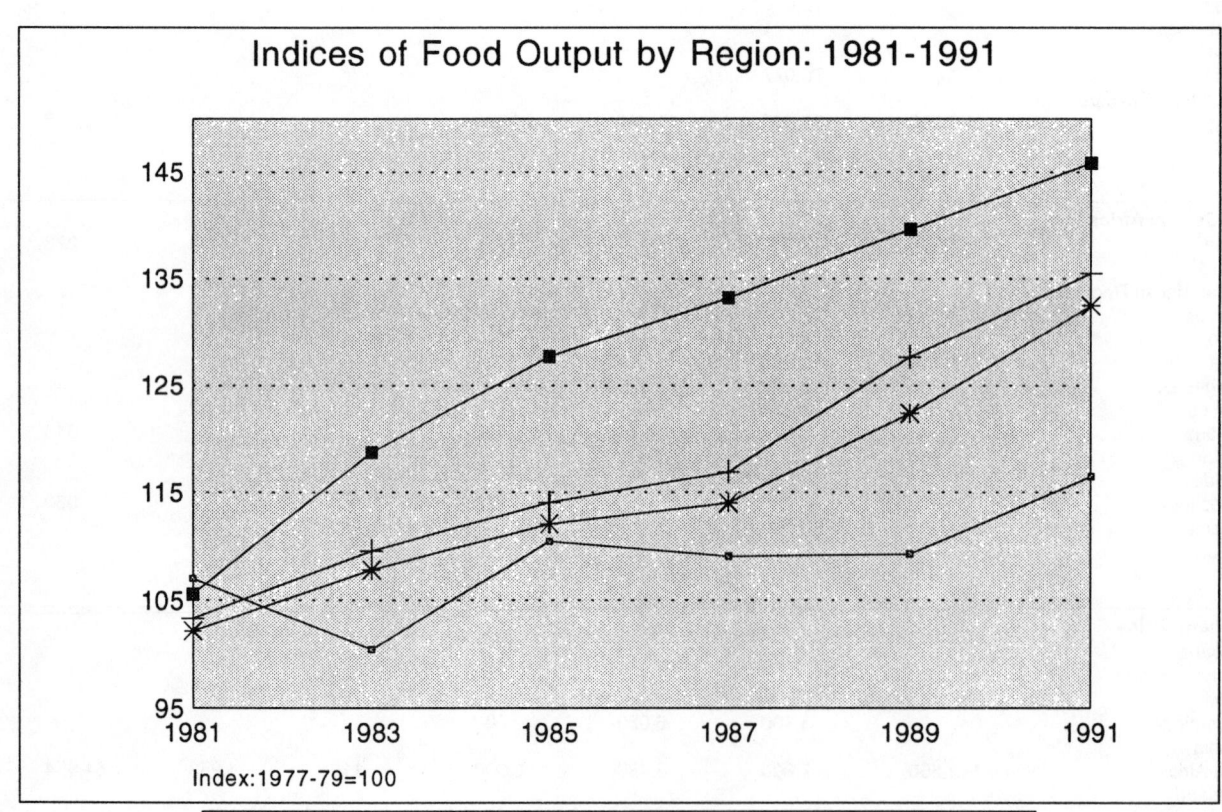

Section Twenty
Communications

TELEPHONES

Table No. 2001

Telephones in Use 1977-1990

Units: '000

	1977	1980	1983	1984	1985	1986	1987	1988	1989	1990
North America										
Canada	14,488.0	16,708.0	18,095.0	18,582.0	19,084.0	19,598.0	20,126.5			
USA	162,076.0	180,424.0							250,000.0	
South America										
Argentina	2,342.0	2,588.0	3,107.9	2,954.0	3,049.0	3,206.0	3,654.7	3,694.1	3,921.6	4,622.4
Bolivia						182.4		183.6	194.2	
Brazil	4,660.8	7,323.4	9,856.0	10,570.2	11,427.9	12,193.3	13,162.0	13,905.3	14,059.5	14,125.4
Chile	467.0	551.0	629.0	679.6	761.1	795.9	815.1	866.7	894.8	1,096.1
Colombia	1,431.2	1,718.2	1,894.5	1,977.9	2,097.0	2,289.1	2,438.2	2,498.8	2,775.3	2,909.2
Ecuador	221.0	272.0	317.8	331.9	339.0	351.9	355.4	691.5	539.6	
French Guiana	10.6	15.8	22.1	24.6	26.5	28.2	30.2	33.3	33.8	30.6
Guyana					33.3	33.0				
Paraguay	43.1	58.7	78.0	83.5	89.5	92.7	100.1	111.5	122.3	128.4
Peru	403.0	475.0	543.5	571.1	600.0			736.2	769.4	
Suriname	18.7		27.5	35.0	36.1	38.3	39.1	40.7	44.5	48.1
Uruguay	268.0	287.0	322.0	337.5	364.4	399.0	437.0	481.6	528.7	579.2
Venezuela	634.0	800.0	1,231.5	1,311.5	1,451.5	1,581.0	1,676.6	1,749.3	1,758.2	1,793.7
Caribbean										
Anguilla			0.9	1.3	1.4	1.4	1.4			
Antigua				11.0						
Aruba						21.7	23.1	19.1		36.4
Bahamas	61.8	71.9	84.1	91.0	97.5	108.1	119.1	128.9	132.9	139.9
Barbados	47.4		75.0				94.3	102.1	110.6	117.5
Bermuda								56.3	51.1	
British Virgin Islands	2.6			4.5	3.7					
Cayman Islands	5.1	7.3		11.9	12.9	13.7	16.1	16.9	18.0	19.4
Cuba	321.0			493.0	515.1	543.2	564.2	536.7	552.8	610.0
Dominica	3.7	4.5	4.5	5.7	6.9				14.6	
Dominican Republic										
Grenada			5.6	6.0	6.4				27.0	
Guadeloupe	30.7	45.1	68.5	81.0	95.7	106.7	100.4	103.4	110.8	121.5
Haiti								50.0		
Jamaica	111.1					152.3	165.8	168.1	168.7	174.5
Martinique	38.5	52.2	83.6	100.2	111.8	120.2	106.9	117.3	124.9	158.7
Netherlands Antilles	50.0	56.0	65.2							
St Kitts					3.8					
St Lucia	7.2			11.6	11.9	14.1		17.6		
St Vincent/Grenadines	5.3			6.5	8.5				16.8	
Trinidad and Tobago	73.2		109.0		165.5	191.7	210.6	211.7		226.0
Central America										
Belize										
Costa Rica	159.6	236.1	292.3	303.7	314.9	343.5	408.8	410.4		450.3
El Salvador	77.5	86.0	116.0	124.0	132.6	128.8	136.2		249.9	
Guatemala					128.2				250.0	
Honduras			35.1	45.5	47.4	52.1	56.3	69.3		91.6
Mexico	3,712.0	4,992.0	6,414.5	6,796.2		7,616.7	8,015.6	8,476.7	9,358.7	10,103.4
Nicaragua	42.9			50.5						
Panama		173.2	202.6	210.3	223.2	231.8	240.0	241.7	251.9	256.1
Puerto Rico										
South Asia										
Afghanistan	28.1	31.7								
Bangladesh	69.0	97.0	140.0	136.0	151.0	164.0	174.0		248.5	
Bhutan					1.8					
India	2,096.0	2,785.0	3,238.2	3,487.9	3,761.2	4,056.9	4,420.1		5,485.9	
Nepal	12.3		18.4	18.2				67.0		
Pakistan	274.0	330.0	474.0	511.0	516.8	623.0	679.4	740.3		
Sri Lanka	68.1	85.3	105.8	108.9	116.8	125.3	132.5	185.0	166.1	166.0

TELEPHONES
Table No. 2001 (cont'd)

Telephones in Use 1977-1990

Units: '000

	1977	1980	1983	1984	1985	1986	1987	1988	1989	1990
Japan										
Japan	46,308.0	53,634.0	61,208.0	63,976.0	66,636.0					
ASEAN/NICs										
Brunei	12.3	17.9	31.3		32.9	35.6	39.5	44.0	49.0	
Hong Kong	1,251.0	1,676.0	2,041.6	2,173.0	2,315.2	2,461.2	2,662.0	2,893.0	3,104.6	3,279.6
Indonesia	349.1	487.3	718.0	788.0	829.0	840.0	864.4	938.2	1,015.3	
Macau			27.3	37.2	49.5	60.5	68.9	80.5	95.4	111.2
Malaysia	376.0	598.0	976.5	1,150.9	1,278.8	1,381.0	1,423.0		2,022.6	
Philippines	567.0	702.0	787.6	811.8	820.3	856.0	866.0	994.3	986.1	1,046.6
Singapore	455.1	702.2	882.6	1,002.6	1,074.0	1,116.0	1,163.8	1,219.6		
South Korea	1,976.0	3,387.0	5,948.0	6,984.6	6,517.4	9,288.0	10,732.8	12,415.0	14,194.8	
Taiwan	1,685.0	3,166.0	4,855.0	5,279.0	5,653.0	6,078.0	6,549.0	7,159.0		
Thailand	367.0	497.0	623.4	733.4	754.6	999.7	1,002.5	1,005.9		
East/SE Asia										
Cambodia										
China	3,770.0	4,355.0	5,072.0	5,539.0	6,260.0	7,059.0	8,057.0	9,418.0	10,893.3	12,735.4
Laos	6.5				8.1				7.1	
Mongolia	34.4	39.8	44.6				55.0	58.3		
Myanmar	32.2		50.6			59.6	65.2	80.6		
North Korea										
Vietnam			102.6	106.1	109.0	115.0				
Australasia										
Australia	5,835.0	7,153.0	8,297.7	8,328.7	8,727.2					
New Zealand	1,673.9	1,779.9	1,939.5	2,010.7	2,105.7	2,203.0	2,315.0	2,402.6		
Pacific										
American Samoa										
Fiji	32.7	42.5	49.5	51.3	53.2	58.4	60.0	62.4	67.1	72.6
French Polynesia	17.3	22.6	33.2	34.0	37.7	41.2	43.7			
Guam										
Kiribati	0.9	0.7	0.9		1.1	1.2	1.2	1.3		
Nauru	1.5	1.6	1.6	1.6	1.6	1.6				
New Caledonia	23.1	26.7	32.0							
Papua New Guinea	39.8	49.3	51.5	54.7	57.9	63.2	69.7	72.2	72.8	63.2
Solomon Islands	1.9	2.5	3.2		4.6	5.0	5.5	7.0		
Tonga		2.1	3.5	4.0						
Tuvalu					0.2	0.2	0.2	0.2	0.2	0.2
Vanuatu	2.4		3.0	3.0	3.0	3.2				
Western Samoa	3.5	5.8	6.3							
Middle East										
Bahrain	38.3	71.9	98.0	108.4	114.9	119.1	121.6	133.6	141.2	153.1
Egypt	473.0		676.7	800.1	1,155.3	1,393.6	1,455.0	1,455.0		2,232.8
Iran	828.6	1,227.3	1,791.8	2,143.8	2,253.0	1,883.6	1,943.7	2,078.6	2,103.8	2,270.0
Iraq			631.1		886.1					
Israel	910.0	1,140.0	1,430.0	1,527.0	1,780.0	1,935.0	2,065.0	2,190.0	2,285.0	2,425.0
Jordan	43.1	62.0	95.0	113.6	147.9	177.9		280.1	320.0	
Kuwait	155.0	215.0	258.0	271.2	287.1	310.1	330.0	362.0		
Lebanon										
Oman	13.0	23.2	62.0	65.2	66.3	74.3	79.9			
Qatar	29.3	53.3	96.0	103.2	110.5	115.5	121.1	129.3	134.8	139.2
Saudi Arabia		443.0	1,624.3	1,752.2	1,800.0					
Syria	211.0	335.0	512.0	582.0	616.0	637.0	653.0	669.0	685.0	694.9
United Arab Emirates	142.1	208.9	307.6	312.8	337.8	358.1	403.6	463.4	544.1	654.7
Yemen										

TELEPHONES

Telephones in Use 1977-1990

Units: '000

	1977	1980	1983	1984	1985	1986	1987	1988	1989	1990
North Africa										
Algeria	297.7	484.9	606.6	708.6	769.2	821.8	888.5	958.8	1,051.9	1,103.4
Chad	6.5				3.0	4.7	5.0	9.9		8.0
Djibouti	3.7	5.2	7.2	7.7	8.1	8.3	8.5	7.6	7.5	14.5
Ethiopia	76.1	86.2	110.3	115.8	122.0	132.2	137.3	138.5	153.0	159.2
Libya					800.0	850.0	900.0			
Mali	8.0	9.0	12.0	12.0	13.0	13.0	14.0	14.6	15.0	14.6
Mauritania	8.0	9.0	11.0	12.0	12.0	12.0	13.0			
Morocco	210.0	231.0	269.9	285.8	311.1	325.3	342.7	361.8	410.0	475.5
Niger	7.1		11.0	11.5	11.8	12.0	13.0			
Somalia										
Sudan	61.6	63.4	71.5	74.6	77.9					
Tunisia	144.0	189.0	232.8	250.6	272.3	291.3	312.0	333.2	370.5	410.5
West Africa										
Benin	14.7				13.1	15.5	16.1	16.2	16.9	16.1
Burkina Faso	7.1		13.9	14.2	14.0	15.0	15.0			
Cameroon			47.2	49.2			61.6			
Cape Verde	1.6	3.0	4.0	4.0	5.0	5.0	6.0			
Côte d'Ivoire	66.6	88.0	103.0	105.0	106.0	106.0	110.0		153.0	
Equatorial Guinea										
Gabon			13.8						25.9	
Gambia	3.0	4.0	5.0	5.0	6.0	6.0	7.0	7.2	9.3	
Ghana	66.5	69.0	74.0	74.0	77.0	72.7	74.9	73.2	77.1	79.2
Guinea	9.5	12.0	13.0	14.0	15.0	15.0	16.0	17.9	19.6	
Guinea-Bissau	4.0	5.0	6.0	6.0	7.0	7.0	7.0			
Liberia	8.0	11.0	18.0	18.0	19.0	19.0	21.0			
Nigeria	123.0	154.0	195.0	210.0	229.0	235.0	245.0			
Sao Tomé e Príncipe	0.8		2.2	2.5						
Senegal		43.0	48.0	50.0	52.0	54.0	55.0			
Sierra Leone	9.0	15.0	22.0	24.0	26.0	27.0	28.0		34.6	
Togo	8.0	9.8	12.0	12.0	13.0	14.0	14.0		21.0	
East/Central Africa										
Angola	23.1	39.6					77.0			
Burundi			6.0			7.9	8.1	9.6	10.4	
Central African Republic				6.7		16.0				
Comoros								4.0		
Congo	11.6		18.1			18.5	19.2	23.4	25.8	
Kenya	143.8	191.7	231.2	248.1		291.6	316.1	337.0	357.3	383.1
Madagascar	32.0	37.7		49.0	51.0	52.0				
Maldives	0.6	1.1								
Mauritius	29.1	37.1	48.3	53.8	64.6		66.9	72.3	74.1	
Réunion	36.2	52.2	85.9					825.0		
Rwanda	3.9	4.3	6.8	9.0	9.1	9.1	10.2	11.2	12.6	14.1
Seychelles	4.9	7.2	9.1	10.7						
Tanzania	70.3	93.2	103.8	104.0	109.0	111.0	122.6	130.5	136.8	140.1
Uganda	48.9	47.1	54.4	57.0	57.0	57.0	59.3	59.7	61.0	57.2
Zaire	31.7	27.3	38.8	38.8	38.8	38.8		32.1		
Southern Africa										
Botswana	9.4		17.9	19.1	19.1	21.4	22.0	41.2	47.9	
Lesotho				11.0	13.7	16.1	18.2	19.1		
Malawi	22.3	31.0	36.8	40.1	40.6	44.7	46.9	50.3	50.2	
Mozambique	44.1		58.8	59.5	60.2	61.8	62.6	63.3	64.1	66.0
Namibia										
South Africa	2,191.0	2,662.0	3,471.5	3,647.7	3,889.8	4,057.7	4,236.0	4,462.0	4,744.0	5,077.2
Swaziland	8.8	12.0		16.1	17.8	20.1	20.7	22.4	23.9	25.3
Zambia	54.3	61.3	71.7	71.2	74.6	85.4	80.9	91.6	95.3	99.8
Zimbabwe	192.4	214.4	246.9	245.1	248.1	256.4	277.5	286.6		300.9

Source: International Telecommunication Union (ITU)/national statistical offices

TELEPHONES   Table No. 2002

Total Telephone Traffic 1977-1990

Units: Million calls

	1977	1980	1983	1984	1985	1986	1987	1988	1989	1990
North America										
Canada	23,305.0	26,935.0	29,548.1	32,865.0	34,742.0	36,660.0	38,628.4			
USA	265,934.0	311,189.0	349,451.1	357,974.3	402,830.1	414,617.3	433,099.3	446,702.6	458,422.4	468,863.1
South America										
Argentina	87,760.0	43,600.0	30,237.0	35,394.0	34,242.0	30,969.0	33,509.0	37,490.0	40,462.0	
Bolivia [a]	1.2					44.5		46.6	48.5	
Brazil		11,466.8	15,134.6	15,355.3	17,494.9	19,636.1	34,400.0	36,900.0	42,200.0	
Chile [b]	1,628.0	2,013.0	1,264.6	1,366.5	1,621.5	5,197.6		5,666.1		
Colombia [a]			1,176.1				8,952.6	10,989.0		
Ecuador										
French Guiana [b]		0.1	0.1	0.1	0.1	0.1	0.3	0.2	0.2	
Guyana				88.1	88.4	88.5				
Paraguay [c]	98.7	164.2	192.5	280.1	273.6	320.4	352.4	416.8		
Peru			314.9	1,397.6	1,989.3	2,640.6		3,452.0	4,208.0	1,930.0
Suriname [b,c]	56.8		73.0	109.0	113.6	121.6	133.4	126.5		
Uruguay	500.9	508.5	572.5	600.0	675.4	697.1	536.0			
Venezuela [a]	2,707.0			12,113.0	10,899.6	12,919.9	11,044.3	12,822.1		
Caribbean										
Anguilla				1.0		1.2				
Antigua				2.3	3.2	3.6	3.9			
Aruba										
Bahamas	148.0	110.1	483.0	1,000.5	1,173.0		2,052.0	1,492.0		
Barbados					1.2					
Bermuda										
British Virgin Islands	4.4									
Cayman Islands [a]	6.4									
Cuba	39.2			116.8	119.5	127.3	151.8	163.3	156.9	
Dominica [d]	4.8			5.0						
Dominican Republic										
Grenada			0.2							
Guadeloupe [b]		245.5	327.4	320.0	321.1	369.6	421.7	489.8	557.6	
Haiti										
Jamaica	2.7									
Martinique [b]		180.1	293.3	280.9	285.8	298.7	349.2	564.0	437.0	257.1
Netherlands Antilles	7.4	13.9								
St Kitts					1.1					
St Lucia [d]	6.3			13.1						
St Vincent/Grenadines [a]	5.4			5.5						
Trinidad and Tobago			11.5							
Central America										
Belize										
Costa Rica	383.0	568.7	711.1	606.5	631.5	1,250.4				
El Salvador [a]	170.4	577.8	410.7	425.2	486.2	650.4				
Guatemala					21.1				1,304.0	
Honduras [b]			272.4	321.2	383.3	427.9	483.2	527.3		
Mexico	8,658.0	11,198.0	11,539.6	12,430.3		13,622.0			13,419.7	6,774.7
Nicaragua [a]	108.5	134.0		272.5						
Panama	470.3	559.8	1,187.1	638.0	591.3	886.6	927.6	930.3	978.6	1,062.7
Puerto Rico										
South Asia										
Afghanistan	0.8	0.1								
Bangladesh	320.0									
Bhutan										
India	146.2									
Nepal [b]	0.1		3.8	4.4	5.4					
Pakistan	82.0	113.6	122.3							
Sri Lanka	200.0	250.0	410.0	550.0	660.0					

TELEPHONES

Total Telephone Traffic 1977-1990

Units: Million calls

	1977	1980	1983	1984	1985	1986	1987	1988	1989	1990
Japan										
Japan										
ASEAN/NICs										
Brunei					7.9	8.3				
Hong Kong				4.1	24.7	27.9	32.4	43.1	134.1	
Indonesia										
Macau					123.0	130.2	171.1	198.2	230.4	266.7
Malaysia [a]	8,529.0	17,961.0	4,575.0	4,886.0	7,679.0					
Philippines	9.6	13.3	19.8	21.8					43.5	72.4
Singapore	2,122.0	3,432.0	4,039.7	4,045.6	4,037.0	3,266.9	3,451.6	4,006.3	4,916.3	4,651.9
South Korea [a]	4,303.0	3,000.0	6,717.0	9,900.0	15,427.0	22,983.0		33,163.0	47,311.0	
Taiwan										
Thailand		775.0	1,072.0	1,174.3		1,651.9				
East/SE Asia										
Cambodia										
China	520.0	641.0	706.0	776.2	862.1	920.9	1,054.0	1,262.0	1,151.7	1,917.5
Laos	0.6				3.9			5.0		
Mongolia										
Myanmar	59.1							460.0		
North Korea										
Vietnam	5.3									
Australasia										
Australia	4,339.6	5,384.7	6,777.0	7,365.1	7,979.8	8,654.7	9,259.2	9,812.4	10,236.7	
New Zealand		84.9	138.7	583.7	705.7	823.3	902.7	1,034.6		
Pacific										
American Samoa										
Fiji			2.2	2.6	3.0	3.5	4.8	6.1		
French Polynesia [a]	12.6	17.1	27.5	35.3	42.2	48.2				
Guam										
Kiribati [a]				0.1	0.1					
Nauru		1.5	1.9	1.8	2.0	2.1				
New Caledonia [a]	13.8	15.8	21.2	24.3	29.5					
Papua New Guinea	38.0	56.4	57.2	59.0	57.3		152.1	148.7		
Solomon Islands					0.5	0.6			1.7	
Tonga [b]			1.6	2.3						
Tuvalu [b]										
Vanuatu										
Western Samoa										
Middle East										
Bahrain [a]			138.6	167.5	193.4	215.3	244.4		466.4	
Egypt				1,642.4	3,245.8	4,633.3				
Iran			9,036.0	9,300.0	11,616.0	8,462.9	11,622.8			
Iraq [a]										
Israel [b]	2,580.0	3,650.0	4,870.0	6,130.0	8,380.0	9,060.0	8,610.0	9,760.0	9,806.0	10,440.0
Jordan									907.3	
Kuwait						9.4	11.3	13.1		
Lebanon										
Oman [b]	0.1	0.2	6.3	8.2	11.7	13.6	15.5	18.1	11.4	
Qatar					300.0	399.0				
Saudi Arabia			676.4						3,492.1	5,610.6
Syria										
United Arab Emirates [a]		135.1	230.8	258.3	416.2	455.2				
Yemen										

TELEPHONES

Total Telephone Traffic 1977-1990

Units: Million calls

	1977	1980	1983	1984	1985	1986	1987	1988	1989	1990
North Africa										
Algeria [b]	501.1	1,243.2	1,994.2	2,038.7	2,311.8	2,421.3				
Chad [a]					4.1	4.8		7.2		
Djibouti [b]	2.9	3.4	4.1		7.2	16.7	22.5			
Ethiopia [a]	182.7	199.8	309.5	293.9	316.8	308.3	382.6	307.9	338.4	
Libya									41.4	
Mali										
Mauritania										
Morocco [b]			906.7	922.9	950.6	963.5				
Niger [e]	0.2									
Somalia										
Sudan	2.7									
Tunisia [a]	350.1	406.9	474.5	513.6	616.7	721.1	742.6	916.4		
West Africa										
Benin	0.6					75.6		75.0		
Burkina Faso [a]				16.0						
Cameroon										
Cape Verde	15.0			0.5						
Côte d'Ivoire										
Equatorial Guinea										
Gabon [a]			48.3							
Gambia					4.5			33.0		
Ghana				0.3		0.4	0.6	0.8	1.8	
Guinea	9.8									
Guinea-Bissau										
Liberia										
Nigeria [a]					86.9					
Sao Tomé e Príncipe			1.8	2.4						
Senegal						10.7				
Sierra Leone [a]						0.6				
Togo [a]						5.9			6.8	
East/Central Africa										
Angola										
Burundi			1.7							
Central African Republic				2.8	9.0					
Comoros										
Congo	33.5		90.0							
Kenya				13.7	14.0	14.2	13.5	6.8	13.0	23.4
Madagascar	34.3	55.4	43.0	9.6	25.2					
Maldives	1.0									
Mauritius	32.9	34.2	60.1							
Réunion [b]		143.4	261.4							
Rwanda										
Seychelles			3.6		4.0					
Tanzania		9.7	9.8	9.6	8.1	9.5	9.8	8.9	13.8	13.9
Uganda	99.2	219.7					78.3	80.3	86.7	166.2
Zaire	0.2	0.2	1.5	1.7	1.8			1.3		
Southern Africa										
Botswana										
Lesotho [a]			54.5	66.2						
Malawi [a]			2.4	2.4	3.3	2.3			4.2	
Mozambique	91.9		77.6							
Namibia										
South Africa [a]	5,904.0	8,208.0	11,060.0	11,806.0	12,636.0	12,058.9				
Swaziland [a]						44.8		92.0	91.2	
Zambia			7.1		10.0	8.8				
Zimbabwe [a]	538.6	704.1	985.6	844.0	930.7	256.9				

Source: ITU/national statistical offices
Notes: see end of section

TELEX   Table No. 2003

Telex Lines in Use 1977-1990

Units: Number

	1977	1980	1983	1984	1985	1986	1987	1988	1989	1990
North America										
Canada	42,115	50,473	50,336	48,800	47,100	42,000	43,900	15,000	11,000	8,500
USA	131,000	159,500	168,300	152,000	117,800	100,500	78,400	81,500	58,700	
South America										
Argentina	2,900	6,400	8,816	10,000	11,200	11,600	12,110	13,020	13,480	12,500
Bolivia	197				1,100	1,170		1,400	1,400	
Brazil	17,794	35,359	56,040	63,120	70,600	88,400	98,300	121,200	135,400	142,900
Chile	1,621	2,632	3,768	4,745	6,000	6,900	7,900	11,600		9,100
Colombia	2,650	4,340	5,310	5,800	6,000	6,900	6,570	6,450	6,100	5,900
Ecuador	1,168	1,474	1,900	2,450	2,600	3,000	3,150		3,600	3,300
French Guiana	88	144	200	200	300	300	310	360	390	400
Guyana				100	100	100				300
Paraguay	272	571	693	793	900	900	990	1,020	1,100	
Peru	2,000	3,000	2,964	3,411	3,300	3,500	3,450	3,450	3,450	3,100
Suriname	112		195	235	300	300	340	350	330	320
Uruguay	723	975	1,332	1,423	1,489	1,600	1,880	2,220	2,250	2,100
Venezuela	7,300		10,400	17,500	17,500	18,000	18,300	18,800	18,800	18,700
Caribbean										
Anguilla			30	32	35	37				
Antigua	33	54		100	100					500
Aruba							200	100		100
Bahamas	229	393	396	391	500	540	500	600	600	500
Barbados	118	189	281	319	350				200	200
Bermuda	311	453		536	530					
British Virgin Islands	18	39	55	58	100					
Cayman Islands	82	164		239	246			200		
Cuba	1,500		3,115	3,500	3,600	3,950	4,800	4,300	4,470	4,600
Dominica	9	13		34	45	100				42
Dominican Republic										
Grenada	14	25	44	49	100	100	100	100	100	50
Guadeloupe	178	340	553	600	600	700	800	800	900	800
Haiti										
Jamaica		311	350	450		500	600	600	500	
Martinique	173	294	422	456	500	560	600	700	700	700
Netherlands Antilles	430	620	783	800	800					
St Kitts	18	34	55	54	100					
St Lucia	46		141	153						
St Vincent/Grenadines	17	53	79	80	100	100				59
Trinidad and Tobago	188	176	267	267	267	267	267	267		
Central America										
Belize	24	51	70	85	100					
Costa Rica	600	1,000	1,439	1,474	1,500	1,600	1,600	1,500	900	700
El Salvador	342	627	683	756	900	900	900		800	800
Guatemala								1,300	1,300	1,200
Honduras	508		600	700	700	800	800	800		770
Mexico	7,500	11,500	23,055	22,569	23,300	23,900	24,500	24,600		24,600
Nicaragua		400					1,000	1,000	1,200	1,500
Panama		1,020	1,523	1,663	1,700	1,700	1,800	1,000	1,300	900
Puerto Rico										
South Asia										
Afghanistan	50	73			125					
Bangladesh										8,800
Bhutan								1,300		
India	13,340		21,502	22,552	26,300	30,200	34,000	37,400	41,300	44,500
Nepal	50		186	217	200	300	400		500	
Pakistan			3,530	3,638	5,200	6,900	7,200	8,000		
Sri Lanka	175	644	968	1,040	1,200	1,300	1,400	1,530	1,500	1,700

TELEX

Telex Lines in Use 1977-1990

Units: Number

	1977	1980	1983	1984	1985	1986	1987	1988	1989	1990
Japan										
Japan	83,000	71,000	57,000	51,000	45,000	47,000	45,000	42,000	40,000	
ASEAN/NICs										
Brunei	52	169	391	400	500	500	500	450	440	
Hong Kong	7,094	13,757	20,868	23,657	26,993	28,831	29,700	27,600	23,800	21,700
Indonesia	2,159	4,745	8,853		10,400		13,400	15,400	14,900	
Macau			391	487	600	600	600	600	500	500
Malaysia	1,733	3,664	7,980	9,774					8,800	8,400
Philippines	4,960	6,417	10,494	12,860			15,800	12,200	10,600	8,400
Singapore	3,490	7,980	14,349	15,975	16,800	17,600	17,900	16,800	15,600	14,200
South Korea	2,321	4,000	8,000	8,210	8,938	9,885	10,300	10,000	9,400	
Taiwan										
Thailand		2,019	3,910	4,856	5,400	5,800	6,200	6,600	6,400	6,100
East/SE Asia										
Cambodia										
China	149	471	1,373	2,019	2,100	5,400	6,900	10,100	12,140	13,100
Laos	19	15	27		30					50
Mongolia										
Myanmar	42		100	100	100	100	100	100	100	
North Korea										
Vietnam										
Australasia										
Australia	19,600	29,700	40,000	43,719	45,900	45,000	37,700	37,700	22,000	18,000
New Zealand	2,578	3,427	4,944	5,451	5,994	6,500	6,500	5,320	3,450	2,240
Pacific										
American Samoa										
Fiji	200	259	448	508	600	700	700	650	560	
French Polynesia	72	113	164	193	200	200	300	300		
Guam										
Kiribati	30		21	26	30					
Nauru	7	10	20	20	20	20	30	30		
New Caledonia	95	117	160	183						
Papua New Guinea	501	1,376	1,119	1,301	1,400	1,400	1,400	1,100	999	900
Solomon Islands										
Tonga			61	74	100	100				
Tuvalu					40	40				
Vanuatu	28		70	70	70	70				
Western Samoa										
Middle East										
Bahrain	687	1,354	1,946	2,075	2,050	2,090	1,900	2,000	1,800	1,700
Egypt			4,820	4,681	5,300	6,100	6,450	6,400	6,600	6,400
Iran	2,160		3,125	3,604	4,079	4,800	6,000	5,500	5,900	8,400
Iraq			1,648		2,200					
Israel	2,600	3,400	4,250	4,540	5,010	6,100	6,400	6,300	5,700	3,600
Jordan							2,600	2,400	2,200	2,300
Kuwait	1,290	2,410	3,692	3,600	3,600	3,300	3,200	3,000		
Lebanon										
Oman	340	645	951	1,111	1,500	1,800	1,500	1,300	1,390	1,070
Qatar	528	834	1,040	1,062	1,100	1,100	1,000	1,000	800	600
Saudi Arabia	900	8,700	16,254	16,733	16,500	15,800	14,960	13,800	12,300	10,900
Syria	433	889	1,803	1,909	2,000	2,100	2,400	2,700	3,100	3,400
United Arab Emirates	2,800	4,700	6,099	5,988	6,100	6,100	6,300	6,310	6,200	5,700
Yemen		71	80							

TELEX

Telex Lines in Use 1977-1990

Units: Number

	1977	1980	1983	1984	1985	1986	1987	1988	1989	1990
North Africa										
Algeria	1,471	3,193	5,895	6,853	7,400	7,800	8,200	9,800	10,500	9,900
Chad	60		58	80	100	100	100	100	100	200
Djibouti	54	106	168	175	200	200	200	200	200	
Ethiopia	310	416	631	630	700	700	800	900	940	998
Libya										
Mali								300	400	330
Mauritania								300		300
Morocco	2,831	3,875	5,061	5,728	6,700	6,700	7,100	7,300		8,700
Niger	142		275	300	300			200		
Somalia										
Sudan	416									
Tunisia	945	1,506	2,111	2,408	3,000			2,930	3,000		3,700
West Africa										
Benin	78				236	300	300	300		300
Burkina Faso	144		223	227	200	300				
Cameroon			1,035			1,900				
Cape Verde	2			79						
Côte d'Ivoire	945	1,330	1,577							1,890
Equatorial Guinea										
Gabon			640							700
Gambia					100	100	100	100	100	100
Ghana	171			310	300	400	470	560	670	710
Guinea	56		195							800
Guinea-Bissau										
Liberia										
Nigeria					4,800			5,900		
Sao Tomé e Príncipe			35	38						
Senegal			779	838	900	900	1,100	900	1,400	900
Sierra Leone	113	189	257	300	300	300				400
Togo	100	139	285	285	400	400	500	500	500	400
East/Central Africa										
Angola	335	587								
Burundi		85	100			200				200
Central African Republic				140						
Comoros			42	329						
Congo		236	317			500	500	500	500	500
Kenya	848	1,170	1,750	1,856		2,300	2,500	2,500	2,300	2,400
Madagascar	244	307	343	341						
Maldives	12		121	142						200
Mauritius	148	247	310	460		600	700	800	800	700
Réunion	91	191	434							800
Rwanda	50	67	100	100	100	100	100	100		140
Seychelles	70	127	143	151						
Tanzania	275	560	1,650			1,300	1,300	1,300	1,700	1,800
Uganda	258	288	419			900		900	900	900
Zaire	690	804	1,600	1,605				1,600		
Southern Africa										
Botswana	90		407	500		700				600
Lesotho				210	200			200		
Malawi	200	339	412	490	500	600				700
Mozambique	385	501	602	618	700	700	800	900		970
Namibia										
South Africa	14,000	18,000	27,585	29,550	32,000	32,500	33,500	31,600	22,600	17,500
Swaziland	128	217		354	300	400	400	400	300	400
Zambia	769	1,146	1,379	1,456	1,500	1,500	1,700	2,520	2,770	2,900
Zimbabwe	773	941	1,584	1,903	2,100	2,100	2,500	2,600	2,800	2,980

Source: ITU/national statistical offices

TELEX

Total Telex Traffic 1977-1990

Units: '000 minutes

	1977	1980	1983	1984	1985	1986	1987	1988	1989	1990
North America										
Canada			14,550.0	15,435.0	15,948.0	14,961.0	13,234.0	9,043.0	5,720.0	
USA			188,699.0	185,908.0	189,245.0	179,234.0	156,463.0	123,326.0	90,247.0	73,104.0
South America										
Argentina										
Bolivia	227.0		2,087.3			2,743.5		3,212.0	3,446.0	
Brazil	99,213.0	176,405.0	276,571.0	393,000.0	476,000.0	420,300.0	500,000.0	561,600.0	637,500.0	
Chile	7,254.0	12,425.0		13,305.7	16,611.4	16,664.7	27,988.0	26,756.0		
Colombia	17,814.0	24,221.0	29,298.0		27,364.0	31,427.0	30,427.0			
Ecuador			6,970.8							1,652.0
French Guiana		280.0	257.0	597.0	677.0	664.0	734.0	754.0	455.0	445.0
Guyana					365.0	365.0				
Paraguay					240.0	267.0	263.6	299.1		
Peru				21,850.2	22,521.0	28,512.6		24,292.3	24,292.0	21,183.3
Suriname			432.5		449.4	1,361.2				1,745.0
Uruguay	1,688.0	2,896.0	2,123.0	2,166.9	2,245.0	2,593.5	2,821.8	3,638.2	2,947.0	2,427.0
Venezuela							208,545.0	192,155.0		
Caribbean										
Anguilla			19.6	24.2	26.9	10.3				
Antigua		90.2		176.2	189.4					
Aruba						303.6	230.5	195.1		
Bahamas	448.8	893.2	1,156.9	992.9	1,316.9	1,127.4	816.6			515.1
Barbados	228.2		595.2	635.3	740.5		746.8	578.4	433.3	423.6
Bermuda					1,616.1					
British Virgin Islands										
Cayman Islands										
Cuba	8,704.0			31,848.9	34,400.0	35,039.0	35,709.0	36,758.0	34,986.0	
Dominica										
Dominican Republic										
Grenada	17.0	46.8	107.8	113.0	117.4					
Guadeloupe	527.3	717.0	743.0	1,119.0	644.0	990.0	1,182.0	1,303.0	638.0	896.0
Haiti										
Jamaica						2,140.0				
Martinique	511.5		672.0	986.0	1,288.0	1,153.0	948.0	1,126.0	580.0	757.0
Netherlands Antilles	969.0	1,643.0	1,784.4							
St Kitts					118.3					
St Lucia										
St Vincent/Grenadines					126.9					
Trinidad and Tobago [a]								364.0	189.0	
Central America										
Belize	48.8	72.1		140.6	137.9					
Costa Rica		2,386.8	3,271.0	3,592.1	2,350.8	2,533.2		3,640.0		3,200.0
El Salvador		1,412.5	1,573.5	1,812.5	2,211.1	4,778.2	5,796.2			
Guatemala								3,540.2		
Honduras				2,072.4	2,722.8	3,638.6	4,818.5	3,198.0		2,054.0
Mexico							77,857.0			42,497.3
Nicaragua	732.3	747.7		1,572.2						
Panama		1,970.0			3,655.9	3,484.7				
Puerto Rico										
South Asia										
Afghanistan [b]					168.9					
Bangladesh	284.0		1,230.0		2,437.2					
Bhutan										
India										
Nepal										
Pakistan				2,376.0	2,936.0	2,960.0	9,138.0	7,800.0		
Sri Lanka [a]	841.0	721.0	1,571.8	1,825.5					6,854.6	9,801.9

TELEX

Total Telex Traffic 1977-1990

Units: '000 minutes

	1977	1980	1983	1984	1985	1986	1987	1988	1989	1990
Japan										
Japan	289,644.0	211,360.0								
ASEAN/NICs										
Brunei	113.1	299.9	659.1	787.4	814.2	811.4				
Hong Kong	17,073.0	37,056.0	60,134.0	69,096.8	75,513.6	83,592.1	83,239.0	72,031.0		
Indonesia [c]	992.2	2,190.5	10,479.6		10,494.7					
Macau			494.7	730.8	882.8	976.5	422.0	348.0	312.0	
Malaysia [c]			3,472.4	3,629.8	3,788.3					
Philippines	5,763.0	10,257.0	14,550.5	11,781.8				11,370.0	10,910.0	5,784.2
Singapore	9,666.0	24,481.0	50,111.3	58,740.0	60,727.0	62,748.7	61,969.0	52,766.0	47,503.0	48,984.9
South Korea [c]		6,005.0	10,974.0	11,358.6	11,423.0		9,692.4			
Taiwan										
Thailand	2,902.0		9,394.0	11,547.5	12,843.4	12,364.0	12,657.0	11,725.6	9,533.4	7,747.3
East/SE Asia										
Cambodia										
China						12,360.0	12,884.0	12,570.0	11,754.0	
Laos									93.0	
Mongolia										
Myanmar										
North Korea										
Vietnam [c]										
Australasia										
Australia [c]	34,304.6	45,816.1	58,114.0	67,024.0	65,094.0	64,797.0	55,897.0	55,879.0	19,380.0	
New Zealand	9,952.0	13,045.0	16,931.9	18,763.7	20,163.2	21,434.2	19,752.0	16,688.0	10,045.0	3,937.4
Pacific										
American Samoa										
Fiji [d]	868.1									
French Polynesia			420.7	549.4	656.9	715.8	810.4			
Guam										
Kiribati			43.7	106.8						
Nauru		28.3	42.2	45.3	50.3	54.3				
New Caledonia	307.4	300.4	419.8	511.7						
Papua New Guinea	1,460.0	2,465.0	3,388.2	3,825.7	3,412.4		3,072.3	2,616.2		
Solomon Islands					264.0				177.7	
Tonga [c]			34.8							
Tuvalu										
Vanuatu [c]						263.6				
Western Samoa										
Middle East										
Bahrain	3,248.3	7,483.1	12,280.8	11,942.2	10,678.5	10,159.8	8,643.7	8,486.9	7,675.5	8,805.0
Egypt			27,302.6	24,211.7	33,700.0	17,985.3				12,250.0
Iran	5,474.0		4,338.5	5,982.8	9,379.9	6,473.8	6,423.0	6,496.0	6,731.5	
Iraq			5,675.4		7,667.7					
Israel	12,472.0	15,901.0	16,900.0	17,280.0	22,437.0	22,846.0	24,749.0	22,538.0	17,422.0	13,075.0
Jordan										
Kuwait			12,513.0	12,549.1	13,434.5	10,907.0	9,899.0	8,338.0		
Lebanon										
Oman	1,339.0	2,181.8	3,807.4	4,556.0	5,217.5	4,716.6	3,334.5	2,879.6	1,945.9	1,904.0
Qatar	1,005.0	1,860.1	2,585.0	2,679.2	2,808.1	2,678.9	2,657.6	2,345.3	1,622.0	1,178.6
Saudi Arabia [c]				15,904.0		14,800.4	12,632.0	8,835.4		
Syria				2,186.0	1,192.0	1,819.0	1,834.0	2,165.0		
United Arab Emirates	6,695.0	12,990.0	20,122.5	19,391.7	19,437.6	18,682.7	17,814.7	16,229.9	13,592.0	10,931.5
Yemen						503.8				

TELEX

Total Telex Traffic 1977-1990

Units: '000 minutes

	1977	1980	1983	1984	1985	1986	1987	1988	1989	1990
North Africa										
Algeria	7,126.0	17,270.0	30,192.1	31,508.3	32,338.0	31,658.0	30,005.0	26,345.0	31,270.0	28,253.6
Chad					236.3	292.4				
Djibouti	222.0	504.5	506.5	535.2	585.3	559.6		658.0	545.0	467.1
Ethiopia	740.0	1,066.0	1,438.5	1,693.4	1,832.8	2,168.9	2,003.0	2,081.0	2,345.3	1,930.7
Libya										
Mali										
Mauritania										384.6
Morocco [c]			3,472.4	3,629.8	3,788.3	4,222.0	5,648.0	6,464.0		
Niger		548.2	478.7	489.6	529.3					
Somalia										
Sudan										
Tunisia	2,382.0	4,181.0	5,239.1	6,896.7	6,724.5	5,452.4	7,431.0	8,632.7	9,356.8	7,545.6
West Africa										
Benin [e]					679.0			9,536.2		
Burkina Faso										
Cameroon										
Cape Verde				169.5						
Côte d'Ivoire										
Equatorial Guinea										
Gabon			2,721.4							8,748.0
Gambia					122.0					234.3
Ghana [b]				76.3		1,081.3	1,320.0	1,181.1	1,620.0	1,430.2
Guinea										
Guinea-Bissau										
Liberia										
Nigeria					3,661.2					
Sao Tomé e Príncipe			53.6	54.8						
Senegal			1,782.0	1,890.5	2,277.5	2,124.4	2,311.0	2,093.1	2,303.2	
Sierra Leone					485.1	702.8				
Togo					922.0	1,718.0			1,058.5	969.0
East/Central Africa										
Angola	428.0	1,293.0								
Burundi						293.6			330.4	339.2
Central African Republic										
Comoros										
Congo [b]	502.0	565.0	797.6			809.0				
Kenya				5,424.1		4,981.2				
Madagascar [f]	490.2	794.1			972.7					
Maldives										
Mauritius			860.8	1,065.3	1,315.3	1,810.0	2,377.1	2,537.4		
Réunion	368.9	602.5	715.0	1,085.0	814.0					1,216.0
Rwanda	263.0	221.0								262.3
Seychelles	120.1	193.0	251.4	288.7						
Tanzania										
Uganda [c]	107.4	167.6	261.9							
Zaire	1,059.0			2,226.7						
Southern Africa										
Botswana	509.0		2,492.8	2,283.1		2,672.1			1,523.0	1,174.0
Lesotho				307.7	287.2					
Malawi										
Mozambique										
Namibia										
South Africa										
Swaziland [f]	3,413.0	2,548.0			1,780.0				804.4	743.7
Zambia	2,386.0	3,286.0	5,377.6	6,239.8	6,102.9	4,997.0	5,036.0	4,710.6	3,515.7	2,957.8
Zimbabwe	9,371.0	22,999.0	72,666.1	120,195.0	89,421.7					

Source: ITU/national statistical offices
Notes: see end of section

Notes to Tables in Section Twenty

Table 2002   a Unit = million minutes
               b Unit = million pulses
               c National calls only
               d From 1984, unit = million pulses
               e From 1983, unit = million minutes

Table 2004   a From 1983, unit = '000 calls
               b International calls only
               c Unit = '000 calls
               d To 1980, unit = '000 pulses
               e From 1986, unit = '000 pulses
               f   From 1984, unit = '000 calls

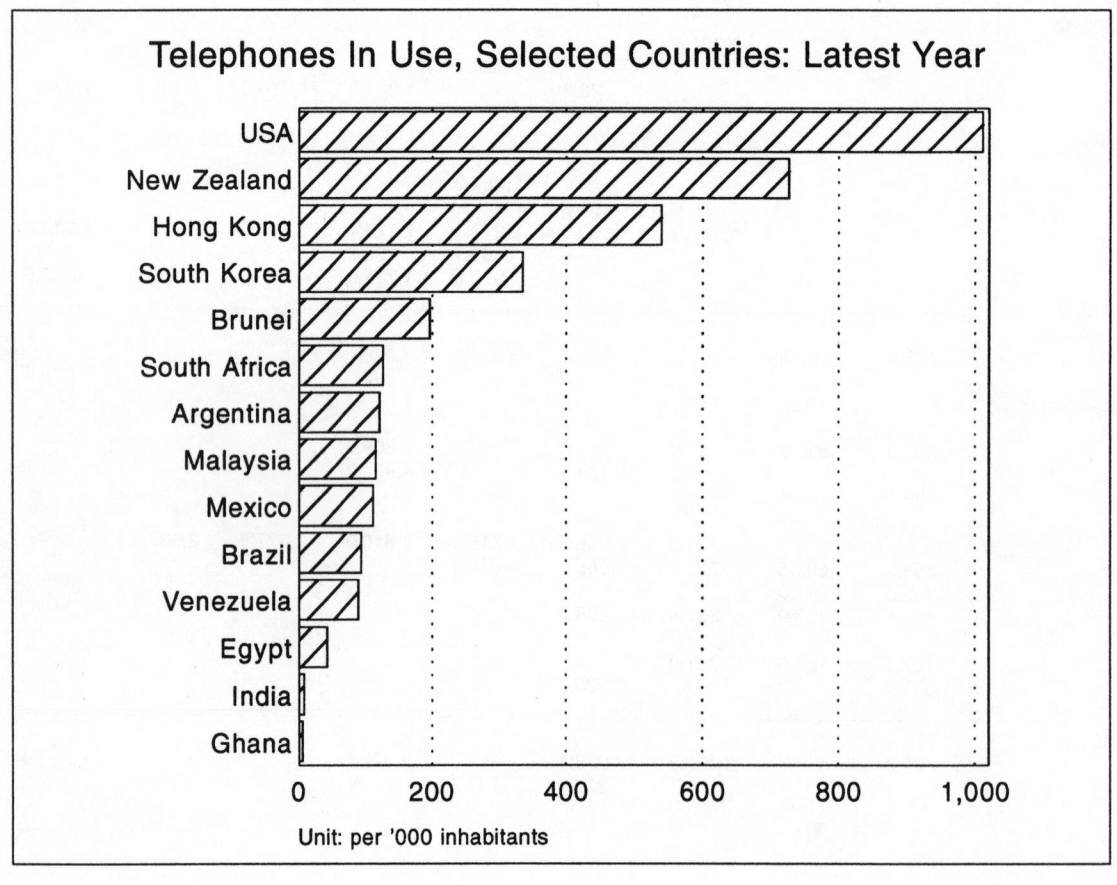

Telephones In Use, Selected Countries: Latest Year

Unit: per '000 inhabitants

Section Twenty-One
Automotives

AUTOMOTIVE REGISTRATIONS — Table No. 2101

New Registrations of Passenger Cars 1981-1992

Units: '000

	1981	1983	1985	1986	1987	1988	1989	1990	1991	1992
Argentina	148.7	125.4	125.6	139.5	163.8	142.4	118.0	83.3	117.4	218.3
Australia	462.7	433.5	530.2	410.9	369.3	418.7	464.3	487.7	416.8	453.2
Brazil	467.2	608.5	602.1	672.6	410.9	556.7	566.6	532.8	583.1	577.7
Canada	909.4	830.5	1,146.3	989.8	1,028.5	1,043.1	974.5	867.8	882.8	783.1
Chile										
China						30.7	58.6	42.3		
Colombia				34.5	42.6	45.7	37.4	32.7	15.4	
Ecuador										
Hong Kong	28.0	12.2	16.3	13.8	20.0	27.1	31.9	33.5	35.8	46.4
India	57.0	67.3	123.9	139.7	183.5	195.1	219.2	216.1	205.5	
Indonesia				33.7	28.9	32.7	31.9	55.7		
Israel										
Japan	2,866.7	3,135.6	3,104.1	3,146.0	3,274.8	3,717.4	4,403.7	5,102.7	4,868.2	4,454.0
Malaysia	86.4	90.0	59.7	47.0	35.3	54.6	75.3	108.4	123.8	110.3
Mexico	340.4	192.1	242.2	160.7	154.2	210.1	274.5	352.6	392.1	445.3
New Zealand	91.4	75.9	84.4	76.1	77.5	71.2	83.9	74.4	55.6	53.0
Nigeria	106.1	53.0		28.4	9.2	15.3	6.7	10.3		
Pakistan						50.0	56.9	54.9		
Peru						3.0	2.0	3.0	20.4	19.8
Philippines	28.6	31.1	4.8	3.6	2.2	16.3	32.8	42.4	32.1	35.2
Singapore	25.3	31.8	14.4	8.7	13.2	25.1	32.7	29.9	27.7	26.5
South Africa	301.5	272.8	204.3	174.5	200.8	230.5	221.3	209.6	197.7	182.9
South Korea	68.8	121.2	255.4	455.3	784.7	888.1	861.8	965.8	1,151.1	1,303.8
Taiwan								415.3	403.4	327.7	283.0
Thailand				22.5	27.1	38.8	47.7	65.9	66.8	121.5
USA	8,443.9	8,924.2	10,888.6	11,139.8	10,277.7	10,479.9	9,852.6	9,103.3	8,234.0	8,056.8
Venezuela	94.2	123.6	77.3	97.6	71.9	74.5	15.1	21.1	33.7	
Vietnam										

Source: Society of Motor Manufacturers and Traders (SMMT)/Automobile International

AUTOMOTIVE REGISTRATIONS — Table No. 2102

New Registrations of Commercial Vehicles 1981-1992

Units: '000

	1981	1983	1985	1986	1987	1988	1989	1990	1991	1992
Argentina	30.2	25.1	20.7	26.5	27.5	21.8	16.7	12.6	25.0	41.3
Australia	143.4	132.1	159.2	115.3	81.5	101.8	133.0	126.5	81.3	89.9
Brazil	113.4	119.2	161.1	194.3	169.5	191.0	195.0	179.9	187.7	162.9
Canada	291.1	223.9	393.4	390.7	450.0	500.5	480.3	416.0	410.1	408.6
Chile						25.0	31.9	24.0		
China										
Colombia				1.9	7.8	21.3	19.1	18.4	7.5	
Ecuador										
Hong Kong	19.6	14.2	20.0	16.3	22.7	21.2	18.3	18.6	17.1	19.9
India	88.0	90.6	98.7	96.5	103.6	117.3	117.0	141.1	139.4	126.2
Indonesia				128.3	130.8	125.8	146.4	218.5		
Israel										
Japan	2,260.3	2,246.7	2,452.7	2,561.8	2,743.6	3,003.6	2,852.9	2,674.8	2,656.5	2,505.1
Malaysia	86.4	15.7	28.2	20.3	13.7	17.0	34.0	57.4	58.1	34.8
Mexico	230.7	80.8	149.5	98.2	93.8	131.9	171.4	197.7	250.9	261.6
New Zealand	25.6	25.0	23.3	18.5	15.2	14.7	17.0	19.0	13.5	13.6
Nigeria	146.5	46.0		28.4		6.0	2.1	5.9		
Pakistan						54.4	43.7	23.5		
Peru						5.2	3.8	5.0	10.2	11.5
Philippines	22.2	48.9	2.1	3.6	2.2	42.0	62.1	93.7	88.9	24.3
Singapore	9.1	9.5	5.4	2.5	3.1	5.3	6.2	5.1	4.8	4.6
South Africa	152.0	132.3	101.0	90.2	108.3	127.4	131.3	125.2	110.3	101.1
South Korea	66.7	99.2	114.0	139.3	181.7	211.5	257.2	335.6	343.4	420.8
Taiwan								73.2	69.9	69.3	139.8
Thailand				56.0	74.5	107.7	160.4	238.2	201.8	241.5
USA	2,185.5	2,976.6	4,681.7	4,869.6	4,912.3	5,211.1	5,110.2	4,798.5	4,344.6	4,809.9
Venezuela	68.2	123.6	46.2	52.5	39.0	48.9	10.9	20.2	37.0	
Vietnam										

Source: SMMT/Motor Vehicle Manufacturers' Association (MVMA)/Automobile International

AUTOMOTIVE REGISTRATIONS · Table No. 2103

New Registrations of Two-Wheelers 1982-1991

Units: '000

	1982	1983	1984	1985	1986	1987	1988	1989	1990	1991
Argentina										
Australia	66.4	61.1	46.7	45.9						
Brazil	160.0	157.5	111.2	114.0						
Canada [a]	689.3	575.0	772.2	722.0	388.1					
Chile										
China										
Colombia	2.3			23.8	16.2	19.3	16.2	15.7		
Ecuador										
Hong Kong					1.1	1.6	2.1	3.2	3.3	4.0
India	526.7	691.6	749.0		1,102.7	1,326.8	1,396.0	1,659.4	1,819.5	
Indonesia	578.1	381.4	290.1							
Israel						4.7	4.4	3.8	4.7	4.7
Japan [b]	268.9	311.2	1,989.7	2,063.7	1,873.6	1,487.5	1,736.6	1,675.5	1,608.1	1,580.7
Malaysia	1.5	1.0	1.1			1.1	1.1	1.0	1.1	
Mexico	194.6	208.0	188.4	159.4	110.6	72.9	94.8	135.3		
New Zealand						11.6				
Nigeria	27.0	19.4	18.7	16.7	16.5	12.6	9.0	5.8	4.9	
Pakistan										
Peru										
Philippines										
Singapore					34.8	30.4	29.7			
South Africa		21.8	27.2		4.9	6.2	8.0	10.0	8.1	8.2
South Korea	50.2		16.7	9.6	8.2	8.4	8.9	6.3		
Taiwan	134.0	118.5	111.5	71.1	100.9	111.8	142.7			
Thailand						241.1	375.6	461.5	417.6	
USA	314.8	306.0	366.9	406.2	370.5		584.2	522.5	645.8	693.2
Venezuela		575.0	722.2	414.1	388.1	296.9	261.6	188.0	269.5	
Vietnam		58.0	39.0	29.0	30.0					

Source: International Road Federation (IRF)

Notes: see end of section

AUTOMOTIVE PRODUCTION · Table No. 2104

Production of Passenger Cars 1977-1992

Units: '000

	1977	1980	1983	1985	1987	1988	1989	1990	1991	1992
Argentina	168.1	227.5	134.4	118.0	166.2	141.8	112.1	86.9	120.8	220.5
Australia	316.4	318.0	317.2	383.8	310.0	317.4	356.9	360.9	278.4	270.2
Brazil	463.9	600.7	748.4	759.1	683.4	782.4	731.0	663.1	705.4	820.1
Canada	1,162.5	846.8	968.9	1,077.9	809.8	1,024.8	1,017.0	1,076.1	1,059.6	1,019.9
Chile [a]					2.4	4.5	6.9	3.0	3.4	4.7
China						36.8	35.5	42.4		
Colombia	27.9	32.3	21.4	28.8	40.6	44.4	48.4	31.5	14.9	23.9
Ecuador										
Hong Kong										
India	47.6	45.6	66.8	129.3	180.9	195.1	219.5	218.6	209.1	192.1
Indonesia							32.1	57.5	47.0	29.4
Israel [a]	3.9	1.6								
Japan	5,431.0	7,038.1	7,151.9	7,646.8	7,891.1	8,198.4	9,052.4	9,948.0	9,753.1	9,378.7
Malaysia [a]	52.5	81.4	100.2	61.2	33.7		28.0	44.5	49.3	37.3
Mexico [a]	7.0	303.1	207.1	297.1	277.4	353.9	438.6	598.1	720.4	778.4
New Zealand					80.3	64.4				
Nigeria										
Pakistan										
Peru [a]						4.7	2.3	0.9	0.6	0.4
Philippines [a]			27.8							
Singapore										
South Africa					204.3	201.8	230.5	222.4		
South Korea	42.3	57.2	122.0	264.5	793.1	872.1	871.9	986.8	1,158.2	1,306.8
Taiwan [b]			113.1	112.9	194.5	213.3	256.4	277.4	327.7	291.0
Thailand					36.1	29.3	59.3	55.3		
USA	9,213.6	6,375.5	6,781.2	8,184.8	7,098.9	7,110.7	6,823.1	6,077.4	5,438.6	5,665.9
Venezuela [a]	98.7	94.3	71.5	71.8	73.7	68.5	16.0	21.5	34.9	44.2
Vietnam										

Source: SMMT/MVMA

Notes: see end of section

AUTOMOTIVE PRODUCTION — Table No. 2105

Production of Commercial Vehicles 1977-1992

Units: '000

	1977	1980	1983	1985	1987	1988	1989	1990	1991	1992
Argentina	67.2	54.3	25.5	19.7	27.2	22.3	15.7	12.7	24.8	41.4
Australia	73.3	47.2	21.6	27.6	20.3	29.7	28.1	23.2	14.9	14.2
Brazil	455.3	323.0	148.1	207.6	236.7	286.3	282.2	251.6	254.8	254.4
Canada	612.9	527.5	555.5	854.8	825.2	924.5	948.2	850.3	828.0	938.1
Chile [a]					4.8	6.0	9.6	8.0	9.4	13.3
China						551.1	494.3	328.8		
Colombia	8.9	10.5	6.8	10.3	4.0	5.4	17.6	17.7	6.5	23.9
Ecuador										
Hong Kong			87.4							
India	41.7	68.3	66.8	101.2	108.1	117.3	117.6	145.6	146.0	132.3
Indonesia							142.3	214.2	207.8	142.9
Israel [a]	2.5	2.3	2.9							
Japan	3,083.5	4,004.8	3,959.8	4,624.3	4,358.1	4,501.4	3,973.3	3,538.8	3,492.4	3,120.6
Malaysia [a]	10.3	19.5	18.2	37.3	15.3	23.8	28.0	75.1	81.1	35.1
Mexico [a]	93.2	187.0	78.3	161.6	117.9	158.9	202.6	222.5	270.0	304.7
New Zealand					80.3	64.4				
Nigeria										
Pakistan										
Peru [a]						8.4	4.7	3.0	3.0	2.0	0.8
Philippines			21.2							
Singapore										
South Africa				101.0	108.3	127.4	131.5			
South Korea	40.7	65.9	99.0	113.7	186.6	211.6	257.6	334.9	339.6	422.9
Taiwan [b]			34.7	38.8	56.9	62.8	77.4	74.2	69.3	145.7
Thailand				74.9	38.8	97.7	105.0			
USA	3,482.3	1,634.3	2,421.5	3,467.9	3,810.7	4,100.6	4,046.5	3,702.8	3,371.9	4,038.2
Venezuela [a]	64.6	60.8	38.3	43.7	41.3	45.4	11.7	21.6	34.9	48.0
Vietnam										

Source: SMMT/MVMA

Notes: see end of section

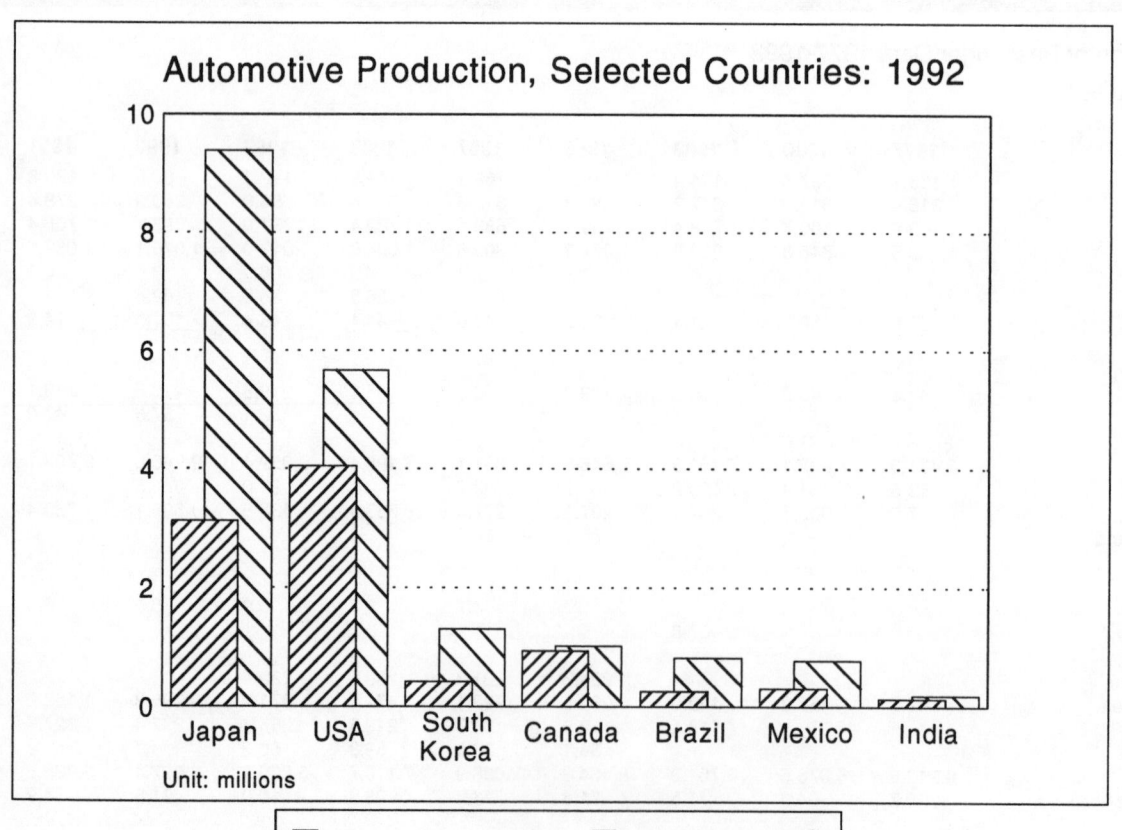

Automotive Production, Selected Countries: 1992

Unit: millions

Commercial vehicles   Passenger Cars

AUTOMOTIVE CIRCULATION | Table No. 2106

Passenger Cars in Use 1977-1992

Units: '000

	1977	1980	1985	1987	1988	1989	1990	1991	1992	Cars in use per '000 persons 1992	% growth 1977-92
North America											
Canada	9,554.3	10,255.5	11,118.1	11,477.3	11,800.0	12,435.0	13,210.0	13,200.0	13,200.0	481.0	38.2
USA	112,287.5	121,630.8	132,108.2	139,041.0	140,655.0	144,375.0	147,000.0	145,000.0	143,823.0		28.1
Regional total	*121,841.8*	*131,886.3*	*143,226.3*	*150,518.3*	*152,455.0*	*156,810.0*	*160,210.0*	*158,200.0*	*157,023.0*		*28.9*
South America											
Argentina	2,649.2	3,005.0	3,700.0	3,928.0	4,061.0	4,186.4	4,186.4	4,325.1	4,315.2	130.4	62.9
Bolivia	32.2	32.1	50.0	74.9	75.0	75.0	75.0	75.0	80.0	10.6	148.4
Brazil	6,926.9	8,302.9	9,500.0	10,025.0	10,250.0	10,250.0	10,250.0	10,500.0	10,500.0	67.2	51.6
Chile	288.8	405.0	550.0	500.0	590.8	706.6	710.0	709.0	765.5	56.3	165.1
Colombia	452.5	551.8	870.0	600.0	650.0	715.3	720.0	798.6	800.0	23.4	76.8
Ecuador	61.0	73.7	79.0	62.7	69.0	70.0	70.0	70.0	70.0	6.3	14.8
French Guiana	15.1	18.3	21.0	22.0	23.0	24.0	24.0	24.0	24.0		58.9
Guyana	31.3	32.5	33.0	20.3	21.0	21.0	22.0	22.0	22.0	20.5	-29.7
Paraguay	27.5	34.5	61.1	62.0	62.0	62.0	62.0	62.0	62.0	13.7	125.5
Peru	312.3	318.7	388.5	390.5	390.5	388.0	387.3	399.9	422.3	18.8	35.2
Suriname	21.6	23.5	31.2	32.5	37.5	38.0	38.0	38.0	38.0	91.3	75.9
Uruguay	166.0	172.9	200.0	180.0	175.0	175.0	179.8	180.0	275.0	87.8	65.7
Venezuela	1,172.4	1,463.8	1,750.0	1,600.0	1,500.0	1,544.2	1,550.0	1,645.7	1,507.3	72.7	28.6
Regional total	*12,156.8*	*14,434.7*	*17,234.1*	*17,497.9*	*17,904.8*	*18,255.5*	*18,274.5*	*18,849.3*	*18,881.3*		*55.5*
Caribbean											
Anguilla											
Antigua	5.8	7.0	7.5	11.8	12.0	12.0	12.0	12.0	13.0	197.0	124.1
Aruba											
Bahamas	37.9	45.7	60.0	66.0	67.5	69.0	70.0	70.0	66.7	249.8	76.0
Barbados	23.8	24.6	30.0	33.5	33.5	34.0	35.0	44.3	41.0	154.7	72.3
Bermuda	13.2	14.2	17.5	21.0	23.0	24.0	20.0	20.0	21.0		59.1
British Virgin Islands											
Cayman Islands			8.0	8.5	8.5	8.5	8.8	8.8	8.8		
Cuba	80.0	80.0	160.0		19.8	19.1	19.0	17.5	17.0	1.6	-78.8
Dominica	2.4	2.5	2.5	2.5	2.5	2.5	2.7	2.5	2.5	34.7	4.2
Dominican Republic	80.0	96.0	104.0	110.0	110.0	115.0	115.0	139.1	140.0	18.7	75.0
Grenada											
Guadeloupe	45.7	53.2									
Haiti	21.0	25.5	30.0	30.0	30.0	32.0	32.0	32.0	30.0	4.4	42.9
Jamaica	107.3	103.6	110.0	100.0	95.0	95.0	95.0	97.5	95.0	36.6	-11.5
Martinique	55.0	62.7									
Netherlands Antilles	49.7	51.1	65.0	67.5	67.5	68.3	68.5	68.7	60.0	301.5	20.7
St Kitts	2.7	2.5	2.5	2.5	2.5	2.5	2.5		3.0	71.4	11.1
St Lucia	4.4	5.0	4.5	6.5	6.5	6.5	6.5	6.5	9.9	70.7	125.0
St Vincent/Grenadines	3.9	4.0	4.0	4.3	4.4	4.4	4.4	4.4	5.0	45.9	28.2
Trinidad and Tobago	112.3	140.9	235.0	240.0	245.0	245.0	250.0	250.2	161.1	127.4	43.5
Regional total	*645.1*	*718.5*	*840.5*	*704.1*	*727.7*	*737.8*	*741.4*	*773.5*	*674.0*		*4.5*
Central America											
Belize	7.5	8.1	3.6	3.5	3.5	3.5	3.5	3.5	12.1	64.0	61.3
Costa Rica	59.9	84.4	90.0	80.0	80.0	85.0	115.0	168.8	125.5	39.7	109.5
El Salvador	53.3	56.6	60.0	55.0	55.0	55.0	55.0	55.0	221.9	40.3	316.3
Guatemala	84.2	95.9	175.0	125.0	100.0	160.0	160.0	155.0	155.0	15.9	84.1
Honduras	23.6	27.5	30.0	30.0	27.0	27.0	27.5	27.5	27.5	5.0	16.5
Mexico	2,829.1	4,032.0	5,000.0	5,200.0	5,183.5	5,400.0	5,425.0	6,819.3	7,053.0	78.8	149.3
Nicaragua	38.0	36.6	40.0	31.5	31.5	31.1	31.2	53.4	50.0	12.1	31.6
Panama	87.2	99.3	125.0	147.6	176.7	150.9	150.9	150.9	150.9	60.0	73.1
Puerto Rico	698.6	931.5	1,150.0	1,125.0	1,150.0	1,285.0	1,300.0	1,300.0	1,350.0	377.1	93.2
Regional total	*3,881.4*	*5,371.9*	*6,673.6*	*6,797.6*	*6,807.2*	*7,197.5*	*7,268.1*	*8,733.4*	*9,145.9*		*135.6*
South Asia											
Afghanistan	36.0	34.1	32.0	30.0	25.0	30.0	32.5	30.0	30.0		-16.7
Bangladesh	26.0	22.0	50.0	31.9	32.8	32.8	35.4	41.4	43.8		68.5
Bhutan											
India	712.9	948.7	1,196.7	1,506.0	1,628.1	1,650.0	2,481.0	2,481.0	2,956.3		314.7
Nepal											
Pakistan	209.0	285.7	380.0	400.0	410.0	590.0	500.0	490.0	633.4	5.3	203.1
Sri Lanka	97.1	120.8	145.0	147.8	155.2	163.8	165.0	180.1	180.0		85.4
Regional total	*1,081.0*	*1,411.3*	*1,803.7*	*2,115.7*	*2,251.1*	*2,466.6*	*3,213.9*	*3,222.5*	*3,843.5*		*255.6*

AUTOMOTIVE CIRCULATION — Table No. 2106 (cont'd)

Passenger Cars in Use 1977-1992

Units: '000

	1977	1980	1985	1987	1988	1989	1990	1991	1992	Cars in use per '000 persons 1992	% growth 1977-92
Japan											
Japan	19,825.7	23,659.5	27,844.6	29,478.3	30,776.2	32,621.0	34,924.2	37,076.0	38,963.8	315.9	96.5
Regional total	*19,825.7*	*23,659.5*	*27,844.6*	*29,478.3*	*30,776.2*	*32,621.0*	*34,924.2*	*37,076.0*	*38,963.8*		*96.5*
ASEAN/NICs											
Brunei	28.2	38.2	72.0	70.0	65.0	93.4	100.1	115.5	120.0	444.4	325.5
Hong Kong	131.7	204.8	185.6	167.0	178.2	193.4	215.7	236.7	265.8	46.2	101.8
Indonesia	443.4	729.5	965.2	965.2	1,073.0	1,199.7	1,293.8	1,475.9	1,574.8	8.4	255.2
Macau											
Malaysia	503.2	729.1	1,000.0	1,125.0	1,165.0	1,200.0	1,225.0	2,018.8	302.2	16.5	-39.9
Philippines	431.0	478.6	350.0	350.0	350.0	413.0	376.6	456.6	460.0	7.2	6.7
Singapore	135.8	164.5	240.0	250.0	250.0	271.2	285.4	300.1	305.0	110.5	124.6
South Korea	125.6	249.1	556.7	844.4	1,211.2	1,557.7	2,074.9	2,727.9	3,461.0	79.3	2,655.6
Taiwan	294.8	337.6	825.0	945.0	1,000.0	1,579.1	1,585.0	1,750.0	2,895.3	145.5	882.1
Thailand	344.0	397.0	575.0	525.0	530.0	550.0	825.0	805.6	890.8	15.4	159.0
Regional total	*2,437.7*	*3,328.4*	*4,769.5*	*5,241.6*	*5,822.4*	*7,057.5*	*7,981.5*	*9,887.1*	*10,274.9*		*321.5*
East/SE Asia											
Cambodia	25.0	15.0	15.0	15.0	15.0	15.0	15.0	15.0	15.0	1.7	-40.0
China	47.0	60.0	110.0	275.0	750.0	1,100.0	1,236.7	1,664.0	2,274.3	2.0	4,738.9
Laos	15.0	15.0	9.0	8.0	8.5	8.5	8.5	8.5	8.5	2.0	-43.3
Mongolia								38.0	20.5	9.1	
Myanmar	34.0	31.5	32.0	30.0	30.0	30.0	27.5	25.0	25.0	0.6	-26.5
North Korea											
Vietnam								60.0	62.3	0.9	
Regional total											
Australasia											
Australia	5,343.8	5,800.6	6,842.5	7,072.8	7,243.6	7,442.2	7,672.3	7,853.5	7,913.2	451.4	48.1
New Zealand	1,210.2	1,307.4	1,500.0	1,550.0	1,550.0	1,550.0	1,500.0	1,500.0	1,575.8	464.8	30.2
Regional total	*6,554.0*	*7,108.0*	*8,342.5*	*8,622.8*	*8,793.6*	*8,992.2*	*9,172.3*	*9,353.5*	*9,489.0*		*44.8*
Pacific											
American Samoa	2.7	3.5									
Fiji	24.6	26.7	32.0	33.0	33.0	33.0	33.0	30.0	30.0	40.5	22.0
French Polynesia	22.0	25.7	30.0	34.0	35.0	36.0	37.5	37.5	37.5	178.6	70.5
Guam	51.0	57.4	90.0	110.0	115.0	120.0	130.0	125.0	72.9	347.1	42.9
Kiribati											
Nauru											
New Caledonia	30.5	37.6	40.0	43.0	45.0	45.0	47.5	47.5	50.0	294.1	63.9
Papua New Guinea	19.0	24.6	27.0	30.0	30.0	30.0	30.0	30.0	14.0	3.7	-26.3
Solomon Islands											
Tonga	0.6	0.6									
Tuvalu											
Vanuatu			3.5	3.5	3.5	3.5	3.8	3.8	4.0	25.0	
Western Samoa											
Regional total											
Middle East											
Bahrain	31.0	45.0	55.0	108.0	85.0	90.0	100.0	104.8	108.8	205.3	251.0
Egypt	269.6	428.3		425.0	430.0	1,030.2	1,167.9	1,170.0	1,200.0	21.8	345.1
Iran	728.1	1,079.1	1,600.0	1,575.0	1,575.0	1,575.0	1,575.0	1,500.0	1,500.0	25.0	106.0
Iraq	97.6	163.4	375.6	350.0	489.6	641.4	650.0	550.0	500.0	25.5	412.3
Israel	312.7	402.5	610.0	655.8	753.5	786.3	790.0	857.4	875.0	176.1	179.8
Jordan	53.3	90.4	135.0	140.0	140.0	170.1	161.9	161.9	161.9	39.1	203.8
Kuwait	273.9	398.9	550.0	575.0	575.0	580.0	500.0	375.0	400.0	190.5	46.0
Lebanon	229.9	362.0	475.0	450.0	400.0	350.0	375.0	380.0	102.5	37.4	-55.4
Oman	35.4	40.0	100.0	112.5	112.1	145.0	150.0	151.0	120.0	76.9	239.0
Qatar	26.9	43.9	80.0	85.4	87.3	105.0	115.1	115.2	120.0	307.7	346.1
Saudi Arabia	376.4	764.5	1,200.0	1,325.0	1,420.0	1,842.5	1,850.0	2,000.0	1,425.0	97.0	278.6
Syria	57.4	65.5	100.0	100.0	117.6	117.6	112.3	120.0	200.0	15.4	248.4
United Arab Emirates	86.7	130.7	200.0	240.0	250.0	260.0	280.0	300.0	265.0	162.6	205.7
Yemen		47.2	92.0	112.0	377.6	428.6	428.6	500.0	500.0	44.3	
Regional total	*2,578.9*	*4,061.4*	*5,572.6*	*6,253.7*	*6,812.7*	*8,121.7*	*8,255.8*	*8,285.3*	*7,478.2*		*190.0*

AUTOMOTIVE CIRCULATION   Table No. 2106 (cont'd)

Passenger Cars in Use 1977-1992

Units: '000

	1977	1980	1985	1987	1988	1989	1990	1991	1992	Cars in use per '000 persons 1992	% growth 1977-92
North Africa											
Algeria	223.9	489.6	650.0	725.0	750.0	775.0	800.0	800.0	950.0	37.0	324.3
Chad	7.3	7.0	7.0	8.0	8.0	8.0	8.0	8.0	7.5	1.3	2.7
Djibouti	5.2	6.5	15.0	10.0	10.0	10.0	10.0	10.0	10.0	23.8	92.3
Ethiopia	43.9	40.4	40.0	44.0	44.0	42.3	40.0	37.5	35.0	0.6	-20.3
Libya	386.0	367.4	400.0	415.0	415.0	425.0	425.0	425.0	450.0	95.5	16.6
Mali	21.0	21.9	12.5	15.0	17.5	18.0	18.0	18.0	18.0	1.9	-14.3
Mauritania	7.5	6.9	8.0	8.0	8.0	8.0	8.0	8.0	7.0	3.4	-6.7
Morocco	326.0	425.0	450.0	450.0	450.0	510.0	525.0	525.0	535.0	20.8	64.1
Niger	11.1	15.8	20.0	18.0	17.0	17.0	17.0	17.0	17.0	2.2	53.2
Somalia	5.0	5.0	20.0	10.0	7.5	7.5	7.5	7.5	7.0	0.9	40.0
Sudan	55.0	57.6	80.0	80.0	90.0	105.0	116.5	120.0	30.8	1.2	-44.0
Tunisia	110.0	112.0	150.0	175.0	200.0	200.0	175.0	180.0	350.0	41.9	218.2
Regional total	*1,201.9*	*1,555.1*	*1,852.5*	*1,958.0*	*2,017.0*	*2,125.8*	*2,150.0*	*2,156.0*	*2,417.3*		*101.1*
West Africa											
Benin	20.0	21.6	17.5	20.0	22.0	22.0	22.0	22.0	22.0	4.5	10.0
Burkina Faso	10.9	12.5	15.0	11.0	10.0	10.0	10.5	10.5	10.5	1.1	-3.7
Cameroon	53.9	66.8	75.0	85.0	85.0	90.0	90.0	95.0	95.0	7.8	76.3
Cape Verde											
Côte d'Ivoire	105.2	127.7	155.0	165.0	150.0	155.0	160.0	160.0	165.0	13.2	56.8
Equatorial Guinea	4.0	4.0	4.0	3.0	3.0	4.0	4.0	4.0	4.0	11.1	
Gabon	18.0	17.0	27.0	17.5	25.0	25.0	25.0	25.0	25.0	20.7	38.9
Gambia [a]						4.5	5.0	5.0	5.5	6.3	
Ghana	66.7	65.9	60.0	60.0	60.0	60.0	82.2	85.0	82.0	5.3	22.9
Guinea	10.0	12.0	12.0	12.0	20.0	20.0	15.0	15.0	15.0	2.5	50.0
Guinea-Bissau	3.2	2.8	2.9	3.0	3.0	3.0	3.0	3.0	3.0	3.1	-6.3
Liberia	18.2	22.2	10.9	8.0	8.0	7.0	7.5	7.5	7.0	2.7	-61.5
Nigeria		522.3	625.0	750.0	785.0	785.0	785.0	800.0	750.0	6.7	
Sao Tomé e Príncipe	355.0										
Senegal [b]	53.0	59.2	35.0	87.5	87.5	83.0	90.0	90.0	90.0	12.0	69.8
Sierra Leone	12.8	23.2	20.0	24.0	25.0	25.0	37.9	35.9	35.9	8.4	180.5
Togo	25.1	20.5	20.0	23.0	24.0	25.0	25.0	25.0	25.0	6.9	-0.4
Regional total	*756.0*	*977.7*	*1,079.3*	*1,269.0*	*1,307.5*	*1,318.5*	*1,362.1*	*1,382.9*	*1,334.9*		*76.6*
East/Central Africa											
Angola	147.0	142.1	110.0	50.0	125.0	125.0	125.0	120.0	110.0	10.7	-25.2
Burundi	5.1	6.0	6.5	7.0	7.0	8.0	8.0	8.0	8.0	1.4	56.9
Central African Republic	12.9	9.0	7.5	8.0	13.0	13.0	13.0	13.0	12.0	3.8	-7.0
Comoros											
Congo	21.0	20.0	24.0	25.0	25.0	26.0	26.0	26.0	26.0	11.1	23.8
Kenya	105.2	126.8	130.0	130.0	130.0	135.0	150.0	150.0	200.0	7.4	90.1
Madagascar	54.7	55.7	53.5	50.0	50.0	27.7	46.6	47.0	50.0	4.4	-8.6
Maldives											
Mauritius	24.5	32.0	34.0	31.0	31.0	32.0	34.0	36.4	38.5	36.0	57.1
Réunion	72.4	75.0	100.0	127.5	130.0	135.0	145.0	145.0	145.0	237.7	100.3
Rwanda			12.0	12.0	20.0	20.0	20.0	20.0	15.0	2.0	
Seychelles	4.8	4.0	3.5	3.6	3.6	4.0	4.0	4.9	4.6	65.7	-4.2
Tanzania	42.8	42.9	45.0	45.0	42.3	45.0	45.0	46.6	47.0	1.8	9.8
Uganda	32.7	33.0	31.0	32.0	12.7	13.0	12.3	12.9	17.8	0.9	-45.6
Zaire	96.7	93.9	92.0	90.0	90.0	95.0	97.5	98.0	95.0	2.6	-1.8
Regional total	*619.8*	*640.4*	*649.0*	*611.1*	*679.6*	*678.7*	*726.4*	*727.8*	*768.9*		*24.1*
Southern Africa											
Botswana	4.6	7.9	13.5	14.0	14.0	14.0	14.0	15.0	22.7	16.3	393.5
Lesotho											
Malawi	15.0	16.2	25.0	14.9	15.0	15.6	15.6	18.0	15.0	1.8	
Mozambique	107.9	50.0	50.0	75.0	85.0	87.5	87.5	90.0	35.0	2.2	-67.6
Namibia									52.8	28.7	
South Africa	2,163.5	2,333.2	2,936.1	3,078.6	3,147.7	3,246.8	3,375.3	3,489.9	3,522.1	97.6	62.8
Swaziland	4.0	13.0	15.0	35.0	35.0	35.0	26.8	21.4	22.0	26.8	450.0
Zambia	104.5	103.0	80.0	95.0	95.0	100.0	100.0	100.0	100.0	11.4	-4.3
Zimbabwe	180.0	172.5	175.0	180.0	200.0	210.0	210.0	220.0	150.0	15.0	-16.7
Regional total	*2,579.5*	*2,695.8*	*3,294.6*	*3,492.5*	*3,591.7*	*3,708.9*	*3,829.2*	*3,954.3*	*3,919.6*		*52.0*

Source: SMMT
Notes: see end of section

AUTOMOTIVE CIRCULATION

Table No. 2107

Commercial Vehicles in Use 1977-1992

Units: '000

	1977	1980	1985	1987	1988	1989	1990	1991	1992	Vehicles in use per '000 persons 1992	% growth 1977-92
North America											
Canada	2,494.3	2,955.3	3,149.7	3,212.1	3,600.0	3,960.0	3,564.0	3,550.0	3,750.0	136.7	50.3
USA	29,805.0	34,165.4	39,582.6	41,948.0	42,813.0	44,294.0	45,000.0	45,698.0	45,871.0		53.9
Regional total	*32,299.3*	*37,120.70*	*42,732.3*	*45,160.1*	*46,413.0*	*48,254.0*	*48,564.0*	*49,248.0*	*49,621.0*		*53.6*
South America											
Argentina	1,138.7	1,187.2	1,350.0	1,440.0	1,482.0	1,493.6	1,493.6	1,483.8	1,519.8	45.9	33.5
Bolivia	42.9	47.6	90.0	135.8	135.0	135.0	135.0	140.0	150.0	19.9	249.7
Brazil	1,875.0	1,987.9	2,100.0	2,250.0	2,300.0	2,400.0	2,400.0	2,450.0	2,450.0	15.7	30.7
Chile	179.9	207.8	275.0	250.0	242.1	240.4	250.0	257.4	402.2	29.6	123.6
Colombia	106.7	270.7	280.0	600.0	650.0	665.3	665.0	670.0	670.0	19.6	527.9
Ecuador	123.2	160.7	175.6	158.0	162.6	165.0	165.0	170.0	170.0	15.3	38.0
French Guiana	3.9	4.8	6.0	6.5	7.0	7.0	7.0	7.0	7.0		79.5
Guyana	12.6	12.9	12.5	8.5	8.5	8.5	9.0	9.0	9.0	8.4	-28.6
Paraguay	17.4	25.5	30.2	31.0	31.0	31.0	31.0	32.0	32.0	7.1	83.9
Peru	158.4	169.9	209.4	222.6	222.6	227.4	230.0	235.7	249.2	11.1	57.3
Suriname	7.3	9.8	12.6	12.5	27.5	28.0	28.0	28.0	28.0	67.3	283.6
Uruguay	91.2	91.2	125.0	85.0	85.0	85.0	146.4	150.0	150.0	47.9	64.5
Venezuela	488.0	659.3	900.0	800.0	750.0	766.7	550.0	589.0	474.5	22.9	-2.8
Regional total	*4,245.2*	*4,835.30*	*5,566.3*	*5,999.9*	*6,103.3*	*6,252.9*	*6,110.0*	*6,221.9*	*6,311.7*		*48.7*
Caribbean											
Anguilla											
Antigua	1.9	1.5	2.5	2.7	2.8	2.8	2.8	2.8	3.0	45.5	57.9
Aruba											
Bahamas	5.7	7.0	12.0	13.0	13.0	14.0	15.0	15.0	14.3	53.6	150.9
Barbados	4.3	5.1	7.5	6.8	6.8	7.0	8.0	8.0	6.7	25.3	55.8
Bermuda	2.6	2.8	3.5	3.5	4.5	5.0	3.3	3.3	3.5		34.6
British Virgin Islands											
Cayman Islands			1.2	1.3	1.3	1.3	1.3	1.3	1.3		
Cuba	40.0	40.0	140.0		32.7	33.2	33.0	33.0	30.0	2.8	-25.0
Dominica	1.2	1.3	1.5	1.5	1.5	1.5	1.6	1.5	1.5	20.8	25.0
Dominican Republic	45.8	63.1	65.0	67.5	67.5	75.0	75.0	80.0	105.0	14.1	129.3
Grenada											
Guadeloupe	20.6	22.9									
Haiti	5.8	9.5	15.0	15.0	17.5	20.0	20.0	20.0	20.0	2.9	244.8
Jamaica	27.3	27.2	30.0	25.0	17.5	17.5	17.5	18.0	17.5	6.7	-35.9
Martinique	20.0	21.6									
Netherlands Antilles	8.1	8.8	14.0	14.0	14.0	14.3	15.0	15.0	13.0	65.3	60.5
St Kitts	0.5	0.7	1.0	1.0	1.0	1.0	1.0	1.0	1.5	35.7	200.0
St Lucia	2.1	2.0	3.0	4.0	4.0	4.0	4.0	4.0	9.1	65.0	333.3
St Vincent/Grenadines	0.8	1.0	2.0	1.3	1.3	1.3	1.3	1.3	1.5	13.8	87.5
Trinidad and Tobago	29.7	39.4	60.0	80.0	80.0	80.0	80.0	80.0	42.5	33.6	43.1
Regional total	*216.4*	*253.90*	*358.2*	*236.6*	*265.4*	*277.9*	*278.8*	*284.2*	*270.4*		*23.2*
Central America											
Belize	3.4	3.8	5.4	3.5	3.5	3.5	3.5	3.5	6.1	32.3	79.4
Costa Rica	57.1	64.1	65.0	70.0	70.0	75.0	60.0	65.0	53.6	17.0	-6.1
El Salvador	31.9	69.0	70.0	65.0	65.0	65.0	65.0	65.0	33.2	6.0	4.1
Guatemala	71.0	93.0	100.0	100.0	100.0	135.0	135.0	140.0	140.0	14.4	97.2
Honduras	38.1	49.3	50.0	50.0	50.0	50.0	50.0	50.0	50.0	9.2	31.2
Mexico	1,118.8	1,622.6	2,100.0	2,260.0	2,215.0	2,400.0	2,400.0	2,500.0	3,345.7	37.4	199.0
Nicaragua	30.0	30.7	35.0	27.5	27.5	43.0	44.1	45.0	14.0	3.4	-53.3
Panama	29.2	37.5	50.0	45.3	49.2	72.7	72.7	73.0	72.7	28.9	149.0
Puerto Rico	147.5	192.4	200.0	215.0	215.0	225.0	230.0	230.0	220.0	61.5	49.2
Regional total	*1,527.0*	*2,162.40*	*2,675.4*	*2,836.3*	*2,795.2*	*3,069.2*	*3,060.3*	*3,171.5*	*3,935.3*		*157.7*
South Asia											
Afghanistan	24.6	28.7	30.0	30.0	25.0	27.5	27.5	25.0	25.0		1.6
Bangladesh	21.0	50.0	35.0	33.4	34.3	34.3	51.2	53.2	55.2		162.9
Bhutan											
India	833.9	700.0	979.9	1,377.0	1,480.4	1,500.0	1,491.0	1,495.0	1,711.4		105.2
Nepal											
Pakistan	97.3	105.5	250.0	275.0	285.0	160.0	275.0	285.0	394.0	3.3	304.9
Sri Lanka	54.4	81.3	120.0	132.7	139.2	136.6	140.0	147.0	150.0		175.7
Regional total	*1,031.2*	*965.50*	*1,414.9*	*1,848.1*	*1,963.9*	*1,858.4*	*1,984.7*	*2,005.2*	*2,335.6*		*126.5*

AUTOMOTIVE CIRCULATION

Commercial Vehicles in Use 1977-1992

Units: '000

	1977	1980	1985	1987	1988	1989	1990	1991	1992	Vehicles in use per '000 persons 1992	% growth 1977-92
Japan											
Japan	12,182.2	14,196.7	18,312.7	20,423.6	21,673.9	22,472.1	22,773.5	22,838.6	22,694.4	184.0	86.3
Regional total	*12,182.2*	*14,196.70*	*18,312.7*	*20,423.6*	*21,673.9*	*22,472.1*	*22,773.5*	*22,838.6*	*22,694.4*		*86.3*
ASEAN/NICs											
Brunei	5.2	7.4	12.0	13.0	13.0	11.5	12.0	13.0	13.5	50.0	159.6
Hong Kong	53.7	69.0	90.0	140.6	154.0	162.5	171.8	178.0	185.6	32.3	245.6
Indonesia	339.5	564.2	1,040.3	1,040.3	1,278.0	1,391.4	1,478.0	1,455.1	1,513.9	8.1	345.9
Macau											
Malaysia	122.6	167.6	250.0	325.0	350.0	355.0	360.0	365.0	128.6	7.0	4.9
Philippines	315.4	374.5	525.0	525.0	520.0	671.7	598.2	827.7	830.0	12.9	163.2
Singapore	54.6	83.8	140.0	145.0	145.0	127.9	142.4	127.7	130.0	47.1	138.1
South Korea	149.7	269.4	556.8	767.0	987.0	1,100.9	1,319.9	1,520.0	1,770.0	40.5	1,082.4
Taiwan	60.8	70.0	415.0	435.0	450.0	541.0	530.0	550.0	727.2	36.5	1,096.1
Thailand	329.3	483.9	850.0	725.0	735.0	750.0	1,425.0	1,795.5	2,125.6	36.8	545.5
Regional total	*1,430.8*	*2,089.80*	*3,879.1*	*4,115.9*	*4,632.0*	*5,111.9*	*6,037.3*	*6,832.0*	*7,424.4*		*418.9*
East/SE Asia											
Cambodia	10.0	15.0	15.0	15.0	15.0	15.0	15.0	15.0	15.0	1.7	50.0
China	700.0	870.0	1,700.0	1,825.0	3,250.0	3,250.0	3,539.7	4,171.9	4,714.5	4.1	573.5
Laos	3.0	3.0	8.0	8.0	8.5	8.5		8.5	8.5	2.0	183.3
Mongolia									26.8	11.9	
Myanmar	41.0	43.2	45.0	45.0	45.0	45.0	40.0	40.0	40.0	0.9	-2.4
North Korea											
Vietnam								60.0	62.3	0.9	
Regional total											
Australasia											
Australia	1,317.7	1,462.5	1,886.5	1,949.8	1,977.5	2,047.1	2,104.3	1,961.3	2,041.3	116.4	54.9
New Zealand	234.1	259.3	302.4	310.0	315.0	315.0	317.5	320.0	327.0	96.5	39.7
Regional total	*1,551.8*	*1,721.80*	*2,188.9*	*2,259.8*	*2,292.5*	*2,362.1*	*2,421.8*	*2,281.3*	*2,368.3*		*52.6*
Pacific											
American Samoa	0.6	1.0									
Fiji	12.6	16.7	25.0	25.0	25.0	25.0	25.0	35.0	35.0	47.3	177.8
French Polynesia	7.0	9.2	14.0	14.0	15.0	15.0	15.0	15.0	15.0	71.4	114.3
Guam	11.0	15.1	25.0	27.0	27.5	28.0	30.0	30.0	29.8	141.9	170.9
Kiribati											
Nauru											
New Caledonia	12.9	14.7	15.0	17.0	17.0	17.0	17.5	17.5	18.0	105.9	39.5
Papua New Guinea	23.8	36.2	50.0	60.0	60.0	60.0	65.0	65.0	25.0	6.6	5.0
Solomon Islands											
Tonga	0.7	0.9									
Tuvalu											
Vanuatu			2.5	2.5	2.5	2.0	2.0	2.0	12.5		
Western Samoa											
Regional total											
Middle East											
Bahrain	10.2	19.0	20.0		5.0	6.0	7.5		31.5	59.4	208.8
Egypt	66.7	127.5	200.0	245.0	245.0	368.7	379.7	380.0	385.0	7.0	477.2
Iran	528.2	406.0	515.0	540.0	550.0	550.0	550.0	600.0	600.0	10.0	13.6
Iraq	83.0	192.7	189.0	195.0	322.7	316.9	320.0	300.0	275.0	14.0	231.3
Israel	107.6	97.1	130.0	132.4	141.3	157.9	160.0	178.2	185.0	37.2	71.9
Jordan	19.4	29.2	60.0	64.0	64.0	65.6	86.4	86.4	86.4	20.9	345.4
Kuwait	100.1	144.0	200.0	205.0	205.0	210.0	200.0	150.0	160.0	76.2	59.8
Lebanon	27.1	40.7	55.0	50.0	45.0	45.0	50.0	65.0	76.8	28.0	183.4
Oman	21.0	45.0	100.0	165.0	62.7	107.0	110.0		75.0	48.1	257.1
Qatar	16.1	30.5	33.4	36.0	40.0	47.5	47.2		50.0	128.2	210.6
Saudi Arabia	500.5	946.6	1,450.0	1,425.0	2,150.0	1,645.0	1,650.0		1,250.0	85.1	149.8
Syria	55.7	69.1	200.0	190.0	138.6	138.6	130.5	150.0	160.0	12.3	187.3
United Arab Emirates	54.8	40.0	75.0	135.0	145.0	150.0	155.0		70.0	42.9	27.7
Yemen		50.3	78.0	168.0	182.4	234.0	234.0		200.0	17.7	
Regional total	*1,590.4*	*2,237.70*	*3,305.4*	*3,550.4*	*4,296.7*	*4,042.2*	*4,080.3*	*1,909.6*	*3,604.7*		*126.7*

AUTOMOTIVE CIRCULATION

Table No. 2107 (cont'd)

Commercial Vehicles in Use 1977-1992

Units: '000

	1977	1980	1985	1987	1988	1989	1990	1991	1992	Vehicles in use per '000 persons 1992	% growth 1977-92
North Africa											
Algeria	134.1	230.8	325.0	480.0	520.0	525.0	535.0	540.0	585.0	22.8	336.2
Chad	7.5	4.0	7.0	10.0	10.0	8.0	8.0	7.5	7.5	1.3	
Djibouti	2.3	2.5	5.0	5.0	5.0	5.0	5.0	5.0	5.0	11.9	117.4
Ethiopia	8.3	14.2	20.0	19.5	20.0	20.0	20.0	17.5	17.5	0.3	110.8
Libya	181.6	278.9	275.0	320.0	320.0	325.0	325.0	325.0	350.0	74.3	92.7
Mali	5.2	6.4	7.5	7.5	7.5	8.0	8.0	8.0	8.0	0.8	53.8
Mauritania	5.5	3.4	5.0	4.5	5.0	5.0	5.0	5.0	4.5	2.2	-18.2
Morocco	140.1	180.0	200.0	200.0	200.0	240.0	235.0	235.0	240.0	9.3	71.3
Niger	13.4	17.3	15.0	18.0	18.0	18.0	18.0	18.0	18.0	2.3	34.3
Somalia	5.5	6.0	20.0	12.5	9.0	9.0	9.0	9.0	8.0	1.0	45.5
Sudan	30.0	71.0	40.0	45.0	54.4	50.0	56.9		35.9	1.4	19.7
Tunisia	78.8	102.8	150.0	175.0	175.0	175.0	175.0	225.0	225.0	26.9	185.5
Regional total	*612.3*	*917.30*	*1,069.5*	*1,297.0*	*1,343.9*	*1,388.0*	*1,399.9*	*1,395.0*	*1,504.4*		*145.7*
West Africa											
Benin	5.0	10.5	12.0	12.0	11.0	12.0	12.0	12.0	12.0	2.5	140.0
Burkina Faso	11.8	13.0	15.0	14.0	13.0	13.0	13.0	13.0	13.0	1.4	10.2
Cameroon	30.8	47.1	50.0	70.0	75.0	80.0	80.0	80.0	70.0	5.7	127.3
Cape Verde											
Côte d'Ivoire	65.5	77.8	80.0	90.0	88.0	90.0	90.0	90.0	90.0	7.2	37.4
Equatorial Guinea	3.0	3.0	3.0	4.0	4.0	4.0	4.0	4.0	4.0	11.1	33.3
Gabon	10.0	14.6	25.0	17.5	15.0	15.0	15.0	15.0	15.0	12.4	50.0
Gambia [a]						1.0	2.5	2.5	2.5	2.8	
Ghana	47.9	47.6	40.0	45.0	45.0	45.0	42.1	42.0	42.0	2.7	-12.3
Guinea	11.0	8.0	12.0	12.0	10.0	10.0	12.5	12.5	12.5	2.1	13.6
Guinea-Bissau	1.0	2.1	2.0	2.0	2.0	2.0	2.0	2.0	2.0	2.0	100.0
Liberia	15.9	19.7	5.8	3.0	3.0	2.8	3.0	3.0	3.0	1.2	-81.1
Nigeria	282.1	458.7	600.0	600.0	620.0	625.0	625.0	630.0	600.0	5.3	112.7
Sao Tomé e Príncipe											
Senegal [b]	32.0	34.2	17.5	25.0	23.0	25.0	25.0	25.0	25.0	3.3	-21.9
Sierra Leone	5.8	10.8	11.0	7.0	15.0	15.0	11.8	12.0	11.8	2.8	103.4
Togo	4.4	10.4	12.0	12.5	12.0	12.5	12.5	12.5	12.5	3.4	184.1
Regional total	*526.2*	*757.50*	*885.3*	*914.0*	*936.0*	*952.3*	*950.4*	*955.5*	*915.3*		*73.9*
East/Central Africa											
Angola	42.0	43.5	50.0	50.0	42.0	42.0	42.0	43.0	37.5	3.6	-10.7
Burundi	2.6	4.0	7.5	8.0	8.0	10.0	10.0	10.0	10.0	1.7	284.6
Central African Republic	3.5	4.8	6.0	6.5	6.0	7.0	8.0	8.0	8.0	2.6	128.6
Comoros											
Congo	13.0	14.0	16.0	18.0	19.0	20.0	20.0	20.0	20.0	8.5	53.8
Kenya	77.7	110.5	125.0	135.0	135.0	145.0	150.0	150.0	110.0	4.1	41.6
Madagascar	48.0	49.2	45.0	45.0	45.0	21.2	33.2	34.0	35.0	3.0	-27.1
Maldives											
Mauritius	12.8	11.0	12.0	12.5	12.5	13.0	14.0		35.1	32.8	174.2
Réunion	25.1	31.2	30.0	40.0	42.5	45.0	50.0	50.0	50.0	82.0	99.2
Rwanda			8.0	12.0	15.0	15.0	15.0		10.0	1.3	
Seychelles	1.2	1.3	1.3	1.3	1.3	1.5	1.5	1.6	1.9	27.1	58.3
Tanzania	47.2	52.1	45.0	50.0	52.3	53.0	53.0		38.0	1.5	-19.5
Uganda	12.4	12.9	15.0	16.0	12.6	13.0	14.9		25.2	1.3	103.2
Zaire	87.1	84.9	70.0	85.0	85.0	85.0	87.5	85.0	85.0	2.3	-2.4
Regional total	*372.6*	*419.40*	*430.8*	*479.3*	*476.2*	*470.7*	*499.1*	*401.6*	*465.7*		*25.0*
Southern Africa											
Botswana	13.4	17.3	25.0	25.0	25.0	23.0	23.0	25.0	48.9	35.2	264.9
Lesotho											
Malawi	13.4	15.4	17.5	16.2	16.0	10.3	10.3	10.0	10.0	1.2	-25.4
Mozambique	24.7	24.7	20.0	22.5	24.0	24.0	24.0		10.0	0.6	-59.5
Namibia									57.2	31.1	
South Africa	900.6	966.3	1,228.7	1,269.7	1,260.8	1,336.5	1,422.3	1,540.8	1,586.1	44.0	76.1
Swaziland	4.5	8.0	15.0	20.0	20.0	20.0	23.5		16.0	19.5	255.6
Zambia	62.5	66.3	50.0	60.0	60.0	65.0	65.0	66.0	65.0	7.4	4.0
Zimbabwe	70.0	70.6	80.0	80.0	75.0	75.0	75.0	76.0	75.0	7.5	7.1
Regional total	*1,089.1*	*1,168.60*	*1,436.2*	*1,493.4*	*1,480.8*	*1,553.8*	*1,643.1*	*1,717.8*	*1,868.2*		*71.5*

Source: SMMT

Notes: see end of section

AUTOMOTIVE CIRCULATION — Table No. 2108

Two-Wheelers in Use 1982-1991

Units: '000

	1982	1984	1985	1986	1987	1988	1989	1990	1991	Number in use per '000 persons 1990	% growth 1982-90
North America											
Canada	473.1	507.1	487.9	465.4	448.1	400.3	378.0				
USA [a]	5,743.5		5,479.8	6,444.4	4,885.8	4,584.3	4,433.9	4,259.3			
South America											
Argentina	641.8	699.9	760.0								
Bolivia	43.1										
Brazil	633.2	923.3	1,088.9	1,367.6	1,420.5	1,666.4	1,666.5				
Chile	31.4	32.0	31.0	34.2	36.0	23.6					
Colombia [b]	184.7	292.7	337.9	386.0	17.8	22.2	24.9				
Ecuador	5.4	11.1	8.7	13.6	11.4						
French Guiana				15.7							
Guyana											
Paraguay											
Peru											
Suriname		1.5	0.4	0.4							
Uruguay											
Venezuela	370.0	434.0	473.0	500.0							
Caribbean											
Anguilla											
Antigua											
Aruba											
Bahamas											
Barbados											
Bermuda											
British Virgin Islands											
Cayman Islands											
Cuba											
Dominica											
Dominican Republic											
Grenada											
Guadeloupe				6.0							
Haiti											
Jamaica		4.6									
Martinique	15.9	17.0									
Netherlands Antilles											
St Kitts											
St Lucia											
St Vincent/Grenadines											
Trinidad and Tobago	8.6	10.5	11.0								
Central America											
Belize											
Costa Rica		33.3	35.0	36.1	37.0	38.2	40.6	41.6			
El Salvador			41.1								
Guatemala											
Honduras	6.5						11.8	8.5			
Mexico	420.4				221.1	218.2	218.7				
Nicaragua			15.5	12.4							
Panama											
Puerto Rico	9.7	16.1	11.3	12.0							
South Asia											
Afghanistan											
Bangladesh											
Bhutan											
India	2,115.3	2,962.7	3,511.9	6,201.0	7,697.2	9,249.5	10,952.7				
Nepal											
Pakistan [c]	310.3	375.0	456.0			635.9					
Sri Lanka		138.6	161.4								

AUTOMOTIVE CIRCULATION   Table No. 2108 (cont'd)

Two-Wheelers in Use 1982-1991

Units: '000

	1982	1984	1985	1986	1987	1988	1989	1990	1991	Number in use per '000 persons 1990	% growth 1982-90
Japan											
Japan [d]	14,557.9	17,353.7	18,180.4	18,668.6	18,636.5	18,450.3	18,207.6	17,771.8	17,295.2	143.9	22.1
ASEAN/NICs											
Brunei					3.3	3.9	3.9	4.0	4.1	14.8	
Hong Kong	27.4	22.4	19.3	17.8	17.1	17.3	18.8	20.7	24.3	3.6	-24.5
Indonesia	3,764.4	4,556.1	4,765.1	5,115.9							
Macau											
Malaysia	1,744.4	2,132.8	2,289.7	2,404.3	2,461.4						
Philippines	218.4	253.3	243.0	288.6	249.6	280.9					
Singapore	136.9	134.7	127.6	119.2	115.5	116.5	119.9	121.3	121.2	44.8	-11.4
South Korea	410.3	640.3	711.4	812.3	924.2	1,066.8					
Taiwan					5,958.8	6,810.5	7,619.0	8,460.1		425.1	
Thailand	1,399.5	1,911.6	1,841.9	1,958.0		3,894.8	4,138.6	4,778.2	5,486.2	85.2	241.4
East/SE Asia											
Cambodia											
China											
Laos											
Mongolia											
Myanmar											
North Korea											
Vietnam											
Australasia											
Australia	390.8	398.4	361.6						284.6		
New Zealand	132.7	126.4	122.8	142.9	118.7			82.3	74.8	24.6	-38.0
Pacific											
American Samoa											
Fiji											
French Polynesia											
Guam											
Kiribati											
Nauru											
New Caledonia											
Papua New Guinea				1.9							
Solomon Islands											
Tonga											
Tuvalu											
Vanuatu											
Western Samoa											
Middle East											
Bahrain					1.7	1.4	1.3	1.4	1.4	2.8	
Egypt	177.3	223.4	247.2	263.4							
Iran	841.1										
Iraq											
Israel					33.8	35.1	36.4	38.1	39.8	8.2	
Jordan	5.8	6.4	6.4	6.5	6.5				1.3		
Kuwait		4.5	4.5	3.9	4.3	4.7	5.0	4.7		2.2	
Lebanon											
Oman											
Qatar											
Saudi Arabia	7.1							12.2	12.6	0.8	71.8
Syria											
United Arab Emirates											
Yemen	27.1	21.7	20.9	19.6	18.6	17.2					

AUTOMOTIVE CIRCULATION — Table No. 2108 (cont'd)

Two-Wheelers in Use 1982-1991

Units: '000

	1982	1984	1985	1986	1987	1988	1989	1990	1991	Number in use per '000 persons 1990	% growth 1982-90
North Africa											
Algeria											
Chad											
Djibouti											
Ethiopia	1.3	1.3	1.4	1.3	1.5	1.7	1.7	1.4	1.5		7.7
Libya											
Mali											
Mauritania											
Morocco	17.7			19.0							
Niger	5.7	7.6	8.1	8.6	8.9						
Somalia											
Sudan	7.0		8.0								
Tunisia	11.7	12.1	12.2	12.2	12.2	12.3	12.5				
West Africa											
Benin											
Burkina Faso	7.2										
Cameroon	43.0	52.6	57.4	58.7							
Cape Verde											
Côte d'Ivoire		22.9									
Equatorial Guinea											
Gabon											
Gambia	2.1		2.0								
Ghana						4.3	4.7				
Guinea											
Guinea-Bissau											
Liberia		0.3	0.2	0.3	0.2						
Nigeria											
Sao Tomé e Príncipe											
Senegal											
Sierra Leone											
Togo		2.5	1.9	1.9	1.9	1.7	1.6	1.5		0.4	
East/Central Africa											
Angola		0.3									
Burundi											
Central African Republic									6.0		·
Comoros											
Congo									2.6		
Kenya	16.9	17.9			20.1	21.3	22.4	23.5		1.0	39.1
Madagascar	3.2	3.2	2.4	3.2	3.1	3.1					
Maldives											
Mauritius		28.1	28.5	29.6			46.4	57.1	68.6	53.4	
Réunion											
Rwanda				6.1	7.3	7.6	8.2	8.0		1.1	
Seychelles											
Tanzania	25.0										
Uganda	3.9		4.8								
Zaire		3.3									
Southern Africa											
Botswana	1.2	1.5	1.6	1.5	1.5						
Lesotho											
Malawi	5.9	7.5									
Mozambique											
Namibia											
South Africa	313.8	336.6	335.9	333.5	322.8	317.3	295.0	303.3		8.6	-3.3
Swaziland				2.4	2.2	2.4	2.5	2.5	2.6	3.2	
Zambia											
Zimbabwe	19.9	24.0	25.1								

Source: IRF
Notes: see end of section

Notes to Tables in Section Twenty-One

Table 2103   a Excludes mopeds
                 b Until 1983, excludes mopeds and
                    motorcycles under 125cc

Table 2104   a Assembly from imported parts
                 b Derived from sales figures

Table 2105   a Change in methodology starting 1980
                 b Assembly from imported parts

Table 2106   There may be wide variations from year to year
                  in SMMT estimates and in other figures
                  due to interpretation of definitions
                 a Included in Senegal prior to 1989
                 b Total included The Gambia prior to 1989

Table 2107   There may be wide variations from year to year
                  in SMMT estimates and in other figures
                  due to interpretation of definitions
                 a Included in Senegal prior to 1989
                 b Included The Gambia prior to 1989

Table 2108   Two-wheelers consists of motorcycles and
                  mopeds
                 a Excludes mopeds
                 b Excludes mopeds from 1987
                 c Includes rickshaws
                 d Includes 3-wheeled vehicles

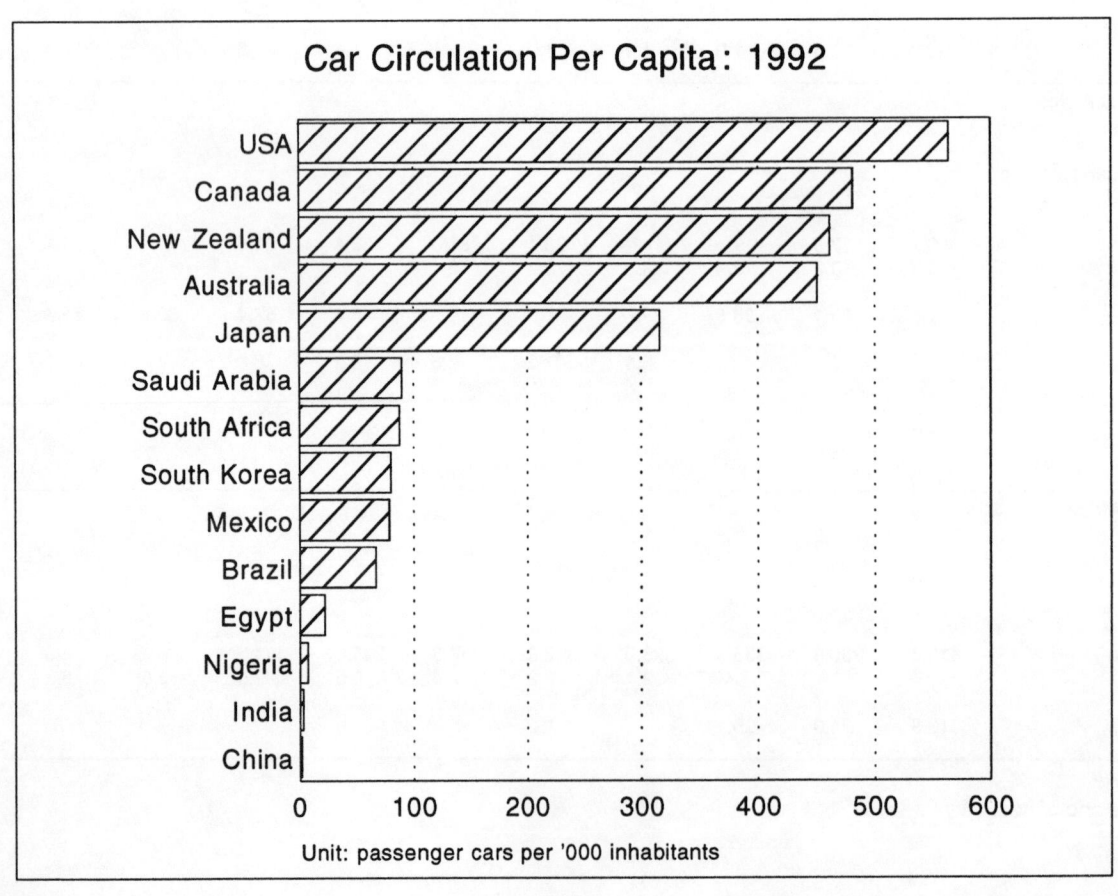

Car Circulation Per Capita: 1992

Unit: passenger cars per '000 inhabitants

Section Twenty-Two
Transport

ROAD TRANSPORT | Table No. 2201

Road Network: Latest Year

Units: '000 kilometres

	Year	Total	Motorway	Highway (national)	Secondary (regional)	Others (local)	% paved	Density (km / km² of land area)
North America								
Canada [a]	1990	825.7	15.0	132.2	134.3	544.2	35.0	0.1
USA	1990	6,243.2	84.9	656.4	702.1	4,884.7	58.2	0.7
South America								
Argentina	1986	211.4	0.4	36.9	174.1		27.1	0.1
Bolivia	1983	41.0		6.1	4.9	29.9	3.8	
Brazil	1990	1,670.1		114.9	219.7	1,335.7	9.8	0.2
Chile	1990	79.6		6.3	16.6	56.6	13.8	0.1
Colombia	1989	129.1		25.7	95.4	8.0	8.0	0.1
Ecuador	1988	37.6		6.3	14.5	16.8	16.8	0.1
French Guiana	1988	1.1		0.4	0.4	0.4	40.0	
Guyana	1985	8.9						
Paraguay	1983	11.3		2.1	9.2		18.5	
Peru	1989	69.9						0.1
Suriname	1990	9.2		1.6	5.5	2.1	26.0	0.1
Uruguay	1981	49.8		9.8	40.0		2.0	0.3
Venezuela	1986	100.6	1.2	35.1	37.9	26.4	33.1	0.1
Caribbean								
Anguilla								
Antigua	1986	1.2						2.7
Aruba								
Bahamas	1985	2.3					72.8	0.2
Barbados	1987	1.6					85.3	3.7
Bermuda								
British Virgin Islands								
Cayman Islands								
Cuba	1986	46.6					27.4	0.4
Dominica	1984	1.2						1.6
Dominican Republic	1982	17.8		1.6	2.0	14.2	28.5	0.4
Grenada								
Guadeloupe	1986	2.1		0.3	0.6	1.2	80.0	1.2
Haiti	1985	3.7					17.4	0.1
Jamaica	1984	16.6		0.8	0.7	15.2	30.0	1.5
Martinique	1984	1.8		0.3	0.6	0.9	83.0	1.7
Netherlands Antilles								
St Kitts	1985	0.3					44.0	1.1
St Lucia	1988	1.0						1.6
St Vincent/Grenadines	1987	1.1					27.2	2.8
Trinidad and Tobago	1985	5.2	0.1	2.0	0.2	3.0		1.0
Central America								
Belize	1987	3.0						0.1
Costa Rica	1991	35.5		7.4	28.2		15.8	0.7
El Salvador	1987	12.2	0.1	0.6	1.1	10.4	14.3	0.6
Guatemala	1990	133.5		18.7	93.4	21.3	12.3	1.2
Honduras	1990	11.4		3.1	2.5	5.8	21.1	0.1
Mexico	1991	242.3	3.2	45.8	61.2	132.1	34.6	0.1
Nicaragua	1986	15.0		1.6	7.8	5.6	10.5	0.1
Panama	1980	8.6		0.7	2.1	5.9	31.7	0.1
Puerto Rico	1986	9.4	0.2	0.8	6.0	2.3	87.0	1.0
South Asia								
Afghanistan	1978	18.8		2.8	14.0	1.9	15.0	
Bangladesh								
Bhutan								
India	1988	1,843.4		32.1	1,460.2	350.9	48.0	0.6
Nepal								
Pakistan [b]	1988	111.2		58.7	52.6		53.0	0.1
Sri Lanka	1985	20.7		4.1	4.9	11.8	41.0	0.3

ROAD TRANSPORT

Road Network: Latest Year

Units: '000 kilometres

	Year	Total	Motorway	Highway (national)	Secondary (regional)	Others (local)	% paved	Density (km / km² of land area)
Japan								
Japan c	1991	1,115.6	4.9	47.0	129.0	939.6	70.1	3.0
ASEAN/NICs								
Brunei	1990	2.0						0.3
Hong Kong	1991	1.5					100.0	1.4
Indonesia	1986	219.2	0.2	12.9	42.5	163.6	62.3	0.1
Macau								
Malaysia	1989	40.2		8.9	27.0	4.2	69.0	0.1
Philippines	1988	157.5		26.1	29.2	102.2	14.2	0.5
Singapore	1991	2.8	0.1	0.5	1.9	0.3	97.1	4.5
South Korea	1988	55.8	1.6	12.3	10.6	31.4	61.4	0.6
Taiwan	1990	19.8	0.4	4.1	15.0	0.4	85.8	0.6
Thailand	1991	52.3	0.2	19.8	32.5		52.9	0.1
East/SE Asia								
Cambodia								
China	1981	17.5	0.4	4.0	2.3	10.8	73.0	
Laos	1991	14.1		3.5	5.7	4.8	24.1	0.1
Mongolia								
Myanmar								
North Korea								
Vietnam								
Australasia								
Australia	1989	798.6		121.2		677.4	33.0	0.1
New Zealand	1991	93.0	0.1	11.5	81.5		73.0	0.4
Pacific								
American Samoa								
Fiji	1982	4.3		1.3	0.6	2.5	13.0	0.2
French Polynesia								
Guam								
Kiribati								
Nauru								
New Caledonia								
Papua New Guinea	1986	19.7		4.9	14.9		6.0	
Solomon Islands								
Tonga								
Tuvalu								
Vanuatu								
Western Samoa								
Middle East								
Bahrain	1991	2.7		0.3	0.4	1.9	75.3	4.1
Egypt	1989	45.5		18.3	14.7	12.5	67.7	
Iran	1984	136.4	0.5	16.6	34.8	84.5	41.0	0.1
Iraq	1989	45.6	1.0	10.1	26.3	8.1	84.3	0.1
Israel	1991	13.4	0.1	4.1		9.2	100.0	0.6
Jordan	1987	5.6		2.6	1.5	1.5	100.0	0.1
Kuwait	1989	4.3	0.3	1.2	2.7			0.2
Lebanon	1982	7.0	0.4	1.2	4.0	1.4	80.0	0.7
Oman								
Qatar								
Saudi Arabia	1990	144.7		20.9	17.6	106.2	43.0	0.1
Syria	1991	31.6	0.7	5.1	18.4	7.4	77.0	0.2
United Arab Emirates								
Yemen	1991	51.5		4.7	2.4	44.3	9.2	0.1

ROAD TRANSPORT
Table No. 2201 (cont'd)

Road Network: Latest Year

Units: '000 kilometres

	Year	Total	Motorway	Highway (national)	Secondary (regional)	Others (local)	% paved	Density (km / km² of land area)
North Africa								
Algeria	1991	90.0	0.4	26.0	22.0	42.0	70.0	
Chad								
Djibouti	1991	2.9		1.1	1.8		12.6	0.1
Ethiopia	1991	28.0		19.0		9.0	15.0	
Libya								
Mali								
Mauritania	1985	7.3		2.2	0.1	5.1	21.5	
Morocco	1991	59.5	0.1	10.9	9.4	39.2	49.5	0.1
Niger	1990	11.3		6.0	2.7	2.6	29.0	
Somalia	1983	21.3		5.0	4.3	12.0	27.6	
Sudan	1985	6.6		3.2	0.7	2.7	59.0	
Tunisia	1989	29.2	0.1	10.8	6.2	12.1	60.0	0.2
West Africa								
Benin	1990	8.4		3.4	2.6	2.4	12.3	0.1
Burkina Faso	1986	11.2		4.6	4.1	2.5	12.0	
Cameroon [b]	1987	52.2		7.5	13.7	31.0	6.0	0.1
Cape Verde								
Côte d'Ivoire	1986	53.7	0.1	6.3	7.5	39.8	7.0	0.2
Equatorial Guinea								
Gabon	1982	7.4		2.9	1.5	2.9	6.8	
Gambia	1990	2.4		0.8	0.5	1.2	32.0	0.2
Ghana	1990	38.1		3.9	10.5	23.6	19.6	0.2
Guinea								
Guinea-Bissau								
Liberia	1987	8.1		1.9	2.0	4.2	9.0	0.1
Nigeria	1980	108.1	0.1	29.7	17.8	60.6	27.8	0.1
Sao Tomé e Príncipe								
Senegal	1986	15.1		3.3	1.3	10.5	30.0	0.1
Sierra Leone	1978	7.4		3.0	4.0	0.3	15.5	0.1
Togo	1990	7.5		1.8	1.1	4.6	24.3	0.1
East/Central Africa								
Angola	1990	72.6		8.0	15.6	49.1	10.9	0.1
Burundi	1990	6.3		1.8	2.2	2.1	17.5	0.2
Central African Republic	1991	23.4		5.4	3.9	14.4	1.8	
Comoros								
Congo	1991	12.7		3.4	4.1	5.2	9.7	
Kenya	1991	62.6		6.3	19.0	37.3	13.3	0.1
Madagascar	1991	34.8		8.5	18.4	7.9	15.4	0.1
Maldives								
Mauritius	1991	1.8		0.9	0.6	0.3	93.0	1.0
Réunion								
Rwanda	1990	13.2		5.2	0.5	7.5	9.0	0.5
Seychelles	1983	0.3		0.1	0.1		51.0	0.6
Tanzania	1984	81.9		17.7	42.0	22.2	3.9	0.1
Uganda	1985	28.1		7.8	18.5	1.8	22.0	0.1
Zaire	1991	145.0		68.0	77.0		1.8	0.1
Southern Africa								
Botswana	1986	13.5		2.0	1.0	10.4	15.0	
Lesotho	1991	4.2		1.9	0.7	1.6	20.0	0.1
Malawi	1989	11.5		2.7	2.8	6.0	21.4	0.1
Mozambique	1989	26.1		4.8	8.1	13.2	19.8	
Namibia								
South Africa [d]	1991	182.3	2.0	53.4	126.9		30.4	0.2
Swaziland	1990	2.8		1.4	1.4	0.8	19.0	0.2
Zambia	1991	37.4	0.1	6.5	8.4	22.4	17.6	
Zimbabwe	1986	77.9		3.6	7.4	66.9	17.0	0.2

Source: International Road Federation (IRF)
Notes: see end of section

ROAD TRANSPORT

Trends in Car Traffic Volume 1977-1991

Units: Million car-kilometres

	1977	1980	1985	1986	1987	1988	1989	1990	1991	% growth 1977/91
North America										
Canada [a]	184,801	205,515	122,676	125,981	135,657					
USA	1,799,900	1,789,412	2,028,249	2,093,653	2,180,726	2,300,139	2,377,730	2,438,230		
South America										
Argentina			31,160	32,095						
Bolivia		219								
Brazil										
Chile	2,240	3,170	7,040	7,018	12,215					
Colombia	3,130		11,688	12,291	13,115	13,940				
Ecuador			308	328	349	373				
French Guiana										
Guyana										
Paraguay										
Peru										
Suriname										
Uruguay										
Venezuela		28,600								
Caribbean										
Anguilla										
Antigua										
Aruba										
Bahamas										
Barbados										
Bermuda										
British Virgin Islands										
Cayman Islands										
Cuba										
Dominica										
Dominican Republic										
Grenada										
Guadeloupe										
Haiti										
Jamaica							1,616	1,468		
Martinique										
Netherlands Antilles										
St Kitts										
St Lucia										
St Vincent/Grenadines										
Trinidad and Tobago										
Central America										
Belize										
Costa Rica				2,405	2,601	2,830	3,055	3,239		
El Salvador										
Guatemala										
Honduras										
Mexico					34,114	34,840	35,224			
Nicaragua										
Panama	10									
Puerto Rico										
South Asia										
Afghanistan	1									
Bangladesh										
Bhutan										
India										
Nepal	380									
Pakistan										
Sri Lanka				1,608	1,658	1,721	1,739	1,787		

| ROAD TRANSPORT | Table No. 2202 (cont'd) |

Trends in Car Traffic Volume 1977-1991

Units: Million car-kilometres

	1977	1980	1985	1986	1987	1988	1989	1990	1991	% growth 1977/91
Japan										
Japan [b]	205,367	241,459	291,403	300,606	308,061	321,496	341,374		365,597	78
ASEAN/NICs										
Brunei					67	70	75	81	87	
Hong Kong [c]	2,133	3,001	3,525	3,497	3,491	3,663	3,937	4,399	4,781	124
Indonesia										
Macau										
Malaysia										
Philippines										
Singapore										
South Korea	2,020	2,861	6,272	7,090	7,134	8,846				
Taiwan	6,985									
Thailand			5,076	8,012	8,937	10,617	11,448	14,178	15,438	17,237
East/SE Asia										
Cambodia										
China										
Laos										
Mongolia										
Myanmar										
North Korea										
Vietnam										
Australasia										
Australia						116,640				
New Zealand	16,824	16,545	18,200							
Pacific										
American Samoa										
Fiji										
French Polynesia										
Guam										
Kiribati										
Nauru										
New Caledonia										
Papua New Guinea										
Solomon Islands										
Tonga										
Tuvalu										
Vanuatu										
Western Samoa										
Middle East										
Bahrain					16,500	16,600	16,970	17,300	17,300	
Egypt										
Iran										
Iraq			17,845	19,260	21,190	17,806	22,806			
Israel	5,466	6,895			10,321	11,384	12,254	12,805	13,574	148
Jordan	1,867	3,165	4,557	4,767	4,944					
Kuwait		7,978	8,590	8,413	8,802	9,385	9,987			
Lebanon										
Oman										
Qatar										
Saudi Arabia										
Syria										
United Arab Emirates										
Yemen		360	883	1,270	2,133	2,919	3,039	3,621	4,352	

ROAD TRANSPORT

Trends in Car Traffic Volume 1977-1991

Units: Million car-kilometres

	1977	1980	1985	1986	1987	1988	1989	1990	1991	% growth 1977/91
North Africa										
Algeria									87	
Chad										
Djibouti										
Ethiopia [d]	36.9	55.0	57	59	58	58	61			
Libya										
Mali										
Mauritania										
Morocco										
Niger						108	112	117		
Somalia										
Sudan										
Tunisia	1,072.0		3,533	3,533	3,815		4,928			
West Africa										
Benin										
Burkina Faso										
Cameroon [e]			918	1,209						
Cape Verde										
Côte d'Ivoire										
Equatorial Guinea										
Gabon										
Gambia										
Ghana							516	547		
Guinea										
Guinea-Bissau										
Liberia	4.6	3.3		87	58					
Nigeria	14,049.0									
Sao Tomé e Príncipe										
Senegal										
Sierra Leone	233.0									
Togo			228	247	275	276	316	296		
East/Central Africa										
Angola										
Burundi										
Central African Republic					172					
Comoros										
Congo	240.0									
Kenya	654.4				879	941	1,034	1,082		
Madagascar					199	185	214	236		
Maldives										
Mauritius										
Réunion										
Rwanda			283							
Seychelles										
Tanzania										
Uganda	283.2	198.0								
Zaire										
Southern Africa										
Botswana										
Lesotho	117.2									
Malawi										
Mozambique									328	
Namibia										
South Africa	28,820.0	34,752.0	44,553	40,364	47,558					
Swaziland										
Zambia										
Zimbabwe										

Source: IRF/national statistical offices
Notes: see end of section

RAIL TRANSPORT
Table No. 2203

Length of Public Railway Network Operated 1977-1990

Units: '000 kilometres

	1977	1980	1983	1984	1985	1986	1987	1988	1989	1990
North America										
Canada	70.0	67.1								
USA [a]	308.4	280.3	250.9	244.6	234.6	234.6	225.4	212.8	213.5	214.3
South America										
Argentina	37.0	34.1	34.1	34.4	34.5	34.4	34.2			
Bolivia	3.6	3.5	3.6	3.6	3.6	3.7	3.7			
Brazil	28.8	28.7	28.1	28.1	28.2	28.1	22.1	22.1		
Chile	6.4	6.3	6.2	6.9	6.7	6.6	8.0	6.3		
Colombia	3.4	3.4	2.8	2.6	2.6					
Ecuador	1.2	1.0	1.0	1.0	1.0	1.0	1.0	1.0		
French Guiana	0.4									
Guyana		0.4	0.4							
Paraguay		0.4	0.4	0.4	0.4	0.4	0.4	0.4		
Peru	2.5	2.1	2.2	2.2	2.2	2.2	2.2	2.2		
Suriname										
Uruguay	3.0	3.0	3.0	3.0	3.0	3.0	3.0	3.0		
Venezuela	0.2	0.2	0.3	0.3	0.3	0.5	0.5	0.5		
Caribbean										
Anguilla										
Antigua										
Aruba										
Bahamas										
Barbados										
Bermuda										
British Virgin Islands										
Cayman Islands										
Cuba	4.2	5.2	5.0	4.9	5.0	4.9	4.8	4.8		
Dominica										
Dominican Republic										
Grenada										
Guadeloupe										
Haiti										
Jamaica										
Martinique										
Netherlands Antilles										
St Kitts										
St Lucia										
St Vincent/Grenadines										
Trinidad and Tobago										
Central America										
Belize										
Costa Rica	1.0	1.3	0.8	0.4	0.7	0.7	0.7	0.6		
El Salvador	0.6	0.6	0.6	0.7	0.7	0.7	0.7	0.7		
Guatemala	0.8	0.9	0.9	0.9	0.9	0.9	0.9	1.1		
Honduras	0.2	0.2	0.2	0.2	0.2	0.2	0.2	0.2		
Mexico	20.0	20.1	20.0	20.0	20.0	20.3	20.4	26.5		
Nicaragua	0.3	0.3	0.3	0.3	0.3	0.3	0.3	0.3		
Panama		0.1	0.1	0.1	0.1	0.1	0.1	0.1		
Puerto Rico										
South Asia										
Afghanistan										
Bangladesh	2.9	2.9	2.9	2.9	2.9	2.8	2.8	2.8		
Bhutan										
India	60.9	60.9	61.4	61.4	61.9	61.8	61.8	62.0	62.1	62.2
Nepal										
Pakistan	8.8	8.8	8.8	8.8		8.8	8.8	8.8	8.8	8.8
Sri Lanka	1.5	1.5	1.5	1.5	1.5	1.5	1.5	1.5	1.5	

RAIL TRANSPORT
Table No. 2203 (cont'd)

Length of Public Railway Network Operated 1977-1990

Units: '000 kilometres

	1977	1980	1983	1984	1985	1986	1987	1988	1989	1990
Japan										
Japan	22.2	22.2	21.3	21.1	20.8	19.9	19.9	21.3	21.0	20.2
ASEAN/NICs										
Brunei										
Hong Kong		0.1	0.1		0.1	0.1	0.1	0.1	0.1	
Indonesia	6.6	6.6	6.4							
Macau										
Malaysia	2.2	2.2	2.1	2.1	2.2	2.2	2.2	2.2	2.2	1.6
Philippines					9.0	8.7	4.5	4.5	4.9	
Singapore										
South Korea	3.1	3.1	3.1	3.1	3.1	3.1	3.1	3.2		
Taiwan		1.1		1.1	1.1	1.1	1.1	1.1	1.1	1.1
Thailand	3.8	3.7	3.7	3.7	3.7	3.7	3.7	3.7	3.7	
East/SE Asia										
Cambodia					0.6	0.6	0.6	0.6	0.6	
China		51.9	51.6	51.6	52.1	52.5	52.6	52.8	53.0	53.2
Laos										
Mongolia		1.6	1.7							
Myanmar	4.3				2.8	2.8	2.8	2.8	2.8	
North Korea	4.4	4.6					4.5	4.5	4.5	
Vietnam										
Australasia										
Australia	40.1	39.5	39.1	39.3	39.0	38.7	38.5	38.2	35.8	
New Zealand	4.7	4.4	4.3	4.3	4.3					
Pacific										
American Samoa										
Fiji										
French Polynesia										
Guam										
Kiribati										
Nauru										
New Caledonia										
Papua New Guinea										
Solomon Islands										
Tonga										
Tuvalu										
Vanuatu										
Western Samoa										
Middle East										
Bahrain										
Egypt		4.4	4.4	4.9						
Iran			4.6	4.6	4.6	4.6	4.6	4.6	4.8	4.8
Iraq			2.1	2.4	2.0	2.0	2.1	2.1	2.1	2.1
Israel		0.5	0.5	0.5	0.5	0.5	0.5	0.5	0.5	
Jordan		0.6	0.3	0.3	0.3	0.3	0.3	0.3	0.3	
Kuwait										
Lebanon			0.4	0.4						
Oman										
Qatar										
Saudi Arabia			0.8	1.4	1.4	1.4	1.4	1.4	1.4	1.4
Syria	1.7		1.5	1.5	1.5	1.5	1.5	1.5	1.5	1.5
United Arab Emirates										
Yemen										

RAIL TRANSPORT · Table No. 2203 (cont'd)

Length of Public Railway Network Operated 1977-1990

Units: '000 kilometres

	1977	1980	1983	1984	1985	1986	1987	1988	1989	1990
North Africa										
Algeria	3.9	3.9	3.8	3.8	4.0	4.0	4.0	4.1	4.1	4.1
Chad										
Djibouti				0.1	0.1	0.1	0.1	0.1	1.0	
Ethiopia	0.8	0.8	0.8	0.6	0.6	0.6	0.6	0.6	0.6	
Libya										
Mali	0.6	0.6	0.6	0.6	0.6	0.6	0.6	0.6	0.6	
Mauritania	0.7	0.7	0.7	0.7	0.7	0.7	0.7	0.7	0.7	
Morocco	1.8	1.8	1.8	1.8	1.8	1.8	1.9	1.9	1.8	1.8
Niger			1.2	1.2	1.2	1.2	1.2	1.2	1.2	
Somalia										
Sudan	4.8	4.8	4.8	4.8	4.8	4.8	4.8	4.8	4.8	
Tunisia	1.7	2.0	2.0	2.1	1.4	1.5	1.5	1.5	1.5	1.5
West Africa										
Benin	0.6	0.6	0.6	0.6	0.6	0.6	0.6	0.6	0.6	
Burkina Faso					0.5	0.5	0.5	0.5	0.5	0.5
Cameroon	1.1	1.2	1.1	1.1	1.1	1.1	1.1	1.1	1.1	1.1
Cape Verde										
Côte d'Ivoire	1.2	1.2	1.2		1.1	1.1	1.1	1.1	1.1	1.1
Equatorial Guinea										
Gabon					0.3	0.3	0.3	0.3	0.3	0.3
Gambia										
Ghana	0.9	0.9	0.9	0.9	0.9	0.9	0.9	0.9	0.9	
Guinea	0.7	0.7	0.7	0.9	0.9	0.9	0.9	0.9	0.9	
Guinea-Bissau										
Liberia	0.5	0.5	0.3	0.3	0.5	0.5	0.5	0.5	0.5	
Nigeria	3.5	3.5	3.5	3.5	3.5	3.5	3.5	3.5	3.5	
Sao Tomé e Príncipe										
Senegal	1.0	1.0	1.0	1.0	1.2	1.2	1.2	1.2	1.2	1.2
Sierra Leone	0.1	0.1	0.1	0.1	0.1	0.1	0.1	0.1	0.1	
Togo	0.4	0.4	0.4							
East/Central Africa										
Angola					2.5	2.5	2.2	2.5	2.5	
Burundi										
Central African Republic										
Comoros										
Congo	0.5	0.8	0.8	0.8	0.9	0.9	0.9	0.9	0.9	
Kenya	1.9	2.7	2.1	2.1	2.7	2.7	2.7	2.7	2.7	2.7
Madagascar	0.9	0.9	0.9	0.9	1.0	1.0	1.0	1.0	1.0	1.0
Maldives										
Mauritius										
Réunion										
Rwanda										
Seychelles										
Tanzania	2.6	2.6	2.6	2.6	2.6	2.6	2.6	2.6	2.6	
Uganda		1.3	1.3	1.3	1.1	1.1	1.1	1.1	1.1	
Zaire	5.3	5.3	4.7	4.7	5.1	5.1	5.1	5.1	5.1	
Southern Africa										
Botswana	0.7	0.7			0.7	0.7	0.7	0.7	0.7	
Lesotho										
Malawi	0.6	0.8								
Mozambique		3.8	3.1		3.2	3.2	3.2	3.2	3.2	
Namibia					2.3	2.3	2.3	2.3	2.3	
South Africa		23.9	23.7	23.8	23.8	23.7	23.6	23.5	23.5	23.5
Swaziland	0.3	0.3	0.3		0.3	0.3	0.3	0.3	0.3	
Zambia	1.3	1.3	1.3							
Zimbabwe	3.5	3.5	3.5	3.4	3.4	3.4	3.4	3.4	3.4	

Source: UN/Union Internationale des Chemins de Fer (UIC)

Notes: see end of section

RAIL TRANSPORT

Table No. 2204

Trends in Railway Passengers Carried 1977-1991

Units: Million passenger-kilometres

	1977	1980	1985	1986	1987	1988	1989	1990	1991	% growth 1977/91
North America										
Canada	2,966	3,280	2,328	2,088	1,920					
USA [a]	16,565	17,695	17,649	19,151	8,640	9,156	9,396	9,864		
South America										
Argentina	12,011	13,510	11,510	13,225	12,480	10,272	10,536	10,512		
Bolivia	397	529	748	657	500	390	386	388		
Brazil	11,699	13,390	17,669	18,444	18,273	17,194	18,000			
Chile	2,382	1,431	1,524	1,275	1,177	1,056	1,104	1,105	1,128	-52.6
Colombia	391	315	230	181	177	156	144	145	85	-78.3
Ecuador	72	65	40	29	29	43	45			
French Guiana										
Guyana										
Paraguay		22	26	26	23	22	22	13		
Peru		496	486	491	279	277	383			
Suriname										
Uruguay	389	418	241	196	141					
Venezuela	39	28	8	12	24	24	36	60	60	53.8
Caribbean										
Anguilla										
Antigua										
Aruba										
Bahamas										
Barbados										
Bermuda										
British Virgin Islands										
Cayman Islands										
Cuba	1,076	1,802	2,256	2,200	2,189	2,628	2,892			
Dominica										
Dominican Republic										
Grenada										
Guadeloupe										
Haiti										
Jamaica	83									
Martinique										
Netherlands Antilles										
St Kitts										
St Lucia										
St Vincent/Grenadines										
Trinidad and Tobago										
Central America										
Belize										
Costa Rica			79	79	65	56	44	43		
El Salvador	24	27	5	5	6	6	5	6		
Guatemala			612							
Honduras		8	8	8	8	8	8			
Mexico	5,040	5,296	5,940	5,880	5,952	5,856	5,976	5,976	4,728	-6.2
Nicaragua	19	15	26	26	26	25	25			
Panama		38	22	22	1	1	1			
Puerto Rico										
South Asia										
Afghanistan										
Bangladesh	4,634	5,119	6,031	6,005	6,024	5,364	5,244	3,792		
Bhutan										
India	176,635	208,558	240,000	250,272	265,704	259,404	263,592	280,848		
Nepal										
Pakistan	13,199	17,315	17,808	16,848	16,920	18,984	20,532	20,373	19,272	46.0
Sri Lanka	2,792	3,799	2,088	2,004	1,992	1,824	1,680	2,484	2,520	-9.7

RAIL TRANSPORT

Table No. 2204 (cont'd)

Trends in Railway Passengers Carried 1977-1991

Units: Million passenger-kilometres

	1977	1980	1985	1986	1987	1988	1989	1990	1991	% growth 1977/91
Japan										
Japan	311,859	313,340	332,772	333,480	341,136	356,460	369,648	383,700	391,032	25.4
ASEAN/NICs										
Brunei										
Hong Kong	279	434	1,776	1,932	2,136	2,364	2,460	2,532		
Indonesia	3,809	6,088	6,768	7,332	7,512	7,860	8,424	9,288	9,768	156.4
Macau										
Malaysia [b]	1,273	1,587	1,404	1,368	1,356	1,524	1,668	1,840	1,752	37.6
Philippines	692	416	144	168	228	228	240	264	228	-67.1
Singapore [c]										
South Korea	17,099	21,640	22,596	23,532	24,457	25,980	25,104	29,864	33,468	95.7
Taiwan				8,305	8,446	8,400	8,350	8,312		
Thailand	5,649	8,861	9,144	9,264	9,576	10,248	11,172	11,832	13,260	134.7
East/SE Asia										
Cambodia			64	73	62	79	62			
China	102,015	138,037	241,380	258,204	283,959	324,096	303,437			
Laos										
Mongolia	227	297	436	467	487					
Myanmar	2,764	3,418	3,864	3,792	4,488	4,068	3,924	4,368	4,476	61.9
North Korea										
Vietnam	4,043									
Australasia										
Australia				928						
New Zealand	497	437								
Pacific										
American Samoa										
Fiji										
French Polynesia										
Guam										
Kiribati										
Nauru										
New Caledonia										
Papua New Guinea										
Solomon Islands										
Tonga										
Tuvalu										
Vanuatu										
Western Samoa										
Middle East										
Bahrain										
Egypt	9,300	10,995	16,854					34,876		
Iran	3,672	2,704		5,585	4,638	3,764	4,661	4,573		
Iraq			1,118	1,005	1,150	1,437	1,642			
Israel	245	252	204	180	168	168	144	168		
Jordan										
Kuwait										
Lebanon										
Oman										
Qatar										
Saudi Arabia	94	82		76	104	120	130	151		
Syria	269	382	948	900	1,032	1,116	1,096	1,140	1,308	386.2
United Arab Emirates										
Yemen										

RAIL TRANSPORT

Trends in Railway Passengers Carried 1977-1991

Units: Million passenger-kilometres

	1977	1980	1985	1986	1987	1988	1989	1990	1991	% growth 1977/91
North Africa										
Algeria	1,506	2,070	1,938	2,011	1,972	2,439	2,724	2,991		
Chad										
Djibouti										
Ethiopia	155	310	383	395	398	410	413			
Libya										
Mali	129	156	153	164	172	180	186			
Mauritania										
Morocco	835	936	1,932	1,956	2,064	2,088	2,150	2,237		
Niger										
Somalia										
Sudan			849	924	982	900	920			
Tunisia	713	862	744	756	795	1,020	1,032	1,019	1,020	43.1
West Africa										
Benin	121	163	150	167	120	190	200			
Burkina Faso								179		
Cameroon	237	234	444	432	468	492	480	457		
Cape Verde										
Côte d'Ivoire	1,172	832	1,008	1,015	1,021	1,035	1,040			
Equatorial Guinea				31	34					
Gabon								54		
Gambia										
Ghana	569	460	130							
Guinea										
Guinea-Bissau										
Liberia										
Nigeria										
Sao Tomé e Príncipe										
Senegal		426	139	143	155	160	163	139		
Sierra Leone										
Togo		82	66							
East/Central Africa										
Angola										
Burundi										
Central African Republic										
Comoros										
Congo	260	337	437	456	400	419	434			
Kenya	1,174	1,056	2,500	2,534	2,608	2,700	2,760	2,805		
Madagascar	278	274	201	211	217	226	230	201		
Maldives										
Mauritius										
Réunion										
Rwanda										
Seychelles										
Tanzania			3,391	3,420	3,521	3,600	3,630			
Uganda			231	250	284	310	315			
Zaire			504	511	522	535	545			
Southern Africa										
Botswana										
Lesotho										
Malawi	59	80	120	108	108	120	108	108	108	83.1
Mozambique		563	508	524	530	500	500			
Namibia										
South Africa			24,009	23,028	21,408					
Swaziland										
Zambia										
Zimbabwe										

Source: UN

Notes: see end of section

RAIL TRANSPORT   Table No. 2205

Trends in Railway Freight Carried 1977-1991

Units: Million net tonne-kilometres

	1977	1980	1985	1986	1987	1988	1989	1990	1991	% growth 1977/91
North America										
Canada	212,416	234,972	232,032	235,524						
USA	1,206,366	1,341,717	1,310,388	1,352,508	1,328,702	1,467,672	1,482,024	1,509,024	1,518,432	25.9
South America										
Argentina	11,567	9,492	9,530	8,793	7,984	8,988	8,232		5,460	-52.8
Bolivia	583	658	458	458	499	420				
Brazil	60,721	40,603	44,529	64,232	63,077	92,838				
Chile	2,508	1,445	2,580	2,556	2,616	2,844	2,952	2,760	2,700	7.7
Colombia	1,215	862	777	694	562	468	360	396	672	-44.7
Ecuador			7,473	6,787	6,787	6,787				
French Guiana										
Guyana										
Paraguay	17	29	13	17	20	17				
Peru		742	744	732	826	794				
Suriname										
Uruguay	307	253	185	203	211	213				
Venezuela	20	21	14	12	12	36	36	16	48	140.0
Caribbean										
Anguilla										
Antigua										
Aruba										
Bahamas										
Barbados										
Bermuda										
British Virgin Islands										
Cayman Islands										
Cuba	2,021	2,358	2,796	2,160	2,100	2,088	2,052			
Dominica										
Dominican Republic										
Grenada										
Guadeloupe										
Haiti										
Jamaica	186									
Martinique										
Netherlands Antilles										
St Kitts										
St Lucia										
St Vincent/Grenadines										
Trinidad and Tobago										
Central America										
Belize										
Costa Rica										
El Salvador	48	55	24	24	40	36				
Guatemala			562	565						
Honduras										
Mexico	36,232	41,323	45,444	40,608	40,812	40,320	38,112	36,384	32,988	-9.0
Nicaragua										
Panama										
Puerto Rico										
South Asia										
Afghanistan										
Bangladesh	701	841	813	612	516	696	660	600		
Bhutan										
India	150,250	147,652	196,488	213,432	217,116	220,956	226,644	233,292		
Nepal										
Pakistan	7,857	8,598	7,200	8,268	7,820	7,968	8,100	7,193	5,796	-26.2
Sri Lanka	225	206	240	216	192	180	168	168	156	-30.7

RAIL TRANSPORT

Trends in Railway Freight Carried 1977-1991

Units: Million net tonne-kilometres

	1977	1980	1985	1986	1987	1988	1989	1990	1991	% growth 1977/91
Japan										
Japan	41,317	39,307	22,104	20,928	20,304	22,872	24,768	26,652	27,348	-33.8
ASEAN/NICs										
Brunei										
Hong Kong	49	67	72	72	72	72	72	72	60	22.4
Indonesia	853	961	1,332	1,452	1,764	2,364	2,928	3,192	3,468	306.6
Macau										
Malaysia [a]	1,209	1,195	1,020	1,044	1,476	1,332	1,404	1,404		
Philippines	49	37	12	15	16	15	13	36	12	-75.5
Singapore [b]										
South Korea	10,294	10,798	12,084	12,660	12,888	13,632	13,536	13,476	14,496	40.8
Taiwan				2,265	2,399	2,500	2,100	1,746		
Thailand	2,912	2,805	2,712	2,568	2,724	2,868	3,264	3,120	3,264	12.1
East/SE Asia										
Cambodia			32	27	31	43	28			
China	455,733	570,732	811,116	874,500	945,565	984,588	1,037,292	1,060,116		
Laos										
Mongolia	2,542	3,449	5,960	6,333	6,180					
Myanmar	435	545	624	576	552	420	456	528	576	32.4
North Korea										
Vietnam	980									
Australasia										
Australia	31,955	36,366								
New Zealand	3,723	3,226								
Pacific										
American Samoa										
Fiji										
French Polynesia										
Guam										
Kiribati										
Nauru										
New Caledonia										
Papua New Guinea										
Solomon Islands										
Tonga										
Tuvalu										
Vanuatu										
Western Samoa										
Middle East										
Bahrain										
Egypt	2,415	2,174	2,594	2,641	2,638	2,650	2,690	2,828		
Iran	5,617	3,428	6,888	7,316	8,625	8,470				
Iraq			1,245	1,294	1,534	1,785	2,683			
Israel	534	819	936	948	1,068	1,032	1,020	1,044		
Jordan										
Kuwait				774	719					
Lebanon										
Oman										
Qatar										
Saudi Arabia	125	261		683	836	775	690			
Syria	426	578	1,248	1,416	1,507	1,572	1,356	1,272	1,236	190.1
United Arab Emirates										
Yemen										

RAIL TRANSPORT

Table No. 2205 (cont'd)

Trends in Railway Freight Carried 1977-1991

Units: Million net tonne-kilometres

	1977	1980	1985	1986	1987	1988	1989	1990	1991	% growth 1977/91
North Africa										
Algeria	1,940	2,461	3,048	2,934	2,937	2,814	2,750	2,674		
Chad										
Djibouti										
Ethiopia	208	131	128	131	136	140	149			
Libya										
Mali	232	132	241	165	174	185	196	202		
Mauritania			6,365	6,411	6,473	6,535	6,610			
Morocco	3,474	3,834	4,560	4,603	4,725	5,712	4,680	5,112		
Niger										
Somalia										
Sudan			1,860	1,813	1,904	1,900	1,920			
Tunisia	1,339	1,698	1,704	1,872	1,986	2,160	2,052	1,836	1,812	35.3
West Africa										
Benin	137	143	179	186	191	205	216			
Burkina Faso								114		
Cameroon	506	612	996	756	677	696	744	751		
Cape Verde										
Côte d'Ivoire	551	598	544	562	578	580	595	541		
Equatorial Guinea										
Gabon					247					
Gambia										
Ghana	192	106	80	101	114	116	119			
Guinea	470	493	534	542						
Guinea-Bissau			534	542	559	580	605			
Liberia										
Nigeria	1,623	1,657	1,709	1,725						
Sao Tomé e Príncipe										
Senegal	306	310	468	492	524	550	565			
Sierra Leone										
Togo		17	10	11	12	13	14			
East/Central Africa										
Angola		2,700	1,615	1,720	1,757	1,780	1,803			
Burundi										
Central African Republic										
Comoros										
Congo	509	538	518	536	449	447	467			
Kenya	2,211	2,281	1,860	1,831	1,702	2,140	2,160	1,983		
Madagascar	210	201	108	112	118	122	125			
Maldives										
Mauritius										
Réunion										
Rwanda										
Seychelles										
Tanzania			1,288	1,248	1,321	1,380	1,420			
Uganda			61	70	74	80	82			
Zaire			1,599	1,624	1,681	1,735	1,788			
Southern Africa										
Botswana	1,056	1,703	1,323	1,378	1,320	1,353	1,370			
Lesotho										
Malawi	210	234	94	125	107	112	113			
Mozambique		1,164	1,134	1,273	1,290	1,310	1,340			
Namibia										
South Africa [c]	69,331	96,523	92,616	90,576	92,184					
Swaziland		2,635	2,624	2,600	2,670	2,730	2,785			
Zambia		1,209	1,407	1,420	1,431	1,470	1,520			
Zimbabwe [d]	4,902	5,283	6,204	6,576	5,932	5,568	5,292	5,700	10,908	122.5

Source: UN

Notes: see end of section

CIVIL AVIATION

Trends in Total Distance Flown, Scheduled Flights 1977-1991

Units: Million kilometres

	1977	1980	1985	1986	1987	1988	1989	1990	1991	% growth 1977/91
North America										
Canada	282.4	337.8	348.5	375.1	370.2	430.6	436.2	432.7	371.9	31.7
USA [a]	3,892.0	4,413.4	5,177.3	5,806.6	6,248.2	6,588.0	6,636.1	7,218.1	7,036.6	80.8
South America										
Argentina	73.0	93.5	79.3	76.7	84.0	79.9	78.8	73.0	68.3	-6.4
Bolivia	9.8	13.5	11.3	11.5	11.3	10.8	11.0	10.9	11.6	18.4
Brazil	171.3	203.4	228.1	255.4	266.6	278.3	291.3	298.8	342.1	99.7
Chile	21.5	24.7	24.4	27.5	32.5	38.7	43.9	50.0	50.4	134.4
Colombia	45.8	44.7	61.3	63.7	65.6	65.0	70.3	71.6	70.8	54.6
Ecuador	14.2	20.4	16.9	18.7	19.7	19.1	19.3	19.5	19.4	36.6
French Guiana										
Guyana [b]	0.6	0.6	2.4	2.4	2.4	2.4	2.7	2.7	2.3	283.3
Paraguay	3.9	4.3	7.9	9.7	10.7	9.2	6.3	5.9	8.8	125.6
Peru	23.9	24.6	22.5	26.4	29.9	27.8	22.6	20.0	18.6	-22.2
Suriname	1.6	2.8	2.6	3.2	2.7	4.0	3.3	3.3	3.3	106.3
Uruguay	3.6	4.3	5.3	4.8	4.8	4.6	4.5	5.1	5.1	41.7
Venezuela	45.5	64.6	43.3	44.5	47.4	73.1	69.1	55.3	64.4	41.5
Caribbean										
Anguilla										
Antigua			6.9	8.3	8.3	8.2	8.3	8.3	8.3	
Aruba										
Bahamas	6.2	10.2	4.8	4.6	4.7	5.0	5.4	5.7	5.7	-8.1
Barbados	1.9	1.3	1.4	1.9	1.0	0.2	0.1			
Bermuda										
British Virgin Islands										
Cayman Islands										
Cuba	11.1	14.7	18.2	19.6	20.8	21.4	22.4	21.2	17.1	54.1
Dominica										
Dominican Republic	6.3	5.7	4.9	4.5	2.9	3.7	4.9	13.2	12.6	100.0
Grenada										
Guadeloupe										
Haiti	0.7	0.7	0.7	0.7	0.7	0.7	0.7	0.7	0.7	
Jamaica	13.3	13.5	11.9	13.3	13.6	13.6	15.9	13.6	12.3	-7.5
Martinique										
Netherlands Antilles										
St Kitts										
St Lucia										
St Vincent/Grenadines										
Trinidad and Tobago	13.7	16.1	16.2	17.7	18.4	20.6	22.4	23.0	25.1	83.2
Central America										
Belize										
Costa Rica	6.7	8.4	7.1	6.9	7.9	9.4	10.1	11.5	11.5	71.6
El Salvador	7.1	3.9	7.1	5.9	6.7	9.0	9.8	10.8	12.0	69.0
Guatemala	4.2	3.7	2.6	2.1	2.7	2.9	3.4	4.1	4.1	-2.4
Honduras	5.3	6.8	6.0	5.2	6.1	6.6	6.6	6.9	5.3	
Mexico	104.6	157.4	185.9	175.8	180.2	136.4	148.9	180.0	190.6	82.2
Nicaragua	2.5	1.6	1.7	1.2	1.2	1.3	1.7	2.1	2.1	-16.0
Panama	8.1	6.7	6.3	6.5	6.7	6.8	6.0	3.6	4.1	-49.4
Puerto Rico										
South Asia										
Afghanistan	5.1	3.3	3.9	3.4	4.0	3.9	3.8	3.9	3.9	-23.5
Bangladesh	8.0	11.8	12.3	12.7	17.1	15.3	12.6	13.3	13.3	66.3
Bhutan						0.3	0.3	0.3	0.3	
India	79.8	84.8	110.2	116.6	126.9	127.1	126.1	113.2	107.5	34.7
Nepal	3.4	5.6	8.8	10.9	8.5	9.3	11.2	11.2	9.0	164.7
Pakistan	39.1	49.7	49.3	51.1	53.2	58.9	61.0	62.6	59.9	53.2
Sri Lanka	6.3	7.5	13.6	11.3	11.0	13.3	15.6	18.4	19.8	214.3

CIVIL AVIATION   Table No. 2206 (cont'd)

Trends in Total Distance Flown, Scheduled Flights 1977-1991

Units: Million kilometres

	1977	1980	1985	1986	1987	1988	1989	1990	1991	% growth 1977/91
Japan										
Japan	296.6	364.8	397.5	417.6	443.2	483.1	496.9	490.6	519.8	75.3
ASEAN/NICs										
Brunei			5.0	4.8	4.5	4.7	5.1	7.3	7.3	
Hong Kong										
Indonesia	72.3	88.4	122.4	127.3	138.2	146.4	147.0	152.5	166.8	130.7
Macau										
Malaysia	29.9	40.9	44.9	47.3	52.6	57.0	71.0	82.9	97.8	227.1
Philippines	43.5	42.4	50.9	53.6	54.5	59.8	59.1	57.4	60.4	38.9
Singapore	46.8	68.9	81.4	86.8	94.4	104.8	114.4	119.9	133.1	184.4
South Korea	42.3	60.7	77.1	85.2	89.1	94.3	117.6	127.6	136.8	223.4
Taiwan										
Thailand	31.8	41.8	61.1	67.0	71.2	84.7	93.4	100.8	107.2	237.1
East/SE Asia										
Cambodia	0.8									
China	23.8	46.5	101.2	126.3	159.1	176.9	166.1	198.5	193.5	713.0
Laos	0.4	0.2	0.2	0.5	0.6	0.6	0.6	1.4	1.4	250.0
Mongolia							6.7	5.2	5.2	
Myanmar	5.3	6.1	7.0	6.9	6.9	7.0	3.9	4.0	4.0	-24.5
North Korea	2.1	2.5	2.9	2.9	3.0	3.1	3.2	3.2	3.2	52.4
Vietnam		0.1	1.5	1.5	1.5	1.5	1.5	1.5	1.5	
Australasia										
Australia	186.7	198.9	211.0	240.8	257.3	284.9	253.0	287.2	334.5	79.2
New Zealand	48.2	52.1	53.3	58.2	62.8	72.6	83.4	94.5	107.0	122.0
Pacific										
American Samoa										
Fiji	3.8	5.5	8.6	7.3	7.1	8.1	9.8	11.1	10.7	181.6
French Polynesia										
Guam										
Kiribati			0.8	0.7	0.6	0.6	0.6	0.6	0.6	
Nauru						3.6	5.2	5.2	5.2	
New Caledonia										
Papua New Guinea	9.9	11.4	13.2	14.0	14.5	17.4	19.1	17.3	16.4	65.7
Solomon Islands			1.7	1.7	1.7	1.8	1.8	1.8	1.8	
Tonga			0.2	0.6	1.2	0.7	0.2	0.8	0.8	
Tuvalu										
Vanuatu			0.4	0.4	0.4	0.5	0.5	0.5	0.5	
Western Samoa										
Middle East										
Bahrain [c]	5.2	7.3	9.3	8.4	8.7	10.2	11.2	12.5	11.0	111.5
Egypt	23.1	30.5	37.8	39.0	37.4	39.7	42.2	42.5	34.7	50.2
Iran	44.0	15.6	25.9	31.2	29.7	27.1	27.3	33.3	33.2	-24.5
Iraq	13.9	12.6	15.1	15.1	15.1	19.8	20.1	12.3		
Israel	33.7	30.2	39.4	40.6	42.3	44.6	46.4	46.1	49.8	47.8
Jordan	13.2	21.4	26.0	26.5	27.6	30.9	31.9	28.3	23.0	74.2
Kuwait	15.7	19.5	26.0	26.2	26.3	26.4	27.9	18.0	13.8	-12.1
Lebanon	42.6	43.4	19.5	11.9	16.3	22.0	14.5	16.2	17.5	-58.9
Oman [c]	5.2	7.3	9.3	8.4	9.6	11.1	12.1	13.4	11.9	128.8
Qatar [c]	5.2	7.3	9.3	8.4	8.7	10.2	11.2	12.5	11.0	111.5
Saudi Arabia	56.1	91.3	113.2	105.3	100.9	100.2	101.0	103.3	87.1	55.3
Syria	11.4	10.5	9.0	9.4	9.2	7.5	8.5	9.6	10.5	-7.9
United Arab Emirates [c]	5.2	7.3	9.3	13.3	18.0	23.7	25.6	30.8	33.7	548.1
Yemen	8.4	9.2	12.5	12.1	11.8	12.5	13.3	13.2	6.9	-17.9

CIVIL AVIATION

Trends in Total Distance Flown, Scheduled Flights 1977-1991

Units: Million kilometres

	1977	1980	1985	1986	1987	1988	1989	1990	1991	% growth 1977/91
North Africa										
Algeria	24.0	27.9	42.2	42.2	39.3	40.5	38.0	31.8	27.4	14.2
Chad [d]	3.1	3.3	2.2	2.3	2.1	2.0	2.0	2.5	2.2	-29.0
Djibouti		1.7	1.3	1.0	1.1	1.1	1.2	1.2	1.2	
Ethiopia	11.2	10.5	16.7	18.2	19.3	21.2	22.5	21.2	20.6	83.9
Libya	10.4	11.7	16.4	14.8	14.0	15.5	16.6	18.5	18.7	79.8
Mali	1.9	2.1	1.8	1.1	0.1					
Mauritania [d]	2.9	3.0	3.1	3.4	3.2	3.2	3.2	3.7	3.3	13.8
Morocco	24.0	20.5	22.9	22.5	23.9	26.1	27.4	29.8	27.3	13.8
Niger [d]	2.4	2.6	1.9	2.5	2.5	2.4	1.8	2.3	1.9	-20.8
Somalia	1.1	3.5	3.2	3.4	3.6	3.3	2.6	2.6	1.4	27.3
Sudan	9.9	10.5	7.6	8.1	10.0	7.9	7.9	10.2	6.0	-39.4
Tunisia	11.5	13.6	14.7	13.0	14.3	14.1	15.2	14.5	13.5	17.4
West Africa										
Benin [d]	1.8	1.8	2.1	2.6	2.3	2.3	1.8	2.3	1.9	5.6
Burkina Faso [d]	1.9	2.3	2.4	3.0	2.6	2.5	2.5	3.0	2.7	42.1
Cameroon	6.2	7.4	6.3	5.4	5.4	5.6	5.7	5.7	5.4	-12.9
Cape Verde	0.7	0.8	1.9	1.4	1.9	1.9	1.9	1.9	1.9	171.4
Côte d'Ivoire [d]	2.6	2.8	3.2	3.2	3.9	3.9	4.1	4.3	3.6	38.5
Equatorial Guinea	0.2	0.2	0.2	0.2	0.2	0.4	0.2	0.2	0.2	
Gabon	3.8	6.4	6.9	6.9	6.3	5.9	6.0	5.6	5.6	47.4
Gambia										
Ghana	3.5	4.3	3.1	3.2	3.4	4.0	3.8	4.1	4.9	40.0
Guinea	1.1	1.1	3.3	0.4	1.0	1.0	1.5	0.8	0.8	-27.3
Guinea-Bissau		0.5	0.5	0.5	0.5	0.5	0.5	0.5	0.5	
Liberia	1.3	1.5	0.6	0.4	0.4	0.4	0.4	0.4	0.4	-69.2
Nigeria	15.7	24.2	31.1	29.4	27.4	14.9	14.2	17.1	13.8	-12.1
Sao Tomé e Príncipe			0.1	0.1	0.3	0.3	0.3	0.3	0.3	
Senegal [d]	2.5	3.2	3.4	1.9	2.5	2.5	2.5	3.0	2.7	8.0
Sierra Leone	0.2	0.9	1.5	1.4	1.1					
Togo [d]	1.8	1.9	2.0	1.9	1.9	1.8	1.8	2.3	1.9	5.6
East/Central Africa										
Angola	3.7	8.4	13.5	11.5	11.5	10.5	13.9	10.1	10.4	181.1
Burundi	0.1	0.2	0.1	0.1	0.3	0.2	0.2	0.2	0.2	100.0
Central African Republic [d]	2.4	2.5	2.6	2.6	2.6	2.5	2.5	3.0	2.7	12.5
Comoros			0.3	0.1	0.1	0.1				
Congo [d]	2.8	2.9	3.6	3.5	2.7	2.7	2.8	3.2	2.9	3.6
Kenya	8.6	11.6	13.1	13.5	13.8	14.4	14.1	15.6	12.5	45.3
Madagascar	6.6	6.7	5.5	5.5	5.6	5.6	5.5	5.8	5.8	-12.1
Maldives	0.5	0.6	1.4	1.5	0.2	0.2	0.2	0.3	0.3	-40.0
Mauritius	1.1	3.4	6.2	6.5	7.5	10.7	11.9	14.7	16.0	1,354.5
Réunion										
Rwanda			0.9	0.3	0.6	0.6	0.2	0.1	0.1	
Seychelles	0.2	0.2	1.6	2.4	2.6	2.5	4.6	3.9	3.4	1,600.0
Tanzania	1.3	7.5	5.2	4.5		5.1	3.5	3.5	4.9	276.9
Uganda		3.7	1.7	1.7	1.6	1.8	3.5	3.5	0.4	
Zaire	11.9	10.0	4.9	5.6	6.5	6.6	7.1	7.4	5.0	-58.0
Southern Africa										
Botswana			1.3	1.4	1.7	2.6	2.6	2.9	3.5	
Lesotho	0.1	0.9	1.0	1.1	1.3	1.6	1.3	0.8	0.9	800.0
Malawi	3.4	2.0	1.9	1.6	1.6	1.7	1.9	2.0	2.7	-20.6
Mozambique	4.0	6.2	3.8	4.1	4.0	4.5	4.6	4.9	5.1	27.5
Namibia									5.3	
South Africa	57.1	67.3	69.8	57.2	56.8	64.1	70.2	66.6	66.7	16.8
Swaziland	0.3	0.8	0.9	1.0	0.9	1.0	0.9	1.0	1.3	333.3
Zambia	8.6	10.5	5.8	5.7	6.1	7.0	9.4	9.7	6.5	-24.4
Zimbabwe			8.3	8.1	9.5	10.7	11.2	11.7	11.6	

Source: International Civil Aviation Organisation (ICAO)

Notes: see end of section

CIVIL AVIATION

Trends in Airline Passengers Carried 1977-1991

Units: Million passenger-kilometres

	1977	1980	1985	1986	1987	1988	1989	1990	1991	% growth 1977/91
North America										
Canada	27,291	36,169	35,684	39,025	40,241	46,917	50,372	47,115	39,042	43.1
USA [a]	310,947	409,066	531,739	582,863	641,733	674,629	693,940	736,107	720,753	131.8
South America										
Argentina	4,874	7,935	7,351	7,942	8,652	8,862	9,253	9,431	9,207	88.9
Bolivia	558	944	894	884	912	955	1,032	1,068	1,022	83.2
Brazil	10,978	15,572	18,494	23,471	22,613	23,712	27,854	28,500	28,537	159.9
Chile	1,433	1,875	1,792	1,961	2,117	2,442	2,807	2,987	3,039	112.1
Colombia	3,376	4,189	4,242	4,260	4,230	4,294	4,537	4,384	4,465	32.3
Ecuador	551	916	969	1,073	1,073	1,051	1,209	1,243	1,201	118.0
French Guiana										
Guyana			163	168	172	185	215	216	214	
Paraguay	220	262	635	987	1,083	891	591	591	1,073	387.7
Peru	1,353	1,974	1,598	2,110	2,670	2,498	2,048	2,025	1,759	30.0
Suriname	114	245	400	304	373	555	404	404	404	254.4
Uruguay	74	178	389	476	459	468	491	471	471	536.5
Venezuela	4,645	4,318	4,370	4,339	5,040	6,907	6,446	5,534	5,939	27.9
Caribbean										
Anguilla										
Antigua			130	160	167	180	190	195	195	
Aruba										
Bahamas [b]	438	539	218	245	260	280	309	346	346	-21.0
Barbados	310	330	213	364	120					
Bermuda										
British Virgin Islands										
Cayman Islands										
Cuba	773	932	1,801	1,856	1,997	2,120	2,017	1,832	1,598	106.7
Dominica										
Dominican Republic	470	550	606	542	213	263	381	1,375	1,350	187.2
Grenada										
Guadeloupe										
Haiti										
Jamaica	1,167	1,202	1,482	1,735	2,125	1,941	1,982	1,463	1,311	12.3
Martinique										
Netherlands Antilles										
St Kitts										
St Lucia										
St Vincent/Grenadines										
Trinidad and Tobago	1,147	1,505	2,058	2,260	2,354	2,507	2,691	2,726	3,129	172.8
Central America										
Belize										
Costa Rica	337	495	570	560	610	786	914	983	1,050	211.6
El Salvador	219	178	575	607	624	838	939	1,066	1,257	474.0
Guatemala	143	155	156	137	165	165	164	213	230	60.8
Honduras	276	394	391	377	484	466	519	468	336	21.7
Mexico	8,586	13,870	17,775	16,885	17,649	14,946	16,059	18,290	18,267	112.8
Nicaragua	92	76	115	85	90	92	77	111	111	20.7
Panama	384	414	534	506	491	511	491	196	272	-29.2
Puerto Rico										
South Asia										
Afghanistan	290	163	175	140	175	165	200	230	205	-29.3
Bangladesh	519	1,179	1,644	1,800	1,876	2,124	2,068	2,190	2,190	322.0
Bhutan						4	4	4	4	
India	8,306	10,765	14,946	15,536	17,280	18,010	17,988	16,722	15,667	88.6
Nepal	120	243	334	302	338	878	688	716	706	488.3
Pakistan	4,088	5,696	7,019	7,126	7,761	8,743	9,129	9,386	9,062	121.7
Sri Lanka	413	691	2,509	2,108	1,940	2,383	2,670	3,424	3,449	735.1

CIVIL AVIATION	Table No. 2207 (cont'd)

Trends in Airline Passengers Carried 1977-1991

Units: Million passenger-kilometres

	1977	1980	1985	1986	1987	1988	1989	1990	1991	% growth 1977/91
Japan										
Japan	39,042	51,217	64,028	66,587	76,506	84,469	93,275	100,501	100,431	157.2
ASEAN/NICs										
Brunei			247	252	275	333	405	487	487	
Hong Kong										
Indonesia	3,917	5,907	9,363	9,808	11,728	14,428	14,930	14,581	15,965	307.6
Macau										
Malaysia	2,099	4,076	6,264	6,252	7,605	8,658	10,056	11,862	14,226	577.8
Philippines	3,594	5,959	8,614	8,920	9,259	10,375	10,592	10,390	11,028	206.8
Singapore	7,869	14,719	21,741	22,876	24,947	28,062	30,466	31,600	33,452	325.1
South Korea	5,475	10,853	12,105	13,406	14,491	14,682	18,163	20,051	20,716	278.4
Taiwan										
Thailand	3,419	6,276	10,778	11,274	13,448	16,682	18,833	19,757	18,246	433.7
East/SE Asia										
Cambodia	42									
China	1,500	3,578	12,114	14,174	18,623	25,615	17,914	23,048	30,132	1,908.8
Laos	10	7	9	18	19	20	21	44	44	340.0
Mongolia							450	411	415	
Myanmar	178	218	229	232	233	237	135	140	140	-21.3
North Korea	73	90	141	150	162	170	179	182	182	149.3
Vietnam		3	80	83	85	86	86	87	87	
Australasia										
Australia	19,239	25,506	28,238	31,827	35,596	40,332	37,026	40,797	44,276	130.1
New Zealand	4,665	5,725	7,925	8,816	9,656	10,850	10,613	11,279	11,299	142.2
Pacific										
American Samoa										
Fiji	125	241	420	478	486	550	820	889	594	375.2
French Polynesia										
Guam										
Kiribati			7	17	4	4	9	9	9	
Nauru						308	365	375		
New Caledonia										
Papua New Guinea	375	520	491	506	542	640	712	681	682	81.9
Solomon Islands			11	11	12	12	13	13	13	
Tonga			1	6	8	7	7	7	7	
Tuvalu										
Vanuatu			25	27	29	33	33	33	33	
Western Samoa										
Middle East										
Bahrain [c]	410	714	1,245	1,160	1,160	1,403	1,492	1,549	1,676	308.8
Egypt	2,037	2,870	4,427	4,023	4,906	5,512	6,186	5,998	5,230	156.8
Iran	4,116	2,071	4,090	4,890	4,874	4,417	4,691	5,755	5,551	34.9
Iraq	1,222	1,161	1,525	1,446	1,451	2,160	2,269	1,370		56.2
Israel	4,820	4,727	6,579	6,799	7,360	6,835	7,595	7,127	7,527	115.5
Jordan	1,132	2,607	3,551	3,244	3,500	3,927	3,679	2,782	2,439	50.2
Kuwait	1,270	2,114	3,803	3,709	3,771	3,670	3,893	2,300	1,908	-25.5
Lebanon	1,544	1,571	930	876	642	892	324	941	1,150	321.7
Oman [c]	410	714	1,245	1,160	1,210	1,453	1,545	1,602	1,729	308.8
Qatar [c]	410	714	1,245	1,160	1,160	1,403	1,492	1,549	1,676	202.3
Saudi Arabia	4,923	9,938	15,458	15,018	15,640	14,935	15,695	16,088	14,881	42.9
Syria	795	948	942	984	792	632	797	1,105	1,136	1,085.6
United Arab Emirates [c]	410	714	1,245	1,671	2,209	3,029	3,351	3,876	4,861	73.8
Yemen	248	375	813	766	772	867	961	929	431	

CIVIL AVIATION   Table No. 2207 (cont'd)

Trends in Airline Passengers Carried 1977-1991

Units: Million passenger-kilometres

	1977	1980	1985	1986	1987	1988	1989	1990	1991	% growth 1977/91
North Africa										
Algeria	1,723	2,300	3,597	3,493	3,303	3,440	3,666	3,463	3,092	79.5
Chad [d]	162	210	241	249	221	216	231	240	211	30.2
Djibouti		53	72	57	61	62	66	67	67	
Ethiopia	535	647	1,016	1,115	1,244	1,404	1,606	1,529	1,568	193.1
Libya	815	1,101	1,672	1,370	1,447	1,283	1,680	1,968	1,251	53.5
Mali	98	97	94	98						
Mauritania [d]	165	218	294	313	288	283	298	307	278	68.5
Morocco	1,757	1,868	2,122	2,058	2,218	2,430	2,695	2,889	2,533	44.2
Niger [d]	154	199	232	260	237	231	224	232	203	31.8
Somalia	19	140	231	283	292	261	248	255	131	589.5
Sudan	555	710	580	448	471	672	494	589	426	-23.2
Tunisia	1,058	1,241	1,499	1,314	1,389	1,483	1,571	1,502	1,407	33.0
West Africa										
Benin [d]	139	178	235	260	228	223	224	232	203	46.0
Burkina Faso [d]	150	183	246	286	243	238	254	264	235	56.7
Cameroon	314	477	580	584	610	640	544	560	301	-4.1
Cape Verde	9	12	32	76	154	159	161	161	161	1,688.9
Côte d'Ivoire [d]	169	215	289	293	287	287	319	317	286	69.2
Equatorial Guinea	6	7	7	7	7	10	7	7	7	16.7
Gabon	129	374		522	404	418	447	445	445	245.0
Gambia										
Ghana	234	324	278	299	286	352	382	366	331	41.5
Guinea	27	34	160	10	29	32	27	29	29	7.4
Guinea-Bissau		8	9	10	10	10	10	10	10	
Liberia	8	17	11	8	7	7	7	7	7	-12.5
Nigeria	979	1,877	2,343	2,261	1,632	1,137	1,007	1,287	1,391	42.1
Sao Tomé e Príncipe			5	4	8	8	8	8	8	
Senegal [d]	152	196	253	238	233	228	243	253	224	47.4
Sierra Leone	49	86	110	110	87					
Togo [d]	140	179	233	238	214	209	224	232	203	45.0
East/Central Africa										
Angola	247	553	1,032	1,000	1,030	950	822	1,189	1,241	402.4
Burundi	1	5	2	1	1	2	2	2	2	100.0
Central African Republic [d]	145	190	243	249	226	221	236	245	216	49.0
Comoros			16	3	3	3	3	3	3	
Congo [d]	152	197	302	308	259	254	272	282	253	66.4
Kenya	563	863	1,150	1,212	1,271	1,322	1,399	1,652	1,479	162.7
Madagascar	280	310	387	395	423	435	442	513	387	38.2
Maldives	10	20	110	120	3	3	3	3	3	-70.0
Mauritius	43	185	642	761	1,179	1,565	1,828	2,279	2,464	5,630.2
Réunion										
Rwanda			1	2	3	2	2	2	2	
Seychelles	2	2	5					440	351	17,450.0
Tanzania	37		257	239	259	274	327	215	284	667.6
Uganda		120	76	104	98	128	278	278	13	
Zaire	693	834	355	382	487	506	501	500	384	-44.6
Southern Africa										
Botswana		15	22	22	24	56	50	63	73	
Lesotho	1	11	17	13	13	27	33	13	14	1,300.0
Malawi	124	68	79	68	64	71	82	80	87	-29.8
Mozambique	378	467	469	492	426	504	494	502	465	23.0
Namibia									423	
South Africa	6,525	8,920	8,745	7,480	7,480	8,805	9,201	9,049	8,413	28.9
Swaziland	5	30	30	26	31	37	40	45	45	800.0
Zambia	499	467	631	654	609	729	916	985	655	31.3
Zimbabwe			653	661	626	674	760	797	817	

Source: ICAO

Notes: see end of section

CIVIL AVIATION

Trends in Airline Freight Carried 1977-1991

Units: Million tonne-kilometres

	1977	1980	1985	1986	1987	1988	1989	1990	1991	% growth 1977/91
North America										
Canada	550.4	689.2	989.8	977.0	1,006.8	1,170.4	1,348.2	1,385.3	1,241.1	125.5
USA [a]	7,922.4	8,371.2	9,648.0	10,712.6	11,937.5	13,874.8	14,649.9	14,791.4	14,486.2	82.9
South America										
Argentina	119.8	179.4	187.1	192.0	197.5	191.0	201.2	199.8	185.3	54.7
Bolivia	27.6	38.2	41.5	27.8	25.5	8.3	8.4	8.4	5.0	-81.9
Brazil	499.3	588.2	909.2	1,013.7	1,013.7	975.8	1,147.9	1,081.6	1,029.0	106.1
Chile	105.7	144.9	114.2	137.2	186.4	242.8	329.5	418.5	428.9	305.8
Colombia	171.9	147.5	375.7	396.8	398.3	403.7	395.3	463.7	526.1	206.1
Ecuador	9.5	33.7	50.7	58.6	70.0	73.6	68.4	63.2	68.0	615.8
French Guiana										
Guyana	0.8	0.8	2.3	2.4	2.5	2.6	2.8	2.8	2.8	250.0
Paraguay	2.1	2.6	13.7	13.7	15.1	7.0	3.9	4.5	5.1	142.9
Peru	34.8	40.1	47.4	70.6	78.7	52.1	33.0	25.6	25.0	-28.2
Suriname	1.1	3.6	11.5	10.4	12.0	22.9	14.5	14.5	14.5	1,218.2
Uruguay	0.2	1.4	1.9	1.7	2.2	2.4	9.4	2.6	2.6	1,200.0
Venezuela	112.6	107.5	83.1	98.9	117.9	213.0	161.4	112.5	132.0	17.2
Caribbean										
Anguilla										
Antigua			0.1	0.1	0.1	0.2	0.2	0.2	0.2	
Aruba										
Bahamas	1.9	3.0	0.2	0.3	0.3	0.3	0.3	0.3	0.3	-84.2
Barbados	0.2	0.5	2.6	4.3	2.6	0.4	0.4	0.4	0.4	100.0
Bermuda										
British Virgin Islands										
Cayman Islands										
Cuba	9.4	10.4	17.1	22.0	25.5	27.8	22.0	19.0	18.0	91.5
Dominica										
Dominican Republic	0.0	10.8	8.5	5.6	3.0	4.0	20.0	70.4	70.2	
Grenada										
Guadeloupe										
Haiti	2.0	1.9	4.8	4.8	4.8	4.8	3.9	3.9	3.9	95.0
Jamaica	11.6	9.4	19.1	18.9	24.2	20.6	16.3	18.8	19.7	69.8
Martinique										
Netherlands Antilles										
St Kitts										
St Lucia										
St Vincent/Grenadines										
Trinidad and Tobago	25.9	17.6	10.0	10.5	11.2	12.5	14.4	15.2	14.8	-42.9
Central America										
Belize										
Costa Rica	18.3	22.4	25.3	24.8	30.0	33.1	32.7	38.7	36.1	97.3
El Salvador	24.5	12.7			3.0	6.5	2.5	4.6	5.1	-79.2
Guatemala	6.7	6.4	9.0	7.2	11.4	11.5	23.4	9.0	9.2	37.3
Honduras	4.2	3.0	2.0	2.2	2.5	2.3	3.0	4.3	3.1	-26.2
Mexico	92.3	131.5	170.0	155.1	169.0	121.5	114.4	143.2	162.7	76.3
Nicaragua	2.0	1.3	1.4	1.0	1.1	1.2	1.8	3.6	3.6	80.0
Panama	3.9	2.9	4.3	6.4	14.8	14.1	14.4	11.3		
Puerto Rico										
South Asia										
Afghanistan	13.9	21.4	19.9	7.5	8.1	8.8	11.5	9.4	8.4	-39.6
Bangladesh	17.0	26.2	68.8	72.1	83.2	76.5	84.1	91.6	91.6	438.8
Bhutan										
India	275.9	366.0	489.7	539.7	645.2	646.3	680.6	662.9	493.5	78.9
Nepal	1.5	5.0	6.7	6.2	5.9	27.9	10.5	11.2	11.2	646.7
Pakistan	161.6	235.4	309.8	319.5	327.9	388.8	418.7	420.5	373.3	131.0
Sri Lanka	2.2	9.7	67.6	54.7	49.1	61.7	75.4	93.4	100.7	4,477.3

CIVIL AVIATION

Trends in Airline Freight Carried 1977-1991

Units: Million tonne-kilometres

	1977	1980	1985	1986	1987	1988	1989	1990	1991	% growth 1977/91
Japan										
Japan	1,147.5	1,870.7	3,071.4	3,608.1	4,326.3	4,774.3	5,126.6	5,084.2	5,233.5	356.0
ASEAN/NICs										
Brunei			4.4	4.5	4.9	6.0	8.6	9.9	9.9	
Hong Kong										
Indonesia	52.1	121.9	153.1	222.0	340.2	445.0	438.2	458.6	474.6	810.9
Macau										
Malaysia	45.0	109.9	200.3	259.3	343.4	373.2	403.7	575.4	712.5	1,483.3
Philippines	129.7	149.8	255.4	235.3	238.7	303.7	327.4	316.0	307.6	137.1
Singapore	248.0	544.1	981.0	1,111.8	1,256.8	1,398.3	1,640.1	1,652.5	1,740.8	601.9
South Korea	394.4	836.0	1,309.1	1,451.2	1,621.1	1,912.9	2,365.1	2,459.4	2,597.0	558.4
Taiwan										
Thailand	104.7	238.6	419.5	464.5	491.9	588.0	612.7	661.0	866.2	727.3
East/SE Asia										
Cambodia	0.4									
China	60.0	120.9	403.0	467.5	647.5	731.8	683.1	818.3	1,009.5	1,582.5
Laos	0.1	0.1	0.2	0.2	0.1	0.1	0.1	0.8	0.8	700.0
Mongolia							1.5	1.5	1.4	
Myanmar	1.2	1.5	2.3	2.4	2.5	2.5	1.1	1.1	1.1	-8.3
North Korea	1.7	2.2	2.4	2.6	2.7	2.9	3.0	3.1	3.1	82.3
Vietnam		0.1	0.8	0.8	0.8	0.8	0.8	0.8	0.8	
Australasia										
Australia	376.1	523.0	814.8	859.3	994.9	1,027.9	1,125.4	1,222.3	1,222.0	224.9
New Zealand	140.7	185.9	305.4	318.6	335.4	320.3	317.4	325.1	379.9	170.0
Pacific										
American Samoa										
Fiji	1.2	2.8	3.8	6.0	10.3	14.9	20.4	21.0	23.3	1,841.6
French Polynesia										
Guam										
Kiribati			0.1	0.1	0.1	0.1	1.0	0.8	0.8	
Nauru						1.4	1.5	1.5	1.4	
New Caledonia										
Papua New Guinea	6.2	8.6	9.6	9.5	9.4	12.9	14.8	14.8	15.0	141.9
Solomon Islands			0.0	0.0	0.0	0.0	0.0	0.0	0.0	
Tonga				0.0	0.0	0.0	0.0	0.0	0.0	
Tuvalu										
Vanuatu			0.1	0.1	0.1	0.1	0.1	0.1	0.1	
Western Samoa										
Middle East										
Bahrain [b]	8.2	26.2	32.6	31.4	31.5	33.9	40.0	44.3	51.2	524.3
Egypt	23.7	29.4	98.5	111.5	112.0	118.8	138.1	144.0	131.6	455.2
Iran	77.2	20.3	104.3	132.0	137.8	120.6	92.3	113.7	86.1	11.5
Iraq	30.0	52.0	54.6	59.2	59.5	70.4	72.9	42.8		
Israel	174.1	295.0	592.1	571.0	642.7	754.4	816.8	831.5	863.3	395.8
Jordan	40.1	80.2	151.8	164.3	186.3	201.5	206.0	222.8	161.5	302.7
Kuwait	32.0	71.6	164.3	222.7	244.0	223.1	233.4	145.0	116.2	263.1
Lebanon	540.2	531.8	199.8	33.1	194.8	309.2	283.5	167.1	169.6	-68.6
Oman [b]	8.2	26.2	32.6	31.4	31.5	33.9	40.0	44.3	51.2	524.3
Qatar [b]	8.2	26.2	32.6	31.4	31.5	33.9	40.0	44.3	51.2	524.3
Saudi Arabia	105.8	165.5	455.1	437.2	453.2	490.0	604.7	609.6	486.6	359.9
Syria	9.4	16.2	15.7	12.5	13.5	9.4	10.0	17.7	14.4	53.1
United Arab Emirates [b]	8.2	26.2	32.6	48.6	68.1	96.2	117.8	145.1	184.4	2,148.7
Yemen	1.9	2.3	12.3	10.4	10.5	12.1	12.8	11.5	5.5	189.4

CIVIL AVIATION

Table No. 2208 (cont'd)

Trends in Airline Freight Carried 1977-1991

Units: Million tonne-kilometres

	1977	1980	1985	1986	1987	1988	1989	1990	1991	% growth 1977/91
North Africa										
Algeria	9.0	12.9	21.0	7.7	13.3	13.9	23.1	14.6	24.3	170.0
Chad [c]	14.0	19.2	18.6	16.5	16.3	15.9	18.0	17.7	16.1	15.0
Djibouti		0.2	0.4	0.3	0.3	0.3	0.1	0.1	0.1	
Ethiopia	20.7	24.8	66.4	82.3	86.3	88.3	92.7	66.6	78.5	279.2
Libya	6.8	11.0	5.4	4.9	8.7	3.8	4.7	10.3	9.4	38.2
Mali	0.5	0.5	0.7	0.8						
Mauritania [c]	13.6	18.6	18.8	16.6	16.5	16.1	18.2	17.9	16.3	19.8
Morocco	22.6	25.6	36.2	43.9	50.9	48.8	34.0	31.5	55.9	147.3
Niger [c]	13.1	18.2	18.4	16.5	16.4	16.0	18.0	17.7	16.1	22.9
Somalia	0.3	0.5	3.3	3.5	3.9	4.4	7.9	8.7	5.0	1,566.6
Sudan	10.1	12.1	7.3	16.2	21.6	11.8	17.0	12.9	11.3	11.8
Tunisia	8.2	11.6	15.9	14.6	18.7	16.8	18.8	19.1	17.8	117.0
West Africa										
Benin [c]	13.0	18.0	18.4	16.5	16.3	15.9	18.0	17.7	16.0	23.0
Burkina Faso [c]		18.0	18.4	16.5	16.3	15.9	18.0	17.7	16.2	
Cameroon	5.8	27.7	56.9	34.8	36.7	38.3	31.8	33.7	37.0	537.9
Cape Verde	0.1	0.2	0.4	0.3	0.5	0.5	0.5	0.6	0.6	500.0
Côte d'Ivoire [c]	13.2	18.2	18.4	16.6	16.3	15.9	18.1	17.7	16.1	21.9
Equatorial Guinea		0.1	0.1	0.1	0.1	0.1	0.1	0.1	0.1	
Gabon	7.8	26.5	36.0	37.4	29.1	27.2	29.4	26.1	26.1	234.6
Gambia										
Ghana	2.7	2.8	9.4	10.1	12.1	13.4	13.6	15.7	19.1	607.4
Guinea	0.2	0.2	0.6	0.0	0.0	0.0	0.4	0.4	3.0	1,400.0
Guinea-Bissau		0.1	0.1	0.1	0.1	0.1	0.1	0.1	0.1	
Liberia		0.1	0.1	0.1	0.1	0.1	0.1	0.1	0.1	
Nigeria	4.1	9.3	28.7	32.4	37.2	29.5	17.0	23.5	27.5	570.7
Sao Tomé e Príncipe				0.0	0.0	0.0	0.0	0.0	0.0	
Senegal [c]	13.1	18.0	18.4	16.5	16.3	15.9	18.0	17.7	16.1	22.9
Sierra Leone	0.9	1.3	2.0	2.2	1.5					
Togo [c]	13.0	18.0	18.4	16.5	16.3	15.9	18.0	17.7	16.1	23.8
East/Central Africa										
Angola	13.4	20.9	33.2	24.8	25.6	26.9	51.6	39.9	41.5	209.7
Burundi		0.1	0.0	0.0	0.1					
Central African Republic [c]	13.1	18.1	18.5	16.6	16.4	16.0	18.1	17.8	16.2	23.6
Comoros		0.1	0.0	0.0	0.0	0.0	0.0	0.0	0.0	
Congo [c]	13.4	18.5	20.0	17.7	16.9	16.5	18.6	18.4	16.8	25.3
Kenya	14.2	18.0	30.4	39.3	54.5	55.2	47.7	52.2	39.2	176.0
Madagascar	6.6	19.9	20.1	19.2	21.0	23.4	29.0	30.2	26.0	293.9
Maldives	0.2	0.3	1.3	1.4	0.0	0.0	0.0	0.0		-100.0
Mauritius	0.2	2.3	15.5	17.0	28.7	58.1	55.1	64.1	81.0	40,400.0
Réunion										
Rwanda			4.4	0.0	9.6	10.3				
Seychelles		0.0	0.4	1.5	1.7	2.0	4.5	10.4	9.1	
Tanzania	0.3	1.9	3.3	2.0		2.7	1.6	1.4	4.2	1,300.0
Uganda		3.0	11.0	14.5	15.3	17.1	21.7	21.7		
Zaire	42.0	34.5	30.5	31.1	52.5	55.3	52.0	57.3	33.2	-20.9
Southern Africa										
Botswana			0.1	0.1	0.1	0.2	0.4	3.1	0.4	
Lesotho		0.0	0.1	0.2	0.3	0.9	0.8	0.1	0.1	
Malawi	6.6	0.8	0.8	0.6	0.6	0.7	0.9	0.9	1.3	-80.3
Mozambique	5.4	8.7	9.1	10.3	8.6	10.2	10.1	9.1	9.4	74.0
Namibia									2.0	
South Africa	173.8	251.2	391.8	308.2	309.5	238.3	205.6	179.2	191.0	9.8
Swaziland		0.1	0.2	0.2	0.2	0.2	0.2	0.3	0.1	
Zambia	32.6	46.9	25.3	24.5	25.7	24.8	24.9	29.6	21.7	-33.4
Zimbabwe			11.1	12.5	73.4	13.4	64.6	64.9	64.1	

Source: ICAO

Notes: see end of section

CIVIL AVIATION

National Airlines: Kilometres Flown, Passengers and Freight Carried 1991

Units: As stated

	Aircraft kilometres ('000)	Aircraft departures (units)	Aircraft hours (units)	Passengers carried ('000)	Freight carried ('000 tonnes)	Passenger load factor (%)	Weight load factor (%)
North America							
Canada	208,100	143,130	333,937	9,879	154	68	56
USA	1,207,799	853,882	1,687,653	75,926	413	62	53
South America							
Argentina [a,b]	43,048	39,800	67,199	2,453	22	64	56
Bolivia	15,136	16,464	24,609	1,269	17	64	66
Brazil	99,313	78,575	160,786	5,236	166	64	52
Chile	25,988	15,923	38,336	694	38	62	61
Colombia [a]	31,413	41,550	58,582	3,235	43	64	62
Ecuador [a,c]	4,341	2,491	5,985	118	7	59	53
French Guiana							
Guyana							
Paraguay [c]		942	9,449	239	2	69	
Peru [a]	9,159	7,715	12,712	554	6	56	49
Suriname [b]	2,075	478	2,764	83	3		
Uruguay [c]	14,465	7,738	8,337	313	1	79	74
Venezuela [a]	14,352	32,697	34,713	1,975	4	51	51
Caribbean							
Anguilla							
Antigua							
Aruba							
Bahamas [c]	3,323	12,952	663		60	46	
Barbados [c]	1,047	387	1,477	31		80	58
Bermuda							
British Virgin Islands							
Cayman Islands							
Cuba [a]	39,492	16,262	49,545	1,155	8	72	75
Dominica							
Dominican Republic [c]	2,395	3,928	6,203	269	3	62	62
Grenada							
Guadeloupe							
Haiti							
Jamaica	10,817	10,767	18,012	846	14	61	58
Martinique							
Netherlands Antilles							
St Kitts							
St Lucia							
St Vincent/Grenadines							
Trinidad and Tobago							
Central America							
Belize							
Costa Rica	11,285	9,198	17,324	465	20	63	75
El Salvador	3,996	3,950	5,918	196	1	67	74
Guatemala [a,b]	2,238	1,890	3,604	80	12	40	40
Honduras	4,141	10,205	7,148	357,603	5	44	45
Mexico [a]	95,699	83,949	134,109	7,855	67	60	51
Nicaragua [c]	1,664	3,631	3,686	109	3	48	46
Panama	2,710	3,745	4,992	266	4	57	56
Puerto Rico							
South Asia							
Afghanistan							
Bangladesh [a,b]	2,077	2,495	3,555	180	4	69	74
Bhutan							
India	54,060	19,350	99,774	7,755	75	74	71
Nepal [c]	8,505	16,591	26,379	409	4	67	57
Pakistan	60,475	66,110	116,940	5,204	98	68	60
Sri Lanka	20,691	8,266	24,751	898	24	72	66

CIVIL AVIATION

National Airlines: Kilometres Flown, Passengers and Freight Carried 1991

Units: As stated

	Aircraft kilometres ('000)	Aircraft departures (units)	Aircraft hours (units)	Passengers carried ('000)	Freight carried ('000 tonnes)	Passenger load factor (%)	Weight load factor (%)
Japan							
Japan	181,747	73,511	255,092	17,340	527	70	65
ASEAN/NICs							
Brunei							
Hong Kong							
Indonesia	85,152	58,902	126,355	5,383	118	62	51
Macau							
Malaysia	71,316	107,469	130,232	8,644	166	70	67
Philippines	52,672	54,136	96,235	4,657	106	71	65
Singapore	133,917	35,283	172,287	7,789	322	73	70
South Korea [c]	109,281	89,687	189,878	11,288	475	75	73
Taiwan							
Thailand	107,584	70,072	173,051	7,743	216	62	63
East/SE Asia							
Cambodia							
China							
Laos							
Mongolia							
Myanmar							
North Korea							
Vietnam							
Australasia							
Australia	134,528	31,381	171,152	4,202	165	65	64
New Zealand	86,265	54,952	101,052	3,763	86	61	54
Pacific							
American Samoa							
Fiji [c]	8,415	6,473	14,357	305	9	59	56
French Polynesia							
Guam							
Kiribati [c]		2,971	1,887	25		49	44
Nauru							
New Caledonia							
Papua New Guinea [b]	10,584	19,980	21,914	700	9	65	58
Solomon Islands							
Tonga							
Tuvalu							
Vanuatu							
Western Samoa							
Middle East							
Bahrain [b,d]	12,647	10,980	19,008	778	14	65	61
Egypt	30,649	21,678	51,817	2,095	41		53
Iran	37,327	39,818	71,022	5,877	76	61	67
Iraq [c]	20,063	12,583	33,179	1,160	18	57	48
Israel	50,360	15,656	71,071	1,751	212	72	72
Jordan [c]	31,936	17,411	48,998	1,204	50	61	55
Kuwait [a,b]	2,401	1,371	3,856	128	5	61	52
Lebanon [c]	4,914	3,431	7,939	183	5	49	48
Oman [b,d]	12,647	10,980	19,008	778	14	65	61
Qatar [b,d]	12,647	10,980	19,008	778	14	65	61
Saudi Arabia	99,816	87,208	165,040	9,766	191	63	49
Syria [b]	10,279	11,561	18,107	656	6	63	58
United Arab Emirates [b,d]	12,647	10,980	19,008	778	14	65	61
Yemen [a,b]	4,427	4,395	7,712	205	2	54	47

CIVIL AVIATION   **Table No. 2209** (cont'd)

National Airlines: Kilometres Flown, Passengers and Freight Carried 1991

Units: As stated

	Aircraft kilometres ('000)	Aircraft departures (units)	Aircraft hours (units)	Passengers carried ('000)	Freight carried ('000 tonnes)	Passenger load factor (%)	Weight load factor (%)
North Africa							
Algeria	27,430	45,587	76,487	3,385	33	73	63
Chad [e]	1,518	343	2,231	50	3	60	53
Djibouti							
Ethiopia	23,345	23,049	38,014	651	50	55	50
Libya [c]	16,558	16,958	28,505	1,610	5	66	58
Mali [c]	57,478	60,672	93,285	3,451	39	62	59
Mauritania [e]	1,518	343	2,231	50	3	60	53
Morocco [a,b]	18,990	12,052	35,096	959	14	68	42
Niger [e]	1,518	343	2,231	50	3	60	53
Somalia [c]	2,578	1,575	5,517	85	3	62	43
Sudan [c]	7,862	8,025	11,690	363	12	35	52
Tunisia	22,302	19,172	38,648	1,861	14	66	53
West Africa							
Benin [e]	1,518	343	2,231	50	3	60	53
Burkina Faso [e]	1,857	1,022	2,683	70	4	57	50
Cameroon [c]	1,518	343	2,231	50	3	60	53
Cape Verde							
Côte d'Ivoire [e]	1,518	343	2,231	50	3	60	53
Equatorial Guinea							
Gabon							
Gambia							
Ghana [b]	4,406	12,678	6,981	196	4	50	58
Guinea [c]	1,481	860	2,420	40	1	11	10
Guinea-Bissau [c]	3,323	12,952	664		60	46	
Liberia							
Nigeria [a]	10,404	11,202	16,491	712	6	54	40
Sao Tomé e Príncipe							
Senegal [e]	1,518	343	2,231	50	3	60	53
Sierra Leone							
Togo [e]	1,518	343	2,231	50	3	60	53
East/Central Africa							
Angola [c]	13,851	6,828	19,355	520	10	76	44
Burundi [c]	12,366	8,743	20,422	1,001	11	68	65
Central African Republic [e]	1,518	343	2,231	50	3	60	53
Comoros							
Congo [e]	1,518	343	2,231	50	3	60	53
Kenya [b]	18,662	13,705	30,144	863	13	61	57
Madagascar	3,559	9,499	9,274	212	4		41
Maldives							
Mauritius [a]	12,484	6,259	17,427	426	9	64	69
Réunion							
Rwanda							
Seychelles [c]	3,853	948	5,214	39	1	53	63
Tanzania	4,975	9,512	12,640	292	3	53	42
Uganda [c]	1,700	1,847	3,300	50	5	64	30
Zaire [a,b]	6,301	4,403	9,372	173	15	52	42
Southern Africa							
Botswana	3,635	6,882	8,592	105	1	35	39
Lesotho [b]	837	4,580	3,694	53		52	51
Malawi	2,228	3,465	3,328	98	2	44	40
Mozambique [b]	5,424	5,738	9,634	290	4	59	57
Namibia							
South Africa	26,969	31,712	1,980	21	57	48	
Swaziland							
Zambia [a]	6,554	2,809	10,655	295	4	62	50
Zimbabwe	2,084	263	2,952		6		74

Source: ICAO/International Air Travel Association (IATA)
Notes: see end of section

MERCHANT SHIPPING

Table No. 2210

Size of Merchant Shipping Fleet 1977-1992

Units: '000 gross tons

	1980	1985	1986	1987	1988	1989	1990	1991	1992	% growth 1980/91
North America										
Canada	3,180.1	3,343.8	3,160.0	2,971.2	2,902.4	2,824.9	2,744.2	2,684.6	2,642.8	-16.9
USA	18,464.3	19,517.6	19,900.8	20,178.2	20,832.0	20,587.8	21,328.1	20,290.5	18,214.2	-1.4
South America										
Argentina	2,546.3			1,901.0	1,876.7	1,832.5	1,890.0	1,708.6	876.5	-65.6
Bolivia	15.1	14.9	14.9	13.8	9.6	9.6	9.6	9.6	9.6	-36.4
Brazil	4,533.7	6,057.4	6,212.3	6,324.1	6,122.8	6,078.2	6,015.7	5,882.5	5,573.2	22.9
Chile	614.4	413.8	566.9	546.7	603.7	589.7	616.3	618.2	601.4	-2.1
Colombia	283.5	365.6	380.1	423.6	412.3	378.9	372.2	313.0	265.7	-6.3
Ecuador	275.1	443.9	437.7	421.4	428.1	401.8	384.9	383.9	369.9	34.5
French Guiana						0.7	0.7	0.7	1.1	
Guyana	18.3	23.4	22.7	22.3	15.0	15.0	15.0	15.6	16.9	-7.7
Paraguay	23.0	42.9	43.3	41.7	38.6	38.7	37.2	35.2	35.2	53.0
Peru	740.5	818.1	754.2	788.2	675.0	638.5	616.7	605.5	498.5	-32.7
Suriname	14.9	15.2	12.7	11.5	11.5	11.5	12.6	12.9	12.9	-13.4
Uruguay	198.5	173.4	149.8	144.4	169.9	101.5	103.8	105.1	128.2	-35.4
Venezuela	848.5	984.9	998.3	999.2	982.1	1,091.7	934.9	970.3	916.4	8.0
Caribbean										
Anguilla	1.1	4.0	4.1	3.7	3.3	2.5	2.5	5.0	5.3	381.8
Antigua	0.4							485.3	611.8	152,850.0
Aruba			128.6							
Bahamas	87.3	3,907.3	5,985.0	9,105.2	8,962.9	11,578.9	13,626.3	17,541.2	20,054.1	22,871.5
Barbados	5.3	8.4	7.6	8.3	8.5	8.3	7.8	7.7	53.4	907.5
Bermuda	499.0	980.7	1,208.3	1,925.3	3,774.3	4,076.1	4,258.3	3,037.0	3,139.2	529.1
British Virgin Islands	5.8	8.6	8.1	8.2	6.8	6.9	6.6	6.6	6.9	19.0
Cayman Islands	256.7	413.8	1,390.0	706.2	476.5	411.0	415.0	395.1	321.6	25.3
Cuba	881.3	965.1	958.6	966.3	912.0	900.3	836.1	770.2	714.9	-18.9
Dominica		1.4	2.0	1.7	2.2	2.9	2.4	2.1	2.1	
Dominican Republic	37.7	46.7	42.2	43.6	48.3	43.7	35.8	12.3	11.6	-69.2
Grenada	0.2	0.4	0.4	0.6	0.2	0.8	0.6	0.6	0.6	200.0
Guadeloupe				2.2	2.8	4.4	4.1	5.3	6.2	
Haiti	1.1	2.7	2.7	0.5	0.5	0.7	0.7	0.7	0.9	-18.2
Jamaica	13.3	9.4	9.4	13.1	14.4	14.4	14.4	14.4	11.1	-16.5
Martinique				7.4	7.4	7.7	8.1	1.2	1.2	
Netherlands Antilles								528.8	848.8	
St Kitts	0.3	0.6	0.3	0.6	0.3	0.3	0.3	0.3	0.3	
St Lucia	2.4	1.8	2.8	2.1	1.9	1.9	1.9	1.9	0.1	-92.1
St Vincent/Grenadines	19.7	235.2	509.9	699.9	900.5	1,486.1	1,936.8	2,709.9	4,381.0	22,138.6
Trinidad and Tobago	17.5	19.0	19.4	18.5	23.9	22.3	22.3	39.6	25.5	45.7
Central America										
Belize	0.6	0.6	0.6	0.6	0.6	0.6	0.6		30.1	4,916.7
Costa Rica	20.3	19.9	13.3	14.8	15.1	13.0	13.9	14.4	12.4	-38.9
El Salvador	0.5			3.8	3.8	3.8	1.5	1.5	1.8	260.0
Guatemala	13.6	16.0	9.4	4.7	4.7	5.0	5.3	1.5	1.8	-86.8
Honduras	213.4	356.6	555.2	506.4	582.2	691.5	711.9	815.9	945.1	342.9
Mexico	1,006.4	1,467.2	1,520.2	1,532.5	1,448.3	1,388.2	1,319.6	1,195.5	1,109.7	10.3
Nicaragua	15.7	18.0	22.9	12.7	13.6	4.6	5.1	5.1	4.1	-73.9
Panama	24,190.7	40,674.2	41,305.0	43,254.7	44,604.1	47,365.4	39,298.1	44,949.3	49,630.0	105.2
Puerto Rico								15.7	10.7	
South Asia										
Afghanistan										
Bangladesh	353.6	358.1	378.7	410.7	431.8	438.8	464.4	456.3	410.4	16.1
Bhutan										
India	5,911.4	6,604.5	6,540.1	6,725.8	6,160.8	6,315.1	6,475.6	6,516.8	6,457.3	9.2
Nepal										
Pakistan	478.0	451.0	434.1	394.4	366.1	365.9	354.1	358.2	363.0	-24.1
Sri Lanka	93.5	634.7	622.2	594.5	410.4	287.1	350.0	333.0	303.9	225.0

MERCHANT SHIPPING

Size of Merchant Shipping Fleet 1980-1992

Units: '000 gross tons

	1980	1985	1986	1987	1988	1989	1990	1991	1992	% growth 1980/91
Japan										
Japan	40,959.7	39,940.1	38,487.8	35,932.2	32,074.4	28,030.4	27,077.9	26,406.9	25,403.3	-38.0
ASEAN/NICs										
Brunei	0.9	1.2	2.0	3.8	3.5	3.5	3.5	360.8	362.1	40,133.3
Hong Kong	1,717.2	6,858.1	8,179.7	8,034.7	7,329.0	6,151.3	6,564.9	5,875.8	6,925.7	303.3
Indonesia	1,411.7	1,936.4	2,085.6	2,120.5	2,126.1	2,035.1	2,178.6	2,336.9	2,338.6	65.7
Macau								2.7	3.0	
Malaysia	702.1	1,773.1	1,743.2			1,668.0	1,717.5	1,755.3	2,015.6	187.1
Philippines	1,927.9	4,594.0	6,922.5	8,681.2	9,311.6	9,384.8	8,514.9	8,625.6	8,448.7	338.2
Singapore	7,664.2	6,504.6	6,267.7	7,098.1	7,209.0	7,272.5	7,927.9	8,488.2	9,247.4	20.7
South Korea	4,334.1	7,168.9	7,183.6	7,214.1	7,333.7	7,832.5	7,783.1	7,820.5	7,518.5	73.5
Taiwan	2,039.1	4,327.5	4,272.8	4,512.7	4,631.5	5,169.3	5,766.3	5,888.1	6,103.6	199.3
Thailand	391.5	586.3	533.1	510.9	515.3	539.2	614.8	724.6	798.1	103.9
East/SE Asia										
Cambodia	3.6	3.6	3.6	3.6	3.6	3.6			3.6	
China	6,837.6	10,568.2	11,567.0	12,431.5	12,919.0	13,513.6	13,899.5	13,888.4	13,946.3	104.0
Laos							0.5	0.5	0.5	
Mongolia										
Myanmar	87.5	116.6	125.5	239.3	272.7	582.2	827.4	1,046.0	977.3	1,016.9
North Korea	230.7	512.6	407.3	406.6	405.8	362.2	442.3	511.2	599.0	159.6
Vietnam	240.9	298.6	338.7	360.5	337.9	358.4	470.3	574.0	562.6	133.5
Australasia										
Australia	1,642.6	2,088.3	2,368.5	2,404.5	2,365.9	2,494.0	2,511.8	2,571.9	2,676.1	62.9
New Zealand	263.5	295.9	314.2	334.2	336.8	256.6	260.2	274.8	253.3	-3.9
Pacific										
American Samoa				0.3	0.3	0.3	0.3	0.6	0.6	
Fiji	14.8	30.6	30.0	35.3	37.2	61.9	55.5	52.2	58.8	297.3
French Polynesia						17.1	20.1	20.4	20.5	
Guam				2.5	2.5	2.5	4.3	0.6	0.8	
Kiribati	1.0	2.1	3.2	3.3	3.5	3.5	3.5	3.5	3.5	250.0
Nauru	54.0	66.7	66.7	65.8	60.1	40.5	32.2	14.8	5.4	-90.0
New Caledonia				12.4	12.1	12.8	14.3	14.1	14.1	
Papua New Guinea	24.9	28.5	30.9	36.3	37.7	37.5	37.2	36.3	44.2	77.5
Solomon Islands	2.7	5.8	6.0	6.4	8.6	8.4	8.2	8.2	7.7	185.2
Tonga	14.9	17.3	16.3	18.3	13.6	34.8	39.6	39.6	10.9	-26.8
Tuvalu	0.4	0.5	0.5	0.5	0.5	1.6	1.2	1.2	12.3	2,975.0
Vanuatu		138.0	165.0	540.1	789.5	920.3	2,163.6	2,172.6	2,154.9	
Western Samoa	4.8	26.1	26.1	26.1	26.1	27.2	27.3	6.3	6.3	31.3
Middle East										
Bahrain	10.2	47.6	51.7	43.8	54.4	54.5	46.6	211.3	155.4	1,423.5
Egypt	555.8	952.6	1,063.0	1,074.2	1,226.7	1,230.3	1,257.1	1,256.6	1,200.1	115.9
Iran	1,283.7	2,380.0	2,911.4	3,976.9	4,336.6	4,732.6	4,738.2	4,583.2	4,558.2	255.1
Iraq	1,465.9	1,011.9	1,016.3	1,002.2	953.1	1,056.2	1,044.4	930.5	918.7	-37.3
Israel	450.2	549.7	556.6	514.8	545.6	505.1	529.5	603.8	652.3	44.9
Jordan [a]	0.5	48.3	42.4	32.9	32.2	32.2	42.2	73.2	61.3	12,160.0
Kuwait	2,529.5	2,349.9	2,580.9	2,087.9	1,735.3	1,865.1	1,854.6	1,373.0	1,910.2	-24.5
Lebanon	267.8	505.0	484.6	460.9	405.3	384.5	307.1	274.3	286.1	6.8
Oman	6.9	17.5	14.8	25.3	25.5	23.6	22.6	22.6	22.3	223.2
Qatar	91.9	353.2	306.7	306.4	308.7	306.1	359.5	484.8	423.7	361.0
Saudi Arabia	1,589.7	3,137.2	2,978.0	2,692.0	2,269.4	2,119.2	1,682.8	1,321.4	1,016.1	-36.1
Syria	39.3	58.0	63.1	63.1	64.1	74.3	79.8	109.5	129.7	230.0
United Arab Emirates	158.2	868.6	653.5	732.0	825.0	838.6	749.6	888.9	928.7	487.0
Yemen	15.2	15.1	19.6	212.2	207.1	207.0		16.7	16.9	11.2

MERCHANT SHIPPING

Table No. 2210 (cont'd)

Size of Merchant Shipping Fleet 1980-1992

Units: '000 gross tons

	1980	1985	1986	1987	1988	1989	1990	1991	1992	% growth 1980/91
North Africa										
Algeria	1,218.6	1,347.4	881.7	892.6	896.7	848.2	905.7	921.3	921.5	-24.4
Chad										
Djibouti	3.1	2.8	3.1	3.1	3.1	3.1	3.1	3.4	3.6	16.1
Ethiopia	23.8	56.7	66.9	73.5	74.1	77.3	74.9	69.5	69.5	192.0
Libya	890.0	853.9	825.2	816.6	830.1	830.5	834.7		727.2	-18.3
Mali	0.2									
Mauritania	0.9	17.1	22.8	29.6	36.9	40.0	40.9	41.9	42.7	4,644.4
Morocco	359.6	460.9	416.5	418.5	437.0	454.2	488.1	483.5	468.1	30.2
Niger										
Somalia	45.6									
Sudan	104.8	95.7	95.7	96.7	96.7	96.7	57.9	45.4	45.4	-56.7
Tunisia	131.1	284.3	285.5	285.5	281.5	281.7	277.6	276.4	279.9	113.5
West Africa										
Benin	4.6	4.9	4.9	4.7	4.7	4.7	4.7	1.7	1.7	-63.0
Burkina Faso										
Cameroon	62.1	76.4	76.7	57.9	57.3	33.2	33.1	34.5	34.8	-44.0
Cape Verde	11.4	14.1	14.1	14.6	17.1	17.6	20.7	21.8	21.7	90.4
Côte d'Ivoire	186.1	141.7	120.7	119.0	119.0	83.0	82.5	82.1	82.0	-55.9
Equatorial Guinea	6.4	6.4	6.4	6.4	6.4	6.4	6.4	6.4	6.5	1.6
Gabon	77.1	97.5	98.0	23.8	24.8	24.5	24.1	24.8	25.2	-67.3
Gambia	3.9	2.6	2.6	3.9	3.5	1.9	1.9	2.8	2.7	-30.8
Ghana	250.4	162.6	165.6	142.4	125.7	126.1	125.5	134.9	133.3	-46.8
Guinea	5.6	7.2	7.2	7.2	7.2	8.0	9.1	9.1	5.4	-3.6
Guinea-Bissau	0.8	3.7	4.1	4.1	4.1	4.1	4.3	4.4	4.4	450.0
Liberia	80,285.2	58,179.7	52,649.4	51,412.0	49,734.0	47,892.5	54,699.6	52,426.5	55,166.9	-31.3
Nigeria	498.2	443.4	563.9	593.6	586.9	499.6	495.9	493.3	503.7	1.1
Sao Tomé e Príncipe		1.5	1.5	1.5	1.5	1.5	1.5	1.5	2.6	
Senegal	34.5	51.0	50.4	46.5	49.1	50.8	52.3	54.9	50.1	45.2
Sierra Leone	3.7	5.9	7.0	8.8	13.7	18.4	21.3	20.7	25.6	591.9
Togo	25.4	54.0	54.9	59.7	47.7	42.5	52.3	21.9	12.2	-52.0
East/Central Africa										
Angola	65.7	91.0	92.3	91.7	91.0	92.9	93.1	93.1	93.9	42.9
Burundi										
Central African Republic										
Comoros	1.1	1.3	1.3	1.8	1.2	2.3	2.3	2.6	2.3	109.1
Congo				8.5	8.5	8.5	8.6	8.6	8.6	
Kenya	17.4	8.1	9.0	7.9	7.9	7.8	7.1	12.5	12.3	-29.3
Madagascar	91.2	74.2	73.7	64.2	91.6	70.1	73.6	72.8	67.4	-26.1
Maldives	136.0	138.3	84.8	100.2	104.4	93.5	77.9		50.3	-63.0
Mauritius [b]	37.7	37.7	152.0	162.8	156.7	130.2	99.2	82.3	102.4	171.6
Réunion						21.3	21.3	21.5	21.5	
Rwanda										
Seychelles	4.6	1.7	3.8	3.2	3.2	3.2	3.2	3.9	4.5	-2.2
Tanzania	55.9	50.6	50.7	31.6	32.1	32.1	31.7	39.4	40.7	-27.2
Uganda	5.5	3.4	5.1	5.1	5.1	5.1	5.1	5.1	3.4	-38.2
Zaire	91.9	84.7	65.8	56.4	56.4	56.4	56.4	56.4	28.1	-69.4
Southern Africa										
Botswana										
Lesotho										
Malawi		0.4	0.4	0.4	0.4	0.4	0.4			
Mozambique	37.9	40.9	42.8	36.0	36.0	38.2	39.6	39.1	37.3	-1.6
Namibia										
South Africa	728.9	632.5	599.6	533.1	485.5	396.9	352.3	340.1	336.7	-53.8
Swaziland										
Zambia										
Zimbabwe										

Source: Lloyd's Register of Shipping, Statistical Tables 1992
Notes: see end of section

MERCHANT SHIPPING — Table No. 2211

Goods Unloaded in International Seaborne Trade 1977-1991

Units: '000 tonnes

	1977	1980	1985	1986	1987	1988	1989	1990	1991	% growth 1977/91
North America										
Canada	58,882	68,342	60,669	61,000	62,000	68,000	79,000			
USA	568,136	468,909	362,481	408,432	424,668	461,364	493,860	495,240	448,860	-21.0
South America										
Argentina	10,619	10,568	5,375	7,140	9,144	9,012	7,440	5,868	6,864	-35.4
Bolivia										
Brazil	62,062	71,855	48,864	58,248	61,872	58,080	57,204			
Chile	7,288	8,792	4,480	4,800	5,752	7,428	9,444	10,848	10,944	50.2
Colombia	3,660	7,276	6,909	5,628	6,096	6,036	5,580	5,784	6,108	66.9
Ecuador	3,823	2,282	2,458							
French Guiana	167	224	249							
Guyana	1,070	757	636							
Paraguay										
Peru	5,784	3,831	3,456	4,200	5,500	5,900	4,000			
Suriname	1,504	1,400	1,435	1,681						
Uruguay	2,437	888	1,518							
Venezuela	7,000	11,966	14,902							
Caribbean										
Anguilla										
Antigua	421	205	104							
Aruba										
Bahamas	10,400	22,426	8,710							
Barbados	547	657	460							
Bermuda	307	702	462							
British Virgin Islands	13	24	52							
Cayman Islands	30	8,093	671							
Cuba	14,036	16,900	18,900	18,445	13,019					
Dominica	30	65	51							
Dominican Republic	3,294	3,714	3,844	3,988	5,048					
Grenada	23	110	52							
Guadeloupe	586	836	929	1,068	1,224	1,332	1,368			
Haiti	646	521	680							
Jamaica	2,712	3,680	3,672	4,100	4,400					
Martinique	940	1,172	1,014	1,320	1,284	1,404	1,260			
Netherlands Antilles	31,065	71,438	11,529							
St Kitts		56	37							
St Lucia	185	208	211	287	386	484	560			
St Vincent/Grenadines	77	127	110	109	211					
Trinidad and Tobago	14,856	9,547	4,267							
Central America										
Belize	155	163	144							
Costa Rica	3,660	7,276	1,653							
El Salvador	2,063	1,482	1,320	1,920	912	876				
Guatemala	1,650	2,405	1,733							
Honduras	1,233	1,252	1,138	1,707	1,865	1,797				
Mexico	8,353	14,557	10,956	9,012	11,244	13,248	44,736	44,856	49,680	494.8
Nicaragua	1,423	1,283	1,453							
Panama	3,419	2,647	2,023	62,676	63,096	67,020	64,244	67,068	63,288	1,751.1
Puerto Rico										
South Asia										
Afghanistan										
Bangladesh	3,393	7,619	7,323	7,572	7,200	9,336	8,940	7,788	6,156	81.4
Bhutan										
India	26,798	40,163	39,490							
Nepal										
Pakistan	7,215	11,259	14,550	15,444	15,936	17,455	19,320	19,716	19,644	172.3
Sri Lanka	3,571	4,442	5,868	4,872	5,400	6,528	6,324	6,708	6,756	89.2

MERCHANT SHIPPING

Goods Unloaded in International Seaborne Trade 1977-1991

Units: '000 tonnes

	1977	1980	1985	1986	1987	1988	1989	1990	1991	% growth 1977/91
Japan										
Japan	582,305	612,726	603,277	597,936	621,108	666,864	703,236	711,612	725,124	24.5
ASEAN/NICs										
Brunei	609	631	920							
Hong Kong	19,116	24,623	37,226	42,984	47,664	53,376	51,264	52,272	61,968	224.2
Indonesia	13,908	18,987	16,830	20,304	23,081	22,284	28,212	30,840		
Macau	446	652	502							
Malaysia	14,551	20,281	22,809	18,420	20,880	24,468	27,204	29,304	31,572	117.0
Philippines	19,543	23,506	16,932	20,736	24,696	24,360	28,668	31,656	31,572	61.6
Singapore	40,471	48,550	59,237	67,116	71,304	84,168	97,308	106,224	116,484	187.8
South Korea	51,498	71,353	101,111	112,056	129,420	144,192	152,988	172,272	208,476	304.8
Taiwan			59,200	67,100						
Thailand	17,009	18,552	17,375	16,440	24,444	25,272				
East/SE Asia										
Cambodia		238	100	100						
China		40,870	70,680	71,136	71,136	67,536	82,404	74,172		
Laos										
Mongolia										
Myanmar	391	540	720	516	480	492	216	612	708	81.1
North Korea		4,820	4,640							
Vietnam		1,868	1,359							
Australasia										
Australia	25,416	26,220	23,582	23,304	20,520	29,208	34,440	31,200	33,180	30.5
New Zealand	10,411	10,425	8,299	5,952	7,368	6,912	7,836	8,316	7,860	-24.5
Pacific										
American Samoa		360	574	132	108	180	132	60	252	
Fiji	784	826	792	576						
French Polynesia	322	449	523	636	660	672	648			
Guam	2,217	83	169							
Kiribati	29	33	25							
Nauru	52	13	59							
New Caledonia	969	842	713							
Papua New Guinea	1,200	1,878	1,562							
Solomon Islands	58	92	305							
Tonga	44	61	55							
Tuvalu										
Vanuatu	51	43	61	62	76					
Western Samoa	93	67	87							
Middle East										
Bahrain	1,200	1,546	3,261							
Egypt	14,506	60,156	74,189	33,852	25,848		23,868	23,808		
Iran	15,046	9,302	12,205	12,700	12,600	12,500	12,400			
Iraq	3,650	8,638								
Israel	38,109	14,443	6,291	9,708	10,608	11,700	8,604	9,852	13,224	-65.3
Jordan	1,389	3,024	6,370	7,152	8,748	9,144	8,700	6,168		
Kuwait	5,500	6,437	7,253							
Lebanon	2,211	2,960	1,053							
Oman	1,545	1,769	4,028							
Qatar	1,845	1,578	2,127							
Saudi Arabia	13,316	25,020	37,521							
Syria	7,735	7,392	9,478	6,864	6,528	3,492	4,308	4,668	5,076	-34.4
United Arab Emirates	5,806	7,457	7,097							
Yemen	3,607	6,943	7,085							

MERCHANT SHIPPING   Table No. 2211 (cont'd)

Goods Unloaded in International Seaborne Trade 1977-1991

Units: '000 tonnes

	1977	1980	1985	1986	1987	1988	1989	1990	1991	% growth 1977/91
North Africa										
Algeria	12,828	14,431	18,972	18,241	16,081	13,900	14,200			
Chad										
Djibouti	900	795	780	753	800	840	890			
Ethiopia	1,067	1,695	2,587	2,885	2,935	3,100	3,200			
Libya	7,820	6,519	6,975							
Mali										
Mauritania	480	381	549	602	599	610	630			
Morocco	8,196	10,251	14,097	14,460	15,108	16,356	16,068	17,604	22,644	176.3
Niger										
Somalia	421	515	1,006	1,200	1,198	1,210	1,340			
Sudan	2,600	2,822	3,340	3,320	3,400	3,480	3,520			
Tunisia	5,743	8,274	6,233	7,860	8,124	10,020	9,900	10,056	9,732	69.5
West Africa										
Benin	973	868	943	910	1,011	1,100	1,200			
Burkina Faso										
Cameroon	1,699	2,394	3,417	3,192	3,402	3,600	3,800	2,448		
Cape Verde	195	149	451	455	472	490	520			
Côte d'Ivoire	4,728	4,918	4,874	4,810						
Equatorial Guinea	150	45	93	95	97	100	102			
Gabon	1,382	387	478	520	570	610	660			
Gambia	162	283	198	204	210	213				
Ghana	3,344	2,450	3,390	3,422	3,490	3,540	3,670			
Guinea	650	593	631	620	654					
Guinea-Bissau	65	104	129							
Liberia	1,330	2,016	1,729							
Nigeria	9,109	14,400	11,490							
Sao Tomé e Príncipe	40	22	19	21	21	22	23			
Senegal	2,337	1,691	2,580	2,491	2,570	2,690	2,710			
Sierra Leone	640	618	490	475	497	510	550			
Togo	516	1,966	688	649	678	750	790			
East/Central Africa										
Angola	1,900	884	980	1,065	1,150	1,230	1,310			
Burundi										
Central African Republic										
Comoros	50	41	98	100	103	107				
Congo	628	743	668	621	518	554	710			
Kenya	3,954	5,577	3,792	4,908	3,276	5,124				
Madagascar	958	1,151	845	768	768	1,100	1,230	984		
Maldives		45	70							
Mauritius	896	1,189	977	1,165	1,284	1,315	1,410			
Réunion	798	937	1,123							
Rwanda										
Seychelles	132	173	235	246	257	260	290			
Tanzania	2,432	3,155	2,602	2,800	2,902	3,100	3,200			
Uganda										
Zaire	1,202	954	779	900	1,200	1,400	1,500			
Southern Africa										
Botswana										
Lesotho										
Malawi										
Mozambique	2,000	4,558	2,427	2,700	2,900	3,100	3,200			
Namibia										
South Africa	25,495	26,128	26,679	9,336	10,440	13,440	95,904			
Swaziland										
Zambia										
Zimbabwe										

Source: UN
Notes: see end of section

Notes to Tables in Section Twenty-Two

Table 2201   Secondary roads include gravel roads
- a   Change in survey methodology
- b   Year ending 30 June
- c   As at 1 April
- d   Year ending 31 March

Table 2202
- a   New series starting 1984
- b   Fiscal year commencing 1st April
- c   Including taxis and passenger vans
- d   Urban traffic not included
- e   Including taxis and pick-up vans

Table 2203
- a   Class 1 Railroads only (approx. 96% of the total)

Table 2204
- a   Excluding commuter railroads from 1987
- b   Includes peninsular Malaysia and Singapore
- c   Included with Malaysia

Table 2205
- a   Includes peninsular Malaysia and Singapore
- b   Included with Malaysia
- c   Includes Namibia
- d   From 1980, includes National Railways of Zimbabwe traffic in Botswana

Table 2206
- a   CAB recognised majors and national carriers only
- b   New series starting 1981
- c   Includes a proportion of the traffic of multi-national Gulf Air
- d   Includes a proportion of the traffic of multi-national Air Afrique

Table 2207
- a   CAB recognised majors and national carriers only
- b   New series starting 1982
- c   Includes a proportion of the traffic of multi-national Gulf Air
- d   Includes a proportion of the traffic of multi-national Air Afrique

Table 2208   0.0 indicates less than 50,000
- a   CAB recognised majors and national carriers only
- b   Includes a proportion of the traffic of multi-national Gulf Air
- c   Includes a proportion of the traffic of multi-national Air Afrique

Table 2209
- a   Statistics refer to six months only
- b   Data refer to 1990
- c   Data refer to 1989
- d   Includes a proportion of the traffic of multi-national Gulf Air
- e   Includes a proportion of the traffic of multi-national Air Afrique

Table 2210
- a   New series starting 1981
- b   New series starting 1986

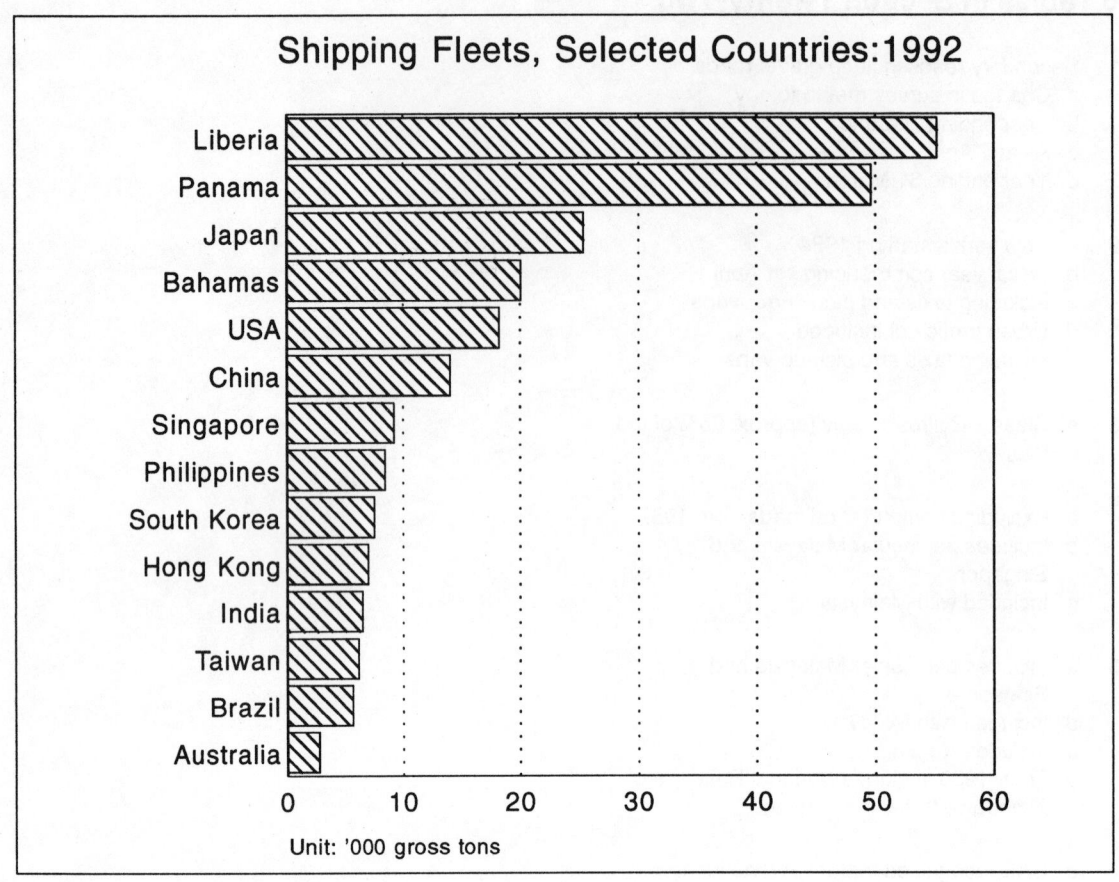

Shipping Fleets, Selected Countries:1992

Liberia
Panama
Japan
Bahamas
USA
China
Singapore
Philippines
South Korea
Hong Kong
India
Taiwan
Brazil
Australia

0   10   20   30   40   50   60

Unit: '000 gross tons

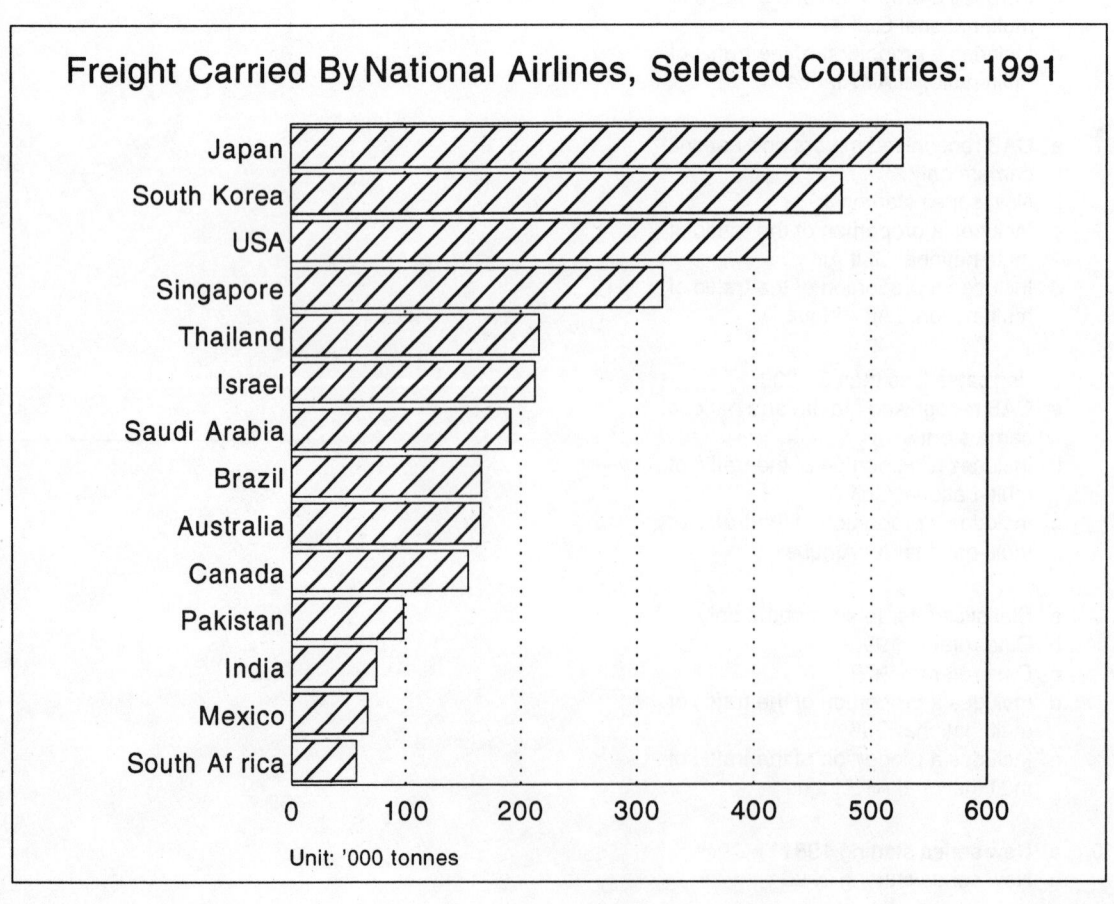

Freight Carried By National Airlines, Selected Countries: 1991

Japan
South Korea
USA
Singapore
Thailand
Israel
Saudi Arabia
Brazil
Australia
Canada
Pakistan
India
Mexico
South Africa

0   100   200   300   400   500   600

Unit: '000 tonnes

Section Twenty-Three
Travel and Tourism

| **TOURISM RECEIPTS** | **Table No. 2301** |

Trends in Tourism Receipts 1985-1991

Units: Million current US dollars

	1985	1986	1987	1988	1989	1990	1991	% growth 1985-91
North America								
Canada [a]	3,103	3,860	3,961	4,603	5,014	5,231	5,537	78.4
USA	17,937	20,454	23,505	28,935	34,432	40,579	45,551	153.9
South America								
Argentina	523	545	614	634	790	1,975	2,336	346.7
Bolivia	30	35	40	65	75	85	90	200.0
Brazil	1,739	1,527	1,502	1,643	1,225	1,559		
Chile	123	183	175	205	407	540	700	469.1
Colombia	287	221	213	461	252	270	410	42.9
Ecuador	133	133	167	173	187	188	189	42.1
French Guiana								
Guyana	18	19	24	30	30	30	30	66.7
Paraguay	105	148	121	114	112	112	145	38.1
Peru	231	302	353	448	402	398	277	19.9
Suriname	5	6	4	8	8	11	11	120.0
Uruguay	235	258	208	203	228	262	333	41.7
Venezuela	416	444	416	291	389	359	365	-12.3
Caribbean								
Anguilla	12	13	19	24	28	35	36	200.0
Antigua	133	156	191	242	267	298	314	136.1
Aruba	117	158	204	276	314	401		
Bahamas	995	1,105	1,146	1,149	1,230	1,333	1,222	22.8
Barbados	309	327	379	459	505	453		
Bermuda	357	422	468	441	451	490	454	27.2
British Virgin Islands	68	89	111	121	125	132		
Cayman Islands	86	93	120	179	180	326	437	408.1
Cuba [b]	96	123	145	189	204	246	300	212.5
Dominica	10	10	11	14	19	25	28	180.0
Dominican Republic	368	464	571	768	818	900	877	138.3
Grenada	26	29	30	29	31	38	42	61.5
Guadeloupe	95	163	188	220	183	231	284	198.9
Haiti	93	82	60	50	50	46	46	-50.5
Jamaica	407	516	595	525	593	740	764	87.7
Martinique	93	108	210	230	272	240	255	174.2
Netherlands Antilles	233	265	280					
St Kitts	31	38	47	54	60	63	74	138.7
St Lucia	56	73	78	152	145	154	173	208.9
St Vincent/Grenadines	23	29	35	39	43	54	53	130.4
Trinidad and Tobago	97	83	92	81	81	95	101	4.1
Central America								
Belize	12	41	47	48	79	91	95	691.7
Costa Rica	118	133	136	165	207	275	331	180.5
El Salvador	43	41	43	61	63	145	157	265.1
Guatemala	67	77	103	124	152	185	211	214.9
Honduras	25	26	26	28	28	29	31	24.0
Mexico	2,900	2,984	3,499	2,902	3,388	3,934	4,355	50.2
Nicaragua	7	8	9	5	4	12	17	142.9
Panama	200	205	188	168	157	167	196	-2.0
Puerto Rico	758	793	955	1,112	1,235	1,367	1,445	90.6
South Asia								
Afghanistan	1	1	1	1				
Bangladesh	23	14	12	13	18	11	9	-60.9
Bhutan	1	1	1	1	2	2		
India	980	1,260	1,430	1,500	1,535	1,437	1,310	33.7
Nepal	39	51	82	94	106	109	126	223.1
Pakistan	186	180	178	147	169	146	163	-12.4
Sri Lanka	82	82	82	77	76	132	156	90.2

TOURISM RECEIPTS   Table No. 2301 (cont'd)

Trends in Tourism Receipts 1985-1991

Units: Million current US dollars

	1985	1986	1987	1988	1989	1990	1991	% growth 1985-91
Japan								
Japan	1,137	1,463	2,097	2,893	3,143	3,578	3,435	202.1
ASEAN/NICs								
Brunei	19	22	25	30	32			
Hong Kong [c]	1,788	2,211	3,184	4,166	4,595	5,032	5,078	184.0
Indonesia	548	647	924	1,283	1,628	2,153	2,515	358.9
Macau	150		686	851	1,087	1,371	1,643	995.3
Malaysia	622	648	690	745	1,038	1,667	1,530	146.0
Philippines [d]	994	1,006	1,029	1,301	1,465	1,306	1,281	28.9
Singapore	1,660	1,767	2,088	2,622	3,307	4,719	5,020	202.4
South Korea	784	1,550	2,299	3,265	3,556	3,559	3,426	337.0
Taiwan	963	1,333	1,619	2,289	2,698	1,740	2,018	109.6
Thailand	1,171	1,421	1,947	3,120	3,754	4,326	3,923	235.0
East/SE Asia								
Cambodia	2							
China [e]	979	1,531	1,693	1,797	1,861	2,218	2,845	190.6
Laos	4	4						
Mongolia								
Myanmar		10	12	8	3	9	13	
North Korea	10	10						
Vietnam		26	30	35	59			
Australasia								
Australia	1,062	1,300	2,105	3,315	3,157	3,660	4,183	293.9
New Zealand	413	622	935	1,014	1,005	1,019	1,021	147.2
Pacific								
American Samoa	7	6	7	8	9	10	10	42.9
Fiji	147	163	121	131	199	227	211	43.5
French Polynesia	98	146	150	157	138	171	150	53.1
Guam	231	308	580	706	804	936	1,093	373.2
Kiribati	1	1	1	1	1	2	2	100.0
Nauru								
New Caledonia			64	65	112			
Papua New Guinea	10	18	21	25	40	42	47	370.0
Solomon Islands	3	3	6	5	5	4	5	66.7
Tonga	5	7	9	9	9	9	10	100.0
Tuvalu								
Vanuatu	19	14	14	18	16	25	30	57.9
Western Samoa	7	9	9	16	17	20	18	157.1
Middle East								
Bahrain	175	83	101	114	116	135	162	-7.4
Egypt [f]	901	785	1,586	1,784	1,646	1,994	2,029	125.2
Iran	27	27	26	25	37	62		
Iraq	181	84	62	61	59			
Israel	1,101	971	1,342	1,347	1,468	1,382	1,306	18.6
Jordan	518	533	579	626	546	511	317	-38.8
Kuwait	103	86	75	108	123	80		
Lebanon								
Oman [g]	52	47	47	49	56	69	63	21.2
Qatar	120							
Saudi Arabia	2,378	2,000	2,600	2,066	2,050			
Syria	395	363	204	332	290	270	300	-24.1
United Arab Emirates	4	4						
Yemen	106	47	48	21	26	20	21	-80.2

TOURISM RECEIPTS

Table No. 2301 (cont'd)

Trends in Tourism Receipts 1985-1991

Units: Million current US dollars

	1985	1986	1987	1988	1989	1990	1991	% growth 1985-91
North Africa								
Algeria	91	137	100	85	64	64		
Chad	7	5	6	7	9	12	10	42.9
Djibouti	5	6	6	5				
Ethiopia	9	5	15	19	21	26	20	122.2
Libya	3	3	3	3				
Mali	25	31	37	38	28	24	12	-52.0
Mauritania	5	8	14	14				
Morocco	606	739	933	1,110	1,146	1,259	1,052	73.6
Niger	6	7	9	11	14	17	16	166.7
Somalia	8	8						
Sudan	62	14	14	29	45	21	8	-87.1
Tunisia	551	488	672	1,234	933	953	685	24.3
West Africa								
Benin	9	14	39	40	20	28	29	222.2
Burkina Faso	5	7	4	5	6	8	8	60.0
Cameroon [g]	45	47	25	21	17	21	15	-66.7
Cape Verde								
Côte d'Ivoire	36	52	59	60	44	48	46	27.8
Equatorial Guinea								
Gabon	9	13	5	7	4	4	8	-11.1
Gambia	19	23	14	23	19	26	26	36.8
Ghana	20	27	36	55	72	81	118	490.0
Guinea								
Guinea-Bissau								
Liberia	6	6						
Nigeria	33	147	77	53	21	25	39	18.2
Sao Tomé e Príncipe	1	1	1	1				
Senegal	85	115	130	147	142	168	171	101.2
Sierra Leone	7	10	14	15	17	19		
Togo	25	34	35	44	41	50	50	100.0
East/Central Africa								
Angola								
Burundi	1	1	1	2	3	4	4	300.0
Central African Republic	2	5	9	8				
Comoros	2	3	3	3	3	2	9	350.0
Congo	6	6	7	6	7	8	7	16.7
Kenya	249	304	354	376	400	443	424	70.3
Madagascar	5	5	10	23	29	43	26	420.0
Maldives	41	43	44	50	66	82	87	112.2
Mauritius	55	88	138	172	183	264	262	376.4
Réunion			169					
Rwanda	7	7	7	7	9			
Seychelles	51	56	67	81	91	120	99	94.1
Tanzania	20	27	31	40	60	65	95	375.0
Uganda	2	3	5	8	9	10	15	650.0
Zaire	8	14	18	7	6	7		
Southern Africa								
Botswana	24	40	49	38	54	65		
Lesotho	7	7	11	12	13	17	18	157.1
Malawi	5	8	9	10	13	11		
Mozambique								
Namibia	15							
South Africa	425	414	589	673	709	1,029	1,046	146.1
Swaziland	13	14	20	22	25	25	26	100.0
Zambia	8	7	6	5	12	41	35	337.5
Zimbabwe	26	29	43	54	40	47		

Source: World Tourism Organisation (WTO), Yearbook of Tourism Statistics
Notes: see end of section

TOURISM EXPENDITURE

Table No. 2302

Trends in Tourism Expenditure 1985-1991

Units: Million current US dollars

	1985	1986	1987	1988	1989	1990	1991	% growth 1985-91
North America								
Canada [a]	4,130	4,294	5,304	6,316	7,370	9,794	10,526	154.9
USA	24,517	26,000	29,215	33,098	34,977	38,671	39,418	60.8
South America								
Argentina	671	853	894	975	1,069	1,171	1,739	159.2
Bolivia	30	27	56	55	59	60	63	110.0
Brazil	1,145	1,464	1,249	1,084	751	1,559	1,224	6.9
Chile	269	319	351	423	397	426	409	52.0
Colombia	169	341	455	536	383	411	593	250.9
Ecuador	196	210	170	167	169	175	177	-9.7
French Guiana								
Guyana								
Paraguay	47	48	51	54	50	58	122	159.6
Peru [b]	163	184	335	344	417	770	881	440.5
Suriname	13	12	8	10	10	12		
Uruguay	162	174	129	138	167	111	100	-38.3
Venezuela	597	543	509	509	640	945	1,011	69.3
Caribbean								
Anguilla								
Antigua	13	14	15	16	16	17	18	38.5
Aruba	17	16	17	27	29	40	47	176.5
Bahamas	123	131	152	171	184	196	205	66.7
Barbados	23	29	28	37	45	47	44	91.3
Bermuda [c]	76	81	77	93	104	119	126	65.8
British Virgin Islands								
Cayman Islands								
Cuba						246		
Dominica	3	3	2	2	4	4		
Dominican Republic	84	90	95	127	136	144	154	83.3
Grenada	3	4	4	5	4	5		
Guadeloupe								
Haiti	43	37	42	34	33	32	33	-23.3
Jamaica	32	35	44	57	54	54	54	68.8
Martinique								
Netherlands Antilles								
St Kitts	5	2	3	3	3	4	4	-20.0
St Lucia		15	15	21	21	18	17	
St Vincent/Grenadines	7	4	4	4	5	7	7	
Trinidad and Tobago	219	165	158	168	119	122	111	-49.3
Central America								
Belize	5	5	5	7	8	7	8	60.0
Costa Rica	53	60	71	72	114	148	149	181.1
El Salvador	89	74	76	75	60	55	60	-32.6
Guatemala	61	82	95	109	126	100	67	9.8
Honduras	27	30	35	37	38	38	37	37.0
Mexico	2,262	2,132	2,366	1,323	1,750	2,171	2,146	-5.1
Nicaragua	6	4	6	2	1	15	28	366.7
Panama	65	73	90	88	86	99	108	66.2
Puerto Rico	411	416	488	533	589	672	798	94.2
South Asia								
Afghanistan	2	1	1	1				
Bangladesh	45	54	52	99	123	78	83	84.4
Bhutan								
India	354	302	352	397	416			
Nepal	29	29	35	43	48	45	38	31.0
Pakistan	202	220	248	338	337	440	555	174.8
Sri Lanka	46	55	63	68	69	79	92	100.0

TOURISM EXPENDITURE   Table No. 2302 (cont'd)

Trends in Tourism Expenditure 1985-1991

Units: Million current US dollars

	1985	1986	1987	1988	1989	1990	1991	% growth 1985-91
Japan								
Japan	4,814	7,229	10,760	18,682	22,490	24,928	23,983	398.2
ASEAN/NICs								
Brunei								
Hong Kong								
Indonesia	591	590	511	592	722	836	949	60.6
Macau			24	26	30	38	42	
Malaysia	1,158	1,178	1,234	1,263	1,377	1,492	1,503	29.8
Philippines	37	56	88	76	77	111	61	64.9
Singapore	613	645	795	930	1,334	1,821	2,019	229.4
South Korea	606	613	704	1,354	2,602	3,166	3,784	524.4
Taiwan						4,984	5,678	
Thailand	280	296	381	602	750	854	1,266	352.1
East/SE Asia								
Cambodia								
China	314	308	387	633	429	448	417	32.8
Laos								
Mongolia								
Myanmar		1	1	1	2	2	1	
North Korea								
Vietnam								
Australasia								
Australia	1,918	2,058	2,427	2,933	3,859	4,148	3,940	105.4
New Zealand	389	506	852	1,253	1,252	1,335	1,408	262.0
Pacific								
American Samoa								
Fiji	18	24	53	35	41	41	45	150.0
French Polynesia								
Guam	226	304	589	589				
Kiribati								
Nauru								
New Caledonia								
Papua New Guinea	21	22	32	48	42			
Solomon Islands	4	6	6	9	9	11	13	225.0
Tonga	3	3	3	3	3	1	2	-33.3
Tuvalu								
Vanuatu	2	2	1	2	1	1	1	-50.0
Western Samoa	1	2	2	1	2	2	2	100.0
Middle East								
Bahrain	125	59	80	77	77	94	98	-21.6
Egypt	106	52	78	43	87	129	225	112.3
Iran	508	247	246	69				
Iraq								
Israel	549	801	1,043	1,161	1,288	1,485	1,783	224.8
Jordan	424	445	444	480	419	336	281	-33.7
Kuwait	1,988	1,941	2,257	2,358	2,318		3,784	90.3
Lebanon								
Oman			47	47	47	47		
Qatar								
Saudi Arabia								
Syria	302	260	131	257	190	200	210	-30.5
United Arab Emirates	409	409						
Yemen	67	27	37	47	81			

TOURISM EXPENDITURE

Table No. 2302 (cont'd)

Trends in Tourism Expenditure 1985-1991

Units: Million current US dollars

	1985	1986	1987	1988	1989	1990	1991	% growth 1985-91
North Africa								
Algeria	606	440	239	296	212	149		
Chad	20	30	47	32	33	36	32	60.0
Djibouti								
Ethiopia	4	5	4	6	10	11		
Libya	487	213	213	210				
Mali	37	49	57	58	56	62	60	62.2
Mauritania	17	18	26	27				
Morocco	88	100	132	164	153	184	190	115.9
Niger	9		34	35	32	44	40	344.4
Somalia								
Sudan	43	32	35	99	144	51	12	-72.1
Tunisia	126	107	158	168	119	112	111	-11.9
West Africa								
Benin	7	9	12	13	10	12	10	42.9
Burkina Faso	20	19	28	30	30	35	34	70.0
Cameroon	130	205	244	283				
Cape Verde								
Côte d'Ivoire	106	195	233	235	216	246	223	110.4
Equatorial Guinea								
Gabon	83	131	132	134	124	143	152	83.1
Gambia	2	2	3	5	5	8		
Ghana	10	11	12	12	13	13		
Guinea								
Guinea-Bissau								
Liberia								
Nigeria	200	90	55	41	416	576	839	319.5
Sao Tomé e Príncipe	1	1	1	1				
Senegal	38	49	55	76	72	105	103	171.1
Sierra Leone	1	6	17	7	3			
Togo	22	27	29	32	37	46	48	118.2
East/Central Africa								
Angola								
Burundi	9	14	17	15	14	16	17	88.9
Central African Republic	24	31	41	41				
Comoros	7	13	5	5	5	6	7	
Congo	63	67	79	126	86	114	93	47.6
Kenya	15	22	24	23	27	38	24	60.0
Madagascar	24	31	26	30	38	40	32	33.3
Maldives	5	6	6	8	10	15	18	260.0
Mauritius	19	26	51	64	79	94	110	478.9
Réunion								
Rwanda	11	14	15	16	16			
Seychelles	9	10	12	13	17	20	12	33.3
Tanzania	16	15	23	23	25	19		
Uganda		9	13	11	10	8	18	
Zaire	35	45	22	16	17	16		
Southern Africa								
Botswana	17	19	26	32	34	39		
Lesotho	5	8	9	11	10	12	11	120.0
Malawi	8	7	6					
Mozambique								
Namibia								
South Africa	413	603	838	958	936	1,065	1,047	153.5
Swaziland	11	12	14	18	10	14	20	81.8
Zambia	22	31	46	49	98			
Zimbabwe	58	38	48	58				

Source: WTO, Yearbook of Tourism Statistics
Notes: see end of section

TOURIST ARRIVALS | Table No. 2303

Trends in Foreign Tourist Arrivals at Frontiers 1987-1991

Units: '000

	1987	1988	1989	1990	1991	% growth 1987-91
North America						
Canada	14,975	15,493	15,111	15,258	14,989	0.1
USA	29,658	33,875	36,604	39,772	42,723	44.1
South America						
Argentina	1,950	2,119	2,492	2,728	2,870	47.2
Bolivia [a]	147	167	194	217	221	50.3
Brazil	1,929	1,743	1,403	1,091	1,352	-29.9
Chile	575	624	797	943	1,349	134.6
Colombia	541	829	733	813	857	58.4
Ecuador	274	347	335	362	365	33.2
French Guiana						
Guyana [b]	60	71	67	64	73	21.7
Paraguay	303	284	279	280	361	19.1
Peru	330	359	334	317	232	-29.7
Suriname [c]	27	21	21	28	30	11.1
Uruguay [b,d]	1,047	1,035	1,240	1,267	1,510	44.2
Venezuela	615	675	412	525	598	-2.8
Caribbean						
Anguilla	21	28	29	31	31	47.6
Antigua	173	187	189	197	197	13.9
Aruba	232	278	345	433	501	115.9
Bahamas	1,480	1,475	1,575	1,562	1,427	-3.6
Barbados	422	451	461	432	394	-6.6
Bermuda	478	427	418	435	386	-19.2
British Virgin Islands	176	176	176	160	147	-16.5
Cayman Islands [e]	209	219	210	253	237	13.4
Cuba	282	298	314	327	408	44.7
Dominica	27	34	37	45	46	70.4
Dominican Republic [d,e]	902	1,116	1,400	1,533	1,321	46.5
Grenada	57	62	69	76	85	49.1
Guadeloupe [a]	293	329	284	288	303	3.4
Haiti	122	133	122	120	119	-2.5
Jamaica	739	649	715	841	845	14.3
Martinique	234	280	312	282	315	34.6
Netherlands Antilles						
St Kitts	66	70	72	76	84	27.3
St Lucia	118	133	135	147	165	39.8
St Vincent/Grenadines [e]	46	47	50	54	52	13.0
Trinidad and Tobago [e]	202	186	194	195	220	8.9
Central America						
Belize	108	151	182	230	223	106.5
Costa Rica	278	329	376	435	505	81.7
El Salvador	125	134	131	194	199	59.2
Guatemala	353	405	437	509	513	45.3
Honduras	158	162	176	202	198	25.3
Mexico		14,142	14,964	17,176	16,560	
Nicaragua	49	55	77	106	146	198.0
Panama	271	199	192	214	279	3.0
Puerto Rico [a]	1,872	2,077	2,450	2,554	2,626	40.3
South Asia						
Afghanistan	9	9				
Bangladesh	107	121	128	115	113	5.6
Bhutan	3	2	2	2	2	-33.3
India [f]	1,484	1,591	1,736	1,707	1,678	13.1
Nepal	248	265	240	255	293	18.1
Pakistan	425	460	495	424	438	3.1
Sri Lanka	183	183	185	298	318	73.8

TOURIST ARRIVALS   **Table No. 2303** (cont'd)

Trends in Foreign Tourist Arrivals at Frontiers 1987-1991

Units: '000

	1987	1988	1989	1990	1991	% growth 1987-91
Japan						
Japan [g]	1,069	1,116	1,499	1,879	2,104	96.8
ASEAN/NICs						
Brunei	523	457	393	377		
Hong Kong [b]	4,502	5,589	5,361	5,933	6,032	34.0
Indonesia [b]	1,060	1,301	1,626	2,178	2,570	142.5
Macau [b,h]				2,513	3,047	
Malaysia [i]	3,359	3,624	4,846	7,446	5,847	74.1
Philippines	781	1,023	1,076	893	849	8.7
Singapore [j]	3,373	3,833	4,397	4,842	4,913	45.7
South Korea [b]	1,875	2,340	2,728	2,959	3,196	70.5
Taiwan	1,761	1,935	2,004	1,934	1,855	5.3
Thailand	3,843	4,231	4,810	5,299	5,087	32.4
East/SE Asia						
Cambodia						
China	26,902	31,695	24,501	27,462	33,350	24.0
Laos	25	25				
Mongolia	186	239	237	147		
Myanmar	48	26	14	21	21	-56.3
North Korea						
Vietnam	139	148	167			
Australasia						
Australia	1,784	2,249	2,080	2,215	2,370	32.8
New Zealand	844	865	901	976	963	14.1
Pacific						
American Samoa	38	39	47	47	37	-2.6
Fiji	190	208	251	279	259	36.3
French Polynesia	143	135	140	132	121	-15.4
Guam	484	586	667	780	737	52.3
Kiribati [b]	4	4	3	3	3	-25.0
Nauru						
New Caledonia [e]	60	61	82	87	81	35.0
Papua New Guinea	35	41	49	41	37	5.7
Solomon Islands	13	11	10	9	11	-15.4
Tonga	17	19	21	21	22	29.4
Tuvalu	1	1	1	1	1	
Vanuatu	15	18	24	35	40	166.7
Western Samoa [e]	46	46	55	48	39	-15.2
Middle East						
Bahrain	178	1,171	1,342	1,376	1,674	840.4
Egypt	1,671	1,833	2,351	2,411	2,112	26.4
Iran	69	67	89	154		
Iraq	739	277	1,025	748	268	-63.7
Israel [k]	1,379	1,170	1,177	1,063	943	-31.6
Jordan [b]	1,898	2,391	2,278	2,633	2,228	17.4
Kuwait	78	80	89	50		
Lebanon						
Oman [a]	112	126	136	149	161	43.8
Qatar	101	113	110	136	143	41.6
Saudi Arabia [b]	2,000	2,089	1,865	1,984	2,290	14.5
Syria [a]	493	421	411	562	622	26.2
United Arab Emirates [a]	584					
Yemen [a]	51	60	65	52	44	-13.7

TOURIST ARRIVALS   Table No. 2303 (cont'd)

Trends in Foreign Tourist Arrivals at Frontiers 1987-1991

Units: '000

	1987	1988	1989	1990	1991	% growth 1987-91
North Africa						
Algeria	778	967	851	1,317	1,193	53.3
Chad	27	21	12	9	21	-22.2
Djibouti	19	27				
Ethiopia [e]	73	76	77	79	82	12.3
Libya	97	98				
Mali [a]	34	36	32	44	38	11.8
Mauritania						
Morocco	2,248	2,841	3,468	4,024	4,162	85.1
Niger [e]	32	33	24	21	16	-50.0
Somalia	39	40				
Sudan	52	37	23	33	16	-69.2
Tunisia	1,875	3,468	3,222	3,204	3,224	71.9
West Africa						
Benin	81	75	75	110	117	44.4
Burkina Faso [a]	51	82	79	74	80	56.9
Cameroon	118	100	87	100	71	-39.8
Cape Verde						
Côte d'Ivoire [e]	175	181	192	196	200	14.3
Equatorial Guinea						
Gabon	21	20	113	108	128	509.5
Gambia	97	102	86	101	114	17.5
Ghana	103	114	125	146	172	67.0
Guinea						
Guinea-Bissau						
Liberia						
Nigeria	177	143	161	190		
Sao Tomé e Príncipe	1	1				
Senegal [a]	236	256	259	246		
Sierra Leone	88	75	86	103	118	34.1
Togo [a]	98	104	115	103		
East/Central Africa						
Angola						
Burundi	80	99	82	109	125	56.3
Central African Republic	5	5				
Comoros	8	8	13	8	17	112.5
Congo [a]	39	39	33	33	31	-20.5
Kenya [l]	661	695	735	814	822	24.4
Madagascar	28	35	39	53	35	25.0
Maldives [e]	131	156	158	195	196	49.6
Mauritius	208	240	263	292	301	44.7
Réunion			182	200	186	
Rwanda						
Seychelles	72	77	86	104	90	25.0
Tanzania	139	130	138	153	187	34.5
Uganda	37	40	41	69	69	86.5
Zaire	36	39	51			
Southern Africa						
Botswana [b]	432	384	691	844	899	108.1
Lesotho	135	110	169	171		
Malawi [l]	76	99	117	130	132	73.7
Mozambique						
Namibia						
South Africa	703	805	930	1,029	1,710	143.2
Swaziland	194	196	248	294	279	43.8
Zambia	121	108	113	141	171	41.3
Zimbabwe [g]	372	449	474	606	664	78.5

Source: WTO, Yearbook of Tourism Statistics
Notes: see end of section

TOURIST NIGHTS   Table No. 2304

Trends in Tourist Nights 1987-1991

Units: '000

	1987	1988	1989	1990	1991	% growth 1987-91
North America						
Canada	84,860	93,309	90,022	93,309		
USA	404,307	468,229				
South America						
Argentina						
Bolivia	494	566	644	710	738	49.4
Brazil	4,852	4,624	4,710	4,713		
Chile	1,008	1,039	1,348	1,561		
Colombia	1,239	1,248				
Ecuador						
French Guiana						
Guyana						
Paraguay	974	907	896	899	1,174	20.5
Peru	1,573	1,571	1,790	1,762		
Suriname						
Uruguay						
Venezuela	4,919	4,958	5,768			
Caribbean						
Anguilla						
Antigua						
Aruba	1,628	2,079	2,014	3,380	3,768	131.4
Bahamas	8,425	8,495	8,978	8,963	8,402	-0.3
Barbados	2,351	2,595	1,948	3,852		
Bermuda	3,118	3,063	2,982	2,739	2,538	-18.6
British Virgin Islands						
Cayman Islands	545	560				
Cuba	3,097	3,064	3,586			
Dominica						
Dominican Republic						
Grenada						
Guadeloupe	938	972	750	697	773	-17.6
Haiti [a]	1,495	1,475				
Jamaica	7,534	6,360	7,579	9,194	9,212	22.3
Martinique	843	898	898			
Netherlands Antilles						
St Kitts						
St Lucia						
St Vincent/Grenadines						
Trinidad and Tobago						
Central America						
Belize						
Costa Rica						
El Salvador	162	153	139	129	165	1.9
Guatemala	1,871	2,389	2,423	3,201	3,437	83.7
Honduras						
Mexico	47,934	54,961				
Nicaragua				79		
Panama	702	481	409	482		
Puerto Rico	2,574	2,793				
South Asia						
Afghanistan						
Bangladesh	1,378	1,359	1,671	1,499		
Bhutan	19	19				
India						
Nepal						
Pakistan	14,650	14,675				
Sri Lanka	2,414	2,305	1,970	3,225	3,633	50.5

TOURIST NIGHTS   Table No. 2304 (cont'd)

Trends in Tourist Nights 1987-1991

Units: '000

	1987	1988	1989	1990	1991	% growth 1987-91
Japan						
Japan	5,781	5,865	5,943			
ASEAN/NICs						
Brunei						
Hong Kong						
Indonesia	6,683	6,705				
Macau	1,861	1,871	1,659	2,293	2,273	22.1
Malaysia	2,395	2,401				
Philippines						
Singapore						
South Korea	6,146	8,288	8,010	9,952	9,483	54.3
Taiwan	11,769	12,855	13,789	12,494	12,782	8.6
Thailand	21,098	31,121	36,683	37,408		
East/SE Asia						
Cambodia						
China	5,097	21,557	15,586			
Laos						
Mongolia						
Myanmar	195	189	78	145	137	-29.7
North Korea						
Vietnam						
Australasia						
Australia	46,384	48,474	57,000	70,900		
New Zealand	17,021	18,329	18,858	20,654	19,289	13.3
Pacific						
American Samoa						
Fiji	1,579	1,730	2,272	2,416		
French Polynesia	855	831	886	917		
Guam		2,343	2,342	2,730	2,551	
Kiribati						
Nauru						
New Caledonia	198	326	383	415	431	117.7
Papua New Guinea	87	100	111	103	96	10.3
Solomon Islands	70					
Tonga						
Tuvalu						
Vanuatu	87	110	153	198		
Western Samoa						
Middle East						
Bahrain	752	696	726	657	834	10.9
Egypt	15,861	17,864	20,582	19,943	16,231	2.3
Iran [b]	264	425	481			
Iraq						
Israel	8,941	7,116	7,030	6,167	4,663	-47.8
Jordan [c]						
Kuwait	303	320	334			
Lebanon						
Oman	258	300	394	544		
Qatar	184	226	238	795	255	38.6
Saudi Arabia						
Syria	1,453	1,240	1,278	1,706	1,715	18.0
United Arab Emirates	1,553					
Yemen	320	334	275	207	175	-45.3

TOURIST NIGHTS

Table No. 2304 (cont'd)

Trends in Tourist Nights 1987-1991

Units: '000

	1987	1988	1989	1990	1991	% growth 1987-91
North Africa						
Algeria						
Chad	14	17	16	17		
Djibouti	61	60				
Ethiopia						
Libya						
Mali	123	134	121	115	81	-34.1
Mauritania						
Morocco	8,424	8,782	8,876	8,367	5,313	-36.9
Niger	78	122	127	105	71	-9.0
Somalia						
Sudan						
Tunisia	17,516	19,602	19,011	18,814	12,443	-29.0
West Africa						
Benin	311	274	314	406	505	62.4
Burkina Faso	110	143	141	133		
Cameroon	304	262	207	254	154	-49.3
Cape Verde						
Côte d'Ivoire [d]	411	391	366	231	262	-36.3
Equatorial Guinea						
Gabon	969	462				
Gambia	501					
Ghana	724	1,024	1,126	1,314		
Guinea						
Guinea-Bissau						
Liberia						
Nigeria						
Sao Tomé e Príncipe						
Senegal [b]	1,027	1,099	1,038	1,068		
Sierra Leone	175	144	377	377	377	115.4
Togo						
East/Central Africa						
Angola						
Burundi	54	48	48	47	58	7.4
Central African Republic						
Comoros	25	20				
Congo	117	127	112	109	105	-10.3
Kenya	3,992	4,090	4,296	5,002	5,422	35.8
Madagascar [e]	183	214	229	173		
Maldives [b]	1,268	1,507	1,462	1,682	1,725	36.0
Mauritius [b]	2,372	3,003	3,197	3,565	3,608	52.1
Réunion						
Rwanda						
Seychelles	817	851	921	1,048	945	15.7
Tanzania	1,470	1,477	1,315	1,265	1,543	5.0
Uganda	19					
Zaire [b]	193	315	330			
Southern Africa						
Botswana	714					
Lesotho						
Malawi [b]	755	834	1,009	1,178		
Mozambique						
Namibia						
South Africa						
Swaziland						
Zambia						
Zimbabwe	842	975	1,144	1,222	1,326	57.5

Source: WTO, Yearbook of Tourism Statistics
Notes: see end of section

LENGTH OF TOURIST STAY   Table No. 2305

Trends in Average Length of Tourist Stay 1987-1991

Units: Days

	1987	1988	1989	1990	1991	% growth 1987-91
North America						
Canada	6	6	6			
USA						
South America						
Argentina						
Bolivia	7	7	7	7	7	-8.5
Brazil	14	17	16	14		
Chile	10	10	11	12	12	17.0
Colombia	11					
Ecuador	9					
French Guiana						
Guyana						
Paraguay	4	4	4	4	4	
Peru	15	16	14	13		
Suriname	29	29				
Uruguay	12	10		10		
Venezuela	8	8	8			
Caribbean						
Anguilla	8	9	10	11	10	37.3
Antigua						
Aruba	7	7	8	8	8	7.1
Bahamas	6	6	6	6	6	
Barbados	10	11	12	11	11	9.0
Bermuda	6	7	8	6	7	10.0
British Virgin Islands	7	7	7	9	10	35.7
Cayman Islands	5	5	5	5	5	8.9
Cuba	10	10	9			
Dominica		9	10	11		
Dominican Republic	8	9	9			
Grenada	9					
Guadeloupe	6					
Haiti						
Jamaica	10	10	11	11	11	6.9
Martinique	5	5			4	-31.4
Netherlands Antilles	5					
St Kitts			7	9	8	
St Lucia						
St Vincent/Grenadines						
Trinidad and Tobago						
Central America						
Belize	6					
Costa Rica	6	7	7	9	9	61.8
El Salvador	4				4	4.9
Guatemala	5	6	6	6	7	34.0
Caribbean						
Honduras	4					
Central America						
Mexico	10	11	11	11	11	8.2
Nicaragua						
Panama	9	9	9	10		
Puerto Rico	3	2	3			
South Asia						
Afghanistan						
Bangladesh	13	13			13	
Bhutan		9	9			
India	30	30	30	30		
Nepal						
Pakistan	37	30	30	30	30	-18.9
Sri Lanka	13	13	11	11	11	-13.6

Trends in Average Length of Tourist Stay 1987-1991

Units: Days

	1987	1988	1989	1990	1991	% growth 1987-91
Japan						
Japan	13	16	14	13	12	-5.4
ASEAN/NICs						
Brunei	7	7	7	9	10	33.8
Hong Kong	4	3	4	3		
Indonesia	13	12		12	12	-7.1
Macau	1	2	1	1	1	
Malaysia	5	5	5	5	5	2.2
Philippines	9	12	12	12	12	34.8
Singapore	3	3	3	3	3	-5.9
South Korea	6	5	5	6	5	-8.8
Taiwan	7	7	7	7	7	5.8
Thailand	6	7	8	7		
East/SE Asia						
Cambodia						
China	3	2	3	2		
Laos						
Mongolia	7					
Myanmar	5	5	5	7	6	18.5
North Korea						
Vietnam	5	5	5			
Australasia						
Australia		28	30	32	29	
New Zealand	21	21	21	21	20	-4.8
Pacific						
American Samoa						
Fiji	8	9	9	9	9	3.6
French Polynesia	10	10	10	11		
Guam	4	4	4	4	4	-12.5
Kiribati						
Nauru						
New Caledonia	12	14	16			
Papua New Guinea	3	2	2	3	3	4.0
Solomon Islands	9	12				
Tonga						
Tuvalu					8	
Vanuatu	14					
Western Samoa						
Middle East						
Bahrain	1	1	2	1		
Egypt	9	9	8	8	7	-18.9
Iran	5	7	6			
Iraq				6		
Israel	19	21	20	18	22	16.1
Jordan	4	5	5	5	5	27.5
Kuwait					5	
Lebanon						
Oman						
Qatar						
Saudi Arabia						
Syria	1	1		3	3	133.3
United Arab Emirates						
Yemen	5	5	5	4		

LENGTH OF TOURIST STAY — Table No. 2305 (cont'd)

Trends in Average Length of Tourist Stay 1987-1991

Units: Days

	1987	1988	1989	1990	1991	% growth 1987-91
North Africa						
Algeria	3			2	2	-21.4
Chad	3	3	4	4	4	23.3
Djibouti						
Ethiopia		7	6	5		
Libya						
Mali						
Mauritania						
Morocco	11	10	10	9		
Niger	4			13	13	230.0
Somalia						
Sudan	4					
Tunisia	9	6	6	6	4	-58.1
West Africa						
Benin	4	4	4	4	5	25.0
Burkina Faso	2	2	2	3	2	14.3
Cameroon	2	2	2	2	2	15.8
Cape Verde						
Côte d'Ivoire						
Equatorial Guinea						
Gabon	12	12				
Gambia	12	12	13	13	13	4.9
Ghana	7	9	9	9		
Guinea						
Guinea-Bissau						
Liberia						
Nigeria						
Sao Tomé e Príncipe						
Senegal						
Sierra Leone						
Togo						
East/Central Africa						
Angola						
Burundi						
Central African Republic						
Comoros						
Congo						
Kenya						
Madagascar	10	16				
Maldives						
Mauritius	11	13	12	12	12	5.3
Réunion			17	17	19	
Rwanda						
Seychelles	11	11	11	10	11	-7.9
Tanzania						
Uganda				5	15	
Zaire	15	15				
Southern Africa						
Botswana	5	5	5	5	5	-4.1
Lesotho	2	2	2	2		
Malawi	10	8	9	9		
Mozambique						
Namibia						
South Africa						
Swaziland	3		3			
Zambia [a]	13	16	12	11	11	-15.4
Zimbabwe	7	6	6	6	6	-13.4

Source: WTO, Yearbook of Tourism Statistics
Notes: see end of section

ACCOMMODATION CAPACITY
Table No. 2306

Trends in Number of Tourist Beds in Hotels and Similar Accommodation 1987-1991

Units: '000

	1987	1988	1989	1990	1991	% growth 1987-91
North America						
Canada						
USA [a]	5,355	5,541	5,602	5,459	5,544	3.5
South America						
Argentina	262	262	265	265	265	1.1
Bolivia	16	18	18	19		
Brazil	250	265	265	274	276	10.4
Chile	48	49	59	57	62	29.2
Colombia	76	86	90	91		
Ecuador	45	46	47	56	58	28.9
French Guiana						
Guyana						
Paraguay	9	10	10	10	10	11.1
Peru	77	86	89	91	92	19.5
Suriname	4	4	4	4		
Uruguay	26			28		
Venezuela	103	114	126	137	143	38.8
Caribbean						
Anguilla						
Antigua					7	
Aruba	6	6	7	7	10	66.7
Bahamas	28	28	28	27	26	-7.1
Barbados	14	14	14	15	15	7.1
Bermuda	10	9	9	9	9	-10.0
British Virgin Islands						
Cayman Islands	5	4	5	6	7	40.0
Cuba	34	34	35			
Dominica						
Dominican Republic	25	33	38			
Grenada	2	2	2	2	2	
Guadeloupe						
Haiti	3					
Jamaica	28	28	30	33	35	25.0
Martinique						
Netherlands Antilles						
St Kitts	2	3	3	4	4	100.0
St Lucia	2	2	2	2	3	50.0
St Vincent/Grenadines						
Trinidad and Tobago						
Central America						
Belize	3	3	4	4	5	66.7
Costa Rica						
El Salvador	6	6	6	6	6	
Guatemala	19	20	20	22	23	21.1
Honduras	10	10	11	11	12	20.0
Mexico	611	621	644	667	690	12.9
Nicaragua			6	6		
Panama	9	9	9	9		
Puerto Rico	14	15	16	16	16	14.3
South Asia						
Afghanistan						
Bangladesh	6	6	6	6	6	
Bhutan	10	9	9	9	9	-10.0
India	69	73	85	89	89	29.0
Nepal	7	8	9	10	11	57.1
Pakistan	32	33	35	37	39	21.9
Sri Lanka	22	21	20	21	21	-4.5

ACCOMMODATION CAPACITY

Table No. 2306 (cont'd)

Trends in Number of Tourist Beds in Hotels and Similar Accommodation 1987-1991

Units: '000

	1987	1988	1989	1990	1991	% growth 1987-91
Japan						
Japan						
ASEAN/NICs						
Brunei						
Hong Kong	10	10	11	12	12	20.0
Indonesia						
Macau	9	9	10	10	10	11.1
Malaysia						
Philippines	30	35	28	27	27	-10.0
Singapore	50					
South Korea	55	66	72	81	85	54.5
Taiwan	38					
Thailand						
East/SE Asia						
Cambodia						
China	401	478	581	634	679	69.3
Laos						
Mongolia				10		
Myanmar	2	3	3	2	3	50.0
North Korea						
Vietnam			15			
Australasia						
Australia	369	403	422	451	465	26.0
New Zealand						
Pacific						
American Samoa			1	1	1	
Fiji	11	11	11	11	12	9.1
French Polynesia	6	6	6	6	6	
Guam						
Kiribati						
Nauru						
New Caledonia						
Papua New Guinea				5	5	
Solomon Islands		1	1	1	1	
Tonga				1	1	
Tuvalu						
Vanuatu	1	1	1	1	1	
Western Samoa				1	1	
Middle East						
Bahrain	4	4	4	5		
Egypt	62	70	82	94	105	69.4
Iran [b]	32	31	31			
Iraq			123	103	74	
Israel	68	66	69	65	60	-11.8
Jordan	14	14	15	15	16	14.3
Kuwait					85	
Lebanon						
Oman	3	3	3	3	3	
Qatar	3	3	3	2	2	-33.3
Saudi Arabia	45					
Syria	27	27	29	29	30	11.1
United Arab Emirates	16					
Yemen	8	7	7	8	9	12.5

ACCOMMODATION CAPACITY

Table No. 2306 (cont'd)

Trends in Number of Tourist Beds in Hotels and Similar Accommodation 1987-1991

Units: '000

	1987	1988	1989	1990	1991	% growth 1987-91
North Africa						
Algeria	48			54	55	14.6
Chad						
Djibouti		2				
Ethiopia	5	5	5	6	5	
Libya						
Mali	2	1	2	2	2	
Mauritania						
Morocco	94	97	103	111	116	23.4
Niger	2	2	3	3	3	50.0
Somalia						
Sudan	9	9	8	7		
Tunisia	100	105	110	117	123	23.0
West Africa						
Benin	3	3	3	3	3	
Burkina Faso	4	4	4	4	4	
Cameroon	10	10	11	11	11	10.0
Cape Verde						
Côte d'Ivoire	12	12	12	12		
Equatorial Guinea						
Gabon	4	4				
Gambia	4	5	5	5		
Ghana		7	9	9		
Guinea						
Guinea-Bissau						
Liberia						
Nigeria						
Sao Tomé e Príncipe						
Senegal	12	12	12	12		
Sierra Leone	2	2	2	2	4	100.0
Togo						
East/Central Africa						
Angola						
Burundi [b]	1	1	1	1	1	
Central African Republic						
Comoros			1	1	1	
Congo	3	3				
Kenya	26	27	27	26	26	
Madagascar	4	5	8			
Maldives	7	8	8	8		
Mauritius	6	7	7	10	10	66.7
Réunion	2	2	2	3	3	50.0
Rwanda						
Seychelles	3	3	3	4	4	33.3
Tanzania	9	10	9	10	10	11.1
Uganda				4	5	
Zaire	15	28	27			
Southern Africa						
Botswana	2	2	2	2		
Lesotho [b]	1	2	2	2	2	100.0
Malawi	1	1	1			
Mozambique						
Namibia	3	3				
South Africa [b]	91	89	87	88	89	-2.2
Swaziland	2	2	2	2	2	
Zambia	6	6	6	6	7	16.7
Zimbabwe		7	7	7	7	

Source: WTO, Yearbook of Tourism Statistics
Notes: see end of section

Notes to Tables in Section Twenty-Three

Table 2301   0 indicates less than 0.5 million
    a Excluding crew spending and international fares
    b Arrivals from market economy countries only
    c Receipts from visitors excluding servicemen, air crew members and transit passengers
    d Receipts from visitors
    e Data for 1988 and 1989 include fares
    f New series starting 1987
    g Receipts from hotel sales

Table 2302   0 indicates less than 0.5 million
    a Excluding crew spending and international fares
    b New series starting 1987
    c Data exclude accommodation (1985-1988)

Table 2303   a International tourist arrivals at hotels and similar accommodation
    b Visitor arrivals
    c 1989: air arrivals only
    d Data include nationals residing abroad
    e Air arrivals only
    f Data include arrivals from within India
    g Data include transit passengers (stays of up to 72 hours)
    h Data exclude ethnic Chinese arriving from Hong Kong
    i Data represent foreign tourist departures and include Singapore residents crossing the border by road
    j Data exclude arrivals of Malaysian citizens by land
    k Data exclude nationals residing abroad
    l Data are estimated from departure figures

Table 2304   a Data include nights spent in selected establishments only
    b Data refer to hotels only
    c Data refer to organised tours only
    d Data include all accommodation establishments
    e Data include nights spent by domestic tourists

Table 2306   a Data refer to hotels with 25 rooms or more
    b Data refer to hotels only

Section Twenty-Four
Cultural Indicators

| | LIBRARIES | | | | Table No. 2401 |

Library Statistics: Latest Year

Units: As stated

	Year	Administrative units	Service points	Book stocks, no. of volumes (millions)	Book stocks per inhabitant	Registered borrowers
North America						
Canada [a]	1989	993	6,157	59.58	2.27	
USA	1988	8,849	15,256	523.49	2.18	
South America						
Argentina	1989	1,528	1,528	9.53	0.35	4,201
Bolivia	1983		99	0.13	0.02	119
Brazil [a]	1989	3,600		18.11	0.14	2,919
Chile	1989	293	293	1.05	0.08	27
Colombia	1985	974	1,036	2.38	0.08	
Ecuador	1987	210	210	0.14	0.01	
French Guiana	1981	1	2	0.02	0.27	0
Guyana [a]	1987					
Paraguay	1990					
Peru	1987	687	687	5.80	0.28	
Suriname	1978	2	68	0.27	0.75	53
Uruguay	1986					
Venezuela	1989	24	567	2.83	0.14	53
Caribbean						
Anguilla						
Antigua						
Aruba						
Bahamas	1987					
Barbados [b]	1989	1	10	0.17	0.68	63
Bermuda	1989	1	4	0.15	2.55	26
British Virgin Islands [b]	1989	1	6	0.05	3.69	8
Cayman Islands	1990	1	2	0.02	0.72	5
Cuba	1989	332	4,671	4.33	0.41	334
Dominica [c]	1981	1	2	0.02	0.20	4
Dominican Republic	1980	68				532
Grenada	1984	1	1	0.03	0.25	7
Guadeloupe	1984	1	2	0.09	0.27	15
Haiti						
Jamaica	1980	1	216	1.11	0.51	614
Martinique	1987					
Netherlands Antilles	1981	1	3	0.10	0.53	9
St Kitts	1984	1	5	0.01	0.17	1
St Lucia						
St Vincent/Grenadines	1985					
Trinidad and Tobago	1986	3	18	0.25	0.21	72
Central America						
Belize	1986	1	34	0.13	0.70	20
Costa Rica [a]	1986	81	87	0.32	0.12	293
El Salvador	1989	44	83	0.06	0.01	21
Guatemala	1987	1	36	0.03		
Honduras	1985					
Mexico	1989	2,269	2,269	9.88	0.11	39
Nicaragua	1987					
Panama	1985	18	18	0.03	0.01	
Puerto Rico						
South Asia						
Afghanistan	1984	55	55	0.35	0.01	11
Bangladesh	1989	57	61	0.52		
Bhutan	1983					
India	1986					
Nepal	1987					
Pakistan	1983	3	3	0.09		
Sri Lanka	1989	15	154	0.48	0.02	98

LIBRARIES

Library Statistics: Latest Year

Units: As stated

	Year	National libraries	Higher education libraries	School libraries	Special libraries	Non-specialised libraries
North America						
Canada [a]	1989	1	168	7,982		
USA	1988	3	3,438	92,438	4,589	1,877
South America						
Argentina	1989	3				
Bolivia	1983	2	17	13		13
Brazil [a]	1989	3				
Chile	1989	1	169	820	4	
Colombia	1985	1	225			
Ecuador	1987		128	1		
French Guiana	1981		1			
Guyana [a]	1987	1	1	31	32	
Paraguay	1990	1	26	145		
Peru	1987	1	2	143		
Suriname	1978		2	3	27	7
Uruguay	1986	1	2	191	15	1
Venezuela	1989	1	78	443	565	
Caribbean						
Anguilla						
Antigua						
Aruba						
Bahamas	1987		2			
Barbados [b]	1989	1	2		1	
Bermuda	1989		1	22	1	
British Virgin Islands [b]	1989	1		2		
Cayman Islands	1990		1	1	1	
Cuba	1989	1	84	3,860	6	
Dominica [c]	1981					
Dominican Republic	1980					
Grenada	1984				1	
Guadeloupe	1984		1			1
Haiti						
Jamaica	1980	1				
Martinique	1987		1			
Netherlands Antilles	1981					
St Kitts	1984		2	2		
St Lucia						
St Vincent/Grenadines	1985	1				
Trinidad and Tobago	1986	1	4	564	31	
Central America						
Belize	1986	1		29	1	
Costa Rica [a]	1986	1	1			
El Salvador	1989	1	110	360		
Guatemala	1987		1		16	
Honduras	1985	1	7		1	
Mexico	1989	1	770	2,988	150	
Nicaragua	1987		13	412		
Panama	1985				1	
Puerto Rico						
South Asia						
Afghanistan	1984		18			
Bangladesh	1989	1	946			
Bhutan	1983				1	
India	1986	8				
Nepal	1987	1				
Pakistan	1983	1				
Sri Lanka	1989	1				

LIBRARIES

Library Statistics: Latest Year

Units: As stated

	Year	Administrative units	Service points	Book stocks, no. of volumes (millions)	Book stocks per inhabitant	Registered borrowers
Japan						
Japan [a]	1987	1,349	1,801	133.61	1.09	12,112
ASEAN/NICs						
Brunei	1988	1	8	0.10	0.52	6
Hong Kong [b]	1989	2	53	3.77	0.65	2,226
Indonesia	1989	30	44	0.46		2,768
Macau						
Malaysia [a]	1989	13	144	4.77	0.28	1,014
Philippines	1989	1	517	5.76	0.10	1,595
Singapore [b]	1987					
South Korea	1990	231	231	5.48	0.13	25,007
Taiwan	1986	201				
Thailand	1989	375	402	1.60	0.03	30
East/SE Asia						
Cambodia						
China	1989	2,512	2,512	283.68	0.25	5,919
Laos	1987					
Mongolia						
Myanmar						
North Korea						
Vietnam	1977	316		4.88	0.10	
Australasia						
Australia	1987	497	1,804	0.03		
New Zealand [a]	1987	209	291	6.08	1.95	1,150
Pacific						
American Samoa	1982					
Fiji	1989	1	4	0.07	0.10	24
French Polynesia	1985	1	2	0.02	0.11	1
Guam	1984	8	9	0.19	1.57	17
Kiribati	1984					
Nauru						
New Caledonia [a]	1985					
Papua New Guinea	1989	19		0.15	0.04	46
Solomon Islands	1985	8	8	0.02	0.08	5
Tonga	1988	3	3	0.20	1.73	3
Tuvalu						
Vanuatu	1988	1	1	0.01	0.10	0
Western Samoa						
Middle East						
Bahrain [d]	1989	1	10	0.22	0.45	51
Egypt	1988	836		8.52	0.16	1
Iran	1989	507	507	3.33	0.06	7,062
Iraq	1988					
Israel	1985	208	655	12.60	2.98	0
Jordan	1989	5	5	0.14	0.04	6
Kuwait	1988	1	23	0.74	0.39	585
Lebanon						
Oman	1987					
Qatar	1989	6	6	0.15	0.36	5
Saudi Arabia	1984	1	50	0.63	0.05	
Syria [a]	1989	14		0.37	0.04	617
United Arab Emirates	1987					
Yemen						

LIBRARIES

Library Statistics: Latest Year

Units: As stated

	Year	National libraries	Higher education libraries	School libraries	Special libraries	Non-specialised libraries
Japan						
Japan [a]	1987	1	1,398	39,685	2,150	928
ASEAN/NICs						
Brunei	1988		1			
Hong Kong [b]	1989	2				
Indonesia	1989	1	45		581	26
Macau						
Malaysia [a]	1989	1	8	7,820	265	
Philippines	1989	1			224	1
Singapore [b]	1987	1	5	380	1	
South Korea	1990	1	270	4,892	334	1
Taiwan	1986					
Thailand	1989	1			277	26
East/SE Asia						
Cambodia						
China	1989	1				
Laos	1987		5	22		1
Mongolia						
Myanmar						
North Korea						
Vietnam	1977	1	58		44	
Australasia						
Australia	1987	1	341			
New Zealand [a]	1987	1	7			
Pacific						
American Samoa	1982		1	1		
Fiji	1989		7	1	68	
French Polynesia	1985				5	
Guam	1984			46		
Kiribati	1984	1				
Nauru						
New Caledonia [a]	1985				3	
Papua New Guinea	1989	1			1	
Solomon Islands	1985	1				
Tonga	1988		1			
Tuvalu						
Vanuatu	1988	1				
Western Samoa						
Middle East						
Bahrain [d]	1989		2	150	1	
Egypt	1988	1	214			
Iran	1989	1	198			
Iraq	1988		106			15
Israel	1985					
Jordan	1989	1				3
Kuwait	1988	1	1	570	13	
Lebanon						
Oman	1987		1	130		
Qatar	1989	1	2	156	1	5
Saudi Arabia	1984					
Syria [a]	1989	1	1		1	
United Arab Emirates	1987		3			
Yemen						

LIBRARIES

Library Statistics: Latest Year

Units: As stated

	Year	Administrative units	Service points	Book stocks, no. of volumes (millions)	Book stocks per inhabitant	Registered borrowers
North Africa						
Algeria [a]	1987					
Chad	1987	1				0
Djibouti						
Ethiopia	1986	4	17	0.12		11
Libya						
Mali						
Mauritania						
Morocco	1986					
Niger	1987					
Somalia	1983					
Sudan	1987					
Tunisia [e]	1989	252	340	1.32	0.16	65
West Africa						
Benin [a]	1989	12	12	0.03	0.01	0
Burkina Faso						
Cameroon	1989					
Cape Verde						
Côte d'Ivoire	1981	1		0.03		2
Equatorial Guinea						
Gabon	1989					
Gambia	1986	4	8	0.09	0.14	1
Ghana	1989	13	47	1.58	0.11	56
Guinea	1988	1		0.01		
Guinea-Bissau	1986					
Liberia [a]	1983					
Nigeria	1989	12	92	1.11	0.01	46
Sao Tomé e Príncipe						
Senegal [a]	1987	10	11	0.02		0
Sierra Leone						
Togo [a]	1989	1	26	0.06	0.02	7
East/Central Africa						
Angola						
Burundi	1989	60	60			20
Central African Republic	1985					
Comoros						
Congo	1989	1	4	0.02	0.01	22
Kenya [a]	1985	2	14	0.51	0.03	97
Madagascar	1986	56	56	0.08	0.01	
Maldives						
Mauritius	1989	2	2	0.02	0.02	8
Réunion	1984					
Rwanda	1987					
Seychelles	1989	1	4	0.04	0.63	16
Tanzania	1985	1	17	0.43	0.02	114
Uganda	1986	1	18			6
Zaire	1977	8	31	0.01		9
Southern Africa						
Botswana [b]	1988	1	18	0.34	0.32	48
Lesotho	1989	1	3	0.02	0.01	0
Malawi [b]	1988	1	6	0.31	0.04	54
Mozambique						
Namibia						
South Africa	1985		700			
Swaziland	1989					
Zambia	1987	4	56			17
Zimbabwe	1988	6	6			18

LIBRARIES

Library Statistics: Latest Year

Units: As stated

	Year	National libraries	Higher education libraries	School libraries	Special libraries	Non-specialised libraries
North Africa						
Algeria [a]	1987	1				
Chad	1987		1			
Djibouti						
Ethiopia	1986	1	5			
Libya						
Mali						
Mauritania						
Morocco	1986				1	
Niger	1987		1			
Somalia	1983		1			
Sudan	1987		1			
Tunisia [e]	1989				29	
West Africa						
Benin [a]	1989	1	10	5		4
Burkina Faso						
Cameroon	1989	1	3			1
Cape Verde						
Côte d'Ivoire	1981	1			1	
Equatorial Guinea						
Gabon	1989	1				
Gambia	1986	1				
Ghana	1989	1			1	
Guinea	1988		6	6		
Guinea-Bissau	1986					1
Liberia [a]	1983		6			
Nigeria	1989	1	46	213		
Sao Tomé e Príncipe						
Senegal [a]	1987	1	1			
Sierra Leone						
Togo [a]	1989	1	1			
East/Central Africa						
Angola						
Burundi	1989		1		2	174
Central African Republic	1985		4		2	
Comoros						
Congo	1989	1	1		1	
Kenya [a]	1985	1	1		1	
Madagascar	1986				24	
Maldives						
Mauritius	1989	1		26		
Réunion	1984		1			
Rwanda	1987		5			
Seychelles	1989			19		
Tanzania	1985	1	7	135	120	
Uganda	1986	1				
Zaire	1977	1				
Southern Africa						
Botswana [b]	1988	1	8	14	1	
Lesotho	1989	1				
Malawi [b]	1988	1	4	1	5	
Mozambique						
Namibia						
South Africa	1985	2	73		325	
Swaziland	1989	1				
Zambia	1987	1			1	
Zimbabwe	1988	1	6		1	

Source: UNESCO/national statistical offices
Notes: see end of section

BOOK PUBLISHING   Table No. 2402

Book Titles Published by Subject: Latest Year

Units: Number

	Year	General	Philosophy	Religion	Social sciences	Philology
North America						
Canada	1983	577	762	454	3,853	
USA [a]	1984	1,448	1,193	2,086	8,760	461
South America						
Argentina	1987		278	368	1,642	31
Bolivia	1988	25	7	26	171	10
Brazil	1985	1,353	711	1,665	6,305	533
Chile	1989	25	36	123	908	42
Colombia	1989	81	44	88	431	34
Ecuador						
French Guiana [b]	1981					
Guyana	1989	1			29	
Paraguay						
Peru	1988	10	12	17	177	8
Suriname						
Uruguay	1989		11	26	330	19
Venezuela	1987	34	64	83	355	30
Caribbean						
Anguilla						
Antigua						
Aruba						
Bahamas						
Barbados	1990	3	1	2	39	
Bermuda						
British Virgin Islands	1982	20				
Cayman Islands	1978				4	
Cuba	1989	98	11	2	525	111
Dominica						
Dominican Republic	1980	46	82	70	1,360	
Grenada [b]	1979				10	
Guadeloupe						
Haiti	1989	9	4	6	104	5
Jamaica	1985	6		2	34	1
Martinique [b]	1981				5	
Netherlands Antilles	1977	3		3	18	
St Kitts	1988				3	
St Lucia [c]	1985	1			11	
St Vincent/Grenadines						
Trinidad and Tobago	1978	3		1	85	
Central America						
Belize [b,d]	1985	2			5	2
Costa Rica	1990	5	1	16	111	5
El Salvador	1988				8	
Guatemala	1981	55		1	203	2
Honduras						
Mexico [e]	1989	525	213	184	1,264	138
Nicaragua [e]	1987				15	
Panama	1981	34	2	4	62	2
Puerto Rico						
South Asia						
Afghanistan	1990	165	25	170	1,045	30
Bangladesh	1988	63	21	60	457	27
Bhutan						
India	1990	294	383	905	2,805	195
Nepal	1989		4	7	19	25
Pakistan [e]	1989	27	20	535	194	27
Sri Lanka	1990	41	17	215	1,232	65

BOOK PUBLISHING

Table No. 2402

Book Titles Published by Subject: Latest Year

Units: Number

	Year	Pure sciences	Applied sciences	Arts	Literature	Geography/ history	Total, inc. others
North America							
Canada	1983	1,805	2,641	1,111	2,248	932	18,373
USA [a]	1984	2,850	7,638	2,793	2,583	2,673	48,793
South America							
Argentina	1987	119	513	177	1,410	298	4,836
Bolivia	1988	24	54	27	56	47	447
Brazil	1985	875	1,757	1,264	2,113	1,072	17,648
Chile	1989	72	296	69	567	212	2,350
Colombia	1989	43	206	58	363	138	1,486
Ecuador							
French Guiana [b]	1981					1	1
Guyana	1989		4	3	4	5	46
Paraguay							
Peru	1988	19	87	17	71	63	481
Suriname							
Uruguay	1989	54	90	19	154	102	805
Venezuela	1987	64	281	66	195	30	1,202
Caribbean							
Anguilla							
Antigua							
Aruba							
Bahamas							
Barbados	1990		7	14	8	3	77
Bermuda							
British Virgin Islands	1982						20
Cayman Islands	1978		1				5
Cuba	1989	200	678	195	315	64	2,199
Dominica							
Dominican Republic	1980	98	227	250	23	63	2,219
Grenada [b]	1979						10
Guadeloupe							
Haiti	1989	8	21	18	81	15	271
Jamaica	1985	2	11	3	8	4	71
Martinique [b]	1981	2	10		1	3	21
Netherlands Antilles	1977	4	4		14	6	52
St Kitts	1988						3
St Lucia [c]	1985		2				63
St Vincent/Grenadines							
Trinidad and Tobago	1978	38	26	7	19	6	186
Central America							
Belize [b,d]	1985		3				12
Costa Rica	1990	13	34	8	35	16	244
El Salvador	1988	1			4	2	15
Guatemala	1981	11	38	155	39	70	574
Honduras							
Mexico [e]	1989	316	330	181	63	276	3,490
Nicaragua [e]	1987		3	2	21		41
Panama	1981	7	14	13	17	16	171
Puerto Rico							
South Asia							
Afghanistan	1990	125	680	95	200	260	2,795
Bangladesh	1988	66	107	14	300	94	1,209
Bhutan							
India	1990	444	3,367	341	3,989	1,214	13,937
Nepal	1989	18	27	3	13	6	122
Pakistan [e]	1989	84	166	13	37	17	1,600
Sri Lanka	1990	47	173	102	400	163	2,455

BOOK PUBLISHING

Book Titles Published by Subject: Latest Year

Units: Number

	Year	General	Philosophy	Religion	Social sciences	Philology
Japan						
Japan	1987	1,190	1,156	630	8,015	1,523
ASEAN/NICs						
Brunei [e]	1990	2			13	2
Hong Kong	1983	231	67	451	1,485	553
Indonesia	1990	188	59	131	394	84
Macau						
Malaysia [e]	1990	108	32	416	1,018	766
Philippines [e]	1990	58	21	32	462	61
Singapore [a]	1983	34	12	216	623	154
South Korea	1990	3,250	1,005	3,042	3,983	2,756
Taiwan	1986	4,115	348	333	1,416	591
Thailand	1990	557	267	520	1,799	154
East/SE Asia						
Cambodia						
China [e]	1990	2,588	1,206		36,231	2,403
Laos						
Mongolia	1990	49			300	2
Myanmar [e]	1985	387	7	216	4	11
North Korea						
Vietnam	1981	143	14	12	638	12
Australasia						
Australia	1987	390	76	391	4,000	624
New Zealand	1984	102	16	91	1,262	18
Pacific						
American Samoa [c,f]	1980				33	
Fiji	1985				7	
French Polynesia	1981		10		26	
Guam [b]	1980				2	
Kiribati						
Nauru						
New Caledonia [b]	1987				4	2
Papua New Guinea						
Solomon Islands						
Tonga	1978			60	105	
Tuvalu						
Vanuatu						
Western Samoa	1978	57	17	41	80	
Middle East						
Bahrain	1983	5			7	
Egypt	1987	15	43	183	232	65
Iran [e]	1989	168	283	1,354	484	632
Iraq [b,g]	1983	6			15	
Israel	1985	25	40	173	230	50
Jordan						
Kuwait	1988	8	9	73	144	134
Lebanon						
Oman						
Qatar	1990	9	5	48	293	22
Saudi Arabia	1980	3		67	27	
Syria	1983		3	1	19	
United Arab Emirates	1990	6	3	37	16	86
Yemen						

BOOK PUBLISHING

Table No. 2402 (cont'd)

Book Titles Published by Subject: Latest Year

Units: Number

	Year	Pure sciences	Applied sciences	Arts	Literature	Geography/ history	Total, inc. others
Japan							
Japan	1987	1,924	6,875	5,046	8,170	1,817	36,346
ASEAN/NICs							
Brunei [e]	1990				8		25
Hong Kong	1983	442	778	213	1,066	395	5,681
Indonesia	1990	50	352	41	119	100	1,518
Macau							
Malaysia [e]	1990	620	433	94	856	235	4,578
Philippines [e]	1990	98	206	20	109	45	1,112
Singapore [a]	1983	123	261	77	376	51	1,927
South Korea	1990	2,918	3,677	6,153	9,992	2,554	39,330
Taiwan	1986	88	1,303	346	1,031	684	10,255
Thailand	1990	135	835	156	1,458	410	6,291
East/SE Asia							
Cambodia							
China [e]	1990	3,087	12,196	5,727	7,756	2,729	73,923
Laos							
Mongolia	1990	45	103		218		717
Myanmar [e]	1985	1	20	3		24	673
North Korea							
Vietnam	1981	70	156	72	329	49	1,495
Australasia							
Australia	1987	596	1,766	994	1,074	1,052	10,963
New Zealand	1984	319	799	348	300	197	3,452
Pacific							
American Samoa [c,f]	1980	8			5		99
Fiji	1985	6					13
French Polynesia	1981						72
Guam [b]	1980				1	9	12
Kiribati							
Nauru							
New Caledonia [b]	1987		1	3		4	14
Papua New Guinea							
Solomon Islands							
Tonga	1978		30			15	210
Tuvalu							
Vanuatu							
Western Samoa	1978		35	5			235
Middle East							
Bahrain	1983				27	7	46
Egypt	1987	73	159	65	403	124	1,276
Iran [e]	1989	387	967	310	1,292	412	6,289
Iraq [b,g]	1983	1			54	6	82
Israel	1985	79	71	44	718	234	2,214
Jordan							
Kuwait	1988	309	74	19	1	22	793
Lebanon							
Oman							
Qatar	1990	56	34	9	19	26	521
Saudi Arabia	1980	1	11	4	63	31	218
Syria	1983	14	18	3	54	7	119
United Arab Emirates	1990	104	17			12	281
Yemen							

BOOK PUBLISHING   Table No. 2402 (cont'd)

Book Titles Published by Subject: Latest Year

Units: Number

	Year	General	Philosophy	Religion	Social sciences	Philology
North Africa						
Algeria	1984	26	15	32	201	13
Chad						
Djibouti						
Ethiopia	1990	32	1	15	179	11
Libya	1988	31	21	20	149	24
Mali	1984				98	19
Mauritania	1977				2	
Morocco						
Niger [e]	1980				3	
Somalia						
Sudan [d,f]	1979	34		16		
Tunisia [a,e,h]	1988	21	8	22	31	8
West Africa						
Benin	1978			1		
Burkina Faso [b]	1985				1	
Cameroon [b,e]	1979	5	4		5	
Cape Verde	1989				2	
Côte d'Ivoire	1983				18	
Equatorial Guinea	1988				8	3
Gabon						
Gambia	1988	1		4	16	
Ghana	1983		1	31	130	16
Guinea						
Guinea-Bissau						
Liberia						
Nigeria	1989	86	18	240	440	66
Sao Tomé e Príncipe						
Senegal [b]	1983		2	3	9	4
Sierra Leone [d]	1984					6
Togo						
East/Central Africa						
Angola [b]	1986					
Burundi	1986			10	28	
Central African Republic						
Comoros						
Congo [b]	1977				24	
Kenya	1990	2		115	47	56
Madagascar	1989	1	2	43	41	3
Maldives	1977	1	1		1	
Mauritius	1990	3	1	4	21	3
Réunion [b]	1985	1		6	15	2
Rwanda [d]	1987	18	5	42	72	9
Seychelles	1980			1	22	
Tanzania	1990		1	18	45	2
Uganda						
Zaire [b]	1979	13	1	142	38	
Southern Africa						
Botswana [b]	1987	5			144	5
Lesotho						
Malawi	1989	11		31	53	2
Mozambique	1984				35	
Namibia	1990	7		2	57	
South Africa	1990	168	47	585	1,128	285
Swaziland						
Zambia	1983	143			231	
Zimbabwe	1990	6		14	153	22

BOOK PUBLISHING

Book Titles Published by Subject: Latest Year

Units: Number

	Year	Pure sciences	Applied sciences	Arts	Literature	Geography/ history	Total, inc. others
North Africa							
Algeria	1984	104	125	22	119	61	718
Chad							
Djibouti							
Ethiopia	1990	74	21	9	32	11	385
Libya	1988	180	24		92	12	553
Mali	1984	17	23			3	160
Mauritania	1977	12			20	6	40
Morocco							
Niger [e]	1980	1			1		5
Somalia							
Sudan [d,f]	1979	28	6	4	31	19	138
Tunisia [a,e,h]	1988	6	16	22	137	22	293
West Africa							
Benin	1978	5			6	1	13
Burkina Faso [b]	1985				3		4
Cameroon [b,e]	1979	3	2		2	1	22
Cape Verde	1989		1		6	1	10
Côte d'Ivoire	1983						46
Equatorial Guinea	1988	1	3			2	17
Gabon							
Gambia	1988	2	18			1	42
Ghana	1983	13	65	33	38	23	350
Guinea							
Guinea-Bissau							
Liberia							
Nigeria	1989	50	246	82	146	92	1,466
Sao Tomé e Príncipe							
Senegal [b]	1983	2			14	8	42
Sierra Leone [d]	1984	6				4	16
Togo							
East/Central Africa							
Angola [b]	1986				130		14
Burundi	1986		19				54
Central African Republic							
Comoros							
Congo [b]	1977	33	3	7	36	24	127
Kenya	1990	26	41	12	23	26	348
Madagascar	1989	5	23	12	11	5	146
Maldives	1977						3
Mauritius	1990	2	6	2	17	18	75
Réunion [b]	1985	2	12	4	18	13	73
Rwanda [d]	1987	20	31	3	4	3	207
Seychelles	1980						33
Tanzania	1990	7	40	3	47	9	172
Uganda							
Zaire [b]	1979	6	7	3	19	2	231
Southern Africa							
Botswana [b]	1987	22	89	4	12	8	289
Lesotho							
Malawi	1989	7	22		11	4	141
Mozambique	1984		17	3	11		66
Namibia	1990	2	18	2	14	4	106
South Africa	1990	420	731	294	1,065	227	4,950
Swaziland							
Zambia	1983	15	13	18		34	454
Zimbabwe	1990	16	70	7	56	5	349

Source: UNESCO/national statistical offices

Notes: see end of section

BOOK PUBLISHING

Table No. 2403

Book Titles Published by Subject: Latest Year (% analysis)

Units: % of total

	Year	General	Philosophy	Religion	Social sciences	Philology
North America						
Canada	1983	3	4	2	21	
USA [a]	1984	3	2	4	18	1
South America						
Argentina	1987		6	8	34	1
Bolivia	1988	6	2	6	38	2
Brazil	1985	8	4	9	36	3
Chile	1989	1	2	5	39	2
Colombia	1989	5	3	6	29	2
Ecuador						
French Guiana [b]	1981					
Guyana	1989	2			63	
Paraguay						
Peru	1988	2	2	4	37	2
Suriname						
Uruguay	1989		1	3	41	2
Venezuela	1987	3	5	7	30	2
Caribbean						
Anguilla						
Antigua						
Aruba						
Bahamas						
Barbados	1990	4	1	3	51	
Bermuda						
British Virgin Islands	1982	100				
Cayman Islands	1978				80	
Cuba	1989	4	1		24	5
Dominica						
Dominican Republic	1980	2	4	3	61	
Grenada [b]	1979				100	
Guadeloupe						
Haiti	1989	3	1	2	38	2
Jamaica	1985	8		3	48	1
Martinique [b]	1981				24	
Netherlands Antilles	1977	6		6	35	
St Kitts	1988				100	
St Lucia [c]	1985	2			17	
St Vincent/Grenadines						
Trinidad and Tobago	1978	2		1	46	
Central America						
Belize [b,d]	1985	17			42	17
Costa Rica	1990	2		7	45	2
El Salvador	1988				53	
Guatemala	1981	10			35	
Honduras						
Mexico [e]	1989	15	6	5	36	4
Nicaragua [e]	1987				37	
Panama	1981	20	1	2	36	1
Puerto Rico						
South Asia						
Afghanistan	1990	6	1	6	37	1
Bangladesh	1988	5	2	5	38	2
Bhutan						
India	1990	2	3	6	20	1
Nepal	1989		3	6	16	20
Pakistan [e]	1989	2	1	33	12	2
Sri Lanka	1990	2	1	9	50	3

BOOK PUBLISHING   Table No. 2403

Book Titles Published by Subject: Latest Year (% analysis)

Units: % of total

	Year	Pure sciences	Applied sciences	Arts	Literature	Geography/ history	Total, inc. others
North America							
Canada	1983	10	14	6	12	5	100
USA [a]	1984	6	16	6	5	5	100
South America							
Argentina	1987	2	11	4	29	6	100
Bolivia	1988	5	12	6	13	11	100
Brazil	1985	5	10	7	12	6	100
Chile	1989	3	13	3	24	9	100
Colombia	1989	3	14	4	24	9	100
Ecuador							
French Guiana [b]	1981					100	100
Guyana	1989		9	7	9	11	100
Paraguay							
Peru	1988	4	18	4	15	13	100
Suriname							
Uruguay	1989	7	11	2	19	13	100
Venezuela	1987	5	23	5	16	2	100
Caribbean							
Anguilla							
Antigua							
Aruba							
Bahamas							
Barbados	1990		9	18	10	4	100
Bermuda							
British Virgin Islands	1982						100
Cayman Islands	1978		20				100
Cuba	1989	9	31	9	14	3	100
Dominica							
Dominican Republic	1980	4	10	11	1	3	100
Grenada [b]	1979						100
Guadeloupe							
Haiti	1989	3	8	7	30	6	100
Jamaica	1985	3	15	4	11	6	100
Martinique [b]	1981	10	48		5	14	100
Netherlands Antilles	1977	8	8		27	12	100
St Kitts	1988						100
St Lucia [c]	1985		3				100
St Vincent/Grenadines							
Trinidad and Tobago	1978	20	14	4	10	3	100
Central America							
Belize [b,d]	1985		25				100
Costa Rica	1990	5	14	3	14	7	100
El Salvador	1988	7			27	13	100
Guatemala	1981	2	7	27	7	12	100
Honduras							
Mexico [e]	1989	9	9	5	2	8	100
Nicaragua [e]	1987		7	5	51		100
Panama	1981	4	8	8	10	9	100
Puerto Rico							
South Asia							
Afghanistan	1990	4	24	3	7	9	100
Bangladesh	1988	5	9	1	25	8	100
Bhutan							
India	1990	3	24	2	29	9	100
Nepal	1989	15	22	2	11	5	100
Pakistan [e]	1989	5	10	1	2	1	100
Sri Lanka	1990	2	7	4	16	7	100

Book Titles Published by Subject: Latest Year (% analysis)

Units: % of total

	Year	General	Philosophy	Religion	Social sciences	Philology
Japan						
Japan	1987	3	3	2	22	4
ASEAN/NICs						
Brunei [e]	1990	8			52	8
Hong Kong	1983	4	1	8	26	10
Indonesia	1990	12	4	9	26	6
Macau						
Malaysia [e]	1990	2	1	9	22	17
Philippines [e]	1990	5	2	3	42	5
Singapore [a]	1983	2	1	11	32	8
South Korea	1990	8	3	8	10	7
Taiwan	1986	40	3	3	14	6
Thailand	1990	9	4	8	29	2
East/SE Asia						
Cambodia						
China [e]	1990	4	2		49	3
Laos						
Mongolia	1990	7			42	
Myanmar [e]	1985	58	1	32	1	2
North Korea						
Vietnam	1981	10	1	1	43	1
Australasia						
Australia	1987	4	1	4	36	6
New Zealand	1984	3		3	37	1
Pacific						
American Samoa [c,f]	1980				33	
Fiji	1985				54	
French Polynesia	1981		14		36	
Guam [b]	1980				17	
Kiribati						
Nauru						
New Caledonia [b]	1987				29	14
Papua New Guinea						
Solomon Islands						
Tonga	1978			29	50	
Tuvalu						
Vanuatu						
Western Samoa	1978	24	7	17	34	
Middle East						
Bahrain	1983	11			15	
Egypt	1987	1	3	14	18	5
Iran [e]	1989	3	4	22	8	10
Iraq [b,g]	1983	7			18	
Israel	1985	1	2	8	10	2
Jordan						
Kuwait	1988	1	1	9	18	17
Lebanon						
Oman						
Qatar	1990	2	1	9	56	4
Saudi Arabia	1980	1		31	12	
Syria	1983		3	1	16	
United Arab Emirates	1990	2	1	13	6	31
Yemen						

BOOK PUBLISHING

Table No. 2403 (cont'd)

Book Titles Published by Subject: Latest Year (% analysis)

Units: % of total

	Year	Pure sciences	Applied sciences	Arts	Literature	Geography/ history	Total, inc. others
Japan							
Japan	1987	5	19	14	22	5	100
ASEAN/NICs							
Brunei [e]	1990				32		100
Hong Kong	1983	8	14	4	19	7	100
Indonesia	1990	3	23	3	8	7	100
Macau							
Malaysia [e]	1990	14	9	2	19	5	100
Philippines [e]	1990	9	19	2	10	4	100
Singapore [a]	1983	6	14	4	20	3	100
South Korea	1990	7	9	16	25	6	100
Taiwan	1986	1	13	3	10	7	100
Thailand	1990	2	13	2	23	7	100
East/SE Asia							
Cambodia							
China [e]	1990	4	16	8	10	4	100
Laos							
Mongolia	1990	6	14		30		100
Myanmar [e]	1985		3			4	100
North Korea							
Vietnam	1981	5	10	5	22	3	100
Australasia							
Australia	1987	5	16	9	10	10	100
New Zealand	1984	9	23	10	9	6	100
Pacific							
American Samoa [c,f]	1980	8			5		100
Fiji	1985	46					100
French Polynesia	1981						100
Guam [b]	1980				8	75	100
Kiribati							
Nauru							
New Caledonia [b]	1987		7	21		29	100
Papua New Guinea							
Solomon Islands							
Tonga	1978		14			7	100
Tuvalu							
Vanuatu							
Western Samoa	1978		15	2			100
Middle East							
Bahrain	1983				59	15	100
Egypt	1987	6	12	5	32	10	100
Iran [e]	1989	6	15	5	21	7	100
Iraq [b,g]	1983	1			66	7	100
Israel	1985	4	3	2	32	11	100
Jordan							
Kuwait	1988	39	9	2		3	100
Lebanon							
Oman							
Qatar	1990	11	7	2	4	5	100
Saudi Arabia	1980		5	2	29	14	100
Syria	1983	12	15	3	45	6	100
United Arab Emirates	1990	37	6			4	100
Yemen							

BOOK PUBLISHING   Table No. 2403 (cont'd)

Book Titles Published by Subject: Latest Year (% analysis)

Units: % of total

	Year	General	Philosophy	Religion	Social sciences	Philology
North Africa						
Algeria	1984	4	2	4	28	2
Chad						
Djibouti						
Ethiopia	1990	8		4	46	3
Libya	1988	6	4	4	27	4
Mali	1984				61	12
Mauritania	1977				5	
Morocco						
Niger ᵉ	1980				60	
Somalia						
Sudan ᵈ,ᶠ	1979	25		12		
Tunisia ᵃ,ᵉ,ʰ	1988	7	3	8	11	3
West Africa						
Benin	1978			8		
Burkina Faso ᵇ	1985				25	
Cameroon ᵇ,ᵉ	1979	23	18		23	
Cape Verde	1989				20	
Côte d'Ivoire	1983				39	
Equatorial Guinea	1988				47	18
Gabon						
Gambia	1988	2		10	38	
Ghana	1983			9	37	5
Guinea						
Guinea-Bissau						
Liberia						
Nigeria	1989	6	1	16	30	5
Sao Tomé e Príncipe						
Senegal ᵇ	1983		5	7	21	10
Sierra Leone ᵈ	1984					38
Togo						
East/Central Africa						
Angola ᵇ	1986					
Burundi	1986			19	52	
Central African Republic						
Comoros						
Congo ᵇ	1977				19	
Kenya	1990	1		33	14	16
Madagascar	1989	1	1	29	28	2
Maldives	1977	33	33		33	
Mauritius	1990	4	1	5	28	4
Réunion ᵇ	1985	1		8	21	3
Rwanda ᵈ	1987	9	2	20	35	4
Seychelles	1980			3	67	
Tanzania	1990		1	10	26	1
Uganda						
Zaire ᵇ	1979	6		61	16	
Southern Africa						
Botswana ᵇ	1987	2			50	2
Lesotho						
Malawi	1989	8		22	38	1
Mozambique	1984				53	
Namibia	1990	7		2	54	
South Africa	1990	3	1	12	23	6
Swaziland						
Zambia	1983	31			51	
Zimbabwe	1990	2		4	44	6

BOOK PUBLISHING

Book Titles Published by Subject: Latest Year (% analysis)

Units: % of total

	Year	Pure sciences	Applied sciences	Arts	Literature	Geography/ history	Total, inc. others
North Africa							
Algeria	1984	14	17	3	17	8	100
Chad							
Djibouti							
Ethiopia	1990	19	5	2	8	3	100
Libya	1988	33	4		17	2	100
Mali	1984	11	14			2	100
Mauritania	1977	30			50	15	100
Morocco							
Niger [e]	1980	20			20		100
Somalia							
Sudan [d,f]	1979	20	4	3	22	14	100
Tunisia [a,e,h]	1988	2	5	8	47	8	100
West Africa							
Benin	1978	38			46	8	100
Burkina Faso [b]	1985				75		100
Cameroon [b,e]	1979	14	9		9	5	100
Cape Verde	1989		10		60	10	100
Côte d'Ivoire	1983						100
Equatorial Guinea	1988	6	18			12	100
Gabon							
Gambia	1988	5	43			2	100
Ghana	1983	4	19	9	11	7	100
Guinea							
Guinea-Bissau							
Liberia							
Nigeria	1989	3	17	6	10	6	100
Sao Tomé e Príncipe							
Senegal [b]	1983	5			33	19	100
Sierra Leone [d]	1984	38				25	100
Togo							
East/Central Africa							
Angola [b]	1986				929		100
Burundi	1986		35				100
Central African Republic							
Comoros							
Congo [b]	1977	26	2	6	28	19	100
Kenya	1990	7	12	3	7	7	100
Madagascar	1989	3	16	8	8	3	100
Maldives	1977						100
Mauritius	1990	3	8	3	23	24	100
Réunion [b]	1985	3	16	5	25	18	100
Rwanda [d]	1987	10	15	1	2	1	100
Seychelles	1980						100
Tanzania	1990	4	23	2	27	5	100
Uganda							
Zaire [b]	1979	3	3	1	8	1	100
Southern Africa							
Botswana [b]	1987	8	31	1	4	3	100
Lesotho							
Malawi	1989	5	16		8	3	100
Mozambique	1984		26	5	17		100
Namibia	1990	2	17	2	13	4	100
South Africa	1990	8	15	6	22	5	100
Swaziland							
Zambia	1983	3	3	4		7	100
Zimbabwe	1990	5	20	2	16	1	100

Source: UNESCO/national statistical offices

Notes: see end of section

| MUSEUMS | Table No. 2404 |

Museums, Museum Visitors: Latest Year

Units: As stated

	Year	No. of museums	Total attend-ances at museums ('000)	Art	Archae-ology and history	Natural history and science	Ethno-graphy and anthro-pology	Other museums
North America								
Canada [a]	1986	1,237	24,964	5,462	3,809	1,435		14,258
USA [b]	1978	4,609	352,736	41,451	84,488			226,797
South America								
Argentina								
Bolivia								
Brazil	1984	778	26,652	2,921	5,405	7,386	397	10,543
Chile	1987	24	634	60	106	201	29	238
Colombia	1979	71	1,440	618	258		286	278
Ecuador								
French Guiana								
Guyana	1979	2	97					97
Paraguay								
Peru	1984	12	201	13	143			45
Suriname								
Uruguay	1987	11	420	91	110	71		148
Venezuela	1979	54						
Caribbean								
Anguilla								
Antigua	1979	3						
Aruba								
Bahamas	1979	7						
Barbados	1987	3	26					
Bermuda								
British Virgin Islands	1984	1	1					1
Cayman Islands								
Cuba [c]	1987	231	9,780	1,500	99	3,270	38	4,873
Dominica								
Dominican Republic								
Grenada	1984	1	8		8			
Guadeloupe								
Haiti	1986	2	36					
Jamaica								
Martinique								
Netherlands Antilles								
St Kitts	1985	1	19					
St Lucia	1979	1	7		7			
St Vincent/Grenadines								
Trinidad and Tobago								
Central America								
Belize	1984	1	1		1			
Costa Rica	1987	15	570	24	350	8		188
El Salvador	1979	4	388	18	241			129
Guatemala	1984	18	58	22	25		3	8
Honduras								
Mexico [d]	1983	91	13,070					
Nicaragua								
Panama								
Puerto Rico								
South Asia								
Afghanistan	1979	7	7					7
Bangladesh	1987	13	254,675					
Bhutan	1979	1	16					16
India	1987	462	204					
Nepal								
Pakistan	1979	10	561		64			497
Sri Lanka								

MUSEUMS

Museums, Museum Visitors: Latest Year

Units: As stated

	Year	No. of museums	Total attendances at museums ('000)	Art	Archaeology and history	Natural history and science	Ethnography and anthropology	Other museums
Japan								
Japan [e]	1978	405	41,468	11,244	13,749	10,646		5,829
ASEAN/NICs								
Brunei	1984	3	112					112
Hong Kong								
Indonesia	1988	131	3,566	31	2,195	44	288	1,008
Macau								
Malaysia	1984	27	5,111					
Philippines	1984	61						
Singapore	1979	3	940			313		627
South Korea	1984	146	665	225	410			30
Taiwan								
Thailand	1979	64	1,103	30	320			753
East/SE Asia								
Cambodia								
China								
Laos								
Mongolia								
Myanmar								
North Korea								
Vietnam	1979	9	1,918	139	1,779			
Australasia								
Australia	1979		5,279	1,200	734			3,345
New Zealand	1987	98	312					
Pacific								
American Samoa	1979	1	52					52
Fiji	1984	1	19		19			
French Polynesia								
Guam								
Kiribati								
Nauru								
New Caledonia	1985	4	20				20	
Papua New Guinea	1979	2	100				20	80
Solomon Islands	1988	1	21					
Tonga								
Tuvalu								
Vanuatu	1987	1	7					
Western Samoa								
Middle East								
Bahrain	1984	2	99		24		75	
Egypt [f]	1984	34	2,076	2,076				
Iran	1987	52	1,581	36	447			1,098
Iraq	1984	13	63		63			
Israel	1984	95	6,780	947	2,997	721	164	1,951
Jordan	1987	11	248	180	68			
Kuwait	1987	16	12					
Lebanon								
Oman	1987	3	21		10	11		
Qatar	1978	1	60					60
Saudi Arabia	1984	1	40		40			
Syria	1987	30	926	64	166	12	191	493
United Arab Emirates	1979	2	23				23	
Yemen								

MUSEUMS	Table No. 2404 (cont'd)

Museums, Museum Visitors: Latest Year

Units: As stated

	Year	No. of museums	Total attend-ances at museums ('000)	Art	Archae-ology and history	Natural history and science	Ethno-graphy and anthro-pology	Other museums
North Africa								
Algeria	1979	28	260	7	240		13	
Chad	1984	5	3					
Djibouti								
Ethiopia	1984	1	6					6
Libya	1979	26	50		14	2	8	2
Mali	1987	2	14					
Mauritania								
Morocco	1984	11	1,580					
Niger	1979	1	600					600
Somalia								
Sudan	1984	7	221		127	45		49
Tunisia	1984	35	367		343		24	
West Africa								
Benin	1984	5	8		5		3	
Burkina Faso	1979	12	5	1				4
Cameroon	1979	42	5	1				41
Cape Verde								
Côte d'Ivoire								
Equatorial Guinea								
Gabon								
Gambia								
Ghana	1979	4	69					69
Guinea	1984	5	21				14	7
Guinea-Bissau	1988	1	1					
Liberia								
Nigeria								
Sao Tomé e Príncipe								
Senegal	1979	3	22	9	10			3
Sierra Leone	1979	19	178					19
Togo	1987	7	221		127	45		49
East/Central Africa								
Angola								
Burundi	1984	2	6				3	3
Central African Republic	1979	65	1		1			
Comoros								
Congo	1984	5	57					57
Kenya	1984	6	531					531
Madagascar	1984	4	21		17		4	
Maldives	1984	1	3					
Mauritius	1987	5	281		19	250		12
Réunion	1984	2	79					
Rwanda								
Seychelles	1987	2	9					
Tanzania								
Uganda								
Zaire								
Southern Africa								
Botswana	1979	1	52					
Lesotho								
Malawi	1984	2	80					80
Mozambique								
Namibia								
South Africa								
Swaziland								
Zambia	1984	6	175		12		25	138
Zimbabwe	1984	9	162		68	40	44	10

Source: UNESCO/national statistical offices
Notes: see end of section

Notes to Tables in Section Twenty-Four

Table 2401   Year specified relates to national libraries only; other data are latest available year
- a   Higher education refers only to main universities or university central libraries
- b   National library serves as public library
- c   Borrowers refers to visits to reading rooms
- d   Borrowers refers to 1986
- e   Book stocks and registered borrowers refer to 1986

Tables 2402/2403

- a   Commercially published works only
- b   First editions only
- c   School textbooks included in total are not identified by class
- d   Textbooks only
- e   Excluding pamphlets
- f   Children's books included in total are not identified by class
- g   Social sciences includes religion; literature includes philology
- h   Excluding school textbooks

Table 2404   Other musems includes: science and technology, specialised, regional, general and others
- a   Archaeology and history includes ethnography and anthropology
- b   Archaeology and history includes following two categories
- c   Total museums includes 103 monuments and sites
- d   Attendances includes visits to monuments and sites
- e   Natural history and science includes science and technology museums
- f   Art includes archaeology and history

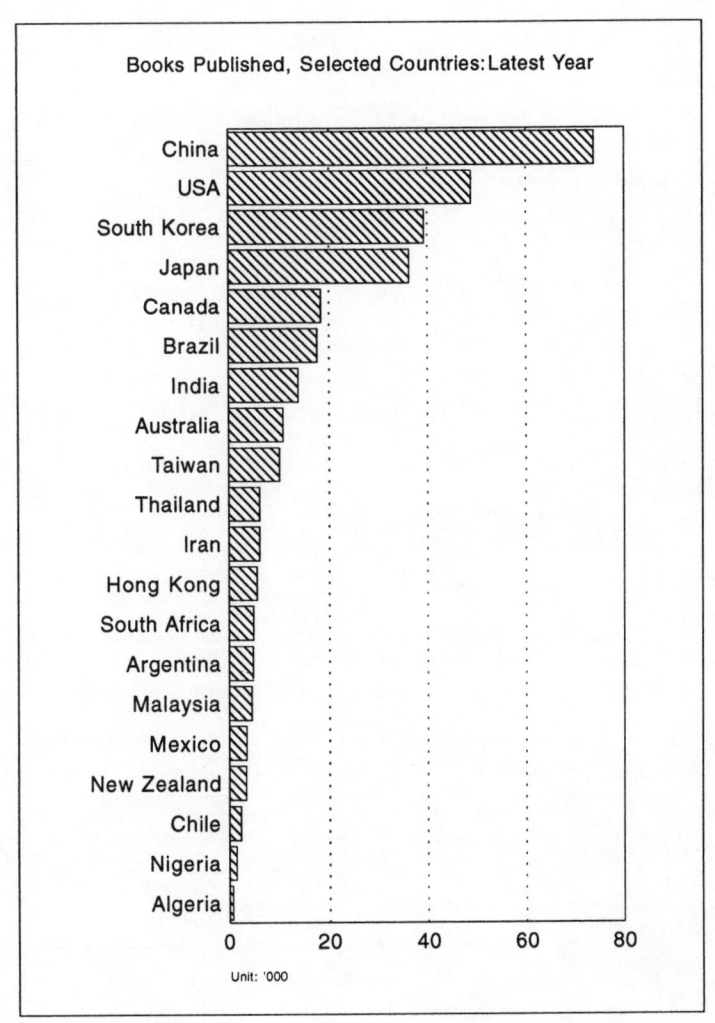

Books Published, Selected Countries: Latest Year
Unit: '000

Section Twenty-Five
Regional Comparisons

POPULATION TRENDS AND FORECASTS — Table No. 2501

Trends in Total Population: National Estimates, 1977-1992

Units: '000

	1977	1980	1985	1987	1989	1990	1991	1992	% growth 1977-92
North America	243,512	251,765	263,551	268,461	273,562	275,999	279,152	282,491	16.0
South America	221,360	239,945	267,838	278,752	290,827	296,558	302,245	305,867	38.2
Caribbean	24,403	25,340	27,714	28,637	29,609	29,974	30,457	30,463	24.8
Central America	87,143	94,794	107,067	111,499	116,227	118,705	120,886	121,004	38.9
South Asia	829,732	892,137	997,588	1,036,729	1,079,469	1,100,996	1,127,664	1,127,664	35.9
Japan	113,871	116,807	121,049	122,264	123,116	123,540	123,921	123,921	8.8
ASEAN/NICs	298,716	318,745	353,697	368,628	383,527	386,760	389,894	390,408	30.7
East/SE Asia	1,067,915	1,113,717	1,191,453	1,225,350	1,262,788	1,275,836	1,276,515	1,276,564	19.5
Australasia	17,312	17,808	19,012	19,605	20,192	20,459	20,710	20,747	19.8
Pacific	4,434	4,724	5,230	5,462	5,722	5,820	5,901	5,901	33.1
Middle East	121,025	133,111	155,480	169,373	177,984	184,833	189,060	189,125	56.3
North Africa	117,819	128,241	147,239	154,402	166,220	171,090	172,911	172,911	46.8
West Africa	127,811	140,357	162,518	172,568	186,439	193,166	168,750	168,750	32.0
East/Central Africa	96,471	106,338	122,838	130,231	140,973	144,637	146,721	146,721	52.1
Southern Africa	55,225	60,234	68,773	71,990	76,004	77,863	77,715	77,715	40.7
Non-European total	*3,426,749*	*3,644,063*	*4,011,047*	*4,163,951*	*4,332,659*	*4,406,236*	*4,432,502*	*4,440,252*	*29.6*
European Community	330,452	333,985	338,331	339,972	342,116	343,750	345,455	347,010	5.0
EFTA	31,113	31,269	31,654	31,847	32,152	32,409	32,672	32,871	5.6
Eastern Europe	373,954	383,015	398,522	405,376	407,442	410,035	412,329	413,757	10.6
Other European countries	42,747	45,440	51,721	54,329	56,204	57,138	58,074	58,628	37.2
European total	*778,266*	*793,709*	*820,228*	*831,524*	*837,914*	*843,332*	*848,529*	*852,265*	*9.5*
International total	*4,205,015*	*4,437,772*	*4,831,275*	*4,995,474*	*5,170,573*	*5,249,568*	*5,281,031*	*5,292,516*	*25.9*

POPULATION TRENDS AND FORECASTS — Table No. 2502

Population Analysis by Broad Age Groups: Latest Official Estimates

Units: '000

	Males total all ages	Males 0-14 years	Males 15-64 years	Males 65+ years	Females total all ages	Females 0-14 years	Females 15-64 years	Females 65+ years
North America	100.0	22.7	66.9	10.4	100.0	20.6	65.1	14.3
South America	100.0	35.9	59.4	4.7	100.0	34.9	59.8	5.3
Caribbean	100.0	33.3	60.3	6.4	100.0	32.6	60.6	6.8
Central America	100.0	42.8	53.8	3.4	100.0	41.1	54.8	4.1
South Asia	100.0	37.4	57.9	4.7	100.0	37.8	57.5	4.7
Japan	100.0	19.6	70.9	9.5	100.0	18.0	68.3	13.7
ASEAN/NICs	100.0	37.1	59.6	3.3	100.0	35.3	60.6	4.2
East/SE Asia	100.0	30.2	65.1	4.8	100.0	29.0	64.9	6.0
Australasia	100.0	21.5	67.9	10.7	100.0	20.3	65.7	14.0
Pacific	100.0	40.6	56.9	2.5	100.0	40.8	56.5	2.6
Middle East	100.0	43.2	53.5	3.2	100.0	43.3	53.3	3.4
North Africa	100.0	46.3	49.5	4.2	100.0	44.2	51.5	4.3
West Africa	100.0	45.9	50.8	3.3	100.0	44.9	51.6	3.5
East/Central Africa	100.0	48.4	48.9	2.6	100.0	46.3	50.7	3.0
Southern Africa	100.0	39.4	55.8	4.7	100.0	42.9	51.6	5.5
Non-European total	*100.0*	*34.5*	*60.5*	*5.0*	*100.0*	*33.6*	*60.4*	*6.0*
European Community [a]	100.0	18.2	67.3	14.5				
EFTA [a]	100.0	17.8	66.5	15.6				
Eastern Europe [a]	100.0	24.2	66.2	9.6				
Other European countries [a]	100.0	35.5	60.0	4.5				
European total	*100.0*	*22.3*	*66.2*	*11.5*				

Notes: see end of section

POPULATION TRENDS AND FORECASTS — Table No. 2503

Birth Rates 1977-1992

Units: Per '000 inhabitants

	1977	1980	1983	1985	1986	1987	1988	1989	1990	1991	1992
Argentina	24.6	24.7	24.0	21.5	21.8	21.3	20.7		21.4		
Australia	15.9	15.3	15.8	15.7	15.2	15.0	14.9	14.9	14.9	14.0	
Brazil	21.8	34.3	20.9	19.3	20.1	18.8	17.9	17.5	28.6		
Canada	15.5	15.4	15.0	14.5	14.2	14.4	14.5	14.9			
Chile	21.6	22.2	22.2	21.6	22.1	22.3	23.3	23.4	23.8		
China						23.3	22.4	21.6	21.0	21.1	
Colombia	33.0	31.7	30.2	29.2	27.8				27.4		
Ecuador	30.0	27.5	23.3	22.4	21.3	26.3	26.7	19.5	32.9		
Hong Kong	17.7	16.9	15.6	14.0	13.1	12.6	13.4	12.3	12.0	12.0	
India						32.2	31.5	30.4	29.9	29.2	
Indonesia				32.9	29.6	28.4	27.2	27.6	27.6	32.2	
Israel	26.4	24.3	24.0	23.5	23.1	22.7	22.5	22.3	22.1		
Japan	15.4	13.5	12.6	11.9	11.5	11.2	10.7	10.1	10.0	9.9	
Malaysia	31.0	31.1	30.4	31.7	31.0	29.5	30.0	27.1	28.0	27.7	
Mexico	37.3	35.3		34.1		34.4	31.4	30.7	31.3		
New Zealand	17.4	16.3	15.8	15.9	16.3	16.8	17.3	17.4	17.9	17.6	17.2
Nigeria							48.0			46.9	
Pakistan		43.7	42.0	43.3	43.3	43.3	40.5	40.9	44.4	39.1	
Peru	27.3	40.0	37.1	36.0	36.0	35.6	35.2	34.6	34.1	29.4	
Philippines	30.2	30.2	28.9	26.3	26.7	27.6	30.8	29.9	31.8	31.2	
Singapore	16.5	17.1	16.2	16.6	14.8	16.7	19.9	17.5	18.4	17.3	
South Africa											
South Korea	21.7	23.4	21.5	15.7	15.0	16.5	16.5	16.5	15.6	16.3	
Taiwan		23.2	20.5	17.9	15.8	15.9	17.1				
Thailand	24.5	23.1	21.2	18.8	18.0	16.5	16.0	16.3	17.0	20.3	
USA	15.1	15.9	15.5	15.7	15.5	15.7	15.9	16.3	16.7		
Venezuela	34.2	32.8	31.4	29.0	28.3	28.3	27.9	27.5	30.7		
Vietnam						33.1	31.7	31.3	30.0	30.6	
European Community	13.2	13.1	12.0	11.9	12.0	11.9	11.9	11.8	12.0	12.0	11.9
EFTA	12.0	12.1	11.9	12.0	12.0	12.1	12.7	12.8	12.9	13.2	13.0
Eastern Europe	18.3	18.1	18.8	18.4	18.7	18.4	18.2	18.0	17.8	17.7	17.5
Other European countries	15.6	14.7	13.7	13.0	12.7	17.8	18.1	17.8	17.7	18.5	19.5

POPULATION TRENDS AND FORECASTS — Table No. 2504

Population Projections 1990-2025: UN Estimates

Units: '000

	1990	1995	2000	2005	2010	2115	2020	2025	% growth 1990-2025
North America	275,745	285,719	294,584	302,814	311,068	319,132	326,241	331,807	20.3
South America	296,714	325,669	354,758	383,628	412,540	440,784	468,002	493,731	66.4
Caribbean	30,124	32,380	34,613	36,816	39,019	41,277	43,557	45,766	51.9
Central America	121,156	134,940	148,971	163,057	177,091	190,988	204,607	217,761	79.7
South Asia	1,145,746	1,285,136	1,426,458	1,567,203	1,702,405	1,827,491	1,937,533	2,047,575	78.7
Japan	123,460	125,904	128,470	130,468	131,035	130,348	129,029	127,496	3.3
ASEAN/NICs	392,587	426,947	460,401	491,117	519,159	546,523	571,692	595,435	51.7
East/SE Asia	1,283,776	1,383,774	1,477,209	1,548,414	1,604,599	1,658,972	1,713,897	1,763,176	37.3
Australasia	20,265	21,435	22,517	23,544	24,523	25,473	26,360	27,155	34.0
Pacific	5,992	6,655	7,349	8,042	8,727	9,392	10,037	10,644	77.6
Middle East	179,137	204,056	233,204	265,227	298,437	332,040	364,527	395,711	120.9
North Africa	169,742	195,395	224,640	256,955	291,642	327,159	361,322	394,706	132.5
West Africa	188,205	221,136	259,415	302,885	351,065	400,787	449,712	496,545	163.8
East/Central Africa	148,268	175,992	208,608	246,071	289,107	334,849	381,475	426,144	187.4
Southern Africa	83,500	95,950	109,757	124,830	140,970	157,582	173,849	189,156	126.5
Non-European total	*4,464,417*	*4,921,088*	*5,390,954*	*5,851,070*	*6,301,387*	*6,742,797*	*7,161,840*	*7,562,808*	*69.4*
European Community	341,521	344,602	347,519	348,576	348,450	347,483	345,864	343,578	0.6
EFTA	32,291	32,834	33,170	33,360	33,423	33,472	33,473	33,358	3.3
Eastern Europe	408,276	424,592	437,051	449,075	460,352	470,262	480,406	489,958	20.0
Other European countries	56,980	62,730	67,972	72,523	76,543	80,794	85,071	89,050	56.3
European total	*839,068*	*864,758*	*885,712*	*903,534*	*918,768*	*932,011*	*944,814*	*955,944*	*13.9*
International total	*5,303,484.9*	*5,785,846*	*6,276,666*	*6,754,604*	*7,220,155*	*7,674,808*	*8,106,654*	*8,518,752*	*60.6*

ECONOMIC INDICATORS   Table No. 2505

Trends in Total Gross Domestic Product 1977-1991

Units: Million current US dollars

	1977	1980	1985	1987	1988	1989	1990	1991	% growth 1977-91
North America	2,178,971	2,973,045	4,390,162	4,957,777	5,393,007	5,799,716	6,097,927	6,266,125	187.6
South America	343,883	488,862	450,220	578,023	643,230	704,018	805,643	799,386	132.5
Caribbean	31,821	38,779	41,115	42,441	43,021	46,082	48,232	47,914	50.6
Central America	114,171	225,882	230,002	193,089	227,847	266,298	303,799	348,321	205.1
South Asia	139,381	219,518	269,607	322,066	356,622	352,764	380,709	349,718	150.9
Japan	690,637	1,059,257	1,343,251	2,408,912	2,898,393	2,871,825	2,932,088	3,346,411	384.5
ASEAN/NICs	182,892	313,403	399,178	507,453	603,310	704,436	788,000	891,094	387.2
East/SE Asia	147,085	257,900	257,270	273,708	342,842	377,611	329,185	328,488	123.3
Australasia	115,890	173,786	184,430	235,033	292,875	325,597	339,166	339,256	192.7
Pacific	5,189	6,875	6,233	8,443	8,925	8,957	8,772	9,386	80.9
Middle East	269,916	450,358	491,089	600,034	389,097	736,247	881,551	1,043,438	286.6
North Africa	74,994	126,682	120,902	139,547	135,507	132,656	139,140	142,067	89.4
West Africa	81,197	142,562	116,935	73,661	78,903	74,258	82,137	77,403	-4.7
East/Central Africa	29,172	50,588	38,274	41,879	44,722	43,842	41,007	41,894	43.6
Southern Africa	49,306	96,362	67,739	96,564	104,262	106,753	120,594	126,742	157.1
Non-European total	*4,454,504*	*6,623,859*	*8,406,409*	*10,478,631*	*11,562,563*	*12,551,058*	*13,297,950*	*14,157,644*	*217.8*
European Community	1,935,872	3,283,170	2,623,747	4,488,849	4,853,215	5,002,066	6,165,037	6,393,629	230.3
EFTA	262,024	417,219	372,174	628,225	689,666	711,429	863,291	871,106	232.5
Eastern Europe	755,004	1,013,954	957,982	1,266,759	1,307,050	1,387,849	1,436,567	1,403,353	85.9
Other European countries	48,712	58,524	56,562	76,344	78,051	85,307	158,855	157,190	222.7
Non-European total	*3,001,612*	*4,772,867*	*4,010,464*	*6,460,177*	*6,927,982*	*7,186,652*	*8,623,751*	*8,825,278*	*194.0*
International total	*7,456,116*	*11,396,726*	*12,416,873*	*16,938,808*	*18,490,545*	*19,737,710*	*21,921,701*	*22,982,922*	*208.2*

ECONOMIC INDICATORS   Table No. 2506

Usage of Gross Domestic Product 1992

Units: % of total GDP

	A	B	C	D	E	F	Total GDP
North America	19.0	68.1	0.0	13.4	12.1	12.6	100.0
South America	11.1	68.7	0.5	15.8	15.2	11.5	100.0
Caribbean	13.3	78.9	0.4	19.9	19.3	31.8	100.0
Central America	8.8	71.1	2.8	18.4	21.5	22.7	100.0
South Asia	11.6	67.3	1.6	20.8	3.7	5.1	100.0
Japan	9.4	57.0	0.5	30.6	10.2	7.8	100.0
ASEAN/NICs	11.7	53.9	0.4	22.4	50.5	38.9	100.0
East/SE Asia	16.3	53.3	7.9	22.5	0.2	0.3	100.0
Australasia	18.6	62.4	0.0	19.0	19.8	19.7	100.0
Pacific	26.6	57.4	0.4	23.8	38.7	46.9	100.0
Middle East	25.2	56.7	0.6	20.3	36.3	39.2	100.0
North Africa	19.7	58.1	0.4	25.0	21.1	24.4	100.0
West Africa	9.9	59.9	0.5	15.1	42.1	27.5	100.0
East/Central Africa	16.7	74.4	0.7	15.6	22.3	29.6	100.0
Southern Africa	20.9	60.2	-1.4	17.5	25.5	22.7	100.0
Non-European total	*15.2*	*63.6*	*0.5*	*19.6*	*14.8*	*13.7*	*100.0*
European Community	18.4	60.0	0.0	19.8	27.9	26.2	100.0
EFTA	21.3	55.4	-0.2	20.8	34.3	31.5	100.0
Eastern Europe	9.6	54.2	16.4	16.5	27.7	24.5	100.0
Other European countries	15.9	61.9	0.0	23.0	24.8	25.7	100.0
Non-European total	*18.4*	*59.4*	*0.5*	*19.9*	*28.6*	*26.7*	*100.0*
International total	*16.4*	*62.1*	*0.5*	*19.7*	*19.8*	*18.5*	*100.0*

Notes: see end of section

EXTERNAL TRADE
Table No. 2507

Trends in Total Imports 1977-1992

Units: Million current US dollars

	1977	1980	1985	1987	1988	1989	1990	1991	1992
North America	202,486	319,564	433,478	517,369	571,820	612,719	640,997	633,139	682,856
South America	36,588	64,835	32,412	40,772	40,789	44,408	48,982	55,139	59,792
Caribbean	12,956	20,395	17,651	18,719	18,529	19,660	20,084	20,304	20,582
Central America	11,188	27,102	20,610	20,120	26,366	32,142	39,910	47,126	48,962
South Asia	11,473	25,801	28,212	28,934	32,719	35,125	39,035	36,699	41,979
Japan	71,252	141,109	130,276	150,297	187,335	210,068	233,814	236,805	233,139
ASEAN/NICs	69,526	135,204	144,881	203,682	265,724	307,337	356,844	416,639	460,123
East/SE Asia	10,170	23,223	47,848	49,429	61,680	64,389	58,286	68,176	81,951
Australasia	16,903	28,071	32,132	36,735	43,372	53,820	51,513	49,989	53,095
Pacific	2,393	3,813	3,268	4,076	4,535	4,613	4,427	4,743	4,660
Middle East	70,558	106,504	96,629	92,473	107,075	104,167	105,947	109,916	120,501
North Africa	18,572	29,631	25,144	22,380	24,924	27,054	32,577	30,618	30,475
West Africa	17,962	27,091	13,744	13,334	13,790	13,691	15,824	19,238	18,670
East/Central Africa	5,179	9,628	7,393	9,234	9,243	10,843	11,601	11,236	10,829
Southern Africa	9,154	25,110	15,287	20,088	24,302	24,858	25,835	26,681	29,207
Non-European total	*566,362*	*987,083*	*1,048,965*	*1,227,643*	*1,432,203*	*1,564,894*	*1,685,676*	*1,766,446*	*1,896,821*
European Community	432,899	781,893	663,328	980,975	1,074,829	1,212,576	1,450,972	1,488,516	1,563,166
EFTA	70,648	124,275	105,853	163,419	178,721	192,097	222,395	209,582	209,400
Eastern Europe	94,533	145,467	152,459	167,913	170,643	175,949	179,029	175,100	175,343
Other European countries	6,273	8,939	12,926	16,661	16,795	19,053	27,180	25,955	27,337
European total	*604,353*	*1,060,573*	*934,566*	*1,328,968*	*1,440,988*	*1,599,674*	*1,879,577*	*1,899,154*	*1,975,246*
International total	*1,170,715*	*2,047,656*	*1,983,531*	*2,556,611*	*2,873,192*	*3,164,569*	*3,565,253*	*3,665,599*	*3,872,067*

EXTERNAL TRADE
Table No. 2508

Trends in Total Exports 1977-1992

Units: Million current US dollars

	1977	1980	1985	1987	1988	1989	1990	1991	1992
North America	164,770	293,345	310,160	352,652	438,990	484,050	520,939	548,835	581,627
South America	37,209	65,610	64,151	60,355	73,274	80,492	86,692	85,223	89,285
Caribbean	13,499	22,542	15,637	14,819	14,388	15,648	16,462	16,175	16,047
Central America	8,948	21,063	26,412	25,293	25,181	27,691	32,089	32,251	32,552
South Asia	9,193	13,799	14,971	18,654	21,181	23,919	27,737	28,490	32,182
Japan	80,623	129,585	175,899	230,337	264,752	274,159	286,325	314,446	339,605
ASEAN/NICs	62,996	128,682	163,700	240,137	291,521	325,613	356,568	413,260	455,781
East/SE Asia	9,602	20,533	30,551	42,643	50,783	56,012	65,770	74,567	84,754
Australasia	16,588	27,690	28,760	33,850	41,857	46,628	49,346	51,547	52,461
Pacific	1,402	2,147	1,805	2,380	3,039	2,367	2,335	2,363	2,843
Middle East	112,800	216,452	99,776	96,403	100,287	110,538	123,285	122,564	154,149
North Africa	21,105	42,393	30,568	23,497	22,933	23,410	24,821	24,920	24,973
West Africa	18,921	36,500	20,878	15,994	15,100	17,028	24,502	23,154	22,709
East/Central Africa	5,428	7,966	7,213	7,142	7,353	8,102	8,147	8,005	7,565
Southern Africa	12,609	30,177	20,070	26,415	26,712	27,810	29,249	29,854	29,248
Non-European total	*575,694*	*1,058,484*	*1,010,552*	*1,190,573*	*1,397,351*	*1,523,467*	*1,654,268*	*1,775,653*	*1,925,781*
European Community	424,523	733,707	682,053	1,016,973	1,104,204	1,225,672	1,461,870	1,455,851	1,544,641
EFTA	63,501	111,753	108,300	159,647	175,644	188,679	223,933	215,863	222,173
Eastern Europe	91,632	145,971	159,339	183,223	181,029	177,320	161,249	161,345	162,299
Other European countries	2,089	3,723	8,927	12,123	13,395	13,625	15,595	16,259	17,396
European total	*581,744*	*995,154*	*958,618*	*1,371,966*	*1,474,271*	*1,605,297*	*1,862,647*	*1,849,318*	*1,946,509*
International total	*1,157,438*	*2,053,638*	*1,969,171*	*2,562,539*	*2,871,622*	*3,128,763*	*3,516,914*	*3,624,971*	*3,872,290*

EXTERNAL TRADE   Table No. 2509

Imports (cif) by Country of Origin 1991

Units: Million current US dollars

	USA	Japan	EC	Former USSR	Africa	Asia	Middle East	South America/ Carib- bean	Austr- alasia	Total (incl. others)
North America	75,025	103,901	102,083	1,100	15,852	116,854	18,174	70,174	4,899	629,710
South America	18,881	4,247	15,957	216	1,462	2,897	3,269	13,504	328	65,990
Caribbean	5,316	919	5,431	18	418	1,100	105	3,425	14	18,045
Central America	36,703	3,360	7,010	97	160	2,081	51	4,170	68	55,800
South Asia	3,494	3,739	10,197	2,597	992	7,691	4,871	778	728	38,788
Japan	53,634		31,971	3,318	3,633	74,533	29,252	9,335	12,965	236,633
ASEAN/NICs	65,758	97,509	56,008	651	3,291	141,766	16,813	5,912	10,186	419,078
East/SE Asia	8,034	10,679	8,997	2,116	382	29,201	822	1,380	1,619	68,258
Australasia	10,861	8,110	9,565	30	152	9,539	1,573	563	1,849	47,017
Pacific	206	355	671		9	536	1	20	1,065	3,252
Middle East	17,167	12,500	46,606	600	1,118	14,714	7,773	2,305	1,408	121,770
North Africa	1,909	1,000	20,241	644	1,456	1,587	1,151	682	62	32,721
West Africa	1,711	1,782	10,529	174	1,610	4,254	344	352	45	22,846
East/Central Africa	520	814	6,898	16	923	1,688	820	304	70	12,763
Southern Africa	2,361	1,875	8,454	1	1,312	1,472	253	362	141	20,607
Non-European total	*301,579*	*250,790*	*340,617*	*11,578*	*32,770*	*409,911*	*85,273*	*113,264*	*35,446*	*1,793,277*
European Community	112,299	65,747	839,346	53,623	45,903	90,488		34,249	7,336	1,465,527
EFTA	14,612	10,470	131,853	9,200	2,537	10,204		3,906	550	215,483
Eastern Europe	5,695	3,481	48,780	29,672	1,193	10,461		2,558	708	119,441
Other European countries	2,872	1,380	13,094	2,126	302	1,133		49	111	27,742
European total	*135,479*	*81,077*	*1,033,073*	*94,622*	*49,936*	*112,286*		*40,762*	*8,705*	*1,828,192*
International total	*437,058*	*331,867*	*1,373,690*	*106,199*	*82,705*	*522,197*		*154,025*	*44,150*	*3,621,469*

EXTERNAL TRADE   Table No. 2510

Exports (cif) by Country of Destination 1991

Units: Million current US dollars

	USA	Japan	EC	Former USSR	Africa	Asia	Middle East	South America/ Carib- bean	Austr- alasia	Total (incl. others)
North America	95,574	54,337	113,033	4,860	6,860	74,216	19,157	65,578	8,997	547,915
South America	22,827	6,250	23,642	1,013	1,250	7,215	2,054	16,743	363	87,786
Caribbean	3,538	232	2,036	29	158	395	39	1,686	10	9,071
Central America	31,147	1,739	4,508	32	64	796	103	2,710	69	44,002
South Asia	4,978	2,658	8,580	3,750	711	5,665	2,239	176	321	32,062
Japan	92,200		59,606	2,117	4,960	105,902	11,841	12,221	6,504	314,892
ASEAN/NICs	93,161	55,398	64,618	742	6,755	134,200	9,546	6,569	6,980	398,654
East/SE Asia	6,221	11,166	7,177	1,870	872	42,286	1,582	681	582	74,949
Australasia	5,499	13,184	6,341	503	332	16,385	1,740	708	1,812	51,629
Pacific	112	553	589			314			727	2,521
Middle East	16,157	26,598	29,584	984	2,355	23,315	10,679	3,115	1,103	127,826
North Africa	2,292	597	24,571	193	795	915	917	480	5	34,031
West Africa	6,523	295	12,074	289	1,840	951	59	992	3	24,825
East/Central Africa	2,756	173	5,177	13	603	445	96	198	12	9,892
Southern Africa	1,835	2,209	8,733		1,812	1,972	321	276	95	30,011
Non-European total	*384,820*	*175,389*	*370,268*	*16,395*	*29,367*	*414,970*	*60,373*	*112,133*	*27,584*	*1,790,065*
European Community	87,840	27,351	846,487	50,079	40,055	63,977		27,915	8,854	1,378,248
EFTA	13,939	5,564	127,463	10,045	2,924	11,287		3,912	1,703	214,943
Eastern Europe	2,428	3,579	46,967	27,909	1,703	8,070		809	147	106,461
Other European countries	969	283	8,024	1,092	350	476		32	23	15,451
European total	*105,176*	*36,777*	*1,028,941*	*89,124*	*45,032*	*83,809*		*32,668*	*10,727*	*1,715,103*
International total	*489,996*	*212,166*	*1,399,209*	*105,519*	*74,399*	*498,779*		*144,801*	*38,311*	*3,505,168*

LABOUR INDICATORS — Table No. 2511

Trends in Total Employment 1977-1991

Units: '000

	1977	1980	1985	1987	1988	1989	1990	1991	% growth 1977-91
North America	101,668	110,011	118,371	124,301	127,213	129,828	130,486	129,217	27.1
South America	60,278	66,310	77,679	83,566	85,650	86,019	87,178	87,553	45.2
Caribbean	5,792	6,021	6,556	6,748	6,858	6,868	6,873	6,869	18.6
Central America	7,857	9,419	11,483	12,686	13,463	14,151	14,728	15,000	90.9
South Asia	51,454	55,725	90,445	92,887	93,374	94,543	95,696	94,702	84.1
Japan	53,420	55,360	58,070	59,110	60,110	61,280	62,490	63,690	19.2
ASEAN/NICs	107,643	123,279	140,390	154,530	160,202	163,224	164,304	167,273	55.4
East/SE Asia	439,634	464,824	548,724	578,537	594,355	604,578	617,823	634,063	44.2
Australasia	7,243	7,559	8,038	8,683	8,900	9,189	9,344	9,164	26.5
Pacific	292	273	288	296	293	316	318	321	9.7
Middle East	13,159	13,860	16,546	16,549	16,598	16,612	16,643	16,735	27.2
North Africa	13,540	15,546	17,609	17,932	18,072	18,214	18,214	18,214	34.5
West Africa	33,540	34,009	38,784	38,715	38,628	38,623	38,608	38,608	15.1
East/Central Africa	23,339	23,602	26,410	26,536	26,603	26,656	26,719	26,719	14.5
Southern Africa	2,026	2,111	2,220	2,256	2,309	2,323	2,356	2,369	16.9
Non-European total	*920,884*	*987,909*	*1,161,615*	*1,223,332*	*1,252,626*	*1,272,422*	*1,291,779*	*1,310,497*	*42.3*
European Community	130,399	132,897	132,152	135,141	137,283	139,570	142,719	142,130	9.0
EFTA	14,061	14,564	15,487	15,787	15,891	16,005	15,650	15,495	10.2
Eastern Europe	161,200	167,911	174,463	174,178	173,715	171,859	168,295	167,045	3.6
Other European countries	2,486	2,528	16,509	18,354	19,288	19,761	19,962	19,880	699.7
European total	*308,146*	*317,900*	*338,611*	*343,460*	*346,177*	*347,196*	*346,626*	*344,550*	*11.8*
International total	*1,229,030*	*1,305,809*	*1,500,225*	*1,566,792*	*1,598,803*	*1,619,618*	*1,638,404*	*1,655,046*	*33.8*

ENERGY — Table No. 2512

Commercial Energy Consumption 1990

Units: Million tonnes of oil equivalent

	Solid fuels	Oil and NGL	Natural gas	Electricity	Total
North America	727	1,159	712	154	2,754
South America	23	159	71	44	298
Caribbean	0	26	7	0	34
Central America	7	126	35	5	174
South Asia	180	86	35	11	314
Japan	114	292	68	36	512
ASEAN/NICs	54	177	29	11	273
East/SE Asia	818	140	21	18	999
Australasia	55	55	29	4	144
Pacific	0	3	0	0	4
Middle East	6	200	125	2	334
North Africa	2	26	27	0	56
West Africa	0	17	3	1	22
East/Central Africa	0	6	0	1	7
Southern Africa	67	12	0	1	81
Non-European total	*2,058*	*2,482*	*1,168*	*293*	*6,002*
European Community	306	577	237	185	1,307
EFTA	8	61	10	48	128
Eastern Europe	436	408	640	78	1,563
Other European countries	21	25	4	2	54
European total	*773*	*1,071*	*893*	*315*	*3,052*
International total	*2,832*	*3,553*	*2,061*	*608*	*9,054*

ENERGY — Table No. 2513

Consumption of Motor Gasoline 1977-1991

Units: '000 metric tonnes

	1977	1980	1985	1987	1988	1989	1990	1991	% growth 1977-91
North America	334,260	313,342	314,000	331,552	340,780	341,482	337,656	331,869	-0.7
South America	26,775	27,880	30,338	30,880	32,580	33,490	36,349	36,841	37.6
Caribbean	2,345	2,891	2,575	2,802	2,858	2,952	2,843	2,754	17.4
Central America	11,351	16,683	16,680	17,982	17,859	18,758	21,275	21,353	88.1
South Asia	2,146	2,313	3,294	3,862	3,960	4,583	5,011	5,481	155.4
Japan	23,127	25,432	26,878	27,987	29,023	30,782	32,624	33,683	45.6
ASEAN/NICs	7,291	8,796	9,333	11,128	12,265	13,394	14,624	16,166	121.7
East/SE Asia	11,373	11,349	15,749	18,151	19,409	21,484	22,039	22,717	99.7
Australasia	12,179	12,560	13,164	13,454	13,950	14,406	14,664	14,183	16.5
Pacific	347	381	341	345	368	372	382	388	11.9
Middle East	10,466	13,644	19,985	21,139	21,663	22,397	23,465	24,185	131.1
North Africa	2,382	3,079	3,754	3,995	3,903	4,286	4,392	4,505	89.1
West Africa	1,947	4,308	4,420	5,143	5,836	5,720	6,009	5,969	206.6
East/Central Africa	1,027	1,098	917	977	966	1,064	1,058	1,072	4.4
Southern Africa	4,048	4,178	4,780	4,700	4,717	4,730	4,714	4,698	16.1
Non-European total	451,064	447,934	466,208	494,097	510,137	519,900	527,105	525,864	16.6
European Community	89,795	91,589	98,262	103,480	108,086	113,581	113,287	115,288	28.4
EFTA	11,475	11,692	13,425	14,200	14,568	14,540	15,003	15,055	31.2
Eastern Europe	74,920	80,118	70,316	73,457	73,277	72,610	73,134	73,070	-2.5
Other European countries	2,358	2,075	2,351	2,880	2,941	3,424	3,318	3,624	53.7
European total	178,548	185,474	184,354	194,017	198,872	204,155	204,742	207,037	16.0
International total	629,612	633,408	650,562	688,114	709,009	724,055	731,848	732,901	16.4

CONSUMER EXPENDITURE — Table No. 2514

Consumer Expenditure by Object: Latest Year

Units: Million current US dollars

	Food/drink/ tobacco	Clo-thing/ footwear	Housing	Fuels	Household goods & services	Health	Leisure & edu-cation	Trans-sport & comms.	Others	Total
Argentina	16,952	2,332	5,031	2,752	2,224	1,835	2,097	2,311	8,156	43,691
Australia	38,530	10,359	33,455	4,054	11,824	13,703	8,585	28,075	27,889	176,475
Brazil	81,934	12,799	72,696	15,484	12,799	13,322	12,930	23,378	17,098	262,442
Canada	57,103	17,601	68,985	12,748	22,849	14,857	25,823	34,250	93,143	347,358
Chile	7,473	1,273	7,228	1,215	992	1,324	1,283	2,321	2,467	25,575
China [a]	82,136	25,353	10,975		17,712	4,480	16,636	3,456	12,902	173,648
Colombia	9,264	1,597	2,232	574	1,578	1,626	1,637	4,295	3,546	26,348
Ecuador [a]	2,553	786	1,088		333	401	400	1,092	1,531	8,184
Hong Kong	8,236	9,983	6,610	743	5,952	1,827	3,946	4,447	8,221	49,965
India [a]	80,866	18,673	14,572		4,461	3,740	4,721	12,654	31,546	171,234
Indonesia [a,b]	34,274	3,580	9,766		5,153		1,240	2,207	7,946	64,166
Israel	10,382	2,245	8,418	1,603	4,409	5,612	3,608	3,808		40,084
Japan	410,727	127,420	98,519	105,997	124,702	219,149	204,691	207,914	593,199	2,092,317
Malaysia	10,244	1,811	1,940	1,139	2,949	542	1,656	3,880	2,044	26,205
Mexico [a]	57,900	12,066	10,095		14,035	5,910	5,800	14,273	51,730	171,810
New Zealand	3,319	1,390	5,401	680	1,871	1,814	2,018	4,632	6,075	27,200
Nigeria [a,b,c]	8,547	914	2,222		619			525	4,198	17,026
Pakistan	16,435	2,724	4,383	2,019	694	1,701	692	1,552	4,684	34,885
Peru [a]	18,927	2,957	4,101		1,814	1,814	2,721	3,391	3,706	39,430
Philippines	22,523	2,990	4,345	2,073	4,186	478	1,794	1,427	48	39,864
Singapore [a]	5,216	1,637	2,374		2,069	1,070	3,376	3,374	704	19,821
South Africa	21,376	4,604	6,312	1,803	5,988	1,880	2,833	5,679	14,467	64,942
South Korea	54,455	6,642	17,849	6,539	9,226	11,615	17,953	17,950	16,288	158,517
Taiwan [a]	27,698	5,267	18,726		5,096	6,031	19,490	15,088	16,606	114,001
Thailand	20,335	7,690	3,961	929	4,862	4,585	8,628	6,829	2,659	60,477
USA	741,340	221,800	600,444	104,689	180,899	635,177	242,308	463,604	905,540	4,095,800
Venezuela [a]	15,501	3,679	3,056		1,853	1,116	1,557	3,708	5,438	35,907
European Community	892,519	310,951	575,501	168,894	315,838	340,111	369,446	626,372	633,336	4,232,968
EFTA	113,615	31,964	87,200	25,201	31,996	30,282	44,252	74,324	60,298	499,046
Eastern Europe	13,912	8,548	4,723	4,234	5,758	4,372	9,330	7,121	46,684	1,123,845
Other European countries	1,615	786	354	144	643	206	349			83,315
European total	1,021,661	352,249	667,778	198,473	354,234	374,972	707,817	423,377	740,318	5,939,174

Notes: see end of section

CONSUMER EXPENDITURE   Table No. 2515

Consumer Expenditure by Object: Latest Year (% analysis)

Units: % of total spending

	Food/drink/ tobacco	Clo- thing/ footwear	Housing	Fuels	Household goods & services	Health	Leisure & edu- cation	Trans- sport & comms.	Others	Total
Argentina	38.8	5.3	11.5	6.3	5.1	4.2	4.8	5.3	18.7	100.0
Australia	21.8	5.9	19.0	2.3	6.7	7.8	4.9	15.9	15.8	100.0
Brazil	31.2	4.9	27.7	5.9	4.9	5.1	4.9	8.9	6.5	100.0
Canada	16.4	5.1	19.9	3.7	6.6	4.3	7.4	9.9	26.8	100.0
Chile	29.2	5.0	28.3	4.8	3.9	5.2	5.0	9.1	9.6	100.0
China [a]	47.3	14.6	6.3		10.2	2.6	9.6	2.0	7.4	100.0
Colombia	35.2	6.1	8.5	2.2	6.0	6.2	6.2	16.3	13.5	100.0
Ecuador [a]	31.2	9.6	13.3		4.1	4.9	4.9	13.3	18.7	100.0
Hong Kong	16.5	20.0	13.2	1.5	11.9	3.7	7.9	8.9	16.5	100.0
India [a]	47.2	10.9	8.5		2.6	2.2	2.8	7.4	18.4	100.0
Indonesia [a,b]	53.4	5.6	15.2		8.0		1.9	3.4	12.4	100.0
Israel	25.9	5.6	21.0	4.0	11.0	14.0	9.0	9.5		100.0
Japan	19.6	6.1	4.7	5.1	6.0	10.5	9.8	9.9	28.4	100.0
Malaysia	39.1	6.9	7.4	4.3	11.3	2.1	6.3	14.8	7.8	100.0
Mexico [a]	33.7	7.0	5.9		8.2	3.4	3.4	8.3	30.1	100.0
New Zealand	12.2	5.1	19.9	2.5	6.9	6.7	7.4	17.0	22.3	100.0
Nigeria [a,b,c]	50.2	5.4	13.1		3.6			3.1	24.7	100.0
Pakistan	47.1	7.8	12.6	5.8	2.0	4.9	2.0	4.5	13.4	100.0
Peru [a]	48.0	7.5	10.4		4.6	4.6	6.9	8.6	9.4	100.0
Philippines	56.5	7.5	10.9	5.2	10.5	1.2	4.5	3.6	0.1	100.0
Singapore [a]	26.3	8.3	12.0		10.4	5.4	17.0	17.0	3.6	100.0
South Africa	32.9	7.1	9.7	2.8	9.2	2.9	4.4	8.7	22.3	100.0
South Korea	34.4	4.2	11.3	4.1	5.8	7.3	11.3	11.3	10.3	100.0
Taiwan [a]	24.3	4.6	16.4		4.5	5.3	17.1	13.2	14.6	100.0
Thailand	33.6	12.7	6.6	1.5	8.0	7.6	14.3	11.3	4.4	100.0
USA	18.1	5.4	14.7	2.6	4.4	15.5	5.9	11.3	22.1	100.0
Venezuela [a]	43.2	10.2	8.5		5.2	3.1	4.3	10.3	15.1	100.0
European Community	21.1	7.3	13.6	4.0	7.5	8.0	8.7	14.8	15.0	100.0
EFTA	22.8	6.4	17.5	5.0	6.4	6.1	8.9	14.9	12.1	100.0
Eastern Europe	1.2	0.8	0.4	0.4	0.5	0.4	0.8	0.6	4.2	100.0
Other European countries	1.9	0.9	0.4	0.2	0.8	0.2	0.4			100.0
European total	*17.2*	*5.9*	*11.2*	*3.3*	*6.0*	*6.3*	*7.1*	*11.9*	*12.5*	*100.0*

Notes: see end of section

MEDIA ACCESS   Table No. 2516

Televisions in Use 1977-1990

Units: '000

	1977	1980	1983	1985	1987	1988	1989	1990	% growth 1977-90
North America	145,000	166,417	197,276	203,128	211,895	214,250	217,459	220,000	51.7
South America	21,378	27,471	30,988	41,427	45,421	47,162	50,550	53,751	151.4
Caribbean	1,463	2,357	3,076	3,442	3,556	3,726	3,870	4,032	175.6
Central America	6,852	7,726	10,341	10,952	12,745	13,337	14,015	15,721	129.4
South Asia	1,388	2,666	4,101	5,670	8,018	8,661	9,737	11,380	719.9
Japan	27,595	62,976	67,200	70,000	71,500	72,000	75,000	76,500	177.2
ASEAN/NICs	8,006	13,748	16,176	24,071	26,822	28,300	30,348	34,580	331.9
East/SE Asia	3,159	6,247	9,283	12,338	20,586	29,674	33,035	38,200	1,109.4
Australasia	5,837	6,462	7,522	7,962	9,020	9,140	9,300	9,700	66.2
Pacific	119	143	162	177	186	190	197	201	69.3
Middle East	6,119	9,362	11,685	14,913	16,228	16,917	18,935	20,443	234.1
North Africa	1,676	3,036	3,839	4,441	4,999	5,237	6,277	6,932	313.7
West Africa	995	1,038	1,176	1,536	1,896	2,011	2,329	2,506	151.8
East/Central Africa	282	400	477	514	688	720	889	990	251.7
Southern Africa	2,132	2,162	2,504	3,251	3,552	3,678	4,045	4,366	104.8
Non-European total	*231,999*	*312,211*	*365,805*	*403,822*	*437,112*	*455,003*	*475,986*	*499,302*	*115.2*

HEALTH
Table No. 2517

Medical Facilities: Latest Year

Units: Number, unless otherwise stated

	Hospital beds ('000)	Doctors	Dentists	Pharmacists	Nursing personnel
North America	1,424	615,575	153,803	172,648	1,768,955
South America	870	374,361	155,467	16,186	117,469
Caribbean	91	43,523	7,512	1,381	71,887
Central America	120	148,814	8,685	3,671	79,039
South Asia	921	410,010	12,941	161,968	258,061
Japan	1,662	199,958	69,499	122,380	365,298
ASEAN/NICs	597	126,395	22,969	63,336	509,659
East/SE Asia	3,161	1,144,474	2,097	111,818	1,210,944
Australasia	191	46,789	8,075	13,223	184,214
Pacific	23	1,386	216	118	7,544
Middle East	234	89,373	21,320	31,660	173,112
North Africa	164	33,754	5,202	3,576	92,093
West Africa	191	20,075	1,341	5,596	70,908
East/Central Africa	215	11,342	1,053	1,509	79,196
Southern Africa	214	22,617	3,584	7,613	100,322
Non-European total	*10,079*	*3,288,446*	*473,764*	*716,683*	*5,088,701*
European Community	2,623	802,552	128,274	158,839	1,719,657
EFTA	273	81,978	21,480	8,399	418,687
Eastern Europe	4,687	1,531,556	34,590	135,460	509,666
Other Europe	116	43,972	10,102	15,111	44,603
European total	*7,700*	*2,460,058*	*194,446*	*317,809*	*2,692,613*
International total	*17,779*	*5,748,504*	*668,210*	*1,034,492*	*7,781,314*

AGRICULTURE
Table No. 2518

Land Use and Irrigation 1990/1991

Units: '000 ha

	Total area	Land area	Arable land	Perma-nent crops	Perma-nent pasture	Forest & wood-land	Other land	Irrigated land	As % of land area
North America	3,238,289	3,059,778	312,920	6,953	392,482	1,075,030	1,272,393	27,501	0.8
South America	1,780,653	1,751,708	97,883	16,016	492,744	829,388	315,677	8,835	0.5
Caribbean	22,493	21,925	4,567	1,694	5,829	4,330	5,508	1,266	5.7
Central America	249,026	242,719	28,721	3,066	88,741	59,083	63,108	5,744	2.3
South Asia	513,319	477,476	206,125	5,570	50,360	81,182	134,239	66,797	13.9
Japan	37,780	37,652	4,121	475	647	25,105	7,304	2,847	7.5
ASEAN/NICs	51,312	51,089	19,000	3,140	780	14,100	14,069	4,300	8.4
East/SE Asia	1,271,008	1,240,367	115,425	5,160	526,529	217,721	425,552	52,396	4.2
Australasia	798,435	791,243	49,132	199	431,132	113,350	197,430	2,180	0.2
Pacific	54,988	53,831	342	764	522	43,880	8,323	1	0.0
Middle East	639,655	637,545	31,147	2,504	159,270	26,191	418,257	13,231	2.0
North Africa	1,395,672	1,364,177	56,651	3,992	389,985	122,160	791,389	4,577	0.3
West Africa	336,402	329,859	49,410	7,837	101,686	115,012	55,974	1,260	0.3
East/Central Africa	696,682	677,307	26,654	5,149	167,311	348,446	129,747	1,246	0.1
Southern Africa	473,803	466,684	28,190	1,179	236,259	99,519	101,537	1,583	0.3
Non-European total	*11,559,517*	*11,203,360*	*1,030,288*	*63,698*	*3,044,277*	*3,174,497*	*3,940,507*	*193,764*	*1.7*
European Community	236,756	233,338	71,683	11,419	56,008	57,475	36,319	11,116	4.7
EFTA	134,029	124,597	7,969	100	6,674	63,974	45,894	303	0.2
Eastern Europe	2,356,954	2,341,861	270,414	6,963	389,567	982,764	692,153	26,881	1.1
Other European countries	78,903	77,920	24,997	3,082	8,504	20,322	21,015	2,406	3.0
European total	*2,806,642*	*2,777,716*	*375,063*	*21,564*	*460,753*	*1,124,535*	*795,381*	*40,706*	*1.5*
International total	*14,366,159*	*13,981,076*	*1,405,351*	*85,262*	*3,505,030*	*4,299,032*	*4,735,888*	*234,470*	*1.6*